DONATION

The Thames through Time

The Archaeology of the Gravel Terraces of the Upper and Middle Thames

Early Prehistory: to 1500 BC

Part 1 – The Ice Ages: palaeogeography, Palaeolithic archaeology and Pleistocene environments

by Anthony Morigi, Danielle Schreve and Mark White

Part 2 – The Mesolithic, Neolithic and early Bronze Age and the establishment of permanent human occupation in the valley

by Gill Hey, Paul Garwood, Mark Robinson, Alistair Barclay and Philippa Bradley

Illustrations prepared by Sarah Lucas

with Magdalena Wachnik and Peter Lorimer

Oxford Archaeology
Thames Valley Landscapes Monograph No. 32
2011

The preparation and publication of this volume has been funded by English Heritage from the Aggregates Levy Sustainability Fund

Published for Oxford Archaeology by Oxford University School of Archaeology as part of the Thames Valley Landscapes monograph series

Designed by Oxford Archaeology Graphics Office

Part 1 edited by Anne Dodd
Part 2 edited by Chris Hayden
Thames Through Time series editor Anne Dodd

This book is part of a series of monographs about the Thames Valley Landscapes
For more information visit www.thehumanjourney.net

ISBN 978-0-9549627-8-4

Typeset by Production Line, Oxford
Printed in Great Britain by Information Press, Eynsham, Oxford

Contents

PART 1 – THE ICE AGES: PALAEOGEOGRAPHY, PALAEOLITHIC ARCHAEOLOGY AND PLEISTOCENE ENVIRONMENTS

CHAPTER 1 – INTRODUCTION AND THE PRE-ANGLIAN GEOLOGICAL, PALAEO-ENVIRONMENTAL AND ARCHAEOLOGICAL RECORDS *by Anthony Morigi, Danielle Schreve and Mark White*

CHAPTER 2 – THE DIVERSION OF THE THAMES, THE HOXNIAN INTERGLACIAL AND ADJACENT COLD STAGES (MIS 12-11-10) *by Danielle Schreve, Anthony Morigi and Mark White*

Contents

PART 2: THE MESOLITHIC, NEOLITHIC AND EARLY BRONZE AGE AND THE ESTABLISHMENT OF PERMANENT HUMAN OCCUPATION IN THE VALLEY

CHAPTER 8: AN INTRODUCTION TO THE HOLOCENE OF THE THAMES *by Gill Hey with Chris Hayden*

CHAPTER 9 – THE THAMES AND ITS CHANGING ENVIRONMENT IN OUR ERA *by Mark Robinson*

CHAPTER 10 – MESOLITHIC COMMUNITIES IN THE THAMES VALLEY: LIVING IN THE NATURAL LANDSCAPE *by Gill Hey with Mark Robinson*

CHAPTER 11 – NEOLITHIC COMMUNITIES IN THE THAMES VALLEY: THE CREATION OF NEW WORLDS *by Gill Hey with Mark Robinson*

Figures

CHAPTER 3

CHAPTER 4

CHAPTER 5

CHAPTER 16

Tables

Preface

This volume is the third in our series The Thames through Time, funded from the Aggregates Levy Sustainability Fund, which seeks to provide an accessible and up to date synthesis of the large quantity of archaeological data recovered over more than a century of quarrying and other development on the gravel terraces of the river Thames. Previous publications have covered the later prehistoric, Roman and Anglo-Saxon periods, from *c* 1500 BC to AD 1000. A final volume, covering the period AD 1000-2000, is currently in preparation.

The present volume reviews knowledge of the earlier prehistory of the Upper and Middle Thames Valley. Archaeological syntheses very often take the Neolithic period as their point of departure, with only a brief and wary glance back over the shoulder at the daunting and unfamiliar world of the Palaeolithic and Mesolithic. This imbalance has, however, been significantly redressed by a number of projects carried out via the Aggregates Levy Sustainability Fund, not least because quarrying has often provided the means by which these ancient deposits and remains can be accessed. In the present volume, therefore, we have been delighted to work with specialists in Quaternary geology and palaeontology, as well as Palaeolithic archaeology, in order to extend the coverage of The Thames through Time as far back as the evidence currently allows, over a period of half a million years and more. As well as introducing fascinating material that may up to now have remained very unfamiliar to most of us, this also enables us to set the Mesolithic and subsequent human occupation of the valley in a much longer (and truer) context. In particular, it illustrates the close relationship between the climate and the environment and natural resources of the valley, which have seen extreme fluctuations over the period covered by this volume. It also points up starkly how fast change happens in modern human societies, and how much we ourselves, only relatively recent arrivals in the region, have moulded and changed its landscape and environment to meet our material and cultural needs.

As in previous volumes, we use colourful double page spreads to summarise and illustrate important aspects of the evidence covered in detail in the main text. For Part 1 this is supplemented by a series of inset pages explaining some of the more specialised techniques and approaches used in Quaternary science and Palaeolithic archaeology, and a glossary of technical terminology is provided at the end of the volume.

Anne Dodd, Series Editor
January 2011

A NOTE ON RADIOCARBON DATES

Any volume dealing with the transitions from the Palaeolithic to the Mesolithic, and from the Mesolithic to the Neolithic, faces the problem of reconciling the different ways in which the scholars of these periods express radiocarbon dates. Radiocarbon dating is effective only for the later part of the Palaeolithic (covered in Part 1, Chapters 6 and 7), and for this period, to avoid potential confusion, we have wherever possible given each date firstly in uncalibrated form and secondly in calibrated form expressed in years BP (Before Present) and years BC. For the Neolithic and later periods, dates are conventionally expressed as calibrated dates BC, and we have followed this practice in Part 2. It is the intervening period – the Mesolithic – which presents the greatest difficulties. For this period, which is covered in Part 2 of this volume, although we have generally cited radiocarbon determinations as calibrated dates BC, in a few cases, especially those concerning the earlier part of the Holocene, we have cited dates as both cal BP and cal BC.

The radiocarbon dates cited in Part 1 have been calibrated using CalPal and the CalPal 2007 Hulu calibration data (www.calpal.de/). (Absolute dates for the earlier parts of the Palaeolithic are obtained using methods other than radiocarbon dating which do not require calibration, and are cited as calendar years BP.)

In Part 2 no attempt has been made to recalibrate dates, which are cited as they are given in the publications from which they have been obtained. Although this means that the calibrated dates have been produced using a range of different calibration data, the differences are usually slight. Where dates have been calibrated for Part 2 of this volume, we have used OxCal (v. 4.1; Bronk Ramsey, C, 2009 Bayesian analysis of radiocarbon dates, *Radiocarbon* **51** (1), 337-360) and the IntCal04 calibration data (Reimer *et al*. 2004, IntCal04 terrestrial radiocarbon age calibration, 0-26 cal kyr BP, *Radiocarbon*, **46** (3), 1029-1058). All calibrated dates have been rounded outwards to the nearest 10 years. In Part 2, some dates are cited which have been estimated using Bayesian models. Since discussion of these models is beyond the scope of this volume, we have not attempted to distinguish such estimated dates from simple calibrated dates. Where possible, the laboratory number and the uncalibrated radiocarbon determination is also given, although, especially in older publications, this information is sometimes not available.

Acknowledgements

We are very grateful for the help we have received in preparing this monograph from a large number of people. Particular thanks are due to Rob Poulton and his colleagues at the Surrey County Archaeological Unit for providing information, text and images, and for reading and commenting on our work as it progressed. We are grateful to Nick Ashton for reading Part 1 of the volume in draft and providing many helpful comments, and to Kate Scott and Christine Buckingham for their help in presenting the work of the Hanson Mammoth Project. Anthony Morigi would like to thank his many colleagues at the British Geological Survey who have assisted him in contributing to this book, especially Steve Booth and John Powell for reviewing the manuscript, and Jon Lee for his invaluable advice and for providing some of the figures. In Part 2 of this volume we have also benefited in particular from advice, information, reports and illustrations from Tim Allen, Martin Barber, Richard Bradley, Jon Cotton, Steve Ford, Frances Healy, Phil Jones, John Lewis, Paula Levick, Paul McCulloch, Stuart Needham, Fiona Roe and Karen Walker. We are grateful also to Adrian Havercroft (of the Guildhouse Consultancy), acting on behalf of Cemex UK Materials Ltd, for allowing us to use information and illustrations of Horton prior to publication.

Our thanks are also due to the many colleagues and institutions, listed in the picture credits, who have been so helpful in providing us with images and allowing us to make use of copyright material, and also to Kelly Powell of OA who carried out the associated administration for us. The French and German summaries were translated by Nathalie Haudecoeur-Wilks and Markus Dylewski respectively and the index was compiled by Chris Hayden.

The preparation and publication of this volume has been funded by English Heritage with grants from the Aggregates Levy Sustainability Fund, and we are grateful to the commissioning team at English Heritage and to the Project Officer, Helen Keeley, for their support and encouragement. Anne Dodd would also like to thank Ian Williamson and Natalie Bennett, then of English Nature, for encouraging us to expand our remit for Palaeolithic archaeology to encompass the palaeontological and geological research that provides its regional context.

Anthony Morigi publishes with the permission of the Executive Director of the British Geological Survey, and the work of Danielle Schreve and Mark White for this volume is a contribution to the AHOB (Ancient Human Occupation of Britain) project.

Summary

The Thames Valley is a rich source of evidence for understanding past climate and environmental change, the effects on plant and animal populations, and the challenges and opportunities these presented for early humans. Much of this evidence has come to light in the course of gravel quarrying on the terraces of the Thames and its tributaries. This volume provides an up to date overview of the early prehistory of the Upper and Middle Thames Valley, set within its wider regional context. The first part of the volume focuses on the geological, palaeontological and archaeological evidence for the Pleistocene, or the epoch of the Ice Ages. This information is synthesised by the authors in chronologically-ordered chapters, beginning more than half a million years ago, and ending with the rapid climatic amelioration that marked the onset of the Holocene epoch, the period of warmer conditions within which we are still living today. Each chapter reviews the evidence for successive glaciations and inter-glacials, their effects on the course of the river Thames itself, the contemporary climatic and environmental conditions, and the plants, animals and hominins present.

The second part of the volume takes up the story from the beginning of the Holocene, around 11500 years ago. Two chapters introduce this era, describing its topography and its changing environment, the character of its archaeological remains and the history of research. The authors review the evidence for early hunter-gatherer populations in the Mesolithic and the transition to a 'Neolithic' way of life at c 4000 cal BC, with the introduction of domesticated plants and animals, pottery and different ways of making stone and flint tools and treating the dead. Three chapters outline present knowledge of the changing character of settlement from the Neolithic to the end of the early Bronze Age, and the creation and development of ceremonial and funerary monuments. The volume ends with three chapters presenting more detailed considerations of the evidence for Neolithic and early Bronze Age ritual, ceremony and cosmology; funerary practices; and procurement, production and exchange of materials throughout the period. An overlying theme is the rich social lives and belief systems of the inhabitants and their gradually increasing impact on the environment.

Zusammenfassung

Das Tal der Themse ist eine reichhaltige Nachweisquelle für das Verständnis früherer Klimate, ökologischen Wandel, die Auswirkungen auf Flora und Fauna sowie die Herausforderungen und Möglichkeiten die diese für die frühen Menschen darstellten. Viele dieser Nachweise kamen beim Kiesabbau in den Flussterrassen der Themse und ihrer Nebenflüsse zutage. Dieser Band beschreibt einen Überblick des aktuellen Forschungsstandes des prähistorischen oberen und mittleren Tals der Themse im regionalen Kontext. Der erste Teil des Bandes befasst sich mit den geologischen, paläontologischen und archäologischen Zeugnissen des Pleistozän, der Eiszeit.

Diese Informationen wurden vom Autor in chronologisch geordnete Kapitel gegliedert, mit dem Beginn vor mehr als einer halben Millionen Jahre und endend mit der rapiden Melioration, welche den Übergang ins Holozän beschrieb, die warme Periode in der wir heute noch leben. Jedes Kapitel überprüft die Nachweise aufeinanderfol-

gender Vereisungen und Zwischeneiszeiten, ihre Auswirkungen auf den Verlauf der Themse, die herrschenden Klimate und Umweltbedingungen, sowie die anzutreffenden Flora, Fauna und die Hominiden.

Der zweite Teil des Bandes beginnt mit dem Anfang des Holozän, vor etwa 11500 Jahren. Zwei Kapitel stellen die Epoche vor, indem sie die Topografie und die sich ändernde Umwelt beschreiben, sowie auf die Beschaffenheit der archäologischen Hinterlassenschaften und die Geschichte deren Erforschung eingehen. Die Autoren begutachten Indizien, die auf frühe Jäger und Sammler Bevölkerungen im Mesolithikum hinweisen und gehen auf den Übergang zur neolithischen Lebensart um etwa 4000 v.Chr. ein, welche durch die Einführung von domestizierten Pflanzen und Tieren, Keramik und der andersartigen Herstellung von Stein- und Flintwerkzeugen, sowie dem Umgang mit den Toten, ihren Ausdruck findet. Drei Kapitel widmen sich dem heutigen

Wissensstand über sich ändernden Siedlungsstrukturen am Übergang vom Neolithikum zur frühen Bronzezeit, sowie der Herstellung und Weiterentwicklung von zeremoniellen und begräbnisorientierten Monumenten. Der Band endet mit drei Kapiteln, welche sich detaillierter mit den Nachweisen neolithischer und früh bronzezeitlicher Rituale, Zeremonien und Kosmologie, Begräbnissitten sowie deren Anwendung auseinandersetzen. Des Weiteren werden Beschaffung, Produktion und Austausch von Materialien während dieser Epoche untersucht. Überspannende Themen sind das reichhaltige Sozialleben und das Glaubenssystem der Einwohner und wie diese sich zunehmend stärker auf die Umwelt auswirken.

Résumé

La Vallée de la Tamise constitue une source riche de témoignages nous aidant à comprendre les changements climatiques et environnementaux passés, leurs effets sur les plantes et les populations animales, ainsi que les défis et les opportunités qu'ils ont présenté pour les premiers humains. Beaucoup de ces témoignages sont apparus lors de l'exploitation des terrasses gravières de la Tamise et de ses affluents. Ce volume fournit une vue d'ensemble de la préhistoire ancienne de la Moyenne et Haute Vallée de la Tamise, présentée dans son contexte régional plus large. La première partie du volume est centrée sur les témoignages géologiques, paléontologiques et archéologiques du Pléistocène, ou de l'ère glaciaire. Cette information est synthétisée par les auteurs dans des chapitres classés chronologiquement, commençant il y a plus de 500 000 ans et s'achevant avec l'amélioration climatique rapide qui a marqué le début de l'Holocène, période aux conditions climatiques plus chaudes durant laquelle nous vivons encore aujourd'hui. Chaque chapitre réexamine les témoignages de glaciations successives et interglaciaires, leurs effets sur le cours même de la rivière de la Tamise, les conditions climatiques et environnementales contemporaines ainsi que les plantes, animaux et hominiens présents.

La seconde partie de ce volume enchaîne sur l'histoire du début de l'Holocène, il y a environ 11500 ans. Deux chapitres introduisent cette ère, grâce à la description de sa topographie et de son environnement en cours de mutation, du caractère de ses vestiges archéologiques et de l'histoire de la recherche. Les auteurs revoit les preuves des populations des premiers chasseurs-cueilleurs au Mésolithique et la transition vers un style de vie `Néolithique' environ 4000 ans av. J.-C., avec l'introduction de plantes et d'animaux domestiqués, la céramique et les différentes manières de fabriquer des objets en pierre ou en silex et de traiter ses défunts. Trois chapitres résument la connaissance actuelle du caractère changeant de l'habitat du Néolithique à la fin du Bronze ancien, ainsi que la création et le développement de monuments cérémoniaux et funéraires. Le volume s'achève par trois chapitres présentant d'autres réflexions détaillées sur les indices recueillis relatifs aux rituels, aux cosmologies et aux pratiques funéraires du néolithique et du Bronze ancien; ainsi que sur l'obtention, la production et l'échange de matériaux tout au long de cette période. Le thème prédominant est celui des vies sociales et des systèmes de croyances riches des habitants et leurs impacts de plus en plus marqués sur l'environnement.

Picture credits

Where illustrations have been sourced from works that are cited in the main text of this volume, the relevant publication is identified in the following list by a short reference and full details can be found in the corresponding entry in the bibliography. Full references are only given in this list for works that are not otherwise cited in the main text.

Fig. 1.1 adapted from Westaway *et al.* 2002, fig 5; Fig. 1.2 *Globorotalia menardii* from *Late Quaternary Environmental Change* by Martin Bell and Michael J C Walker 2nd ed. 2005 Pearson Education Ltd, fig 2.11; Specmap and Gisp2 ice core from Grootes *et al.* 1993 reprinted by permission Macmillan Publishers Ltd; pollen, British Geological Survey; *Aphodius holdereri* from an original image by Scott Elias, Royal Holloway, University of London; mammoth excavation image courtesy of Kate Scott and Christine Buckingham, the Hanson Mammoth project; magnetostratigraphy diagram adapted after Lowe and Walker 1997 fig 5.26; Fig. 1.3 from Gibbard 1988 fig. 2; Fig. 1.4 palaeogeography of the pre-Anglian 'Ancient' Thames after J Rose, Early and Middle Pleistocene landscapes of eastern England, *Proc Geologists' Assoc* 120 (2009), fig. 8; Fig. 1.5 sea-level/orbital forcing after *Global environments through the Quaternary: exploring environmental change*, by D E Anderson, A S Goudie and A G Parker (2007), fig. 7.11 modified after Chappell and Saddleton 1986, by permission of Oxford University Press; maps after K. Lambeck 1995 Late Devensian and Holocene shorelines of the British Isles and North Sea from models of glacio-hydro-isostatic rebound. *Journ. Geol. Soc.* London, Vol. 152, 437-448, fig 3; Fig. 1.6 after Gibbard 1988 fig. 3; Fig. 1.7 after Gibbard 1988 fig. 4; Fig. 1.8 British Geological Survey Make a Map; Fig. 1.9 IPR/117-40C British Geological Survey. © NERC 2009. NEXTMap Britain Elevation Data from Intermap Technologies. All rights reserved; Fig. 1.10 from M G Sumbler *British Regional Geology: London and the Thames Valley* (4th edition), British Geological Survey, 2006; Fig. 1.11 adapted from Bridgland 2000; Fig. 1.12 stratigraphy adapted from Bridgland 1994, pollen diagram from Bridgland 1994 after Turner 1983; Fig. 1.13 photo Danielle Schreve; Fig. 1.14 adapted from Preece and Parfitt 2000; Fig 1.15 photo S Parfitt; Figs 1.16, 1.17, 1.18 adapted from Parfitt *et al.* 2005 reprinted by permission Macmillan Publishers Ltd; Fig. 1.19 adapted from Bridgland 1994; Fig. 1.20 hominin skulls adapted from C Scarre *The Human Past*, London, 2005; Fig. 1.21 from M B Roberts, S A Parfitt, M I Pope and F F Wenban-Smith, Boxgrove, West Sussex: Rescue excavations of a Lower Palaeolithic Landsurface (Boxgrove Project B, 1989-91), *Proceedings of the Prehistoric Society* 63, 303-358, figs 24-26, 1997 with permission; Fig. 1.22 from Ashton *et al.* (eds) 1992, figs 3021 (plate 5), 3047 (plate 10), 3094 (plate 21), 3078 (plate 17) British Museum; Fig. 1.23 from Wymer 1999, 51, fig. 13, with permission Wessex Archaeology; Fig. 1.24 core types from Ashton *et al.* 1998, 291, fig. 4, flake tools from Ashton *et al.* (eds) 1992, figs 3010 (plate 2), 3131 (plate 29), 3147 (plate 33) and 3137 (plate 31) British Museum, handaxes from J Evans On the occurrence of flint implements in undisturbed beds of gravel, sand and clay, *Archaeologia* 38, 280-307, 1860; Fig. 1.25 main image reconstruction by Peter Lorimer Oxford Archaeology, flints from Wymer 1999, fig. 13 with permission Wessex Archaeology; Fig. 2.1 British Geological Survey; Fig. 2.2 BGS 2005 Beaconsfield: England & Wales Sheet 255 Solid and Drift geology 1:50000 (Keyworth Notts, British Geological Survey), after Gibbard 1985; Fig. 2.3 background images Sarah Lucas Oxford Archaeology, schematic map as Fig 2.2, Skilak Lake US Fish and Wildlife Service, Steve Hillebrand, Greenland ice sheet Hannes Grobe (Creative Commons CC-BY-SA-2.5), steppe mammoth Sam Brown, Norfolk Museums and Archaeology Service; Fig. 2.4 map courtesy of S Elias, specimen image courtesy of S Kuzmina; Fig. 2.5 photo Danielle Schreve; Fig. 2.6 from Schreve 2004; Fig. 2.7 adapted from Bridgland 1994; Fig. 2.8 photo Danielle Schreve; Fig. 2.9 photo Danielle Schreve; Fig. 2.10 from White 2000, 3, fig. 1; Fig. 2.11 from Wymer 1968, fig. 49 objects 107, 108, 113, 114, with permission; Fig. 2.12 after Hardaker 2001, fig. 19.1; Fig. 2.13 adapted from Gibbard 1985 Cambridge University Press with permission; Fig. 2.14 from White and Plunkett 2004, 108, fig. 7.11; Fig. 2.15 Swanscombe waterhole painting and the Clacton spear © Natural History Museum London, reconstruction of straight-tusked elephant – artwork by Mauricio Anton, Southfleet Road Ebbsfleet elephant under excavation photo Oxford Archaeology © Union Railways (North) Ltd, flint core and handaxe photos F Wenban-Smith © Union Railways (North) Ltd; Fig. 3.1 British Geological Survey; Figs 3.2, 3.3 from Schreve *et al.* 2002; Figs 3.4, 3.5, 3.6 photos Danielle Schreve; Fig. 3.7 from Wymer 1968, fig. 56 nos 123 and 126 and fig. 57 no 129, with permission; Fig. 3.8 adapted from Bridgland 1994; Fig. 3.9 from Roe 1981, 120-1, fig. 4.12 objects a1-3, images © Pitt Rivers Museum Oxford; Fig. 3.10 photos © Natural History Museum London, drawing after Wymer 1968 fig 79 no. 215, with permission; Fig. 3.11 after Wymer 1968 fig 74 no. 203, fig 78 no 214 and plate ix, with permission;

Fig. 3.12 photos N Branch; Fig. 3.13 handaxes from Glasshouse St and Yiewsley © Museum of London, handaxe from Lower Clapton - Bromley Museum Service (Bromley Museum, Orpington) photo C Juby; Fig. 3.14 idealised Levallois core and preparation from Wymer 1999, 9, fig. 3 (1) and (3) with permission Wessex Archaeology, Boeda's Levallois concept modified after Boëda 1995; Fig. 3.15 Sonning Railway Cutting and Creffield Rd from Wymer 1999, 81, fig. 26, 83, fig. 28 with permission Wessex Archaeology; Butt's Hill Pit and Hillingdon Pits after Wymer 1968, fig. 63 no 152 and fig. 85 nos 223-5 and 230, with permission; Fig. 3.16 main image reconstruction by Peter Lorimer Oxford Archaeology; Levallois core and flake from Baker's Hole, Kent © Trustees of the British Museum, Levallois core from Yiewsley, © Museum of London; Fig. 4.1 British Geological Survey; Fig. 4.2 Mark White; Figs 4.3, 4.4 photos Danielle Schreve; Fig. 4.5 © Natural History Museum London; Fig. 4.6 photo Jeff Veitch; Fig. 4.7 Natural History Museum, photo courtesy of Beccy Scott; Fig. 4.8 adapted from Kennard 1944; Fig. 4.9 photo Danielle Schreve; Fig. 4.10 adapted from Scott and Buckingham 1997; Fig. 4.11 Stanton Harcourt from Hardaker 2001 fig. 19.4, Berinsfield from Macrae 1982, figs 1-3, reproduced by permission of the Oxfordshire Architectural and Historical Society; Fig. 4.12 photo Danielle Schreve; Fig. 4.13 Dix Pit Stanton Harcourt information and images courtesy of Kate Scott and Christine Buckingham, the Hanson Mammoth Project; Fig. 5.1 British Geological Survey; Fig. 5.2 from Hardaker 2001, fig. 19.8(a) and 19.9 (a, b); Fig. 5.3 US Fish and Wildlife Service, Tim Bowman; Fig. 5.4 photo Danielle Schreve; Fig. 5.5 from M R Bates, Pleistocene sequences at Norton Farm, Chichester, West Sussex, in J B Murton *et al*. (eds), *The Quaternary of Sussex*, Field Guide. London: Quaternary Research Association, fig. 5.14; Fig. 5.6 Mary Evans Picture Library; Fig. 5.7 adapted from Preece 1999; Fig. 5.8 photo Danielle Schreve; Fig. 5.9 from Trimmer 1813; Fig. 5.10 adapted from Maddy *et al*.,1998, fig 9a; Fig. 5.11 Sarah Lucas Oxford Archaeology; Fig. 6.1 British Geological Survey; Fig. 6.2 after Grootes *et al*., 1993 reprinted by permission Macmillan Publishers Ltd; Fig. 6.3 adapted from Coope *et al*., 1997; Fig. 6.4 Marlow from Wymer 1968, 58, fig. 25, with permission, Coygan Cave from White and Jacobi 2002, 111, fig. 2; Fig. 6.5 background mapping IPR/117-40C British Geological Survey. © NERC 2009. NEXTMap Britain Elevation Data from Intermap Technologies. All rights reserved. Archaeological data after Tyldesley 1987, 19; Fig. 6.6 Ancient Human Occupation of Britain (AHOB) project; Fig. 6.7 reconstruction by Peter Lorimer Oxford Archaeology; Fig. 6.8 flint images courtesy of Roger Jacobi: leaf point, Kent's Cavern Torquay Museum, Joanna Richards; blade points, Kent's Cavern lhs Natural History Museum, rhs Torquay Museum, Joanna Richards; nosed scraper, Kent's Cavern Torquay Museum, Hazel Martingell; busked burin Ffynnon Beuno Cave

Natural History Museum, Hazel Martingell; Gravettian Font Robert point Mildenhall British Museum, Hazel Martingell; Creswell Point Gough's Cave Cheddar Man Museum, Hazel Martingell; Cheddar points Gough's Cave Cheddar Man Museum, Hazel Martingell; Penknife points Risby Warren British Museum Hazel Martingell; backed blade Pin Hole Manchester Museum, Hazel Martingell; Fig. 6.9 *Homo sapiens sapiens and Homo neanderthalensis* skeletal comparisons adapted from C Scarre (ed.) *The Human Past*, London, 2004, 147; Fig. 6.10 burial of the Red Lady of Paviland Amgueddfa Genedlaethol Cymru National Museum of Wales; Fig. 7.1 adapted from Lowe and Walker 1997 fig 7.22, Pearson Education Ltd © Addison Wesley Longman Ltd 1997; Fig. 7.2 all photos © Natural History Museum London; Fig. 7.3 Specimens from Gough's Cave photo © Natural History Museum, modern antelope photo Xavier Bayod, FLIKR; Fig. 7.4 © Surrey County Council (Surrey County Archaeological Unit); Fig. 7.5 from Barclay *et al*. 2003, 54-5, figs 4.11, 4.12 Oxford Archaeology; Fig. 7.6 background image Sarah Lucas Oxford Archaeology, all other images © Surrey County Council (Surrey County Archaeological Unit), Church Lammas text courtesy of Phil Jones, SCAU; Fig. 8.1 background mapping IPR/117-40C British Geological Survey. © NERC 2009. NEXTMap Britain Elevation Data from Intermap Technologies. All rights reserved; Fig. 8.2 Oxford Archaeology; Fig. 8.3 portrait of William Camden National Portrait Gallery, London; Fig. 8.4 John Aubrey, 1665-96, *Monumenta Britannica*; Fig. 8.5: from Plot 1677; Fig. 8.6: from Lambrick 1988. Reproduced by permission Ashmolean Museum, University of Oxford; Fig. 8.7 Rolleston 1884; Fig. 8.8 Thurnham 1860a; Fig. 8.9: English Heritage National Monuments Record; Fig. 8.10: Reproduced by permission Ashmolean Museum, University of Oxford; Fig. 8.11: English Heritage National Monuments Record; Fig. 8.12: Oxford Archaeology; Fig. 8.13 English Heritage National Monuments Record; Fig. 8.14: Google Earth; Fig. 8.15: Data provided courtesy of NERC, ARSF, The Natural Environment Council's Airborne Research and Survey Facility, and processed by Paula Levick; Figs 8.16, 8.17 Oxford Archaeology; Fig. 8.18 mace head Ashmolean Museum, University of Oxford, Atkinson *et al*. 1951; polished flint axe Prehistoric Society, Robertson-Mackay 1987; Carinated and Plain Bowls Benson and Whittle 2007; Grooved Ware Barclay 1999b; Leaf-shaped arrowheads, Decorated Bowl and Collared Urn CBA/Ashmolean Museum, Case and Whittle 1982; flat axe reproduced by kind permission of the Bristol and Gloucestershire Archaeological Society, Needham and Saville 1981; Mesolithic flint: we are grateful to the Society of Antiquaries of Scotland for permission to reproduce the image of the early Mesolithic microliths from Barton and Roberts 2004, fig. 18.2 (© Society of Antiquaries of Scotland); Mesolithic flint Butler 2005; Beakers Clarke 1970; Shafthole Axe

Gerloff 1975; Fig. 8.19 flat axe reproduced by kind permission of the Bristol and Gloucestershire Archaeological Society Needham and Saville 1981; flanged axe reproduced courtesy of Surrey Archaeological Society, Needham 1987; Beaker and early Bronze Age daggers Gerloff 1975; spearheads Ehrenberg 1977; other artefacts: Oxford Archaeology; Fig. 8.20 calibration data from: Reimer, P J, Baillie, M G L, Bard, E, Bayliss, A, Beck, J W, Bertrand, C J H, Blackwell, P G, Buck, C E, Burr, G S, Cutler, K B, Damon, P E, Edwards, R L, Fairbanks, R G, Friedrich, M, Guilderson, T P, Hogg, A G, Hughen, K A, Kromer, B, McCormac, G, Manning, S, Bronk Ramsey, C, Reimer, R W, Remmele, S, Southon, J R, Stuiver, M, Talamo, S, Taylor, F W, van der Plicht, J, and Weyhenmeyer, C E, 2004 IntCal04 terrestrial radiocarbon age calibration, 0-26 cal kyr BP, *Radiocarbon* 46(3), 1029-58. Prepared using OxCal v. 4.1: Bronk Ramsey, C, 2009 Bayesian analysis of radiocarbon dates, *Radiocarbon* 51(1), 337-60; Fig. 9.1 Oxford Archaeology; Fig. 9.2: after D E Anderson, A Goudie, and A Parker, 2007 *Global environments through the Quaternary: exploring environmental change*, by permission of Oxford University Press; Data from the World Data Centre for Paleoclimatology and NOAA Paleoclimatology Program; Fig. 9.3 background mapping IPR/117-40C British Geological Survey. © NERC 2009. NEXTMap Britain Elevation Data from Intermap Technologies. All rights reserved; Fig. 10.1 Early Mesolithic microliths: We are grateful to the Society of Antiquaries of Scotland for permission to reproduce the image of the early Mesolithic microliths from Barton and Roberts 2004, fig. 18.2, © Society of Antiquaries of Scotland; all other artefacts Butler 2005; Fig. 10.2 Oxford Archaeology; Fig. 10.3 Oxford Archaeology; Fig. 10.4 Newbury and District Field Club, J Wymer, 1962, Excavation at Thatcham (second interim report), *Trans Newbury and District Field Club* 11, 2, 41–52; Fig. 10.5 Prehistoric Society, Healy *et al.* 1992; Butler 2005; Fig. 10.6 artist's reconstruction Wymer 1991; bone and antler from Thatcham, Prehistoric Society, Wymer 1962; flint Newbury and District Field Club, Wymer 1958; animal bone Prehistoric Society, Ellis *et al.* 2003; Fig. 10.7 Oxford Archaeology; Fig. 10.8 Newbury and District Field Club Sheridan *et al.* 1967; Fig. 10.9 reproduced by permission of the Oxfordshire Architectural and Historical Society Bradley and Hey 1993, figs 5 and 11-12; Fig. 10.10 Oxford Archaeology; Fig. 10.11 Framework Archaeology; Fig. 10.12 Oxford Archaeology; Fig. 10.13 RCHME Lambrick 1988; reproduced by permission Ashmolean Museum, University of Oxford; Fig. 10.14 Runnymede British Museum, Needham 2000a; reconstructions of tools David 1998; Fig. 10.15 Upper left and centre Wymer 1991; others Oxford Archaeology; Fig. 10.16 English Heritage, after Saville 1990a; Fig. 10.17 Berkshire Archaeological Society Froom 1972; Fig. 10.18 Prehistoric Society, Wymer 1962; Fig. 10.19 reproduced by permission of the Oxfordshire Archi-

tectural and Historical Society, Boismier and Mepham 1995, fig. 3; Fig. 10.20 © Museum of London; Fig. 10.21 Wessex Archaeology, Barnes *et al.* 1997; Fig. 11.1 after Holgate 1988, with additions; Fig. 11.2 © Museum of London; Figs 11.3, 11.4 Oxford Archaeology; Fig. 11.5 Horton reconstruction courtesy of CEMEX UK Materials Ltd and Wessex Archaeology, copyright reserved Wessex Archaeology; Yarnton Oxford Archaeology; Figs 11.6, 11.7 Oxford Archaeology; Fig. 11.8 Hey and Barclay 2007; Horton courtesy of Wessex Archaeology and CEMEX UK Materials Ltd; Fig. 11.9 Benson and Whittle 2007; Fig. 11.10 Benson and Whittle 2007; Fig. 11.11 Wessex Archaeology, courtesy of CEMEX UK Materials Ltd; Figs 11.12, 11.13 Oxford Archaeology; Fig. 11.14 British Museum, courtesy of Stuart Needham; Fig. 11.15 Wessex Archaeology, Butterworth and Lobb 1992; Figs 11.16, 11.17 Oxford Archaeology; Fig. 11.18 British Museum, courtesy of Stuart Needham; Fig. 11.19 Benson and Whittle 2007; Fig. 11.20 reproduced by permission of the Oxfordshire Architectural and Historical Society, Pine and Ford 2003, fig. 3; Figs 11.21, 11.22, 11.23, 11.24 Oxford Archaeology; Fig. 11.25 after Holgate 1988a, with additions; Fig. 11.26 Oxford Archaeology; Fig. 11.27 after Benson and Whittle 2007; Figs 11.28, 11.29, 11.30 Oxford Archaeology; Fig. 12.1 Benson and Whittle 2007; Fig. 12.2 Oxford Archaeology; Fig. 12.3 photos Alistair Barclay; Fig. 12.4 Daniel 1950; Figs 12.5, 12.6 Benson and Whittle 2007; Fig. 12.7: HMSO, Grimes 1960; Fig. 12.8 Smith and Brickley 2006, radiocarbon determinations calibrated using OxCal v4.16; Bronk Ramsey, C, 2009 Bayesian analysis of radiocarbon dates, *Radiocarbon* 51(1), 337-60, with IntCal09; Reimer, P J, Baillie, M G L, Bard, E, Bayliss, A, Beck, J W, Blackwell, P G, Bronk Ramsey, C, Buck, C E, Burr, G S, Edwards, R L, Friedrich, M, Grootes, P M, Guilderson, T P, Hajdas, I, Heaton, T J, Hogg, A G, Hughen, K A, Kaiser, K F, Kromer, B, McCormac, F G, Manning, S W, Reimer, R W, Richards, D A, Southon, J R, Talamo, S, Turney, C S M, van der Plicht, J, and Weyhenmeyer, C E, 2009 IntCal09 and Marine09 radiocarbon age calibration curves, 0-50,000 years cal BP, *Radiocarbon* 51(4), 1111-50; Plan: HMSO Grimes 1960; Fig. 12.9 HMSO, Piggott 1962; Fig. 12.10 British Museum, Kinnes 1992; Fig. 12.11 Berkshire Archaeological Society, Wymer 1965-6; Fig. 12.12 © English Heritage Photo Library; Fig. 12.13 Oxford Archaeology; Fig. 12.14: Prehistoric Society, Bradley 1992; Fig. 12.15 Thames Valley Archaeological Services, Ford and Pine 2003; Fig. 12.16 photo Jeff Wallis, Abingdon Area Archaeological and Historical Society; Fig. 12.17 Prehistoric Society, Whittle *et al.* 1992; Fig. 12.18 Oxford Archaeology; Fig. 12.19 English Heritage National Monuments Record; Fig. 12.20 CBA/Ashmolean Museum, Case and Whittle 1982; Fig. 12.21 reproduced courtesy of Surrey Archaeological Society, Jones 1990; Fig. 12.22 aerial photographs and plans of Sites I and II, Ashmolean Museum, University of Oxford, Atkinson *et al.* 1951; artefacts and burial

Prehistoric Society, Whittle *et al.* 1992; Fig. 12.23 aerial photograph English Heritage National Monuments Record; plan English Heritage, Oswald *et al.* 2001; Fig. 12.24 English Heritage National Monuments Record; Fig. 12.25 Prehistoric Society, Robertson-Mackay 1987; Fig. 12.26 English Heritage, after Oswald *et al.* 2001; Fig. 12.27 English Heritage, Oswald *et al.* 2001; Fig. 12.28 CBA/Ashmolean Museum, Case and Whittle 1982; background map reproduced from the Ordnance Survey on behalf of the controller of Her Majesty's Stationery Office, © Crown Copyright, AL 1000005569; Fig. 12.29 Whittle *et al.* 1999; Fig. 12.30 Oxford Archaeology; Fig. 12.31 Framework Archaeology; Fig. 12.32 aerial photograph Ashmolean Museum, University of Oxford; plan and section CBA/Ashmolean Museum, Case and Whittle 1982; Fig. 12.33 Framework Archaeology; Fig. 12.34 Oxford Archaeology; Fig. 12.35 Prehistoric Society, Whittle *et al.* 1992; Fig. 12.36 Oxford Archaeology; Fig. 12.37 © English Heritage Photo Library; Fig. 12.38 Gillings *et al.* 2008; Fig. 12.39 Mark Fearon Photography, www.pitmatic. com; Fig. 12.40 Oxford Archaeology; Fig. 12.41 Ashmolean Museum, University of Oxford, Atkinson *et al.* 1951; Fig. 12.42 plan Ashmolean Museum, University of Oxford, Atkinson *et al.* 1951; artefacts HMSO, Clarke *et al.* 1985; Fig. 12.43 Gillings *et al.* 2008; Fig. 12.44 Prehistoric Society, Pollard 1992; Fig. 13.1 Oxford Archaeology; Fig. 13.2: after English Heritage Stonehenge World Heritage site website; Figs 13.3, 13.4, 13.5 Oxford Archaeology; Fig. 13.6 © GeoPerspectives; Figs 13.7, 13.8, 13.9 Oxford Archaeology; Fig. 13.10 reproduced by permission of the Buckinghamshire Archaeology Society, Richmond *et al.* 2006; Fig. 13.11 © Museum of London; Figs 14.1, 14.2 Oxford Archaeology; Fig. 14.3 Staines, Prehistoric Society, Robertson-Mackay 1987; Devils's Quoits, Oxford Archaeology; Fig. 14.4 Wayland's Smithy photo Paul Garwood; Windmill Hill English Heritage National Monuments Record; Fig. 14.5 Staines, after Robertson Mackay 1987; Dorchester, after Atkinson *et al.* 1951, Ashmolean Museum, University of Oxford; Fig. 14.6 The Sanctuary, Prehistoric Society, Pollard 1992; others, Oxford Archaeology; Fig. 14.7 Anon; Fig. 14.8: Windmill Hill, after Whittle *et al.* 1999; Eastleach, English Heritage, after Oswald *et al.* 2001; Staines, Prehistoric Society, after Robertson Mackay 1987; Drayton, Oxford Archaeology; Dorchester-on-Thames, Prehistoric Society, after Whittle *et al.* 1992; Avebury, after Gillings *et al.* 2008; the Big Rings, Prehistoric Society, after Whittle *et al.* 1992; Westwell, Condicote and Cutsdean, Oxford Archaeology; West Kennet, after Whittle 1997b; Barrow Hills, Radley, Oxford Archaeology; Figs 14.9, 14.10 Oxford Archaeology; Fig. 14.11 Upper Kennet Valley, after Gillings *et al.* 2008; Drayton-Abingdon-Dorchester area, Oxford Archaeology; Fig. 14.12 Avebury after Gillings *et al.* 2008; Dorchester, Prehistoric Society, after Whittle *et al.* 1992; Fig. 14.13 Oxford Archaeology; Fig. 14.14

photo Gill Hey; Fig. 14.15 Benson and Whittle 2007; Fig. 14.16 Oxford Archaeology; Fig. 14.17 Prehistoric Society, Whittle 1991; Fig. 14.18 after Gillings *et al.* 2008; Fig. 14.19 English Heritage, after Oswald *et al.* 2001; Fig. 14.20 Whittle *et al.* 1999; Fig. 14.21 Framework Archaeology; Fig. 14.22 Oxford Archaeology; reconstruction by Mark Gridley Oxford Archaeology; Fig. 14.23 Standlake, CBA/ Ashmolean, Case and Whittle 1982; Hodcott Down, Berkshire Archaeological Society, Richards 1986-90; Radley Oxford Archaeology; Fig. 14.24 Oxford Archaeology; Fig. 14.25 Ashmolean Museum, University of Oxford; Fig. 14.26 Oxford Archaeology; Fig. 14.27 base plan, Berkshire Archaeological Society, after Case 1956a; additional information Paul Garwood; Fig. 14.28 Oxford Archaeology; Fig. 14.29 reproduced by permission of the Oxfordshire Architectural and Historical Society, after Boston *et al.* 2003, fig. 1 with additions; background map reproduced from the Ordnance Survey on behalf of the controller of Her Majesty's Stationery Office, © Crown Copyright, AL 1000005569; Fig. 14.30 aerial photograph, Ashmoean Museum University of Oxford; Plan, CBA/ Ashmoleam Museum, Case and Whittle 1982; Figs 14.31, 14.32 Oxford Archaeology; Fig. 14.33 courtesy of Museum of London Archaeology; Fig. 14.34: Dorchester, Ashmolean Museum University of Oxford, Atkinson *et al.* 1951; Barrow Hills, Radley, Oxford Archaeology; Fig. 14.35: skull, Oxford Archaeology; mace heads, Smith 1918; all other artefacts © Museum of London; Figs 14.36, 14.37,14.38 Oxford Archaeology; Fig. 15.1 Ascott-under-Wychwood, Benson and Whittle 2007; Wayland's Smithy, Prehistoric Society, Whittle 1991; Hazleton North, English Heritage, Saville 1990a; West Kennett, HMSO, Piggott, S, 1962 *The West Kennet long barrow: excavations, 1955-56*, London; Fig. 15.2 Windmill Hill, Whittle *et al.* 1999; Shepperton, Jones 2008; Radley and Eton, Oxford Archaeology; Fig. 15.3 Whittle *et al.* 1999; Fig. 15.4 Oxford Archaeology; Fig. 15.5 Linch Hill Corner, reproduced by permission of the Oxfordshire Architectural and Historical Society, after Grimes 1943-4, fig. 14; Newnham Murren, CBA/ Ashmolean Museum, after Moorey 1982; Radley and Mount Farm, Oxford Archaeology; Fig. 15.6 Linch Hill Corner, reproduced by permission of the Oxfordshire Architectural and Historical Society, Grimes 1943-4, fig. 15; Barrow Hills, Radley, Oxford Archaeology; Fig. 15.7: Prehistoric Society, A Barclay, N Beavan, P Bradley, G Chaffey, D Challinor, J I McKinley, A Powell and P Marshall, 2009 *Past*, 4; Fig. 15.8 Oxford Archaeology; Fig. 15.9 Hemp Knoll, Prehistoric Society, after Robertson-Mackay 1980; Radley, Stanton Harcourt, Yarnton, Oxford Archaeology; West Overton, Prehistoric Society, after Smith and Simpson 1966; Dorchester, Prehistoric Society, after Whittle *et al.* 1992; Winterbourne Monkton, Wiltshire Archaeological and Natural History Society, after Pollard 1994; Fig. 15.10 West Overton, Prehistoric Society, Smith and

Simpson 1966; Hemp Knoll, Prehistoric Society, Robertson-Mackay 1980; Yarnton and Stanton Harcourt, Oxford Archaeology; Stanton Harcourt, Clarke 1970; Fig. 15.11, Oxford Centre for Gene Function, reproduced by permission of the Oxfordshire Architectural and Historical Society, after Boston *et al.* 2003, fig. 5; Mount Farm and Gravelly Guy, Oxford Archaeology; Fig. 15.12: Hemp Knoll, Prehistoric Society, after Robertson-Mackay 1980; Lambourn, Berkshire Archaeological Society, after Case 1956a; West Overton, Prehistoric Society, Smith and Simpson 1966; Radley, Oxford Archaeology; Fig. 15.13 Oxford Archaeology; Fig. 15.14 Dorchester, Prehistoric Society, after Whittle *et al.* 1992; Linch Hill Corner, reproduced by permission of the Oxfordshire Architectural and Historical Society, after Grimes 1943-4, figs 14 and 17; Fig. 15.15 Lambourn, Berkshire Archaeological Society, after Case 1956a; Gravelly Guy, Oxford Archaeology; Fig. 15.16 Prehistoric Society, Smith and Simpson 1966; Fig. 15.17 Oxford Archaeology; Fig. 15.18 Shorncote, reproduced by kind permission of the Bristol and Gloucestershire Archaeological Society, Barclay and Glass 1995; Radley Oxford Archaeology; Fig. 15.19 Eynsham, Case 1977; Cassington, reproduced by kind permission of the Society of Antiquaries of London from the *Antiquaries Journal*, Recent Bronze Age discoveries in Berkshire and Oxfordshire, E T Leeds, 1934 ©; Fig. 15.20 Oxford Archaeology; Fig. 15.21: Field Farm, Wessex Archaeology, Butterworth and Lobb 1992; City Farm, reproduced by permission of the Oxfordshire Architectural and Historical Society, Case *et al.* 1964-5, fig. 5; Burn Ground, HMSO, Grimes 1960; Radley, Oxford Archaeology; Figs 15.22, 15.23 Oxford Archaeology; Fig. 15.24 artefacts, Wiltshire Archaeological and Natural History Society (©Wiltshire Heritage Museum, Devizes); burial, Cunnington 1907; Fig. 15.25 Hodcott Down, Berkshire Archaeological Society, after Richards 1986-90; Stanton Harcourt, Oxford Archaeology; Fig. 15.26 Stanton Harcourt and Radley, Oxford Archaeology; Snowshill, Gerloff 1975; Fig. 15.27 Field Farm, Wessex Archaeology, Butterworth and Lobb 1992; Aldbourne, British Museum, Kinnes and Longworth 1985; Fig. 16.1 Ros Lorimer Oxford Archaeology; Fig. 16.2 HMSO, Clarke *et al.* 1985; Fig. 16.3: Manton artefacts, Wiltshire Archaeological and Natural History Society (©Wiltshire Heritage Museum, Devizes); Yarnton and Radley, HMSO, Clarke *et al.* 1985; Gravelly Guy, Oxford Archaeology; Fig. 16.4 Oxford Archaeology; Fig. 16.5 Wiltshire Archaeological and Natural History Society (©Wiltshire Heritage Museum, Devizes); Fig. 16.6 © Museum of London; Fig. 16.7 photos, Alistair Barclay Oxford Archaeology; lower right, Michael Dudley Ashmolean Museum, University of Oxford; Figs 16.8, 16.9 Oxford Archaeology; Fig. 16.10 Ascott-under-Wychwood, Benson and Whittle 2007; Oxford Centre for Gene Function, reproduced by permission of the Oxfordshire Architectural and Historical Society, Boston *et al* 2003, fig. 5; Radley, Oxford Archaeology; Fig. 16.11 Gerloff 1975; Fig. 16.12 Chelsea 'club', © Museum of London; Horton bark container, Thames Valley Archaeological Services, Pine and Preston 2004; Yarnton, Oxford Archaeology; Dagenham idol, Colchester Castle Museum (Colchester and Ipswich Museum Service); Fig. 16.13 Oxford Archaeology; Fig. 16.14 Ascott-under-Wychwood, Benson and Whittle 2007; Abingdon, reproduced by kind permission of the Society of Antiquaries of London from the *Antiquaries Journal*, A Neolithic site at Abingdon, Berks (second report), E T Leeds, 1928 ©; Fig. 16.15 Pierowall, we are grateful to the Society of Antiquaries of Scotland for permission to reproduce the image of the decorated stone from Pierowall, from N Sharples, 1984 Excavations at Pierowall Quarry, Westray, Orkney, *Proceedings of the Society of Antiquaries of Scotland*, vol. 114, illus. 28 (© Society of Antiquaries of Scotland); Knowth, Royal Society of Antiquaries of Ireland, Eogan and Richardson 1982; Barrow Hills, Radley, Oxford Archaeology; Fig. 16.16 reproduced by kind permission of the Bristol and Gloucestershire Archaeological Society, Needham and Saville 1981.

Chapter 1 – Introduction and the Pre-Anglian geological, palaeoenvironmental and archaeological records

by Anthony Morigi, Danielle Schreve and Mark White

The importance of the river Thames to English culture and history imparts to it an impression of permanence and timelessness: throughout the tumultuous events of our history it has appeared constant, changeless. Indeed, it seems possible that the river has an ancestry that stretches as far back as the Palaeocene epoch some 55 million years ago (Gibbard 2003), though for much of that time the traces are few and the evidence scant. In contrast, the river has left in the landscape and its deposits of the last 2 million years or so a wealth of evidence that shows that, far from being changeless, it has constantly altered its character, extent and course; on occasions dramatically so. It is this period of the history of the river Thames and its relationship to changing climate, fauna, flora and human occupation that is the subject of this volume.

CHRONOSTRATIGRAPHY (Fig. 1.1; Table 1.1)

Post-war ideas on the nature of the Quaternary succession in Britain culminated in 1973 in a chronostratigraphical scheme proposed by the Geological Society of London (Mitchell *et al.* 1973). The scheme adopted palaeobotanical interpretations of temperate deposits and, together with geological evidence for the deposition of other sediments under extremely

Table 1.1: Former chronostratigraphical scheme for the subdivision of British Pleistocene glacials and interglacials (after Mitchell et al. 1973; West 1980a; Zalasiewicz and Gibbard 1988 and Gibbard et al. 1991)

Holocene (= Flandrian, UK only)	
Devensian	
Ipswichian	
Wolstonian	
Hoxnian	
Anglian	
Cromerian	
	HIATUS
Beestonian	
	HIATUS
Pastonian	
Pre-Pastonian d	
Pre-Pastonian c	
Pre-Pastonian b	
	HIATUS
Pre-Pastonian a	
	HIATUS
Baventian	

cold or even glacial conditions, proposed a subdivision of the Pleistocene based on climate change. Although now mostly superseded, the scheme highlighted the contemporary need for a standardisation of glacial and interglacial stages and was to shape the development of Pleistocene studies in Britain for the next decade. Only four interglacials were recognised by Mitchell *et al.* (1973) in the Middle and Late Pleistocene (in descending age order): the Pastonian, Cromerian, Hoxnian and Ipswichian, interspersed by evidence for cold 'stages' (Table 1.1). West (1980a) later added the Pre-Pastonian a-d. It is clear from comparisons with the continental record that the British Early and early Middle Pleistocene contain several important hiatuses (Zalasiewicz and Gibbard 1988; Gibbard *et al.* 1991).

However, the 1973 scheme was never intended to be immutable and flaws rapidly began to appear. The fragmentary nature of the terrestrial stratigraphical evidence and the lack of adequate type sites resulted in considerable problems when comparing and correlating widely separated deposits that usually contained only partial pollen sequences (or in some cases, none at all). These deficiencies led to a serious lack of precision within the formal chronostratigraphic record, which was complicated still further by the increasing recognition that additional warm and cold-climate episodes were present that were not formally named. In particular, the evidence from fossil mammals revealed the possibility that more interglacials were present than the pollen record had allowed (Sutcliffe, 1975; Sutcliffe and Kowalski, 1976). Today, the stratigraphical evidence obtained from deep sea cores is widely used as a yardstick to define the Pleistocene succession (Shackleton and Opdyke, 1973; Hays *et al.*, 1976) and as many as 19 individual warm and cold stages are recorded back to the Brunhes-Matuyama palaeomagnetic boundary at 780 ka (Fig. 1.1). The recognition that there have been considerably more climatic fluctuations during the Pleistocene has therefore provided much greater flexibility in the interpretation of the British stratigraphical record (Fig. 1.2).

NORTH-WESTERN EUROPEAN SETTING OF THE RIVER THAMES SYSTEM (Figs 1.3-1.7)

The history and development of the Thames and its ancestors bear a broad similarity to many of the great rivers of north-western Europe although in detail there are significant differences. Gibbard

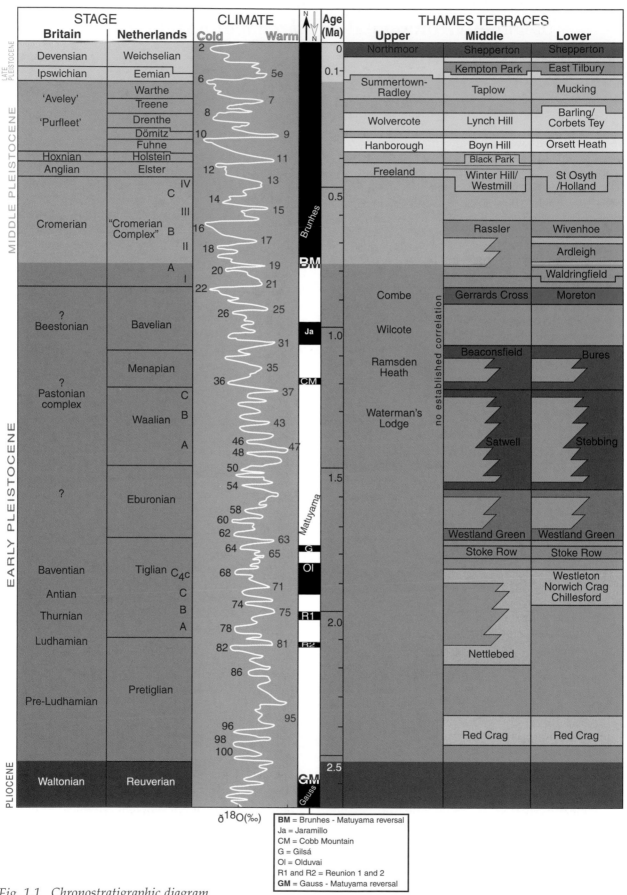

Fig. 1.1   Chronostratigraphic diagram

(1988) reviewed the Late Pliocene and Pleistocene history of these rivers and much of this section, with additions, follows his account. During the late Pliocene to early Pleistocene a land bridge existed across the straits of Dover. North of this bridge the southern North Sea occupied much of East Anglia and the London Basin to the west and most of the Netherlands to the east. The ancient Thames, the Bytham River that drained central and eastern England, the Rhine-Meuse (or Maas) systems and a so-called Baltic River system that flowed westward from the eastern Fennoscandian Shield and Baltic Platform across northern Germany and the north east Netherlands all debouched into the southern North Sea Basin (Figs 1.3, 1.4). These large and vigorous braided river systems developed in response to the onset of glaciation in northern latitudes that was triggered by a marked cooling of the global climate about 2.6 Ma ago (Fig. 1.5). The rivers deposited extensive terrestrial sequences and built large deltas out into the southern North Sea Basin, where contemporaneous marine sediments include the Red and Norwich Crag Formations of East Anglia and their equivalents throughout the basin.

By the Middle Pleistocene (Fig. 1.6) the Baltic River system appears to have waned and deposition was dominated by the Meuse, Rhine and other north German rivers, with continuing input from the Thames and Bytham River. At this time due to a lowering of sea level the coast lay far to the north of its early Pleistocene position and the area formerly occupied by the southern North Sea Basin was emergent. Drainage was still predominantly to the north, however. By the onset of the Anglian glaciation (Elsterian in Europe) an ice sheet filled much of the North Sea area while a large proglacial lake occupied the southern North Sea Basin (Fig. 1.7). This glaciation destroyed the Bytham River and either diverted or destroyed some north German river systems, but the Rhine-Meuse, Scheldt and Thames continued to discharge into the lake. There has been much debate about the mechanism and timing of such an event but there appears to be general agreement that the proglacial lake later overflowed, incising a channel through the land bridge at the Dover Straits (Smith, 1989; Bridgland and D'Olier, 1995; Gibbard, 1995a; 2007; Ashton and Lewis, 2002; Gupta *et al*. 2007) and draining to the south-west through a postulated Channel River system. Subsequent sea level variation notwithstanding, this general pattern appears to have been maintained throughout the remainder of the Pleistocene until rising sea level after the last glacial maximum (LGM) resulted in the current geographic configuration. Gibbard (1988) has suggested that the formation of the Dover Straits may have been polycyclic with repeated episodes of marine erosion during marine transgression and fluvial dissection during periods of low sea level.

TOPOGRAPHY AND GEOLOGY OF THE THAMES CATCHMENT: AN OVERVIEW
(Figs 1.8, 1.9)

The distribution and composition of the deposits of the river Thames are closely related to the nature and structure of the bedrock of southern England. The catchment of the present-day river Thames drains a region that is underlain by gently south-eastward dipping Mesozoic and Cenozoic strata (Fig. 1.8). In the west, the Thames rises near the Cotswold Hills, formed largely of Jurassic limestone, and is fed by tributaries that flow down the dip slope of the Cotswolds. As the river meanders eastwards across a low-lying Oxford Clay vale it is flanked by broad spreads of river terrace deposits (Fig. 1.9) before traversing the more resistant Cretaceous Chalk Group of the Chilterns via the narrow, almost gorge-like, Goring Gap. This topographic feature has been a significant factor in the evolution of the Thames and its terraces as it forms a natural constriction that divides the Upper from the Middle Thames. On exiting the Goring Gap the river once again crosses a low-lying vale, here underlain by the soft sands and clays of the Palaeogene Lambeth and Thames Groups that occupy a broad, shallow syncline known as the London Basin.

Extensive river terrace deposits again flank the river and its tributaries, which flow from the Chalk uplands of the Chilterns, Berkshire Downs, the North Downs and the Weald beyond them (Fig. 1.9). The gravels of the younger river terrace deposits that lie above the Goring Gap are composed mainly of limestone derived from the Cotswolds while downstream from the Gap their principal component is durable flint from the Chalk Group. However, the presence in the gravels of many of the older river terrace deposits of relatively large proportions of far-travelled rocks, such as quartzite, quartz and acid volcanic rocks, with a provenance beyond the present catchment, attests to the existence of a more extensive catchment earlier in the history of the river Thames.

An overview of the river terrace deposits of the Thames (Figs 1.10, 1.11)

The river terrace deposits of the Thames form a staircase of bench-like features rising up the valley sides above the present floodplain. Each terrace is underlain mainly by sand and gravel deposits typically between 3 m and 7 m thick but very rarely over 20 m thick. In the Thames Valley there are about 18 different terraces along the pre-Anglian course of the ancient Thames, although they are not all present in any one section of the river valley. The best preserved flight or staircase of terraces is in the Middle Thames between

Fig. 1.2 (overleaf)   Climate change and dating

Climate Change and Dating

Sources of evidence

It is now known that the last 2.6 million years have been a period of climatic instability. A long sequence of alternating cold and warm climate episodes have been identified in which the earth many times moved from the ferocious cold and aridity of glaciations to the warm, temperate conditions of interglacials, and back again. A range of sources of evidence are used by scientists to identify, characterise and date these events. Some of those most relevant to the present volume are described here.

Deep Sea Cores — Oxygen Isotopes

Oxygen isotope ($^{18}O/^{16}O$) ratios preserved in the shells of very small protozoa known as foraminifera from Pacific deep sea bed cores show variations throughout the depth of the cores. These oxygen isotope ratios reflect those of oceanic water during the lifetimes of the organisms. 'Light' water, $H_2^{16}O$, evaporates more easily than 'heavy' water, $H_2^{18}O$. During glaciations evaporation of seawater increases and as it condenses and falls as snow in higher latitudes, it supports the growth of ice sheets. As a result, the remaining sea water, which is at its lowest level at glacial maximums, is 'enriched' in ^{18}O and so its $^{18}O/^{16}O$ ratio increases. The melting of the ice sheets during the subsequent interglacial returns the 'light' water to the ocean decreasing its $^{18}O/^{16}O$ ratio. The record of oxygen isotope variation in deep sea cores is thus an indirect indicator (or 'proxy') for ice volume and climate change through time. The variation of $^{18}O/^{16}O$ ratios is usually expressed as the change, $\delta^{18}O$, relative to a standard ratio and shown graphically to produce a 'climate curve'.

* Right - Scanning electron micrograph image of the foram Globorotalia menardii

* Facing page - Pollen of Scots pine (Pinus sylvestris), *actual size 76 microns across*

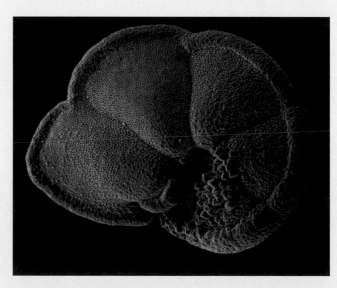

Periods of relatively low or high $\delta^{18}O$, respectively representing warm or cold climate episodes, have been assigned to Marine Oxygen Isotope Stages (MIS). Over 100 such stages numbered from the present MIS 1 to the oldest MIS 100 and higher, have been identified in deep sea cores covering the last 2.6 million years, including up to 50 cold/temperate cycles (see Fig. 1.1).

Climate Change and Dating
Ice Cores

Deep sea sediment cores provide evidence for warm/cold climatic fluctuations over the last 2.6 million years. On land, a similar record, of shorter timespan but greater resolution, is provided by cores drilled through layers of snow and ice that have accumulated as ice sheets and glaciers at the poles and in high mountain regions. In the northern hemisphere the most important records come from Greenland, where two ice cores known as GRIP and GISP2 have been drilled down to depths of over 3 km.

Many important indirect (or 'proxy') indicators of past climate are preserved in the compacted snow and ice. Changing ratios of heavier and lighter oxygen and hydrogen isotopes are a key indicator of changing global temperatures. Dust particles provide information about past wind strength and aridity. Chemical analysis identifies change in the relative acidity or alkalinity of the ice over time. Air bubbles in the ice contain trapped atmospheric gases, showing us the changing proportions of 'greenhouse' gases such as carbon dioxide and methane in past atmospheres.

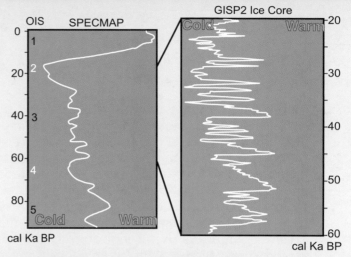

The climate curve from deep sea cores (left) compared with the high resolution record of rapid climatic variation seen in the Greenland ice cores (right)

Because the ice sheets form layer by layer with each passing year, they provide a very high resolution image of climate change over short periods of hundreds or even tens of years. The ice cores provide key information for a very unstable climate during the course of the last 120 000 years, with rapid swings between warmer and colder conditions over very short periods of time.

Pollen

Pollen analysis, or palynology, is one of the most powerful methods used by archaeologists and Quaternary scientists to aid reconstruction of past environments. Pollen grains and spores are dispersed in vast quantities by wind and can also be carried by water, insects, birds and animals. Although tiny (mostly between 20 and 40 microns in size) they have an exine, or outer layer, which is extremely tough and so are often preserved in sediments, especially peat and lake deposits. Following their recovery from sediment samples using a variety of laboratory separation techniques, pollen grains are examined under the microscope. The size and shape of pollen grains and spores are characteristic of the plants that produced them and can generally be identified to genus level. Under the microscope the pollens are counted in order to establish the relative proportions of different taxa represented in the sample. This mixture of pollen, which may reflect the vegetation present at that location and time, is termed the pollen assemblage or pollen spectrum. Employing the

principle that the present is the key to the past, comparing the results of analyses of fossil pollen to the present-day distribution of vegetation gives an indication of the environments prevailing at the time the pollen-bearing sediments were deposited.

When pollen grains and spores yielded by samples from a stratigraphic sequence are analysed in this way, different pollen assemblages at various levels may be interpreted as indicating changes in vegetation, environment and climate through time. The variation in pollen assemblages is often expressed graphically as a pollen diagram, one type of which is shown in Figure 2.13 of this volume. Such diagrams are commonly divided into groupings of characteristic pollen types known as pollen zones. An individual pollen diagram may be divided into local assemblage zones, while a number of pollen diagrams for regionally disposed stratigraphic sequences of the same age may be compared in order to establish regional pollen assemblage zones.

Figure 1.2

Palaeoecology

The fossil remains of mammals, birds, fish, snails and insects preserved in ancient sediments also provide key evidence for past climatic stages. Different types of animals inhabit very different environments, and the species represented in ancient assemblages provide an indirect ('proxy') indicator of the conditions prevailing at the time they were alive. Mammals, as warm-blooded organisms, are less useful indicators of prevailing temperatures than reptiles or amphibians but can nevertheless reveal significant aspects of the local environment. For example, species of temperate deciduous or mixed woodland such as fallow deer and straight-tusked elephant, and open grassland such as horse and narrow-nosed rhinoceros, were found at Swanscombe in Kent and are evidence for a fully temperate stage known as the Hoxnian Interglacial (Chapter 2). By contrast, the cold-adapted species woolly mammoth, woolly rhinoceros and reindeer found at Lynford in Norfolk indicate a cold, treeless and grassland-dominated environment during the Middle Devensian (Chapter 6).

Although rare as fossils, birds can provide useful insights into local environmental conditions depending on the species represented, whereas remains of fish can shed light on the depth, flow and level of oxygenation of rivers and lakes. The presence of 'exotic' snails, which may today be found as far afield as northern Scandinavia or the Mediterranean, is significant for interpreting past climatic change, as well as charting variation in vegetation and aquatic characteristics (woodland, grassland, marsh, flowing water etc). However, it is fossil beetles that provide arguably some of the best indications of past climatic and vegetational conditions because many species are closely tied to particular temperature regimes or certain plants. Since most species of beetles that appear in Britain during the Pleistocene are still living, their present-day habitat requirements can be compiled in a Mutual Climatic Range reconstruction, thereby allowing mean maximum and minimum temperatures to be generated for the warmest and coldest months.

Biostratigraphy

The species represented in mammalian and snail assemblages in particular also change over time, as species evolve, become extinct or appear and disappear in the British record. Both the overall composition of the assemblage and the evidence from individual species or lineages is significant, in particular evolutionary trends through time. Two of the best-studied cases of evolutionary trends occur in the water vole and mammoth lineages, where change through time in response to environmental fluctuations is clearly apparent in the teeth of these animals. By studying assemblages found in stratified sediments, whose relative ages are clear from the sequence in which they were laid down, researchers have been able to identify groups characteristic of different climatic stages. These are known as Assemblage-Zones and they have played an important role in identifying previously unrecognised climatic stages in the terrace sequences of the Thames Valley and elsewhere.

More than 1000 bones of a distinctive small form of mammoth known as Mammuthus cf. trogontherii were excavated at Dix Pit, Stanton Harcourt

The Earth's magnetic field is known to have reversed its polarity many times during Earth history. The cause of these polarity reversals is poorly understood (and is beyond the scope of this account) but is thought to be related to flow in the iron-rich liquid outer core of the Earth and its interaction with the solid core.

Ferromagnetic particles in sedimentary or volcanic rocks may be aligned to the Earth's magnetic field during deposition or on cooling, rather like tiny magnetic compasses that have become fixed in time. Thus a record of polarity reversals is preserved in the rocks. This magnetic property, known as permanent remanent magnetism, can be measured and the rock's 'fossil' polarity determined.

Polarity reversals have occurred about four times every million years in the last ten million years although there have been much longer periods in Earth's history when there were no reversals. There is no periodicity to the reversals so their frequency and duration is unpredictable. The time taken for a reversal to occur is thought to be only about 5, 000 to 10,000 years. Long periods during which one polarity was dominant are termed Polarity Epochs, or 'Chrons', while shorter periods of less than 100, 000 years are known as Polarity Events, or 'Subchrons'. Periods are said to have 'normal' polarity if the prevailing magnetic field was aligned towards the present geographic North Pole, as it is now, or 'reverse' polarity if it was towards the South Pole.

Observations of polarity reversals of the Earth's magnetic field recorded in rocks dated by independent methods (e.g. radiometric dating, biostratigraphy) have enabled the construction of a Geomagnetic Polarity Timescale (right). By convention epochs - 'Chrons' - and events -'Subchrons' - are named (the present normal polarity epoch is known as the 'Brunhes Chron' after the French geophysicist Bernard Brunhes): normal polarities are coloured black on the timescale and reverse polarities are white.

'Fossil' polarities identified in rocks and sedimentary sequences can be related to the Geomagnetic Polarity Timescale and this has proved an extremely useful tool in determining their age.

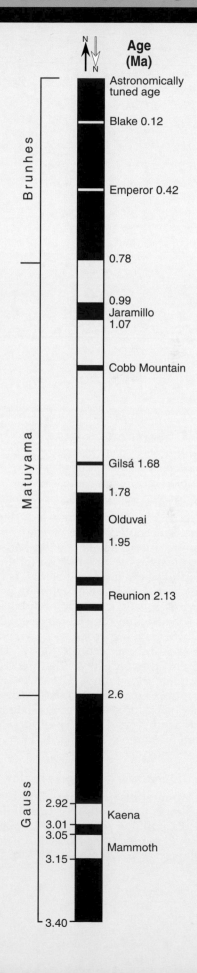

Figure 1.2

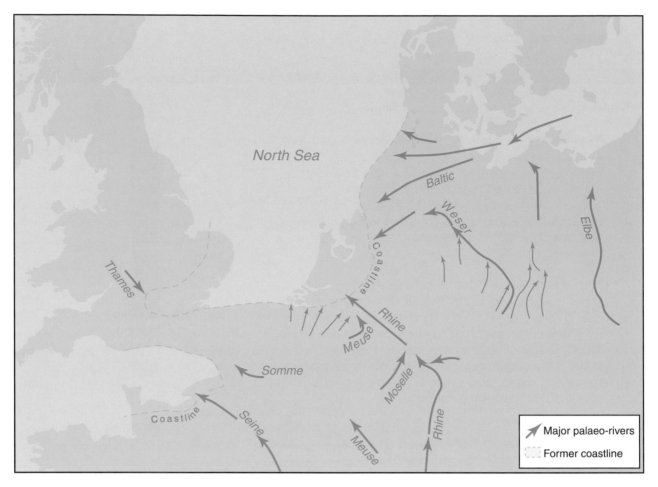

Fig. 1.3   The palaeogeography of the 'North Sea' and main rivers during the early Pleistocene, c 2.5 million years ago. This is a schematic reconstruction of the main river systems of the region at the start of the long period of extreme climatic fluctuations known as the Pleistocene

Reading and Rickmansworth where up to 13 terraces have been recognised (Fig. 1.10). It is generally accepted that extreme climatic change – glacial to interglacial – is the driving force for terrace formation and that simultaneous progressive uplift of the land (see below) is necessary for a staircase of terraces to develop. In essence they are the remnants of former floodplains of the river abandoned when the river incised, or eroded, to a new lower level, a process known as rejuvenation. Thus the highest terraces (above the floodplain) represent the oldest of the deposits while the lowest are the youngest. However, such a bald description belies the potential for complexity of the deposits: in order to appreciate this it is necessary to understand how river terrace deposits are formed (see below and Fig. 1.11).

Climatic controls on Thames terrace formation

Development of the Thames terraces was initiated in response to a cooling of the climate that began about 2.6 million years ago. Although the Thames river system may have existed for as long as 2.2 Ma (Westaway *et al.*, 2002), the bulk of fluvial deposi-

tion and terrace formation has occurred in the last 1.81 Ma (Rose *et al.*, 1999). During this period there were over 30 cold-warm cycles in the global climate and at least 12 glacial episodes that directly influenced fluvial deposition in the Thames river system (eg McGregor and Green, 1978; Hey, 1980, 1991; Green *et al.* 1982; Bowen *et al.*, 1986; Rose *et al.*, 1999). Until relatively recently it was assumed that river terrace deposition, a process known as 'aggradation', happened as one event and in one temperate climate episode (stage). This was because fossil temperate fauna and flora were often found seemingly in the gravel. It is now widely accepted, following the work of Bridgland (1996; 2000) that gravel aggradations occur mainly under cold, periglacial conditions and that river terrace deposits form over multiple climatic stages. Fossiliferous deposits that were laid down during periods of temperate climate between gravel aggradations, are largely silt, clay and peat that are preserved, if at all, as beds or channel-fill within the terrace structure (see Fig. 1.11). Bones of temperate climate animals have been found within the gravel units themselves but this apparent contradiction is explained by reworking from

8

older temperate deposits. The terrace gravels contain evidence of the periglacial conditions that prevailed during their deposition, such as cryoturbation, ice-wedge casts, frost-shattered pebbles (Gibbard, 1985), and cold-climate snails (Briggs and Gilbertson, 1973).

Under periglacial conditions the availability of large volumes of meltwater and sediment, coupled with a lack of vegetation that otherwise may reduce river flow, leads to the formation of wide, shallow and fast-flowing, braided rivers. Braided, in this context, means rivers in which the flow diverges and rejoins around ephemeral bars on a scale of the order of channel width (Reading, 1978). The Denali River in Alaska is a modern example of this type of river. Sand and gravel are the principal deposits of such rivers with the sediments exhibiting an assemblage of characteristic features that aid in their

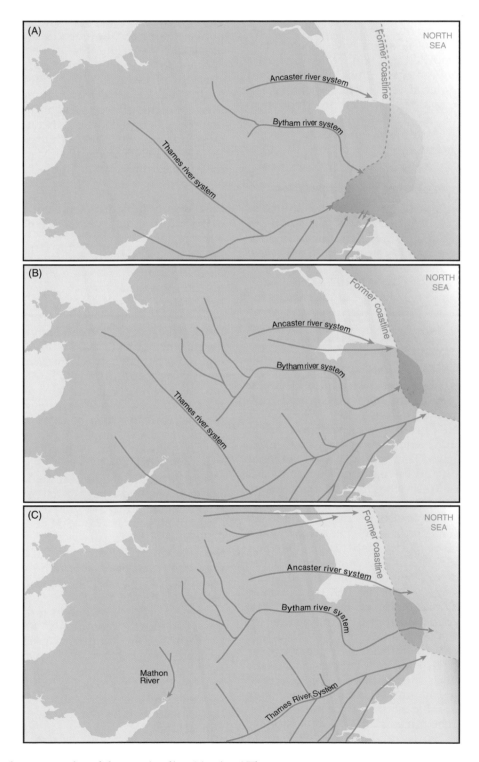

Fig. 1.4 The palaeogeography of the pre-Anglian 'Ancient' Thames

recognition: these include lenses of sand and gravel with erosional bases, imbrication of the gravel, commonly planar-bedding but sometimes cross-bedding, reactivation surfaces, ripple cross-lamination, and silt and clay channel fill remnants (Reading, 1978). The sand and gravel beds that underlie the terraces of the Thames were deposited in this way. During interglacials, or warm climatic episodes, rivers are generally slow flowing and muddy with a single meandering channel, just as the Thames is at the present time. This interaction of climate and sedimentation has resulted in terrace deposits in which the remnants of silt- and clay-filled channels deposited in a temperate climate are 'sandwiched' between two units of gravel laid down under periglacial conditions (see Fig. 1.11). Throughout this volume, detailed information is presented on the relationship between climate change and the formation of specific terrace deposits of the Thames.

Tectonic controls on Thames terrace formation

During the last 3 million years the south of England has been uplifted while the southern North Sea Basin has subsided. The hinge line for this tilt lies along a roughly north-south axis close to the present coast of Suffolk and Essex (Rose *et al.*, 1999). The rate of uplift has been calculated at an average of around 0.07 m ka[-1] in the west of the region (eg Maddy, 1997) while over the same period the southern North Sea basin has subsided at an average rate of 0.15 m per thousand years. This pattern of uplift and tilting has been a major factor in the formation of the terraces. Rates of uplift have varied along the course of the Thames: uplift history modelled at five sites located from west to east along the Thames valley (Westaway *et al.* 2002) indicated a gradual westward increase in average rate of uplift contrasting with slow subsidence at the coast. The rate of uplift has not remained constant and the pattern of uplift at each of the sites differs. Westaway *et al.* (2002) modelled, for example, net uplift at Reading in the order of 128 m between 3.0 to 1.9 Ma, 79 m from 1.9 to 0.9 Ma, and 58 m from 0.9 Ma to the present, whilst in East Suffolk it was respectively between -45 m and -95 m, -10 m and +90 m. The cause of uplift has been attributed to orogenic movements and erosion driven isostacy (Maddy, 1997) or the onset of upland glaciation in mainland Europe at 3.1 Ma, followed by cyclic loading by continental ice sheets from about 0.87 Ma (Westaway *et al.*, 2002). A general southward shifting of its course over time is a characteristic of the Thames and is the result of tilt towards the south-east. The effects of tilting are particularly marked in Suffolk and Essex where the progressive southward course of the early Thames can be traced in the pre-diversionary terrace deposits. The southward shift appears to have resumed in the Lower Thames after diversion (see Figs 3.1, 4.1, 5.1, 6.1)).

Nomenclature of the river terrace deposits

Traditionally the Thames terraces have been grouped according to whether they are located in the Upper, Middle or Lower Thames, with a different nomenclature for each sector (see Fig. 1.1). The Upper and Middle Thames terraces, which are the focus of this volume, are separated by the Goring Gap. The lack of continuity through the Gap has posed difficulties of correlation and, although there have been many attempts, complete agreement has still yet to be achieved. The development of a nomenclature for the terraces has been somewhat haphazard reflecting the tendency of many past authors to conduct their research within limited stretches of the river, often defined by the Upper, Middle and Lower sectors. In recent years there have been concerted efforts to establish cross-sector correlations (e.g. Bridgland, 1994) and catchment-wide classifications (Hey, 1986; Whiteman and Rose, 1992; Rose *et al.*, 1999; Bowen, 1999; Macmillan *et al.*, 2006): these are summarised in Figure 1.1.

Palaeogeography of the ancient Thames and the distribution of its river terrace deposits

The extent of the Thames catchment has varied greatly through this period (see Fig. 1.4). At times it has been limited to an area similar in extent to that of the present river: at others it extended its headwaters beyond the Cotswold Hills into the West Midlands and possibly as far as North Wales. In its earliest evolution the Thames discharged into the sea near the Essex/Hertfordshire border (see Fig. 1.4A) but later, as relative sea levels fell and the coast moved eastward, it followed it over the older marine sediments (see Fig. 1.4B). Upstream the main drainage was south-eastward through Goring. Downstream the river took an east-north-easterly course, some distance to the north of Reading, through Marlow and Watford and on through the Vale of St Albans to Essex and Suffolk.

The earliest unequivocal evidence for the river Thames is a deposit of sand and gravel at Nettlebed, Buckinghamshire. This deposit lies high in the Chiltern Hills at an elevation of about 206 m above OD and about 150 m above the present floodplain of the Thames. Westaway *et al.* (2002) have suggested that the Nettlebed Formation was deposited between MIS 82 and 68, indicating an age range between 2.2 and 1.85 Ma (see Figs 1.1, 1.9).

These high-level sediments form part of a suite of gravel deposits (commonly known as 'Pebble Gravel') that are comprised predominantly of the rounded flint pebbles that typically make up the Palaeogene pebble beds. Pebble Gravel of fluvial origin, such as that found at Nettlebed, is preserved north of the Vale of St Albans, where it forms the highest elements of the Thames terrace 'staircase'. Pebble Gravel is also known to cap the hills in north

Fig. 1.5 (facing page)   Climate change and sea level

Orbital forcing and Milankovitch Cycles

It is generally accepted that changes in the Earth's orbit and axis are the principal causes of Quaternary climate change: this process is known as Orbital Forcing.

An astronomical theory usually credited to Milutin Milankovitch, a Serbian mathematician of the early 20th century, relates climate change to variations in the amount of solar radiation received on the earth's surface (insolation) resulting from cyclic changes in the Earth's orbit and axis. Milankovitch identified three main periodic cycles: eccentricity, a 100 ka cycle due to the predictable change of the Earth's orbit from near circular to slightly elliptical (about 5%) and back; obliquity, a 41 ka cycle caused by changes in the tilt (through 2.4°) of the Earth's axis relative to the Plane of the Ecliptic; and precession, a 21 ka cycle due to the Earth slowly wobbling as it spins on its axis causing a change in direction of the Earth's axis of rotation relative to the sun at perihelion and aphelion. It is not the total radiation received by the Earth that is significant but the changes in amount and location that affect seasonality.

It was not until the much later work on oxygen isotopes in deep-sea sediments that the validity of Milankovitch's theory was recognised. A time series curve derived from a combination of the three cycles shows a remarkable similarity to oxygen isotope variation in deep-sea sediment cores (Lowe and Walker 1997). However, a detailed comparison of the climatic record with that expected from the effects of Milankovitch

Cycles shows an imperfect fit. A glacial episode has not always been triggered at the expected time and climatic events have occurred at slightly different times from those calculated. It is thought that Milankovitch cycles alone are insufficient to cause glaciation. Other factors, perhaps inducing positive feedback mechanisms, may be involved. These factors include the distribution of landmasses at or near the poles (as at the present time), tectonics, changes in the extent of ice cover and oceanic circulation. For example, when the interaction of the cycles brings about a cool summer in the Northern Hemisphere with landmasses near the North Pole (as they have been distributed during the Quaternary), snow and ice on the continents may persist to the next winter, eventually allowing the growth of ice sheets. The albedo effect (reflection of solar radiation) of the ice sheets will in turn promote further cooling and increased ice sheet growth.

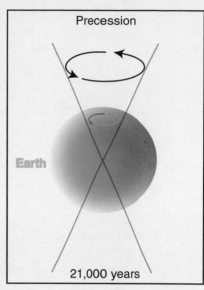

Eccentricity

100,000 years

Precession

Earth

21,000 years

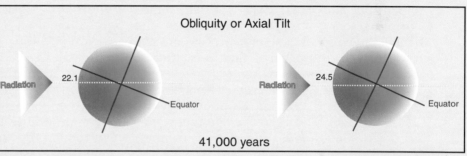

Obliquity or Axial Tilt

Radiation 22.1 Equator

Radiation 24.5 Equator

41,000 years

Figure 1.5

Sea Level change in the Quaternary

Sea level change through the Quaternary, particularly from the Middle Pleistocene onwards, has profoundly affected ancient human occupation and the diversity of fauna and flora in Britain. These effects are reflected in the archaeology and palaeontology of the terrace deposits of the river Thames.

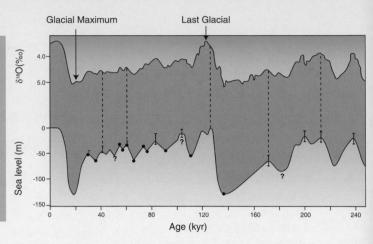

There have been two major causes of sea level change around Britain during the Quaternary. **Glacio-eustasy** is global sea level change that results from the expansion and contraction of ice sheets during glacial/interglacial cycles and the accompanying removal of water from, and its return to, the oceans. **Glacio-isostasy** is local or regional vertical tectonic movement caused by the Earth's crust responding to the loading and unloading imposed by ice sheet advance and retreat. At times they occurred simultaneously and their complex interaction was such that, strictly, it is the effect of relative sea level change that has been observed.

During the Early Pleistocene south-eastern Britain was connected to continental Europe by a structural feature known as the **Weald-Artois Ridge**. For most of this period the 'Channel' was a marine embayment open to the Atlantic Ocean but separated from the North Sea Basin by the ridge. Occasionally, sea level may have been low enough to allow the rivers of southern England and northern France (e.g. Solent, Somme and Seine) to merge in a westward-flowing drainage system that occupied the floor of the 'Channel'. In contrast, the rivers east of the Weald-Artois (e.g. the Rhine, Meuse, Scheldt and Thames) flowed northwards into the southern North Sea basin carrying a vast amount of sediment that was deposited as large, northward-building deltas in the subsiding North Sea Basin. The deltas grew rapidly reaching a considerable thickness (several hundred metres) and becoming the dominant local influence on sea level. By early **Cromerian Complex** times, extensive wetlands covered the whole of the southern North Sea basin and the shoreline was far to the north.

Following a brief rise in sea level in late Cromerian Complex times, onset of glaciation during the **Anglian** resulted in a major fall in sea level. At the maximum of the glaciation, the ice sheet advanced into the southern North Sea area, trapping water from the north-west European rivers in a large, proglacial lake. Eventually, the lake overtopped the Weald-Artois Ridge, bringing about its catastrophic destruction and in so-doing created the Straits of Dover. Some of the rivers, including the Thames, that had previously flowed northwards into the North Sea now flowed south-east through the Straits of Dover, and then westward via the 'Channel River' drainage system enlarged by the floodwaters. But rising sea level that accompanied amelioration of the climate during the succeeding **Hoxnian** interglacial led to inundation of the low-lying land by a shallow sea that, at its maximum, submerged the Straits of Dover.

There is some uncertainty about the sequence of events, the range of sea level change and the detailed palaeogeography in the interval between the **Hoxnian** and the **Ipswichian** (that is, MIS 10 to 6). It has been suggested that there was at least one further catastrophic flooding event similar to the one already described. There was undoubtedly continuing sea level change related to glacial/interglacial cycles and there is evidence that Britain may have been isolated from the continent several times.

Sea Level change in the Quaternary

Palaeogeography of the Holocene

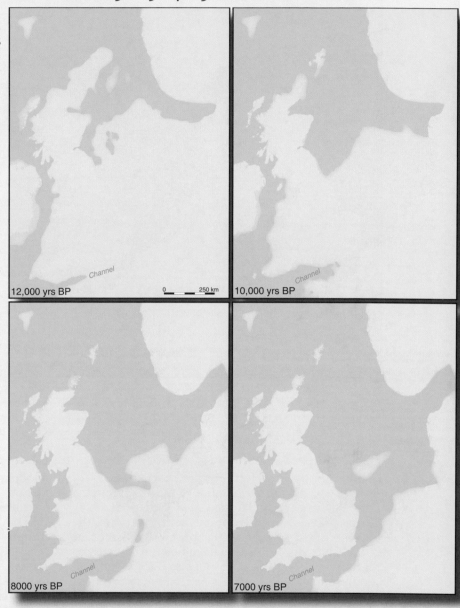

Early in the **Ipswichian** interglacial the return to a warm temperate climate was accompanied by high sea levels, probably at a level slightly higher than at the present day and sufficiently high that Britain again became an island. Global sea level fell during the late Ipswichian and, except for an oscillation early in the early **Devensian**, continued to fall until the lowest sea level (-135 m) coincided with the last glacial maximum (at about 22 ka BP). During this period, much of the southern North Sea basin was a periglacial plain. The sea no longer separated Britain from mainland Europe but the 'Channel River' had by now developed to its maximum extent. With most of the major rivers that formerly flowed into the southern North Sea basin (including the Thames and the Rhine) diverted through the Straits of Dover this river system formed a significant barrier.

The ice sheets began to melt about 19 ka BP and this was accompanied by a rapid rise in global sea level. However, the region around the North Sea, including Britain, Scandinavia and parts of north-west Europe, was affected by **glacio-isostatic recovery**. In other words, the crust in the northern part of the region that had been depressed by the weight of glacial ice rebounded as the ice melted. The amount and rate of rebound, or uplift, varied: it was greatest where the ice had been at its maximum thickness. By contrast, the southern North Sea basin subsided. During the glacial maximum it lay to the south of the ice sheet but was affected by a phenomenon known as **glacio-isostatic forebulge** which caused the crust near the ice margin to bulge up. The subsidence was due to a combination of the collapse of the forebulge following the melting of the ice sheet and tectonic movements in the southern North Sea Basin.

The changes that resulted from the complex interplay of all these factors in late glacial times are illustrated above. At the beginning of the Holocene (11,500 ka BP) most of the southern and central North Sea area was land and Britain was a peninsula of Europe. This land area, which now lies beneath the sea, has been named **'Doggerland'**. It is known to have been occupied by man because artefacts, such as flint handaxes, have been dredged up in fishing nets. As relative sea level rose so 'Doggerland' was progressively submerged. At around 7000 ka BP the last vestiges of 'Doggerland' disappeared beneath the waves and the geography of the North Sea region began to resemble that of the present day.

Figure 1.5

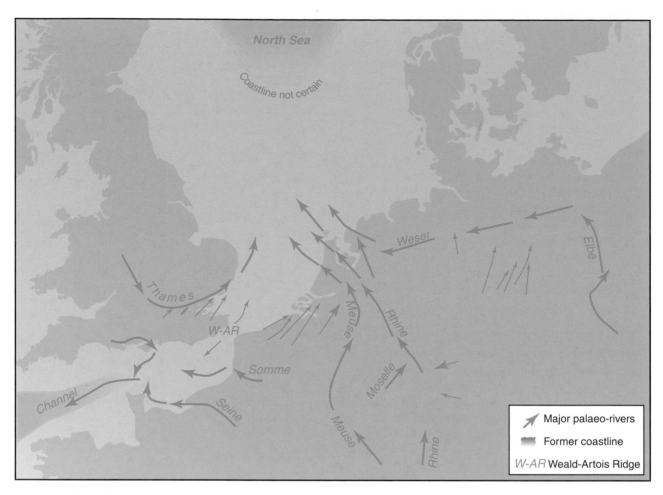

Fig. 1.6   The palaeogeography of the 'North Sea' and main rivers during the early Middle Pleistocene 'Cromerian Complex'. This is a schematic reconstruction of glacial palaeogeography, when cold conditions led to the formation of ice sheets and falling sea level. Such conditions existed on numerous occasions during the period c 750,000-500,000 years ago.

London and south Hertfordshire, having been laid down by south-bank tributaries of the Thames in the Late Pliocene/early Pleistocene (Bridgland, 1994). These gravels should not be confused with the deposits also referred to as 'Pebble Gravel' that occur in the Chilterns and which have been interpreted as marine or littoral in origin (Wood; 1868; Whittaker, 1889). Similar deposits on the North Downs of Surrey at Netley Heath contained the poorly-preserved casts of marine shells that imply evidence of correlation with the Red Crag of East Anglia, the latter now considered to be of late Pliocene-early Pleistocene age, 3.5-2 million years old (Cambridge, 1977; Zalasiewicz and Gibbard, 1988). These marine gravels are unrelated to the evolution of the Thames system (Bridgland, 1994). The Nettlebed Gravel comprises about 1.5 metres of gravel with a sandy matrix, lacks bedding structures and, although it may not be entirely *in situ*, is considered to be a fluvial deposit (Horton, 1977; Gibbard, 1985). The elevation of this deposit relative to similar deposits suggests that they lie on a gradient of about 90 cm km[-1], slightly steeper than that of the present day

floodplain of the Thames, and implying that the Thames flowed from Oxfordshire north-east across the mid Thames region (Horton, 1977; Gibbard, 1985). According to Gibbard, the Nettlebed deposit comprises sand derived from the Palaeocene Reading Formation and a gravel fraction that consists mainly of rounded flint (also derived from the Reading Formation), and angular flint (from the Chalk Group), with up to 15% vein quartz, 4% quartzite and a trace of Palaeozoic chert in some gravel fractions. The presence of quartz and quartzite was considered particularly significant because they were thought to be far-travelled from a source in the Triassic strata of the Midlands, thus implying an extensive catchment for the Thames (or, more properly at this stage, the ancient or 'proto-Thames') beyond the Cotswolds. However, other workers (Moffat, 1986) produced different estimates of gravel composition that indicate an entirely local derivation for the gravel and so the extent of the earliest Thames catchment remained unclear. Recently, Riding *et al.* (1998, 2000) have reported Silurian palynomorphs in the marine Norwich Crag Formation of southern

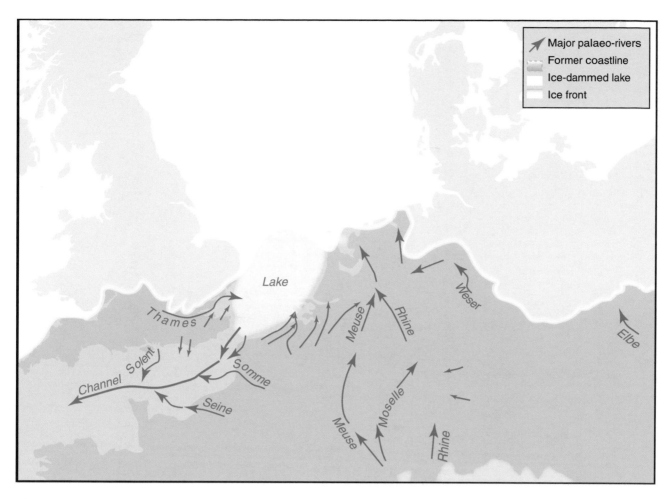

Fig. 1.7   Schematic palaeogeography of the Anglian glacial maximum, showing the extent of the ice sheet, the proglacial lake that formed in the southern North Sea Basin and the breaching of the Dover Straits.

East Anglia, the time equivalent of the Nettlebed Formation. These are considered to have been transported from the Welsh borders (the nearest occurrence of Silurian strata) by the ancient Thames thus supporting the view that, even at this early stage in the evolution of the Thames, its headwaters extended well beyond the Cotswold escarpment. The next youngest terrace, the Stoke Row Gravel, reaches its highest elevation at 174 m OD and is underlain by deposits that contrast markedly with the Nettlebed Gravel since they contain a significant proportion of exotic material including up to 50% quartz and 4% quartzite (Hey, 1965; Gibbard, 1985). This sudden influx of evidently far-travelled material is the earliest unequivocal evidence that the headwaters of the ancient Thames lay to the north of the Cotswolds.

Six lower and therefore sequentially younger terraces of the Middle Thames were deposited in the 1.3 Ma or so that elapsed prior to the Anglian glaciation: the Westland Green Gravel, Satwell Gravel, Beaconsfield Gravel, Gerrard's Cross Gravel, Rassler Gravel and Winter Hill Gravel. They are characterised by gravel fractions with a high proportion of quartz and quartzite (Gibbard, 1985) considered to have been derived from the Triassic Kidderminster

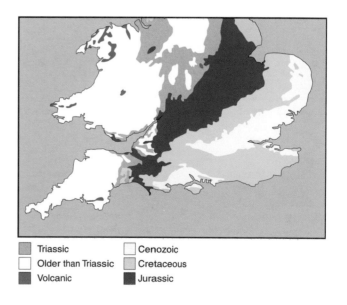

Triassic	Cenozoic
Older than Triassic	Cretaceous
Volcanic	Jurassic

Fig. 1.8   Bedrock geology of the Thames catchment and adjacent areas

15

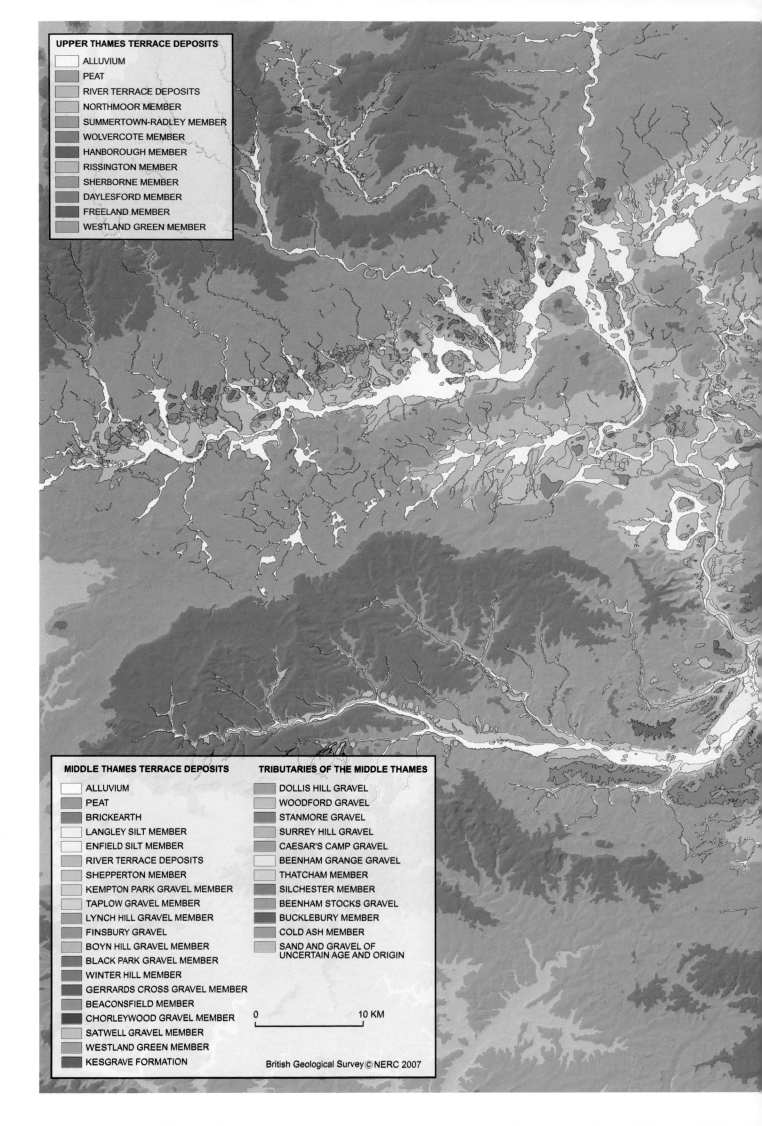

UPPER THAMES TERRACE DEPOSITS

- ALLUVIUM
- PEAT
- RIVER TERRACE DEPOSITS
- NORTHMOOR MEMBER
- SUMMERTOWN-RADLEY MEMBER
- WOLVERCOTE MEMBER
- HANBOROUGH MEMBER
- RISSINGTON MEMBER
- SHERBORNE MEMBER
- DAYLESFORD MEMBER
- FREELAND MEMBER
- WESTLAND GREEN MEMBER

MIDDLE THAMES TERRACE DEPOSITS

- ALLUVIUM
- PEAT
- BRICKEARTH
- LANGLEY SILT MEMBER
- ENFIELD SILT MEMBER
- RIVER TERRACE DEPOSITS
- SHEPPERTON MEMBER
- KEMPTON PARK GRAVEL MEMBER
- TAPLOW GRAVEL MEMBER
- LYNCH HILL GRAVEL MEMBER
- FINSBURY GRAVEL
- BOYN HILL GRAVEL MEMBER
- BLACK PARK GRAVEL MEMBER
- WINTER HILL MEMBER
- GERRARDS CROSS GRAVEL MEMBER
- BEACONSFIELD MEMBER
- CHORLEYWOOD GRAVEL MEMBER
- SATWELL GRAVEL MEMBER
- WESTLAND GREEN MEMBER
- KESGRAVE FORMATION

TRIBUTARIES OF THE MIDDLE THAMES

- DOLLIS HILL GRAVEL
- WOODFORD GRAVEL
- STANMORE GRAVEL
- SURREY HILL GRAVEL
- CAESAR'S CAMP GRAVEL
- BEENHAM GRANGE GRAVEL
- THATCHAM MEMBER
- SILCHESTER MEMBER
- BEENHAM STOCKS GRAVEL
- BUCKLEBURY MEMBER
- COLD ASH MEMBER
- SAND AND GRAVEL OF UNCERTAIN AGE AND ORIGIN

0   10 KM

British Geological Survey © NERC 2007

Fig. 1.9   The terraces of the Thames

ELEVATION

0-75 m

75-150 m

Above 150 m

Formation (formerly the Bunter Pebble Beds) of the West Midlands. A suite of fluvial sediments with similarly distinctive characteristics, the pre-Anglian glaciation Kesgrave Formation, has been described in Eastern Essex (Rose *et al.*, 1976; Rose and Allen, 1977) and is correlated with this group of Middle Thames deposits on the basis of lithology, elevation and the limited biostratigraphical data available (Hey, 1980; Bridgland, 1988a, 1996; Whiteman and Rose, 1992; Rose *et al.*, 1999). Carboniferous and Devonian sandstones from South Wales and the Pennines have been recorded in the Kesgrave Formation gravels (Hey and Brenchley, 1977; Bridgland, 1988b) as well as sporadic occurrences of acid volcanic rocks from a Welsh source (Hey and Brenchley, 1977; Whiteman, 1983, 1990). The presence of Cretaceous Greensand chert in the Kesgrave Formation shows that material was supplied by left bank tributaries, such as the Mole-Wey and Darent-Medway, which drained the Weald. The Kesgrave Formation, as originally defined (Rose and Allen, 1977), lies outside the study area but is referred to briefly here because of the implications for the evolution of the Thames.

Whiteman and Rose (1992) proposed a new catchment-wide classification scheme in which precedence was given to lithological distinctiveness. They noted a marked reduction in quartz and quartzite content below a level that could be traced across the entire catchment. This reduction was observed within the Anglian-age Winter Hill Gravel

and Freeland Member. It was interpreted as reflecting a contraction of the headwaters of the Thames catchment to the south of the Cotswold escarpment thus cutting off the supply of quartzose gravel (see Fig. 1.4C). The reduction was also noted in the Wivenhoe, Ardleigh and Waldringfield Gravels of Essex which are correlated with the earlier Middle Thames Rassler Gravel by Westaway *et al.* (2002). A pre-Anglian glaciation north of the Cotswolds (Whiteman and Rose, 1992) and truncation of the headwaters of the Thames by the Bytham River during an extension of its catchment (Sumbler, 2001) have both been invoked as possible explanations. Sumbler considered this explanation plausible because the elevation of the Combe Member (see below) is much higher (30 to 40 m) than occurrences of the compositionally similar Stretton Sand that lies beneath glacigenic deposits of Anglian age to the north of the watershed in the Evenlode valley. The Stretton Sand is a deposit of the north-eastward draining Bytham River. It contains a temperate fauna (Shotton, 1973a; Lister, 1989) and so must date from at least the late Cromerian Complex (ie MIS 13 or older). Truncation of the extended river Thames must, then, have occurred prior to this time (Sumbler, 2001).

Correlating the Middle and Lower Thames terraces with possible equivalents in the Upper Thames has proved problematical, mainly because of lack of continuity through the Goring Gap and the paucity of biostratigraphical evidence. Spreads of

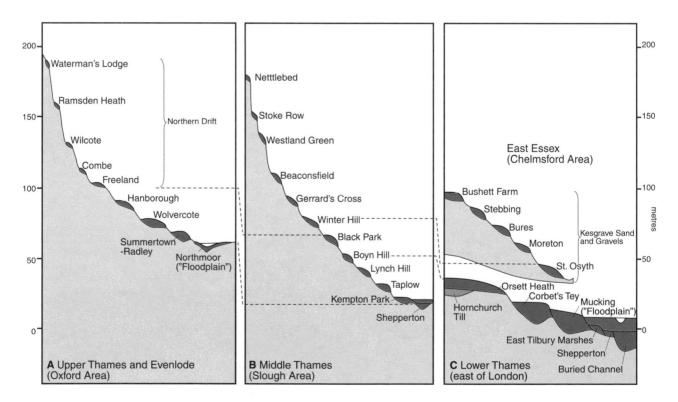

Fig. 1.10   Schematic of the terraces of the river Thames

Fig. 1.11 (facing page)   River terrace formation

River Terrace Formation

It is generally accepted that extreme climatic change – glacial to interglacial - is the driving force for terrace formation and that simultaneous progressive uplift of the land is necessary for a staircase of terraces to develop. In recent years Bridgland (1994; 2000) has refined a theory of terrace formation. In its latest evolution he proposed the six-phase process that is illustrated here.

In **Phase 1** the river abandons its floodplain and cuts down to a new lower level. This event is triggered by the high discharge of water that is due to melting of permafrost during the transition from a cold, glacial climatic stage to an interglacial, and results in the generation of a pair of river terraces.

Later in the same warming episode, incision is followed by **Phase 2**, aggradation - the laying down of gravel and sand on the new riverbed.

During the succeeding interglacial, **Phase 3**, deposition of silt, clay and organic material is dominant.

Such deposits are seldom preserved because of renewed erosion as the climate cools once more: **Phase 4**. Incision in this phase does not generate terraces because interglacial stages tend to be too short for significant uplift.

In **Phase 5** as the climate cools further the gravel bedload of the river increases in response to a reduction in vegetation that liberates more sediment. This is the main phase of aggradation during which the river is likely to braided.

During the next glacial stage, **Phase 6**, potential discharge is locked in permafrost and the river passes through a period of stability.

As the climate begins to warm again so the cycle recommences with **Phase 1**.

Each six-stage cycle generates one river terrace so that if climate-driven cycles recur many times against a background of progressive uplift a staircase of river terraces is formed.

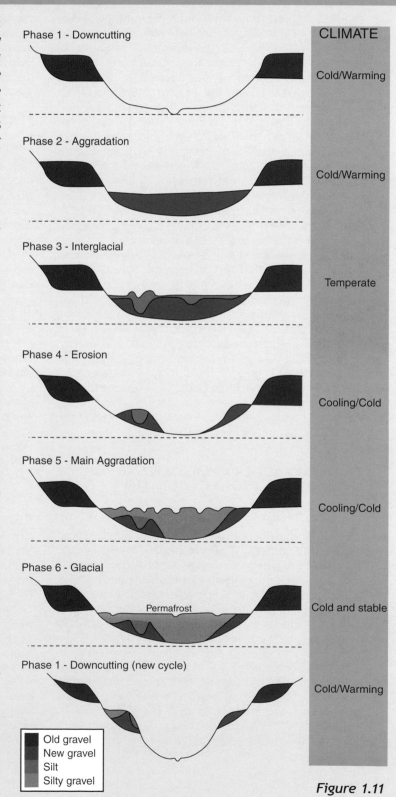

Phase 1 - Downcutting

Phase 2 - Aggradation

Phase 3 - Interglacial

Phase 4 - Erosion

Phase 5 - Main Aggradation

Phase 6 - Glacial

Permafrost

Phase 1 - Downcutting (new cycle)

Old gravel
New gravel
Silt
Silty gravel

CLIMATE

Cold/Warming

Cold/Warming

Temperate

Cooling/Cold

Cooling/Cold

Cold and stable

Cold/Warming

Figure 1.11

clayey gravels in the valley of the river Evenlode that are known as the 'Northern Drift' contain quartz and quartzite comprising more than 93% of the gravel fraction (Hey, 1986; Whiteman, 1990). They were once thought to be glacial in origin, but Hey (1986) showed that the Northern Drift in fact represents a flight of five high-level, degraded and decalcified river terrace deposits of the early Upper Thames. In descending order of both age and elevation these are known today as the Waterman's Lodge, Ramsden Heath, Wilcote, Combe and Freeland members of the Northern Drift Formation (Bowen, 1999). However, it should be noted that Sumbler (2001), on the basis of composition (including flint pebbles), elevation and distribution, considers the Freeland Member to represent outwash from the Moreton glacigenic deposits, and therefore not related to the early Thames terrace deposits of the Northern Drift Formation. Accordingly he reassigned the Freeland Member to the Upper Thames Valley Formation of Bowen (1999). The occurrence of these terrace deposits along the Evenlode valley suggests that for some considerable time this was the main conduit for the early Thames through which it drained a catchment that included parts of the West Midlands (Hey, 1986; Bowen *et al.*, 1986; Bridgland, 1988b; 1996; Whiteman, 1990; Bowen, 1999). Clayey gravels at Sugworth have been tentatively correlated with the Freeland Member (Hey 1986). Fossiliferous interglacial deposits that fill a channel beneath these gravels have been assigned by Shotton *et al.* (1980) to the Cromerian Complex (ie between MIS 19 and 13). Although a younger date has been suggested by others (Gibbard, 1985; Sumbler, 1995; Bowen *et al.* 1989) the weight of the evidence favours a Cromerian Complex age (see below). This implies a minimum Anglian (MIS12) age for the Freeland Member so it has been correlated with both the Winter Hill and Black Park gravels (see Chapter 2; Hey, 1986; Whiteman and Rose, 1992; Rose *et al.*, 1999) and the Black Park Gravel alone (Sumbler, 2001).

THE EARLY MIDDLE PLEISTOCENE ENVIRONMENT AND OCCUPATION

The Early Pleistocene (Fig. 1.12)

The Early Pleistocene palaeoenvironmental record in Britain is generally poorly known and it is clear that there are substantial gaps within the sequence. In this respect, the evidence from the Thames Valley is no exception. The oldest interglacial deposits to be preserved within the Thames catchment are those at Priest's Hill, Nettlebed, which lie a few metres below the level of the terrace deposits. The Nettlebed interglacial site has only been investigated via boreholes and temporary exposures. Beds of dark brown humic silt and humic pebble-free clay were observed to overlie white, silty pebbly sand occupying a depression in the Reading Beds (Horton, 1977, 1983) (Fig. 1.12). The humic beds have yielded pollen spectra that are characteristic of

the first half of an interglacial, with dominant *Betula* (birch) and *Pinus* (pine) and lower amounts of *Picea* (spruce) giving way to abundant *Quercus* (oak) and *Ulmus* (elm), followed by the arrival of *Carpinus* (hornbeam) and an expansion of *Corylus* (hazel) (Turner, 1983). The relationship of the interglacial deposits to the Early Pleistocene Nettlebed Gravel is unclear (Bridgland, 1994) but features of the pollen succession led Turner (1983) and later Gibbard (1985) to propose a late Early Pleistocene or early Middle Pleistocene age. Certainly the stratigraphical position of the deposit, at a very high level within the Thames terrace system, clearly predating unequivocal early Middle Pleistocene 'Cromerian Complex' sites such as Sugworth (see below), imply a considerable age, most likely within the Early Pleistocene.

The early Middle Pleistocene

The earliest occupation of Britain

The first unequivocal evidence of early human occupation in Britain occurs during the early Middle Pleistocene, during the extended, climatically variable period now referred to as the 'Cromerian Complex' *c* 780-450 ka (but see recent paper by Parfitt *et al.*, 2010, which proposes an Early Pleistocene age). Examination of the oxygen isotope record derived from deep-sea sediments suggests that the early Middle Pleistocene is approximately equivalent to Marine Oxygen Isotope Stages [MIS] 19-13 inclusive (*c* 780-450ka) (Bassinot *et al.* 1994), thereby indicating that four full interglacial cycles are present, not to mention the numerous smaller temperate substages that occur within these. Recent stratigraphical and palaeontological investigations (Turner, 1996a, 1996b; Preece and Parfitt, 2000; Stuart and Lister, 2001) in East Anglia have shed some light on the complex nature of this period and identified a succession of temperate-climate episodes with diagnostic faunal assemblages, within which periods of early human occupation may be identified. One of the key divisions between these early Middle Pleistocene assemblages is based on the evolutionary stage of the water vole remains that are present. Sites have accordingly been divided into an earlier group with *Mimomys savini* (in which the molars are rooted in older individuals), and a later group with *Arvicola terrestris cantiana* (in which the molars are always unrooted) (Fig. 1.13).

In Britain the early Middle Pleistocene is principally represented by the richly-fossiliferous Cromer Forest-bed Formation (CF-bF) of Norfolk and Suffolk, a complex, extensive and spatially varied sequence of freshwater and marine sediments. The CF-bF is underlain by an older series of principally marine deposits (parts of the Norfolk Crag Formation) but is separated from them by an extensive temporal hiatus of at least one million years (Lister, 1998). The Cf-bF is directly overlain by glacio-

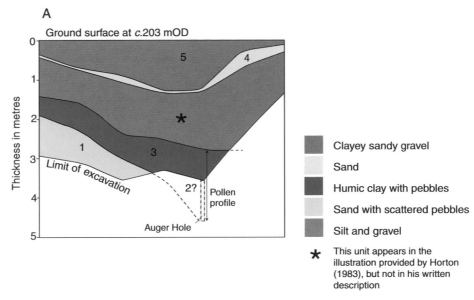

A

Ground surface at *c.*203 mOD

Thickness in metres

Clayey sandy gravel
Sand
Humic clay with pebbles
Sand with scattered pebbles
Silt and gravel

* This unit appears in the illustration provided by Horton (1983), but not in his written description

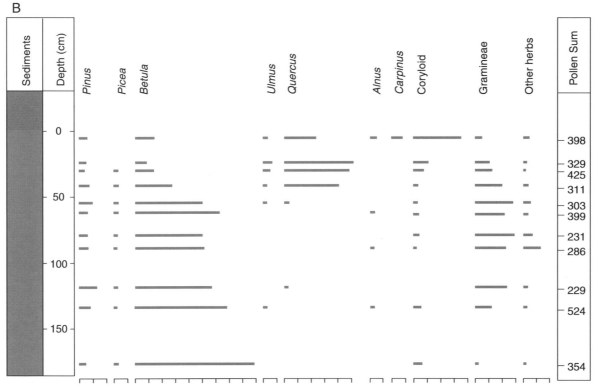

B

Sediments

Depth (cm)

Pinus *Picea* *Betula* *Ulmus* *Quercus* *Alnus* *Carpinus* Coryloid Gramineae Other herbs

Pollen Sum

— 398

— 329
— 425

— 311

— 303
— 399

— 231
— 286

— 229

— 524

— 354

Horizontal scale in increments of 10% of total land pollen

Fig. 1.12   A: The stratigraphy of the deposits at Nettlebed; B: Pollen diagram from Beds 2 and 3 at Nettlebed

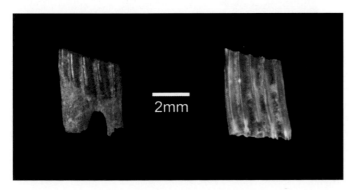

2mm

Fig. 1.13   Lateral (side) views of a rooted molar of the archaic water vole Mimomys savini *(left), shown next to an unrooted molar of its descent,* Arvicola terrestris cantiana *(right)*

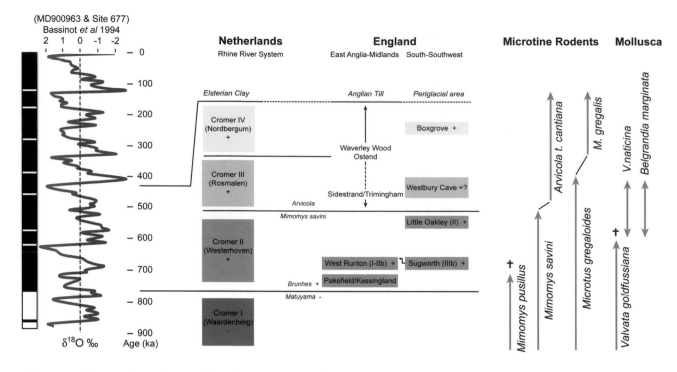

Fig. 1.14 *Proposed correlation of English Cromerian Complex temperate deposits with the marine oxygen isotope record and magnetostratigraphy. Links are based on palynology, the position of the Brunhes-Matuyama boundary, evolutionary transitions in microtine rodents, presence/absence of molluscan species and marker deposits of the Anglian/Elsterian ice advance. Direct correlation should not be inferred with the four interglacials of the Dutch early Middle Pleistocene sequence*

genic deposits (tills and outwash), which have traditionally been regarded as representing phases of a single cold stage, the Anglian (see Chapter 2, below). The Anglian was the most far-reaching glaciation in Britain (extending as far south as north London) and was responsible for the major remodelling of the drainage systems of eastern England. It is widely correlated with MIS 12 of the deep sea sequence (Rowe *et al.*, 1999; Grün and Schwarcz, 2000), *c* 450ka.

The type locality of the Cromerian interglacial is at West Runton in Norfolk. The sediments there were regarded by West (1980a) as representing a single interglacial stage, subdivided into four pollen zones (Cr I-Cr IV). However, it is now clear that the type Cromerian is just one of a number of interglacials that occur within an extended 'Cromerian Complex'. In the Netherlands, for example, a series of four distinct Cromerian Complex interglacials (Interglacials I-IV) separated by periods of cold climate, has been recognised on the basis of palynology, lithology and heavy mineral analysis (Zagwijn, 1985, 1996). However, this sequence is based entirely on information from boreholes and in no one site is the complete interglacial cycle represented for any one of the component stages. The earliest, Interglacial I, is unique in that it is magnetically reversed and has a highly diagnostic pollen zone characterised by *Carpinus* (hornbeam) and *Eucommia* (Chinese rubber tree) that is unknown from any subsequent interglacial event.

Correlation of the British and Dutch sequences remains extremely problematic. All British Cromerian Complex interglacials are normally polarised and must therefore post-date the Dutch Interglacial I. However, in the UK, as many as six discrete temperate episodes are now recognised on the basis of mammalian and molluscan biostratigraphy (Preece and Parfitt, 2000; Stuart and Lister, 2001; Fig. 1.14). The oldest of these temperate climate periods, *c* 700ka, is represented at Pakefield, in Suffolk, a site that has recently yielded the oldest

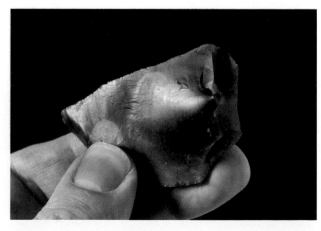

Fig. 1.15 *An example of a humanly-struck flint flake from Pakefield*

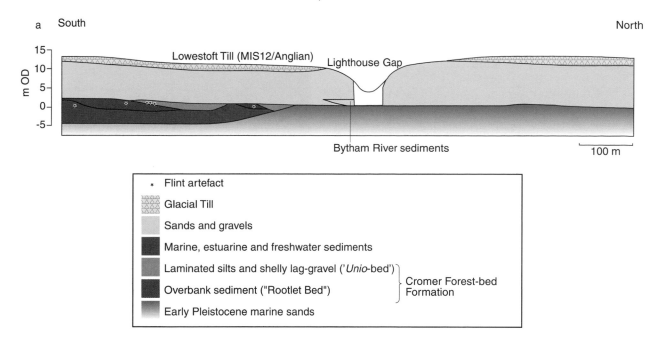

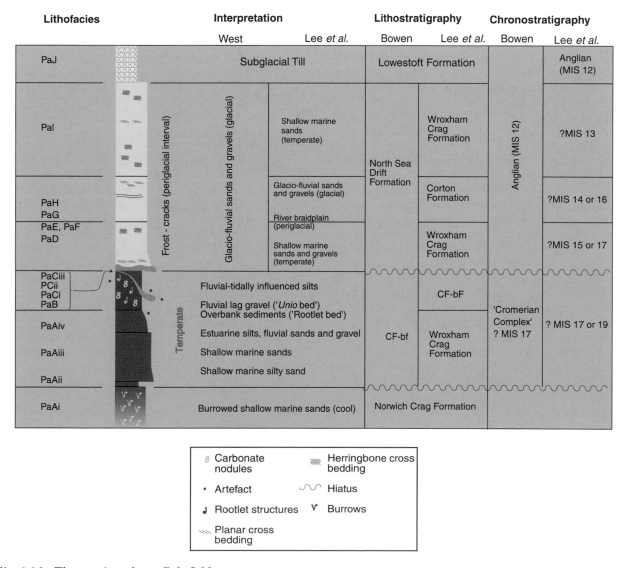

Fig. 1.16   The stratigraphy at Pakefield

evidence of human occupation in Britain (Parfitt *et al.*, 2005), thereby radically overturning the long-held view that colonisation did not occur until *c* 500ka.

The Pakefield sediments consist of an interglacial infill of a channel incised into Early Pleistocene marine deposits and overlain by a sequence of marine sands, glaciofluvial sediments and Lowestoft Till (the last laid down by the Anglian glaciation, *c* 450ka). The artefacts comprise a small assemblage of 32 worked flints, including a simple flaked core, a crudely retouched flake and a quantity of waste flakes (Parfitt *et al.*, 2005) (Fig. 1.15). The artefacts are all in very sharp condition and are made of good quality black flint. Unworked flint surfaces are water-worn, suggesting that the raw material may have been collected from the adjacent river channel sediments. These contain a significant quartz and quartzite component, pointing to deposition by the erstwhile Bytham River that drained the English Midlands at this time. The lithic assemblage is consistent with a Mode 1 technology (ie flakes, pebble tools and choppers made with hard hammers and lacking formal tools) (Parfitt *et al.*, 2005). The artefacts have come from several different levels within the channel infill (Fig. 1.16), with the oldest from the upper levels of an estuarine silt bed that has yielded marine and brackish-water ostracods, foraminifera and rare marine mammals such as dolphin and walrus. The remainder were found in sediments attributed to the CF-bF, which comprise (from the base to the top) the 'Rootlet bed' (overbank sediments with well-developed soil features including numerous fossil root-casts and pedogenic carbonate nodules), the '*Unio*-bed' (a lag gravel cutting into the overbank sediments) and laminated silts at the edge of the channel. Sediments overlying the channel infill were originally interpreted as Anglian glaciofluvial deposits laid down during MIS 12 but are now thought to represent a complex succession of marine sands, Bytham River sands and gravels, and glaciofluvial sands and gravels from a pre-Anglian glaciation, the Happisburgh Glaciation (Lee *et al.*, 2004, 2005). The reinterpretation of Lee and colleagues invokes a longer chronology on the basis of sedimentological evidence, suggesting that the CF-bF may be separated from the Anglian MIS 12 till by two separate high sea-stands and two cold episodes, thereby placing the Pakefield interglacial deposits in MIS 17 (about 680ka) at the latest and possibly as early as MIS 19, *c* 750ka (Lee *et al.*, 2004).

The dating of the site to a very early phase within the CF-bF has been corroborated by mammalian biostratigraphy and amino acid geochronology. Certainly, the presence of southern warm-loving plants such as the water chestnut (*Trapa natans*), floating water fern (*Salvinia natans*) and the Portuguese crowberry (*Corema album*) and exotic beetle species (*Cybister lateralimarginalis*, *Oxytelus opacus* and *Valgus hemipterus*) provides an immediate point of difference between Pakefield and the Cromerian stratotype at West Runton, which lacks

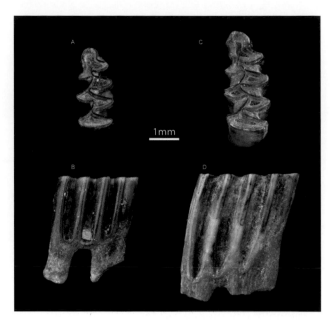

Fig. 1.17   Occlusal (A) and lateral (B) views of Mimomys pusillus *and occlusal (C) and lateral (D) views of* Mimomys savini

these warm-loving components and apparently had temperatures no warmer than at present. In addition, the composition of the mammalian assemblage suggests a difference in age between these two sites. In the large mammal assemblage, several species of large mammal are known from Pakefield, including hippopotamus (*Hippopotamus* sp.), giant deer (*Megaloceros dawkinsi*) and straight-tusked elephant (*Palaeoloxodon antiquus*) that have never been found at West Runton, despite the much more extensive collections from the latter locality. Furthermore, two species of the water vole genus *Mimomys* occur at Pakefield, the archaic *M. savini*, which is also present at West Runton, and *M.* aff. *pusillus*, which is not present (Fig. 1.17). Again, the prolific amount of collecting that has been carried at West Runton strongly supports the notion that *M. pusillus* is a genuine absentee, despite the apparent palaeoenvironmental suitability for this species at the site. Although this is the only known record from Britain, *M. pusillus* is present in Europe from the Early Pleistocene to its latest occurrence in the early Middle Pleistocene Ilynian Complex in Russia (Pevzner *et al.*, 2001). The Ilynian Complex is overlain by the Don Till, commonly correlated with MIS 16, consequently suggesting a minimum age for the Pakefield '*Unio*-bed' of at least MIS 17 and corroborating the longer chronology proposed by Lee *et al.* (2004). The implication of the evidence from the microtine rodents at Pakefield is that all younger early Middle Pleistocene sites (including the West Runton typesite) that lack *M. pusillus*, should be accommodated within MIS 15 and 13. However, as can be seen from the marine oxygen isotope record (see Fig. 1.14), these stages contain numerous short-lived sub-Milankovitch warm episodes, to which these sites might convincingly be related.

The palaeogeography of Britain was substantially different at this time, with Britain connected to what is now mainland Europe and East Anglia being located at the southwestern margin of a large coastal embayment around the North Sea basin (Fig. 1.18). This allowed the free movement of flora, fauna and early humans across the landbridge until the Straits of Dover were cut, either during the Anglian glaciation (Gibbard, 1995a) or even later (Ashton and Lewis, 2002). A particularly interesting aspect of the Pakefield 'Rootlet bed' is the evidence from pedogenic carbonate nodules contained within it. Stable isotope analysis of the nodules has revealed intense soil moisture evaporation during their formation (Parfitt *et al.*, 2005). Together with palaeotemperature information derived from the beetle assemblage, indicating higher summer temperatures than at present (18-23°C) and mild winters (-6 – +4°C), the strongly seasonal precipitation regime is thought to be indicative of a warm, seasonally dry Mediterranean climate (Parfitt *et al.*, 2005). In this respect, the hominin presence may reflect a fleeting period of occupation during a particularly warm period, with large scale coloni-

sation not taking place until much later. Suitable founder populations with a similar technology are known to have been present in Mediterranean Europe at this time, for example at Atapuerca in northern Spain (Carbonell *et al.*, 1999). The combined palaeoenvironmental evidence from the site indicates the presence of a meandering river with adjacent marshes, reeds and alder trees, with oak woodland and dry grassland nearby that supported a range of large browsing and grazing mammals including *Mammuthus trogontherii* (steppe mammoth), *Stephanorhinus hundsheimensis* (Hundsheim rhinoceros), two species of giant deer and *Bison* cf *schoetensacki* (bison) (Parfitt *et al.*, 2005). The floodplain would therefore have provided a diversity of plant and animal resources for early humans, in addition to raw material from the flint-rich river gravels.

The early group of Cromerian Complex sites that are characterised by the presence of the ancestral water vole *M. savini* therefore includes several East Anglian sites located outside the immediate study area (Pakefield, West Runton and the Essex locality of Little Oakley) but also, within the study area, the

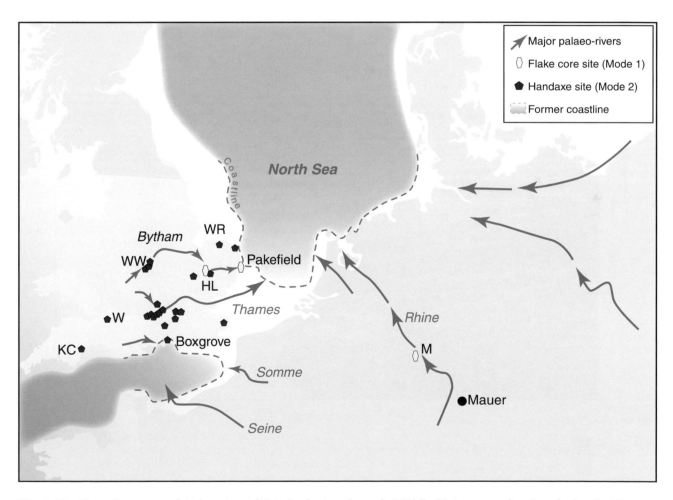

Fig. 1.18 The palaeogeographical setting of Britain during the early Middle Pleistocene, showing the landbridge connection to the continent. Archaeological sites of pre-Anglian age are also indicated. KC= Kent's Cavern; HL=High Lodge; M = Miesenheim; W = Westbury-sub-Mendip; WW = Waverley Wood; WR = West Runton

site of Sugworth, near Abingdon, in Oxfordshire. Here, the ancestral river Thames laid down a series of sand and gravel-filled channels cut into Jurassic Kimmeridge Clay (Fig. 1.19). These have yielded organic-rich fossiliferous sediments containing pollen, plant macrofossils, beetles, molluscs, ostracods and vertebrate remains although no archaeology has yet been recovered. The pollen spectra indicate deposition during a late temperate substage of an interglacial, probably the same one but slightly later than that represented at West Runton (Gibbard and Pettit, 1978). This would accord well with the presence of frost-sensitive plants at Sugworth, including *T. natans* and the water fern *Azolla filiculoides*, thereby suggesting that Sugworth represents the thermal optimum of this particular interglacial (Preece and Parfitt, 2000). The molluscs from the site include several biostratigraphically-diagnostic elements that point to an early Middle Pleistocene age, such as *Valvata golfussiana*, *Bithynia troscheli* and *Tanousia runtoniana*, and imply a close match with West Runton. The vertebrate fauna also bears strong similarities to the Cromerian type-site (Stuart, 1980), including (in addition to *M. savini*), *Stephanorhinus*

etruscus (Etruscan rhinoceros) and two species of large, extinct shrew, *Sorex savini* and *Macroneomys brachygnathus* (Preece and Parfitt, 2000).

The relative abundance of Lower Palaeolithic sites (see Fig. 1.18) dating to *c* 500,000 years ago (late 'Cromerian Complex') are believed to represent a major dispersal event into Northwest Europe at this time (Roebroeks and van Kolfschoten, 1994; Dennell and Roebroeks, 1996; Fig. 1.20). Well preserved and/or well studied sites dating to this period (see Fig. 1.18 for locations) include the open-air localities at Boxgrove, West Sussex (Roberts and Parfitt, 1999), High Lodge, Suffolk (Ashton *et al.*, 1992) and Waverley Wood, Warwickshire (Shotton *et al.*, 1993), and the cave sites at Kent's Cavern, Devon (Campbell and Sampson, 1971) and Westbury-sub-Mendip (Andrews *et al.*, 1999). Wherever small mammals have been recovered, all of these sites are united in the ubiquitous presence of the unrooted species of water vole, *A. t. cantiana*, the likely descendant of *M. savini*. The sites may be further divided on the basis of the evolutionary stage observed in the narrow-skulled lineage, with the replacement of *Microtus gregaloides* (which had featured in the early

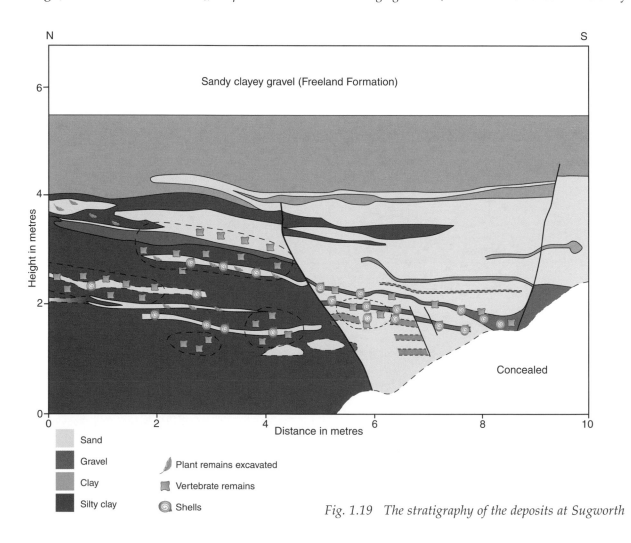

Fig. 1.19   *The stratigraphy of the deposits at Sugworth*

Fig. 1.20 *(facing page)   The Middle Pleistocene people of Britain and Europe*

Britain and Europe

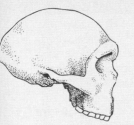 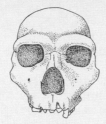

HOMO HEIDELBERGENSIS

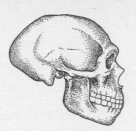 

HOMO NEANDERTHALENSIS

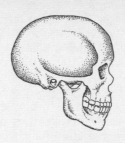 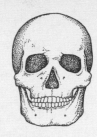

HOMO SAPIENS SAPIENS

The first 'successful' colonisers of Europe, who appeared *c* 600—500,000 years ago bringing along their characteristic handaxe and flake assemblages, are known by the taxonomic name of *Homo heidelbergensis*, after a lower jaw found near Heidelberg, Germany in 1907.   Other important European fossils assigned to this taxon include the skulls from Petralona, Greece and Arago, France.   These show strong similarities to African specimens such as Kabwe, Zambia and Elandsfontein, South Africa, from whom it is widely believed they were descended.   Only two British sites have produced fossils referred to this *Homo heidelbergensis*: Boxgrove and Swanscombe, which produced two incisor teeth and a tibia, and three skull fragments respectively.   The latter is considered by some workers to represent an early or proto-Neanderthal.

In their body shape, *Homo heidelbergensis* was similar in size and proportions to modern humans, although they were remarkably more robust, probably reflecting their highly physical lifestyle. Cranially, they were quite different. Their skulls were very thick with massive forward projecting faces, strong arched browridges and low receding foreheads. Their jaws were robust and chinless with large teeth.

In terms of brain size, *Homo heidelbergensis* ranges from 1225-1300cc, increased over earlier species but lower than the modern human average of 1400cc.

Earlier attempts at colonising Europe, including Britain (i.e. at Pakefield) may go back as far as 800,000 years or even earlier.   The most notable fossil evidence for such visitations is found at Gran Dolina TD6, Atapuerca, Spain and Ceprano, Italy. The former site produced bones from a minimum of 6 individuals that have been assigned to the species *Homo antecessor*. This find is thus far unique, but if the recently suggested dates for occupation on the Suffolk coast are to be believed then similar populations may also have visited Britain at around the same time.

Homo heidelbergensis is generally believed to be the direct ancestor of the archetypal archaic Europeans — the Neanderthals. Fully developed, classic Neanderthal features are evident by about 70,000 years ago, but Neanderthal affinities are detected in specimens as early as 400,000 years ago at Sima de los Huesos, Spain, Swanscombe, Kent and Steinheim, Germany. The Neanderthals occupied a range extending throughout Western Eurasia: west-east from the Atlantic seaboard to the Ukraine and north-south from the North Sea to the Red Sea. Classic Neanderthals are characterised by highly prognathous (forward projecting) faces with swept-back cheekbones, large nasal apertures (big noses) and pronounced arched browridges. Their skulls were configured very differently to those of modern humans, showing a large receding forehead, a pronounced swelling (occipital bun) at the rear and a tendency to bulge outwards at the sides. Their jaws were large and chinless, with large teeth. In their postcranial skeletons, Neanderthals were short and stocky, with massive trunks and relatively short distal limbs. In Britain only the Welsh cave site of Pontnewydd has produced skeletal material physically and temporally within the Neanderthal range.

Figure 1.20

Middle Pleistocene interglacials with *M. savini*) by its descendant *Microtus gregalis* (see Fig. 1.14). As previously, access to Britain continued to be fairly straightforward. Although the late Cromerian Complex saw high sea-levels, which submerged the western English Channel, the Straits of Dover had not yet been breached and Britain remained a peninsula of Western Europe. A significant landbridge – the Weald-Artois anticline – would have linked the present south coast of Britain to France, and significant fluvial deltaic sedimentation may also have left areas of the southern North Sea potentially crossable (Funnell, 1995). Hominins may have traversed the tops of these landbridges or 'coasted' around the seashores, moving inland via major river valleys.

Outside the study area, Boxgrove in West Sussex is one of the earliest and best preserved Lower Palaeolithic localities in Europe and has been excavated at a landscape scale (Pitts and Roberts, 1997; Roberts and Parfitt, 1999). The site represents a coastal embayment in the South Downs that existed during a period of warm climatic conditions and high sea level some 500,000 years ago. The key sediments are the nearshore marine Slindon Sands, which rest on a wave-cut platform abutting the base of a chalk sea-cliff, and the overlying lagoonal Slindon Silts. The silts represent a regressive phase of marine deposition at the mouth of a broad Solent River estuary and pass upwards into a thin palaeosol, which marks the

onset of fully terrestrial conditions (Preece and Parfitt, 2000). The terrestrial deposits have produced a rich vertebrate assemblage, including the earliest known British records of *Meles* sp. (badger) and *Oryctolagus cuniculus* (rabbit), as well as *Capreolus capreolus* (roe deer), *Sus scrofa* (wild boar), *Dama dama* (fallow deer), two species of giant deer (*M. dawkinsi* and *Megaloceros* cf *verticornis*) and two species of extinct rhinoceros, *S. hundsheimensis* and one currently undescribed (Roberts and Parfitt, 1999). Together, these mammals indicate a mosaic of vegetational conditions, including grassland, scrub and deciduous or mixed woodland. At the top of the sequence lies gravel, a mass-movement deposit derived from the adjacent South Downs emplaced under cold climate conditions. Mammals from this phase show a marked shift towards cold-adapted species, including *Lemmus lemmus* (Norway lemming) and *Clethrionomys rufocanus* (grey-sided vole).

Archaeology is preserved throughout the sequence, the best being in the Slindon Silts and in the chalk scree at the base of the cliff, from which flint raw material was procured. Particularly rich concentrations of artefacts were recovered from silty sediments that accumulated in a waterhole fed by freshwater springs from the downland block. The archaeology generally consists of extensive scatters of handaxes, handaxe manufacturing debitage, plus a few flake tools and cores. Much of the lithic

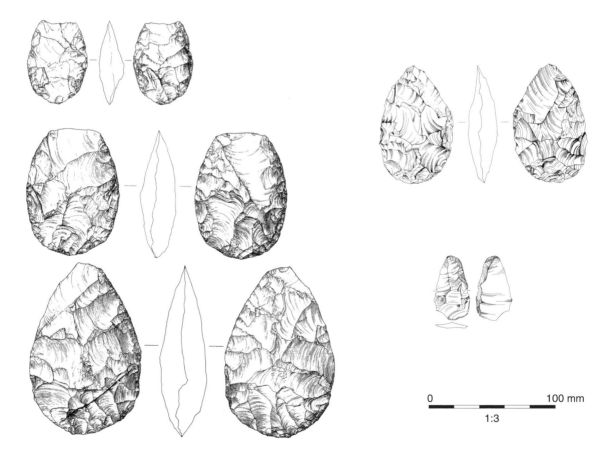

Fig. 1.21   Handaxes and (bottom right) tranchet flake from Boxgrove

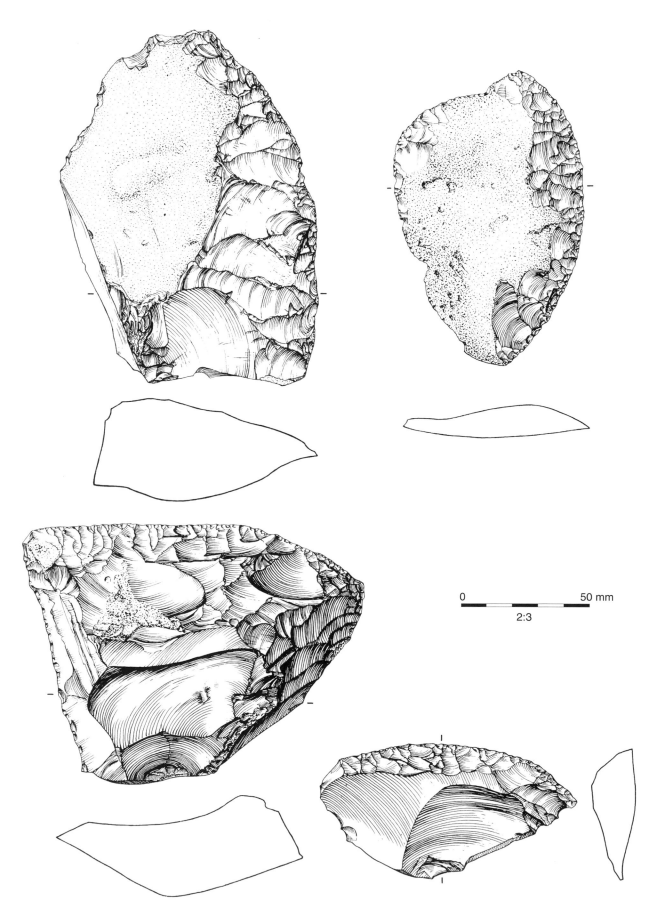

Fig. 1.22   Scrapers from High Lodge, Suffolk

material appears to be *in situ* and extensive refitting groups have been reconstructed. In addition, a number of antler and bone soft-hammers that were used to manufacture the handaxes have also been found. The handaxes from Boxgrove are particularly well made, and their initial discovery did much to erode the old idea that a simply linear evolution in handaxe form should exist in the archaeological record: contrariwise, the oldest in Britain are in fact some of the best (Fig. 1.21).

The flint artefacts are frequently in association with the bones of large terrestrial herbivores including horse, Hundsheim rhinoceros and red deer, some of which bear extensive cutmarks testifying to butchery by humans. Boxgrove is also one of only three sites in Britain to have yielded archaic hominin fossils – a tibia and two incisors – which have been assigned to *Homo heidelbergensis* (Roberts *et al.*, 1994; Roberts and Parfitt, 1999; see Fig. 1.20). Roberts (1996a and b) interprets Boxgrove as a hunting ground on a coastal grassland plain, to which hominins repeatedly went to exploit the rich combination of herd animals and raw materials. Indeed, the site has preserved evidence for several hunting episodes, involving at least one rhinoceros and a horse (the latter apparently bearing a projectile wound in its shoulder). The sequence of events involved in the horse-hunting episode shows that hominins co-operatively brought down the animal (probably wearing it out first in the marshes), then collected flint nodules from the Chalk, from which they made handaxes on the spot and finally butchered the carcass. The whole event seems well-organised and unhurried. Handaxes and presumably a large amount of meat were subsequently removed from the site, for further processing and consumption elsewhere. Refitting material has also been found in the overlying mass-movement cold climate gravels, perhaps suggesting continued occupation into the early Anglian glaciation.

The site at High Lodge, Suffolk (Ashton *et al.*, 1992), represents part of the extinct Bytham River system, which once flowed west-east from the Midlands to south Lincolnshire, then through Norfolk and Suffolk into the North Sea basin. Here an assemblage dominated by flakes, cores and flake tools was found in a series of low energy fluviatile silts and clays, representing the floodplain deposits of a gently flowing river surrounded by pine-spruce woodland and areas of marshy ground. Some of the material refits and the archaeology may be essentially *in situ*, although the sediments in which it is contained have been picked up, moved *en masse* and deformed by Anglian ice. The flake tools include a number of refined scrapers with semi-invasive, scalar retouch (Fig. 1.22). Their morphology is so refined that they were originally believed to be Middle Palaeolithic. Another assemblage dominated by handaxes was also recovered from glaciofluvial outwash gravels that mantle the transported silty clays; given their condition they probably came from a nearby source and are considered by some to have

originally been contemporary with the scraper assemblage, which perhaps once occurred in different activity areas along the same stretch of river valley. Another important pre-Anglian site occurs only 2 km away at Warren Hill, where a very rich handaxe assemblage has been found in deposits now believed to form part of the Bytham river system (Wymer *et al.*, 1991).

One final site outside the main study area is worth mentioning. At Waverley Wood Farm Pit, Warwickshire, a series of non-flint artefacts including three andesite handaxes were recovered from the base of the Bagington-Lillington Gravel (Shotton *et al.*, 1993; Wise, 1993; Keen *et al.*, 2006). Further discoveries have been made at the pit more recently, including a flint handaxe (Keen pers. comm.). The gravels containing the artefacts have been assigned to the Bytham River, and based on a number of lithostratigraphical correlations and biostratigraphical analysis of the mammalian and molluscan faunas from organic deposits underlying the gravels, are probably of late Cromerian (MIS 13) date (Preece and Parfitt, 2000), although a date of MIS 15 (*c* 565,000 BP) was previously suggested on the basis of aminostratigraphy (Bowen *et al.*, 1989). Organic sediments were present in several shallow channels at the site, yielding pollen of boreal character, fluvial molluscs including *B. troscheli*, *Unio crassus* and *P. clessini*, and a limited vertebrate assemblage containing *Microtus oeconomus* (northern vole), common mole (*Talpa europaea*), *Microtus subterraneus* (European pine vole) and the water vole *A. t. cantiana*, amongst others (Shotton *et al.*, 1993). Few large mammal fossils are known from the site and when present, they are frequently of *Palaeoloxodon antiquus* (straight-tusked elephant), although horse, bison and a large cervid have also been encountered. Archaeologically the most interesting thing about the Waverley Wood artefacts is that they have been made on non-local raw materials. The andesites have been compared with the Langdale series in the Lake District, a distance of some 300 km. If hominins were procuring this directly, then not only is this evidence of extensive transport beyond that generally seen in the Lower Palaeolithic (see below), but it also provides evidence for humans advancing much further north than presently known (Keen *et al.*, 2006). The possibility that the andesite was obtained from erratics brought into the Midlands by earlier ice advances, must also be considered, however. Given that flint could be had within much shorter distances than this, simply by following the route of the Bytham River, this seems a very plausible solution, although of course, hominins returning from hypothetical northern excursions could easily have carried a curated andesite tool kit with them.

Upper and Middle Thames

Despite the growing number of Cromerian Complex sites now known from Britain, it is intriguing that not a single primary context archae-

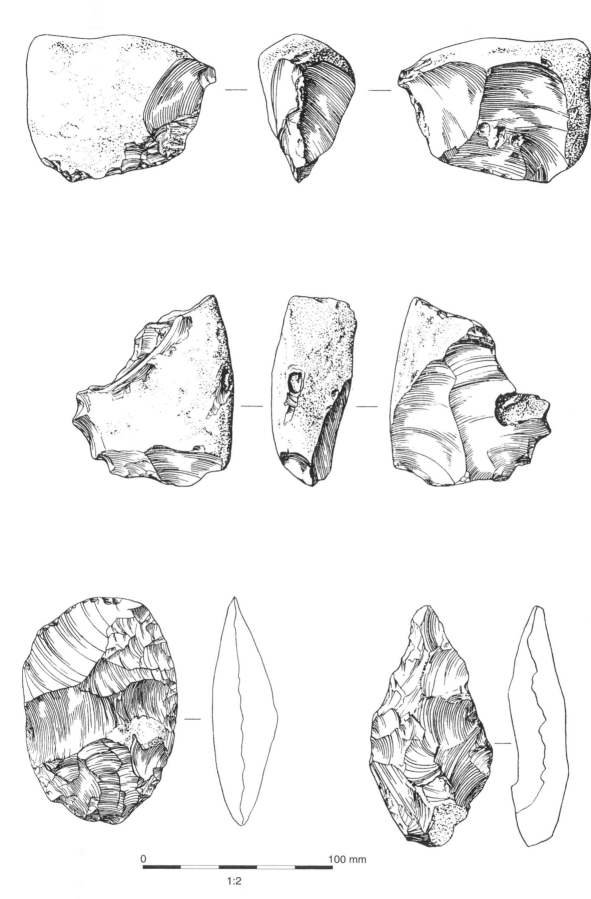

Fig. 1.23   Tools from Highlands Farm, Oxfordshire   Fig. 1.24 (overleaf)   Lower Palaeolithic stone tools

LOWER PALAEOLITHIC STONE TOOLS

Lower Palaeolithic stone tool technology is based entirely on direct percussion, an object stone being struck directly with a percussor or hammer to detach flakes. Two types of hammer were used: hard hammers, usually another piece of stone; and soft hammers, usually of antler or bone, and perhaps wood. There are three basic elements to the British Lower Palaeolithic tool kit: cores and flakes, handaxes and various flake tools.

Lower Palaeolithic stone tool technology

In simple core and flake working a stone nucleus was struck with a hard hammer to remove flakes of various, largely uncontrolled, shapes and sizes. The knapper selected a striking platform with angles suitable for flake removal (<90°), and after minimal if any preparation to this platform proceeded to work the core via a number of fundamental knapping modes (single flaking, parallel flaking, and alternate flaking). A single core can show several different episodes of flaking using a variety of modes: the resultant cores vary enormously in form, although they are generally fairly globular and chunky. The resultant flakes generally show exaggerated percussion features, with large butts and strong ripple marks. Whilst not random, progression often appears relatively unstructured, responding to events as they unfolded in the hand, moving from one area of the core to another in the search for suitable striking platforms and knapping angles.

Today it is widely assumed that the primary aim of core and flake working was to produce flakes with sharp edges, which could be used for a number of cutting and slicing purposes, the cores being waste. However, there are some cores, referred to as choppers or chopper-cores, which have a sharp zig-zag edge opposite an unworked face. There is some question as to whether these were unplanned waste-products generated by the

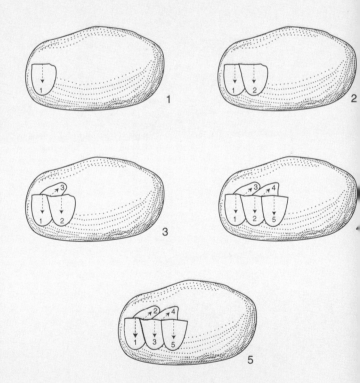

use of alternate flaking along one side of a core only or whether they were intentionally created to be used in heavy-duty chopping activities.

* Above — Stages in the reduction of cores ('core episodes'): 1 single removal; 2 parallel flaking; 3 simple alternate flaking; 4 complex alternate flaking; 5 classic alternate flaking

FACING PAGE
* Above — Flake tools. Top row left to right, scraper, notch, denticulate; below, flaked flake

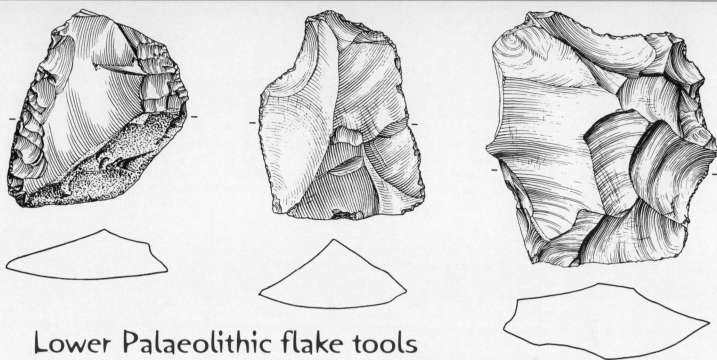

Lower Palaeolithic flake tools

At the basic level Lower Palaeolithic flake tools are simply flakes which have been subjected to some form of edge modification. Several rudimentary types are recognised in the Lower Palaeolithic – simple scrapers, notches, denticulates and flaked flakes. Flake tools are not particularly rare, although it is sometimes difficult to differentiate between anthropogenic and naturally altered edges. Lower Palaeolithic scrapers tend to be more crudely made and less diverse in form than their Middle Palaeolithic counterparts, often just a thick flake with a few retouch removals along one edge.

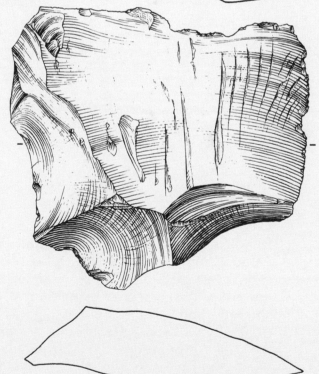

Different combinations of these tool forms are used by archaeologists to define different stone tool industries. In Britain, two Lower Palaeolithic industries are recognised: the *Clactonian* and the *Acheulean*. At the most basic level, the difference between these two industries is the presence or absence of handaxes. The Clactonian is defined as a core and flake industry, with a variety of flake tools including scrapers, flaked flakes, denticulates and notches, chopper cores, but no handaxes. The Acheulean has all these elements plus handaxes. Although historically the Clactonian was also believed to represent an early 'crude' form of lithic technology, recent studies have failed to support any technological differences in the underlying core and flake working, although Acheulean scrapers may be more sophisticated in their manufacture than those seen in the Clactonian.

Figure 1.24

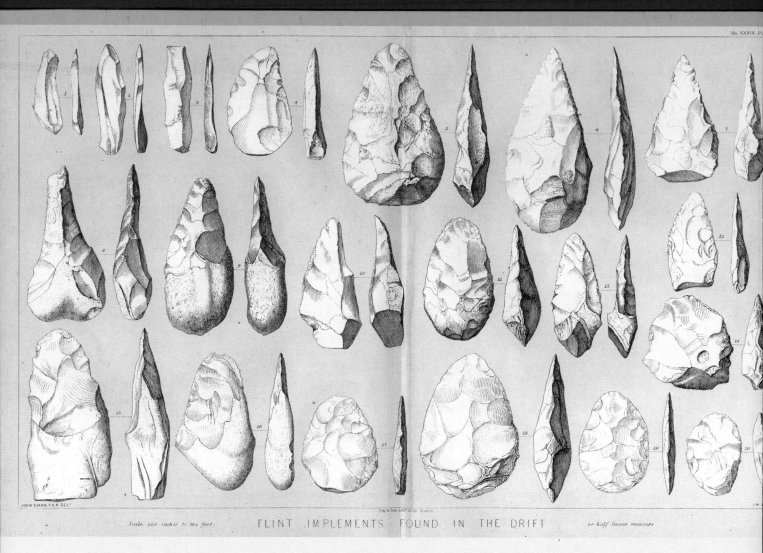

FLINT IMPLEMENTS FOUND IN THE DRIFT

Scale, six inches to the foot.   or half linear measure

JOHN EVANS, F.S.A. DEL.

Handaxes

Handaxes are the quintessential Lower Palaeolithic tool, in which there is clearly repetitive design intent. Handaxes are generally described as symmetrical, pear-shaped implements possessing a sharp bifacially-worked edge around all or part of the circumference, although they vary enormously in shape, symmetry, manufacture and refinement. Handaxes can be made on nodules, pebbles or flakes. Technological studies have suggested that many handaxes were initially roughed-out with a hard hammer, after which they were thinned and finished using a soft hammer. The roughing out phase produces flakes practically identical to simple core

working, but the thinning and later phases often produce very distinctive thin flakes with small butts, diffuse knapping features and complex knapping patterns (reflecting previous bifacial working) on their dorsal surfaces. Handaxes are often described as the Palaeolithic Swiss Army Knife, although most use-wear analyses in Britain have found traces of animal butchery only.It was once believed that handaxes showed an evolution in sophistication of form through time, but a number of recent discoveries have shown this not to be the case. Variation in handaxe form is a heated and complex topic (see main text).

Figure 1.24

The Ancestral River Thames

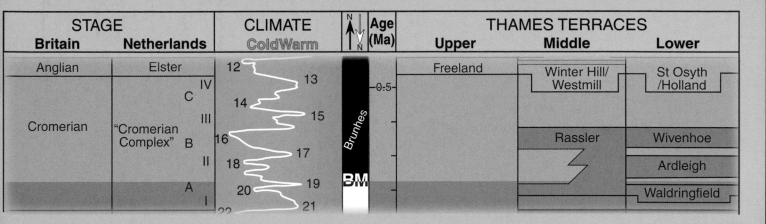

STAGE		CLIMATE	Age (Ma)	THAMES TERRACES		
Britain	Netherlands	Cold Warm		Upper	Middle	Lower
Anglian	Elster	12 / 13		Freeland	Winter Hill/ Westmill	St Osyth /Holland
	IV C	14 / 15	0.5			
Cromerian	"Cromerian Complex" B	16 / 17	Brunhes		Rassler	Wivenhoe
	II	18				Ardleigh
	A I	20 / 19 / 21	BM			Waldringfield
		22				

The Thames river system has largely developed over the last 2 million years. During this time its course and character have been subject to major changes under the influence of succeeding cold-warm climate cycles.

Today the Thames rises in Gloucestershire, and its upper reaches drain the limestone hills of the Cotswolds. However it is clear that the Thames once drained a much wider area than this. Quartz and quartzite are present in the early gravel terraces of the Middle Thames. There are no bedrock sources of this material within the modern Thames catchment and its presence provides evidence that the river once flowed from the West Midlands and possibly drained an area extending as far as North Wales. This ancestral river flowed into our region through the Evenlode Valley and then along approximately its modern course as far as Goring.

Downstream from Goring, however, the ancient Thames once again took a very different, north-easterly course, flowing to the north of Reading, through Marlow and Watford, and on through the Vale of St Albans to Essex and Suffolk. The terrace deposits of the ancient Middle Thames can be followed on Figure 1.9 (Kesgrave Formation to Winter Hill Member).

By about 500,000 BP, the headwaters of the Thames had contracted to the south of the Cotswold escarpment but the main course continued to run through the Evenlode Valley.

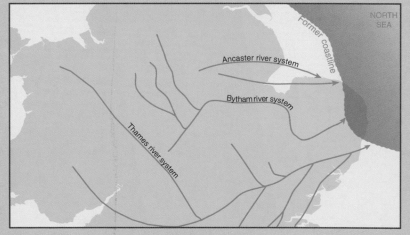

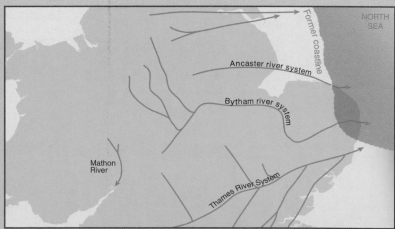

Figure 1.25

THE ANCIENT THAMES VALLEY

Occupation and Environment: The "Cromerian Complex" c 780–500,000 BP

Rare evidence for the environment of the Thames Valley in this remote period has been found at Sugworth, near Abingdon, in an ancient channel of the Thames. This can probably be equated with either MIS 15 or 13, dating to approximately 600-500,000 BP. Warm-loving plants such as water chestnut and water fern grew around the channel, and animals living nearby included Etruscan rhinoceros and two species of large, extinct shrew.

It is very likely that early hominins would have been present in the Thames Valley at times during this period but no *in situ* evidence has yet been found. Large numbers of flint tools have been discovered in the gravels that accumulated during the Anglian glaciation, many of them from an ancient channel of the Thames between Caversham and Henley. It is possible that some of these flints, which include handaxes, cleavers, cores, chopping tools and flake tools, are of Cromerian Complex age and were subsequently incorporated into later gravels.

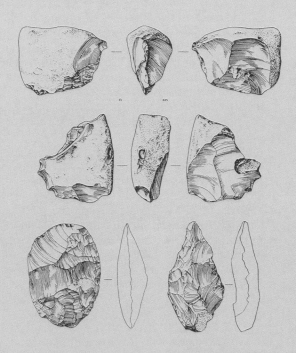

Left – Artist's impression of a Homo heidelbergensis occupation site in wooded uplands, c 500 000 years ago

Above – Early flint tools from the Middle Thames Valley. These flints, from Highlands Farm Pit, were found in the Black Park terrace, dating from the Anglian glaciation (see Chapter 2)

Figure 1.25

ological site of definite pre-Anglian age has been identified in the Thames Valley (Wymer, 1999). With the notable exception of Sugworth, this applies equally to sites of palaeontological or palaeoecological interest. Moreover, the occurrence of artefacts within the various Thames gravels of Anglian age does not allow us to infer any major pre-Anglian occupation in the valley itself. There is practically nothing in the Upper Thames, and the earliest artefacts in the Middle Thames are found in the late Anglian Black Park gravel, the earlier Anglian Winter Hill gravel being famously barren (Wymer, 1999). A few isolated finds have been documented on the older, higher level gravels (Winter Hill and equivalent) surrounding the 'Ancient Channel' at Caversham and in the Thames/Kennet Valley near Tilehurst further west, but these were considered by Wymer to be surface finds of later date and of little significance in terms of the earliest occupation of the valley (Wymer, 1999). The critical point here is that any artefacts derived from early Middle Pleistocene landsurfaces should logically occur in the Winter Hill gravel as well as the Black Park, leading Wymer to suggest that the material in the Black Park belongs to a hypothesised mid-Anglian interstadial, a short period of climatic amelioration long enough, and with a climate favourable enough, to allow humans ingress to the British Isles.

The earliest evidence for occupation of the study area, then, comes from a series of accumulations in late Anglian gravels. The richest come from the abandoned 'Ancient Channel' between Caversham and Henley (Wymer, 1968, 1999; see above). The gravels within this channel belong to the Black Park terrace of late MIS 12 age and have produced a number of prolific Palaeolithic sites – including those at Highlands Farm Pit, Kennyland's and Farthingworth Green – which together have yielded several thousands of artefacts (Fig. 1.23). These include handaxes of various forms, cleavers, cores, chopping tools, flake tools and a number of soft and hard-hammer flakes (Wymer, 1968, 192-3). The material is described as relatively fresh (although it actually occurs in a variety of preservational states) and there is no stratigraphical rationale to divide the various elements into separate industries. Wymer (1968) suggested that the artefacts in the channel represent a mixture of Clactonian and Acheulean industries, although many would now dispute this conclusion (see Fig. 1.24 and further discussion in Chapter 2, below). Another collection of 23 handaxes came from the Silchester Gravel (according to Bridgland (1994) a Black Park equivalent) at Hamstead Marshall, Newbury.

The temporal distribution of artefacts within these gravels is actually quite mysterious, as there are few obvious reasons why during the early Middle Pleistocene, the Upper and Middle Thames

should not have been host to human populations large enough to leave a visible archaeological record, especially when humans are known to have been present both north and south of the river. There is even some evidence for human activity in the Thames' southern tributaries during this period: the oldest terrace (Terrace A) of the Wey at Farnham, for example, having produced a series of crude handaxes believed to be of at least Anglian age if not much older (Oakley, 1939; Gibbard, 1982; Wymer, 1999). Also the numerous artefacts in the Wallingford Fan Gravels, situated on the slopes of the Chilterns about four miles from the modern river in Oxfordshire, seem to testify to occupation of the adjacent upland zone at this time (Roe, 1986, 1994). Horton *et al.* (1981) concluded that the majority of the Wallingford Fan Gravel accumulated under cold conditions, partly by solifluction from the Chilterns and partly by fluvial deposition in a tributary of the Thames. The gravels are correlated with the Upper Winter Hill gravel of the Thames, making the derived archaeology they contain earlier than anything in the Thames itself, possibly representing the sweepings from landsurfaces of Cromerian Complex age.

The lack of evidence in the present Lower Thames area can be explained by the fact that the valley did not exist as a Thames route prior to the Anglian, but good evidence for human occupation in the pre-diversion low-level Kesgrave gravels in Essex is equally missing (Wymer, 1999). Perhaps the studied exposures are just of the wrong age to contain artefacts, the artefact-bearing beds having been scoured out by later fluvial activity, although if so, this was a remarkably thorough and selective period of reworking. It is therefore highly probable that the Thames Valley was a focus for activity during the Cromerian Complex and that the posited 'inter-Anglian' sites actually contain derived material of this age. At present however, there is no way to confirm this.

Hominin Behaviour in the Lower Palaeolithic

The types and basic function of the stone tools of this period are outlined in Figure 1.24. The following section offers a brief discussion of how the archaeological record allows us to go further into understanding the lives and behaviour of the earliest Lower Palaeolithic inhabitants (ie those who intermittently occupied Britain from at least MIS 13 until MIS 9). Although the study area has not produced a rich archaeological record for this time, the evidence from elsewhere in Britain and across Europe allows us to build up a more detailed picture of how these people may have lived. Note that this discussion is also of relevance to the following two chapters, where the various themes will be taken up further in relation to specific cases.

Fig. 1.25 (previous spread)   The Ancient Thames Valley: occupation and environment of the Cromerian Complex

Britain represents the extreme northwestern edge of the Palaeolithic world. For a tropical African hominin, it would have presented a number of challenges. Apart from the differences in annual temperature, hominins would have had to learn to cope with reduced daylight foraging hours, greater seasonality of resources (especially vegetation which may have increased reliance on meat resources), reduced species diversity and a generally lower biomass. In order to survive in such conditions, one might speculate that a number of pre-existing behavioural characteristics were in place, such as the controlled use of fire and the ability to actively hunt a range of medium- to large-sized game (Dennell, 1982).

Throughout the 1980s and 1990s, the early inhabitants of Europe were generally conceived as being marginal scavengers, reliant on large carnivores such as lions, sabre-toothed cats and hyaenas to provide sufficient carcasses for them to survive (Binford, 1985; Turner, 1992). However, the faunal evidence from sites such as Boxgrove has now begun to show that hominins were accomplished hunters, and the incredibly preserved wooden spears from the 300,000-400,000 year old site at Schöningen, Germany (Thieme, 1997) provide unique insights into the types of hunting weapons used. These spears – of which a dozen or so are now known – are ~2 m long, crafted from spruce and are apparently weighted like a modern Olympic javelin. Whether they were truly used for throwing or thrusting remains uncertain, but either way they would have been essential survival tools in the predation of a range of animals, including the horse, red deer and rhino that seem to have been among the favoured prey of these early humans. Palaeolithic archaeologists have been very cautious in accepting claims for controlled fire at such an early date. However, survival in northern latitudes would seem to demand it – for warmth, defence, deterrence, and light. Several of the more convincing claims for Lower Palaeolithic hearths again include Schöningen (Thieme, 2005) and also the site of Beeches Pit, Suffolk (Gowlett and Hallos, 2000).

Most known Palaeolithic findspots, no matter how rich, do not appear to have been residential camps, however. The lives of these early hominins have been characterised as being based on high frequency mobility around a home range, groups and sub-groups frequently moving between a number of well-known locations that provided them with a range of resources (Gamble, 1996). Most 'sites', then, are places where the means, motive and opportunity (Kuhn, 1995) to carry out a number of basic subsistence and social activities came together, and which therefore formed magnet locations that were repeatedly visited over long periods, with each visit being fairly fleeting (how long sites were actually occupied may never be known). The activities carried out at these sites seem also to have been fairly repetitive – stone tool manufacture and use, animal processing, plus a range of invisible but reasonably inferred activities such as plant processing and woodworking etc – all tasks based around habit and predictability. So, the grassy plains at Boxgrove and riparian floodplains of the major river valleys were probably rich hunting grounds that also provided access to lithic raw materials and other resources. In the case of river valleys, they may also have provided natural routeways through the landscape (Ashton *et al.*, 2006). Pope (2002; Pope and Roberts, 2005) has also suggested that sites where large accumulations of artefacts built up would have helped hominins understand their landscape, highlighting places rich in ecological affordances and marking out earlier (and future) social gatherings for fissioned sub-groups.

Judging from the distances over which raw materials moved during the Lower Palaeolithic, hominin home ranges were quite limited in size, life was spatially and socially local (Gamble, 1996, 1999). In general, raw materials were immediately available or were situated within a 5-10 km radius of a site (Feblot-Augustin, 1999). Only very occasionally do materials move longer distances, and then only in small quantities. Evidence that handaxes and other artefacts were moving though landscapes (Hallos, 2005; Pope, 2005) shows that hominins equipped themselves with tools for use elsewhere, but for how long and how far these would have been carried before the need or opportunity to replace them arose is uncertain. Given that none seem to have been used or reworked to the point of exhaustion, days rather than weeks seems more likely.

Does this mean that campsites did not exist? Some have certainly expressed this opinion (eg Gamble, 1996), and when claims for camps, replete with huts and hearths, are made – for example at Terra Amata, Nice (de Lumley, 1969) and Bilzingsleben, Germany (Mania, 1991) – they often fail to stand up to scrutiny or are received with extreme scepticism. One question that needs to be asked, though, is whether the types of environment where most of our Palaeolithic evidence is recovered – river valleys, lakesides and coastal plains where large carnivores were highly active – would have been suitable places to make camp, or whether hominins might not have chosen more protected places as centres of social life. Indeed, Roberts (1996a) has argued that at Boxgrove any hypothetical camps would have been situated on the forested downland block, not on the open coastal plain. Such places would certainly have provided far better protection and shelter but being outside major sedimentary traps would also have greatly reduced chances of preservation or discovery. Also, given the high levels of mobility inferred above, investment in structures was unlikely, meaning that any fleeting and probably unstructured camps that were constructed would leave little archaeologically clear signature and would be unlikely to be preserved (cf Verpoorte, 2006).

In this regard, Wymer's (1999) observation that in the Thames Valley many of the densest accumulations seem to be situated on the confluences of the main river and major tributaries takes on added significance. Not only do these represent junctions between different natural routeways, providing access to wide plains with an abundance of resources and access to different parts of a group's home range, but the interfluves might also have provided relatively safe havens from which the surrounding open valleys could be monitored and surveyed, allowing choices about where to go and when. Wymer (1999, 48) similarly suggests that the Chalk hinterlands would have been favoured locations, providing access to raw materials, well-drained soils with attractive grazing for herbivore prey (whose feeding habits would have kept the area relatively open) and easy access to the more heavily wooded clay-with-flint and tertiary uplands for shelter and cover. This certainly provides several reasons why the Upper Thames is so impoverished compared to the Middle and Lower Thames, although problems of ancient preservation and modern recognition of different raw materials should also be considered. These themes will be taken up further in later chapters.

Chapter 2 – The diversion of the Thames, the Hoxnian interglacial and adjacent cold stages (MIS12-11-10)

by Danielle Schreve, Anthony Morigi and Mark White

THE ANGLIAN GLACIATION

The Anglian British Ice Sheet was the most extensive glaciation of the past 500,000 years. At this time, ice advanced as far south as Finchley in north London, obliterating the Bytham river system and diverting the Thames into its modern course. The preceding chapter described how the early Thames flowed through the Vale of St Albans to the north of London. However, some 430,000 years ago a marked change in climate triggered what is perhaps the most significant event in the history of the river, a diversion into its present day course. During the Anglian stage (MIS 12) the climate cooled sufficiently to allow ice sheets to advance into northern Europe. In Britain ice reached as far south as London, with lobes of ice extending to the vicinity of Watford, Finchley and Hornchurch at the glacial maximum (Fig. 2.1). The evidence for this is the widespread glacial deposits in the region, which include glacial till, glaciolacustrine and glaciofluvial deposits that together constitute the Lowestoft Formation. It is the stratigraphic relationship between these glacial deposits and the terrace deposits of the river Thames that has provided the key to the cause and timing of diversion. The following account draws particularly on the work of Gibbard (1974, 1977, 1985) and Bridgland (1994).

The diversion of the Thames

Earlier workers had speculated upon the reasons for the diversion (eg Salter, 1905; Sherlock and Noble, 1912), including the suggestion that overspill from a proglacial lake in the Vale of St Albans was the cause (Sherlock and Pocock, 1924). Gibbard (1974, 1977) found evidence to support this view in a sequence of deposits at Moor Mill Quarry near Watford, which comprises gravels overlain by laminated clays, followed by till, which in turn is overlain by gravel. The basal gravel is rich in quartz and quartzite, and imbrication and other sedimentary structures indicate palaeocurrent flow towards the northeast. Gibbard showed it to be the equivalent of both the downstream Westmill Gravel and the upstream Winter Hill Gravel, thereby demonstrating the continuation of the Winter Hill/ Westmill terrace from the Middle Thames into the Vale of St. Albans. He interpreted the overlying laminated clays as glaciolacustrine deposits of a proglacial lake, the Moor Mill Lake, which formed during an advance of ice into the Vale. He also attributed an apparent flattening of the gradient of the Winter Hill Gravel upstream of Watford to the formation of a delta in Moor Mill Lake, although Cheshire (1986) has suggested that slight uplift resulting from isostatic rebound following ice retreat may have been the cause. Gibbard reasoned that the course of the Thames through the Vale of St Albans had been blocked by the Moor Mill Lake. The till, correlated by Gibbard with the Eastend Green Till, represented the second of two ice advances into the Vale of St Albans, the first not having reached the Moor Mill area. The upper gravel, his Smug Oak Gravel, contrasted markedly with the basal gravel in composition and sedimen-

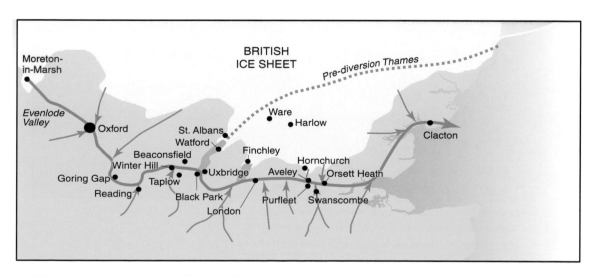

Fig. 2.1   The palaeogeography of the Thames during the Anglian glaciation

tary features indicated a palaeocurrent direction to the southwest; the opposite direction to the river that deposited the Winter Hill/Westmill Gravel. The Smug Oak Gravel can be traced southwestwards to Uxbridge along a course similar to that of the present day River Colne (Gibbard, 1979). At this point it passes into the Black Park Gravel, the earliest terrace deposited by the post-Anglian-glaciation river Thames (Fig. 2.2).

Deposits at Westmill Quarry near Ware, to the northeast of Moor Hill Quarry, have been the subject of detailed investigations (Gibbard, 1974, 1979; Cheshire, 1983b, 1986). This locality is some distance outside the area that is the focus of this volume but as it is important to an understanding of the diversion of the Thames a brief reference is desirable. Here a complex sequence comprises two gravel units separated by a till, and a second till that overlies the upper gravel unit. Thin laminated clays occur locally beneath the lower till. Gibbard correlated both the lower gravel unit and the greater part of the upper gravel with the basal gravel at Moor Mill Quarry. The intervening till he considered the equivalent of the Ware Till, deposited by an earlier ice advance, which in the surrounding area rests

upon laminated clays. The uppermost few metres of the upper gravel unit were taken by Gibbard, because of an upward change in composition and palaeocurrent direction, to be outwash from the ice that deposited the upper till at Westmill Quarry, which he assigned to his Eastend Green Till.

According to Gibbard (1974, 1977, 1979) the deposits at Moor Mill, Westmill and other nearby localities represent the following sequence of events. During the early Anglian, the Thames flowed northeastwards through the Vale of St Albans, depositing the Winter Hill/ Westmill Gravel. Ice advanced into the eastern part of the Vale near Ware and a proglacial lake formed in the path of the River Thames. This ice advance did not interrupt the passage of the river which continued with the deposition of the Westmill Gravel. Ice re-advance into the Vale emplaced the Eastend Green Till at Westmill and also over the deposits of a second proglacial lake in the Watford area, Moor Mill Lake. This advance of ice into Moor Mill Lake caused an overspill of the lake into the Mole-Wey valley in the vicinity of Uxbridge. Following the draining of Moor Mill Lake the Smug Oak Gravel was deposited by a southwestward flowing river

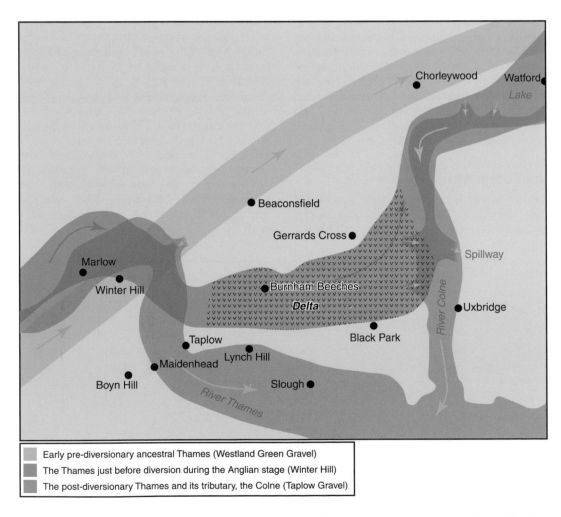

Fig. 2.2 *Schematic representation of the stages of the diversion of the Thames from the Vale of St Alban's*

which flowed out through the spillway. The Thames was re-routed through existing valleys via a series of spillways until it joined the river Medway near Southend-on-Sea. From there the Thames-Medway followed the existing early course of the River Medway to join the earlier course of the Thames near Clacton (Bridgland, 1980) before discharging into a large proglacial lake that occupied the southern North Sea basin during the Anglian stage (see Fig. 1.7).

However, detailed stratigraphic studies of fluvial and glacial deposits in the Vale of St Albans by Cheshire (1981, 1983a, b and c, 1986) resulted in a different interpretation involving a more complex sequence of events leading up to diversion of the river. Cheshire considered that the first ice advance into the Vale of St Albans interrupted the course of the Thames near Harlow forming a proglacial lake in the Ware-Harlow area and emplacing the Ware Till. He suggested that a tributary of the Darent-Medway had captured the Mole-Wey (which at this time joined the early Thames in the Vale of St Alban's) at a point further upstream and that overspill from this proglacial lake led to southward flow in the abandoned reach of the Mole-Wey thus initiating the river Lea. If this interpretation is correct then the Thames underwent an initial, albeit short-lived, diversion to the Medway via the Lea. Bridgland (1994) has speculated that the earliest post-diversionary deposits of the Thames to the east of London, correlated with the Black Park Gravel but buried by the later Boyn Hill/Orsett Heath Gravel (Bridgland. 1988a) may be coeval with the youngest part of the Winter Hill/Westmill Gravel and so contemporaneous with this short-lived diversion. Cheshire argued that Ware Till ice then extended into the western part of the Vale of St Albans emplacing the till at Moor Mill Quarry (which he correlated with the Ware Till rather than Gibbard's Eastend Green Till) and precipitating the overspill of the Moor Mill Lake as described by Gibbard.

Palaeogeography of the terrace deposits (Table 2.1)

In the early Anglian, prior to glaciation and diversion, the Thames continued to flow from its headwaters in the Evenlode Valley following contraction of its catchment (see Chapter 1), more-or-less following the course of the present day Thames through the Goring Gap, and on to Marlow (see Fig. 2.1). Now somewhat more sinuous in character (Whiteman and Rose, 1992), it looped south of Beaconsfield before turning northeast past Watford and then via the Vale of St Albans and through northern Essex where equivalents of the Winter Hill Gravel form part of the Kesgrave Formation (Table 2.1). In the lower part of the Thames catchment continuous southward migra-

tion of the river due to basin-ward tilting of the land is evident from the distribution of the terrace gravels which young southward. The adoption by the Thames of its post-diversionary course below Uxbridge was described in the account of the diversion above. Following diversion the course of the Middle Thames, though broadly similar to today's, was still via a channel in the Caversham area to the north of Reading. Black Park Gravel deposits that occupy this 'Ancient Channel' have proved a rich source of Palaeolithic artefacts derived from an earlier, pre-Anglian period (see Chapter 1). Following subsequent rejuvenation, by Boyn Hill Gravel times the Thames had abandoned the 'Ancient Channel' as it continued its low southward migration. The distribution of the Hanborough Gravel, the correlative of the Boyn Hill Gravel, in the Upper Thames indicates that up until this time, at least, the main course of the Thames was still through the Evenlode Valley and then along the Thames Valley to the Goring Gap.

Correlation of the terrace deposits

The Black Park Gravel was the first deposit of the post-diversionary Thames. Correlation of this deposit with deposits in the Lower Thames has proved extremely controversial. As the Lower Thames falls outside the principal interest of this volume, a detailed history of the controversy is beyond its scope. For a thorough account, the reader is referred to Bridgland (1994) but briefly, the nub of the debate is the status of deposits beneath a relatively high-level terrace at Dartford Heath. Gibbard (1979; Gibbard *et al.*, 1988) followed earlier authors (eg Zeuner, 1945) in correlating these deposits with the Black Park Gravel while Bridgland (1980) accepted the view that projecting the slope of the Black Park Gravel downstream placed it beneath the level of the younger Boyn Hill Gravel (Evans, 1971). Bridgland therefore argued that the deposits at Dartford Heath were likely to equate with the Boyn Hill Gravel (= Orsett Heath Formation) while the Black Park Gravel may be represented within the fill of a channel system that underlies the Orsett Heath Formation in eastern Essex (Bridgland, 1980, 1983a, 1983b, and 1988a). However, during a re-survey of the Romford district by the British Geological Survey, spreads of gravel lying topographically above the Orsett Heath Formation at several locations were classified as Black Park Gravel. Consequently, Ellison (2004) suggested that the height ranges of the Black Park and Orsett Heath (Boyn Hill) gravels overlap supporting the view that the deposits at Dartford Heath include gravels equivalent to both of these terrace deposits. As elsewhere in this volume Bridgland's view is followed.

Fig. 2.3   The Anglian glaciation and the diversion of the Thames

THE DIVERSION OF THE THAMES

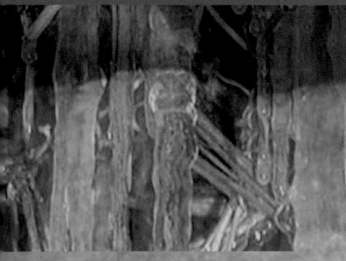

The Anglian glaciation was the most extensive of the last half million years. Dating to around 430,000 BP, it is equated with MIS 12. At this time the climate cooled sufficiently to allow ice sheets to advance far into northern Europe. In Britain the ice extended as far south as Watford, Finchley and Hornchurch on the northern side of the Thames Valley. The advance of the ice blocked the course of the ancient Thames in the Vale of St Alban's, where a 'proglacial' lake formed in front of the ice.

Before the Anglian glaciation the ancient Thames had followed a much more northerly course than today, flowing north-eastwards through the Vale of St Alban's. When the ice advanced into the eastern part of the vale it interrupted the course of the river, blocking it and creating a 'proglacial' lake.

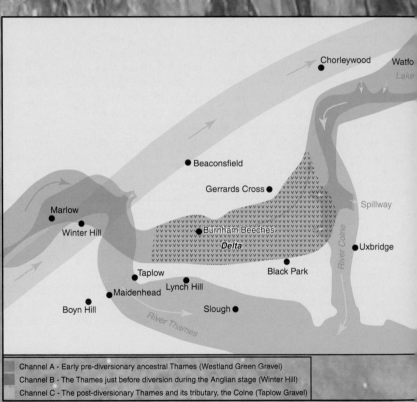

Channel A - Early pre-diversionary ancestral Thames (Westland Green Gravel)
Channel B - The Thames just before diversion during the Anglian stage (Winter Hill)
Channel C - The post-diversionary Thames and its tributary, the Colne (Taplow Gravel)

Channel A shows the general north-easterly trend of the ancient Thames.

By the onset of the Anglian glaciation, the Thames had moved slightly southwards, flowing around the loop represented by Channel B. A delta formed as the Thames slowed and deposited sediment at the edge of the proglacial lake. Ice advanced further into the lake and the water overflowed, draining the lake southwards along tributary valleys such as that of the modern river Colne.

To the west, the Thames established a new course south of the delta, represented by Channel C. It still follows this course through the Middle Thames Valley today, but in Anglian times it returned to a north-easterly alignment north of London and met the sea at Clacton.

THE ANGLIAN GLACIATION

STAGE		CLIMATE		Age	THAMES TERRACES		
Britain	**Netherlands**	Cold — Warm	N ↑ ↓ N	**(Ma)**	**Upper**	**Middle**	**Lower**
	Fuhne				Hanborough	Boyn Hill	Orsett Heath
Hoxnian	Holstein	11		0.4		Black Park	
Anglian	Elster	12			Freeland	Winter Hill/ Westmill	St Osyth /Holland
	IV C	13		0.5			

The Contemporary Environment

Directly in front of the Anglian ice sheet, polar desert conditions would have prevailed, with tundra further south, presenting a very hostile environment for most mammals (including hominins).

There have been very few finds made from this period because such severe environmental conditions do not favour fossil preservation. At Hall's Pit near Benson (Oxon) two species of snail were present that are today extinct in Britain and found only in arctic and alpine environments. At Long Hanborough pit in the Evenlode Valley, sub-arctic species of snail were also found, together with mammals such as steppe mammoth and horse. It is highly unlikely that hominins could have survived in Britain during the coldest parts of the Anglian glaciation.

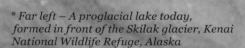

* Far left – A proglacial lake today, formed in front of the Skilak glacier, Kenai National Wildlife Refuge, Alaska

* Left – Schematic representation of the diversion of the Thames

* Top right – The Greenland ice sheet is now the second largest body of ice in the world, after the Antarctic ice sheet. The ice is generally more than 2 km thick. During the Anglian glaciation ice sheets extended far into Britain and northern Europe

* Right – Artist's reconstruction of the extinct steppe mammoth Mammuthus trogontherii; remains of steppe mammoth have been found at Long Hanborough in the Evenlode Valley

Figure 2.3

Correlation of the Black Park and Winter Hill Gravels with possible Upper Thames equivalents also poses some difficulties. Gibbard (1985) correlated the Black Park Gravel with the Freeland Member and the higher and therefore older Combe Member with the Winter Hill Gravel by projecting longitudinal profiles upstream. If Hey's (1986) interpretation of the stratigraphical relationship between the Sugworth Channel Deposits and the Freeland Member (see Chapter 1) were correct then these correlations would imply an implausible Anglian age for the former. The suggestion of a younger Hoxnian age for the Sugworth Channel Deposits, based on their elevation (Gibbard, 1985) runs counter to unequivocal biostratigraphical evidence for a Cromerian age (see Chapter 1). Bridgland (1994) has suggested that the difficulty can be resolved if the Freeland Member is considered coeval with both the Winter Hill and Black Park Gravels.

The Hanborough Gravel crops out in the Upper Thames and its tributaries the Evenlode and Cherwell. It is the highest of the four limestone-rich terrace deposits present in the Oxford area. The stratigraphical position of this terrace deposit in relation to glacigenic deposits in the Evenlode Valley near Moreton-in-Marsh is important because it has a bearing on the age of the Hanborough Gravel and may have wider implications for the age of glaciation in the Midlands. Arkell (1947) believed that the Hanborough Gravel underlay and therefore pre-dated the Moreton glacigenic deposits because he equated it with the apparently similar Paxford Gravel Member that lay beneath those deposits higher in the Evenlode Valley. The reported absence of flint in the Hanborough Gravel (while present in the younger Wolvercote Gravel) seemed to support this conclusion because flint, absent from the local bedrock, could only have been brought into the area by glaciation. More recently, however, Maddy *et al.* (1991) considered the lithological composition of these two terraces to be similar (see Chapter 3). If, as is now generally accepted, the Moreton glacigenic deposits are assigned to the Anglian Stage and Arkell's interpretation of their relationship to the Hanborough Gravel is correct, the latter must pre-date MIS 12. Nevertheless, it is clear from altitudinal

evidence that the Hanborough Gravel probably correlates with the Boyn Hill Gravel, and so must post-date the Anglian glaciation. This juxtaposition raises the possibility that the Moreton glacigenic suite could be younger than MIS 12 and the product of a later glaciation (Bridgland, 1994).

Careful mapping by Sumbler (2001) has shown unequivocally that the Paxford Gravel Member is interdigitated with the Moreton glacigenic deposits and is unrelated to the Hanborough Gravel, thus negating Arkell's interpretation. Based on his mapping and all other available evidence, Sumbler proposed a controversial chronology in which the older part of the Moreton glacigenic deposits, the Paxford and Moreton members, were deposited north of the col at the head of the Evenlode by ice-advance during MIS 12, with the Freeland Member representing outwash from this event. In Sumbler's chronology the younger parts of the glacigenic sequence, the Oadby (ie the 'chalky boulder clay' of the Midlands) and Wolford Heath (outwash sandur of the Oadby ice-sheet) members date from MIS 10. Evenlode Valley equivalents of the Hanborough and Wolvercote gravels (Spelsbury – in part – and Daylesford members) equate to glacial outwash during this period. Arising from this interpretation Sumbler (2001) further suggested that 'two separate phases of ice-advance and outwash are represented in the Moreton Drift [glacigenic deposits]' and thus the 'Anglian Glaciation' spanned MIS 12 to 10.

Traditionally, the Hanborough Gravel has been correlated with the Boyn Hill Gravel of the Middle and Lower Thames, although Gibbard (1985) thought the Boyn Hill Gravel and the next youngest terrace deposit, the Lynch Hill Gravel, converged upstream of Reading. Projecting long profiles of both into the Upper Thames indicated that both intersected the Hanborough Gravel near Oxford. He therefore suggested that the Hanborough Gravel might be composite and equate to parts of both Boyn Hill and Lynch Hill gravels. Bridgland (1994, 1996) confirmed the conventional Hanborough – Boyn Hill correlation, arguing that it is supported by unequivocal altitudinal evidence. The Boyn Hill Gravel is an important and widespread marker throughout the Middle and Lower Thames principally because of its association with Hoxnian interglacial deposits at

Table 2.1   *Correlation of Quaternary deposits of the Thames MIS 12-10*

Marine Isotope Stage	Quaternary deposits of the Thames		
	Upper	*Middle*	*Lower*
10	Hanborough Gravel	Boyn Hill Gravel	Orsett Heath Formation (top)
11			**Swanscombe Member**
12	Freeland Member	Black Park /Smug Oak gravels	Orsett Heath Formation (base)
	Moreton glacigenic deposits	*Lowestoft Formation*	*Lowestoft Formation*
	Freeland Member?	Winter Hill/Westmill gravels	St Oyth/Holland Members (Eastern Essex)

(Glacigenic deposits in italics, interglacial deposits in bold). Sources: Bridgland (1996); Bowen (1999).

Swanscombe (see below). In the Lower Thames, where it has been redefined as the Orsett Heath Formation (Bridgland, 1988a, 1994), it forms the highest (and therefore oldest) of the three terraces above the floodplain. Significantly, it directly overlies the Hornchurch Till, the southernmost representative of the Anglian Lowestoft Till, thus fixing all Lower Thames terrace gravels as post Anglian in age (Holmes, 1892 and many others). Several complex interpretations of the Orsett Heath Formation have been proposed some of which are discussed below. However, Bridgland (1996) considers that the Swanscombe Hoxnian interglacial deposits provide the key evidence for assigning the Hanborough Gravel/Boyn Hill Gravel/Orsett Heath Formation to MIS 12 to 10.

ARCHAEOLOGY AND PALAEONTOLOGY OF THE ANGLIAN GLACIATION

The debate over the correlation of the Anglian with the marine oxygen isotope record notwithstanding (cf Sumbler, 1995), most authors now agree that MIS 12 is the most likely correlative for this glaciation (Shackleton, 1987; Bridgland, 1994; Scourse *et al.*, 1999). Directly in front of the Anglian ice sheet, polar desert conditions would have prevailed, with tundra further south, presenting very hostile conditions for most mammals. Indeed, very few vertebrate or invertebrate records are known from this period anywhere in Britain. Within the study area, the site of Hall's Pit, near Benson in Oxfordshire, has yielded cool-climate non-marine Mollusca such as *Pisidium obtusale lapponicum* and *Columella columella*, two arctic-alpine species that are today extinct in Britain. The molluscs are indicative, in the lowest levels, of a lake with well-vegetated calcareous water giving way to a treeless grassland environment (Horton *et al.*, 1981). Rare vertebrate remains were also present, including frog or toad (*Rana* or *Bufo* sp.), Norway lemming (*Lemmus lemmus*), water vole (*Arvicola terrestris cantiana*), tundra vole (*Microtus gregalis*) and horse (*Equus ferus*) (Horton *et al.*, 1981). These remains came from a calcareous silt bed within the Wallingford Fan Gravels (see Chapter 1), an extensive sheet some 6 m thick of soliflucted chalky flint gravels and fluvial angular gravels and sands with interbedded finer-grained sediments (Horton and Whittow, 1977). The Wallingford Fan Gravels are aggraded to the level of the Winter Hill terrace of the Middle Thames and are therefore also of presumed Anglian age. Further evidence of cold-climate conditions comes from Long Hanborough gravel pit in the terrace system of the river Evenlode, in the form of non-marine molluscs indicative of a sub-arctic environment (Briggs and Gilbertson, 1973). Mammals from the site comprise a mixed assemblage including temperate forest species such as straight-tusked elephant (*Palaeoloxodon antiquus*) and open ground indicators such as steppe mammoth (*Mammuthus trogontherii*) and horse (*Equus ferus*) (Sandford, 1925). Of these, the relatively archaic aspect of the straight-tusked elephant teeth led Sandford to suggest that they had been reworked from early Middle Pleistocene interglacial deposits. Outside the study area, the few examples of Anglian mammals include the crushed skeleton of a ground squirrel (*Spermophilus* sp.) from freshwater silts below glacial till at Mundesley in Norfolk (Newton, 1882) (although Lee *et al.* [2004] would suggest an earlier, MIS 16, age for this till) and remains of red deer (*Cervus elaphus*) from late Anglian deposits at Hoxne, Suffolk (Spencer, in West, 1956).

Fig. 2.4   The present-day distribution of the Arctic beetle Diacheila polita

Late Anglian beetle remains from Hoxne include species with incompatible geographic ranges at the present day (Coope, in Singer *et al.*, 1993). The assemblage from Hoxne Stratum F, a lacustrine clay-mud directly overlying Anglian Lowestoft Till, contains not only a group of cold-indicative, boreal or boreo-montane inhabitants, including *Diacheila polita* (today living no nearer to the British Isles than the Kola peninsula of arctic Russia; Fig. 2.4) and tundra species, but also relatively southern species. The most plausible explanation for this assemblage is that it reflects rapid climatic amelioration, with mean July temperatures estimated to be 10° C, rising rapidly to 15° C. Anglian pollen and spore records from East Anglia indicate a regional sub-arctic or sub-alpine vegetation with groves of *Picea*, *Betula* and *Pinus* and substantial non-arboreal pollen frequencies in the early Anglian (West, 1977), giving way to assemblages with dominant grasses, sedges and *Hippophaë* (sea buckthorn) at the end of the glaciation (West, 1980b; Mullenders, in Singer *et al.*, 1993). These latter assemblages are considered to reflect a climate similar to that found today above the timberline, in the shrub zone between grassland and sub-arctic forest (Mullenders, in Singer *et al.* 1993). It is highly unlikely that archaic hominin populations would or could have survived in Britain during the very coldest parts of this glacial episode and sites such as Boxgrove (see Chapter 1) probably represent the final phases of occupation in the early part of this cold stage, prior to a protracted absence. As the climate ameliorated into the ensuing interglacial, however, hominins returned to Britain and the archaeological record shows a consistent (although not necessarily continuous) human presence throughout this warm period.

THE HOXNIAN INTERGLACIAL

The Hoxnian interglacial is one of the best represented and well studied episodes in the British Pleistocene sequence, with a number of well known sites both within and outside the Thames Valley. The archaeology of the period can be characterised as wholly Lower Palaeolithic in nature. It is dominated by Acheulean assemblages with a diverse array of different handaxe types and some flake tools, although a non-handaxe industry known as the Clactonian is also found at a small number of localities (see Fig. 1.24, above). There is probably a temporal element to the occurrence of these two industries. Where present, the Clactonian belongs to the terminal Anglian and earlier part of the interglacial only, with the Acheulean and its characteristic handaxes appearing later.

Sites outside the main area

The most famous Hoxnian site in Britain is Barnfield Pit at Swanscombe in Kent (Swanscombe Skull National Nature Reserve, see Fig. 2.15, below), situated in the Lower Thames Valley (eg Wymer,

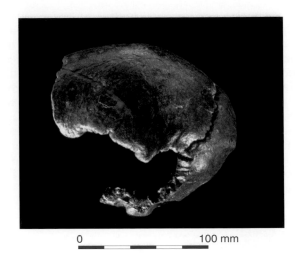

0   100 mm

Fig. 2.5   Partial skull of a pre-Neanderthal female from Barnfield Pit, Swanscombe, Kent

1968; Conway *et al.*, 1996; Bridgland, 1994; Schreve, 2004a). This site contains a remarkably full and very rich archaeological and palaeontological sequence, with evidence for human occupation stretching through 14 m of sediment from the terminal part of the Anglian, through the interglacial and into the ensuing cold phase. Barnfield Pit is also remarkable for having produced three refitting bones from a hominin skull (Fig. 2.5), found in separate pieces in 1935, 1936 (Marston, 1937) and 1955 (Wymer, 1964). The skull has been assigned to *Homo heidelbergensis*, and is argued to possess a number of incipient Neanderthal characteristics, suggesting that Neanderthals evolved in Eurasia from *Homo heidelbergensis* ancestors (Stringer and Hublin, 1999).

The Swanscombe deposits have been mapped as Boyn Hill Gravel (= Orsett Heath Gravel of Bridgland, 1994) (Fig. 2.6). They consist of gravels, sands and loams, which rest on an eroded surface of Thanet Sand and Chalk at about 22.5 m OD and reach a maximum height of 35.5 m OD. At Hornchurch in Essex, the Boyn Hill/Orsett Heath gravels overlie Anglian glacial till or 'Chalky Boulder Clay'. The interglacial sediments within the Boyn Hill/Orsett Heath terrace are therefore thought to represent the first immediately post-Anglian interglacial, correlated with MIS 11 (Bridgland, 1994; Schreve, 2001a). Traditionally, the Swanscombe deposits have been correlated with the Hoxnian interglacial of the British chronostrati-graphical scheme and they have long been regarded as the best representative for that interval in the Thames Valley (King and Oakley, 1936; Sutcliffe, 1964; Kerney, 1971). Correlation with the Hoxnian interglacial has been based primarily on comparisons of the Swanscombe pollen, molluscan and mammalian records with those of Clacton-on-Sea (see below), also assigned to the Hoxnian interglacial on palynological grounds (Pike and Godwin, 1953; Turner and Kerney, 1971). By comparing the molluscan faunas from Swanscombe and Clacton, Kerney (1971) was able to correlate the various fossiliferous parts of the Swanscombe sequence with the pollen biozones established at the Hoxne type site in Suffolk by West (1956) and also recognised at Clacton (Turner and Kerney, 1971). Subsequent work on mammalian assemblages from all three sites has also demonstrated their contemporaneity (Schreve, 2001a). The recognition of Anglian till at the base of the Boyn Hill/Orsett Heath sequence thus provides a *terminus ante quem* for the chronology of the ensuing terrace succession in the Lower Thames Valley. The stratigraphical succession and inferred environments at Swanscombe have been described

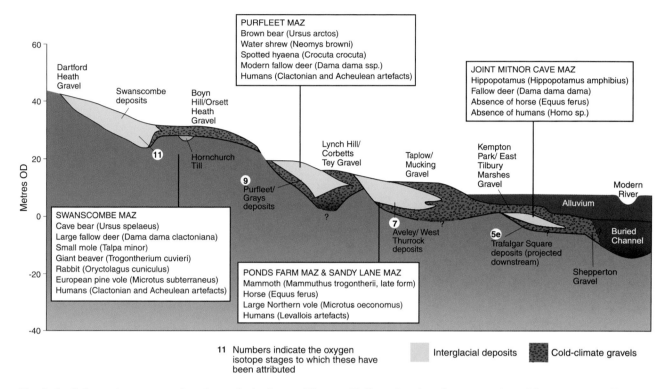

Fig. 2.6   Schematic cross-section through the Lower Thames Valley, showing the succession of four post-Anglian terraces. Interglacial deposits are indicated and key features of their mammalian assemblages are also given

Table 2.2   The stratigraphic sequence at Swanscombe after Conway and Waechter (1977), Bridgland (1994) and Conway et al. (1996). Principal beds are shown in bold type. Archaeological industries and prevailing climate are shown where known.

Members (beds)	Thickness	Industry	Climate
Phase III		-	
IIIe Higher Loams	up to 1m	-	?
IIId **Upper Gravel**	2m	Acheulean (derived handaxes)	Cold
IIIc **Upper Loam**	1m	Acheulean (mostly ovate handaxes)	Temperate
IIIb 'Upper Sands' channel deposits	0-2m	-	?
IIIa Soliflucted clay	0-1m	-	?
Phase II			
IIb **Upper Middle Gravel**	1.5-3m	Acheulean (mostly pointed handaxes)	Cool
IIa **Lower Middle Gravel**	2-2.5m	Acheulean (mostly pointed handaxes)	Temperate
Phase I			
1e Weathered surface of Lower Loam	0.5m	-	
1d Lower Loam	2-2.5m	Clactonian (non-handaxe)	Temperate
1c Lower Gravel 'midden'	0-0.75m	Clactonian (non-handaxe)	Temperate
1b Lower Gravel	up to 5m	Clactonian (non-handaxe)	Temperate
1a Basal Gravel	0-0.5m	-	Cold or temperate?

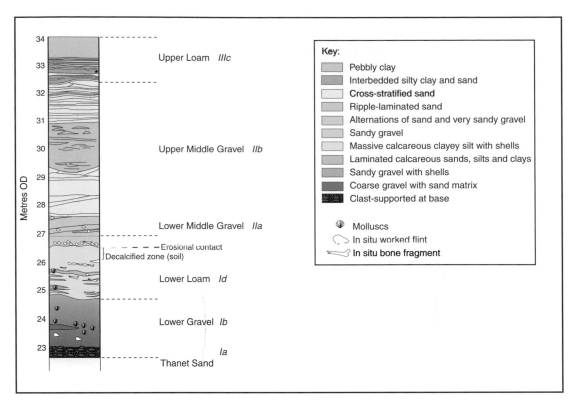

Fig. 2.7   The stratigraphy of the deposits at Barnfield Pit, Swanscombe

in detail by numerous previous authors and are summarised below, along with their stone tool industries (Table 2.2; Fig. 2.7):

The mammal remains from Swanscombe form a particularly diagnostic suite, the Swanscombe Mammal Assemblage-Zone (MAZ) (Schreve, 2001a) that may be used to characterise the MIS 11 interglacial (Hoxnian *sensu stricto* and subsequent parts of the interglacial) in Britain (see Fig. 2.6) and correlate with other sites. Important features of this faunal grouping are (1) the first appearance in the UK of aurochs (*Bos primigenius*), Merck's rhinoceros (*Stephanorhinus kirchbergensis*), narrow-nosed rhinoceros (*Stephanorhinus hemitoechus*) and giant deer (*Megaloceros giganteus*), (2) the last appearance in the UK of the extinct small mole (*Talpa minor*), the giant

beaver-like rodent (*Trogontherium cuvieri*), European pine vole (*Microtus subterraneus*) and rabbit (*Oryctolagus cuniculus*), and (3) the occurrence, uniquely in this interglacial in Britain, of cave bear (*Ursus spelaeus*) and the large-bodied subspecies of fallow deer (*Dama dama clactoniana*).

Fossil remains from Phase I indicate fully temperate climatic conditions. The molluscs and ostracods are characteristic of a swift-flowing river with a stony bed in the Lower Gravel, in turn succeeded by slowly moving or stagnant water with reed swamps and marshes surrounded by grasslands and calcareous woodland in the Lower Loam. The mammal fauna is dominated by animals inhabiting temperate deciduous or mixed woodland, such as the 'Clacton' subspecies of fallow deer (Fig. 2.8)

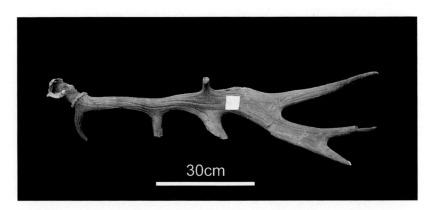

Fig. 2.8   Antler of the Hoxnian large fallow deer, Dama dama clactoniana, *from Barnfield Pit, Swanscombe*

and straight-tusked elephant, with plenty of open grassland in the vicinity to support numerous large grazers, including horse, narrow-nosed rhinoceros and aurochs. Water vole and European beaver (*Castor fiber*) indicate aquatic habitats. As seen in Table 2.2, this part of the sequence is characterised by an exclusively non-handaxe (Clactonian) assemblage. A soil at the top of the Lower Loam represents an old land surface (Kemp, 1985), on top of which were observed white-patinated flint flakes, land snails and a large number of mammalian footprints, including those of wild cattle and horses (Waechter 1970).

The Lower Middle Gravel of Phase II is extremely poor in vertebrate remains but the presence of southern species in the molluscan assemblage indicates the persistence of warm conditions. Most striking is the occurrence of a diagnostic suite of aquatic species, including *Theodoxus serratiliformis* (Fig. 2.9), *Pisidium clessini*, *Viviparus diluvianus* and *Corbicula fluminalis*, some of which first appear at the top of the Lower Loam. Certain members of this assemblage have central European distributions at the present day and were thus termed a 'Rhenish' fauna, thought to indicate a connection with the river Rhine at this time (Kennard, 1942a and b). This has significant implications for the movement of Palaeolithic populations from the continent, since it highlights the availability of a landbridge at this time, and indeed, there is a concomitant change in the archaeological record, with the appearance of a handaxe (Acheulean) industry (Table 2.2). The Upper Middle Gravel reflects a change in climatic and environmental conditions, with a steep decline in woodland-adapted species and a rise in taxa indicative of open grassland, such as field vole (*Microtus agrestis*), northern vole (*Microtus oeconomus*) and horse. The unusual occurrence of the Norway lemming, currently a boreal and arctic species, may reflect slightly cooler conditions as well as more open vegetation. The environmental context of Phase III is not well known, although pollen of frost-sensitive species such as *Hedera* (ivy) and *Ilex* (holly) from the Upper Loam suggests that temperate conditions prevailed. No mammalian remains have been recorded from the Upper Loam or Upper Gravel, with the exception of musk ox (*Ovibos moschatus*) from the latter, thus implying a return to cold climatic conditions at the top of the sequence.

The Swanscombe site therefore preserves a long and complex succession of environmental fluctuations that appear to span most of the MIS 11 interglacial. Although high-resolution records are traditionally difficult to obtain from ancient fluvial sites, this may be one of the rare occasions where periods of past climatic change can be related not only to isotope stages of the oceanic record but even to smaller-scale fluctuations within an individual interglacial (Schreve, 2001b).

Evidence for a human presence along the banks, floodplains and beaches of the Thames at Swans-

Fig. 2.9 Shell of Theodoxus serratiliniformis, *one of the 'Rhenish' suite of molluscs*

combe thus extends over a long period, during which the climate and concomitant environment varied considerably. However, there is no simple correlation between these factors and the stone tools produced. For a long time, the Barnfield sequence of industries was taken to form the 'type series' for the British Palaeolithic, with the changes from non-handaxe to handaxe signatures, as well as differences in handaxe shape, thought to represent cultural or evolutionary trends through time. Such interpretations are now out of favour, and other reasons for assemblage variation, which will be discussed at the end of this section, have been put forward. Some of the faunal material from Swanscombe has revealed traces of cutmarks testifying to at least butchery and maybe hunting of large mammals (cutmarks are also present on faunal material from Clacton and Hoxne – see below, also Binford, 1985; Stopp, 1993; S. Parfitt, pers. comm.).

Another important site in the Lower Thames is that at Clacton-on-Sea, Essex, the type site for the Clactonian industry (Fig. 2.10) (Wymer, 1968; Bridgland, 1994; White, 2000). Here a series of relict channels of the Thames have preserved late Anglian and early Hoxnian freshwater beds, overlain by later Hoxnian estuarine deposits, the sedimentology and invertebrate fauna of the latter testifying to brackish conditions and thus indicating high-sea levels in the southern North Sea at this time. A rich Clactonian industry in both primary and secondary contexts has been recovered from the Freshwater Beds at a number of localities at Clacton but artefacts in the Estuarine beds are very rare, the Thames estuary probably not presenting an ideal habitat for human activity. The Clacton deposits have further provided the lectotypes (type specimens) of *Dama dama clactoniana*, the large-bodied fallow deer that is unique to this interglacial (Schreve, 2001a), and of the narrow-nosed rhinoceros, in addition to yielding an important mammalian assemblage of Hoxnian age. Clacton is also famous for having produced the only unequivocal wooden implement from the British Palaeolithic – the point of a broken wooden spear of yew (*Taxus*) wood, recovered by Warren (Warren, 1911). The significance of this implement for the non-lithic technology and hunting practices of early hominins is immense, but remarkably it seems to have languished as something of a curio until the

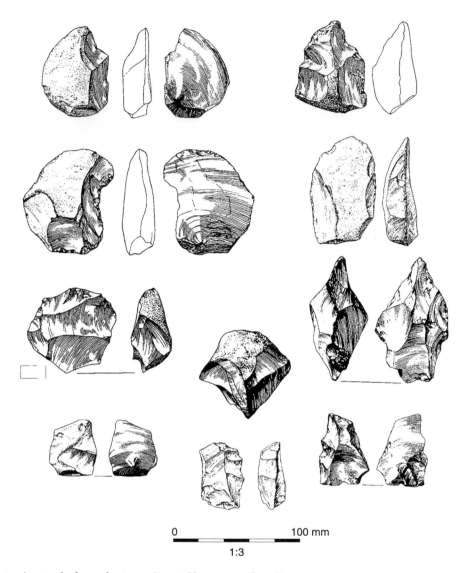

Fig. 2.10   Clactonian tools from the type site at Clacton-on-Sea, Essex

discovery of a series of spears from a lignite mine at Schöningen (Germany) in the 1990s (Thieme, 1997) reignited interest in such artefacts.

A number of other very important sites in East Anglia are worth mentioning as they aid our understanding of human behaviour during this long period. At the interglacial type-site at Hoxne, a deep sequence of lake deposits, overlain by fluvial clays and gravel have yielded evidence for at least two separate primary context handaxe assemblages – a lower one with predominantly ovate handaxes and an upper one with pointed handaxes and scrapers. This is the reverse of the 'classic' Swanscombe succession, and its discovery precipitated the demise of Swanscombe as the 'standard' for the British Lower Palaeolithic and brought forth a number of alternative explanations to explain variation in these stone tool assemblages. Recent work at Hoxne (Ashton *et al.*, 2006) would also seem to show that even though Hoxne is widely cited as a lake-side occupation site, humans were absent or very infrequent visitors to Hoxne during the lake phase, only becoming visibly active there once the site became part of an established drainage network. A similar situation occurs at the sites of Elveden and Barnham, Suffolk (Ashton *et al.*, 1998; Ashton *et al.*, 2005), the latter being important because, like Swanscombe, it contains evidence for both non-handaxe and handaxe industries in different geological contexts (Paterson, 1937; Wymer, 1985; White, 2000). However, the chronological resolution at Barnham is insufficiently precise to discern whether these represent temporally discrete industries (as is the case at Swanscombe) or whether they were contemporary (Ashton *et al.*, 1998).

Key sites in the Upper and Middle Thames

Curiously, the richness of the overall Hoxnian archaeological and palaeontological record is not reflected in the Upper Thames. The Hanborough

Gravel Formation, the oldest of the limestone terrace gravels of the Upper Thames (see above), has produced just one isolated handaxe, from Duke's Pit at Hanborough itself. The Middle Thames is more productive, with over thirty listed findspots for the Boyn Hill Terrace between Reading and Ealing (Wessex Archaeology, 1994-5). Almost all known artefacts are handaxes, probably reflecting collector bias. The majority of these findspots have produced fewer than 10 pieces, and only three locations have yielded large assemblages: Toot's Farm, Caversham; Kidmore Road, Caversham, and Cooper's and Deverill's Pits at Burnham.

Toot's Farm Pit is the richest site in the Middle Thames Valley above Maidenhead and produced a large number of handaxes between 1892-1904, most of them pointed in form. Existing museum collections number *c* 250 but the original number was probably much higher, with Treacher estimating that some 600 came from a quarter acre area (Fig. 2.11) (Wymer, 1968, 137). Artefacts were concentrated in a sandy gravel about 1 m above the Chalk; numerous flakes and broken implements, as well as some quartzite handaxes were noted (Treacher, 1904). About two thirds of the material is in fresh to slightly rolled condition, which in conjunction with the presence of handaxe thinning flakes, led Wymer to suggest that the artefacts represent the remains of a disturbed activity site that once existed a short distance upstream. A horse tooth and very poorly-preserved bone fragments are the only faunal remains noted from this locality. The other major findspot at Kidmore Road Gravel Pit, Caversham produced at least 121 handaxes in association with handaxe manufacturing debitage.

The area around Caversham has rather more numerous findspots, possibly due to preferential preservation in an old meander loop (Wymer, 1999, 59). Today it is also located near to a number of river confluences, but as Wymer reminds us, at the time of the Boyn Hill terrace formation few of the modern rivers flowed in their current courses and it is practically impossible to reconstruct the palaeo-geography of the area as archaic hominins would have experienced it. For some as yet unestablished reason, the area seems to have been a favoured location during the post-Anglian period, or else much material has been derived from the older and artefact-rich Caversham Ancient Channel.

Located immediately south of Burnham Beeches, Cooper's and Deverill's Pits were two adjacent quarries separated by a shallow dry valley. As both showed the same stratified gravel overlain by solifluction deposits, they are generally considered to be part of the same sequence (Wymer, 1968). In total some 240 handaxes were recovered from these pits (22 definitely came from Cooper's, 24 from Deverill's), plus a core, 3 retouched flakes and some 30 flakes. The majority of the handaxes are in a rolled preservational state, and a large variety in shape and sophistication of manufacture is evident (Lacaille, 1939). For a period the commercial excava-

tions were carefully monitored by Lacaille (1939), but it was Treacher, who had a well-known predilection for handaxes (Cranshaw, 1983), who was the major collector and this no doubt accounts for the large number of handaxes at the expense of all other types. Most of the flakes from the site were collected by Wymer from a small cutting made in 1954, after the pits had been abandoned commercially (Wymer, 1968, 231); Lacaille (1939, 171) refers to large numbers of flakes but these have not been traced.

Compared to the Lower Thames and parts of East Anglia, the Upper and Middle Thames are decidedly impoverished for all periods of the Palaeolithic. Hardaker (2001) reports a total of 1126 finds from the entire Upper Thames for the whole Middle Pleistocene. Some of this is probably due to taphonomic processes – the mechanics of fluvial aggradation, differences in the deposits through which the river has cut and the manner in which the river has changed its course and eroded older deposits – all contributing to the chances of preservation and discovery. For example, in the Middle Thames between Medmenham and Marlow, the river is deeply incised into its Chalk valley and little remains here of the Boyn Hill gravel (or, in fact, of the later Lynch Hill gravel), any artefacts originally present presumably being washed away. Further downstream past Bourne End, however, the river on its west bank began to cut into Reading Beds and London Clay, which aided the preservation of large deposits of sand and gravel. Artefacts therefore occur in much greater abundance there, partly because the preservational environments existed and also because more gravel meant more opportunities for extraction and discovery (Wymer, 1999, 60). However, it is not all about the actions of rivers, as human landscape use (for instance, the perceived preferences for riparian plains, confluences and the Chalk hinterland) probably also had a role in structuring the distribution of major sites.

Upstream of the Goring Gap, other factors also come into force. This is an area devoid of any good quality primary flint resources, the flint that does exist being heavily derived, of poor quality and occurring in forms deemed unsuitable for artefact manufacture (MacRae, 1988; Roe, 1994). In this region, as in the British Midlands in general, hominins probably substituted a number of locally abundant rocks for flint, most notably quartzites. This alone may be contributing very significantly to the apparently low human presence in this part of the valley, due to several compounding factors:

1) Quartzite artefacts are much harder to spot than their flint counterparts and often display far less unequivocal evidence for human workmanship

2) Most collectors, past and present, consciously or subconsciously target flint artefacts because that is what they are most familiar with and have consequently trained themselves to spot. They do not have their 'eye in' when it comes to

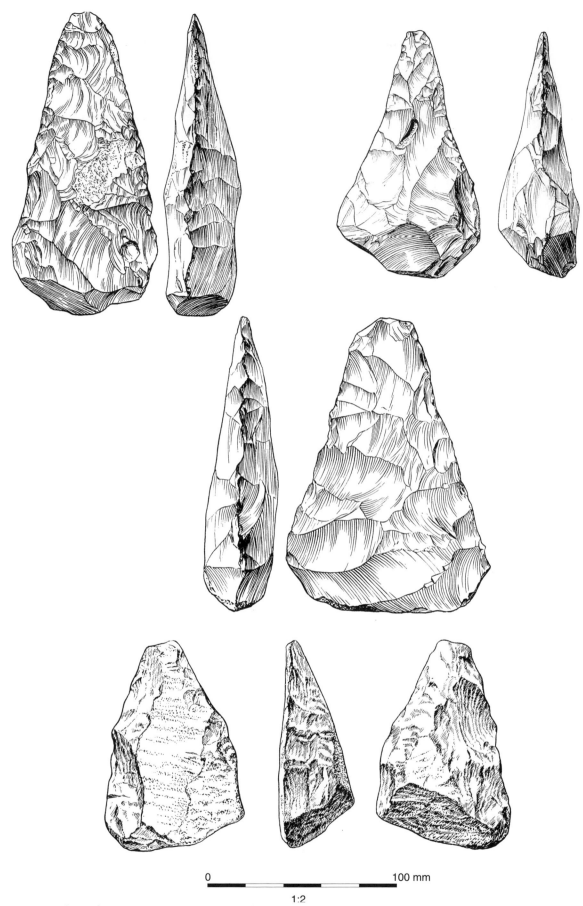

0   100 mm

1:2

Fig. 2.11   Handaxes from Toot's Farm Pit, Caversham

non-flint artefacts. Indeed, the work of R J MacRae and Terry Hardaker has shown just how many non-flint tools begin to emerge once collectors actively start to look for them (eg MacRae, 1982; MacRae and Maloney, 1988; Hardaker, 2001). Since 1989 these authors have actually found twice as many quartzite artefacts as flint ones, quadrupling the number of quartzite objects in the study area (from 101 to 392) and significantly reducing the dominance of flint tools (Fig. 2.12).

3) Flint is more durable than quartzite, and when discarded in rivers with a significant non-flint bedload, will retain its shape even after several episodes of reworking (this is particularly noticeable in the Trent system of central England). Quartzite artefacts on the other hand may return to an unrecognisable form relatively rapidly, which, given the lack of primary context sites in both the Middle and Upper Thames, may be rendering archaic

humans practically invisible in the archaeological record.

Given recent findings from Waverley Wood (see Chapter 1), the dearth of evidence for humans north of the Severn-Wash line (Evans, 1897) and in areas such as the Upper Thames, may yet prove to be an illusion created by these and other factors. As we become more aware of these biases, and begin to understand more about the dynamics of quartzite artefacts as clasts, this situation may change. Students of the Palaeolithic are encouraged to bear this is mind when scanning exposures and quarries.

KEY DEBATES IN HOXNIAN ARCHAEOLOGY

Having such a rich record, albeit not well expressed in the Middle and Upper Thames, the archaeology of the Hoxnian interglacial has sparked several debates regarding archaic human behaviour.

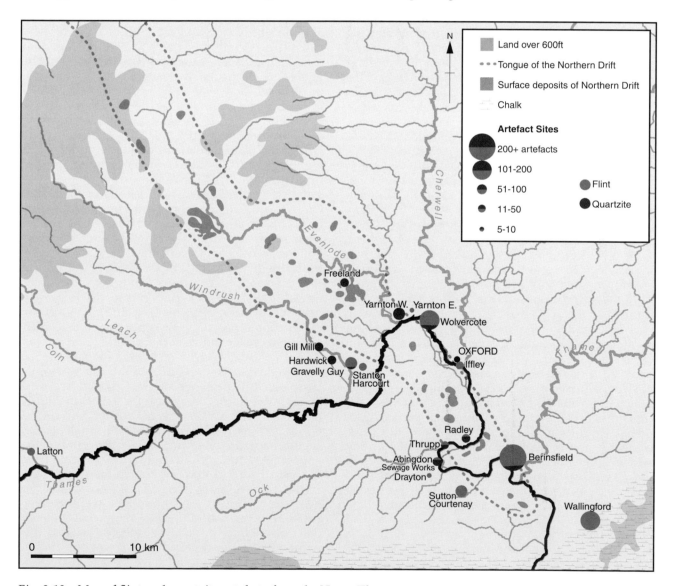

Fig. 2.12   Map of flint and quartzite artefacts from the Upper Thames

Clactonian-Acheulean

The relationship between the Acheulean and Clactonian is an evergreen debate in British Palaeolithic archaeology. The classic interpretation maintains that these industries were the products of two distinct cultural traditions, one that habitually made and used handaxes and one that did not. In the past, the Clactonian has at various times been linked with the 'chopper-tool' industries of East Asia, with some further believing that the two traditions represented the work of different species (Warren, 1924; Paterson, 1945; Oakley, 1949). Over the past 20 years, such accounts have become increasingly unfashionable. At the extremes, some modern scholars have even wondered whether the Clactonian is anything more than a sampling error (eg McNabb, 1996). Most, however, would accept the basic division, but have proposed alternative hypotheses to explain the presence/absence of handaxes in some contexts (see White, 2000, for a detailed consideration).

These hypotheses revolve around a number of common themes. The most widespread is that the Clactonian is a facies of the Acheulean, representing situations in which otherwise handaxe-making hominins did not or could not make handaxes. This may be due to a number of factors, singly or in combination, such as inadequacies or local variations in raw materials (McNabb, 1992; Ashton and McNabb, 1996; Ashton, 1998) or places where specific tasks that did not require the use of handaxes were carried out (McNabb, 1992; Ashton and McNabb, 1994). In a slightly different vein, Ohel (1979) proposed that localities where the Clactonian was found represented places where hominins prepared roughouts for handaxes that were subsequently taken away for thinning and use elsewhere.

Another common interpretation is that the two industries represent adaptations to different environments. Collins (1969) thought that the Acheulean represented the tool kit of mobile hunters on the open grassland, while the Clactonian was the product of non-hunting, forest dwelling communities. Picking up on these ideas, Mithen (1994) suggested that the ecological contrasts between wooded and open environments would have engendered differences in hominin group size, which in turn would have impacted upon the social transmission of learnt behaviour. So, open environments would encourage larger groups with more elaborate and stronger channels of social learning and facilitate the transmission and maintenance of a more sophisticated tool kit. As interesting and ingenious as these ideas are, there is no strong evidence that such a simple woodland-grassland division exists.

Most recently, White and Schreve (2000), in attempting to incorporate the clear temporal division noted above (ie Clactonian appearing first in the interglacial, Acheulean appearing later), have resurrected the old idea that they may represent different populations of hominin entering Britain from different parts of Europe at different times. It is also possible that the Acheulean developed out of the Clactonian as populations became larger and more established. In fact, this pattern apparently recurs in the following climatic cycle (MIS 10-8), which also seems to start with a phase of non-handaxe assemblages. It has to be said however that this is far less well established and more open to question than the Hoxnian occurrence (see Chapter 3). At present the jury is still out on the Clactonian, none of the suggestions outlined here fully explaining this phenomenon.

Hominin Landscapes and Habitats

Although a number of sites are widely believed to represent occupation around lake basins (see Wymer, 1999, 155ff), recent studies have shown that humans did not in fact have much of a presence around these basins while they were actually lakes (Ashton *et al.*, 1998; Ashton *et al.*, 2006). Rather, at locations such as Hoxne, Barnham and Elveden, hominins only became visibly active once the lakes had silted up and the sites had become part of an established drainage network. In Britain, this pattern is particularly clear during the Hoxnian interglacial, and especially in East Anglia. There, following the retreat of the Anglian ice, the landscape would have been covered in glacial till and outwash, with numerous lakes formed in kettle holes and over-deepened sub-glacial valleys, but with a heavily disrupted fluvial drainage system that may have taken centuries or millennia to stabilise. In the study area, the site of Slade Oak Lane, near Denham, represents one such hollow (probably a large doline) in Anglian till, infilled with sand, lacustrine clay muds and silty clay. Pollen spectra from the site have been attributed to the Hoxnian interglacial by Gibbard *et al.* (1986) and suggest deposition in the second half of the interglacial (pollen zone Ho IIIa) in response to a rise in the water table at this time (Fig. 2.13). This appears to be contemporary with other water level rises across southern and eastern England (Gibbard and Aalto, 1977; Gibbard *et al.*, 1986) and may reflect increased precipitation during the latter part of the Hoxnian. The presence of fresh water, access to game drinking at the water's edge and plant resources such as beech mast, water fern (*Azolla filiculoides*) and sedges (*Dulichium arundinaceum*) should have provided hominins with a productive environment in which to operate at Slade Oak Lane, yet no archaeology has been noted there.

The pattern of activity so far observed does not necessarily imply that hominins were actively avoiding lakes, but rather that they were preferentially active in river valleys, probably because they represented natural corridors for moving through the landscape that would have presented rich and diverse sets of floral, faunal and mineral resources. As mentioned in Chapter 1, Wymer (1999) goes

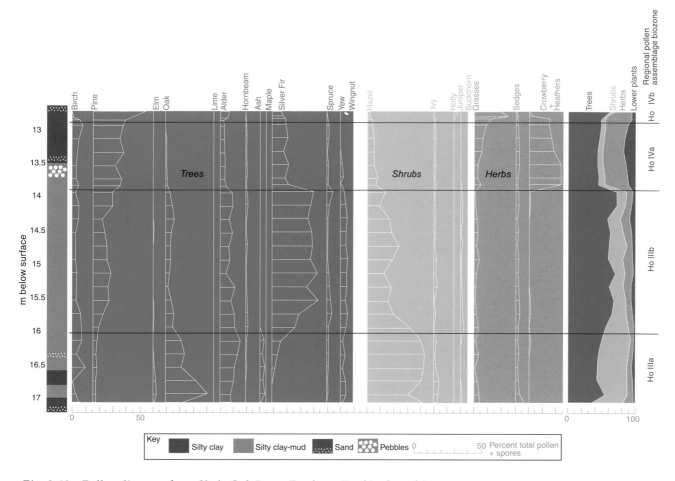

Fig. 2.13   *Pollen diagram from Slade Oak Lane, Denham, Buckinghamshire*

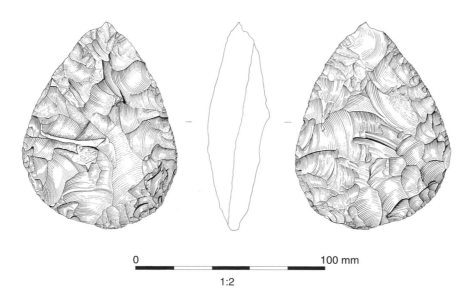

0   100 mm
1:2

Fig. 2.14   *Twisted ovate handaxe from Foxhall Road, Ipswich*

Fig. 2.15 (overleaf)   *Swanscombe and the Hoxnian interglacial*

SWANSCOMBE

The return of warm (interglacial) conditions at the end of the Anglian glaciation marks the beginning of the period known as the **Hoxnian interglacial.**
This is generally equated with MIS 11 and dates to *c* 400,000 BP.

Above – An artist's reconstruction of the Swanscombe waterhole

Top – The Clacton spear: the point of a broken wooden spear of yew, found at Clacton in 1911. The spear provides very rare evidence that early hominins made tools out of wood, and that they were hunting with spears rather than simply scavenging carcasses.

Right – Artist's reconstruction of the extinct straight-tusked elephant Palaeoloxodon antiquus. This elephant flourished in deciduous and mixed woodland during the warmer temperate stages of Pleistocene interglacials.

THE HOXNIAN INTERGLACIAL

| STAGE | | CLIMATE | N | Age | THAMES TERRACES | | |
Britain	Netherlands	Cold Warm	N	(Ma)	Upper	Middle	Lower
	Domitz	10 9			Hanborough	Boyn Hill	Orsett Heath
	Fuhne					Black Park	
Hoxnian	Holstein	11		0.4			
Anglian	Elster	12 13			Freeland	Winter Hill/ Westmill	St Osyth /Holland

The Hoxnian interglacial is one of the best understood episodes of the British Pleistocene. It takes its name from the type site at Hoxne (rhyming with 'oxen') in Suffolk but arguably the most famous Hoxnian site in Britain is Barnfield Pit at Swanscombe, Kent, now designated the Swanscombe Skull National Nature Reserve.

At Swanscombe, a 14 m thick sequence of deposits provides a rich source of archaeological and palaeontological evidence showing the transition from the cold of the Anglian glaciation into a long warm period, giving way in turn to colder conditions as the climate cooled once again, around 350,000 BP.

The earlier part of the sequence sees a transition from a swift-flowing river with a stony bed typical of cold-climatic conditions, to a large slow-moving or stagnant lowland river typical of a warm period, with reed swamps and marshes surrounded by open grassland and deciduous or mixed woodland. Large grazing animals such as narrow-nosed rhinoceros and aurochs roamed the grassy plains, with fallow deer and straight-tusked elephants browsing in the woodlands. Footprints of wild cattle and horses have been found at the site, associated with an ancient soil horizon.

The animals attracted hominins in search of food, and three fragments of skull of *Homo heidelbergensis* with very early Neanderthal features have been found at Swanscombe. Cut marks on bones from the site show that hominins were butchering animals here, and quite probably hunting them too. Flint tools characteristic of a Clactonian industry were present in the lower part of the sequence.

The middle part of the Swanscombe sequence shows an important change in the type of flint tools being used at the site, with the appearance of pointed handaxes typical of an Acheulean industry. At around the same time, new species of aquatic snail appear in the river deposits, implying connection of the Thames with the river Rhine at this point. The changes seen in the archaeology and in the fauna strongly suggest the arrival of new groups of hominins and animals coming into Britain across the landbridge from the continent.

Towards the top of the sequence, remains of musk ox suggest that the climate was starting to cool significantly once again.

Much less evidence is known for human activity in this period in the Upper and Middle Thames. This does not necessarily mean that humans were absent, or less active, in these regions. The recognition of past human presence depends largely on finding their flint tools. However the Upper and Middle Thames regions have no good quality flint sources and it appears that humans in these areas may have used other stone types from the river deposits, such as quartzite, instead.

These do not survive as well as flint and they are much harder to identify in the archaeological record.

Figure 2.15

SWANSCOMBE

Further important remains dating from the Hoxnian interglacial have recently been found nearby at Southfleet Road, Ebbsfleet. Here, work in 2004 in advance of the Channel Tunnel Rail Link unearthed the partial skeleton of a straight-tusked elephant (Wenban-Smith *et al.* 2006). The elephant was preserved in mud near what was then the edge of a small lake. Its bones were surrounded by 3 flint cores and around 50 flakes knapped on the spot. This tells us that hominins were butchering the elephant carcass with tools they were making on the spot. They may have been scavenging a carcass they had discovered, but there is evidence to suggest that early hominins would also have been capable of hunting an elephant with wooden spears.

As at Barnfield Pit, Swanscombe, the earliest parts of the sequence at Southfleet Rd contained flint tools characteristic of a Clactonian core and flake tool industry. At both sites, handaxes only appeared in higher overlying layers of later date. Over 50 handaxes were found in overlying gravel at Southfleet Rd.

THE HOXNIAN INTERGLACIAL

* Left – The remains of the straight-tusked elephant under excavation

* This page – A Clactonian flint core under excavation

*This page, inset – One of around 50 handaxes found in later gravels overlying the elephant remains

Figure 2.15

further, suggesting that the distribution of artefacts within river valleys is not only a function of preservation and deposition, but also reflects hominin preferences for certain areas within them, such as the confluences of the main river and its major tributaries and the Chalk hinterland.

Indeed, early in their development, many of these lake sites probably represented isolated basins that may simply have been 'off the beaten track' and not a key location in the hominins' habitual landscapes. Examples such as Hoxne, situated on wooded higher-level interfluves, may have effectively been 'forest oases', known about perhaps, but visited very rarely. However, at a number of other sites, such as Caddington, Round Green and Gaddesden Row on the Chalk uplands of the Chilterns, humans were active around isolated pools (White, 1997). These sites though, seem to have been occupied towards the end of interglacials, perhaps when the upland environment had become more open, thereby revealing the presence of these basins as visible features in the landscape.

Handaxe variation

Another key question for the Lower Palaeolithic period is why handaxes show such a wide variety of forms. It was long assumed that variation in handaxe morphology between assemblages represented both an evolution in sophistication and form through time, combined with the effects of local traditions of manufacture, some groups historically making different shapes from others. As discussed above, the assumption that Swanscombe formed a type sequence for the development of handaxes in Hoxnian Britain, from crude pointed to refined ovates, was overturned by the discovery of precisely the opposite pattern at Hoxne (Wymer, 1983), just as the notion that there should be an early phase of the Acheulean comprising very crudely made forms was dismissed by the evidence for very well-made ovate handaxes from the pre-Anglian site at Boxgrove (discussed in the previous chapter). Similarly, the idea that inter-site variation represents different cultural norms has been called into question as the true level of intra-site variation has become more appreciated; there is often a modal

tendency, but the range of variation around this is enormous.

Alternative explanations have concentrated on hominin behaviour and landscape use, trying to put the tools back into action in the hands of mobile, intelligent hominins. Ashton and McNabb (1994) argued that the difference between pointed and ovate handaxes related to the form of the original blank, with hominins guided by the path of least resistance rather than cultural norms. Pointed forms were seen to have been most frequently produced on smaller pebble blanks, the original form of which was often reflected in the shape of the finished artefact, while more refined ovates were usually made on large nodules or flakes where a more free-flowing knapping trajectory was possible. White (1998a) linked this to raw materials in the landscape, noting that ovate-dominated assemblages were more likely to occur where hominins had access to sources of large flint nodules, whereas pointed forms tended to be more prolific when raw materials were obtained from a gravel source. McPherron (1994) has suggested that different handaxe shapes represent not finished ideal forms, but different stages in the reduction history of the object, the form of a piece changing as it was moved around, used and resharpened. Such hypotheses are particularly relevant in the flint-poor Upper Thames, where hominins may have practised higher levels of curation. It is also highly likely that a large part of the variation relates to the idiosyncrasies of individuals, who having learnt how to make handaxes by virtue of their cultural milieu, each developed their own style based on the social relationships they formed through life (White and Plunkett, 2004).

On the other hand, one potentially interesting observation with possible cultural connotations is that sites with a notable proportion of ovate handaxes with a twisted edge (Fig. 2.14), all seem to date from the terminal Hoxnian (White, 1998b). None of these have yet been found in the Middle or Upper Thames, but it is something that demands further investigation since it has considerable importance for understanding the size of hominin home ranges and the scale of the social networks through which ideas, objects and people may have been flowing.

Chapter 3 – The 'Purfleet' interglacial and adjacent cold stages (MIS 10-8)

by Mark White, Danielle Schreve and Anthony Morigi

The period covered in this chapter has only been relatively recently recognised in the British chronostratigraphical scheme, since it covers an interglacial (pre- and post-dated by episodes of cold climate) that occupies an intermediate position between the traditional Hoxnian and Ipswichian interglacials (cf Mitchell *et al.*, 1973). In Britain, the evidence from the Thames Valley has been critical in the recognition of this new warm stage (Bridgland, 1994) and in furnishing diagnostic multiproxy palaeobiological information that may be used for correlating with other sites (eg Bridgland *et al.*, 2001; Schreve, 2001a and Keen, 2001).

PALAEOGEOGRAPHY OF THE TERRACE DEPOSITS

The relatively wide occurrence in the Evenlode Valley of terrace deposits of this age, the Wolvercote Gravel, suggests that the main drainage of the Thames system at this time still flowed south-eastwards from its headwaters in the Evenlode Valley to the Oxford area (Sumbler, 2000). Like the other younger terraces in the Upper Thames the Wolvercote Gravel consists mainly of limestone. Flint is also present but in much lower quantities than are present in the Lynch Hill Gravel (the Middle Thames equivalent). As there is no bedrock source for flint above the Goring Gap a glacial origin for the flint in the Wolvercote Gravel has been suggested (but see below and Chapter 2). From Oxford the river followed its present course through the Goring Gap to Reading and then on to Maidenhead. Below here the distribution of the deposits, the Lynch Hill Gravel, indicates an easterly

course to Brentford and then a slightly more northerly route to central London. The terrace surfaces here are much wider (up to 6 km in places) and more continuous than they are above Maidenhead. With the exception of small spreads around Wandsworth and Clapham, they are on the north bank of the present river. East of London the river continued on a rather sinuous course (see below) eastwards through Essex before turning north-east along the course of the early river Medway and towards Clacton-on-Sea (Fig. 3.1). By MIS 8, the lower reaches of the river appear to have migrated south-eastwards, continuing a trend already well-established in this region (see Fig. 4.1, below).

Correlation of terrace deposits

The correlation of the Thames terraces of the period follows the scheme of Bridgland (1994, 1996), in particular the concept that interglacial deposits in the Corbets Tey Formation can be assigned to a previously unrecognised and un-named interglacial (Table 3.1). However, the age and relationships of these deposits have long been controversial and are still disputed. Indeed the resulting literature is so extensive that the history and detail of the debate cannot be encompassed within this volume. The Lower Thames Corbets Tey Formation, defined by Gibbard (1985; Gibbard *et al.* 1988), was originally mapped as the Taplow Gravel and accordingly some authors have assigned the associated interglacial deposits to the Ipswichian (MIS 5e). Similarly, many have correlated the Upper Thames Wolvercote Gravel Formation with the Taplow Gravel (Sandford, 1932;

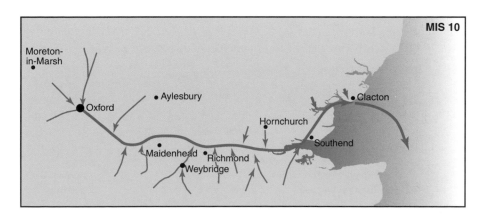

Fig. 3.1 The palaeogeography of the Thames MIS 10-8

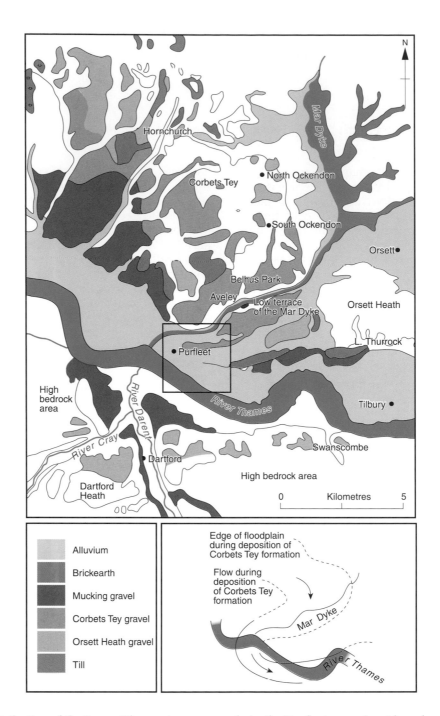

Fig. 3.2   The distribution of the Lower Thames terrace gravels in the Purfleet area. Inset box shows the former course of the river during the MIS 9 interglacial, occupying a now-abandoned reverse loop

Table 3.1 Correlation of Quaternary deposits of the Thames MIS 10-8

| Marine Isotope Stage | Quaternary deposits of the Thames | | |
	Upper	Middle	Lower
8 (early)	Wolvercote Gravel Formation (top)		Corbets Tey Formation
9	**Wolvercote Channel Deposits**	Lynch Hill Gravel	**'Purfleet'**
10 (late)	Wolvercote Gravel (base)		Corbets Tey Fm (base)

(Interglacial deposits in bold). Sources: Bridgland (1996); Bowen (1999).

Arkell, 1947; Evans, 1971; Gibbard, 1985), or even assigned it to the Anglian (MIS 12) stage (Bowen, *et al.* 1986). At Wolvercote (just north of Oxford), the terrace contains a fossiliferous channel fill deposit, the Wolvercote Channel Deposit. It is generally accepted that the channel cuts through the Wolvercote Gravel but the stratigraphical and age relationships are again far from clear and have been much debated. The Wolvercote Channel Deposits are believed by some to be of Ipswichian age (Sandford, 1932; Shotton, 1973b; Briggs and Gilbertson, 1974) and Hoxnian to 'Saalian' (MIS 11 to 6) by others (Bishop, 1958; Wymer, 1968; Roe, 1994). The salient aspects of the chronostratigraphy adopted for this volume are discussed in relation to alternative interpretations later in this chapter.

A key locality within the Lynch Hill/Corbets Tey Gravel Formation is the site of Greenlands Pit at Purfleet, Essex, on the north bank of the Thames (Fig. 3.2). The site, which gives its name informally to this intermediate interglacial, was for a long time the subject of considerable debate over its age with both Hoxnian and Ipswichian ages advanced (Snelling, 1975; Palmer, 1975; Hollin, 1971, 1977; Gibbard, 1994). However, the potential significance of Purfleet as a site where an additional, previously unrecognised interglacial might be represented was identified by Allen (1977), who considered that the height of the terrace deposits there and the composition of the molluscan fauna could not easily be correlated with any established Middle or Late Pleistocene interglacial. In the revised stratigraphical scheme for the Thames terrace sequence proposed by Bridgland (1994) and following new investigations at the site in the late 1990s (Schreve *et al.*, 2002), correlation was advocated between the interglacial deposits at Purfleet and MIS 9, the second of four post-Anglian temperate episodes.

THE ARCHAEOLOGY AND PALAEOENVIRONMENT OF THE 'PURFLEET' INTERGLACIAL

Archaeologically, this period is amongst the most interesting and most complex within the British sequence. It contains evidence for three separate stone tool industries, and heralds at its close the emergence of a new form of core working – the Levallois method – which represents the first major innovation within the European technological landscape for some 300,000 years and which defines the beginning of the Middle Palaeolithic (see Fig. 3.14, below). This time span also has the distinction of having the richest record for any time period within the Upper and Middle Thames, although the evidence from these regions alone does not reveal the whole story.

The archaeological sequence for this period comprises:

Late MIS 9/   Levallois industry
    Early MIS 8

MIS 9   Acheulean handaxe industry

Late MIS 10/   Non handaxe (cf Clactonian
   Early MIS 9   type) industry

Stratigraphically the earliest stone tool industry belonging to this period is of the non-handaxe core and flake type (cf Clactonian). It is not represented in the Upper or Middle Thames, the two most notable occurrences being in the Lower Thames at Essex: Greenlands and Bluelands Pits, Purfleet and Globe Pit, Little Thurrock (Schreve *et al.*, 2002; Bridgland and Harding, 1993). In order to understand the importance of the archaeological sequence, it is first necessary to explain the stratigraphical and environmental setting of these localities. The palaeogeography of Purfleet and Globe Pit is particularly significant, since the Thames fluvial sediments in this area lie banked against the eroded northern flank of the ridge formed by the Purfleet Anticline, an arch-shaped fold in the Chalk bedrock of the region. The Purfleet deposits form part of the Corbets Tey Formation of the Thames, occupying an intermediate position between the Orsett Heath Formation at Swanscombe and the Mucking Formation at Aveley (see Fig. 2.6; also Chapter 4, below). Previous work at the site was influenced by the fact that bedding structures within the gravels there indicate currents flowing towards the west and south-west, ie clearly contrary to the present-day course of the river. Accordingly, it was suggested that the Purfleet deposits had been laid down by the modern, small westward-flowing tributary, the Mar Dyke, which drains the area to the north of the Chalk ridge and joins the Thames at Purfleet (Dewey *et al.*, 1924; Wymer, 1968, 1985; Palmer, 1975). Gibbard (1994, 1995b), who had attributed a Last (Ipswichian) Interglacial age to Purfleet, also followed this interpretation by explaining the anomalously high level of the deposits (15 m OD when compared to other Last Interglacial deposits at or below sea level) as evidence of deposition by a tributary and not the Thames. However, mapping of the fluvial deposits over a wider area of southern Essex by Bridgland (1994) revealed that the Thames formerly followed a course resembling a reversed letter 'S', as first recognised by Wooldridge and Linton (1955) (see Fig. 3.2). In the area of South Ockendon, the river turned south-west and then ran east to reach Little Thurrock, thereby explaining the (apparently anomalous) palaeocurrent directions. Following deposition of the Corbets Tey Gravel, the Ockendon-Purfleet loop was abandoned by the river and the next terrace in the sequence, that of the Mucking Formation, follows the modern, shorter route, passing to the west of Aveley. Recent investigations at Purfleet have demonstrated first that the sediments were deposited by a substantial river up to 1 km wide and 5 m deep, and second, on the basis of clast lithological analysis, that this river was unequivocally the Thames (Schreve *et al.*, 2002).

The sequence at Greenlands Pit, Purfleet, reveals the edge of the main Pleistocene river channel

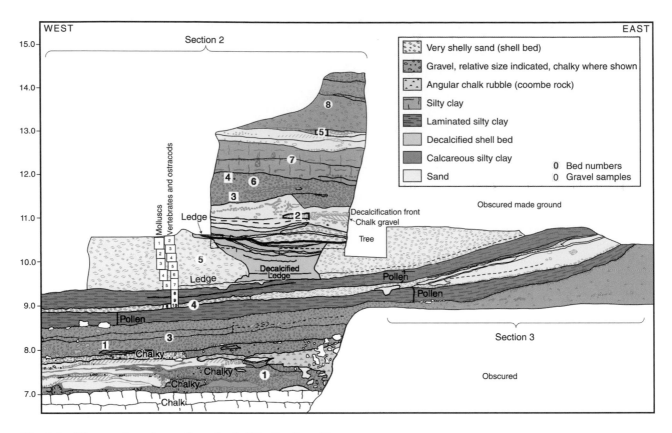

Fig. 3.3   The stratigraphy at Greenlands Pit, Purfleet, Essex

adjacent to a steeply-sloping river cliff cut in Chalk. Brecciated Chalk bedrock at the base is overlain by the following sequence (after Schreve *et al.*, 2002) (Fig. 3.3; Table 3.2). Major beds are indicated in bold type and their contained archaeological industries denoted.

These units represent the typical 'sandwich' of deposits representing successive cold, warm and cold climatic episodes that is observable in the Lower Thames terraces (cf Bridgland 1994, 1995, 2000). The most significant palaeoenvironmental evidence comes from Beds 4 (silty clay) and 5 (Greenlands shell bed). Bed 4 consists of silty clay, which is laminated throughout and possibly reflects tidal sedimentation during a period of high sea level, although the saline influence is very muted. Ostracods from Bed 4 are predominantly temperate freshwater species, although species tolerant of elevated levels of salinity have also been encountered, including *Cyprideis torosa*. In addition, intertidal foraminifera such as *Ammonia beccarii* and *Haplophragmoides* spp. were recorded (Schreve *et al.* 2002). In summary, the environment at Purfleet appears at this time to reflect the uppermost tidal reaches (presumably at the time of the interglacial climatic optimum when maximum high sea level stands would have been reached) of a deep, slow-flowing river. The immediate floodplain consisted of fen or marshland habitats with areas of standing water. Pollen from Bed 4 is dominated by arboreal taxa (up to 70% of total pollen), including *Alnus*

(ash), *Picea* (spruce) and *Quercus* (oak) and fully temperate climatic conditions are denoted by thermophilous taxa such as *Tilia* (lime), *Fraxinus* (ash) and *Ulmus* (elm). The pollen evidence supports an interpretation of mixed forest with open areas, the latter perhaps maintained by proximity to the river or by grazing, browsing or fire. Remains of green frog (*Rana ridibunda/lessonae/esculenta*) from this bed indicate mean July temperatures of at least 15-17° C (as warm as southern Britain today) and suggest the presence of a mature, vegetated water-body (Schreve *et al.* 2002).

The deposition of the Greenlands Shell Bed (Bed 5) reflects an increase in flow energy and the development of a sand flat. The sand is horizontally-

Fig. 3.4   Detail of the Greenlands Shell Bed

Table 3.2: The stratigraphical succession at Purfleet (Essex), with details of contained archaeological industries and inferred climatic conditions (after Schreve et al., 2002)

Members (beds)	Thickness	Industry	Climate
Botany Member			
8. Botany Gravel	2m	Levallois	Cold
Purfleet Member or Botany Member			
7. Grey-brown silty clay	<0.75m	-	Temperate
6. Bluelands Gravel	up to 6m	Acheulean	Cold?
Purfleet Member			
5. Greenlands Shell Bed	up to 2m	-	Temperate
4. Silty clay	<0.25m	-	Temperate
Little Thurrock Member			
3. Shelly gravel	<0.75m	Non-handaxe (?Clactonian)	Temperate
2. Little Thurrock Gravel	<0.4m	Non-handaxe (?Clactonian)	Cold
1. Angular chalk rubble	1m	Non-handaxe (?Clactonian)	Cold

bedded and contains a spectacular abundance of shells (Fig. 3.4), mostly bivalves (predominantly *Unio* spp. and *Corbicula fluminalis*), most of which are articulated and in life-position. Again, species indicative of slowly moving, large rivers dominate, although those characteristic of more rapidly moving waters are well represented but occur in smaller numbers. The limited terrestrial taxa indicate a mosaic of marsh or swamp close to the river channel, grassland and shaded habitats ranging from scrub to woodland (Schreve *et al.*, 2002). In contrast to Bed 4, there is no indication of any salinity. Preece (1995b) recorded the extinct hydrobiid '*Paladilhia radigueli*', for which a brackish habitat is inferred, but where present, this species is very rare in the deposits, further suggesting that during deposition of the Corbets Tey Formation, the distance to the mouth of the estuary must have been greater than at present. Bed 5 has yielded abundant fish remains that are indicative of slow-flowing

water with high summer temperatures (at least 18° C) for spawning. The mammalian assemblage from the shell bed also reflects fully interglacial conditions, in particular the presence of *Crocidura* sp. (a white-toothed shrew), *Dama dama* (fallow deer) and *Palaeoloxodon antiquus* (straight-tusked elephant), all of which were restricted to periods of temperate climate during the Pleistocene. The small mammals indicate a range of habitats, including woodland, grassland, riparian and aquatic environments, whereas the larger mammals, in particular *Macaca sylvanus* (macaque monkey) (Fig. 3.5), *Castor fiber* (European beaver), *Capreolus capreolus* (roe deer) and *P. antiquus*, suggest the proximity of deciduous or mixed woodland (Schreve *et al.*, 2002).

The vertebrate assemblage from Purfleet has been designated as the 'type' for the Purfleet Mammal Assemblage-Zone (MAZ) and attributed to MIS 9 by Schreve (2001a). In terms of composition, the vertebrate fauna from Purfleet and from the neighbouring site of Grays Thurrock occupies an intermediate evolutionary position between the older faunas of the Boyn Hill/Orsett Heath terrace and the younger ones of the Taplow/Mucking terrace (see Chapter 4). Important features of the Purfleet MAZ include the absence of several 'indicator species' that characterised the preceding Hoxnian (MIS 11) interglacial, such as the extinct small mole (*Talpa minor*), the giant beaver-like rodent (*Trogontherium cuvieri*), the European pine vole (*Microtus subterraneus*), the rabbit (*Oryctolagus cuniculus*), the cave bear (*Ursus spelaeus*) and the large-bodied subspecies of fallow deer (*Dama dama clactoniana*). These species have not been recovered from any post-Hoxnian interglacial deposit either in the Thames Valley or elsewhere in Britain, despite appropriate climatic and environmental conditions and extensive sampling, thus suggesting that their extinction from the record at this time is genuine (Schreve, 2001a). Further features of the Purfleet

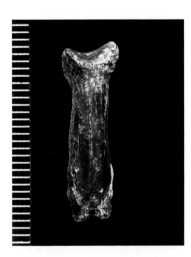

Fig. 3.5 Toe bone of macaque monkey (Macaca sylvanus) from Purfleet

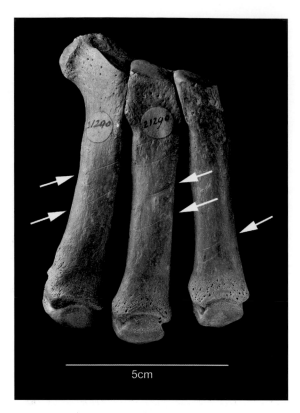

Fig. 3.6 Brown bear paw bones from MIS 9 interglacial deposits at Grays Thurrock, Essex. White arrows denote cutmarks made by flint tools

MAZ include the first appearance of the brown bear (*Ursus arctos*) (Fig. 3.6) in Britain, the reappearance of spotted hyaena (*Crocuta crocuta*) and the presence of more evolved forms of water vole (*Arvicola terrestris cantiana*) than previously witnessed.

The Bluelands Gravel (Bed 6) and the Botany Gravel (Bed 8) are considered to have been deposited under cooling climatic conditions at the end of MIS 9 and into MIS 8. The mammalian assemblage from these beds (although very limited) is at least consistent with more open conditions, in particular the presence of *Equus ferus* (horse). This detailed sequence of palaeoenvironmental change consequently provides an excellent backdrop for the analysis of the archaeological assemblages that have been recorded both from Purfleet itself and elsewhere.

Purfleet is unique in the Thames Valley in having all three putative archaeological industries (Clactonian, Acheulean and Levallois) in stratigraphical superposition. The non-handaxe assemblage, which comes from Beds 1-3 inclusive, is numerically small, being represented by about ninety artefacts (cores, hard-hammer flakes and a few scrapers) from several different excavations. Those from the 'coombe rock' are generally in mint condition, while those from the overlying gravels of Beds 2 and 3 tend to show a mixture of preservational states. At the nearby site of Little Thurrock, the downstream continuation of Greenlands Bed 2 (Bed 1 at Little

Thurrock) has yielded a much richer artefactual assemblage, with several hundred pieces collected in densities of up to 60 per cubic metre (Wessex Archaeology, 1994-5; Wymer, 1999, 71). Most are in fresh or mint condition. Their stratigraphic position (arguably) suggests that these non-handaxe occurrences represent the initial re-occupation of the British Isles following its abandonment during the height of the MIS 10 cold episode. There are no organic remains from these 'coombe rock' and gravel contexts that may allow us to reconstruct more precisely the palaeoclimatic conditions at these sites during this initial (re)occupation, but the nature of the sedimentology suggests that conditions were still cold and that hominins were probably attracted to both Purfleet and Little Thurrock because of the immediate supply of good quality flint being eroded by an active river from the Chalk. Possible reasons for the absence of handaxes suggested in relation to the Clactonian *sensu stricto* discussed in the last chapter equally apply here.

No pure non-handaxe assemblages of this age have been identified in the Middle or Upper Thames. However, several sites in the Middle Thames have been suggested to contain a mixture of Acheulean and 'Clactonian', for example Denton's Pit, Tilehurst and Grovelands Pit, Reading where large numbers of handaxes were found in association with 'crude' flakes, cores and flake tools, all in a similar range of preservational states (Fig. 3.7) (Wymer, 1968). The problem with such claims is that they are based on the belief that 'Clactonian' core and flake working is technologically distinct from that seen in the Acheulean, a supposition that has been severely criticised in recent years (McNabb, 1992; McNabb and Ashton, 1995). In fact, as outlined in Figure 1.24, above, it is only the presence or absence of handaxes and their characteristic manufacturing flakes that divide the two assemblage types, the core and flake working in both assemblages being basically the same. Unless there is a clear difference in condition, it is unwise to arbitrarily divide assemblages into different elements, for even if they were originally discrete entities, once mixed, there remains no technological or typological grounds on which to divide them. This does mean, though, that true non handaxe assemblages may be severely underrepresented simply by virtue of archaeological systematics, because once adulterated with a handaxe industry, one would have to assume by default that it is all Acheulean!

As a consequence of the problems of admixture and the fashion in which archaeologists currently divide assemblages based on presence and absence of key markers, Acheulean assemblages are much better represented than non-handaxe ones. Furthermore, the Middle Thames is far richer than the Upper Thames. TERPS identified at least 192 find spots with artefacts from the Lynch Hill terrace of the Middle Thames, but only 3 belonging to the Wolvercote Terrace, the upstream equivalent

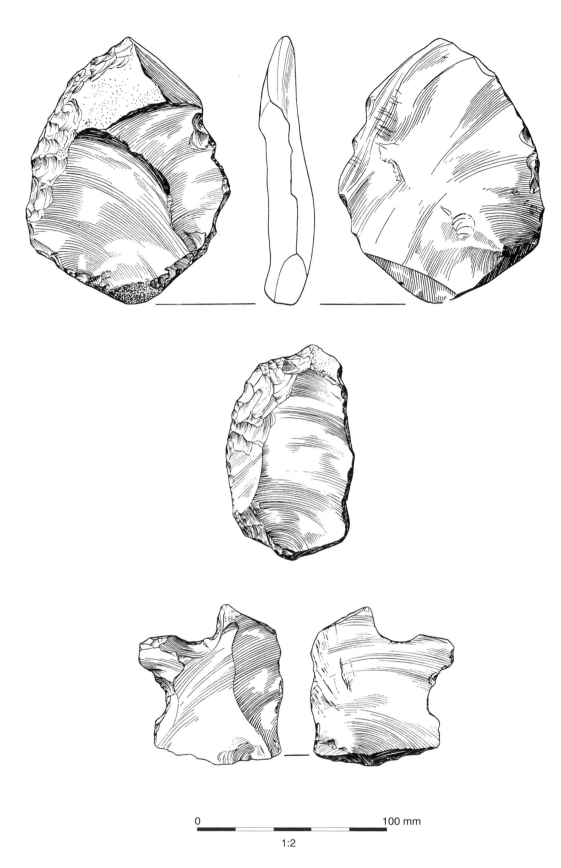

0   100 mm

1:2

Fig. 3.7   Tools from Grovelands Pit, Reading

in the Upper Thames. Indeed, in terms of sheer number of artefacts, Wymer (1988, 1999) identified the Lynch Hill Terrace phase as the richest in the Thames sequence, once again raising the question of why the Upper Thames is so sparse. The richness of the archaeology in the Middle Thames Lynch Hill terrace is unfortunately not paralleled in the palaeoenvironmental record, particularly when compared to the Lower Thames sequences described above. Only a small number of fossiliferous sites are known from the Reading area, including records of undetermined rhinoceros, *Bos primigenius* (aurochs), horse and *Cervus elaphus* (red deer) from sands lying above basal gravel at the aforementioned Grovelands Pit (Stevens, 1882; Shrubsole, 1890). Wymer (1968) also listed a tusk and mandible of mammoth and a molar of straight-tusked elephant reportedly from this site, although it is not known whether these species were found in association with one another or from different parts of the sequence. Shrubsole (1884, 1890) further described a radius of aurochs from Grovelands Pit as deliberately split, although it unfortunately does not survive in museum collections today (Wymer, 1968).

The best and most famous site of this age in the Upper Thames is in the Wolvercote Channel, approximately 3 km to the north of Oxford, on the west bank of the river Thames and north of its confluence with the river Cherwell. Here, over 50 flint and 10 quartzite handaxes in association with sparse manufacturing flakes and palaeoenvironmental remains were collected during the late 19th and early 20th century (Sandford 1924; Tyldesley 1986a) from a 4.5 m deep channel consisting of calcareous, sandy gravels and laminated silty clays, cut into bedded gravels overlying Oxford Clay (Fig. 3.8). The quartzite pieces clearly show that where necessary non-flint materials were used, but it is the flint handaxes from Wolvercote that have

attracted particular attention. Amongst what may be described as 'standard' array of pointed handaxes (ie with partial edges, pebble butts, concentrated working at the tip) are a number of large, well-made plano-convex forms with a characteristic 'slipper-shaped' planform (Fig. 3.9). Roe (1968) considered these to be so distinctive that he assigned them to their own subgroup, which he believed might be related to the European Micoquian industry and which he considered on typological grounds to be of a fairly young age, possibly MIS 7 or MIS 5 (Roe, 1994). This is much younger than the MIS 9 date suggested by Bridgland (1994) and used throughout this volume (although see below for further discussions on the age). Tyldesley (1986b) thought that the classic forms might all be the product of a single knapper and could easily have been made in a single day (given access to enough suitable quality flint).

Others have attempted to explain the Wolvercote assemblage in technological or behavioural terms and relate it to the paucity of flint in the area. White (1998a) observed that many of the plano-convex handaxes had been made on flakes or naturally flat plaquettes of flint, and suggested that the 'Wolvercote-type' might simply represent the careful crafting of specific forms out of occasional better locally found blanks. Ashton (2001) attempted to put them in a more dynamic context, proposing that they had been selectively transported into the Upper Thames from the flint-rich regions to the south-east. This is why they are larger than the others, whilst reworking of the tips as they became blunt or broken through use could also explain the unique Wolvercote shape. Furthermore the need to transport large maintainable handaxes while minimising the associated increases in weight may help understand the plano-convex rather than more 'normal' biconvex profile. Doubling the dimensions of a handaxe will cause an eight-fold increase in weight,

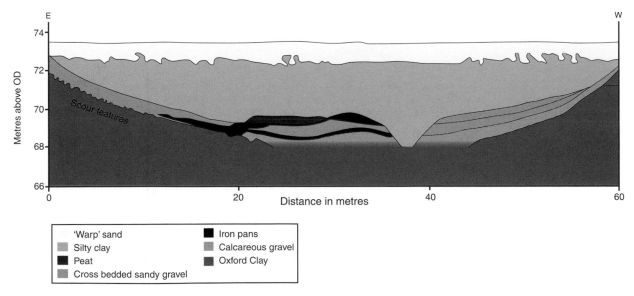

Fig. 3.8   The stratigraphy of the Wolvercote Channel, Oxfordshire

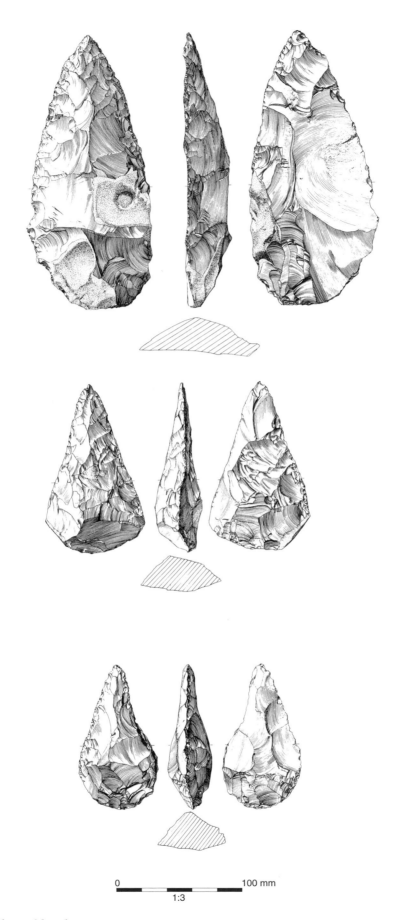

0   100 mm
1:3

Fig. 3.9   Wolvercote Channel handaxes

but if one side is created flat the thickness and therefore weight will be half that of a 'normal' biconvex piece of the same length and width, making it far less of a burden to carry. Flakes and plaquettes may have been selected to allow this.

Early reports on the molluscan, mammalian and plant macrofossil remains from the Wolvercote Channel were provided by Bell (1894a, b, 1904), Pocock (1908), Sandford (1924, 1926) and Arkell (1947). Unfortunately, no extensive exposures of the deposits have been available since the 1930s so very little modern work has been carried out and the age of the site remains controversial. The Pleistocene succession in the Upper Thames established by Bridgland (1994) placed the Wolvercote Gravel Formation as the second oldest of the various limestone-rich terrace gravels, after the Hanborough Gravel Formation. The Wolvercote Gravel was originally suggested by Tomlinson (1929) and later Bishop (1958) to be the first deposit to contain fresh flint introduced into the basin by the glaciation of the Cotswolds. However, on the basis of comparisons of the Wolvercote Gravel with the higher Hanborough Gravel, later authors concluded that the Cotswolds glaciation occurred between the aggradation of the two formations (Briggs and Gilbertson, 1973; Briggs *et al.*, 1985). The Cotswold glaciation had previously been correlated with the 'Wolstonian' (ie the British equivalent of the continental Saalian Stage) by Shotton (1973b, c), although re-evaluation of the sequence in the Midlands has suggested that the ice advance that reached the Cotswolds occurred during the Anglian (Sumbler, 1983a, b; Rose, 1987, 1989). In addition, the veracity of the input of flint into the Upper Thames system between the Hanborough and Wolvercote Gravels has also now been called into question by Maddy *et al.* (1991), who see no justifiable basis for the separation of the Wolvercote Terrace from older terraces on lithological grounds. Given the current uncertainties over the age of the Hanborough Gravels (see Chapter 2), the attribution of the Wolvercote Terrace to MIS 9, or even 11, remains equally in the balance.

The mammalian assemblage from the Wolvercote Channel is considered to reflect still temperate but cooling conditions towards the end of an interglacial and contains straight-tusked elephant, *Ursus* sp. (undetermined bear), horse, *Stephanorhinus hemitoechus* (narrow-nosed rhinoceros), red deer, aurochs and possible bison (Schreve, 1997). Unfortunately, these species cannot confirm or refute the MIS 9 age, since they are not diagnostic of any particular interglacial but the predominance of horse at the site strongly suggests that the Wolvercote Channel is not of Ipswichian age (*contra* Roe, 1994). Plant macrofossils (Bell, 1894a; 1904; Reid, 1899; Duigan, 1956) and beetle remains (Blair, 1923) from a thin peat within the channel suggest a transition from cold conditions at the base of the channel to a cool-temperate higher up, based upon the occurrence of the arctic-alpine hoary whitlow-

grass *Draba incana* (Duigan, 1956), the northern weevil *Notaris aethiops* and mosses of cold climate affinities (Bell, 1904). The cooling climatic conditions were also reflected in sparse pollen assemblages obtained (probably) from the laminated silty clay at the top of the channel (Briggs *et al.*, 1985), which show a transition from pine-dominated forest to open conditions.

As previously noted, the Middle Thames boasts a large number of sites belonging to this period – figures produced by TERPS (Wessex Archaeology, 1994-5) suggesting at least 192, now probably far more. Of these, many are single find spots or small derived collections from gravel deposits. Several areas, however, have produced very substantial collections, often an artefact of collector and quarrying activities rather than past human landscape use.

One of the most prolific areas for Acheulean finds anywhere in the British Isles lies between Cookham and Maidenhead on the right bank of the river, and between Burnham and Farnham Royal on the left bank. Here quite extensive gravel extraction in Lynch Hill deposits has produced over 2000 handaxes and other artefacts, with notably large collections coming from Danefield Pit at Cookham, Cannoncourt Farm Pit at Furze Platt, Bakers Farm Pit at Farnham Royal and the Lent Rise Pits at Burnham (Wymer, 1968). Wymer (1999) identifies this as one of the 'favoured' Chalk Hinterland zones (see Chapter 2). Due to collector biases, handaxes dominate these assemblages at the expense of all else, but other artefacts were recovered, including flakes and handaxe manufacturing flakes. The artefacts tend to be in a mixed preservational state, although those from Cannoncourt Farm and Bakers Farm Pits are generally described as being in fresh or only slightly worn condition. Combined with the evidence of handaxe manufacture, this has led many authors to assume that the material has not moved far from its point of origin, although it is unlikely to be in true primary context. Cannoncourt Farm also has the distinction of producing the largest handaxe in the British Isles, the 32.3cm long 'Furze Platt Giant' (Fig. 3.10). Such large pieces were probably functionally redundant, and may have had more social significance. Kohn and Mithen (1999) have argued that the over-elaborate symmetry and refinement of many handaxes in general, and the various giant forms in particular, show that handaxes were used by humans as a way of expressing their sexual fitness to potential mates. This would be especially true in an area where raw materials usually dictated the manufacture of smaller, cruder pointed forms (see below). The gravels in the Maidenhead area have yielded only very rare and fragmentary faunal remains, including a fragment of antler of giant deer (*Megaloceros giganteus*) (Lacaille, 1940).

An interesting characteristic of the handaxes assemblages throughout this area is that they are mostly point dominated with an important cleaver and ficron element (Fig. 3.11). Roe (1968) suggested that this reflected a combination of local tradition and activities, the ficrons and cleavers serving somewhat different purposes to other bifaces. White (1998a) on the other hand argued that the dominant shape and frequency of ficrons reflected the use of elongated nodules on which other forms would have been extremely difficult to make. The frequency of cleavers in all these assemblages is equally intriguing. White (2006) has recently argued that these are not a unique form, but rather a resharpened variant of the round-ended imple-

ments frequent in all these sites, with hominins reworking the tips to extend their use-life in an area where raw materials, despite being widely available often came in less than ideal packages.

An equally important series of sites occurs in the Hackney-Stoke Newington area (Smith, 1894; Green *et al.*, 2004, 2006). These represent deposits of the River Lea, quite close to its confluence with the main river, and have been suggested by Gibbard (1995b) to form part of a large meander situated within an open grassland environment with areas of alder carr. Recent investigations at the Nightingale Estate,

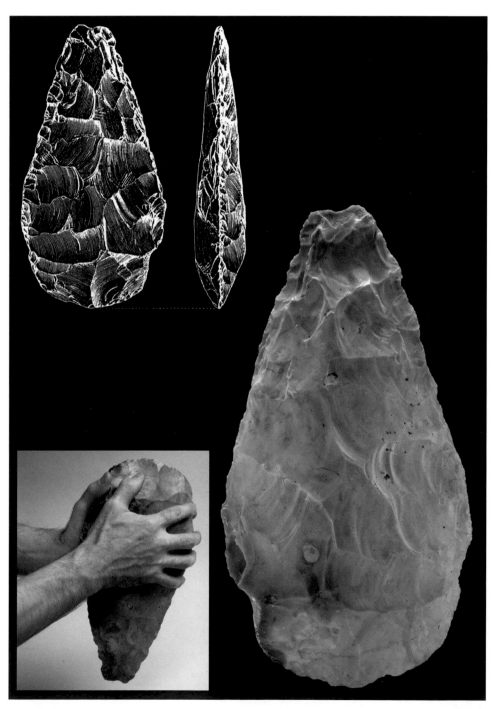

Fig. 3.10   The Furze Platt Giant

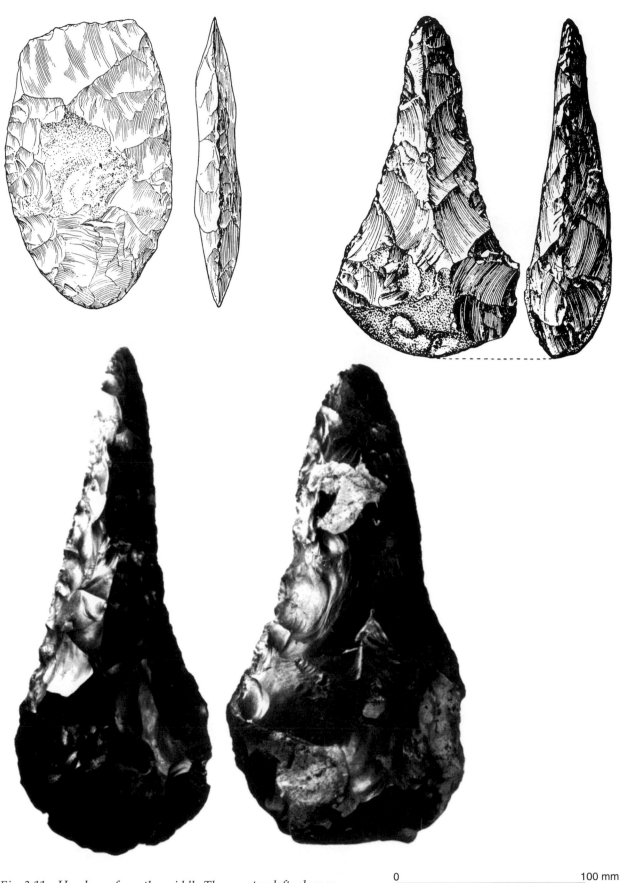

Fig. 3.11   Handaxes from the middle Thames: top left, cleaver from Dean's Pit, Marlow; top right and below, three ficrons from Cannoncourt Farm Pit, Furze Platt

0   100 mm

1:2

Fig. 3.12   The excavations at Hackney Downs, London: Top left: the Nightingale Estate; Bottom left: palaeo-environmental sampling; Right: core showing grey interglacial silts overlain by orange cold-climate gravels

Hackney (Fig. 3.12) revealed a thick series of organic deposits (the Highbury Silts and Sands) with spectacularly rich associated palaeoenvironmental evidence, apparently representing a short time interval, perhaps no more than a few years, within the MIS 9 interglacial (Green *et al.*, 2006). The pollen assemblage from the site was dominated by oak (40–50%), with smaller percentages of alder and pine, followed by beech, ash, hazel and grasses. Herbaceous and aquatic plants were also recorded, including umbellifers (Apiaceae), sedges (Cyperaceae), *Plantago lanceolata* (ribwort plantain), *Ranunculus* type (buttercup or crowfoot), *Rumex* (dock), *Typha latifolia* (bulrush) and Filicales (ferns). Within the beetle assemblage, 254 taxa were identified, including a predominance of species characteristic of shallow running water with a stony bed and numerous species of dung beetle. Other habitats, including marsh and wet grassland with scarcer patches of woodland and dry ground, were also indicated. Increasing percentages of terrestrial Mollusca towards the top of the sequence suggested a reduction in the influence of fluvial conditions and the development of marshland, most likely attributable to shallowing of the river channel or to the progressive infilling of a floodplain pond. Only a small number of vertebrate remains were recovered from the organic deposits including stickleback (*Gasterosteus aculeatus*), perch (*Perca fluviatilis*), slow worm (*Anguis fragilis*) and palmate newt (*Triturus helveticus*). Most significantly, the fossil plant, insect, mollusc and vertebrate remains from the interglacial deposits all indicate climatic conditions with summers of 18–19°C, ie warmer than at present in south-east England, and winters with a similar thermal climate. The presence of deposits apparently representing the thermal optimum of an interglacial invites possible correlation with the silty clay (Bed 4) at Greenlands Pit, Purfleet, since this deposit appears to reflect maximum high sea level stand in the same interglacial. The Highbury Silts and Sands are overlain by the Hackney Downs Gravel. These predominantly unfossiliferous sands and gravels are thought to represent deposition on the floodplain of a braided river under cool or cold climatic conditions (Green *et al.*, 2006). A single record of woolly rhinoceros (*Coelodonta antiquitatis*) is known from this part of the sequence but is otherwise unlocalised (Schreve, 1997).

Large collections of artefacts were made during the 1870s by Worthington Smith, a particularly careful collector who retained everything he found, leaving the collections remarkably complete for an assemblage of this vintage. Smith found most of his artefacts on a sandy Palaeolithic 'floor' just below brickearth (*c* 24 m OD), which he suggested extended from Abney Park Cemetery to Clapton. The artefacts are mostly in fresh or mint condition, and there are a number of conjoining pieces. They include both pointed and ovate bifaces (many of which are very small), roughouts, biface manufacturing flakes, scrapers, hammers, anvils, cores and flakes. This area was undoubtedly a favourite spot for humans, again probably attracted by the confluence of the two rivers and the wide floodplain of the meander loop, with its rich animal and vegetal

Fig. 3.13 Handaxes from the London area. Left to right: Glasshouse St, Piccadilly; Lower Clapton (Hackney); Yiewsley (Hillingdon)

resources. The Lea would also have provided a key route north into the Chilterns, another area of exceptionally preserved evidence for human activity in the Chalk uplands (Smith, 1894). Interestingly, the assemblages from both Stoke Newington and the Chilterns contain some evidence for the use of quartzite and other non-flint raw materials, with Caddington and Stoke Newington Common each having produced at least one quartzite handaxe. Smith's perceptive eye and the increased use of non-flint resources as one moves north and west are just two of the factors that probably contribute to this.

No artefacts were found during the recent excavations at the Nightingale Estate, Hackney (Green *et al.*, 2006) and the sediments observed did not resemble those described by Smith (1894) in association with the Palaeolithic 'floor'. In addition, Smith's 'floor' was located approximately 3 m above the level of the ground surface at the Nightingale Estate and 7 m above the top of the organic unit there. The higher level of the Stoke Newington sediments therefore suggests that although they may form part of the Lynch Hill/Corbets Tey complex, they represent a depositional phase separate from and earlier than that represented at the Nightingale Estate (Green *et al.*, 2004).

Figure 3.13 shows a selection of handaxes from the London area.

Levallois technology and the Early Middle Palaeolithic

Towards the end of the MIS 9 interglacial, a major change occurs in the archaeological record and, for the first time, the sustained use of Levallois technology is seen (Fig. 3.14). In archaeological terms, this marks the transition from the Lower to Middle Palaeolithic, during which a number of technological and behavioural changes begin to emerge.

The earliest occurrence in Britain is probably that at Botany Pit, Purfleet where a prodigious number of cores and flakes were recovered from gravel dated to *c* 320,000 years BP (Wymer, 1985; White and Ashton, 2003). The industry shows an 'undeveloped' form of prepared core working, described by Wymer (1968, 1985) as Proto-Levallois and by Roe (1981, 228) as a reduced Levallois with simplified preparatory stages. According to White and Ashton (2003) the nature and antiquity of the Purfleet material is a reflection of the gradual development of the Levallois technique within Europe, fusing technological concepts from earlier types of core working and handaxe production to enable the consistent production of medium-large sized flakes. Botany Pit also produced a number of classic Levallois cores, and further Levallois material has been recovered from the Upper Gravel at Bluelands and Greenlands Pits at Purfleet. Botany Pit further yielded several handaxes that, according to the gravel diggers at the site (Wymer, 1968, 312-314),

were found on the Chalk beneath the gravel and may therefore pre-date the Levallois material (Wymer, 1985, 312). These possibly also postdate the core-and-flake assemblage, representing the final occurrence of the Acheulean industry found in the other Purfleet pits, or they may be contemporary and represent the last use of handaxes before Levallois became the dominant technology.

The sheer number of artefacts found at Botany Pit led Wymer (1968, 1985) to conclude that it was a 'quarry or workshop', and it is interesting that a shift in hominin focus of activity seems to have occurred, away from the previously favoured Greenlands/Bluelands areas to the east, and towards the Botany site. Changes in topography are one key factor in understanding this shift: the Botany Pit contains only the upper part of the overall sequence, the river having shifted its channel westwards, so the lack of earlier material is understandable in these terms. However, the shift away from Bluelands/Greenlands Pits probably also reflects the fact that Botany Pit presented a more attractive location: it is situated on the inside of a large bend where the channel margins were very gently inclined and where they cut through a major flint seam. Access to raw materials and a wide riparian plain may have made this a prime location and preferable to the (now) fairly steep and less flint rich margins to the east. The appearance of the earliest Levallois in Britain coincides with a deterioration in climate that is undoubtedly responsible for the increased vigour of the river at this time, leading to the deposition of coarse gravels and the excavation of new sources of raw material from the Chalk. Palaeoenvironmental records for this time period are very few, although a limited vertebrate assemblage was recorded from the Botany Pit gravel by A J Snelling in the 1960s, including remains of horse, red deer and an indeterminate large bovid.

Two key Early Middle Palaeolithic/Levalloisian localities exist in the Middle Thames. The most famous is that at Creffield Road, Acton, where J. Allen Brown (1887) amassed significant collections during the late 1800s (Fig. 3.15). The finds came from four small and closely spaced pits in Lynch Hill gravel, within which Brown identified three black find horizons that he interpreted as ancient landsurfaces. The main assemblage came from the top horizon, which sat at 6 ft beneath the surface immediately beneath a capping of brickearth. This produced over 500 artefacts characterised by Levallois points and flakes, plus a very small number (n=~10) of heavily reduced cores. Handaxes are absent, the two listed by Roe (1968) not actually being associated with the pits described by Brown. Brown believed the site to represent a flint workshop and noted the presence of flint nodules >30cm diameter, but such an interpretation does not explain all the complexities of the assemblage. The collection is dominated by debitage resulting from either end of the reduction process –

Fig. 3.14 (overleaf) Levallois technology

LEVALLOIS TECHNOLOGY

Levallois technology appears in Britain c300,000 years ago. Levallois is a form of prepared core technology, which differs from earlier core technology in that the faces and striking platforms of the core are carefully dressed to produce flakes of a desired — or predetermined — shape and size. The precise level of actual predetermination in flake morphology is hotly debated, although most archaeologists would agree that there is clear design intent from the outset, even if the final form of the flake is not absolutely controlled.

Classic Levallois is associated with 'tortoise-cores', whereby a core is carefully prepared in a radial fashion on both sides and a large single flake removed from one side - the flaking surface - the shape and size of the final flake being controlled by the scar pattern imposed on this surface.

Another well-known variant is the Levallois point core, in which the shaping of the surface was based on a series of converging scars with a central ridge that guided the production of strongly pointed flakes. In both the striking platform may or may not be carefully shaped and facetted to further control the force and direction of the hammer blow. Until recently Levallois was considered to be a very wasteful technique, a large volume of material expended to produce a single desired product, although refitting and experimental work has now shown this to be a fallacy, with many cores having their flaking surfaces reprepared to produce several Levallois flakes.

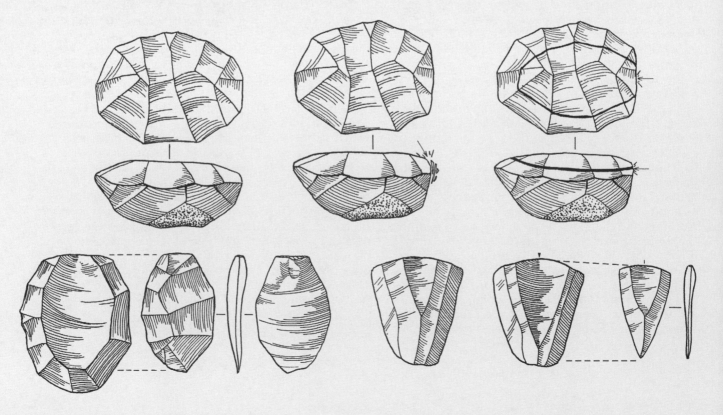

Today, many workers use **Eric Boeda's 'Levallois Concept'** as a basic tool for understanding and recognising Levallois technology.

Boeda's scheme sees Levallois as a volumetric method of exploitation, with 6 defining criteria. This method of analysis takes into account a much larger range of variation and accepts that Levallois cores could have been reprepared several times to produce a number of products.

Levallois production may be 'lineal', with each flaking surface producing only a single desired flake, or it may be 'recurrent', with several Levallois flakes being detached from a single surface. In addition a number of preparation and exploitation techniques are recognised, including **centripetal**, **unipolar** and **bipolar** forms.

* Opposite page — (top line and below left) idealised Levallois core and preparation; (below right) idealised point core and preparation

* This page — Boëda's Levallois concept

Criterion 1:
The core is conceptually divided into two surfaces separated by a plane of intersection

Criterion 2:
The roles of the two surfaces are fixed, one being a dedicated striking surface, the other a dedicated flaking surface

flaking surface

striking platform surface

Criterion 3:
The flaking surface is shaped in a fashion that predetermines the morphology of the desired flakes. This is achieved by the management of distal and lateral convexities

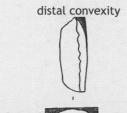

distal convexity

left lateral convexity   right lateral convexity

Criterion 4:
The plane along which the desired flakes are removed is parallel to the plane of intersection

Criterion 5:
The axis of flaking of the desired flakes are at 90° to the intersection of the striking surface and flaking surface

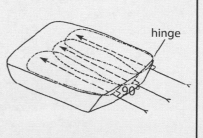

hinge

Criterion 6:
Hard hammer percussion

Figure 3.14

large cortical flakes from initial core preparation combined with end products and cores reduced to the point of exhaustion – but material from the intervening stages of the reduction sequence is underrepresented. One possible interpretation is that Creffield Road represented a re-tooling station, where hominins discarded their exhausted cores and used Levallois points – tools that had seen earlier service as part of a transported, curated toolkit elsewhere in the landscape – and replaced them with new cores prepared on the spot and subsequently taken away (Scott, 2006; White *et al.*, 2006).

Notable quantities of Levallois material were also collected from gravel pits exploiting Lynch Hill terrace deposits around West Drayton and Yiewsley, Hillingdon (Brown, 1895, Lacaille and Oakley, 1936; Collins, 1978, Ashton *et al.* 2003). Contextual information for most finds within what was eventually an enormous quarry complex is minimal, but where available indicates the Levalloisian material was recovered from the surface of coarse fluvial gravel, sealed by solifluction gravel and brickearth (Langley Silt) (Brown, 1895, Ashton *et al.*, 2003). The fresh condition of the Levallois material, and the fact that

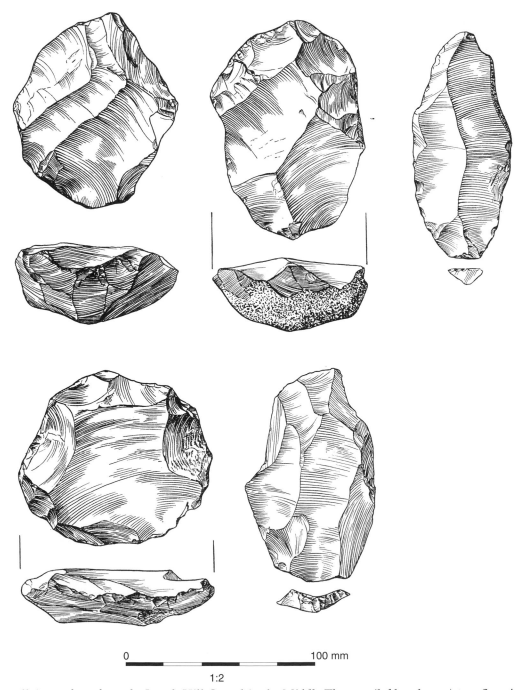

0   100 mm

1:2

Fig. 3.15 Levallois artefacts from the Lynch Hill Gravel in the Middle Thames: (lefthand page) top, Sonning Railway Cutting, Reading; below, Creffield Road; (righthand page) top left, Butt's Hill Pit; others, Hillingdon

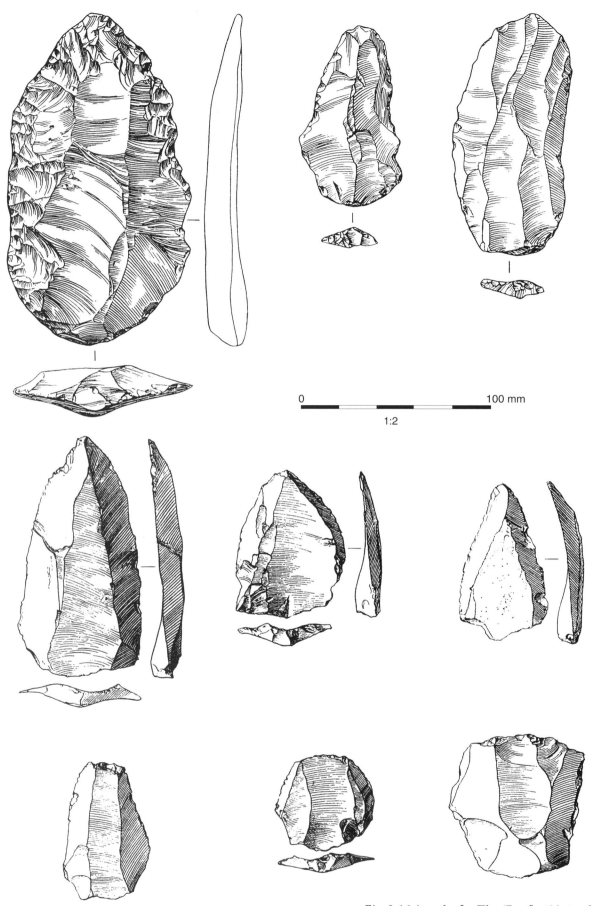

Fig. 3.16 (overleaf)   The 'Purfleet' interglacial

0   100 mm
1:2

PURFLEET AND WOLVERCOTE

The existence of an interglacial that can be equated with MIS 9, roughly 300,000 BP, has only been recognised quite recently. Much of the key evidence has come from Purfleet, Essex, which gives its name informally to this period.

Deposits in the area show a transition from the cold environment of MIS 10 into the warm temperate period of MIS 9, which then gave way in turn to colder conditions as the climate started to cool again.

At this time, the river continued to follow the course it had adopted during the preceding interglacial, although it flowed in a reverse 'S' loop in the Purfleet area that it later abandoned.

The lowest part of the Purfleet sequence is characteristic of cold conditions but there is evidence of rapid climatic warming in the gravels, which have yielded around 100 flints assigned to a Clactonian industry. These flints record the return of hominins to Britain at the start of the MIS 9 interglacial. They would have been attracted to the area because the river was eroding good quality flint from the local Chalk bedrock. Although we have no fossils of the hominins themselves, they are likely to represent a transitional form between *Homo heidelbergensis* and *Homo neanderthalensis* (Neanderthals).

During the main part of the interglacial, the Thames at Purfleet was around 1 km wide, 5 m deep and flowing slowly through a floodplain of fen or marshland with areas of standing water. Ash, spruce, oak, lime and elm trees were growing in the vicinity and the temperature was as warm as, or slightly warmer than, southern Britain today. Abundant fish remains have been recovered from the site, along with fossils of green frog, macaque monkey and straight-tusked elephant. Gravels from the middle part of the sequence, possibly representing a short-lived cooler period, contain flints of the Acheulean industry, which is characterised by the presence of handaxes.

THE 'PURFLEET' INTERGLACIAL

STAGE		CLIMATE	N↑ N↓	Age (Ma)	THAMES TERRACES		
Britain	**Netherlands**	Cold Warm			**Upper**	**Middle**	**Lower**
'Aveley'	Treene	8 7		0.2			Barling/ Corbets Tey
'Purfleet'	Drenthe				Wolvercote	Lynch Hill	
	Dömitz	10 9		0.3			
	Fuhne				Hanborough	Boyn Hill	Orsett Heath
Hoxnian	Holstein	11		0.4		Black Park	

Over 50 flint and 10 quartzite handaxes of this tradition were collected at Wolvercote, near Oxford, from a 4.5 m deep ancient channel of the river. This channel is also thought to date broadly from the later part of the MIS 9 interglacial. Pollen grains show pine forest giving way to bleaker open conditions as the temperature dropped.

Some of the best finds of Acheulean artefacts from this period have come from the Middle Thames between Cookham and Maidenhead. The largest handaxe known in Britain was found at Furze Platt. It was probably not made for practical use but as a prestige item.

* Purfleet interglacial – hominins butcher a brown bear carcass on the banks of the Thames, c 300 000 years ago (MIS 9)

Figure 3.16

THE 'PURFLEET' INTERGLACIAL

Levallois flint technology and the dawn of the Middle Palaeolithic

The top of the sequence at Purfleet shows a key change. Prodigious numbers of flint cores and flakes employing a new technology, the Levallois industry, were being deposited around 250 000 BP under cooling conditions. At Purfleet, as at a number of west London sites such as Creffield Road in Acton, West Drayton, and Yiewsley in Hillingdon, the quantities of discarded Levallois artefacts suggest the presence of abundant raw material and working areas. It is certain that as the temperature cooled the Thames would have flowedmore vigorously, thereby exposing new sources of flint as it increased its erosion of the chalk bedrock.

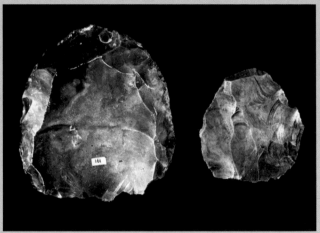

* Above – Levallois core and flake from Baker's Hole, Kent

* Left – Levallois core from Yiewsley, Hillingdon

The appearance of the Levallois industry conventionally marks the transition from the Lower to the Middle Palaeolithic. It is thought to be associated with significant changes in hominin behaviour and is attributed to the earliest true Neanderthals in Britain.

Levallois flint working (see Figure 3.14) was based on the careful manipulation and reduction of flint cores to form flake tools of a desired or predetermined size and shape. It was much more versatile than the older traditions, and provided a wider range of tool forms, and there is evidence for change in hunting strategies, and in the mobility, size and organisation of hominin groups. Some of the richer sites yield very dense concentrations of manufacturing debris, suggesting that hominins were either making frequent repeated visits to key resources, or were periodically taking part in large gatherings.

Figure 3.16

similar accumulations have not been recovered from equivalent sub-Langley Silt contexts on lower terraces, suggests rapid burial shortly after discard. Handaxes were also recovered from these localities, but these came from well within the gravel and are in a different preservational state. The Levallois material, which includes Levallois flakes, blades and points as well as a variety of cores show a much wider range of exploitation strategies than Creffield Road, perhaps suggesting that a more diverse range of activities was organised from here. These sites fall close to the confluence of the Thames and Colne, and this may be one of the reasons why so much activity seems to have been concentrated around this area.

Once again, the Upper Thames is remarkably poor and cannot boast a single Early Middle Palaeolithic site. Why this should be so, given the excellent evidence for human presence in the Wolvercote Channel, is presently unclear.

Behavioural changes at the Lower-Middle Palaeolithic Transition

The appearance of Levallois is accompanied by other significant changes in human behaviour, in hunting, forward planning, resource use and organisation within the landscape. These are discussed further in the next chapter. It is important to note that there are differing views on the significance of the appearance of Levallois. For Foley and Lahr (1997), the appearance of prepared core technologies in Europe around 300-250,000 years BP represents a dispersal event from Africa, during which the last common ancestor of modern humans and Neanderthals appeared on the European landscape, bringing with them new technological practices. Others, such as White and Ashton (2003), see Levallois as being an indigenous development, the technological changes being based on incipient properties of earlier core and core-tool technologies that formed part of a wider behavioural transformation amongst Neanderthals related to changing habitats and landscape use. Indeed, prepared core technologies had occurred sporadically and without lasting impact in earlier periods, for example at Rickson's Pit, Swanscombe and at Cagny la Garenne in the Somme Valley. The flourishing of Levallois during the terminal part of MIS 9 and MIS 8 may relate to population dynamics, for if the richness of the record of MIS 9 is any guide to population density, then human populations may have been at their highest during this period (Wymer, 1988; cf Ashton and Lewis, 2002; Hosfield, 2005). If so, then the behavioural changes that emerge here may relate to stronger and more dynamic channels of social learning, with more innovation and the more lasting, widespread uptake of new ideas.

Chapter 4 – The 'Aveley' interglacial and adjacent cold stages (MIS 8-6)

by Anthony Morigi, Mark White and Danielle Schreve

Traditionally, only the Hoxnian (MIS 11) and Ipswichian (MISs 5e) interglacials have been recognised in Britain for the period between the Anglian and Devensian glaciations. Recently, this concept has been challenged by the suggestion that deposits in the terraces of the river Thames provide evidence for two previously unrecognised interglacials during this time (Bridgland, 1994, 1996). The preceding chapter recounts the evidence for an interglacial in MIS 9, based primarily on an interpretation of sediments at Purfleet and related deposits in the Thames terrace staircase of the Lower Thames. This chapter presents evidence for an additional interglacial in MIS 7 that is represented by fossiliferous deposits at Aveley (and correlatives), also in the Lower Thames. Later in the chapter, the significance of the recognition of these new stages for the chronostratigraphy of terraces throughout the Thames is discussed. We acknowledge, though, that the scheme presented here has been controversial: as so often with interpretations of the Thames terraces there is always scope for disagreement. Gibbard (1994) for example, based on pollen biostratigraphy assigned the Aveley deposits (Aveley Member of Bowen, 1999) to the Ipswichian (MISs 5e). Nevertheless, the recognition of these new stages has achieved widespread acceptance.

PALAEOGEOGRAPHY OF THE TERRACE DEPOSITS

By this time the palaeogeography of the river Thames was close to adopting its now familiar pattern. The distribution of the Summertown-Radley Formation in the Upper Thames Valley west of Oxford, where the terrace is well preserved around Stanton Harcourt, indicates that the main drainage had switched from the old EvenlodeThames route to the present day course of the river along the foot of the Cotswold dip slope. In the Middle Thames downstream of Maidenhead its course was slightly to the north of its present position, passing through Slough and Heathrow. Between here and Twickenham the Middle Thames correlative of the Summertown-Radley Formation, the Taplow Gravel, is very extensively developed – Heathrow Airport is situated on the widest terrace. In eastern Essex, the river had migrated from its north-easterly course along the lower reaches of the Medway to a more easterly course through Southend on the north side of the Thames Estuary (Fig. 4.1).

Correlation of the terraces

Leaving aside the debate over the age and relationship of the Aveley interglacial deposits, which is reviewed in detail later in this chapter, there is general agreement that the Mucking Formation (Mucking Member of Gibbard, 1988 and Bowen, 1999) equates with the Taplow Gravel of the Middle Thames. On the other hand, correlation between the Taplow Gravel and its equivalent in the Upper Thames is problematic. The difficulties relate principally to the status of fragmentary terrace deposits in the Reading area (the Reading Town Gravel of Gibbard, 1985) and the complexity of the Summertown – Radley Formation in the Upper Thames. In this respect, understanding that the deposits underlying the Summertown-Radley terrace span multiple climatic stages has proved

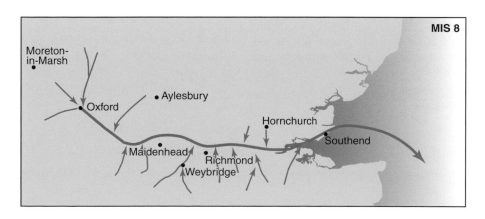

Fig. 4.1   The palaeogeography of the Thames MIS 8-6

crucial. The Summertown-Radley Formation is an excellent example of the complexities that may lie beneath an apparently simple 'bench' in the valley side. The recognition that more than one climatic stage is represented in these deposits has long been established since Sandford (1924) noted a lower gravel unit containing a cold-climate fauna and an upper gravel unit with a temperate fauna. Later investigations at other localities resulted in the gradual understanding that these deposits were even more complex and probably accumulated over multiple climatic stages (Briggs and Gilbertson, 1980; Shotton, 1983; Briggs *et al.*, 1985; Briggs, 1988; Bowen *et al.*, 1989). The history of research of the Summertown-Radley Formation is extensive and beyond the scope of this volume but for a detailed account the reader is referred to Bridgland (1994). The latest interpretation, and the one adopted in this volume, suggests that the deposits underlying the Summertown-Radley span five successive climatic stages (Bridgland, 1994). This chapter covers the early part of the sequence (Table 4.1), while Chapter 5 deals with the later stages.

Gibbard (1985) correlated the Taplow Gravel with the Wolvercote Gravel based on upstream projection of its gradient but in this account Bridgland's correlation of the Taplow Gravel with the Summertown-Radley Formation is preferred. The reasons for this are reviewed in some detail in Chapter 5 but a brief summary is useful here. Gibbard (1985) equated the lower of two terraces in the Reading area (his Reading Town Gravel) with the 'Summertown-Radley gravels' based on downstream projection. The higher, he correlated with the Taplow Gravel. However, Bridgland (1994, 1996) argues that the Taplow Gravel of the type area, when projected upstream, intersects with the Reading Town Gravel, thereby confirming the correlation of the Taplow Gravel with the Summertown-Radley Formation.

ARCHAEOLOGY AND PALAEONTOLOGY

From an archaeological perspective this period can be defined as the Early Middle Palaeolithic (White and Jacobi, 2002). Technologically and typologically it is characterised by the dominance of the Levallois technique as the main method of blank production, which formed the basis for a number of retouched and unretouched tools such as points, scrapers and some bifacial forms. The handaxe, which dominated the hominin tool kit during earlier periods, all but disappeared, its role probably being usurped by large, sometimes bifacially worked Levallois flakes. This represents a major change in the way hominins conceived flint raw materials, moving away from the production of core tools and towards a greater emphasis on flake tools, although the range of tasks to which stone tools were put probably remained broadly the same. On a European scale, these technological changes may reflect wider developments in the way that hominins were organising themselves and their technology in the landscape, as discussed at the end of this chapter (see White and Ashton, 2003).

Finds outside the study area

As has been the experience throughout this volume, the best evidence from this period occurs in the Lower Thames and East Anglia, although even here evidence is sparse (Fig. 4.2). The hundreds of find

1 Aveley, Essex	7 Pontnewydd Cave, Clwyd
2 Baker's Hole/Ebbsfleet, Kent	8 Purfleet, Essex
3 Brandon, Suffolk	9 Selsey, West Sussex
4 Crayford & Erith, Kent	10 Stanton Harcourt, Oxford
5 Cuxton, Kent	11 Stoke Bone Bed, Ipswich, Suffolk
6 Holbrook Bay (Stutton & Harkstead), Suffolk	12 West London sites
	13 West Thurrock, Essex

Fig. 4.2 Distribution of possible Early Middle Palaeolithic sites

Table 4.1 Correlation of Quaternary deposits of the Thames MIS 8-6

| Marine Isotope Stage | Quaternary deposits of the Thames | | |
	Upper	Middle	Lower
6 (early)	Summertown–Radley Formation* (part)	Taplow Gravel	Mucking Formation (top)
7			**'Aveley'***
8 (late)			Mucking Formation (base)

(*Details in text; interglacial deposits in bold). Sources: Bridgland (1996); Bowen (1999).

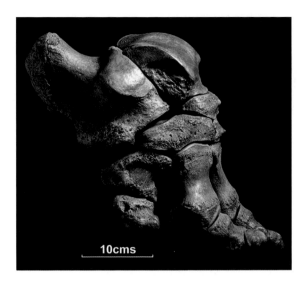

Fig. 4.3 Complete right hind foot of straight-tusked elephant (Palaeoloxodon antiquus) *from Aveley, Essex*

spots reported for earlier periods now diminish to just a handful. Possible reasons for this paucity are outlined below.

In the Lower Thames, the locality at Aveley (Essex), on the north bank of the river Thames, serves as a useful type-site and gives its name informally to the interglacial represented within the Mucking Formation, the downstream equivalent of the Taplow Formation (and terrace) of the Middle Thames (Bridgland, 1994). The site is renowned for the discovery at Sandy Lane Quarry in the 1960s of skeletons of straight-tusked elephant (*Palaeoloxodon antiquus*) (Fig. 4.3) and mammoth (*Mammuthus trogontherii*) (Blezard, 1966). More recently, during the late 1990s, a new mammalian assemblage, in association with abundant multiproxy environmental evidence and a limited amount of archaeology, was recovered from cuttings created during construction of the A13 dual carriageway between Purfleet and Wennington (Bridgland *et al.*, 1995; Schreve, 2004b; Schreve *et al*. in prep.).

Aveley played a key role in early debate concerning the existence of what is now recognised as the penultimate (MIS 7) interglacial. Together with Ilford (also in Essex) and Trafalgar Square in central London, Aveley was originally assigned to the Ipswichian (Last) Interglacial on the basis of its palynology (West, 1969; Mitchell *et al.*, 1973; Hollin, 1977). However, it was apparent from the outset that the temperate-climate deposits at Aveley and Ilford were situated at a higher terrace level than Trafalgar Square (see Fig. 2.6, above) and contained very different mammalian assemblages that, according to Sutcliffe (1975), were impossible to reconcile with the view that all three sites should be placed within the same (Ipswichian) interglacial. The combined evidence from the mammals and differences in the heights of the interglacial deposits thus led Sutcliffe (1975) to conclude that the Trafalgar Square deposits were indeed laid down during the Ipswichian but

that the Aveley and Ilford deposits accumulated during an older, post-Hoxnian, pre-Ipswichian temperate interval, now correlated with MIS 7 of the marine oxygen isotope record. This view has been subsequently upheld by the model of terrace succession in the Lower Thames put forward by Bridgland (1994) which places the interglacial deposits at Aveley and Ilford within the Mucking Formation, the third of four terraces indicated within the post-Anglian succession (see Fig. 2.6). Further corroborative evidence has also come from mammalian biostratigraphy (Schreve, 2001a), molluscan biostratigraphy (Preece, 2001; Keen, 2001), coleopteran biostratigraphy (Coope, 2001) and aminostratigraphy (Bowen *et al.*, 1989; Schreve *et al.*, 2006). In contrast, the palynological signatures from the successive interglacials correlated with MIS 7 and the Ipswichian appear to be highly similar and cannot, as yet, be confidently separated.

The sediments at Aveley record a complex climatic signal within a single interglacial, with two (and possibly three) temperate-climatic episodes identified, separated by breaks in deposition. As at Swanscombe (see Chapter 2), these are considered to reflect climatic oscillation at the isotope substage level (Schreve, 2001b). The mammalian fauna from Aveley may be subdivided into two discrete groups, termed the Ponds Farm MAZ and the Sandy Lane MAZ, and considered to reflect the earlier part of the interglacial and the later part of the interglacial respectively (Schreve, 2001a, b).

The Ponds Farm MAZ coincides with the oldest temperate-climate sediments in the Mucking Formation, the lower part of the Aveley Member sands, silts and clays (Schreve, 2001a). These have yielded a vertebrate assemblage of fully temperate woodland character characterised by straight-tusked elephant and including obligate thermophiles such as European pond terrapin (*Emys orbicularis*) and a white-toothed shrew (*Crocidura* sp.), both of which today have predominantly southern European distributions. Molluscs from this part of the sequence indicate a slow-flowing, well-oxygenated river with water depths of 1-5 m but also some areas of shallower water with a muddy substrate and surrounding marshland (D. Keen, pers. comm.). The proximity of more open grassland conditions is indicated by the presence of horse (*Equus ferus*) and bison (*Bison priscus*) but mammoth was apparently absent. A younger age for this faunal grouping, when compared with the Purfleet MAZ of the preceding interglacial (see Chapter 3), is indicated by molars of water vole *Arvicola*, which present a more evolved morphology.

A major break in deposition is then apparent, marked by soil development, representing a land-surface during an inferred period of cooler conditions (Schreve, 2001a, b; Schreve and Bridgland, 2002). A return to temperate-climatic conditions is indicated by two organic clays, in turn overlain by further silts and clays. The organic clays (Fig. 4.4) have proved to be a rich source of plant macrofossil remains, dominated by waterside and damp ground species, and insect remains, including large numbers of dung beetles (G. Coope, pers. comm.). The clays and silts have yielded a second mammalian grouping, the Sandy Lane MAZ (Schreve, 2001a), which contrasts sharply in terms of its composition with the Ponds Farm MAZ of the earlier part of the interglacial. The Sandy Lane MAZ is defined by a predominance of species favouring open grassland, in particular a late form of steppe mammoth (*Mammuthus trogontherii*) and horse. The mammoth is represented frequently (but not exclusively) by the

'Ilford type' form (Fig. 4.5), characterised by a combination of smaller size and lower plate count in the molars when compared to last cold stage woolly mammoth (*Mammuthus primigenius*), namely 19-22 plates in the M3 of the former as opposed to an average of about 24 plates in the latter (Lister and Sher, 2001). A significant element of the small mammal fauna of the Sandy Lane MAZ is a large form of northern vole (*Microtus oeconomus*) and an important absentee from this biozone is fallow deer (*Dama dama*). In parallel with the pollen evidence from Sandy Lane (West, 1969), which marks a transi-

Fig. 4.4   The upper part of the sequence at Aveley, showing interglacial organic deposits and silty clays

Fig. 4.5   Complete skull and tusks of a late form of steppe mammoth (Mammuthus trogontherii) from Ilford, London Borough of Redbridge

tion from woodland to grassland in this part of the sequence, the mammalian assemblages also reflect an opening up of the environment at this time, with a reduction in woodland-favouring forms and an increase in herds of large grazers.

The pronounced turnover in the mammalian fauna between the Ponds Farm and Sandy Lane MAZs, both present at Aveley, lends support to the idea of an intervening cooler episode during the MIS 7 interglacial. The resultant marine regression would have permitted the immigration from mainland NW Europe of taxa such as *M. trogontherii* that are characteristic of continental environments. The timing of the suggested reconnection has previously been proposed as substage 7d of the marine isotope record (Schreve, 2001b), when increased global ice volume probably lowered sea level enough to rejoin Britain to mainland Europe. However, new Uranium-series dating from the correlative site at Marsworth indicates that substage 7b is more likely (Candy and Schreve, 2007).

Until recently, Aveley had produced no evidence of human occupation but since 1996 a small number of artefacts have been recovered from two different stratigraphical contexts. Five flakes have been recovered from the lower part of the Aveley Member (sands, silts and clays, Ponds Farm MAZ), while a further four flakes and a Levallois core were found in association with the upper part of the Aveley Member (silts and clays, Sandy Lane MAZ) (Schreve *et al.*, in prep). Although a very small collection, these artefacts are nonetheless very valuable in helping to show human presence during both the early and later parts of this interglacial, in association with different environmental regimes.

The nearby deposits at the Lion Pit Tramway Cutting at West Thurrock also form part of the Mucking Formation. The sequence has been exposed at a number of different locations and comparable sections of fossiliferous river terrace sands and silty clays ('brickearths'), under- and overlain by gravel and resting against a buried Chalk cliff (rising to 16 m OD), were described by Whitaker (1889), Abbott (1890), Hinton and Kennard (1900) and Hinton (1901). Near the cliff, the terrace deposits are aggraded to an elevation of 15 m OD and are capped by colluvial deposits (Hollin, 1977). The geological sequence established from the 1984 and 1995 excavations can be summarized as follows (Bridgland and Harding, 1994, 1995; Schreve *et al.*, 2006):

6. Colluvial overburden

5. West Thurrock Gravel (present only in the southern part of the cutting)

4. Upper Sand, up to 2m

3. Silty clay (brickearth), 0.5-3m

2. Lower Sand, up to 8.5m

1. Basal gravel, up to 1m

0. Angular chalk rubble ('coombe rock'), 1m

The basal gravel (Bed 1) has been attributed to the end of MIS 8 (Bridgland, 1994; Schreve *et al.*, 2006). Very small scale investigations in the gravel have produced over 250 artefacts, including eight Levallois cores, Levallois flakes and associated debitage (Fig. 4.6) (Warren, 1926; Bridgland, 1994; Bridgland and Harding, 1995; Schreve *et al.*, 2006). The archaeology was in primary context on top of the coarse basal gravel and a number of artefacts could be conjoined, although some movement and fluvial winnowing of smaller debitage had probably occurred. The archaeology belongs to the transitional period spanning the end of a cold stage into a period of temperate climatic conditions, at which time the gravel formed both a platform on which to work and source of raw materials. Vertebrate remains from the interglacial sediments of Beds 2 and 3 include wood mouse (*Apodemus* sp.), brown bear (*Ursus arctos*), straight-tusked elephant and Merck's rhinoceros (*Stephanorhinus kirchbergensis*). These taxa indicate nearby deciduous or mixed woodland, although by far the most important local habitat appears to be open grassland, presumably adjacent to the river. This is indicated by the presence of large grazing or semi-grazing herbivores, such as aurochs (*Bos primigenius*), steppe mammoth and horse. No artefacts have been reported from the interglacial sediments themselves but a pelvis bone of narrow-nosed rhinoceros (*Stephanorhinus hemitoechus*) bears cutmarks suggestive of butchery by hominins (Schreve *et al.*, 2006). Several samples of brickearth from the tramway cutting were sampled for pollen by Hollin (1977). Pollen abundances were very low but were dominated by *Alnus* (alder) and Filicales (ferns), with *Carpinus* (hornbeam), *Corylus* (hazel) and lower frequencies of *Pinus* (pine), *Quercus* (oak), *Tilia* (lime) and *Fraxinus* (ash) (Hollin, 1977). The vegetation adjacent to the river has therefore been reconstructed as alder fen carr, with the develop-

100 mm

1:2

Fig. 4.6   Levallois cores from Lion Pit Tramway Cutting, West Thurrock

ment of hornbeam forest occurring on nearby dry calcareous soils (Gibbard, 1994).

Crayford is another primary context Levallois site in the Lower Thames, probably belonging to the later part of the MIS 7 interglacial when conditions were beginning to deteriorate towards the MIS 6 cold stage. Here prodigious quantities of mint condition laminar Levallois were recovered from an *in situ* knapping 'floor', some in direct association with animal bones (Fig. 4.7) (Spurrell 1880a, b; Chandler 1914, 1916). Many of the artefacts could be refitted, the site having been subjected to so little disturbance that whole nodules could be reconstructed. At Crayford, the stratigraphical sequence follows a phase of deep erosion, which cut a bench in the Chalk/Thanet Sand at around zero O.D. The Pleistocene deposits are banked against this steep cliff and can be sub-divided into three well-marked divisions (Morris, 1838; Chandler, 1914; Kennard, 1944; Fig. 4.8):

3. The Upper Brickearth (including the 'trail'), up to 6 m

2. The Lower Brickearth (including the Corbicula Bed), the former up to 9 m thick, the latter up to 1.5 m

1. The Crayford Gravel, up to 4.5 m, separated from Bed 2 by a depositional hiatus

The Crayford Gravel consists of sand and coarse gravel, containing some derived artefacts and vertebrate remains. It clearly pre-dates the brickearths and was probably deposited soon after the cutting of the bench (Kennard, 1944). The inferred environment of deposition for this unit is in a fast-flowing river of considerable size. Kennard (1944) supposed that the surface of the gravel had formed an older landsurface related to the initial downcutting to this terrace level. Hominins were undoubtedly attracted to the site for a number of reasons, but access to

prey and stone resources were highly significant in their choice of location. Spurrell's main floor was within the Lower Brickearth, where it banked up against the Chalk and a seam of flint. The Lower Brickearth also yielded the majority of organic remains for which Crayford is known, including large mammals such as wolf (*Canis lupus*), lion (*Panthera leo*), narrow-nosed rhinoceros, Merck's rhinoceros, aurochs, horse and woolly mammoth, together with indicators of colder climates, such as musk ox (*Ovibos moschatus*) (Schreve, 1997). Lenticular patches of sand and pebbles, thought to represent transient currents, have been observed

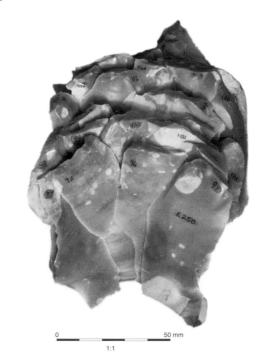

0   50 mm

1:1

Fig. 4.7   Refitting laminar Levallois sequence from Crayford

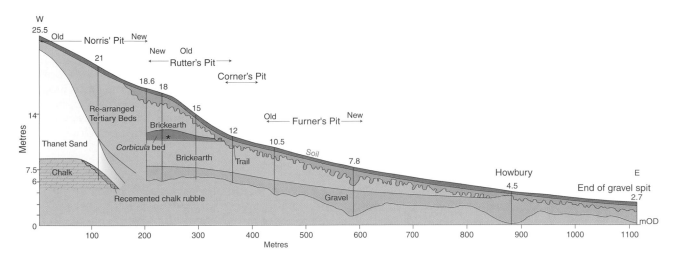

Fig. 4.8   *The stratigraphy of the brickpits in the Crayford area*

within this unit, although the brickearth itself is clearly the product of slow-moving water. Mollusca are uncommon, although it is noteworthy that the larger bivalves (*Anodonta*, *Corbicula* and *Unio*) are often in life-position, thereby suggesting that deposition of the Lower Brickearth occurred rather rapidly. The sole palaeobotanical record from Crayford is of *Castanea sativa* (sweet chestnut), which was found in the Lower Brickearth and is today common in the Mediterranean.

The Lower Brickearth is overlain by the '*Corbicula* Bed', up to 1.5 m thick. As the name suggests, it contains numerous molluscan remains (especially *Corbicula fluminalis*), together with abundant remains of small mammals, including grassland voles and lemmings. The apparent disharmonious co-occurrence of 'warm' and 'cold' mammalian and molluscan species within the Lower Brickearth, for example temperate molluscs and aurochs with lemmings and musk ox, makes palaeoenvironmental and palaeoclimatic reconstruction particularly complex. The overall picture suggested by the mammalian assemblages is one of an interglacial, continental climate with an open, steppe-like

environment and cold winters, possibly marking the onset of the climatic deterioration of MIS 6. The Upper Brickearth, which overlies the *Corbicula* Bed, is present only on the higher ground to the west (Bull, 1942) and is more thinly-bedded and clayey than the Lower Brickearth (Leach, 1905; Chandler, 1914). Tylor (1869) proposed that the sediments were not fluvial but the result of sludging from higher ground during a period of heavy rainfall. The Upper Brickearth has yielded a few mammalian fossils and rare, isolated artefacts (Kennard, 1944).

No discussion of this period would be complete without at least some mention of the prolific quantities of Levallois material recovered from deposits infilling the Ebbsfleet valley, a south bank tributary of the Lower Thames, near Northfleet. Thousands of artefacts in fresh condition were collected from the basal Chalky breccia, including very large Levallois cores, retouched and unretouched Levallois flakes and other debitage (Smith, 1911; Wenban-Smith, 1995; Scott, 2006). The sedimentology and elements of the fauna (ie *Coelodonta antiquitatis*, Fig. 4.9) from these units indicate cold and open conditions at the very end of MIS 8.

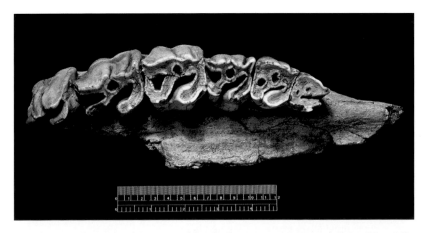

Fig. 4.9   *Right upper tooth row of woolly rhinoceros* (Coelodonta antiquitatis) *from Northfleet, Kent*

Hominins were engaged in major exploitation of the substantial flint nodules obtained from the weathered chalk slope, and while the cores have frequently been argued to show the profligate use of flint, each producing only a single flake, there is actually some evidence of core re-preparation and recurrent flaking techniques. Several hundred Levalloisian artefacts in fresh condition were also recovered from the overlying fluviatile gravel and silt (Burchell, 1957; Kerney and Sieveking, 1977), which judging from their contained vertebrate and molluscan faunas belong to a fully temperate but still largely open-woodland phase at the beginning of the MIS 7 interglacial (Schreve, 2001b). The freshwater silts higher up in the sequence, belonging to a later phase within MIS 7 (Kemp, 1995; Wenban-Smith, 1995), contain only rolled archaeology derived from elsewhere. Molluscan and ostracod remains from the silts suggest that deposition occurred in a marshy swamp, surrounded by open grassland and with nearby shady woodland. Fully temperate conditions continued to prevail. The invertebrate evidence is echoed by the mammalian assemblage from the silts, which offers much the same information, being dominated by large grazers such as mammoth, horse and red deer (*Cervus elaphus*). Possible stands of woodland in the vicinity are indicated by the tentative identification of a pine grosbeak or parrot cross-bill (Wenban-Smith, 1995) and aquatic habitats are suggested by records of water vole, three-spined stickleback (*Gasterosteus aculeatus*), carp family (Cyprinidae), pike (*Esox lucius*) and eel (*Anguilla anguilla*) (Wenban-Smith, 1995). These reflect the presence of still or slow-flowing water, with summer water temperatures of at least 18° C (Wheeler, 1969).

At the Lion Pit Tramway Cutting, Crayford and Ebbsfleet, humans were highly active and at their most archaeologically visible while a source of readily available raw materials existed, but seem to have moved their focus elsewhere once these had been concealed by sedimentation. These rich sites may therefore have formed major extraction ('workshop' or 'quarry') locations, foci for primary flint knapping tasks as well as other social and subsistence activities. A number of other sites with smaller collections of artefacts also exist, for example at Stoke Tunnel, Suffolk, where only a handful of isolated flakes and cores were found.

These probably represent more ephemeral 'stopovers' where artefacts produced at the workshops and transported in anticipation of future needs were used and ultimately lost or discarded. Judging from the inferred age of these sites, people were present throughout later MIS 8 and both the early wooded and later open phases of MIS 7. However, population density at this time may have been remarkably small. This point is discussed further below.

Sites in the Main Area

Evidence for human occupation of the Upper and Middle Thames during this period is sparse, the majority of finds being isolated implements or small collections. Indeed, The English Rivers Project (Wessex Archaeology, 1994-5) lists only 40 archaeological findspots from the Taplow Terrace in the Middle Thames, which together produced only 240 artefacts, most of them rolled handaxes that were probably derived from older deposits. Only three Levallois cores and ten Levallois flakes are reported, but the original provenance or terrace attribution of several of these may be open to question (Ashton *et al.*, 2003). The Summertown-Radley terrace in the Upper Thames is even poorer in number of sites, although by virtue of the efforts of some indefatigable local collectors, has produced more artefacts.

Four sites warrant further attention, all in the Upper Thames. The most important of these is Dix Pit, Stanton Harcourt where highly organic interglacial channel deposits at the base of the Summertown-Radley Formation have produced major floral and faunal collections. The Summertown-Radley aggradation actually contains five members and although these have never been recorded in direct superposition, the combination of supporting information points clearly to a cold-warm-cold-warm-cold succession (Bridgland, 1994). Within the Summertown-Radley terrace, two interglacial episodes are therefore thought to be preserved, the older attributed to the penultimate interglacial (MIS 7) and the younger to the last (Ipswichian) interglacial (MISs 5e). The lithostratigraphic classification of the Summertown-Radley terrace deposits is presented below (after Bridgland, 1994; Table 4.2):

Systematic investigations carried out at the site in the 1990s yielded large collections of mammalian

Table 4.2: The stratigraphy of the Summertown-Radley terrace in the Oxford area, with inferred climatic conditions and proposed correlation with the marine oxygen isotope record.

Formation	Member	MIS	Climate
Summertown-Radley	Unnamed upper gravel at Eynsham	5d-2?	Cold
	Eynsham Gravel	5e	Temperate
	Stanton Harcourt Gravel	6	Cold
	Stanton Harcourt Channel Deposits	7	Temperate
	Unnamed lower gravel at Summertown	8	Cold

material from the Channel Deposits. These temperate-climate deposits consist of silt, sand, gravel and organic sediments, frequently overlying a boulder or cobble bed and occupying a shallow, SW-NE trending, linear depression (60-70 m wide and up to 1.5 m deep) in Oxford Clay bedrock (Briggs and Gilbertson, 1980; Briggs *et al.*, 1985; Bridgland, 1994; Buckingham *et al.*, 1996). Gravel at the base of the Channel deposits is dense and poorly-sorted, with a sandy or silty matrix, and lying above cobbles and boulders (Buckingham *et al.*, 1996). It is overlain by moderately-sorted, cross-bedded gravel, often showing signs of iron-staining. As the gravel thins laterally, silt and sand beds dominate. Large vertebrate remains and chunks of wood form part of the cobble and boulder bed at the base (Fig. 4.10). These are more frequent in the marginal areas of the channel and are often imbricated, stacked on underlying silt and sand units. The preferred orientation of the clasts within the Channel Deposits suggests that dominant flow was towards the north or north-east. This is consistent with the former position of the Thames in this area (Buckingham *et al.*, 1996). Large herds of grazers such as a late form of steppe mammoth, bison and horse were present together with straight-tusked elephant, red deer, brown bear, lion and wolf (Kate Scott, pers. comm.). Pollen from the Channel Deposits is poorly preserved, although 30 taxa have been recorded, consisting mainly of aquatic and waterside plants (Buckingham *et al.*, 1996; Scott and Buckingham, 1997). Pollen from terrestrial species includes *Alnus* (alder), *Betula* (birch), *Pinus* (pine), *Prunus* (blackthorn) and *Sambucus* (elder), with other thermophilous species, such as *Quercus* (oak), indicated by abundant pieces of wood. However, the predominant environment is one of herb-rich grassland.

The molluscs from the Channel indicate the presence of fresh water and an absence of dense forest in the vicinity, while the Coleoptera are, for the most part, inhabitants of thinly-vegetated, sunny ground, only a few shade-loving species being present. The occurrence of the molluscs *Corbicula fluminalis* and *Potomida littoralis* suggests warm conditions at the time of deposition of the Channel sediments (Keen, 1990), as does the insect fauna, which is dominated by species which today have a mainly southern distribution, thereby suggesting a climate as warm as, or possibly warmer than, the present day (Buckingham *et al.*, 1996). Fish remains have also been recovered from the Channel, including stickleback, pike, perch and eel (Buckingham *et al.*, 1996), together with specimens of frog and bird (K. Scott pers. comm.).

In terms of archaeology, finds have been very sparse. To date 27 artefacts have been recovered, including eleven handaxes, a Levallois-like core and two chopping tools (Buckingham *et al.*, 1996; Scott and Buckingham, 2001; K. Scott pers. comm.). Although most are in an abraded condition, the core and some of the flakes are practically mint and may represent a human presence contemporary with the channel deposits (Buckingham *et al.*, 1996). Given that raw materials are locally very poor, this is the type of situation where one might again expect humans to have come prepared with a tool kit that they subsequently took away with them; hence the large quantities of tools and knapping waste seen in the Lower Thames are absent. Another MIS 7 site has recently been described at Latton, Wiltshire, very close to the headwaters of the Thames, although the fossiliferous and artefact-bearing sediments exposed there probably represent deposits of the river Churn, close to its confluence with the main river (Lewis *et al.*, 2005). This site produced only a small number of artefacts, in association with a mammoth-dominated assemblage, including eight rolled handaxes, which again are likely to have been reworked from older accumulations.

Few other fossil finds are known from the Summertown-Radley terrace, although plant remains including hoary whitlowgrass (*Draba* cf *incana*) and sea pink were reported from this terrace by Duigan (1955), with additional specimens of *Cerastium arvense* (field chickweed), *Leontodon autumnalis* (autumnal hawkbit), *Polygonum aviculare* (dock), *Ranunculus repens* (creeping buttercup) and *Carex rostrata* (bottle sedge) amongst others by Turner (1968).

Above the Channel, exposures of Stanton Harcourt Gravel have been described by Briggs (1973, 1976), Goudie and Hart (1975), Gilbertson (1976), Briggs and Gilbertson (1980), Bryant (1983), Briggs *et al.* (1985) and Seddon and Holyoak (1985) and have been interpreted as being deposited by a braiding river under cold, periglacial conditions (Bryant, 1983; Seddon and Holyoak, 1985). The Stanton Harcourt Gravel usually overlies, unconformably, Jurassic Oxford Clay, except in parts of Dix Pit, for example, where it overlies the Stanton Harcourt Channel Deposits mentioned above. Two divisions are noted within the gravel (Briggs *et al.*, 1985). The lower part is coarser and has a maximum thickness of 1.5 m, whereas the upper part is finer and is separated from the lower by a well-defined zone of cryoturbation (Bridgland, 1994). Signs of cryoturbation are present at the top of both divisions, in the form of involutions, festooning, small-scale slumps and load structures, often associated with ice-wedge casts (Fig. 4.12). These imply the periglacial conditions at the time of deposition (Bridgland, 1994; Buckingham *et al.*, 1996).

Both divisions of the Stanton Harcourt Gravel contain thin, intermittent sand and silt beds, from which molluscan remains of cold-climate affinities have been obtained (Briggs *et al.*, 1985; Seddon and Holyoak, 1985). Pollen and plant remains, characterised by arctic and alpine herb species, were also recovered from the silt bands (Seddon and Holyoak, 1985). Mammals from the Stanton Harcourt Gravel comprise mammoth, horse, bison, woolly rhinoceros and bear (Schreve, 1997). As a whole, the

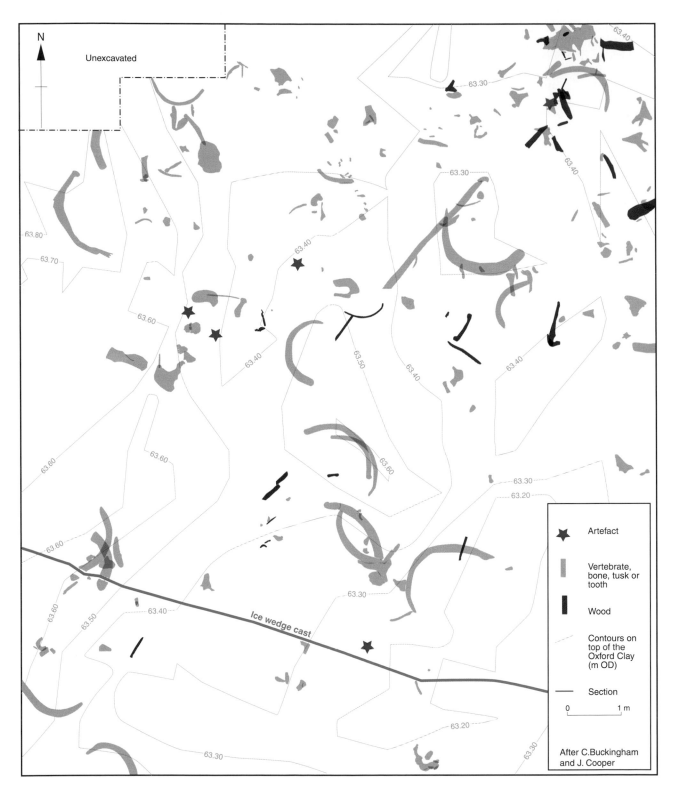

Fig. 4.10 Plan view of part of the Stanton Harcourt Channel deposits, Oxfordshire, showing the distribution of bones and wood

Fig. 4.11 (facing page) Handaxes from the Upper Thames: top row left and middle, Stanton Harcourt; others Berinsfield

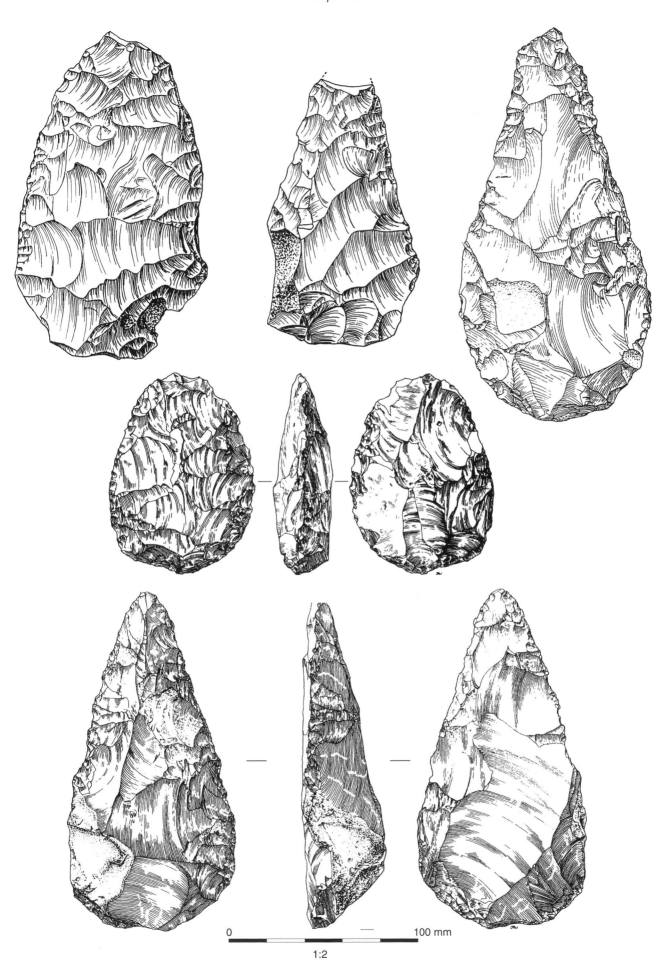

0   100 mm

1:2

Fig. 4.12   Examples of cold-climate cryoturbation features in the Stanton Harcourt Gravel, Oxfordshire

assemblage is indicative of open environments, as attested by the presence of horse, in association with other large grazing or part-grazing herbivores. All of the above-named taxa are known from cold and temperate episodes but the absence of any obligate thermophiles from the assemblage suggests that at the time of deposition of the gravel, the prevailing climate was cold.

Current measurements for the Stanton Harcourt Gravel Member suggest that the main flow direction was to the east or south-east (Bryant, 1983). This contrasts with the evidence from the underlying Channel deposits, which indicates flow towards the north or north-east, and suggests that during the time of deposition of the Stanton Harcourt Gravel, water entered the area from the valley of the River Windrush, a left-bank tributary of the Thames (Seddon and Holyoak, 1985).

Much larger collections of artefacts come from the sites of Berinsfield near Dorchester-on-Thames and Gravelly Guy/Smith's Pit, Stanton Harcourt (MacRae 1982, 1991) (see Fig. 4.11). At the latter MacRae collected some 99 artefacts of both flint and quartzite, including handaxes, chopping tools and cleavers, from the base of the Stanton Harcourt Gravel or on the surface of the Oxford Clay. The artefacts are water-worn and are likely to originate from eroded older landsurfaces (Hardaker, 2001; Scott and Buckingham, 2001). According to Lee (2001) the Gravelly Guy/Smith's pit artefacts are very similar in condition and form to those from the MIS 7 channel deposits at Dix's Pit, Stanton Harcourt (Buckingham *et al.*, 1996), which are themselves mostly abraded, suggesting that they

may *all* be earlier than the oldest deposits in which they were found (ie pre-MIS 7).

The Stanton Harcourt Gravel is also the most probable source of the artefacts from Mount Farm Pit and Queensford Pit at Berinsfield (MacRae, 1982; Lee, 2001), which produced over 200 artefacts of both flint and quartzite. These are mostly abraded and frost damaged handaxes, but some flakes (including handaxe thinning flakes) and, most notably, two Levallois cores and seven Levallois flakes were also recovered. The rolled condition of the artefacts again suggests derivation from older deposits, but Roe (1986) makes the important point that the Levallois material is fresher than the handaxes, and may therefore be younger. The lack of any decent raw material in this area (the closest primary source is the Chiltern foothills 6 miles to the south) led Wymer to infer that, the handaxes manufacturing flakes notwithstanding, hominins must have been importing finished handaxes (as well as perhaps roughouts and other blanks) into the area. Indeed, preferential transport may explain why a region apparently so lacking in flint and decent archaeological assemblages has managed to produce a number of very large handaxes (cf Roe, 1994).

So, while the Upper and Middle Thames are not the most informative of regions for this period, they once again provide insights into the transport of materials and use of non-flint resources. What is also clear, however, is that the evidence available from sediments of this age in these regions may not actually belong where it was found, either in space or time. Most of the artefacts are rolled pieces (mostly handaxes) that likely derive from the previous climatic cycle(s). In both the Upper and Middle Thames it is therefore remarkably difficult to actually pin down any primary evidence for MIS 7 human presence, the best being a couple of possible artefacts from Dix Pit and some fresher Levalloisian pieces from Berinsfield.

The Middle Thames is notably poor in vertebrate remains. Isolated records include a musk-ox skull from the Station Pit at Taplow, found low down in thick gravel deposits above Coombe Rock (Owen, 1856; Prestwich, 1956) and an apparently complete, articulated mammoth skeleton from Southall, West London (Brown, 1889) from a sandy loam horizon between two coarse gravel beds. Brown (1889) reported the presence of a Levallois point and other artefacts allegedly found in association with the mammoth bones.

Human behaviour and population dynamics of MIS 7

The much poorer record for this period – both within the main study area and elsewhere – raises the very important question of the palaeodemography of Britain, currently the focus of much attention. As discussed in previous chapters, part of the paucity is probably a function of differential preservation, suitable exposures or terrace remnants being better represented further east, perhaps exacerbated by the river flushing artefacts from higher reaches and depositing them further downstream. For the Middle Thames, David Bridgland (pers. comm.) has suggested that most of the Taplow Gravels cropping out at this terrace level most probably represent aggradation at the end of the climatic cycle – ie MIS 6 deposits – a period during which Britain was completely abandoned. In the absence of primary MIS 8 or MIS 7 sediments the absence of rich Levallois sites and predominance of rolled handaxes should therefore not come as much of a surprise. It should always be borne in mind, though, that hominins may have been preferentially active in the lower lying, flatter Chalk landscapes of the eastern lower reaches, where wide valley floors provided a range of habitats and resources and access to Chalk flint within a tightly clustered mosaic. As discussed in previous chapters different raw materials affecting hominin technological practices, preservation potential and under-representation due to collector bias may also be important factors.

Recently, Ashton and Lewis (2002) have suggested that the paucity of archaeological evidence actually reflects a population crisis during MIS 7. Using the relative density of handaxes and Levallois products in different terrace formations as a proxy for population size, these authors have attempted to model the demography of Britain during the Lower and Middle Palaeolithic. According to their model, MIS 9-8 is seen as the last period to witness a large human population, which declined gradually or dramati-

cally in MIS 7 and underwent a complete crash in MIS 6. According to Ashton and Lewis, the demographic events of MIS 8 to MIS 7 relate to changing habitat preferences, away from the warm maritime west favoured before 300,000 and towards the cooler continental east. Breaching of the Straits of Dover at some point after the Anglian (later than previously believed) may also have restricted unhindered access to Britain for the first time. This would have been instrumental in keeping populations low, as short term or local crashes could not be replaced by populations from adjacent parts of Europe (cf Preece, 1995a; White and Schreve, 2001; Bates *et al.*, 2003).

Ashton and Lewis have highlighted an intriguing pattern in the archaeological record of southern Britain, the low density of finds in the Taplow compared to earlier terraces being particularly noticeable. Reduced population size driven by changing habitat preference and fewer opportunities to enter Britain are among a number of plausible explanatory mechanisms. However, as well as the basic preservation issues already discussed, other factors seem likely to have exacerbated the patterns described, the most important for our present concerns being human technological organisation.

At a European scale, the Early Middle Palaeolithic was a period of increasing behavioural complexity, heralding a number of changes in hominin behaviour that are critical to our understanding of Neanderthals. There is evidence that Levallois technology was used as part of a more sophisticated scheme of stone tool transport and curation. In comparison to Lower Palaeolithic handaxes, which appear to be predominantly involved in butchery tasks (Keeley, 1980; Mitchell, 1995; Austin *et al.*, 1999) and were somewhat limited in their range of possibilities by their form and restricted patterns of edge modification, Levallois technology can be regarded as more versatile. Levallois gave hominins a new set of options: it was adaptable (one core could produce many varied products), maintainable (it could be reworked to provide new opportunities) and portable. The products of one Levallois core could thus potentially take the place of many handaxes and a range of other tool forms.

There is also evidence from across Europe that the lithic chaîne opératoire had become extended in time and space. Although the actual transport of raw materials *per se* does not dramatically increase across the Middle-Lower Palaeolithic transition (Feblot-Augustin, 1999), the selective curation and transport of Levallois products is marked. Geneste (1989) demonstrated that in south-west France Levallois products often occur on raw materials showing longer transport distances and hence greater levels of curation. At about the same time,

Fig. 4.13 The 'Aveley' interglacial

THE 'AVELEY' INTERGLACIAL

The 'Aveley' Interglacial

Recent research has led to the identification of a warm interglacial period that can be equated with MIS 7, roughly 200,000 BP. Key evidence comes from Aveley, Essex, which has given its name informally to this period.

By this time the Thames was close to adopting its familiar modern course. The main drainage had switched from the Evenlode Valley to the present-day course of the river along the foot of the Cotswold dip slope. In its middle and lower reaches it passed slightly to the north of its present position, flowing through Slough and Heathrow, and along what is now the north side of the Thames Estuary, through Southend.

The human record for this period is much poorer than for earlier periods. Finds of Levallois cores and flakes, indicative of Neanderthal presence, are known in small quantities from various locations, including Stanton Harcourt in the Upper Thames Valley. Larger quantities of Levallois flints have been found in the Lower Thames region, at West Thurrock, Crayford and Ebbsfleet.

Various different explanations of this 'sparse archaeological record are reviewed in the main text of this chapter. It is possible that human populations may have been relatively low during MIS 7, but other factors also need to be taken into account. During the earlier part of the interglacial, when temperatures were still cool, the river was actively cutting down into bedrock and exposing sources of flint that provided opportunities for hominins to acquire and work their tools and leave behind highly visible remains. Once the temperature had risen, however, the river became more sluggish. The flint sources were concealed by silting and alluviation, and humans may have been more concerned to conserve and re-use tools, thus leaving less debris behind for us to find.

STAGE		CLIMATE		Age	THAMES TERRACES		
Britain	**Netherlands**	**Cold**	**Warm**	**(Ma)**	**Upper**	**Middle**	**Lower**
Ipswichian	Eemian	6	5e	0.1	Summertown-Radley	Taplow	Mucking
'Aveley'	Warthe		7				
	Treene			0.2			Barling/Corbets Tey
'Purfleet'	Drenthe	8		0.3	Wolvercote	Lynch Hill	

Dix Pit, Stanton Harcourt

The excavations of the Hanson Mammoth Project took place at Dix Pit, Stanton Harcourt (Oxon) during the 1990s, and involved large numbers of volunteers working at the base of a disused gravel quarry. Important collections of material were recovered from an ancient channel of the Thames that is equated with the MIS 7 interglacial.

When this channel was active, temperatures were similar to today and the surrounding landscape was predominantly herb-rich grassland. Large herds of grazers, such as a late form of steppe mammoth, bison and horse were present, together with straight-tusked elephant, red deer, brown bear, lion and wolf. Stickleback, pike, perch and eel swam in the waters of the channel.

The Stanton Harcourt gravel, which has been seen to overlie the channel deposits at Dix Pit, signals a return to colder conditions at the end of MIS 7.

Stone tools were also found during the excavations. Because these were in a river channel rather than on a land surface they could have been carried by the river from elsewhere. However, a number were in a relatively fresh condition and may be evidence for the actual presence of hominins in the vicinity. Some of the tools were made of quartzite rather than flint. The Upper Thames Valley is very poor in flint as it does not occur in the local bedrock. It is likely that early hominins visiting the area will have been careful to preserve flint tools they brought with them from elsewhere rather than discarding them. They also made tools from locally available materials such as quartzite. It is possible that we are underestimating levels of hominin activity in the region simply because their tools were made of materials that are much harder for us to identify today.

THIS PAGE
* Right – Tooth of the distinctive small form of mammoth (Mammuthus cf. trogontherii) found at Dix Pit

* Centre left and right – shells and mammoth and elephant bones from the excavations

* Below – Driftwood from the ancient channel of the Thames

FACING PAGE
* Top – Specialists from the Quaternary Research Association visit Dix Pit in 1997

* Main photos – Excavation shots: More than 1000 bones of mammoth were recovered from the pit

* Two handaxes of quartzite found at Dix Pit (shown here at half size).

Figure 4.13

a growing importance of the rich grassland environments of the mammoth-steppe and an extension of occupation to the north-east may be observed (cf Guthrie, 1990; Ashton and Lewis, 2002; Gamble, 1995). The distribution and movement of herds in these more open landscapes would have required greater mobility by human populations and new strategies for dealing with the exploitation of such resources. This is reflected in the faunal record. Gaudzinski (1999) sees MIS 7 as a period during which specialised hunting becomes much clearer in the archaeological record, with repeated use of natural traps and ambush sites such as La Cotte de St Brelade, Jersey (Scott, 1980) and the younger occurrence at Salzgitter-Lebenstedt, Germany (Gaudzinski and Roebroeks, 2000) providing a vivid picture of fully 'tooled-up' Neanderthals moving through the landscape targeting herds and individual animals where they were most vulnerable.

These shifts in hunting, mobility and settlement might also have been accompanied by changes in group organisation and size (Ashton and Lewis, 2002). Some multiple kill sites have been argued to reflect relatively large (seasonal) gatherings of people (Farizy and David, 1992) and something similar might also be recognisable in the lithic record. Some of the richer sites tend to yield very dense concentrations of manufacturing debris suggesting either frequent repeat visits to key resources or exceptionally large gatherings. If the latter, then the skilled execution of a Levallois reduction sequence might have operated just as much in the social world as in the functional one, perhaps being used by individuals to express identity, skill and social role, helping define people and their place in society through their deeds (cf Kohn and Mithen, 1999; Gamble, 1999).

Returning to the question of low archaeological visibility throughout MIS 7 in Britain, it might now be suggested that this is because of the changes in the way that technology was organised in the landscape rather than the number of people making stone tools. The greater curation and reworking of Levallois products once they had left the major extraction sites led to reduced levels of discard at and between sites. This might be especially relevant to flint-poor regions such as the Upper Thames, where artefacts simply would not have been discarded in any great numbers when they could not be easily replaced. Examination of cutmarks on faunal sites, showing humans were present but left little evidence in the form of lithic refuse, may take on added significance here.

However, it is also true that most of the richer sites belong to the earlier part of the period, late MIS 8 and earliest parts of MIS 7, with most later MIS 7 sites producing very poor assemblages (Ashton and Lewis, 2002; White *et al.*, 2006). If site richness can be used as a proxy for population size, this would ostensibly support the notion of depopulation during this period (Ashton and Lewis, 2002). However, it is here necessary to again factor in human technological organisation around the changing landscapes of this long period, especially with regard to climatically driven adjustments in fluvial regimes and raw material resource availability.

During the colder episodes, highly erosive and gravel-laden rivers afforded greater opportunity to exploit large reservoirs of raw materials in the form of coarse gravels and Chalk exposed during downcutting, whereas during the relatively quiescent interglacials and other periods of low-energy deposition these opportunities were curtailed. So, humans may have created richer, highly visible signatures during the colder and early interglacial phases, simply because raw material was more plentiful and more easily available. Concomitantly, there are relatively fewer rich sites relating to the main part of the interglacial but a greater number of smaller, episodic sites with higher levels of curation. This argument is supported by the evidence from a number of sites discussed above: for example at Ebbsfleet, Crayford and West Thurrock where the rich archaeological horizons occur only as long as the targeted source of raw material (Chalk and gravel outcrops) was available and the sites acted as extraction localities. Once these sources become concealed by further deposition, evidence of human presence at all these sites is restricted to just a few pieces, although significantly they are still present; leaving only discrete signs of debris as evidence of their movement through the landscape. At sites lacking in adequate raw materials, large assemblages simply do not occur at any point during the cycle. This is not to say that human populations during MIS 7 were not relatively low, merely that the previously suggested dramatic depopulation may be partly illusory. Indeed, if we were to take the number of sites rather than the artefact density as the important factor, humans are equally well represented throughout MIS 7, although certainly not everywhere.

Chapter 5 – the archaeology of absence in the Late Pleistocene (MIS 6-4)

by Danielle Schreve, Mark White and Anthony Morigi

PALAEOGEOGRAPHY OF THE THAMES TERRACES

The Northmoor Gravel and Summertown-Radley Formation are the most extensive terrace deposits in the Upper Thames with their terraces respectively lying 2 to 3 and 8 to 13 metres above the alluvium of the present river (Bridgland, 1994). They flank the present day valley of the river above and below Oxford so, clearly, by this time the drainage pattern of the Upper Thames seen today was already well established. The Northmoor Gravel also underlies the Holocene alluvium where it fills a largely buried channel. Below the Goring Gap the course of the river, as represented by the Taplow Gravel, continued largely as before (see Chapter 4) but with a small southward shift downstream of Marlow indicated by the distribution of the Kempton Park Gravel. The Kempton Park Gravel is not seen above Marlow but is extensively developed downstream of here with 6 km wide terraces around the type locality at Kempton Park itself. In London, it under-lies parts of Westminster and the City where it contains (or according to some authors, overlies) the famous Ipswichian interglacial deposits at Trafalgar Square. Over much of its extent, the Kempton Park Gravel is the lowest terrace above the floodplain but east of Woolwich it passes beneath the alluvium and so is concealed: 'submerged' equivalents are, however, recognised in the Lower Thames (see below). The correlative of the Northmoor Gravel, the Shepperton Gravel, forms the floodplain terrace in the Middle Thames and similarly occupies a channel beneath the alluvium.

Fine-grained silt deposits quite extensively overlie the Kempton Park Gravel, the Taplow Gravel and the earlier Lynch Hill Gravel. These deposits, which are classified collectively as the Langley Silt Complex (Gibbard, 1985), are almost certainly of polygenetic origin as they contain loess with indications of reworking by water. The presence of loess and ice wedge casts implies deposition in a cold climate but the age of the deposits is uncertain. Where Ipswichian deposits are present, the Langley Silt always overlies them and so it would seem reasonable to assume that it is mainly Devensian in age (Gibbard, 1985).

Correlation of the terrace deposits

The detailed chronostratigraphy of the Upper Thames Summertown-Radley Formation and evidence for its correlation with the Middle Thames Taplow Gravel were discussed in Chapter 4. For both terrace deposits, Bridgland (1994) considered the cold-climate gravels that comprise the bulk of the sequence probably accumulated during MIS 8 and 6. He suggested that deposits with the wide range of ages similar to those encompassed by the Summertown – Radley Formation might also be expected in the Taplow Gravel above Marlow (see below). Gibbard (1985) traced the Kempton Park Gravel upstream as far as Marlow. Bridgland (1994) suggested that following aggradation of the Taplow Gravel in MIS 6, incision to the lower Kempton Park Gravel level occurred in the Marlow area but did not affect upstream areas. Thus, the Kempton Park Gravel may be considered coeval with the younger stages of both the Summertown Radley Formation and the Taplow Gravel (Table 5.1). In the Lower

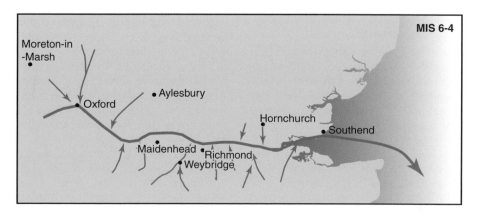

Fig. 5.1   The palaeogeography of the Thames MIS 6-4

Table 5.1 Correlation of Quaternary deposits of the Thames MIS 6-4

| Marine Isotope Stage | Quaternary deposits of the Thames | | |
	Upper	Middle	Lower
5a -4	Northmoor Gravel (base)	Shepperton Gravel (base)	Shepperton Gravel (submerged)
5d-2	Summertown-Radley Formation* (upper part)	Taplow Fm (top)/Kempton Park Gravel (top)	East Tilbury Marshes Gravel (submerged)
5e		**Trafalgar Square Member †**	
6 (late)		Taplow Formation (part)/Kempton Park Gravel (base)	

(*Details in text and Chapter 4; interglacial deposits in bold; †and other localities, see text). Sources: Bridgland (1994); Bowen (1999).

Thames the East Tilbury Marshes Gravel that underlies the alluvium has been equated with the Kempton Park Gravel (Bridgland, 1988a; Gibbard *et al.*, 1988). The relationships of the various interglacial deposits to these terrace sequences are described later in this chapter.

ARCHAEOLOGY AND PALAEONTOLOGY

In the preceding chapter it was noted that there is a marked decline in the richness of the British Palaeolithic record from around 250 000 BP (during the MIS 7 interglacial) and several plausible reasons for this pattern were reviewed. The climatic deterioration that began at the end of the penultimate interglacial was ultimately to result in catastrophe for Neanderthal populations, since by 180,000 BP all hominin populations appear to have died out or abandoned Britain completely. Humans would not return until *c* 60,000 BP, after an absence of some 120,000 years. During this time, Britain witnessed two major periods of cold climate conditions (with apparent accompanying glaciation in one, if not both episodes) in MIS 6 and MIS 4, as well as a full interglacial (MISs 5e) and other smaller-scale climatic events. Two major questions must be asked here:

1) How certain is it that there was no human presence during this period?
2) How can this absence be explained?

Is the absence real or imaginary?

One of archaeology's most well-worn axioms is that the 'absence of evidence is not evidence of absence'. Nevertheless, it remains equally true that few of the most frequently cited causes of apparent but arguably illusory absences, such as insufficient research activity or a paucity of sites of the correct age, do not apply here. Britain is one of the most extensively researched areas of the Pleistocene world with a 150 year history of both amateur and professional endeavour. It also has a whole host of sites now firmly attributed to the period concerned but still no convincing evidence that humans were present.

Previous claims for human occupation during the Ipswichian (MIS 5e) and the Early Devensian (MIS 5d-4) were based on the 1973 Geological Society's chronological framework (Mitchell *et al.*, 1973), which expounded a simplified and compressed sequence for the past 500,000 years. Thus, many sites of different ages were conflated into a single 'Ipswichian' interglacial. Nowadays, using improved chronostratigraphical schemes, together with the expanded marine and ice core isotope chronology, most if not all of these archaeological sites can be re-assigned on the basis of lithostratigraphy, biostratigraphy or direct dating to other glacial or interglacial periods, generally MIS 7 or MIS 3 (see Schreve, 1997, 2001a; Currant and Jacobi, 2002).

It is true that some sites and sequences belonging to different parts of this interval do contain artefacts or other claimed evidence for human presence, but none of these has any real archaeological merit. Indeed, in their separate reviews, Ashton (2002) and Currant and Jacobi (2002) systematically rejected all the putative evidence for occupation of Britain during the period MIS 6-3. They found that artefacts from sediments of this age were generally in rolled condition and unlikely to be contemporaneous with the deposits in which they were found, had very uncertain provenances and associations or were not, in fact, anthropogenic at all (see Table 5.2).

A good example is the site of Cassington in the Upper Thames (see below), where Hardaker (2001) reported eight flint, 92 quartzite and one andesite artefact (Fig. 5.2). These were found in association with a Devensian terrace gravel dated to MIS 5a (see below), although their condition suggested to Hardaker that they are derived from earlier deposits. Hardaker even suggested that the spatial separation of the quartzite and flint implements may show that they were introduced into the area by different rivers; the flint carried by the main Thames river, the quartzites coming from the north via the Cherwell/Rowell Brook tributary system. Although not *in situ*, these artefacts once again serve to show the importance of non-flint resources upstream of the Goring Gap. Scott and Buckingham (2001) are certain that the Upper Thames was uninhabitable during MIS 6, for reasons to be discussed further below.

How can the absence be explained?

As the fact that such a long period of abandonment existed has gradually become accepted over the past 20 years, archaeologists have begun to seek ways in which to explain it. Most recently, it has been highlighted as one of the seven key questions of the *Ancient Human Occupation of Britain Project* (a major five-year multidisciplinary project funded by the Leverhulme Trust http://www.nhm.ac.uk/hosted_sites/ahob/), although neither a consensus view nor simple monocausal explanation has been forthcoming. This is not surprising, however, given that the hiatus spans multiple climatic fluctuations of varying magnitude. Currently favoured models, which are not mutually exclusive, revolve around several ecological, geographical and social factors:

1) Neanderthals could not or would not cope with the climatically severe or glacial environments of MIS 6 and MIS 4, and therefore shunned the British Isles in favour of warmer refugia elsewhere

2) Absence during the warmer periods was due to the abrupt termination of the MIS 6 glaciation and rapid flooding of the Channel and North Sea basins following the melting of the ice sheets, resulting in insularity and restricted access to Britain from MIS 5e to MIS 5a inclu-

Table 5.2 Some Late Middle and Upper Pleistocene occurrences apparently showing evidence for human activity, with reasons for their rejection (data principally taken from Ashton 2002 and Currant and Jacobi 2002, with additions). The list is not exhaustive, but to date no convincing evidence of primary context archaeology has been forthcoming for any of these periods in Britain.

	Archaeology Present	Reason for rejection (see key)
MIS 6		
Taplow Gravel	stone artefacts	1
Stanton Harcourt Gravel	stone artefacts	1
Warwickshire Avon Terrace 4	stone artefacts	1
River Trent, Egginton Common Sands & Gravels	stone artefacts	1
MIS 5e		
Barrington, Cambridgeshire	small flint core	2
Cardo's Pit, Barrington	Flake	2
Lavenham, Suffolk	stone artefacts	2
Newmarket Railway Station, Cambs	Flints	3
East Mersea	Flake	2
Victoria Cave	Biface	4
Milton Hill Fissure	butchered & burnt bone	5
MIS 5d-a		
Kempton Park Gravel	stone artefacts	1
Cassington, Unit 1	stone artefacts	1
Bacon Hole, grey clay, silts and sands	split & polished bone	3
MIS 4		
Banwell Bone Cave	modified bone & antler	3
Banwell Bone Cave	human tooth	2 (modern)
Bosco's Den	split pebble	3
Steetley Wood Cave	human mandible	2 (modern)
Tornewton Cave, Reindeer Strata	stone hammer	3
Windy Knoll	stone artefacts	4 (from Creswell)
River Trent, Beeston Gravel	stone artefacts	1
Kempton Park Gravel	stone artefacts	1

Key

1) Derived, abraded artefacts clearly not contemporary with deposits in which they were found and likely to have originated from older deposits in the region

2) Finds of late or post-Pleistocene type and/or other evidence that they came from deposits of different age

3) Non-anthropogenic

4) Do not actually belong at the site to which they have been attributed (based on preservational state, archival records etc)

5) Re-examination failed to verify

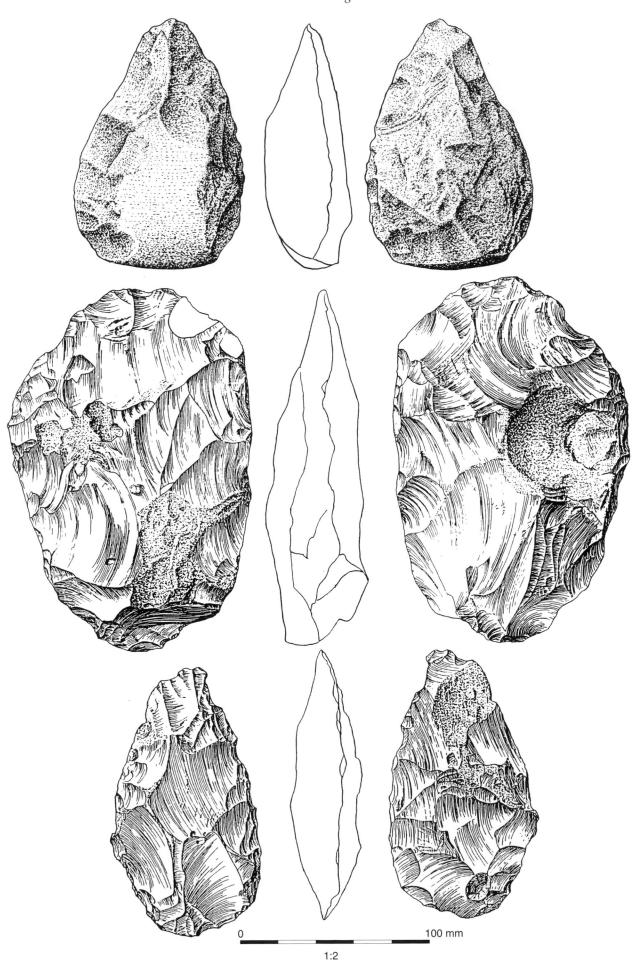

0   100 mm

1:2

sive (cf Shackleton, 1987; Keen, 1995; Ashton, 2002; Gupta *et al.*, 2007)

3) Absence during the last interglacial, MIS 5e, reflects an absence of human populations from NW Europe as a whole, with Neanderthals avoiding, for ecological, behavioural and social reasons, fully temperate dense deciduous forests (Gamble, 1986, 1987, 1995; Ashton, 2002; see also Roebroeks *et al.*, 1992; Speleers, 2000 and Roebroeks and Speleers, 2002 for criticisms of this argument).

Each of these hypotheses has its own merits but also problems, as will be discussed below.

The assumption that the glacial climates and associated cold tundra environments of MIS 6 and MIS 4 – which together account for about 55% of the entire period of absence – were just too hostile for archaic humans to cope (or bother) with is not in itself unreasonable (Fig 5.3). Even culturally sophisticated modern humans abandoned Britain during the more extreme parts of the last glacial period (MIS 2) (Housley *et al.*, 1997; Gamble *et al.*, 2004). Judging from the oxygen isotope record, MIS 6 appears to have been one of the most extreme glaciations of the last half million years with, apart from a slight amelioration at the beginning, very severe conditions throughout (Shackleton, 1987). Indeed, in the Netherlands, this period (the Saalian) appears to have been even more severe than the MIS 12 glaciation, in terms of the southerly extent of the ice sheets.

In Britain, it has been posited that deposits in the West Midlands, Eastern England and East Anglia are evidence for glaciation in England during MIS 6, for example the gravels and till of the Welton-le-Wold Formation of Lincolnshire. Bowen *et al.* (1986) suggested that the Welton Member, a till, was emplaced by a glaciation between the Anglian and Devensian but it is accepted that this correlation is only tentative (Bowen, 1999). Sandy till containing Scandinavian erratics and seen along the Northumberland and Durham coast is thought to be of MIS 6 age or older (Francis, 1970; Bowen, 1999). Catt (1991) has suggested the glacigenic Bridlington Member (formerly the 'Basement Till' of Catt and Penny (1966)), which is currently assigned to the Devensian Holderness Formation (Bowen, 1999), may date from MIS 6. The Briton's Lane Formation of north Norfolk includes extensive gravel deposits that cap the Cromer Ridge in north Norfolk. They are thought, on the basis of stratigraphic position, the presence of Scandinavian erratics, and the freshness of associated landforms, to represent outwash from a MIS 6 ice sheet that also deposited the aforementioned tills (Hamblin *et al.*, 2000). However, in the absence of an unequivocal date for any of these deposits the correlations remain uncertain.

Not only may glaciation in MIS 6 have acted to push Neanderthals towards local extinction in

Britain but a further point of note is the apparent presence of high sea levels on the south coast of England during at least part of this time. At the site of Norton Farm, near Chichester (West Sussex), a series of laminated fine-grained silts has been described overlying marine sands of the Brighton-Norton raised beach (Bates *et al.*, 2000). The laminated silts have been interpreted as tidal mudflats and the sequence as a whole records a declining marine influence. It is clear from molluscan bivalves, such as *Pisidium obtusale lapponicum* and *Pisidium stewarti*, not only that cold climatic conditions prevailed but also (from marine microfossils such as *Elphidium clavatum* and *Cassidulina reniformis*) that high sea levels persisted at this time. The palaeontological evidence therefore suggests that there may have been a significant lag between the onset of cold climatic conditions and a glacio-eustatic fall in relative sea level (Bates *et al.*, 2000). This clearly presents an interesting palaeogeographical situation, since the combination of a severe climate and high sea level would have acted in combination to exclude early humans and other animals from entering Britain at this time.

The climatic deterioration in MIS 6 certainly affected the contemporary flora and fauna. The beginnings of the decline are apparent at Crayford (see Chapter 4), with the immigration of taxa such as musk ox (*Ovibos moschatus*), ground squirrel (*Citellus citellus*), and collared and Norway lemmings (*Dicrostonyx torquatus* and *Lemmus lemmus*). Vertebrate faunas from pre-Devensian cold-climate episodes are generally very poorly known in Britain, so the evidence is sparse. However, a rich mammalian assemblage attributed to a pre-Ipswichian cold episode has been recovered from a series of gravels pits in the Balderton Sand and Gravel, which underlies the Balderton Terrace between Newark and Lincoln (Brandon and Sumbler, 1991). Lister and Brandon (1991) identified wolf (*Canis lupus*), brown bear (*Ursus* cf *arctos*), lion (*Panthera leo*), straight-tusked elephant (*Palaeoloxodon antiquus*), *Mammuthus primigenius* (woolly mammoth), *Equus ferus* (horse), narrow-nosed rhinoceros (*Stephanorhinus* cf *hemitoechus*), woolly rhinoceros (*Coelodonta antiquitatis*), red deer (*Cervus elaphus*), reindeer (*Rangifer tarandus*), possible bison (cf *Bison priscus*) and musk ox (*Ovibos moschatus*). The assemblage is broadly indicative of a largely open environment and on the basis of the presence of reindeer (an inhabitant of tundra and boreal forest at the present day) and musk ox (presently restricted to the arctic tundra of North America and Greenland), the balance of evidence suggests that it was probably cold. However, the presence of *O. moschatus* within the Lower Brickearth at Crayford, in association with temperate-climate *Corbicula* (Dawkins, 1872), hints that its appearance during the Pleistocene may have been governed less by climatic constraints than by the availability of suitable vegetation. The presence of two temperate-indicator species, straight-tusked elephant and a stephanorhine rhinoceros (probably narrow-nosed

Fig. 5.2 (facing page)   Artefacts from Cassington

rhinoceros), seems somewhat at odds with the rest of the assemblage. *P. antiquus* has been reported from interstadial deposits within the Anglian Baginton-Lillington gravels at Snitterfield (Lister *et al.*, 1990) and at Waverley Wood, both in Warwickshire (Shotton *et al.*, 1993), although it is absent from typical cold stage mammalian assemblages (Stuart, 1982). The specimens of *P. antiquus* and *S.* cf *hemitoechus*

Fig. 5.3   Severe cold conditions returned around 180,000 BP (MIS 6). Humans seem to have abandoned Britain completely, and were not to return for some 120,000 years. Animal remains found at British sites of this period are consistent with very cold conditions such as exist today in the arctic tundra of North America and Greenland. The photograph shows a musk ox in the modern tundra. Conditions like this may well have existed in the Thames Valley during periods within MIS 6

Fig. 5.4   Astragalus of small-bodied horse from MIS 6 cold-climate deposits at Bacon Hole, Gower, West Glamorgan (left), compared to a specimen from MIS 9 interglacial deposits at Grays Thurrock, Essex

apparently show no more evidence of rolling or abrasion than any of the other specimens (Lister and Brandon, 1991) and it thus seems unlikely that they have been derived from a much earlier deposit. It is therefore possible either that the Balderton assemblage represents an amalgamation of several climatic phases within a cold stage, or that it reflects interstadial conditions sufficiently warm to accommodate the more temperate elements (Lister and Brandon, 1991). The pollen spectra imply the presence of rich, open herbaceous vegetation without significant trees or shrubs, and with grasses dominating sedges (Peglar *et al.*, in Brandon and Sumbler, 1991). Molluscs (Preece, in Brandon and Sumbler, 1991) and ostracods (Robinson, in Brandon and Sumbler, 1991) imply a wider range of temperatures, whereas Coleoptera from silt-filled channels beneath the Balderton gravels are indicative of open habitats with a cold climate more continental than that of modern Britain. Mean July temperatures are estimated to be around 10°C and January temperatures at or below -20°C (Coope and Taylor, in Brandon and Sumbler, 1991).

The few other British sites with palaeobiological evidence that can be related to MIS 6 are, however, distinguished by very low-diversity vertebrate assemblages with accompanying evidence for the dwarfing of large mammals, in this case horse. At several sites in southern and western Britain, including Bacon Hole in West Glamorgan, Clevedon Cave in Somerset, Norton Farm, Portslade and Brighton in East Sussex and Marsworth in Buckinghamshire, there is evidence for a small-bodied horse associated with cold-climate deposits from stratigraphical contexts pre-dating the Last Interglacial (Schreve, 1997; Parfitt *et al.*, 1998; Murton *et al.*, 2001). At these localities, the horse has undergone a noticeable reduction in size and an increase in stockiness, compared to the large forms encountered in late Middle Pleistocene interglacials. The extent of this size decrease is shown clearly in Figure 5.4, in which an example of the small MIS 6 horse from Bacon Hole is shown against a typical Middle Pleistocene interglacial specimen from MIS 9 deposits at Grays Thurrock, Essex. Average withers height reconstructions for the MIS 6 horses are only 1.27 m compared to 1.47 m in MIS 7 horses (Parfitt *et al.*, 1998). Size decrease in mammals is frequently believed to occur in response to climatic warming in accordance with Bergmann's Rule (but cf Lister, 1992). However, the reverse seems true of the Middle Pleistocene caballine horses, which tended to be particularly large during temperate periods. The decrease in body size exhibited by the MIS 6 horse may have been an adaptation to the harsh climate and poor vegetational conditions of this period (cf Forstén, 1996). This compares well with both the oxygen isotope curve and other lithological evidence, which suggests that the MIS 6 cold episode was extremely severe. The length of time required for the dwarfing is unknown but studies of island populations of red deer on Jersey, which became isolated and then dwarfed during the Last

Interglacial, showed a 50-60% reduction in body size after about 6000 years (Lister, 1995).

As well as the small-bodied horse, a second species of biostratigraphical importance is present in the form of a large northern vole, *Microtus oeconomus*. During MIS 7 and MIS 6, this species was the dominant grassland vole in Britain, apparently resulting in an increase in size (expressed in the length of the first lower molar) and an increase in morphological variation in that tooth (Stuart, 1982; Schreve, 1997; Bates *et al.*, 2000) (Fig. 5.5). These particular teeth have therefore proved extremely useful in identifying and correlating deposits of this age. However, as mentioned above, preservational factors have made deposits of MIS 6 age difficult to identify and with the exception of very occasional finds from sites in the Stanton Harcourt Gravel and the Taplow Gravel, mentioned in the previous chapter, there is nothing notable in the vertebrate record to report from either the Upper or Middle Thames.

The impact on the flora and fauna of this severe climatic deterioration is therefore clear. With the possibility of ice sheets extending as far south as the West Midlands and north Norfolk, one can infer a wide band of polar desert and semi-barren tundra stretching across the study area that would have been equally inhospitable for humans. However,

extreme glacial conditions would have existed for only part of the time, and it is known from recurring patterns of occupation during previous glacial cycles that hominins were often present in Britain during the cooling (early) and warming (later) intermediate phases of the coldest episodes. What is intriguing, then, is why hominins failed to return during the intermediate warming phase from MIS 6-MIS 5e, despite having successfully re-colonised Britain during this phase in all previous Middle Pleistocene glacial-interglacial transitions. Their absence from the warm interstadial periods of MIS 5c and 5a is equally interesting.

One very significant factor is the sudden termination of MIS 6 around 130 000 years ago and the subsequent rapid flooding of the Channel and North Sea, cutting Britain off from Europe. It has widely been assumed (von Koenigswald, 1992; Ashton, 2002) this happened so quickly that hominins, migrating northwards and westwards from their southern (Mediterranean) and eastern (steppe) refugia in response to climatic amelioration, were unable to re-enter Britain in time before it was cut off; indeed Shackleton (1987) estimated that this sharp rise in sea level may have occurred within a mere 3000 years. It is interesting to speculate that with possible high sea levels on the south coast during some parts of MIS 6, opportunities for access may have been very limited indeed. Following the rapid sea level rise of the Ipswichian, Britain may have remained isolated for the remainder of MIS 5. Keen (1995) suggests that during MIS 5d and 5b sea-levels dropped by only ~25 m, while the English Channel and North Sea Basins at this time were in the order of −40 m and −50 m respectively. Together, avoidance of extremely cold environments during MIS 6 and the effect of rapidly occurring, sustained insularity during MIS 5 can thus provide a tidy explanation for human absence. However, this did not prevent other animals from exploiting the 3000 year 'window of opportunity' and successfully colonising the British landscape.

MIS 5E: THE IPSWICHIAN INTERGLACIAL

Evidence for the Last (Ipswichian) Interglacial is well-preserved within the Thames valley, including in the study area. Arguably the most famous Middle Thames deposits are those from Trafalgar Square, in central London, which have been known since the early 1700s although never published in full. Although isolated finds of mammalian fossils, including straight-tusked elephant and hippopotamus (*Hippopotamus amphibius*), have come to light in a variety of locations in the area (St James Square, Pall Mall, Spring Gardens, Cockspur Street and Lower Regent Street), the best-known sections were exposed in 1957 during the construction of Uganda House on the south side of Trafalgar Square and in 1958 during foundation work for New Zealand House in Lower Regent Street (Franks *et al.*,

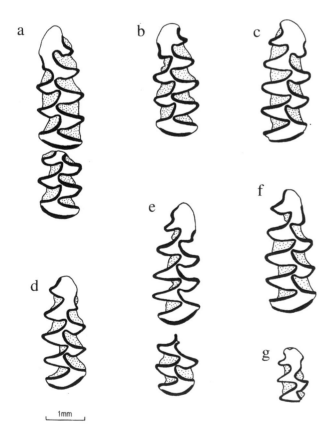

1mm

Fig. 5.5 Examples of occlusal views of molars of northern vole (Microtus oeconomus)

WHEN LIONS REALLY CROUCHED WHERE NELSON NOW STANDS: THE TRAFALGAR

Trafalgar Square, with its huge Nelson monument, Landseer's bronze lions and its fountains and pigeons, is one of the best-known Squares in the world. It is unlikely that passers-by, political demonstrators, photographers (or pigeons) have much, if any, idea of the appearance of the Square 100,000 years ago. But recent discoveries have now provided us with sufficient material to build up a picture of the scene as it once appeared. In his drawing on these pages our Special Artist, Mr. Neave Parker, with the co-operation of experts, has reconstructed the gently undulating landscape of parkland

type, such as existed in Central London during the Last Interglacial when the climate was warmer than it is to-day, and some of the abundant flora and fauna. In the foreground, standing on a grassy promontory, is a Straight-Tusked Elephant, an extinct warmth-loving species distinct from the Woolly Mammoth of colder times, remains of which have also been found in London. Nearby a Rose Chafer beetle, so called from its habit of feeding on the wild rose, which was a common plant at this time, is seen in flight. Three hippopotamuses, also warmth-loving animals, wallow in a marshy

Drawn by our Special Artist, Neave Parker, F.R.S.A., with the co-operation

Fig. 5.6   *Reconstruction of the Trafalgar Square area during the Ipswichian Interglacial as portrayed in the* Illustrated London News, *1958*

SQUARE OF 100,000 YEARS AGO, ITS FLORA AND FAUNA AND INTERGLACIAL LANDSCAPE.

backwater of the Thames, in which grow Yellow Water Lilies, Water Chest-nuts, Sedges and Reed-Mace. In these still waters live numerous river snails, aquatic beetles and other forms of life. Near the water's edge stands a large wild ox (*Bos primigenius*), a remote ancestor of our present-day domestic cattle. The rising ground beyond is grassland, interspersed with scattered trees of yew and oak and with patches of low scrub of hazel, maple and other plants. Here two lionesses are seen disturbing a group of Red Deer which are moving away (left). A herd of Fallow Deer, not unlike those found in

English parks at the present day, is visible in the distance. A lion is resting, in a Landseer pose, in the shade, and (right, centre) a bear shambles into view in search of food. If space permitted, our artist could have included a rhinoceros and perhaps a prowling hyæna. Fossil remains of all these animals, which flourished during a warm phase between two glacial periods, probably about 100,000 years ago, have come to light as the result of the recent excavations in old deposits of the Thames in Trafalgar Square. These finds are described in the article on page 1011.

of the authors of the article on page 1011 *and Professor F. E. Zeuner.*

1958; Franks, 1960, Fig. 5.6). Later sampling was undertaken at Canadian Pacific House in Trafalgar Square and at the Tennessee Pancake House site on Whitehall (Gibbard, 1985; Preece, 1999). The Trafalgar Square Sands and Silts have been interpreted alternately as an erosional remnant buried by the later emplacement of the Kempton Park Gravel (Gibbard, 1994) or as an integral part of the Kempton Park terrace aggradation, the youngest of four post-Anglian terraces in the Middle and Lower Thames valleys (Bridgland, 1994) (see Fig. 2.6), the latter following the model of climatically-generated terraces adopted in previous chapters of this volume. Both authors are in agreement with the Ipswichian age for the temperate-climate deposits originally proposed by Franks (1960), a correlation supported by molluscan (Preece, 1999) and mammalian biostratigraphy (Currant and Jacobi, 2001) and by aminostratigraphy (Bowen *et al.*, 1989).

At Uganda House, Kerney (1959) recorded a basal coarse gravel (0.9 m thick), overlain by dark grey sandy clays and silts with lenses of plant material (1.5 m), then by brown and yellow well-bedded sands with thin shell beds (4.9 m) and finally by laminated silty clays (brickearth). Today, the interglacial sediments lie predominantly below sea level with a base on London Clay between -0.5 and -3.3 m O.D. and a surface at *c* +7.5 m O.D. (Preece, 1999). Slight variations in this sequence

were noted at other localities, reflecting changing sedimentation rates in shallow floodplain channels or depressions. This variability is echoed by the molluscan assemblages, which indicate a large, slow-flowing calcareous river with changing frequencies of moving water, slum and terrestrial taxa (Fig. 5.7). Species characteristic of aquatic vegetation, damp marshy ground and dry, open calcareous grassland are also well represented (Preece, 1999). Pollen spectra from the Canadian Pacific House site (Gibbard, 1985) indicate fully temperate climatic conditions with forests dominated by *Quercus* (oak), smaller amounts of *Acer* (maple), *Fraxinus* (ash) and increasing amounts of *Corylus* (hazel). In addition, a diverse range of dry grassland and disturbed ground taxa are present, including Poaceae, *Plantago* (plantain), Chenopodiaceae, Compositae (Liguliflorae) and Umbelliferae, as well as some local wet woodland, indicated by *Alnus* (alder), and damp marshland communities near the channel itself. The presence of frost-sensitive taxa such as *Hedera* (ivy), *Ilex* (holly) and *Viscum* (mistletoe) indicates that winters were mild and a muted brackish influence is highlighted by the occurrence of species such as *Armeria maritima* (sea thrift) and *Plantago maritima* (sea plantain) (Gibbard, 1985). In the plant macrofossil record, additional exotic thermophiles such as *Trapa natans* (water chestnut) and *Acer monspessulanum*

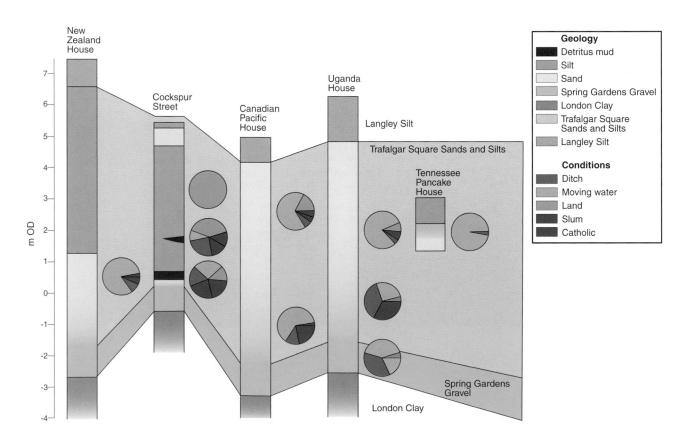

Fig. 5.7   Reconstruction of changing environmental conditions as seen in the molluscan records from various sites in Trafalgar Square, central London

(Montpellier maple) were noted by Franks (1960). The palaeobotanical evidence thus indicates optimal climatic conditions and presumably also maximum high sea levels stands, equating well with the original pollen zonation of Franks (1960). This sits well with the information from Ipswichian beetle assemblages, which are dominated by species living today in relatively warm areas, almost all of them in central and southern Europe. Mutual Climatic Range estimates based on the beetles indicate that mean July temperatures were around 4°C above those in southern England at the present day (Coope, 2001).

The mammalian remains from Trafalgar Square include isolated bones and teeth of hippopotamus (Fig. 5.8), straight-tusked elephant, lion, fallow deer (*Dama dama*), red deer, aurochs (*Bos primigenius*), an undetermined rhinoceros and possible bear. Franks *et al.* (1958) also reported fossil coprolites, thought to indicate the presence of spotted hyaena (*Crocuta crocuta*), a species present in abundance in many other Last Interglacial sites in Britain. The faunal list was increased with the finding of bison during construction of the British Council building in Spring Gardens in 1972 and water vole (*Arvicola* sp.) from the Canadian Pacific House site in 1980 (A P Currant, pers. comm., 2007). Notable absentees from this assemblage and from others of equivalent age are horse, Merck's rhinoceros (*Stephanorhinus kirchbergensis*) and hominins (Neanderthals). The assemblage composition places this fauna within the Joint Mitnor Cave Mammal Assemblage-Zone (MAZ) of Currant and Jacobi (2001), considered by those authors to be characteristic of MIS 5e in Britain. In particular, hippopotamus is considered an important indicator of age, since it is not known from any other post-Anglian interglacial in Britain. A Last Interglacial age has been supported by Uranium-series direct dating of flowstone encasing hippopotamus remains at Victoria Cave (North Yorkshire) to 120 000 ± 6 000 BP (Gascoyne *et al.*

1981). This has since been corroborated at other Last Interglacial sites by further Uranium-series age-estimates, for example a date of 129 000-116 000 BP obtained from stalagmite fragments from Bacon Hole (Schwarcz, 1984; Stringer *et al.* 1986; Sutcliffe *et al.* 1987). An Ipswichian age for the Trafalgar Square deposits is also proposed on the basis of the molluscan assemblages by Preece (1999), on the basis of the combined presence of *Belgrandia marginata*, *Potomida littoralis* and *Margaritifera auricularia*, coupled with an absence of species well known from older Pleistocene interglacials such as *Pisidium clessini*, *Unio crassus* and *Corbicula fluminalis*. The last of these, the bivalve *C. fluminalis*, is particularly interesting since although it coexists in the Nile and other African rivers at the present day with hippopotamus, these two species have never been found together, in an un-reworked context, in Britain in the fossil record (Preece, 1999; Keen, 2001).

The mammalian assemblage supports the prevalence of full temperate conditions and indicates a combination of some deciduous or mixed woodland bordering an extensive grass-dominated floodplain. Indeed, the importance of hippopotamus and other large grazers as environmental 'modifiers' has been suggested by Gibbard and Stuart (1975). At Barrington, Cambridgeshire, where hippopotamus remains were extremely abundant, the sediments had a notably high mineragenic content (implying inwashing of soils from bare trampled ground) and the pollen spectra consisted of 90% herb pollen, implying local deforestation by megaherbivores (Gibbard and Stuart, 1975). This pattern has also been observed at other sites with Ipswichian pollen profiles (Stuart, 1982), further highlighting the impact of these very large mammals on their landscape. A lack of tree pollen was also noted in the spectra from the Tennessee Pancake House, despite the presence of thermophilous molluscs indicating continued temperate conditions in this, slightly later, part of the Trafalgar Square succession (Gibbard, 1985). This absence may reflect either the aforementioned local deforestation activities of the large herbivores or the effects of a deep water channel receiving extensive inputs of inwashed pollen from adjacent grass and marsh vegetation (Gibbard, 1985).

Within the Upper Thames, the site at Eynsham Station Pit near Oxford is probably the best known Ipswichian locality. The Eynsham Gravel (Bridgland, 1994) overlies the Stanton Harcourt Gravel of the Summertown-Radley Formation (see Chapter 4) and is thus separated from the older interglacial deposits represented by the Stanton Harcourt Channel Deposits (MIS 7) by an intervening period of cold-climate conditions. Sandford noted this relationship in 1924, reporting teeth of mammoth at the base of the Eynsham pit sequence, with 'the very common occurrence of *Hippopotamus*' in the overlying gravels (Sandford, 1924, 140). Other sites yielding hippopotamus in the Summertown-

Fig. 5.8 Canine (tusk) of hippopotamus (Hippopotamus amphibius) *from Trafalgar Square, central London*

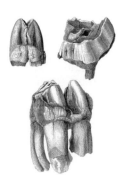

Fig. 5.9   Teeth of hippopotamus, (Hippopotamus amphibius) (top left and bottom) and of narrow-nosed rhinoceros (Stephanorhinus hemitoechus) from Ipswichian deposits at Brentford, Middlesex

Radley Terrace include Wytham, Iffley, Abingdon, Dorchester and Radley (Sandford, 1924, 1925; Briggs *et al.*, 1985). The record of *Corbicula fluminalis*, found at Radley in the same deposits as hippopotamus, is however, only a single valve and most probably reworked (Preece, 1999).

Other Last Interglacial sites in the Middle Thames include Brentford and Brown's Orchard in Acton. At Brentford, large vertebrate remains including hippopotamus, narrow-nosed rhinoceros (Fig. 5.9) and straight-tusked elephant, together with molluscs and plant remains, were recovered from the interface of a shell-rich sandy loam with a basal gravel unit overlying London Clay (Trimmer, 1813; Morris, 1838). Further remains of hippopotamus, together with a large cervid (probably red deer) and an undetermined large bovid (aurochs or bison) were collected from the Great West Road in 1958 (Zeuner, 1959). A faunal assemblage reported by Lane-Fox (1872) from Brown's Orchard in Acton includes a mixture of temperate and cold-climate indicators with very different preservation types. Of these, the preservation of the remains of hippopotamus, fallow deer, red deer and most probably straight-tusked elephant appear to form a discrete grouping of credible Last Interglacial age. These are commingled with remains of (younger?) horse and reindeer that share a second preservation type, and remains of a large bovid and possible roe deer (*Capreolus capreolus*) that cannot currently be attributed to either group (A P Currant, pers. comm. 2007).

Further remains of hippopotamus were reported from a pit at Kensington Road, Reading (Shrubsole and Whitaker, 1902), within the 'Reading Town Gravel' of Gibbard (1985), although the original authors unfortunately provide no context for these finds. Gibbard (1985) cited the occurrence of these (reworked) hippopotamus teeth within this gravel body as evidence of an early Devensian age for the 'Reading Town Gravel', banked up against residual Ipswichian deposits. However, the nearby downstream site at Redlands Pit has yielded a very different mammalian assemblage and biostratigraphical attribution of this assemblage to the Ipswichian is extremely problematic. On the basis of reassessment of the altitudinal distribution of gravel remnants within the Reading area and projection of the Taplow Gravel from the type area upstream, Bridgland (1994) suggested that the Redlands Pit deposits fall within the predicted elevation of the Taplow Formation and that the 'Reading Town Gravel' therefore is the true upstream correlative of the Taplow. An age for the Redlands Pit fauna within MIS 8-7-6 is consequently more likely. Nevertheless, the presence of hippopotamus remains at Kensington Road led Bridgland (1994) to conclude that Ipswichian deposits do indeed occur within the Taplow Formation in the Reading area, thereby implying that no MIS 6 rejuvenation took place in this part of the valley, in contrast to the sequence of events reconstructed for the Lower Thames. This is significant, since it demonstrates that the Taplow Formation in the Reading area has much in common with the Summertown-Radley Formation of the Upper Thames, an aggradation that also covers a complex succession of deposits apparently spanning MIS 8-5e inclusive and possibly incorporating early Devensian gravels as well.

It is clear from the palaeoclimatic and palaeoenvironmental parameters described above that if hominins were able to access Britain before island isolation took hold, the Last Interglacial environment was both equable and stocked with plentiful plant and animal resources, suggesting that conditions should have been favourable for occupation. The third hypothesis concerning the dearth of archaeology therefore proposes that the absence of humans from Britain during this warm period reflects a more general absence or at best paucity of human populations throughout NW Europe: simply put, there was no one in adjacent areas of Europe to fill our empty landscape. Gamble (1986, 1987) has long argued that humans were unable to cope with the dense deciduous forests that existed here during MIS 5e, which far from being well-stocked larders, are actually difficult places to make a living with unevenly-spaced resources in inconvenient packages. Success in such environments demands complex solutions, involving technical and planning skills, extended alliance networks and channels of information exchange that apparently did not match those of Neanderthal societies. Neanderthals were much better able to deal with mosaics of open woodland-steppe environments, which were ecologically more varied and provided localised access to a range of resources of different size and character. The spatial structure of these mosaics also made them more resilient and quick to recover from disruption from fire or overgrazing, with any temporary local interruptions quickly filled by resources in adjacent areas (Gamble, 1995).

According to Ashton (2002), throughout the Middle Pleistocene hominins were actually becoming progressively specialised to life on the wide open grassland of the mammoth-steppe (Guthrie, 1990), an adaptation that depended on greater mobility, more developed hunting practices and greater social flexibility. This can be linked to the isotopic evidence for hyper-carnivory in Neanderthals (Bocherens *et al.*, 1999; Richards *et al.*, 2000), with a reliance on access to large herds and ambush hunting techniques (Gaudzinski, 1999). During forested interglacial periods the focus of occupation would thus have been in the east, the west only being colonised during cooler periods when more continental, Mammoth Steppe conditions extended right up to the Atlantic Seaboard (Currant and Jacobi, 2001).

The presence of dense forests keeping humans at bay for social or adaptive reasons is another plausible piece to the jigsaw, but it is not without its problems (see Roebroeks *et al.*, 1992 for adequate evidence of human settlement during climax forest phases). There is good evidence for exploitation of forested environments during MIS 5e, for example Lehringen, Gröbern and Taubach in Eastern Germany (Roebroeks *et al.*, 1992; Bratlund, 1999), where individual straight tusked elephants and woodland rhinoceroses were targeted by humans. Still, these sites are in the more continental areas of central Europe, and severe doubts remain over claims for occupation further west (see Ashton (2002) and references therein). Nevertheless, the recent report of a Last Interglacial Palaeolithic occupation site from tufa deposits at Caours in the Somme valley of northern France (Antoine *et al.*, 2006) provides perhaps the first indication that this part of NW Europe was successfully occupied. There is evidence for suitable founder populations during the later phases of MIS 5, for example at Seclin (France) and Maastricht Site J (the Netherlands), but according to the second hypothesis, Britain was probably already an island by this time; perhaps humans arrived just too late to make the crossing.

On the other hand, some scholars contend that the paucity of humans from NW Europe is simply an illusion of preservational bias (Roebroeks *et al.*, 1992; Speleers, 2000; Roebroeks and Speleers, 2002). The types of preservational environment where sites are found in central and Eastern Europe – thick travertines and deep glacial landforms – are virtually absent in the west and fluvial deposits of relevant age are usually deeply buried under modern floodplains, a problem exaggerated by the progressive down-warping of the North Sea basin. There is also the complication that many MIS 5e land surfaces, such as those on the raised beaches of Northern France underwent erosion during MIS 5d and later cold events, making their precise age attribution very difficult. However, it should be remembered that a number of suitable sites exist in Britain but still no evidence of human presence has been found.

Another sticking point is that the floral as well as vertebrate and invertebrate faunal evidence indicates that the MIS 5e environment was probably more open than often portrayed (Stuart, 1995; Gao *et al.*, 2000). Indeed, the very presence of hippopotamus – the classic MIS 5e indicator species for Britain and a heavyweight grazer – requires open grassland. As outlined above, these large herbivores played an active role in creating and maintaining open environments, particularly in river valleys. As such, river valleys, such as the Upper and Middle Thames, would have remained the prime habitats and conduits to movement across the landscape that they had always been (Ashton *et al.*, 2006).

One may therefore conclude that MIS 5e environments in Western Europe were not the uniform, densely-wooded habitats that Neanderthals might have found difficult to exploit and that palaeogeographical and other factors may have been responsible for the failure of early human populations to recolonise Britain after MIS 6. The Early Devensian

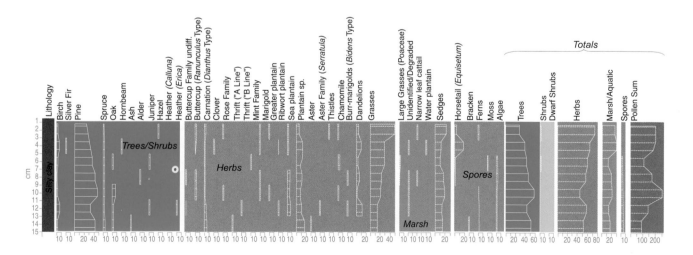

Fig. 5.10   Pollen diagram from Cassington, Oxfordshire

TRAFALGAR SQUARE

The climatic deterioration that began at the end of the previous interglacial (MIS 7, see Chapter 4) was ultimately to result in catastrophe for Neanderthal populations, since by 180,000 BP all hominin populations appear to have died out or abandoned Britain completely. Humans would not return until around 60,000 BP, an absence of some 120,000 years.

During this time Britain saw two major periods of cold climate conditions in MIS 6 and MIS 4, with a full interglacial, MIS 5e, in between. This interglacial, the Ipswichian, is well preserved within the Thames Valley. At this time the modern drainage pattern of the Thames was well established in the Upper Thames Valley. Below the Goring Gap the river generally flowed slightly to the north of its present course.

The cold period equated with MIS 6 appears to have been one of the most extreme glaciations of the last half million years. Ice sheets may have reached as far south as the West Midlands, with a wide band of polar desert and semi barren tundra extending across much of the Thames Valley. For much of the time mean July temperatures would have been no higher than 10° C, falling to a mean of -20° C in January.

During previous glacial cycles, hominins returned to Britain as temperatures began to improve but this does not appear to have been the case as the MIS 6 glaciation gave way to the Last Interglacial (MIS 5e). One reason that has been suggested for this is that temperatures increased sharply at this time, leading to rapid flooding of the Channel and the North Sea basin. This happened so quickly that hominins migrating from warmer southern and eastern areas were unable to re-enter Britain before it was cut off by sea level rise. However, this did not prevent other animals from exploiting the 3000-year 'window of opportunity' and successfully colonising the British landscape.

THE IPSWICHIAN INTERGLACIAL

STAGE		CLIMATE	Age (Ma)	THAMES TERRACES		
Britain	Netherlands	Cold Warm		Upper	Middle	Lower
Devensian	Weichselian		0	Northmoor	Shepperton	Shepperton
Ipswichian	Eemian	5e	0.1	Summertown-Radley	Kempton Park	East Tilbury
'Aveley'	Warthe	6			Taplow	Mucking
	Treene	7	0.2			

S ome of the most famous MIS 5e interglacial deposits were found in Trafalgar Square in London during the 1950s. These show a large, slow-flowing river in a landscape of dry grassland and oak forest, with maple, ash and hazel. Mean July temperatures were probably around 4°C higher than in southern England at the present time.

A nimals present included hippopotamus, straight-tusked elephant, lion, fallow deer, bison and narrow-nosed rhinoceros. Hippopotamus remains are very common in deposits of this period and have been found at Iffley near Oxford, Abingdon, Dorchester and Radley, in the Reading area, and at Brentford and Acton.

• Main picture - Hippos wallowing in the Ipswichian Thames near Reading to keep cool, around 120 000 years ago (MIS 5e)

Figure 5.11

interstadials (MIS 5c and 5a) may have been equally suitable for occupation but the continued isolation of the island meant that access to Neanderthals was still denied. Little is known of the environmental conditions of later parts of MIS 5, although the cave site of Bacon Hole has furnished a mammalian faunal assemblage (the 'type assemblage' of the Bacon Hole MAZ of Currant and Jacobi, 2001), attributed to MIS 5c, which appears still temperate in aspect but notably lacks hippopotamus.

MIS 5D-4: THE EARLY DEVENSIAN

During the terminal parts of MIS 5 and MIS 4, as climatic deterioration worsened, there is no solid evidence for ice-sheets on the British mainland and ice probably extended no further than the southern and western margins of the Baltic Sea. Nevertheless, the British record from this time is characterised by a low-diversity assemblage of high Arctic-adapted mammals (Lowe and Walker, 1997; Currant and Jacobi, 2001; van Andel, 2003). This grouping of mammals has been termed the Banwell Bone Cave Mammal Assemblage-Zone (MAZ) by Currant and Jacobi (2001), after its type-site in the Mendip Hills of Somerset. The MAZ is chiefly characterised by a dominance of great numbers of bison and reindeer, with additional remains of Arctic hare (*Lepus timidus*), wolf, red fox (*Vulpes vulpes*), Arctic fox (*Vulpes lagopus*), a very large-bodied form of brown bear (bigger even than the contemporary bison!), and wolverine (*Gulo gulo*). The only small vertebrate so far recognised as a member of this fauna is the northern vole (Currant and Jacobi, 2001). Dating of the Banwell deposits and their characteristic fauna is difficult but they clearly post-date the Last Interglacial (at Bacon Hole and at Tornewton Cave in Devon, distinctive elements of the Banwell fauna have been found overlying deposits containing a Last Interglacial mammal assemblage (Currant and Jacobi, 2001)) and pre-date classic Middle Devensian faunas (see Chapter 6). Although attributed to MIS 4, *c* 80-70 000 years ago, by Currant and Jacobi (2001), the real age of the Banwell Bone Cave MAZ may in fact be slightly older. Uranium-series dating of mammalian remains attributed to the Banwell Bone Cave MAZ from between *in situ* stalagmitic flowstones at Stump Cross Cavern (North Yorkshire) has produced age-estimates of 79.2±2.4 kyr (SC-90-6A: Baker *et al.*, 1996) indicating that the bones pre-date the time of the boundary between MIS 5a and 5b. Most recently, uranium-series dates on another Banwell Bone Cave MAZ assemblage from Wood Quarry (Nottinghamshire) have given age-estimates of 66.8±3.0 kyr, placing the assemblage within or just before MIS 4 (Pike *et al.*, 2005). The greatest age of these bones thus remains poorly constrained, but is clearly within MIS 5 (Sutcliffe *et al.*, 1985).

Within the study area, the Upper Thames site of Cassington, near Oxford, in the Northmoor Member of the Upper Thames has furnished an important palaeoenvironmental record from the terminal parts of MIS 5. Here, channel deposits of silts, sands and gravels up to 4 m thick indicate deposition in a braiding river system. Pollen profiles (Fig. 5.10) have yielded abundant *Pinus* (pine), with *Picea* (spruce) and *Abies* (silver fir) and smaller numbers of thermophiles such as oak (possibly the result of long-distance transport). Grasses and sedges are also well represented. The overall picture of the vegetation is one of open woodland of boreal Fennoscandian character (Maddy *et al.*, 1997, 1998). The large mammalian assemblage is composed almost exclusively of bison and reindeer, including some articulating material, with a single individual each of wolf and brown bear. Remains of horse, woolly mammoth and woolly rhinoceros have a different preservation type and are thought to have come from deposits higher up. A climatic deterioration is apparent upwards through the sequence, with mean temperatures falling from 17°C to 18°C in summer and -4°C to +4°C in winter, to 7 to 11°C in summer and -10 to -30°C in winter, as savage cold developed (Maddy *et al.*, 1998). A combination of aminostratigraphy, Optically-Stimulated Luminescence age-estimates within the range of 65-148 000 years BP and problems of biostratigraphical correlation with other recognised Late Pleistocene climatic episodes led Maddy *et al.* (1998) to propose an age for the Cassington deposits within the latter half of MIS 5, most plausibly in MIS 5a, with the climatic deterioration correlating with the MIS 5-4 transition.

'Bison-Reindeer' faunas in the Middle Thames are known from Willment's Pit at Isleworth and Kew Bridge in the Kempton Park Gravel of the Upper Floodplain Terrace. The Willment's Pit remains were collected in the 1950s and early 1960s from an organic silty clay bed, thought to have accumulated in slowly-flowing or still water in an abandoned channel or floodplain pool (Gibbard, 1985). The abundance of shed male reindeer antlers led Stuart (1982) to conclude that herds were present predominantly during the winter months. The organic silt also yielded pollen spectra characteristic of treeless conditions with abundant grasses, sedges, herbs and marsh plants (Kerney *et al.*, 1982), while taxa characteristic of bare and disturbed ground, such as *Plantago* spp. (plantain) and *Coronopus squamatus* (greater swinecress) suggest that vegetation near the pool may have been trampled by large herbivores (Gibbard, 1985). Small mammals, including northern vole (*Microtus oeconomus*) and narrow-skulled vole (*Microtus gregalis*) were also reported by Sutcliffe and Kowalski (1976). The beetles are not especially cold-adapted, in that 91% of the assemblage (225 species)

Fig. 5.11 (previous spread)   The Ipswichian interglacial

is still native to Britain. Coope and Angus (1975) drew comparisons with faunas from the north German plain and invoked a more continental climate than in Britain today, with summer temperatures of around 18°C and winter temperatures around 0°C, suggesting deposition during an interstadial period. A radiocarbon date of 43 140 (+1520/-1280) BP (Coope and Angus, 1975) implies a rather younger, Middle Devensian, age for the deposits than other geochronometric or biostratigraphical age estimates of the 'Bison-Reindeer' fauna have proposed (see above) although this may be explained by the date produced being so close to the limit of the radiocarbon technique. Remains from Kew Bridge include a purported specimen of polar bear (*Ursus maritimus*), although re-examination has revealed that this is yet another example of the exceptionally large brown bear that characterises the Banwell Bone Cave MAZ.

Thus, in summary, cold conditions would have acted to keep populations at a minimum during the stadials of MIS 5 and, later, MIS 4, although insularity may also be a factor (Keen, 1995). So far, there is no evidence that people were here during any part of this extended period.

Individually none of the above hypotheses is entirely convincing, but together they provide a reasonable set of contingencies – involving harsh glacial climates, impenetrable forests, the absence of founder populations and the need for sea-crossings – that could have worked to keep humans out of Britain for such a long period. As will be seen in the next chapter, however, when they did return, conditions were certainly far from easy.

Chapter 6 – The Middle and early Late Devensian (MIS 3-2)

by Mark White, Anthony Morigi and Danielle Schreve

PALAEOGEOGRAPHY OF THE TERRACES

By this time, during the formation of its youngest terrace, the river Thames had finally adopted the present day course throughout its catchment (Fig. 6.1). Nevertheless, its character was still far-removed from the placid muddy river familiar today. The gravels themselves and the many indications they contain of deposition by a swiftly flowing braided river in a periglacial climate attest to this. The terrace surfaces of the Northmoor Gravel in the Upper Thames and the Shepperton Terrace in the Middle Thames lie low on the valley floor just above the level of the alluvium. The deposits beneath these terraces are continuous beneath the alluvium where they fill what is in effect a buried valley. Gibbard (1985) traced the Shepperton gravel in boreholes as far downstream as Charing Cross and Waterloo but at some point east of here it becomes effectively 'submerged' beneath the alluvium. In the late Devensian sea level was some 120 m lower than today causing incision of the river channel to depths of about 20 m below OD in the Lower Thames. Initially, the channel was filled with sand and gravel deposited by the braided river but about 15,500 years ago, river flow declined and the regime changed to one of sand deposition in restricted channels (Ellison, 2004).

Correlation of the terraces

For once, the correlation of the Northmoor and Shepperton gravels is straightforward as in both the Middle and Upper Thames they form the floodplain of the river. Indeed, traditionally they were known as the 'Floodplain Terrace' a term often retained in casual usage (Table 6.1).

THE LATE MIDDLE PALAEOLITHIC

This period witnessed the return of archaic human populations to the British landscape after an absence of some 100 000 years. Although Britain has thus far yielded no skeletal remains of this age, the fossil evidence from Eurasia indicates that this new wave of colonists would have been classic Neanderthals. The earliest dates pertaining to this re-colonisation are from Lynford Quarry, Norfolk, for which preliminary OSL dates of ~64 000 BP have been obtained (Boismier et al., 2003), indicating that Neanderthals took their first steps onto the British landscape at the end of MIS 4/beginning of MIS 3. Radiocarbon dates are given as BP, and cal BC where appropriate (from CalPal http://www.calpal-online.de).

The palaeoenvironmental evidence from Lynford suggests that conditions would have been difficult, if not downright hostile, for Neanderthals during the winter months. The site is located on the lowest terrace of the River Wissey and represents the remnants of a former meander cut-off or oxbow lake that may have been used as a watering hole. The main palaeochannel sediments consist of dark brown organic-rich sands. These are indicative of deposition under still or slow-flowing water conditions, although there is evidence of bank collapse and debris or mud flows in the southern and eastern parts of the channel (Boismier et al., 2003). The combined palaeobiological datasets (pollen, plant macrofossils, beetles, molluscs and vertebrates) indicate open conditions dominated by grasses, sedges and low-growing herbaceous communities with small stands of birch or scrub, acid heath and wetlands adjacent to a source of permanent water less than 1.5 m deep (Boismier et

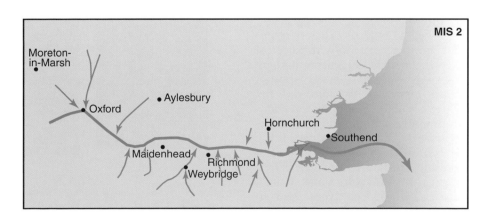

Fig. 6.1   The palaeogeography of the Thames MIS 2

Table 6.1 Correlation of Quaternary deposits of the Thames MIS 3-2

| Marine Isotope Stage | Thames terrace deposits | | |
	Upper	*Middle*	*Lower*
3-2	Northmoor Gravel	Shepperton Gravel	Shepperton Gravel (submerged)

Sources: Bridgland (1994); Bowen (1999)

al., 2003). Terrestrial herb pollen and plant macro-fossils include those of meadow rue (*Thalictrum* sp.), chickweeds (*Stellaria* spp.) and dandelion (*Taraxacum officinale*), with bilberry (*Vaccinium myrtillus*) or crowberry (*Empetrum nigrum*) also present. The slow-flowing water in the channel and its marshy margins supported flora such as spiked and whorled water milfoil (*Myriophyllum spicatum* and *M. verticillatum*), pondweed (*Potamogeton* sp.) and water buttercup (*Ranunculus* sp.), as well as fish and amphibians, including three-spined stickleback (*Gasterosteus aculeatus*), perch (*Perca fluviatilis*) and common frog (*Rana temporaria*). The beetle evidence gives a clear picture of the prevailing climate, with mean July temperatures calculated as 13°C or lower (around 3°C lower than summer temperatures in eastern England today) and mean January temperatures below -10°C (Boismier *et al.*, 2003). The reconstructed temperatures for the coldest months mean that spring or summer occupation of the site by Neanderthals is more likely, perhaps linked in to annual migrations to summer grazing grounds by large herbivores.

In terms of its mammalian species composition, the Lynford assemblage compares closely with the Middle Devensian Pin Hole Mammal Assemblage-Zone of Currant and Jacobi (2001), correlated with MIS 3 of the oceanic record. The principal characteristics of this biozone include the return to Britain of woolly mammoth (*Mammuthus primigenius*), woolly rhinoceros (*Coelodonta antiquitatis*), horse (*Equus ferus*), spotted hyaena (*Crocuta crocuta*) and Neanderthals themselves, after the protracted absence noted previously. Mammoth is by far the most abundant species at Lynford (over 91% of the assemblage) with at least 11 individuals represented, including one juvenile (Schreve, 2006). Reindeer (*Rangifer tarandus*) is the next best represented, with smaller numbers of woolly rhinoceros, horse and bison (*Bison priscus*), supplemented by individual remains of wolf (*Canis lupus*), spotted hyaena, brown bear (*Ursus arctos*) and red fox (*Vulpes vulpes*) (Schreve, 2006). The palaeoenvironmental evidence from Lynford and other contemporary sites fits well with reconstructions of the 'Mammoth Steppe' (Guthrie, 1990), a broad belt of steppe-tundra extending from northern Eurasia into North America during the last cold stage. Unlike the modern tundra, which is relatively poor in nutrients and supports only low herbivore biomass, the 'Mammoth Steppe' has no precise modern analogue, being substantially more arid with

increased evaporation, higher seasonality and deeper summer thaws than prevail today (Guthrie, 1990). This led to the repressing of growth of woody plants and the development of rich grasslands supporting many millions of herbivores, the grazing and dunging actions of which in turn contributed to the maintenance of the open landscape and nutrient recycling. Although the Middle Devensian is a relatively warmer part of the last glaciation (compared to the Early and Late phases), evidence from ice cores in Greenland has revealed that the climate was subject to sharp fluctuations at this time. These are reflected by rapid (often millennial-scale) climatic oscillations (Fig. 6.2), which would have placed living organisms (including Neanderthals and early modern humans) under intense ecological stress. In the GISP2 ice-core (Grootes *et al.*, 1993), numerous abrupt alternations are apparent between 'warm' excursions (the so-called 'Dansgaard-Oeschger interstadial events'), which were 6-7°C warmer than the intervening cold episodes, the latter equalling those of the last glacial maximum towards the end of MIS 3. The impact of these sharp climatic fluctuations on the landscape, vegetation and animals (in particular megafaunal species), should not be underestimated. Indeed, it is at this time that many large mammalian species (and indeed Neanderthals) began to go extinct (see Fig. 6.9, below).

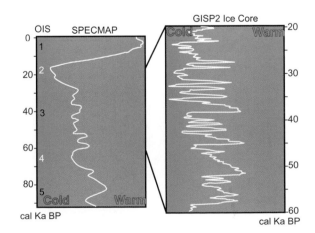

Fig. 6.2 Rapid climatic variations during MIS 3 as seen in the Greenland ice cores: (left) SPECMAP, the standard chronology for oxygen isotope records; (right) GISP2, data from the Greenland Ice Sheet Project 2

The Middle Devensian is well represented in the Middle Thames by sites within the Kempton Park Gravel (Upper Floodplain Terrace) (Table 5.1; Fig 1.1). At the type locality, Kempton Park quarry, near Sunbury (Surrey), Gibbard *et al.* (1982) reported plant remains, molluscs, ostracods and insects from a grey clayey silt bed within gravel, the top of which was dated to 35 230 ± 185 BP (40 215 ± 839 cal BP/ 38 265 ± 839 cal BC). In combination with the invertebrate assemblages, the plant macrofossils suggest deposition in a well-vegetated stream with slowly flowing and still water. Dwarfed trees are present, including *Salix herbacea* (dwarf willow) and *Betula* cf *nana* (cf dwarf birch) but otherwise the palaeobotanical assemblage is dominated by grasses, sedges, sun-loving herbs such as *Campanula rotundifolia* (British harebell), *Potentilla anserina* (silverweed) and *Rhinanthus* sp. (rattle) and aquatic and marshy taxa such as *Groenlandia densa* (oppositeleaved pondweed), and *Zannichellia* sp. (horned pondweed) (Gibbard *et al.*, 1982). A rapid deterioration in climate is apparent upwards through the sequence from the insect assemblage. Initially this was interpreted as reflecting the transition from the Upton Warren Interstadial to colder conditions, although it is now recognised that this may be just one of the many interstadial-stadial transitions apparent in MIS 3.

A Middle Devensian pollen record from a bed of interstratified sand, silty clay and sand (up to 2.3 m thick) found within gravels (Fig. 6.3) during construction of the Ismaili Centre in South Kensington (London) produced a very similar palaeobotanical reconstruction. Two pollen assemblage biozones were recognised: the lowest (ICa, -0.04 m to +0.9 m OD) dominated by grasses and

sedges with low values of arboreal pollen except for local stands of dwarf birch (Gibbard, 1985). The spectra include plants characteristic of dry grasslands, such as *Artemisia* (sagebrush) and *Sanguisorba officinalis* (greater burnet), with nearby stony ground (*Saxifraga oppositifolia*, purple saxifrage). Very high values of *Armeria maritima* (sea thrift) pollen (today found on mountain tops, coastal cliffs and salt marshes), together with *Silene maritime* (bladder campion), which has similar environmental preferences, suggest that there were highly saline soils locally, possibly induced by high evaporation rates as a result of permafrost (Gibbard, 1985). The upper pollen zone at the Ismaili Centre (ICb, +0.9 m to +1.56 m OD) displays a much more diverse development of grassland plants as part of a tall herb community, witnessed by an increase in Umbelliferae pollen and plant macrofossils such as *Anthricus sylvestris* (caraway) and cf *Oenanthe* sp. (water dropwort). Tree pollen remains at very low levels although there is a slight increase in *Pinus* (pine), a known 'far travelling' and buoyant pollen grain. The rapidity and intensity of climatic changes at this time is clearly demonstrated by the beetle assemblages from the Ismaili Centre silts. These indicate the presence of two distinct climatic regimes within a single channel deposit; a lower unit that accumulated when the climate was arctic and an upper unit laid down when temperatures were at least as warm as those of the present day. Palaeotemperature reconstructions using the Mutual Climatic Range method demonstrate a transition from mean July temperatures of 9 ± 2°C and mean January temperatures of -22 ± 10°C in the lower silts to +17°C and -4°C respectively in the upper silts (Coope *et al.*, 1997).

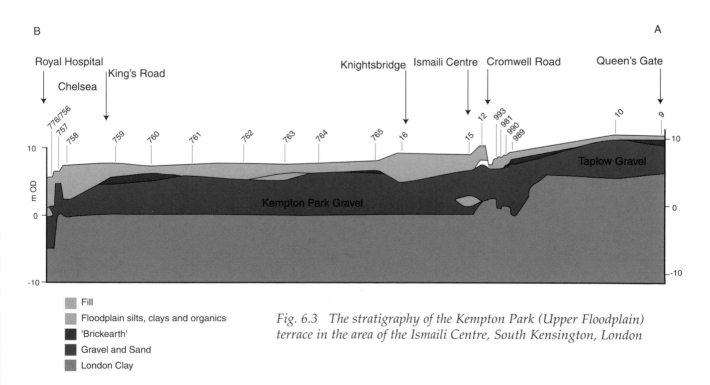

Fig. 6.3 The stratigraphy of the Kempton Park (Upper Floodplain) terrace in the area of the Ismaili Centre, South Kensington, London

An isolated bone of *Bison* was found during the Ismaili Centre excavations, one of several to have come from the South Kensington and Earl's Court areas, presumably from coeval sediments. Other large mammal finds from central London include woolly rhinoceros and woolly mammoth remains from Battersea Park and the Old Kent Road, and a beautifully preserved juvenile woolly rhinoceros skull from Salisbury Square.

At Marlow, Shotton and Williams (1971) reported the presence of an organic silt from within sand and gravel of the Kempton Park Gravel. Analyses of the plant macrofossils, pollen and beetles (Bell, 1968, 1969; Coope pers. comm. in Gibbard, 1985) initially invited comparison with the Upton Warren Interstadial, although radiocarbon dating yielded only a finite age of >31 000 BP (Coope *et al.*, 1997). As with other Middle Devensian sites, the prevailing environmental conditions appear to have been treeless and dominated by grasses and herbs. However, a notable diversity of chalk grassland plants is present, including *Arenaria ciliata* (fringed sandwort), *Leontodon autumnalis* (autumn hawkbit), *Diplotaxis tenuifolia* (rocket) and *Allium scheonoprasum* (chives) (Gibbard, 1985). In common with sites such as the Ismaili Centre, a range of salt-tolerant taxa is present, suggesting highly saline soils and permafrost conditions (Bell, 1968, 1969).

The tool kit that the Neanderthals brought with them upon their return to Britain is of classic Middle Palaeolithic type and can be described as Mousterian of Acheulean Tradition (MTA), a variant of the Mousterian characterised by the presence of small cordiform/sub-triangular handaxes (Mellars, 1974, 1996a). The MTA is particularly well represented in France, which thus forms the obvious area for the parent Neanderthal population(s). However,

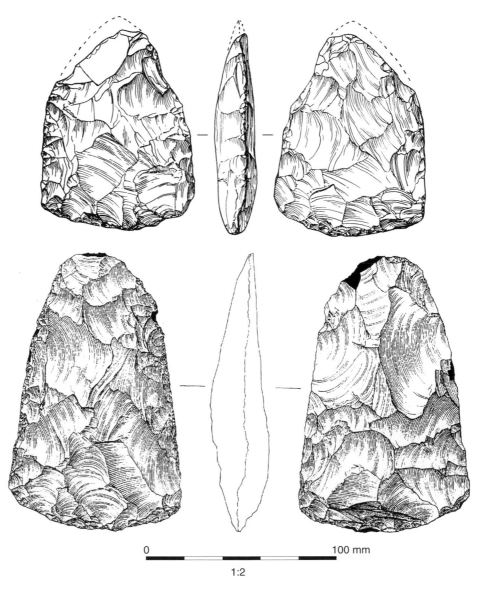

0   100 mm

1:2

Fig. 6.4   Bout coupé handaxes: above, Marlow; below, Coygan Cave, Carmarthenshire

the British record contains an apparently unique handaxe variant – the so-called *bout coupé* – that is not found in France and which has been argued to be something of a 'marker fossil' for the British Late Middle Palaeolithic (Roe, 1981; Tyldesley, 1987; White and Jacobi, 2002; M. Soressi, pers comm. 2005). As with all typologies there is some variation in different authors' definitions but most agree that bout coupés are refined, symmetrical cordiform or sub-rectangular (elongated d-shaped) pieces with a straight or slightly convex butt, slightly convex sides and a rounded tip. There is a marked discontinuity of curvature (ie two clear angles) at the intersection of the sides and the base (Roe, 1981; Tyldesley, 1987: Fig. 6.4).

One of the most remarkable aspects of the British Late Middle Palaeolithic is that these distinctive bout coupé handaxes occur as isolated discards or as parts of very small assemblages only; very rarely are large assemblages from this time period found. Unlike its Lower Palaeolithic counterpart, which is regarded as the tool in and of itself, the Middle Palaeolithic handaxe has been described as a support for other tools where different ways of modifying edges render them suitable for different tasks (Soressi and Hays, 2003). This would have made the Middle Palaeolithic handaxe a very adaptable and flexible instrument (the well-worn analogy of the Swiss Army Knife might actually find an appropriate home here!), which might have been curated for longer periods and over longer distances than earlier forms, being discarded only rarely and then usually in ones or twos. Indeed, the evidence from Lynford shows that some were repeatedly repaired, modified and rejuvenated, while other examples, such as the two from Coygan Cave, near Laugharne in south Wales, were found in an out-of-the-way spot close to the cave wall and could represent small caches that the hunter intended to retrieve later.

The British record contains at least 180 pieces that have been described as bout coupé, from both cave and open-air sites. Not all of them have good provenances that can securely date them to this period, but some 10% of the total comes from the Upper and Middle Thames. Examples from probable MIS 4-3 stratigraphical contexts (Fig. 6.5) have been found at:

- Radley, Tuckwell's Pit, Oxfordshire
- Abingdon, Oxfordshire
- Marlow, Bucks
- Marlow Brickpit, Bucks
- Berrymead Priory, Acton
- Sipson Lane, Hillingdon
- Eastwood's Pit, West Drayton (brickearths)
- Summerleaze Pit, Maidenhead

Others which on the basis of typology might also be considered to be of this age (but which quite conceivably could belong to other periods) have been found at:

- Sulhamstead Abbots, Abbots' Pit, Berkshire
- New Road, Bourne End, Bucks
- Brickhill Road, Fenny Stratford, Bucks
- Lavender Pit, Iver, Bucks
- Mead's Bridge Pit, Iver
- Clayton's Pit, Yiewsley
- Isleworth (from Thames)
- Creffield Road, Acton
- Acton brickearth (no further provenance)

If all these pieces are genuinely of MIS 4-3 age, then Neanderthals are well represented in the study area, proportionally better than for most other periods, although again the Upper Thames upstream of the Goring Gap has a poorer signature. Still, Neanderthals were demonstrably active in the region, and the lack of a stronger signal may once again be due to a reluctance to discard tools in this flint-poor region. Furthermore, when larger Middle Palaeolithic assemblages are found these show that a wider variety of handaxe forms were used in the Late Middle Palaeolithic (many similar to those from earlier periods) and that bout coupés provide only a partial and very restricted view of the true scale of Neanderthal presence. Perhaps only certain individuals could or would make them.

More significant findspots of this age are incredibly rare, and there is nothing of note in the Upper or Middle Thames. As well as the aforementioned examples from Lynford, other good examples are known from Little Paxton, near St Neots, Cambridgeshire (Paterson and Tebbutt, 1947). In addition to handaxes these assemblages contain a range of scrapers and other flake tools, cores (although curiously not Levallois, its role as a mobile flexible technology perhaps being taken up by the different approach to handaxes in the Later Middle Palaeolithic) and debitage. Detailed technological study at Lynford has shown that the flint-work is dominated by debitage from the later phases of handaxe production, handaxe modification and reworking; cores and the earlier phases of production are underrepresented (White, in press). This has been interpreted as showing that Neanderthals repeatedly visited Lynford, and that each time they went fully 'tooled up' and expecting to find a limited range of prey animals. Whilst there they had occasion to finish, mend or modify their tools; they also appear to have taken some large flakes, blanks on which to make new handaxes should the others fail. Again, a highly mobile, curated tool kit with low levels of discard and high levels of transport planning is indicated.

Environmental reconstructions of MIS 3 Britain leave us with something of a conundrum in terms of wider Neanderthal cultural capabilities. The environmental proxies discussed in earlier sections provide a rather dismal picture: treeless grasslands (part of the north Eurasian Mammoth Steppe) with only moderate summer temperatures, cold blasting winds and long harsh winters during which temperatures may have fallen below -20°C and

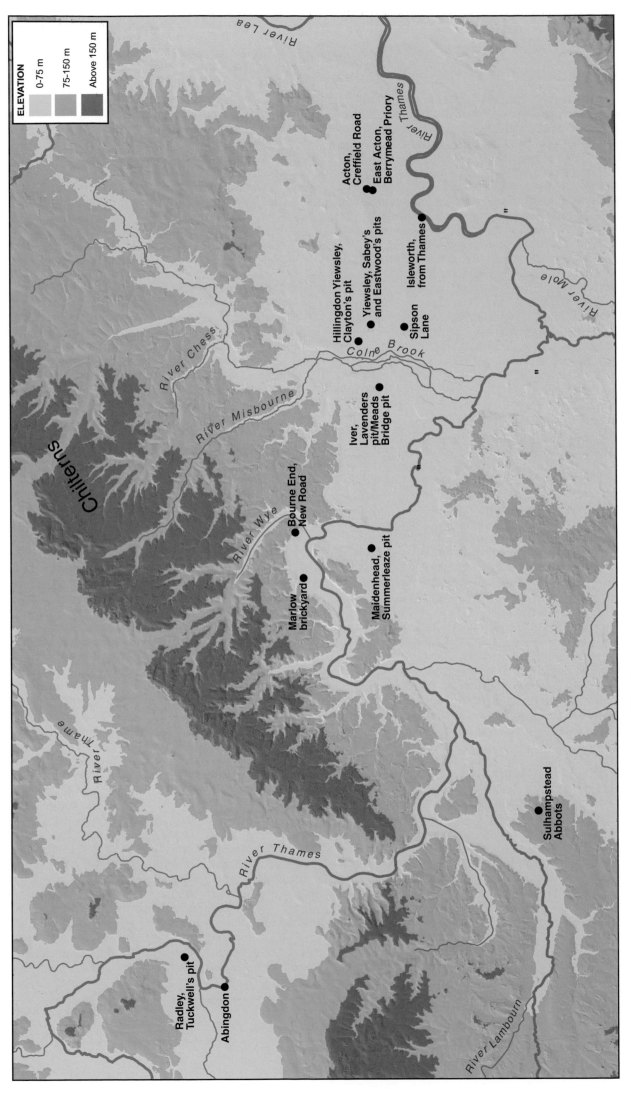

ELEVATION
0-75 m
75-150 m
Above 150 m

Chilterns

River Lea

River Thames

River Wye

River Chess

River Misbourne

Colne Brook

River Thame

River Thames

River Lambourn

River Mole

River

Acton, Creffield Road

East Acton, Berrymead Priory

Hillingdon Yiewsley, Clayton's pit

Yiewsley, Sabey's and Eastwood's pits

Isleworth, from Thames

Sipson Lane

Iver, Lavenders pit/Meads Bridge pit

Bourne End, New Road

Marlow brickyard

Maidenhead, Summerleaze pit

Sulhampstead Abbots

Radley, Tuckwell's pit

Abingdon

Fig. 6.5   Distribution map of selected Middle Palaeolithic findspots

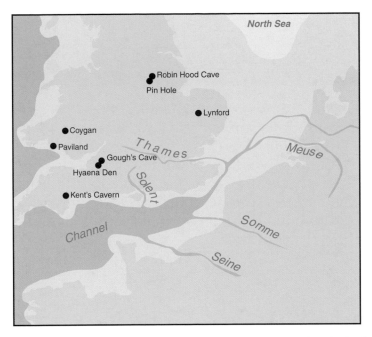

Fig. 6.6 The palaeogeographical setting of Britain during the Middle Devensian (MIS 3), showing a landbridge across the North Sea basin created by lowered sea levels. Key archaeological sites are indicated

snow may have covered the ground for up to six months. Over much of the known south-eastern distribution of Late Middle Palaeolithic sites, caves and other natural shelters are relatively rare, and where they are more abundant – at Creswell, the Mendips and South Wales – they generally do not contain signatures indicative of prolonged residential occupation but small and restricted assemblages suggesting very temporary, perhaps task specific, stop-off points.

Long regarded as surviving the harsh conditions of glacial NW Europe by virtue of their robust physical adaptation and culturally very poorly equipped (cf Stringer and Gamble, 1993), new work on Neanderthal physiology has cast some doubt on whether this really gave them much of an advantage (Aiello and Wheeler, 2003). Indeed, some form of loosely tailored clothing would seem to be essential, as would fire, shelter and a ready supply of animal protein to meet all the additional energetic requirements of life in a cold climate. The problem is that without adequate wood resources, access to sufficient fuel, building materials, hunting weapons – and hence meat and unravaged furs – would seem to have been rather restricted. Perhaps Neanderthals were only occasional summer visitors to Britain bringing most of their survival tools with them. At this time Britain would have been a steppic upland plateau at the north-westernmost edge of the Eurasian landscape (Fig. 6.6), home to a great array of (migratory) prey animals (see above) and a great place to hunt, but nevertheless a very poor place to live.

EARLY UPPER PALAEOLITHIC (EUP)

The latest dates for a Middle Palaeolithic presence in Britain fall *c* 40 000 BP. Following this a succession of Upper Palaeolithic industries appears, although the record in the Thames Valley is remarkable only for its extreme paucity. A brief survey of the Upper Palaeolithic record from the rest of Britain is provided below, mostly for reference should anything surface at a later date (Fig. 6.8). For more detailed accounts the reader is referred to the extensive writings of Nick Barton and Roger Jacobi, which form the basis of what follows.

The earliest Upper Palaeolithic industries in Britain are sometimes called Lincombian (Campbell, 1977) and are characterised by leaf points and blade points; about 31 findspots are currently known (Jacobi, 1990). A number have associated organic materials (eg Bench Tunnel Cavern, Brixham, Devon; Soldier's Hole, Cheddar Gorge, Somerset and Pin Hole Cave, Creswell Crags, Derbyshire) and recent radiocarbon dating programs on these have suggested a time-range of 36-38 000 years BP (Jacobi, 1999, pers. comm.; Aldhouse-Green and Pettitt, 1998). Perhaps the best locality is Beedings, Sussex (Jacobi, 1986, 1990, 2007) where some 40 leaf points and associated lithic materials were found in a series of gulls in the local bedrock; they are probably not *in situ*, although a number of refits suggest that they do belong together. Many are represented solely by the base, and only one tip is present. Assuming that these formed parts of hafted hunting weapons, then the tips were probably lost at the kill sites, with Beedings representing a station to which shattered

Fig. 6.7 (overleaf) The last Ice Age: the Devensian glaciation

127

THE LAST ICE AGE

Following the Last Interglacial Britain entered a prolonged period of predominantly cold conditions known as the **Devensian**, which is equated with MIS 5d-2. As the temperature cooled, the river regime changed to a braiding system of numerous vigorous channels. At Cassington, near Oxford, deposits from this period reveal a brief period of slightly warmer conditions (interstadial) with the presence of open boreal woodland with abundant pine, spruce and silver fir, inhabited by bison, reindeer, wolves and brown bears.

Neanderthal hunters stalk woolly mammoths across the Thames Valley tundra c 50 000 years ago (MIS3)

THE DEVENSIAN GLACIATION

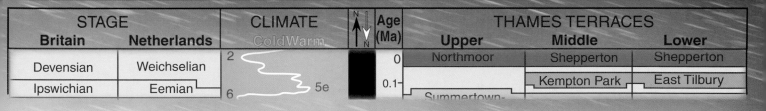

STAGE		CLIMATE		Age (Ma)	THAMES TERRACES		
Britain	**Netherlands**	Cold Warm	N↑ N↓		**Upper**	**Middle**	**Lower**
Devensian	Weichselian	2		0	Northmoor	Shepperton	Shepperton
Ipswichian	Eemian	6 5e		0.1	Summertown-	Kempton Park	East Tilbury

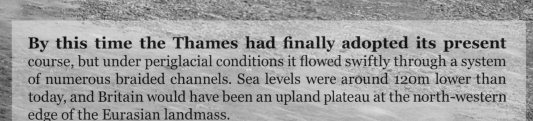

By this time the Thames had finally adopted its present course, but under periglacial conditions it flowed swiftly through a system of numerous braided channels. Sea levels were around 120m lower than today, and Britain would have been an upland plateau at the north-western edge of the Eurasian landmass.

After 100 000 years of absence Neanderthal populations finally returned to Britain around 64 000 BP. At this time, the climate fluctuated rapidly, with periods of relative warmth interspersed with times of severe cold. The broad environmental picture is one of a rather bleak and inhospitable landscape of treeless grasslands with cold blasting winds and long harsh winters during which temperatures may have fallen below -20°C with snow on the ground for up to six months. However, the rich grasslands were able to support huge herds of large herbivores including woolly mammoth, woolly rhinoceros, horse and bison. It would have been a great place to hunt but a very poor place to live.

Figure 6.7

UPPER PALAEOLITHIC INDUSTRIES IN BRITAIN

BLADE POINTS

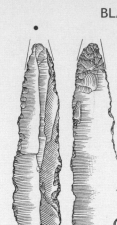

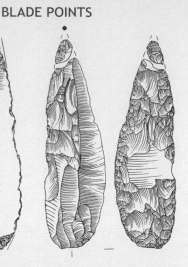

BUSKED BURIN

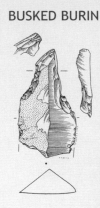

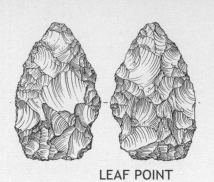

LEAF POINT

NOSED SCRAPER

Upper Palaeolithic lithic technology is heavily based around the production and retouch of blades and bladelets from prismatic cores, a trait that was once believed to be a defining feature of behavioural modernity, although a number of much older industries, associated with non-modern humans, are now known from across the Old World. Modern humans also made much more use of bone and antler as a plastic medium from which to craft a range of tools and weapons, some elaborately decorated. Upper Palaeolithic industries also changed much more rapidly in time and space than Lower and Middle Palaeolithic ones. The classic cultural framework for the Upper Palaeolithic in Western Europe is based upon finds from cave sites in SW France. Those found in Britain, and their most characteristic tools, are shown on this page:

LINCOMBIAN:
leaf-points and blade points

AURIGNACIAN:
shouldered nosed scrapers, busked-burins and split-based bone points

GRAVETTIAN:
stemmed (Font-Robert) points

CRESWELLIAN:
characterised by trapezoidal backed blades with a double truncation (Cheddar Points) and backed blades with a single truncation (Creswell Points). Other typical forms include end-scrapers on long blades, sometimes with additional lateral retouch

FINAL UPPER PALAEOLITHIC:
Penknife points, curved backed points and curve backed blades. Notched bone/antler points

LATE GLACIAL INDUSTRIES:
Long blades (>12cm), bruised blades, microliths

CRESWELL POINT

GRAVETTIAN FONT ROBERT POINT

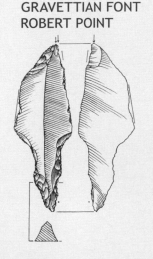

CHEDDAR POINTS

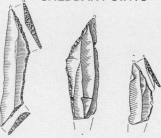

BACKED BLADE

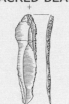

PENKNIFE POINTS

Figure 6.8

(possibly still hafted) pieces were brought back for replacement. Jacobi has suggested that flint was in short supply and that humans were recycling to a very high degree. The Beedings site is unlikely to have been a residential camp, but did afford stunning views of the Weald and may have been a hunters' camp. A more recent example from Glaston in Rutland (Thomas, 2001) would seem to support such an interpretation. Although this site is probably part of a hyaena den, a leaf-point, a core and some debitage was found in association with butchered horse bones that had been split for marrow. The leaf point industries may therefore represent a hunter's mobile tool kit.

Within the study area, the importance of topographic setting is echoed by a small flint assemblage comprising a handful of robust white-patinated flint blades from the Cargo Distribution Services site on the southern edge of Heathrow airport, one of a limited number of Early Upper Palaeolothic (EUP) sites in the study area. The Heathrow assemblage was found on a slight eminence at the edge of the Taplow Gravel, overlooking a southward flowing palaeochannel (Cotton, 2004), again highlighting the significance of these wide vistas to Upper Palaeolithic groups.

The British leaf- and blade-point industries are reminiscent of several of the so-called 'Transitional' industries from central and eastern Europe, such as the Jerzmanovician and Szeletian, and probably fall within a similar time-frame. At this early phase of the Upper Palaeolithic there are two human species present in Europe – Neanderthals and modern humans – and there is considerable debate concerning the authorship of some of these industries and how far the Neanderthals adapted their earlier technology to copy that of modern humans (eg D'Errico et al., 1998; Mellars, 1999). Unfortunately, in the absence of any 'smoking gun' associations it is impossible to determine whether the leaf and blade point industries are the product of Neanderthals or modern humans. By 29 000 BP Neanderthals had become extinct across Europe (Finlayson et al., 2006); when they actually disappeared from Britain for the last time is currently unclear, although they may have lingered longer at the margins of their previous territory than at the core (Pettitt, 2000).

The unequivocal arrival of modern humans across Europe is believed to be marked by the Aurignacian, although there are few reliable skeletal associations to confirm this, the best at present perhaps being the findings from Mladec (Czech Republic) though tools are sparse at this site (Churchill and Smith, 2000). Once considered a 'Human Revolution' (Mellars and Stringer, 1989), the Upper Palaeolithic in Europe is associated with widespread changes in behaviour.

The most important for present purposes are a shift to blade-based lithic technologies, the appearance of complex tools of bone and ivory, and overtly symbolic material culture expressed through such media as personal adornments and mobile and parietal (cave) art (Mellars, 1996b). Several of these have now been shown to have much longer roots in Africa (McBrearty and Brooks, 2000), the sudden rupture in Europe around 40-36 000 BP being the replacement of one cultural system (that of the Neanderthals) with another (that of modern humans). How far these changes relate to differences in the cognitive, linguistic and social skills of the different hominin species involved is still hotly debated (Mithen, 1996; Mellars and Gibson, 1996; Gamble, 1999), but this largely falls outside the scope of this volume (Fig. 6.9).

In Britain, Jacobi (1999) recognises only seven Aurignacian findspots. All of these are in Western Britain, which might testify to settlement northwards along the Atlantic Seaboard. There is also little evidence for any typological seriation within the British Aurignacian, which all seems to belong to Aurignacian II and for which a modal date of c 32-29 000 BP might be posited. The sparse yet homogenous record suggests that early modern humans were present for a short period, and in a very restricted part of the country, perhaps only seasonally. The largest sample of Aurignacian material comes from Paviland Cave, Gower, the definitive monograph for which has recently been published by Aldhouse-Green (2000). Further examples come from Uphill Cave and Wookey Hole Hyaena Den in Somerset (Jacobi and Pettitt, 2000). Again there is no evidence from the Thames Valley.

Certain evidence for the Gravettian in Britain is equally sparse, with just nine find spots in the entire British Isles (Jacobi, 1990, 1999). Most of the British evidence probably belongs to the earliest phase of the Gravettian, although there are few associated radiocarbon dates for these points to unequivocally demonstrate this. The most notable find of Gravettian age is the burial at Paviland (Fig. 6.10), for which a radiocarbon age of 26 350 ± 350 BP (31 146 ± 412 cal BP / 29 196 ± 412 cal BC) has been obtained (Hedges et al., 1989; Aldhouse-Green and Pettitt, 1998). This male inhumation was reported to have been stained with red ochre and accompanied by shells, ivory rods and fragments of a bracelet. Further radiocarbon determinations on a range of unmodified bone as well as bone and ivory artefacts range from 28-21 000 BP (Aldhouse-Green and Pettitt, 1998), suggesting brief intermittent visits to the cave over a prolonged period, perhaps for special purpose visits such as burial or ivory collection (Barton, 1997; Aldhouse-Green, 2000).

Fig. 6.8 (left)   Upper Palaeolithic industries in Britain

*Fig. 6.9 (overleaf)   Modern human origins, and Fig. 6.10
The last Ice Age: the Upper Palaeolithic and the arrival of modern humans*

Modern Human Origins

The origin of modern humans is one of the most hotly contested questions in human evolutionary studies. The debate, which tackles the critical issue of when and where members of our own species first emerged, has become polarised between two camps, each favouring a remarkably different hypothesis:

1 THE MULTI-REGIONAL HYPOTHESIS

Championed by **Milford Wolpoff, Alan Thorne** and others. This hypothesis argues that modern *Homo sapiens* emerged gradually from the various archaic populations that had established themselves in different parts of the old world — Neanderthals in Europe, *Homo erectus* in Asia, Archaic *Homo sapiens/heidelbergensis* in Africa etc. Sufficient levels of gene flow between these neighbouring populations ensured that the evolving regional populations remained genetically a single species while physiologically developing local racial characteristics.

2 THE SINGLE ORIGIN, REPLACEMENT OR OUT OF AFRICA HYPOTHESIS

Championed by **Christopher Stringer** and others. This hypothesis argues that all modern humans can trace their ancestry to a single geographical origin, most often argued to have been somewhere in Africa. Modern Humans migrated from their homeland and replaced the local archaic populations, beginning sometime after 100,000 years ago.

Scholars such as **Fred Smith** and **Gunter Brauer** have proposed models which take an intermediate view, accepting an essentially African origin for biologically modern humans but allowing for varying levels of hybridisation between the African migrants and the existing local populations. Today, most archaeologists and palaeoanthropologists would probably accept that Neanderthals were replaced, but with some interbreeding.

Genetics has played a large role in the development of the debate. Studies of mitochondrial DNA, inherited only through the female line, have shown a remarkably small divergence between all living populations, pointing to a fairly recent origin in Africa sometime around 200,000 years ago. The recent results of the Neanderthal genome project, however, have demonstrated that modern Europeans and Asians share some 1-4% of our DNA with the Neanderthals, suggesting that some interbreeding took place. This possibly occurred quite early on when the two species met in the Near East, prior to the major spread of modern humans east and west. Still, in Europe itself, Neanderthals may have experienced a long period of isolation and development from *H. heidelbergensis*.

Archaeologically, there is also dramatic change after *c* 36,000 BP. Often referred to as the Human or Upper Palaeolithic Revolution, this period sees the replacement of the 'monotonous' Neanderthal cultural repertoire and the appearance of much more sophisticated ways of doing things. During the Upper Palaeolithic we see more rapid developments and standardisation in lithic technology; the appearance of art and personal adornments; tools of bone, antler and ivory; complex multi-part technology; routine long distance transfers of objects; convincing dwelling structures, elaborate fire-places; and storage. These were once thought to represent a sudden evolutionary event at around this time – perhaps a major cognitive event or the development of complex language due to genetic mutation. Many of these changes are now argued to emerge piecemeal and gradually in Africa from 250,000 years onwards; another trajectory was followed in Europe. The situation in Europe simply reflects the total replacement of one long-evolved culture with another.

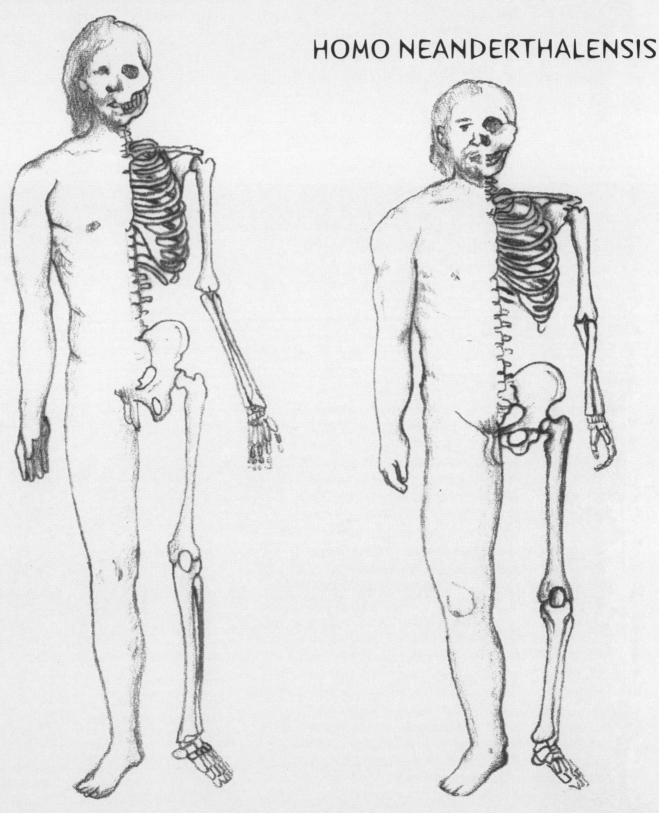

HOMO SAPIENS SAPIENS

HOMO NEANDERTHALENSIS

Figure 6.9

Between 40 000 and 36 000 years ago new stone tool industries appeared in Europe, based on the production and retouch of blades and bladelets from prismatic cores (see Fig. 6.8). For archaeologists, this marks the transition from the Middle to the Upper Palaeolithic. Around the same time modern humans, *Homo sapiens sapiens*, moved into the area for the first time, initially living alongside the older Neanderthal populations (see Fig. 6.9). We still do not know for certain if the new Upper Palaeolithic tools were made exclusively by *Homo sapiens sapiens*, or if Neanderthals also produced the new leaf and blade-points, perhaps copying the technology of the new arrivals.

By 29 000 BP the Neanderthals had become extinct across Europe. Exactly how and why this happened is still not known for certain. However, the Greenland ice cores show us that this was a time of very rapid and sometimes extreme climatic fluctuations. This would have placed all living organisms in the region – plants, animals and humans – under intense ecological stress. It is possible that the Neanderthals were simply unable to adapt as successfully as the more inventive *Homo sapiens sapiens*.

The spread of modern humans across Europe during the Upper Palaeolithic is associated with widespread changes in behaviour by comparison with earlier hominin populations. Modern humans made and used a much wider range of tools, in bone, antler and ivory as well as wood and stone. They also expressed themselves in art: in shell and ivory jewellery, carved decoration and most famously in paintings and engravings on cave walls.

There is very little evidence for a human presence in the Thames Valley during the earlier part of the Upper Palaeolithic, c 40 000–20 000 BP. Indeed, very few sites of this period are currently known in Britain, and they have a mainly westerly distribution, as if modern humans often approached along the Atlantic coast, rather than across a Channel landbridge.

The best-known site of this period in Britain is the burial called the Red Lady of Paviland, found in 1823 in Goat's Hole Cave, Paviland, on the Gower Peninsula in South Wales. The burial, now known to be that of a young man, was described by its finder as stained with red ochre and accompanied by ornaments of seashells and ivory rods. Recent radiocarbon dating of the remains from the cave suggests that the man was buried c 29 000 BC, but that Upper Palaeolithic people made intermittent visits to the cave over thousands of years.

THE UPPER PALAEOLITHIC AND THE ARRIVAL OF MODERN HUMANS

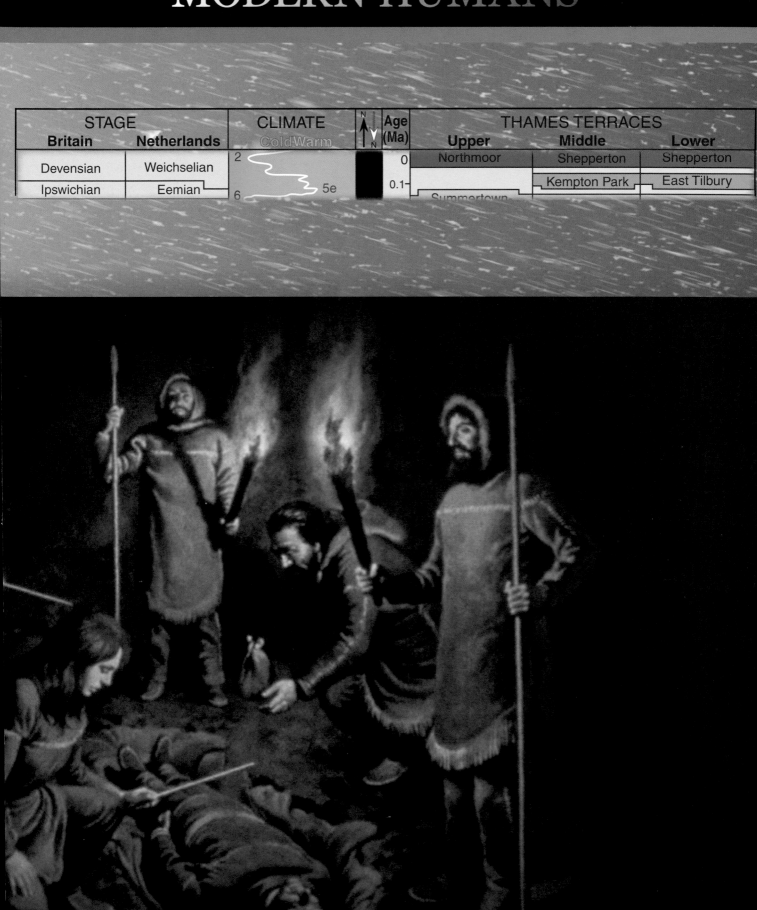

STAGE		CLIMATE	N↕N	Age (Ma)	THAMES TERRACES		
Britain	Netherlands	Cold Warm			Upper	Middle	Lower
Devensian	Weichselian	2		0	Northmoor	Shepperton	Shepperton
Ipswichian	Eemian	6 5e		0.1	Summertown-	Kempton Park	East Tilbury

Figure 6.10

Chapter 7 – The terminal Pleistocene-early Holocene transition (MIS 2-1)

by Danielle Schreve and Mark White with contributions by Gill Hey, Philip Jones, Anthony Morigi and Mark Robinson

PALAEOGEOGRAPHY OF THE TERRACES

As previously discussed in Chapter 6, the river Thames was, by this time, well established in its current course. The rapid and high frequency climatic oscillations during the terminal part of the Pleistocene, as witnessed for example in the Greenland ice core record (Fig. 7.1), undoubtedly affected the depositional regime of the river, with coarse gravels and sands alternating with quieter-water deposits, but unfortunately the degree of resolution currently available in the fluvial record is not sufficient to identify the individual Greenland stadials and interstadials. The transition from a braided river system, which was reworking and probably lowering part of the floodplain terraces, to a system of multiple, broad, incised channels occurred towards the end of the last cold stage but before full climatic amelioration. Following the climatic warming that marked the start of the Holocene, sea level rose flooding the lower valley of the Thames. The accompanying marine (or estuarine) deposition buried parts of the earlier fluvial sequence.

Correlation of the terraces

In the study area, deposits recording the terminal Pleistocene and earliest part of the Holocene (the present warm stage) are preserved within the Northmoor Terrace of the Upper Thames Valley (also referred to in the literature as the First or Floodplain Terrace) and the Shepperton Terrace of the Middle Thames Valley (also referred to as the Lower Floodplain Terrace).

LATEGLACIAL HUMANS AND THEIR ENVIRONMENT

The Last Glacial Maximum

With the climatic downturn at the last glacial maximum (LGM) around 20,000 years ago, humans abandoned large parts of northern Europe, including the British peninsula, for several thousand years. This hiatus may have been punctuated by short-term forays into some northern latitudes (Terberger and Street, 2002), but the earliest evidence for a continuous presence does not occur until much later, about 13,000 radiocarbon years BP (c 15,000 years ago; see Fig. 7.1) in Britain

(see below; Housley et al., 1997; Barton et al., 2003). The vertebrate fossil record from this time period is notably sparse, leading Currant and Jacobi (2001) to coin the term 'Dimlington Stadial Faunal-Interzone' to characterise the absence of evidence during the LGM. Conceivably only reindeer (Rangifer tarandus) and perhaps horse (Equus ferus) would have occupied Britain on a seasonal basis but preservation of remains is very poor. It is noticeable, however, that the relative paucity of dung beetles in LGM deposits suggests that the abundance of large herbivores was low in comparison to earlier parts of the Devensian, such as MIS 3. A handful of Middle Thames localities in the Shepperton Gravel have produced assemblages of inferred Late Devensian (MIS 2) age, including Battersea Gas Works (Coombs, 1873), Peascod Street, Home Park and the Infantry Barracks, all in Windsor (Whitaker, 1860, 1889; Dawkins, 1880; Dewey and Bromehead, 1915), and Hurley (Whitaker, 1889). A range of cold-adapted species, such as woolly mammoth, woolly rhinoceros and reindeer, is present together with taxa suggestive of open grassland conditions, such as horse and bison. However, the reported finding of hippopotamus from the last site (Whitaker, 1889) strongly suggests that if the identification is verified, there are evidently reworked elements of Last Interglacial fauna also present. In addition, it is equally possible that some of the other remains of cold-adapted species mentioned above are reworked from older Devensian deposits in the Thames. The environment at this time was still relatively open herb-grassland, with only limited forest development at best.

The return of humans in the Lateglacial (Windermere) Interstadial

The Late Upper Palaeolithic

The earliest period of reoccupation, which archaeologists consider to mark the start of the Late Upper Palaeolithic, is dated to the end of the LGM, c 15 000 years ago (see Fig. 7.1), and is assigned to the Creswellian, a local variant of the European Magdalenian characterised by Cheddar points and Creswell Points (see Fig. 6.8, above). A number of 'Magdalenian' bone, antler and ivory artefacts, some decorated, are associated with this period (Barton, 1999; Barton et al., 2003); the recently

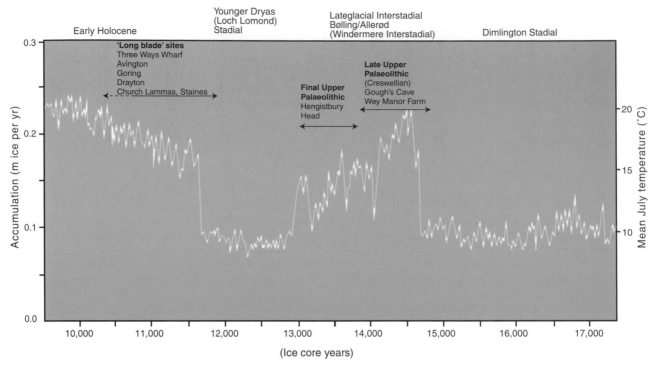

Fig. 7.1   The terminal Pleistocene-early Holocene transition. Climatic variation and the archaeology of the Late and Final Upper Palaeolithic

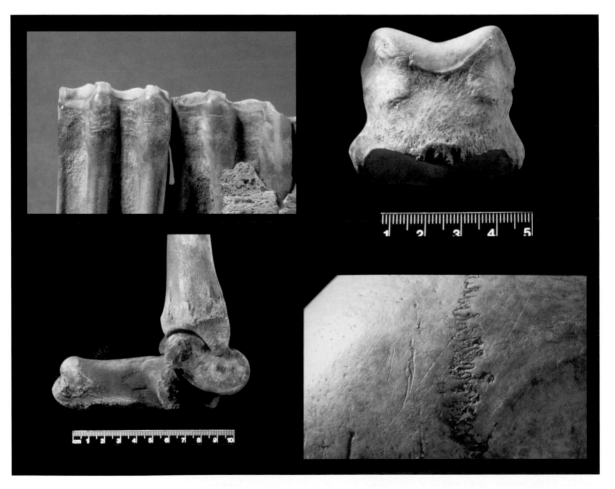

Fig. 7.2   Gough's Cave, Cheddar, bones showing butchery cutmarks. Clockwise from top left: cutmarked horse teeth; cutmarked horse second phalanx, probably for removal of tendons; cutmarked human skull; articulating bones of lower hindlimb of red deer

138

discovered engravings in Church Hole, Creswell may also on stylistic grounds belong here (Ripoll *et al.*, 2004). The evidence for human occupation during this period is better than for the Early Upper Palaeolithic (see Chapter 6), with some 24-35 findspots regarded as having Creswellian affinities (depending on what is accepted as a Creswellian marker), although only five of these can be considered as unmixed (Kent's Cavern and Three Holes Cave, Devon; Sun Hole Cave and Soldier's Hole, Cheddar; and Robin Hood Cave, Creswell Crags) (Barton *et al.*, 2003).

Most known Late Upper Palaeolithic findspots are in the upland margins of central and western Britain, the majority being cave sites. One or two open-air sites are recognised, but the evidence from the Thames Valley for the Creswellian remains limited (see below). It seems very unlikely that the river valleys such as the Thames were entirely unexploited, leading some to suggest that much evidence for open-air activity has been destroyed by periglaciation during the terminal Last Glacial (the Younger Dryas or Loch Lomond stadial, see below) (Jacobi, 1991) or that the evidence lies buried under the modern floodplains.

It would appear from European comparisons that the topographic settings of the known find spots may reveal significant behavioural patterns. Most known sites are associated with the edges of the upland zone, which may have presented a range of tightly spaced microclimates affording diverse animal and vegetal resources, as well as good vantage points from which to monitor the landscape for game (Barton *et al.*, 2003; Jacobi, 2004). Jacobi (2004) has recently published an extensive consideration of Gough's Cave, Cheddar, which provides a vivid picture of 1000 years of use of this cave during the Lateglacial Interstadial (see Fig. 7.1), between 14,600 and 13,600 years ago. The cave was occupied by hunters and their families during both the summer and winter months. Thousands of lithic artefacts were produced and discarded,

carcasses were skinned, dismembered and butchered and bone awls and needles were made to produce skin-clothing (including arctic hare, *Lepus timidus*). Horse, red deer (*Cervus elaphus*) and human bones and teeth make up the majority of the bone assemblage. Most specimens bear cutmarks from butchery with flint tools and large numbers have been deliberately smashed, presumably for marrow extraction (Fig. 7.2). Carnivores (including lynx, *Lynx lynx*, wolf, brown bear, red fox and Arctic fox, *Alopex lagopus*) and herbivores show the same patterns of damage. Material from all species, including the human remains, has been discarded together under overhangs in the cave wall, possibly representing deliberate and systematic disposal of rubbish (Currant, 2004).

Non-lithic artefacts from Gough's Cave include a baton of reindeer antler and a double bevelled ivory rod of mammoth ivory, the age of which is close to that of the occupation, suggesting the use of fresh rather than fossil ivory. Transport distances of both lithic and non-lithic materials and partial reduction sequences (with an over-representation of finished items) seen at this and other Creswellian sites can be taken as evidence for high rates of long distance mobility, although Gough's might best be interpreted as a base camp from which to exploit the environs of the Mendips to which selected raw materials were logistically introduced in the form of partly worked blanks. The site also yielded a collection of human bone bearing cut and scrape marks, with some evidence of burning, possibly testifying to cannibalism or perhaps to ritual or practical defleshing as part of a burial rite. A major AMS radiocarbon dating programme was initiated on the human bones, on artefacts made from bone, antler and ivory and on cutmarked bones. The dates indicate that Late Upper Palaeolithic human use of the cave occurred during the first half of the Lateglacial Interstadial – the Bölling and Older Dryas Chronozones (between 12,500 and 11,800 radiocarbon years BP, or approximately 14,600-13,600 years ago) (Currant, 2004.)

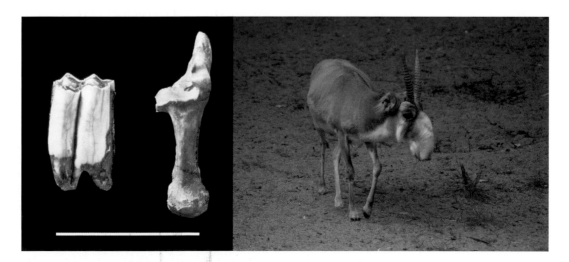

Fig. 7.3   Saiga antelope with (left) remains found at Gough's Cave, Cheddar

The presence of animals requiring woodland, such as lynx, European beaver (*Castor fiber*) and aurochs (*Bos primigenius*) – the last always associated with temperate episodes in the Pleistocene – reflects a significant climatic amelioration during the Lateglacial Interstadial. Small quantities of alder (*Alnus*), birch (*Betula*), willow (*Salix*) and hazel (*Corylus*) pollen were reported by Leroi-Gourhan (1986) from the cave deposits, although tree pollen did not exceed 10% in any sample. However, there is also some indication of short-term environmental instability at this time, in the form of a molar and calcaneum of saiga antelope (*Saiga tatarica*) (Fig. 7.3), an extremely unusual record for Britain. The remains have been radiocarbon dated to 12,380 ± 160 BP (Currant 1991; 14,593 ± 417 cal BP / 12,643 ± 417 cal BC). This small antelope is now restricted to the arid steppe regions of the southern part of the former Soviet Union. Its sudden dispersal to Britain seems to be broadly contemporaneous with similar records from elsewhere in Europe and even as far afield as Alaska, thereby implying a short-lived but dramatic climatic deterioration, possibly a very severe drought in southern Asia (Currant, 1987). Within the study area, a skull of saiga antelope has also been found in gravel at Twickenham (Leeson, 1891).

Undisturbed Upper Palaeolithic sites are rare outside the sealed stratigraphies of caves or rock shelters in Britain, but one of Creswellian age in the volatile environment of a lowland floodplain was a unique and unexpected discovery in 2004 at Wey Manor Farm, Addlestone, Surrey (P. Jones and L. Cooper, pers. comm.; Fig. 7.4). Here, stripping by machine of overburden from river clays was halted when the pressure of the bucket released flint long blades from their buried positions: they audibly 'pinged' upwards when it touched them. Further excavation revealed a nucleated cluster of struck flints focused within an area of *c* 40m², which petered-out to the north-west into a less dense array of mostly larger blades. There would, almost certainly, have been an animal bone component to the cluster, but because of the acidity of the river clay the only finds were of struck flints, some small fragments of calcined flint and occasional river pebbles.

Preliminary examination of the assemblage suggests it represents a single, short-lived butchering site of Late Upper Palaeolithic date. The flint is of good quality and almost certainly from a source on the Chalk, the nearest outcrop of which is 12 km distant on the North Downs, and the *c* 370 struck pieces include some that are burnt, suggesting activities around a hearth. The collection includes 28 formal tools, amongst which are complete or part examples of nine shouldered, Cheddar and Creswell points, eight burins, two truncated blades and six scrapers; and there are eight utilised blades and by-products of tool manufacture that include three burin spalls, a Krukowski microburin and two core fragments. It is suspected, however, that many of the blades may have been brought to the site ready-made.

A feature of Creswellian long blade production is the use of single platform cores that tend to produce blanks with pronounced curvature. Because of this the sweep of the bucket blade at Wey Manor Farm had triggered their upward movement, bringing about the discovery of a site that might otherwise have been missed.

Currently the only other known Creswellian-stage find from the study area is a Cheddar point which was found with an end scraper in redeposited contexts at Mingies Ditch, Oxfordshire (Barton 1993). The end scraper may be a Final Upper Palaeolithic implement. There is no sign of use on the point, but the end scraper appears to have been deliberately snapped. The use of intentional breakage in tool manufacture and repair is known from continental and indigenous Upper Palaeolithic contexts (*ibid.*; Bergman *et al.* 1987).

The Final Upper Palaeolithic

The evidence for the Final Upper Palaeolithic is far richer (*c* 80 findspots) and occurs over a more extensive and ecologically diverse area, with more open-air sites recognised (Barton 1999; Jacobi 2004). They are generally assigned to the period 12,000-11,000 radiocarbon years BP (or approximately 13,900 to 12,900 years ago), corresponding with the beginning of a more forested phase of the Lateglacial Interstadial (see Fig. 7.1), although only a few have provided direct radiocarbon determinations to support this (eg Mother Grundy's Parlour, Creswell and Pixie's Hole, Devon). Final Upper Palaeolithic industries appear to be much more regionally diverse (Barton and Roberts 1996), with a greater variety of tools present than in the Creswellian phase, including curve-backed, straight-backed, tanged and Penknife points and blade-end scrapers (see Fig. 6.8, above). Assemblages seem to be made on locally-available lithic raw materials and have a different manufacturing technology from Creswellian industries. Whether the apparently simultaneous occurrence of these forms is indicative of different populations, chronology, function or style is unknown, but there is certainly more variety represented in the archaeological record than in the Creswellian. A number of sites of this age have produced organic artefacts, the majority being undecorated uniserial barbed points (Barton 1999).

Current knowledge about this period is based on data from both caves and open air sites, but especially the well-known open-air site of this period at Hengistbury Head, Dorset (Barton 1992). The evidence suggests a pattern of short-lived and seasonal settlement, with open-air sites that seem to represent places where people congregated close to the spring or autumn migration routes of herding animals (Barton 1997, 128). It is possible that, at first, there was long-distance mobility, with groups moving in and out of Britain (Jacobi 1981) but, with

Fig. 7.4 Wey Manor Farm. Clockwise from bottom left: location of the site in the Wey valley, just south of the confluence with the Thames; the Creswellian flint scatter being excavated; distribution plan of the scatter, with the flints shown as found; late Magdalenian (Creswellian) burins on blade supports (actual size)

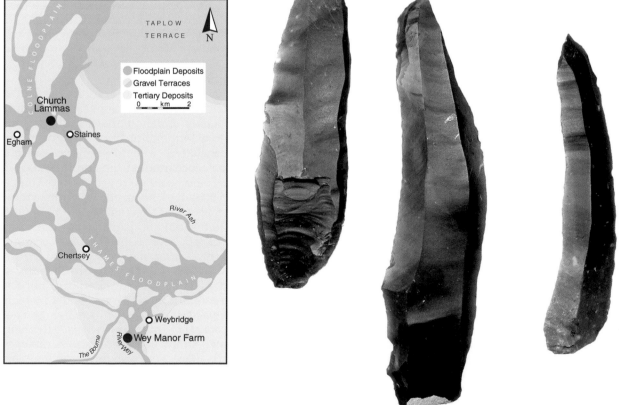

141

more closed habitats, people may have become less wide-ranging.

At present there are only a few diagnostic artefacts from the area of the Thames Valley, most of which have come from gravel extraction sites, for example curve-backed and Penknife points and an opposed platform blade core from Hardwick Pit, Harwick-with-Yelford, Oxfordshire (Terry Hardaker pers. comm.). A possible tanged point was recovered at '100 Acres' pit in the lower Colne Valley, also in a riverine environment (Lacaille 1963; Wymer 1977). Alison Roberts has recently identified a number of Final Late Upper Palaeolithic artefacts in the Ashmolean Museum collections which came from a wider range of contexts (pers. comm.) but, to date, all seem to have been recovered from the valley itself; given the context of their discovery, perhaps this is unsurprising.

The last cold event: the Younger Dryas/Loch Lomond stadial

Britain appears to have been all but abandoned again during the Younger Dryas/Loch Lomond stadial (*c* 10,800-10,000 radiocarbon years BP or approximately 12,800-11,500 years ago); a climatic downturn seen in the terminal Pleistocene terrestrial record and broadly equivalent to the final phase of Greenland Interstadial 1 and Greenland Stadial 1 of the ice core record (see Fig. 7.1). The seasonally very cold conditions followed by partial summer thaw, combined with the lack of complete vegetational cover led to much surface instability in the Thames Valley and subsequent large-scale erosion and sedimentation. The flat topography of the gravel terraces meant that they did not experience slope erosive processes although some frost wedges possibly belong to this period. Channel migration in the valley bottom caused much erosion and deposition of gravel. Soils on the gravel terraces would have been rudimentary but there was a covering of fine material above the gravel, often a red-brown silt loam, the silt component possibly a reflection of a loessic contribution. A low sand mound on the First Gravel Terrace of the Upper Thames at Thrupp proved on excavation to be a dune probably belonging to this period.

Lateglacial environments

Only snippets of environmental information can be gleaned for this time period within the study area. Organic remains preserved within channel-fill sediments in the tributary valley of the Lower Colne (Dewey and Bromehead, 1915; Hare, 1947) at West Drayton and Colnbrook (Coope, 1982; Gibbard and Hall, 1982) have yielded plant and insect remains indicative of extremely severe cold-climate conditions with radiocarbon age estimates of 11,230 ± 120 BP and 13,405 ± 170 BP respectively (Gibbard, 1985) (13,124 ± 152 cal BP/11,174 ± 152 cal BC and 16,312 ± 464 cal BP/14,362 ± 464 cal BC).

Following the Loch Lomond/Younger Dryas ice readvance, pollen analyses suggest increasing aridity and continentality, and mammals such as reindeer, horse, wolverine (*Gulo gulo*) and steppe pika (*Ochotona pusilla*) reflect the prevalence of cold, arid and open environments up until about 10,000 radiocarbon years BP (or *c* 11,500 years ago) (Jacobi, 1987; Currant, 1991). A molluscan assemblage from the tributary river Kennet in Berkshire yielded species characteristic of bare ground and open environments, including *Pupilla muscorum* and *Columella columella*, also thought to be of Younger Dryas age (Holyoak, 1983).

In the Upper Thames Valley, a radiocarbon date of 10,860 ± 130 BP (HAR-8356; 12,842 ± 122 cal BP/10,892 ± 122 cal BC) was obtained on waterlogged twigs from a minor channel within the cross-bedded gravels of the Lower Windrush at Mingies Ditch (Allen and Robinson, 1993), while organic sediments at the base of a major incised channel of the Thames at Farmoor, which remained open into the Holocene, were dated to 10,600 ± 250 BP (BIRM-590; Lambrick and Robinson, 1979; 12,387 ± 344 cal BP/10,437 ± 344 cal BC). Biological analyses at both sites suggested the presence of tundra. Along with seeds of aquatic and marsh plants such as *Menyanthes trifoliata* (bogbean) and *Carex* spp. (sedges), both deposits contained many seeds of *Betula nana* (dwarf birch), a low-growing arctic shrub. Twigs of *Salix* cf *repens* (creeping willow) were present at Mingies Ditch along with the leaf beetle *Chrysomela collaris* which feeds on the woolly species of willow such as *Salix lapponum* or *S. lanata*. *C. collaris* was also identified at Farmoor. Calyces of what is now a coastal plant, *Armeria maritima* (sea pink or thrift), were found at Farmoor while a bare, harsh environment with tufts of low-growing herbaceous plants or moss was suggested by the weevil *Otiorhynchus nodosus*.

Pollen evidence from two sites in the Middle Thames Valley, Moor Farm, Staines (Keith-Lucas 2000) and Thames Valley Park, Reading (Keith-Lucas 1997) extends our knowledge of the Lateglacial vegetation. The Moor Farm sequence was from a palaeochannel at the confluence of the rivers Colne, Colne Brook, Wraysbury and Thames. The Thames Valley Park sequence was from a minor palaeochannel of the Thames which apparently spanned all of the Late Devensian. Both sites showed the presence of a low shrub community which included *Betula nana* (dwarf birch) and *Juniperus communis* (juniper), with *Ephedra* sp. (somlatha) at Thames Valley Park. A tall-herb meadow-like community was represented by plants such as *Sanguisorba officinalis* (greater burnet), *Filipendula ulmaria* (meadowsweet), *Centaurea scabiosa* (greater knapweed) and *Lychnis flos-cuculi* (ragged robin). There were also low-growing plants of sparsely-vegetated habitats including *Dryas octopetala* (mountain avens) and *Plantago maritima* (sea plantain). A low concentration of pollen of *Pinus* sp. (pine) at both sites is difficult to interpret in relation to the local vegetation because pine is a prolific producer of pollen which is dispersed over a wide area.

The harsh periglacial environment of the area during the final cold episode of the Lateglacial probably resulted in the gravel terraces of both the Upper and the Middle Thames Valley supporting a discontinuous low-shrub tundra of dwarf birch and juniper growing no more than 0.4 m high. Between the areas of shrubs was sparsely-vegetated ground where grew low xerophile plants, including some which are now to be found only in exposed coastal habitats. The inland occurrence of these coastal plants was a widespread phenomenon in Britain during the Lateglacial possibly related to the desiccating effect of the wind against the background of low rainfall resulting in slight salination of the ground surface. 'Sub-arctic meadow' vegetation of herbaceous plants grew in moister areas, possibly on parts of the floodplain or where there was a greater thickness of fine deposits above the gravels. On the floodplain, the rapid migration of minor channels would have left cut-off lengths holding stagnant water where sedges grew while small shrubby willows were probably established in slacks between gravel ridges left by the channel movement. Some Scots pine trees and perhaps birch trees grew in stunted clumps in particularly sheltered localities on the valley sides.

A particularly good source of information on the prevailing climate is preserved insect remains. The assemblages comprise arctic faunas which today occur north of this region or above the tree line. They do not contain so many of the species of Eastern Siberia and the mountains of Central Asia as commonly occur in Middle Devensian cold faunas; most of the species can now be found in Northern Scandinavia with some species restricted to the Arctic Circle and the tops of mountains further south. The most abundant beetle recovered from Farmoor was *Helophorus glacialis*, a species that no longer occurs in Britain but can be found in arctic Europe, the Alps and Pyrenees, where it lives in pools of snow meltwater. Its presence implies patches of snow lasting, at least on shaded slopes, into the early summer. Another beetle of the genus from the deposit was *H. obscurellus*, which occurs in arctic Russia as far east in Siberia as the Lena River and also on the Altay and Tien Shan Mountains, on the border between Kazakhstan and China. A total of 17 species, indicative of cold conditions, which no longer occur in Britain were identified from the site and others, for example *Notaris aethiops*, have a northerly distribution in Britain and are now absent from the region. Coope *et al.* (1977) suggested that the average July temperature was close to 10°C and that the average January temperature was no warmer than -10°C. Somewhat similar cold-indicative insect assemblages have been identified from Mingies Ditch (Allen and Robinson, 1993) and from other palaeochannels on the floodplain of the Upper Thames Valley, for example at

Northmoor, radiocarbon dated to 11,250 ± 100 BP (Briggs *et al.* 1985) (13,146 ± 134 cal BP/11,196 ± 134 cal BC).

Human occupation: Final Upper Palaeolithic 'long blade' industries

Significantly for the present volume, some of the few plausible instances of human presence during the final cold period of the last glacial (the Younger Dryas/Loch Lomond stadial) are from the study area. The technology of this period is characterised by 'long blade' industries. These occur at the very end of the Pleistocene and beginning of the Holocene, and may overlap with the earliest Mesolithic (see below), although technologically they are allied to the Final Upper Palaeolithic (Barton and Roberts 2004, 342). They were defined for Britain by Barton (in Wymer 1977) and are mainly found in floodplain or river valleys close to the sources of high-quality, *in-situ* flint (Barton 1986). The technology is characterised by the production of very long blades, commonly heavily edge-damaged blades known as 'bruised blades', but assemblages also include end scrapers and burins as well as microliths (Barton and Roberts 2004). The absence of hearths and quantities of burnt flint associated with these sites has led Barton to suggest that they represent short-term occupation events (Barton 1997).

It has been proposed that the edge damage found on 'bruised blades' is the result of working hard materials such as wood or antler (Barton 1986), although they may also have been used to replenish the ends of sandstone hammers for flint knapping. Other tools suggest a bow-hunting technology.

A curve-backed point, a blade end-scraper and a core discovered during the Drayton Cursus excavations are typical 'long blade' industry products (Fig. 7.5; Holgate *et al.* in Barclay *et al.* 2003, 126-7, figs 4.11-12). At Three Ways Wharf, Uxbridge, in the Middle Thames a flint scatter (Scatter A) comprised long blades (>12cm in length), small truncated microliths and 'bruised blades' from a grey clay horizon overlying fluvial gravels of the river Colne (Lewis, 1991). Faunal remains associated with the scatters include horse, reindeer, and other burnt bone, suggesting processing for food; horse bone from the site has been radiocarbon dated to 10,270 ± 100 BP (OxA-1778) and 10,010 ± 120 BP (OxA-1902) (ibid., 253; 12,080 ± 269 cal BP/10,130 ± 269 cal BC and 11,582 ± 234 cal BP/9632 ± 234 cal BC respectively). The flint assemblage from this site, which is *in situ* and contained refits (Lewis 1991; Lewis *et al.* 1992), is broadly comparable to that from Avington VI (see below). A second scatter on the site produced *c* 7000 early Mesolithic flints and animal bone, including red deer.

'Long blade' assemblages from 28 localities in south-eastern England, most in riverine settings with access to raw materials, were discussed by

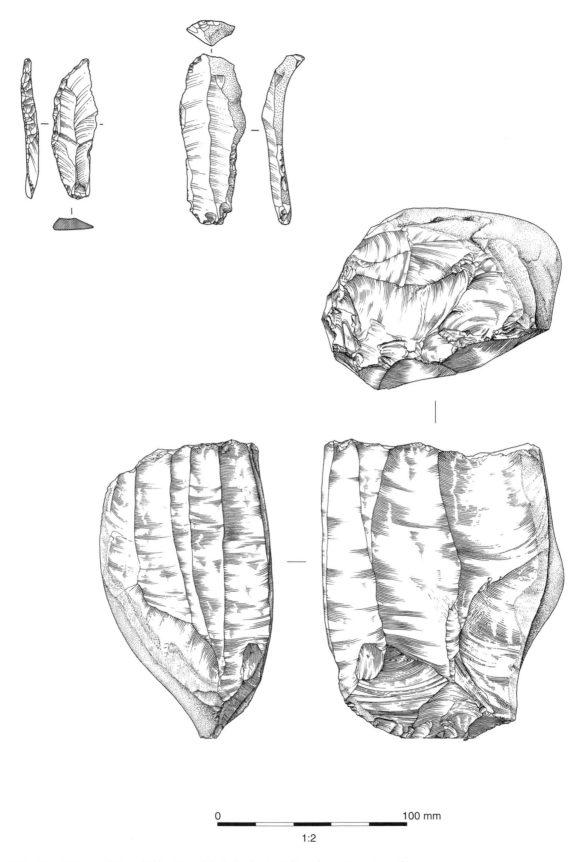

0   100 mm

1:2

Fig. 7.5   Final Upper Palaeolithic 'long blade industry' flint from Drayton, Oxon:
top row (left) partially backed blade, (right) end scraper; below, core with faceted platform

Fig. 7.6 (right)   The late Devensian: the end of the ice

THE LATE DEVENSIAN
THE END OF THE ICE

Towards the end of the last (Devensian) glaciation, the climate continued to swing rapidly between very cold and warmer conditions. Much of the evidence for these climatic fluctuations has come from the Greenland ice cores, which provide us with a very detailed record of short-term changes at this time.

Modern humans, *Homo sapiens sapiens*, had replaced Neanderthals in Europe around 29 000 years ago. However, they abandoned our region following a severe climatic downturn around 20 000 years ago, known as the Last Glacial Maximum. Much of Britain would have remained largely uninhabitable over the ensuing 5000 years, its cold, open and relatively barren grasslands perhaps seasonally visited by herds of reindeer and horses.

The climate warmed again around 15 000 years ago, with the onset of the Lateglacial interstadial. This 2000-year interlude of more favourable conditions saw the return of humans to Britain, bringing with them the characteristic Creswellian flint tool industry. For archaeologists this marks the start of the Late Upper Palaeolithic. The best-known Creswellian occupation site is Gough's Cave, Cheddar, where hunters and their families produced bone awls and needles to make clothes from the skins of animals such as the arctic hare. Open-air sites of this period are very rare, but flint tools have been found within our study area at Wey Manor Farm near Addlestone, in Surrey, and at Mingies Ditch in Oxfordshire.

Towards the end of the Lateglacial interstadial a greater variety of flint tools appear (including curve-backed, straight-backed, tanged and penknife points and blade-end scrapers). For archaeologists, this marks the transition to the Final Upper Palaeolithic. Many more sites of this period are known in Britain, although only a few have been recognised in the Thames Valley.

A sudden and severe climatic deterioration led to the return of bitterly cold conditions by 12 500 years ago (the Younger Dryas, or Loch Lomond, stadial). Once again, the Thames gravel terraces could have supported only sparse vegetation. The insects that lived in our region at this time are types that are nowadays found in Northern Scandinavia, within the Arctic Circle or on high mountain tops.

Despite the harsh climate, humans were present in our area during this final cold period. Their technology is characterised by 'long blade' industries, which occur at the very end of the Pleistocene and the beginning of the Holocene, and may overlap with the earliest Mesolithic. 'Long blade' sites are increasingly being recognised within our study area.

Glacial conditions came to an end around 11 500 years ago. A rapid rise in temperature is evident in many different types of record from this time. This upturn marks the end of the Pleistocene (the epoch of the Ice Ages) and the start of the Holocene epoch, the period of warmer climatic conditions in which we are still living today. It remains possible that the climate will cool again in the future, taking the world into another glaciation. How this might be affected by global warming due to human use of fossil fuels (the 'greenhouse effect') is not yet clearly understood.

Figure 7.6

Final Upper Palaeolithic occupation in the Thames Valley: The 'long blade' sites at Church Lammas, Staines

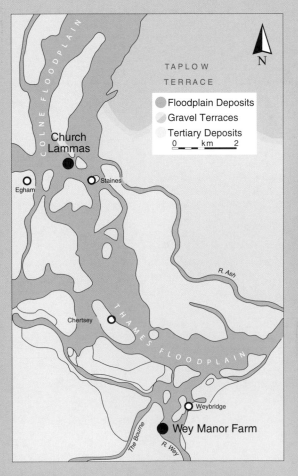

The potential of the Colne valley for understanding the subsistence strategies employed by people dependent upon migrating reindeer herds and horse in the open tundra landscape at the end of the last glaciation was first realised from excavations at Three Ways Wharf in Uxbridge (Lewis 1991). Twelve kilometres downstream, in the confluent delta of the Colne with the Thames, that potential was reinforced by the discovery and excavation of parts of two small, discrete scatters of struck flints and animal detritus of similar age in 1995.

The best-preserved scatter was of 245 pieces of a long blade tradition, amongst which are characteristic crested or edge-damaged 'bruised' blades (*lame machuré*), opposed platform cores and a restricted tool range that includes two fine burins. Several re-fits, including some of core debris, indicate *in situ* flint-knapping and some of the debitage is burnt, although the seat of fire was not located. The assemblage is very similar to those of Scatters A and C (east) of Three Ways Wharf, which probably belong to the end of the Devensian glaciation or the earliest pre-Boreal. It has been suggested that the relatively small size of much of the debitage of the main Church

• Left — Location of the Church Lammas site in the Colne valley, north of the confluence with the Thames

• Above — An artist's impression of the temporary camp made by hunters in the tundra landscape of 11,000 years ago

• Above right — The photo shows how the archaeological excavation at Church Lammas, Staines, was surrounded on all sides by rapidly-approaching mineral extraction. This rare Late Upper Palaeolithic camp was found only just in time

• Above left — Beautifully worked long blades from the site

Lammas scatter and those of Uxbridge scatters A and C (east) may reflect a paucity of suitable raw materials in the district for the production of long blades and the development of a 'stunted' facies of the tradition within the Colne valley (Lewis 2002). In addition to the flints the principal Church Lammas scatter was associated with fragmentary bones and teeth of reindeer, red deer and wild horse, of which several were burnt.

The second, smaller, scatter lay 65m south-east of the first, but less of it had survived quarrying. It included c 90 struck flints of a similar 'long blade' tradition, of which eight flakes are burnt, and a burin as the only modified piece. It, too, was associated with fragments of animal bone, including parts of a radius shaft from a reindeer.

The Church Lammas scatters, which probably represent encampments of very short duration, were on a relict floodplain of glacial outwash sands that had survived the subsequent carving of new palaeochannels by south-flowing braided streams of the Colne. One of these lay west of the larger scatter, and another flowed east of the smaller scatter. The fluvial infills of the eastern palaeochannel were sampled immediately north of Church Lammas, and the basal part of its peat sequence provided evidence of an open tundra landscape and an uncalibrated C^{14} date of 9710 ± 150 (Keith Lucas 1997). This suggests an approximate contemporaneity with the two encampments, and even closer to the larger of these were two linear hollows that probably represent spring thaw scourings of minor palaeochannels of slightly later date. One contained some struck flints and bones of reindeer or red deer, and the other provided a palynological assemblage representing a landscape dominated by pine forest with some birch and hazel.

Figure 7.6

Barton (1999). As already noted, long blade sites are mainly found on the floodplain or in river valleys close to the sources of high-quality, *in situ* flint (Barton 1986). A site at Gatehampton Farm, Goring, Oxfordshire is, thus, in a classic location. It was interpreted by Barton (1995) as a kill/butchery site and its position in the narrow Goring Gap where the Thames has forced its way through the Chalk ridge may not be coincidental. The flint assemblage at Gatehampton Farm was preserved in a palaeosol which developed in the upper fill of a palaeochannel (Allen 1995). A high degree of refitting was found amongst the blades, cores and flakes showing local manufacture (Barton in Allen 1995). However, a few of the long blades showed 'bruising' an attribution suggestive of chopping bone or antler. Pollen from the long blade layer at Gatehampton Farm suggested open conditions with pollen fron Gramineae (grasses) predominating (Parker 1995). Other taxa from the sequence appropriate to sub-arctic conditions included *Helianthemum* sp. (rockrose), *Thalictrum* sp. (meadow rue) and *Juniperus* sp (juniper). Pollen of thermophilous trees was present towards the top of the profile above the long blade layer suggesting the opening of the Holocene.

A number of important long blade sites occur not far from Goring, in the Kennet Valley, including Avington VI which has three OSL dates of at least 10,300 years ago (Froom 1970; 2005; Barton and Froom 1986; Barton 1989; Barton *et al.* 1998). Six thousand artefacts were recovered seemingly *in situ* on and within possible colluvial or soliflucted clay with a fine (overbank) alluvial input and unusually this site also yielded small tanged points. Unfortunately, bones were not preserved but pollen and molluscs from the same level as the *in situ* knapping floor (Barton and Froom 1986) were indicative of cold conditions and open, disturbed ground (Holyoak 1980). The absence of hearths, burnt flints and high percentage of knapping waste to retouched tools led Barton (1999) to suggest that these sites may have been occupied for short periods and were principally used for primary collection and reduction of stone resources. Barton (1999, 31) draws parallels with the Ahrensburgian of northern Germany, although he notes the absence of characteristic small tanged points from British occurrences. A similar long blade industry lacking tanged points has been described in the Somme Valley and Basin, the available radiocarbon assays overlapping with those for Three Ways Wharf.

Other Kennet Valley long blade sites include Wawcott XII (Froom 1970, 2005) and Crown Acres (Campbell 1977; Barton 1986; Froom 2005). As with Goring, they were open sites with a high proportion of blade waste to retouched pieces. At Crown Acres, the long blade horizon appears to lie in sandy marl below a site of early Mesolithic date, both being sealed by peat (Barton 1986, 84).

Further down the Thames Valley, recent work by MoLAS at the Sanderson site, between the Colne and the Colnbrook in Buckinghamshire, has yielded relatively large flakes which may be of Upper Palaeolithic date within an otherwise early Mesolithic assemblage (Lakin 2006), and at Denham nearby, *in situ* long blade material has been found during evaluations by Wessex Archaeology (2005). This site was sealed by peat over 2 m deep radiocarbon dated to 9300±50 BP (10,494 ± 72 cal BP/8544 ± 72 cal BC), showing a late cold stage indicated by a herb/juniper assemblage.

A recent new discovery has been a long blade assemblage from Church Lammas, near Staines (Surrey) (Fig.7.6), incorporating both bruised edge blades and retouched pieces (broad blade microliths and burins), uncovered together with remains of reindeer and horse. These finds complement earlier discoveries made at nearby Brockhill, on the outskirts of Woking, comprising straight-backed and shouldered points, end scrapers and burins, probably indicative of a short-stay hunting camp geared towards the processing of large animals (Cotton, 2004). In many respects, the technological repertoires of these terminal Palaeolithic hunter-gatherers bear many similarities to those of the early Mesolithic, albeit with a different range of faunal and floral resources to exploit.

Since 2000, work in advance of the Channel Tunnel Rail Link has recovered a further long blade assemblage consisting of some 176 pieces of Lateglacial flintwork from around the springs at Springhead in Kent (Lamdin-Whymark forthcoming). The assemblage contains blades in excess of 120 mm in length, with evidence of a complete reduction and use sequence, and includes heavily utilised 'bruised' flakes and blades. These new finds complement earlier evidence from excavations nearby to the north, where substantial blades reaching 180 mm in length were discovered by James Burchell in the 1930s (1938; Barton 1999).

Under the harsh conditions of tundra, the range of food resources exploited by these settlements is likely to have been narrow. Horse and reindeer were noted from Three Ways Wharf, Uxbridge but they are likely to have been the only large game in the region. A continued paucity of dung beetles suggested the abundance of large herbivores remained low in comparison to earlier parts of the Devensian. The broad expanse of the floodplain prior to the stabilisation of the gravels would, however, have attracted large populations of migratory wildfowl in the summer, although there is no direct evidence for their exploitation. The range of edible plants would also have been narrow. The gravel terraces themselves were probably not acidic enough for *Vaccinium* spp. (bilberry etc), nor were there likely to have been large areas of bog which would have favoured other species of *Vaccinium* spp. (cranberry etc) or *Rubus chamaemorus* (cloudberry).

In a handful of cases, sites within the study area preserve evidence of the transition to the Holocene and accompanying climatic amelioration. At

Mingies Ditch, a temperate biological assemblage radiocarbon dated to 9380 ± 110 BP (HAR-8366; 10,626 ± 174 cal BP/8676 ± 174 cal BC) and indicative of Holocene climatic warming was found in a channel cutting the gravels (Allen and Robinson 1993), whereas in the Middle Thames at Dorney, pollen evidence from a palaeochannel cut into the Shepperton Gravel suggests the transition from an open tundra environment to pine-hazel woodland, the latter radiocarbon dated to 9070 ± 40 BP (CAMS-54440; Parker and Robinson, 2003) (10,231 ± 17 cal BP/8281 ± 17 cal BC). A radiocarbon date of 8960 ± 130 BP (Branch and Green 2004) (10,023 ± 190 cal BP/8073 ± 190 cal BC) was given by wood from palaeochannel sediments above the Shepperton Gravel at Meadlake Place, downstream from Staines. This date, which was from towards the top of the sequence, indicated that this channel was already largely filled in by the early Holocene.

Chapter 8 – An Introduction to the Holocene of the Thames

by Gill Hey with Chris Hayden

INTRODUCTION TO THE HOLOCENE OF THE THAMES

The second part of this volume covers the period from the beginning of the Mesolithic in the very early Holocene (c 11,550 cal BP or c 9600 cal BC) up to the middle Bronze Age (c 1500 cal BC). Although the river Thames had flowed along its present course from before the end of the Last Glacial Maximum and subsequent geomorphological change was relatively minor (Fig. 8.1), the transformation in the environment of the river valley was dramatic, from tundra dotted with dwarf birch and juniper to climax, mixed woodland 6,000 years later, at the end of the Mesolithic (see Chap. 9). During this period of time, Britain was occupied by hunter-gatherer groups who adapted to the changing landscape around them. Their relationship to Final Late Upper Palaeolithic people using long-blade technology (see above, Chapter 7) is uncertain; early Mesolithic dates appear to be later, but there may be some overlap (Barton and Roberts 2004, 340-2). It is possible that the same population changed its subsistence strategies and tool kits to cope with the new environment (Jacobi 1987b). Alternatively, new groups from more southerly climes may have arrived who were already adapted to the opportunities of warmer and more wooded conditions, in which different plant foods and a more varied fauna, including mammals that were much smaller than those of the end of the Pleistocene, were available. The big game hunters may have gone elsewhere.

The final 2,500 years covered by this book witnessed a much more fundamental, cultural shift. From around 4000 cal BC farming was introduced to Britain along with a range of new materials including pottery and new kinds of stone tools. Foods that had never been consumed before, such as cereals, mutton and lamb, and milk, became available. Domesticated cattle and pigs were herded and no longer had to be hunted, and tracts of woodland were cleared in order to provide browse for these animals and for arable plots. Rather than accommodating themselves to the landscape around them like all earlier human populations, Neolithic people played a much more deliberate, and effective, role in altering the environment. They built monuments to the dead, and constructed increasingly dramatic ceremonial structures in which to gather and participate in communal and religious events. They thus made a permanent mark on the landscape for the first time, a mark that would have a lasting impact on the physical world

of their successors. In the process, they also created a more complex society, for these increasingly large-scale and sophisticated projects were conceived, designed and executed, and the events within them orchestrated, as a result of the collaboration of ever greater numbers of people, the activities requiring organisation and negotiation, or perhaps coercion, and thus creating the potential for the acquisition of power by a few. Habitation sites also become more visible, and the use of greater quantities and a greater range of material for containers and tools means that their activity areas are more visible today than are those of their predecessors. Towards the end of our period, from around 2400 cal BC, metalworking – that magical process whereby skilled individuals transformed intractable lumps from the earth into jewellery, weapons and tools – was introduced.

The catchment of the valley contains a number of diverse and well-known areas of prehistoric activity: the Upper and Middle Thames gravels, Avebury in the Upper Kennet Valley, Thatcham in the Middle Kennet Valley, the Cotswolds, the Berkshire Downs, the Lower Colne Valley and the Surrey Greensand (Figs 8.1-2; Holgate 1988a). Flint scatters of Mesolithic, Neolithic and early Bronze Age date are found throughout the region indicating the extent of the area visited in this period. There are distinct clusters of finds, however, both in the river valleys and some more upland areas which, in addition to other settlement features such as pits and occasional structures, show that some parts of the Thames Valley were favoured over others. In low-lying areas near to the major rivers, intact ground surfaces have survived with *in situ* finds scatters and midden deposits from which not only flint and other stone types have been recovered but also pottery, bone and, occasionally, organic artefacts.

Funerary and ceremonial monuments are found from the earliest Neolithic onwards and they too are clustered; some geographical zones have concentrations of monuments while others are almost devoid of the same types of structures. At the western corner of our study area is the impressive Avebury monument complex, with some of the largest monuments to be found anywhere in Britain, and a history of monument building that lasted for over 2,000 years. More modest monument complexes are found on the Upper Thames gravel terraces, in particular those around Lechlade, Stanton Harcourt, Abingdon and Dorchester-on-Thames, with a number of small monument groups in the 40 km stretch between

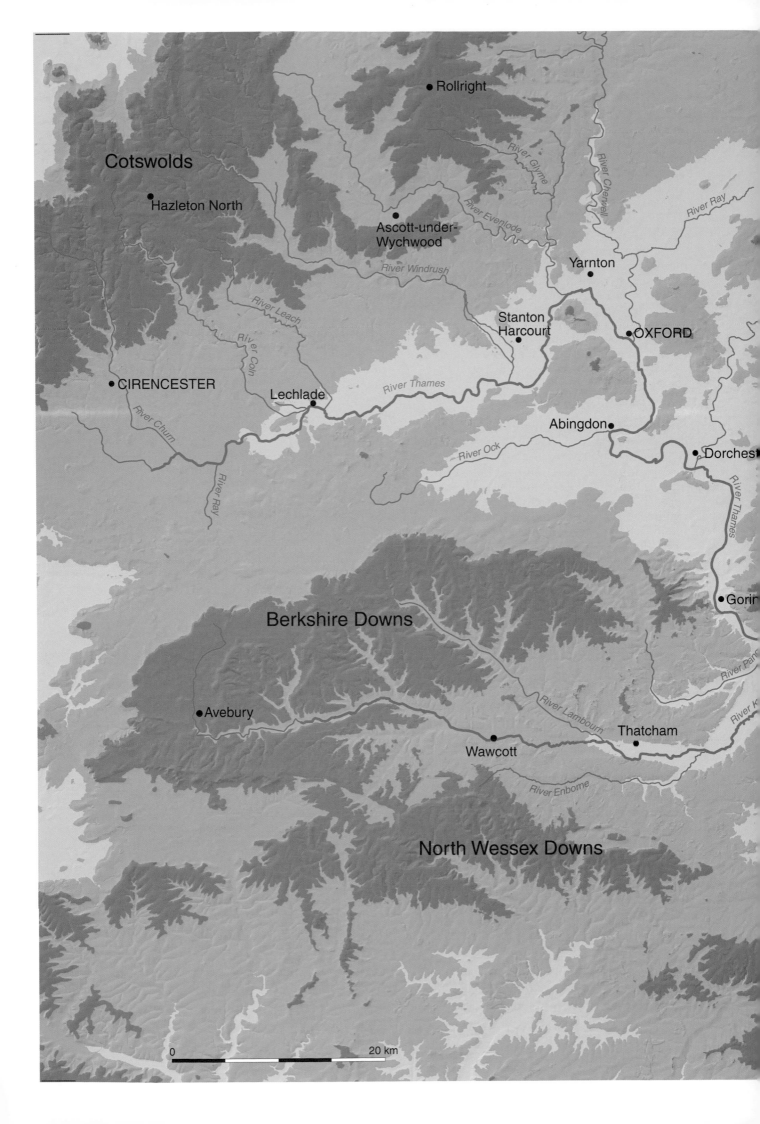

Cotswolds

● Rollright

River Glyme

River Cherwell

River Ray

● Hazleton North

Ascott-under-
Wychwood ●

River Evenlode

Yarnton ●

River Windrush

Stanton
Harcourt ●

● OXFORD

River Leach

River Coln

River Thames

● CIRENCESTER

Lechlade ●

Abingdon ●

● Dorches

River Churn

River Ray

River Ock

River Thames

Berkshire Downs

● Gorin

River Pan

River K

● Avebury

River Lambourn

Thatcham ●

Wawcott ●

River Enborne

North Wessex Downs

0   20 km

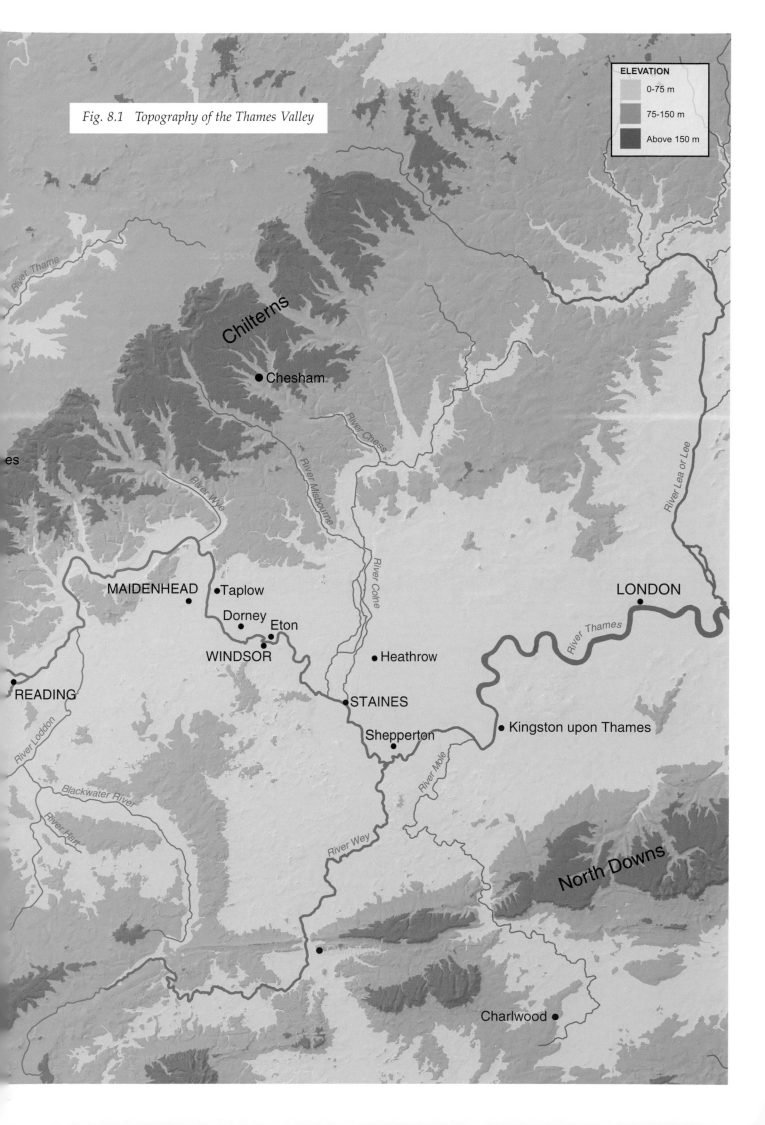

Fig. 8.1 Topography of the Thames Valley

ELEVATION
0-75 m
75-150 m
Above 150 m

River Thame

Chilterns

Chesham

River Chess

River Wye

River Misbourne

River Lea or Lee

es

River Colne

MAIDENHEAD   Taplow

Dorney   Eton

WINDSOR

Heathrow

LONDON

River Thames

READING

River Loddon

STAINES

Shepperton

Kingston upon Thames

River Mole

Blackwater River

River Hart

River Wey

North Downs

Charlwood

Abingdon and the Goring Gap. South of here, monuments and monument complexes are relatively scarce, with the notable exception of the Staines causewayed enclosure and the nearby Stanwell bank barrow in the Lower Colne Valley. The latter appears to have replaced monuments of a more modest scale. Votive offerings in watery places, principally the river, are found all along the valley but occur in marked concentrations in the Middle and Lower Thames.

THE HISTORY OF RESEARCH

The Thames Valley has witnessed archaeological endeavour from the days of early antiquarian investigations, much of it because of the presence of the university and Ashmolean Museum in Oxford. Interest was fuelled by a few spectacular standing monuments, such as Avebury and the Rollright Stones, but also by the proximity of gravel workings which provided a supply of artefacts as well as a fruitful source of information.

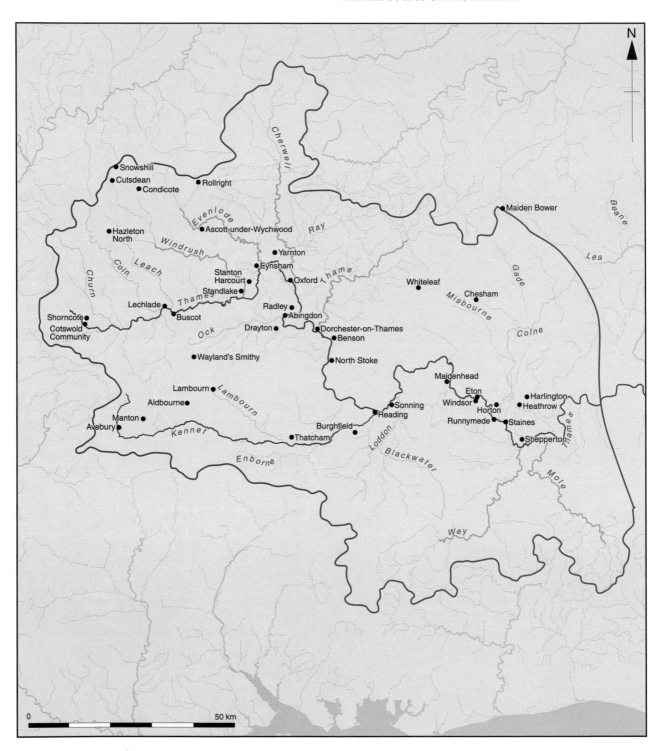

Fig. 8.2   Location of major sites mentioned in the text

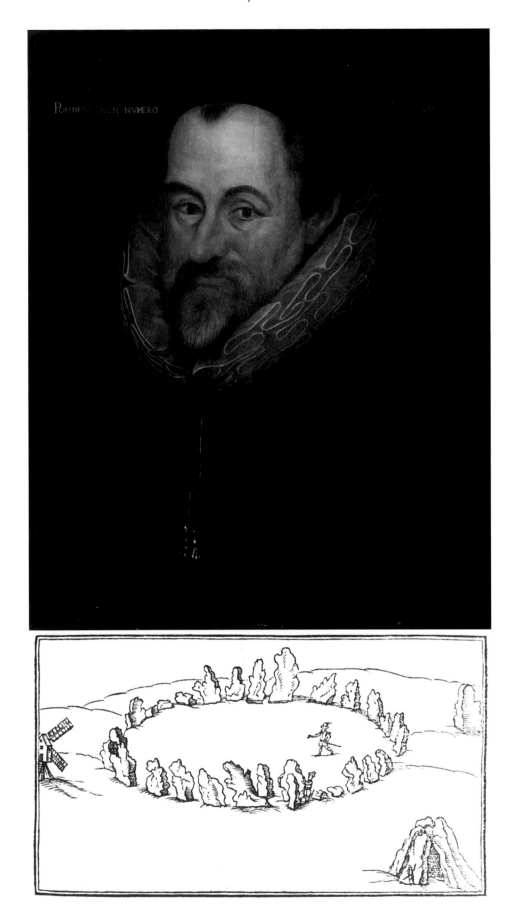

Fig. 8.3   above: William Camden, by Marcus Gheeraerts the Younger; below: the Rollright Stones from Camden's
Britannia *(1607 edition)*

Early antiquaries included William Camden who published an engraving of the King's Men stone circle at Rollright in his *Britannia* of 1607 (Fig. 8.3), and John Aubrey who visited and mapped the remains at Avebury for his *Monumenta Britannica, c* 1675 (Fig. 8.4). Aubrey also provided our first account of three surviving standing stones of the Devil's Quoits stone circle and henge and the nearby Stanton Harcourt barrow which was levelled in the 18th and 19th centuries (Grimes 1960, 145). Dr Plot (1677) wrote the first history of the antiquities of Oxfordshire, which included drawings by Loggan of the Rollright Stones monuments amongst the illustrations of an eclectic mix of sites and finds of different periods (Fig. 8.5). He noted circular marks in the grass in the University Parks at Oxford, marks which we now know were the ploughed-out remains of round barrows, but which he thought were created by lightning bolts striking the earth or witches, elves or fairies dancing (Piggott 1989). In the 18th century, William Stukeley visited and drew many of these monuments, including Avebury and Windmill Hill, and attempted to provide accurate plans of some (Stukeley 1743; Fig. 8.6).

Nineteenth-century railway construction and gravel digging provided additional new information, and important contributions were made to regional and national research at this time by Boyd Dawkins, George Rolleston, Sir Henry Dryden, the Reverend William Collings Lukis and Stephen Stone. Rolleston (Fig. 8.7) reported on two ring ditches that were dug away at Yarnton in order to provide ballast for a railway embankment, one of which yielded a very early copper neck ring or diadem (Fig. 16.3; Rolleston 1884). Dryden and Lukis drew plans of the site (Lambrick 1988, 14; figs 13-16). Stephen Stone excavated and recorded a ring ditch in addition to later settlement features at Standlake in Oxfordshire with scientific precision (Akerman 1855; Stone 1857). These early archaeologists were also observant of standing remains. Lukis and Dryden, for example, drew plans and elevations of the Rollright Stones and surrounding monuments in 1840 and 1842 (Fig. 8.8). On and near to the Berkshire Downs, excavations of barrows were undertaken by that most active of barrow diggers, Canon Greenwell (1890), and others in north Wiltshire were excavated by Thurnham (1860a; 1860b; 1871). Dean Merewether carried out excavations at Silbury Hill and of barrows there and at Avebury (Merewether 1851a; 1851b). Our earliest photographs of monuments were taken in the late 19th century; the Oxford photographer, Henry Taunt was particularly active (Fig. 8.9).

The light ploughsoils of the Surrey Greensand yielded highly-visible scatters of prehistoric flint-work which attracted collectors from the 19th century onwards. Indeed, Shelley's even earlier collection of microliths from Redhill station must be among the earliest of preserved collections (Bird 2006). The work of Hooper and Rankine on collections from this area later played an important part in the recognition of the Mesolithic period (Rankine 1953). These substantial assemblages, sometimes associated with hearths, were compiled into a database and studied by Roger Jacobi; they formed the basis for his chronology of the British Mesolithic (Jacobi 1978; 1981; Wymer 1977), which has been little altered since (Gardiner 2006; Reynier 2000). Important Mesolithic sites were brought to light by Lacaille in the Colne Valley and by Froom around Wawcott in the Middle Kennet, but the work of John

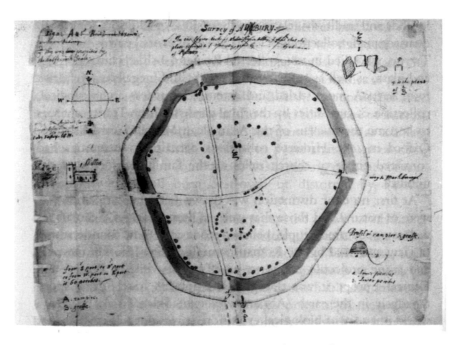

Fig. 8.4 Plan of Avebury from Aubrey's Monumenta Britannica *(1665-93)*

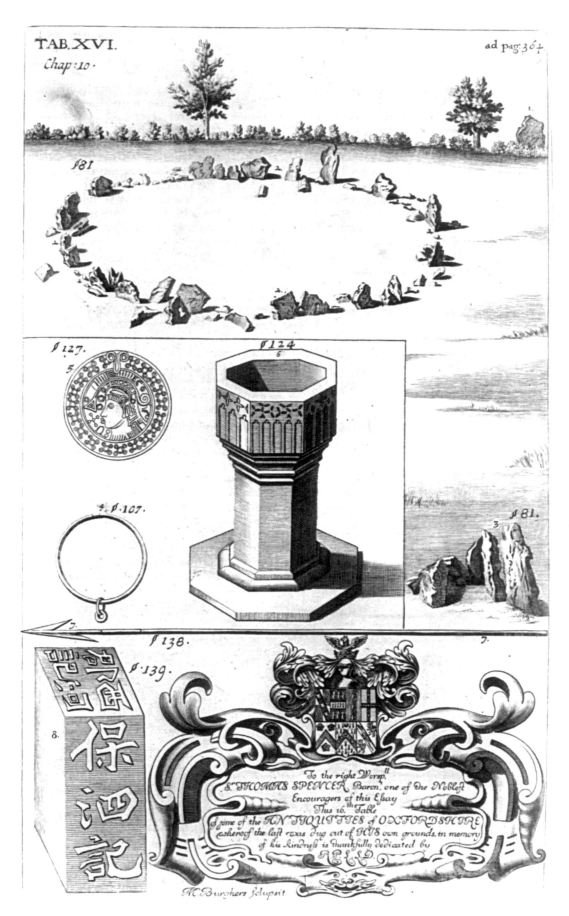

Fig. 8.5   The Rollright Stones and the Whispering Knights from Dr Plot's Natural history of Oxfordshire *(1677)*

Wymer at Thatcham has had a particular role in shaping our understanding of the Mesolithic period.

The Thames Valley has also had its share of important 20th-century archaeologists, working largely on Neolithic and early Bronze Age sites: E T Leeds, Major G W Allen, Professor W F Grimes, Derrick Riley and Humphrey Case, amongst many others. E Thurlow Leeds is a towering figure in the archaeology of the Upper Thames Valley, and his work as Assistant Keeper and then Keeper of the Ashmolean Museum (1908–1945) included the examination of sites of all periods. He was an indefatigable investigator of gravel quarries, co-opting the assistance of gravel diggers, who provided him with information on their discoveries. It was through his efforts that the substantial Beaker flat grave cemeteries at Cassington and

Fig. 8.6 Stukeley's drawing of the Whispering Knights from the east

Fig. 8.7 Portrait of George Rolleston (1884)

Fig. 8.8 Thurnham's (1860) view of the gallery of West Kennet from the chamber looking through the entrance

Fig. 8.9 *The entrance to Wayland's Smithy, photographed from the west by Henry Taunt*

Fig. 8.10 *A cropmark at Burcot Pit near Dorchester-on-Thames, photographed in section by Major G W Allen*

Foxley Farm, Eynsham were recognised and at least partially excavated, and elements of the Drayton cursus were examined in advance of extraction, but he was also a keen promoter of the then new technique of air photography which has played such a crucial role in the understanding of the Neolithic and Bronze Age of the Thames Valley. Major G W Allen started to fly in the early 1920s, and, using his own specially adapted camera, photographed many monuments, providing some of the best images of cropmarks that we possess (Figs 12.22 and 14.25; Allen 1984). His family owned gravel pits near Dorchester-on-Thames, and it was in the course of observing a quarry section at Allen's Pit that he was able to demonstrate how cropmarks formed (Fig. 8.10). His work was in many ways continued by Derrick Riley who trained pilots at the Stanton Harcourt airfield during the Second World War, and also by J K St Joseph as Director of the Cambridge University Air Photography Unit. These pioneering air photographers enabled the recognition of many important sites which had been ploughed flat and, in some cases, their excavation in advance of gravel extraction. The major monument complex at Dorchester-on-Thames was identified from the air and, although its destruction occurred in the days before professional archaeological groups and large area excavations, the photographs did enable key sites to be targeted and examined in advance of destruction. This work was largely undertaken by staff from the Ashmolean Museum and students from Oxford University under the direction of Richard Atkinson. Air photographs also enabled W F Grimes to identify elements of the Devil's Quoits henge and stone circle near Stanton Harcourt and investigate them during the course of rescue work to remove the one remaining standing stone in advance of runway construction during the Second World War. Grimes' work for the Ministry of Public Works during the war also entailed very detailed excavations and recording of chambered cairns in the Cotswolds (Grimes 1960), as well as sites with Neolithic pits in the Lower Colne Valley which, although much less spectacular, are in many ways just as important because they were so rare (ibid.).

There are, perhaps, two distinctive features of the history of archaeological investigations in the region. Firstly, relatively few excavations have been entirely research based; even research excavations conducted from university departments were often carried out in advance of development, as, for example, in the case of Richard Atkinson's excavations at Dorchester-on-Thames (Atkinson *et al.* 1951), Humphrey Case's work at North Stoke and Cassington Mill (Case and Whittle 1982) and Richard Bradley's work at the Radley oval barrow (Bradley 1992). Even the meticulous excavations by Don Benson at the Ascott-under-Wychwood long mound in the 1960s were prompted by imminent roadworks, even if these never went ahead (Benson

and Whittle 2007). In Berkshire, most work on early sites has been concentrated in the middle stretches of the river Kennet, focusing on a few large sites such as Thatcham and Wawcott (Wymer 1962; Lobb and Rose 1996), as this is where the pressure for gravel and other development was originally most intense. Research projects have followed because of the known quality of the resource. In Buckinghamshire, most work has been conducted in the south of the county, on the outskirts of London, especially in relation to gravel extraction in the lower Colne Valley, for example at the well-known Mesolithic sites at Iver (Lacaille 1963). Further south in the Colne Valley, the early work in the Heathrow area by Grimes should be mentioned (Grimes 1960). However, there have been research excavations, such as those at Wayland's Smithy, White Horse Hill and the Lambourn barrows (Whittle 1991; Miles *et al.* 2003; Case 1956a; Wymer 1965-6). Furthermore, because of the scale of gravel workings, even in the earlier 20th century there has perhaps been more of a focus on landscape archaeology than on site-specific work.

In the last 50 years, and particularly since the introduction of PPG 16 in 1990, the vast majority of archaeological endeavour in the region has been undertaken in advance of development. Once again, most of this work has been related to gravel extraction or to the development of urban centres such as Oxford and Reading. For this reason, we know much more about our river valleys than we do about the surrounding uplands and valley slopes, even though upstanding monuments only survive in these higher topographies. Nevertheless, the exposure of large areas in advance of quarrying has provided significant and unexpected discoveries ranging from Neolithic buildings to early Bronze Age cremation burials; it has enabled us to appreciate the wider contexts of settlement sites and has challenged our preconceptions of the nature of the early occupation of the Thames Valley. It is not an exaggeration to say that it has revolutionised the way that we think about these early periods.

THE NATURE OF THE EVIDENCE

Preservational environments

The topography of the gravel terraces and their suitability for agriculture means that ploughing has usually destroyed all traces of ancient soils and occupation spreads and has flattened earthwork monuments. However, colluvial sediments derived from past cultivation have accumulated on terrace edges in a few localities, and sequences of alluvial sediments occur on the floodplain, sealing non-alluvial palaeosols and interstratified archaeological deposits. Silted-up palaeochannels also occur on the floodplain.

Carbonised plant remains are usually present on settlement sites, and the soils are often well-suited to flotation processes for their recovery. Bone preservation in the Upper Thames Valley is often satisfactory, even if the soil itself is not calcareous, because the incorporation of limestone gravel into archaeological contexts buffers rainwater leaching, although bones are often lost from shallow soil-filled deposits of Bronze Age and earlier date. Under the more acidic conditions on the terraces of the Middle Thames bones survive less well. Shells of land and freshwater molluscs do not survive on gravel terrace sites in the Thames Valley except where there are locally calcareous conditions. However, the waters of the river Thames are calcareous and palaeochannel sediments usually are as well, and both contain abundant shells. Overbank alluvium is sometimes decalcified but where this has not occurred, shells survive within it. Pollen is not preserved in non-waterlogged sediments on the gravels of the Upper Thames but some non-waterlogged sites on the terraces of the Middle Thames have deposits which are sufficiently acidic for the preservation of pollen. The results must, however, be treated with caution because conditions are rarely sufficiently acidic for earthworm activity to be entirely absent.

While river gravels are well-known for the occurrence of organic remains preserved by waterlogging at the bottom of deep archaeological features, such deposits are extremely rare in the Upper and Middle Thames Valley prior to the middle Bronze Age. Thereafter, changes to the character of settlements and rises in the water-table resulted in waterlogging in archaeological features becoming more common. However, palaeochannels with waterlogged sediments containing pollen, macroscopic plant remains including seeds, leaves, twigs and wood, and insect remains are frequently present on the floodplain, and many channels appear to have experienced sedimentation from the Neolithic onwards. The various categories of biological remains that can be found in non-waterlogged deposits are also preserved in the waterlogged sediment although the decay of organic material sometimes causes local acidification which results in the loss of shells.

A wide range of evidence is thus available from the Thames gravels and floodplain for the past environment. While this region has neither the degree of organic survival of a wetland landscape with developing peat surfaces, nor the extent of preservation of mollusc shells and palaeosols to be found in some Chalk landscapes, the many lines of evidence give a more balanced picture than is available from some other regions.

The state of preservation of archaeological remains

A few archaeological features in the Thames Valley dating from the early Neolithic period onwards (from *c* 4000 cal BC) survive as upstanding remains. Of these, the earliest are the long cairns and other stone tombs of the Cotswolds (Figs 12.1 and 12.3),

and funerary monuments remain the types of sites most commonly visible throughout the Neolithic and early Bronze Age, although their size and shape varied through time and space. Inevitably, such monuments have survived in those parts of the landscape that have seen relatively little ploughing and development: the limestone of the Cotswolds, and the Chalk of the Berkshire Downs and Chilterns. Very rarely, Bronze Age round barrows are visible on the floodplain of the Thames as slight rises in the ground surface, for example on Port Meadow, Oxford where a combination of alluvial cover and historic use as common pasture has ensured the survival of some traces of round barrow mounds (Atkinson 1942; Lambrick and McDonald 1985). Inhumation or cremation burials that were not apparently marked in any way are found in the Thames Valley, usually by chance during the course of development, as they are hard to detect by non-intrusive means. Large-scale work over the last 20 years has shown that they are more common than had been thought.

Large ceremonial monuments began to be constructed at around *c* 3600 cal BC, and the causewayed enclosures of Windmill Hill and Knap Hill are the earliest of these which are visible above ground (Fig. 12.24). Such sites have mainly survived at the headwaters of the Kennet, where the monument complex around Avebury developed, and the large henge and its stone circles, other upright stones and Silbury Hill can still be seen today (Fig. 8.11). These, with the Kings Men stone circle at Rollright on the Cotswolds, are exceptional survivals in our area. Other ceremonial monuments lie in the river valleys and have been flattened by agriculture and, in many cases, damaged by gravel extraction or urban development.

The state of preservation of settlement features is very variable, but none are visible above ground. Activity areas, middens, hearths and (very rarely) floor surfaces are occasionally preserved but such features are only found where they lie protected beneath later structures such as barrow mounds or natural deposits such as alluvium or hillwash (colluvium). Features cut into the ground such as pits and postholes, are more common, though they are usually truncated by ploughing. The ground plans of wooden structures can sometimes be discerned amongst posthole groups. Most evidence of Mesolithic, Neolithic and early Bronze Age settlement has come from artefacts from habitation sites which are sufficiently durable to have survived on the surface of ploughed fields.

Objects of flint, stone and bone are found from all these periods, flint being particularly important because it was widely used, is susceptible to dating because tool types and methods of manufacture changed through time, and because it survives so well, whether in ploughsoils or other disturbed contexts. As already discussed, the survival of bone depends on its burial environment which varies throughout the valley; in general, it survives reason-

Fig. 8.11   Avebury and Silbury Hill, photographed by H A Wingham

ably well. Pottery was made from the early Neolithic period, and forms and styles of decoration changed over the course of time. It is reasonably robust, being found in most types of contexts, but was not sufficiently well fired to enable it to survive many ploughing events. Gold, copper and bronze appear at the transition from the late Neolithic to the early Bronze Age (*c* 2500 cal BC) and objects made from these metals are found in most topographies, from graves cut into chalk to objects dredged from the river itself. They are very datable, but rare. Objects of wood, bark and leather would probably have been in common day-to-day use, and all have all been found in the valley, but in very small numbers as the waterlogged and anaerobic environments needed to preserve organic artefacts are very unusual until the middle Bronze Age (see above).

Investigating Mesolithic, Neolithic and early Bronze Age remains

As we have already seen, upstanding stone and earthwork monuments have proved to be a focus for investigation from at least the 17th century, and the drawings of antiquaries have been of great importance for the understanding of sites which have since been damaged. Detailed survey of earthworks and other sites has been undertaken on most of the monuments in the area, and even at well-known sites it is possible to make unexpected

discoveries. A detailed survey of the Rollright Stones, for example, showed that the stones stood on a bank, 0.1-0.2 m tall, through which there was a wide entrance to the south-east.

Traditionally, fieldwalking has provided much of our information about Mesolithic to early Bronze Age activity (Fig. 8.12). This method can cover substantial areas relatively quickly and as long as issues such as the subsequent burial of earlier deposits are taken into account, can provide useful

Fig. 8.12   Fieldwalking at Yarnton

162

data about the relative intensity of activity across the landscape at particular periods of time (cf Holgate 1988a). Fieldwalking has been especially important for the recovery of early habitation sites, for these were usually insubstantial and easily damaged by later activity. All that remains of most Mesolithic sites lies within the ploughzone. Nevertheless, where sites are identified and the surviving finds retrieved by sieving, a considerable amount can be said about the range of tasks that might have taken place and the dating of these activities, as was possible, for example, at Tubney Wood (Bradley and Hey 1993) and Windmill Hill, Nettlebed (Boismier and Mepham 1995). A study of a number of major infrastructure projects in south-east England showed that, with the exception of widespread stripping of sites, fieldwalking was the most effective technique for detecting the existence of Neolithic and Bronze Age settlement (Hey and Lacey 2001, 60).

As we have already seen, air photography has been of immense importance for the recovery and understanding of Neolithic and Bronze Age remains, particularly of funerary and ceremonial monuments. Although the Thames Valley was at the heart of the development of this technique, and a considerable amount of flying was done, new sites continue to be detected from the air, as fields are photographed in different conditions. The English Heritage National Mapping Programme (NMP) reviewed all air survey data in the Thames Valley in 1992 as one of its pilot areas, and 45% of the sites they found had no previous archive record (http://www.english-heritage.org.uk/server/show/nav.8662). New discoveries have been made since that time, including a causewayed enclosure near Banbury (Featherstone and Bewley 2000, plate 4) and numerous ring ditches throughout the valley (Fig. 8.13). The NMP has been extended to cover the Avebury World Heritage Site, the Lambourn Downs and the North Gloucestershire Cotswolds among other areas, as can be seen on the English Heritage website; even Google Earth has played its part (Fig. 8.14). Standard air photography has recently been joined by LiDAR survey. LiDAR (Light Detection and Ranging) is a technique similar to radar, which, however, uses lasers rather than radio waves. By taking very large numbers of readings of the reflection of lasers off the ground surface the technique can reveal extremely subtle variations in topography. This has shown that earthworks sometimes do survive where nothing is visible to the eye, as long as ploughing has not been too severe. It is proving particularly effective on the Berkshire Downs (P Levick, pers. comm.; Fig. 8.15).

Fig. 8.13   Aerial photograph of the causewayed enclosure in the parish of Aston Cote, Shifford and Chimney, Oxfordshire

Fig. 8.14   A ring ditch and other cropmarks in Minchin Recreation Ground, Dorchester-on-Thames, shown in an image from Google Earth

Geophysical survey – mainly magnetometry in the case of Neolithic and Bronze Age sites – has been used increasingly, both to ascertain whether sites are present in advance of development and to provide information on sites where intrusive work is not possible or desired. Many of the geologies in the study area are suitable for such survey; chalk, limestone and the limestone gravel terraces can provide clear and detailed results (Fig. 8.16). Other geologies such as clay are less responsive, though results can be obtained. Deeply-buried sites like those on the floodplain often lie below the limits of detection. Success depends not only upon appropriate geologies and site depth, but also on the type of site. Ceremonial and funerary monuments, often with substantial subsurface features and soils enhanced by burning, are much easier to find than evidence of settlements with pits and postholes where individual features are small and may contain little magnetically-enhanced material. Ground penetrating radar has been used at, for example, the West Kennet Avenue at Avebury to

locate buried sarsen stones (Shell and Pierce 1998-99), but has not otherwise been applied widely in the area.

Dredging of the Thames, and construction on its banks, has also been been a significant source of Neolithic and early Bronze Age finds (Adkins and Jackson 1978; Lawrence 1929; Ehrenberg 1980; York 2002). The collection of material by these means is biased in several ways, as a result of the locations and manner in which dredging has taken place, variations in the incentives to collect material, such as paying dredgermen for certain items, and in the recording of the material which was found. The distribution and kinds of finds may, therefore, be a very inaccurate reflection of what originally found its way into the river. Archaeological interest in this material has also varied. Bradley and Gordon have noted, for example, that finds of human skulls from the river, although they initially attracted much attention, received increasingly less attention in the archaeological literature (Bradley and Gordon 1988). One of the reasons for this is no doubt the

Fig. 8.15 LiDAR image of Green Down and Stancombe Farm, showing probably early Bronze Age round barrows and Roman field systems.

Fig. 8.16 Magnetometer survey of the barrow cemetery at Barrow Hills, Radley

difficulty of interpreting material from the river, and in particular of determining whether it consists of material which was deliberately deposited there, perhaps as parts of rituals, or consists of material which has accidentally fallen or eroded into the river (Bradley 1990). Nonetheless, the river has been the source of an intriguing range of material. As well as the skulls, some of which are Neolithic, there are finds of flint and stone axes, daggers and maceheads (Adkins and Jackson 1978), antler maceheads (Loveday *et al.* 2007), pots, and bronze daggers, axes and spearheads (York 2002; Ehrenberg 1977; 1980).

Gravel extraction has also played an important role in shaping our knowledge of the archaeology of the region (Brown 2009; Fulford and Nichols 1992). Whilst that contribution was not, in the past, always positive, the extent of quarrying was an important spur encouraging excavation, as, for example, in the case of the Beaker cemeteries at Eynsham and Cassington (Leeds 1938), Beaker pits at Sutton Courtenay (Leeds 1934a) and the monument complex at Dorchester-on-Thames (Atkinson *et al.* 1951), and ultimately in the development of rescue archaeology. The extensive areas which have more recently been excavated as a result of gravel extraction, near Somerford Keynes, Fairford, Lechlade, Stanton Harcourt and Yarnton in the Upper Thames, as well as at the Eton Rowing Course (where gravel extraction was only a secondary concern; Fig. 8.17) and along the river Colne in the Middle Thames,

have provided completely new pictures of the nature of Neolithic settlement, which complement that of the more obvious monuments that first attracted the interest of antiquaries. The sparse scatters of pits and postholes, which the extensive stripping of quarries now shows are characteristic of much Neolithic and early Bronze Age occupation, are much less conspicuous as cropmarks and in the context of archaeological evaluations (which usually involve narrow test trenches) than the remains of later periods. Such extensive stripping has led to the discovery of structures, such as the early Neolithic houses at Yarnton and Horton, and middens at the Eton Rowing Course, which previously were unknown within the Thames Valley.

Some of the most significant advances in our understanding of the Mesolithic, Neolithic and early Bronze Age have come from the application of new scientific techniques. Studies using such techniques often analyse samples from a wide range of sites, but material from the Thames Valley has played an important role in some of them. For example, analysis of stable isotopes from prehistoric human skeletal remains has been used to examine diet. The stable carbon isotopes (^{12}C and ^{13}C) from Neolithic skeletal remains from a range of sites in the Thames Valley including Ascott-under-Wychwood, Hazleton North, Barrow Hills, Radley, Dorchester-on-Thames, Millbarrow, West Kennet, Lambourn and Windmill Hill, were used in a recent important study. This indicated that the transition

Fig. 8.17   Open-area excavation of a ring ditch and other features at Eton Rowing Course

from the Mesolithic to the Neolithic was characterised by a marked and quite rapid change in diet, rather than by a gradual transition, in which marine foods were abandoned in favour of a terrestrial diet, consisting probably of the new domesticated species which were introduced at the beginning of the Neolithic (Richards *et al.* 2003). Such analyses can provide insights which the other sources of evidence for diet in the Neolithic, consisting largely of plant and animal remains, leave uncertain. Given the uncertainties surrounding the circumstances which have led to the deposition and preservation of plant and animal remains, it is difficult to use this evidence to evaluate the relative contribution which plants and animals may have made to the Neolithic diet. Analysis of stable carbon and nitrogen isotopes from Hazleton North, however, suggest that the diet of the individuals there contained a very high proportion of meat or animal products (75% by weight of protein; Hedges *et al.* 2008).

Further evidence for diet in the Neolithic has been provided by the analysis of lipids which have been absorbed into the fabric of pots. Again, such analyses often involve samples from a wide range of sites, but Neolithic sherds from Yarnton, Abingdon causewayed enclosure, Windmill Hill, Eton Rowing Course and Runnymede Bridge were used in studies which provided evidence for the use of milk products, and probably butter fat in particular (Copley *et al.* 2005a; 2005b), from the beginning of the Neolithic, and of the cooking of pork, especially in Grooved Ware vessels (Mukherjee *et al.* 2007). Whilst animal fats predominate in the analysed sherds, plant fats have also been detected in a small number of sherds, including some from Yarnton and Windmill Hill, although they are often associated with animal fats.

Beeswax, which may have been used to seal the fabric of the pots or derive from the use of honey, has also been identified in pots from the Eton Rowing Course and Runnymede (Copley *et al.* 2005a; 2005b).

The analysis of DNA has also begun to shed light on the Neolithic. Most studies of the genetic evidence for the role of migration or acculturation in the spread of the Neolithic across Europe and into Britain have been based on samples from the present population (eg Balaresque *et al.* 2010), and very little prehistoric human DNA (eg Haak *et al.* 2005), none of which is from the Thames Valley, has so far been analysed. Possible aurochs bones from Windmill Hill were, however, used in a study of the mitochondrial DNA of prehistoric aurochs (*Bos primigenius*) and domesticated cattle (*Bos taurus*) which suggests that the domestic cattle derive from the Near East and remained genetically quite distinct in Europe and Britain from the native aurochs (Edwards *et al.* 2007). In contrast to results obtained for pigs (Larson *et al.* 2007), which do indicate significant interbreeding within Europe, there was no indication that the aurochs was

domesticated within Europe nor that it had interbred to any significant extent with domestic cattle. (It is perhaps worth adding that the ancestors of domestic sheep were not present in Europe and there is, therefore, no doubt that they were introduced from the Near East (Tresset and Vigne 2007).)

The analysis of strontium isotopes is another technique which, although it has not yet been used in the Thames Valley, has provided significant evidence for the movement of individuals elsewhere in England, in, for example, the Beaker period (eg Evans *et al.* 2006) and in Europe in the Neolithic (eg Nehlich *et al.* 2009).

CHRONOLOGY AND DEFINITIONS: AN OVERVIEW

The role of material culture

Material culture studies remain central to an understanding of the period covered in this volume, for understanding the date and purpose of sites and the character of the activities that took place upon them. Traditional chronologies have been based on flint and, to a greater extent, pottery, and these remain the main tools for dating sites, especially given the paucity of organic material (Fig. 8.18).

Early Mesolithic flint assemblages are characterised by simple microlith forms with a range of other tools, including end scrapers, microdenticulates, burins, awls and bifacially-flaked axeheads or adzes (Barton and Roberts 2004, 342). Large assemblages can be recognised as belonging to three or four different, chronological styles, described below in Chapter 10. Small, geometric and more varied microlith forms are the diagnostic elements of late Mesolithic finds groups, and rod microliths are seen as indicative of very late dates (ibid.). Flint working techniques remain similar throughout, as do many tool types and, as a result, it can be difficult to distinguish between early and late Mesolithic assemblages. Indeed, methods of manufacture were sufficiently similar in the early Neolithic that, where diagnostic elements are absent, it can be difficult to discriminate between late Mesolithic and early Neolithic material.

The Neolithic or New Stone Age was originally defined by the presence of polished stone tools, and this distinction, with the absence of such tools in the Mesolithic, remains valid. The early Neolithic is also characterised by other new types of stone tools such as leaf-shaped arrowheads and knives. Early Neolithic assemblages are often blade-based and there was an emphasis on finer secondary working rather than careful core reduction. In terms of material culture, the Neolithic is, however, more readily defined in the Thames Valley, if not elsewhere, by the presence of pottery. The first pottery, known as Carinated Bowl pottery, in use from around 4000-3650 cal BC, consists of round-based bowls and cups with simple rims and shoulders which tend to be open with tall concave necks.

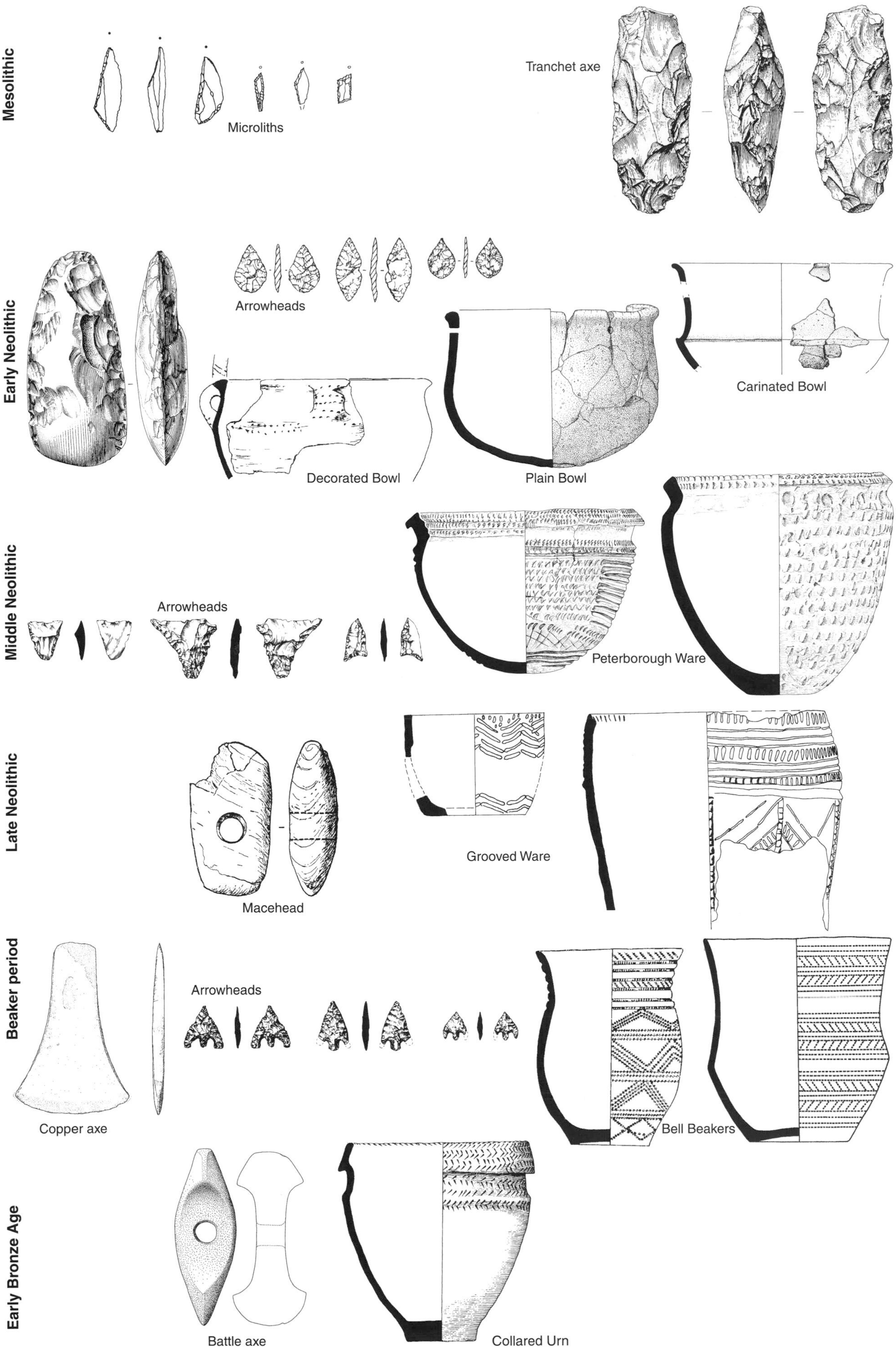

Mesolithic

Microliths

Tranchet axe

Early Neolithic

Arrowheads

Decorated Bowl

Plain Bowl

Carinated Bowl

Middle Neolithic

Arrowheads

Peterborough Ware

Late Neolithic

Macehead

Grooved Ware

Beaker period

Copper axe

Arrowheads

Bell Beakers

Early Bronze Age

Battle axe

Collared Urn

Slightly later vessels tend to have more upright necks and less angular shoulders and were sometimes decorated. The middle of the 4th millennium cal BC is marked by the appearance of Plain and Decorated Bowl pottery, including highly decorated vessels associated with causewayed enclosures (Barclay 2002) such as those which have been used to define Abingdon Ware.

In ceramic terms, the middle Neolithic is characterised by Peterborough Ware. This style, although not as well understood as other Neolithic pottery styles, may first appear from around the 36th century cal BC, but only became more common between *c* 3300 cal BC and *c* 2900 cal BC (Gibson and Kinnes 1997; Barclay 2007). The earliest substyle, Ebbsfleet Ware, is defined by round-bodied bowls and jars which are often only minimally decorated, but by about 3300 cal BC this style had developed into a range of cups, bowls and jars, known as Mortlake Ware and Fengate Ware, which can be highly decorated.

The flint assemblages of the Middle Neolithic are characterised by chisel, oblique and *petit tranchet* arrowheads, discoidal and edge-polished knives and maceheads. During the mid to late Neolithic there was a shift in flint production strategies from the use of soft hammers (such as antler) to those made of stone and other hard materials. Extensive, invasive retouching also became a feature on flint tools, particularly from the early Bronze Age. This does not mean that flintwork became crude. Barbed and tanged arrowheads are characteristic of Bronze Age lithics, along with occasional fine forms with serrated edges which seem to have been made for display purposes. A range of neatly retouched knives, scrapers including 'thumbnail' types, and fabricators were also used at this time.

The late Neolithic, from around 2900 cal BC, is characterised by Grooved Ware pottery. The sometimes large, flat-bottomed pots which belong to this period fall into three substyles: Woodlands and Clacton with open tub-shaped forms which are similar within this region, and Durrington Walls which is represented by plain, cordoned jars or cordoned jars with decorated panels (Wainwright and Longworth 1971, 235-68; Barclay 1999b).

From the 25th century cal BC, the often highly decorated Beaker pottery appears and becomes more common towards the end of the 3rd millennium. Although most Beakers have been found in funerary contexts, similar fine vessels are also found, with coarser, often rusticated pots, in pits and on domestic sites. Beaker pottery was replaced by Food Vessels and Collared Urns in the period *c* 1850-1660 cal BC.

The first metalwork, consisting of copper and gold objects, appeared associated with Beaker pottery. Tools made of relatively pure copper, which is quite soft, were however, quite quickly replaced by tougher artefacts made of bronze, an alloy made of copper mixed with tin (Needham 1996; 1999a). Like the pottery of the early Bronze Age, most metal artefacts have been recovered from funerary contexts, although some finds have been dredged from the river (Fig. 8.19).

The impact of radiocarbon dating on our understanding of the period

Radiocarbon dating has overturned some of the orthodoxies of the chronology of the period and has also extended its range. It has been very important for setting artefact sequences into a more precise chronological framework. Its application to samples of Mesolithic age is relatively recent and many more dates are needed in order to clarify the chronological framework of the period. Results for the Neolithic and early Bronze Age, however, are more numerous and have begun to transform our understanding of these periods, especially the early Neolithic.

The precision of radiocarbon dates varies from period to period depending upon the shape of the calibration curve (Fig. 8.20). Thus, whilst the curve is quite steep over much of the early Neolithic, and thus produces quite precise calibrated results, in the late Neolithic, there are several wiggles affecting the period from *c* 2800-2400 cal BC for example. This means that dates for this period often have wide calibrated ranges.

For some sites it has been possible to use Bayesian modelling to reduce the date ranges for samples from stratigraphic sequences (Buck *et al.* 1991; Buck *et al.* 1996; Bayliss and Bronk Ramsey 2004), although this technique has only recently been applied to archaeological material and has only been undertaken on a few sites within our study area. Important examples are a number of chambered cairns (Whittle, Barclay, Bayliss *et al.* 2007) and a current project to date causewayed enclosures (Whittle *et al.* forthcoming).

A brief overview

A number of dates exist for the Mesolithic period, in particular for Thatcham. These show that activity associated with a Mesolithic material culture started in the area within perhaps 500 years of the start of the Holocene (dates on bulked charcoal gave results of 10,900-9,700 cal BC; Q-659: 10,365±170 BP; and 9700-8750 cal BC; OxA-732: 9760±120; Wymer 1962; see Chapter 10 below). Thatcham and Star Carr in the Vale of Pickering are the earliest Mesolithic sites so far recorded in Britain (ibid.; Mellars and Dark 1998; Dark 2000). It has been suggested that there may have been either an overlap between Final Upper Palaeolithic culture and early Mesolithic activity at Thatcham and the nearby Chamberhouse Farm site, or continuity of habitation at these sites (Wessex Archaeology 2005; cf Chisham 2006).

Fig. 8.18 (facing page)   The evolution of material culture from the Mesolithic to the early Bronze Age

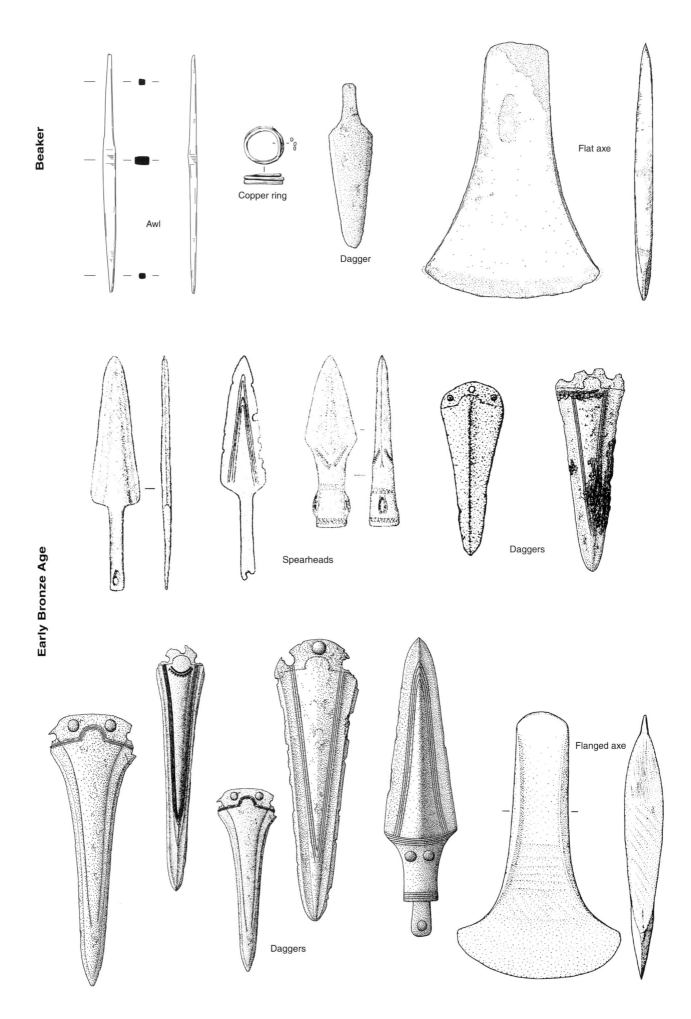

Beaker

Awl

Copper ring

Dagger

Flat axe

Early Bronze Age

Spearheads

Daggers

Daggers

Flanged axe

170

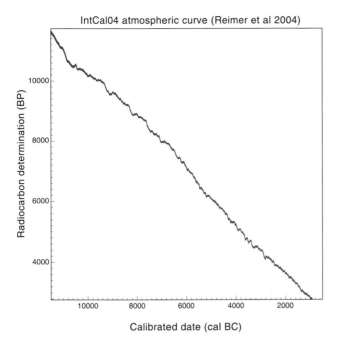

Fig. 8.20 The radiocarbon calibration curve IntCal04, from c *11,000 cal BC to* c *1000 cal BC*

Mesolithic dates are scarce but span the period from then until the 5th millennium. Late dates come from beneath the Ascott-under-Wychwood long mound (Bayliss, Bronk Ramsay, Galer *et al.* 2007), and the very late Mesolithic date of 4360-3780 cal BC (BM-449: 5260±130 BP; Froom 1972) from a hearth at Wawcott (Lobb and Rose 1996).

Our earliest Neolithic dates come from the midden deposits beneath the chambered cairn at Ascott-under-Wychwood (*c* 3900 cal BC), and other sites with Carinated Bowl pottery could date from this time or very slightly later. Dates from the earliest phase of the Neolithic (3800-3600 cal BC) also come from the main phase of use of Ascott-under-Wychwood, Yarnton, Wayland's Smithy and Lambourn long barrow (Benson and Whittle 2007; Bayliss and Hey in prep.; Whittle, Bayliss, and Wysocki 2007; Schulting 2000).

The Abingdon causewayed enclosure was in use in either the mid 3600s or the mid 3500s cal BC (Whittle *et al.* forthcoming) and is associated with its eponymous Decorated Bowl pottery and, as far as it is possible to judge from the limited number of results available, the causewayed enclosures at Staines and Goring are contemporary. Windmill Hill, in the Upper Kennet Valley, was constructed at the same time, although seems to have been in use for a much longer period, albeit perhaps not continuously, up to the end of the 3rd millennium (ibid.). It seems likely that the Drayton Cursus was

constructed at a slightly later date, but perhaps sufficiently near in time for an older person present at the construction of the cursus to have participated in events at the Abingdon cause-wayed enclosure when young. Other cursus monuments are not well dated, but the evidence is consistent with their use in the second half of the 4th millennium cal BC (Barclay *et al.* 2003). A number of burials and funerary monuments belong to this period, including Whiteleaf, Barrow Hills, Dorchester-on-Thames long enclosure Site 1, Mount Farm and Wayland's Smithy (Hey *et al.* 2007; Barclay and Halpin 1999; Whittle *et al.* 1992; Lambrick in prep.; Whittle 1991; Whittle, Bayliss and Wysocki 2007).

Pit deposits are hard to date with precision and the mid to late Neolithic periods tend to produce radiocarbon results with wide error terms. A group of pits at South Stoke produced eight radiocarbon determinations within the range of 3630-3350 cal BC (Timby *et al.* 2005, table 4). A number of pits usually associated with Peterborough Ware pottery have produced dates in the range of *c* 3300-2900 cal BC (eg Yarnton, Maidenhead, Windsor and Eton Flood Alleviation Scheme and Cippenham, Slough). Pits with Grooved Ware pottery date to the period *c* 2900-2400 cal BC (Yarnton, Drayton, Barrow Hills, Radley). Other features with late Neolithic radio-carbon dates include a house at Yarnton, flat graves at Barrow Hills, a penannular enclosure and a post circle (Site 3) at Dorchester-on-Thames, tree-throw holes at Drayton, a henge at Gravelly Guy, the Devil's Quoits henge ditch and stone circle and numerous monuments in the Upper Kennet Valley (Bayliss and Hey in prep.; Barclay and Halpin 1999; Whittle *et al.* 1992; Lambrick and Allen 2004; Barclay, Gray and Lambrick 1995; Whittle *et al.* 1999; Pollard and Reynolds 2002).

The large number of Beaker burials, including some impressive examples, have yielded a good crop of radiocarbon dates for the earliest Bronze Age (Barrow Hills, Gravelly Guy, Yarnton) which provide date ranges between 2500 and 1900 cal BC. Non-funerary deposits have been much less commonly dated (and, indeed, excavated) though they do exist (for example pits at Yarnton and Gravelly Guy).

Early Bronze Age dates have also usually been obtained on burials and funerary monuments, such as Barrow Hills, Radley, the Devil's Quoits complex, Yarnton and Dorchester-on-Thames Site 4. The very few dates from domestic contexts include those from the houses, waterholes, pits and burnt stone deposits at Yarnton. Biconical Urn deposits date from around 1900 cal BC.

Fig. 8.19 (facing page) The development of metalwork in the Beaker period and early Bronze Age

Chapter 9 – The Thames and its changing environment in our era

by Mark Robinson

FLOODPLAIN CREATION AT THE END OF THE DEVENSIAN

Both the Upper and Middle Thames are flanked by extensive gravel terraces, in places more than 3 km wide (Fig. 9.1). The last glacial period provided the prerequisites of high discharge from melting winter snow and surface instability of rock upstream for the erosive process of downcutting, removing parts of earlier gravel terraces, and for the formation of a new terrace from a new and lower floodplain level. In the case of the Upper Thames, oolitic limestone from the Cotswolds formed the Northmoor gravel terrace over Oxford (and Gault) Clay in the Devensian (Bridgland 1994, 86). In the Middle Thames Valley, the Devensian Shepperton Terrace mainly comprises flint from the Chalk of the Chilterns and Downs, with lesser quantities of material coming from some of the Tertiary beds (Bridgland 1994, 90-1). These youngest terraces are sometimes called the floodplain terrace, although all terraces represent former floodplains (see above,

Chapters 2-6). In both the Upper and Middle Thames, part of the lowest terrace was reworked and lowered during the very Late Glacial (towards the end of Late Devensian Zone III which spans *c* 13,000-11,500 cal BP/11,000-9,500 cal BC) when channel flow was becoming established. This area now tends to have a covering of fine alluvial overbank sediments and the term floodplain, as it is used today, is restricted to this area.

The channels of the Thames seem to have been incised to their greatest extent at the start of the Holocene. Thereafter, the regime has been one of channel silting and simplification from multiple to single channel systems (Robinson 1992a, 47-8). There has been little Holocene channel migration. In the Upper Thames, pedological processes predominated over alluvial accretion on the floodplain during the Early and Middle Holocene (Robinson and Lambrick 1984); any flooding was of limited extent. The present covering of up to 2 m of alluvial clay is the result of sedimentation over the past 2,000 years,

Fig. 9.1   Aerial photograph of excavations in Cassington Quarry showing the wide gravel terraces of the river Thames

and postdates the period covered by this volume. In contrast, at least some parts of the floodplain of the Middle Thames began to experience fine overbank alluvial sedimentation in the Early Holocene (Parker and Robinson 2003), and there is a zone of Holocene organic sediments and clays, the Staines Alluvial Deposits, which extends up the Middle Thames Valley as far as Pangbourne (Gibbard 1985). These deposits, which range from Mesolithic to Bronze Age in date, represent palaeochannel fills.

The Upper and Middle Thames have entirely lowland catchments and arable agriculture now extends to the watersheds. The modern soils of the Upper Thames Basin are mostly calcareous or circumneutral and only in a few areas of acid soils and plateau gravels are there serious problems of soil fertility. The limestone of the Cotswolds gives soils that are easily worked although they are often shallow and brashy, sometimes with problems of steep slopes. The Oxford Clay is relatively intractable and suffers from impeded drainage but cultivation is possible and it is mostly ploughed. The light, free draining soils of the gravel terraces were originally stone-free and developed into argillic brown earths which shows that they had experienced a somewhat acidic phase. Limestone gravel has been incorporated into them by cultivation, and with this input they have become well suited to agriculture. Such effects may have been limited until at least the middle Bronze Age when arable became more extensive. The floodplain has thin soils over gravel and is regularly inundated today, though this would not have been the case during the periods examined in this volume (see below).

The soils of the Middle Thames Basin tend to be more acidic and less fertile than those of the Upper Thames Basin. Although the Chalk gives rise to light calcareous soils, much of the dip slope of the Chilterns is covered with acidic clay-with-flints where woodland is quite extensive. The gravel terraces have light, free-draining soils which, because the gravel is flint, are usually acidic. London Clay also gives soils more acidic than those of the Oxford Clay, though the Middle Thames floodplain has similar alluvial clay soils to the Upper Thames. In the Lower Kennet Valley there are extensive peat-filled backswamps beneath a thin layer of alluvial clay. Light acidic soils are present on some of the other Tertiary and also Cretaceous (Greensand) deposits in the region.

The modern river Thames has been substantially channelised by dredging, embanking and the insertion of locks and weirs for navigation. It has also experienced much natural silting which has tended to simplify a complex system of linked multiple channels (an anastomosing system) to a single channel. However, along part of its length, for example at Oxford, a complex channel system survives. The river Thames has a gradient of less than 1 m per km and a nonflashy flow.

During the last glaciation (or Ice Age) sea levels were much lower than they are today, and much of the North Sea and the Channel would have been dry land (see Chapter 1, Fig. 1.5). At this time, the Thames was a tributary of the greater Rhine river and to the east of Thanet joined the main river and flowed south into the Channel. It was only in the 7th or 6th millennium cal BC that the connection between Britain and mainland Europe was breached by rising sea levels; the tidal reach of the Thames was, even in the Neolithic period, way below where it is today, perhaps at Erith (Sidell and Wilkinson 2004).

PALAEOHYDROLOGY

The Late Devensian to Holocene transition *c* 11,500 cal BP/9500 cal BC

The lowest and most recent terraces of the Thames, the Northmoor or Floodplain Terrace in the Upper Thames Valley and the Shepperton or Lower Floodplain Terrace in the Middle Thames Valley, were laid down in the Late Devensian (Fig. 1.9). The Thames was a braided system of many migrating channels depositing gravel on the inside of bends as the channels moved. This is reflected in a pattern of crossbedding when the gravels are viewed in section at right angles to the direction of flow. The transition from a braided system which was reworking and probably lowering part of the floodplain terraces to a system of multiple, broad, incised channels occurred towards the end of the Late Devensian but before full climatic amelioration.

In the Upper Thames Valley, a radiocarbon date of 11,150-10,650 cal BC (HAR-8356: 10,860±130 BP) was obtained on waterlogged twigs from a minor channel within the crossbedded gravels of the Lower Windrush at Mingies Ditch (Allen and Robinson 1993), while organic sediments at the base of a major incised channel of the Thames at Farmoor which remained open into the Holocene were dated to 11,200-9600 cal BC (BIRM-590: 10,600±250 BP; Lambrick and Robinson 1979, 141-2). As noted above (Chapter 7), both deposits produced fruits of *Betula nana* (dwarf birch), an arctic alpine shrub, and fragments of *Helophorus glacialis*, a beetle of snow meltwater pools which is now extinct in Britain. A temperate biological assemblage was found in a channel cutting the gravels at Mingies Ditch which was dated to 9150-8300 cal BC (HAR-8366: 9380±110 BP).

In the Middle Thames at Dorney, a pollen assemblage from fine sediments at the base of a palaeochannel which cut the Shepperton Gravel suggested an open Late Glacial environment (Parker and Robinson 2003). Further up the sequence, a radiocarbon date of 8330-8230 cal BC (CAMS-54440: 9070±40 BP) on a sample with pollen evidence for pine-hazel woodland showed that the channel spanned the Late Devensian to Holocene transition. A radiocarbon date of 8500-7650 cal BC (8960±130 BP) was given by wood from palaeochannel sediments above the Shepperton

Gravel at Meadlake Place, downstream from Staines (Branch and Green 2004, 9-11). This date, which was from towards the top of the sequence, indicated that this channel was already largely filled in by the early Holocene.

The early and mid Holocene hydrological sequences for the Upper and Middle Thames Valley diverge, the floodplain of the Upper Thames Valley becoming dry whereas the lower areas of the flood-plain of the Middle Thames Valley soon became waterlogged. The lowest areas of the floodplain of the Upper Thames Valley tend to have a clay covering above the gravel, perhaps the result of alluviation shortly after the transition to channel flow. The higher points of the floodplain have palaeosols above the gravel more similar to those on the Northmoor Terrace where it has no alluvial covering, being sandy loams, silty clay loams and silty clays. These soils often have a high silt and chlorite content suggesting a substantial loess content (Limbrey and Robinson 1988). There is no evidence of extensive flooding or alluviation of the floodplain in the early Holocene. In contrast, the floodplain of the Middle Thames Valley, or at least the lowest areas of floodplain, remained wet. Alluviation soon built up levees alongside the major palaeochannels at Dorney (Parker and Robinson 2003, 44).

The character of the floodplain of the Upper Thames Valley was clearly displayed by the excava-tions over an area of about 100 ha to the north of the Thames at Yarnton, between the A40 and the Summertown-Radley Gravel Terrace further to the north (Fig. 9.1). The removal of the covering layer of Holocene alluvial clays showed that what underlies the modern floodplain is an irregular eroded surface of the Northmoor Terrace. There are lower areas which had resulted from the migration of palaeochannels dissecting the floodplain and higher 'islands' between them, although they do not stand to the full height of the uneroded Northmoor Terrace. As the river regime changed to one of multiple broad incised channels, so minor channels began to cut down more deeply before they became isolated. One such channel at Yarnton was about 100 m wide, asymmetric and, on its deeper bank, eroding into a gravel island. The deepest point of the gravel bed of the palaeochannel was 2 m below the surface of the gravel island. Once channel migration ceased, a little inorganic sandy silt was deposited on the bed. An OSL date of 9450-6850 cal BC (at 95% confidence) was obtained on this sediment (Hey in prep.) placing it at the end of the Late Devensian or the start of the Holocene. There was no further sedimentation in this channel until the late Bronze Age.

The Mesolithic c 9600-4000 cal BC

There is little evidence for the Mesolithic part of the palaeohydrological sequence for the Upper Thames Valley, partly because conditions remained stable.

Very little channel migration occurred, so there are few palaeochannel sediments from this period. Little, if any, flooding was occurring on the flood-plain. Tree-throw holes showed that woodland had extended onto the lowest part of the palaeochannel bed at Yarnton (Robinson in prep.). A radiocarbon date of 4460-4250 cal BC (OxA-10713: 5535±50 BP) was obtained on decayed roots of *Alnus glutinosa* (alder) from one of them.

In the Middle Thames Valley, the Staines Alluvial Deposits accumulated. They comprise a strati-graphic unit of mixed organic alluvial sediments, sometimes with a component of inorganic alluvial clay. They extend from the Lower Thames Valley as far upstream as Pangbourne (Gibbard 1985). The unit overlies the Shepperton Terrace and much of the deposition can be dated to the early Mesolithic (Branch and Green 2004, 8-13). It appears to repre-sent both palaeochannel sedimentation and flood-plain alluviation. Much of the evidence for the Staines Alluvial Deposits has been derived from boreholes. However, it was possible to gain a better understanding of this unit from seeing it exposed in plan and section at Dorney (Parker and Robinson 2003, 44-7). The levees at the margins of palaeochan-nels prevented drainage of the floodplain and created large expanses of backswamp where fine-grained clays, marls and peats were deposited under low-energy conditions. Peat accumulated rapidly until its upper surface reached the level of the permanent water table. Thereafter, clay alluvia-tion continued on the floodplain without organic preservation. A radiocarbon date of 9220-8690 cal BC (OxA-9411: 9560±55 BP) was obtained on sedge seeds from the base of the peat behind a levee and it is possible that the majority of the sedimentation had occurred during the first 1,000 years of the Holocene. A tree-throw hole from towards the top of the alluvium gave a radiocarbon date of 5230-4940 cal BC (OxA-9412: 6130±45 BP). Little channel migration or sedimentation occurred at Dorney during the Mesolithic. However, at Runnymede there were episodes of channel incision and sedimentation particularly in the 7th millennium cal BC (Needham 2000a, 188-194). It is likely that the Staines Alluvial Deposits represent a zone within which limited Mesolithic channel migration occurred and where backswamps formed on the floodplain between the channels.

Similar zones of Mesolithic palaeochannels and peat-filled backswamps occur along the Lower Colne Valley (Gibbard 1985) and along the Lower Kennet Valley.

Some channel simplification occurred in the Middle Thames Valley. A minor parallel channel of the Thames found in both the Maidenhead, Windsor and Eton Flood Alleviation Scheme and at the Eton Rowing Course was active in the Late Devensian but in the early Holocene flow became sluggish and peat began to accumulate (Robinson in T G Allen *et al.* forthcoming). By the late Mesolithic, oak fen woodland entirely covered the palaeochannel at Marsh Lane East, being represented by preserved roots growing down into the peat.

The Neolithic *c* 4000-2500 cal BC

Channel developments in the Upper Thames Valley during the Neolithic were limited. Some silting occurred, for example a palaeochannel filled with Neolithic sediments was found at Buscot Lock (Robinson and Wilson 1987). Channel migration at Whitecross Farm, Cholsey, created a long narrow island (eyot) of sands and gravel in the Neolithic or earlier Bronze Age (Robinson 2006). However, there is no evidence for large scale channel movement and pedological processes predominated over alluvial accretion on the floodplain. The palaeosol sealed beneath the bank of the Drayton Cursus was a well-oxidised stony calcareous brown earth only 0.08 m thick above the Devensian gravels of the floodplain (Robinson 1992b, 201; Barclay *et al.* 2003, 164-6). A flint scatter suggested Neolithic activity extending well onto the bed of a dry palaeochannel at Yarnton (Hey in prep.).

There was evidence from Dorney for a change in river activity in the Middle Thames Valley from around 4000 cal BC onwards (Parker and Robinson 2003, 47). Whereas the channel pattern was very stable in the later Mesolithic, there were episodes of bank erosion and sedimentation which began at the start of the Neolithic and probably continued until the middle Bronze Age. These channel sediments comprised calcareous organic silts and sands, with abundant broken shell and tufa or carbonate encrustations. The high proportion of calcareous material suggests that much of the material being reworked was generated within the channel system rather than having been eroded into the river from the terrestrial landscape. One of the Neolithic episodes at Dorney resulted in the undermining of *Quercus* (oak) trees which had been growing along the bank, causing them to topple into the channel. Their trunks were rapidly covered with organic sediments and preserved. No large woody debris in the palaeochannel could be attributed to clearance activities, although it is likely that such material was entering the river system and causing obstructions to the flow. Some beaver-gnawed wood was, however, recorded. The erosion and sedimentation were confined within a relatively narrow zone of the floodplain, and these developments certainly must not be seen as having been part of a more general channel migration across the floodplain.

Similar processes were occurring at Runnymede, where there was Neolithic occupation extending out over palaeochannel sediments in the mid 4th millennium cal BC (Needham 2000a, 196-9). However, the Runnymede sequence provided evidence for a major high-energy flood event in which a substantial body of gravel was deposited over the Neolithic surface towards the end of the 4th millennium cal BC. It is possible that the same flood was responsible for the creation of the eyot at Whitecross Farm, Cholsey. The extent of flooding is, however, unknown, although the evidence from Runnymede, with Neolithic settlement extending over palaeochannel sediments, suggests there were periods of little flooding and, with the exception of extreme events, flooding was probably confined to the area of the Staines Alluvial Deposits. The insect evidence from Runnymede suggests that there was an abrupt transition from the aquatic habitats of the river to well-drained terrestrial habitats with only a narrow marginal reedswamp zone (Robinson 1991).

The early Bronze Age *c* 2500-1500 cal BC

Hydrological conditions in the early Bronze Age remained similar to those of the Neolithic. Evidence for a seasonally low water table on the floodplain of the Upper Thames Valley is given by sites with early Bronze Age pits or ditches which extend below the present permanent water table yet which have ungleyed fills, whereas later archaeological features on these sites of a similar depth have gleyed fills, perhaps with preserved organic remains at the bottom. For example, at Port Meadow, Oxford, the fills of Bronze Age ring ditches were found to be nongleyed but water-logged macroscopic plant remains were present in Iron Age enclosure ditches at the same depth (Robinson and Lambrick 1984). Nonalluvial palaeosols are present beneath Bronze Age barrows on the floodplain, as, for example, at Kings Weir (Bowler and Robinson 1980).

The earliest evidence that the water table was rising in the Upper Thames Valley during the Bronze Age came from a pair of middle Bronze Age ditches on a low area of the floodplain at Yarnton. The preservation of organic remains was very poor in the initial cuts of these ditches, but well-preserved remains were found in recuts (Robinson in prep.). Six radiocarbon dates were obtained from the bottoms of the recuts which ranged from 1620-1320 cal BC (OxA-6287: 3200±60 BP) to 1410-1120 cal BC (OxA-6617: 3045±40 BP). An adjacent palaeochannel bed, dry in the Neolithic, had become reactivated by the late Bronze Age. Waterlogging within a minor palaeochannel at Latton, near Cricklade, occurred slightly later, at the end of the 2nd millennium cal BC (Robinson 1999a, 497-500).

In the Middle Thames Valley at Runnymede Bridge, there were changes in river behaviour after 2000 cal BC (Needham 1992, 256-7). Channels became more confined, and there was widespread alluviation within the palaeochannel zone. At Dorney, a substantial timber bridge with a double row of oak piles was built across one of the palaeochannels in the 3rd quarter of the 2nd millennium cal BC. The absence of piles from the central part of the bridge suggested that episodes of peak flow were capable of carrying away obstructions, but there was no further evidence of channel erosion.

Aquatic conditions

Both the Upper and Middle Thames had the characteristics of an unmanaged, well-vegetated river with clean calcareous water in all its aspects, both rapids and almost still pools, throughout the Mesolithic, Neolithic and Bronze Age. Detailed studies of the Neolithic fauna and flora of the Thames were undertaken at Runnymede (Evans, Greig, E Robinson and M Robinson in Needham 1991). Similar results were obtained for the Thames at Runnymede in the late Bronze Age (ibid.) and also for the Upper Thames at Buscot Lock in the Neolithic (Robinson 1981, 308-13) and at Whitecross Farm, Cholsey, in the late Bronze Age (Cromarty *et al.* 2006, chap. 4). The mesotrophic nutrient levels were sufficient to enable the development of a rich aquatic flora, but there was no hint of eutrophication (an oversupply of nutrients leading to polluted conditions). The macroscopic plant and insect remains from Neolithic Runnymede suggested a submerged flora of *Ranunculus* S. *Batrachium* sp. (water crowfoot) and *Myriophyllum verticillatum* (whorled water-milfoil), a floating-leaved community in slowly moving water of *Potamogeton* spp. (pondweeds), *Nymphaea alba* (white waterlily) and *Nuphar lutea* (yellow waterlily), and a marginal reedswamp which included *Schoenoplectus lacustris* (true bulrush), *Phragmites australis* (common reed), *Sparganium* sp. (bur-reed) and *Sagittaria sagittifolia* (arrowhead). The most abundant water beetles from these sites were from the family Elmidae. They occur in clean flowing water, clinging to stones and aquatic plants. Most of those from the Neolithic and Bronze Age sediments, such as *Esolus parallelepipedus*, if they occur at all in the modern river, are restricted to weir outflows and fast-flowing tributary streams. One of them, *Stenelmis canaliculata*, now has a very restricted distribution in Britain and is extinct in the Thames. The aquatic molluscs from the Neolithic palaeochannel sediments at Runnymede include *Gyraulus acronicus* (Evans in Needham 1991, 267), a water snail which in Britain is restricted to the Thames drainage basin.

The transition from a braided river system to fewer more deeply incised channels towards the end of the Late Devensian was probably related to climatic factors. The channels of the Thames were probably eroded to their greatest size and were most mobile at the start of the Holocene when there were periods of high, short-lived discharges caused by seasonal snow melt (Robinson and Lambrick 1984). As the climate ameliorated and there was less seasonal variation in river flow, so there was no longer sufficient energy for channel migration. It is uncertain why the floodplain of the Upper Thames Valley became dry whereas backswamps developed on the floodplain of the Middle Thames Valley in the early Holocene. It is unlikely to have been related to sea level because at the start of the Holocene, sea level was lower than at present and

the Middle Thames was far from the tidal reach of the river. It is possible that most of the alluviation within the backswamps at Dorney occurred within the first 1000 years of the Holocene, before the spread of dense woodland throughout the catchment had fully stabilised the Pleistocene sediments. Perhaps there was less loess cover in the basin of the Upper Thames than in the Middle Thames Valley. The change in channel activity at Dorney from around 4000 cal BC, with episodes of erosion and sedimentation, implies higher-energy fluvial conditions (Parker and Robinson 2003, 37). It is uncertain whether this was related to Neolithic and Bronze Age clearance activities.

VEGETATIONAL SUCCESSION

The early Mesolithic (Flandrian Zone I, 9400-6000 cal BC)

The transition from the Late Devensian to the Holocene was marked by a very rapid rise in temperature (Fig. 9.2). Insect evidence from the English Midlands suggests that the change from arctic conditions to mean summer temperatures similar to those of the present day could have occurred over a period of 50 years or less (Osborne 1980). While no such closely dated sequences spanning the Devensian-Holocene transition have been found in the Thames Valley, arctic species were absent from a palaeochannel on the Upper Thames floodplain at Mingies Ditch dated to 9150-8300 cal BC (HAR-8366: 9380±100 BP; Allen and Robinson 1993). However, the deposit did contain one northern species, the carabid beetle *Patrobus assimilis*, which now only occurs as far south as Cannock Chase, Staffs. As well as being warmer, the Holocene climate was also wetter than the Late Glacial climate.

The response to the climatic amelioration was vegetational succession dependent upon not, as originally thought, a gradually warming climate but upon the ease with which the species concerned were able to colonise. At Mingies Ditch, for example, in the Upper Thames Valley, the deposit noted above gave pollen evidence for open woodland of *Betula pendula* or *pubescens* (a tree species of birch) and *Salix* sp. (willow or sallow; Allen and Robinson 1993, 9). Bud scales of *Populus* cf *tremula* (aspen) provide evidence of another tree which was probably important in the pioneering woodland. However, a high proportion of Gramineae (grass) pollen showed that tree cover was by no means complete. There were various chafer and elaterid beetles with larvae that feed on the roots of grassland plants such as *Sericea brunnea* and *Agrypnus murinus* while the presence of pollen of *Papaver* sp. (poppy) suggested there were still some exposed areas of soil on which annual weeds grew. A Flandrian Late Zone I deposit alongside the river Windrush at this site dated to 6600-6250 cal BC (HAR-8354: 7590±80 BP) gave evidence for *Salix*

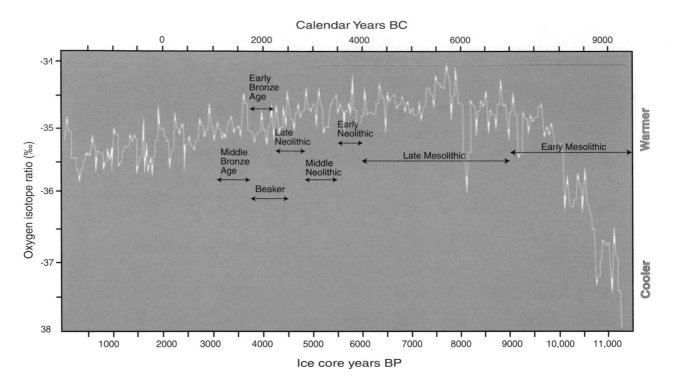

Fig. 9.2   Climate change in the Holocene as recorded by Oxygen isotope ratios in the NorthGRIP ice core

carr growing on the peat fringing the river and *Quercus* (oak)-*Ulmus* (elm)-*Corylus* (hazel) woodland on the floodplain. While the abundance of seeds of *Thelycrania sanguinea* (dogwood) suggested that the tree canopy alongside the river was relatively open, there was little evidence for grassland. Although this deposit did not yield a full old-woodland insect fauna, there were beetles of decaying trees such as *Melasis buprestoides* and so far the only British record of the ant *Dolichoderus quadripunctatus*, which nests in hollow branches and under bark. It is still to be found in woodland in Belgium.

Several pollen sequences from the Middle Thames Valley illustrate the early Holocene vegetational succession well (Fig. 9.3). At Moor Farm, Staines, a radiocarbon date of 9300-8830 cal BC (OxA-6469: 9710±75 BP) was obtained for the part of the sequence just before a rapid rise in pollen frequencies for *Betula* sp. and *Pinus* sp. (pine; Keith-Lucas 2000). Woodland of *Pinus sylvestris* (Scots pine) probably predominated, and the proportion of herb pollen declined as the ground conditions became more shaded. However, by 7600-7350 cal BC (OxA-6474: 8460±65 BP), pine was beginning to decline as *Quercus* sp. and *Ulmus* sp. started to displace it. *Corylus avellana* formed the understorey to the woodland. A similar but undated succession was noted at Thames Valley Park, Reading (Keith-Lucas 1997). Branch and Green (2004, 11-12) summarise early Mesolithic pollen evidence from Staines ABC Cinema and Meadlake Place and the

work by Scaife (2000) at Runnymede Bridge to propose the following sequence:

10,000-9000 uncal BP (*c* 9500-8250 cal BC) *Pinus*-dominated woodland on drier ground with sedge and reedswamp on wetland areas which is gradually replaced by *Salix* woodland.

9000-8000 uncal BP (*c* 8250-7000 cal BC) *Quercus*, *Ulmus*, *Betula* and *Corylus* invade the areas occupied by *Pinus* woodland resulting in the formation of mixed deciduous woodland. *Salix* remains dominant on wetland although there is evidence for isolated trees of *Alnus glutinosa* (alder).

Not all sites in the Middle Thames show quite the same sequence. At Dorney, the pollen sequence from a palaeochannel of the Thames suggested that *Pinus* was able to out-compete *Betula* on the drier ground between 9000 and 8000 uncal BP (*c* 8250-7000 cal BC; Parker and Robinson 2003, 55). There was also an unusually early rise of *Alnus* pollen beginning around 8410-8230 cal BC (CAMS-54440: 9070±40 BP), rising to 15% of total land pollen before declining by 7750-7540 cal BC (CAMS-57206: 8610±50 BP). The colonisation of Britain by alder occurred at the start of the Holocene but its expansion to become the dominant wetland tree was delayed by about 2000 years for uncertain reasons. It is likewise unknown why this tree should have briefly flourished at an early date at Dorney.

Pollen has been analysed from several organic sequences at Thatcham from a backswamp of the

Fig. 9.3 (facing page)   Topography of the Thames Valley showing sites with important environmental evidence

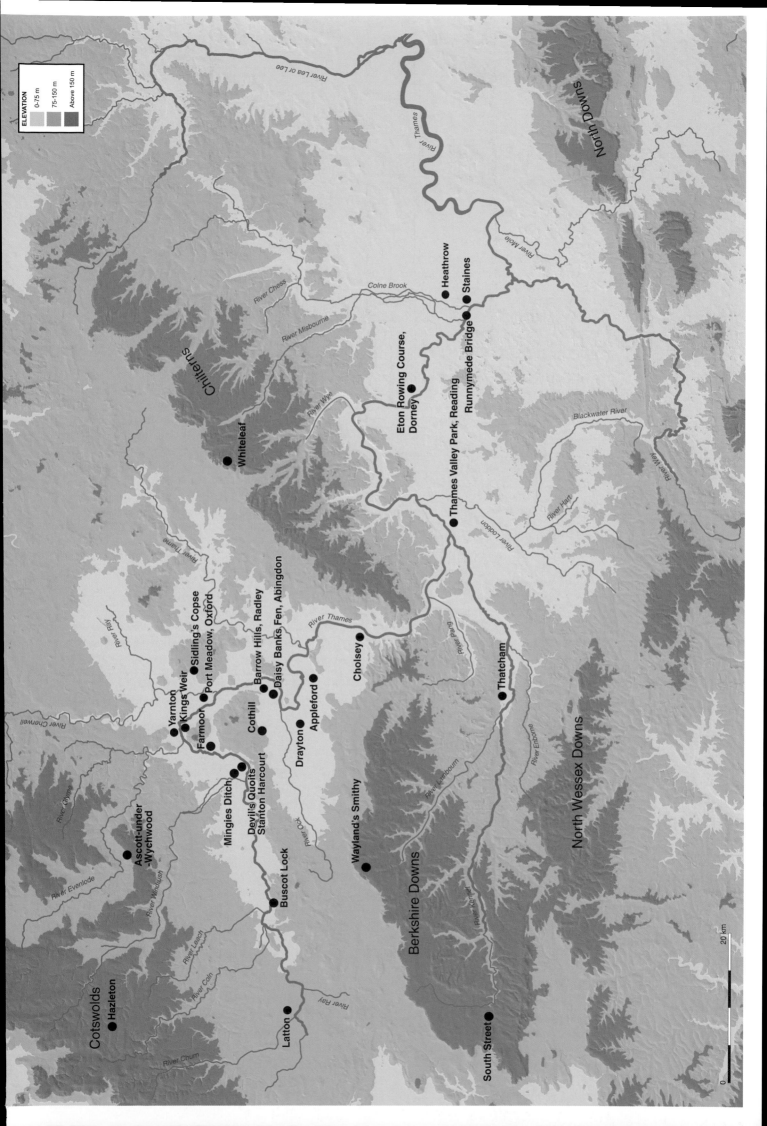

ELEVATION

0-75 m

75-150 m

Above 150 m

North Downs

Chilterns

Cotswolds

Berkshire Downs

North Wessex Downs

River Lea or Lee

River Thames

River Mole

River Chess

River Misbourne

River Wye

Colne Brook

Blackwater River

River Wey

River Hart

River Loddon

River Thame

River Ray

River Cherwell

River Windrush

River Evenlode

River Churn

River Coln

River Leach

River Ock

River Thames

River Pang

River Lambourn

River Kennet

River Enborne

Heathrow

Staines

Runnymede Bridge

Eton Rowing Course, Dorney

Thames Valley Park, Reading

Whiteleaf

Sidling's Copse

Port Meadow, Oxford

Kings Weir

Yarnton

Farmoor

Barrow Hills, Radley

Daisy Banks Fen, Abingdon

Cothill

Stanton Harcourt

Devil's Quoits

Mingies Ditch

Appleford

Drayton

Cholsey

Wayland's Smithy

Thatcham

Buscot Lock

Ascott-under-Wychwood

Hazleton

Latton

South Street

20 km

0

Kennet adjacent to an early Mesolithic settlement (Dimbleby 1958; Churchill 1962; Scaife 1992). They showed a typical Flandrian Zone I succession with open birch-willow woodland giving way to denser pine-hazel woodland which then experienced colonisation by oak and elm. A more detailed consideration of the ecology of the settlement, including the wild vertebrates being exploited and possible human impact on the vegetation, is given below in Chapter 10.

The greater ease with which pine woodland will burn in comparison to deciduous woodland means that the period when Scots pine predominated is likely to have the greatest evidence of clearance by fire. Indeed, microscopic particles of charcoal are often found in pollen preparations from deposits of this period. It has been argued from such evidence at Cothill Fen, a valley fen in the Corallian ridge to the west of Oxford, that Mesolithic peoples were using fire to manage woodland (Day 1991).

In summary, the main vegetational developments in the region during Flandrian Zone I were the establishment and succession of woodland in response to the climatic amelioration which defines the beginning of the zone. Initially tree cover was sparse, and some areas probably remained open grassland for 500 years or more, but the canopy gradually became complete. The cessation of periglacial processes and the vegetational cover both made major contributions to greatly increased surface stability, and allowed soil formation to progress. A full woodland fauna colonised the region facilitated by the land connection to mainland Europe, across what is now the southern part of the North Sea, for at least the first 2000 years of the Holocene. There was a human presence in the Thames Valley from the start of the Holocene but there is only slight evidence for human impact on the vegetation in the valley bottom.

The late Mesolithic (Flandrian Zone II, 6000-4000 cal BC)

Whereas the start of Flandrian Zone I was defined by a rapid climatic amelioration, the transition to Flandrian Zone II was a more gradual process defined by the culmination of vegetational succession with a community of mixed woodland. There followed a long period of stability. Mature brown earth soils had developed extensively in the regions. By the end of Flandrian Zone I the climate was 1-2°C warmer than that of the 20th century AD giving rise to the term Post-Glacial Climatic Optimum, and these warmer conditions prevailed throughout Flandrian Zone II. Precipitation levels increased at the start of Flandrian Zone II and this warm wetter episode was given the name the Atlantic climatic period by the early vegetational stratigraphers in NW Europe (Godwin 1975, 27; Fig. 9.2).

Few waterlogged deposits from this period have been discovered in the Upper Thames Valley. However, a second organic deposit from a channel of the Windrush at Mingies Ditch was dated to 5630-5340 cal BC (HAR-8355: 6540±80 BP). It gave strong evidence for dense alder woodland on the floodplain. Over 50% of the pollen of nonaquatic plants was from *Alnus* sp., fruits of *A. glutinosa* were the most abundant type of seeds and alder was also represented by catkins, wood and galls of *Eriophyes laevis inangulis*, a leaf mite confined to *Alnus*. Remains of *Agelastica alni* (alder leaf beetle), which is also restricted to alder, confirmed the importance of this tree. *A. glutinosa* is on the edge of its ecological range in Britain, and requires substantial areas of alder woodland to maintain a viable population. As alder woodlands became fragmented as a result of clearance activities so the beetle declined in abundance. However, the warming climate today has enabled it to compete more effectively, despite the fragmentation of its habitat, and it has become re-established in England.

While alder was probably predominant on the wettest areas of floodplain at Mingies Ditch, the pollen evidence suggested mixed woodland elsewhere in which *Quercus* sp. (oak) and *Fraxinus excelsior* (ash) were major trees of the woodland canopy while *Corylus avellana* (hazel) was an important shrub. Finds of insects such as the oak leaf weevil *Rhynchaenus quercus*, the ash leaf beetle *Hylesinus crenatus* and the hazelnut weevil *Curculio nucum* confirm this picture. There was also an example of the bark beetle *Ernoporus caucasicus* which is dependent on *Tilia cordata* (small-leaved lime). This tree tends to be underrepresented in the pollen record because it is insect-pollinated. It has been argued that once pollen productivity is taken into account, the pollen evidence shows that it was the dominant woodland tree over much of southern England and the Midlands during Flandrian Zone II (Greig 1982; Rackham 1987, 68-71). *T. cordata* was certainly a significant member of the woodland in the valley bottom during the Neolithic (see below), and its pollen attained values of up to 20% of the pollen of terrestrial plants between 6230-5890 cal BC (OxA-3509: 7180±85 BP) and 4330-3940 cal BC (OxA-3560: 5250±75 BP) in a sequence from Sidlings Copse, a valley fen in the limestone above the Thames Valley near Oxford (Day 1991; Preece and Day 1994). It is thought likely that *T. cordata* was also an important tree on the gravel terraces of the Upper Thames Valley during Flandrian Zone II.

Many of the Coleoptera (beetles) from the Mingies Ditch deposit were species associated with dead wood and old moribund trees. Some are now characteristic of old woodland and are very rare in Britain. For example, *Gastrallus immarginatus* is now only known in Britain from Windsor Great Park, and *E. caucasicus*, the lime bark beetle, is restricted to a few old parkland and woodland lime trees in the Midlands. Many of these old-woodland insects have very poor dispersive powers across nonwoodland obstacles but were able to spread into the region when there was almost continuous tree cover across Britain. There was little indication of open habitats. Scarabaeoid dung beetles which feed on the droppings of larger herbivores comprised less than 1% of the terrestrial Coleoptera which would be appropriate to a slight presence of woodland browsers.

The results from the Middle Thames Valley present a picture very similar to that of the Upper Thames Valley. Flandrian Zone II pollen sequences from Thames Valley Park (Keith-Lucas 1997), Staines Moor (Keith-Lucas 2000), Meadlake Place (Branch and Green 2004) and Runnymede (Scaife 2000) all had very high percentages of *Alnus* pollen, suggesting dense alder woodland on the wetter parts of the floodplain and alder carr (woodland on peat) on the palaeochannel fills of the Staines Alluvial Deposits. However, alder did not predominate everywhere and oak fen woodland grew on the peat filling a palaeochannel at Marsh Lane East (T G Allen *et al.* forthcoming).

Insect results very similar to those from Mingies Ditch were obtained from one of the palaeochannels of the Thames at Runnymede, which was dated to 6500-5950 cal BC; Robinson 2000b). Wood and tree-dependent species formed 20% of the terrestrial Coleoptera, and *Agelastica alni* (alder leaf beetle) was again present. An old fauna of insects included the wood-boring weevil *Dryophthorus corticalis*, which is now restricted in Britain to Windsor Forest. There was no evidence for open conditions.

A hypothesis has been advanced that stable dense woodland of mixed deciduous trees was not the climax community of Flandrian Zone II (Vera 2000). Vera has argued instead for instability, with cycles of woodland being replaced by grassland which in turn underwent scrub colonisation followed by woodland succession. The hypothesis was based on observations of old woodlands in NW Europe, some of which were experiencing grazing whilst grazing animals had been excluded from others. The Vera hypothesis has gained wide currency in conservation circles in Britain and, if correct, has considerable implications for an understanding of the British Mesolithic.

In more detail, Vera points out that the woodland floor beneath a closed canopy of mature oak trees is too shaded for oak seedlings to become established. Those trees whose seedlings can develop under low levels of illumination, for example small-leaved lime, are more palatable to herbivores than oak, and are prevented from becoming established by the browsing of animals such as deer and aurochs. Eventually, the oak trees begin to die of old age and the woodland disintegrates leading to a parkland effect of open areas between a few individual trees. As the ground becomes better illuminated, so grass is able to colonise, which attracts herbivores and, while light levels become suitable for oak seedlings, the increased grazing presence prevents any regeneration of woodland trees. However, seedlings of light-demanding thorn-scrub species such as hawthorn and sloe are able to become established despite grazing. Clumps of thorny shrubs provide

protection for oak seedlings, which are able to grow and eventually shade-out their protectors, completing the cycle.

Pollen sequences from Britain including the Thames Valley show no clear evidence of 'Vera cycles' although pollen of grasses and some light-demanding herbaceous plants is never entirely absent in Flandrian Zone II sediments. Vera (2000, 61-101) does not regard pollen analysis as entirely reliable as a means of detecting open areas in woodland, and correctly notes that the thorn-scrub species which are part of his proposed succession are insect-pollinated shrubs which scatter little pollen. The two main arguments against the widespread occurrence of Vera cycles in the Thames Valley during Flandrian Zone II are, firstly, that pollen and other lines of palaeoecological evidence have proved perfectly capable of revealing episodes of temporary and small-scale clearance activity during the Neolithic (see below), and secondly, that oak was not the only important tree in the Thames Valley, and despite any pressures from browsing herbivores, succession was able to proceed to lime woodland.

Flandrian Zone II was a period when the vegetation of the regions had reached a balance with the prevailing climate. There was a human presence but any human impact was slight. The overall impression in both the Upper and Middle Valley is of woodland: alder woodland alongside river channels and on the wettest part of the floodplain, and oak-ash-lime to lime-dominated woodland on the gravel terraces with an understorey of hazel. Living in the woodland was a very diverse fauna of invertebrates. The mammal fauna was less diverse but only as a result of the marine barrier to colonisation. Red deer, roe deer, aurochs (wild cattle), wild boar, bear and wolf were all present and, alongside finds from archaeological sites (see below, Chapter 10), bones of most of these species have been recovered during dredging operations on the Thames (although the dating of these bones to this period is insecure).

The Elm decline and the earliest Neolithic, *c* 4000 cal BC

There is no evidence for any environmental change before the Elm Decline of around 4000 cal BC, at around the time of the beginning of the Neolithic, although the Elm Decline itself was not necessarily related to human activity. The Elm Decline is shown by several pollen diagrams from the area and is characterised by a substantial fall in the proportion of *Ulmus* sp. (elm) pollen. It is often coincident with a rise in the proportion of Gramineae (grass) pollen and the appearance of pollen of light-demanding herbaceous plants such as *Plantago lanceolata* (ribwort plantain). It is a widespread phenomenon over much of NW Europe the causes of which remain enigmatic (Parker *et al.* 2002). The Elm Decline is often followed by the earliest evidence for agricultural activity in a region, as is the case in the Thames Valley, but the relationships between possible causal factors such as disease of elm trees, climatic change and tree clearance are uncertain. Indeed it is even possible that the adoption of agriculture was a response to the changes brought about by the loss of elm trees rather than its cause.

In the Upper Thames Valley, sedimentation began in the late 5th millennium cal BC at Daisy Banks Fen, a narrow valley crossing the Summertown-Radley Gravel Terrace adjacent to the archaeological sites of the Abingdon causewayed enclosure and Barrow Hills, Radley (Parker 1999). The earliest part of the pollen sequence (Fig. 11.3) suggests a fairly wooded environment with the local woodland dominated by *Ulmus* sp. and *Tilia* sp. (lime) along with lower proportions of *Corylus avellana* (hazel) and *Quercus* sp. (oak). At a point dated to 4350-3750 cal BC (OxA-4559: 5240±110 BP), there was a sharp decline in elm pollen to a very low level (Fig. 11.3). The Elm Decline at Daisy Banks was accompanied by substantial and permanent clearance. Cereal pollen was present from the Elm Decline and rapidly rose to 7% of the nonaquatic pollen. Wheats and barleys are notorious for their poor pollen dispersal, and such a value would be very high for an early Neolithic landscape. Either cereal cultivation extended up to the edge of Daisy Banks or cereal processing remains were being discarded from a nearby settlement into one of the streams which fed the fen. No other pollen sequences crossing the Elm Decline have been investigated from the gravels of the Upper Thames Valley but the Elm Decline was recorded in the Sidlings Copse sequence from a valley fen on the Corallian geology 16 km north-east of Daisy Banks (Preece and Day 1994). It occurred in lime-dominated woodland and was dated to 4350-3950 cal BC (OxA-3560: 5250±75 BP) but, in contrast to Daisy Banks, pollen and molluscan evidence suggested no more than a slight reduction in shading of the woodland.

The Elm Decline is evident in two pollen sequences from the Middle Thames Valley, Thames Valley Park, Reading (Keith-Lucas 1997) and Moor Farm, Staines (Keith-Lucas 2000). Unfortunately the sequences were rather compressed at this point and were undated. However, at Thames Valley Park, the occurrence of cereal-type pollen, weeds of cultivation such as Chenopodiaceae (fat hen, orache etc) and grassland plants such as *Plantago lanceolata* (ribwort plantain) suggested the beginning of Neolithic arable and pastoral agriculture. There was only slight evidence for woodland disturbance at Moor Farm. Pollen-stratigraphic records from Meadlake Place (Branch and Green 2004) and Runnymede Bridge (Scaife 2000) provided no evidence for a decline in the proportion of elm in the woodland. There was, however, some evidence of interference with the woodland at Runnymede.

A radiocarbon date of 4040-3790 cal BC (BM-2657: 5130±50 BP) was obtained from this part of the Runnymede sequence. The Coleoptera very much emphasised the occurrence of woodland of old-woodland character, with the presence of beetles such as *Rhyncolus truncorum* (Robinson 2000a; Robinson 2000b). Wood and tree-dependent beetles comprised 14% of the terrestrial Coleoptera. The macroscopic plant remains suggested dense alder woodland alongside the Thames without any hint of clearings. However, scarabaeoid dung beetles such as *Aphodius* cf *sphacelatus*, which mostly occur in the dung of the larger herbivores as droppings on the ground, make up 6% of the terrestrial Coleoptera. This is well above the proportion which would be expected from wild mammals in the woodland and well above previous levels on the site. It is possible that this represents some of the earliest Neolithic activity in the region, with domestic animals being herded in woodland where the canopy was largely intact. The two most likely domestic animals to have been grazed under these conditions are cattle and pig.

Thus the period around 4000 cal BC saw a range of vegetational changes in the Thames Valley following the Elm Decline. In many places there was no more than an adjustment of woodland composition and little immediate evidence of human impact, although domestic animals were probably being grazed widely in the woodland. In others there was small-scale and probably temporary clearance for agriculture. At Daisy Banks adjacent to the Abingdon causewayed enclosure, however, clearance for cereal cultivation was on a larger and more permanent scale. This is the only place to provide evidence for human impact on the soil; it is possible that clearance caused the erosion of the sediments which were then deposited in the fen.

The Neolithic (*c* 4000-2500 cal BC)

While there was limited Mesolithic interference with woodland, there is no doubt that there was significant tree clearance in the Thames Valley during the Neolithic. Clearance could have been achieved by felling trees with axes, and where completely open areas needed to be created in a short time, for example for cereal cultivation, this was probably the preferred method. However, cutting down trees a metre in diameter with a polished stone axe, although possible, would have been very hard work. Evidence for another means of clearance during the Neolithic was identified at Drayton on the floodplain and Northmoor Terrace of the Upper Thames (Barclay *et al.* 2003; Robinson 1992a, 50-51). Numerous bowl-shaped depressions were found which had resulted from the disturbance to the ground by tree root clusters when trees fell over. The tree-throw pits were circular or oval in plan, about 2 m in diameter and often had a crescent shape of dark soil defining part of the edge, the crescent shape being soil of the former ground surface which had been held together by the root plate whilst being rotated through 90 degrees by the fall of the trees. Some of the Drayton tree-throw pits were perhaps the result of trees being uprooted naturally by strong winds or toppling over after death, although in dense Flandrian II woodland many dead trees would probably have stayed where they stood. The reason for associating the majority of these features at Drayton with clearance was that 15 of the 17 pits investigated for carbonised plant remains contained charcoal, some in considerable quantities. Most of the charcoal in each pit was from a single taxon, and in some instance could be recognised as root-wood. Some of the tree pits showed reddening from burning which suggested that the trees had been burnt after falling, and there were also signs of much burning on the surface of the floodplain. Radiocarbon dating of the charcoal from the tree-throw pits showed them to belong to periods of Neolithic activity on the site, with early to middle Neolithic clearance related to the construction of the cursus, and at least one other phase of clearance in the late Neolithic-early Bronze Age when there was occupation at the site (Barclay *et al.* 2003; Robinson 1992a, 51). It is argued that where areas were to be cleared for grazing, which could begin under partly wooded conditions, large trees were killed, perhaps by ring barking, regrowth was prevented and dead trees were either allowed to topple or were deliberately pulled over once their roots had decayed. The fallen trunks were then burnt out. Smaller trees could have been felled with axes. It is possible that this process was the main means of clearance in the Thames Valley (although the wood felled by this method would not have been suitable for use in structures or for objects because its greenwood properties would have been lost (M Taylor pers. comm.)).

It is suggested that the dead trees were burnt once they had fallen, which could have provided a spectacular event in itself. It must be stressed that the deciduous woodland of the Thames Valley could not have been cleared by the use of fire alone (Rackham 1987, 71-3). Trees would have needed to be killed, allowed to dry and had their branches gathered together before they became easily combustible.

Any process of clearance which created tree-throw pits would have had a significant impact on the soil. At Drayton 30% of the floodplain was occupied by tree-throw holes (Barclay *et al.* 2003, 62). Gravel would have been brought to the surface amongst the tree roots which, in the Upper Thames Valley, would have tended to recalcify the soil, and soil would have been lost into the tree-throw holes.

The pollen sequence from Daisy Banks Fen suggested that conditions on the Summertown-Radley Gravel Terrace of the Upper Thames remained open in the vicinity of the Abingdon causewayed enclosure monument complex throughout the Neolithic (Fig. 11.3; Parker 1999). There was woodland regeneration on the fen itself from about 3500 to 2800 cal BC, with trees such as *Alnus glutinosa* (alder), *Salix* sp. (willow) and

Corylus avellana (hazel) becoming established on the peat. However, this woodland was removed at the start of the late Neolithic and values of tree pollen were low from 2800 cal BC onwards. Cereal pollen was sufficiently well-represented from all the Neolithic samples to suggest cereal cultivation throughout. In the late Neolithic there was a rise in the pollen of grassland plants, particularly *Plantago lanceolata* (ribwort plantain), which was perhaps a reflection of the development of more extensive grassland on the Summertown-Radley Terrace.

Another monument complex showing evidence for permanently open conditions from the time of its construction was the Devil's Quoits, on the Summertown-Radley Terrace at Stanton Harcourt (Evans 1995). Open-country snails predominated in the ditch sediments of the henge from the initial stages of infilling in the early 3rd millennium cal BC onwards. The more usual pattern for the Neolithic of the Thames Valley was for episodes of clearance to be followed by periods of woodland regeneration, as seen for the Drayton Cursus above. There is molluscan evidence for woodland regeneration on a high area of the floodplain of the Upper Thames Valley at Yarnton. Shells were preserved in ditch fills of a probable early Neolithic enclosure which had been recut twice, once in the middle Neolithic and again in the middle Bronze Age. The shells from the early fills of the initial ditch suggested dry open conditions, with *Vertigo pygmaea*, *Vallonia costata* and *V. excentrica*. While *V. costata* can occur at low frequencies in woodland, the other two species are entirely restricted to open habitats but were evidently able to colonise. These species were also able to colonise a middle Neolithic oval barrow at Radley (Robinson 1999b, 241). The upper fill of the early Neolithic ditch at Yarnton, however, contained a high concentration of shells amongst which, apart from a single example of *V. costata,* species of open habitats were entirely absent. Instead there were snails of shaded habitats and woodland such as *Carychium tridentatum*, *Discus rotundatus* and various Zonitidae. The old-woodland snail *Ena montana* was also present. Shells of both open and wooded habitats were present in the initial fills of the middle Neolithic recut but woodland species predominated in the subsequent fill of the recut, and *E. montana* was again present. The snails from the middle Bronze Age recut suggested a return to more open conditions. At present, *E. montana* shows poor dispersive powers and has little ability to colonise newly created woodland. It is suggested that during the Neolithic, clearances were on a relatively small scale and that when woodland regeneration occurred, there were sufficient adjacent refugia retaining an old-woodland fauna from which *E. montana* could recolonise once the secondary woodland had reached an appropriate stage of maturity.

The prevalence of collected edible wild plants such as *Corylus avellana* (hazelnut) and *Malus sylvestris* (crab apple) in assemblages of charred food plant remains suggests many settlements had a background presence of woodland. A full range of open-country molluscs was present in some late Neolithic pits at Barrow Hills, Radley including *Helicella itala* and *Truncatellina cylindrica* (Robinson 1999c, 241). *T. cylindrica* is a snail of short-turfed dry grassland which is now very rare and no longer occurs in the region (Kerney and Cameron 1979, 68-263). It was of much more widespread distribution during the Neolithic and Bronze Age (Evans 1972, 140). However, there was also a lesser presence of woodland species. The charcoal from Neolithic sites where there is evidence for settlement activity, such as Barrow Hills, Radley (Thompson 1999) and Yarnton (Robinson in prep.), tends to be mixed, with thorn-scrub species including *Prunus* cf *spinosa* (sloe), *Rhamnus catharticus* (purging buckthorn) and Pomoideae (hawthorn-type) as well as the more typically woodland taxa of *Quercus* sp. (oak), *Corylus avellana* (hazel) and *Acer campestre* (maple). This charcoal is thought more likely to have been representative of the local vegetation than wood brought to sites for ceremonial purposes.

Much woodland remained on the gravels of the Upper Thames Valley in the late Neolithic. A deposit from a former channel of the Thames at Buscot Lock, on the Oxfordshire-Gloucestershire border, dated to 2900-2250 cal BC (4010±90 BP) contained evidence of human activity, including part of a well-worn antler pick and bones of domestic animals showing signs of butchery (Robinson and Wilson 1987, 31-2). However, it had been laid down under largely wooded conditions. Pollen and macroscopic plant remains suggested alder woodland alongside the river, while fruits of *Tilia cordata* (small-leaved lime) were probably from lime-dominated woodland on better-drained soils. A woodland insect fauna was present and there were seeds of a woodland ground flora including *Mercurialis perennis* (dog's mercury). A reminder that the woodland retained its large mammal fauna was given by the discovery of a particularly fine aurochs horn core. Tree cover was not complete. Macroscopic remains of the light-demanding shrubs *R. catharticus* and *P. spinosa*, a little pollen of *Plantago lanceolata* (ribwort plantain) and shells of the grassland snail *Vallonia pulchella* suggested there were grassy areas surrounded by thorn scrub within the woodland. Scarabaeoid dung beetles made up 2.5% of the total terrestrial Coleoptera, suggesting limited grazing by domestic animals.

The pollen, macroscopic plant remains and insects from two organic sequences from palaeochannels of the Thames in the Middle Thames Valley at Dorney (Parker and Robinson 2003) and Runnymede (Greig 1991; Robinson 1991) which spanned much of the Neolithic have been investigated. At Dorney, the pollen flora was dominated by a woodland association, with high frequencies of *Corylus avellana* (hazel), along with *Alnus glutinosa* (alder), *Quercus* sp. (oak), *Ulmus* sp. (elm) and a little *Tilia* sp. (lime). Numerous seeds, female catkins and

other remains of *A. glutinosa* and the beetle *Agelastica alni* (alder leaf beetle) confirmed the presence of alder woodland on the floodplain while one of the channels contained the trunks of several oak trees, which had toppled from the riverbank, preserved within it. The other trees probably comprised the regional woodland and were not well represented amongst the host-specific insects, although there was an example of *Scolytus scolytus* (elm bark beetle) in the sample dated to 3700-3380 cal BC (CAMS-57208: 4800±40 BP). The pollen showed evidence of several disturbance phases to the woodland with a marked decrease in arboreal pollen types and an increase in the pollen of herbaceous plants, particularly Gramineae (grasses) and *Plantago lanceolata* (ribwort plantain). The peak of one event was dated to 3640-3370 cal BC (CAMS-57207: 4730±40 BP) while further disturbance and clearance occurred around 2800 cal BC. There were a few seeds of grassland plants in these samples including *Prunella vulgaris* (self-heal), and light-demanding thorn-scrub species which withstand the presence of grazing animals were also present. Beetles with larvae which feed on the roots of grassland plants, such as *Phyllopertha horticola* and *Agrypnus murinus* comprised around 5% of the terrestrial Coleoptera while the scarabaeoid dung beetles which are favoured by droppings of domestic animals were well represented, forming 8% of the terrestrial Coleoptera. The landscape was perhaps a mosaic of woodland and small clearings, some of which were becoming overgrown with thorn scrub.

Evidence for somewhat similar conditions was given by a sequence at Runnymede which extended from about 3500 cal BC to 2000 cal BC. The pollen suggested a strong presence of woodland throughout the sequence with the woodland becoming slightly more closed with time. As might be anticipated, the macroscopic plant remains suggested alder predominated alongside the river. Beavers were active in this woodland. A bundle of twigs and small branches of *Cornus sanguinea* (dogwood), some with beaver-gnawed ends and their bark stripped, was found in the palaeochannel (Coles 2006, 96-7). The wood was radiocarbon dated to 2450-2050 cal BC (ibid., 97). The woodland on drier ground was interpreted, taking pollen productivity into account, as being dominated by lime, oak and pine with a significant presence of elm and ash, and an understorey of hazel. It is uncertain whether the occurrence of pine was a reflection of the acidity of the terrace gravels or whether the trees were growing on the Tertiary sands beyond the river gravels. The insects included a full old-woodland fauna, with some species restricted today to a very few localities in Britain including, in the case of *Teredus cylindricus*, nearby in Windsor Great Park, where it occurs on old oaks infested by wood-boring beetles. Two of the beetles are now extinct in Britain. *Dromaeolus barnabita* occurs in dry dead wood of deciduous trees in scattered localities throughout Central and Southern Europe while

Pelta grossum is a large beetle which occurs in rotten wood in various parts of Europe including Scandinavia, the Alps and the Pyrenees.

Open areas were also a significant feature of the Neolithic landscape around Runnymede. Although the pollen included *Plantago lanceolata* (ribwort plantain) throughout the sequence, and there were a few seeds of grassland plants such as *Prunella vulgaris* (self heal), some of the best evidence was given by the insects. Confirmation of the occurrence of *P. lanceolata* was given by the weevils *Gymnetron labile* and *G. pascuorum* while *Hydrothassa glabra* suggested the presence of *Ranunculus* spp. (buttercups) and *Hypera punctata* feeds on *Trifolium* spp. (clovers). There was a group amongst the open-country species of beetles which tends to be associated with sun-warmed habitats on sandy and sometimes chalky soil with only patchy vegetation. Some now tend to have a coastal distribution. They included *Rhinocyllus conicus*, which is now only known from a few localities on the south coast, and *Caenopsis waltoni* which is monophagous on *Plantago coronopus* (stags-horn plantain), a plant that although mostly coastal, does also occur inland on bare sandy and gravelly soils. It is possible that these beetles were favoured by tree clearance on the gravel terraces exposing the subsoil to erosion. Scarabaeoid dung beetles, particularly *Aphodius granarius* and *A.* cf *sphacelatus*, comprised about 6% of the terrestrial Coleoptera, suggesting that the areas of grassland were being used as pasture for domestic animals. Most of these beetles are still common in dung around Windsor but one, *Onthophagus taurus*, is now extinct in Britain, and another, *Copris lunaris*, is extremely rare.

A shorter pollen sequence was given by the sediments of a middle Neolithic pit at Heathrow Terminal 5 (Wiltshire in Lewis *et al.* 2006, 61-5). Although the sediments were not waterlogged and there can be problems with preservation or earthworm mixing in aerobic soils which are not strongly acidic, the results seem reliable. They showed that the landscape supported mixed deciduous woodland in which oak, lime and hazel were important, but there appear to have been some relatively small grassy areas and some areas of cereal cultivation. It is suggested the pit was located within a woodland clearing or at the edge of a transition from woodland to more open landscape. Pollen from a late Neolithic pit on the site suggested open conditions but preservation was poor and the interpretation was regarded as tenuous (Lewis *et al.* 2006, 85).

Snail assemblages from the Whiteleaf Neolithic barrow show that from the time of the construction of the barrow in the middle of the 4th millennium cal BC to the late Neolithic period, the hill remained quite densely wooded, with relatively undisturbed, mature, broadleafed deciduous woodland and abundant leaf litter (Stafford in Hey *et al.* 2007, 61-8). Snails recovered from the primary fill of the

barrow ditch on the west side of the mound, for example, included no open-country species, and although more catholic species were present further up the profile, shade-loving species dominate all the assemblages. The evidence suggests that, after clearance undertaken for the construction of the barrow and later disturbance around the mound, these snails were able to recolonise quickly from nearby, substantial refugia. This situation may have prevailed until the Bronze Age. By the time a cross-ridge dyke and curvilinear earthwork were constructed on the site, probably towards the end of the Bronze Age or the Iron Age, there were some indicators of established short-turfed or grazed grassland.

The results from Runnymede and the other Middle Thames sites fall into a familiar pattern for the Neolithic, suggesting a landscape that was a mosaic of woodland and temporary clearings. It is uncertain why this should have been so rather than the Thames Valley experiencing progressive permanent clearance throughout the Neolithic. The Daisy Banks Fen clearance was atypical: the usual fate of clearances was that they would experience regeneration even though it was most unlikely that their soils were so exhausted that they could not even support permanent pasture (and there was no evidence from the soils themselves for such deterioration). Some Neolithic clearances were made for the construction of ceremonial monuments, and it is possible that there might have been social or religious reasons why they could no longer be cultivated, grazed or kept open for ceremony. Another possibility is that an explanation can be found by considering human influence on the vegetational ecodynamics. It has already been argued that during the Neolithic domestic animals were being grazed under partly wooded conditions and that at least some clearance was being achieved by killing trees by ring barking and allowing them to fall or pulling them over once their roots had decayed, hastening the opening up of the tree canopy as a result of the natural death of old trees. Grazing pressure from domestic animals in some areas of woodland would have prevented regeneration. Once park woodland, that is isolated mature trees or clumps of trees with grass in between, or fully open grassland had been created, stability could be maintained by regular scrub cutting. However, if grazing alone were being used to keep conditions open, the light-demanding thorn-scrub species would gradually become established. As the clumps of scrub expanded, so the area of useful grazing would decline. There would come a stage when, if grazing was to continue to be provided, either the scrub had to be cut or the animals moved to a new area. Possibly it was considered easier to open up established woodland than to clear scrub. Thus the grazing pressure of domestic animals in woodland, and the deliberate killing of trees, were possibly able to provide the impetus to enable Vera cycles to occur, with mature woodland being replaced by grassland which was invaded by thorn scrub and then gave way to woodland succession, completing the cycle.

The overall impression of the landscape of the Middle and Upper Thames Valley throughout the Neolithic is of a patchwork of stands of relatively undisturbed woodland: alder on the wettest areas of the floodplain, mixed but with lime and oak usually prominent on the gravel terraces; more open woodland in which domestic animals sometimes grazed; areas of grassland, some grazed, others with ceremonial monuments; a very few cultivation plots; and areas of thorn scrub. This picture was not stable, it was an ever-changing mosaic of clearance and vegetational succession in which relatively few areas remained permanently open. Despite the degree of disturbance, an old-woodland invertebrate fauna managed to persist in the region because habitat loss was compensated for by nearby areas of secondary woodland reaching the appropriate stage of maturity for colonisation to occur. Conversely, there were sufficient refugia and routeways to enable plants and animals of open habitats to colonise newly cleared areas. The colonists included some molluscs of apparently poor dispersive prowess which have never been recorded from woodland. More woodland would have experienced disturbance as the Neolithic progressed but the only evidence for an increase in the open area with time is given by a rising proportion of sheep bones in relation to cattle and pig bones. Sheep require pasture whereas the other two animals can be grazed in woodland. It is possible that the only permanently open areas were associated with major monument complexes. In the Upper Thames Valley, the Barrow Hills area was open from the early 4th millennium cal BC following the construction of the Abingdon causewayed enclosure and at Stanton Harcourt at least the immediate environs of the Devil's Quoits stayed open following the construction of the henge in the early 3rd millennium cal BC. The Dorchester-on-Thames ceremonial complex is another candidate for an area which remained open although no palaeoenvironmental evidence is available. In contrast, the area around the Drayton Cursus did experience woodland regeneration in the mid to later Neolithic.

The early Bronze Age (2500-1500 cal BC)

There is surprisingly little evidence for the early Bronze Age environment of the Upper Thames Valley. The uppermost radiocarbon date on the pollen core from Daisy Banks Fen (Fig. 11.3), in the narrow stream valley crossing the Summertown-Radley Gravel Terrace adjacent to the Barrow Hills, Radley monument complex, was 2500-1750 cal BC (OxA-4558: 3680±120 BP; Parker 1999). The sequence, however, probably continued to the middle of the 2nd millennium cal BC. Values for tree pollen in the early Bronze Age part of the

sequence remained low and there appears to have been no more than a background presence of mixed oak, lime and hazel woodland in the catchment. A small quantity of *Crataegus* sp. (hawthorn) pollen hinted at areas of thorn scrub. This shrub is insect-pollinated, and so tends to be greatly underrepresented in pollen assemblages. Grassland was a major component of the open landscape, and there were high values for pollen of *Plantago lanceolata* (ribwort plantain) and Gramineae (grass). Cereal pollen was also present at around 1% of the dryland pollen sum, so it is likely that at least limited cereal cultivation on the gravel terraces adjacent to the fen continued from the Neolithic.

Although the preservation of mollusc shells is poor in the Bronze Age soils of the Upper Thames Valley, a few assemblages have been found, all indicative of open conditions. An uncultivated soil of late Beaker or early Bronze Age date sealed beneath a round barrow on the floodplain at King's Weir just north of Oxford contained a small group of shells including *Pupilla muscorum* and *Vallonia excentrica* suggesting grassland. Some early Bronze Age barrow contexts from the Barrow Hills site contained open-country faunas with *P. muscorum*, *V. excentrica* and, in one sample, *Truncatula cylindrica* (Robinson 1999b). The earlier Bronze Age sediments in the ditch of the Devil's Quoits henge contained open-country molluscs (Evans 1995).

The degree of clearance on the gravel terraces of the Upper Thames Valley during the early Bronze Age remains uncertain. There are many early Bronze Age ring ditches on the river gravels, and they tend to contain a layer of fine soil above their primary silting and any deposits related to rebuilding (Robinson 1992a, 53). This contrasts with the gravelly ploughsoil of Iron Age or Roman date which often fills the top of these features. This layer of fine stone-free soil indicates that there was a long stable phase which is assumed to have been grassland. Tubers of the grass *Arrhenatherum elatius* var. *bulbosus* (onion couch) seem to be particularly characteristic of Bronze Age cremations (Robinson 1988, 109) including those associated with the ring ditches and their barrows. Examples include Barrow Hills (Moffett 1999), Gravelly Guy (Moffett 2004) and Ashville (Jones 1978). The grass is characteristic of ungrazed or very lightly grazed grassland. It does not withstand heavy grazing. Perhaps the ring ditches were set amidst lightly grazed grassland from which tussocks of *Arrhenatherum* were collected for the funeral pyres.

It is unlikely that woodland had entirely disappeared from the Upper Thames Valley during the early Bronze Age. Indeed older woodland was being cleared from the floodplain of the Windrush at Mingies Ditch in the late Bronze Age (Allen and Robinson 1993, 14-15). While it is unlikely that there was much clearance in the early Bronze Age, the absence of evidence for woodland is a reflection of biases in the sources of evidence. If early Bronze Age organic palaeochannel deposits had been available for study, this bias would have been redressed.

Palaeochannel deposits which span the early Bronze Age have been analysed from the Middle Thames Valley but unfortunately they are not closely dated. At Thames Valley Park, Reading, it was argued that the beginning of the early Bronze Age was marked by a decline in pollen of *Tilia* sp. (lime; Keith-Lucas 1997). Other forest trees appeared to be unaffected, and it was suggested that there was selective felling of lime in the regional woodland. There was also evidence of an expansion of pastoral activity and, to a lesser extent, arable farming. A high level of *Pteridium aquilinum* (bracken) suggested more acidic soil on the gravel than on the terraces of the Upper Thames Valley. In contrast, at Moor Farm, Staines, the first major clearance did not occur until well into the Bronze Age (Keith-Lucas 2000). Unfortunately there is a gap in the pollen sequences from Runnymede, although by the late Bronze Age a largely open landscape had replaced the substantially wooded landscape of the Neolithic (Greig 1991; Scaife 2000). There was also a gap in the sequence at Dorney.

It has been argued that there were early Bronze Age hedged fields on the Taplow Terraces at Heathrow Terminal 5 (Lewis *et al.* 2006, 102-4). This argument, which was based on the species diversity of plant remains found in middle Bronze Age water-holes on the site, is completely rejected (see below). It is believed that these fields had their origins no earlier than 1600-1300 cal BC (Lambrick with Robinson 2009).

If the Neolithic can be characterised by cycles of woodland clearance and regeneration, the early Bronze Age can be seen as a period of larger-scale clearances that were more likely to be permanent, especially on the gravel terraces of the main river valley. However, clearance resulted in a landscape of lightly grazed grassland with thorn scrub. There were few cultivation plots and there was no evidence for field systems except possibly just before 1500 cal BC. Much woodland probably remained on the gravel terraces between monument complexes and in the tributary valleys, Likewise, the hinterland to the Thames Valley, particularly the clay slopes of the Upper Thames Valley and the various geologies of the Middle Thames Valley, probably retained much woodland.

Middle Bronze Age postscript (1500 cal BC onwards)

In the Upper Thames Valley, there is strong evidence for the continuity of open conditions around major monument complexes, even if the monuments themselves were falling into disuse. The molluscan sequence from the ditch of the Devil's Quoits henge, on the Summertown-Radley Terrace at Stanton Harcourt, showed an open environment throughout the silting of the ditch (Evans 1995). Likewise, slow silting of stone-free

soil continued in the ring ditches on the river gravels. At Yarnton, by the 3rd quarter of the 2nd millennium cal BC, few wood and tree-dependent Coleoptera were present but some seeds of *Alnus glutinosa* (alder) and a few leaf fragments of *Quercus* sp. (oak) showed that trees were not entirely absent. The occurrence of seeds of grassland plants and phytophagous insects suggest that grassland predominated and evidence from scarabaeoid dung beetles indicates that it was being grazed (Robinson in prep.).

The macroscopic plant remains from middle Bronze Age waterholes at Eight Acre Field, Radley, Appleford Sidings and Yarnton are dominated by species of mixed scrub, though pollen and insect evidence suggest largely unwooded landscapes (Parker 1995b; Robinson 1995; Robinson in prep.). Scarabaeoid dung beetles show that domestic animals were being grazed in the area. Waterlogged seeds of *Linum usitatissimum* (flax) and carbonised cereal remains were found on all three sites. The apparent discrepancy between the different lines of evidence was probably due to the macroscopic plant remains being from the vegetation surrounding the waterholes, whereas the pollen and insects were derived from the wider landscape. It is suggested that once each of the waterholes began to fall out of use and therefore fill with organic sediments, scrub was allowed to become established around them, perhaps colonising from nearby hedges. However, there had been no general abandonment on these sites to scrub regeneration; the middle Bronze Age landscape of the gravel terraces and floodplain was largely grassland with at least small areas of cultivation.

There was, however, still some woodland on the gravel terraces and floodplain, for example in the Lower Windrush, until the late Bronze Age (Allen and Robinson 1993), and woodland also remained towards the top of the Upper Thames Valley on the floodplain and on the Northmoor Terrace (Scaife 1999; Robinson 2002).

Around 1500 cal BC, the middle Bronze Age saw the beginning of major changes to the landscape of the Thames Valley. Much, probably most, of the gravel terraces and floodplain of the main valley had been cleared by this date. Middle Bronze Age fields were present on some of the settlements mentioned above, and several groups of small rectilinear fields have been identified from aerial photography. Cereals were certainly being cultivated in the area before this date although on a very small scale. Likewise, domestic animals were being raised and perhaps grazed extensively but the pressure of grazing was light. The organisation of the open landscape in the Neolithic and early Bronze Age seems to have been related as much to earlier ceremonial monuments as to agricultural produc-tion. After this date, more intensive agriculture began within the small, probably hedged, fields which were laid out around an increasing number of settlements. Many had pond-like waterholes within them. The main use of the fields seems to have been pasture but cereal and other crops were also being cultivated on a larger scale than previously. The areas between the settlements were perhaps lightly grazed rough pasture on which limited thorn scrub was presumably present. Even by the end of the middle Bronze Age there was certainly some woodland remaining on the gravels at the top of the Upper Thames Valley, in the tributary valleys and perhaps in some of the gaps between settlements. The hinterland to the Thames Valley, particularly the clay slopes of the Upper Thames Valley and the various acid geologies of the Middle Thames Valley, probably retained much woodland.

ORIGIN AND DEVELOPMENT OF AGRICULTURE IN THE THAMES VALLEY

No evidence has yet been found in the region to suggest agricultural activity prior to the beginning of the 4th millennium cal BC. The pollen results from Daisy Banks Fen, Radley (Fig. 11.3) suggested cereal cultivation on the Second Gravel Terrace of the Upper Thames from 4350-3750 cal BC (OxA-8559: 5240±110 BP) onwards (Parker 1999). In the Middle Thames Valley at Runnymede, an insect assemblage suggestive of the grazing of domestic animals was found in a deposit of detrital peat dated to 4040-3790 cal BC (BM-2657: 5130±50 BP; Robinson 2000b, 150-2; Robinson 2000a, 31-2) although pollen evidence for cereals did not appear until later in the sequence (Scaife 2000, 174-5). As has already been noted (and see below, Chapter 11), there is no evidence from the region for a gradual transition from a Mesolithic to a fully Neolithic subsistence economy.

Wheat and barley are cultivars derived from wild desert-edge grasses of the Near East, and they require all the available daylight for them to be grown under British conditions. They also need to be sown in a seedbed which has been sufficiently well cultivated to eliminate most potentially competing weeds. This means that clearings for growing cereals would have had to have been of an area of at least 1 ha, probably more, otherwise large proportions would have been shaded by surrounding trees. The clearings would also have needed to have their soil broken up either by ploughing or by spade cultivation. The chalk beneath the South Street Long Barrow in the Upper Kennet Valley had been scored by two sets of plough marks running at right angles to each other (Evans 1971) showing that ard (scratch plough) cultivation was practised in early Neolithic England. Cultivated soil may also have been present beneath the Wayland's Smithy long barrow (Whittle 1991), and it has been suggested that middens were used, perhaps even deliberately created, in order to cultivate plots (Guttman 2005).

Cereals could have been sown either in autumn or spring. If they were autumn-sown, the seedlings would not have needed much attention until mid-March and if grazed, the plants would have responded by tillering (producing side shoots). However, from late March onwards, which is also when spring crops would have been sown, crops would have needed to be protected from grazing. It is also likely that some weeding would have been necessary. Therefore, even if Neolithic society were mobile, there would have been at the very least a presence in the vicinity of cultivation plots from mid March until harvest time, perhaps in August.

Cereals appear in the earliest dated fourth millennium cal BC contexts in this region, at Hazleton North long cairn, from the Area 6 midden at the Eton Rowing Course and a pit deposit at Yarnton, for example (Allen *et al.* 2004, 91; Bayliss and Hey in prep.; Meadows *et al.* 2007). The pollen evidence from Daisy Banks Fen suggested that cereal plots were located on the adjacent Second Terrace of the Upper Thames at Barrow Hills, Radley at the start of the Neolithic (Fig. 11.3; Parker 1999; Robinson 1999b). Unusually, this area remained open, and cultivation continued throughout the Neolithic. Cereal cultivation also apparently occurred in some smaller and impermanently cleared areas, as, for example, at Runnymede in the Middle Thames (Scaife 2000, 174-5). However, there is no evidence from the region for 'slash and burn' agriculture where plots were cleared and burnt, crops grown for a couple of seasons in the soil, the fertility of which had been enhanced by the ashes, the plots then utilised for grazing for a few more years before being abandoned to woodland regeneration.

Charred crop remains are very sparse from earlier Neolithic settlements but the following have been identified from all parts of the valley: *Triticum dicoccum* (emmer), a free-threshing variety of *Triticum* sp. and *Hordeum* sp. (hulled barley). The free-threshing *Triticum* was probably a short-grained variety of *T. aestivum* sl. (bread-type wheat) but *T. turgidum* (rivet wheat) is also a possibility. The charred cereal remains are supplemented by seed impressions on pottery: impressions of *T. dicoccum*, *Hordeum vulgare* (six-row barley), *M. sylvestris* and *P. spinosa* were noted in sherds from the Abingdon Causewayed Enclosure (Helbaek 1952, 334; Murphy 1982).

Charred plant remains from earlier Neolithic contexts from a substantial area of floodplain of the Upper Thames at Yarnton have been studied in detail (Robinson 2000c; Hey *et al.* 2003; Robinson in prep.). The earlier Neolithic features included a substantial rectangular building, a rectangular ceremonial structure and some pits. The flotation of all the soil from the postholes of the Neolithic yielded only three hazelnut shells and no cereal remains. Only one context, a pit, contained a high concentration of remains with almost two items per litre. Summary results are given in Table 9.1. Two cereals were present, *Triticum dicoccum* (emmer wheat) and *Hordeum* sp. (barley). There were also fragments of *Malus* sp. (apple) and *Corylus avellana* (hazel) nut shell fragments. Cereal chaff and weed

Table 9.1: Summary of charred plant remains from early Neolithic contexts at Yarnton and the Eton Rowing Lake, Dorney

Species		Number of items	
		Yarnton pit	*Dorney midden*
Triticum dicoccum - grain	emmer wheat	3	14
T. dicoccum or *spelta* - grain	emmer or spelt	2	2
Triticum sp. - free-threshing grain	rivet or bread-type wheat	-	-
Triticum sp. - grain	wheat	2	5
Hordeum sp. - hulled grain	hulled barley	-	1
Hordeum sp. - grain	barley	2	1
Indeterminate cereal grain		38	73
Total cereal grain		47	96
Prunus spinosa - stone	sloe	-	3
Crataegus cf *monogyna* - stone	hawthorn	1	-
Malus sp. - endocarp and skin frags	crab apple	2	-
Corylus avellana - nutshell frags	hazel	118	53

seeds were absent.

A most interesting discovery was made from the pit. There were two fragments of charred bread, vesicular material containing partly crushed cereal grains including *Hordeum* sp. Two separate assays on the bread gave a combined radiocarbon date of 3620-3350 cal BC (OxA-6412: 4675±70 BP; NZA-8679: 4672±57 BP).

Probably the richest earlier Neolithic charred assemblage of food plant remains from the Middle Thames Valley was from midden material in the upper fill of a palaeochannel of the Thames at Dorney (Robinson 2000c). Emmer wheat and hulled barley were found with a few grains of a free-threshing wheat. Hazelnut shell fragments were well-represented but unusually they were outnumbered by cereal grain.

The Yarnton evidence showed that the cereals were rough ground to make a type of bread. From at least the late Bronze Age onwards, hulled wheats including emmer were parched to facilitate dehusking the grain. The resultant chaff was often either used to fuel the parching process or was discarded onto the fire as waste. In addition, grain being parched was sometimes accidentally burnt. Many late Bronze Age and Iron Age settlements in the Thames Valley have rich assemblages of charred remains which resulted from this process. However, chaff was entirely absent from the early Neolithic sites so far investigated in the Thames Valley and almost absent from the later Neolithic sites. It is possible that other means, such as pounding and rubbing alone, were used to dehusk grain.

Hazelnuts would have been widely available in woodland. (The paucity of nuts from some modern hazel woodland is the result of depredations by the introduced grey squirrel which eats developing nuts; the native red squirrel only feeds on mature

nuts.) The cropping capacity of hazel is much reduced when it is growing as an understorey to tall-growing trees such as lime on oak. It is possible that some of the opening up of woodland which was occurring in the earlier Neolithic was intended to enhance the nut harvest (as perhaps it was in the Mesolithic) as well as to improve browsing for domestic animals, although there is no direct evidence for this. Gathered food plant remains are found on settlement sites, including *Corylus avellana* (hazel), *Malus sylvestris* (crab apple), *Crataegus* cf *monogyna* (hawthorn) and *Prunus spinosa* (sloe). Indeed, charred cereal grains are usually outnumbered by carbonised hazelnut shell fragments.

The relative importance of cereals and hazelnuts in the Neolithic diet is a topic of much debate (Moffett *et al.* 1989; Jones 2000; Robinson 2000c). It must be made clear that what we are not seeing is a gradual transition in which the earliest settlements have the highest proportion of gathered wild food plant remains. The use of cereals was a usual part of the Neolithic economy over much, if not all, of England and Wales from the start of the Neolithic but so was the collection of wild food plants, particularly hazelnuts, from woodland or scrub (Moffett *et al.* 1989, 247). Gathered plant foods are commonly found in middens and pit deposits, where hazelnut shells are abundant, but apple/pear, blackberries and sloes have also been found. The collection of wild food plants in addition to cereal cultivation continued throughout the Neolithic. Indeed higher proportions of cereal grain to nut shell fragments tend to be a feature of earlier Neolithic settlements (Robinson 2000c, 87).

It is not possible to give an accurate estimate of the contribution wild edible plants made to the Neolithic diet because different factors operated in the preservation of their remains in comparison to those of cereals. The hazelnut shells were waste, and it is not surprising that they were burnt. In contrast, any charred grain would have been burnt accidentally. However, concentrations of wild food plant remains in relation to cereal remains were certainly much lower on post-Neolithic sites in the Thames Valley than on Neolithic sites, so whatever the proportion they comprised of the Neolithic diet, it was probably much greater than it was in later periods.

The domestic mammals which were introduced at the start of the Neolithic were also domesticated in the Near East. However, two of them, cattle and pig, had a very wide distribution in Western Asia and Europe and were native to England. Both are well adapted to partly wooded conditions. Sheep were not native to England and require some grass-land to graze. Some grazing presumably occurred in areas which had been fully cleared. However, the evidence noted above from Runnymede suggested that animals were being grazed under largely wooded conditions at the start of the Neolithic, and in a landscape with a major presence of woodland in the middle Neolithic. The high proportion of cattle and pig in contrast to the low proportion of sheep in bone assemblages would be consistent with much grazing being under partly wooded conditions. The deliberate killing of some trees would have greatly increased illumination of the woodland floor thereby facilitating more lush growth with a higher energy content within the reach of cattle and pigs. While stocking levels for domestic animals would not have been as high as for an area which had been completely cleared by felling the trees, the return per unit of effort expended on cutting would probably have been greater. It is possible that domestic animals were managed by transhumant herders over extensive areas. However, the control of cattle was such that there does not seem to have been interbreeding with aurochs. Bones of animals intermediate in size between domestic and wild cattle have not been reported. Pigs were probably herded into areas of closed woodland when fungi or tree seeds or mast were available. Indeed, isotopic evidence suggests that fungi formed a major component of the diet of pigs in the Thames Valley during the Neolithic in contrast to later periods (Hamilton *et al.* 2009)

Table 9.2: Summary of animal bone from the Abingdon causewayed enclosure

Species	% Fragments	% Minimum no. individuals
Cattle	56.5	43.2
Sheep/Goat	8.7	13.5
Pig	34.1	37.8
Red Deer	0.5	2.7
Dog	0.2	2.7
Total no.	616	37

The only large published assemblage of earlier Neolithic animal bones from the region is from the Abingdon causewayed enclosure, on the Summertown-Radley Gravel Terrace of the Upper Thames (Table 9.2; Cram 1982). There is little published information from the Middle Thames Valley. Three new domestic animals join dog, which was present in the Mesolithic: cattle, pig and sheep. In addition, goat was identified from the Abingdon causewayed enclosure (Cram 1982, 43) although Wilson (in Robinson and Wilson 1987, 34) raised the possibility that the bone could have been intrusive, and doubt has similarly been cast on a horse scapula from the Drayton cursus (Ayres and Powell 2003, 158).

Bones of wild mammals are also usually present in earlier Neolithic bone assemblages. Species from the region include aurochs, red deer and roe deer (Robinson and Wilson 1987, 35). In contrast to the ratio between wild food plant remains and crop remains, the bones of wild mammals are usually greatly outnumbered by the bones of domestic animals.

There is often the problem with Neolithic bone assemblages of deciding whether they reflect 'typical' domestic activity or whether they were derived from ritual events, perhaps including feasting. Although this applies to the bones from the Abingdon causewayed enclosure, these bones still provide useful evidence for earlier Neolithic exploitation of animals. These were very few bones of wild animals. It is possible that some of the cattle bones were from aurochs but all the pigs were apparently domestic (Cram 1982). The limited evidence from tooth eruption and wear, and from bone epiphyses fusion suggested that around a quarter of the cattle were killed in their first year but that many animals lived for more than four years. This need imply no more than the retention of some older animals for breeding purposes, but it is at least possible that dairying was occurring. The pig teeth suggested animals were being slaughtered at all ages. The range of bones suggested that animals were killed and butchered at the site. Cut marks on the bones suggested that carcasses were disarticulated by cutting ligaments and tendons with knives. Some bones had apparently been split to extract marrow. Cattle and pig were the main animals eaten. Once carcass weight is also considered, it is clear that beef comprised the majority of the meat at around 80% of the total. Pig made up around another 15% with mutton and venison only playing a minor part in the diet.

The packing of a large post pit of the Yarnton building contained material which was interpreted as resulting from feasting, with prime meat-bearing bones of domestic animals and some articulated pig bones (Hey *et al.* 2003, 81). Charcoal from the pit gave a radiocarbon date of 3950-3640 cal BC (OxA-6772: 4970±60 BP).

Further evidence for diet in the Neolithic is provided by the analysis of lipids from sherds.

Samples from a range of sites, including Ascott-under-Wychwood, Runnymede Bridge, the Eton Rowing Course, the Abingdon causewayed enclosure, Yarnton, and Windmill Hill have been analysed in this way (Copley *et al*. 2003; Copley *et al*. 2005a; 2005b; Copley and Evershed 2007). High proportions of dairy fats were found at all of these sites (Copley *et al* 2005), although other lipids, from the pigs and the carcasses of ruminants, were also present. Experiments conducted by Copley *et al*. (2005a; 2005b) suggest that the dairy fats are more likely to derive from butter fats than from milk, and they suggest that many of the traces of dairy lipids may derive from the melting of butter during cooking. Although dairy and ruminant adipose fat remained common, analysis of a sample of late Neolithic Grooved Ware sherds, including some from Yarnton, has shown that they contained a higher proportion of pork fat than is present earlier in the Neolithic (and in later periods; Mukherjee *et al*. 2007). This is consistent with the evidence provided by animal bones discussed above. There is much less evidence for plant-derived fats, probably because plants contain significantly lower proportions of fats than do animal products. Nonetheless a couple of sherds from Windmill Hill and three from Yarnton did contained plant-derived lipids (Copley *et al*. 2005a), although in all cases these were associated with animal fats. Beeswax has also been identified on five vessels from the Eton Rowing Course and one from Runnymede Bridge.

Chapter 10 – Mesolithic communities in the Thames Valley: living in the natural landscape

by Gill Hey with Mark Robinson

HUNTER-GATHERERS

From early in the Holocene, southern England was inhabited by small groups of people who hunted wild animals, birds and fish, and gathered plant foods that grew naturally in the varied ecological niches of the valley bottom, slopes and surrounding upland areas. A conservative estimate of population density towards the end of this period, based on that of ethnographically known hunter-gatherers in similar environments, is 0.1 individuals per km² (Milner *et al.* 2004, 13). This would equate to a population of only around 1000 people in the Thames and its catchment. The main evidence that we have for these people and their lifestyles consists of the flint tools that have been recovered from later features and modern ground surfaces and, much more rarely, from occupation sites and activity areas. These flint artefacts are typified by small objects such as microliths and blades, but larger tools such as tranchet adzes are also found (Fig. 10.1). There is also limited evidence for the use of bone, antler and stone other than flint and, very occasionally, ornaments such as beads are found. Some material was acquired from quite distant sources: the Dorset chert that was used for an axe found at Wawcott in the Middle Kennet Valley (Froom 1963a), for example, and tools made from Chalk flint which were recovered on the Cotswolds at the northern limit of our area. Activity at Thatcham, Berkshire is known from the 10th or possibly the 11th millennium cal BC (Wymer 1962; Gowlett *et al.* 1987; Chisham 2006), and a hunting and gathering way of life continued until around the turn of the 4th millennium cal BC when domesticated plants and animals were introduced, and pottery and new types of flint implements began to be made. Probably the latest dates associated with Mesolithic activity are the very late 5th millennium cal BC dates obtained from beech charcoal recovered from beneath the Ascott-under-Wychwood long barrow in Oxfordshire (Benson and Whittle 2007, 25-7) and late 5th millennium or, just possibly, very early 4th millennium dates on a red deer antler mattock from Staines (4360-3970 cal BC, OxA-1158: 5350±100 BP; Bonsall and Smith 1989) and charcoal in a hearth at Wawcott (4350-3790 cal BC, BM-449: 5260±130 BP; Froom 1972).

The hunter-gatherer population would have been highly knowledgeable about their surrounding landscape, and very sensitive to changes within it. They would have maintained a complex and shifting web of relationships both with the natural environment and with neighbouring groups. Sparse evidence suggests that in the realm of social relations, belief and expression, their lives were rich (Milner and Woodman 2005; Conneller and Warren 2006). When we attempt to study Mesolithic people, however, we face a number of fundamental difficulties. Sites are few, their use is often short lived, and they are seldom well preserved; activity is usually only represented by artefact scatters in the modern ploughsoil. It is thus difficult to assess the range of activities that may have been undertaken in any one place at any one time, the longevity of occupation there, and the functional and chronological relationships between adjacent sites. Furthermore, we are looking at a long period of around 6,000 years, the chronology of which is only poorly understood (Barton and Roberts 2004, 340-1; Warren 2006). The paucity of intact surfaces and stratified sequences means that material suitable for scientific dating is rare and chronological control weak. There are no more than 35 radiocarbon dates on Mesolithic samples in the catchment, the majority coming from Kennet Valley sites. Our dating thus relies on artefact typologies, the chronology of which is known only approximately.

Diagnostically early Mesolithic flint assemblages are represented by simple microlith forms (oblique points and broad triangles) with a range of other equipment, including end scrapers, microdenticulates, burins, awls and bifacially-flaked axeheads or adzes (Fig. 10.1; Barton and Roberts 2004, 342). Where assemblages are of reasonable size, it is sometimes possible to distinguish chronological traits within early Mesolithic groups (Reynier 1998). Earliest, 'Star Carr' assemblages, represented by microliths with broad oblique points, isosceles triangles and trapezoids, have been found as far south as Thatcham in the Middle Kennet Valley. Slightly later, 'Deepcar' assemblages, perhaps dating to around 9400 years ago, have more slender oblique points, with few isosceles triangles and trapezoids. Still later early Mesolithic 'Horsham' assemblages (after around 9000 years ago), with distinctive basally-retouched microlith forms, are more common and widely dispersed (Barton and Roberts 2004).

Small geometric and more varied microlith forms are the defining characteristics of late Mesolithic assemblages (Fig. 10.1); smaller microliths, and rod microliths in particular, are seen as indicative of very late dates (ibid.). Axes and adzes also appear to be more common (Gardiner 1988). There are, however, many sites of uncertain date within the Mesolithic period because of the lack of diagnostic elements within the associated artefact assemblages. End scrapers, microdenticulates, burins,

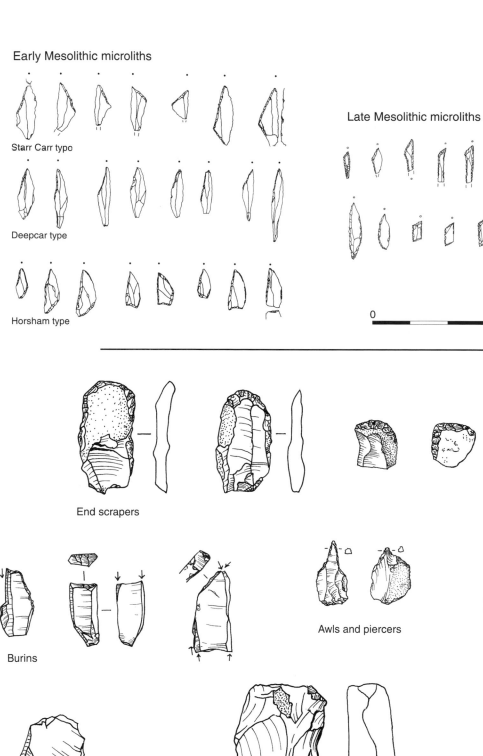

Early Mesolithic microliths

Starr Carr type

Deepcar type

Horsham type

Late Mesolithic microliths

0 ——————————————— 100 mm

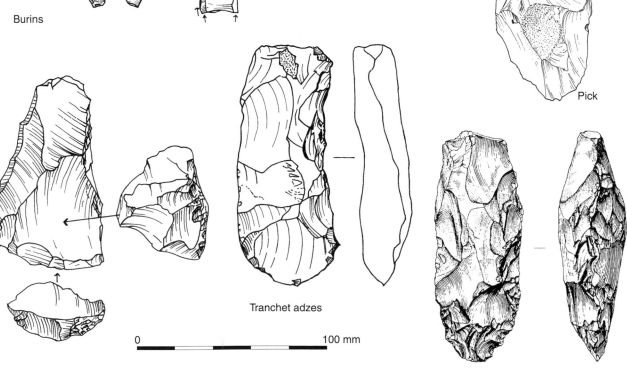

End scrapers

Burins

Awls and piercers

Tranchet adzes

Pick

0 ——————————————— 100 mm

194

awls and bifacially flaked adzes and axeheads, and picks, for example, are found throughout the period, even if the proportions in which they occur change (Barton and Roberts 2004; Butler 2005). Additionally, there can be difficulties in distinguishing between late Mesolithic and early Neolithic assemblages that lack diagnostic microliths or leaf-shaped arrowheads (Holgate 1988a, 54-60; 2004b); both have types of tranchet axe (Gardiner 1990).

As discussed in the previous chapter, Mesolithic populations lived at a time when the region was still changing geomorphologically. At the beginning of the Mesolithic, Britain was still part of the European mainland and became an island only around 7000 or 8000 years ago. Such transformations would, of course, have had a more profound effect on people living further down the Thames as landscapes drowned and marine influences began to have an impact on dry-land environments, but it may also

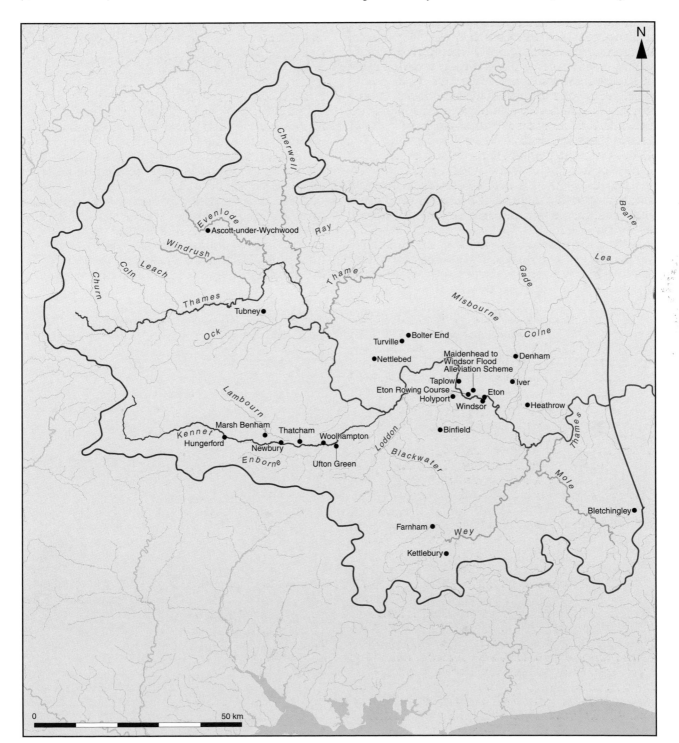

Fig. 10.1 (facing page) Mesolithic flintwork   *Fig. 10.2 (above) Early Mesolithic sites in the Thames Valley*

have affected communities in the Middle Thames, both in terms of changing hydrology and in their contacts with more distant neighbours. Probably of far greater consequence in our area would have been the alteration of the inland landscape as it gradually changed from one of open grassland with some pine and birch woodland to much more closed deciduous woodland in response to the warmer and wetter climate. This would have affected not only the appearance of the area and the experience of living in it, but would also have had practical effects for the people moving through the landscape and obtaining their food and other resources from it. Gathered foods from woodland, particularly fruits and nuts, would have formed an increasingly important part of the diet. Animal populations would also have changed in response to environmental shifts, with the highly gregarious reindeer and horse being replaced by mammals which form smaller social groups such as deer, boar and wild cattle. The Mesolithic tool assemblage includes specialist woodworking equipment such as transversely sharpened axes and adzes, and more flexible tool kits with portable items suited to a mobile lifestyle and hunting small game within a more enclosed setting (cf Childe 1931; Clarke 1976a).

Within the wooded environment of the Thames Valley and its catchment, early and later Mesolithic activity is surprisingly widespread (Holgate 1988a)

and the distribution of sites along the river valley is striking (Figs 10.2 and 10.12). It is uncertain what proportion of these sites are of early date, but certainly by the later Mesolithic travel by boat would have been the easiest way to move about (Reynier 1998). Even in the early Mesolithic, river and other waterside locations seem to have been preferred in the Thames region. Long-distance movement between coastal and inland areas has been proposed for some parts of southern Britain (eg Barton *et al.* 1995), but there is no evidence for this in the Thames Valley.

MOVEMENT AND HABITATION IN THE EARLY MESOLITHIC

The Kennet Valley

The Kennet Valley provides a good model for Mesolithic habitation in the Thames Valley catchment. The greatest concentration of Mesolithic sites known in the region is found in the middle of the valley on or near the valley floor (Fig. 10.3). Of these, the site of Thatcham has been most extensively excavated (Fig. 10.4). Discovered at the Newbury Corporation Sewage Works beneath peaty deposits, and first excavated in 1920 and 1921 by Peake and Crawford (1922), it was examined more extensively by John Wymer between 1958 and 1969 at his sites I

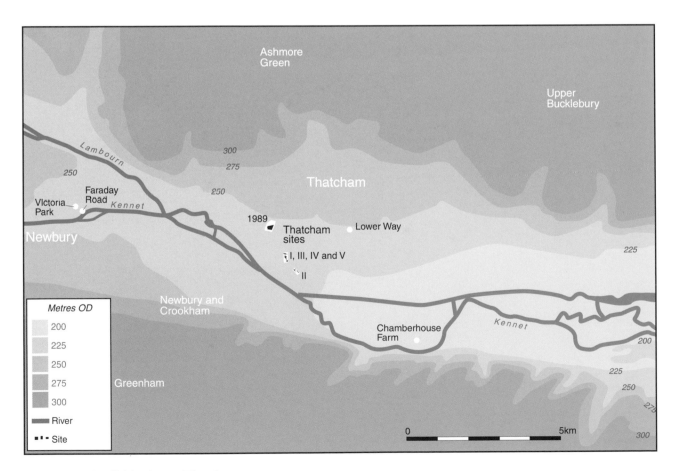

Fig. 10.3   Mesolithic sites at Thatcham

196

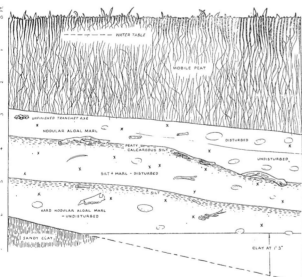

Fig. 10.4   Work in the coffer dam (Site V) below the bluff at Thatcham

– V (Wymer 1962). Later excavations were undertaken by Wessex Archaeology in 1989 in the sewage works themselves (Healy *et al.* 1992), and are referred to here as sites WA1 and WA2.

People first came to the Thatcham site early in the Mesolithic period. A date provided by a worked antler beam from an adjacent swampy area (Site IV, 9660-8780 cal BC, OxA-732: 9760±120 BP) suggests

activity may have begun as early as the 10th millennium cal BC. Earlier dates (10,400-9220 cal BC, Q-658: 10030±170; 10,850-9550 cal BC, Q-659: 10365±170; Reynier 2000) were obtained from a hearth on Site III, but these were derived from bulked samples of wood charcoal. The sites lie on a gravel bluff at the edge of a fen, immediately overlooking a stream that was part of the meandering river system of the Kennet (Wymer 1962; Healy *et al.* 1992). The occupied area itself seems to have consisted of fairly open dry grassland with low-growing herb and grass flora. It was, however, situated within a broader mosaic of pine and hazel woodland with, increasingly, areas of deciduous oak and elm, and, within the fen, stands of birch, pine and willow (Churchill 1962; Holyoak 1980; Scaife 1992; Allen and Healy 1992). The variety of environmental niches in the surrounding area was probably one of its attractive features.

At least seven separate occupation or activity areas, some associated with hearths and spreads of charcoal, have been identified, although there were probably many more. Further deposits have been recovered from below the gravel bluff (Fig. 10.4). The hearths had been scraped out of the gravel, and one was lined with large flints and sarsen stones (Wymer 1962, 333). Calcined bone and flint and burnt pebbles in the area also testified to cooking activities. Wymer suggested that the charcoal spreads, which were around 20 m in diameter, represented hut sites, perhaps of a band of a few dozen individuals who returned to this place periodically (ibid. 336-7).

These sites represent events over a considerable period of time. Patinated flints of 'Star Carr' type have come from the earliest occupation levels (on Site III). Most occupation, however, was slightly later in date, and seems to belong to the 'Deepcar' tradition, in which longer and more slender microliths were made (Reynier 2000). Mastic found on a flake of this type has been radiocarbon dated to 8640-8260 cal BC (OxA-2848: 9200±90 BP; Roberts *et al.* 1998), and burnt elk antler from a deposit below the bluff of the main occupation provided a date of 9250-8550 cal BC (OxA-894: 9490±110 BP; Gowlett *et al.* 1987). Sections through these low-lying deposits revealed the presence of small numbers of flints throughout the stratigraphic sequences suggesting that the nearby occupation was long lived. Wymer did not, however, believe that settlement was continuous, but that there was a clear succession of occupations (Wymer 1962, 333). Many visits of different duration may have taken place. More recent work, further north in the sewage works, has indicated activity from at least two separate events, with charred hazelnut shells from the earlier site (WA1) yielding a radiocarbon result of 8600-8000 cal BC (BM-2755: 9100±80 BP; Healy *et al.* 1992). The flint assemblage was similar to those excavated further south. The more northerly concentration (WA2) lay over a relict stream channel, and did not yield

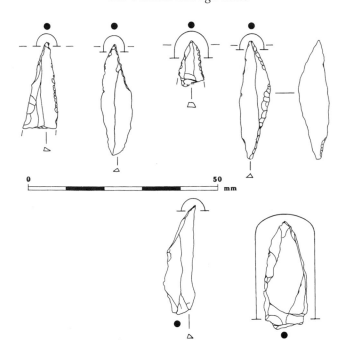

Microliths used with a rotational motion

a) Cutting soft material

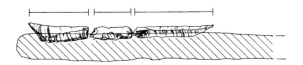

b) Cutting medium material

Flakes, blades and bladelets used for cutting and scraping

Key Reconstruction of hafting

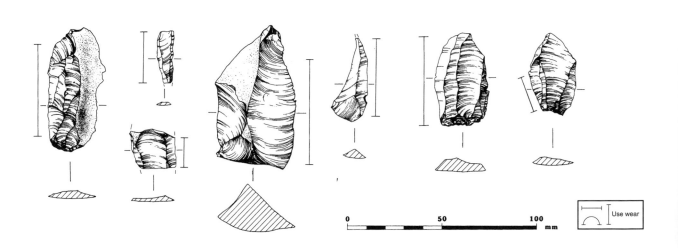

material suitable for dating. It appears, however, to be typologically later, perhaps hundreds of years later, with geometric points and smaller microliths (ibid., 52-3).

Over 18,000 struck flints were recovered from the Thatcham sites, of which the vast majority (roughly 97%) was waste generated from knapping tools, and the impression that a good deal of flint working was taking place is reinforced by the identification of refitting flakes amongst the assemblage (Wymer 1962, 339). One intriguing discovery was a red deer skullcap with antlers, found inverted and standing proud of the Mesolithic surface on Site II (Fig. 10.18). The antlers had probably been used as anvils during flint tool preparation, and the battered beam of another antler which had been used as a hammer was found lying propped up against them, with a concentration of waste flint lying to one side (ibid.). The survival of this group of objects and perhaps the use of red deer suggests that they had special significance. Analogies drawn from historically documented hunting groups show that hunters often share particular affinity with their quarry, especially the animals that require the greatest knowledge and skill to hunt (Chatterton 2006; Jordan 2006; cf Conneller 2004). Thus, the bones of red deer may have imbued the flint tools with qualities which might have been seen to make them particularly successful in the hunting of deer and other animals (Warren 2006, 21–5).

The tools which remained on the site, as opposed to those which were made here for use elsewhere, included microliths, scrapers, burins, awls, hammerstones and axes/adzes. There were also resharpening flakes from these tools. Traditionally these would be seen as representing a 'home-base', with tools made for a range of tasks including hunting, domestic activities and woodworking although, as we have seen, the palimpsest of occupation events shows that the assemblage as a whole may represent different activities from many different visits. A study of the edges of tools from the two most northerly Thatcham sites (WA1 and WA2) showed that five of the six microliths, tools normally thought to be part of composite arrowheads for hunting, had been used in a rotational motion, one for piercing soft material and three for medium-density material such as wood (Fig. 10.5; Grace 1992, 60–1). Flakes, which are usually considered to be waste, had been used for cutting soft material such as vegetable matter, and for scraping, as had unretouched blades and bladelets (ibid., 58-60). One flake on Site III had traces of mastic adhering to it suggesting that it had been hafted with other blades into wood as a composite tool (Roberts *et al.* 1998). It may have been part of a grating board for plant foods or, perhaps, for flaying birch bark (ibid.). Grace also proposes that flakes and blades were hafted to form composite cutting tools (Grace 1992, fig. 17). Flint material was used expediently here, and there was no clear correlation between tool type and function.

The importance of processing plant foods is reinforced by the presence of numerous burnt hazelnut shells on all sites, especially in association with charcoal patches (Churchill 1962; Scaife 1992), although Scaife has questioned whether the quantities really indicate that this was a significant food source rather than a snack (ibid.). Otherwise there was no surviving plant food material. Indirect evidence from the usewear analysis indicated the processing of tuberous foods, such as wild carrots and parsnips, rather than grasses (Grace 1992, 59).

Animal bone was very poorly preserved on the northern sites, but Wymer's excavations on more low-lying ground yielded large assemblages. Red deer was the meat of choice here, and it has been calculated that one red deer might provide a substantial meal for 50–75 people (Miracle 2002, 83). There were smaller amounts of roe deer and wild pig, occasional aurochs, wild cat, fox and wolf, with very occasional horse and elk (King in Wymer 1962, 355-61; see below). There were also bones from a range of birds and fowl, rodents and other small mammals reminding us of the wide variety of protein sources available even if not all these animals were eaten. Dogs were also present, and probably assisted in the hunt. Wymer originally suggested that a small gully on Site III was a fish trap (Wymer 1962, 336) but it is now thought to be a beaver-cut channel (Wymer 1991, 27). Only a single pike vertebra was recovered, although the paucity of fish bones on site does not necessarily mean fish was not eaten (Milner 2006, 75). Fragile fish bones may not have survived (although other small bones had been preserved) or may have been removed for disposal elsewhere. It is possible, for example, that they were returned to the water whence they came. Some support for the suggestion that consumption of fish was very limited is provided, however, by isotopic analysis on a human femur from the site the results of which indicated a diet lacking in freshwater fish as well as marine resources (including salmon which have a marine isotopic signature). Similar results were obtained from a dog bone also found at the site (Schulting and Richards 2000). Two samples are hardly representative, but they do provide a solid piece of evidence in the debate, which persists throughout the prehistoric period in the Thames Valley, over whether the absence of fish on sites is the result of a taboo against eating fish or the result of decay or discard practices.

The left humerus fragment from an adult, probably female, from a flood deposit below the occupation sites at Thatcham (Brothwell in Wymer 1962, 355), is the only human bone from the Thames region which is certainly of Mesolithic date. Three human skulls were reported by Silus Palmer in the

Fig. 10.5 (opposite) Usewear on flints from Thatcham

Fig. 10.6 (overleaf) The Mesolithic in the Kennet Valley

THE MESOLITHIC IN

The Kennet Valley provides a good model for Mesolithic habitation in the Thames Valley. The greatest concentration of Mesolithic sites in the region is found in the middle of the valley on or near the valley floor. Of these, the site of **Thatcham** has been most extensively excavated.

The sites lie on a gravel bluff at the edge of a fen, immediately overlooking a stream that was part of the meandering river system of the Kennet. The occupied area seems to have consisted of fairly open dry grassland with low-growing herb and grass flora. It was, however, situated within a broader mosaic of pine and hazel woodland with, increasingly, areas of deciduous oak and elm, and, within the fen, stands of birch, pine and willow. The variety of environmental niches in the surrounding area was probably one of its attractive features.

At least seven separate activity areas, some associated with hearths and spreads of charcoal, have been identified. The hearths had been scraped out of the gravel, and one was lined with large flints and sarsen stones. Calcined bone and flint and burnt pebbles testify to cooking activities. The charcoal spreads, around 20 m in diameter, may have represented hut sites, perhaps of a band of a few dozen individuals who returned to this place periodically.

Tim Taylor's reconstruction of a Mesolithic settlement

THE KENNET VALLEY

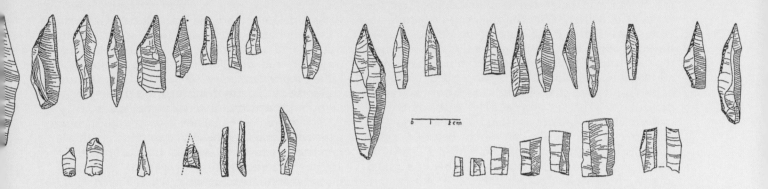

These sites represent events over a considerable period of time. Patinated flints of 'Star Carr' type have come from the earliest occupation levels, but most occupation was slightly later in date, and seems to belong to the 'Deepcar' tradition, in which longer and more slender microliths were made.

These sites also provide evidence for the range of other activities. Analysis of the mastic adhering to a flake showed that it had been prepared with resin, probably of birch, mixed with clay and a lipid or beeswax (Roberts *et al.* 1998). If the latter, the availability of honey is implied. Antler and bone had been used to make a range of objects: bone points, an arrowhead, pins, chisels, the point of a bodkin, a punch, and other tools, including an unusual spearhead resembling a Palaeolithic type.

The Thatcham sites form one concentration within a wider spread of early Mesolithic sites, mainly located on low terraces and bluffs of the Kennet and its tributaries, where a range of activities took place. At the adjacent sites of Faraday Road and Greenham Dairy Farm in Newbury, the focus of activity seems to have been on the processing and consumption of wild boar, although some aurochs, red deer, roe deer, wild cat and beaver were also found. Charred hazelnut shells were also numerous amongst the cooking remains and the paucity of hazel trees in the pollen diagrams demonstrate that these were for food rather than the result of burning the local vegetation.

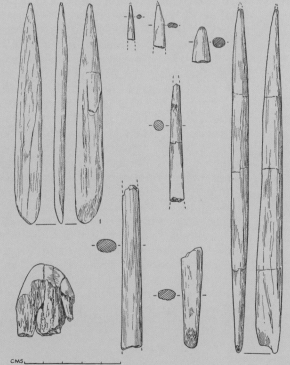

Top: Mesolithic flint from Sites 1 and 2 at Thatcham: microliths, microburins and segmented blades

Middle right: A concentration of animal bone from the surface of the Mesolithic layer at Faraday Road

Above: Spearheads, points, pins and other objects in bone and antler from Sites II, III and IV at Thatcham

19th century as coming from the peat near Newbury, one found accompanied by 'rude instruments of stone … at the contact of peat with the underlying shell-marl' and another at Halfway close to red deer antlers (Palmer 1872-5). These skulls have not been dated and their whereabouts is unknown. It is uncertain whether the Thatcham bone had eroded from the site or had been deliberately deposited in the water (Conneller 2005). The majority of the animal bone was also recovered from offsite 'refuse areas' at the edge of the fen, and the quantities present might represent the remains of feasting rather than, or in addition to, everyday consumption. Such collections of bone and other material indicate more than casual deposition. What is disposed of and where is a cultural choice, and bones from both feasting events and day-to-day meals can often be seen to be carefully managed (Miracle 2002; Milner 2006, 75). These places of deposition may then become sacred in their own right (Jordan 2006, 95-8). Rituals are often also associated with the treatment of hunted animals: if prey are treated with respect they will be more co-operative in the hunt (Chatterton 2006, 104). The Thatcham deposits might represent a special site at which bone was placed, and one which, as it was wet, might have discouraged gnawing animals. At nearby Ham Marsh, Newbury, the skeleton of an aurochs with microliths embedded into its sinus region was found alongside the horn of a red deer and this, too, might indicate an animal allowed to lie where it fell for a special reason (Palmer 1872-5, 133; Chatterton 2006, 104).

The Thatcham site is also striking because of the evidence for the range of other activities that have been found. Analysis of the mastic adhering to a flake showed that it had been prepared with resin, probably of birch, mixed with clay and a lipid or beeswax (Roberts *et al.* 1998). If the latter, the availability of honey is implied. Antler and bone had been used to make a range of objects: bone points, an arrowhead, pins, chisels, the point of a bodkin, a punch, and other tools, including an unusual spearhead resembling a Palaeolithic type (Wymer 1962, 351-3; Fig. 10.6). Abrasion on some of the flints from the northern site (WA2) indicated that bone working may have taken place here, in addition to hide scraping (Grace 1992, 59). The bone tools from the southern sites also indicate the preparation of clothes and fabric for bedding and shelters, such as tents. Skins and hides would have come from the larger animals, with fur and sinews being provided by the small mammals found (Chisham 2006). Small, natural, perforated pebbles may have been for clothing or strung as jewellery. Woodworking is indicated by abrasion on flints on both northern sites, with an emphasis on boring, grooving and whittling on the earlier of these sites (Grace 1992, 60-1). The presence of tranchet adzes on Wymer's southern sites, and resharpening flakes from these tools, demonstrates more heavy-duty woodworking such as the construction of shelters; these larger tools were absent from the sites excavated in 1989.

Undoubtedly, Thatcham was a favoured place in the landscape and one to which people returned frequently. People were not always undertaking the same tasks when they came, and there is no reason to assume that their visits were of the same duration or undertaken at the same times of year. Sedge (*Carex*) nutlets preserved by the burning of the landscape suggest a late summer presence (Chisham 2004) and the hazelnut shells autumn, although there could have been some storage of nuts. An assessment of the age of death of six immature red deer teeth by Carter suggested that killing took place at least in late summer or autumn and in winter; periodic visits through the year were favoured but not in a set seasonal pattern (Carter 2001 reported in Chisham 2006). Modern hunter-gatherers have been observed to return to the same or adjacent sites at a variety of times during the year and in different family or gender groupings to undertake different activities (Conneller 2005, 43-6).

The Thatcham sites form one concentration within a wider spread of early Mesolithic sites, mainly located on low terraces and bluffs of the Kennet and its tributaries, where a range of activities took place (Figs 10.6-7; Lobb and Rose 1996; Chisham 2006). Numerous cores found in trial trenching at Lower Way on the floodplain near Thatcham indicate large-scale flint knapping, and at nearby Chamberhouse Farm the exploitation of wild boar took place (Fig. 10.3; Wymer 1977; Wessex Archaeology 2005; Chisham 2006). At the adjacent sites of Faraday Road and Greenham Dairy Farm in Newbury (Fig. 10.8), the focus of activity also seems to have been on the processing and consumption of wild boar (as represented by 80% of the identifiable bone), although some aurochs, red deer, roe deer, wild cat and beaver were also found (Sheridan *et al.* 1967; Ellis *et al.* 2003). Multiple cut marks on one of the beaver bones shows that this animal was exploited for its meat as well as for its fur. The relative scarcity of head, trunk and feet bones shows that the major meat bearing bones of wild boar had been brought to the site after the animals were killed and partially dismembered elsewhere, although some complete skeletons were present. The animals were both disarticulated and filleted on site, with butchery and skin processing taking place on one part of the site along with flint knapping, and final processing, cooking and eating elsewhere, in addition to possible smoking or drying for consumption later. Charred hazelnut shells were also numerous amongst the cooking remains and the paucity of hazel trees in the pollen diagrams demonstrate that these were for food rather than the result of burning the local vegetation. It was only possible to date two items: a hazelnut shell (8850-8450 cal BC at 91.7% confidence, R-24999/2: 9418±60 BP) and a butchered bone of wild boar (7610-7460 cal BC, R-24999/1: 8510±60 BP). At face value, this suggests that the site was in use for over a millennium. Nevertheless, the range of tools was restricted compared to the Thatcham sites, and the range of activities at Faraday Road seems to have varied little over time. Wild boar processing also seems to have been the main activity at Marsh Benham (Reynier forthcoming), a site of similar age (8300-7750 cal BC, OxA-5195: 8905±80 BP; Hedges *et al.* 1996; Chisham 2006). A more temporary, specialised kill and butchery site seems to be represented by the evidence at Ufton Green, a site on the floodplain sealed by peat (Allen and Allen 1997; Chisham 2004).

There is good evidence to suggest that human activity was also having an impact on the surrounding environment. As river valleys in the region became increasingly wooded, the area around Thatcham remained quite open, and included grassland clearings (Allen and Healy 1992). Indeed, in his samples from the WA1 and WA2 sites, Scaife recorded an increasing number of herb taxa through time, in addition to plants of disturbed ground which suggested deliberate clearance (Scaife 1992, 67). Human interference in the landscape is also implied by repeated burning of the vegetation as is shown by successive charcoal lenses within the floodplain (Holyoak 1980, 235), with a

peak in landscape burning associated with burnt sedge (*Carex* sp.) nutlets dated to 8550-8240 cal BC (AA-55306: 9134±65 BP; Chisham 2004). A similar picture emerges from the contemporary sequence at nearby Woolhampton (Chisham 2004), and also possibly at Charnham Lane, Hungerford (Keith-Lucas 2002), though not at the more temporary site at Ufton Green (Chisham 2006). Such burning would have allowed animals such as deer and aurochs to graze near to habitation sites, further maintaining clearings as they did so, and also have encouraged the growth of woodland-edge plants such as hazel and fruiting shrubs, attractive to animals and people alike. It would also have enabled people to move more freely through the landscape, between sites and to the river.

The area of the Kennet, Lambourn and Enborne confluences seems to have been a hub within a wider network of more dispersed sites, a focus for routeways up and down the river valleys and into other landscapes with different resource potentials (Lobb and Rose 1996, 73). It is no longer believed that Mesolithic populations followed herds of migrating animals, but it would have made sense

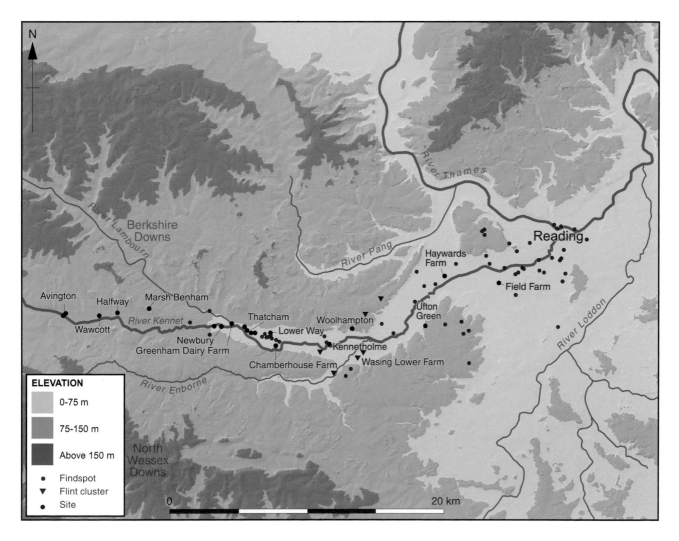

Fig. 10.7 Mesolithic sites in the Kennet Valley

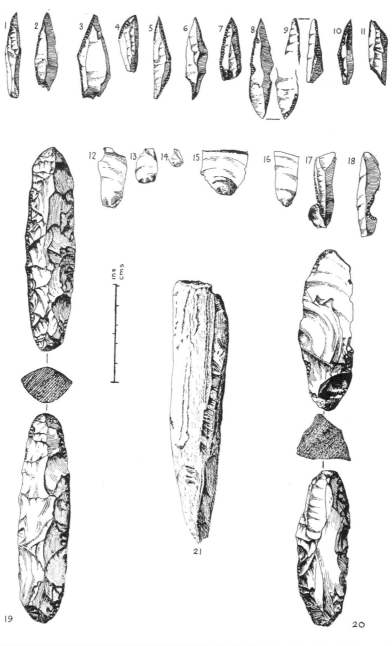

Fig. 10.8 Finds (above) recovered from the Greenham Dairy Farm site (below)

for people to spread their hunting sites out across the landscape in order to conserve viable herds.

There were also other reasons for people to travel further afield. Flint found on the Kennet Valley sites includes some material derived from the gravels, but most is good-quality Chalk flint for which journeys onto the nearby Berkshire Downs would have been necessary. Survey on the surrounding upland areas and the Upper Kennet Valley suggests that they were only lightly used, however (Richards 1978; Holgate 1988a; Whittle 1990), and the presence of tool types such as tranchet adzes may indicate specialised activity (S Allen 2005) or smaller settlements (Ford 1992). There also seems to have been only transitory use of the lower Kennet and the headwaters of the Lambourn and Loddon, although the number of visits may have increased through time (Richards 1978; Ford 1987a; 1997). As people moved around the landscape they would not just have been searching for food; the maintenance and creation of social networks would also have been an important consideration. The middle valley sites may represent the bases of more closely related family groups. Different people may have been encountered in upland areas, people from other valley systems, providing opportunities for extending contacts, creating new family ties, exchanging objects and sharing food.

Early Mesolithic habitation elsewhere in the Thames Valley catchment

Elsewhere in the Thames catchment, a similar pattern of activity 'hot spots' can be seen, surrounded by areas which were used more occasionally (Fig. 10.2).

There is a noted concentration of early Mesolithic sites on the Corallian Ridge (Case 1952-3). Many of these are situated near the scarp overlooking the Thames Valley, and they may have provided single locations within easy reach of a variety of environmental niches. Tubney Wood is a good example (Bradley and Hey 1993; Norton 2007). The site seems to have been visited on a number of occasions, but there was evidence of more permanent occupation with a range of domestic activities taking place, including hide preparation, woodworking, the working of plants and fibrous materials such as textiles and cord, as well as hunting (Bradley and Hey 1993; Lamdin-Whymark 2007; Fig. 10.9). Some early activity is also present in the river valley itself, for example around Abingdon at the confluence of the Thames with the Ock, but this seems to have been small scale in the early Mesolithic, as does the more specialised activity represented by tranchet adzes in other parts of the Upper Thames Valley at this time (Case 1952-3). Sites on the Cotswolds, like Ascott-under-Wychwood (Benson and Whittle 2007), and the Chilterns, such as Windmill Hill, Nettlebed (Boismier and Mepham 1995), Kimble Farm, Turville (Peake 1917) and Marline's Sandpit, Bolter

End (Millard 1965) are not numerous and are further away from the main river valley, although in the case of the Cotswolds they are often near to tributary rivers and streams. As on the Chalk, it seems probable that woodland cover was not as dense in these higher areas as on the intermediate valley slopes, and clearings would have provided important areas of resource aggregation. The large number of microliths in the flint assemblage from Ascott-under-Wychwood (Cramp 2007), including one with impact damage, suggests a hunting encampment, albeit one that may have been used on a number of occasions.

Further down the Thames, Mesolithic finds have been discovered during a variety of fieldwork projects in the Eton area (Fig. 10.10). This includes early and later Mesolithic material at Holyport, Bray, the Eton Rowing Course, and various sites along the Maidenhead, Windsor and Eton Flood Alleviation Scheme, especially around Taplow (Allen *et al.* 2004; forthcoming). There was evidence that reedswamp vegetation adjacent to an early Mesolithic site at the Eton Rowing Course had been burnt (Parker and Robinson 2003, 55), although it is not clear whether the vegetation was being modified in order to improve the browsing for game or to increase the yield of nuts. Mesolithic flint scatters at Binfield, near Reading, 7 km from the river, indicate repeated use of the site, perhaps over a prolonged period of time (Roberts 1995). The assemblage composition suggests a variety of activities, perhaps signifying that smaller groups of people were carrying out a similar range of tasks to those that occurred at the larger, riverside sites. An early to late Mesolithic riverside site was also found at Jennings Yard, Windsor (Fig. 10.2), where the 817 pieces of flint included blades, a few cores, retouched pieces and burnt flint (Healy 1993). It was not possible to tell whether this material was from one occupation event or several short visits, when fires were lit, water heated, a few tools used and discarded and flint nodules were collected and tested for use elsewhere (ibid., 12).

Major Mesolithic sites have come to light in the braided river system of the lower Colne Valley and on the Buckinghamshire-Middlesex border (Fig. 10.2), where finds have been recovered in quarries since the 19th century. The river is fed by the Chess, Misbourne and Alderbourne rivers which cut through the Chilterns Chalk. They all contained infilled late and post-glacial sediments. Much work was undertaken by Lacaille, mainly on quarries at Denham and Iver where earlier Mesolithic sites seemed to have been situated near to a lake in the Colne Valley (Lacaille 1963; Wymer 1977). Recent evaluation work by Wessex Archaeology at Denham uncovered early Mesolithic flintwork in association with animal bone (Wessex Archaeology 2005). A sample of wild boar was dated to 8470-8250 cal BC (9131±45 BP). At Heathrow, a number of pits have recently been excavated which would have been situated near to a stream, and which contained

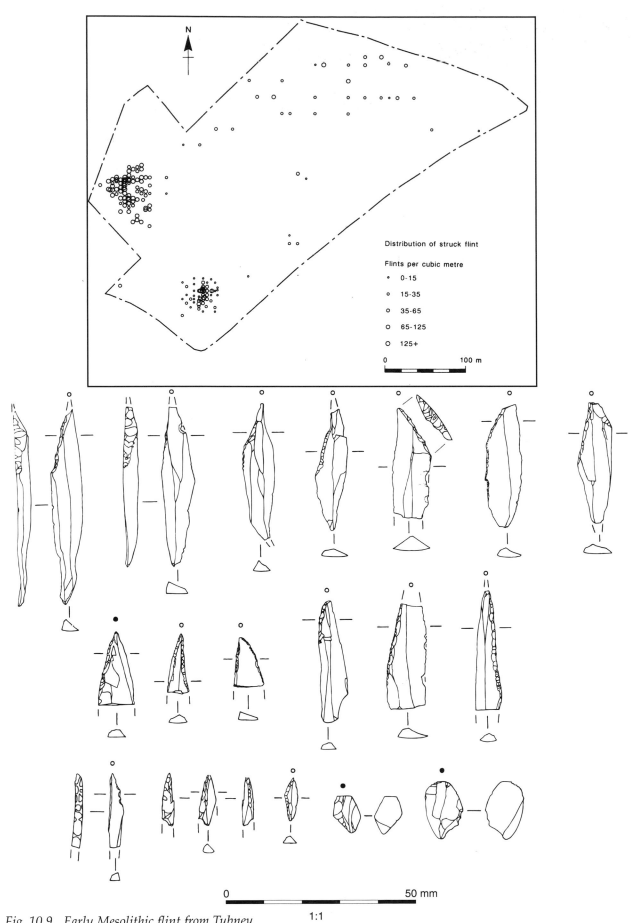

Fig. 10.9   Early Mesolithic flint from Tubney

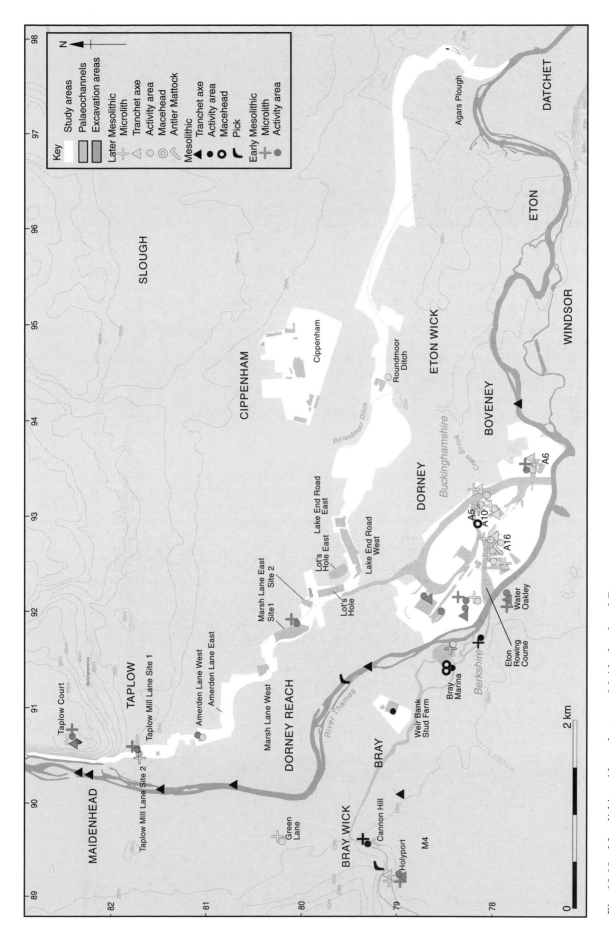

Fig. 10.10 Mesolithic evidence between Maidenhead and Eton

Fig. 10.11 Mesolithic pits from the Terminal 5, Heathrow excavations

a few pieces of worked flint with stone which had been burnt in the 7th millennium cal BC (Fig. 10.11; Lewis *et al*. 2006, table 2.1, 43-4).

A further concentration of Mesolithic finds has been found on the Surrey Greensand, including apparently multiperiod assemblages suggestive of repeated visits to the same sites (Holgate 1988a, map 9). There are some substantial groups of material, often containing Horsham points, and sometimes associated with hearths and charred hazelnut shells (Mellars 1976). This material formed the basis of current typologies for the British Mesolithic (Jacobi 1978; 1981; Wymer 1977). Mesolithic finds have also been made in smaller numbers on the surrounding Weald Clay, London Clay and the Chalk (Cotton 2004; Field 2004). One attraction of the Greensand may have been that these different environments all lay within easy reach. The sandy soils would, however, have been well-drained and would have provided ideal conditions for settlement and for the growth of a range of foods such as hazel, bracken, the root of which can be eaten, and a range of fungi (Clarke 1976a). These foods would have attracted animals and humans, and the presence of large numbers of microliths amongst some of these assemblages, at Abinger Common, Farnham and Kettlebury, for example, suggests that these would have been good hunting grounds (Mellars 1976).

Other parts of the Thames catchment such as the Vale of Aylesbury, the Vale of the White Horse and the boulder clay of East Berkshire appear, on present evidence, to have been little used in the early Mesolithic (Wymer 1977; Ford 1987a). As already noted, only light scatters of Mesolithic flint have been recovered from the Berkshire Downs (Richards 1978) and other slopes away from the Thames (Ford 1987b; 1992, 263).

In summary, most early Mesolithic activity seems to have taken place on scarps, bluffs and slopes overlooking watercourses, within the river valleys themselves or along springlines. Sandy geologies such as the Corallian Ridge in Oxfordshire and the

Surrey Greensand were also favoured. These naturally acidic soils would have produced distinctive combinations of vegetation and resources, encouraging repeated occupation of traditional hunting and foraging grounds (Gardiner 2006). All would have provided optimal environments for the exploitation of a range of resources and for the congregation of communities, probably at specific times of the year, in areas with a good and constant water supply. Large assemblages probably represent the repeated use of favoured sites over many generations.

LATER MESOLITHIC HABITATION IN THE THAMES VALLEY

Use of the landscape, habitation and resource exploitation seem to have changed during the course of the later Mesolithic period. Smaller sites are found over a much wider range of geologies and topographies (Fig. 10.12), although the presence of nearby water remained an important factor in site selection. A greater variability within flint assemblages has also been noted (Mellars 1976). There is some evidence that the Thames river valley became more heavily utilised.

By the 7th millennium cal BC, the Thames Valley was quite heavily wooded, and closed alder woodland prevailed on the floodplain by the mid 6th millennium. Mixed deciduous woodland appears to be present over much of the valley by the 5th millennium, with alder growing in the valley bottoms, and lime, oak, hazel, ash and elm on the better drained gravel terraces and higher slopes (Day 1991; Needham 1992; Allen and Healy 1992; Robinson 1993, 9-12; Scaife 2000; Keith-Lucas 2000; Branch and Green 2004). Under climax vegetation, channels in the Upper Thames ceased to flow, many subsidiary river channels silted up, and the floodplain became quite dry; alder trees were growing in the base of channels at Yarnton by 4460-4250 cal BC (OxA-10713: 5535±50 BP; Robinson in prep.). The hydrology of the Middle Thames was affected by sea-level rises, the changing gradient of the river creating wetter valley-bottom conditions and encouraging peat formation, with tufa deposits in stream channels. Periodic flooding occurred in the Middle Kennet Valley, and the early habitation sites were covered with peat.

Excavations near to the river in the Upper Thames Valley show that later Mesolithic sites are often present in these lower-lying areas, but are hard to identify because they are small and often sealed beneath alluvium. Good groups have come to light recently at Gravelly Guy, Stanton Harcourt (Holgate 2004a) and, especially, in the Abingdon area (information from the Abingdon Area Archaeological Society; Allen and Kamash 2008, 67). A small assemblage of both early and late Mesolithic flintwork which is thought to represent seasonal visits to a short-stay camp near to the river at the woodland edge was recovered from the various excavations in and around the Drayton Cursus (Holgate 1988a, fig. 6.9, chapter 3; Holgate *et al.* 2003). Another cluster of Mesolithic sites is known around the Lower Cherwell Valley (eg Lock Crescent, Kidlington (Booth 1997) and the small collection of blades and blade-like flakes that have come from the recent excavations at Oxford Castle (Mullin forthcoming)). Robin Holgate's (1988a) model of late Mesolithic activity in the Thames Valley postulated short-stay or base camps on the terrace edges adjacent to rivers with increasing utilisation of

upland areas reflecting the increased importance of hunting ungulates as part of food-gathering strategies. Recent work has shown that there was more activity on the floodplain than he anticipated and few large sites in any location, although microliths are more numerous in upland assemblages, which contain fewer tranchet adzes and axe-sharpening flakes (ibid., 74-6). At Rollright, high up on the Cotswolds, a knapping scatter is interpreted as representing one or more individuals carrying a flint-

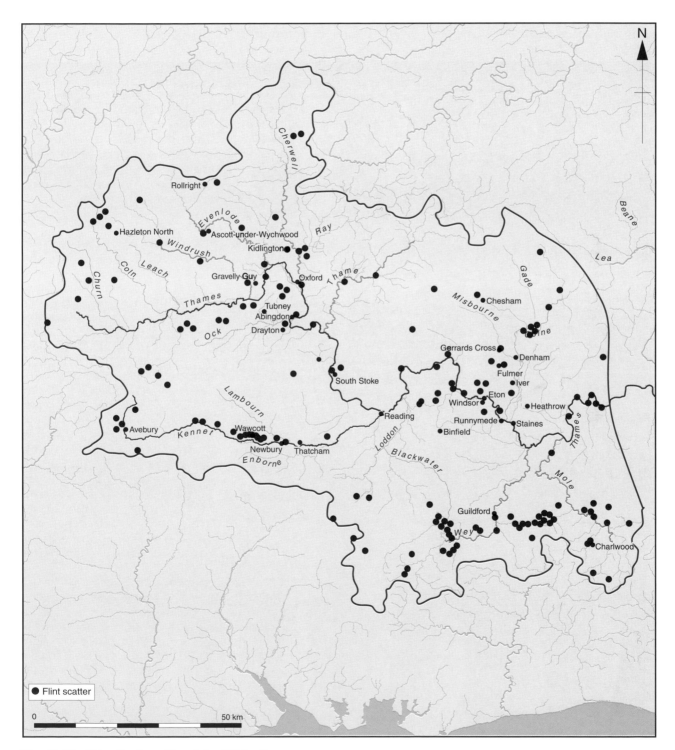

Fig. 10.12   *Distribution of late Mesolithic sites*

working toolkit and manufacturing or repairing hunting equipment on the spot (Holgate 1988b, 90; Fig. 10.13). Sites around South Stoke and Goring in the Goring Gap, may represent more frequent hunting visits and locations where hunting tools were prepared and maintained using raw materials derived from the nearby Chalk downs (Ford 1987b; Brown 1995), while individual microliths found in the landscape may represent tools lost during hunting expeditions. The evidence is, perhaps, more consistent with smaller and more mobile groups exploiting many different environments according to resource availability, need and inclination.

There seems to be less activity in the middle Kennet Valley in the late Mesolithic than there had been earlier in the period, although finds of this period are frequent in the area around Wawcott (Fig. 10.12). Several substantial assemblages suggest long-term use, notably Wawcott Sites XV and XXX (Froom 1976; Froom *et al.* 1993), but other small discrete clusters are thought to represent short-term events with a broad range of activities being undertaken. The remains of small structures or shelters are thought to have sometimes survived at sites such as Wawcott I and Wawcott III, where a radiocarbon date of 5400-4700 cal BC was obtained on

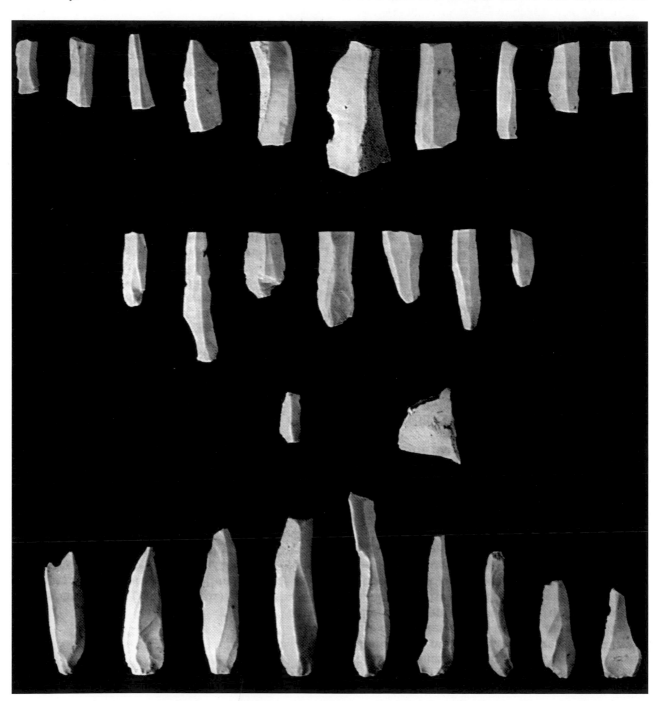

Fig. 10.13   Mesolithic flint blades, bladelets, and other worked flint from the Rollright Stones

'carbonaceous material and fragments of hazelnut shells' in the bottom of a pit or tree-throw hole (BM-767: 6120±134 BP; Froom 1963b; 1976; Mellars 1976, 389-91).

Conversely, sites are more common in east Berkshire and around Avebury near the source of the Kennet than they had been in the early Mesolithic (Holgate 1988a). The increase in water-logging and woodland within the valley bottoms (Healy *et al.* 1992; Evans *et al.* 1993), while it might not have created conditions unfavourable to settle-ment and exploitation (cf Whittle 1990), may have changed patterns of settlement and land use. Once again, the picture seems to be of smaller groups, moving over more extensive and varied territories. The very small assemblages or individual finds in the Upper Kennet Valley are best interpreted as the result of hunting forays with small parties camping nearby and undertaking small-scale extraction and working of flint to meet immediate needs (Whittle 1993; Pollard and Reynolds 2002, 23-4). The excep-tion to this pattern is the site at Cherhill, just west of Avebury in the catchment of the Bristol Avon, where dense deposits of flint, including tested nodules, knapping waste and discarded tools, and animal bone, mainly aurochs and pig, could represent a base or seasonal camp (Evans and Smith 1983; Grigson 1983, 70) or the repeated use of a favoured locality for a variety of activities over a long period of time (Whittle 1990, 105). A number of find spots and small sites have also been plotted by Lobb and Rose in the Lower Kennet Valley (1996, fig. 13), but slightly more activity seems to be represented by the flints recovered at Thames Valley Park, Reading on the floodplain near the Thames/Kennet conflu-ence, where some animal bone was also found, including the possible kill site of an aurochs (Fig. 10.21; Barnes *et al.* 1997).

At the Eton Rowing Course, by 5000 cal BC, lakes and reed fen on the floodplain had silted up and a series of channels flowed through the area on the banks of which levees had formed. Alder carr devel-oped over the backswamps (Allen *et al.* 2004). Late Mesolithic flint scatters have been discovered which, although not dense, were widespread and were mainly found on the levees close to the channel, as well as occasionally stretching back on to the floodplain, perhaps indicating trails leading through the woodland (T Allen, pers. comm.; Fig. 10.10). Twenty-three geometric microliths and an antler mattock were found on the floodplain itself, and these seem to represent either knapping events or the performance of one specific task (Lamdin-Whymark 2008, 58-9). A similar picture emerges at Runnymede, a site occupied repeatedly for short periods of time (Needham 2000a). A cluster of eight late Mesolithic straight-backed flints found at this site may represent the remains of a composite side-hafted arrow or harpoon, similar to that illustrated by David (1998, fig. 26.5) for a similar group of tools from Seamer Carr (Fig. 10.14; Needham 2000a, 71; Cotton 2004, 23). Small collections of finds have also

come from sites around Staines, such as Hengrove Farm, the Ashford Prison site, Staines Police Station and Staines causewayed enclosure (Ellaby 1987; Carew *et al.* 2006, 10; Healey and Robertson-Mackay in Robertson-Mackay 1987, 116), and the late 5th-millennium perforated antler-beam mattock, referred to above, was dredged from the river here (Fig. 10.15; Bonsall and Smith 1990).

Late Mesolithic sites are also present in the tributaries of the Colne Valley. At Fulmer in the Alderbourne Valley, a cluster of apparently undis-turbed material survived within a thin spread of generally sharp and unabraded flints which included tranchet adzes, rod and crescent microliths and blade cores, but no scrapers (Farley 1978). Layers of tufa containing Mesolithic flints which included edge-blunted microliths, axe-trimming flakes and many snapped blades associ-ated with animal bone were found at Misbourne Railway Viaduct near Gerrard's Cross (Farley 2007). Animal bone was also present at Stratford's Yard, Chesham, a site where much flint working had taken place, including the production of microliths; over 49 were recovered from a small area beneath a demolished cottage (Stainton 1989).

Sandy substrates appear to have been less favoured in the late Mesolithic, with relatively few sites known on the Corallian Ridge in Oxfordshire. There also seems to have been a reduction in use of the Surrey Greensand, although late sites are found, for example at Woodbridge Road, Guildford where pits are reported to have been present (Holgate 1988a; Cotton 2004, 23-4). Sites are also present on the adjacent Wealden Clay, such as Charlwood where claims of pits have also been made, and there were certainly tree-throw holes with charcoal dating to 4340-3940 cal BC (HAR-4532: 5270±90 BP).

MESOLITHIC LIFEWAYS

The pattern of habitation that emerges from the description above is of a much more complex Mesolithic in the Thames Valley than that allowed by traditional explanations of home bases in the valleys and seasonal hunting sites on higher ground. Recent archaeological and ethnographic work elsewhere, which emphasises the wide variety of potential uses of sites and the adaptability and flexibility of hunter-gatherer groups in the landscape (eg Spikins 2000), is supported by the evidence from our region, as illustrated particularly well by the Middle Kennet Valley sites discussed above. Here, activities as varied as core reduction and tool preparation, the working of skins and fibres, and a whole range of other 'domestic' activi-ties as well as hunting and kill sites are all repre-sented on the river terraces and the floodplain. Even away from the valley bottoms, sites of varying sizes existed on which a range of activities seem to have taken place. At Windmill Hill near Nettlebed on the edge of the Chilterns, for example, people seem to

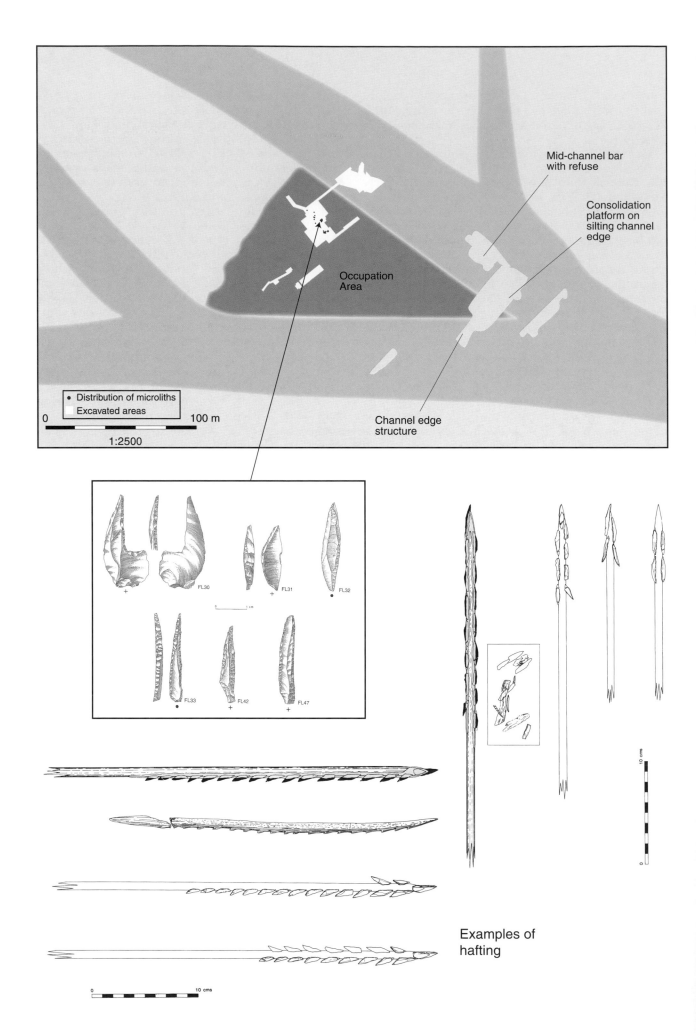

Mid-channel bar
with refuse

Consolidation
platform on
silting channel
edge

Occupation
Area

Channel edge
structure

- Distribution of microliths
  Excavated areas

0   100 m

1:2500

FL30

FL31

FL32

FL33

FL42

FL47

0   1 cm

Examples of
hafting

0   10 cms

0   10 cms

212

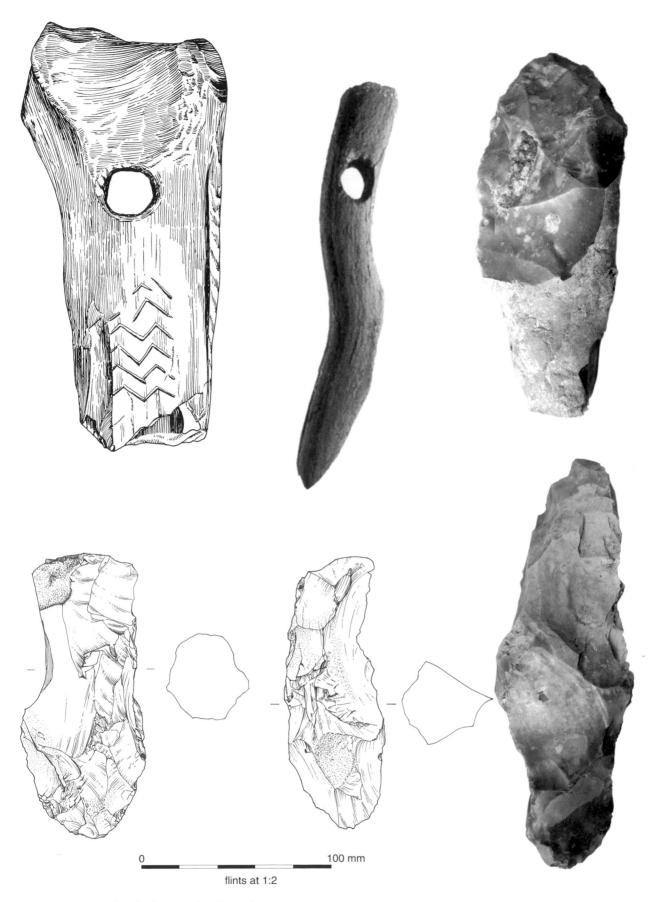

0 100 mm

flints at 1:2

Fig. 10.15 *Mesolithic finds from the river Thames*

Fig. 10.14 (facing page) *Mesolithic occupation at Runnymede, with reconstructions of composite tools based on finds from Seamer Carr, Yorkshire*

213

have visited on a variety of occasions to prepare and reduce flint cores, and to make, use and rejuvenate tools for working bone, antler or wood, and for processing skins (Boismier and Mepham 1995). A series of knapping events and small task-specific sites has been found in the head of a shallow valley at Bletchingley on the Lower Greensand (Anon 2005; Cotton 2004, 23-4), and the varied activities that took place at Cherhill, on Chalk drift near Avebury (Evans and Smith 1983), have already been mentioned. On the Cotswolds limestone, on the other hand, the generally small size of flint assemblages and the dominance of microliths or blades for microlith manufacture within the larger collections, as, for example, at Syreford, Rollright, Hazleton North and Ascott-under-Wychwood (Saville 1984, 71; Lambrick 1988; Saville 1990a; Benson and Whittle 2007), does suggest that these uplands might have been traditional hunting grounds. Mesolithic groups were highly knowledgeable exploiters of their environment, moving across the landscape according to tradition and inclination, taking advantage of seasonal and other natural resources but also of more occasional fluctuations in the availability of different foods. Occasional abundance may have provided opportunities for gatherings of larger numbers of people.

For small, mobile populations, the importance of food sharing and eating with others should not be underestimated (Milner and Miracle 2002). Feasting would have drawn people together and afforded opportunities for social interaction at many different scales (Clark 1940; Miracle 2002; Milner 2006). The process of accumulating, preparing and cooking food would have provided an experience which participants would have shared and which would have bound them together. Rich animal bone deposits at sites like Thatcham and Faraday Road, Newbury may represent feasting events as well as everyday meals and snacks. Smaller, celebratory meals or meals eaten by work parties would have been a focus for gatherings of fewer people. Preserving foods for future use and gearing up for journeys would have enabled people to plan activities together (Conneller 2005).

The dense deposits of animal bone found at Thatcham (see above) probably represent the conscious and deliberate accumulation of the residue from feasts and other meals. Middening is a well-known phenomenon of the Mesolithic period in coastal regions but is much more difficult to identify in disturbed, agricultural landscapes. It is possible that the clusters of material found at sites like Runnymede (Needham 2000a, 240), the Eton Rowing Course (T G Allen *et al.* forthcoming), Ascott-under-Wychwood (Benson and Whittle 2007) and Hazleton North (Saville 1990a; Fig. 10.16) represent the remains of smaller-scale accumulations of material, although the scatters on the floodplain at the Eton Rowing Course appear to be *in situ*, in contrast to the Neolithic midden material on the same site which had been brought from elsewhere (Lamdin-Whymark 2008, 59). These sites may have become important locales in themselves, representing a 'conscious decision to accumulate rather than to scatter' (Thomas and Tilley 1993, 228), and their physical presence, lying within clearings and emphasised by the different vegetation that would have grown over them, would have been a reminder of the events, such as feasting, that had

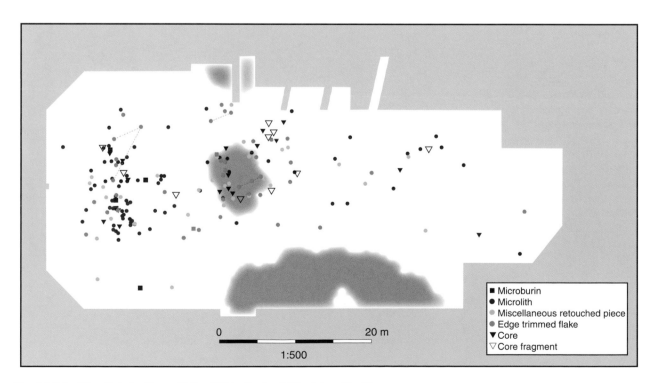

Fig. 10.16 The distribution of Mesolithic finds at Hazleton North

created them. Their integration into the network of local paths would have reinforced their importance even as their physical traces faded from view (Saville 1990a, 254).

Middens represent one of the very few Mesolithic 'structures' we find in the Thames Valley. Houses and shelters are only rarely documented in the national record, and there are no clear-cut examples from our region. A large pit dug into gravel at Wawcott I in the Kennet Valley was interpreted by Froom (1972, 25-7) as a structure. It had four postholes around its sides and spoil and flint nodules piled up around the edge, and a hearth had been placed within it when it had nearly filled (Fig. 10.17). In section, this feature resembles a tree-throw hole but it could have been used as a shelter. It has also been claimed that hollows and possible pits on the Wawcott III and IV sites were the remains of structures (Froom 1965; 1976). 'Pit dwellings' at Farnham, Surrey (Clarke and Rankine 1939) have recently been discredited as tree-throw holes (Evans *et al.* 1999), although they were undoubtedly filled with much Mesolithic material. It is, perhaps, not surprising that the shelters of small groups of people moving frequently across the landscape and making structures from wood, hides and other natural materials have left no physical remains. Hearths, the focus of domestic and other sedentary activities, are encountered more commonly than structures, though they are not common. They are found on both early and late sites, as the examples at Thatcham and Wawcott show, and have been noted particularly on the Lower Greensand and elsewhere in Surrey (Mellars 1976; Cotton 2004, 23).

Pits provide another, very occasional, physical indicator of the persistent use of particular places in the landscape at this time (Mithen 1999, 43), and they represent one of the earliest signs of deliberate human intervention in the ground. In the Thames Valley, four small possible pits or postholes were identified at Stratford's Yard, Chesham (Stainton 1989). A possible marker post, 0.85 m deep, was found at Runnymede which was reminiscent of the 8th-millennium cal BC post pits found in the Stonehenge car park (M Allen 1995, 43-7; Needham 2000a, 193; Allen and Gardiner 2002). Smaller pits were also found at Heathrow Terminal 5, as already mentioned (Fig. 10.11; Lewis *et al.* 2006), and several have been claimed on sites in Surrey, including Charlwood and Frank's Sandpit (Cotton 2004, 23-4; Ellaby 2004; Williams 2004), though these have been challenged (Evans *et al.* 1999; Lamdin-Whymark 2008, 93). The slight evidence suggests that they do exist and that they became more common through time. Some pits seem to have been cut and backfilled straight away (Cotton 2004, 24), which may be an indication that the excavation of features into the ground in order to receive deposits or offerings has a Mesolithic origin, but the evidence is, as yet, very slight.

There is better evidence that tree-throw holes began to be used for the deposition of material towards the end of the Mesolithic period. Tree-throw holes at Gatehampton Farm, Goring yielded almost entirely Mesolithic flintwork and, on some parts of the site, exclusively later Mesolithic material, even though overlying activity from the early fourth millennium cal BC onwards was present (Brown 1995, 80-1). As already discussed, substantial assemblages from features at Farnham and Charlwood in Surrey were probably also mainly from tree-throw holes (Clark and Rankine 1939; Ellaby 2004, 15-6). Analysis of the character and contents of 85 tree-throw holes excavated at Eton Rowing Course and on the Maidenhead, Windsor and Eton Flood Alleviation Scheme showed that certainly four and probably nine of these features had late Mesolithic material deposited within them (Lamdin-Whymark 2008, 82-100). Although there was no evidence of formal structuring of these finds, this activity was clearly deliberate and reflects the intimate relationship between people and their natural woodland environment (Allen *et al.* 2004, 91). It may have been seen as a way of putting something back into a place from which something else had been removed, replacing like for like perhaps, to give thanks or propitiate for any harm done (Carew *et al.* 2006). It has been suggested that Mesolithic people, like a number of groups studied by ethnographers, may have had a fear of woodland and felt the need to protect themselves from malign influences within it (Davies *et al.* 2005).

Examples of modern and historically documented hunter-gatherer groups suggest that ritual, magic and superstition would have pervaded Mesolithic life, although, as encounters were with a natural world and did not involve the construction of permanent monuments, this is very hard to evidence. It is possible that the substantial postholes found at Stonehenge and, perhaps, Runnymede, were for totem poles or similar uprights, and they could thus represent an exception. The inverted red deer skullcap and antlers, antler beam hammer and knapping waste found above the ground surface at Thatcham, in the Middle Kennet Valley, has already been cited as a possible example of the inclusion of ritual practice into a more mundane task (Fig. 10.18; Warren 2006, 24-5; Wymer 1962). It has been suggested that the deliberate deposition of objects into the Thames and other rivers was a practice that began in the Mesolithic period (Ford 1987b, 60). Mesolithic picks and adzes downstream of Goring and similar finds from London are reasonably common (Figs 14.36 and 16.8; T Allen 1995, 117-8; Field 1989; Haughey 2000, 225-8). In addition to the perforated antler-beam mattock dredged from the river at Staines (Bonsall and Smith 1990), a number of other bone and wooden objects have been retrieved from the river between Staines and Hammersmith which could be Mesolithic in date (Fig. 10.15). These include a perforated aurochs radius with incised decoration from Hammersmith which Wymer suggested was a handle for a flint axe or pick (Wymer 1991, 53). It has been argued that

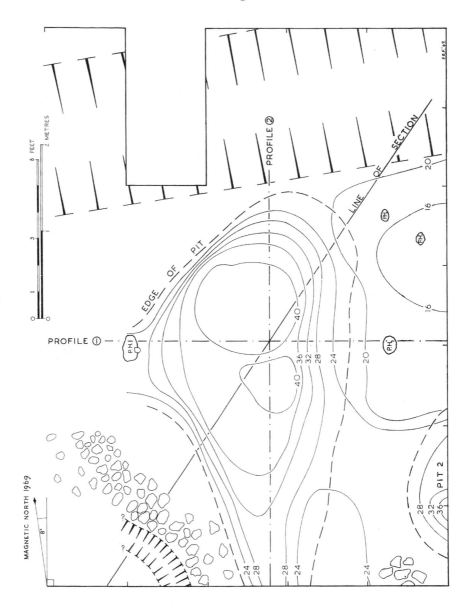

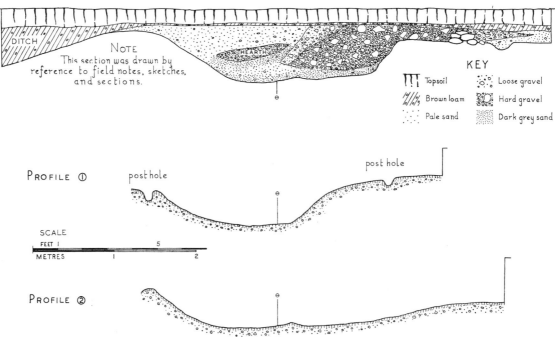

PROFILE ①

PROFILE ②

Fig. 10.18 (left)   Red deer skull and knapping deposit at Thatcham

Fig. 10.19 (below)   Flint from Windmill Hill, Nettlebed

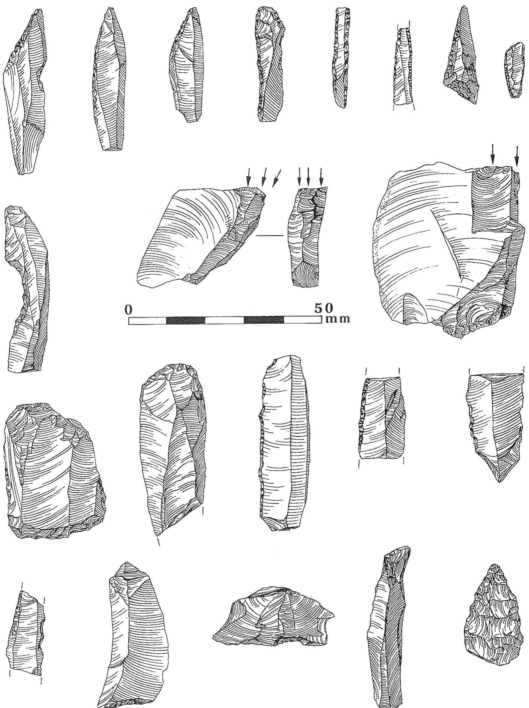

0   50 mm

Fig. 10.17 (facing page)   The possible late Mesolithic structure at Wawcott Site I

river finds could simply be accidental losses, and their distribution is, indeed, strongly biased towards those places where dredging has often occurred, but the fact that only some artefact types belonging to some and not all periods are recovered suggests that these objects had greater significance and represent material that had been placed in the river. Other tool types have also been found which are more clearly associated with a river environment, including two bone harpoons from Battersea and Wandsworth. The reason for their presence is more uncertain (Haughey 2000, 227).

HUNTER-GATHERERS AND NATURAL RESOURCES

Although there is some use of larger flint nodules from the river gravels, good-quality flint occurs on most Mesolithic sites. There is no evidence for flint mines during this period, and the material could all have been recovered by 'harvesting' surface deposits such as Clay-with-Flints, Chalk exposures on hillsides and exposures of river gravels. The Kennet Valley assemblages are dominated by high-quality flint from the Chalk, requiring short-distance importation from exposures and outcrops, with most material being brought to sites as pre-prepared cores (Ford 1997, 3-5; Healy 1993, 12), although there is some use of local, lower-quality material here as on many river valley sites. Flint taken from the London Clay and from river gravels was also noted at Holyport, Bray and Jennings Yard, Windsor, for example (Ames 1993; Healy 1993). Sites on the Chilterns, such as Windmill Hill, Nettlebed and Stratford's Yard, Chesham could be related to exploitation of flint on valley slopes of the Chilterns (Fig. 10.19; Stainton 1989; Boismier and Mepham 1995). In the north of the region, however, there is no local supply of flint. Even so, sites on the Cotswolds like Rollright produce tools made of high-quality flint (Fig. 10.13). Thus people moved over long distances to acquire important resources or they exchanged materials with neighbouring groups. Knowledge of the whereabouts of flint and other natural materials would doubtless have been prized. Occasionally chert objects are found at some distance from their source. The black chert axe found at Wawcott, the stone for which probably came from near Shaftesbury, Dorset (Froom 1963a) provides one example, but there is very little other evidence for the long-distance transport of exotic stone.

Although they dominate the archaeological record, flint and stone are only the durable items amongst what would have been a range of possessions made of many different materials. Plants and animals would have been exploited for clothing, tools, ornaments and other items. Hides, wood, bark and plant fibres, such as reeds, would have been used for containers, ropes, bedding, shelters and more permanent structures. Although it is extremely rare to find such remains, charred fibres were discovered in Mesolithic peat during evaluation by Wessex Archaeology at Culham Reach near Abingdon, and we have already seen that usewear analysis at Thatcham was able to demonstrate the working of a variety of materials (Fig. 10.6). We also have the evidence of flint tools designed for cutting, scraping, boring and piercing, engraving and hide preparation, as well as hunting and food preparation, as, for example, at Tubney Wood and Gravelly Guy, Oxfordshire (Bradley and Hey 1993; Holgate 2004a; Lamdin-Whymark 2007).

Zvelebil has drawn attention to the sophisticated use of wild plant resources by hunter-gatherer groups, ranging from opportunistic and incidental plant use to tending and managing wild resources, including burning the woodland (Zvelebil 1994, 37-40). Plant acquisition would have been one of the factors which influenced settlement strategies. There is very limited evidence of plant use for food in the Thames Valley by hunter-gatherer communities, except for occasional evidence from usewear analysis on flint tools, and the presence of charred hazelnut shells on sites where conditions were conducive to preservation such as Thatcham, where nuts had apparently been opened by crushing (Churchill 1962, 367; Grace 1992; Scaife 1992). The more densely wooded environment of the late Mesolithic, especially in the Middle and Upper Thames Valley, would have provided increasingly challenging conditions for human groups, as the resource base for plant foods able to make a major calorific contribution to the human diet became narrower. Although hazelnuts would have remained predominant amongst these food sources, the yield of nuts also declines when hazel grows as an understorey to tall woodland trees such as oak and lime. This may have provided an impetus for creating and maintaining woodland clearings. Other trees would not have provided major food sources. Although many species of oak have nutritious acorns which were undoubtedly eaten by hunter-gatherers, the two species native to Britain, *Quercus robur* and *Q. petraea*, have particularly toxic acorns and there is no evidence for their consumption in the Mesolithic (nor indeed in the Neolithic). Presumably some bulbs, roots and tubers were eaten, although many common woodland plants with large underground storage organs, such as bluebell, are toxic.

It would have been advantageous for people to have attempted to manage their environment, particularly by creating clearings or at least by maintaining natural openings in the woodland, in order to encourage new plant growth, more vigorous hazelnut production and animal aggregation. This issue has been widely discussed in recent years (eg Tipping 2004), and it is referred to above in relation to the Thatcham area. There are, however, significant difficulties in identifying such activity. Natural events causing treefall and the maintenance of clearings by wild animals will generally have much the same signature as those created and used by human groups (Brown 1997). Aside from Thatcham and the possible deliberate burning of vegetation at the Eton Rowing Course, environmental evidence at Runnymede indicates the existence of some clearings in the late Mesolithic woodland within more dense alder carr (Needham 2000a, 193-5), and an increase in herbaceous plant taxa and reduction in tree pollen can be seen in the early 5th millennium cal BC woodland at Meadlake Place, Surrey (Branch and Green 2004, 12-3, fig. 1.6). There is some evidence to suggest that clearings existed within the woodland in the Upper Thames too. Horizons of early Mesolithic age containing charcoal were seen in pollen samples at Cothill Fen on the Corallian Ridge (Day 1991) near to a number of broadly contemporary sites, including Tubney Wood (Bradley and Hey 1993). Clearings are also known along the major river corridors (for example at Corporation Farm, Abingdon, and Gravelly Guy) and on higher ground, especially on the Cotswolds (for example at Ascott-under-Wychwood and Rollright), although there is no evidence that these were necessarily long-lived or were created or enhanced by early populations (Holgate *et al.* 2003, 133; Holgate 2004a; Benson and Whittle 2007; Lambrick 1988). The impact of the very small population in a large landscape remains hard to quantify but the close association between such environments and hunter-gatherer sites seems inescapable (Bell and Walker 1992, 156-8; Zvelebil 1994).

Thatcham provides us with the only early Mesolithic site where useful quantities of animal bones have been found in a settlement context, including an important assemblage of bones of medium and large-sized mammals, most of which were probably from animals hunted for consumption and for their skins (Table 10.1; King 1962).

Bird bones included crane, teal or garganey, mallard, goldeneye and perhaps smew. The diverse mammal fauna suggested the exploitation of a landscape in transition from the more open birch-willow woodland of the Pre-Boreal to the denser woodland of the Boreal in which pine and hazel were major elements. The large ungulates of more open conditions, elk and horse, only comprised a small proportion of the early assemblage. Red deer and pig bones predominated with red deer providing the main source of meat consumed at the site (Fig. 10.20). The birds were mostly wetland species which would have found suitable conditions in the valley bottom, as would the relatively abundant beavers. The absence of fish has already been noted.

From the early post-glacial period, and as tree-cover became more dense, the species diversity of medium and large ungulates and the carrying capacity for ungulates declined. The main sources of meat would have become restricted to red deer, aurochs and wild pig. This is demonstrated by the later Mesolithic animal bone assemblages from Stratford's Yard, Chesham, Wawcott Sites IV and XXIII and Misbourne Railway Viaduct (Stainton 1989; Holgate 1988a, 98; Farley 2007). Wild cattle, red deer, wild pig and roe deer were found at Stratford's Yard, Chesham (Grigson 1989) along with charred hazelnut shells. A radiocarbon date of

Fig. 10.20   *Artist's reconstruction of a Mesolithic woodland hunting scene*

5010-4500 cal BC (BM-2404: 5890±100 BP) was obtained on a *Bos primigenius* (aurochs) bone (Stainton 1989). At the Misbourne Railway Viaduct site, on the floor of the Misbourne, small flint assemblages were found associated with aurochs, red deer, wild pig, roe deer and small amounts of beaver, wild cat, otter, badger and possibly pine

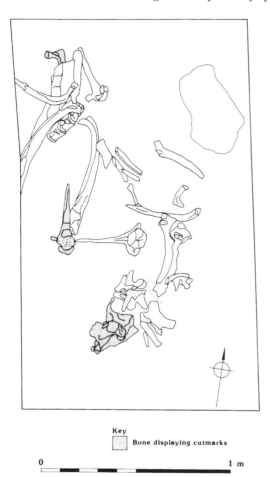

Key

▨ Bone displaying cutmarks

0 ——————— 1 m

Fig. 10.21 The aurochs kill site at Thames Valley Park, Reading

Table 10.1: Summary of animal bone from Thatcham (data from King 1962)

Species	%
Wolf	0.4
Dog	0.2
Fox	1.0
Pine Marten	0.2
Badger	2.0
Wildcat	1.0
Wild Horse	0.6
Wild Pig	25.0
Red Deer	31.0
Elk	0.6
Roe Deer	15.0
Aurochs	2.0
Beaver	20.0
Fragment no	*c* 500

marten (Farley 2007). Seven radiocarbon dates were obtained, three of which were late Mesolithic, but others are both very early, late glacial, and post-Mesolithic in date. At Thames Valley Park, Reading 35 bones of a semiarticulated aurochs skeleton were found in a channel in a layer which suggests that it was Mesolithic in date (Barnes *et al.* 1997, 97-9). One rib bone and three of the vertebrae had cut marks which were consistent with the use of a flint blade (Fig. 10.21), and the absence of the main meat-bearing bones suggested that it was a kill site.

The smaller size of later Mesolithic sites, compared to those of the earlier Mesolithic, suggests that people moved in smaller groups or stayed in one place for shorter periods of time. Small groups would have been more effective at resource maximisation in the increasingly wooded ecosystem described above, as is suggested for other valley systems in Europe (Whittle 1996, 153; Barton and Roberts 2004, 350).

Chapter 11 – Neolithic communities in the Thames Valley: the creation of new worlds

by Gill Hey with Mark Robinson

WORLDS IN TRANSITION: CHANGING LANDSCAPES OF THE EARLY 4TH MILLENNIUM CAL BC

A fundamental shift occurred in lifestyles and settlement in the period between *c* 4000 and 3500 cal BC, arguably one of the most important changes to have occurred in the history of human occupation of the British Isles and one which, ultimately, provided the possibility of a settled existence. Some changes are immediately apparent: the introduction of domesticated plants and animals, and of pottery. These appeared quite suddenly at the beginning of the 4th millennium cal BC. But in other ways this was a gradual and complex transition and one which is very difficult to trace clearly. As we shall see, there were few if any settled agricultural communities, even by the end of the period under study.

This transformation from the Mesolithic hunter-gatherer lifestyle of the 5th millennium to the Neolithic agricultural society of the 4th, has received a great deal of attention in recent years (eg see articles in Whittle and Cummings 2007), but there is still disagreement about how and why this change took place. The extent to which incoming farmers from the nearby Continent (whether Brittany or the Pas de Calais/Belgium region) played a role in the transition or were solely responsible for it, and the relative importance of acculturation of indigenous Mesolithic groups continues to be hotly debated. It is not even certain whether the same model of change applies across Britain and Ireland or whether there were many, regionally-specific transitions.

In the Thames Valley, the problem is compounded by our inability to recognise with certainty Mesolithic sites dating to the very end of that period and sites which were continuously occupied across the period of transition (Hey and Barclay 2007). This may be partly an artefact of the constantly shifting nature of settlement throughout this period, but late Mesolithic sites with assemblages of microliths, blades and adzes, the remains of animals that had been hunted and gathered plant foods such as hazelnuts have not yet been found to contain occasional Neolithic artefacts, domesticated plants or animals. Equally, where Neolithic sites yield diagnostic Mesolithic tools there are, so far, good grounds to believe that these are residual finds.

In addition, there is a great deal of disagreement about what the Neolithic 'revolution' actually involved. Was it a cultural change manifested in the artefacts that people used on sites, an agricultural revolution in which domesticated plants and animals were introduced and grown, or was it an ideological shift involving changing beliefs about the treatment of the dead and the way that people and events were commemorated and marked in the landscape? All these changes occurred during the course of the early 4th millennium, but did people bring or adopt a 'Neolithic package' meaning that all these elements appeared, to all intents and purposes, simultaneously, or were different aspects introduced more gradually and piecemeal?

Inherited landscapes

Whatever differences emerged during this period, late Mesolithic and early Neolithic people would have shared a common experience of the landscape and its natural vegetation, one that would have been dominated by the river and by woodland (Field 2004; Hey and Barclay 2007). This would have been mixed deciduous woodland, with alder growing in the valley bottoms and lime, oak, hazel, ash and elm on the better-drained soils of the gravel terraces and higher slopes (see above, Chapter 9; Day 1991; Parker 1995a; Robinson 1992a, 49-50). In contrast to the environment with which we are familiar, in which woods and forests are limited entities within a generally open landscape, in the late Mesolithic and early Neolithic, clearings would have been the small and defined spaces within a background of trees, albeit of varying densities (Evans *et al.* 1999, 241-2). The nature of the environment would have had a profound influence on people's social lives and belief systems as well as a practical impact on their day-to-day existence (Bloch 1998).

At a time of dense woodland in the valley, the Thames and its tributaries would have been major communication networks, as well as environments which provided a rich and varied source of plant and animal food. There is no direct evidence for river transport such as boats, but this can be inferred from early settlement patterns (Fig. 11.1), the position of monument complexes and the recovery of finds from rivers and their banks. Some of the earliest Neolithic monuments in the Thames Valley catchment, such as Ascott-under-Wychwood and Rollright on the Cotswolds, are sited near to the river or in, or at the heads of, tributary valleys (Fig. 14.9), and the continuing importance of these arteries can be seen in the positioning near river confluences of causewayed enclosures and cursus monuments in the middle and later 4th millennium cal BC respectively, and of monument complexes in the 3rd (Barclay *et al.* 1996; Barclay and Hey 1999, 68-70). Indeed, it has been observed that cursus monuments often run parallel to river courses (ibid.; Last 1999; cf Loveday 2006, 133-6).

Doubtless there were overland routes too. Traditionally it has been postulated that the Jurassic Way over the Cotswolds, the Ridgeway along the Berkshire Downs and the Icknield Way along the Chilterns scarp would have been important trackways, but there is no evidence to support this idea,

and the pre-Roman antiquity of the Icknield Way, for example, has recently been questioned (Harrison 2003). High-level routes might, nevertheless, have traversed less densely-vegetated areas (cf Allen and Gardiner 2009), but it seems clear that rivers would have provided the best means of communication, and this is supported by the distribution of material brought over a distance, such as Neolithic stone axes (Bradley and Edmonds 1993, figs 3.1 and 3.2).

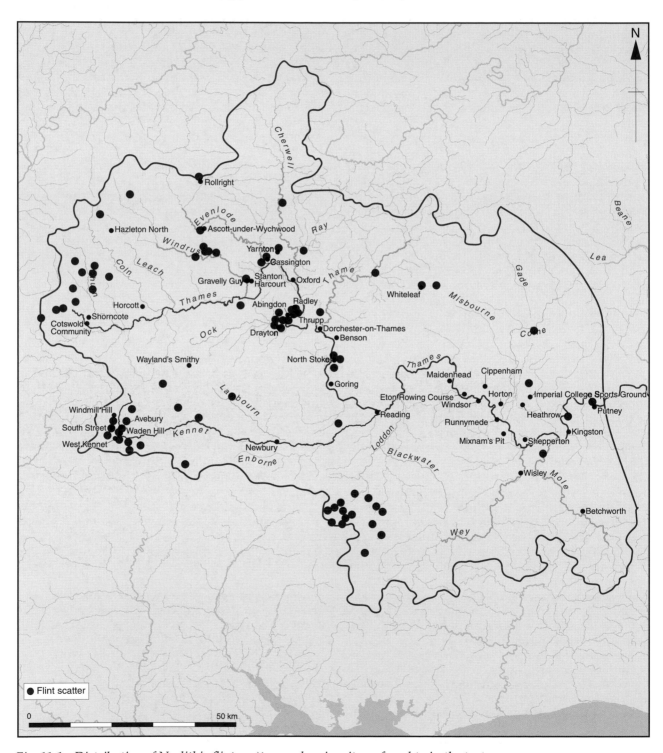

Fig. 11.1   Distribution of Neolithic flint scatters and major sites referred to in the text

Changing landscapes

Woodland clearance

We have already seen that woodland clearings were important to Mesolithic populations in the Thames Valley, and may have been augmented and maintained by local groups to maximise resource aggregation. Human interference in this wooded landscape is clearly demonstrable from the beginning of the 4th millennium cal BC and increased visibly from this time (Fig. 11.2). The scale and character of this activity show that it was deliberately undertaken and maintained. The Abingdon causewayed enclosure was constructed in an area that had been cleared of trees early in the 4th millennium (Fig. 11.3; Parker 1999) and it remained open, calcareous, well-drained grassland with some cereal plots until a phase of woodland regeneration perhaps around 700 years later (Cain 1982; Parker 1999). This example shows that Neolithic clearances were not necessarily for settlement or for agriculture; in some cases they may have been made for the siting of ceremonial monuments.

A number of Mesolithic clearings, for example those at Hazleton North, Ascott-under-Wychwood and Runnymede, witnessed activity in the Neolithic too (Saville 1990a, 240-1; Benson and Whittle 2007, 344-8; Needham 2000a). This may reflect the comparative ease of tree removal, and the favourable siting of these places, but could indicate the continuing use of traditional locales in the landscape and, by implication, continuity amongst the people who used them. Early Neolithic settlement at Yarnton, on the other hand, was set in small woodland clearings in areas with only slight evidence for pre-4th millennium activity (Hey in prep.).

Few clearings were long lasting, however, and they were almost always small in scale. Woodland recolonisation subsequently occurred at both Ascott-under-Wychwood and Hazleton (Benson and Whittle 2007; Saville 1990a), and an early Neolithic long enclosure at Yarnton appears to have had a similar history of clearance in advance of construction followed by woodland regeneration (Robinson in prep.). There was no practical reason why grassland around monuments should not have been grazed, and the Abingdon example and, later in the Neolithic, long-lived grassland at the Devil's Quoits henge, Stanton Harcourt, suggests that this was the case at some sites (Parker 1999; Evans 1995). However, evidence from other regions suggests that the grassland within which monuments were set did not always experience much grazing (Robinson 2000a, 34) and, in the Thames Valley, even cleared areas associated with ceremonial monuments usually experienced episodes of woodland regeneration. The Drayton Cursus, downstream from Abingdon, was constructed in a cleared landscape where earlier

Fig. 11.2   Artist's reconstruction of tree clearance in the Neolithic

monuments were present, but there were several phases of regeneration and clearance in the middle and late Neolithic (Barclay *et al.* 2003). Where more extensive grassland existed, this lay next to monuments which were the scenes of large-scale gatherings, such as causewayed enclosures and cursus monuments (Barclay and Hey 1999). The overall impression of the Upper Thames landscape by the mid 4th millennium cal BC is of a mosaic of woodland and clearings the location of which shifted across the landscape (Robinson 2000a, 33), but with few permanently open areas.

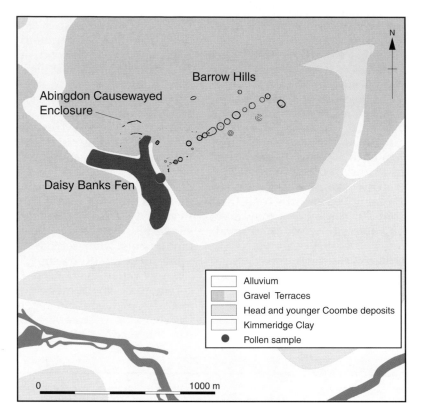

Fig. 11.3 (above and below)   The Daisy Banks Fen pollen sequence

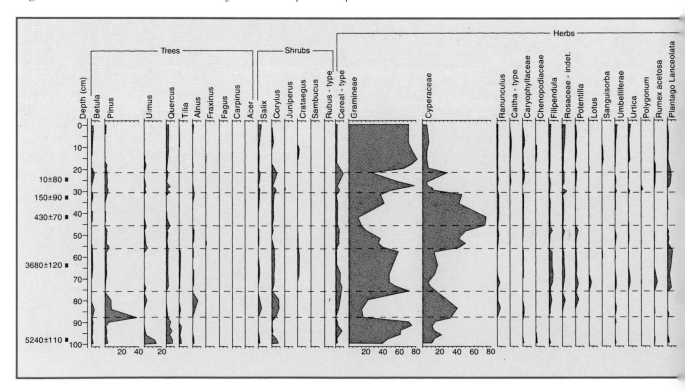

A similar picture emerges from the Upper Kennet Valley, where the landscape at the beginning of the 4th millennium was of closed, oak-dominated deciduous woodland (Pollard and Reynolds 2002, 30-1). Subsequent clearance was patchy but included some areas which remained clear, including, for example, the area around Avebury itself where clearance was followed by some arable cultivation and then transformation into dry grassland, as well as others, such as Easton Down (Whittle *et al.* 1993), where woodland regeneration occurred (Evans *et al.* 1993, 189; Whittle 1993, 40). Once again, it is suggested that the landscape throughout the 4th millennium remained largely wooded but contained small and shifting clearings with only a few more long-lived open areas developing.

At the Eton Rowing Course in the Middle Thames, there is no evidence for widespread clearance in the early 4th millennium, despite the presence of middens, and evidence of other contemporary activity nearby, although there are some suggestions of localised openings in the woodland (Parker forthcoming). A similar picture emerges at Runnymede, where pollen dating to the early 4th millennium cal BC indicates deliberate interference in the tree canopy, although plant macrofossils continue to suggest dense alder woodland (Needham 2000a, 193-5; Robinson 2000a, 31-2). A clearance event at the Eton Rowing Course is recorded at around 3640-3370 cal BC (CAMS-57207: 4730±40 BP), although it seems to have been quite localised (Parker forthcoming). In the London area, land clearance is associated with cereal cultivation on some sites in the early 4th millennium cal BC, although adjacent areas appear to have remained wooded (Sidell and Wilkinson 2004, 42).

As has been argued above (Chapter 9), the cycle of woodland being replaced by open conditions which then experienced regeneration is seen as being driven by limited killing of trees and the grazing pressure of domestic animals:

- some trees are killed by ring barking in old high woodland from which any thorn scrub has been shaded out, and domestic animals are introduced

- grass begins to grow on the woodland floor but the grazing prevents regeneration of the woodland trees. Some trees die of old age, others are killed by ring barking, and the dead trees either collapse or are pulled over and burnt

- any remaining trees are felled, leaving grassland which is either grazed or cultivated for cereals

- thorn scrub gradually invades the pasture, reducing the potential for grazing

- woodland trees begin to become established amongst the thorny bushes, where they are protected from grazing

- as the woodland regenerates, the stock is moved to a new area

Unfortunately, because of the relatively low water table at the time (see above, Chapter 9), little organic material from this period has been preserved, and so any form of woodland management is hard to detect. Evidence elsewhere, especially from the Fens, suggests coppicing from an early period (Taylor 1988), and it has been

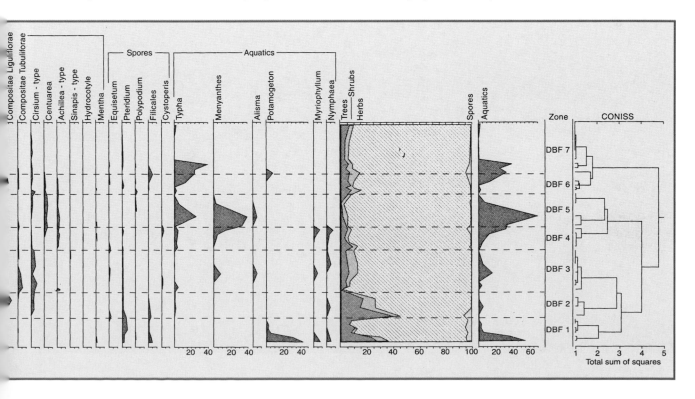

suggested that hazel was managed in order to yield large quantities of nuts as a crop (F Pryor pers. comm.).

Charcoal is relatively common on early Neolithic sites, although no obvious pattern has been discerned in the choice of wood for fuel. Both woodland taxa, particularly *Quercus* sp. (oak), and bushes of thorn scrub such as Pomoideae indet. (hawthorn-type) and *Prunus spinosa* (sloe) tend to be well-represented. The postholes of the building at Yarnton contained some oak charcoal but it is unclear whether this was from the burning of the structure itself (Robinson in prep.).

The evidence from tree-throw holes

Tree-throw holes are common features on Neolithic sites in the Thames Valley and provide physical evidence of clearance (Fig. 11.4), although it is difficult to demonstrate which are the result of human

effort and which natural tree fall (Brown 1997). At Reading Business Park, however, it was noted that the direction of tree fall was contrary to that of the generally prevailing winds, suggesting that deliberate felling played some part in clearance there (Moore and Jennings 1992, 13). The different shapes and sizes of holes probably reflect different tree species (Lamdin-Whymark 2008, 76-9). Evidence in some tree-throw holes of the deliberate chopping of roots suggests that stumps were being grubbed out (M Taylor pers. comm.), and it has been claimed that charcoal within some, including charcoal from roots, derives from the burning of stumps and debris *in situ* (Hey 1997, 110; Robinson in Lambrick and Robinson 2003, 166-8). Tree-throw holes were numerous on the Yarnton floodplain but, rather than being evenly spread, they formed distinct clumps which tended to correspond to the distribution of Neolithic features (Hey in prep.). The implication is that these relate, at least in part, to

Fig. 11.4   Tree-throw holes: formation and excavation

deliberate clearance for specific episodes of use. Lower down the Thames Valley, numerous tree-throw holes were discovered during the works associated with Terminal 5 at Heathrow, many of which contained early Neolithic material (Lewis *et al.* 2006, 64-7). Nevertheless the prevailing environment was wooded, and clearings must have been quite small and short-lived. At the Eton Rowing Course the tree-throw holes were more dispersed (Lamdin-Whymark 2008, 94).

As in the later Mesolithic, material such as struck flint was placed in tree-throw holes. Indeed, this seems to have become a more common practice in the early 4th millennium, as is shown by sites on the Eton Rowing Course and Maidenhead, Windsor and Eton Flood Alleviation Scheme where deposition associated with Carinated and Plain Bowl pottery was most common; charred plant remains were also found (Allen *et al.* 2004, fig. 9.2 and 91; Lamdin-Whymark 2008; T G Allen *et al.* forthcoming). At the Eton Rowing Course, tree-throw holes yielded finds that are indistinguishable in character from those from hollows on adjacent ground surfaces, and their composition shows that they had probably come from nearby middens (Lamdin-Whymark 2008, 94). Some material, on the other hand, seemed to have been deliberately placed in these features, including, for example, a section of cattle vertebrae in one feature and a discrete deposit of pottery with complete leaf and chisel arrowheads amongst other flints in another (ibid.); flintwork from these contexts was usually quite fragmented.

Excavation of the Drayton Cursus revealed a number of tree-throw holes that were filled with burnt and redeposited material, most of which was mundane and appeared to derive from household activities, although there were also some more special items which may represent offerings, such as large pieces from an Ebbsfleet Ware bowl (Barclay *et al.* 2003, 60-7, fig. 4.22). At Yarnton, a large part of a polished flint axe, a leaf-shaped arrowhead and a small quantity of burnt stone appeared to have been deliberately placed in a tree-throw hole just to the north-east of an early Neolithic structure (feature 3384; Hey in prep.), and further examples come from Shorncote near Cirencester and Horcott Pit near Fairford (Powell *et al.* 2010; Brady and Lamdin-Whymark in press). At Horcott, large parts of at least five Grooved Ware pots were stacked in a 0.3 m diameter circle part way up the fill of a probable tree-throw hole. It has been proposed that material was deliberately deposited in tree-throw holes in other parts of southern England as a means by which people registered occupation events within a natural forest environment in the context of shifting settlement (Evans *et al.* 1999), the deposits perhaps representing the clearing up and closing down of a phase of habitation. At the Eton Rowing Course and the Maidenhead, Windsor and Eton Flood Alleviation Scheme it is possible to interpret a number of these deposits in the same way, as perhaps marking the temporary abandonment of an occupation site.

The extent to which deposition within tree-throw holes represents continuity from Mesolithic practice is hard to establish, not least because the material available to be deposited had changed. It was suggested in Chapter 10 (following Carew *et al.* 2006) that, in the late Mesolithic, material placed in tree-throw holes could, in some cases, represent offerings for things which had been retrieved from the holes, particularly flint nodules. By the early Neolithic, this practice had become much more widespread and has been found in areas like the Upper Thames where the underlying gravels would not yield usable flint. Ideas of reciprocity, however, might have been transferred to other benefits derived from tree removal: the cleared area, timber, firewood and nuts (Lamdin-Whymark 2008, 99), or may have become customary on the deliberate, as opposed to fortuitous, fall of trees. Evans *et al.* (1999, 251, following Bloch 1998) proposed that the life cycle of trees, their growth, development and their death, may have created a perceived 'kinship' between trees, humans and animals.

THE CREATION OF NEW WORLDS

Houses

Some early 4th millennium clearings were used for habitation, but this activity took a variety of forms and, new materials notwithstanding, can be nearly as elusive and difficult to interpret as its Mesolithic counterpart. Indeed, some characteristics of settlement remained remarkably similar, particularly its impermanence. On the other hand, radically new features of domestic life appeared early in the 4th millennium, the most conspicuous of which were houses (Fig. 11.5). The earliest radiocarbon dates come from Ascott-under-Wychwood, where a structure or structures was built in the latter part of the 40th century cal BC or the first part of the 39th (Bayliss, Bronk Ramsey, Galer *et al.* 2007). Buildings at Hazleton North and Sale's Lot are likely to be of similar age or marginally later (Bayliss and Whittle 2007), and a longhouse at Yarnton belongs to the end of the first quarter of the 4th millennium cal BC, probably the 38th century (Bayliss and Hey in prep.).

When found, these rectangular wooden buildings are well defined and can be substantial in size; they have no parallels from earlier periods in this country. Their distant origins lie in the early Neolithic structures of the *Linearbandkeramik* cultures of central and northern Europe, although those buildings are earlier in date, larger and most often found in groups rather than dispersed as in Britain (Whittle

Fig. 11.5 (overleaf) Neolithic buildings

NEOLITHIC BUILDINGS

The discovery of a longhouse at Yarnton was particularly exciting. It is rare to find traces of Neolithic structures of any kind in south-east Britain, and even more unusual to uncover the remains of longhouses, which are regarded as fairly typical of Neolithic settlement in highland Britain and elsewhere in Europe.

The remains at Yarnton comprised the postholes of a building which had a basic rectangular shape, 20 m long and 11 m wide, and was divided centrally into two approximately square modules. Some of the postholes were substantial and would have accommodated thick posts supporting a wide roof; it is not impossible that there was an upper storey but there would at least have been a large loft. A line of smaller posts which diverged from the main axis of the building could represent a pentice or a funnelled entranceway, or could indicate that the building was, in outline, trapezoidal. This tantalising evidence makes the building hard to reconstruct with confidence.

The reconstruction shown here uses the rectangular model, and suggests that the walls would have been of wattling covered with daub. A small amount of burnt clay was found in the postholes which could have come from wall cladding. Planking might also have been used, as wood would have been plentiful. It seems likely that reeds, or possibly straw, would have been used to thatch the roof; a turf roof with this span would have been immensely heavy.

Alternative reconstructions are, however, possible, several of which are shown in Figure 11.13. Given the ambiguities in the surviving evidence, it is difficult to evaluate the plausibility of these reconstructions. For example, the arrangement of the postholes is

* *Above — Reconstruction of Yarnton longhouse by Peter Lorimer*
* *Opposite — Photograph of Yarnton longhouse under excavation*
* *Yarnton reconstruction in progress*
* *Reconstruction of the Neolithic Building at Horton,* © *WA*

compatible with the structure having been trapezoidal, but the roof on a framework of this shape would have been less stable structurally than that of a rectangular structure, and would have had to span up to 15 m. Figure 11.13 demonstrates how these reconstructions have been built up using the precise positions of postholes as they were found on the site.

The Yarnton house remains the only certain longhouse so far discovered in the Thames Valley, but other types of buildings have been found. The clearest was a smaller rectangular building, 8 m by 5 m, recently found at Horton in the Lower Colne Valley. The frame of this building seems to have been built around three pairs of upright posts, and dark staining within the wall trench indicated at least some plank walling. The structure was divided internally into two roughly equal parts.

Early Neolithic building 3871

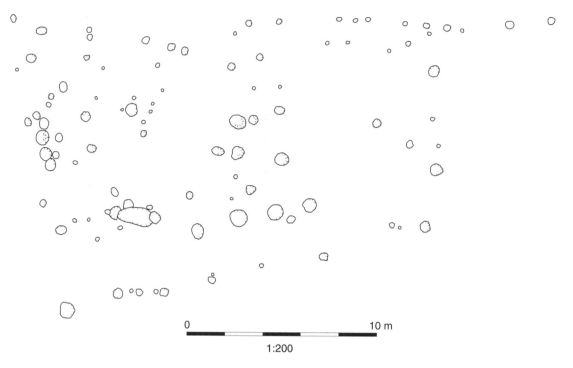

0   10 m

1:200

Fig. 11.6   Plan of the rectangular early Neolithic building at Yarnton, Oxon

Fig. 11.7   Photograph of the rectangular early Neolithic building at Yarnton, Oxon

1996; Last 1996; R Bradley 2007, 38-46). The precise relationship between *Linearbandkeramik* structures and those belonging to the early 4th millennium, both in Britain and Ireland and the near Continent, is not fully understood (Last 1996) and, as we shall see, there is considerable variation amongst them but, without doubt, these buildings were constructed with a Continental template in mind.

Only the Yarnton building resembles the substantial longhouses that have been found with much greater frequency in the north and west of the British Isles (Fig. 11.6). It was orientated east–west and built of earthfast posts arranged in a basic rectangle 21 m x 11 m, divided into two modules (Hey in prep.). Some of the postholes were substantial and presumably held posts which would have supported the roof; one had post packing associated with a foundation deposit of cremated human and pig bone. There was also an outer line of smaller posts on the south side which may have created an outer trapezoidal shape and a maximum width of 15 m (Fig. 11.7). With the exception of the foundation deposit, finds were extremely scarce: a few flint flakes and fragments of animal bone, some fired clay, burnt stone and wood charcoal. A very small quantity (16 g) of cremated human and animal bone was found in three other postholes. The paucity and character of the finds, in conjunction with the massive size of the structure, naturally raise questions about its use. It has been argued that such buildings may have been cult houses or halls for feasting (Thomas 1996; Cross 2003). Whilst there is no indication of feasting, the absence of obviously domestic material within the postholes does not suggest intensive occupation either. This is also true of later Bronze Age buildings on the Yarnton floodplain, on the other hand, the character of which has not been questioned. Residues of meals, sweepings and things that were broken may have been carefully gathered together and placed on a midden for use at a later date. The presence of human and animal bone in the postholes associated with the building is interesting, but does not necessarily preclude its use as a domestic structure, for these may have been seen as appropriate foundation deposits for the building. Given the range of evidence, it is perhaps best to think of this house as having multiple uses, with formal and domestic activities occurring within the same space (Bradley 2003; 2005).

The structures found beneath the long cairns of Sale's Lot and Ascott-under-Wychwood are not so easy to define. The full extent of the postholes at Sale's Lot was not fully revealed, but it is possible to discern a rectangular building more than 6 m x 4.5 m in size with a central hearth (O'Neil 1966; Darvill 1996, 104; Fig. 11.8). The postholes at Ascott-under-Wychwood have been interpreted by the excavator as belonging to two separate buildings 3.5 m x 1.5 m and 3 m x 1 m in size with a hearth lying between these structures (McFadyen *et al.* 2007, 27-31). The evidence could, however, be interpreted as a single rectangular structure, *c* 8.25

m x 3.5 m, with a central hearth (ibid., fig. 2.4; Figs 11.9-10). The buildings on both of these sites were associated with middens and were then overlain by chambered cairns containing human burials. A similar sequence was found at Hazleton North, nearby on the Gloucestershire Cotswolds, where a linear arrangement of postholes and a hearth were found to the west of a midden which lay beneath the later tomb (Saville 1990a, fig. 13). Darvill (1996, 85-8 and fig. 6.5.2) has suggested that these features were related to a ridge-roofed building. Given the subsequent monumentalisation of these sites, was the original purpose of the structures ceremonial too? It is known that these were places which had been visited over generations, but the evidence, particularly middens which contained domestic items (see below), suggests settlement activity, even if this material had been gathered together in a formal way. It seems more likely that these were important places in the landscape, where people had congregated and lived for some periods of time. They were then chosen as appropriate locales at which to bury and to commemorate the dead (Pollard and Reynolds 2002; Bradley 2005, 57-64).

Regular arrangements of postholes found preserved beneath the outer bank of the Windmill Hill causewayed enclosure during several different phases of work may indicate that a similar building had been present there in the early Neolithic period (Whittle *et al.* 1999, 350-2, fig. 220.C). In this case, the significance of the site was monumentalised as a causewayed enclosure in the middle of the 4th millennium. A recent review of the evidence has, however, suggested that the postholes could have been associated with the laying out of the earliest phase of the bank (Whittle, Bayliss and Healy forthcoming).

Although it too was rectangular, a different kind of building was found at Gorhambury. It was defined by gullies and was constructed in two conjoining modules, each *c* 6 m x 4 m (Fig. 11.8; Neal *et al.* 1990, 8-9). It was associated with a little Neolithic Plain Bowl pottery and four flint blades, and resembles the house excavated at Fengate by Francis Pryor (Pryor 1974). One radiocarbon date on mature oak from the upper fill of one of the wall trenches yielded a date of 3770-3370 cal BC (3770-3490 at 79.1%; HAR-3484: 4810±80 BP). A similar building has recently been excavated at Horton in the Lower Colne Valley by Wessex Archaeology. It was *c* 8 m x 5 m and divided into two roughly equal parts (Fig. 11.11; A Barclay pers. comm.). The frame seems to have been built around three pairs of upright posts and dark staining within the wall trench indicated at least some plank walling. Fragments of early Neolithic Bowl, animal bone, flint, part of a Group VI Langdale axe, charred hazelnut shells and a few charred cereal grains in the wall footings suggest sweepings from occupation, and are similar in character to the finds made at the White Horse Stone Neolithic structure in Kent (Figs 11.5 and 11.8; Hayden and Stafford 2006).

A similar structure has been recorded at Cranford Lane, Hayes some 9 km to the north-east, associated with Plain Bowl pottery (N Elsden pers. comm.). The dating from the Horton house suggests that it was constructed around a hundred years after the Yarnton building, but still belongs to the first half of the 4th millennium.

All the buildings discussed above were rectangular in shape, albeit of different sizes, but a small, circular structure recently dated at Yarnton shows that there was some variety in architectural form. The building was initially thought to be late Bronze Age, but radiocarbon dating places it firmly within the second quarter of the 4th millennium cal BC (*c* 3600

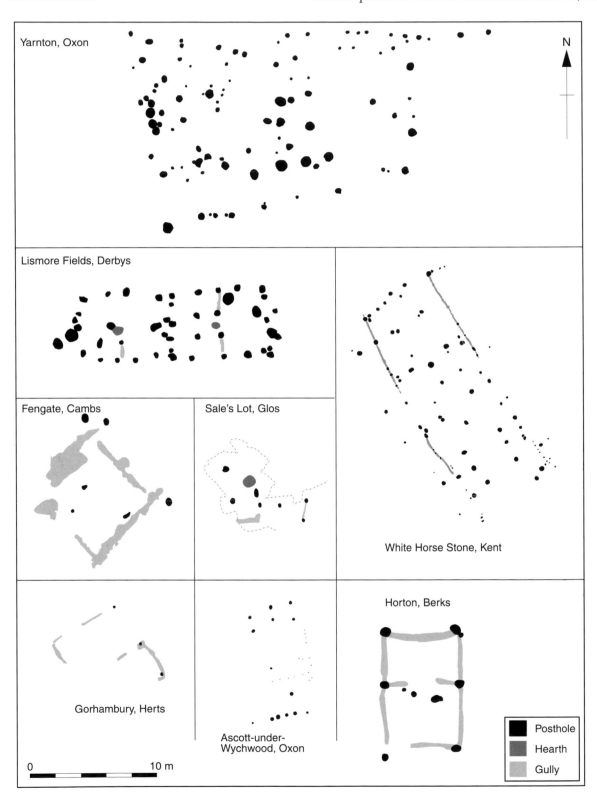

Fig. 11.8   Comparative plans of early Neolithic houses in England

Fig. 11.9 (above) A hearth and pit below the cairn at Ascott-under-Wychwood

Fig. 11.10 (right) Timber structures, axial stakeholes and cists below the cairn at Ascott-under-Wychwood

Fig. 11.11 (below) Photograph of the early Neolithic house at Horton

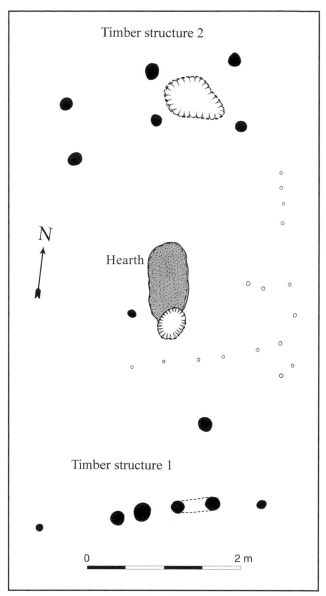

Timber structure 2

N

Hearth

Timber structure 1

0   2 m

cal BC; Bayliss and Hey in prep.), around 100-150 years later than the longhouse. The ring of posts was well defined but had a diameter of only 2.5 m; the posts presumably supported a ring beam and the wall would have lain beyond, as has been suggested for circular Bronze Age and Iron Age houses (Fig. 11.12). Ephemeral circular stake-built structures were also found beneath the outer bank of the Crickley Hill causewayed enclosure further north on the Gloucestershire Cotswolds (Dixon 1988).

We have very little information about how these rectangular houses might have appeared above ground (Fig. 11.5). It is assumed that they would have had some sort of thatch, or perhaps turf, roof, though turf would have been very heavy and perhaps only practical on the smaller structures. Wattle-and-daub walling was suggested by the charcoal and burnt daub in the wall trenches at Gorhambury (Neal *et al.* 1990, 9) and burnt clay was also found in some of the Yarnton postholes, though the evidence from Horton indicates plank walls there. None of these houses has a surviving floor, although those which were subsequently buried

below monuments did have hearths, which often appear to be central to these structures. Figure 11.13 presents a reconstruction based on the Yarnton house.

These Neolithic houses have two particularly striking features. First, given that we are looking at a small group of rectangular wooden buildings, there is quite a lot of variation in size, layout and, apparently, method of construction. It is possible to divide them into large post-built structures like Yarnton, smaller and sometimes less-regular post-built structures as at Ascott-under-Wychwood and post-in-trench constructions like Horton and Gorhambury, but that puts very few buildings in each category. It is also the case that, where buildings are large, they seem to have been subdivided into smaller and more square spaces, or were expanded from square modules. In truth, however, there are no two buildings found in the Thames Valley catchment so far which are very alike (Fig. 11.8). This would suggest that, although the purpose and use of the buildings might have been similar, there were no rigid principles that people felt they had to follow or, perhaps, that they were not built by closely-related communities.

Secondly, given the known extent of early settlement in the Thames Valley, we still have very few houses of Neolithic date. It used to be thought that this was because of the much more extensive and intensive farming regimes in southern English valleys compared to other parts of the British Isles, but the survival of the structures described above, not all of which were buried beneath monuments, along with the numerous, flimsy later Bronze Age and Iron Age houses with which the valley is dotted (Lambrick with Robinson 2010), provide good evidence that the absence of Neolithic buildings is not entirely a factor of subsequent plough destruction (Thomas 1996, 2-3). It must, however, indicate that most buildings or shelters were constructed in ways that did not leave traces below the topsoil. Even careful examination of the buried ground surfaces preserved at the Eton Rowing Course, where evidence of activity was widespread, failed to reveal structures (Allen *et al.* 2004).

If early Neolithic houses are rare, in common with the rest of Britain, those post-dating the middle of the 4th millennium are even more so. There are just three possible structures in our area which belong to the middle Neolithic and one which is late Neolithic in date.

A pair of structures may be represented by post- and stakeholes associated with mid 4th millennium cultural material found on an island between palaeochannels at Runnymede (Fig. 11.14; Needham 2000a). Although it was not easy to define individual buildings amongst the numerous features present in the confined excavation area

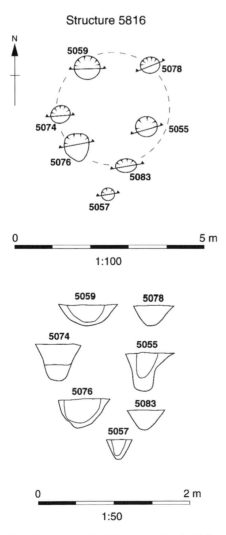

Fig. 11.12 *The early Neolithic circular building at Yarnton*

Fig. 11.13 (facing page) *Reconstruction of the early Neolithic building at Yarnton*

(Area 20), linear arrangements can be seen, including, for example, the line of stakeholes running away from the camera in Figure 11.14 (S Needham pers. comm.).

At Field Farm, Burghfield, a group of post- and stakeholes could have been the remains of a small structure approximately 2.20 m x 1.70 m, though its shape is not well defined (Butterworth and Lobb 1992, 11-3). These features lie to one side of a hearth which has been dated by archaeomagnetism to 3900-3000 cal BC (at 68% confidence; AJC-63) and appear to be associated with Mortlake Ware pottery (Fig. 11.15).

The associations of a subrectangular house at Yarnton (see Fig. 11.28) were with late Neolithic Grooved Ware pottery, and radiocarbon dates showed that it belonged to the third quarter of the 3rd millennium cal BC (probably the 25th or 24th centuries cal BC; Bayliss and Hey in prep.). It was *c* 9 m x 7 m in size, but its precise form was hard to determine, as a number of postholes and pits lay around its perimeter. Parallels for such a structure do, however, exist outside the region at Gwithian (Phase 1), Cornwall (Darvill 1996, fig. 6.8) and, possibly, Wyke Down on Cranborne Chase (Green 2000, fig. 47).

If houses are such rare phenomena, how do we recognise Neolithic settlement and what characterises it?

Middens

The creation of middens is an important feature of early Neolithic social practice, and the character of the deposits within them provides a strong link to domestic activities. They have been found associated with structures beneath the Cotswold long cairns of Hazleton North and Ascott-under-Wychwood, but also at a number of other sites near to the Thames and the headwaters of the Kennet (Saville 1990a; Benson and Whittle 2007; Allen *et al.* 2004; Lamdin-Whymark 2008; Pollard 2005). They comprise dark soils with much charcoal, worked flint, pottery, animal bone, cereals and other food remains. The character of some of these finds, and the manner of their deposition, sometimes indicate separate episodes of activity and, where soil analysis has been possible, it can be seen that trampling took place as people and animals worked over the material. Whether the presence of higher organic phosphates detected within some middens is a result of the latter or deliberate manuring in

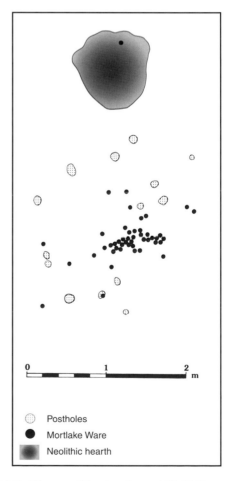

Fig. 11.14   Neolithic features at Runnymede

Fig. 11.15   The possible structure at Field Farm, Burghfield

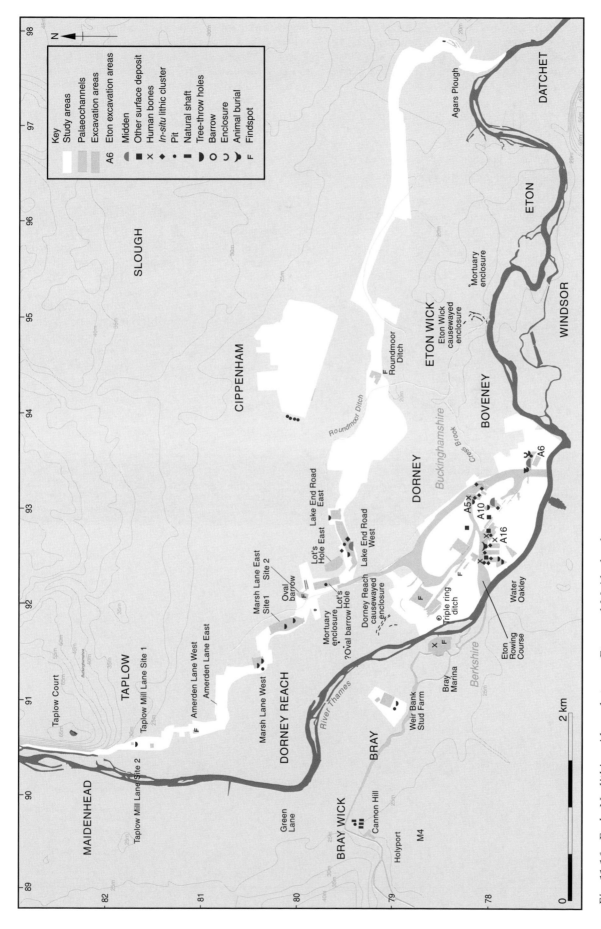

Fig. 11.16   Early Neolithic evidence between Eton and Maidenhead

order to cultivate these fertile locations (Guttman 2005; Macphail in Benson and Whittle 2007, 70-3; see below) is uncertain, but the midden beneath the Hazleton North cairn, and possibly also the example under the Ascott-under-Wychwood cairn, had been ploughed.

The Middle Thames Valley has provided an important group of midden sites close to the river which were sealed beneath alluvium (Fig. 11.16). Three middens were excavated at the Eton Rowing Course and on the adjacent Flood Alleviation Scheme which appear to have had a main period of

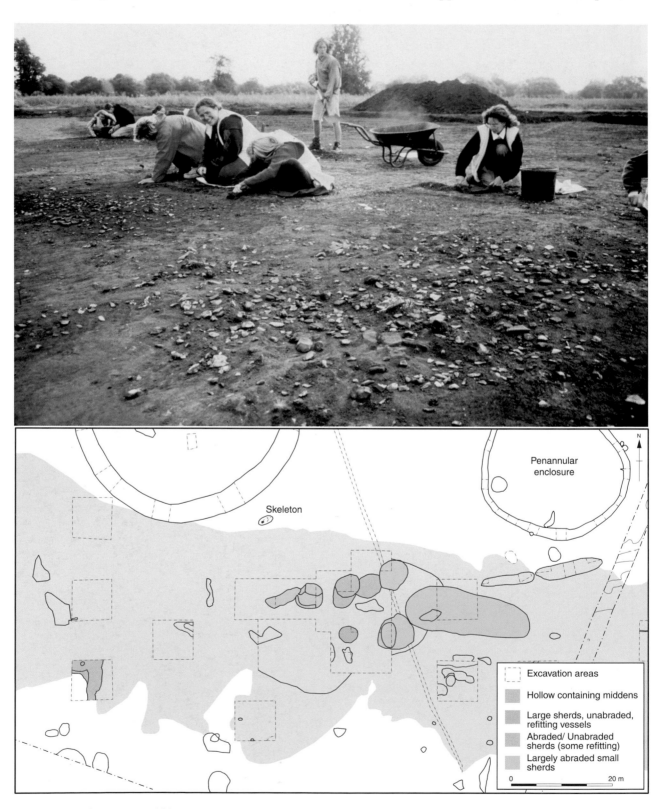

Fig. 11.17   The Area 6 midden at Eton Rowing Course

use from around *c* 3800-3500 cal BC, although material may have been added to them throughout the Neolithic (Allen *et al.* 2004). One midden was up to 80 m long and all lay within a distance of 3 km, close to the river and in an area with much other contemporary activity (Fig. 11.16). The associated pottery was highly fragmented with few refitting sherds amongst the many hundreds retrieved, and the struck flint showed much evidence of re-use, by a factor two to three times greater than that recovered from other sites in the area which seem to have been used during much shorter visits (Fig. 11.17; T G Allen *et al.* forthcoming). Additionally, soil micromorphology indicates considerable trampling over the midden areas, suggesting frequent visits to these sites which may have been areas of provisional discard (Allen *et al.* 2004, 85-91). This was not casually-deposited material, but items that had been collected and brought from elsewhere and then had been reworked (Lamdin-Whymark 2008). As a result of this complicated deposit-formation process, it is very hard to assess whether this material is the residue of special events or ordinary domestic activity. The evidence does, however, point to the episodic but repeated use of this site, with perhaps 60 or so separate depositional events. It was

evidently an important focus of activity at this time, and is an indicator of the relative mobility of settlement in the Neolithic. Other middens excavated in this area, for example on the Maidenhead, Windsor and Eton Flood Alleviation Scheme and at Runnymede, shared these characteristics (T G Allen *et al.* forthcoming.; Needham and Spence 1996; Needham 2000a, 240; Serjeantson 2006). At Runnymede, hearths and more dispersed areas of burning were found in association with these rich refuse spreads (Fig. 11.18; S Needham pers. comm.).

In the very different landscape of the Cotswolds, the abraded and fragmentary character of the finds, and the occasional refits scattered over the area of the midden at Hazleton North, were also believed to be the result of the redeposition of rubbish accumulated elsewhere (Saville 1990a, 240-1). A wide range of pottery vessels was recovered, indicating drinking, cooking and storage. Cereals and hazelnut shells were found and there was evidence for the slaughter and consumption of sheep, cattle and pigs nearby; some human bone was also present. The site then appeared to have been ploughed. The midden at Ascott-under-Wychwood has recently been re-evaluated and published (Fig. 11.19; Benson and Whittle 2007), and its composition suggests that, on this site too, the presentation and sharing of food was an important activity. Its formation seems to belong the last half of the 40th century or the 39th century cal BC, and it incorporated much pottery (from which at least 17 vessels have been recognised), animal bone (cattle, pig, sheep, dog, red and roe deer and fox) and struck flint (including many diagnostic pieces and many early Mesolithic microliths), the result of at least two episodes of deposition and probably more (Whittle in Benson and Whittle 2007, 328). The origin of some of the finds indicates that people may have gathered here from diverse places (Barclay 2007). A period of around 50 years seems to have elapsed before the chambered cairn was constructed on the site (Bayliss, Bronk Ramsey, Galer *et al.*2007).

Fig. 11.18   Hearths at Runnymede

Fig. 11.19   The midden below the cairn at Ascott-under-Wychwood

Middening is also an activity witnessed in the Avebury landscape where Pollard (2005, 109-11) has drawn attention to the long-term accumulation of deposits such as the site excavated by Keiller on the line of the West Kennet Avenue. Although much of this material appeared to have been the result of occupation, there were a number of unusual and fancy items, and some objects appeared to have been carefully placed, suggesting much more than casual discard (ibid.). The midden may have been marked or enhanced by posts and material from it may have been placed within pits, perhaps at the end of its use, in order to close-down the site.

Other sites in the Thames Valley have provided evidence for spreads of finds which may suggest the previous existence of middens. One such area was found on the floodplain at Yarnton, 450 m from the Neolithic house, and included finds and activity contemporary with it (Bayliss and Hey in prep.). Other spreads have been examined at Drayton Cursus (Barclay *et al.* 2003) and lower down the Thames in Surrey at Sefton Street, Putney and Eden Walk, Kingston (Field and Cotton 1987). The site at Mixnam's Pit near Staines, examined by Grimes during the Second World War, may be another example (Grimes 1960, 181-5).

Pollard has suggested that middens are a physical demonstration of long-term commitments to particular locales (Pollard 1999, 82). They would have provided a visible marker of occupation events, created a sense of place, and have been a material link between the past and the present. In a recent analysis of the Eton Rowing Course evidence, Lamdin-Whymark (2008, 46-50 and 56) has proposed that, because of the presence of charred cereals and quern fragments, middens were associated with the processing of crops. They would, of course, have been very fertile places, covered with distinctive vegetation including plants growing from seeds that had been middened (Bell and Walker 1992, 112), and this would have enhanced their significance. It may be no coincidence that at least some middens were cultivated (Guttman 2005; Whittle 1990, 107; Saville 1990a, 254-5). They would have conveyed connotations of fecundity and abundance (Hey and Barclay 2007).

In general, the creation of middens belongs to the early Neolithic period, and occurred at much the same time as the construction of the houses with which they were sometimes associated. This is shown by the presence of Carinated Bowl from the lowest part of the deposits at the Eton Rowing Course and the midden at Ascott-under-Wychwood, and by the radiocarbon dates from both sites. At a number of sites this activity was superseded and sometimes sealed by later monuments; in other places accumulation continued, though at a less intense rate than before. The cessation of intensive midden use coincides with the construction of the first large-scale monuments in the Thames Valley, and links between deposits of curated material within middens and those found in the base of ditch segments at causewayed enclosures have been noted (Pollard 2005, 109-111; Whittle 1990, 107; Whittle *et al.* 1999; Oswald *et al.* 2001; Benson and Whittle 2007, 345; Lamdin-Whymark 2008). Indeed, midden sites at which people seem to have gathered together and perhaps feasted, may form the precursors to causewayed enclosures (ibid.; R Bradley 2007).

Whereas houses were demonstrably a new feature of the archaeological evidence in the early 4th millennium, the creation and augmentation of middens, with their representation of past events and association with feasting, seem to have been features of both 5th and early 4th millennium cal BC populations (Hey and Barclay 2007). They demonstrate that people made repeated visits to particular locales, probably not on an annual cycle but as part of a traditional routine, and that these patterns of activity were as important to early farmers as to earlier hunter-gatherer groups. Indeed, it is not unusual to find Mesolithic material in or near early Neolithic middens, as the examples from Hazleton North, Ascott-under-Wychwood and the Eton Rowing Course demonstrate (Saville 1990a, fig. 163; Benson and Whittle 2007, fig. 2.8; T G Allen *et al.* forthcoming). Their presence could be taken to indicate the same population doing the same things albeit with different material, but this might be misleading. The only substantial Mesolithic midden deposits in the Thames Valley belong to the early Mesolithic period (and the sites in the Middle Kennet Valley specifically – see above, Chapter 10), and there is very little that is comparable in the late Mesolithic of the Thames Valley, although sites in adjacent areas, such as Cherhill and Oakhanger Warren, may represent modest accumulations of material as may some of the more dense late Mesolithic Thames Valley sites (Rankine and Dimbleby 1960; Evans and Smith 1983; see above Chapter 10). The practice may be similar, therefore, but the scale and visibility of these events in the Neolithic were of a different order. Pollard has suggested that this may be the result of a conscious reassertion of older ways of doing things at a time of profound social change (Pollard 2005).

Artefact scatters

The most obvious manifestation of early settlement activity is found in the modern ploughsoil, but comparatively little attention has been devoted to Mesolithic and Neolithic finds scatters in recent years. This is partly because of the extensive and still extremely useful earlier surveys undertaken in the Thames Valley by Robin Holgate and others (Hingley 1980; Ford 1987b; 1992; Holgate 1988a; Fig. 11.1) and the fact that fieldwalking currently tends to be omitted from requirements for developer-funded evaluation. There is also the significant difficulty of both dating surface find scatters and of identifying the activities they represent. Pottery very rarely survives within the ploughsoil and, with the exception of a few diagnostic artefacts, it is hard to distinguish between later Mesolithic and early Neolithic flintwork (see above, Chapter 10), or between mid to late Neolithic and early Bronze Age flint. Flint tools can be used for a variety of purposes and, where detailed studies have been carried out, it is clear that many scatters are, in fact, composite assemblages produced as a result of several different episodes of activity. Some material is mundane, but exceptional artefacts are recovered, such as arrowheads and polished flint and ground stone axes. If some of these scatters derive from middens and pits, as some must, it is easy to see why these difficulties of interpretation arise.

There are, however, sites within the Middle Thames Valley where intact ground surfaces survive. At the Eton Rowing Course, in addition to middened material, a wide variety of depositional practices was apparent across the floodplain landscape. These varied from surface scatters related to large-scale camps with associated hearths, some of which were visited on more than one occasion, to individual knapping events (Fig. 11.16; T G Allen pers. comm.; Lamdin-Whymark 2008, 58-72). Unlike middens, these scatters contained relatively little pottery and animal bone and less obviously-used flint (ibid., 70-2). The results of fieldwalking around North Stoke suggest a similar pattern (Ford 1987a), as does the spread of early and later Neolithic finds recovered from sand layers near to the Thames at Sefton Street, Putney, which was associated with two hearths and a series of postholes (Warren in Field and Cotton 1987, 75). Recent careful analysis has identified different types and phases of activity within a single, disturbed assemblage, from the Maidenhead Thicket site (Boismier 1995). The finds from sites such as the Eton Rowing Course can aid in the interpretation of artefact scatters which are not *in situ*, and further work is needed to compare fieldwalking scatters with the variety of settlement assemblages which have now been excavated.

The distribution of sites indicated by finds scatters suggests that early Neolithic settlement shared a focus on the river and its tributaries, stretching up onto the Cotswolds, similar to that evident in the Mesolithic. Thrupp, Corporation Farm and Gravelly Guy are examples of sites with evidence of 4th-millennium use where there had previously been hunter-gatherer encampments at the forest margin overlooking the Thames floodplain (Holgate 1988a, 87; 2004a), and early Neolithic activity at Hazleton and Rollright on the Cotswolds was preceded by smaller-scale episodes of use in the Mesolithic, perhaps for hunting (Lambrick 1988, 111-2; Saville 1990a, 240). Goring, lower down the Thames, provides a similar example (T G Allen 1995), and the juxtaposition of Mesolithic and early Neolithic sites has also been noted by Field for the Thames further downstream and on the Greensand of the Weald to the south (Field 2004, 156). Although the early Neolithic pattern is more dense than that

of the the 5th millennium, the sites are similarly small and appear to have been short-lived.

At the Eton Rowing Course in the early 4th millennium cal BC, activity was more widespread than it had been previously but still mainly followed the channel edge, and exhibited a similar pattern of land use (cf Figs 10.10 and 11.16; Allen *et al.* 2004, 85). Although few sites have been investigated over such a scale as the Eton Rowing Course, continuity in the location of settlement in riverside locations is apparent elsewhere, along the Maidenhead, Windsor and Eton Flood Alleviation Scheme, for example (T G Allen *et al.* forthcoming). At Runnymede, although the earlier material remains were not dense, the evidence suggests repeated use of the site throughout this period (Needham 2000a, 71 and 240). The proximity of early Neolithic to Mesolithic sites has also been noted in the Thames Estuary (Bates and Whittaker 2004, 59; Field 2004, 156).

In other areas, the location of Mesolithic and Neolithic sites seem to be complementary rather than overlapping, a good example being in the Upper Kennet Valley, an area where Mesolithic sites were dispersed and small in size, but which became an important centre of Neolithic activity (Whittle 1990; Barclay 2000; Pollard 2005). At Yarnton, the picture is more ambiguous. Later Mesolithic flint was recovered during fieldwalking over the central gravel island on which early 4th millennium cal BC features were present from a range of activities. It was found in very small quantities, but its correlation with areas of early Neolithic activity is marked. It does not, however, indicate continuity in any meaningful sense.

Pits

If pits are an occasional feature of Mesolithic sites (Mithen 1999), their Neolithic counterparts have become a relatively common discovery in the Thames Valley, and have been found in all parts of the region and on all topographies in recent years. Indeed, it could be said that pits are the most ubiquitous of Neolithic and early Bronze features in the Thames Valley. These generally bowl-shaped and relatively shallow features have been encountered in small numbers over many years, mainly in the course of examining larger-scale ceremonial sites or the remains of other periods. Holgate (1988a, 259-76) listed approximately 128 to 132 pits from 37 sites within our area (excluding pits with burials and those associated with the West Kennet Avenue stone row; the number of pits at three sites was uncertain), but over the last 20 years perhaps thousands have been excavated in development-led excavations in the Thames Valley and surrounding areas, including over 150 at Yarnton alone (Fig. 14.1; Hey in prep.).

They date from the early Neolithic (at Benson and South Stoke, for example; Pine and Ford 2003; Timby *et al.* 2005) to the early Bronze Age (at

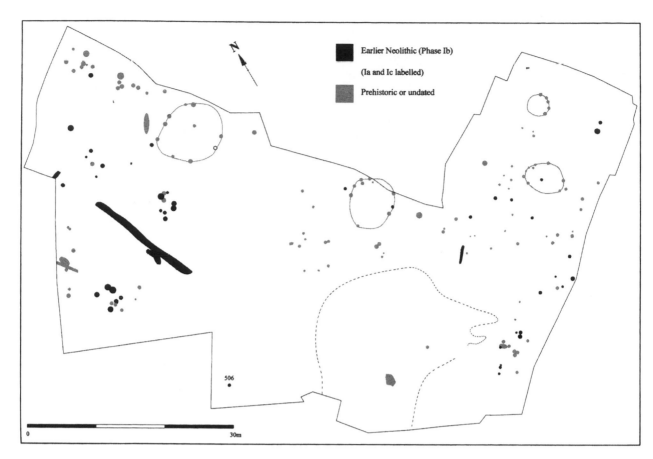

Fig. 11.20   Plan of Neolithic pit groups at Benson

Thames Valley Park, Reading, for example; Barnes *et al.* 1997), although middle and late Neolithic pits are most common. Sometimes they occur over extensive areas as at Yarnton (Hey in prep.), Drayton (Barclay *et al.* 2003) and Stanton Harcourt/Gravelly Guy (Barclay 1995b), but even on these sites they tend to cluster in very small groups, mainly in pairs, or are isolated features. The dense early Neolithic pit sites that characterise the settlement evidence in the east of England (Clark *et al.* 1960; Healy 1988; Garrow *et al.* 2006) are not a feature of the Thames Valley. The group of 23 early Neolithic pits found at Benson (Pine and Ford 2003) is, to date, atypical (Fig. 11.20).

Pits are found associated with monuments and monument complexes throughout the Thames catchment, at New Wintles Farm in West Oxfordshire, at Barrow Hills, Radley, at Horton in the Middle Thames and in the Upper Kennet Valley, for example (Kenward 1982; Barclay and Halpin 1999; Ford and Pine 2003; Pollard and Reynolds 2002, 33-7; Pollard 2005). They are not always, or even usually, contemporary with the monumental phase of the site, however, but tend to precede or follow it, as the example of the pits and midden incorporated into the West Kennet Avenue demonstrate (Pollard 2005, 110-1); the sequence of events here mirrors that for some structures and middens. The vast majority of pits that have been discovered, on the

other hand, are not demonstrably associated with funerary or ceremonial sites, but are found in the wider landscape in small groups or individually, sometimes with scattered postholes (Fig. 11.21). They appear to reflect settlement activity.

It might be thought that the interpretation of pits should be straightforward. It used to be believed that they were either rubbish pits or storage pits belonging to settlements (Field *et al.* 1964), the remains of which had otherwise been eroded or ploughed away (Holgate 1988a, 31-3). Mark Robinson suggests that some may have been dug

Fig. 11.21   Yarnton: scatter of pits and postholes

for the storage of hazelnuts with any ceremonial function being secondary, as the nuts are amenable to storage in small pits and the hazelnut shell fragments which are commonly found in them were, perhaps, waste from nuts which had been recovered, roasted and opened nearby. The finds from such pits are, however, by no means confined to hazelnut shells. Case (1973) and Richards and Thomas (1984) drew attention to the unusual character of many of these features which appeared to have been dug and backfilled quickly with charcoal-rich deposits including a high proportion of fine artefacts (Fig. 14.31). Thomas suggested that this material was deliberately placed within pits which had been specifically dug for the purpose (Thomas 1999, 64-74). Pits in the Thames Valley share many of the characteristics which Thomas noted and this is discussed further below in Chapter 14. It is important here, however, to comment on their relationship to settlement sites.

It is undoubtedly true that a number of pit deposits include some very fine and unusual objects made of a variety of materials, but consisting mainly of pottery, flint and stone. Fancy flint and stone tools include a complete polished flint axe from an early Neolithic pit at Cippenham, Slough (Ford 2003), part of a polished flint macehead and flint knives at Yarnton (Roe in prep.; Bradley and Cramp in prep.) and ground stone axes from sources as far away as North West England at Cassington (Case 1982b, 121-4). Substantial assemblages of flintwork have also been found in some pits including, for example, two of the early Neolithic pits at Horcott near Fairford which provided evidence of on-site flint knapping; a quartzite axe polisher also came from this site (Brady and Lamdin-Whymark in press).

Pits sometimes contain highly-decorated pottery vessels, such as the unusual Mortlake Ware bowl from Lake End Road West on the Maidenhead, Windsor and Eton Flood Alleviation Scheme (Fig. 14.31; Allen *et al.* 2004), pottery of the same substyle at Cippenham (Ford and Taylor 2004, fig. 10.4), the spiral-decorated Grooved Ware sherd at Barrow Hills, Radley (Fig. 16.15; Barclay and Halpin 1999, fig. 4.33), and Beaker pottery from Cotswold Community, Somerford Keynes, near Cirencester at the headwaters of the Thames (Powell *et al.* 2010). Although the fills of early Neolithic pits at South Stoke were simple and no obvious placing of material was noted, one pit did contain a minimum of ten vessels comprising at least two large bowls, two cups and a decorated bowl, suggesting that the finds were the remains of an important meal or feast (Timby *et al.* 2005, 231). A pottery burnisher was buried within a pit at Horcott (Brady and Lamdin-Whymark in press).

Other objects include a fossil shell bead in an early Neolithic pit at Horcott (ibid.), a canal coal bead with Grooved Ware at Yarnton (Sheridan in Hey in prep.), a bone scoop in a Grooved Ware pit at Lower Mill Farm, Surrey (Jones and Ayres 2004), and an awl

made from the ulna of a white-tailed eagle at Barrow Hills, Radley (Barclay and Halpin 1999, fig 4.35). Human bone is also an occasional addition to pit contents, presumably providing extra potency to the deposit or referencing a particular person or event. Examples include a fragment of an adult human skull in an early Neolithic pit at the Eton Rowing Course (Lamdin-Whymark 2008, 117) and part of the skull of an adult female, a complete shed deer's antler and parts of another in one of three Peterborough Ware-associated pits near Bourton-on-the-Water in the Cotswolds (Dunning 1932). One of the seven Beaker pits found beneath the Avebury G55 bell barrow contained the dismembered body of an infant (Smith 1965b, 37-40).

In addition to exotic items, some deposits reveal a highly-structured arrangement of material. There are examples of pits lined with broken sherds at Horcott, Gravelly Guy and Yarnton (Brady and Lamdin-Whymark in press; Lambrick and Allen 2004; Hey in prep.). At Horcott, these were placed with the decorated sherds facing the sides of the pit, so that the pit mimicked a vessel. At Yarnton, the sherds were placed around the circumference of the pit, and another pit at the same site had a large cobble placed on its base over which sherds of a Mortlake Ware vessel had been smashed (Fig. 14.31). An almost complete Peterborough Ware bowl (Mortlake substyle) was found standing upright in a pit at Mixnam's Pit in the Lower Colne Valley, as though it had been placed with food or drink within it (Grimes 1960, 186, fig. 75); an adjacent pit contained an inverted oval bowl. E T Leeds described the varied flint assemblage found in a charcoal-rich, 'flint-worker's pit' (Pit P) at Sutton Courtenay, near Drayton, as having the large pieces of flint placed around the edges and base of the feature, where most of the charcoal was concentrated (Leeds 1934a, 264-5). A quartzite and two flint hammerstones, part of a polished stone axe, five scrapers, 'a few' flint saws, a chisel arrowhead and a bone point or awl were found, along with several sherds from a Grooved Ware vessel in which a repair had been made. Three similar pits were found nearby, part of a wider scatter of pits in the northern part of the Drayton South Cursus (Barclay *et al.* 2003, 20-4, 98-9).

Pits are often found in small groups of three or in pairs and, not uncommonly, the pits contain a complementary range of material (Lamdin-Whymark 2008, 102-16). Examples include pairs of Peterborough Ware pits at Yarnton and at Horcott. The two Yarnton pits contained strikingly similar pottery assemblages, but one contained the majority of the pottery and a single cereal grain, whereas the other yielded most of the other finds including flints, animal bone, charred hazelnut shells and burnt and worked stone (Hey in prep.). This reinforces a pattern of a 'rich pit' paired with a 'poor pit' observed in the Middle Thames Valley (Lamdin-Whymark 2008). At Blewbury, Oxfordshire, a flint scraper had been snapped and the two halves placed in different, adjacent pits (Halpin 1984), and refitting flakes and knapping waste were found in different pits at South Stoke (Cramp and Lamdin-Whymark in Timby *et al.* 2005, 265-6).

The burnt soils within which these objects are recovered frequently contain food remains. These include cereals, although gathered foods from the woodland edge are more common (Moffet *et al.* 1989; Robinson 2000c). The contents of pits on the south slopes of Windmill Hill suggested the possibly deliberate burning of cereals in the early Neolithic (Fairbairn in Whittle *et al.* 2000, 175-6), and burnt bread of much the same date was recovered from a pit at Yarnton (Robinson in prep.). Animal bone, occasionally forming substantial deposits, is also found. The dismembered carcass of a young adult aurochs was discovered in a deep, oval pit excavated at Holloway Lane, Harmondsworth (Cotton *et al.* 2006), the five barbed and tanged arrowheads around its skeleton and one in the layer below suggesting an early Bronze Age date for this deposit (the condition of the bone was too poor to allow radiocarbon dating). The animal had been butchered and the remains had been carefully arranged around the partly-filled pit while the flesh was still attached (Fig. 14.33). Fatty residues (presumably from the aurochs) and beeswax (perhaps a component of the mastic used to attach the arrowhead to its haft) were found on the arrowheads. No traces could be found of the upper leg bones and horns which might have been removed before burial. A large collection of animal remains in a pit at Horcott was also interpreted as butchery remains (Evans in Brady and Lamdin-Whymark in press). This deposit included a large number of skull and foot bones mostly of cattle, and was sealed by a layer of charcoal containing cereals, hazelnut shells and fruits including crab apple. This pit highlights some of the difficulties in interpreting the contents of these features: are they offerings, the remains of special meals, or refuse from the domestic hearth or middens?

Where a number of pit groups are examined, a reasonable proportion of the pits are found to contain few or no finds, or to have material which is abraded and mundane. This was noted at Horcott where some pits contained large deposits and fresh, unabraded pottery and flint which did not appear to have travelled far between last use and final deposition. Many other pits, however, contained fragmentary and abraded material, sometimes only a single sherd (usually one to six sherds per pit; Brady and Lamdin-Whymark in press). Just 2% of the pits found in the Cotswold Community excavations contained special deposits (Powell *et al.* 2010), and at Yarnton, the majority of the pits could only be dated by association with other, nearby features with richer assemblages; some features contained nothing at all (Hey in prep.).

Undoubtedly, some of these pits could have held organic material, deposited as votive offerings, which has since decayed: perishable foods such as dairy produce or filleted meat, vegetables and fruits, flowers or objects made of wood. The presence of bark objects in the lower lying sites of Horton, Yarnton and Runnymede, or the mineralised early Neolithic bucket from Yarnton are valuable reminders of what might have been lost (Fig 16.12; Ford and Pine 2003; Hey in prep.; Needham 1991, 28, plates 17 and 18). Nevertheless, the spectacular should not blind us to the commonplace.

There appear to be links between material found in pits and that recovered from middens (T G Allen *et al.* forthcoming; Lamdin-Whymark 2008). Analysis of the contents of individual pits rarely reveals large parts of individual vessels or reconstructable flint tool reduction processes, but usually produces fragments which appear to have come from material collected elsewhere. In addition, there are instances where the contents of different pits, sometimes set some distance apart, seem to have derived from the same parent deposit, as has been suggested at Taplow Mill on the Maidenhead, Windsor and Eton Flood Alleviation Scheme (Barclay in T G Allen *et al.* forthcoming). At Lake End Road West, on the same scheme, ten pits – one group of four pits, one of three and three isolated features – were found spread over an area of 50 x 100 m. The contents were carefully excavated in spits and all finds were recorded three-dimensionally. This revealed that pottery, flint, bone, burnt stone and charred plant remains were all jumbled throughout the ashy fill of each pit. The pottery was generally in very fresh condition, almost as if some of the pots had been deliberately smashed or broken, but the material was clearly collected from a dump or midden and then placed within the pits, rather than being placed separately and specifically within each pit. Refits were found amongst the pottery that came from the pits in the group of four and in one of the isolated pits located some 40 m away. This suggests that all five pits received material from the same parent occupation deposit and perhaps that they were open at the same time.

Additionally, there are a number of examples in our region where the material within pits indicates a varied history prior to deposition. Unburnt pottery, for example, was found with burnt flint and animal bone in a hearth pit at Ascott-under-Wychwood (Benson and Whittle 2007, 32-3), and there are instances of burnt and unburnt conjoining sherds at Yarnton (Barclay in Hey in prep.). These various aspects of pit deposits have led to the suggestion that, as with tree-throw holes, the material within them was placed there from middens at the end of a phase of occupation in order to close down the settlement in a formal manner (Evans *et al.* 1999).

Pits may not necessarily, therefore, have been dug next to houses and shelters as part of domestic activity areas, but they do reflect occupation events and are good indicators of the location of settlements within the landscape, as well as the character of some of the activities that went on there. Scraping hides, woodworking and plant food preparation were all indicated at Shorncote (Powell *et al.* 2010). The distribution of pits, whether extensive or clustered, and whether numerous or small in scale, should also be a good indicator of the intensity and frequency of use of a site and, perhaps, the size of the groups that visited particular locales. The lack of similarity between artefactual assemblages from different pits or small pit groups was noted at Shorncote, indicating that each related to a separate episode of activity (ibid.). It was suggested, using Hill's (1995) study of ethnographic parallels and following Garrow (2006), that each pit-digging event equated to between one and seven months of activity.

The occasional fancy items selected for deposition and, even more rarely, carefully placed within pits, may denote special events in the lives of individual communities and their members (Hey *et al.* 2003; Bradley 2005), and as such they represent individual and very personal acts. The variety of deposits within them presumably reflects what was appropriate in a particular set of circumstances. However, the material selected and the positioning of these features within the landscape suggest that these special acts fell within the domestic sphere and usually formed part of everyday life. That some became part of monument complexes may not have been foreseen when they were first dug, and may be an accident of the later history of the site.

In the changing world of the early 4th millennium, the presence of pits on settlement sites may be seen to represent continuity with a Mesolithic practice but, as with middens, this similarity is more apparent than real. Pits are only occasional features on Mesolithic sites in the Thames Valley, they rarely contain many finds, and no placed deposits have so far been recognised (Chapter 10). Neolithic pits with all the diversity described above, on the other hand, are a common and distinctive feature of 4th millennium and later settlement. That pit digging became a more common practice in the middle Neolithic period perhaps underlines its novelty.

New objects and materials

One of the reasons why Neolithic settlement looks so different from that of the Mesolithic period is, of course, the presence of new objects and new foods. Regardless of the type of settlement – Yarnton with its timber house or the Eton Rowing Course with middens and activity areas on the floodplain but with no structures – people still grew cereals and ate beef and dairy products from pottery vessels. The use and/or adoption of these new items must have made a fundamental difference to people's lives and changed their relationship with the environment in which they lived.

The term 'Neolithic', or New Stone Age, was first coined to differentiate the period when people started to use ground and polished flint and stone

Fig. 11.22   Leaf-shaped arrowheads from Yarnton

axes (Fig. 8.18) from the Old Stone Age when axes were struck and chipped from these materials (see above, Chapter 8). In southern Britain, polished axes are still good indicators of Neolithic sites, with fragments of early flint axes known from the late 40th or 39th century cal BC pre-cairn middens at both Ascott-under-Wychwood and Hazleton North long barrows (Benson and Whittle 2007, 35; Saville 1990a, 165) and polished stone axes from slightly later sites such as causewayed enclosures (for example Windmill Hill; Smith 1965a; Whittle *et al.* 1999), but they are not common artefacts. Leaf-shaped arrowheads (Fig. 11.22) are found more frequently and in the same very early Neolithic contexts, along with a range of other tools which are much more difficult to distinguish from those in Mesolithic assemblages (see Chapter 16). Many assemblages without diagnostic elements, especially those recovered by fieldwalking as already discussed, can be difficult to date, even though there are differences in flintworking techniques (Butler 2005, 119-22; see Chapter 16). On the one hand there seems to be some continuity in flintworking, suggesting at least a shared repertoire of techniques, if not the same people following traditional methods of tool manufacture but making a few different tools (Holgate 2004b). On the other hand, polished axes and larger arrowheads are both features of the Continental Neolithic, and the inspiration to use them came from there, if not the people who made them.

A commonly-held view is that people started to make leaf-shaped arrowheads in order to hunt more effectively in a more open environment. As we have seen, there is little to suggest that the environment changed substantially over the course of the 4th millennium, and hunting would have taken place in wooded landscapes very similar to those of the previous millennium. Ground stone and polished flint axes may be more efficient at chopping down trees than tranchet axes or adzes (which were probably used for working timbers rather than felling trees), but as discussed above, tree clearance is most likely to have been achieved through ring barking or pulling trees over and chopping through their roots as they were grubbed out. Undoubtedly axes were used to chop up wood, but they were also prestige items, and are found in a range of formal deposits, as has already mentioned in the context of pits. The adoption of these new objects seems to represent a cultural rather than a purely practical choice. The change to a more varied tool kit with less emphasis on composite tools, along with a shift from soft to hard-hammer methods of manufacture, seems to be a more gradual process (see Chapter 16).

Pottery is an undeniably new material in the Neolithic, and it is first found as simple but finely-made Carinated Bowl vessels which recall Continental forms (Fig. 8.18; see Chapter 16; Herne 1988). It has been recovered in small quantities from the earliest dated Neolithic deposits, such as the midden beneath the Ascott-under-Wychwood long cairn (Barclay 2007, 279-81) and the the Eton Rowing Course middens (Allen *et al.* 2004), and seems to have been adopted very quickly over an extensive area of Britain (Sheridan 2007). The similarity of these very well-made vessels over such a wide area, and the speed with which they spread, certainly implies the arrival of some skilled individuals who had learned how to make these pots on the Continent, rather than many local groups mimicking processes they had heard about third hand.

Pots presumably replaced organic containers for serving and eating food, but their presence may also imply a change in cooking methods, enabling more liquid meals, such soup, stews and porridges to be consumed. Pottery may also indicate more formal ways of sharing food, with large vessels for cooking, serving and presenting meals, but also smaller individual dishes from which to eat them (Barclay 2007). Its appearance complements the arrival of new forms of food to cook.

New foods

Animals and dairying

Domesticated animals are present in the earliest Neolithic assemblages and, from that time, form the largest element of animal bone assemblages. Cattle seem to have been the most common animal raised in the Thames Valley catchment throughout the Neolithic and early Bronze Age (Fig. 11.23; see Chapter 9), providing not only beef but also dairy foods and a whole host of other secondary products, such as hides, horn and sinew for ropes. Lipids from dairy products, probably milk, have been found in early Neolithic pots from Ascott-under-Wychwood, Yarnton and the Eton Rowing Course (Copley *et al.* 2005a; 2005b; Copley and Evershed 2007). Domesticated pigs are also found in the earliest deposits, particularly in funerary or ceremonial contexts, and sheep and goats are also present. Cattle and pigs, being originally woodland creatures, do well in a wooded environment whereas sheep need some open grassland (see Chapter 9), but it is worth noting that, although sheep were available and eaten from the earliest Neolithic, people tended to raise and eat the domesticated versions of the animals – cattle and pigs – which were present in the wild in this country.

A strong relationship with woodland persisted into the Neolithic, and red and roe deer were hunted, as were wild boar, although many finds are of antlers which could have been collected when shed. The presence of dogs in funerary contexts shows that they continued to be kept and were, presumably, used in the hunt as well as for herding. However, the following and hunting of wild animals in woodland was replaced in the main by

Fig. 11.23   Neolithic burial of a cow at Yarnton

the herding of domestic animals under partly-wooded conditions. This would have given much higher yields of meat than the exploitation of woodland game which probably did not form an important part of the Neolithic and early Bronze Age diet (Mulville in prep.); wild animals are absent at both Runnymede and the Staines causewayed enclosure (Field and Cotton 1987, 91-2; Serjeantson 2006). There is no evidence at all for the consumption of fish, and birds make only a rare appearance in special deposits, such as the white-tailed eagle bone from a Grooved Ware pit at Barrow Hills, Radley already mentioned (Barclay and Halpin 1999, 74), but there is no direct evidence that they were hunted.

Cereals

Cereal cultivation is also evident from the earliest Neolithic period, and is evidenced, for example, in the middens beneath the Ascott-under-Wychwood long cairn and on the Eton floodplain (Allen *et al.* 2004; Benson and Whittle 2007). Wheat and barley were present from the beginning of the Neolithic (see Chapter 9). The speed and success of the introduction of early grain crops in Britain, as elsewhere in Europe, could partly have been because initially there would have been relatively few pests and diseases (Dark and Gent 2001), as well as the novelty and nutritional value of the food. Cereals could have been used to make a variety of foods and drinks, including porridge and beer, but we can be certain that they were making bread because the charred remains of barley bread were found in a pit at Yarnton dated to 3620-3350 cal BC (OxA-6412: 4675±70 BP; NZA-8679: 4672±57 BP; Fig. 11.24; see Chapter 9). Nevertheless, the tradition of collecting woodland fruit and nuts continued from the Mesolithic, and these foods appear to have formed an important part of the Neolithic diet (Moffett *et al.* 1989; Robinson 2000c).

Physical evidence of cultivation is rare, but does exist beneath some later monuments. At both Ascott-under-Wychwood and Hazleton North the sub-barrow soil profiles suggested patches of

0   10 mm

5:1

Fig. 11.24   Charred early Neolithic bread, made from barley, from Yarnton

ground which had seen slightly different histories (Evans *et al.* 2007). Those at Hazleton had been ploughed, and consisted of separate plots of cultivated midden, recently cultivated and still bare ground, cultivated areas which had revegetated and shrub-covered areas (Evans *et al.* 2007, 76-7). Criss-cross plough marks were observed beneath the South Street long barrow where a lower buried soil horizon also appeared to be a ploughed soil (Ashbee *et al.* 1979, fig. 36, 282). There was one other phase of cultivation, perhaps spade digging with an input of manure (Ashbee *et al.* 1979, 296), but the immediately pre-barrow environment was grazed grassland (ibid., 264). McOmish suggested that the criss-cross ploughing could have been part of a lengthy, if piecemeal, process of tilling (McOrmish 2005, contra Thomas 1999, 24), and that the line of sarsens which formed the axis through the barrow may have originated as a linear clearance cairn, and might even represent a field boundary (McOrmish 2005, 133). Pre-barrow clearance and probably ploughing had taken place at Easton Down, too, but seems to have been short lived as a thin calcareous turfline had developed before barrow construction (Whittle *et al.* 1993, 230). Cultivation was also witnessed at Horslip, West Kennet, Silbury Hill and Avebury in the Upper Kennet Valley, and also probably at Wayland's Smithy, leading Whittle *et al.* (1993, 231) to suggest that burial mounds had been preferentially sited in grazed locations near to cultivated land.

Becoming 'Neolithic'

It has been suggested that part of the attraction of 'the Neolithic package' lay in its potential to provide the wherewithal for the feasting that would have taken place as an important part of the hunter-gatherer lifestyle (Robb and Miracle 2007). In addition to the prestige of being able to serve novel meals in exotic dishes, domesticated animals and plants would have been a much more reliable source of food, with the opportunity to increase the supply as necessary. It is also suggested that such a change might have been prompted by the ever-declining carrying capacity of the woodland landscape. This is an interesting and attractive theory, although it remains a moot point whether the new 'Neolithic' items would have been acquired by Mesolithic people who maintained contact with the near Continent, or were brought by incoming farmers. Possessing domesticated plants and animals would have enabled people to have more control over their food supply and, at the same time, enhanced the community focus of their activity. Any of the drawbacks of being tied into an agricultural routine may have been outweighed by the importance of provisioning events such as feasts or other ceremonies and the prestige they may have brought. The social consequences would not have been obvious.

As we have seen, there were a number of features of late Mesolithic and early Neolithic life which were shared: a common experience of a woodland landscape in which the rivers would have been dominant features, a mobile lifestyle with repeated visits to particular locales, the creation of occupation spreads and the accumulation of domestic material in middens which might have formed important visible markers in the landscape. Tree-throw holes continued to be utilised and pits continued to be dug, and the formal deposition of material within them not only continued but increased. It is possible that some other patterns of activity were also inherited from earlier times, including, for example, votive deposition in the Thames (see below; T G Allen 1995; Bradley 1990). On the other hand, the similarity of some of these practices are less convincing when examined in detail, and in particular the evidence of middening and deposition within pits. Other aspects of the archaeological record were undoubtedly new: the construction of houses, the use of pottery and new types of stone and flint tools, and the raising of domesticated animals and cultivation of cereals. Formal treatment of the dead also becomes apparent at this date, although monuments were not built in the earliest Neolithic period in our region (see below, Chapters 12 and 15). These new materials and practices must have made a fundamental difference to people's lives and, as noted above, changed their relationship with the environment in which they lived.

It seems most probable that some incomers were involved in this process, migrant farmers from the near Continent bringing a new way of life with them, and it is tempting to see Yarnton, with its house, evidence of human remains and new technology as the site of a pioneer settlement. It can be imagined that the impact of even a small number of new arrivals with such a radically different lifestyle would have had a profound effect on those living a traditional way of life. Alternatively, or in addition, long-lived or increasing contact with the Continent may have introduced British hunter-gatherers to a Neolithic way of life which may have become increasingly attractive, especially as a way of gaining a more reliable food supply in a fragile ecosystem – whether for feasting or everyday subsistence. Imported elements and new settlers may have arrived at the same time, the desire for the former producing a climate which made the latter possible. If Yarnton represents the settlement of incomers, the Eton Rowing Course with its middens and *in-situ* activity areas where no structures have ever been found, may represent the continuity of a more traditional way of life, but one in which new technologies and subsistence strategies had been adopted.

NEOLITHIC HABITATION: LIVING IN AN ALTERED LANDSCAPE

The early Neolithic settlement of the Thames Valley

It is has already been noted that many 4th millennium cal BC sites in the Thames Valley lie close to the river and that there are some distinct clusters of activity, such as those around Abingdon and in the Upper Kennet Valley (Fig. 11.1; Holgate 1988a, 244). It is also evident that people were utilising upland areas, particularly the Cotswolds and the North Wiltshire Downs where tree cover may not have been so dense (ibid.; Allen and Gardiner 2009). Numerous and sometimes dense flint scatters which tend to be scraper dominated but sometimes include finer objects such as flint axes and arrowheads are found on the Lower Greensand too (Field and Cotton 1987). The Berkshire Downs and the Chilterns do not seem to have been so heavily used, though early 4th millennium sites are present on both (Schulting 2000; Hey *et al.* 2007: Holgate 1988a, 244). Settlement represented by flints and the heavily-weathered sherds from nine or ten 'Windmill Hill' bowls has been found beneath the bell barrow at Farncombe Down, Berks, for example (Rahtz 1962), but this is a rare example.

One area with a particularly marked concentration of sites, which were not detected in field-walking surveys, is along the Middle Thames around Eton, Cippenham, Bray Weir Bank Stud Farm, Bray Marina, Cannon Hill and the Maidenhead, Windsor and Eton Flood Alleviation Scheme. All of these sites cluster in an area 6 km by 4.5 km near to the river (Fig. 11.16; Allen *et al.* 2004; Barnes and Cleal 1995; Bradley *et al.* 1975-6; Ford 2003; Holgate 1988a, 278). The contrast with the adjacent brickearths to the west of Slough where little has been found in survey (Ford 1987b; Ford and Taylor 2004, 99) highlights this density near to the river. The character of the remains in the Eton area suggests that a variety of activities were taking place. This includes middens, *in-situ* activity areas with hearths, small flint-knapping sites, tree-throw holes and pits (see above), and at Cannon Hill a possible shaft was identified in which a deliberate deposit of hearth debris was found including Carinated Bowl and cup fragments and animal bone (Bradley *et al.* 1975-6). Despite the intensity and diversity of activity, each individual site is quite small, and episodes of habitation appear short lived. People were moving around this landscape and utilising its rich resources according to availability and need. Doubtless there would have been a routine to this movement, as the repeated visits to places like the the Eton Rowing Course midden suggest, but people were not tied to particular sites.

Evidence has emerged in recent years of early Neolithic habitation in the Lower Colne Valley, though the picture is less coherent than that around Eton and the area may have been less intensively

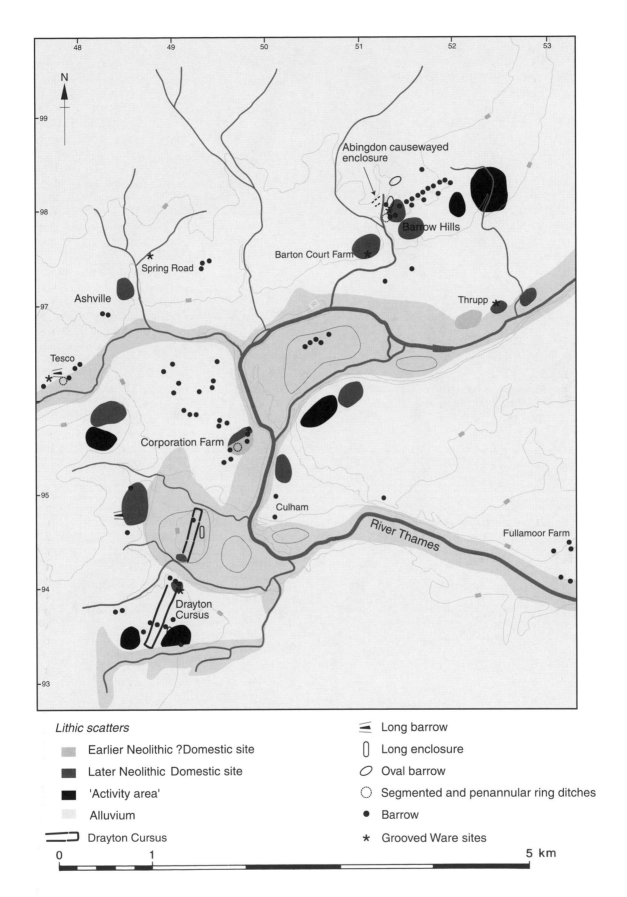

Fig. 11.25   Neolithic and early Bronze Age lithic scatters and monuments in the Abingdon area

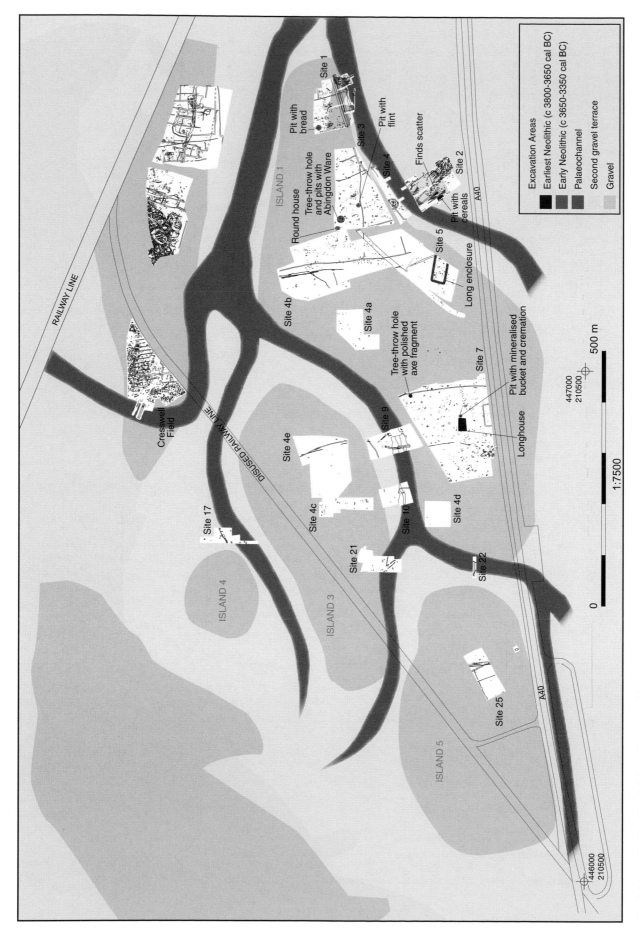

Legend:

Excavation Areas

Earliest Neolithic (c 3800-3650 cal BC)

Early Neolithic (c 3650-3350 cal BC)

Palaeochannel

Second gravel terrace

Gravel

Fig. 11.26 Earlier Neolithic evidence at Yarnton

used. At Runnymede, people created small clearings and were grazing animals in the local woodland. Some worked timbers from a palaeochannel of the Thames yielded early 4th millennium radiocarbon dates (Needham 1991, 26-7, 53-5), but the possible posthole structures were associated with slightly later, middle Neolithic cultural material. A rectangular plank-walled house was constructed at Horton (see above), though the few associated pits appear to be slightly later in date (*c* 3600-3500; A Barclay pers. comm.), and features were also found at Heathrow which predate the middle Neolithic Stanwell bank barrow (Lewis forthcoming).

Less work has been done in the Abingdon area, but the results so far indicate that a similar 'hot spot' of activity may have been present there, around and just upstream of the confluence with the river Ock. This is evidenced mainly by finds scatters (Fig. 11.25; Holgate 1988a, 78-87, figs 6.5-9; records held by Abingdon Area Archaeological Society), but also the results of pollen analysis near to the causewayed enclosure (Parker 1999). The only feature which has been found to predate the enclosure, however, is a deep pit with an antler at its base dated to 4240–3700 cal BC (OxA-1881: 5140±100 BP; Barclay and Bradley 1999, 28–31).

The early 4th-millennium cal BC house at Yarnton in the Upper Thames was situated less than 0.5 km from the river on a gravel island in the floodplain (Fig. 11.26; Hey in prep.). A pit containing a mineralised bucket and a cremation lay adjacent to the house, but very little other contemporary material was found nearby, a situation similar to that at Horton, and perhaps indicating pioneer settlement in both cases (see above; A Barclay pers. comm.). A finds spread was, however, present nearly 500 m away at Yarnton, at the edge of an adjacent floodplain island, and this may have been

a midden which was exposed and later trampled. A small number of early Neolithic pits were also found on these two islands which became the locus for an increasing number of depositional events. The smaller timber buildings and structures at Ascott-under-Wychwood, Sale's Lot and Hazleton North were much more closely associated with middens (Fig. 11.27), even though the precise chronological relationship is not always clear; conjoins between finds in the postholes and in the midden provide convincing evidence of contemporaneity at Hazleton North (Saville 1990a, fig. 20). These sites seem also more obviously associated with earlier activity than is apparent at Yarnton. Too little is known of Neolithic activity around Gorhambury to place the house constructed there (Neal *et al.* 1990) into its contemporary landscape.

Intermittent and repeated occupation of particular places in the landscape, as represented by material found within buried ground surfaces, is evidenced at a number of places in the Upper Kennet Valley. A spread of material found beneath the Avebury G55 bell barrow (Smith 1965b, 32-6), for example, included Neolithic Decorated Bowl and some later pottery, in addition to contemporaneous flintwork and animal bone. Further northeast, on the northern edge of the Marlborough Downs, a buried ground surface which contained early Neolithic Plain Bowl and struck flint was found below the Burderop Down disc barrow (Cleal and Harding in Gingell 1992). Molluscs suggested that the pre-barrow environment of dry grazed grassland was preceded by open but shrubby conditions. It was suggested that clearance originally took place at the time of Neolithic occupation, but that light grazing, probably related to the small scale and short-term nature of the activity, had allowed shrub regrowth (Allen 1992, 147-9) as, perhaps, at Roughridge Down and Hemp Knoll to

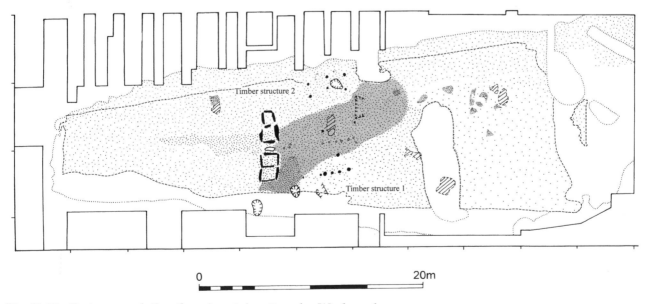

Fig. 11.27   *Features predating the cairn at Ascott-under-Wychwood*

the south of Avebury (ibid.). Small quantities of Peterborough Ware, a pit and finds related to Grooved Ware suggest long-term, if only occasional, use of the Burderop Down site.

Most evidence of early Neolithic settlement in the Thames Valley, however, is represented by pits, such as, for example, the small group found south of and just below the Windmill Hill causewayed enclosure which contained material from domestic activity, including pottery, bone, antler, sarsen and flint (Whittle *et al.* 2000, 141-2). Interestingly, more cereals were recovered in these pits than from later pits containing Grooved Ware, and it was suggested that this new food substance might have been deliberately burnt and then deposited here (Fairbairn in Whittle *et al.* 1999, 139-56).

Very occasionally habitation is represented by tightly-defined clusters of pits, such as the nine pits discovered at South Stoke, South Oxfordshire (Timby *et al.* 2005). These perhaps indicate more intensive but less long-lived use of single sites. The contents of these pits, deposited between 3650-3350 cal BC (on the basis of eight radiocarbon dates; ibid., table 4), allow us to say something of the activities which took place on the site. On-site knapping is indicated by hammerstones, refitting pieces and the very fresh condition of the material, and specific activities are suggested by the restricted range of tools dominated by edge-retouched flakes and serrated flakes, some of which had edge gloss suggesting the working of plant materials, perhaps rushes and reeds, to provide fibres for textiles or for other purposes. Scrapers are under represented in the assemblage and arrowheads absent. The remains of at least ten pottery vessels indicate that some special meals had taken place; they included two relatively large bowls, a smaller decorated bowl and two cups. It is uncertain whether these were deposited straight into the pit following a feasting event or whether they had been placed in a midden first. Cattle and some sheep/goat and pig had been eaten, and also a little wheat and some hazelnuts. A larger number of pits was discovered nearby at Benson (Fig. 11.20; Pine and Ford 2003), consisting of 23 certain and seven less-certain examples and around ten postholes. The pits seemed to belong to at least three or four separate episodes of activity, with four early pits containing Carinated Bowl pottery, three of which were in a group, and two spatially distinct later groups containing Plain Bowl pottery which have been dated to *c* 3640-3370 cal BC. The site at Benson lay very close to the Thames, supporting the picture of more intense early Neolithic activity on the Thames floodplain which was suggested by Ford's earlier fieldwalking surveys (Ford 1987b).

At Horton in the Lower Colne Valley, a cluster of pits was found which dates from slightly later in the early Neolithic than the house (*c* 3650-3500 cal BC). No contemporaneous building was found with these pits, but their arrangement could suggest that they somehow respected a space where a less substantial, perhaps temporary shelter had once

stood. The pits contained a similar range of refuse to the earlier house, with the notable absence of cereal grain (A Barclay pers. comm.).

More commonly, however, pits are recovered as isolated features or in pairs, indicating a single visit. Examples include pits in Oxford at Mansfield College (Booth and Hayden 2000), at Little Wittenham (Allen and Lamdin-Whymark 2006) and at Appleford Sidings, where pottery from Neolithic Plain Bowl vessels was found with thin flakes and blades, a number of which showed evidence of use (Booth and Simmonds 2009). Similar features have been found in the Middle Thames at the Eton Rowing Course (Allen *et al.* 2004) and Cippenham, Slough (Ford 2003). Early Neolithic pits have also come to light in recent years in zones where they had previously been scarce. For example, in north Oxfordshire, near the Cherwell and the causewayed enclosure at Wykeham, Banbury, an early Neolithic pit was found with sherds from at least three finely-made Carinated Bowl vessels which, although broken when deposited, and short of rim and shoulder sherds, appear to have been quite rapidly buried as they were still in good condition (Cuenca 2006). Six pits were also found at Horcott, near Fairford in the upper reaches of the Thames (Brady and Lamdin-Whymark in press).

In conclusion, the settlement evidence suggests that, in the early Neolithic, the Thames Valley was lightly populated by small groups of people, perhaps extended family groups. The investment of effort required to build some of the timber houses in the region might suggest that people lived on these sites for appreciable periods, but the paucity of associated finds and features does not support this view. Indeed, there is remarkably little evidence for occupation of any great duration and, except in rare instances, there is little to indicate that individual settlement events lasted for more than a few months. On the other hand, evidence for the re-use of sites on an episodic basis is common, as the examples from Yarnton, Benson, Windmill Hill and the Eton Rowing Course show (Hey 1997, 106-8; Pine and Ford 2003; Whittle *et al.* 2000; Allen *et al.* 2004). In addition, there are some areas, like the Upper Kennet Valley, the Abingdon area and that around Eton, which seem to have been favoured locations, perhaps suggesting a greater population density. Other parts of the Valley catchment, for example the Thames Valley upstream of Abingdon and the Cotswolds, may have been more lightly populated, and it cannot be assumed that, even if the material culture is similar in these areas, the lifestyle was the same (Whittle, Barclay and McFadyen *et al.* 2007, 330-1).

Middle and late Neolithic settlement of the Thames Valley

The evidence for settlement in the later 4th and early 3rd millennium cal BC is both more extensive but also different in character to that of the early

Neolithic. As already discussed above, the majority of Neolithic houses belong to the earliest phases of Neolithic settlement, and most of these to the first 300 years of habitation. A small possible structure associated with Peterborough Ware pottery and a 4th-millennium archaeomagnetic date was found at Field Farm, Burghfield in the Lower Kennet Valley (Fig. 11.15; Butterworth and Lobb 1992, 11-3). Possible post-built structures of middle Neolithic date also survived at Runnymede in the Lower Colne Valley (Fig. 11.14; Needham 2000a), and a subrectangular Grooved Ware house came to light at Yarnton in the Upper Thames (Fig. 11.28; Hey in prep.). Otherwise, there are no known buildings belonging to the one thousand years or so of middle and late Neolithic occupation in the Thames Valley.

Middens are also largely a feature of early Neolithic settlement. As with houses, however, there are exceptions, with accumulations of material at places like Waden Hill in the Upper Kennet Valley (Smith 1965a, 210-6) and at Runnymede in the Middle Thames (Needham and Spence 1996). Finds spreads of this period were also found at Yarnton (Hey in prep.). The Eton Rowing Course middens were augmented at this time (Allen *et al.* 2004), although the main period of midden creation there belongs to the first half of the 4th millennium. These sites are discussed further below. Deposits in tree-throw holes seem also to become less common after the middle of the millennium across the valley (Lamdin-Whymark 2008). In the middle and late Neolithic the majority of the evidence for habitation is derived from artefact scatters and pits (Fig. 11.29).

Whereas the range of features appears to diminish, the evidence from pits suggests increased activity during the 4th millennium; there are many more pits with Peterborough Ware than with early Neolithic pottery, and they are spread over a much wider area. Indeed, many areas of the Thames Valley seem to have been cleared and inhabited for the first time in the middle Neolithic (see Chapter 9). The river undoubtedly continued to be a focus of activity, as is shown not only by the distribution of sites but also the increasing movement of imported stone axes – polished stone axes from Cornwall and the Lake District, jadeite axes from the Continent – as well as Portland chert, along Thames (see Chapter 16; Clough and Cummins 1979; Field and Cotton 1987, 83-5), but sites are also found in a wider range of topographies than in the preceding period.

Expansion of settlement in the middle Neolithic is very evident at a number of places where habitation seems previously to have been slight. In the upper reaches of the Thames, near Cirencester, for example, the earliest features found on the large areas examined near Shorncote were 13 pits containing Peterborough Ware (Powell *et al.* 2010), and 11 pits of this date were excavated at Horcott Pit near Fairford. These features consisted of one group of three pits, three pairs of pits and two isolated features, plus five other possibly contemporary pits and two tree-throw holes sitting on a spur of elevated ground overlooking the valley floor (Brady and Lamdin-Whymark in press). Deliberate deposition within these pits, and the complementary assemblages of finds recovered from the pairs and group, have been discussed above. The small number of pottery vessels (around one to six in each pit), and the low minimum number of individual animals present in these pits, suggest that these deposits derive from small parent accumulations perhaps resulting from short periods of occupation (ibid.).

The finds spreads on the edge of the floodplain island at Yarnton were created from the early Neolithic into the early Bronze Age, but most material was associated with middle Neolithic Peterborough Ware and this may be related to the increasingly frequent or intensive use of this area at the time (see above; Hey in prep.). More than 25 pits containing Peterborough Ware pottery have been excavated (ibid.), and these were spread extensively over the two gravel islands where early Neolithic activity had been focused but also on the edge of the adjacent gravel terrace. These features are mainly found individually, in pairs or in small groups, sometimes with postholes (Fig. 11.21) indicating separate episodes of habitation, but they are also absent from some parts of the floodplain, giving an impression of the extent of surviving woodland. Occasional pits of this date have also come to light further west in Cassington as a result of gravel extraction, largely in the early and mid 20th century (Leeds 1940; Case 1982b). The features in this area may represent part of the same spread of repeated occupation events along the broad terraces and floodplain north of the Thames. Good grazing land

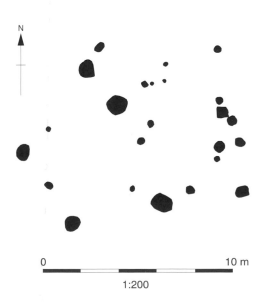

0   10 m

1:200

Fig. 11.28 The late Neolithic house at Yarnton

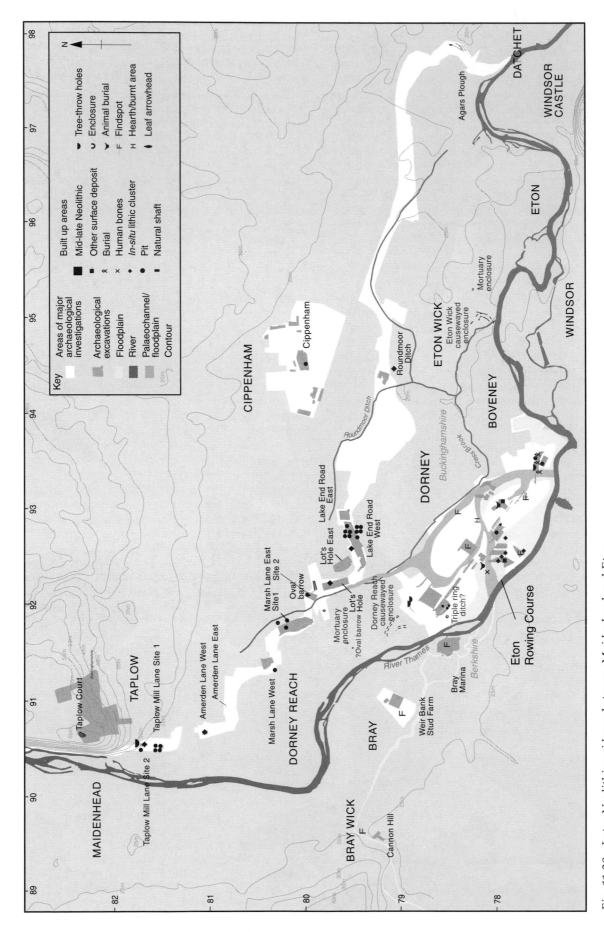

Fig. 11.29 Later Neolithic evidence between Maidenhead and Eton

would have been provided by the soils on these relatively-easily cleared locations.

Considerably more activity also seems to be represented in the Lower Colne Valley than is the case for earlier periods, with over 80 pits found associated with Mortlake Ware at Imperial College Sports Ground and in adjacent development areas, near to small early and late Neolithic funerary monuments (Barclay *et al.* 2009). Smaller numbers of pits associated with Peterborough Ware were found during recent development work at Heathrow Terminal 5 (Lewis forthcoming) and at Ashford Prison Hospital (Cowie 2008), but not all discoveries have been recent. The two pits found during wartime work at Heathrow (Grimes 1960, 186-97), with their interesting and important deposits of Mortlake Ware, have been discussed above.

The site at Runnymede appears to be of a different character. Possible post-built structures were associated with hearths and dense deposits of middle Neolithic material (Figs 11.14 and 11.18; Needham and Spence 1996; Needham 2000a), and wooden piles and areas of horizontal brushwood and timber found in the adjacent palaeochannels seem to have been broadly contemporaneous (Needham 1991). Feasting appears to have been taking place at this Thames-side site, primarily on beef, but also pork and lamb (Serjeantson 2006). Although, at first sight, the evidence for feasting might appear unusual for a middle Neolithic context in the Thames Valley, finds recovered from pits elsewhere in the valley have also, in a number of instances, been interpreted as the remains of special events such as feasts (see above). It is uncertain whether Runnymede was a site where the remains of feasting were left *in situ,* and feasting was thus more visible than is the case elsewhere, or whether the deep burial environment of the site, beneath alluvium, led to the preservation of a ground surface that would normally have been ploughed away.

Although activity in the Eton area is less visible in the middle Neolithic than it was in earlier periods, a number of pit groups have been found recently, and it may be that the location and character of habitation had changed rather than that there had been a decline in settlement activity (T Allen pers. comm.). Work on the Maidenhead, Windsor and Eton Flood Alleviation Scheme, for example, uncovered ten pits of this date at Lake End Road West (Allen *et al.* 2004), and other pits were exposed at Cippenham, Slough (Ford and Taylor 2004). In addition, material was added to the the Eton Rowing Course middens through the middle and late Neolithic, as is evidenced by a little pottery and transverse arrowheads; a few barbed and tanged arrowheads were also present (Allen *et al.* 2004), and human remains of this period have been discovered (Allen 2000).

Pits containing Peterborough Ware have also been found in small numbers throughout much of the Thames Valley, and their distribution is widespread if not as dense as in the areas just mentioned (Holgate 1988a, maps 16 and 17). Examples include earlier 20th-century discoveries at Wisley, Surrey, Enborne in the Kennet Valley, and at Eynsham and Asthall in the Upper Thames (ibid., 266-76), as well as those coming from more recent work, such as the pits found in the Wallingford area (Network Archaeology 2005; Richmond 2005), and at least two of the pits at Mount Farm, Berinsfield which were associated with sherds of Peterborough Ware and a range of worked flint (Lambrick 2010).

In the Upper Thames Valley at least, few middle Neolithic pits have been found associated with the ceremonial monuments and monument complexes which began to develop in this period (Bradley and Holgate 1984). A number of Upper Thames monument groups were damaged by gravel extraction or housing development in the early and mid 20th century and, understandably, rescue work was focused on the monuments themselves. Only four Peterborough Ware pits were recorded in the Stanton Harcourt area, for example, and just four pits of this date were associated with the Drayton North and South cursus monuments. No pits of this date were reported at Dorchester-on-Thames, even though middle Neolithic activity is known in all areas and Grooved Ware pits are present in greater numbers (Barclay 1995b; Barclay *et al.* 2003; Whittle *et al.* 1992). Barrow Hills, Radley, next to the Abingdon causewayed enclosure, was, however, excavated more recently and stripped in order to examine the spaces between the monuments. Even though Grooved Ware and Beaker pits were found, only two pits with Peterborough Ware were identified (Barclay and Halpin 1999). A further pit of this date was excavated at the nearby Barton Court Farm site (Miles 1986). The paucity of pits in these locations may indicate that settlement was deliberately sited away from monuments in this period or, perhaps more likely, that habitation near monuments did not involve the kinds of activities that resulted in the deposition of material within pits.

Although there is not the same evidence for expansion in the Cotswolds as is found elsewhere in the Valley, there is evidence of activity in this period, including, for example, the three bowl-shaped pits found in a gravel pit near Bourton-on-the-Water (Dunning 1932). Two of these pits contained Peterborough Ware and the third, a complete shed deer's antler, parts of another and part of the skull of a young woman. The Berkshire Downs and Chilterns continued to be little used, although the burial monuments constructed in both areas continued to be visited and enhanced, as is shown by the construction of the later parts of Wayland's Smithy chambered tomb and the heightening of the barrow mound at Whiteleaf (Whittle, Bayliss and Wysocki 2007; Hey *et al.* 2007; see below). There is much less evidence for the use of Cotswold tombs at this time, and most Peterborough Ware seems to be associated with tomb blocking (Darvill 2004, 183-5).

In the Upper Kennet Valley much of the evidence for late Neolithic settlement comprises flint scatters, small groups of pits and occasional post- and stake-holes, suggesting seasonal transhumance and short-term occupation of particular locations (Pollard and Reynolds 2002, 122-4). Continuing use of early Neolithic sites in the Upper Kennet landscape is evidenced by the presence of Peterborough Ware in addition to earlier material beneath the Avebury G55 bell barrow (Smith 1965b, 32-6). Some sites suggest quite intensive occupation activity, especially on the slopes around the valley floor, as, for example, on the eastern flank of Waden Hill where a midden and related pits and postholes belonging to a late Neolithic settlement contained over 600 sherds of Peterborough Ware and Grooved Ware which still survived on the ground surface when excavated by Keiller in the 1930s (Smith 1965a, 210-6). A wide variety of flint tools was present, suggesting that a range of domestic activities were undertaken, and some imported stone from sources as far-flung as Wales, Cornwall and the Continent demonstrate extensive exchange networks (Pollard and Reynolds 2002, 124). The presence of daub could indicate the existence of buildings and a few pits and postholes were found. One pit contained a cattle skull, antler, other cattle and pig bone, sherds from three Grooved Ware vessels, an arrowhead and other flint tools and several pieces of sarsen (ibid.; Smith 1965a, 210-16). The West Kennet Avenue later incorporated the site, and a gap in the west stone alignment corresponded to the thickest part of the midden (ibid. fig. 37). A dense and extensive flint scatter was also recovered from the south slopes of Windmill Hill, including over 500 transverse arrowheads (Holgate 1988a, 242). Two pits and a shallow scoop excavated during test pitting yielded animal bone, Grooved Ware pottery and worked flint from ashy soil (Whittle *et al.* 2000, 143-4). In contrast to the ceremonial sites in the area (see Chapter 12), cattle was the main animal represented, alongside some pig, sheep/goat and wild pig and aurochs. The plant foods were mainly wild (hazelnuts and aquatic plants) with only occasional cereals. There was continuing episodic use of the causewayed enclosure site itself (Whittle *et al.* forthcoming), though there is little to suggest that this was special and is anything other than part of the general use of the landscape at this time (Whittle *et al.* 1999, 371-80). A settlement site might also be represented by spreads of Fengate and Grooved Ware pottery under barrows on Overton Hill (Pollard and Reynolds 2002, 123). A flint scatter on Hackpen Hill, which included large numbers of polished discoidal and plano-convex flint knives could be the product of flint extraction on this site (Thomas 1999, 211).

In the Upper Thames Valley, the general expansion of habitation described above for the middle Neolithic intensified in the first half of the 3rd millennium cal BC. Grooved Ware pits have been found over a large area, albeit mostly on the low-lying gravel terraces next to the Thames (Barclay 1999b, illus. 2.1). Artefact scatters from this period, such as those around Abingdon, are also more dense and extensive (Fig. 11.25; Hingley 1980; Holgate 1988a, figs 6.9 and 6.11), and environmental evidence from a number of sites shows that more tree clearance took place, with more areas maintained as open grassland than in earlier periods (see Chapter 9). Such areas include those around some of the major monuments like the Devil's Quoits at Stanton Harcourt, Daisy Banks Fen next to Barrow Hills, Radley, and the Drayton Cursus, but also areas without a major monument focus like Shorncote at the headwaters of the Thames.

There are some important Grooved Ware pit groups (Barclay 1999b). Extensive spreads of pits are present at Yarnton, for example, where over 50 examples date to this period, demonstrating the longevity of use of this area (Hey in prep.). The pits are found in association with small monuments (see below, Chapter 12), as small isolated groups and, occasionally, as individual features. Although these features are found on the same gravel islands as the pits from earlier periods, their discrete groupings and the fact that they tend to occupy zones separate from those in which Peterborough Ware pits occur, may show separate episodes of woodland clearance (Fig. 11.30). As has already been discussed, many of these pits contain mundane domestic material, but the presence of more special items such as a bead of canal coal and spiral-decorated pots, and the occasionally careful positioning of artefacts, demonstrates that important events were being commemorated by these deposits (Hey *et al.* 2003; Barclay in Hey in prep.). Seven pits were found at Cassington Mill, less than a kilometre to the west, three of which formed a group (Case 1982b, 121-9). They contained Grooved Ware, struck flints, two polished stone axes (one Group VIII and one porphyritic augite andesite) and a bone awl, though only one contained a large deposit of material. Case suggested that, rather than representing simple rubbish disposal, the fills of these pits may have been concerned with taboos or beliefs connected with settlement rubbish or remains of personal possessions (ibid., 124).

Pit digging seems to have become more frequent around monuments too (Barclay 1999b, 15). A large number of late Neolithic pits were excavated at Barrow Hills, Radley, including an area 40 m x 17 m of intercutting pits (Barclay and Halpin 1999, 64-97), as well as five nearby at Barton Court Farm (Miles 1986) and another at Thrupp (Holgate 1988a, 260). At Drayton, 18 late Neolithic pits were found, mostly focused around the east ditch of the south cursus (Barclay *et al.* 2003, 20, fig. 3.2), and more late Neolithic pits were found in the Stanton Harcourt area (Barclay 1995b). There was relatively little activity in the latter area until the henge was built in the late Neolithic period, however, and most pits were associated with Beaker pottery (see below, Chapter 13).

Grooved Ware pits are also found more extensively in the Upper Thames catchment, and are not necessarily associated with either monuments or areas of earlier habitation. They are found at the upper reaches of the Thames, for example at Roughground Farm and the Loders near Lechlade (Jones 1976), near Banbury (Cuenca 2006), on the Corallian Ridge at Tubney (Bradley and Hey 1993), and further down the Upper Thames at Mount Farm, Berinsfield (Lambrick 2010). Pits have also been found slightly further downstream in the Lower Kennet Valley, with several groups at Reading Business Park (Moore and Jennings 1992; Brossler *et al.* 2004), and on the Berkshire Downs (Howell and Durden 1996; Miles *et al.* 2003, 143). On the Marlborough Downs, a shallow pit containing a large amount of struck flint including scrapers, a fabricator and a petit tranchet arrowhead, a flake

from a stone axe, sarsen, a bone point, animal bone and sherds from probably one Grooved Ware pot was found near the Burderop Down disc barrow (Gingell 1992, 41). Further Grooved Ware lay nearby. The environment seems to have been characterised by long grass with occasional bushes (Allen 1992, 148).

In contrast, it has been suggested that there was a decline in activity in the late Neolithic period in the Middle Thames, where relatively few pits and finds spreads associated with Grooved Ware have been found (Field and Cotton 1987, 89). In recent years, however, archaeological work in advance of development has begun to change this picture. Occasional pits were found at Eton Rowing Course (Allen *et al.* 2004, 92), including, for example, a pit with Grooved Ware, burnt stone, animal bone and a worked and polished bone awl (T G Allen 2005),

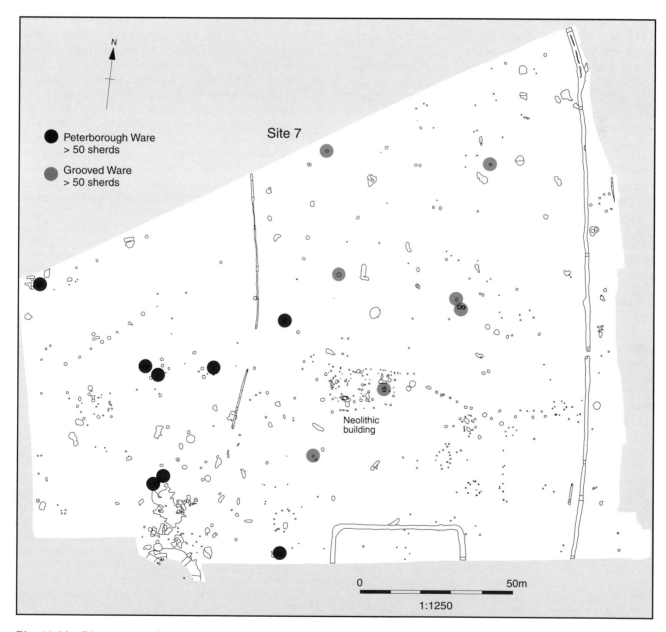

Fig. 11.30 Pits associated with Peterborough Ware and Grooved Ware at Yarnton

and some deposits were made on the earlier middens. In addition, pollen and plant macrofossils show a gradual opening up of the landscape through the later Neolithic and the early Bronze Age (Allen *et al.* 2004, 97-8), and activity in the palaeochannels and burning on the banks have provided radiocarbon dates which span the 3rd millennium cal BC.

In the Lower Colne Valley at Lower Mill Farm, Stanwell, a group of late Neolithic cooking pits and hearths was uncovered (Cotton 2004, 25; Jones and Ayres 2004). One pit contained a bone scoop made of aurochs bone and many sherds from a tub-shaped Grooved Ware vessel profusely decorated with grooves defined, in places, by panels, as well as flint and other animal bone (Jones and Ayres 2004). A scatter of Grooved Ware was found on the Holloway Lane site, Harmondsworth, including one concentration with a minimum of 15 vessels and a number of scrapers (Cotton *et al.* 1986, 36; Cotton *et al.* 2006), and at Staines Road Farm, Shepperton (Jones 2008).

Further south in Surrey, three circular pits which contained sherds from around 20 different vessels as well as struck flints including many scrapers were found at Franks' Pit, Betchworth. Several sherds had charred residues and four were radio-carbon dated to the early and mid 3rd millennium cal BC (Williams 2004). In addition, late Neolithic/ early Bronze Age find scatters have recently been recovered from a wide range of geologies in Surrey on Chalk and Weald clay (Cotton 2004, 25).

Later Neolithic land use and the social landscape

In conclusion, Neolithic sites suggest short-term settlement by a small, mobile population, perhaps staying for months rather than years; there are no known sites which were occupied for long periods of time. The only possible evidence for relatively sedentary occupation may be provided by the long-term clearance of the landscape at Abingdon (Parker 1999), but even in this area the evidence for permanent rather than repeated occupation is thin. Undoubtedly, cereal cultivation would have tied at least some family members to one place for a few months of the year, but this could have been a relatively short period of only four or five months.

We have seen that there seems to have been a general expansion of settlement activity in the Upper and Middle Thames in the middle Neolithic which continued, at least in the Upper Thames and Upper Kennet Valleys, in the early 3rd millennium cal BC. However, we need to be a little cautious before interpreting this as entirely the result of an increase in population. A number of other changes occurred at this time which may suggest that, rather than becoming more settled, people were pursuing a more mobile lifestyle which might, in itself, have resulted in more extensive woodland clearance and a more widespread site distribution.

One of these changes was the apparent reduction in the range of settlement features found, suggesting less long-lived occupation, but other evidence comes from slight changes in the economy and land-use patterns of later Neolithic farmers.

The range of cereal crops grown in the Thames Valley in the later Neolithic seems to be the same as it was in the earlier part of the Neolithic. Very little chaff is represented. Although there are finds of glumes of *Triticum dicoccum* (emmer wheat) from Yarnton, in the Upper Thames Valley (Robinson in prep.), it is even rarer than grain. It is likely that flax, which has been identified from impressions in pot sherds elsewhere in England (Helbaek 1952), was also grown in the Thames Valley but its seeds rarely become charred and enter the archaeological record, although burnt seeds have recently been recognised and dated to the early Neolithic at Lismore Fields, Derbyshire (Garton 1987; 1991). As well as being grown for its fibrous stems, the high oil content of its seeds makes them very nutritious. Gathered wild food plants tend to represent an even higher proportion of assemblages of charred plant remains in the later than in the earlier Neolithic (Moffet *et al.* 1989; Robinson 2000c). Indeed, the evidence from Yarnton suggests that not only did the proportion of wild foods to cereals increase from the early Neolithic to the middle and late periods, but that absolute numbers of cereals fell too, with around 80% of all Neolithic cereals coming from early contexts, even though middle and late Neolithic features were more numerous (Robinson in prep.). The proportions changed from *c* 37% cereals and 63% wild foods in the early Neolithic to between 1-2% cereals later, rising to around 7% in the Beaker period. A similar pattern emerged at the Eton Rowing Course, suggesting that cereal production might have reduced at this time (Robinson in T G Allen *et al.* forthcoming.). Traces of ploughing have been found beneath early or middle Neolithic monuments, but there is little or no comparable evidence of later Neolithic cultivation.

Some of the largest later Neolithic assemblages of wild food remains have been from pits. The composition of assemblages from three groups of pits in the Upper Thames Valley which between them span that period are summarised in Table 11.1. The Drayton Highways Depot pit and those at Barton Court Farm were on the Summertown-Radley Gravel Terrace and contained middle Neolithic Fengate Ware pottery and late Neolithic Grooved Ware respectively (Barclay *et al.* 2003, 23-31; Miles 1986). The Barton Court Farm pits gave radiocarbon dates of 2900-2300 cal BC (HAR 2387: 4030±70 BP) and 2580-2190 cal BC (HAR 2388: 3910±70 BP); the charred remains were identified by Martin Jones (ibid., microfiche 9: A2-B3, F2-4). The Drayton North Cursus pits were on the floodplain and contained sherds of Beaker pottery (Barclay *et al.* 2003, 86-9, 168-9).

Table 11.1 Summary of charred plant remains from pits at the Drayton Highways Depot, Barton Court Farm and the Drayton North cursus

| | | Number of items | | |
		Drayton Highways Depot (mid Neolithic)	Barton Court Farm (late Neolithic)	Drayton North Cursus (Beaker)
Triticum dicoccum - glume	emmer wheat	-	1	-
T. cf *dicoccum* - grain	emmer wheat	-	2	-
Triticum sp. - free threshing grain	rivet or bread type wheat	2	3	1
Triticum sp. - grain	wheat	2	9	-
Hordeum sp. - hulled grain	hulled barley	1	-	-
Hordeum sp. - grain	barley	1	3	1
Indeterminate cereal grain		11	4	1
Total cereal grain		17	22	3
Malus sp. - seeds	apple	-	23	-
Corylus avellana - nut shell frags	hazel	317	84	111

Similar evidence has been recovered from the Middle Thames Valley. For example, charred hazelnut shell fragments were recovered from a late Neolithic pit on the Maidenhead, Windsor and Eton Flood Alleviation Scheme. More generally, it has been observed that pits containing Grooved Ware in the West London area also contained wild autumnal fruits (Lewis *et al.* 2006, 87).

Detailed studies have been made of charcoal from Grooved Ware and also Beaker Pits in the Upper Thames Valley at Barrow Hills (Thompson 1999), Drayton (Barclay *et al.* 2003, 168-9) and Gravelly Guy, Stanton Harcourt (Gale 2004). All showed a diverse range of taxa being used for fuel, with an average of four taxa per pit at both Barrow Hills and Drayton. *Quercus* sp. (oak) and *Corylus avellana* (hazel) dominated the assemblages at Barrow Hills, but thorn-scrub species were also present. In contrast, most of the charcoal from Drayton was from Pomoideae (hawthorn etc) and *Prunus* cf *spinosa* (sloe), particularly from relatively small-diameter branches, but oak and hazel charcoal was also present. It is likely in the case of Drayton that most fuel was obtained from woodland edge or thorn-scrub habitats.

When Wilson undertook his useful review of later Neolithic and Beaker bone assemblages in the Upper Thames in the 1980s (Wilson in Robinson and Wilson 1987, 35), many later Neolithic bone assemblages were from ceremonial monuments or pits on sites with monuments, and some of the bones were undoubtedly related to ritual activity. One particularly clear example of this was the initial deposit in a late Neolithic ring ditch at Barrow Hills, where the floor of the ditch was scattered with eight naturally-shed red deer antlers. There were also two diametrically opposed cattle limbs within the ditch (Levitan and Serjeantson 1999, 239). At Barton Court Farm, Mount Farm, Berinsfield, and Dorchester-on-Thames, 35-66% of later Neolithic animal bones were of domesticated pig, with 19-35% of cattle,

10-19% sheep and much smaller numbers of wild animals (Robinson and Wilson 1987, 35). Particularly high proportions of pig were also found in pits containing Grooved Ware at Barrow Hills which were analysed after Wilson's survey, where pig bones comprised around 60% of the total (Levitan and Serjeantson 1999, 238-9). Since that time, however, a number of other important sites which provide much larger assemblages have been published or excavated. Of these the most notable are the feasting deposits at Runnymede and 'domestic' assemblages at Yarnton which suggest that cattle were the main species raised, in terms of numbers of fragments but particularly in weight of meat produced (Serjeantson 2003; 2006; Mulville in prep.). Although pigs seem to have increased in importance elsewhere in southern England in the late Neolithic period (cattle being the dominant animals in the early and middle Neolithic; Pollard 2006; Serjeantson 2006), at Yarnton, even in late Neolithic contexts, pigs only form 26% of the animal bone assemblage (Mulville in prep.).

It has been argued that the rise in carbonised hazelnut shell fragments in relation to cereal remains which is seen throughout much of Neolithic Britain is possibly a taphonomic feature (Jones 2000) but, as already discussed, there is certainly no evidence for an increase in the scale of arable activity. This observation has been linked to woodland regeneration on abandoned agricultural land (Grigson 1982). It could, however, also be seen as resulting from more intensive exploitation of woodland. As the Neolithic progressed, an ever-greater swathe of the valley would have experienced at least one cycle of clearance and regeneration. The increase of secondary woodland was not the result of wholesale abandonment of cleared land but was a feature of the Neolithic system of subsistence. The gradual increase in the ratio of sheep/goat bones to cattle bones through the Neolithic also supports this proposition. Robinson and Wilson (1987, 35) noted that the percentages of sheep/goat in relation to the total number of sheep/goat and cattle bones rises in their sample from the earlier Neolithic (14%) to the later Neolithic (34%), and increases further still in the Beaker period (46%). As sheep favour grassland and not woodland, the results suggest a slow increase in grassland, not an overall regeneration of woodland. The decline of aurochs and the rise in proportion of red deer at the end of the Neolithic was perhaps also a reflection of greater pressure on woodland resources.

The analysis of lipids which have been absorbed into the walls of pots, provides an additional strand of evidence for eating habits through the Neolithic. The method has provided us with the first clear evidence for the consumption of dairy products (see above). During the course of the middle to late Neolithic period, however, the numbers of sherds containing lipids from dairy products seems to fall, whereas lipids from cooking meat, and especially pig, seems to increase (Copley *et al.* 2007). This may suggest a greater reliance on meat production, and, as people moved with their herds, they would have covered more ground and cleared more of the landscape.

By the end of the Neolithic, a range of cereals had been grown and domestic animals raised for around 1500 years, yet the area under cultivation was very small, much of the landscape remained wooded,

even where the soils were fertile, and there was still a major reliance on woodland resources. Open areas seem to have been organised as much around ceremonial activities as for agriculture. Certainly the Thames Valley was not being exploited to its full agricultural potential given the available technology and domesticates. Agriculture can support much higher population levels than a hunter-gatherer way of life, but primitive agriculture is hard work and has a narrow resource base, which makes those dependent on it vulnerable to severe episodes of famine if adverse weather causes crop failure. Continued use of wild foods would have provided a broader resource base. However, there would have been a host of other reasons for people to continue to live in and rely upon woodland, reasons which were social and religious in nature and not linked to economic choices. Indeed, it is highly unlikely that Neolithic communities would have distinguished between these aspects of their existence. Additionally, they may not have perceived their lifestyle as being significantly changed, the herding of domestic animals under partly-wooded conditions taking over a significance formerly given to hunting, and perhaps a continued importance being given to an autumn 'rutting' ceremony. In this fluid landscape, permanence would have been represented by funerary and ceremonial monuments.

Chapter 12 – Inscribing the landscape:
Neolithic funerary and ceremonial monuments

by Gill Hey and Alistair Barclay

CONSTRUCTING MONUMENTS AND BURYING THE DEAD

The construction of permanent monuments began in the early Neolithic period. Mesolithic populations would undoubtedly have recognised many significant places in the landscape, both natural and created by themselves – clearings in the woodland, sites of earlier occupation events and gatherings or accumulations of feasting debris – and these may even have been marked in some way, perhaps by posts, as has been suggested was the case for the postholes at Stonehenge and elsewhere (Cleal et al. 1995, 43-56; Allen and Gardiner 2002). Through time the evidence of activity at these places would have faded from view, and we can no longer observe them except as occasional artefact scatters in the ploughsoil or on buried ground surfaces. From early in the 4th millennium cal BC, however, people built structures which were intended to be seen and to endure: monuments of stone or with wooden posts bedded into the ground, which can be examined by excavation, and are sometimes still visible above ground today. These were followed by cairns, mounds of earth and earthwork enclosures of varied forms. The desire to mark indelibly the landscape represents a significant change in the way in which people interacted with the world around them (Bradley 1993; 1998). At the same time, people began to treat at least some of their dead in a different way, and in a way that allows us to recover human remains today (see Chapter 15). This stands in contrast to the almost complete absence of Mesolithic human bone from the whole of the Upper and Middle Thames catchment (see above, Chapter 10).

Monuments may not, however, have been constructed at the very beginning of the Neolithic (Whittle, Barclay, Bayliss et al. 2007). The earliest dated monuments, such as the Cotswold-Severn tombs of Ascott-under-Wychwood and Hazleton North (dating to the 38th century and early 37th century cal BC respectively; Bayliss, Bronk Ramsey, van der Plicht and Whittle 2007), overlay phases of Neolithic activity represented by small wooden structures and middens (Benson and Whittle 2007; Saville 1990a; see above, Chapter 11). Nor were ideas of monumentality adopted simultaneously across our area. The Cotswolds has a large number of early sites (Fig. 12.1), with simple stone monuments like the Whispering Knights portal dolmen at Rollright, in addition to the cairns such as Ascott-under-Wychwood and Burn Ground. However, like a number of other monument groups (for example the Medway Megaliths in Kent), the Cotswold tombs appear to represent a precocious phase of monument building that was restricted to only a few areas of Britain at this time (Whittle 2003, 118). Similar monuments may have been constructed in the Avebury area and on the Berkshire Downs at a slightly later date, during the 37th century cal BC (Whittle, Barclay, Bayliss et al. 2007), and current evidence suggests that monument building began on the Thames gravels later in that century.

There are a large number of these monuments along the north and west of the Thames catchment, mainly on the Cotswolds and around Avebury, with a few on the Berkshire Downs (Fig. 12.2), although, as discussed by Whittle, Barclay, Bayliss et al. (2007, 136-8), if people were only buried within them for a few generations, the number in use at any one time may not have been very great. Indeed, as is discussed in Chapter 15, the overall number of burials suggests that only part of the population would have been placed within them. Nevertheless, the impression they give of a greater intensity of early Neolithic activity in these areas is reinforced by the relative density of early flint recovered (Holgate 1988a), and the higher proportion of earliest Neolithic Carinated Bowl pottery which has been found when compared to other parts of the Thames Valley (Barclay 1997; 2007).

At a slightly later date, notable clusters of monuments began to be built on the gravels too, around Abingdon and Dorchester-on-Thames, for example, mainly along the river corridor and its tributaries. Large tracts of the landscape are, however, devoid of such structures or contain only isolated examples (Barclay 2007). Relatively few mortuary structures are known in the Middle Thames, where only a few isolated examples have been found at Imperial Sports Ground, Harlington, for example, and around Eton and Sonning (Crockett 2001; Lamdin-Whymark 2008; Ford 1987b). Monuments appear to be almost absent from the south side of the river Thames in this area despite the presence of evidence for other types of activity (Holgate 1988a; R Poulton pers. comm.).

Monuments in the river valleys appear to be of different kinds to those on higher ground. Whereas portal dolmens and long cairns are found mainly in the Cotswolds, and long barrows on the Chalk, mortuary enclosures and cursus monuments occur almost exclusively on the gravels, along with a whole range of small oval and circular monuments. The sheer variety of funerary structures of this date is very striking. Other monuments such as causewayed enclosures and round barrows are more widespread.

The position of long barrows and cairns in the landscape can be revealing. Very often they overlook tributary rivers and streams and, at least sometimes, areas of settlement. Helen O'Neil has noted, for example, that the horned entrance to the Sale's Lot cairn, situated on the steepest part of the slope, would have looked very impressive as it was approached uphill (O'Neil 1966, 7). Nevertheless, most of these monuments seem to have been sited within woodland clearings – Whiteleaf is a good example (Childe and Smith 1954; Hey *et al.* 2007) – and extensive views to and from them may not have been important. The presence of earlier activity on these sites, on the other hand, seems to have been a significant factor in their selection. A number of clearings used for early burial monuments seem to have been long-standing. Ascott-under-Wychwood and Hazleton North barrows were both constructed on sites where there is evidence of use going back into the Mesolithic period, even though these clearings had become overgrown from time to time (Saville 1990a; Benson and Whittle 2007; see above, Chapters 10 and 11). Middens and structures also lay beneath the Ascott-under-Wychwood and Hazleton North mounds, and a wide range of barrow sites – from Hazleton on the Cotswolds to South Street and Horslip in the Upper Kennet and (probably) Wayland's Smithy on the Berkshire

Downs (Ashbee *et al* 1979; Macphail in Saville 1990a, 255; Whittle 1991; see above, Chapter 11) – had seen earlier phases of cultivation. The history of clearance, stability, cultivation and then grassland at South Street suggests long use of a clearing in a landscape which otherwise appears to have been scrub woodland, perhaps with other small clearings but with few signs of cereal cultivation or open grassland (Ashbee *et al.* 1979, 296-7). Pits, stake-holes, flint knapping debris and burning were variously found beneath Horslip, Beckhampton Road and South Street (Ashbee *et al.* 1979). These monuments seem to be referencing the past and important places or events in the history of the community which then chose to bury some of their dead on these sites (Pollard 2005). Pollard describes how such sites may have evolved from being places of routine activity to special places which were then appropriate settings for monument construction (ibid, 105-8; Pollard and Reynolds 2002, 106-8).

THE EARLIEST MONUMENTS

The earliest monuments to be built were structures associated with the burial of human remains, the dominant rite being the inhumation of complete skeletons of people who had died not long before (Whittle, Barclay, Bayliss *et al.* 2007, 129-30). It was

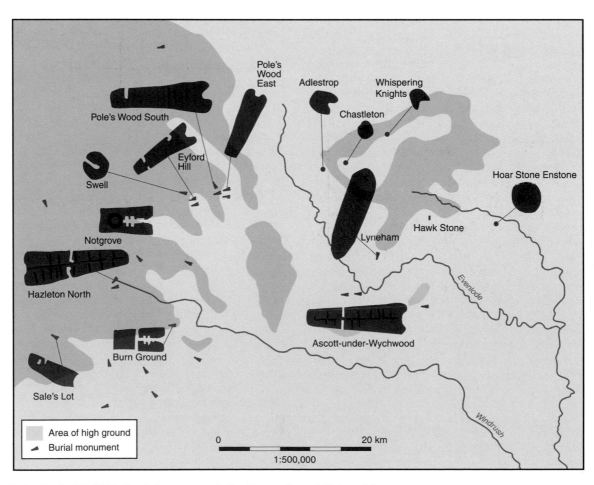

Fig. 12.1   Early Neolithic burial monuments in the north-east Cotswolds

not only the use of structures for burials that was new, however. As we have already seen, apart from one possible individual in the Burn Ground cairn (Smith and Brickley 2006), the only pre-4th millennium human bone so far discovered in the region is a single humerus from the early Mesolithic site of Thatcham. This suggests that in the early Neolithic people began to think about, treat and commemorate their dead in a different way; perhaps there was 'a new awareness of human mortality' (Whittle, Barclay, Bayliss *et al.* 2007, 139; see below, Chapter 15). Individual human bones are sometimes found within early Neolithic midden deposits, including, for example, the skull fragments and teeth at Hazleton North (Saville 1990a, 16 and 197), and there are small cremation deposits of human bone in postholes and pits (for example, in the longhouse at Yarnton; Hey in prep.), but the dead also began to be brought together in formal burial monuments.

The Cotswolds monuments

Sites on the Cotswolds include small simple tombs and dolmens (Fig. 12.1) such as the Whispering Knights at Rollright, and these may represent our earliest monuments, although none is securely dated (Barclay 1997; Darvill 2004, 46-66). By analogy with excavated sites in Wales, such as Dyffryn

Ardudwy (Powell 1973), they ought to be early in the sequence, although it should be noted that recent dating of portal dolmens in western Britain and Ireland suggests that these monuments may have been in active use, if not constructed, throughout the first half of the 4th millennium cal BC (Kytmannow 2008). The exact purpose of these simple monuments is unclear as so few have been excavated, but a link with funerary activity is assumed. Only the Whispering Knights has seen limited excavation in modern times, although this did not extend into the chamber area (Lambrick 1988). Human bone found more recently in a rabbit burrow on the western edge of the monument provided a radiocarbon date of 1630-1370 cal BC at 94% confidence (R 26652: 3202 ± 60 BP), indicating use of the site in the Bronze Age (Hey 2001), as is also seen at monuments further west (Kytmannow 2008). The Whispering Knights has a south-east facing portal consisting of a broad slab bracketed by two taller stones (Fig. 12.3). At the back is a much smaller stone, while a now fallen stone of roughly triangular shape almost certainly formed all or part of the capstone. Like sites in Western Britain and Ireland the capstone would have tilted down from front to back. Surrounding this arrangement of stones was a platform or low cairn, no more than 10 m across, of collected stone, which the excavator

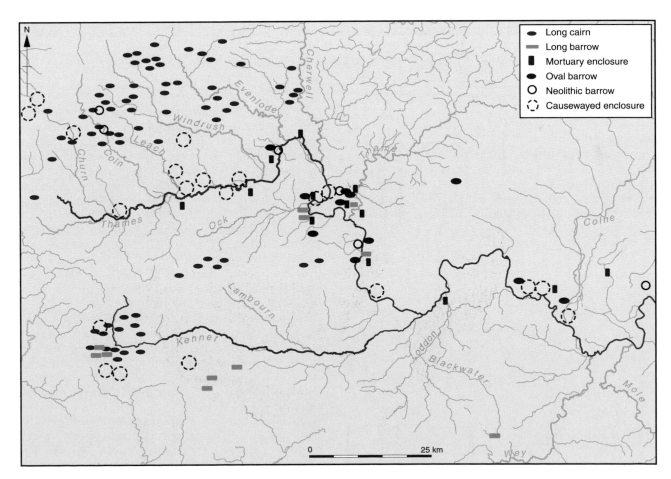

Fig. 12.2   Earlier Neolithic funerary monuments and causewayed enclosures in the Thames Valley

Fig. 12.3 Early Neolithic tombs: left: Enstone; upper right: Adlestrop; bottom right: the Whispering Knights at Rollright

suggests may have been material from a ramp used to raise the capstone (G Lambrick pers. comm.). Two other sites nearby, Enstone and Chastleton, may have been of similar design (Darvill 2004, 49-52), while Adlestrop appears to have been slightly different, with a simple chamber, forecourt and enclosing low oval mound (Fig. 12.3; Donovan 1938; Barclay 1997). A small amount of human bone was

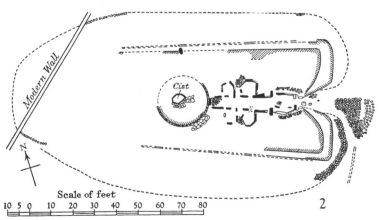

Fig. 12.4 The long barrow and earlier rotunda at Notgrove

recovered from Chastleton during field survey in 1970-71 (Benson and Fasham 1972, 5-6), and at Adlestrop the chamber contained the disarticulated remains of at least eight people: three adults, an adolescent and four children (Cave 1938).

It has been suggested that rotunda graves, small circular stone monuments some of which contain human remains, are also early in date (Darvill 2004, 60-2). The rotunda at Notgrove, within which were found the remains of an adult male, was subsequently incorporated into a classic transepted Cotswold-Severn tomb (Fig. 12.4; Clifford 1936), and a similar structure was found beneath the Sale's Lot barrow (O'Neil 1966). However, neither of these long cairns need be particularly early in the sequence. Recent re-examination and dating of human bone from these sites by Smith and Brickley (2006) suggest that the rotundas were short-lived constructions post-dating *c* 3650 cal BC which were overlain by cairns built one or two centuries either side of 3500 cal BC.

Burial monuments with long cairns of stone or of earth and stone, covering burial chambers, certainly began to be built from around 3800 cal BC. The Ascott-under-Wychwood tomb in the Evenlode Valley in north Oxfordshire is estimated to have been built between 3760-3695 cal BC (95% probability; Bayliss, Bronk Ramsey, Galer *et al.* 2007). Around 21 individuals, in various stages of completeness, with semi-articulated and very incomplete remains present as well a cremated body, were found within the four stone chambers of this burial monument and their side passages (Figs 12.5 and 15.1; Galer 2007). The recent analysis suggests that most of these bodies were probably intact when they were placed within the tomb, and the jumble of bones which confronted the excavators was largely a product of movement and

reworking of bones when new burials were introduced and, perhaps, on other occasions; some bones had been removed (Whittle, Barclay, McFadyen *et al.* 2007, 358), a situation that appears to have been mirrored at Hazleton North (Saville 1990a). It is possible that the stone chambers in which the bones lay predated their incorporation within an earth and stone mound, but more likely that the construction process was continuous and short-lived. The monument was only used for burial for three to five generations before the mound was enlarged and

Fig. 12.5   The long barrow at Ascott-under-Wychwood from the west; the road circles to the south of the monument

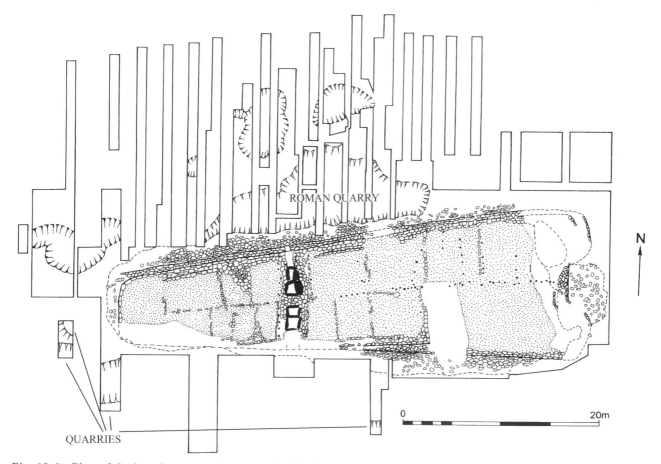

Fig. 12.6   Plan of the long barrow at Ascott-under-Wychwood

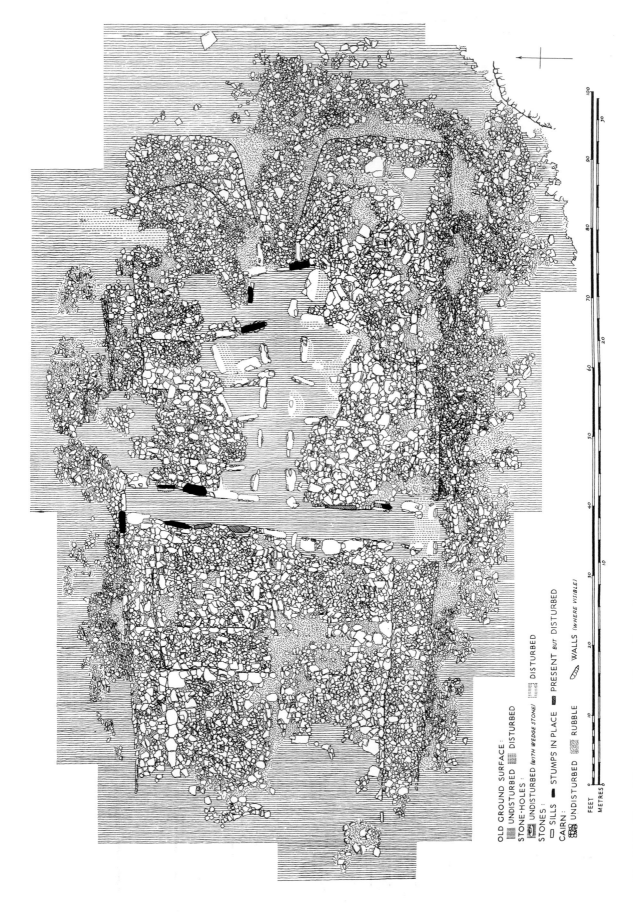

OLD GROUND SURFACE:
▦ UNDISTURBED ▩ DISTURBED
STONE-HOLES:
▒ UNDISTURBED *(WITH WEDGE STONE)* ░ DISTURBED
STONES:
▢ SILLS ▬ STUMPS IN PLACE ▨ PRESENT *BUT* DISTURBED
CAIRN:
▨ UNDISTURBED ░ RUBBLE ◇ WALLS *(WHERE VISIBLE)*

Fig. 12.7   Plan of the long barrow at Burn Ground

OLD GROUND SURFACE:
|||||| UNDISTURBED ||||| DISTURBED
STONE-HOLES:
|||||| UNDISTURBED *(WITH WEDGE STONE)* ||||| DISTURBED
STONES:
⬭ SILLS ▬ STUMPS IN PLACE ▨ PRESENT *BUT* DISTURBED
CAIRN:
▨ UNDISTURBED ▨ RUBBLE ▨ WALLS *(WHERE VISIBLE)*

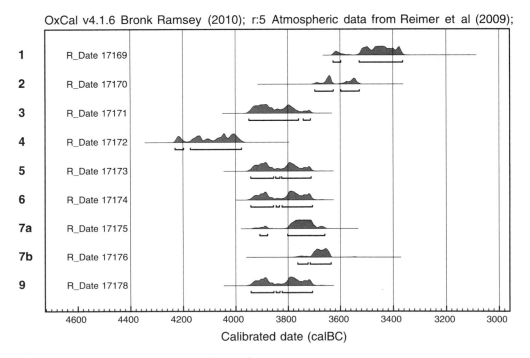

OxCal v4.1.6 Bronk Ramsey (2010); r:5 Atmospheric data from Reimer et al (2009);

1	R_Date 17169	
2	R_Date 17170	
3	R_Date 17171	
4	R_Date 17172	
5	R_Date 17173	
6	R_Date 17174	
7a	R_Date 17175	
7b	R_Date 17176	
9	R_Date 17178	

4600 4400 4200 4000 3800 3600 3400 3200 3000
Calibrated date (calBC)

Fig. 12.8   The chronology of burials at Burn Ground

entry into the chambers was blocked (Fig. 12.6). One vessel appears to have been placed in the south passage, possibly freshly broken for this purpose (Barclay 2007, 278-9).

The Hazleton North long cairn is also a Cotswold-Severn tomb of lateral type – a monument with small burial chambers set into each side of a long mound (Saville 1990a). It is slightly later in date than Ascott-under-Wychwood, and may only have been used for two to three generations (Meadows *et al.* 2007). Animal remains, including partly-articulated animals, were also found at Hazleton where they appear to post-date the human burials (ibid.). Transepted tombs – monuments with chambers leading off a passage entered from the broadest end of the mound – have been thought to be slightly later in date (Thomas and Whittle 1986; Thomas 1988; Whittle, Barclay, Bayliss *et al.* 2007), with earthen long barrows constructed from a similar period of time, but the dated sample is very small. A number of transepted tombs are found amongst the Cotswold group, of which Notgrove and Burn Ground are notable examples (Clifford 1936; Grimes 1960). Whereas the recent dating of some of the human remains from Notgrove and Sale's Lot (O'Neill 1966) supports the suggestion that tombs accessed from the terminal end of long cairns or mounds may be later, the dating of samples from Burn Ground suggest that this site is very early in the sequence, perhaps earlier than Ascott-under-Wychwood (Smith and Brickley 2006; Whittle *et al.* forthcoming). The layout of this monument is complex. It has both a lateral passage running the full width of the cairn and a conjoining passage running from the east end of the monument with five side chambers (Fig. 12.7; Grimes 1960). At face value, the human remains from the transepted chambers, which appear to represent complete or near-complete burials, were at least as early as those from the lateral passage (Fig. 12.8). Indeed, one individual was dated to 4230-3970 cal BC (Wk-17172; 5255 ± 35; Smith and Brickley 2006, table 1) perhaps representing curated remains, although this surprising result merits redating (and isotope analysis if confirmed).

Early monuments on the Chalk

An important cluster of early burial monuments, including around 30 long barrows, lies on the North Wessex Downs at the headwaters of the river Kennet around Avebury, and at the south-western fringes of our study area (Barker 1985; Whittle 1993; Thomas 1999, 203-8; Pollard and Reynolds 2002, 63-70). Unlike the Cotswold monuments, however, these are very varied in their method of construction, with both earthen barrows and chambered tombs present. Probably the most famous of these is the West Kennet long barrow which is of Cotswold-Severn transepted type (Fig. 12.9). Its passage and five chambers, constructed of sarsen orthostats, are found at the east end of a huge, *c* 100 m x 25 m (to

12 m) mound of chalk rubble overlying a core of small sarsen stones (Piggott 1962). Recent re-analysis of the human bones suggests that 36 individuals were buried within the chambers (Wysocki and Whittle in prep.), probably from 3670-3635 cal BC (at 81% probability; Bayliss, Whittle and Wysocki 2007). Although there have been a number of interpretations of the disarticulated and mixed remains, current views follow those of the excavator in proposing successive interment of complete bodies followed by later re-arrangement with some removal of bones once flesh had decayed. This happened over a period of around 1-55 years (probably between 10 and 30 years; ibid. 96-7). There then followed a period of around 100 years, when there are no signs of activity in and around the tomb, although bones of the gradually decomposing bodies may have been rearranged and removed over this period of time. The chambers then began to be backfilled with rubble within which were found deposits of human bone, mainly children, animal bone and artefacts. Recent radiocarbon dating suggests that this process continued for between 775 and 1420 years (Bayliss, Whittle and Wysocki 2007, table 2), although Piggott (1962), and later Case (1995, 8), believed that the infilling was rapid based on the absence of stratigraphy within the deposit and parallels elsewhere.

Other megalithic long barrows are situated mainly to the north and east of West Kennet, and although few of these have seen excavation in recent years, it is apparent that they share many of the design elements of Cotswold-Severn tombs with terminal chambers of simple or transepted form, but with each tomb displaying unique features which demonstrate the distinctive individual histories of each place. At Millbarrow, for example, there appears to have been a stone facade and kerb and at least one stone chamber which received a number of human burials which had become disarticulated and quite fragmented, though partly as a result of agricultural disturbance, antiquarian activity and animal burrowing (Whittle 1994). At least ten individuals were present, of whom five were children (Brothwell in Whittle 1994, 36-8). The monument appeared to be later than West Kennet in date, but overlay a possible timber phase and pits from which came at least three adults and a child. The entire monument was enlarged in its final phase by the digging of a second set of flanking ditches, indicating longevity of use of this site.

The dates of the earthen long barrows are not so precisely known, but they could be as early as West Kennet in the sequence. Rather than containing collective burials, human remains seem to have been treated differently at these sites with one or a few individuals being interred which are mainly found as articulated remains (Barker 1985; Pollard and Reynolds 2002, 68-9). Some had timber mortuary chambers, as seems to have been the case at King's Play Down (Cunnington 1909-10). Three excavated long barrows – Horslip, South Street and

Beckhampton Road (Ashbee *et al.* 1979) – appear to have contained no burials at all and pose the question of whether the monumental aspect of some barrows was not more important than their funerary role (Thomas 1999, 207); they have been referred to as cenotaph barrows (Pollard and Reynolds 2002, 69). Although they had no megalithic elements, South Street and Beckhampton Road had mounds constructed in individual bays, each containing contrasting materials as is the case with a number of Cotswold-Severn tombs (Thomas 1999, 207-8; Pollard and Reynolds 2002, 62). Both mounds overlay settings (sarsens in the case of South Street and stakeholes at Beckhampton Road)

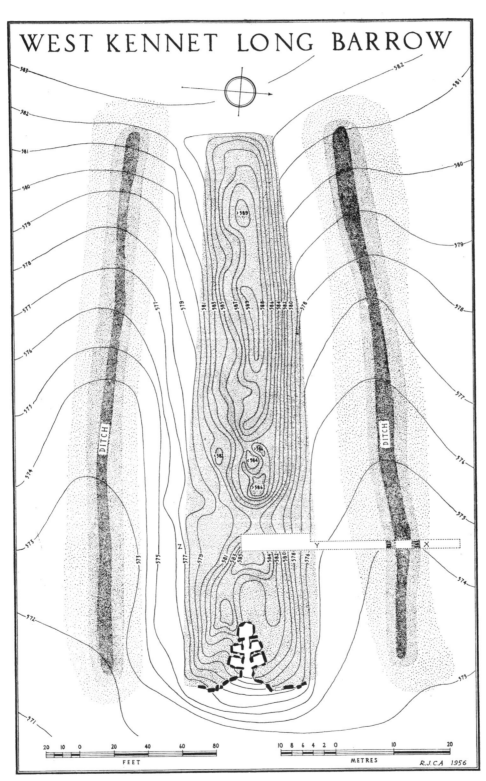

Fig. 12.9 Plan of the West Kennet long barrow

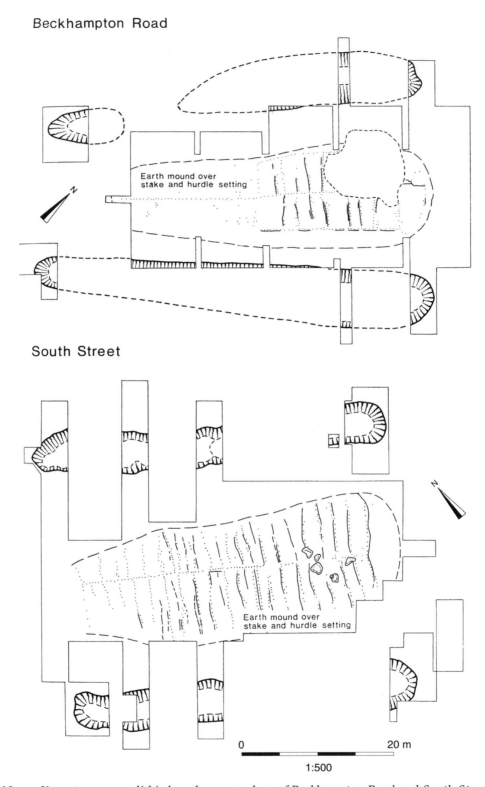

Beckhampton Road

Earth mound over
stake and hurdle setting

South Street

Earth mound over
stake and hurdle setting

0　　　　　　　　20 m

1:500

Fig. 12.10　Upper Kennet non-megalithic long barrows: plans of Beckhampton Road and South Street

associated with cattle bone, and both were constructed in areas which had seen a long history of earlier use (Fig. 12.10; Ashbee *et al.* 1979; Pollard and Reynolds 2002, 60-2).

Just a few long barrows are known on the Berkshire Downs (three certain and two possible examples; Brown 1978; Darvill 2004, 242-3), an area from which Neolithic evidence in general is sparse (see above, Chapter 11) and where there appears to have been little woodland clearance. These sites include the Lambourn long barrow, an earthen mound 68 m x 18 m, which seems originally to have had sarsen chambers, or at least settings, at its east end (Fig. 12.11; Wymer 1965-6). The barrow had

270

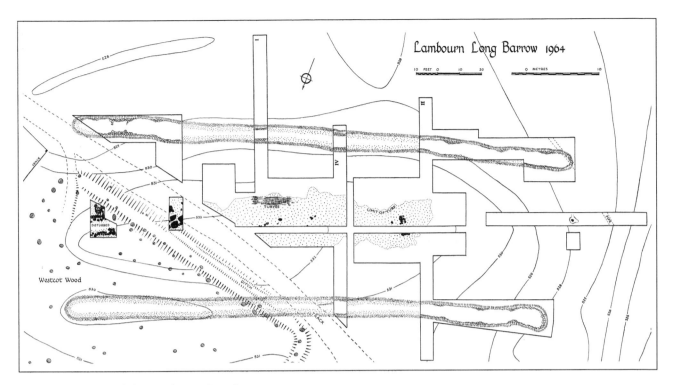

Fig. 12.11   Plan of the Lambourn long barrow

been opened in the middle of the 19th century by the local farmer and then by Martin Atkins when 'human remains and a quantity of black earth were found' (Case 1956a, 16). Several sarsens still protruded from the mound in the 1930s suggesting the presence of chambers (Grinsell 1936) but these were no longer visible and the site had been badly disturbed by agriculture when John Wymer undertook rescue excavations of its most damaged parts in 1964 (Wymer 1965-6). Recent reassessment of the site by Rick Schulting has included radiocarbon dating of part of a human cranium and a femur recovered from the ditch silts in 1964, and results from these, along with an antler pick from the floor of the north ditch, indicate that the construction and primary use of the monument lay in the second half of the 38th or the first half of the 37th century cal BC (Schulting 2000). Later dates, at the end of the 4th or early 3rd millennium, were obtained on an articulated burial found on a sarsen cairn during the 1964 excavations (Wymer 1965-6, 8-9), suggesting that the monument remained a focus for burial or saw a later phase of activity. In its initial phases, Lambourn is an early monument, of similar age to the well-dated examples on the Cotswolds and earlier than West Kennet, demonstrating that, however lightly settled the Berkshire Downs were in the Neolithic period, there was activity here from its earliest stages.

The existence of another earthen barrow has recently been confirmed at White Horse Hill, Uffington (Miles *et al.* 2003). Situated between the chalk-cut horse and the hillfort, this monument became the site of a Romano-British cemetery. It was extensively excavated by Martin Atkins in the

19th century and has been badly disturbed by rabbit burrowing; little of the original structure of the mound remains (ibid., 38-46). Recent excavations did show, however, that the monument was of earth and chalk construction with no obvious signs of stone chambers.

Wayland's Smithy, on the other hand, lying only 2 km to the west, is a 'classic' Cotswold-Severn chambered cairn of transepted type (Whittle 1991; Atkinson 1965). Its passage and five stone chambers, entered through the south-eastern end of the 55 m long mound, contained disarticulated human remains, although, because of tomb robbing and poorly-recorded early 20th-century excavations, the number of individuals is uncertain. The imposing SSE-facing facade of large upright sarsen slabs resembles that at West Kennet (Fig. 12.12). Recent dating suggests, however, that it was constructed at a somewhat later date, in the mid to late 35th century cal BC (3460-3400), possibly 150-200 years after West Kennet (Whittle, Bayliss and Wysocki 2007); it may even have been built to resemble this ancient and venerated monument (ibid., 118-9). It was not the earliest burial monument on the site, however. Lying beneath the central part of the present mound was an earlier, small oval barrow which covered a post and sarsen chamber 4.6 m x 1.2 m with a paved sarsen floor (Fig. 14.18). This chamber was thought by the excavators to have had a tent-like superstructure (Atkinson 1965) but the evidence has been reinterpreted and it is now thought to have been a large box-like structure with a lid, probably of wood, enabling access for successive burials over a period of time (Whittle 1991). An articulated adult male was found crouched at the

Fig. 12.12   The restored facade of Wayland's Smithy

north end of the chamber, and the remains of 13 individuals (ten males, two females and a child) were found apparently piled one over another; a number of these were largely complete, though some appeared to be incomplete when deposited (Whittle, Bayliss and Wysocki 2007, 107). In addition to the leaf-shaped arrowhead found embedded in a hip bone (Fig. 16.10; Wysocki and Whittle in prep.), arrowheads with broken tips were found in the pelvic areas of three other individuals during the excavations (Atkinson 1965, 130), suggesting that some of these people may have died from wounds sustained in conflict. Intriguingly, the probability is that the use of the mortuary structure only lasted for between 1-15 years (at 68% confidence; Whittle, Bayliss and Wysocki 2007), the mound being constructed 40-100 years later. Wayland's Smithy I is also somewhat later than might have been antici-pated, having been in use in the 36th century cal BC.

There are a number of parallels for the split posts which formed the ends of the early burial chamber at Wayland's Smithy, including those excavated below the oval barrow at Whiteleaf, Bucking-hamshire in the Chilterns (Fig. 12.13; Childe and Smith 1954; Hey *et al.* 2007). The fragmentary remains of a male found within and beyond the chamber here have recently been dated to 3760-3640 cal BC (OxA-13567: 4900 ± 33 BP), probably the first half of the 37th century (at 68% probability; Bayliss and Healy 2007). Around 45-150 years later, these remains were encased by an oval barrow, 20.25 m x

14.6 m, which incorporated much pottery, flint and animal bone, possibly feasting debris (Childe and Smith 1954, 216-7). The barrow was enlarged towards the end of the 4th millennium (Hey *et al.* 2007). There are few Neolithic monuments on the Chilterns and the Whiteleaf barrow seems to have been constructed in a densely wooded landscape (ibid.). This and the evidence from the Berkshire Downs suggests that the Chalk scarps were only lightly used in the Neolithic period, either by very small groups or on a seasonal basis by people based in the adjacent river valleys.

On the North Downs, at the southern fringe of the Thames catchment, the remains of a long barrow came to light in the 1930s in a chalk quarry at Badshot Lea, Surrey when it was already much damaged (Keiller and Piggott 1939; Holgate 1988a, map 37). It was 25 m wide and at least 45 m long. Small quantities of early Neolithic Plain Bowl pottery and flints came from the primary silting in addition to a deposit containing cattle bone, red deer antlers and two leaf-shaped arrowheads. Two radiocarbon dates on animal bone suggest this material dates from the mid to late 4th millennium cal BC (BM-2273: 4480±100 BP; BM-2274: 4600±120 BP; Field and Cotton 1987, 73). Peterborough Ware pottery, further animal bone, flint and a polished axe fragment were recovered from secondary fills, dated to the end of the 4th millennium (BM-2272: 4420±90 BP). Otherwise, little is known of Neolithic activity in this area (Holgate 1988a).

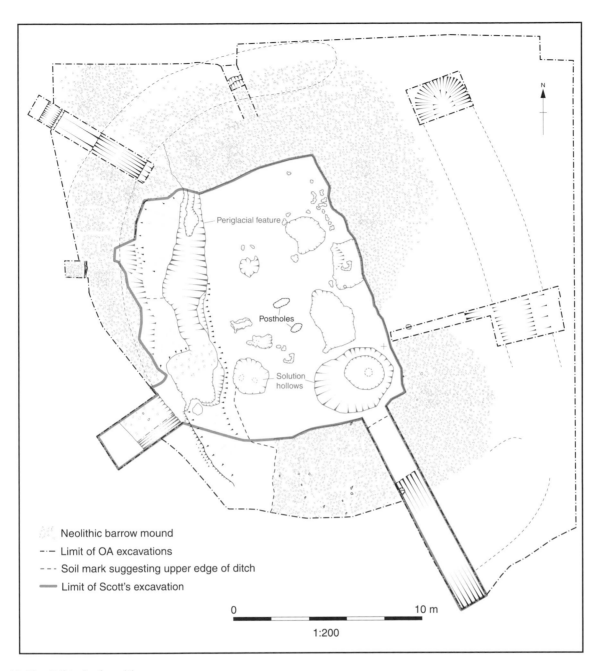

Periglacial feature

Postholes

Solution
hollows

Neolithic barrow mound
--·-- Limit of OA excavations
- - - Soil mark suggesting upper edge of ditch
Limit of Scott's excavation

0   10 m

1:200

Fig. 12.13   Whiteleaf oval barrow

Funerary and other small monuments of the 4th millennium on the river gravels

The greatest expansion of monument building in the Thames Valley probably belongs to the middle of the 4th millennium, but so few sites are dated that it is important to treat this statement with caution. These monuments seem to differ from those found on higher ground and are very varied in form: they include rectangular, U-shaped, oval and circular ditched enclosures which would, before they were ploughed, have had banks or internal mounds. Some monuments may have had external banks as has been suggested was the case for Ring Ditch 1 at Corporation Farm (Shand *et al.* 2003). Ditches were often discontinuous and, even

where continuous lengths are present, can often be seen to have been dug originally in segments which were later joined. As with their counterparts on higher ground, a number of these monuments had complex histories; Radley in the Upper Thames and Horton in the Middle Thames are good examples of sites with extended monument-building sequences. Radley oval barrow began as a rectangular enclosure, was remodelled twice as a U-shaped enclosure, and only became an oval barrow in its final phase of use (Fig. 12.14; Bradley 1992). The phase or phases to which its central grave pit and two burials belonged remains uncertain (ibid.; see Chapter 15). Horton was, at first, a U-shaped enclosure which was later encased within an oval barrow similar to that at Radley though a little larger (Fig. 12.15; Ford and Pine 2003). There was no central burial. The distinctions that we make between different monument categories become blurred in this context and should make us cautious about using precise morphological classifications; for Neolithic communities it was appropriate to modify and rebuild as circumstances dictated. As we shall see in Chapter 14, the diverse biographies of individual monuments can be revealing about the social and ritual practices of Neolithic communities.

The interpretation of many river valley monuments is made more difficult by the fact that most have been truncated by ploughing, usually removing all above-ground traces, or have been damaged by other forms of development. Additionally, they are not all associated with human remains, or have yielded only fragmentary deposits. Nevertheless, these broadly contemporaneous structures, with shared repertoires of building form and sequence, appear to be part of a

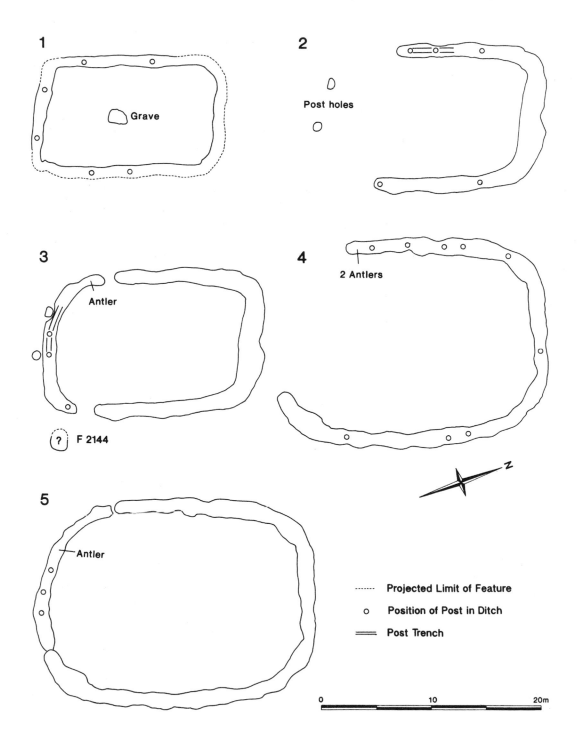

Fig. 12.14 The sequence of construction of the oval barrow at Radley

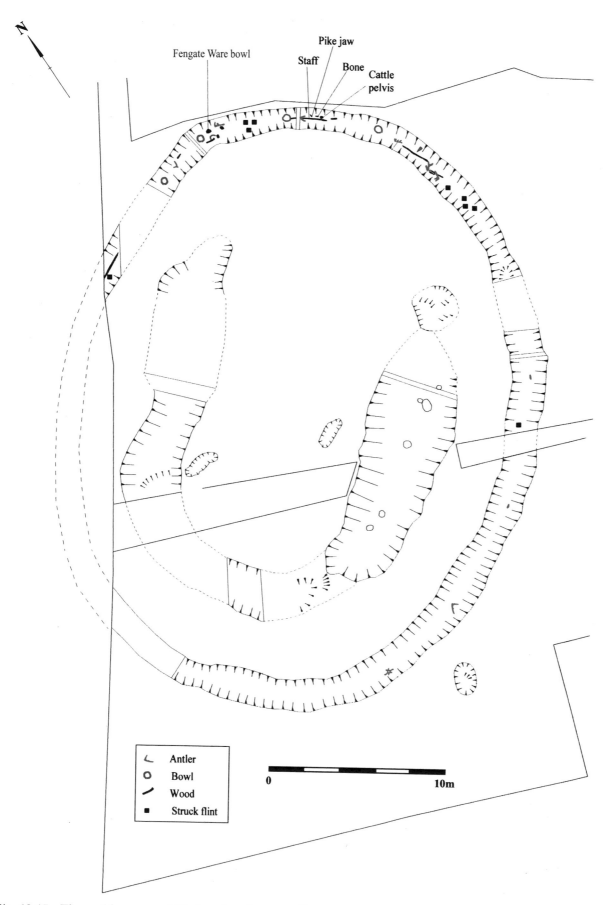

Fig. 12.15   The oval barrow and U-shaped enclosure at Horton

common tradition within which the presence of human remains is often, though not always, a feature (see below, Chapter 14).

There are a few long barrows in the more intensively-ploughed river valleys, such as those known from air photographs near Drayton to the southwest of Abingdon, at Frilford and Wheatley, and others may exist at Drayton St Leonard and Benson (Fig. 12.16; Barclay *et al.* 2003), but these are unusual. They have been identified from the air because of their familiar side ditches, although they tend to be shorter than their upland equivalents; whether they are of a similar age is not known as none has been excavated. There is a distinct cluster

Fig. 12.16   *Aerial photograph showing long and round barrows at Abingdon*

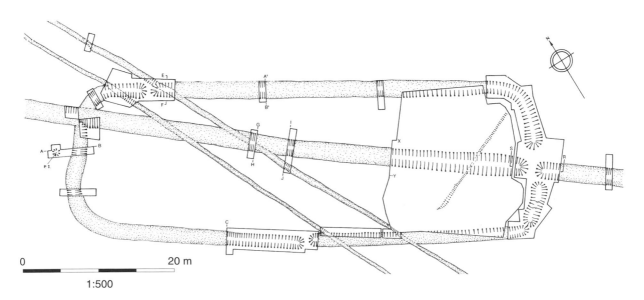

Fig. 12.17   *Site VIII at Dorchester-on-Thames, cut by the southern ditch of the cursus (and by parallel later Bronze Age ditches)*

in the area to the south-west of Abingdon (Fig. 12.2).

There are a few burial monuments which may date to the earlier part of the 4th millennium. Of these, the most securely dated are ditched rectilinear enclosures with either continuous or interrupted ditches, generally referred to as mortuary or long enclosures. These vary in size from the massive (135 m x 53 m) Dorchester-on-Thames Site 1 (Whittle *et al.* 1992) to the considerably smaller (15 m x 9 m) first phase enclosure at Radley (Bradley 1992). They have right-angled or rounded corners, some but not all have breaks in the ditch suggesting entrances and, where the evidence survives, they appear to have had internal banks, for example Yarnton Site 5 (Hey in prep.) and Imperial College Sports Ground (Crockett 2001). The Imperial College Sports Ground enclosure also had an internal division in its eastern end. Dorchester Site 1 and Site VIII were rectangular enclosures which pre-dated the construction of the cursus (Fig. 12.17) and were associated with small quantities of human bone; a pit with the disarticulated remains of a young adolescent was cut by the former and a lower human jaw bone was found within the latter (Whittle *et al.* 1992). A radiocarbon date of 3950-3300 cal BC (at 94% probability) was obtained from the burial within the pit (OxA-119: 4800±130 BP; ibid., table 12). Other excavated rectangular enclosures are less well dated and less clearly linked with human remains. The Yarnton Site 5 enclosure contained middle Neolithic Peterborough Ware pottery in recuts of the ditch, along with some Neolithic Bowl, but nothing from the primary fills, and, although it became the focus for the deposition of human remains from the middle Neolithic into the Bronze Age and an inhumation burial lay within it which cannot be dated (Fig. 12.18), no human bone was found within the ditch itself (Hey in prep.). The grave that lay in the centre of the Radley enclosure, which contained the bodies of a man buried with a jet or shale belt slider, and a woman with a polished flint knife, is believed by the excavator to belong to the earliest, rectangular stage of the monument (Bradley 1992, 132). Six posts had been set into the primary fill of the ditch here. The inhumations produced anomalously late and inconsistent radiocarbon dates (ibid., 138). The long enclosure at Imperial Sports Ground, Hillingdon was more typical being associated with no human remains, although late 4th-millennium cremation burials were found with a double ring ditch and a U-shaped enclosure on the same site (Crockett 2001; Barclay *et al.* 2009). Nevertheless, the similarity of these monuments to those which have been found beneath long barrows (Kinnes 1992), and the explicit relationship with human remains in some cases, strongly implies that these monuments were linked to funerary practices; it has been suggested that excarnation took place within them (Atkinson 1951). Many other monuments of rectangular form are known from air photographs, with examples along the valley at Buscot, Stadhampton, Sonning and Heathrow (Fig. 12.19; Benson and Miles 1974; Gates 1975; Canham 1978); a significant number are found near to cursus monuments (see below).

Related to this type of monument, though they tend to be somewhat smaller and have more rounded corners, are U-shaped ditched enclosures which are open along one of their narrow sides. Several examples have been excavated across the region, including those at Horton, Imperial College Sports Ground and Perry Oaks, all in the Lower Colne Valley (Ford and Pine 2003; Lewis *et al.* 2006;

Fig. 12.18   Undated burial within the rectangular enclosure at Yarnton

Barclay *et al.* 2009), and in the Upper Thames at North Stoke, Yarnton Cresswell Field, Yarnton Site 1 and Radley (Case 1982a; Bradley 1992; Hey in prep.). None of these examples has been closely dated, although the Horton enclosure lay below the late 4th-millennium oval barrow and contained early Neolithic pottery, whilst at North Stoke, the enclo-sure was abutted (and post-dated) by a bank barrow which has been dated to 3630-3350 cal BC (BM-1405: 4672±49 BP; Case 1982a). Two graves lying within the Imperial College Sports Ground enclosure produced dates in the last few centuries of the 4th millennium cal BC (Barclay *et al.* 2009). The enclo-sure ditch at Horton contained fragments of the

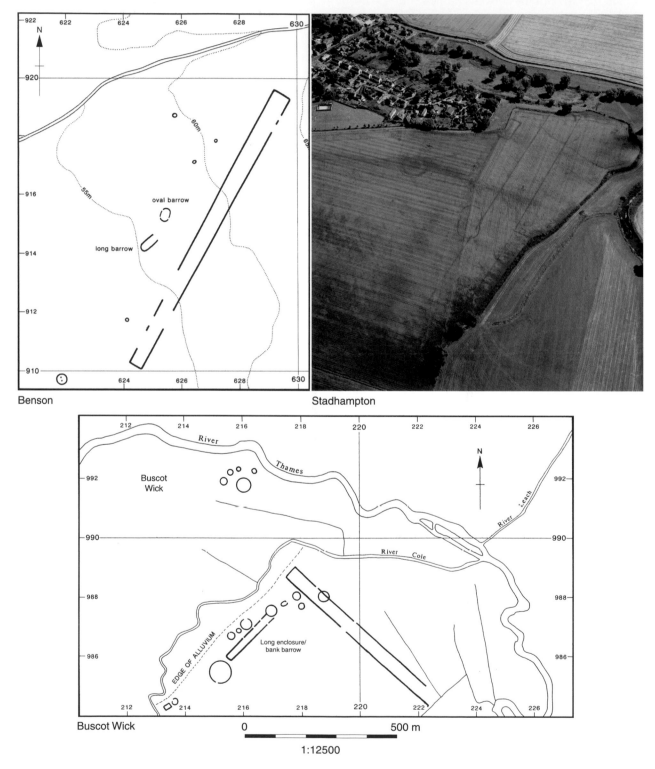

Fig. 12.19   Cursus monuments and associated oval, U-shaped or rectangular ditched enclosures at Benson, Stadhampton and Buscot Wick

278

skulls of children and also feasting debris (clusters of bone, Plain Bowl pottery, struck flint and animal bone, mainly cattle), which are perhaps indications of the ceremonies that may have attended the deposition of human remains (Pine and Ford 2003). Posts seem to have been set within the ditch in places (Fig. 12.15). At Radley, antlers placed in the ditches to the south-west of the monument yielded dates in the later 4th millennium (Bradley 1992, 134-5). A little human bone was recovered from the upper fills in the same area, and posts had also been placed around the perimeter of the ditch, cut into the earliest fills (Fig. 12.14). Other U-shaped enclosures have been much less productive of finds.

As we have seen, oval barrows formed the final phase of construction at a number of monument sites. They may indicate a formal end to a phase of active use of the site, physically preventing access to the deposits which they enclosed. A small segmented oval enclosure at New Wintles Farm, Eynsham, for example, probably provided the soil to cover the remains of a split-post setting, a structure strongly reminiscent of those already described for Wayland's Smithy and Whiteleaf, flanked by side ditches (Fig. 12.20). Small quantities of the cremated bone of children, including skull fragments, possible pyre

debris and some Neolithic Decorated Bowl came from the inner ditches and three associated pits, all of which would have been sealed by the mound (Kenward 1982). This monument may belong to the 37th–36th century cal BC. Oval barrows overlying U-shaped enclosures have already been described for sites as widely distributed as Radley in the Upper Thames and Horton in the Colne Valley (Bradley 1992; Ford and Pine 2003), and another possible example is known from air photography at Eton Wick (Ford 1991-3). At Horton, the outer barrow ditch had a series of placed deposits, including birch bark containers, wooden objects, a complete Fengate Ware vessel and four flakes from a Group VI axe from Cumbria (Fig. 12.15; Ford and Pine 2003). The bark vessels date to 3340-2890 cal BC, 3340-2850 cal BC and 3610-3040 cal BC (OxA-3577: 4390±75 BP; OxA-3008 4320±120 BP and OxA-3576: 4584±75 BP; Ambers in Ford and Pine 2003).

Some oval barrows have more straightforward histories, with inhumation burials sealed beneath barrow mounds in what appear to be single events. The remains at Mount Farm, Berinsfield seem to fall into this category (Lambrick 2010). The grave of an adult male was found with a polished flint knife and blades within an oval ditched enclosure which

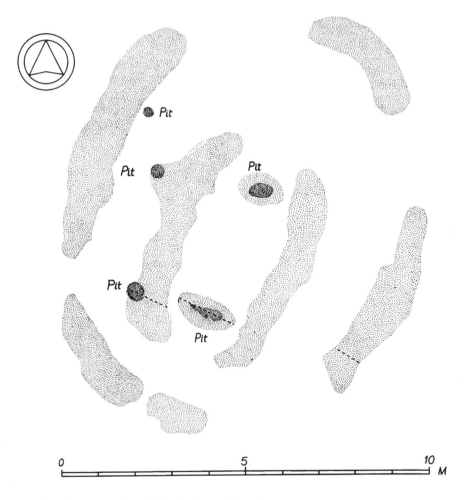

Fig. 12.20 The oval enclosure at New Wintles Farm, Eynsham

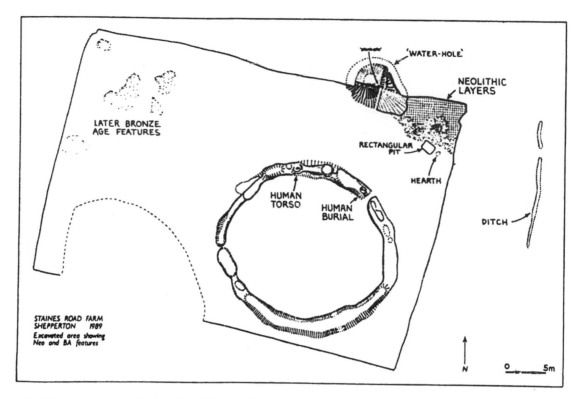

Fig. 12.21   The enclosure at Staines Road Farm, Shepperton

measured 12.5 m x 10 m. The inhumation has recently been redated to 3640-3370 cal BC (OxA-15748: 4738±35 BP); a date obtained at Harwell in the 1980s (HAR-4673) which indicates a later date is believed to be inaccurate (Lambrick 2010). Other undated features were present within the enclosure ditch on this multi-period, plough-damaged site, including a possible empty grave, but a Beaker burial was also found nearby, and the empty grave may well belong with this phase of funerary activity. Recent resistivity survey over a cropmark at Dorney Reach, north of the causewayed enclosure, has shown it to be an oval barrow (Lamdin-Whymark 2008, 166 and fig. 56).

Morphologically, oval barrows form a continuum with those which are subcircular and circular in shape. The enclosure at Staines Road Farm, Shepperton, for example, was 23 m x 21.5 m with an entrance to the north-east. It contained a complex sequence of deposits within its segmentally-dug ditch, which had probably been recut (Jones 1990; 2008). Deposits of antler picks, part of an inverted Mortlake Ware bowl and other large pottery fragments, a piece of red ochre, wolf and fox remains and a number of other animal skull parts had been placed at the base of the recut, as had two adult inhumation burials, one the crouched burial of a woman but the other only represented by a torso, neck and mandible (Fig. 12.21). The crouched burial dated to 3600-3340 cal BC (OxA-4061: 4645±85 BP) with three other mid 4th millennium dates and a slightly earlier date of 3780-3530 cal BC (OxA-4060: 4860±85 BP) coming from bone found in the primary

and main fills of the ditch (Bayliss and Jones in Jones 2008, 73). A large quantity of animal bone, representing at least four cows and three pigs, was found in the main fill of the ditch (Smith in Jones 2008, 59); the uniform condition of the bone, and the absence of gnawing may suggest that the remains of feasting had been placed within the ditch and then buried, as has been suggested was the case at Horton. At nearby Ashford Prison a smaller ring ditch, 17.5 m in diameter, had an indentation on the north-east side of its perimeter and had been dug as a series of segments. It appeared to have had a central mound or bank. A pit and an arc of small pits or postholes containing Peterborough Ware lay in the centre and around the entranceway, some cutting the fill of the ditch (Carew et al. 2006). Two middle Neolithic flat graves lay adjacent to, and may have been contemporary with, a circular enclosure at Area 6 on the Eton Rowing Course (Allen et al. 2004).

Double-ditched circular enclosures with central burials have been excavated in the Upper Thames at Linch Hill Corner, Stanton Harcourt and Newnham Murren near Wallingford (Grimes 1960; Moorey 1982). At the former, a woman was buried with a jet belt slider and a polished flint knife (Grimes 1960, 154-7; Figs 15.5-6), the belt slider being similar to that found with the man buried within the Radley oval barrow and the knife with that found with the woman in the same grave. The knife from the Mount Farm burial (above) was of similar type, though more worn (Bradley 2010). These finds provide important links between mid to late 4th millennium burials of individuals placed within monuments of slightly varied type (see Chapter 15). The tightly-contracted middle-aged woman buried within the double ring ditch at Newnham Murren is likely to be earlier in date: she was buried with a sherd of Abingdon Ware and two flakes, one of which was serrated. Her thumbs and ankle bones were missing. A double ring ditch with no surviving burial at Cassington is of uncertain date, but it can be noted that it had been dug in segments which were then conjoined, suggesting 'gang-work' (Leeds 1936, 13-5). A double ring ditch at Imperial College Sports Ground in the Lower Colne Valley contained pyre debris and was associated with a series of unurned cremation burials, four of which dated to the late 4th millennium cal BC (Fig. 15.7; Barclay *et al.* 2009).

A wide range of small, round to slightly oval enclosures, with continuous, penannular and segmented ditches are present in the valley. These monuments are less commonly associated with human remains and, although this may partly be the result of subsequent ploughing, they may also have had a more ceremonial purpose (see below, Chapter 14). A segmented subcircular ring ditch at Corporation Farm near Abingdon was formed by a pair of ditches with entrances to the north-east and south-west. It had sherds of Carinated Bowl and early flintwork within its lower fills, although later Neolithic Grooved Ware deposits were found in the upper fills, and the early material could have been redeposited (Barclay *et al.* 2003, 32-5). Another small ring ditch nearby contained three early Ebbsfleet Ware sherds (ibid.). Segmented ring ditches are also known in the Lower Kennet Valley at Green Park, Reading (Brossler *et al.* 2004) and in the Middle Thames at Eton Wick (Ford 1991-3) and Heathrow Airport (Canham 1978). Some mid to late Neolithic ring ditches can be seen to have kinks in their perimeter, suggesting that they were initially U-shaped, penannular or segmented but were later 'closed off', just as others were encased within oval and round barrows (R Bradley 2007).

There are also a number of small penannular ring ditches, such as the enclosure 15 m diameter across at Thrupp Farm, Radley, which contained Abingdon Ware, some flint and animal bone (Thomas and Wallis 1982, 184; Case 1986, 23). A similar monument was found at Yarnton (Site 2) on low-lying ground near a river channel, with deposits of earlier Neolithic struck flint and burnt stone in its interior; an oak tree within it may have been of later date (Hey in prep.). Such sites are very widespread even though relatively few have been excavated. Isobel Smith noted the presence of a number of small circular and penannular features, some with multiple ditches, in her survey of ring ditches in central and eastern Gloucestershire, mainly found in the Cirencester to Lechlade area by aerial photography (Smith 1972), and similar sites are known at Cassington (Leeds 1934a, 269-70), Marlow (Gates

1975), Eton Rowing Course Area 6 (Allen *et al.* 2004) and in the Colne Valley (O'Connell 1990). Not all of these sites need be of early or middle Neolithic date.

In addition, there are a number of burials of early to middle Neolithic date that have been found on the river gravels which do not appear to have been marked in a conspicuous way, although it is evident from their subsequent histories that the positions of many could be recognised and they may have been memorialised by marker posts or small, scraped-up mounds which have since been ploughed flat. The structures and features associated with some of these burials resemble those which underlie burial mounds. The linear mortuary structure at Barrow Hills, Radley is reminiscent of timber mortuary structures between split posts at Wayland's Smithy, Whiteleaf and New Wintles Farm that have been described above. Unlike these sites, the Radley example was housed within a suboval trench dug 0.65 m into the ground (Barclay and Halpin 1999, 28-31). The trench overlay a deep, steep-sided pit which contained a pair of antlers in its lower fill, one of which yielded a radiocarbon date of 4250-3700 cal BC (OxA 1881: 5140±100 BP). Traces of a wooden chamber 2.95 m x 0.75 m were found. It was supported by conglomerate blocks, and contained the remains of three individuals: the articulated body of an adult male in the west of the grave and the disarticulated and semi-articulated remains of two adult females, one in the centre and the other in the east (Figs 14.26 and 15.4). Radiocarbon dates (BM-2716: 4600±70 BP; BM-2714: 4470±70 BP; BM-2709: 4270±100 BP) suggest that these people may have died and been buried sequentially, the man representing the earliest burial event between 3650 and 3050 cal BC (at 95% confidence; Whittle *et al.* forthcoming). There was no surviving evidence for a barrow mound over the mortuary structure, but the different dates of the burials suggest that it must have been marked in some way. It is much less certain whether there had been any sort of monument placed over the graves of three individuals who had been buried at much the same time around 750 m to the north-west (Barclay and Halpin 1999, 31-34), but all three had been dug into at a later date, disturbing one burial quite badly, and implying that their positions could be discerned from ground level. Two of the inhumations, a child, perhaps buried in a wooden coffin, and a disturbed adult, probably a female, date to the 3rd quarter of the 4th millennium (OxA-1882: 4650±80 BP; OxA-4359: 4700±100 BP). Radiocarbon dates from an adult male who lay in the third grave show that he had been buried later (3370-3030 cal BC; BM-2710: 4530±50 BP). The graves lay at the edge of the excavated area and may represent part of a larger cemetery.

There are a number of other 'flat' graves or pit graves in the surrounding area. At Curtis' Pit, Abingdon, the crouched inhumation of a man was found buried with four worked flints of earlier

Fig. 12.22 (overleaf) The monument complex at Dorchester-on-Thames

DORCHESTER

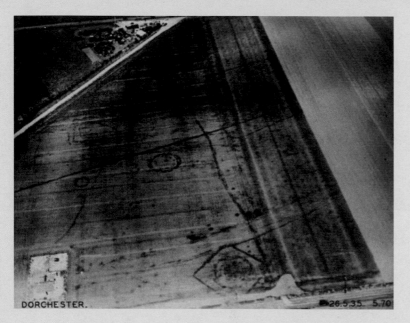

DORCHESTER. 26.5.35. 5.70

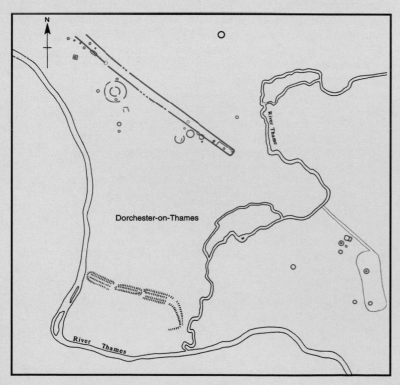

River Thame

Dorchester-on-Thames

River Thames

N

When people first began to farm in Britain, around 6000 years ago (*c* 4000 BC), the landscape was heavily wooded and extensive views would have been few. Routeways would mainly have been along rivers and many early settlements lay near to the riverbanks. Dorchester, lying in a loop of the River Thames, at its confluence with the Thame and opposite the prominent hills at Wittenham Clumps, may have been seen as a particularly propitious site.

In the Neolithic and early Bronze Age, Dorchester-on-Thames became a prestigious ceremonial centre in the Thames Valley. The earliest monuments were quite small scale and seem to be associated with funerary rituals, but between around 3400 and 3200 BC a long and impressive linear ditched enclosure, known as a Cursus, was constructed which stretched for over 1.8 km across the narrow neck of land between the Rivers Thames and Thame. Cursus monuments are enigmatic features, but are believed to be associated with ritual processions. The Dorchester Cursus linked a number of the earlier funerary monuments and may have been constructed to commemorate the dead in a dramatic way.

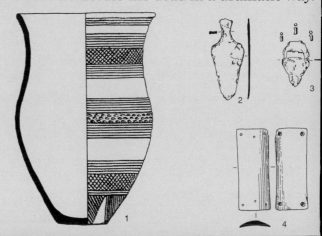

1 2 3 4

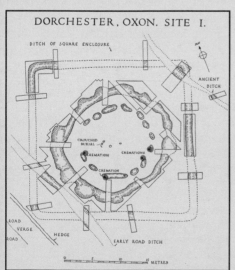

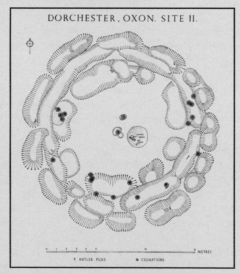

The Cursus provided the focus for several exotic monuments with recut ditches and circles of pits and postholes. Many cremation burials were placed within these features towards the end of the Neolithic (*c* 2900 - 2500 BC). Cremation was not very common at this time and the number of these deposits and manner of their deposition makes Dorchester very unusual.

At the end of the Neolithic the Dorchester Big Rings Henge monument was built. This was nearly 200 m in diameter and would have provided a wonderful arena for a large number of people to congregate and to witness and participate in ceremonies and rituals. It would have performed a similar function for the surrounding area as Avebury, for example.

A large number of round barrows were built in the area in the early Bronze Age (*c* 2200 - 1600 BC), within which important people would have been buried.

Sadly, many of these monuments were destroyed by gravel extraction in the 1940s and 1950s, and also by the construction of the bypass of the 1980s. However, we are lucky in having a very good collection of early photographs taken from the air, primarily by Major Allen. These show many important features very clearly.

DORCHESTER, OXON. SITE I.

DORCHESTER, OXON. SITE II.

* Above — Aerial photograph (Major Allen) of the Big Rings henge monument and, to the right, the cursus
* Above — Plans of circular structures containing burial pits
*Right — Detailed plan of crouched Beaker burial

Facing page
* Top— Aerial photograph (Major Allen)
* Left —Plan showing cropmarks of circular and rectangular monuments
* Left — Finds from the burial (see plan on the right).

Neolithic character (Wallis *et al.* 1992). A multiple inhumation of a woman, a child and an infant in a pit, and a pit deposit comprising 10 human skulls along with a small number of other bones, mostly limbs, were discovered during gravel extraction close to the Drayton cursus and reported to E T Leeds (Leeds 1934a, 266-8; Barclay *et al.* 2003, 16-20). It has been suggested that collective interment in pits may be an early Neolithic feature, paralleling the disarticulated character of remains which are found beneath cairns and earthen barrows (ibid., 19-20), although the original form of these burials may have been complete (Whittle, Barclay, Bayliss *et al.* 2007, 129-30; and see Chapter 15). Another possible example of the burial of disarticulated human bone is a 19th-century discovery in pits covered with sarsen slabs to the west of Millbarrow in the Avebury area (Pollard and Reynolds 2002, 69).

At Pangbourne, a woman, 'well-on in years' was found buried with a large Abingdon Ware bowl, a cut red deer antler and other bones of deer and pig (Piggott 1929). No traces of a mound could be found. Further downstream, at the Eton Rowing Course, two graves were found in the Area 6 midden, one containing the crouched burial of a man and the other of a juvenile (Allen *et al.* 2004, 96-7). They have been dated to 3370-3020 cal BC (BM-3173: 4500±50 BP) and 3330-2900 cal BC (BM-3179: 4400±50 BP) respectively. A partial animal burial nearby was of a similar date, although a human skull found at the edge of a palaeochannel seems to be earlier (3660-3370 cal BC; OxA-8220: 4795±50 BP).

These burials resemble the first stage of a sequence of events which we usually see beneath more formal structures. They tend to be a river gravels phenomenon but, as most only come to light by chance during development, particularly gravel extraction, this may be a reflection of the location of modern development; they may be more common in upland contexts than we think. Indeed, the presence of so many small monuments of diverse form on the gravels raises the question of whether the differences reflect the different histories of research on these different topographies. Work in upland areas has focused on above-ground monuments, which have not tended to survive in the well-settled and cultivated river valleys. On the gravels, on the other hand, air photography has brought to light an enormous variety of ditched monuments and development has provided the opportunity to examine a range of such sites, but has also exposed a wide range of monuments and burial sites that could not be seen from the air and were totally unexpected. It has also, perhaps, focused attention on the primary elements at the core of burial monuments. Differences still exist, however, and these cannot be totally accounted for by availability of raw materials. Earthen long barrows are as likely to have survived the ravages of ploughing as other monuments and yet these remain few.

A number of small sites at Dorchester-on-Thames share the morphological characteristics of the 4th millennium monuments just described, with penannular, annular and oval ditches present, often dug in segments (Figs. 12.22 and 12.35; Atkinson *et al.* 1951; Whittle *et al.* 1992). Many have complex sequences of construction, with pit and post circles, and cremation burials; one monument lay within a square enclosure (Fig. 12.22). These exotic monuments, mostly investigated in the late 1940s and all in advance of gravel extraction or road building, mainly cluster at the north-west or south-east ends of the *c* 1.8 km long Dorchester cursus (see below), near the earlier rectangular enclosures (Sites VIII and 1) described above, and provide a good example of the development of monument complexes on the Thames Valley gravels. They are not, however, well dated. The quantities of associated finds are small, and the apparent longevity of use of some sites, and the uncertainty regarding their sequence of construction, makes the interpretation of the surviving evidence extremely difficult; there are a number of different views (Atkinson *et al.* 1951, 64-7; Whittle *et al.* 1992, table 10; Bradley and Chambers 1988; Thomas 1999, 192-5; Loveday 2006, 146-52). On balance, at least the later phases of most of these monuments appear to belong to the first half of the 3rd millennium cal BC (see below), but some may have been first used in the 4th millennium.

Site I (Atkinson *et al.* 1951, 5-18) was a monument with an outer square ditch, a segmentally-dug oval ditch and an inner ring of oval pits with an entrance to the north-west (Fig. 12.22). It is possible that the pits held posts. Twenty-eight sherds of Abingdon Ware came from the primary silt of the square enclosure and the first cut of the oval ditch and the pits, with Peterborough Ware and Grooved Ware from upper fills and recuts. A crouched inhumation burial lay on the ground surface within the entrance to the pit circle facing the interior of the site, and four cremation burials were found next to pits on the south side of the circle; two were accompanied by bone pins. The square enclosure is unusual in a Neolithic context, but does have a possible parallel just outside the Windmill Hill causewayed enclosure (Smith 1965a, 30-3). Other examples may be present on King Barrows Ridge overlooking Stonehenge (Wessex Archaeology 2002), and at Aston on Trent and Maxey (R Loveday pers. comm.).

Bradley and Chambers (1988) drew attention to the shared alignment of Sites II and XI with that of rectangular enclosure VIII (Fig. 12.22). As Site VIII was cut through by the cursus when its ditch had nearly filled (Fig. 12.17; Whittle *et al.* 1992, 148 and 152), these three sites should belong to the early or mid 4th-millennium, at least in their initial phases. Site II, at the north-west end of the alignment, comprised three successive circuits made up of ditch segments or pits which were often conjoining, and which seem to have provided the soil for internal banks or a mound (Fig. 12.22). Site XI was also a multiphase monument with three continuous oval ditches and an internal pit, or more probably, a post circle with a possible entrance to the north-east (Whittle *et al.* 1992, 161-6). There is nothing to indicate an earlier Neolithic date for Site II; two antler picks from the primary fill of the inner ditch of Site XI suggested dates at the beginning of the 3rd millennium cal BC, or possibly the end of the 4th millennium (BM-2440: 4320 ± 90 BP; BM-2442: 4320 ± 50 BP; Whittle *et al.* 1992, table 12). A number of cremations were found on both sites, cutting or respecting the final structural phase of these monuments (see below).

Six other monuments of probable Neolithic date have been excavated at Dorchester-on-Thames: Sites IV, V and VI to the north-west, Sites 2 and 3 to the south-east and Site XIV beneath the later site of the Big Rings henge monument (Fig. 12.22; Atkinson *et al.* 1951; Whittle *et al.* 1992; see below). Cremations were found on all these sites. Sites IV, 3 and 2 were all found within the line of the mid 4th millennium cursus and were all aligned on the long axis of that monument.

CAUSEWAYED ENCLOSURES

Not all early Neolithic monuments were specifically associated with burial. From around the middle of the 4th millennium cal BC, probably the 37th century, a number of causewayed enclosures were built in the Thames Valley region, part of a phenomenon which spread across southern and western Britain at this time (Oswald *et al.* 2001; Whittle *et al.* forthcoming). These large monuments, up to 600 m across, though generally 100-200 m in the Thames Valley, are characterised by an enclosed subcircular space, defined by one or more sets of interrupted ditch and bank systems (Fig. 12.23). Originally interpreted as enclosed settlements, over 80 years of research has revealed the complex nature of such sites where the sometimes large accumulations of material which include exotic objects appear to represent many individual, deliberate and formal acts of deposition. It is now thought that these were places where a dispersed population gathered together, feasted and participated in a variety of ritual activities, at least some of which entailed placing groups of material within the enclosure ditches (see below, Chapter 14; Edmonds 1993; Bradley 1998a; Edmonds 1999; Oswald *et al.* 2001, chap. 7; R Bradley 2007, 69-77), an idea first propounded by Isobel Smith (Smith 1965a, 19-20). The deposits comprise differing amounts and combinations of animal bone, plants, pottery and stone, often resembling material found on settlement sites but also including material brought from afar as well as human remains.

Abingdon was the first causewayed enclosure to be found on the lowland gravels of southern England (Curwen 1930) and, when it was first discovered in a gravel quarry in the 1920s, it appeared anomalous because similar sites had otherwise been found on the Chalk. Today, 14 enclo-

sures are known along the Thames corridor and its Cotswold tributaries, with four other probable or possible candidates (Fig. 12.2), in addition to the four enclosures known at the headwaters of the Kennet, mainly – like Knap Hill – surviving as well-defined earthworks on Chalk downland (Fig. 12.24). Of these sites, only Staines and Windmill Hill have seen much excavation (Fig. 12.25; Robertson-Mackay 1987; Smith 1965a; Whittle *et al.* 1999). Some parts of the Abingdon enclosure were excavated in advance of development (Leeds 1927; 1928; Case 1956b; Avery 1982) and small trenches have been dug into Eton Wick, Goring, Knap Hill, Rybury and Crofton (Ford 1991-3; T G Allen 1995; Cunnington 1911-12; Connah 1965; Bonney 1964; Lobb 1995). The majority of Thames Valley causewayed enclosures remain unexamined.

Causewayed enclosures are not evenly distributed across the region. One of the most dense concentrations known in Britain occurs on the southern slopes of the Cotswold Hills and the adjacent gravel terraces of the river Thames (Fig. 12.26; Oswald *et al.* 2001, fig. 6.4). Here, five enclosures lie along the river corridor, with a further six along the tributaries flowing south from the Cotswolds, including a site that has recently been discovered through air photography near Banbury on the Cherwell (Oswald *et al.* 2001, 154). In the Middle Thames, a small cluster of three sites occurs close to the Thames around and up river from its confluence with the Colne (Fig. 12.2), and Windmill Hill, Knap Hill, Rybury and Crofton lie in the upper reaches of the Kennet (Whittle, *et al.* 1999; Oswald *et al.* 2001, fig. 6.2). There are other more isolated sites, the best example of which is Abingdon. A small and unexamined enclosure perhaps of this type is, however, known nearby at Radley (Fig. 12.27), although its form is perhaps more similar to the later circular enclosures of Stonehenge and Flagstones than to causewayed enclosures (R Bradley pers. comm.). Other probable candidates lie in more isolated positions at Goring in the narrow gap where the Thames cuts through the Chalk ridge (T G Allen 1995), and at Eye and Dunsden, South Oxfordshire.

We still do not fully understand the siting of causewayed enclosures in the Neolithic landscape. From being considered settlements (see, for example, discussions of the Abingdon evidence in Leeds 1927 and 1928), they came to be thought of as centres of population and emerging chiefdoms (Renfrew 1973; Oswald *et al.* 2001, 32-4), perhaps even elite residences (Bradley 1984b, 27-33). Recent work on causewayed enclosures across England, including new work at Windmill Hill, and re-evaluation of earlier excavation results, has tended to regard these sites as lying at the margins of everyday settlement (Thomas 1982; Evans *et al.* 1988; Whittle *et al.* 1999; Healy 2004b; R Bradley 2007, 75). Their location in areas where late Mesolithic/earliest Neolithic settlement seems sparse (as in the case of the enclosures upstream of Oxford and in the

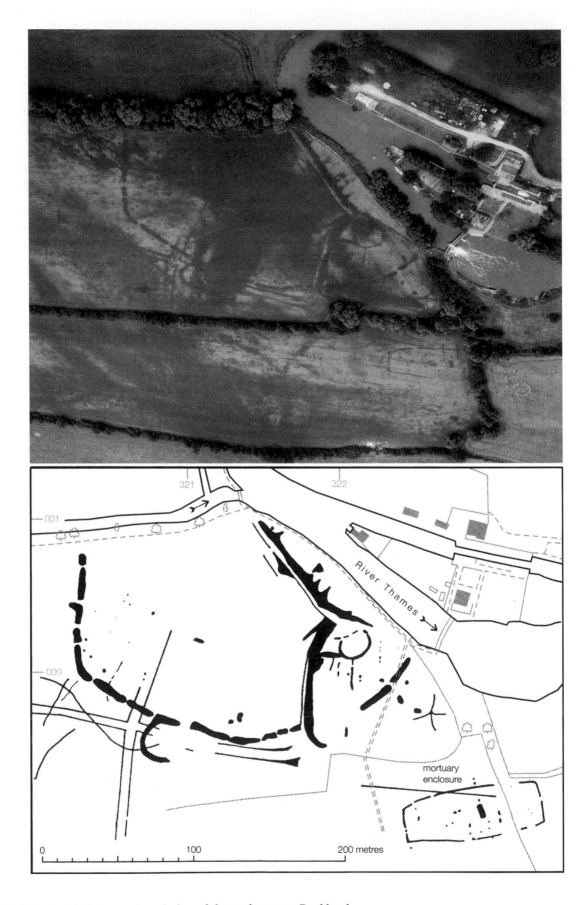

Fig. 12.23 Aerial photograph and plan of the enclosure at Buckland

Fig. 12.24   Aerial photograph of the causewayed enclosure at Knap Hill

Fig. 12.25   The Staines causewayed enclosure under excavation

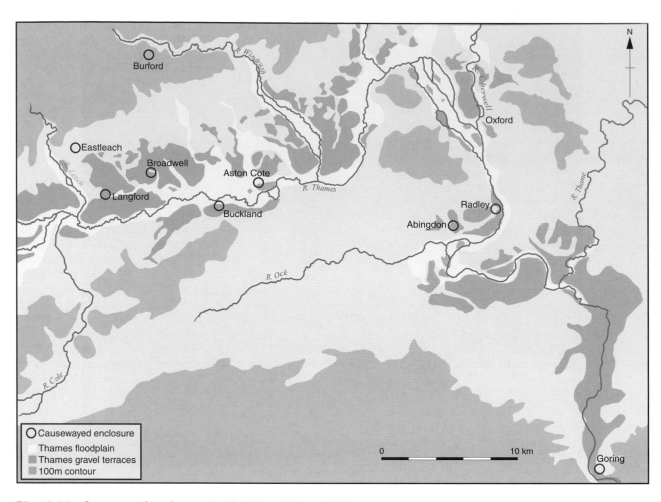

Fig. 12.26   Causewayed enclosures in the Upper Thames Valley

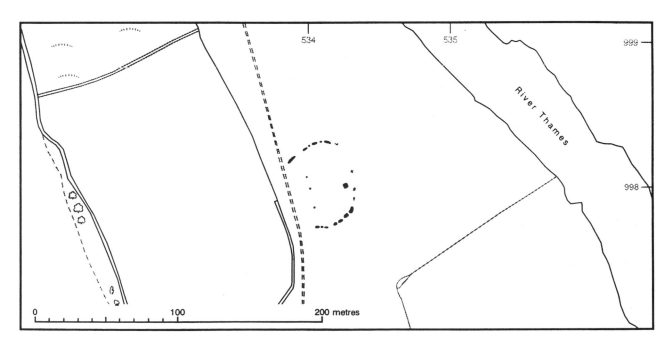

Fig. 12.27   The possible causewayed enclosure at Radley

Upper Kennet) supports this argument, and the environmental evidence from some, such as Windmill Hill, shows that they were clearly at the edge of uncleared woodland. These sites can, perhaps, be understood within the context of a relatively small population moving around the landscape over distances of 50 km or more, and gathering in these places as part of a routine. Objects found within the ditches, particularly stone artefacts, suggest that people were bringing material acquired from a wide geographical area, although the vast majority of the pottery could have been made locally (Williams 1982; Robertson-Mackay 1987, 67; Zienkiewicz 1999, 269). Isotopic analysis of human remains from the causewayed enclosure of Hambledon Hill in Dorset has shown that the diets of these individuals varied, in contrast to the much more uniform diet of the people buried at the Hazleton North and West Kennet long barrows, implying that the Hambledon Hill dead had come from several different social groups (Richards 2000).

The Dorney Reach and Eton Wick causewayed enclosures, on the other hand, were situated at either end of divided channels of the Thames within which there is quite a lot of evidence of late Mesolithic activity and earlier Neolithic settlement, including middening (Figs 10.10 and 11.16; Allen *et al.* 2004; Hey and Barclay 2007; Lamdin-Whymark 2008). Even though activity on these sites seems to have declined in the middle Neolithic, and perhaps had moved a little to the north-west, it is evident that the causewayed enclosures were situated in an area which had seen frequent and relatively dense activity rather than being built away from settlement (Allen *et al.* 2004, 96; contra Thomas 1999, 38-41).

The Staines causewayed enclosure, too, was positioned very close to the earlier Neolithic site at Runnymede. Other early Neolithic sites are also known nearby. The evidence for Abingdon is a little more ambiguous. Although only a small quantity of redeposited Mesolithic flint was found during the admittedly limited excavations, collection over the years, mainly by the Abingdon Area Archaeological Society, has revealed quite substantial assemblages of late Mesolithic and early Neolithic flintwork in the area, and the environmental evidence suggests that the site lay in an already cleared, grassland landscape where there had probably already been some cereal cultivation (Parker 1999; Cain 1982).

One result of the recent radiocarbon dating of enclosures research programme is to reveal that most sites were relatively short lived (Whittle *et al.* forthcoming). This could mean that, as with long cairns, the location of specific activities shifted across the landscape within a few generations and could explain why there are so many sites close together in the Upper Thames region. Alternatively, some of these sites, such as the cluster of sites between Lechlade and Standlake, those at Dorney and Eton Wick, and at Rybury and Knap Hill, could have been paired and had complementary functions.

Such pairing could also have been the result of emulation and competition (Edmonds 1999, 136-7; Oswald *et al.* 2001, 112-3). The diversity of form seen amongst the enclosures of Eastleach, Langford, Broadwell, Buckland and Aston Cote perhaps favours the latter explanation (Fig. 12.34).

Thames Valley causewayed enclosures are generally small to medium in size compared to others in Britain (Oswald *et al.* 2001, 54-79), and tend to have between two and four circuits, with closely and widely spaced examples. The majority lie close to the river and its tributaries; indeed, a notable aspect of the Thames Valley examples is the number which are incomplete and/or designed to incorporate natural features, particularly rivers and streams, and bluffs overlooking the floodplain. This is a well-known feature of the Abingdon and Staines causewayed enclosures, but Broadwell, Buckland and Dorney are also good examples of this phenomenon (eg Figs 12.33 and 14.19). The causewayed enclosure at Crofton straddles a water course, whereas the other Upper Kennet enclosures are sited prominently on the Chalk facing out across the landscape (eg Fig. 12.24; Oswald *et al.* 2001, 97 and fig 5.24).

Where enclosures have been extensively excavated, it is apparent that deposits are not found uniformly within the ditch fills, but occur in discrete deposits separated from others (Fig. 14.20), with different types and densities of material in different ditch segments and circuits (see below and Chapter 14). Thus, where sites have only been sectioned, it is impossible to tell how typical the deposits uncovered might be. For example, a trench excavated at Eton Wick by Steve Ford across the inner of three concentric arcs of ditch yielded, in addition to an antler comb, deposits rich in animal bone, pottery, lithics and charcoal (Ford 1991-3), whereas only a small assemblage of pottery was recovered from the one section that was fully excavated at Goring, although lenses of dark soils with charcoal were interleaved with cleaner slips or dumps of gravel and sand, and some possible recutting was present (T G Allen 1995, 23-8). The articulated skeleton of a child was found half way up the ditch, dating to 3100-2890 cal BC (BM-2835: 4360±45 BP).

More extensive excavation took place on the Abingdon enclosure before it was destroyed by gravel extraction in the first part of the 20th century or was covered by housing in the 1960s (Leeds 1927; 1928; Case 1956b; Avery 1982). It comprised two discontinuous ditch circuits 55 m apart which cut off a promontory of higher gravel terrace above the Thames floodplain, between and overlooking the confluence of two converging streams, with an area of *c* 3 ha (Fig. 12.28). The excavations by Leeds in the 1920s, and in the 1960s by Avery, revealed the discontinuous character of the inner ditch, and showed that recutting had occurred within the different segments. Finds mainly derived from the recuts. Although the distribution of the finds was not discussed in any detail, it is evident that amongst the large quantities of animal bone, flint,

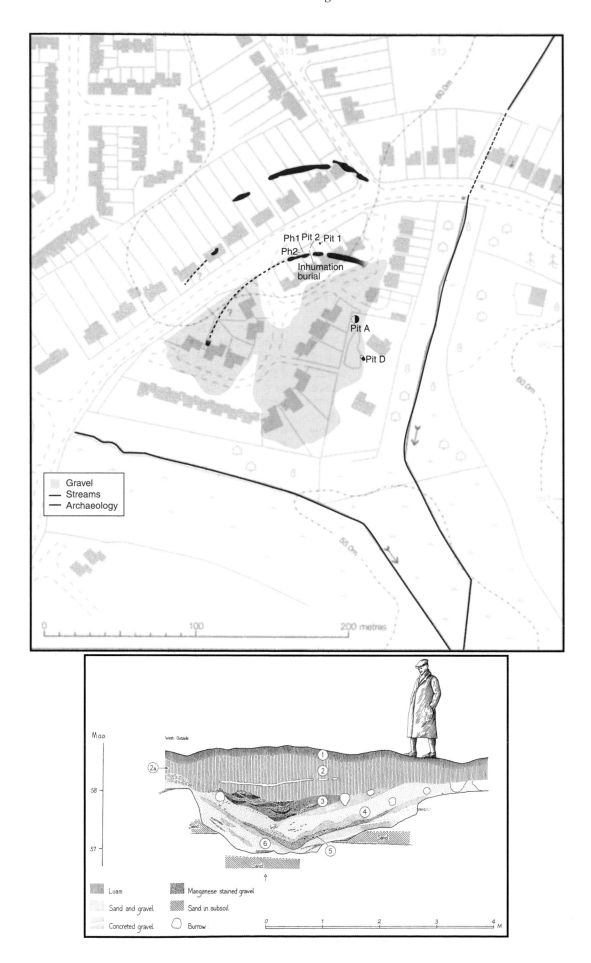

pottery and charcoal were distinct groupings of pottery (Leeds 1927, 443) and bone (Leeds 1928, 466). Rings of large river-worn pebbles appeared to represent hearths within which lay charcoal, and worked flint seemed to be specifically associated with these, including a dump of flintworking debris. Other 'parcels' of flint were also noted (Leeds 1927, 445). The significant collection of antler combs and other bone tools, along with unworked deer bone, came very largely from the work of the 1920s rather than the 1960s (Avery 1982, 43), and the same is true of the Group VI polished axe fragments. In addition to slips of gravel from the sides of the ditch, there were also hints that some material had been deliberately covered with gravel, and this feature of the ditch fills was particularly evident in the excavations in the 1960s, when alternating dumps, possibly basketfuls, of organic soils and natural gravel were found (Fig. 12.28; Avery 1982, 15-8).

The section through the outer ditch excavated by Humphrey Case in 1954 revealed a very different pattern of ditch digging and deposition (Case 1956b). This circuit appeared to comprise much longer lengths of continuous and much more substantial ditching, with an internal bank which appeared to have been revetted with turfs. The ditch contained fewer finds and seemed to have silted naturally.

Despite the wide spacing of the two circuits at Abingdon, and their different character, recent work on the radiocarbon evidence indicates that this was a short-lived monument with no detectable difference in the dates of the ditches, both belonging to either the middle of the 37th or the middle of the 36th century cal BC (Whittle *et al.* forthcoming). The contrast between the ditch forms and fills, over which there has been considerable speculation, seems therefore to be related to the different meanings attached to the two ditches, and the differential use of space, as was originally suggested by Richard Bradley (1986a), and as now proposed for Windmill Hill by Whittle *et al.* (1999).

Much more of the enclosure at Staines was excavated in 1961-3 by Robertson-Mackay in advance of gravel extraction, including at least a quarter of the interior, 30% of the inner ditch and 15% of the outer (Robertson-Mackay 1987; Fig. 12.25). This monument, comprising two circuits 25 m apart and enclosing an area of 2.4 ha, ran parallel to a watercourse on its south-west, flattened side. As at Abingdon and Windmill Hill, finds were more dense in the inner than the outer ditch, though abundant throughout, and individual dumps of material, mainly of animal bone and pottery, were identified, especially in the segment butts. These deposits often consisted primarily of one category of material (ibid., 34). More recent work on the distribution of this material suggests that there are differences in the way that deposits were made in different parts of the enclosure (P Bradley 2004; Lamdin-Whymark 2008; see below, Chapter 14).

The Windmill Hill causewayed enclosure was also largely examined in the 1920s, first by H G O Kendall, but mainly by Alexander Keiller. This work was supplemented and brought to publication by Isobel Smith (1965a). Further research, involving both further excavation and also re-examination of the site archive, was undertaken in 1988 to obtain environmental and dating samples, and to gain better information about the character of deposits made on the site (Whittle *et al.* 1999). Not only was it possible to identify substantial deposits of material within the ditches, principally animal bone, but also to characterise this as belonging to numerous individual and small-scale events (see Chapter 14).

The interiors of causewayed enclosures have attracted little systematic investigation. Keiller excavated approximately half of the area within the inner ditch at Windmill Hill and discovered a number of pits (Smith 1965a, chap 2; Whittle *et al.* 1999, 69-70). Two pits were discovered in the edge of the gravel workings within the inner enclosure at Abingdon, although it is conceivable that one of these represents an additional ditch circuit as Humphrey Case suggested (1956b, 11). Additional trenches in the inner area excavated by Michael Avery failed to locate other features, although a trench dug between the inner and outer ditches revealed a pit, two postholes, a possible gully and an inhumation burial which has not been dated. Much more activity was revealed within the Staines causewayed enclosure, including pits, postholes and gullies, some of which could represent the remains of structures. Quite substantial quantities of Neolithic finds came from these features, although Bronze Age to medieval material was also present, and at least some of the structures yielded early medieval radiocarbon dates.

Given the density of material and variety of deposits, it is surprising that the radiocarbon dates suggest that some of these monuments were so short lived. The ditches at Abingdon in particular seem to have been filled within 125 years, possibly in less than 30 years (57% probability; Whittle *et al.* forthcoming), although we must remember that some gatherings may have left little or no trace, as we will see was the case for later monuments. At Goring, the burial of the infant part of the way up the ditch fill shows that the site was at least revisited at the end of the 4th millennium or the beginning of the 3rd. Windmill Hill, on the other hand, appears to have continued in use throughout the late 4th millennium, with some significant deposits having been made in those periods. This probably includes the articulated burial of a man who appears to have been left exposed for a time in a grave at the main south-eastern entrance to the site (3650-3370 cal BC; OxA-2403: 4745±70 BP; ibid.).

The reasons for the sudden and widespread appearance of causewayed enclosures, both in our

Fig. 12.28 (opposite)   The Abingdon causewayed enclosure (The figure on the inner edge of the ditch is E T Leeds)

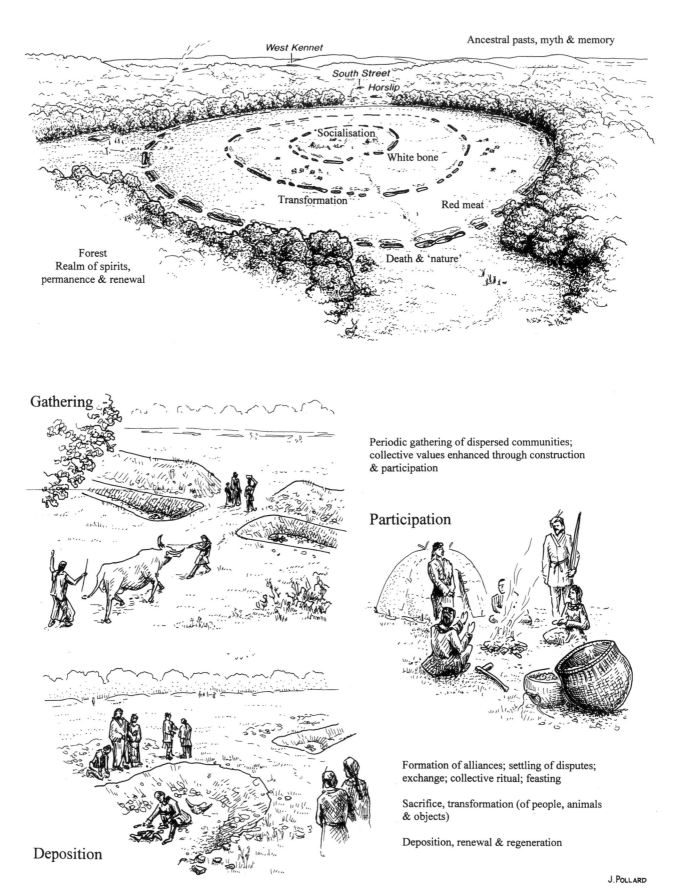

West Kennet

Ancestral pasts, myth & memory

South Street

Horslip

Socialisation

White bone

Transformation

Red meat

Death & 'nature'

Forest
Realm of spirits,
permanence & renewal

Gathering

Periodic gathering of dispersed communities;
collective values enhanced through construction
& participation

Participation

Formation of alliances; settling of disputes;
exchange; collective ritual; feasting

Sacrifice, transformation (of people, animals
& objects)

Deposition, renewal & regeneration

Deposition

J. POLLARD

Fig. 12.29   Interpretation of the Windmill Hill causewayed enclosure

area and elsewhere, in the mid 4th millennium BC, and their apparently equally rapid demise in the Thames Valley around 50-100 years later remain uncertain. With the exception of Windmill Hill and possibly Goring, they seem to have ceased to be used at much the same time that new and very different rectilinear monument forms – cursus monuments and bank barrows – appeared in the southern British landscape, some of which were built on a scale never before witnessed, necessitating the clearance of considerable areas of woodland or scrub. Radiocarbon dating suggests that the Drayton cursus was built not long after the nearby Abingdon causewayed enclosure, potentially within the lifespan of a single individual (Whittle *et al.* forthcoming). It is interesting to note, in the context of the continuing use of Windmill Hill, that cursus monuments were not constructed in the Upper Kennet Valley.

CURSUS MONUMENTS AND BANK BARROWS

Cursus monuments are a type of monument very different from causewayed enclosures. The form of these long, linear earthworks suggests that people moved along them rather than gathering at one place within them (Last 1999), and there are few signs that large deposits of material, whether from feasts or ritual activities, were ever made within their interiors or their ditches. Nevertheless, they appear to post-date and effectively replace causewayed enclosures as the large communal sites of the later 4th millennium within the valley (with Windmill Hill the only causewayed enclosure known to have remained in active use).

Cursus monuments were first identified as a distinct class of site in the 18th century, but it was only during the pioneering days of air photography on the Thames gravels in the 1930s that their frequency, variety of form and possible date gained national recognition (Leeds 1934b; Crawford 1935; Harding and Barclay 1999; Loveday 2006). The Upper Thames has one of the greatest concentration of these sites in Britain, with at least nine along a 60 km stretch of the river Thames between Lechlade and Goring, mainly clustering around the area where the rivers Ock and Thame meet the Thames (Fig. 12.30; Barclay and Brereton 2003, fig. 10.1). An additional site at South Stoke, *c* 200 m long and between 30 m and 50 m wide, could be categorised as a cursus or as a long enclosure (ibid., 232). In contrast, the Middle Thames has only two known sites: one near Reading at Sonning, and the impres-

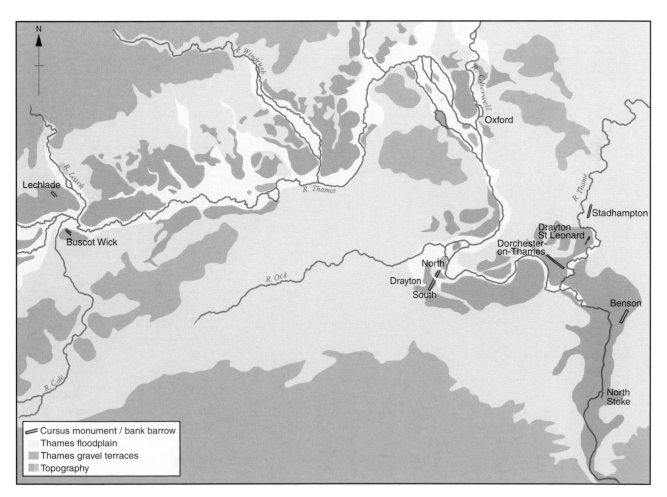

Fig. 12.30 Distribution of cursus and related monuments in the Upper Thames Valley

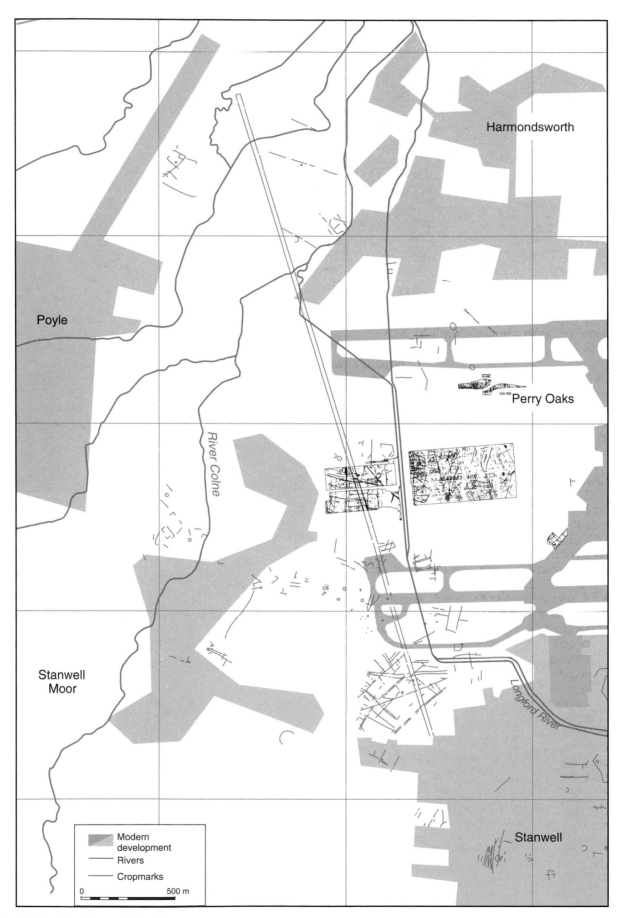

Fig. 12.31   The Stanwell bank barrow

sive Stanwell (Heathrow) cursus or bank barrow further to the east (Fig. 12.31; Gates 1975, 38; O'Connell 1990; Lewis *et al.* 2006). The majority of cursus monuments are only known from the air, and only five of these monuments have ever seen excavation (Barclay *et al.* 2003; Lewis *et al.* 2006; Whittle *et al.* 1992).

These linear monuments are defined by parallel ditches, usually between 45 m and 75 m apart, and can stretch for several kilometres across the landscape; the Stanwell bank barrow is at least 3.6 km long, although most are between 0.5 km and 1.5 km (Barclay and Brereton 2003, table 10.2; Lewis *et al.* 2006; Loveday 2006). Compared with long enclosures, which in the Thames Valley are distinctly smaller, they represent a significant increase in the time and effort that people were prepared to expend on monument construction. Where cursus terminals are visible (and many are not), the ditches often form square ends, as at Stadhampton, Benson and the east end of the Sonning cursus (Fig. 12.19), but the ends can be more rounded, as at the south-east of the Dorchester-on-Thames cursus (Figs 12.22 and 12.35), or the north terminal of the Stanwell bank barrow (O'Connell 1990, 9). Loveday (2006) has commented on the geometric precision of some of these monuments. Occasionally, cursus monuments are open-ended, as the Stonehenge Lesser cursus is known to be (Richards 1988, 72-8), and some of the incomplete cursus monuments of the Thames Valley may be of this form. The Drayton North and South cursus monuments are open ended where they face each across a tributary stream. Whether open monuments represent projects that were never completed, were intentionally built to be different, or were monuments which fell out of use before they had been formally 'closed up', is a matter of debate (Johnston 1999; Last 1999; Barclay *et al.* 2003, 240-1; R Bradley 2007; see Chapter 14). Interruptions can often be seen in the ditches, and these have been confirmed by excavation in a few cases, for example at the Drayton North cursus and at Dorchester-on-Thames (Atkinson *et al.* 1951, fig. 1, 62-3; Barclay *et al.* 2003, plate 4.3). Excavation has also shown that, as with other cursus monuments in Britain, the ditches usually provided soil for internal banks.

Closely allied to cursus monuments are bank barrows, monuments which are defined as having much more closely-spaced ditches, and internal mounds rather than parallel banks. They also tend to be shorter in length. Indeed, the name bank barrow derives from their resemblance to elongated long barrows. The bank barrow at North Stoke, 240 m long with ditches 11 m apart, examined by Humphrey Case in 1950-52, is a good example of this class within the Thames Valley, and is similar to sites in Wessex and elsewhere in northern Britain and Scotland (Fig. 12.32; Case 1982a; Loveday 2006). In practice, it is difficult to distinguish between bank barrows and cursus monuments, as the two categories merge at their extremes. Stanwell may be the longest cursus/bank barrow in the region, but it

is also the narrowest, with ditches only 20 m apart. Perhaps of greater significance is the fact that both North Stoke and Stanwell are monuments which had internal mounds rather than parallel banks, a fact that is related to the proximity of the ditches no doubt, but one that can hardly have been accidental. It would have had important implications for the way in which the site was used, providing a platform for display or to achieve a panorama, as has been suggested for Stanwell (Lewis *et al.* 2006), rather than an enclosure within which to focus and delimit action (see below, Chapter 14).

In physical terms, cursus monuments resemble extremely long versions of long enclosures, and they are very often associated with these monuments, along with other 'mortuary' enclosures: U-shaped enclosures, long barrows and oval barrows. This relationship can be seen in the cases of Benson, Stadhampton and Buscot Wick (see above and Fig. 12.19). Drayton and Benson were each associated with a long barrow, an oval barrow and a long mortuary enclosure, while a long enclosure or bank barrow was aligned on the north-west terminal of the Buscot Wick cursus. The Stanwell bank barrow also lay near to a horseshoe-shaped enclosure (Fig. 12.33; Lewis *et al.* 2006, 72-80). At Dorchester-on-Thames, the cursus incorporated a D-shaped long enclosure within its south-eastern terminal, and cut across a long enclosure 1.2 km further north-west, although the south cursus ditch was carefully aligned to run through the entrance to this enclosure (Figs 12.17 and 12.22; Whittle *et al.* 1992, 160-2; see below). Geophysical survey in 2008 by the Dorchester Project revealed more of the north ditch of the cursus to its north-west, showing that it intersects with what seems to be a small ring ditch (Wintle 2008). The bank barrow at North Stoke similarly post-dated the U-shaped enclosure which it adjoined to the south, and air photographs show it running into an oval enclosure in the north (Fig. 12.32; Case 1982a). Thus, a formal link is implied between cursus monuments and bank barrows on the one hand and, on the other, sites which seem to be associated with the dead. This connection is, in some instances, manifested by the direct physical relationship between these monuments. It is reinforced by a general paucity of finds in both monument types; these are sites in which people did not stay, and formal acts of deposition seem not to have been appropriate. In most excavated examples, cursus monuments were a secondary development, perhaps connecting dispersed agglomerations of monuments over several kilometres.

The distribution of cursus monuments suggests that there were groupings of monuments within the class too, with smaller monuments being satellites to more substantial neighbours such as, for example, in the case of Lechlade and Buscot Wick (Fig. 12.30). The cursus monuments of Stadhampton and Drayton St Leonard may have been related in a similar way to the Dorchester-on-Thames cursus (Loveday 1999).

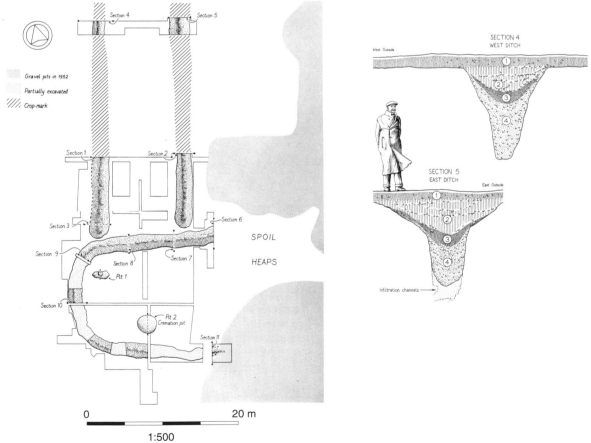

Fig. 12.32   The North Stoke bank barrow

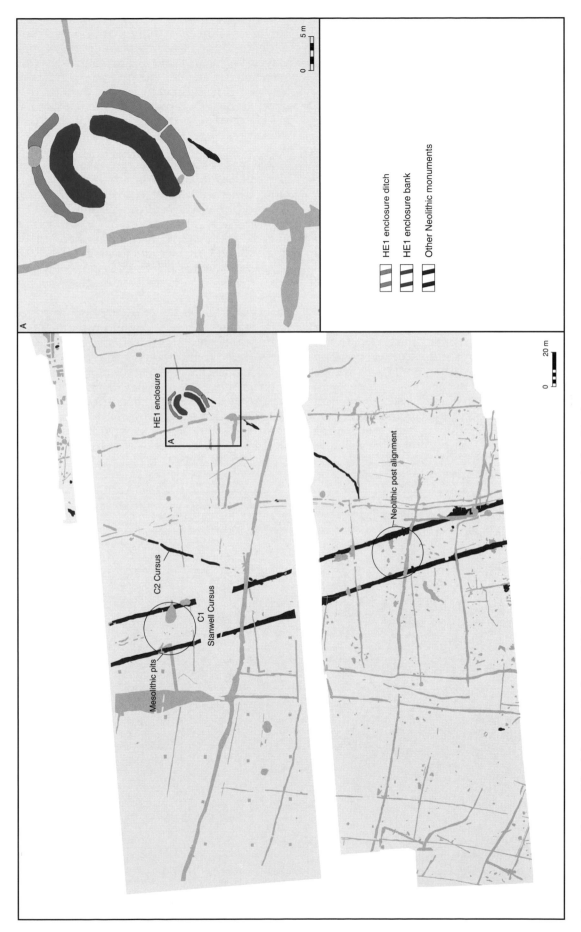

Fig. 12.33   The Stanwell bank barrow, Enclosure HE1, and other features at Terminal 5, Heathrow

The Thames Valley cursus monuments are all situated near to the river or its major tributaries, often near their confluences, on fairly level ground (Fig. 12.30), and it has been noted that the largest monuments are to be found near to confluences with the Thames, whereas smaller monuments were built further up the tributaries (Barclay *et al.* 2003, 223). Many reflect the linear direction of the river, the dominant landscape feature in the valley, either running roughly parallel to it, or continuing a particular orientation (Barclay and Hey 1999), although their form is strictly linear in contrast to the meandering flow of the river (Last 1999). A number of monuments end at tributary streams – the north-west terminal of Dorchester-on-Thames, for example – or encompass streams within their course, as, for example, at Drayton. The Stanwell bank barrow appears to have crossed the rivers Colne and Wraysbury before terminating to the north-west, close to the bank of another tributary stream (Fig. 12.31; O'Connell 1990, 9). It is hard to escape the link between the flow of the river and the line of the monuments, and the metaphorical link with cleansing and processes of regeneration and transformation (see Chapter 14). However, rivers also provided the major routeways through this landscape, and paths may often have run parallel to their courses. Cursus monuments may have formalised these pathways which led along the river, between important pre-existing monuments (Last 1999).

Proximity to the river (Fig. 12.34) is a feature that cursus monuments share with earlier Neolithic settlement; the close relationship between causewayed enclosures and water courses has already been noted. Generally, however, the correspondence between cursus monuments and the sites of earlier domestic activity is poor. The Drayton North cursus lies only 5 km to the south-east of the Abingdon causewayed enclosure, and a cluster of early finds was present around it (Barclay *et al.* 2003, 59-67; Wallis *et al.* 1992). The North Stoke bank barrow is also situated in an area where flint scatters suggest quite dense settlement activity (Ford 1987b) but, otherwise, there is very limited evidence of settlement activity around cursus monuments. This mirrors the pattern found elsewhere in eastern England and further afield (Last 1999, 93; G J Barclay *et al.* 1995, 323-4). The contrasting distribution of cursus monuments and causewayed enclosures is also very striking (Barclay *et al.* 1996), particularly given the current evidence suggesting that at least some cursus monuments were constructed only shortly after causewayed enclosures ceased to be used (Whittle *et al.* forthcoming), and when it seems that cursus monuments were the only major aggregation sites in the period following the use of causewayed enclosures (after *c* 3400 cal BC). By the same token, causewayed enclosures did not become the sites of cursus monuments in this area, unlike some sites in eastern England, such as Maxey (Pryor 1985).

Fig. 12.34 Photographic reconstruction of the Drayton Cursus looking towards the South Cursus from the North Cursus across the stream which separates the two

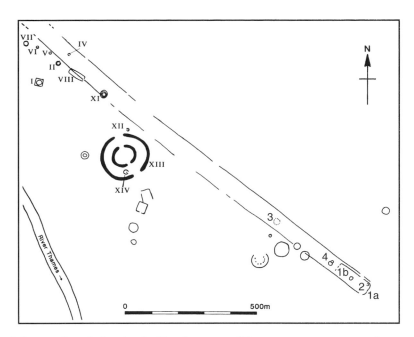

Fig. 12.35   Location of the numbered sites in the Dorchester-on-Thames monument complex

It is of note that the design of cursus monuments, some of which are very straight (eg Benson) and long (eg Stanwell) or have particular orientations (eg Dorchester-on-Thames), implies fairly extensive open vistas, at least of linear form, in a landscape that we know was generally heavily wooded. Even if the monuments were constructed piecemeal over a period of time, their unity of plan indicates that they were laid out in relatively open ground from an early stage and/or that tree clearance formed part of the project. Additionally, cursus monuments sometimes appear to reference monuments that are at some distance from them, such as the long barrow *c* 800 m to the south-east of the Drayton North cursus which appears to be aligned on the northern terminal of the cursus (Barclay *et al.* 2003, 8). Of course, the varied mortuary monuments that are found around cursus monuments, some at least of which are earlier in date, demonstrate that tree clearance had already taken place to some extent, but these were probably small clearings in the woodland landscape, perhaps linked by paths and tracks (see above, Chapter 11). Nevertheless, tree clearance must have taken place on a fairly large scale which, in some cases, would have represented projects at least as vast as the construction of the monuments themselves. At Dorchester-on-Thames, for example, even assuming quite large clearings to the north and south, this might represent around 200 hectares of trees. Tree clearance pre-dating the construction of both the Stanwell and Drayton cursus monuments has been recognised in the form of tree-throw holes either cut by ditches or sealed beneath banks (Barclay *et al.* 2003), but it is difficult to be precise about how recently these trees had fallen before monument construction began. The soil beneath the Drayton cursus bank suggested recent disturbance (Robinson 2003, 164-8), although the charcoal beneath part of the east bank included some charred grasses indicating at least locally open conditions along its length (ibid., 170). It is also apparent in this case that woodland regeneration requiring new clearance took place at least once during the use of the monument. The evidence from the Lechlade area is similarly ambiguous. Snails from the lower fill of the Lechlade east cursus ditch were characteristic of short-turfed grassland and suggest dry open conditions (Robinson in Barclay *et al* 2003, 208-9), but waterlogged deposits only 1 km from the nearby Buscot Wick cursus showed a largely wooded environment even in the 3rd millennium, although grasses formed 20% and herbs 6% of the pollen spectra (Robinson and Wilson 1987, 31).

The role of large-scale tree clearance in the creation of these monuments, and the extent to which cursus monuments defined and monumentalised these areas could have been significant. Of the few finds that are associated with cursus monuments, two categories stand out: axes and cattle bones. Polished flint axe fragments and a worked-down stone axe came from the Drayton North cursus buried ground surface (Barclay *et al.* 2003, 56 and 99), and a greenstone axe was found by a gravel worker in the area of the Drayton South cursus (Leeds 1927, 62). A polished flint axe also came from the primary fill of the cursus ditch at Dorchester-on-Thames (Whittle *et al.* 1992, 160). Cattle dominated the animal bone assemblage in both of the Drayton cursus ditches and

Fig. 12.36 (overleaf)   Henges in the Thames Valley

HENGES

Large henge monuments are not especially common nationally - just 42 such sites were listed in a recent survey - but the Thames Valley encompasses four large henge monuments - the Big Rings at Dorchester-on-Thames, the Devil's Quoits at Stanton Harcourt, Westwell near Burford and Condicote in Gloucestershire. There are also two probable examples, one, known only from cropmarks, at Cutsdean in Gloucestershire, and another, a small part of which was recently found in Blackhall Road, near Keble College in Oxford.

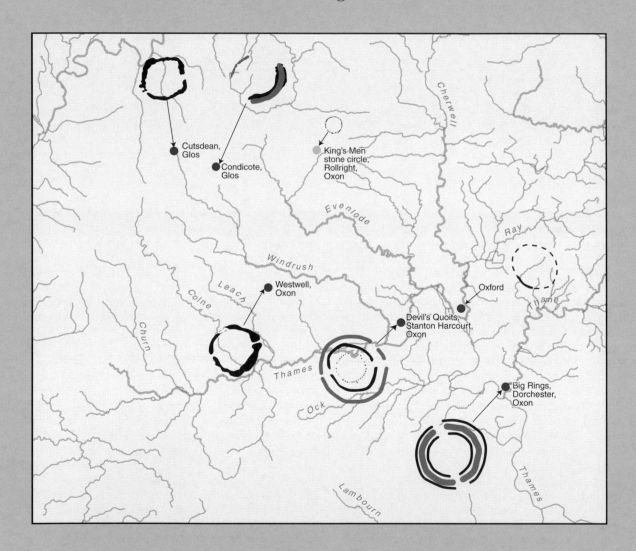

Henges, named after Stonehenge, are large circular enclosures defined by a bank and, usually, an internal ditch. With the exception of Condicote, where the entrances have not been certainly identified, all of these monuments are Class II henges: monuments with two opposing entrances. Both the Big Rings and Condicote had two ditches which lay on either side of the bank (type IIa henges); the others - the Devil's Quoits, Westwell and Cutsdean - had the more usual form consisting of a single ditch which lies within the bank. Too little of the Oxford henge has been exposed for its form to be clear. These latter sites also share a ENE - WSW orientation. It is uncertain whether this reflects a particular celestial alignment, or whether the entrances incorporate important pathways or face particular landscape features. The Bigs Rings, however, is again exceptional: its entrances were oriented NNW and SSE.

HENGES

In the absence of recent and full excavation, dating the Upper Thames monuments is difficult. The only radiocarbon dates have been obtained from the Devil's Quoits. Otherwise, excavations across ditches at Condicote, Westwell and Dorchester-on-Thames have only yielded Beaker pottery from upper fills, corroborating the use of henges through the Beaker period but not dating their earliest construction and use. The dates from the Devil's Quoits, and analogy with better dated sites elsewhere, suggest, however, that these monuments belong to the late Neolithic, around 2500 cal BC or possibly a little earlier, a similar period to the main phase of work at Avebury.

* Left – Distribution of major henges in the Thames Valley
* Above — Reconstruction of Devil's Quoits henge

The Upper Thames Valley henges are situated along the Windrush Valley, from its headwaters (Condicote and Cutsdean) to its confluence with the Thames (the Devil's Quoits), and further south down the Thames, near the confluence with the Cherwell (Oxford), and near the confluence with the Thame (Dorchester-on-Thames). Significantly, the sites occur at regular intervals of around 20 km. The sites thus connect the Thames gravels with an area of the Cotswolds that had a rich history of monument building, and long and distant connections with western Britain. It is possible that gatherings took place progressively from one monument to another as cult members or larger communities moved between Dorchester-on-Thames and the Cotswolds, perhaps as part of a ritual cycle or pilgrimage.

the adjacent buried ground surface (Ayres and Powell 2003), and cow skull fragments came from both of the Stanwell cursus ditches (Lewis *et al.* 2006, 59). The possible link between tree clearance, the herding of cattle, and cursus monuments is discussed further in Chapter 14.

Dorchester-on-Thames stands out for several reasons. Firstly it is the only site to incorporate a solar alignment within its design (Bradley and Chambers 1988), and secondly it became the focus for a major monument complex. The small post and ditch monuments which were created around and within the cursus (some possibly pre-dating its construction), have already been described above, but in the mid 3rd millennium cal BC a more dramatic addition was built: the Big Rings henge monument.

HENGES

The Big Rings henge was a monument very different from the cursus monuments discussed above (Figs 12.22 and 12.35). It was positioned to one side of the Dorchester-on-Thames cursus rather than over it, near the point at which the cursus changed its alignment, where there appeared to have been a number of causeways; the henge appears to reference rather than challenge the presence of the cursus. It was considerably larger than the circular monuments previously constructed in this area, being over 190 m in diameter in total. It was defined by two concentric ditches between which there was a bank *c* 15 m wide. It had two widely-spaced entrances, one to the SSE and the other facing to the NNW in the general direction of the cursus, though not towards the point where the two were closest, but rather to the small monuments to the north, and particularly to Site XI which sat within one of the cursus ditch causeways (Fig. 12.35). Barclay (2000) suggests that this could have become a formal entrance to the cursus at that time.

The internal area of the Big Rings (109 m in diameter) would have provided a large arena for ritual and display, and it is tempting to think of an audience, which could have been of considerable size, sitting on the bank observing proceedings. There is no obvious sign of large gatherings of people, however, and indeed, the paucity of finds from Thames Valley henges compared with those in Wessex is striking. At Dorchester-on-Thames, a deposit of animal bones was found with Beaker pottery on the eastern side of the north entrance, and more animal bone, including cattle bone, came from the western side of the south entrance. It is, however, unlikely that the ditch was ever bottomed (R Bradley pers. comm.; Whittle *et al.* 1992, fig. 27), and this material is probably associated with the elaborate mortuary rituals connected with the later Beaker burial and barrow found just to the north of the site. At the Devil's Quoits henge, hearths and deposits of bone in the ditches next to the entrance do seem to have been contemporary with its use,

marking liminal places in the monument (see below, Chapter 14; A J Barclay *et al.* 1995).

Large henge monuments are not especially common nationally, and in their survey of these monuments in Britain Harding and Lee list just 42 'classic' sites (Harding and Lee 1987, 30-1, fig. 23). Nevertheless, Dorchester Big Rings is not the only large henge in the Upper Thames Valley. There are three other certain henges of similar proportions, at the Devil's Quoits, Stanton Harcourt, Westwell near Burford and Condicote in Gloucestershire (Fig. 12.36; A J Barclay *et al.* 1995, 70-1), with two less certain examples: Cutsdean which is only known from cropmarks (Darvill 1987, 90; Saville 1980, 27) and Oxford, where the monument was recently discovered by Thames Valley Archaeological Services in advance of a development adjacent to Keble College. Where known, these Upper Thames Valley monuments had two opposing entrances (Atkinson's (1951) Class II henges), although those at Condicote have never been certainly identified. Condicote shares the Big Rings layout of a double ditch with a bank between (O'Neil 1957; Saville 1983), whereas the other three sites, the Devil's Quoits, Westwell and Cutsdean, have the more usual (Class I) form of a single ditch with an external bank. These latter sites also share a ENE–WSW orientation (Fig. 12.36). It is uncertain whether this reflects a particular celestial alignment, or whether the entrances incorporate important pathways or face particular landscape features (A J Barclay *et al.* 1995, 73-7). Only one portion of the Oxford henge has been located and its form is, so far, uncertain.

The Devil's Quoits is the only henge in the Thames Valley known to have been associated with a stone circle (Figs 12.36 and 14.22). It comprised a widely-spaced ring, 75 m in diameter, of 28 conglomerate stones with one further stone offset to the south-east. It also had a setting of posts at its centre (A J Barclay *et al.* 1995). It is, however, the only site to have seen extensive excavation. A little less than a quarter of the interior of the Big Rings was examined before the site was quarried away, and only two possible postholes came to light (Whittle *et al.* 1992, fig. 27). A small central post circle or setting could have been present, but it is very unlikely that anything of proportions similar to the Devil's Quoits circle existed. A possible stone socket was found within the inner ditch at Condicote during Alan Saville's small-scale excavations there (Saville 1983); Atkinson's section at Westwell did not expose the interior of the monument (Atkinson 1949).

The Upper Thames Valley henges are situated along the Windrush Valley, from its headwaters (Condicote and Cutsdean) to its confluence with the Thames (the Devil's Quoits), and further south down the Thames, near the confluence with the Cherwell (Oxford) and near the confluence with the Thame (Dorchester-on-Thames). They are fairly evenly spaced along this possible routeway from the Cotswolds (and the west of Britain) to the main river valley (Fig. 12.36). Dorchester-on-Thames would have been an ancient and revered site by this time. The other henges were placed in areas with less evidence of earlier monumental construction. The Devil's Quoits was situated near to an alignment of three Neolithic mortuary monuments and not far from the Linch Hill Corner middle Neolithic burial, with two other small, possibly earlier Neolithic ring ditches to the north-west (A J Barclay *et al.* 1995, 106-7); the Westwell henge lay around 1 km from the Burford causewayed enclosure. Snails from the Condicote inner ditch suggested a shaded environment, created almost certainly by open woodland and tall grass (Bell in Saville 1983, 39-45) with little else in the surrounding area, although some early Neolithic and later flint has been found (O'Neil 1957, 147).

Rather than functioning as separate sites, these henges may have been visited in succession as an important route was followed, perhaps indicating an increasing or renewed interest in routes through the Cotswolds to northern and western regions. The nearest parallels to the Upper Thames sites are to be found in Yorkshire, notably the Thornborough henges (Harding and Lee 1987; Harding 2003), and henge construction may be a physical manifestation of these strengthening links. In contrast, no large henges are known downstream of Dorchester-on-Thames, and the contrast between the Upper and Middle Thames that appeared to be emerging in the middle Neolithic becomes striking towards the end of this period.

The Avebury henge monument lies at the very edge of the area under study (Gray 1935; Smith 1965a; Burl 2000; Pollard and Reynolds 2002, 81-96; Gillings *et al.* 2008). It is massive, even when compared with the Upper Thames Valley monuments, and has much more in common with the elaborate henge monuments found elsewhere in Wessex (Fig. 12.37). These differences reinforce the impression of changing social and political group-

Fig. 12.37   Avebury henge

ings at this time. The henge itself with its huge ditch and external bank described an area around 420 m in diameter, estimated to have taken around a million worker hours to construct (Startin and Bradley 1981). In its final form (Fig. 12.38), it had two opposing entrances, to the WSW and ENE as at Cutsdean, Westwell and the Devil's Quoits, and another pair to the NNW and SSE, as at the Big Rings. The ditch was ringed internally by a stone circle of 95-100 substantial sarsen boulders which had gaps opposite the west and east entrances but was continuous to the north and south. Within this outer circuit lay two separate inner stone circles, both around 100 m in diameter, and themselves containing stone settings including the Cove to the north and the (now fallen) Obelisk and stone alignment to the south. Aerial photography and geophysical surveys have revealed other features within the henge, including a subrectangular enclosure (possibly a barrow) and a timber circle.

This huge and complex monument (each inner stone circle enclosed areas similar to those of the Upper Thames Valley henges; see below, Chapter 14 and Fig. 14.8) must have been constructed over a period of time, as part of an ongoing project, but with a main phase of construction around 2900-2600

cal BC (Pitts and Whittle 1992). Traces of an earlier ditch and bank are thought to survive beneath the existing earthworks (ibid., 206). These features have not been dated but, potentially, they put the origin of the enclosure early in the 3rd millennium, perhaps as early as Stonehenge (at 3020-2910 cal BC; Cleal *et al.* 1995), with important implications for the chronological relationship between the henge and the earlier nearby circular causewayed enclosure on Windmill Hill which is now believed to have been in active use throughout the late 4th millennium (Whittle *et al.* forthcoming).

In the absence of recent and full excavation, dating the Upper Thames monuments is more difficult. The Devil's Quoits has five radiocarbon results from the ditch, although two are from combined samples which include material from more than one deposit, and two are from stone holes (A J Barclay *et al.* 1995, table 6). Otherwise, excavations across ditches at Condicote, Westwell and Dorchester-on-Thames have only yielded Beaker pottery from upper fills, corroborating the use of henges through the Beaker period but not dating their earliest construction and use. The dates from the Devil's Quoits, and analogy with better dated sites elsewhere, suggest these monuments belong to the

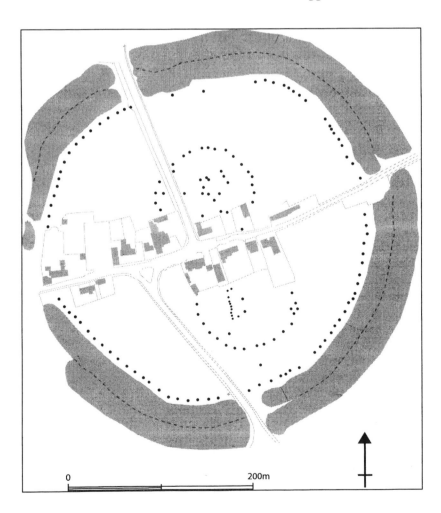

Fig. 12.38   Plan of Avebury henge

late Neolithic, around 2500 cal BC or possibly a little earlier (Harding 2003), a similar period to the main phase of work at Avebury.

The relative chronology of earthworks and stone and timber circles has recently been questioned (Gibson 2005). In the cases of both Avebury and the Devil's Quoits, the relationship between the earthwork monuments and stone circles remains uncertain. On the latter site, the dating tends to suggest that they were either broadly contemporary or that the stones were a slightly later addition (A J Barclay *et al.* 1995, 45-6). At Avebury, current thinking favours a model of the existing earthworks enclosing earlier central stone settings and

replacing a less substantial enclosure. The outer stone ring seems have been erected soon after (Pollard and Cleal 2004; Gillings *et al.* 2008, 203-4).

STONE AND TIMBER CIRCLES

A number of other stone and timber circles are known around Avebury, including circles such as the Sanctuary, which comprised concentric rings of both wood and stone (see below), which appeared to have formed an integral part of the monument complex. Other stone circles may have existed around 5.5 km away, both upstream at Winterbourne Bassett and downstream at Clatford, as well

Fig. 12.39　The Rollright Stones

as further afield at Broome just to the south of Swindon (Fig. 14.11; Burl 2000, 311; Pollard and Reynolds 2002, 110-2). In the context of the Thames Valley, however, stone circles are very rare. Apart from the Devil's Quoits, the only site known is the King's Men stone circle at Rollright which is quite different in size and form to the circle at the Devil's Quoits (Lambrick 1988). It is only *c* 30 m in diameter and was constructed of closely-set stones which are set in a slight bank (Fig. 12.39). There is no surrounding ditch and bank. Its closest parallels lie, not in the Thames Valley and Wessex, but to the north, principally with Cumbrian stones circles (ibid.). Its position high up in the Cotswolds, at the watershed between the Thames and the Severn drainage may, therefore, be significant, as may its proximity to 'northern-style' henges in the Upper Windrush Valley (Fig. 12.36).

Within the Thames Valley, a number of post circles and penannular post settings have been found during the course of rescue excavations. These are reminders that stone was not widely available in the area, timber circles may have been common, and that such features are difficult to find; they may not be revealed by aerial photography or geophysical survey. In general they are small monuments, of around 10 m to 20 m in diameter.

Sometimes post circles lay near to larger monuments. The Gravelly Guy penannular setting of 23 postholes lay to the north of the Devil's Quoits (Lambrick and Allen 2004), and the egg-shaped setting of 12 posts at Site 3, Dorchester-on-Thames lay within, and was orientated upon, the line of the cursus (Fig. 12.35; Whittle *et al.* 1992, 169-75). Both had postpipes and some split timbers; the posts at Dorchester had been burnt *in situ*. Other small circular monuments at Dorchester were probably, in their earliest phases, timber circles (Gibson 1992). Other post settings, such as the small oval setting of 14-15 posts at Mount Farm, Berinsfield, near Dorchester (Fig. 12.40; Lambrick 2010), and a small post circle of which only eight post pits survived at the Cotswold Community site, near the headwaters of the Thames (Powell *et al.* 2010) were more isolated.

MONUMENT COMPLEXES

We have observed the growth of monuments over the course of over 2,000 years. Abingdon, for example, had a causewayed enclosure by 3600 cal BC and was still a significant place in the landscape in the early Bronze Age. Why were these places chosen and what made them special so that people returned? Of course, they may have been the sites of particularly memorable events, significant incidents in the lives of the community or important people, which were commemorated by a single monument and then embellished. And so the aura of the place would have developed, and visiting would have

Fig. 12.40 The post circle at Mount Farm, Berinsfield

become a part of the routine of life. However, there are some consistent patterns in the siting of monuments that suggest that their location was not random. Furthermore, having become a focus, something about some of these sites brought people back, and encouraged monument enhancement and replacement with new forms of monuments when ideas changed or events dictated.

Abingdon is of great interest in this respect. Having been one of the most important places in the region when its causewayed enclosure was in use, it seems to have lost its central ceremonial role in the later 4th millennium when cursus monuments were constructed at Drayton and around Dorchester-on-Thames. It never became the site of a henge monument. Nevertheless, as we have already seen above, a U-shaped enclosure was built here which was superseded by an oval barrow, and a number of other burials, included Grooved Ware-period flat graves, were placed here and pits were dug, all suggesting that it never entirely lost its significance. From the end of the Neolithic, it became the site of a complex linear barrow cemetery with the richest and most elaborate burials in the region. However, from the middle Neolithic onwards, its focus was on the dead and, by the Beaker period it may have become revered as an ancient site (see below, Chapters 14 and 15).

Dorchester-on-Thames is also a very good example of the development of a monument complex, though of a different kind. By the middle of the 3rd millennium cal BC it had become the most impressive monument complex in the Thames Valley. Possibly formalising an existing route, we have already traced its development from small mortuary enclosures, to the massive cursus, the embellishment of the site with small but complex monuments within and around which cremation deposits were made, and the creation of the Big

Rings henge. Sites IV, V, VI, 2, 3, XIV and possibly II and XI (see above) were small monuments constructed after the cursus (Fig. 12.35), but during the time that the monument was in active use, perhaps at the end of the 4th millennium or the beginning of the 3rd millennium cal BC. They could represent small shrines or sanctuaries, perhaps for the use of smaller groups of people among a larger community who gathered at the site, though whether these would be separate family groups or more specialised members of the community is not known. Their final use for the placement of cremation burials may suggest the former.

As with Sites II and XI already discussed above, Sites IV, V and VI (Fig. 12.41; Atkinson *et al.* 1951) had all been small post circles between 7.3 m and 8.9 m in diameter, their posts, eight to twelve in number, having been set into large pits which conjoined to varying degrees to form a more-or-less continuous ditch (Gibson 1992); the soil seems to have been used to form external banks. In total, 95 cremation burials were placed on these three sites, post-dating the visible structural elements; 21 cremations were found on Site II and three deposits of cremated bone were found associated with the inner post ring of Site XI. A number of the cremations were accompanied by artefacts, such as the bone pins, maceheads and flint objects on Site II. Two discrete deposits of aurochs bones, including an articulated leg, and possible sweepings from a funeral pyre were also found in its ditches and central pits (Fig. 12.42).

Slightly different monument forms are represented by Site 2, a small penannular ring ditch within the southern terminal of the cursus; Site 3, a post circle 20 m in diameter lying within the centre of the cursus; and Site XIV, a circular ring ditch, 13 m in diameter, to the west of the cursus and beneath the bank of the Big Rings henge monument

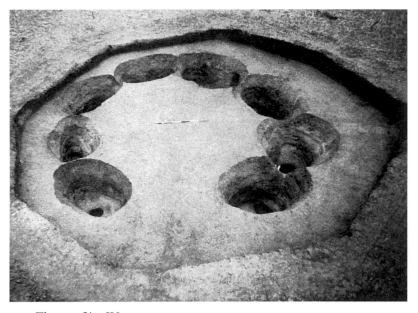

Fig. 12.41   Dorchester-on-Thames Site IV

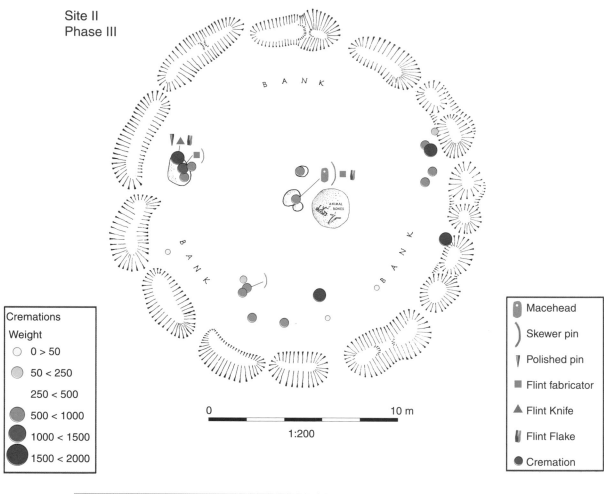

Site II
Phase III

BANK

BANK

BANK

BANK

ANIMAL BONES

Cremations
Weight

○ 0 > 50

● 50 < 250

250 < 500

● 500 < 1000

● 1000 < 1500

● 1500 < 2000

0   10 m

1:200

Macehead

Skewer pin

Polished pin

Flint fabricator

Flint Knife

Flint Flake

Cremation

Fig. 12.42   Dorchester-on-Thames Site II

(Whittle *et al.* 1992). Twenty-eight later cremation burials were found on Site 2 with two burnt bone pins and a burnt blade; antler from the primary fill of the ditch just to the north of the entrance provided a date of 2920-2630 cal BC (BM-4225N: 4230±50 BP). Six cremations were placed in the hollows resulting from the deliberate burning of the Site 3 posts (ibid., 169-75). Site XIV appeared to have had an inner bank or mound sealing a square posthole setting and a pit. Seventy marine shells came from the base of the ditch, and a fragmentary cremation deposit and a Group I (Cornish) stone axe from the upper fills.

It seems most probable that the cremations on Sites I, II, IV, V, VI, 2 and, possibly, XIV were broadly contemporary and were later in date than the sites within which they were placed (see below, Chapter 15). Very tentatively, they may belong to the early to mid 3rd millennium cal BC. Nevertheless, they do respect the final form of the earlier monuments which, although small in scale, must have remained visible. Two cremations within Site XI appear to have been contemporary with the inner pit circle and may, therefore, be earlier in date than the rest, whilst those in the Site 3 post circle may be slightly later in date (Whittle *et al.* 1992; table 12), although there may not have been a large interval of time

between the burning of the posts and the placing of the cremations on the site.

Avebury provides the focus for the most striking monument complex (Fig. 12.43). It was linked physically to the Beckhampton enclosure by the Beckhampton Avenue and to the Sanctuary by the West Kennet Avenue, both stone rows of considerable length with stones every 20-30 m, perhaps dating from *c* 2600-2300 cal BC (Pollard and Reynolds 2002, 100-5). Following a sinuous course, perhaps to create anticipation as people approach the major monuments (Barrett 1994, 13-20), or to follow a pre-existing pathway (Gillings *et al.* 2008, 201-2), they also provided a view of earlier monuments and features along the line. For example, the Beckhampton Avenue ran towards the Beckhampton long barrow, through the Beckhampton enclosure up to the Longstones Cove which was reconfigured at this time, and the West Kennet Avenue ran over an earlier midden or occupation site and near to Falkener's Circle, and respected and included natural sarsens (ibid.; Pollard and Reynolds 2002, 96-106). Stoneholes examined so far have yielded few finds, except for occasional deliberate deposits including human bone and stone axe fragments. To the west, the Beckhampton enclosure was an oval earthwork

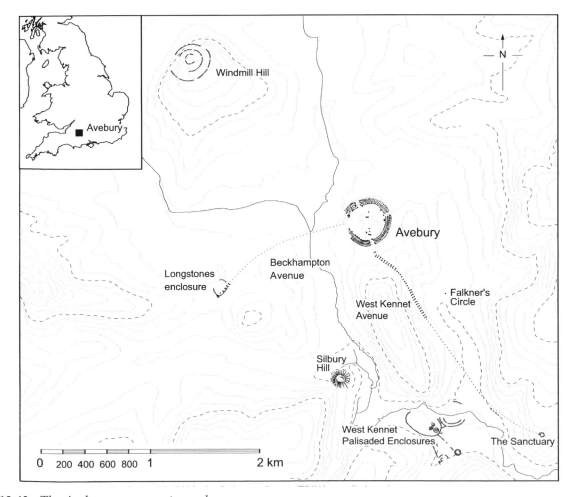

Fig. 12.43 The Avebury monument complex

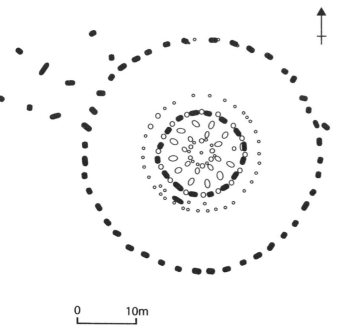

0   10m

Fig. 12.44   The Sanctuary

which had feasting debris deposited within its ditch, rather like a causewayed enclosure. Its date, however, is unequivocally mid 3rd millennium cal BC. The Sanctuary, on the other hand, lying to the south-east, was a complex circular monument with concentric timber and stone settings (Fig. 12.44). Deposits at this site suggested much meat consumption (cattle and pig) and flint working, including the production of arrowheads (Cunnington 1931; Pollard 1992; Pitts 2001).

Between the Beckhampton enclosure and the Sanctuary lay the West Kennet palisaded enclosures and Silbury Hill (Fig. 12.43). One of the West Kennet enclosures actually straddled the river Kennet, and the other, which was possibly slightly later but may have been in contemporary use, lay adjacent (Whittle 1997b). A huge number of unshaped oak trunks had been used in their construction and also in the smaller concentric palisade and post-ring structures and radial palisade lines that were found inside or linked to the second enclosure (ibid., fig. 28). Once more, quantities of animal bone were recovered, including deliberate deposits of articulated joints, many from right hand sides of animals, and the Grooved Ware pots were of types suitable for the cooking, serving and consumption of food. Specialised flintworking was also evidenced.

Silbury Hill, at 37 m high, is the tallest prehistoric mound in Europe. At least three separate phases of construction have been identified (Whittle 1997b),

though recent work has shown that it is a much more complex monument than was previously thought (Leary and Field in press). A new dating programme has shown that its first phase was constructed in the 24th or 23rd centuries cal BC, and it could either have been completed quite quickly after that or throughout the end of the 3rd millennium (Bayliss, McAvoy and Whittle 1997).

The greater similarity of the Avebury henge to those in Wessex, rather than those in the Upper Thames Valley, has already been discussed, and these parallels are reinforced by the character of the complexes that developed around these sites. These similarities lie not only in the monumental stone settings at Avebury, which may in part reflect the availability of local raw materials, but also the presence of large enclosures in which meat consumption and deposition played an important part. As we have seen, the Thames Valley henges are, with occasional exceptions such as the ditch terminals at the entrances to the Devil's Quoits, relatively clear of finds. Avenues of either stone or wood have not yet been discovered, and Silbury Hill is unique.

Monument complexes in the Middle Thames Valley are few, and their main structural elements date to the middle Neolithic period. The small Sonning complex, for example, comprises a cursus and what appears from the air to be a number of small funerary monuments (Slade 1963-4; Gates 1975; Lamdin-Whymark 2008, 152-4). The Eye and Dunsden causewayed enclosure lies 2 km away to the north of the river. The Stanwell bank barrow seems also to have provided the focus for the construction of small enclosures although it may post-date some of them (Lewis *et al.* 2006). Within the general area are a number of long and U-shaped enclosures, segmented ring ditches and oval barrows, such as those at Imperial College Sports Ground, Staines Road, Shepperton and Horton (Barclay *et al.* 2009; Jones 2008; Ford and Pine 2003). This is, however, a very dispersed distribution of monuments (Lamdin-Whymark 2008, fig. 53) with virtually no construction dating to the 3rd millennium. This contrast with adjacent areas to north and west, despite a shared material culture, is remarkable. In contrast, river deposition appears to increase in the Middle Thames at this time (see below; Lamdin-Whymark 2008), and Hugo Lamdin-Whymark suggests that this points to a distinct cultural identity in this part of the Thames corridor, perhaps indicating a more dispersed and egalitarian society where social relations were negotiated through portable artefacts rather than the construction and use of ceremonial monuments (ibid., 210-1).

Chapter 13 – Domesticating the landscape: settlement and agriculture in the early Bronze Age

by Gill Hey with Mark Robinson

During the course of the 2nd millennium cal BC, the Thames Valley was transformed into a landscape extensively cleared of trees, with small farmsteads, some associated with fields, paddocks and water-holes, a few larger and more organised settlements, and occasional high-status hilltop and valley enclosures, suggesting emerging settlement hierarchy (Fig. 13.1; Lambrick with Robinson 2009; and see below). There are no hints of these changes in the early part of the Bronze Age. At the end of the 3rd millennium, the valley was still largely wooded, and the environment was generally dry, with few waterlogged deposits, even on the floodplain. Occupation sites are rare, and although they appear to have been impermanent, the character of settlement remains difficult to define. As in the Neolithic, people seem to have been quite mobile, moving with their animals between woodland clearings.

In other aspects of life, however, there was considerable change at the beginning of the Bronze Age in the middle of the 3rd millennium. Metalworking was first introduced into this country, and gold, copper and bronze became available for prestige items like jewellery and weapons, as well as for tools (see Chapter 16). Pottery styles and methods of production changed, as did the methods of working and use of flint and stone tools. The consistent exploitation of high-quality raw materials to make portable, flexible tools gave way to a much more profligate use of stone and flint, suggesting that people utilised whatever raw materials came to hand (Edmonds 1999, 143-4). At the same time, a more varied range of flint implements was produced, including some very fine and carefully-made examples, probably for use in ritual and ceremonial contexts (see Chapter 16). Funerary practices also changed, as is marked particularly by the widespread burial of individuals with grave goods in graves often sealed beneath round barrows (see Chapters 14 and 15).

THE END OF THE NEOLITHIC, THE BEGINNING OF THE BRONZE AGE, AND THE BEAKER PHENOMENON

Archaeologists do not agree about what to call the transitional period at the end of the Neolithic and beginning of the early Bronze Age, and the terms late Neolithic/early Bronze Age, Chalcolithic, early Bronze Age and Beaker period are all used (M Allen *et al.* forthcoming). In the classic 'Three Age System', the Bronze Age denoted the period during which bronze became available and was worked. During

the course of the first half of the 20th century, it also came to be seen as a period when other important changes took place: many of the large Neolithic ceremonial monuments fell out of use, and individuals were buried beneath round barrows, sometimes accompanied by rich and exotic grave goods. These changes appeared to be correlated with a change in pottery styles and an intensification in agricultural activity. Discoveries and research over the last ten to fifteen years have shown that this was a very complex period, marked in some respects by rapid change, but in others by much more gradual evolution. The most dramatic changes, however, appear after the transition from the early to the middle Bronze Age (R Bradley 2007, 178-81).

Bronze objects are found in this country from around 2400 cal BC (Barber 2002; Needham 2005). The earliest dated items have been found in graves (and subsequently in hoards and river contexts; see Chapters 15 and 16), and their impact on day-to-day life may not, initially, have been great. This, and the unchanging character of settlement, has led to the use of the term late Neolithic/early Bronze Age to refer to this period. On the other hand, it may be wrong to underestimate the speed with which metal made a wider impact. There is evidence from Ireland, at Corlea, County Longford, that wood used in a trackway across a bog had been worked with metal tools at around 2270-2250 cal BC (O'Sullivan 1996; Prior 2004, 266). Given the paucity of waterlogged environments in the Thames Valley before *c* 1700 cal BC, by which time bronze tools were certainly being used to fashion wooden objects (Taylor in prep.), it is impossible to rule out the possibility that their use may have been widespread before this date. The correlation between changing flint and stone tool technologies, and the adoption and availability of bronze tools may not be coincidental.

Bronze was not, however, the earliest metal in use. Around 100 or 200 years earlier, gold and copper items were placed in the earliest Beaker burials. On the Continent this phase of copper use is of much longer duration and is often referred to as the Chalcolithic (from the Greek for copper and stone). The addition of tin (mined in south-west England) to copper produces the stronger, more durable and gold-like metal bronze, and, once discovered, its manufacture rapidly replaced that of copper. Some people have advocated the use of the term Chalcolithic in Britain in order to identify the metal-using period prior to the widespread adoption of bronze as distinct and different. However, this brief period can only be identified in some early burials, and not in other kinds of evidence, such as those related to occupation sites, the development of the landscape and land use, or, indeed, to most ritual activity. Thus, until and unless our dating becomes much more precise, its application has limited utility (see papers in M Allen *et al.* forthcoming for both sides of this argument). In this volume, we have generally used the term 'early Bronze Age' to describe this period. Where it is not possible to distinguish between late Neolithic and early Bronze Age material, as is the case, for example, in flintwork, the term late Neolithic/early Bronze Age has been used.

The arrival of metalworking is inextricably linked to the introduction of Beaker pottery and the exotic paraphernalia that is found in Beaker graves. Weaponry and archery equipment feature prominently: flat axes, daggers, knives, barbed and tanged arrowheads and stone wristguards. Personal ornaments are also an important and early feature of

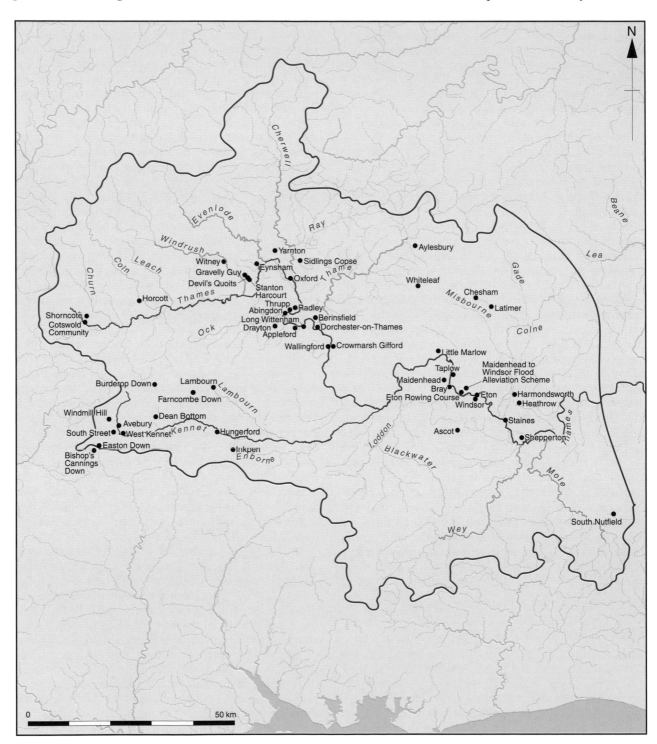

Fig. 13.1   Location of Beaker period and early Bronze Age sites discussed in Chapter 13

the 'Beaker package': rings, earrings, hair rings and neck rings or diadems, along with pins and awls (Burgess and Shennan 1976; Case 2004a; Needham 2005; see Chapters 15 and 16). In the cultural archaeology of the first half of the 20th century, this material was seen as having been brought by and buried with 'Beaker Folk' who arrived from the Continent, either from the west Atlantic seaboard or northern France and the Low Countries. Although invasion hypotheses began to be questioned by the 1960s, the idea that large numbers of Beaker people arrived in the early Bronze Age remained remarkably persistent (Clark 1966; and see R Bradley 2007, 142-58 for a clear and up-to-date account). Folk movement theories had, however, fallen from favour by the 1970s, being replaced by the idea of a Beaker network (Clarke 1976b), and the adoption by indigenous populations of attractive objects, perhaps associated with new belief systems (Burgess and Shennan 1976; Case 2004b). Those able to obtain these novel items formed a new elite, based on personal prestige, warfare and hunting, which was able to pose a challenge to traditional authority. Individuals became rich and powerful, as is reflected in the material placed in their graves, and the community-based projects of the late Neolithic, represented by large ceremonial monuments, were appropriated by a few. The difficulties posed by interpreting grave assemblages in this way are discussed in Chapters 14 and 15.

New advances in scientific techniques for analysing human remains have shown that there were undoubtedly some incomers from the Continent at the beginning of the Bronze Age, as is demonstrated by the Amesbury Archer who was brought up in central Europe, and was buried, accompanied by exceptionally fine grave goods, near Stonehenge very early in the Bronze Age (Fitzpatrick 2003). There was certainly exchange of material in this period, with exotic goods being both exported and imported (Needham 2000b; 2005; 2007). It may have been the renown of the big henge sites that attracted people from afar. Perhaps more significantly, the construction, use and elaboration of such monuments may have provided the mechanism through which some people gained pre-eminent positions in society, as leaders and custodians of knowledge (Barrett 1994, 24-9 and chap. 4). An emerging elite may have tried to reinforce their position by acquiring both new kinds of objects made of unfamiliar materials, and the specialists who made them (Needham 2000b; R Bradley 2007, 153-8). The exchange of goods and, perhaps, of marriage partners, in this way would have encouraged interaction and created alliances with people on the Continent. It is now certain that there was some movement of people, and it has been suggested that the danger of travel, the acquisition of exotic items and knowledge of remote places would have conferred prestige on the voyager (Helms 1998). However, whether large numbers of people came to, and settled in, this country remains to be proved.

Beaker pottery was not only used in funerary contexts and on ceremonial sites but also in domestic situations where it is found in both a more coarse and robust fabric and as fineware (Gibson 1982; Boast 1995; see Chapter 16). It replaced Grooved Ware, though whether there was a period when both styles were in use, or whether there were specific contexts in which Grooved Ware continued to be employed when it was no longer in common currency, remains uncertain (Garwood 1999a, 159-62; Barclay 1999b, 15). Because of the shape of the radiocarbon calibration curve in this period, calibrated radiocarbon dates have particularly large error terms, and, as a result, this question will be difficult to resolve. Certainly, Beaker pottery was being used by around 2400 cal BC, and there are no convincing Grooved Ware dates in the 2nd millennium cal BC. By around 1800 cal BC, Biconical Urn and Collared Urn pottery was in general use in the Thames Valley.

Both the round barrows and flat graves associated with Beakers represented a break with the funerary traditions of the late Neolithic, although both had been in use in the 4th millennium (see Chapters 12 and 14). Round barrows became important features of the early Bronze Age landscape, including a few, such as that which contained the rich Wessex Culture burial at Stanton Harcourt (Harden and Treweeks 1945), of considerable size, as well as a range of smaller monuments of diverse forms (bell barrows, disc barrows, pond barrows etc, although often they are preserved only as ring ditches; Fig. 13.2; Barrett 1990; Garwood 2007a).

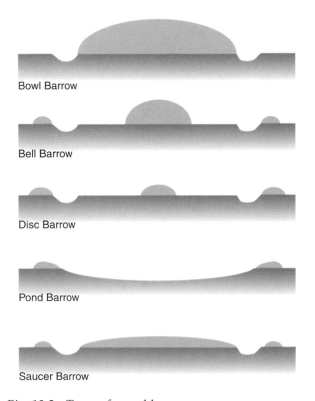

Bowl Barrow

Bell Barrow

Disc Barrow

Pond Barrow

Saucer Barrow

Fig. 13.2   Types of round barrows

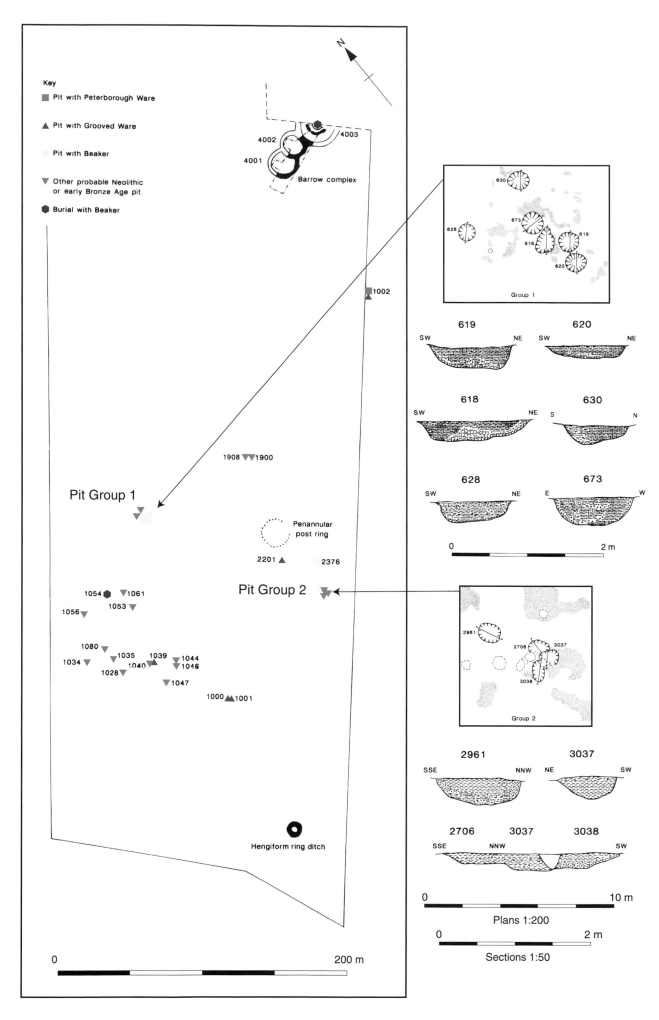

Key

■ Pit with Peterborough Ware

▲ Pit with Grooved Ware

○ Pit with Beaker

▼ Other probable Neolithic or early Bronze Age pit

⬢ Burial with Beaker

Barrow complex

4002   4003
4001

N

■▲ 1002

1908 ▼▼ 1900

Pit Group 1
▼

Penannular
post ring

2201 ▲   2376

1054 ⬢ ▼ 1061
1056 ▼   1053 ▼

1080 ▼
1034 ▼   ▼ 1035   1039   ▼ 1044
1028 ▼   1040 ▼   ▼   ▼ 1016
▼ 1047

1000 ▲▲ 1001

Pit Group 2 ▼▼

Hengiform ring ditch

0   200 m

Group 1

630
628   673   619
618
620

619   620
SW   NE   SW   NE

618   630
SW   NE   S   N

628   673
SW   NE   E   W

0   2 m

Group 2

2961   2706   3037
3038

2961   3037
SSE   NNW   NE   SW

2706   3037   3038
SSE   NNW   SW

0   10 m

Plans 1:200

0   2 m

Sections 1:50

314

From the beginning of the Bronze Age, both inhumations and cremations occur as primary burials although cremations are less common. Barrows also, however, formed the focus for secondary burials, again consisting of both inhumations and cremation burials, which were placed both within and around the barrow. These developments, and the way in which Beaker and early Bronze Age burial practices functioned within their wider social, cultural and ritual context, are considered in more detail in Chapters 14 and 15.

SETTLEMENT AT THE BEGINNING OF THE BRONZE AGE

There is great variety in the type and scale of early Bronze Age sites, which range from large communal gathering places and ceremonial sites to short-term, task-specific activity areas. The different landscape contexts in which assemblages are found indicates extensive use of the diverse resource niches of the Thames Valley (Brück 1999a, 65-6). Brück has suggested that there was considerable fluidity in the membership of co-resident groups (Brück 2000, 281-5). The slight evidence of early Bronze Age domestic settlement we have, however, is represented, as in the later Neolithic, by scatters of surface finds and occasional postholes and pits. Clusters of flint, which can only be categorised as generally late Neolithic/early Bronze Age, are found quite extensively in the valley, and this provides what is probably the best indication of the wide spread of habitation at this time.

Early Bronze Age pits, which are often found in small groups of two or three, sometimes include deposits which seem to have been deliberately placed. It has been claimed that distinguishing such sites from those of ritual character is difficult, partly because this distinction is a modern concept and not one that would have been made in the past (Brück 1999b). Nevertheless, these sites usually lie apart from ceremonial monuments, and the material evidence suggests day-to-day activity. If they do represent ritual activity, it was ritual as a practice or performance taking place in the context of daily life (Bradley 2003, 12). The selection of particular items and their structured deposition in special contexts may mark the formal beginning or end of episodes of occupation or other important events in family life (Evans *et al.* 1999; Hey *et al.* 2003).

Gravelly Guy provides a good example of early Bronze Age domestic activity in the Upper Thames Valley (Lambrick and Allen 2004). There, 1 km north-west of the Devil's Quoits henge, scatters of mainly Beaker and late Neolithic/early Bronze Age pits were found over an area of *c* 4 ha, including two quite well-defined groups (Fig. 13.3; Lambrick *et al.* 2004). Struck flints and occasional pot sherds were also retrieved from overlying soils and later

Fig. 13.3 (opposite) Beaker pits at Gravelly Guy

features. Some pits, like pit 2961, were richer in finds than the others, with sherds from five or six rusticated Beakers, and a range of retouched flint tools including knives and a barbed and tanged arrowhead as well as debitage, and the bones of two piglets (ibid., 43). Generally, however, the pits contained small amounts of mundane material, the residues of everyday life, with no indication that the finds had been deliberately placed. The distribution of features and the character of their contents suggest extensive, episodic occupation which, the environmental evidence indicates, lay in grassland at the forest margins. In common with Neolithic assemblages, the charred plant remains were mainly of hazelnut shells, although there were also a few wheat and barley seeds and weed seeds from disturbed ground (Moffett 2004, 422-8).

Similar, though less concentrated evidence has come from further up the Thames Valley at Horcott, near Fairford, where four pits containing Beaker pottery, flint and burnt stone in a charcoal-rich mix (similar to the Neolithic pits in this area) were found (Pine and Preston 2004, 5; Lamdin-Whymark *et al.* forthcoming). A scatter of Beaker sherds over the site, some within tree-throw holes, may represent an episode of woodland clearance. The pattern is repeated further down the valley at Drayton (Barclay *et al.* 2003, 89) and in the Wallingford area near Duxford and at Crowmarsh Gifford, for example (Barber and Bateman 2003; Ford *et al.* 2006). One isolated pit at Drayton, to the south-west of the North Cursus was associated with fine, Wessex Middle Rhine Beaker, but the other seven pits which lay in two groups to the west of the cursus contained a wide range of more typical domestic material.

More intensive activity seems to be represented at Cotswold Community, near Cirencester (Powell *et al.* 2010). At least 30 pits which contained Beaker pottery and assemblages of contemporary flintwork were found, mainly in the south of the area excavated (ibid., 20-2). Some pits were isolated, but pairs and groups of three pits were common, and these contained a range of artefacts which were thought to indicate single occupation events (ibid., 30). One of the pits in a group of three near the southern edge of the site contained a multipurpose stone tool used as a hammerstone and polisher, over 20 flint flakes, eight scrapers, four knives, including an exceptional plano-convex example, two arrowheads, a core, a piercer and a notch, as well as Beaker pottery (Fig. 13.4). An adjacent pit yielded a Neolithic polished stone axe of Cornish origin, presumed to be an heirloom or a prehistoric discovery which had been prized. Another pit, in a different cluster of three, contained a human long bone shaft and small fragments of human skull. The associated environmental evidence indicates clearings amongst woodland.

The picture of a generally wooded landscape with patches of clearance, as at Gravelly Guy and Cotswold Community, seems typical of the Upper Thames Valley at this time. Similar evidence was

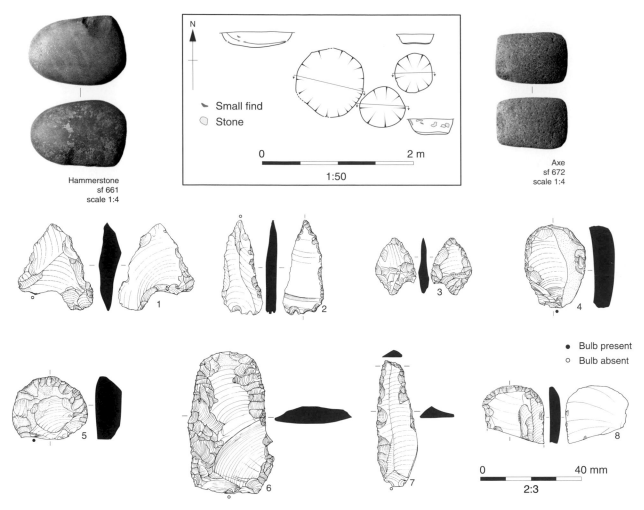

Fig. 13.4   Early Bronze Age pits at Cotswold Community

found at Yarnton and Drayton. At Sidlings Copse on Otmoor, as on the floodplain of the Lower Windrush Valley, however, there is no sign of clearance in the 3rd millennium (Allen and Robinson 1993; Day 1991). That is not to say that the valley was entirely wooded. There were extensive cleared areas around certain ceremonial and burial complexes, some of which were long lived, including, for example, the areas around the Devil's Quoits henge monument (Evans 1995) and at Dorchester-on-Thames, but particularly around the Abingdon/Barrow Hills complex which was clear from the early Neolithic up to the beginning of the Bronze Age (Parker 1999). It is evident from Holgate and Hingley's fieldwalking data, and from chance discoveries during the course of development and gravel extraction, that there continued to be quite dense settlement in the area around the causewayed enclosure and between it and the Drayton Cursus (Fig. 11.25; Holgate 1988a). Pit digging, however, usually occurred away from barrows and barrow cemeteries, perhaps running up to them but not encroaching upon them (Barclay et al., 1996; Barclay et al. 2003, 89). Only one Beaker pit was found at at Barrow Hills, Radley despite

extensive excavation in the area (Barclay and Halpin 1999, 66-7 and 320).

There is also evidence that during the early Bronze Age people continued to use many monuments first constructed in the later Neolithic, and particularly henges. Beaker-period finds were recovered from the Dorchester Big Rings henge, for example (Whittle et al. 1992, 190-1), and from the Devil's Quoits (A J Barclay et al. 1995, 20-3). The larger henge monuments had the capacity to accommodate quite large numbers of people, and the permanently-grazed grassland that encircled them suggests that substantial herds were gathered there on a fairly regular basis. There is, however, no evidence of pressure on land and resources in other parts of the landscape; monument complexes were the exceptions rather than the norm. In general, the population appears to have been relatively small, and their efforts were invested in communal, ceremonial monuments, perhaps reflecting large community or kin groups, and not in settlements and activities at a household level (Barrett 1994, chap 6; Brück 1999a, 64). In this respect, the evidence from the earliest Bronze Age of the Upper Thames Valley is very similar to that of the late Neolithic.

Settlement in the Upper Kennet Valley in the late 3rd millennium seems, similarly, to have been intermittent and semipermanent (Pollard and Reynolds 2002, 136-7). Surface finds and pits discovered on the southern slopes of Windmill Hill (Whittle *et al.* 1999, 371-80) probably represent such activity, as do finds associated with at least seven pits found below the Avebury G55 barrow (ibid.; Smith 1965b, 37-40). There is, however, evidence for clearance in the wider landscape (Evans *et al.* 1993) – at Easton Down, for example (Whittle *et al.* 1993, 232; and see below) – and for the expansion of settlement onto downland to the south and east. Further hints of more intensive use of the landscape are represented in the Kennet Valley by ploughmarks (associated with Beaker pottery) cutting into upper ditch fills at the South Street long barrow (Ashbee *et al.* 1979, 289), and evidence for increased alluviation in the valley bottom (Evans *et al.* 1993). The burial of material and human remains in the henge ditch, and the erection of some stone settings, show that use of the Avebury henge continued. Some Beaker burials were also placed at the foot of earlier stone uprights.

Beaker occupation is also widespread on the adjacent Marlborough Downs (Gingell 1992), suggesting exploitation of new land (Pollard and Reynolds 2002, 136). Nevertheless, settlement appears to have been short-lived, and no evidence of structures has been found (Cleal 1992a, 152-3). Habitation at Dean Bottom, for example, was represented by a scatter of Beaker sherds, a pit, a scoop and a posthole. The pit appeared to have been backfilled from a midden, and contained the remains of at least 20 decorated and plain Beaker vessels, a range of worked bone objects and a scraper-dominated flint assemblage (Gingell 1992, 27; Cleal 1992b, 62-7; Cleal 1992c). The environmental evidence suggested recent woodland clearance, the grazing of sheep and cattle, and, probably, some cereal cultivation (Allen 1992, 146). A scatter of Beaker sherds and a barbed and tanged arrowhead from Bishops Cannings Down, and Beaker pottery from Burderop Down suggest similar transitory use of these sites (Gingell 1992). In the case of Burderop Down, the pottery came (with early and middle Neolithic material) from what appears to be a ploughsoil manured with material from a midden which was subsequently sealed beneath the bank of a disc barrow (ibid., 54-5).

The general impression given by this evidence is of more extensive use of at least the Upper Thames and Kennet Valleys and adjacent areas, with greater land clearance, and hints of more intensive agriculture (see below).

There is much less evidence for late 3rd millennium settlement activity in the middle Kennet Valley and on the Berkshire Downs, though some sites are known. These include the Beaker found inside a four-legged bowl in pit near Inkpen, Berkshire, just to the south of Hungerford in the 1930s (Peake 1936). Sherds from more than 20

Beaker vessels were found beneath the Farncombe Down barrow, with small flint knives and scrapers, fragments of animal bone and charcoal suggesting settlement here before the barrow was built (Rahtz 1962). Molluscs in the buried ground surface indicated a grassland environment interspersed with scrub.

Evidence of earliest Bronze Age activity in the Middle Thames and on the Chilterns is also scarce, continuing a trend observed towards the end of the late Neolithic. At Whiteleaf in the Chilterns, although no features of early Bronze Age date were found, flint nodules seem to have been collected and tested, with initial preparation taking place (Hey *et al.* 2007). In most parts of the Middle Thames Valley, sites with Neolithic pits and small funerary monuments were usually succeeded by middle or late Bronze Age field systems, as witnessed, for example, at Ashford Prison, Middlesex (Carew *et al.* 2006) and Reading Business Park (Moore and Jennings 1992; Brossler *et al.* 2004). Beaker funerary evidence is as rare as that of settlement (see Chapter 15), but whether this reflects people making different cultural choices or limited use of the valley is uncertain. More material has come to light during development projects in recent years, such as the very occasional Beaker sherds and diagnostic flints which came from later features at Heathrow (Lewis *et al.* 2006, 36) and Beaker pot and struck flint found on the Thames floodplain, at, for example, the Eton Rowing Course and along the Maidenhead, Windsor and Eton flood alleviation scheme (T G Allen *et al.* forthcoming), as well as on sites overlooking the headwaters of tributary streams such as the Hogsmill and Wandle (Cotton 2004, 26; Cotton *et al.* 2006, 163). A radiocarbon date on hazelnut shell of 2580-2340 cal BC (SUERC-9149: 3975±35 BP) and Beaker sherds from two of the pits at Chessvale Bowling club, Chesham indicate activity in the very late Neolithic or earliest Bronze Age (Halsted 2008). Further evidence for activity in this period is provided by an aurochs burial comprising a dismembered aurochs with six barbed and tanged arrowheads which was found at Holloway Lane, Harmondsworth (Fig. 14.33; Cotton *et al.* 2006, 153-4; see Chapter 14).

BRONZE AGE SETTLEMENT IN THE EARLY 2ND MILLENNIUM CAL BC

A similar pattern of settlement appears to have existed in the early 2nd millennium cal BC, with habitation represented by small groups of pits, and continuity of use of sites such as Yarnton, Drayton and Avebury which had seen recurrent episodes of earlier occupation (Hey in prep.; Barclay *et al.* 2003; Pollard and Reynolds 2002, 136-7). However, early Bronze Age sites seem particularly difficult to find; there was, for example, only one certain pit with Collared Urn and one with possible Biconical Urn at Drayton (Barclay *et al.* 2003, 24). Presumably, some sites of this date are present amongst late Neolithic/

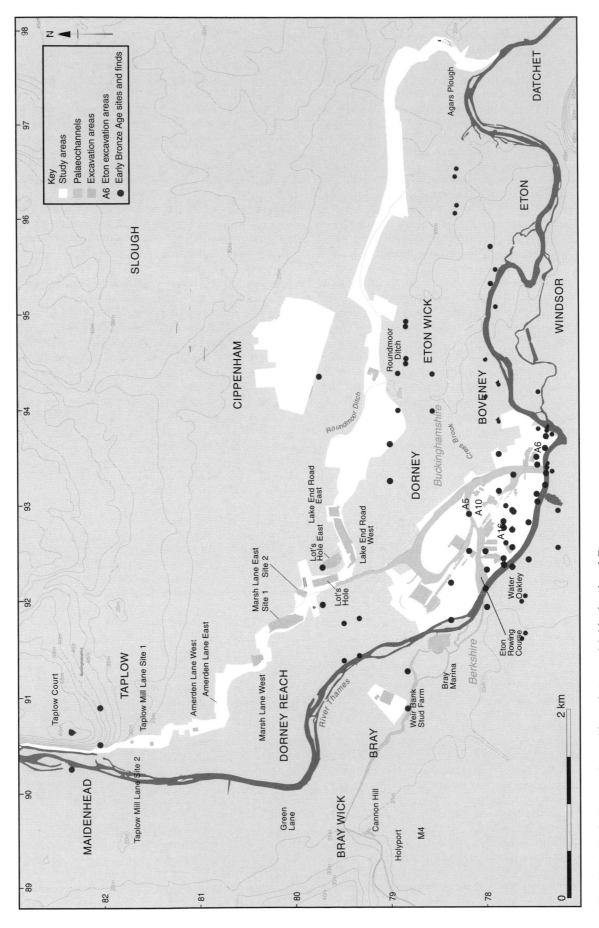

Fig. 13.5 Early Bronze Age evidence between Maidenhead and Eton

early Bronze Age flint scatters, but it is only occasionally possible to identify those of specifically early Bronze Age date, like that at Brockhurst Farm, Latimer on the river Chess in Buckinghamshire (Biddulph 2006).

In the Upper Thames Valley, pits of early Bronze Age date have been found at sites without previous evidence of activity, such as Downs Road, Witney (Colls 2002). A complex of early Bronze Age pits, one with sherds of Collared Urn, was found at Walton Lodge Lane, near Aylesbury (Bonner 1994; Biddulph 2006). At Thames Valley Park, Reading, 26 sherds of unclassified early Bronze Age pottery and 12 flint flakes were recovered (Barnes *et al*. 1997), and early Bronze Age deposits were also found at Charnham Lane, Hungerford near to a pit circle (Ford 2002).

Evidence of early 2nd millennium cal BC non-funerary activity has also come to light recently in the Middle Thames Valley (Fig. 13.5). Excavations at Taplow Court, on a spur of the Burnham Plateau overlooking the Thames (Fig. 13.6), revealed hollows containing sherds of Collared Urn with worked flint, fired clay, charred wheat and barley grains and wood charcoal from a range of species, perhaps indicating settlement at the forest edge (Fig. 13.7; Allen *et al*. 2009). The intercutting character of these features suggests some duration of use of the site, although each had similar contents. A range of flint tools seems to have been made, and the predominance of scrapers and the presence of an awl may

suggest that hide preparation was one of the activities that took place. The fired clay could have come from hearths. On the valley floor, for example, around 1 km away and further downstream along the Maidenhead, Windsor and Eton Flood Alleviation Scheme and at the Eton Rowing Course, sherds of Collared Urn have been found amongst lithic scatters and associated with hearths (Allen *et al*. 2004, 98), and there is some evidence for increasing woodland clearance (Parker and Robinson 2003, 56).

Very limited evidence of settlement, represented only by flint scatters and a small amount of metalwork, has come from the Weald on the southern fringes of our area. A decorated axe was found in the Weald clay at South Nutfield near Redhill (Cotton and Williams 1997, axe B), and a few other small flat axes have been found since (Bird and Bird 1987), but no other early Bronze Age metalwork has been recovered (Cotton 2004, 27).

The spread and position of Bronze Age barrows across the valley could be another way of assessing the extent and distribution of settlement. Case suggested that the distribution of Beaker burials, whether under small mounds or unmarked, and whether found in small clusters or as more scattered graves, reflected the extent of settlement, and indicated a continued infilling of the landscape (Case 1986, 32-4); the burials often correlated with surface finds scatters. He also proposed a link between areas of grazing, ring ditches and

Fig. 13.6   Aerial view of Taplow Court

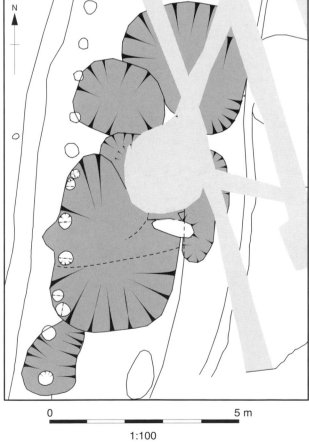

Modern features

Early Bronze Age hollows

Fig. 13.7   Early Bronze Age hollows at Taplow Court

the evidence of the long-term use of some cemeteries (Case 1963). Bronze Age barrows do seem most likely to have been constructed in or near to areas of settlement, and it has been suggested that individual monuments and small barrow groups may be the cemeteries of individual communities throughout the early Bronze Age (R Bradley 2007, 168-9). Their distribution certainly suggests that this may have been the case. The larger barrow cemeteries, which tended to attract exotic later monuments, may have had a less local emphasis. Even here, however, worked flint scatters suggest a greater intensity of domestic activity in the areas around the barrows – as is evidenced, for example, at Barrow Hills, Radley, and the Lambourn barrow cemetery (Richards 1978; Gaffney and Tingle 1989; Bradley forth-coming) – than occurred elsewhere.

Surrey has a good number of round barrows, suggesting that settlement in this area was more extensive than is indicated by the evidence from occupation sites. The barrows are often found on the heathlands, and it has been claimed that heathland was created by the expansion of farming into this area in the Bronze Age (Bird 2006). The bell barrow at Ascot, Berkshire, however, was constructed on a buried surface which had seen previous human interference, culminating in cereal cultivation (Bradley and Fraser 2010; Bradley and Keith-Lucas 1975). Charcoal from this surface provided a radiocarbon date of 1920-1530 cal BC (HAR-478: 3430±70 BP). The mound was built of turves, some of which may have been stripped from the site prior to construction, so it is possible that grassland had already developed above the ploughing horizon.

On the Chalk of Wessex and the South Downs, some of best preserved Beaker/early Bronze Age settlement evidence has been found beneath hillwash in valley bottoms (M Allen 2005), and it is possible that occupation sites in the Upper Kennet Valley, the Chilterns and the North Downs may lie hidden in similar locations. Settlement may similarly exist on river floodplains buried beneath alluvium. At the Eton Rowing Course in the Middle Thames, only one early Bronze Age pit was found but, as has already been mentioned, there were numerous early Bronze Age lithic clusters on the floodplain, often associated with hearths, and sometimes intermingled with spreads of domestic pottery, both Beaker and Collared Urn (Allen *et al.* 2004, 97-8). At Yarnton in the Upper Thames, the floodplain was preferentially occupied at this period rather than the nearby gravel terraces, although these were where round barrows were sited. Round barrows are quite commonly found in terrace-edge locations in the Upper Thames, and it has been suggested that, if settlement was often on the floodplain, this position would have given the barrows an impressive appearance on the sky line from contemporary domestic sites (Barclay *et al.* 1996).

EVIDENCE FOR CHANGE IN EARLY BRONZE AGE SETTLEMENT

Settlement in the early Bronze Age may have been as transitory as that of the Neolithic, but there are indications of change in the character of domestic activity and in the use of the landscape over this period. One place which had been the focus of repeated occupation events since the early Neolithic was the floodplain at Yarnton where both individual and small groups of Beaker and early Bronze Age pits, postholes and other features were discovered on several sites over an area of around 100 ha (Hey in prep.).

There seem to have been particular foci of activity in each period, but these changed over time, and new areas of the floodplain were brought into use in the 2nd millennium which had not seen activity before; presumably they had previously been wooded (Fig. 13.8). There were similar numbers of pits in each phase, and placed deposits were found in a number of these, but, whereas nearly all the Beaker pits contained rich deposits of material, this was true of only a few of early Bronze Age (2nd millennium cal BC) date which seem to have been used for a range of other purposes. However, what distinguishes features with Beaker material from those of both the late Neolithic and the early 2nd millennium is their frequent association with funerary and ritual activity. This includes the burial of six individuals in flat graves and one neonate in a finds-rich pit. Four of these burials and several of the pits lay adjacent to early Neolithic monuments which seem to have retained (or regained) their significance; one male was buried with a pair of Beakers and barbed and tanged arrowheads. In addition, a ring ditch, a penannular ditch with internal burnt deposits, a small three-sided enclosure with a pit, and a pit alignment (one pit in which contained a human cremation burial) were constructed. This suggests greater use of domestic areas for small-scale, formal ceremonies and for the burial of the dead. The presence of ring ditches nearby may indicate the continuity of this pattern into the early 2nd millennium, and that family groups began to focus on, and invest more effort in, places in the landscape that were becoming associated with them (Hey in prep.).

Small signs that more time was being spent at Yarnton include the presence of a house, built sometime in the first two centuries of the 2nd millennium cal BC. It was circular in shape with a ring beam 4 m in diameter, and an entrance porch, suggesting a building with an outer wall 5 m in diameter (Fig. 13.9; Hey in prep.). Biconical Urn was found in the entrance posts. A group of five small, circular post-built structures 400 m to the west may also date from the early Bronze Age, but their chronology is more uncertain. Small pits, postholes and fencelines lay around these structures.

Evidence of intensification of settlement on the Marlborough Downs in the earliest Bronze Age has been discussed above, and the evidence suggests

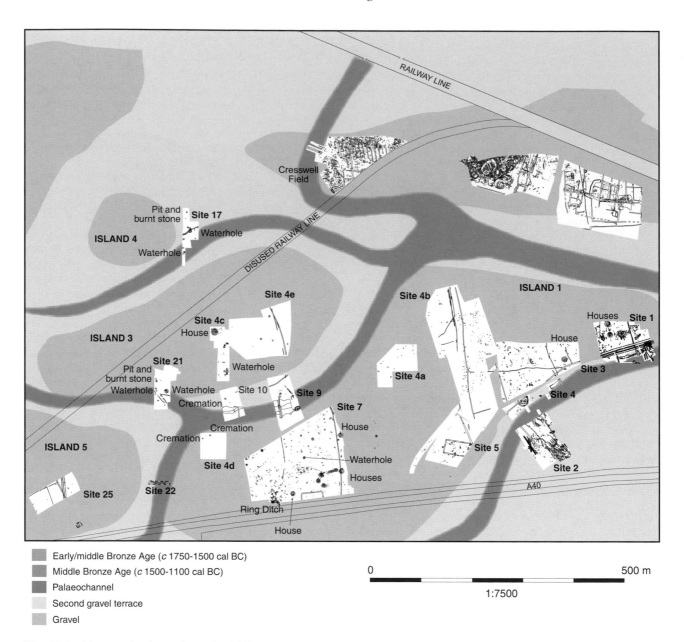

Legend:
- Early/middle Bronze Age (*c* 1750-1500 cal BC)
- Middle Bronze Age (*c* 1500-1100 cal BC)
- Palaeochannel
- Second gravel terrace
- Gravel

0   500 m
1:7500

Fig. 13.8 Yarnton in the early and middle Bronze Age

that, as at Yarnton, this continued in the 2nd millennium (Gingell 1992, 7-14). The Bishops Cannings Down settlement, which comprised two successive houses and other structures, seems to have belonged to the very end of the early Bronze Age or the beginning of the middle Bronze Age. The similarity in the layout, if not size, of these houses to that excavated at Yarnton is worth noting (ibid., fig. 3); a number of middle Bronze Age houses have similar forms (Brück 2000). Otherwise, no early Bronze Age structures have been found in the Thames Valley and its catchment.

The practice of burning wood, wood charcoal and stone near to water sources, leaving what are often called 'burnt mounds', first appears in the early Bronze Age (if not earlier). At Yarnton, such burnt mounds usually consisted of spreads of burnt stone and charcoal on the edges of small seasonal

water courses. They appear to lie apart from areas of domestic activity. Similar burnt material also accumulated in hollows, tree-throw holes and pits (Fig. 13.8; Hey in prep.). Some spreads could date from as early as the late Neolithic, but they can only be more definitely dated to the Beaker period. They seem to have become more widespread over time, and more clearly associated with dug features, including waterholes.

Burnt mounds are found across Britain and, although not especially common, they are found elsewhere in the Thames Valley in the early Bronze Age. Two pits filled with burnt flint and an adjacent waterhole were excavated at Ashford Hospital. Unidentified charcoal from one pit gave dates of 1970-1520 and 2030-1520 cal BC (Beta-193984: 3450±90 BP; Beta-195870: 3460±100 BP; Cowie 2008). A particularly early example was found at a stream-

Fig. 13.9   The early Bronze Age house at Yarnton

side site at Little Marlow, Buckinghamshire, where three separate spreads of black earth and fire-shattered flint, which seemed to represent separate phases of activity, albeit of a similar kind, were uncovered (Fig. 13.10; Richmond *et al.* 2006). A possible trough-like feature and other pits and gullies were associated with the spreads, one of which appears to be middle Bronze Age in date. The other two spreads, lying on the south side of the stream, are earlier, with one sample of unidentified charcoal from each dating to 2480-2140 cal BC and 2140-1920 cal BC (Beta-130863: 3860±60 BP; Beta-130864: 3660±40 BP). If the charcoal was contemporary with the burnt mounds, these results provide our earliest evidence for such activity in the Middle and Upper Thames Valley. Collared Urn sherds found in association with the later spread may indicate that the charcoal was from older trees; a rubbing stone and flint objects, possibly weights, were also found. Evidence for the contemporaneous environment from a variety of sources, including pollen from peat between the deposits and the stream, showed no human impact on the woodland environment, despite the obviously extensive burning of wood (ibid., 86-93).

The type of activity which generated burnt mounds remains a subject of debate (see papers in Buckley 1990). They have been compared to Irish *fulachtaí fiadh*, which have been thought to be associated with cooking. Experiments have shown that heating stones and casting them into a trough is a very effective means of bringing liquids to the boil and cooking joints of meat (O'Drisceoil 1988). The difficulty with this interpretation for deposits in this country, and particular for those in the Thames Valley, is the absence of any signs of feasting, or, indeed, of food remains of any sort. At Little Marlow, for example, there was no animal bone, and only one wheat seed, one hazelnut shell and a fragment of sloe or blackthorn. In this context, the authors questioned the use of the site for cooking and feasting and, following Barfield and Hodder (1987), suggested instead ritual bathing as an activity undertaken episodically at a favoured location (Richmond *et al.* 2006, 94). Some kind of craft process, such as soaking and steaming hides, is also possible.

As has already been mentioned, waterholes are associated with burnt stone spreads at some Thames Valley sites. At Yarnton, the earliest examples were dug in the beds of water channels, presumably to tap water when the channels were dry. Although they may have been dug in order to provide water for steaming or cooking (perhaps associated with burnt mounds), it seems more likely that their main purpose was to provide a ready and reliable source of water for cattle which were increasingly being herded in one place for longer periods of time. They are another indication that people were investing more time and effort in their domestic landscape, and they are an increasingly common feature of Bronze Age sites in the Thames Valley (see below). They also provide the environment for the survival of our earliest wooden artefacts, including a wooden bowl, a weaving sword, a birch bark container and an alder log

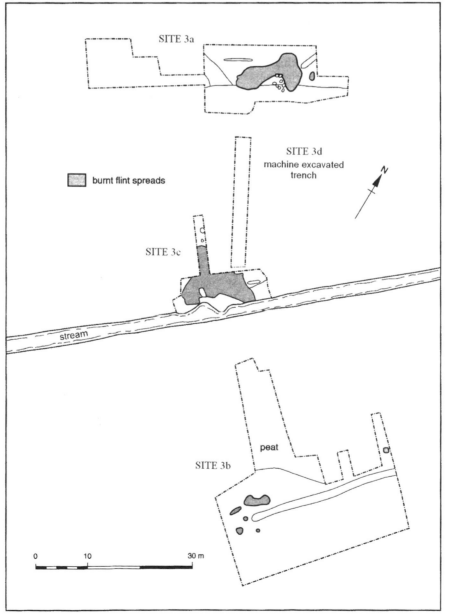

ladder (Fig. 16.13; Taylor in prep.). It is also from this period that we acquire waterlogged deposits which provide important evidence for the surrounding landscape. At Yarnton, by the second quarter of the second millennium cal BC, two water-holes provide evidence of a more open grassland flora than is evidenced in earlier periods, although trees and shrubs still represent 55% of the pollen. By the 15th century cal BC, this had dropped to *c* 6%-12% (Hey in prep.).

LANDSCAPE, LAND USE AND FARMING

Clearance occurred for the first time in the early Bronze Age in some places such as Sidlings Copse in the Upper Thames (Day 1991), and in some parts of the Lower Colne Valley, as at Moor Farm, Staines (Keith-Lucas 2000). Beaker period clearance is also suggested by the evidence from the side ditches at South Street long barrow (Ashbee *et al.* 1979, 289), and at Easton Down, radiocarbon dating suggests the clearance of secondary woodland at 2480-2140 cal BC (OxA-3761: 3860 ±60 BP; Whittle *et al.* 1993, 232). An early Bronze Age pond at Staines Road Farm, Shepperton, in a clearing on the gravels of the river Ash, a tributary of the Middle Thames, showed that provision was made for the watering of domestic animals. The Coleoptera, which were from sediments dated to 2280-1750 cal BC (GU-5278: 3630±90 BP, confirmed the presence of domestic animals (Robinson in Jones 2008), and other environmental evidence, and the general rarity of ploughsoils, suggest that clearances were mainly used for grazing animals (see below).

Cattle continued to be the main animal reared (Robinson and Wilson 1987; Mulville in prep.). The only new species of domestic animal to be confirmed is horse. The date of horse bones from Yarnton is not certain, as their context on a buried ground surface was not secure (Hey *et al.* 2003, 82), but horse bone was identified amongst human bone

in a Beaker cremation from Barrow Hills (Harman in Barclay *et al.* 2003, 59).

The Beaker-period animal bone assemblages from the Upper Thames Valley sites of The Hamel Oxford, Thrupp and, Mount Farm, Berinsfield were, unfortunately, very small (Robinson and Wilson 1987, 35). The range of variation for these sites is shown in Table 13.1. The relative importance of sheep continued to increase in this period, as it had since the early Neolithic. The relative proportion of sheep/goat bones in relation to cattle bones in a range of samples from these and other sites was: earlier Neolithic 14% sheep/goat; later Neolithic 34% sheep/goat; and Beaker 46% sheep/goat (ibid.). This pattern is repeated at Yarnton (Mulville in prep.). As sheep favour grassland and not woodland, the results suggest a slow increase in grassland, rather than the regeneration of woodland. Woodland resources continued to be of importance in the Beaker period, however, and there may have been an increase in the hunting of deer. The decline of aurochs and the rise in proportion of red deer are perhaps also reflections of greater pressure on woodland resources (Fig. 13.11). Unfortunately, little bone evidence is available from the Middle Thames Valley for this period.

The main domestic animals of the early 2nd millennium cal BC remained cattle, sheep and pig. Dog was also kept. However, site assemblages are small and are mostly from funerary contexts. Many were apparently placed for ceremonial purposes, and it is not possible to build up an overall picture of the pastoral economy. The early Bronze Age material from Barrow Hills, Radley illustrates this well (Levitan and Serjeantson 1999, 238-9). One barrow ditch contained much of a cattle skeleton. A second contained an unusual range of species including an aurochs bone, most of the skeleton of a duck (probably a mallard) and a pair of pike jaws. An inhumation was accompanied by a set of seven red deer antlers, all of which had been smashed from the skulls of slaughtered animals (rather than having been naturally shed).

Evidence of cereal cultivation is particularly sparse for the early Bronze Age, but one new crop, *Hordeum vulgare* var. *nudum* (six-row naked barley) is first recorded in the Upper Thames Valley from the start of this period. Impressions of its grains were found in a late Beaker sherd from Eynsham (Murphy 1982). This crop has the same ecological requirements as six-row hulled barley but it is free-threshing so the grains do not need to be rubbed to remove the lemma and palea (husks). A second new crop, *Triticum monococcum* (einkorn wheat), was identified from the impression of a single grain in a Collared Urn from Long Wittenham (Jessen and Helbaek 1944, 18). Whereas there are sufficient records of six-row naked barley from the British Isles for there to be little doubt that it was grown as a crop (indeed it seems to have been rather charac-

Table 13.1: Range of variation in the proportion of animal bones of differing species in Beaker period assemblages from The Hamel, Oxford, Thrupp, and Mount Farm, Berinsfield (data from Robinson and Wilson 1987, 35)

Species	Range (as % of no. of fragments)
Cattle	30-35
Sheep / Goat	26-30
Pig	26-30
Red Deer	5-9
Roe Deer	0-9
Dog	0
Total Fragments	20-23

Fig. 13.10 (opposite) Early Bronze Age burnt mounds at Little Marlow

Fig. 13.11   Artist's reconstruction of an aurochs hunt

teristic of the early Bronze Age), the status of einkorn is uncertain. Einkorn was a crop grown over much of Europe in prehistory, but there are so few charred identifications of einkorn from prehistoric Britain – all of single grains – that there is no strong reason to believe it was grown as a crop in its own right. It is possible either that einkorn grew as a weed in other cereal crops or that the identified examples were, in fact, aberrant grains of *Triticum dicoccum* (emmer wheat).

Most of the charred food plant remains which have been identified from the early Bronze Age were recovered from ring ditches and cremation burials. They do not seem to have been food offerings, and their presence was probably the result of chance occurrence in kindling material. They provide little more than a basic crop record. *Hordeum* sp. (barley) and free-threshing *Triticum* sp. (rivet or bread-type wheat) have been identified from Bronze Age ring ditches in the Upper Thames Valley at Ashville, Abingdon (Jones 1978). A few indeterminate cereal grains were the only cereal remains from early Bronze Age cremations at Barrow Hills, Radley (Moffett 1999). Probably the richest deposit of charred remains comes from a pit dated to towards the end of the early Bronze Age on the Summertown-Radley Terrace of the Upper Thames at Drayton Highways Depot (Table 13.2; Barclay *et al.* 2003, 23-31). These remains show the use of emmer wheat and six-row hulled barley. Gathered woodland food plant remains were absent. There are, nonetheless, some records of gathered woodland food plants. Hazelnut shell fragments outnumbered grain in some early Bronze

Age pits at Yarnton (Robinson in prep.). These pits were, however, very similar in character to nearby pits containing sherds of Beaker pottery, and it is possible that they were not very different in date. Overall, the impression is that gathered woodland plants comprised a much smaller part of the diet than had been the case in earlier periods. However, it must be stressed again that even in comparison to the Neolithic, evidence for Bronze Age edible plants in the area is limited. With the exception of cremation deposits, the concentration of charred plant remains is usually so low that doubt must be

Table 13.2: Summary of charred plant remains from an early Bronze Age pit (119) at the Drayton Highways Depot (data from Barclay et al. *2003, table 3.5)*

Species		Number of items
Triticum dicoccum - grain	emmer wheat	1
T. cf *dicoccum* - grain	emmer wheat	1
Triticum sp. - grain	wheat	1
Hordeum vulgare - hulled grain	six-row hulled barley	2
Hordeum sp. - hulled grain	hulled barley	8
Hordeum sp. - grain	barley	20
Indeterminate cereal grain		77
Total cereal grain		110
Arrhenatherum elatius v. *bulbosum* - tuber	onion couch grass	2

expressed as to whether, on some sites, they were indeed contemporaneous with the deposits rather than representing a low background presence of intrusive material from later activity.

Carbonised tubers of *Arrhenatherum elatius* var. *bulbosus* (onion couch grass) have been found in many early Bronze Age cremation burials including Ashville (Jones 1978) and Barrow Hills (Moffett 1999), as well as the above-mentioned pit at Drayton Highways Depot. It was initially thought that they were food remains but it is now believed that they are more likely to be either from kindling material or the turves used in the pyre.

The main evidence for the exploitation of woody plants in the early Bronze Age also comes from human cremation burials. Both woodland species such as *Quercus* sp. (oak) and *Corylus avellana* (hazel), and species of thorn scrub were used as fuel. It seems that sometimes particular kinds of wood were chosen for use in pyres. Charcoal from the six early Bronze Age cremations at Barrow Hills were dominated by a single taxon, in five cases oak and in one case hawthorn-type (Thompson 1999), contrasting with the range of taxa already noted from the later Neolithic pits on the site. In these cases, it is possible that a single tree or bush was burnt.

The location of cereal plots remains elusive. Pollen evidence from Daisy Bank Fen, adjacent to the Barrow Hills monument complex in the Upper Thames Valley, suggests cereal cultivation on the Summertown-Radley Terrace during the Neolithic, but cereal pollen values had declined by the start of the Bronze Age (Parker 1999). A possible early Bronze Age ploughsoil was found in the top of the Yarnton long enclosure (Hey in prep.). As has already been mentioned, criss-cross ploughing took place up to the edge of the South Street long barrow and perhaps over the mound itself (Ashbee *et al.* 1979, fig. 39, 289, 298), and Beaker-period ploughing was identified beneath the disc barrow at Burderop Down (Gingell 1992). At Ascot on the Greensand in Berkshire, a series of spade furrows was found beneath the bell barrow. However, soils sealed beneath Bronze Age monuments only rarely show signs of cultivation, especially in the Thames Valley itself, and it has already been noted that the soils which developed in ring ditches usually provide evidence for a long stable phase with no soil from cultivation being eroded into them.

It has been suggested that in the Upper Kennet Valley there was intensified land-take during the Beaker period, though the land was perhaps not initially consolidated into fields (Evans *et al.* 1993). Gingell was certainly of the opinion that the Marlborough Downs field systems post-dated the Beaker period, although in some cases they overlay areas of Beaker clearance which had probably seen limited cultivation (Gingell 1992, 155). Some of the earliest boundaries may belong to the later part of the early Bronze Age, but most date from the mid to late Bronze Age. Case (1993) suggested that they

were perhaps at first attached to traditional patterns of land tenure, and formed part of a way of life which included respect for ancestral monuments. He thought that this broke down at the end of the 3rd millennium (the climax of the Beaker period), and that a new pattern of land tenure evolved, or was imposed, necessitating destroying previous traces of settlement (eg middens), bringing new farming areas into use (Case 1993, 15), and establishing the first permanent boundaries (Gingell 1992, 155). Settlement material from the associated destruction could have been used, for example, to block the monument at West Kennet long barrow (see Chapter 12).

There is no evidence for early Bronze Age field systems in the Upper Thames Valley. Ford *et al.* (2006) have suggested that a pair of parallel gullies, 2 m apart with a hollow way between them, at Howbery Park, Crowmarsh Gifford, were part of an early Bronze Age droveway attached to a field system. Two decorated Beaker sherds came from one of the features, along with four less distinctive sherds and a little undiagnostic flintwork. In the absence of more certain evidence of field boundaries of this date in this area in particular and the region generally, it seems most likely that the pottery was related to an earlier phase of activity; other redeposited finds were recovered from the site.

It has also been claimed that early Bronze Age fields existed at Heathrow Terminal 5, Perry Oaks, on the Taplow Terrace of the Middle Thames Valley (Lewis *et al.* 2006, 93-104). If correct, this implies a major change in the organisation of agriculture which was previously thought to have occurred at the start of the middle Bronze Age in this area. There is no doubt that there was a ditched middle Bronze Age system consisting of fields of 0.5 to 1 ha on the site. The earliest of the ditches respected the Stanwell bank barrow ditches, whereas the later field ditches cut through them. The pottery assemblages from the field ditches included much middle Bronze Age Deverel-Rimbury pottery, but very few sherds of early Bronze Age Collared Urn. The earliest radiocarbon date on organic material from a waterhole within one of the enclosures was 1610-1390 cal BC. Such results would be entirely consistent with the field system being laid out at around 1500 cal BC, perhaps as early as 1600 cal BC, as is suggested by Lewis *et al.* (2006, 97) when discussing the radiocarbon dates. The claim that the field system had its origin prior to 1600 cal BC is based on the botanical evidence from the waterholes (ibid., 102-4). The pollen and waterlogged macroscopic plant remains from these contexts comprise material from a diverse range of shrubs including field maple, hazel, dogwood, purging buckhorn, hawthorn, sloe and guelder rose. Not unreasonably, at least some of this scrub community was interpreted as having grown in hedgerows, and some of these shrubs, when they occur in present-day hedges, are characteristic of hedges that are at least 500 years old (provided the hedges have not been created by mixed planting or the selective clearance of woodland). Maple, for example, is not an early member of scrub succession.

The occurrence of the remains of these shrubs in middle Bronze Age waterholes in the Thames Valley is not unusual. Where maple is present – for example at Shorncote in the Upper Thames Valley (Robinson 2002) – it has been interpreted either as a survivor from woodland which had largely been cleared or as a member of long-established scrub. It is entirely plausible that once the Stanwell bank barrow lost its major ceremonial function towards the end of the Neolithic, limited scrub and even woodland regeneration occurred on parts of the site, facilitated by the nearby presence of established woodland, and that over time, maple became a member of the community. When the Bronze Age ditched land-boundaries were laid out, perhaps as early as 1600 cal BC, selective scrub clearance and the transplanting of local shrubs could have resulted in mixed hedges alongside the ditches, and perhaps the retention of some scrub as a source of fuel. The creation of an agricultural system based around enclosed fields, probably both for crops and stock, may thus have begun at Heathrow Terminal 5 before 1500 cal BC, perhaps starting around 1600 cal BC. This change can be seen as part of the start of the transition in agricultural practices which mainly occurred in the middle Bronze Age (Lambrick with Robinson 2009).

In summary, the general environmental evidence for the gravel terraces of the main valley of the Thames, particularly the Upper Thames Valley, is for monuments set in open expanses of grassland which was only very lightly grazed. The exploitation of woodland for gathered food plants and for the grazing of domestic animals appears to have declined in importance. However, early Bronze Age population levels remained low in relation to the agricultural potential of the area (Yates 1999; 2001). The agricultural economy should perhaps be seen as based around transhumant herders taking their stocks over unenclosed rough grassland and scrub, but perhaps spending longer periods of time in some places with adjacent, small cultivation plots.

A CHANGED LANDSCAPE

In the middle of the 2nd millennium, the landscape of the Thames Valley would still have been a mosaic of woodland and clearings, but some of those clearings would have been quite long lived by the middle Bronze Age. In addition, some areas of more extensive forest clearance had become permanent grazed grassland, principally around monument complexes like Stanton Harcourt, but also at some domestic sites, such as Yarnton. People were tied into a farming system which, although primarily focused on animal rearing, seems increasingly to have involved cereal cultivation.

As we have seen from the pollen evidence, by 1700-1600 cal BC at Yarnton, trees and shrubs had been reduced to around 55% of the vegetation cover within a largely open grassland flora. By the 15th century cal BC, trees and shrubs formed only 6%-12% of pollen from a waterhole, and the environment was much more open. A similarly open landscape is suggested by pollen and waterlogged material from contemporary linear ditches and three waterholes, each on different gravel islands on the floodplain, which have been dated to the 14th and 15th centuries cal BC. It is not just the rapid reduction in tree cover that is noteworthy, but the rise in water levels over the same period. This is shown very clearly by two adjacent waterholes, one dug between 1650 and 1500 cal BC in the bed of the channel when the water table must have been below *c* 58 m OD, and the other in the 15th century cal BC, perhaps 100 years later, when the water table, as represented by the preservation of organic deposits, seems to have risen by over 0.50 m. The watertable continued to rise by another 0.60 m or so during the course of the 14th century cal BC.

Crop remains do not become common, but they are certainly more abundant from around 1500 cal BC. In part this is because waterholes, which preserve a wider range of plant evidence, are present on some middle Bronze Age settlements. Sites with both waterlogged and charred crop remains in the Upper Thames Valley include Eight Acre Field, Radley, Yarnton, Appleford Sidings and Bradford's Brook, Wallingford (Robinson 1995; in prep.; 2009; 2006). *Triticum dicoccum* (emmer wheat) and hulled *Hordeum vulgare* (hulled six-row barley) remained the main crops in cultivation from the early Bronze Age, but at Yarnton and Appleford Sidings these were joined by *T. spelta* (spelt wheat). A carbonised grain of spelt from a well at Yarnton was dated to 1690-1400 cal BC (OXA-6548: 3255±70 BP; Hey in prep.). Free-threshing wheat (*T. turgidum* or *aestivum*) possibly fell out of cultivation at the end of the early Bronze Age. The earliest records of *Linum usitatissimum* (flax) in the region are also from the middle Bronze Age, although it is likely that it had been in cultivation from the Neolithic as is shown by the charred flax from the Neolithic house at Lismore Fields, Derbyshire (OxA-2436: 4970±70 BP; Hedges *et al.* 1991). Waterlogged seeds of another potential crop, *Papaver somniferum* (opium poppy) were quite well represented at Bradford's Brook (Robinson 2006). In the Middle Thames, similar results were obtained at Weir Bank Stud Farm, Bray on the floodplain (Clapham 1995), where the main cereal crops identified were emmer, spelt wheat and hulled barley. Interestingly, there were also a few grains of another cereal, *Secale cereale* (rye), and a large quantity of charred flax was found. Charred fragments of hazelnut shells were also abundant at the site showing that wild food plants were still being exploited. Waterlogged spikelets of emmer and spelt wheat, along with a few chaff fragments of barley and capsules of flax, were present in middle Bronze Age waterholes set amidst small rectangular fields at Heathrow

Terminal 5 (Carruthers in Lewis *et al.* 2006, 155-6).

Cattle, sheep and pig remained the main domestic animals during the middle Bronze Age, and cattle continued to dominate bone assemblages (Robinson and Lambrick 2009, 240-1). Dogs were also present at most settlements but horse was rare. Bones of wild animals are occasionally found, including aurochs and red deer, serving as a reminder that some hunting was occurring over remote, partly-wooded areas.

It has already been noted that small rectangular ditched fields were probably laid out at Heathrow Terminal 5 by around 1500 cal BC. Similar fields, also with waterholes, were created in the Upper Thames Valley during the middle Bronze Age. Crops are likely to have been grown in some of these fields although it is uncertain whether cultivation was by ard (scratch plough) or spade. Assemblages of charred weed seeds from crop processing are small but they do include *Galium aparine* (goosegrass) which tends to be a weed of autumn rather than spring-sown crops. Both emmer and spelt are suitable either for autumn or spring sowing, but flax is spring-sown. Small rectilinear fields also seem to have been used for pasture, and the ready provision of water within them, for example at Appleford Sidings in the Upper Thames and Heathrow Terminal 5 in the Middle Thames Valley, would have facilitated the raising of domestic animals (Booth and Simmonds 2009; Lewis *et al.* 2006). Indeed, it is possible that this was the main use of the fields (Yates 1999; 2001). The position of waterholes in areas where field boundaries are not apparent, as, for example, at Yarnton, may either indicate open grazing or that field boundaries were not ditched and have left no trace.

Between these more intensively managed fields were areas of open grassland which were experiencing sufficient grazing to ensure that woodland regeneration did not occur but which were not being used to their full agricultural potential. An advantage of this combination of intensive and extensive systems is that stock allowed to graze widely by day and enclosed in the fields overnight would bring nutrients to the fields from the landscape in their dung. Such grazing is likely to have been light, and there would have been no shortage of winter grazing (Lambrick with Robinson 2009). The organisation of the agricultural landscape in areas without field systems is more uncertain. It is possible that there was a more extensive system of agriculture with less of a focus on crop production. However, evidence from waterholes suggests that animals were herded nearby, and it is possible that fences and hedges formed boundaries which have left no archaeological trace.

The middle Bronze Age marks a period of significant change in the relationship of people to their environment and landscape. Before this date, the landscape had mainly been organised around ceremonial activities and monuments, with people moving through the landscape rather than settling

within it. Barrett (1994, chap. 6) suggests that a long fallow system, in which people had generalised rights to land as a result of their membership of wider kin groups, may have existed. Cultivation plots and grazing grounds would have formed part of a mosaic of resources over which the community exercised rights, and which could be used, abandoned and cleared afresh as was needed. After this date, evidence for the organisation of the landscape around agricultural production becomes much more widespread, as do indications of a greater investment in settlements, all of which may have been related to the adoption of a short fallow system (ibid.). Middle Bronze Age houses are relatively common discoveries, often surrounded by a range of domestic features, and possibly representing single generation households (Lambrick with Robinson 2009). Field systems were small, and it is probable that agriculture was conducted at a family level with habitation areas being adjacent to the waterholes found within fields. Whether field systems were present or not, people seem to have lived in settlements on a more permanent basis than had been the case in earlier periods, and access to land seems to have been held by smaller social groups who invested effort in, and claimed tenurial rights to, particular places in the landscape.

The origins of this transformation seem to lie in the early Bronze Age. Although the changes are gradual, almost imperceptible, the visibility of domestic structures, the investment in a range of features associated with habitation areas, such as waterholes and burnt mound deposits, are all new aspects of the early Bronze Age archaeological record. There is also evidence for increasing attention to arable cultivation. In addition, burial of the dead and small-scale ceremonial activity was increasingly focused on areas close to occupation sites rather than on the large ceremonial monuments of the late Neolithic. There are no signs in the Thames Valley that these monuments were still in use by the middle of the 2nd millennium.

The reasons for the increasing emphasis on agricultural production were not technological; there was the potential for these developments to have occurred more than a thousand years earlier (Moffett *et al.* 1989). The main domestic animals and, with the exception of spelt wheat, the main crops had been present in Britain since the introduction of agriculture. The introduction of spelt wheat, although perhaps improving cereal yields, could hardly have been the cause of an agricultural revolution. Ard cultivation was a technique which had been practised since the Neolithic (Evans 1971). It seems, instead, that the changes are most likely to have arisen out of the break up of the social systems of the 3rd millennium. The use of large ceremonial monuments seems to have become more specialised, and those buried nearby may represent an elite (see Chapters 14 and 15). The wider community may have begun to undertake ceremonies on a smaller scale, whether among an extended family group or at a household level, and to bury their important dead elsewhere, resulting in a fragmentation of ritual practice. The places people chose to undertake these activities would have become increasingly central to the existence of particular groups and their social identities. People's sense of belonging would have been attached to one locale and to a smaller social network, forming 'a landscape which was viewed from the centre of a domain, with distinct boundaries', between the internal world of the household and the external world of others (Barrett 1994, 147).

How the positions of boundaries were set, and the rights to fields and to live in one place were negotiated with other people in the wider community (who would originally have shared traditional rights to that land) is uncertain, and such changes would probably have put a strain on the cohesion of larger kin groups (Barrett 1994, 136-47; Brück 2000;

Lambrick with Robinson 2009, 380-4). It seems most likely that the mechanisms varied from place to place depending on the relative size of the population and the extent to which previous land use had become customary. Where people had longer-lived and more widely recognised claims to parcels of land, there may have been no need to create physical boundaries. Whatever the process involved, the evidence we have in the Thames Valley suggests that family enterprise, rather than communal endeavour, was operating by the end of the early Bronze Age. It is, however, also clear that in some areas, such as that around the Devil's Quoits at Stanton Harcourt, communal organisation of land continued over a large area up to the early Roman period, with grazing focused on the Devil's Quoits henge itself (Lambrick 1992). Field boundaries are not seen in this area until the end of the early Roman period.

Chapter 14 – Ritual, ceremony and cosmology

by Paul Garwood with Gill Hey and Alistair Barclay

RITUAL PRACTICES AND CEREMONIAL MONUMENTS

Interpreting ritual and ceremony

Our understanding of social activity and cultural life in the Neolithic and early Bronze Age of the Thames Valley, along with the rest of Britain, is dominated by the material outcomes of ritual practices (Bradley 2005; Pollard 1995) and by the architectural forms ('monuments') built to facilitate and guide such practices (Bradley 1993; 1998b). These practices appear to have ranged from very large-scale, formal ceremonial events to more informal, personalised and immediate shamanistic or magical performances. As has been described above (Chapters 11 and 13), settlement and production sites, in contrast, are still comparatively rare and materially ephemeral.

Although the status and characterisation of 'ritual' and 'ceremony' have been the subject of considerable debate in archaeology over the last 30 years, there is still little agreement about basic definitions or even the value of ritual as an archaeological concept at all (Brück 1999b). In contrast, although there is also considerable disagreement among anthropologists about the nature of ritual, a basic working definition of ritual as a kind of social activity involving 'prescribed formal behaviour for occasions not given over to technological routine, having reference to beliefs in mystical beings or powers' (Turner 1967, 19) remains in widespread use. There is also some level of consensus about the purpose of ritual action. Van Gennep's (1909) 'rites of passage' model, which represents ritual as a means of achieving and sacralising transitions in social identity, is consistent with Turner's (1974) view that ritual is a kind of 'redressive action' required at times of social stress, such as deaths and marriages, when everyday social life has to be suspended, the 'crisis' resolved, and social order formally reconstituted. This, in turn, is not dissimilar from Geertz's (1973) idea that ritual is the means by which people come to terms with the fundamental conditions of existence and make sense of moral conflicts and contradictions.

It has been suggested that all rites of passage share a tripartite structure and that their beginnings (rites of separation), middles (rites of liminality) and ends (rites of re-aggregation) have similar attributes from one ritual and cultural context to another (van Gennep 1909; Metcalf and Huntingdon 1991, 30). The apparent universal structure of this process can be explained with reference to the relationship between everyday life in the present, and what is sacred and belongs ultimately to a state of being or place that is not of the 'here and now'. Rituals in this light provide a practical means of engaging with the sacred. Rites of separation set aside daily life and guide participants to a place where ordinary social matters are excluded. In the liminal stage, people in sacred conditions or places perceive themselves to be in the presence of supernatural forces or entities (gods, ancestors or spirits), in a domain where social norms are suspended. Finally, rites of re-aggregation provide a way for people to leave the sacred and return safely to living society (bringing back something of the sacred – absolution, purity or power – with them). It is easy to see how architecture and the spatial organisation of social practices have a special part to play in the articulation of rituals – as a means of both separating and bounding sacred and secular locales, in guiding or delineating passages between them, and in physically structuring the ordering and participation of people in the performance of ritual actions.

Recent approaches to ritual in archaeology have focused on aspects of ritual performance, structured practices and the process of ritualisation (eg Bradley 2005, Hill 1995), but have also been diverted by debates concerning the dichotomisation of ritual and practical behaviour and whether ritual is visible archaeologically (eg Hill 1995, 95-101; Brück 1999b; Insoll 2004; Bradley 2005, 28-36). In many ways, however, the problems identified in these studies seem more methodological than theoretical or interpretative, especially as recent appraisals of ritual in anthropology have no difficulty seeing ritual as a distinct form of action (eg Bell 1992, Humphrey and Laidlaw 1994; James 2003, 100-25; Schechner 1994). These studies broadly agree that social actors have prior conceptions of 'ritual-actions-to-be', which they mark out as separate from other activities (Bell 1992, 140) and to which they consciously commit themselves in terms of practical conduct (Humphrey and Laidlaw 1994, 5, 106). The political significance of ritual and ceremony is also widely recognised, not just as a medium for forging social relations, but also in the way expressions of power appear to be a quality of ritual performance. Bloch, for example, argues that ritual has an ideological dimension because it '…transforms and reduces events so that they lose their specificity and re-presents them as part of a timeless order' (1986, 185). If elites can identify themselves with the content or performance of a ritual, they can thus legitimise their authority by presenting it as if it is something unchanging and incontestable.

There are, then, some consistent themes running through the anthropological literature. Ritual is seen as a mode of self-conscious, intrinsically performative, formalised and socially-prescribed social action and ritualised actions are performed because they are understood to be efficacious in some way (Schechner 1994). In addition ritual is recognised as *separate* from other activities, its meaning lying not in the intention of the actor but in the intended (sacred) purpose of the action to which the actor is committed. These features have a range of material implications for the recognition and interpretation of ritual and ceremonial practices. These are considered in more detail in the following sections, but it is worth emphasising qualities such as formality, order, performance, purposefulness, separateness, cosmological signification and power. With these ideas in mind, the materiality of ritual and ceremony during the Neolithic and early Bronze Age in the Middle and Upper Thames Valley is considered in this section in three main ways: first, by considering the symbolic significance of material culture and the deliberate deposition of material objects and substances in the course of ritual actions; second, through the architectural forms designed to direct and stage ceremonial performances; and, third, by examining the way in which ceremonial activities can be organised on a large spatial scale (ie in relation to ideas of cosmography and 'sacred landscapes').

Ritual and material culture: special objects and structured deposits

Central to recent discussions of the material culture of ritual performance in archaeology is the idea of 'structured deposition'. This idea was first outlined by Colin Richards and Julian Thomas (1984), who argued that ritual is not just symbolic behaviour but also communicates a sense of order in the form of timeless categories and fundamental principles of existence. Their approach was derived from the work of anthropologists such as Leach and Tambiah, who equated 'symbolic communication' with ritual, arguing that ritual is not a kind of behaviour but an *aspect* of behaviour. Ritual, according to Tambiah (1979, 119), consists of 'patterned and ordered sequences of words and acts …whose content and arrangement are characterised in varying degree by formality (conventionality), stereotypy (rigidity), condensation (fusion), and redundancy (repetition)'. In Richards and Thomas' view, it follows that ritual should be visible in the degree of formality, repetition and salience evident in material patterns; that is, in the degree of 'structured deposition' visible in the placement and spatial distribution of artefacts and other materials (1984, 190-92). This idea was elaborated in a detailed analysis of depositional patterns at Durrington Walls henge, and has been applied very

widely (methodologically, at least) in British prehistoric studies since, especially in relation to Neolithic depositional practices at causewayed and henge enclosure sites and in pit contexts (eg Barrett *et al.* 1991, 92-106; Edmonds 1993; Pollard 1992, 1995; Whittle and Pollard 1998; cf Thomas 1999, 62-88).

The problem, of course, is that because meaning is conveyed in all action, human behaviour in this view always has some 'ritual' aspect, and the concept thus loses its value as a way of interpreting specific practices. There is certainly no question that it is difficult to distinguish between structured deposition in ritual contexts and other kinds of action resulting in patterned material deposition. This, as J D Hill (1995, 96) observes, is because: 'all human activities are symbolically structured, drawing on and reproducing cultural norms and structures … Ritual, as practice, draws on the same structures as any other, daily, practice'. The solution may be a matter of degree, not in quantitative terms as Richards and Thomas (1984) suggested (in the 'amount' of structure) but rather in qualitative terms: in the relative intentionality, formality and propositionality of expressions of meaning. Hill argues that in everyday activities 'generative principles, metaphors, and symbolic structures' are drawn upon and reproduced largely unreflectively (ie habitually), in contrast with ritual activities which reveal the underlying 'religious' basis of actions more overtly (1995, 99). This characterisation is clearly consistent with the features of ritual outlined previously, especially in terms of the emphasis on formality, purposefulness and separateness. In this light, there are two principal attributes which can be used to identify ritualised actions in the manipulation of objects and materials in the past, both of which are readily identifiable in many site contexts in the Middle and Upper Thames Valley.

First, it is possible to recognise the deliberate selection and careful placement of distinct material types in a range of depositional contexts. Apart from the most obvious category of burials, these include pits and ditches that contain deposits of ceramic and lithic artefacts, as well as other materials such as charcoal and animal and human bone. Notable examples include the pits containing Peterborough Ware at Yarnton (Hey in prep.), and at Lake End Road West, Dorney (Fig. 14.1; Allen *et al.* 2004, 92-3), and the pits containing Grooved Ware at Roughground Farm, Gloucestershire (Allen *et al.* 1993), Barrow Hills, Radley (Barclay 1999a, 73-87; 1999b, 319-20), and Lower Mill Farm, Surrey (Jones and Ayres 2004). In each of these cases, great care was evidently taken in the way assemblages of materials were brought together and laid within pits, some of which were then quickly backfilled.

Far more spatially-extensive ordering of depositional events, of the kind often associated with henges and timber circles, can be seen at a wide range of Neolithic monumental sites throughout the region. This is evident at early Neolithic enclosures

Fig. 14.1   A pit containing Peterborough Ware under excavation at Yarnton

such as Windmill Hill (Whittle and Pollard 1998; Whittle *et al.* 1999, 354-71; cf Pollard 2004), and Staines, where a spatial contrast between the 'front' (south-east) and 'back' (north-west) parts of the ditch circuits and interior can be seen in the scale, distribution and material qualities of both pit-digging and structured depositional events (Lamdin-Whymark 2008, 145-51; cf P Bradley 2004; Robertson-Mackay 1987). This is very similar to the front-back division evident in the distributions and depositional contexts of late Neolithic pottery, worked flint and human remains at The Sanctuary in Wiltshire (Pollard 1992). Similar oppositions are also apparent within the Radley oval barrow ditch deposits (Fig. 14.2), where a long-term division of cultural materials existed on either side (left:right) of the long axis of the monument: between the south/east where lithic artefacts were mainly found, and the north/west where all human bone and antler fragments were deposited (ibid.; cf Bradley 1992).

Second, ritual actions may be evident in the physical separation of formal depositional practices from less formal ones (emphasising self-conscious attempts to separate ritual actions, and their interpretation, from the everyday), and in the choice of 'special' or 'important' places for depositional acts, highlighting the special staging of ritual performances, their separateness and cosmological signif-

Fig. 14.2   *Spatial structuring of material within the Radley oval barrow ditch deposits*

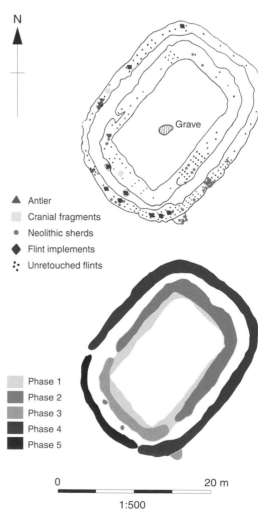

N

- ▲ Antler
- ▨ Cranial fragments
- ● Neolithic sherds
- ◆ Flint implements
- ⁝ Unretouched flints

Grave

- ▨ Phase 1
- ▨ Phase 2
- ▨ Phase 3
- ▨ Phase 4
- ▨ Phase 5

0 — 20 m

1:500

icance. This is most immediately apparent where monumental architecture served to demarcate spaces or provide focal points for ceremonies (the architectural setting of ritual performances is discussed in more detail in the next section). The tripartite structuring of rituals, in particular, involves a series of transitions which are highly significant for negotiating profound (and perhaps dangerous) transformations in conditions of sacredness and personal identity, with particular emphasis on boundaries, passages and thresholds. The deposition of a range of cultural materials in the terminals of some of the ditch segments at the early Neolithic Staines causewayed enclosure in Surrey, especially pottery sherds and fragmentary human skeletal remains in both the outer ditch (eg trenches 17 and 42-6) and the inner ditch (eg trench 37), suggests events marking important moments of transition while traversing boundaries between spaces outside and inside the enclosure (Fig. 14.3; Robertson-Mackay 1987, 59, fig.10; cf P Bradley 2004, 115-18, fig.13.2). Similarly, hearths and deposits of charcoal, ash, flint artefacts, bone fragments and large stones found on the top of the primary fills in both ditch terminals at the south-west entrance of the Devil's Quoits henge in Oxfordshire (Fig. 14.3; Gray and Lambrick 1995, 11-23; cf Barclay 1995a, 77) suggest burning and depositional events at the threshold between 'outside' and 'inside', perhaps understood in terms analogous to 'profane' and 'sacred' (or perhaps as part of a sequence of transitions between those two domains).

Viewed in these ways, it is possible to recognise highly formalised, purposeful and spatially-defined actions involving material deposition at every turn in the earlier prehistoric material record of the Middle and Upper Thames Valley. Although there must, inevitably, be some ambiguity with regard to how specific assemblages of material culture and other substances were accumulated, manipulated and deposited, and whether these should be interpreted as the outcome of overt ritual actions (eg in midden and tree-throw contexts; cf Allen *et al.* 2004, 91-2; Pollard 1995), this does not negate the fact that much of the evidence we are concerned with came into being as a consequence of deliberate, structured, ritual performances.

Sacred places: space, knowledge and ceremonial architecture

Architecture, too, provides a way of engaging directly with ritual action. Monuments have always been regarded as a typical feature of the Neolithic and early Bronze Age cultural landscape of the British Isles, closely associated with the origins of agricultural communities (see discussions in R Bradley 1998b; 2004; Thomas 1993; 1999, 6-33) and the later development of complex societies (for example, as an expression of power relations in terms of the mobilisation of labour and other resources: cf

Renfrew 1973; cf Barrett 1991, 155-72; Whittle 1997b, 139-70; Richards 1998). Indeed, in the absence of other sources of evidence, monuments, their contents and their landscape contexts often provide most of the evidence we have for cultural life in these periods. There is also a general assumption (at least implicitly) that the wide range of architectural forms described as monuments were intended as places for the performance of ceremonies such as mortuary rituals or larger-scale communal celebrations. More recently, there has been considerable discussion of the way in which monuments may have been built to embody symbolic schemes in their spatial designs and structural forms (ie as micro-cosmographic representations of certain kinds of symbolic order: eg Richards 1996; Whittle 1997a; Whittle and Pollard 1998). In contrast, the nature of the relationship between architecture and ritual has received relatively scant attention.

The main issue to address is the purpose architectural structures serve in relation to ritual actions. Turner, in particular, observed that rituals have expressive and performative attributes that are repeated from one occasion to the next, involving both key performers and participants (1982, 61-88; cf Lewis 1985). This is very similar to theatre, but there are also significant differences. Turner argued that the qualities and conditions of ritual and theatre pervade all performances, but occupy opposed points in a spectrum of variation in public performance, distinguished in terms of their purpose, context, and expected outcomes (Turner 1982; 1990). As Schechner (1994, 622) argues: 'The relationship between ritual and theatre takes the form of an interplay between efficacy and entertainment …Whether a specific performance is 'ritual' or 'theatre' depends mostly on context and function'. In both cases, there is an architectural – or at least spatial – dimension to performance, usually but not always durable, that demarcates the domain of action, accommodates and organises the participants, and practically guides or constrains how forms of movement and expression should be conducted and properly repeated each time they are enacted. From this perspective, the prehistoric monumental architecture of the Middle and Upper Thames Valley can be interpreted as carefully designed spaces and edifices for the appropriate staging of ritual performances.

There is, in addition, a more fundamental condition of architectural forms that has important implications for understanding the relationship between ritual and built structures. The main point is summarised incisively by Parker Pearson and Richards, who observe that 'architectural space may be defined as a concretisation of …existential space' (Parker Pearson and Richards 1994, 4). In other words, built structures 'on the ground' are physical realisations of social purposes and structures of meaning (practical, categorical, functional, cosmological and so forth) that people hold in their minds. Once built, such structures delineate a spatial order

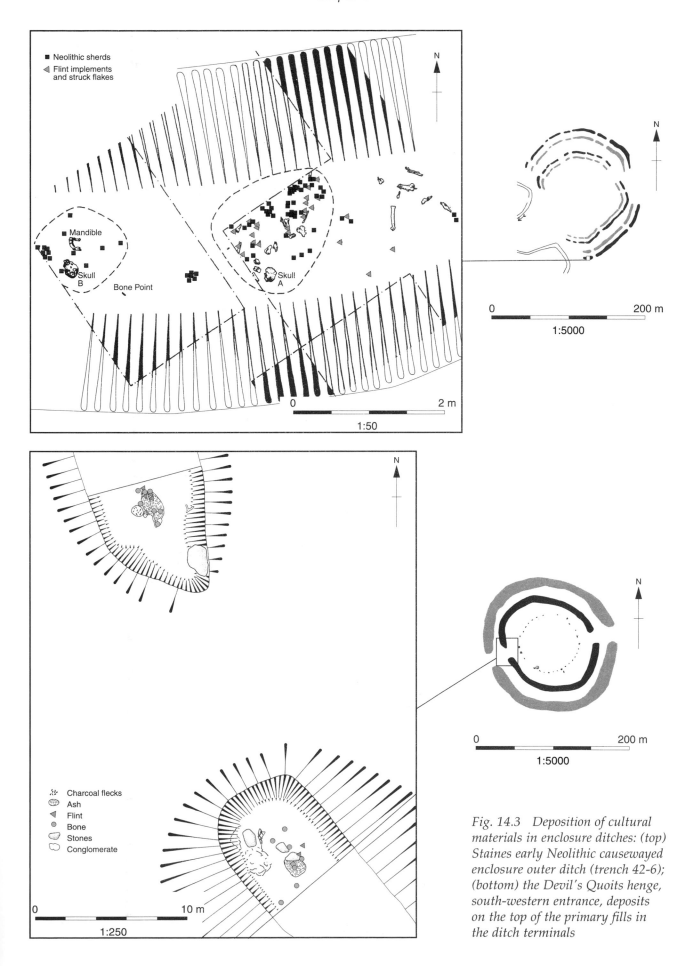

Fig. 14.3 *Deposition of cultural materials in enclosure ditches: (top) Staines early Neolithic causewayed enclosure outer ditch (trench 42-6); (bottom) the Devil's Quoits henge, south-western entrance, deposits on the top of the primary fills in the ditch terminals*

that guides, constrains and conditions social actions and the meanings given to these. From this perspective, to study an ancient built structure involves a *direct* encounter with a set of spatial and formal design elements (eg kinds of spaces, boundaries, forms and orientations) that were assembled specifically to facilitate particular social practices while reifying the classificatory schemes and beliefs that made such practices (and buildings) meaningful.

The symbolic significance and practical purpose of prehistoric monumental architecture can thus be discerned in much the same way that it is possible to recognise symbols and metanarratives of sacredness and transformation embodied in the designs of medieval parish churches, and to see how these buildings and the rituals that took place within them constituted a spatial technology for the practical reproduction of fundamental religious concepts (Gilchrist 1999, 83-7). It is not difficult, in fact, to give meaning to some of the design principles and symbolic referents evident in prehistoric monuments: in the case of cursus monuments, for example, the extended linear enclosure form, suggesting processional practices, and their alignment in some cases on ancient structures associated with the dead (eg the Stonehenge Cursus and the Dorset Cursus), can be interpreted as an architectural framework that facilitated and guided a metaphorical journey – from life to death, or from living to ancestral domains (and perhaps back again) – that was played out in the course of ritual performances. Qualitatively, the very nature of ritual actions – intended to reveal meanings originating beyond the everyday world – may also be evident in the strangeness that we sometimes perceive in ancient monuments, as these were deliberately fashioned to evoke just such a sense of difference and otherworldliness (Barrett 1991, 5).

With these ideas in mind, it is possible to differentiate between the various kinds of monumental architecture found in the study area with reference to design forms, sensory qualities and performative scale (ie in relation to the possible social scale of ceremonial events). Major distinctions can be seen in terms of what Bradley (1998b, 124-6) has termed the permeability of monuments – defined in terms of relative ease of access, penetrability of physical barriers, and the visibility of activities inside for those outside the monument. There are also clear differences in terms of the internal organisation of space, with some structures organised in a compartmental manner, others taking linear forms, and many with circular and concentric spaces. Finally, there are contrasts between kinds of monumental architecture that define arenas of various shapes and sizes, and those that have a distinct focal character (although these two aspects are not exclusive; cf Parker Pearson and Richards 1994, 12-14). The differences between enclosure architecture and mound and tomb architecture illustrate these points in an extreme way (Fig. 14.4). Chambered tombs such as Notgrove, Wayland's Smithy and West

Kennet, for example, consist of spatially constricted, lineally-organised compartmentalised spaces with focal end-chambers with very little space for participants. These were housed within massive mound structures that hid internal activities while at the same time providing a material presence for tombs as focal points in the wider landscape (Darvill 2004, 132-57). In contrast, contemporary enclosures such as Windmill Hill, Abingdon and Staines were concentrically organised spaces, spatially more open, with a relatively high level of physical and sensory permeability, and extensive central arenas that could accommodate large numbers of people (cf Oswald *et al.* 2001, 67-75, 120-32).

The Neolithic earthwork enclosures of the Middle and Upper Thames mostly appear to lack a built focus (Avebury is a notable exception, with multiple foci in the obelisk and cove at the centres of the south and north circles respectively), suggesting that they accommodated ceremonial performances

Fig. 14.4 Contrasts between 'hidden' chambered tomb structures with spatially constricted internal spaces for ritual participants (Wayland's Smithy), and 'open', concentrically-organised causewayed enclosures with central arenas that could accommodate large numbers of people (Windmill Hill)

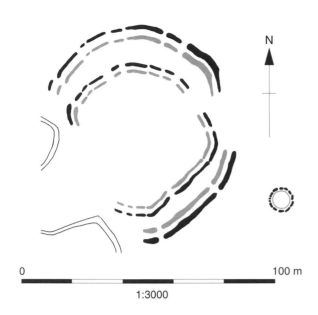

0   100 m

1:3000

Fig. 14.5 Early and middle Neolithic circular arenas and the spatial structuring of ceremonial practices: Staines causewayed enclosure (left); Dorchester-on-Thames Site II phase 3 (right)

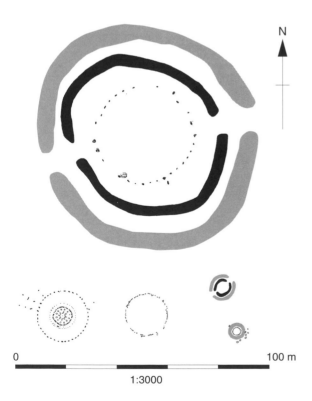

0   100 m

1:3000

Fig. 14.6 Late Neolithic and early Bronze Age circular arenas and the spatial structuring of ceremonial practices: Devil's Quoits (top); (bottom, left to right) The Sanctuary; The King's Men, Rollright; Corporation Farm henge; Radley pond barrow 4866

that were spatially extensive and relatively fluid. The larger enclosures in many cases consisted of series of nested spaces, mostly organised concentrically, which may imply degrees of access, and spatial divisions of people involved in ceremonies, and certainly indicates multiple points of transition as boundaries were traversed in the course of movement into and out of internal spaces. The main points of difference between earlier and later Neolithic enclosures relate to contrasts in architectural permeability: in the way in which entrances were positioned, both with respect to other entrances and to earthwork circuits, and in the constraints on visibility determined by the height of enclosure banks.

In the case of the Staines causewayed enclosure, major gaps in the outer enclosure circuit on the eastern side are mostly offset in relation to gaps in the inner circuit, suggesting multiple access routes that wove their way between the exterior, intra-circuit and interior spaces of the site (Fig. 14.5; Robertson-Mackay 1987). This contrasts with the spatial arrangement of entrances on the north and west sides, where gaps in the outer circuit are aligned with those in the inner circuit, suggesting direct avenues of ingress and/or egress. This complex variation is not evident at later Neolithic henge enclosures such as the Devil's Quoits (Fig. 14.6; A J Barclay *et al.* 1995), which has simple opposed entrances aligned with gaps in the internal stone circle. Although thresholds at points of transition from outside to inside are clearly demarcated by gaps in the bank, ditch and stone circle, movement through entrances was more constrained with fewer points of access, and was also far more direct, with a single alignment or route for movement to and from the central arena. Different again are later Neolithic unembanked stone circles (such as the King's Men at Rollright: Figs 14.6-7; cf Lambrick 1988) and simple timber circles (for example, at Gravelly Guy; Lambrick and Allen 2004, 61-3) which consist of relatively insubstantial single boundaries, often. but not always permeable

Fig. 14.7 The King's Men: the late Neolithic stone circle at Rollright, Oxfordshire

(for example, at Rollright the stones were contiguous, and access was possible only through a single entrance), which delimited small easily-visible arenas. From this perspective, at least as far as enclosures are concerned, the change suggested by Bradley (1998b) from less to more permeable monumental architecture over time is too general a description; instead, we may be seeing more complex shifts of emphasis in terms of different kinds of accessibility, ritual performance and sensory appreciation over time.

The striking contrasts evident in the physical scale of ceremonial architecture provide a crude measure of the social scale of ritual performances. It is clear, for example, that a broad distinction can be made between large and small enclosures throughout the Neolithic and early Bronze Age (Figs 14.5-6). This suggests not only major differences in the significance of these enclosures in symbolic and cosmographic terms, but also in how they were conceived as stages for ritual performances that were conducted in particular ways by social groups of known or expected sizes. The design similarities of enclosures of very different scales, at least in a visual sense *in plan*, has tempted some archaeologists to interpret them in similar terms – in the way that they were used and in what they signified – but this disguises the profound differences evident in terms of the sheer scale of the ceremonies that they seem to have been intended for.

It is also instructive to compare the different forms of the largest ceremonial structures built in the Middle and Upper Thames in the 4th to 2nd millennia cal BC. It is common in the archaeological literature to focus on architecture of one period or another, and to characterise the scales of structures in very general terms (eg huge, large-scale, massive, etc), yet such estimations of size are relative and the comparative scales of construction under-appreciated. As Figure 14.8 shows, apart from very rare, exceptionally large enclosures such as Windmill Hill and Avebury, the most impressive architectural edifices are middle Neolithic cursus monuments, which dwarf most causewayed enclosures and henge sites in terms of their scale, ambition and impact on the landscape, and which make things like mortuary enclosures appear physically insignificant. It is also perhaps surprising that monument complexes such as linear round barrow groups, which from the 19th century cal BC were being elaborated as coherent ceremonial centres comprising avenues and arenas (Garwood 1999b), are easily comparable in scale to cursus monuments, large henges and palisaded enclosures. Most striking of all, perhaps, are the great differences of

emphasis in basic design principles between those kinds of ceremonial architecture that defined linear pathways (embodying qualities of movement, journeying and dramatic or historical narrative), and those that defined circular spaces and concentric and symmetrical spatial orders (embodying qualities of focus, fixity and atemporality). This suggests profound contrasts in the kinds of signification invested in the ritual performances that took place on such stages, and also the special complexity of architectural settings where both linear and circular elements were combined (for example, in the articulation of the Avebury monuments, discussed below; Fig. 14.12).

The creation of sacred landscapes: ritual and cosmography

The nature of monument concentrations and their relationship to settlement, especially the distinction sometimes made between sacred and secular landscapes, have been prominent themes in British Neolithic and Bronze Age studies since the 19th century. The idea of symbolic or structural order in prehistoric landscapes, in particular, has tended to focus attention on the way that groups of monuments are distributed and articulated spatially, imposing particular kinds of order on the landscape and on practices within it (Tilley 1994). In this context, there has been a persistent interpretative division between those who see monument groups and settlement areas as being more or less co-extensive (eg Barnatt 1999; Barnatt and Collis 1996; Malim 2000), and those who see them as largely separate (eg Fleming 1971; Field 1998). Whilst there is agreement that some occupation sites existed within or around monument groups, it is far less clear whether habitation was continuous or discontinuous, how it was organised spatially and temporally, and whether it differed in character from occupation in areas without monuments (see Chapters 11 and 13).

It is likely that there was considerable variation in the relationships between ceremonial activity, monuments and occupation practices from one part of Britain to another, and from one landscape context to another. These relationships may also have changed over time in different ways and at different tempos. In the case of Avebury, for example, it has been suggested that settlements and monuments occupied different parts of the landscape, with repeated occupation episodes at hillside locations overlooking major monuments (Pollard 2005, 109-10; Holgate 1988a, 91-7), although both here and at Stonehenge there is some evidence that occupation

Fig. 14.8 (opposite) Neolithic and early Bronze Age monumentality and ceremony: comparative perspectives on the design and spatial scale of ceremonial architecture: (1) Windmill Hill, (2) Eastleach and (3) Staines causewayed enclosures; (4) Drayton and (5) Dorchester-on-Thames cursus monuments and associated monuments; (6) Avebury, (7) the Big Rings, (8) the Devil's Quoits, (9) Westwell, (10) Condicote and (11) Cutsdean henges; (12) the West Kennet palisaded enclosures; (13) Barrow Hills, Radley round barrow group

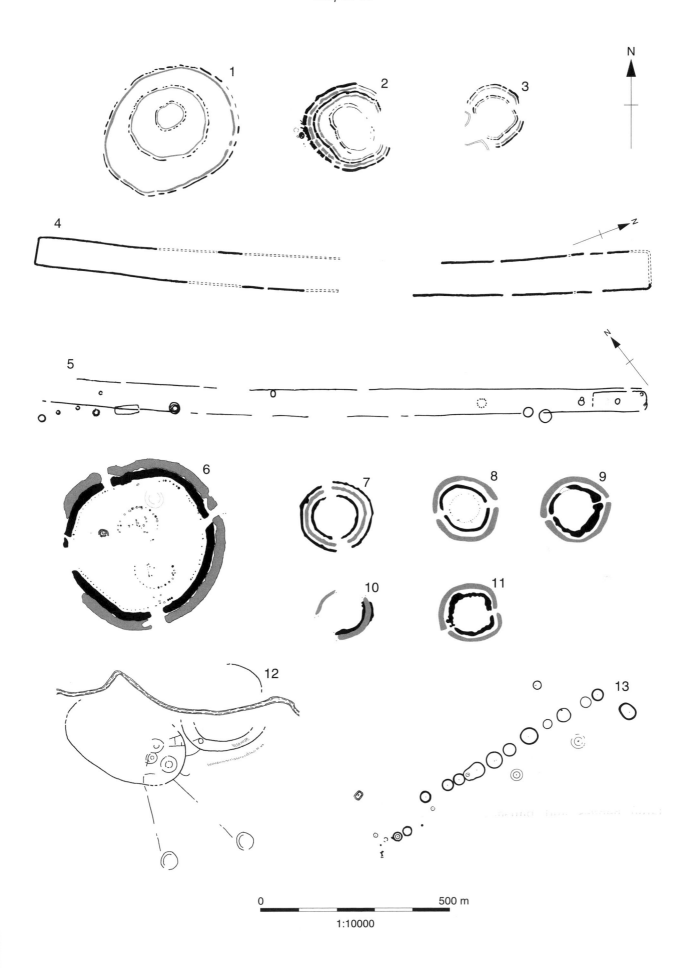

sites were also interspersed among the monuments (Thomas 1999, 174-77). In the Upper Thames Valley, separate ceremonial, funerary and occupation areas at Yarnton may have endured for many centuries (Thomas 1999, 190; cf Hey 1997), yet not far away settlements and monuments at Stanton Harcourt appear to have been closely integrated (A J Barclay *et al.* 1995, 112). To some extent these contrasts are less pronounced if landscapes are studied at a larger scale: in the Abingdon to Dorchester-on-Thames area, for example, changes in the nature and intensity of activity at one monument group may have been complemented by changes at others (Garwood 1999b, 292-98; Thomas 1999, 195). This suggests that settlement may be best understood at a regional level: separate monument groups or settlement foci, when seen at a larger spatial scale, in fact appear to

be constituent parts of more extensive organised landscapes.

Whether monuments and everyday settlements were closely interrelated spatially or not, the idea that prehistoric landscapes were structured cosmographically is now widely accepted (Bradley 2000; Darvill 1997; Field 1998; 2004; Garwood 2003; Parker Pearson and Ramilisonina 1998; Richards 1996; Woodward and Woodward 1996). This is seen in two main ways, to some extent at two different scales of spatial analysis.

First, there is recognition of very large-scale structuring of the cultural landscape as a kind of reification of symbolic and classificatory order: both as an outcome of routine, habitual practices in social space, and as deliberate construction (in the placing of built structures, or in the explicit spatial separa-

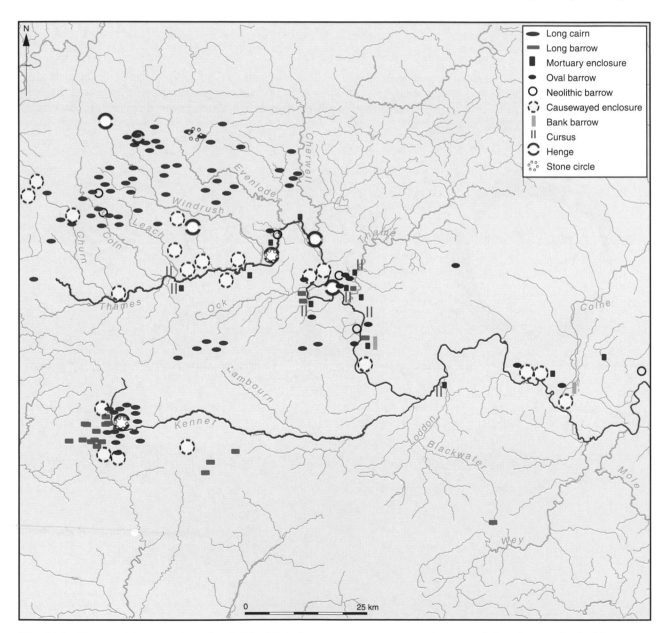

Fig. 14.9   The spatial separation of early Neolithic funerary monuments and ceremonial enclosures in the Upper Thames Valley

tion or bounding of some activities in relation to others; Field 1998; Ruggles 1999, 130-39; Thomas 1999, 167-77). This process may be apparent, for example, in the spatial separation of early Neolithic funerary monuments and ceremonial enclosures in the Upper Thames Valley (Fig. 14.9), the latter being found mostly around the fringes of the funerary monument distribution in the Cotswolds, either in the low-lying areas near the Thames to the south, or on hilltops to the north-west (cf Whittle, Barclay, McFadyen *et al.* 2007, 338-42). The spatial concentration of middle and late Neolithic monuments in specific landscape zones in the Middle and Upper Thames Valley (Fig. 14.10), with relatively empty spaces between each monument group, also suggests large–scale structuring of ceremonial activities, the existence of core 'sacred landscapes' belonging to distinct religious communities or polities (eg Renfrew 1973; cf Garwood 2007c), or areas occupied by groups who were unable or chose not to become part of the wider 'ceremonial universe' of the day.

Interpretations of this kind have for some time focused on the well-preserved monument groups on the Wessex chalklands (Renfrew 1973; Whittle 1997b), giving the impression that these were both more impressive and built on a far larger scale than

ceremonial centres elsewhere. This order of difference is not so apparent, however, when the Upper Thames monument concentrations (Fig. 14.11) at Drayton-Abingdon-Dorchester (Barclay and Halpin 1999; Barclay *et al.* 2003; Garwood 1999b; Loveday 1999; Thomas 1999, 195) and Stanton Harcourt-Eynsham-Cassington (A J Barclay *et al.* 1995; Healy 2004a) are compared with the Avebury complex (Fig. 14.11; cf Gillings *et al.* 2008, 188-96; Thomas 1999, 199-220). The main contrast, in fact, does not relate to overall geographical scale, architectural diversity or spatial complexity, but in the sequence, spatial distribution and intensity of construction events: the Upper Thames Valley monument concentrations, for example, have multiple centres that developed over a long period, partly in succession (cf Garwood 1999b, 292-98; Thomas 1999, 195), whereas the Avebury monument group seems to have had a far stronger focus in one core area of construction, with an especially intense period of monument-building in the mid 3rd millennium cal BC (see below).

Second, there is recognition of far more purposeful, physical constructions of symbolic order in the articulation of monuments and practices within smaller landscape areas (ceremonial centres), and in the ways these were interrelated (eg aligned, juxta-

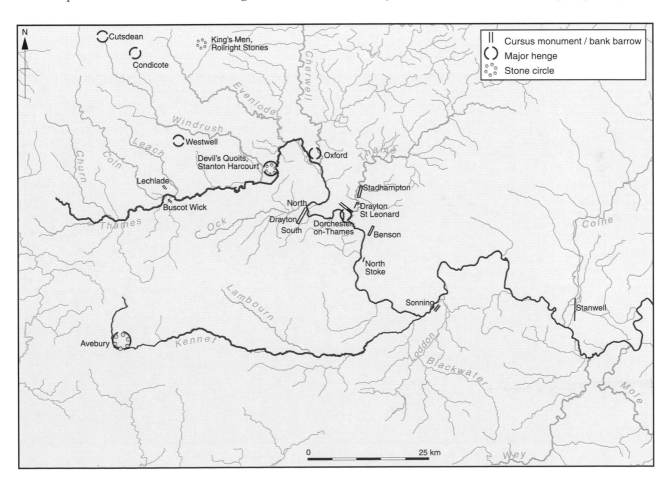

Fig. 14.10 The distribution of middle and late Neolithic monuments and 'empty' landscape zones in the Middle and Upper Thames Valley

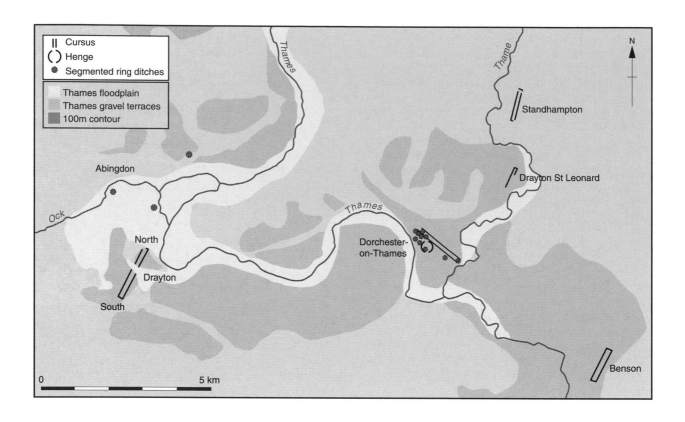

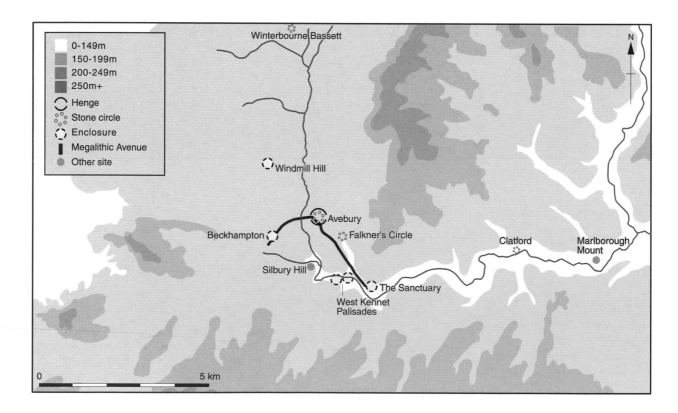

Fig. 14.11   The geographical scale and complexity of middle thand late Neolithic monuments in the Drayton-Abingdon-Dorchester area (top) and in the Upper Kennet Valley (bottom)

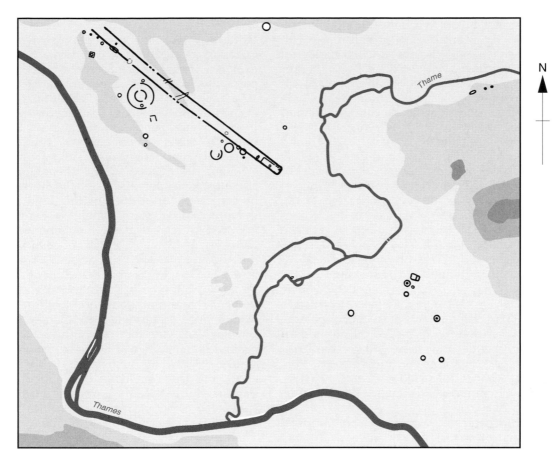

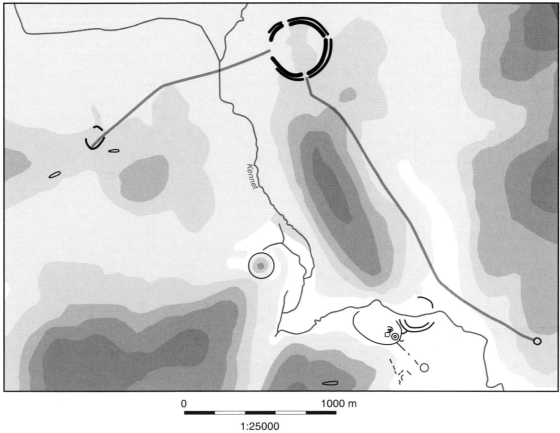

Fig. 14.12 *The 'ceremonial centres' at Dorchester-on-Thames (top) and Avebury (bottom)*

posed, physically linked, visually inter-referenced, etc) to create a powerful sense of coherence with reference to a single religious and cosmological scheme (cf Bradley 1993; 1998b, 119-31; Parker Pearson and Ramilisonina 1998; Thomas 1999, 45-61). Well-known examples in the study area include the monument groups at Dorchester-on-Thames (Bradley and Chambers 1988; Whittle *et al.* 1992; Loveday 1999; Barclay *et al.* 2003, 225-8) and Avebury (Whittle 1997b; Pollard and Reynolds 2002; Thomas 1993). It is striking that the relative scales of the middle to late Neolithic monument construction zones in both these cases are very similar (Fig. 14.12). There are, however, clear contrasts in the chronologies of the main monument-building phases: the largest construction events at Dorchester-on-Thames took place in the mid to late 4th millennium cal BC (the cursus) and in the mid-3rd millennium cal BC (the Big Rings henge; Whittle *et al.* 1992, 196-98; Harding 2003, 28, 31), whereas the construction dates for the large monuments at Avebury span the middle and later centuries of the 3rd millennium cal BC (Avebury henge and stone circles, the West Kennet and Beckhampton Avenues, Silbury Hill, and the West Kennet palisaded enclosures; Bayliss, Bronk Ramsey, van der Plicht and Whittle 2007; Gillings *et al.* 2008).

In each landscape area we thus see a palimpsest of spatial patterns relating to several distinct phases of monument-building and landscape organisation, patterns that can all too easily be conflated into single symbolic-structural models of supposedly long-term spatial order (eg Parker Pearson and Ramilisonina 1998). Indeed, it is extremely difficult to interpret such spatial patterns in terms of particular cosmological schemes because the fundamental principles underlying the constitution of sacred landscapes changed radically during the 4th to 2nd millennia cal BC, especially in relation to the nature of cosmologies, and in the ways that beliefs and identities were represented architecturally and ceremonially (Garwood 2007c). In the early Neolithic, for example, there appears to have been an emphasis on local, traditional belief systems and bounded religious-ethnic identities (Thomas 1988; 1999, 226). In the middle and late Neolithic, in contrast, these local identities and belief systems seem to have co-existed with increasingly dominant and universalising religious cults that attracted devotees from far afield, focused first on major cursus monuments (Loveday 1999) and later on large henges (Harding 2003, 96-106). In the early Bronze Age, great numbers of small funerary monuments and individual burial practices again suggest local, personal and exclusive, lineage-focused expressions of identity, but in ways that may have been subordinate to elite expressions of political status, cult membership or wider religious beliefs (evident, perhaps, in widespread traditions of mortuary practice related to distinct funerary artefact sets: Burgess 1980, 98-111, 122-31; Clarke *et*

al. 1985, 182-92, 204-20; Woodward 2000, 101-22).

In this light, the perception, experience, and material constitution of ceremonial space is best explored in terms of specific kinds of agency at particular locales over short timeframes (eg Barrett 1994; Tilley 1994; Thomas 1993). Spatial order is created in the course of social actions at significant places where people appreciate (visualise) and interpret wider spaces and try to mould them materially and cognitively in particular ways. Whether investigated from a phenomenological or structurationist perspective, the architectural points of departure for studies of this kind are usually monumentalised places where the kinds of agency involved were essentially ceremonial in character. However, with the exception of several studies of the Avebury complex (eg Barrett 1994, 13-20, 29-32, 55-65; Parker Pearson 2000; Pollard 1992, 2005; Thomas 1993), symbolic-structural and phenomenological interpretations of Neolithic and early Bronze Age monuments and landscapes in the Thames Valley are rare. The only significant recent examples are studies of Drayton cursus (Barclay *et al.* 2003, 93-100), the Stanwell landscape (Lewis *et al.* 2006), the Devil's Quoits henge (Barclay 1995a), Barrow Hills, Radley round barrow group (Garwood 1999b, 305-9), and the large-scale symbolic construction of landscape in the Middle Thames valley (Lamdin-Whymark 2008).

Despite the flat nature of the terrain on the terraces of the Thames, a cursory glance at the topographies of several of the linear arrangements of monuments in the Upper Thames Valley suggests some consistent patterns in the way that these would have been experienced in the course of processional movements along them. At both Drayton cursus (moving south to north) and Barrow Hills, Radley (moving east to west), the ceremonial routes start by traversing a relatively elevated area of land, followed by a shallow valley, and then the top of another elevated area before coming to an end at a location providing relatively wide vistas, as well as close-up views of ancient monuments that would have been at least partly hidden by the lie of the land or architectural barriers until that point (Fig. 14.13). This suggests a shared aesthetic of journey and revelation, with similar experiential qualities to those suggested for movement along the Dorset Cursus (Barrett *et al.*1991, 36-58.; Tilley 1994, 170-201), the West Kennet Avenue (Thomas 1993), the Stonehenge Cursus (eg Exon *et al.* 2000, 44-52; cf Bender 1998, 78-86), and the Stonehenge Avenue (Barrett 1994, 43-7). These routes may perhaps be interpreted as symbolic pathways that reified acts of pilgrimage and rites of passage. There is clearly considerable potential for more detailed phenomenological studies of the monuments of the Thames Valley using digital terrain modelling, viewshed analysis and virtual landscape techniques, as well as more conventional fieldwork (cf Exon *et al.* 2000).

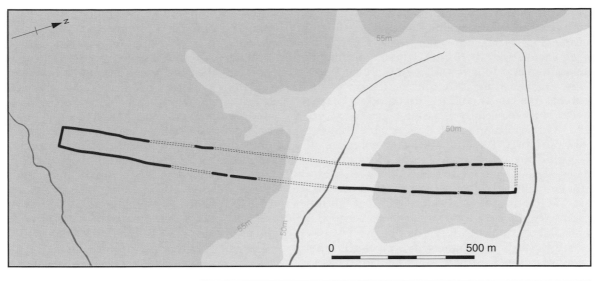

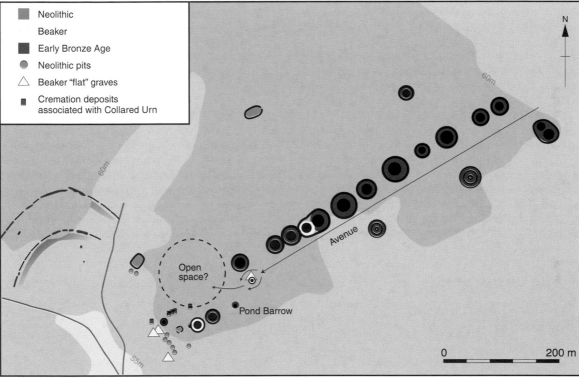

Fig. 14.13   The topographies of ceremonial routes in the Upper Thames Valley: Drayton cursus (top) and the Radley Barrow Hills linear round barrow group (bottom)

INTERPRETING NEOLITHIC CEREMONIAL MONUMENTS AND DEPOSITIONAL PRACTICES

The diversity and often unique character of ceremonial and funerary monuments evident in different parts of the Thames Valley and its catchment, despite sometimes reflecting the availability of raw materials (such as stone), seems to be the result of very specific choices about how to build such structures. We are presented with a complex mosaic of construction practices, which suggest varied rationales and responses among different communities in relation to a range of cultural and material situations. A high degree of creativity, and a concern for aesthetic qualities, is implied by the variability of scale, morphology, complexity and the incorporation of many different combinations of materials, as is a desire to commemorate and inscribe a particular view of the world on the landscape.

The simple tombs of the north-east Cotswolds

Arguably, the earliest monuments in our area are the simple stone-built tombs which are found only in the north-east Cotswolds, some of which bear a striking resemblance to the portal dolmens of western Britain (see above Chapter 12; Darvill 2004, chap. 3). They are stark and simple statements in the landscape (Fig. 14.14). For other areas of Britain it has been argued that the form of these monuments mimicked tors and hills (Bradley 2000; Tilley 1994). This line of reasoning is harder to follow in the context of the gently rolling topography of the Cotswold Hills, especially at a time when they were cloaked with woodland, yet it is notable that the sites at Rollright, Chastleton and Adlestrop were all sited around the upper edge of one of the highest points in the Cotswolds, a ridge that was subsequently embellished with a stone circle, cairns and at least one standing stone. It is possible that this hill held some significance as a sacred place because it commanded views north towards the Avon Valley and south towards the Thames, as well as glimpses of distant places as far afield as the Malvern Hills to the north-west and the Chilterns to the south. The connection with prominent hills should not, therefore, be dismissed.

As Whittle points out, the most remarkable feature of portal dolmens is the raised capstone which he suggests could have had a mythical or metaphorical significance, embodying 'a version of creation, in which the earth was raised to the sky or how... earth and sky were once joined' (2003, 120). In the case of the Whispering Knights, the capstone would have sloped from the south-east down towards the north-west, possibly capturing the sunset near to midsummer. In this case the tilted stone could also represent the movement of the sun as it descended to earth, the tomb thus embodying notions of cyclical time and regeneration.

These are small monuments, and there is little in the architecture to suggest large gatherings of people. Although none is complete now, they may have been permeable monuments (Bradley 1998b; see above), permitting views through them, providing easy, if constricted, access to the enclosed space, and allowing the addition of human remains over a long period of time. They had one dominant façade which would have provided a focus for ceremony and display, although it is uncertain whether the 'portals' which were present on this main side, at least at the Whispering Knights and Enstone (Fig. 12.3), were part of the original design or were intended to 'close down' the monument. Whatever the case, these uprights did not prevent access to the interior from the sides and back of the monument, as is demonstrated by the Bronze Age human remains at Rollright (Hey 2001).

Their size seems most appropriate for the use of a small kin group, probably reflecting the small size of the tomb-building communities in the region at the beginning of the 4th millennium. They may have been intended to advertise the individual character and group identity of the people who built them, people who may have had family links with the west of Britain rather than with the Thames Valley.

Long barrows, cairns and mortuary structures

Unlike sites elsewhere in Britain, there is little evidence for the 'entombing' of early Neolithic simple tombs by long cairns, with the exception of the rotundas within the mounds at Notgrove and Sale's Lot which seem to be atypical for the region (Clifford 1936; O'Neil 1966; Darvill 2004, 60-2; Barclay 2007). One connection between simple tombs and long cairns is the slight similarity of the stone boxes of portal dolmens to the chambers at

Fig. 14.14   The Whispering Knights portal dolmen in its landscape setting

sites such as Ascott-under-Wychwood (Fig. 14.15) and Hazleton North (the south chamber). In addition, there is a striking similarity between so-called 'false portals' set into the facades of laterally-chambered tombs, and the appearance of some portal dolmens when viewed from the front. Some long cairn chambers may also have existed for a while as free-standing structures that subsequently became incorporated into a long mound (Benson

and Whittle 2007). It is still uncertain, however, whether portal dolmens generally predate the construction of long cairns or represent a different tradition of monument building (Darvill 2004; Barclay in Benson and Whittle 2007; Whittle, Barclay, Bayliss *et al.* 2007).

The long cairns and long barrows built across the hills of the Cotswolds, the Avebury area, and to a lesser extent the Berkshire Downs and Chilterns

Fig. 14.15   The cists at Ascott-under-Wychwood

were often constructed in old clearings and places where earlier gatherings and settlement had occurred (see Chapter 12). A number of these places had also seen episodes of cultivation. This has interesting implications for our understanding of how sites became 'special', and how the past was referenced and then monumentalised at particular locales (Saville 1990a; Benson and Whittle 2007; Pollard and Reynolds 2002). The links between the placing of dead materials on middens, cultivation and new growth, and the selection of these places for the burial of dead people is surely significant (Bloch and Parry 1982; R Bradley 1998b). The construction of monuments above earlier sites seems much less common, however, in the context of the river valley of the Upper and Middle Thames where a different range of structures, such as long mortuary enclosures and oval barrows, often situated near to the river itself, is present. Some of these monuments are, nonetheless, found near to earlier sites, as the Yarnton long enclosure (near to the timber longhouse) and the Radley oval barrow (across a stream from the causewayed enclosure) show (Fig. 14.16; Bradley 1992; Hey *et al.* in prep.). They may similarly have invoked memories of past times and events.

Burial of the dead within permanent structures suggests a change in the perception of personal and group identity. Not only is a new consciousness of self and of individual mortality implied, but also new awareness of the importance of individuals to the community and of the significance of their commemoration in a permanent form (Whittle in Benson and Whittle 2007, 361-4). Only some people,

however, were commemorated in this way, whether because they were more important, their deaths had particular significance or because they died at a time and place that was opportune and appropriate for formal treatment (see Chapter 15). People were motivated to invest time and effort for particular people in particular places, and to create opportunities for ritual and display before, during and after the burial event (see above). A collective decision would have to have been taken to undertake such projects, to decide how and when they would be accomplished, and to come together to achieve them (McFadyen 2007). The ground would have to have been prepared, trees and other vegetation cleared, and the tomb laid out. The preponderance of cattle skulls and the left-hand sides of animals in the barrow construction deposits at Ascott-under Wychwood and pre-barrow settings under some of the Upper Kennet Valley monuments show that such events were accompanied by formal, ritual acts (Pollard and Reynolds 2002, 62-9; Darvill 2004, 96-101; Benson and Whittle 2002, 62-9).

In the case of cairns and other monuments with enclosed stone cists, only a few of those present at the funeral would have been able to enter the burial chamber and conduct rituals associated with laying out the dead and moving any burials already present. Larger-scale and more inclusive ceremonies could, however, have taken place outside. The forecourts and 'horns' found at the ends of many long cairns and barrows would have provided a dramatic backdrop to such events, as well as impressing other groups. More open burial chambers, like those at Whiteleaf, the Radley long

Fig. 14.16   The long mortuary enclosure at Yarnton, Oxfordshire

mortuary structure and the chamber of Wayland's Smithy I, would have provided space for more people to observe the final acts of burial (Whittle 1991; Barclay and Halpin 1999; Hey *et al.* 2007).

Grave goods only rarely seem to have been placed with the dead at this time (Darvill 2004, 165-72). The flint core and quartz hammerstone associated with the male inhumation in the north chamber area at Hazleton North, small pottery vessels from West Kennet, and beads, including an example in shale, found at Notgrove may be examples (though the latter may have been worn on the garment of the deceased; Saville 1990a; Piggott 1962; Clifford 1936). Recent radiocarbon dating and Bayesian modelling of results at Hazleton indicate that deposits of animal bone found in the south chamber and passageway were later offerings (Meadows *et al.* 2007).

The construction of a mound may have occurred either immediately after burial or after a period of time during which other events may have taken place, many of which may have left no trace. Radiocarbon dates at Whiteleaf suggest that between 45 and 150 years elapsed between the death of the man found in the mortuary structure and the raising of the first phase of the mound (Hey *et al.* 2007), and 40 to 100 years separate the burials in the Wayland's Smithy I mortuary structure and the construction of the barrow (Whittle, Bayliss and Wysocki 2007). Building the mound was another act which required communal effort and provided the opportunity to think about those buried and the importance of the place. Animal bone, quantities of quite freshly-broken pottery vessels, struck flint and charcoal suggest that the core of the Whiteleaf barrow incorporated feasting debris (Childe and Smith 1954). The remains of feasting seem also to have been present in the ditch fills of the oval barrow at Staines Road Farm, Shepperton where they were found above placed deposits of antler, pottery vessels, animal remains and some human bone (Jones 2008). For most earthen barrows, raising the mound would have been the final act, closing the opportunity to see the dead and add other individuals to the grave beneath, although there is plenty of evidence that barrow mounds continued to be visited and enhanced at a later date, as is seen at Whiteleaf (Hey *et al.* 2007) and more dramatically at Wayland's Smithy where the phase 1 oval barrow was embodied within the Cotswold-Severn long mound (Fig. 14.17; Whittle 1991). Even when ceremonies had ceased to take place, the monument would have prompted personal memories and, increasingly, would have embodied collective social histories, of people and places, about which stories may have been told. The cenotaph barrows of the Upper Kennet Valley, where no human remains appear to have been buried, demonstrate the importance of the monument structure itself (Thomas 1988).

Monuments constructed of stone, like dolmens and chambered cairns, lent themselves to greater longevity of use, and returning and reusing them may always have been possible, even if many now seem to have been used for only a few generations (Bayliss and Whittle 2007). Monuments of wood, on the other hand, had much shorter lifespans, and timber mortuary houses would have decayed comparatively rapidly; some may have left no trace. Although they are not numerous, an important group of monuments incorporated, or consisted solely of, structures built of split tree trunks. These are found in quite diverse parts of the landscape, from Whiteleaf on the Chilterns and Wayland's Smithy I on the Berkshire Downs, to New Wintles Farm on the gravels near Eynsham (Kenward 1982; Whittle 1991; Hey *et al.* 2007). The symbolic importance of the use of trees and their association in each case with the burial of the dead (including cremated human remains in addition to inhumation burials) is apparent. This pattern is also seen elsewhere in southern Britain, at Fussell's Lodge in Wiltshire, for example, and Aldwincle in Northamptonshire (Ashbee 1966; Jackson 1977). The architectural contexts and use-histories of these structures, however, varied considerably: the Whiteleaf example was encased within an oval barrow; the New Wintles structure was surrounded by a small segmented enclosure, possibly embanked; and the split tree-trunk chamber at Wayland's Smithy was covered by an oval barrow *c* 40-100 years after the initial deposits were made, and the oval barrow was, in turn, covered some 1-35 years later by the Cotswold-Severn tomb (Whittle, Bayliss and Wysocki 2007).

The Wayland's Smithy I structure was similar to the linear mortuary structure at Radley, situated close to the Radley oval barrow and the Abingdon causewayed enclosure, and dating to the mid- or late-4th millennium BC (Barclay and Bradley 1999, 28-31; Garwood 1999b, 276-77). Although the Radley mortuary structure was not a 'box' built on the surface but a timber structure supported by conglomerate blocks constructed within a pit, it also contained a sequence of inhumations which suggests that it was possible to re-access the wooden coffin or chamber. This underlines a preoccupation, also seen at Whiteleaf, with placing some of the dead within containers which could then be re-entered, and which were only later closed and sealed. This is demonstrated most clearly in the Cotswold Severn tombs, in the entrance of the northern chamber passageway at Hazleton, for example (Saville 1990a). Although the bones are jumbled, only three adult burials were present, probably placed as successive deposits of complete bodies, together with one or more children and some cremated human bone.

These site biographies suggest a common repertoire of practices and architectural options which were widely shared and which people could employ as seemed appropriate in a range of different situations (Thomas 1999). Burial practices and the 'housing' of the dead, in particular, appear to have been similar, while later monumentalisation and embellishment were very varied, and it seems unlikely that the final forms of these monuments were anticipated at the beginnings of their very different 'lives' (cf McFadyen 2007). These monuments appear to be the outcome of very specific choices made on a local level, perhaps as expressions of individual communities and their particular ceremonial and representational needs.

In the Upper Kennet Valley, tombs of Cotswold-Severn type are found to the east and north of Avebury, and earthen barrows to the south and west (Thomas 1999, 203-4, fig. 9.1), a distribution which relates only approximately to the availability of stone for chamber- and wall-construction. Pollard has suggested that this spatial pattern might reflect a grand cosmological scheme encompassing different domains of existence and the transformations from one domain to another (Fig. 14.18): from west to east, from earth to stone, and from the fleshed remains of the recently-dead to the defleshed disarticulated remains of the ancestors (Pollard and Reynolds 2002, 69-70). This assumes an ordering of events over a large area for a considerable period of time. In the absence of good dating evidence for many of these monuments, however, it

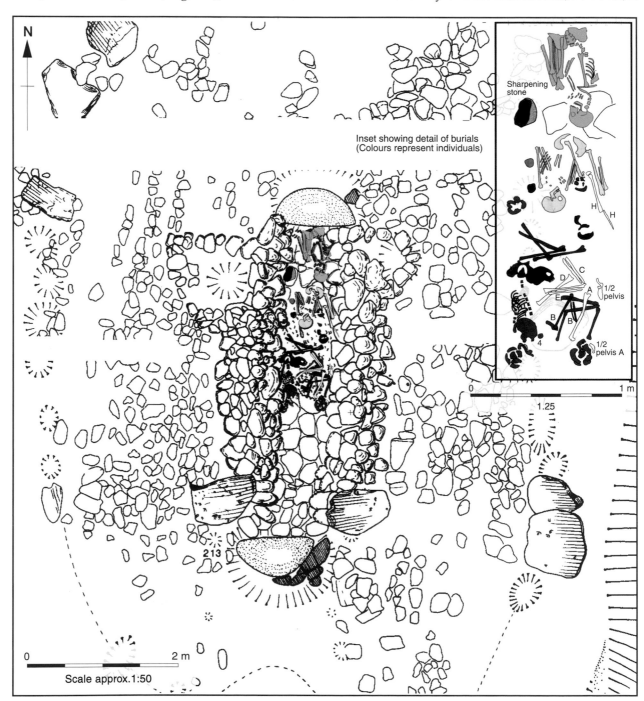

Fig. 14.17 The burial chamber of Wayland's Smithy I

350

is difficult to be certain of the extent to which some of the contrasts may have been related to changes in practices over time or the possibility that different monuments were built by people with different funerary traditions. If Avebury in the early Neolithic was a liminal landscape at the margins of the main areas of settlement, where people came together from different geographical and cultural regions for ceremonies, festivities and exchanges unbound by usual social norms (Whittle and Pollard 1999), chambered tombs and earthen barrows may have been built by different groups of people at the limits of their respective territories. The chambered tombs of the Avebury area are certainly found closest to the large groups of stone-built tombs in the Cotswold region to the north, while the earthen barrows in the area occur closest to the dense distributions of similar monuments on the chalklands to the south. In this context, competition between groups, mixing of ideas and innovation may explain some of the exotic features of these monuments, and the presence of 'foreign' material such as imported stone and pottery (Thomas 1999, 208; cf Bayliss, McAvoy and Whittle 2007, 99).

In fluid social environment of the time, more successful, competitive or ruthless groups may have sought to display and legitimate their prominence through elaborate mortuary rituals and then through even more eye-catching monument constructions (Whittle, Barclay, Bayliss *et al.* 2007, 135). Nevertheless, these were structures that seem to have been built by small groups of people, perhaps once in a generation.

Causewayed enclosures

If barrows, cairns and other funerary structures reflect the concerns of small communities, causewayed enclosures were monuments built and used by much larger groups. They were constructed on a much larger scale than burial monuments, and were plainly designed to delimit spaces in which communal events could take place, with permeable boundaries to facilitate movement between different areas (see above). These events included treatment of the dead, but the deposits found within them show that people were also undertaking a much wider range of other activities. As Whittle and Pollard remark in their concluding chapter on Windmill Hill, it is 'hard to think of a dimension of the earlier Neolithic way of life in the region which is not made present at this enclosure' (Whittle *et al.* 1999, 384).

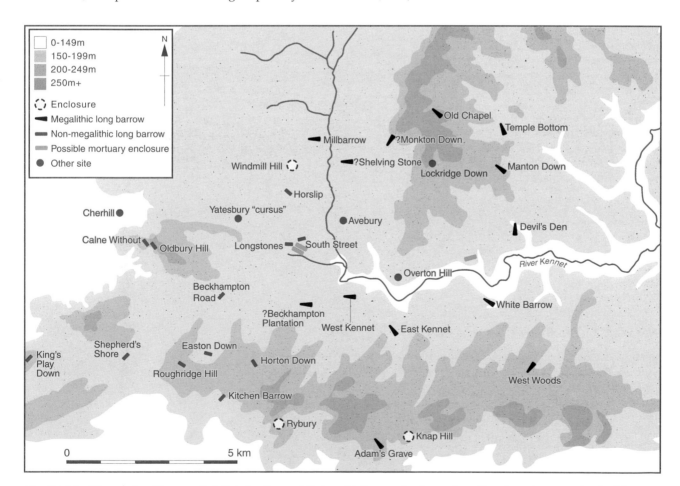

Fig. 14.18   The contrasting spatial distributions of Cotswold-Severn tombs and earthen long barrows in the Upper Kennet Valley

The enclosures on the Chalk in the Upper Kennet Valley appear to be positioned to have wide views over particular parts of the landscape. It has been suggested that they may have drawn people from a wide area, perhaps as people moved their herds between the Chalk uplands and the clay vales. It is possible that marginal locales were deliberately chosen to reflect the nature of activities that were performed in these arenas, such as communal gatherings to witness rites of passage and events concerned with the dead and the ancestors (Whittle *et al.* 1999), and as places where the transformation of material would be both possible and more potent (Edmonds 1993; Thomas 1999, 41). Valley enclosures are located either at or near major confluences (eg Abingdon and Staines) or close to major topographical changes, as with the cluster of enclosures near the Thames on the south edge of the Cotswolds and at Goring. In these cases, liminal positions away from settlement may not have been as important as locations where routeways crossed and, thus, people met. It is also notable that some enclosures, like Buckland and Staines, were situated by rivers, and could have been prone to flooding, bringing water into the enclosed sphere of the site. This suggests that waterways were not only important as people travelled around the landscape but

also in terms of what they had come to symbolise: the 'confluence' of different groups of people as they moved (or flowed) through the landscape, and shared understandings of the otherworldliness of 'watery' places.

The sizes of the enclosures certainly suggest gatherings of large groups of people, while the absence of evidence for dense settlement close by suggests that people congregated at these places from a wide area on an occasional basis. They could have provided a permanent focus for people to gather together for social reasons, to feast, to maintain family bonds, exchange information, negotiate and deal with disputes, form alliances, find marriage partners, and exchange valued items such as stone axes and breeding animals. The presence of small bowls for serving food and drink, for example, as well as quantities of animal bone, quernstones and the evidence of cereals, lends weight to this interpretation.

The creation of an enclosure, of course, implies a series of significant decisions and actions which would not only have demonstrated the importance of the site but would also have reinforced group co-operation and commitment. These were large projects involving shared interests, agreement, mobilisation of labour, design and construction

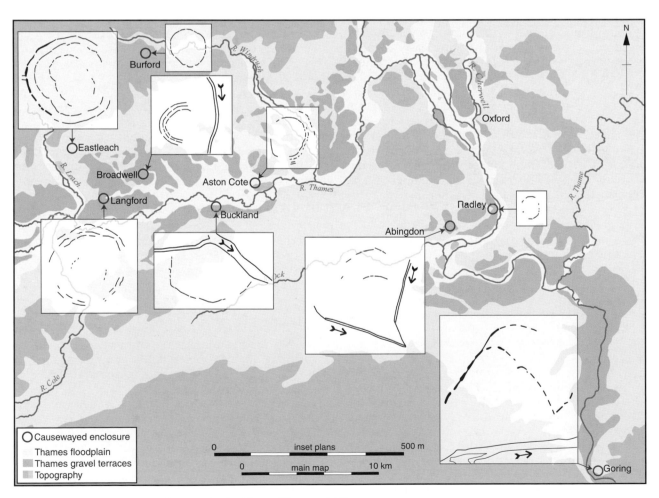

Fig. 14.19   Causewayed enclosures in the Upper Thames Valley

even before the use of the site (Whittle *et al.* forth-coming). As has long been suggested, the cause-wayed plan (Fig. 14.19) may imply that different groups dug their own ditch lengths, and the cause-ways themselves created a permeable architectural form, suggesting that entry and egress was open. The banks would not have been high, and some at least of the ditches were filled quickly. Activities would not have been screened from public view; on the contrary, they were intended to be visible. Many could have participated and, unlike later ceremonial monuments, there is no obvious suggestion that a few would be actively engaged while the majority watched. These were not private spaces, therefore, although multiple ditch circuits, as at Windmill Hill, would have created a hierarchy of spaces through which perhaps only certain categories of people could have passed (see above).

The temporality of these enclosures also needs to be borne in mind: not only did they have their own extended histories but they may have referenced memories of much more ancient and distant enclosures, communal village spaces or past communities and mythical settlements (Bradley 1998a). Indeed, it is possible that these enclosures 'invoked a tradition of communal living that no longer existed, but which continued to have resonance' (R Bradley 2007, 87). Their apparent appearance around 300 years after the beginning of the Neolithic must reflect the changing social and ritual needs of a growing and changing early Neolithic population, perhaps the result of an 'intense dialogue about the right way to live within the larger community' (Whittle, Barclay, Bayliss *et al.* 2007, 138). At a practical level, the design and construction of enclosures also involved repetitive actions over time: the digging and recutting of ditch segments, repeated deposition of cultural materials and acts of backfilling, thus creating a boundary that could be filled and then renewed again (Thomas 1999, 41-2), closing down and recreating the monument afresh. Such physical and visible engagements with the site would have helped keep the site 'alive' through a process of renewal, creating further memories and distinctive histories of place.

The deposits found within enclosure ditches often demonstrate careful and deliberate selection of materials and their careful placement. Animal bone, predominantly skull and limb bones, forms a consistently high proportion of the deposits, indicating specific and repeated series of actions related to the treatment of the animal remains, and reflecting the importance of animals in the lives of these people (Fig. 14.20; Ray and Thomas 2003). The animals are mostly domesticates, principally cattle, although occasionally wild animals are found, most commonly the remains of deer, although aurochs, fox and cat are also represented. At Windmill Hill, a deliberate mix of animals seems to have been selected for deposition in some ditch segments (Whittle *et al.* 1999, 358-61). At

Fig. 14.20 Placed animal bone deposits in Middle Ditch segments IB and VII at Windmill Hill

Abingdon there were also carefully placed bone deposits in some ditch segments, often in bundles and sometimes articulated (Avery 1982). These practices suggest the conspicuous non-consumption of meat. Other deposits comprised broken and fully-processed bone, including split long and skull bones, as well as bones disturbed and damaged by scavengers. The dark soil within which they are often found suggests that they came from middens. Occasional human remains at these sites, again usually represented by skull and limb bones, often weathered, may indicate the 'potency of ancestral remains' (Bloch and Parry 1982). Occasional complete inhumations are also found at causewayed enclosure sites, including two children and an adult at Windmill Hill (Whittle *et al.* 1999), and undated burials at Abingdon (Avery 1982), Knap Hill and Staines (Edmonds 1993, 121-2). The significance of these burial events is uncertain (see Chapter 15), although Edmonds notes that such burials are mainly of children, with fewer women and even fewer men.

In some cases, different ditch circuits, at Abingdon and Staines for example, appear to have been used for the deposition of different combinations of objects apparently representing different concerns (Bradley 1986a; P Bradley 2004; Lamdin-Whymark 2008). The outer circuit at Windmill Hill contained deposits of articulated animal bone groups, unworked antler, wild plants and axe fragments, and also the dead, including infant burials, which were thus related to the natural surroundings beyond the enclosure. The ditch seems to mark a liminal zone, crossed as people entered from the outside world to the sociality of the interior, providing also a reminder of the departed and, perhaps, ancestors and the past (Fig. 12.29; Whittle *et al.* 1999). The inner two circuits had deposits which seem to relate to the meals, feasts and rituals which took place within the monument, with the most fragmented material coming from the inner circuit, some of which could have derived from middens. This material includes more pottery and flint flakes and knives as well as querns and rubbers. The recent causewayed enclosure dating programme has shown that these three ditch circuits were not all dug at the same time, and, in particular, that the middle ditch, probably cut *c* 3655-3605 cal BC, may have been excavated after the inner and outer ditches (*c* 3685-3635 cal BC and 3685-3610), although the period of construction as a whole probably lasted less than 75 years (Whittle *et al.* forthcoming).

This evidence suggests that while carefully arranged depositional events occurred repeatedly, and regular patterns can be seen in the general categories of things used, there is very little consistency in the combinations found or in the manner of deposition. These were not formulaic practices. Instead, we can recognise a 'constant play on materials' (Whittle *et al.* 1999, 363), involving guiding principles in the way ritual practices were enacted, and strong shared ideas of what was appropriate, but no rigid set of prescriptive rules.

Cursus monuments and related structures in the Thames Valley

Cursus monuments are almost as much of an enigma now as they were when William Stukeley first identified them in the 18th century, interpreting the Stonehenge cursus as an ancient British chariot-racing course (1740, 41). In the intervening years, they have been described amongst other things as Bronze Age rectangular enclosures of unknown purpose (Leeds 1934b, 416) and as British trackways (Crawford 1935), but the idea of movement and

procession along them has persisted (Harding and Barclay 1999), based on their linear form and scale, stretching in some cases beyond the visible horizon (Fig. 14.21). Indeed, human processions would have been dwarfed by the proportions of many of these monuments (Loveday 1999).

It is also notable that cursus monuments were often built incrementally, sometimes with changes of design, so that the final form may never have been visible at any one moment of time while some sections may already have been heavily eroded before other parts were built (Barclay *et al.* 2003, 93-7; Pryor 1985, 299-304). Indeed, the construction project may have been as important as the use of monument itself (as has been suggested for the Cleaven Dyke on Tayside; G J Barclay *et al.* 1995), while woodland clearance and the creation of animal grazing may have formed part of the overall design (see above, Chapter 12). Additions to monuments and their elaboration would have kept alive their special significance, and might have become part of the ritual activity enacted there (Pryor 1985; Bradley 1993).

Nevertheless, there is a unity of design which suggests that moving through and linking places in the landscape, including natural features and earlier monuments with histories of their own, was an underlying motivation for the people who conceived and constructed them (Bradley 1993). The journey would have enabled the participants to see places of importance in their shared past, and remember significant people and events, while the physical form of the monument would have acted as an avenue directing and restricting movement and discourse (*ibid.*; Barrett 1994). This would have

Fig. 14.21 Reconstruction of a procession along the top of the Stanwell bank barrow, as viewed from the HE1 enclosure

been a shared journey which brought people together, perhaps from a wide area, to witness and participate in communal ceremonies, some of which may have referenced solar events (eg at Dorchester-on-Thames; Bradley and Chambers 1988). At the same time, they may have acted as symbolic and physical boundaries, possibly between domestic and wild (Barrett 1994), or at least between interior and exterior spaces (Bradley 1991; G J Barclay *et al* 1995, 325).

The extent to which tree clearance was involved in the creation of these monuments has already been noted in Chapter 12, where it was noted that amongst the small number of finds recovered from cursus monuments axes and cattle stand out. The strong link between tree clearance, cursus construction and the herding of cattle has been discussed elsewhere (Barclay and Hey 1999), and between Neolithic monuments and herding domesticates more generally (Tilley 1994, 206-8). This was not a new aspect of the archaeological record. As we have seen, formal deposits of cattle can be seen at a number of causewayed enclosures and funerary monuments, perhaps even being treated as equivalents to human bones (Thomas 1988; Ray and Thomas 2003; Whittle 2003), but the construction of these very large features in extensively cleared landscapes occurred at a time when settlement in the Upper Thames Valley seems to have become more extensive, and lifestyles more mobile and more centred around cattle herding. Creating and maintaining ceremonial spaces on the one hand and grazing animals on the other would have been intertwined activities, reinforcing the metaphorical link between humans and cattle.

Last has suggested that cursus monuments monumentalised previous routes, and represent the beginning of a symbolic focus on routes themselves (Last 1999). He argues that the absence of material in cursus ditches and from fieldwalking over cursus sites suggests that people were moving through these places rather than to them, and that there was less focus on acts of deposition, and more emphasis instead on formal choreographed movement and perhaps an association with the dead. In this context, the close spatial and temporal relationship with earlier funerary monuments is important. It is notable that a variety of small oval, U-shaped or rectangular ditched enclosures, which are believed to have had a mortuary function, are often found close to cursus monuments, including the examples at Buscot Wick and Stadhampton (Fig. 12.19). At Dorchester-on-Thames, the cursus linked two axially-aligned sites of this kind, spaced over 1 km apart (Bradley and Chambers 1988; Whittle *et al.* 1992), thereby formalising a processional path between two earlier monuments, and creating a sacred space or precinct with only a limited number of entrances for channelling movement (Fig. 14.8). At Stanwell it has been argued that ceremonies were articulated between such places and the area marked by the cursus or

bank barrow (Lewis *et al.* 2006), and a similar scenario may have existed at sites like North Stoke and Benson where similar monuments occur in close proximity (Barclay and Brereton 2003, 223, 230-1). Cursus monuments may thus have created physical and symbolic links between the living and the dead (Bradley 1993), perhaps even representing extended 'houses of the dead' (Loveday 2006).

The ability to view other sites and topographical features probably influenced their design. Roy Loveday has argued that many of the cursus monuments near Dorchester-on-Thames were aligned on a group of low but prominent hills (1999), and Barclay and Hey (1999) have noted that movement along the Drayton cursus – with its combination of subtle and dramatic changes in topography – would have involved a journey of changing experiences. Their association with rivers and water may also have been important (Barclay and Hey 1999, 73-4; Last 1999, 94). Although cursus banks would not necessarily have been high, they would nevertheless have focused the attention of participants and viewers in a linear direction, and in the case of bank barrows such as North Stoke and Stanwell would have provided central linear platforms for processions. Such architecture would have elevated and made visible anyone partaking in ceremonies. Other interpretations favour the idea that people were excluded from cursus monuments, thus explaining the long stretches without entrances and the frequent terminal ditches: they were places for the dead and not the living (Johnston 1999; R Bradley 2007, 65-6).

Several cursus monuments, including the example at Drayton, were later blocked by the building of round barrows. Only at Dorchester-on-Thames is there clear evidence of a cursus being appropriated and adapted for ceremonial use by subsequent generations. A post circle was constructed within the cursus, and other small palisade enclosures were built inside and outside it, a number of which were then reused as cremation cemeteries (see Chapters 12 and 15). It is tempting to see these monuments as physical manifestations of ritual acts that would have taken place during pauses or stations in the journey as people passed along the cursus, but it is possible that Dorchester-on-Thames was always special. It stands out within the Thames valley for several reasons: it is the only site to incorporate a solar alignment within its design (Bradley and Chambers 1988), it integrates two earlier Neolithic enclosures, and it is surrounded by a small cluster of other cursus monuments. It is perhaps not surprising, therefore, that it was reused by subsequent generations, perhaps most dramatically when the double-ditched Big Rings henge was constructed just outside the line of the cursus later in the Neolithic.

Fig. 14.22 (overleaf) The Devil's Quoits

DEVILS QUOITS

The Devil's Quoits is a late Neolithic henge monument which lies to the south of Stanton Harcourt, not far from the Thames. As is typical of such monuments generally, the ditch at the Devil's Quoits lies inside the bank, and like most of the other large henges in the Thames Valley, the Devil's Quoits is a Class II henge, with two diametrically opposed entrances, which here are 115 metres apart and are aligned roughly ENE-WSW.

A widely-spaced circle, 75 m in diameter, of 28 stones - the Quoits - lay within the henge. It is the only henge in the Thames Valley known to have been associated with a ring of stones. The stones are conglomerate, a concretion of sand and gravel pebbles which occurs in rafts in the gravel terraces of the Thames. It outcrops on this site and can still be seen in situ at the western entrance. Excavations suggest that there was also a setting of posts in the centre of the monument.

A further single stone lay offset from the circle on its southern side. This stone may have been a marker from which observations were made, but it is uncertain whether the position of this stone, or that of the entrances to the monument, reflect particular celestial alignments, or whether the entrances incorporate important pathways or face particular landscape features.

The henge was, however, built in an area which had already been largely cleared of trees, and consisted of lightly grazed grassland with areas of scrub. It was also already a significant place in the landscape. A number of earlier funerary monuments lay nearby, including an important middle Neolithic burial at Linch Hill Corner.

The area retained its significance in later periods too. Over the following millennium over 60 burial monuments were constructed in the surrounding area, which also provided the location for a number of unmarked graves, a timber circle and many pits containing special deposits, making it one of the densest monument complexes in Bronze Age Britain. In the Iron Age, rather than being ploughed, it seems to have become traditional grazing land for the nearby farming settlements.

DEVILS QUOITS

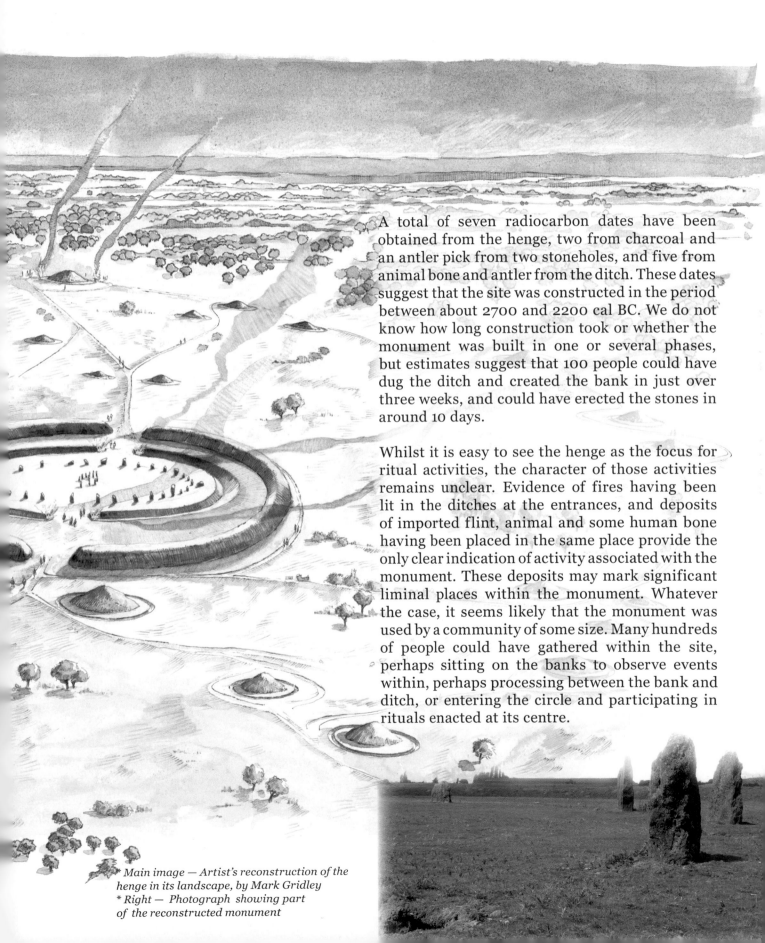

A total of seven radiocarbon dates have been obtained from the henge, two from charcoal and an antler pick from two stoneholes, and five from animal bone and antler from the ditch. These dates suggest that the site was constructed in the period between about 2700 and 2200 cal BC. We do not know how long construction took or whether the monument was built in one or several phases, but estimates suggest that 100 people could have dug the ditch and created the bank in just over three weeks, and could have erected the stones in around 10 days.

Whilst it is easy to see the henge as the focus for ritual activities, the character of those activities remains unclear. Evidence of fires having been lit in the ditches at the entrances, and deposits of imported flint, animal and some human bone having been placed in the same place provide the only clear indication of activity associated with the monument. These deposits may mark significant liminal places within the monument. Whatever the case, it seems likely that the monument was used by a community of some size. Many hundreds of people could have gathered within the site, perhaps sitting on the banks to observe events within, perhaps processing between the bank and ditch, or entering the circle and participating in rituals enacted at its centre.

Main image — Artist's reconstruction of the henge in its landscape, by Mark Gridley
Right — Photograph showing part of the reconstructed monument

DEVILS QUOITS

Further insights into the character of the monument have recently been gained as a result of its reconstruction. Although it is impossible to replicate the form of the monument exactly, it has nevertheless been possible to turn a plan into three-dimensional reality. The huge size of the internal area is probably the first impression to strike the observer, and it is also possible to appreciate the sense of enclosure achieved by even a modest bank which, at full height, would have excluded much of the external view, and would have focused attention on action taking place in the interior. More surprising is the width of the berm, which would have provided space for processions, subsidiary activities or a segregated area for those who were not allowed to proceed through the inner entrance. The standing stones are relatively small and widely spaced (c 6.5 m apart) and do not form a barrier to visibility, but they do demarcate another area between the inner ditch and the interior.

* Above — Re-erecting the quoits
* Below left — Some of the quoits lying incumbent prior to reconstruction (and being used as a picnic table).
* Below right — Reconstructing the henge ditch using modern excavation techniques.

Henges

Dorchester-on-Thames was one of six places in the Upper Thames Valley where massive henges were constructed, along with sites at Oxford, Stanton Harcourt (the Devil's Quoits), Westwell, Condicote and Cutsdean (Barclay 1995c; Figs 14.6 and 14.8). Significantly, these sites occur at regular intervals of around 20 km (Fig. 14.24). The sites connect the Thames gravels with an area of the Cotswolds that had a rich history of monument building and long and distant connections with western Britain. It is possible that gatherings took place progressively from one monument to another as cult members or larger communities moved between Dorchester-on-Thames and the Cotswolds, perhaps as part of a ritual cycle. Not surprisingly, these sites became the foci for later burials, many of which involved the deposition of rare, powerful and novel objects (for example, at Snowshill, Gravelly Guy and Dorchester-on-Thames). In the context of the Yorkshire henges, Jan Harding has suggested that they may have been pilgrimage sites (Harding 2003) and this could also be proposed for the Upper Thames henges; they may have replaced ceremonial routes represented by cursus monuments, but with Dorchester-on-Thames retaining its pivotal role.

Little is known about the architectural design and ceremonial qualities of most of these henges with the notable exception of the Devil's Quoits, the reconstruction of which has been an informative experience (Hey 2009). Although it is impossible to replicate the form of the monument exactly as so much detail has been lost, it has nevertheless been possible to turn a plan into three-dimensional reality (Fig 14.22). The huge size of the internal area is probably the first impression to strike the observer, and it is also possible to appreciate the sense of enclosure achieved by even a modest bank which, at full height, would have excluded much of the external view and focused attention on action taking place in the interior. More surprising is the width of the berm, which would have provided space for processions, subsidiary activities or a segregated area for those who were not allowed to proceed through the inner entrance. The standing stones do not form a barrier to visibility as they are relatively small and widely spaced (c 6.5 m apart), but they do demarcate another area between the inner ditch and the interior. The monolith positioned just outside the circle clearly had a significant ceremonial role within this space (although it appears to have no relation to any particular celestial alignment; A J Barclay *et al.* 1995, 73). Analysis of the stone holes suggests that the inner area would have been entered through the stone circle between taller uprights which lay opposite each of the main entrances. The postholes found in the centre of the monument may also have formed a structure such as a screen or cove that would have allowed special activities to remain hidden from people beyond. Opposed entrances

suggest movement through the monument, as has been suggested by Barclay in relation to the Dorchester-on-Thames Big Rings (2000), where the entrances are aligned on Site XI, a multiple ring ditch and pit circle lying in an entrance into the cursus (Fig. 12.22). On the other hand, the presence of an internal ditch and external bank, apparently 'defending' the exterior of the monument, has led others to propose that these monuments were constructed to contain malign spirits or 'the wild' (Hodder 1990; Gibson 2005; Harding 2003, 39-41).

Very few objects have been found associated with the Thames Valley henges. The terminals of the ditches at the Devil's Quoits contained placed deposits of animal bone and some human bone, and animal bone and pottery was found in the ditch of the Dorchester-on-Thames Big Rings (Whittle *et al.* 1992; Barclay *et al.* 1995), but these were not substantial deposits; they seem more likely to derive from acts of ritual deposition. Very little cultural material was found in the surrounding areas to suggest large gatherings and feasting nearby. There is a sense of other-worldliness about these places. Hearths and evidence of burning at the terminals of the Devil's Quoits ditches suggest that fires were lit at these liminal places, perhaps enhancing the mystery and danger of moving into the centre of the monument (Fig. 14.22). Posts were also set here.

The henge at Avebury presents a contrast to the Thames Valley monuments. It was much larger and contained much more complex and elaborate inner settings (see above and Chapter 12), and it was closely connected to other sites in the landscape (Gray 1935; Smith 1965a; Burl 2000; Pollard and Reynolds 2002, 81-96; Gillings *et al.* 2008; see Chapter 12). Its stone avenues may have been a physical manifestation of unmarked and traditional paths that would have been present at other henges, but which at Avebury became formal and dramatic. As with all the monuments in this area, considerable time and effort was expended in constructing ever more elaborate, awe-inspiring and ostentatious structures.

The West Kennet Avenue linked the henge to the Sanctuary and the Beckhampton stone avenue led to the Beckhampton enclosure (Fig. 12.43), both sites where feasting deposits were recovered (Cunnington 1931; Pollard 1992; Pollard and Reynolds; Gillings *et al.* 2008). At the nearby West Kennet palisaded enclosures large quantities of animal bone were found along with pottery vessels for cooking, serving and consuming food (Whittle 1997b; see Chapter 12). These were places where large groups came together and feasted, principally on meat, near to the henge during its construction or use. In this, as in other respects, Avebury is much more similar to other Wessex henges like Durrington Walls and Marden, than it is to the Thames Valley monuments.

As people moved down the stone avenues from the outer ceremonial sites and feasting places towards Avebury, they would have experienced a changing vista of earlier monuments and other important places (Barrett 1994, 13-20 Pollard and Reynolds 2002), and the misalignment of the stone avenues as they approached the Avebury monument may have heightened the anticipation of arrival (Gillings *et al.* 2008). Once there, they would have been in the centre of a circular world, defined by the henge bank and ditch but also by more distant views of low hills (R Bradley 1998, chapter 8; 2007, 136-7). The stone circle and internal post settings at the Devil's Quoits suggest a nested sequence of spaces in which ceremonies could take place but, with the possible exception of the inner settings of posts, these may largely have been visible to those within the bank of the henge. The complex structural elements at Avebury, on the other hand, suggest very specialised and elaborate ceremonies undertaken within a range of alternative sites. Many of these could not easily have been observed except by those permitted to participate (Gibson 2005). What remains today is the result of a long sequence of development over the 3rd millennium, with many changes and embellishments over time. The unwitting outcome of what may have begun as a large communal project, may have been the creation of inequalities between those who could and could not attend, and between those who were observers and those who performed the rites. This may have enabled knowledgeable and forceful individuals to become specialists and orchestrate events, and a few to become preeminent within their societies (Barrett 1994, 29-32).

Neolithic round barrows, ring ditches and pit circles

The wide range of small circular monuments dating to the period before *c* 2500 BC, including various kinds of round barrows, continuous and segmented ring ditches and pit circles is far less well understood (see Chapter 12). There are numerous excavated sites of these kinds in the study area, including: Stanton Harcourt Ring Ditch XXII 6 (Taylor 1995), Radley Barrow Hills segmented ring ditch (Barclay and Halpin 1999), Corporation Farm Ring Ditches 1 and 2 (Shand *et al.* 2003), Dorchester-on-Thames Sites I, II, IV-VI, XI and 2 (Atkinson *et al.* 1951, Whittle *et al.* 1992), Reading Business Park segmented ring ditch (Area 3017; Brossler *et al.* 2004, 5-7, 117), Perry Oaks Horseshoe Enclosure 1 (Lewis *et al.* 2006, 72-80), Ashford Prison Ring Ditch 1, Middlesex (Carew *et al.* 2006), and Heathrow Airport Site A, Middlesex (Canham 1978, 6-7). The categorisation of these monuments, however, varies greatly from one site report to another, and is further complicated by uncertain interpretations of the presence or absence of mounds at plough-truncated sites and vague and inconsistent use of terms such as 'henge' and 'hengiform'. There is also no agreed typology for pit circles and related structures. Neolithic round mounds remain relatively

little-studied (Kinnes 1979; Lamdin-Whymark 2008, 162-70; Leary *et al.* 2010), and the formal similarity of some of these sites to early Bronze Age round barrows, at least when seen as truncated ring ditches, prevents type identification based only on air photographs.

As dating evidence is sparse, and the monument forms and depositional practices represented are so varied, it is not possible at present to suggest anything more than a tentative dating scheme for these circular ditched monuments (cf Barclay 1995c, 107-8) as part of a more extended chronology of round barrow forms in the Middle and Upper Thames Valley spanning the 4th to 2nd millennia cal BC. Unsurprisingly, there is also very little agreement about the use of these sites except for a broad 'ceremonial' interpretation, based on their architectural forms and frequent evidence for deliberate deposition of cultural materials (Lamdin-Whymark 2008, 162-70). Very few appear to have had a funerary role at any stage during their use (the segmented ring ditch at Staines Road Farm, Shepperton, is a rare exception, with secondary burials of middle Neolithic date in the ditch recut; Jones 1990; 2008). What they do share, of course, is an architectural scale that suggests only small numbers of people were needed for their construction, and – at least in terms of enclosed spaces – that they accommodated only small groups engaged in rituals (see Figs 14.5-6; see also Lamdin-Whymark 2008, figs. 54, 55). The contrast with cursus monuments and henges could not be greater, reinforcing the sense of different scales of ceremonial activity, probably dedicated to very different aspects of cosmological representation and religious expression.

DEATH, CEREMONY AND MONUMENTAL ARCHITECTURE IN THE BEAKER PERIOD AND EARLY BRONZE AGE

Round barrows as ceremonial architecture

Round barrows have usually been regarded literally as 'monuments'; that is, as simple memorials to the dead (see Fig. 14.24 for an overall distribution map), although the complexity of construction sequences and free-standing premound architecture have been recognised for some time (eg Ashbee 1960, 60-5; 1978, 27-34; cf Barrett 1990; Lynch and Waddell 1993). Only very recently has this architectural complexity been considered in relation to the spatial organisation of ceremonial practices such as funerary rituals, and in terms of the potential symbolic significance of constructional forms and features. Concentric stake- and post-rings, for example, have been interpreted as ways of delineating space for guiding and organising funerary events (Garwood 1991, 15; Last 1998; Owoc 2001b), while ring cairns and pond barrows have been seen as arenas for repeated ceremonial performances (ibid.; Lynch 1993, 134-43; Garwood 1999b, 286-88; 2007a). Some mound structures were certainly also

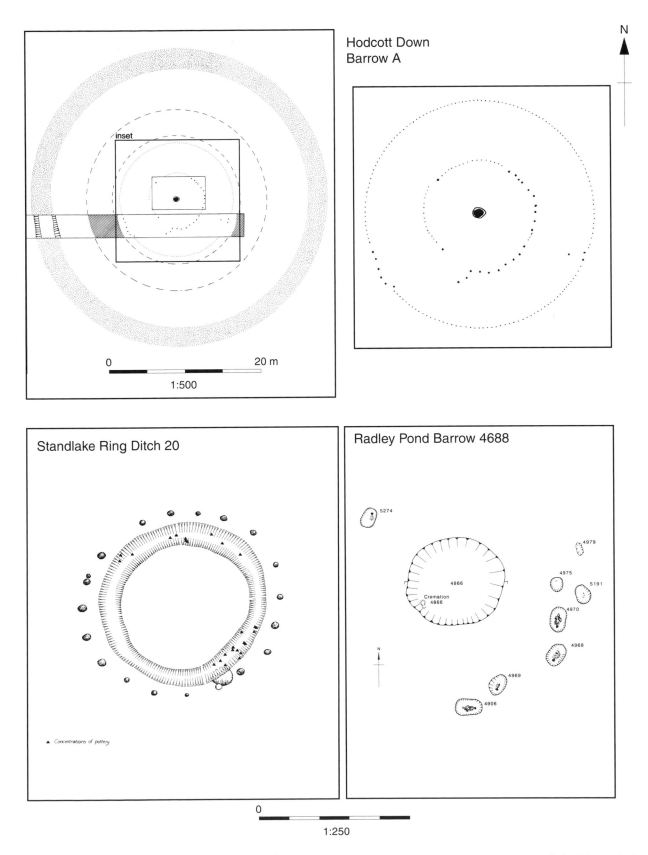

Fig. 14.23 Early Bronze Age 'open arena' stake/post structures at Hodcott Down Barrow A, Standlake Ring Ditch 20, and Pond Barrow 4688 at Barrow Hills, Radley

flat-topped or truncated to create elevated ceremonial platforms (Garwood 2003, 51; 2007a). There are a number of well-documented examples of these architectural forms in the Middle and Upper Thames Valley (Fig. 14.23), including stake or post circles at Hodcott Down Barrow A, Berkshire (Richards 1986-90), and Standlake Ring Ditch 20, Oxfordshire (Catling 1982), a stake circle that possibly acted as a revetment for a flat-topped mound at Farncombe Down, Berkshire (Rahtz 1962,

4-11, fig.7), and pond barrows at Radley (4688: Barclay 1999a, 115-28) and Berinsfield, Oxfordshire (Barclay and Thomas 1995). Structures of these kinds may have been designed in many cases with reference to cosmological schemes, especially in relation to the symbolic use of spatial divisions and orientations that could be identified or realised in ritual acts (see Owoc 2001a). This may be apparent, for example, in the arrangement of burials at Radley 4866 (Garwood 1999b, 286-88). In comparison,

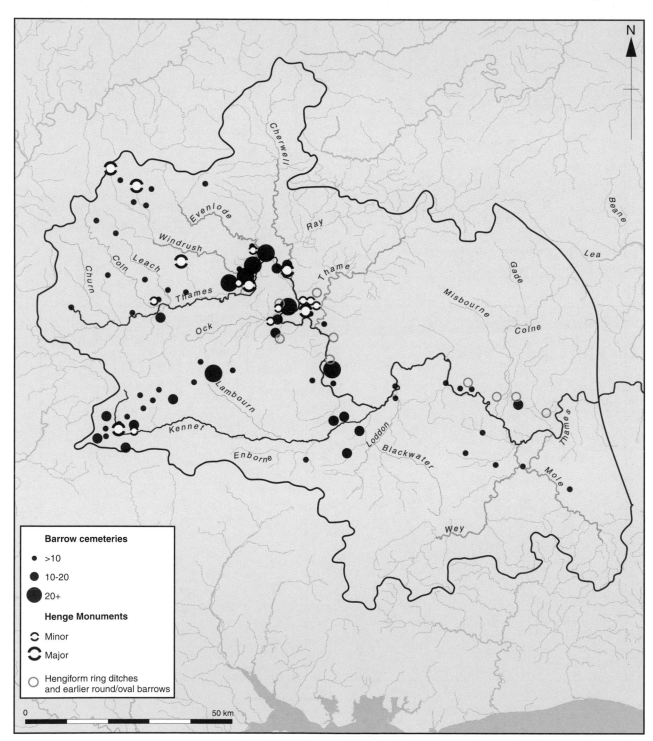

Fig. 14.24   Distribution of henge monuments and barrow cemeteries in the Upper and Middle Thames Valley

smaller free-standing and possibly roofed structures such as 'mortuary houses' or shrines are extremely rare in the Bronze Age of the Middle and Upper Thames Valley, although small stake-built structures were built above or around the central burial deposits at both Cassington Barrow 6 (Atkinson 1946-7) and Clifton Hampden (Leeds 1936, 15-16).

Recognition of the ceremonial and symbolic significance of round barrows is not restricted to architectural features defining arenas, platforms and free-standing buildings. Construction materials, in particular, may have been media for highly visible symbolic representation. The use of wood for building purposes, and the incorporation of unmodified trees (living or dead) within mound fabrics, may have been especially significant (Healy and Harding 2007). Similarly, the choice of materials for mound bodies, surface layers and coatings may have been important in terms of colour symbolism and properties such texture and lustre (Owoc 2002). There is also little question that great care went into moulding the more elaborate and distinctive mound forms such as bell and disc barrows (Barrett 1990; Garwood 2007a), of which there are several examples around Avebury (Pollard and Reynolds 2002, 131), on the Berkshire Downs (at Lambourn Seven Barrows; Case 1956a: see Fig. 14.25), and elsewhere at places such as Ascot, Berkshire (Bradley and Keith-Lucas 1975), and Horsell Common, Surrey (Needham 1987, 106). Among the most striking monument forms of this kind are double- and triple-mound structures, some of which may have been designed as coherent single-phase entities (eg double-bell barrows or double- or triple-mound disc barrows), although precise dating evidence to show that mound construction events were contemporaneous is not available for any of the Thames Valley sites. Excavated examples include Radley 16 (Barclay and Halpin 1999, 162-66) and possibly Latton Lands enclosure 2255, Wiltshire (Powell and Laws, in prep.). Another is clearly

visible on aerial photographs of the North Stoke complex (Case 1982a, fig.33).

That many mounds were routinely revisited for ceremonial purposes is most apparent in the case of multiphase structures that involved series of building events, usually accompanied by multiple burials and other deposits (see Chapter 15). Examples in the Middle and Upper Thames include Radley 12 (Barclay 1999a) and probably the barrow excavated at Teddington in the 19th century (Akerman 1855). A variation on this theme, with horizontal rather than vertical elaboration of monument structures, can be seen in groups of contiguous barrows with linked or intersecting ditches, as, for example, at Gravelly Guy (Stanton Harcourt XV Barrows 2-4A; A J Barclay *et al.* 1995, 89-93; Lambrick *et al.* 2004, 51-61), Dorchester-on-Thames Site 4 (Whittle *et al.* 1992, 192-94), and Crooksbury Common and West End Common, Surrey (Needham 1987, 106). It is possible that some of these may have been built in single construction episodes, but dating is not precise enough to distinguish these from examples involving successive mound building events. These groups of mounds, and larger linear alignments, are the most prominent examples of round barrow clusters that formed articulated monument complexes, some of which plainly incorporated avenues and arenas that acted as stages for repeated, frequent ceremonial activities (discussed in more detail below; cf Garwood 1999b, 298-309; 2003, 60-1).

The interpretation of round barrows and related monuments, in this light, should proceed from the assumption that these included open arenas or provided prominent architectural foci for lively ceremonial activities (whether these places were revisited routinely, or only on significant sacred dates in the ritual calendar), rather than dusty, lonely memorials to the dead (ibid.). At the same time, the extraordinary diversity of architectural forms and features suggests considerable variation in the design principles and ceremonial uses of different kinds of round barrows and other circular monument forms. This diversity may, to a considerable extent, relate to chronological variation in the currencies of particular monument-building practices and designs. This is evident in a recent reassessment of the dating evidence for British late Neolithic and early Bronze Age round barrow architecture and funerary practices (Garwood 2007a), which proposes a three period chronological framework for the period *c* 2500-1400 cal BC. This scheme shows that there was not only variation in the designs and ceremonial purposes of different kinds of monuments, but that there were also significant transformations in the ritual use and symbolic significance of both open arena and mound architecture over time (ibid.).

Fig. 14.25 Aerial photograph of the Lambourn Seven Barrows, Berkshire, by Major Allen, showing elaborate bell- and disc-barrow forms and the spatial organisation of the monument complex

Fig. 14.26 (overleaf)
The monument complex at Barrow Hills, Radley

The complex of monuments at Barrow Hills,

Radley is the most thoroughly researched in the Thames Valley. It extends for over 1 km, to the north of the Thames, close to Abingdon. Aerial photographs and gravel quarrying in the 1920s first revealed the existence of the monuments. Although now partly covered by housing, a series of excavations have provided us with a rich record of the site's development. Whilst there is considerable chronological overlap, the floruits of monument construction at Barrow Hills and Dorchester are, to some extent, complementary. The two major floruits at Radley, represented by the causewayed enclosure, oval barrow and single graves in the early Neolithic, and the graves and barrows in the Beaker period and the early Bronze Age, largely precede and post-date the most spectacular monuments - the cursus and the Big Rings henge - at Dorchester-on-Thames.

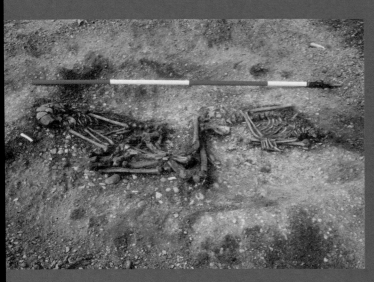

Top left — Barrow 4a, gold earrings, beaker and arrowheads

Top right — Barrow 16, miniature Collared Urn and Food Vessel, copper knife-dagger and jet/shale, faience and amber beads

Middle — Oval barrow, burials in central grave 2126

Bottom left — Early Neolithic flat grave 5354

Bottom right — Grooved Ware with intricate decoration from pit 3196

RADLEY BARROW HILLS

The causewayed enclosure at Abingdon consists of two discontinuous ditch circuits 55 m apart which cut off a promontory above the Thames floodplain, between two converging streams. Despite the wide spacing of the two ditches, and their different character, radiocarbon dates indicate the site was a short-lived monument and that both ditches date from the same period, either in the middle of the 37th or the middle of the 36th century cal BC.

The oval barrow at Radley began as a rectangular enclosure, was remodelled twice as a U-shaped enclosure, and only became an oval barrow in its final phase. The phase to which the two central inhumation burials belong to is uncertain. No radiocarbon dates could be obtained for the first phase, but dates from the later phases indicate that they belong to the last third of the 4th millennium cal BC.

The linear mortuary structure consisted of a wooden chamber supported by conglomerate blocks set within a suboval trench. It contained the remains of an articulated adult male and the disarticulated and semiarticulated remains of two adult females. Radiocarbon dates suggest that these people may have been buried sequentially, the man representing the earliest burial event between 3650 and 3050 cal BC, and one of the females the latest, between 3350 and 2550 cal BC.

Top left — Barrow 12, hengiform ring ditch 611 and the segmented ring ditch

Top right — Hengiform ring ditch 611 with Barrow 12 in the background

Bottom — Early Neolithic linear mortuary structure 5352

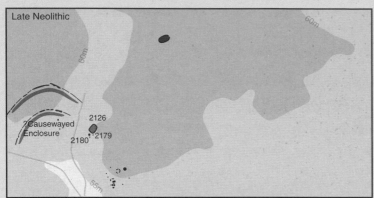

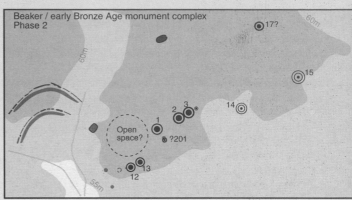

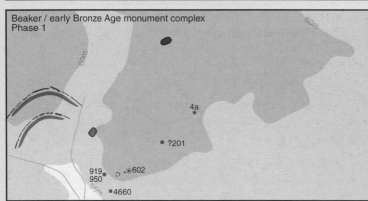

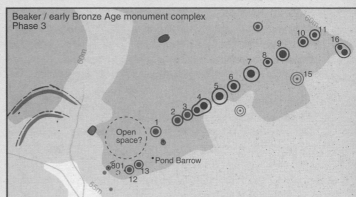

Evidence for later Neolithic activity is less extensive but includes a number of Grooved Ware pits - including one which contained an exceptionally rich group of finds consisting of Grooved Ware sherds, some with unusual lattice and spiral motifs, flint artefacts, worked bone (including a pin made from the ulna of a white-tailed eagle), and animal bone - and a hengiform ring ditch, dated to 2600 - 2200 cal BC, the ditch of which contained placed deposits of antlers and cattle limbs.

The site is, however, perhaps most significant for the evidence it provides for the development of a **Beaker period and early Bronze Age monument complex**. This development began, *c* 2500-2100 cal BC, with several inhumation graves, most with Beakers. In Phase 2, *c* 2100-1850 BC, two of the Phase 1 graves provided foci for the construction of new monuments on different alignments, including a multiphased mound with concentric ditch circuits (Barrow 12), and the pond barrow (4866), both associated with multiple burials. Finally in Phase 3, *c* 1850-1600/1500 BC, the main close-set linear array of large single-phase round barrows, most associated with single burials, developed from west to east, defining - with another line of more widely-spaced barrows to the south - an 'avenue' leading to an open space fringed by earlier, and in some cases already ancient, monuments.

Above — The development of the monument complex
Left — Barrow 12, central burial 605

Round barrow groups as ceremonial complexes

We can now also make sense of the chronological development of *groups* of Beaker period and early Bronze Age funerary monuments. This is possible, above all, because of the precise phasing of the Radley Barrow Hills monument complex in Oxfordshire (Garwood 1999b), which provides the first richly-detailed picture of the changing forms and spatial organisations of monuments and burial deposits within one large linear round barrow group (Fig. 14.26). This sequence has significant implications for re-evaluating similar barrow groups elsewhere. In Phase 1 (site phase 4), *c* 2500-2100 cal BC, several inhumation graves, most with Beakers, including four in a widely-spaced linear arrangement, were built close to a number of earlier Neolithic monuments. In Phase 2 (site phase 5a), *c* 2100-1850 cal BC, two of the Phase 1 graves provided foci for the construction of new monuments on different alignments, including a multiphased mound with concentric ditch circuits (Barrow 12), and the pond barrow (4866), both with multiple burials. Finally in Phase 3 (site phase 5b), *c* 1850-1600/1500 cal BC, the main close-set linear array of large single-phase round barrows, most with single burials, developed from west to east, defining (with another line of more widely-spaced barrows to the south) an 'avenue' leading to an open space fringed by ancient monuments (round mounds to the south, and an oval barrow and the Abingdon causewayed enclosure to the west).

It is possible to recognise similar sequences at other linear round barrow groups wherever there is sufficient dating evidence to unravel the chronology of at least some elements of their spatial layouts. The Normanton Down group to the south of Stonehenge, for example, is comparable in many respects to Barrow Hills, Radley, except for the lack of definite evidence for multiphase mounds (Garwood 2007a; cf Woodward 2000, 88; Exon *et al.* 2000, 92-3, 102-4), and similar development sequences have been glimpsed at Shrewton (Green and Rollo-Smith 1984) and Snail Down, Wiltshire (Thomas, N, 2005). Elsewhere in the Middle and Upper Thames Valley, complex developmental histories and significant changes over time in the architectural design and symbolic-spatial and practical configuration of round barrow groups are discernible at Lambourn Seven Barrows, Berkshire (Case 1956a; Richards 1986-90; cf Woodward 2000, 84-5), and at Stanton Harcourt (A J Barclay *et al.* 1995), and are clearly implied at sites such as North Stoke and Foxley Farm (Case 1982a), and Standlake, Oxfordshire (Catling 1982).

At Lambourn Seven Barrows (Figs 14.25 and 14.27), a dispersed group of early monuments including a long mound, two middle Beaker burial monuments (Barrows 17 and 31, dating to the end of the 3rd millennium cal BC) and a multiphase monument (Barrow 1, probably dating to the period *c* 2000-1800 cal BC), was given a new focus with the development of a double line of bell, bowl and disc barrows forming what appears to be an avenue or processional way (Barrows 4-13). The linear barrow group is not well-dated but almost certainly developed in the period *c* 1800-1600 cal BC (Garwood 2007a), possibly from south-east to north-west beginning with Barrow 9, which had a primary cremation burial in an early Collared Urn placed upright in a sarsen cist (Case 1956a, 21; cf Woodward 2000, 84-5). The more extensive Stanton Harcourt group of monuments in Oxfordshire (Fig. 14.28) has a greater number of well-dated monuments and funerary deposits but is far more complex in spatial terms, making it very difficult to establish a developmental sequence. Nonetheless, it is possible to suggest a broad chronological scheme based on direct dating evidence (summarised in Barclay 1995b; see also Lambrick and Allen 2004) and recent reassessments of wider chronological frameworks for round barrow construction sequences and spatial arrangements (Garwood 2007a).

This reappraisal of round barrow cemeteries, as ceremonial centres with complex histories that acted as stages for dramatic ritual performances, offers scope for wider reinterpretation of the structuring of these monument complexes, the kinds of social agency represented, and the cultural concerns realised in architectural forms and ceremonial practices. It is especially notable that the distinctive spatial organisations of many of these mound groups often made particular reference to things representative of the past. The alignment of the Radley barrows on a group of ancient monuments (described above) is not unusual. At Standlake the main linear group of barrows (Ring Ditches 13-18) is aligned on the Devil's Quoits henge, located some 2.5 km to the east on the other side of the river Windrush. Even more striking is the orientation of barrow groups on celestial phenomena (cf Garwood 2003; 2007a). Although there is evidence for earlier concerns with solar orientations at individual round barrows, especially those with open arena structures (eg sites in Cornwall; Owoc 2001b, 195), the spatial design of several linear barrow groups after 1900 cal BC suggests that there was a shift to mound groups as the principal context for the referencing of solar alignments. This may be evident at Lambourn Seven Barrows, where the large linear barrow group arranged in two lines appears to be oriented approximately on a point on the horizon where the sun sets on Midsummer's Day. This is similar, although in a very different topographic context, to the solar referencing embodied in the spatial arrangements of the Devil's Jumps and the Heyshott barrow groups in West Sussex (Garwood 2003, 60-1).

These kinds of spatial arrangements, and the wider character of early Bronze Age linear mound group architecture, suggest deliberate attempts to reify cosmological schemes in highly visual and physically-imposing ways. This involved especially

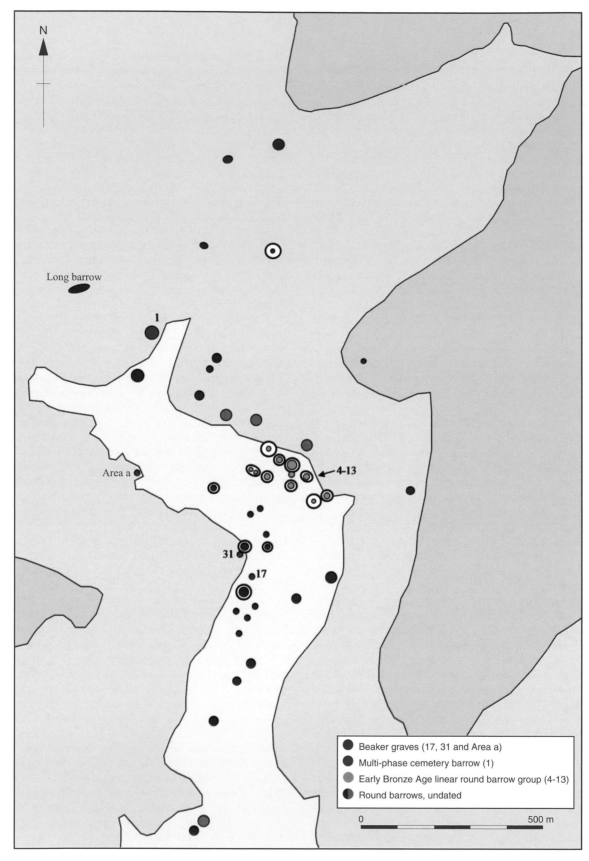

N

Long barrow

1

Area a

4-13

31

17

Beaker graves (17, 31 and Area a)
Multi-phase cemetery barrow (1)
Early Bronze Age linear round barrow group (4-13)
Round barrows, undated

0   500 m

Fig. 14.27   Plan of Lambourn Seven Barrows

Fig. 14.28 (opposite above)   Distribution of barrows and the location of the Devil's Quoits in the Stanton Harcourt area

Fig. 14.29 (opposite below)   Round barrows, ring ditches and burials in Oxford

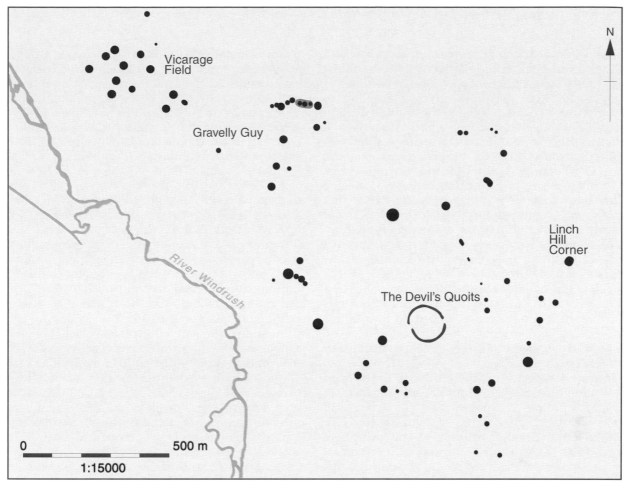

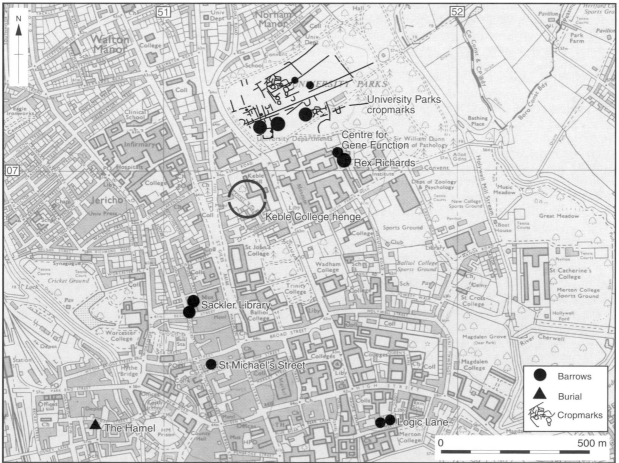

powerful invocations of perceived historical and metaphysical relationships between things redolent of the past, such as ancient monuments (with reference, perhaps, to ancestors, mythological heroes and glorious events) and the living and the dead in the present. Lines of mounds suggest narratives of dynastic succession and moral and political success, while their orientation on ancient monuments and natural phenomena symbolising eternal cycles suggests a desire to give these narratives and the elites they describe a sense of permanence that transcended immediate social and political concerns. These fundamental cosmological relationships would have been recognised and given a sense of reality in the course of ceremonial performances. Such performances were guided by the barriers, spaces and alignments of mound group architecture, structured with reference to the kinds of symbolic representations embodied in mounds and graves, and oriented at significant times on places and events that affirmed timeless natural and cultural order.

In many respects, it is more difficult to interpret the ceremonial and symbolic significance of dispersed groups of barrows as these have rarely been excavated on a large scale using modern methods (the Brenig group is a rare exception: Lynch 1993; cf Garwood 2007a; 2007b). It is increasingly apparent, however, that dispersed groups usually include monuments with diverse architectural forms, of many different periods, with evidence for significant changes over time in the way that new monuments were spatially and practically related to earlier ones. Indeed, there is the suggestion of significant lacunae in monument-building and burial events between periods of more intensive and sustained activity (often marked by a high level of consistency in funerary practices from one event to the next). There is certainly considerable variation in the spatial distribution of mounds within such groups. In some cases, mounds are scattered and isolated, while in others there are localised concentrations (sometimes as paired, nucleated or short linear arrangements of mounds) amidst the wider dispersed group of monuments.

The most extensively investigated dispersed round barrow group in the Middle and Upper Thames Valley is at Oxford (Fig. 14.29), where at least 25 round barrows, ring ditches and burials have been recorded on the river terraces between the Cherwell and the higher ground to the west of the Thames (Hassall 1986, 116; Dodd 2003, figs. 2.1-2). This concentration of sites, now associated with the recently-discovered henge enclosure in the area of Keble College (TVAS 2010), appears to bear close similarity to the Stanton Harcourt monument complex in both scale and spatial organisation (Fig. 14.28). The scatter of early Bronze Age monuments and burial sites, some revealed in the course of development in the urban and university areas of

Oxford, includes a small linear barrow group on Port Meadow, and small nucleated clusters of monuments in the University Parks Science area and at Binsey. There have been excavations of round barrow sites at Port Meadow (Atkinson 1942), St. Michael's Street (Barclay and McKeague 1996), the Sackler Library (Poore and Wilkinson 2001, 15-17), the Rex Richards Building (Parkinson *et al.* 1996), the Gene Function Centre (Boston *et al.* 2003) and Logic Lane (Radcliffe 1960), as well as a child burial associated with Beaker pottery at The Hamel (Palmer 1980) and further beaker burials in North Oxford (Dodd 2003, 9). Although in most cases very little evidence of mound superstructures survived, it is apparent that some of these must originally have been very substantial, especially the Sackler Library site (Poore and Wilkinson 2001, 15-17), and the multiphased monument at the Rex Richards Building (Parkinson *et al.* 1996).

A rather different kind of dispersed pattern of monument building and funerary activity is evident in recent excavations just north of the Thames on the Gloucestershire-Wiltshire border at Shorncote (Barclay and Glass 1995; Darvill 2006, 37-9; Hearne and Adam 1999; Powell *et al.* 2010). In an area extending some 1.25 km north-south and about 0.9 km east-west there is a scatter of at least 11 ring ditches, both circular and penannular, of sizes ranging from 5 m (internal diameter, eg Shorncote 1000) to *c* 20 m (Cotswold Community 4944), together with a probable post circle (Cotswold Community 9100). Only one of these monuments was associated with a surviving central grave: the Beaker burial with flint dagger and knives at Shorncote Ring Ditch 103 (Barclay and Glass 1995, 25-9). It is possible that four more Beaker flat graves may have had low mounds: Shorncote Grave 1007 (ibid., 29-31) and Cotswold Community 7611, 9551 and 8933 (Powell *et al.* 2010). Although some of these monuments and burials were clustered in small groups there was no obvious attempt to organise them in an ordered spatial form. The limited dating evidence, including small amounts of Peterborough Ware, Grooved Ware, Beaker and early and middle Bronze Age pottery from monuments, burials and scattered pit deposits, suggests diverse but episodic activity spanning the 3rd and 2nd millennia cal BC. In this context, it is impossible to identify extensive or durable structuring of the 'ceremonial complex'. This highlights the difficulties inherent in interpreting such apparent concentrations of activity in a holistic manner, as if they represent related practices or cultural continuity over long spans of time. It is equally possible, in fact, that these concentrations represent unconnected series of activities that happen to have occupied the same space for entirely unrelated reasons.

At a larger spatial scale, it has been suggested that the cosmographic structuring of late Neolithic and early Bronze Age landscapes extended far

Fig. 14.30 (opposite)   The North Stoke monument complex, Oxfordshire

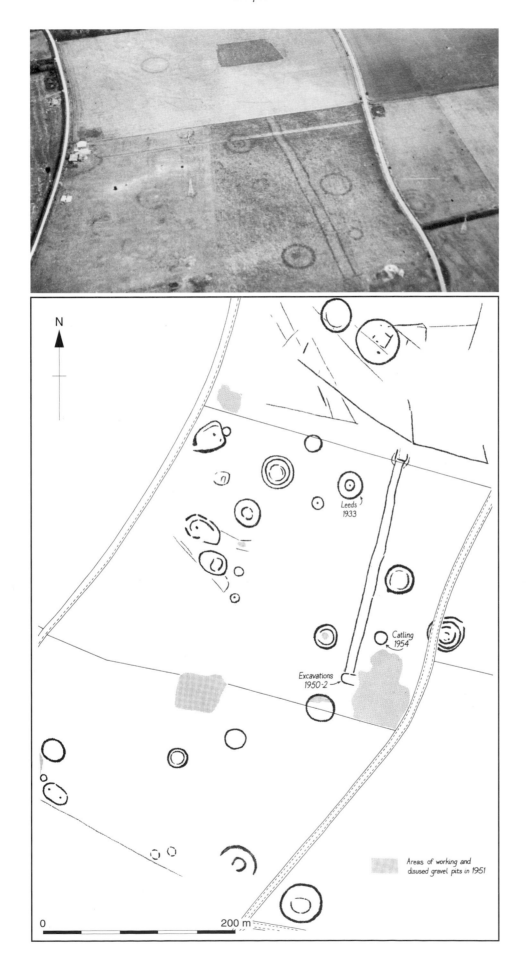

N

Leeds
1933

Catling
1954

Excavations
1950-2

Areas of working and
disused gravel pits in 1951

0   200 m

beyond local groups of monuments. This is most readily apparent where there are concentric distributions of monumentalised and non-monumentalised areas in relation to major ceremonial foci, such as Stonehenge (Woodward and Woodward 1996; Cleal and Allen 1995; Parker Pearson and Ramilisonina 1998), or where monuments are concentrated in lineally-banded landscape zones defined by striking terrain features such as downland ridges, notably the South Downs in Sussex (Field 1998; cf Garwood 2003) and the Dorset Ridgeway (Tilley 1999, 185-238). These studies suggest the delineation of sacred landscapes or even wider symbolic organisations of space that integrated different areas of practice and signification within universal schemes of cultural, natural and cosmic order. The very large-scale zonation of social practices suggested by these studies has not been proposed for any part of the Middle and Upper Thames, except in a fairly muted way for the Avebury landscape where it may be possible to identify some degree of concentric patterning of monuments (Woodward and Woodward 1996, 279-81; Pollard and Reynolds 2002, 130-31, fig. 46; Watson 2001, 208-9). This interpretation appears overly monolithic and deterministic, however, once the radial distributions of many of the early Bronze Age round barrow groups in the Avebury area are recognised, especially along the Ridgeway and in Bishops Cannings Vale to the east and south-west of Avebury respectively. Other major round barrow concentrations in upland areas within the Middle and Upper Thames region could perhaps be interpreted in ways similar to those suggested for Sussex and Dorset, although dense linear aggregations of round barrows are less apparent in both the Chilterns (Dyer 1961; Holgate 1995) and the Cotswolds (cf Darvill 1987, 95-9).

Elsewhere, in the Upper Thames Valley, the relationship suggested between the Barrow Hills, Radley and Dorchester-on-Thames monument complexes, in terms of shifts in ceremonial focus and relative tempos of monument-building (Garwood 1999b, 293-98; Thomas 1999, 195) may perhaps be extended to include the North Stoke complex (Fig. 14.30). Barrow Hills, Radley and North Stoke are located roughly the same distance from Dorchester-on-Thames, to north and south respectively, and both consist of dense groupings of late Neolithic/early Bronze Age funerary monuments that developed at a time when monument-building and burial events at Dorchester were increasingly rare and spatially dispersed. It is very tempting to see this in terms of a very large-scale structured early Bronze Age ceremonial landscape, consisting of an ancient ceremonial core that was respected, episodically occupied or visited, and conceptualised with reference to ideas of cosmogony, ancestral origins and perhaps collective identity, flanked to north and south by separate funerary complexes that marked out the sacred and political identities of elite groups and their mytho-historical narratives of dynastic succession and moral order.

ACTS OF RITUALISED DEPOSITION IN PITS, TREE-THROW HOLES AND MIDDENS

An especially thorny issue in considering ritual and ceremony during the Neolithic and early Bronze Age is the extent to which pits, tree-throw holes and middens were contexts for ritualised activity and were ceremonial foci in their own right, or were primarily used as places for everyday occupation practices that sometimes included the conscious selection and managed placement of materials (whether in explicitly meaningful ways or not). These different kinds of practice are not necessarily exclusive, of course, and indeed a continuum of variation can be recognised between more or less ritualised action, but the interpretative emphasis one way or another can still predetermine our understanding of depositional practices, with potentially contrasting representations of what the evidence reveals about prehistoric cultural life (see Lamdin-Whymark 2008, 73-128, for a recent evaluation of the evidence). The wider character and chronological and landscape contexts of these practices and their relationship to settlement occupation have been discussed in Chapters 11 and 13, but it is also helpful to consider the more formal and structured range of depositional acts in the light of the preceding discussion of the nature of ritual and ceremonial performance.

Recent interpretations of Neolithic pit deposits have focused on the structured nature of social practices, and the use of depositional acts as symbolic media (cf Bradley 2000, 117-31; J Harding 2006; J Thomas 1999, 62-8). The selection and careful placement of materials in 'special' places certainly suggests purposeful and reflective performances separate from those enacted on a day-to-day basis. Interpreting depositional practices in these terms, however, is difficult because many ceremonial acts are performed as ritualisations of everyday practices, drawing upon the domestic sphere (of reproduction, production and consumption, for example) both materially and as a source of metaphors and symbols for conveying fundamental meanings about the nature of the world (J Thomas 1999, 87; Pollard 2004). In this light, it is unsurprising that interpretations of pit deposits are often ambiguous.

As noted in Chapter 11, early and middle Neolithic pits in the Upper and Middle Thames Valley mostly tend to contain occupation material consisting of deposits of used and broken pottery and flintwork, charred food remains, animal bones and hearth residues. In general, this evidence suggests short-lived residential episodes and repeat visits to individual sites. Very rarely is there any indication that material was either carefully selected or placed. Yet is it also apparent that individual pits rarely contain large parts of individual ceramic vessels or evidence for flint tool reduction

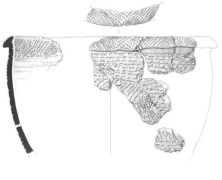

Fig. 14.31   *Middle Neolithic pit deposits (top and centre: Lake End Road, Dorney; bottom: Yarnton)*

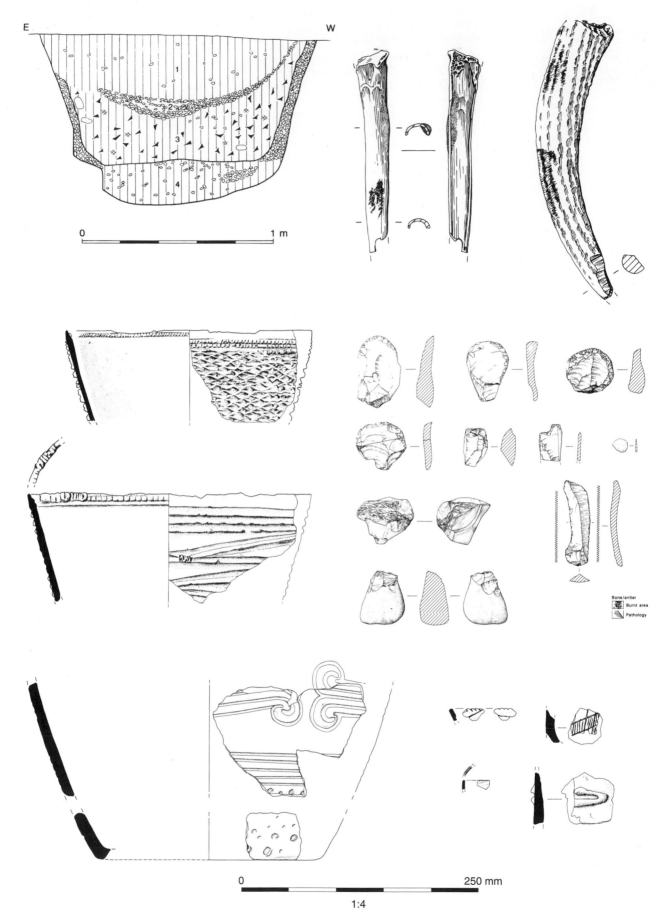

Fig. 14.32   Section of Grooved Ware pit 3196 at Barrow Hills, Radley, with some of the associated artefacts

sequences, but rather fragmentary remains – both abraded and unabraded – which appear to have been collected from deposits elsewhere. There are also instances where the contents of different pits suggest they derived from the same parent deposit (eg where refits are identifiable between pit assemblages), as has been suggested at Taplow Mill and Lake End Road West (Barclay, in Allen *et al.* in prep.). These aspects of pit deposits appear to indicate purposeful redeposition of middens, perhaps at the end of occupation phases as acts of settlement closure (Evans *et al.* 1999).

There is also no question that in some cases the size, coherence and apparent spatial structuring of artefact assemblages in single depositional contexts suggest highly reflective, deliberate and contrived actions that indicate some kind of abstract symbolic communication or more narrative or qualitative expressions of meaning. One of the early Neolithic pits at South Stoke, for example, contained fragments of at least ten pottery vessels of various sizes, perhaps marking a feasting event (Timby *et al.* 2005, 231). Similarly, the unusual scale and character of the late Neolithic assemblage in Pit P at Sutton Courtenay, and the complex form of the pit itself, the edges and base of which were lined with flint and charcoal (Leeds 1934a, 264-5; cf Barclay *et al.* 2003, 20-4, 98-9), suggests conscious selection of materials and careful attention to the architecture and aesthetics of deposition (cf Pollard 2005).

The presence of semicomplete vessels, some of which appear to be of unusual or unique design, may also indicate self-conscious selection of significant symbols, substances or tokens (Fig. 14.31). Middle Neolithic examples include the Mortlake ware vessel found at Lake End Road, Dorney, near Maidenhead (Allen *et al.* 2004), and another similar vessel at Yarnton (Barclay and Edwards in prep.). In both cases the vessels may have been purposefully smashed before burial. Evidence from Yarnton indicates that at least some sherds were carefully arranged within pits, or at least that particular elements of vessels were sometimes deliberately chosen for burial. One pit, located just outside an entrance into a ditched enclosure of slightly earlier date, appeared to be lined with large decorated sherds from several Fengate style vessels, placed in an alternating pattern either face up or face down (Hey in prep.). Examples of similar practices have been recorded at Horcott Pit and Gravelly Guy (Brady and Lamdin-Whymark in press; Lambrick and Allen 2004). It is unlikely that these were anything other than deliberate deposits. More widely, detailed analysis of the pit groups at Yarnton has revealed spatial patterning of vessel elements that suggests these were often deliberately selected for burial, presumably because they had particular symbolic significance.

Grooved Ware and Beaker pits in the study area share many of the same characteristics as Peterborough Ware-associated pits, with the majority containing what appears to be occupation debris but also cases where special deposition is evident. One exceptional pit deposit within the long mortuary enclosure at Yarnton contained part of a bowl with internal decoration and a possible external spiral motif, associated with a small quantity of refitting flint debitage. Even more striking is the extremely large assemblage deposited in a multiphased sequence in Pit 3196 at Barrow Hills, Radley consisting of Grooved Ware sherds, flint artefacts, worked bone (including a pin made from the ulna of a white-tailed eagle), and animal bones (Fig. 14.32). The Grooved Ware from the pit included several large sherds decorated with unusual lattice and spiral motifs (Barclay 1999a, 73-7). The whole pit deposit, the richest assemblage of its kind found anywhere within the study area, appears to represent a selected and structured set of unusual materials and objects brought to the site specifically for deposition.

Significant formal deposits of Beaker period and early Bronze Age date are rarer. A pit assemblage from Horton, consisting of eight barbed and tanged arrowheads, a copper awl, a stone object (possibly an anvil) and other flintwork, may represent an arrow-makers toolkit, and was perhaps a votive deposit. This is not unlike the body-less Beaker 'burial' found close to the Thames at Reading (Smith 1997, 24-6), which may also represent some

Fig. 14.33 The aurochs pit burial, associated with six barbed and tanged arrowheads, at Holloway Lane, Harmondsworth

kind of offering. It is notable that this was found only a few kilometres upriver from Sonning, where a stone wristguard was recovered from the river. Most dramatic of all is the deposit of a young adult aurochs associated with six barbed and tanged arrowheads, found at Holloway Lane, Harmondsworth, near Heathrow (Cotton *et al.* 2006), the butchered sections of which had been carefully arranged around a deep partly-filled pit (Fig. 14.33).

This striking burial event represents one extreme of a range of ritualised depositional acts that appear to have evoked particular relationships between humans and animals (cf Whittle 2003, 78-106; Bradley 1998b, 34). Although the

presence of animal bones in pits and other contexts are as open to alternative interpretations as any other category of material, being variously interpreted as butchery waste, food refuse, remains of special meals, offerings, and sometimes salient symbolic media (depending on context, associations, and the interpretative perspectives adopted), there is certainly no doubt that animals could be used to convey complex ideas in the course of ritual performances. Cattle skulls, in particular, are sometimes found in pits, the ditches of monuments, and occasionally in contexts normally associated with human remains (Hodder 1990, 250). At Beckhampton long barrow near Avebury,

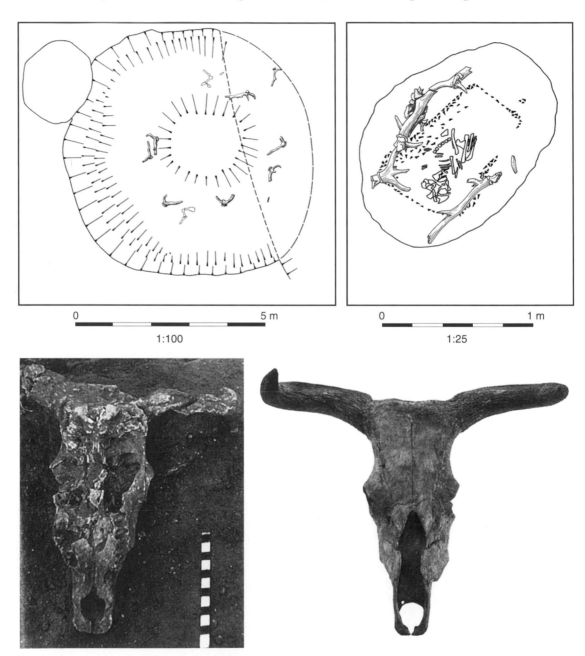

Fig. 14.34   Deposits of animal bones: upper left: Hengiform Ring Ditch 611 at Barrow Hills, Radley, showing the ring of antlers and cattle limbs around the base; upper right: Grave 4969 at Barrow Hills, Radley; below: the aurochs skull (in situ *and restored) from Site II at Dorchester-on-Thames*

for example, three domestic cattle skulls were placed along the long axis of the mound. In other contexts, deer antlers and articulated parts of animal skeletons occur widely, perhaps most strikingly at Radley (Barclay 1999a) where a ring of antlers and two articulating cattle limbs were placed around the base of a hengiform ring-ditch (611: Fig. 14.34). Animal remains have also been found in pit contexts directly associated with human remains. Indeed, in some cases, fragments of both animals and humans appear to have been treated in the same ways, or at least in ways that mutually referenced animal and human: at Bourton-on-the-Water, for example, a Peterborough Ware-associated pit contained part of the skull of an adult female alongside a complete shed deer antler and parts of another (Dunning 1932).

At a larger spatial scale, our understanding of ritualised depositional practices in pits and other contexts may well be modified in the light of a more detailed understanding of geographical variation in material culture, depositional practices and landscape organisation. Grooved Ware deposition in pits, for example, is very rare in the Middle Thames Valley, where only seven Grooved Ware pit deposits are known, in contrast with far more frequent deposits in the Upper Thames (Lamdin-Whymark 2008, 121-23). A similar pattern may be evident in parts of south-east England, such as the Sussex Downs, Thanet and the Ebbsfleet Valley, where extensive fieldwork has revealed almost no evidence for Grooved Ware at all. The situation could not be more different in regions such as Wessex where complex Grooved Ware pit deposits are widespread. Such geographical contrasts may indicate regional cultural differences in the way that material culture categories and associated practical and symbolic repertoires were adopted and perceived, as well as possible variation in settlement distributions and population densities.

The temporalities of such practices also need close scrutiny. It is notable that in south-east England well-dated Grooved Ware assemblages all belong to the period *c* 2900-2500 cal BC. Although the number of finds is still low, it is possible that Grooved Ware in this region lost its significance or was replaced by Beaker ceramics in the mid 3rd millennium cal BC, some time before this occurred in areas such as Wessex (where pit digging may have reached a peak during the late Neolithic: J Thomas 1999, 69) and the Upper Thames Valley (cf Garwood 1999b). This might also partly explain the lack of evidence for complex Grooved Ware-associated pit deposition in the Middle and Lower Thames Valley. Indeed, the shift from 'simple/domestic' to 'complex/ceremonial' forms of Grooved Ware deposition, marked by increasing formality and more frequent display of fine and exotic items was realised most fully in Wessex in the *late* 3rd millennium cal BC (Thomas 1999, 69-73, 86-8; Pollard 2001, 322-28), by which time Grooved Ware may already have disappeared from material

culture repertoires or been overtaken by the adoption of new types of material culture in other parts of southern Britain.

RIVER DEPOSITS AND VOTIVE OFFERINGS

As is discussed in Chapter 11, the Thames and its tributaries had a strong influence over the siting of both settlements and monuments. Indeed, many monuments appear to have been deliberately located beside rivers, sometimes incorporating them in their designs, or were aligned so that their axes ran parallel or at right angles to river courses. In this broad context, Barclay and Hey have suggested that some rivers, and perhaps especially the Thames, may have had exceptional cosmological significance as dominant natural features of the landscape (1999). Similar examples of natural features acting as symbolic foci in prehistory are noted by Bradley (1993), although none compare with the scale of the river Thames.

Moreover, of all British rivers, the Thames stands out as being the most prolific in terms of both the range and quantity of objects which have been recovered from it. Although the finds from the stretch of the river between Kingston and London Bridge are most striking, other parts of the Thames as far upstream as Gloucestershire have produced significant numbers of artefacts, as have some of its tributaries. These finds represent aspects of complex and long-lived practices that appear to have their origins in the Mesolithic (Cotton and Green 2004, 123; Chatterton 2006, 103-12), with later periods of intensive material deposition during the Neolithic and Bronze Age. Stone axe and bronze finds from the river dating from the 4th to the 1st millennia cal BC are especially well known (Bradley 1990), but a far wider range of objects has been recovered, including stone shafthole implements, flint daggers, worked bone maceheads, pottery, wooden objects and animal and human bones (Fig. 14.35). Many of these objects can be considered 'special' in one way or another, either with respect to their unusual formal and decorative properties, their rarity, or their special depositional contexts elsewhere. Perhaps the most evocative of all the objects from the river, however, is the late Neolithic wooden carved idol recovered from peat deposits in the Lower Thames Valley at Dagenham (Coles 1990; J Cotton pers. comm.).

The deposition of axes in the river started during the Mesolithic period and continued right through the Neolithic. Holgate (1988a) lists over 350 finished axes of flint and stone recovered from the Thames, including a number of exotic continental axes of jade and nephrite that are otherwise almost absent from the study area (Fig. 14.35; Holgate 1988a; Cotton and Green 2004, 129). The range and variety of these axes compares well with assemblages recovered from larger Neolithic enclosure sites. It is also evident that the concentrations of Mesolithic, early Neolithic and late Neolithic axe finds in the

river valley, and changes in these over time (Fig. 14.36), cannot be easily explained in terms of accidental losses or fluvial processes, and point instead to the special selection of axes for deposition in watery contexts at significant locales. Moreover, these patterns of deposition can be related to much larger-scale regional distributions of finds, especially in relation to the general absence of monument-building traditions from large parts of the Middle and Lower Thames (in contrast with the concentration of monuments in the Upper Thames Valley). In the case of the Middle Thames, it seems almost as if the river itself, the dominant nature feature of the landscape, negated the need to build monuments by becoming a focus for rituals and ceremonies itself.

Shaft-hole implements ranging from Mesolithic axes to early Bronze Age battle axes have also been recovered from the river in significant numbers (Fig. 14.35). Of these, later Neolithic crown antler and ovoid- and pestle-shaped stone and flint maceheads (Roe 1968, 161) are particularly prolific: of 58 crown antler maceheads listed by Simpson (1996, 295), for example, 41 come from one short stretch of the Thames . These two macehead types may belong to separate regional traditions: those of stone are found predominantly in western Britain while those of antler tend to be found in eastern Britain. This point is reinforced by the occurrence of two almost identical examples decorated with multiple ground facets in the Thames at Hammersmith and Sion Reach, one made from antler and the other from flint. It is unusual for maceheads to be decorated,

and it is therefore likely that these objects were not for everyday use or were the property of important individuals, as is supported by the evidence from Liff's Low, Derbyshire, and Knowth (Bateman 1848; Clarke *et al.* 1985, plate 3.34; Eogan 1986, plate X). Late Neolithic maceheads are less numerous than other types (Roe 1968) but again probably represent special objects deposited in exceptional circumstances. It is notable, for example, that only one macehead was recovered from the Dorchester-on-Thames cremation cemeteries (see Chapters 12 and 15), and that some of the finest cushion-type maceheads found anywhere were recovered from the Thames. Rarer Beaker period and early Bronze Age axe-hammers and battle axes were also deposited in the river in some numbers, especially between Kingston and London Bridge (Roe 1979, fig 4). Of particular interest is the single example of a picrite battle axe, very similar to examples found with early Bronze Age burials at Lambourn and Snowshill in the Upper Thames Valley (see Chapter 15), again pointing to a close relationship between the objects found in burials and rivers.

Finds of Beaker and early Bronze Age metalwork from the Thames are extremely rare, especially in comparison with flint and stone axes, shafthole implements, and later Bronze Age rapiers, swords and other items. A few early Bronze Age axes, knives, daggers and halberds (including one from County Hall, Lambeth) have been recovered from the river (Needham 1988), as well as a small number of skeuomorphic bone daggers that are assumed to be of this date (Gerloff 1975). The status of such

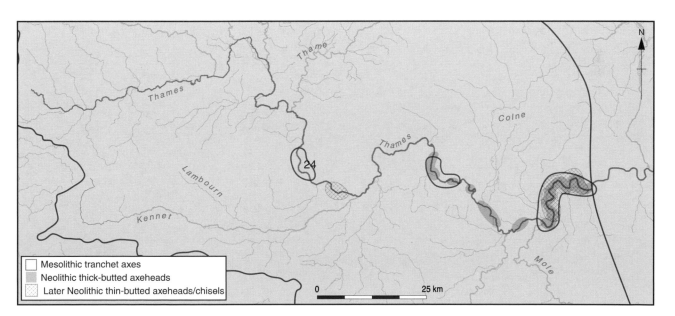

Fig. 14.36   Distribution of river finds: Mesolithic tranchet axes/adzes; Neolithic thick-butted axe; and later Neolithic thin-butted axeheads/chisels

Fig. 14.35 (opposite)   Middle Neolithic, late Neolithic and late Neolithic/early Bronze Age objects recovered from the Thames: stone battle axe and hammer, human skull, crown antler maceheads, Peterborough Ware vessel, flint and metal daggers and a bone skeuomorphic dagger

objects is difficult to determine, although the watery context could be significant. In addition, a remarkable bone barbed and tanged 'arrowhead', found on the Thames foreshore at Bermondsey, Surrey, could be a copy of a fancy Green Low/Kilmarnock type that is sometimes found in rich early Bronze Age graves (Cotton and Field 2004, 138-9 and fig. 13; see Chapter 12). A significant number of flint daggers have also been recovered from the Middle Thames (see Chapter 16), which contrasts with the extreme rarity of such objects in burials in the region, with just two recorded examples at Lambourn, Berkshire, and Shorncote, Gloucestershire (Case 1956a; Barclay and Glass 1995).

Over 35 earlier prehistoric pottery vessels are recorded as coming from the river Thames: Holgate lists 25 Neolithic pots, to which at least 11 Beakers can be added (Holgate 1988a, 283; Clarke 1970; Cotton and Wood 1996, 12, fig. 8; summarised in Barclay 2002). The few finds of early Neolithic pottery may well have resulted from rubbish disposal from riverside occupation or the erosion of bankside settlements, but most of the 21 Peterborough Ware vessels appear to be votive deposits. Mortlake Ware is most prevalent (Fig. 14.37), with most find spots concentrated in the middle reaches of the Thames, although there are some notable outliers at Crowmarsh (near Wallingford), Oxfordshire, Hedsor, Buckinghamshire, and Weybridge, Surrey (Barclay 2002). The remaining vessels are all from Greater London. Some sites have multiple find spots, including Crowmarsh where a large bowl and two smaller cups or bowls have been recovered. Stone axes were also found in the same stretch of river, and it is striking that the concentration of pots in Greater London corresponds with concentrations of other artefact types such as axes and maceheads.

The range of Peterborough Ware vessels recovered from the Thames is made up of either large or small bowls, while the medium-sized bowls found in pit deposits are largely absent (Barclay 2002). This supports the idea that these are not accidental losses, although the precise contexts of deposition are little understood. At Mongewell, just south of Wallingford, a substantial Mortlake Ware bowl and two small, cup-sized bowls were dredged from the riverbed (Smith 1924, 127-8, plate 26.1). Two small cups have also been recovered from the river in Greater London (Curle 1924, 150 and plate 28, nos 1-2), one probably at Mortlake and the other probably at the site of a 'pile-dwelling' in the Thames at Putney. There is the suggestion that some of these vessels were placed at the river edge, and if the wooden piles at Putney were indeed contemporary then maybe offerings were placed against such structures. Elsewhere, a Fengate Ware bowl with unusual body decoration consisting of concentric lines was recovered from the Thames near Hammersmith Bridge, Wandsworth. This vessel, like the cups described above, is relatively small and suggests individual use, in contrast to the communal use suggested by several much larger Mortlake Ware bowls found at sites such as Mongewell (Barclay 2000; 2002).

The river Thames has also yielded an important range of Beaker finds, in sharp contrast with the near absence of Grooved Ware (see Cotton and Green 2004, 134). Most striking in this respect, however, is the geographical division between the core area of Beaker burials and domestic activity in the Oxford region, and the rest of the valley, especially downstream (Fig. 14.38). The rarity of Beaker pottery in the Middle Thames Valley, in particular, is not just a simple reflection of a lack of

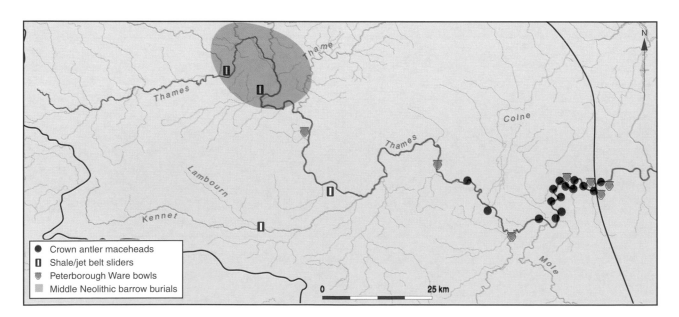

Fig. 14.37 Distribution of middle Neolithic single graves and river deposits: crown antler maceheads, shale/jet belt sliders, Peterborough Ware bowls and middle Neolithic barrow burials in the Upper and Middle Thames Valley

archaeological fieldwork (Lewis *et al.* 2006). At the same time, it is notable that a small number of Beaker vessels have been recovered from the stretch of the river in the London area, which is well-known for its concentration of artefact deposits (Bradley 1991; Clarke 1970; Field and Cotton 1987) including categories that are commonly associated with Beaker burials such as flint daggers and stone battleaxes (Needham 1987).

The significance of discoveries of human bone along the river is especially problematic (Lamdin-Whymark 2008, 197). In addition to recent finds of human bones from a silted former channel of the river Thames at the Eton Rowing Course, associated with what appeared to be placed deposits of animal bone (T Allen pers. comm.), there are human remains from the London area, especially skulls (J Cotton pers. comm.), including two that have produced earlier prehistoric radiocarbon dates (Bradley and Gordon 1988; Cotton and Green 2004, 136). It is possible that some of these finds relate to formal acts of river burial, but many other potential interpretations could account for their presence. They might, for example, represent victims of accidental drowning, erosion of riverside cemeteries, and votive or sacrificial deposition of whole or complete bodies.

In conclusion, deliberate deposition in the river Thames almost certainly had its origins in the Mesolithic period and was a long-lived practice that continued throughout prehistory. Stretches of the river appear to have been used for votive deposition as opposed to other forms of practice that involved the building of monuments. This is perhaps most notable with the deposition of Peterborough Ware, a type of pottery that was often deposited at earlier monuments, as well as with various special-purpose perforated implements, belt sliders and waisted axes that were placed in graves and monuments. The river also appears to have been a place where human remains were deposited, a suggestion that may receive some support from discoveries of a small but important range of Beaker-associated artefacts usually found in burial contexts. In the early Bronze Age, river deposition appears to have become more selective as the emphasis shifted towards the deposition of particular types of bronzework.

RITUAL, CEREMONY AND COSMOGRAPHY

It is plain from the foregoing discussion that ritual, ceremony and cosmography should be seen as pervasive aspects of cultural life throughout the Neolithic and early Bronze Age, finding expression in a very diverse range of practices, artefacts, materials, architectural forms and landscape organisations. The categories and qualities of archaeological evidence that, in one way or another, can be understood with reference to the kinds of social action and cognition characterised broadly as 'ritualised' and 'religious' are indeed so varied that formal classification and even definition are often elusive. The interpenetration and interreferencing of the sacred and the everyday, practically, materially and in terms of the meanings which were evoked, also demands subtle interpretations of the evidence that do not depend on simple dichotomisations of ritual/sacred *versus* practical/profane. Indeed, the key to distinguishing 'ritual' from 'non-ritual' lies not in universalising models but in analyses sensitive to the particular cultural contexts being explored: 'what must be comprehended are the ways in which *indigenous actors* in the past and

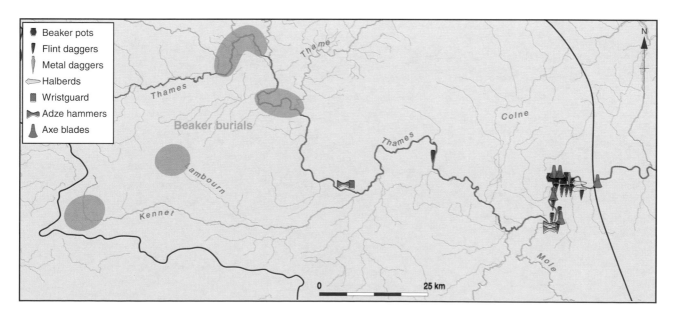

Fig. 14.38   Principal areas of Beaker burials and selected river finds

present make distinctions between different forms of practice' (Owoc 2001a, 28).

Although ritual appears to be such a transient phenomenon that it easily evades archaeological recognition, the performance of ritual – as the Thames Valley evidence demonstrates forcibly – has an intrinsic materiality comprising many different kinds of physical acts, built stages, representations and objects. Our recognition of symbolically-charged material kinds and conditions of deposition, and the ritualised actions that brought these into being, thus seems less challenging than arriving at an interpretation of what such materials and practices signified to the people involved. One of the greatest problems in arriving at such an understanding is that rites of passage are best understood as whole, transformative processes – each stage effective and sensible only in relation to the others – yet not every stage may be equally visible materially. Most discussions of ritual in archaeology are thus selective and incomplete, focusing on specific parts or elements of the ritual process that can be seen, such as thresholds, votive deposits or architecturally-defined liminal spaces, while failing to recognise the overall processes involved or the meanings these conveyed.

This issue is highlighted if the full range of ritual practices evident in the Middle and Upper Thames Valley is considered at a regional scale. In each period, it is apparent that such practices were highly varied, materially, contextually, geographically and temporally. Each distinct kind of practice recognised on this basis tends to be treated more or less separately, such as pit deposition, river deposition, ceremonies within enclosures, processions, burials of the dead, and numerous variants or categories of each of these. Yet, as the possible connections made above between cursus monuments and funerary rituals or between river deposition and burials on land suggest, it is equally likely that much of this diversity represents alternative ways of ritually achieving the same ends, perhaps by different communities or sects, or represents specific components or stages of the *same* ritual processes. The great advantage of a regional scale of enquiry, of the kind provided by the Middle and Upper Thames, is that it offers opportunities to discern the complexities and interrelationships of the different categories of evidence available. This theme is developed more fully in the next chapter, on the making of the dead, the mortuary treatment, deposition and memorialisation of which provide us with perhaps the most compelling insights into the nature of Neolithic and early Bronze Age rituals and what these meant to the people who performed them.

Chapter 15 – Making the dead

by Paul Garwood with a contribution by Alistair Barclay

FUNERARY RITUAL AND SOCIETY

The prehistory of the 4th to mid-2nd millennia cal BC, more than any other period in British archaeology, is dominated by the evidence from funerary monuments and graves (for general discussions of the evidence and its interpretation see: R Bradley 1984a; 2007; Barrett 1988; 1990; Brück 2004a; Garwood 1991; 2007a; Shanks and Tilley 1982; Thomas 1991; 1999; 2000). Understanding of this evidence, however, is fraught with empirical and theoretical difficulties that are all too often ignored in social interpretations. Simplistic 'reflectionist' approaches to the reading of the mortuary data in social and demographic terms has been widely discredited for some time (eg Shennan 1982; cf Bloch and Parry 1982; Hodder 1982, 195-201), yet the expectation that it is somehow possible to reconstruct social organisation, as if mortuary evidence directly reflected prehistoric social categories, remains remarkably durable. Contrasting approaches that emphasise the social construction of the dead with reference to ideal categories of dead and living people, particular moral, aesthetic and political schemes of meaning or representation (eg Thomas 1991; Treherne 1995), and different kinds of personhood (eg Brück 2004a; Díaz-Andreu et al. 2005; Fowler 2004), provide far more convincing and compelling interpretative insights. Even these, however, take insufficient notice of the constitution of the dead in the course of *ritualised* actions. This has far-reaching significance for how we understand burials in all cultural contexts.

The 'meaning' of ritual action (as discussed above; cf Bell 1992, 140-41; Humphrey and Laidlaw 1994, 5, 106) rests in the intended purpose of the ritual and its relationship to cosmological, moral and political order. The 'meaning' of burials, therefore, lies not in how they reflect lived social types, but rather in how they realise sacred categories and concerns, and also in how these are manipulated to political ends (Verdery 1999). The distinct stages that make up tripartite rites of passage, and their implications for understanding representations of identity in mortuary rituals, are also insufficiently appreciated by archaeologists. In the ritual process, when everyday social relationships and identities are suspended, the dead and the living alike are transformed into sacred or ideal stereotypes and invested with particular qualities or significance appropriate to the frames of reference evoked in the ritual. Unlike the living participants, however, the dead remain behind and are not transformed again into living social kinds, thereby retaining the identi-

ties or qualities conferred during the ritual. As a consequence, the images of human existence and personhood constructed in funerary settings may bear little relation to everyday social practices or relationships (cf Bloch 2005, 21). Indeed, human bodies or body parts may be subject to such radical substitutions of meaning in the course of ritual acts that they cease to represent 'people' at all (Garwood 2007c).

An equally striking feature of the mortuary evidence, especially in the light of its dominant role in social interpretation, is the *absence* of the dead from large geographical and temporal swathes of British prehistory. This can come as a surprise to those who imagine that burial practices involve a simple translation of living society into the community of the dead, and that 'normal' treatment of the dead should result in complete body deposition. This surprise rests not only on a lack of recognition of the highly destructive and disaggregative nature of some mortuary practices in relation to human bodies, and their uneven application in relation to different social categories, but also a profound misappreciation of the nature of funerary ritual and of depositional acts involving human remains. Indeed, given that the majority of people who died in the Neolithic and Bronze Age do not seem to have been *buried* in formal funerary settings of any kind, and that mortuary practices can take any imaginable form that people care to devise (eg Metcalf and Huntingdon 1991; Parker Pearson 1999), it is perhaps most surprising that there should be burials to study at all.

It is true that earlier prehistoric burials may be especially difficult to see materially in comparison with more recently buried human remains: they are more likely to be chemically and biotically eroded, or in various ways concealed, disturbed or destroyed by a range of post-depositional natural geomorphological processes or social practices such as ploughing. Even so, it is clear that formal interment practices during the Neolithic and early Bronze Age, whether in built structures such as tombs or in burial pits, appear never to have been representative of the entire living population, and for long periods were exceptionally rare events if they happened at all. In studying the remains of the dead we are never, therefore, dealing with more than parts of the communities of the living, and indeed parts that were selected and treated in distinctive ways on the basis of religious and social criteria about which we are at best uncertain and more usually entirely ignorant. There is little question that these criteria varied culturally in space, and changed over time, as did the religious and sociopolitical contexts of funerary rituals and mortuary practices, with the dead having markedly different significance in relation to cultural and political agenda or fields of discourse in different places and at different times. Moreover, what are sometimes described as 'burials' on closer inspection often appear to be either partial deposits derived from more complex mortuary practices, or the outcomes of votive acts that involved fragments of dead people as a material resource, rather than as formal treatment of individuals as discrete 'persons'. It should come as no surprise, therefore, that interpretative frameworks that are used to make sense of mortuary deposits in one cultural context may be unhelpful if not detrimental to understanding those of other places and times.

In the following sections, therefore, the nature and significance of Neolithic and early Bronze Age funerary practices in the Middle and Upper Thames Valley will be surveyed chronologically, because it is only by investigating the mortuary evidence in specific cultural and temporal contexts that the meanings, significance and uneven and diverse presence of the dead becomes explicable. Similarly, it is necessary to contextualise consistent kinds of practice and signification with reference to their cultural landscape settings, other monuments and funerary events, other kinds of contemporary mortuary practices, and the wider social and cultural worlds of which such burial events were a part.

The specific meanings of burial events, conveyed in the course of highly 'theatrical' ritual performances (Turner 1982; Schechner 1994; Pearson and Shanks 2001, 119-25), are of course very difficult to reconstruct. Yet the very structure of funerary ritual embodies a need for clear and emphatic communication of the existential status of the dead at key transformative stages in the ritual process. Body display and deposition, for example, are often given special visual prominence and dramatic expression during culminating or closing acts that bring the funerary process to completion, when ideal or sacred identities and qualities are confirmed and crystallized. At these points, participants in funerals require especially overt and unambiguous representation if they are to appreciate the 'messages' intended, especially within the usually short timeframe of burial deposition (Thomas 1991, 34). We should assume, therefore, that in most cases the selection, sequence and arrangement of bodies and other objects or substances were very carefully and explicitly staged for the audience to see and understand, in ways that sometimes produced material forms that we can recognise archaeologically. Interpretation, however, rests with the interpreter and their knowledge of people, places, artefacts, materials and the uses and meanings of these as symbolic media. The difficulty for the archaeologist is not so much a matter of identifying the material forms and relationships intended, but in approximating the pre-understandings of people in the past in such a way that aspects of past meaning can be recognised and translated into terms sensible in the present.

EARLY NEOLITHIC MORTUARY PRACTICES: IMAGINING, MAKING AND CELEBRATING THE DEAD

Interpretations of early Neolithic mortuary evidence in Britain have been dominated by the evidence from chambered tombs and related structures and, to a lesser extent, earthen long barrows (see especially: Ashbee 1970; Renfrew 1976; Kinnes 1981; 1992; Shanks and Tilley 1982; Thorpe 1984; R Bradley 1984a; 2004; Barrett 1988; Thomas 1988; 1999, 131-51; 2000; Saville 1990a; Barber 2000; Schulting 2000; King 2001; 2003; Fowler 2004; Darvill 2004, 140-65; Jones 2005; Kirk 2006; Field 2006, 125-40; Smith and Brickley 2006). In almost all cases, at least since the early 1980s, attention has focused on disarticulated human remains (Fig. 15.1), their spatial organisation within and between chambered structures or across old land surfaces in premound contexts, and the complex and distinctive nature of mortuary practices. These are assumed to have involved various combinations of defleshing processes, secondary burial, movement or circulation of human remains, and selective and structured deposition. It is notable that most of the chambered tomb sites in southern Britain from which this evidence is derived are located within the Middle and Upper Thames study area, either on the Cotswolds or on the Berkshire and north Wiltshire downs. These include: Ascott-under-Wychwood (Chesterman 1977; Benson and Whittle 2007) and Wayland's Smithy (Whittle 1991; Whittle, Bayliss and Wysocki 2007) in Oxfordshire, Hazleton North (Saville 1990a; Meadows *et al.* 2007), Notgrove (Clifford 1936), Rodmarton (Saville 1989), Burn Ground (Grimes 1960), and Sale's Lot (O'Neil 1966) in Gloucestershire, and West Kennet in Wiltshire (Piggott 1962; Thomas and Whittle 1986; Bayliss, Whittle and Wysocki 2007). Several of the most recently excavated or reevaluated long barrows in southern Britain can also be found in the study area, both with and without mortuary evidence, notably Beckhampton Road, South Street and Horslip near Avebury, Wiltshire (Ashbee *et al.* 1979), and Lambourn, Berkshire (Schulting 2000).

Closely associated with these early Neolithic burial contexts are 'linear mortuary structures', consisting of elongated pits or wooden 'boxes', in some cases probably lidded, containing human skeletal remains mostly in a disarticulated state. These may have been left open or accessible for some time, and some may have been revetted or covered by low mounds (Thomas 1999, 131-34; 2000, 658). Examples of these structures in the Middle and Upper Thames area include Radley feature 5352 (Barclay and Bradley 1999: discussed further below), and Wayland's Smithy I, Berkshire (Whittle 1991; Whittle, Bayliss and Wysocki 2007). These have similarities in terms of architectural forms and mortuary deposits with structures at Nutbane, Hampshire (Morgan 1959a, 1959b), Aldwincle Site 1, Northamptonshire (Jackson 1976), the Fengate 'flat grave' (Pryor 1976), Haddenham, Cambridgeshire (Evans and Hodder 2006), and Street House, Cleveland (Vyner 1984; Bowman *et al.* 1990).

By far the most powerful concept used to explain the cultural significance and specific meanings of the mortuary practices evident at these sites, especially the collective deposits of disarticulated skeletal remains and their long-term ritual handling and spatial organisation, is the idea of 'ancestors'. This was first used in an explicit way by Bradley (1984a, 15-20) and Barrett (1988), and was derived especially from anthropological discussions of mortuary ritual (eg Metcalf and Huntington 1991, 93-118) and particular ethnographies (especially of the Merina of Madagascar: Bloch 1981a; 1982). The usual assumption is that tombs were built to house the dead of a sacred community or descent group (eg a lineage), whose durable and prominent presence in the landscape was perceived to be important in terms of claims to territory, a sense of belonging, reproductive capacities, and cultural and social identity (Bradley 1984b; cf R Bradley 2004). Although the idea of ancestors has attracted some criticism, notably by Whitley (2002), it remains the most widely used and favoured means of characterising an imagined relationship between the living tomb-building community and their forebears (Whittle, Barclay, Bayliss *et al.* 2007, 133-34). There is, however, clearly a need to reexamine some of the basic premises that underlie this interpretative metaphor in early Neolithic studies, especially in the light of reassessments of the evidence from Severn-Cotswold tombs and from other sites in the Middle and Upper Thames region.

Most important in this respect, is a far-reaching reevaluation of some of the most well-known and most intensively investigated chambered tomb and earthen long barrow sites in southern Britain (summarised in Whittle, Barclay, Bayliss *et al.* 2007), most of which are located within the study area (West Kennet, Wayland's Smithy, Ascott-under-Wychwood and Hazleton North). This work, which relies heavily on Bayesian modelling of series of high quality radiocarbon dates, suggests that early Neolithic funerary monuments were built rapidly as short-term realisable construction events (rather than as long drawn-out 'projects'), during a relatively narrow span of time within the period *c* 3750-3400 cal BC (ibid., 125-27). Moreover, it is argued that mortuary deposition at each monument was of short duration, rarely lasting more than a century (ie over some three to five generations; ibid., 129), and that most bodies were placed in tombs as complete articulated corpses, with varying degrees of disarticulation and sorting or removal of skeletal remains occurring only after initial depositional events. Well-documented examples of already disarticulated bone deposits appear to be extremely rare (Thomas 2000, 660), and even in these cases there may be several different explanations for the practices involved. It is also striking that there appears to be no strong evidence from chambered tombs for the inclusion of ancient human remains alongside the newly dead (Whittle, Barclay, Bayliss *et al.* 2007, 132-33).

This interpretation runs counter to interpretations of tombs as 'ossuaries' (cf Ahlström 2003; Darvill 2004, 147-53; Whittle, Barclay, Bayliss *et al.* 2007), and must cast doubt on the idea that tomb deposits were the culmination of very long-term practices involving the circulation and reorganisation of 'ancestral' remains, their curation, or collection from excarnation or other mortuary contexts (eg Smith and Brickley 2006, 348). In fact, the reverse seems to be the case: tombs appear less like final repositories for ancestral skeletal materials (whether reworked *in situ* or introduced from outside for incorporation in collective deposits), but rather places in which such materials were first created, and from which they were sometimes removed for use and deposition elsewhere (eg in pits, causewayed enclosure ditches, and perhaps long mortuary structures). In this way, chambered tombs can be seen as sources of 'ancestral' substances, as well as a means of housing and perhaps protecting such resources.

In the light of this recent work, there is now also an opportunity to reinterpret the composition of the 'communities of the dead' who occupied chambered tombs. Whittle, Barclay, Bayliss *et al.* (2007, 134) suggest that the mortuary deposits studied indicate successive interments of only small numbers of people, in total, no more than 15-40 over five generations or less in each case. They argue that 'it is clear that we are not dealing with complete social units or all the members of even [a] nuclear family unit' (ibid.). Although great caution is expressed in asserting the possibility that tomb groups represent social elites of some kind, there seems little question that the identity of the dead was 'special' in some way, and that burial events were relatively rare and especially significant events. However these people were defined, it is apparent that in tomb contexts we encounter not the 'everyday dead' but the 'significant dead', whose very presence realised their exceptional sacred or political identities, biographies and/or personal characteristics, and whose funerals and mortuary treatment were media for diverse kinds of cosmological, eschatological and ideological manipulation and representation (cf Shanks and Tilley 1982).

The bodily remains of people perceived in these ways, transformed into hard skeletal material,

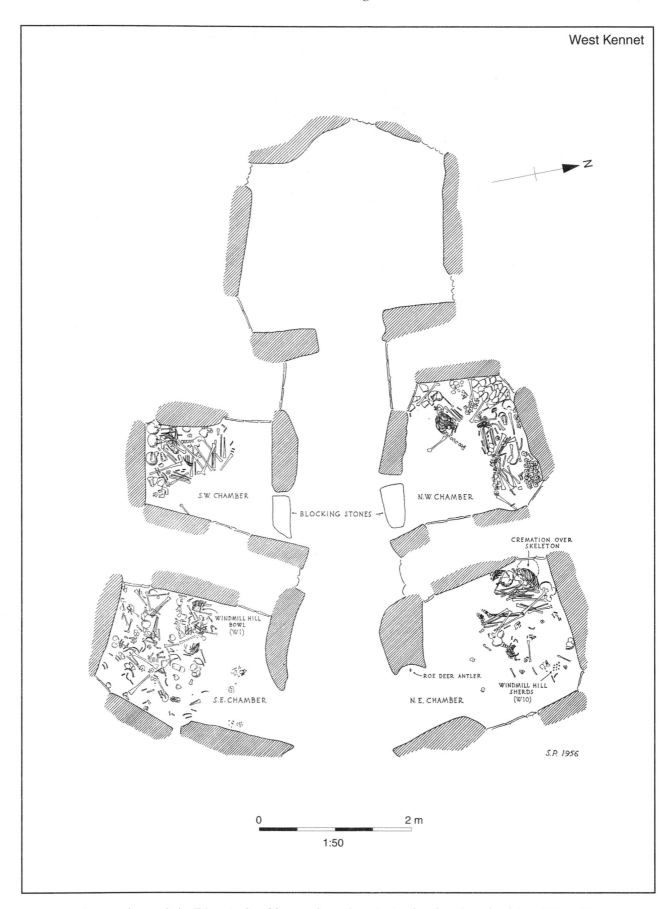

Fig. 15.1 (above and opposite)   Disarticulated human bone deposits Tin chambered tombs: (above) West Kennet; (opposite) Wayland's Smithy I, Hazleton North (north chamber) and Ascott-under-Wychwood (northern inner cist)

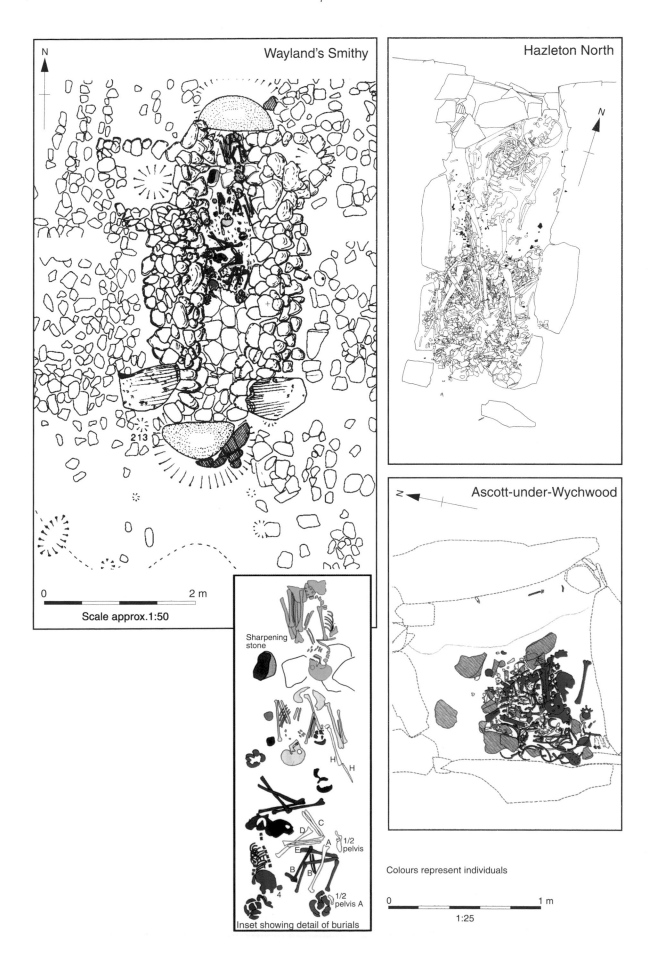

Wayland's Smithy

0   2 m

Scale approx.1:50

213

Sharpening
stone

H   H

D
E
A
1/2
pelvis

C

B B

4

1/2
pelvis A

Inset showing detail of burials

Hazleton North

N

Ascott-under-Wychwood

N

Colours represent individuals

0   1 m

1:25

might thus easily have been regarded as substances imbued with special qualities or powers: to be celebrated in their own right, strategically drawn upon to be redeployed as striking symbolic media in ritual performances, and consumed in powerful depositional acts in other social contexts (for example, in sacrificial, devotional and gift-giving events). It is indeed likely, given the rarity and perhaps episodic nature of burial events, that these took place not according to a continuing tradition of religious observance, but at times when such acts were thought to be necessary according to salient religious and political agenda, and in reaction to perceptions of events and changing circumstances in the lived world. These circumstances must inevitably have altered from one depositional episode to the next. This is consistent with the sheer variety and inconsistency of person-types (by age, gender, health and diet) selected for placement in tombs (Whittle, Barclay, Bayliss *et al.* 2007, 134), and

the considerable variation in the ways their bodies were organised spatially and subject to differing treatment after death.

This theme is brought into still sharper focus by the wide range of mortuary and depositional practices evident in non-monumentalised contexts. Although it is difficult to categorise these in any simple manner, in part because many deposits appear to have been reworked over time, it is possible nonetheless to identify a range of different strategies and modes of conduct in the treatment and deposition of bodies and skeletal materials. This differentiation is most evident in the following ways:

(i) Predepositional treatment of human remains (especially in terms of whether bodies were kept intact for burial or consisted of already disarticulated bones, and the selection of specific age and sex categories);

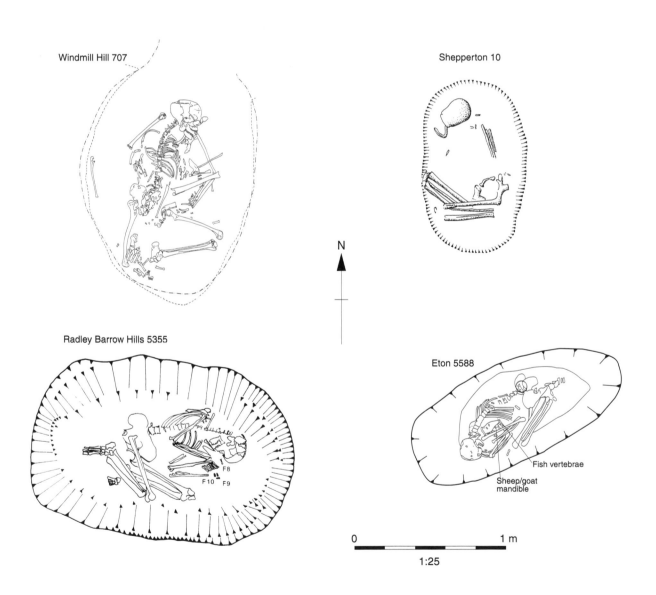

Fig. 15.2   *Earlier Neolithic single graves in the Upper Thames and Upper Kennet Valleys*

(ii) Modes of deposition (eg single event individual articulated burials, single event multiple articulated burials, multi-event articulated burial sequences, single- or multi-event deposits of disarticulated bone collections; and depositional acts undertaken with, or without, the intention of returning to re-access the mortuary deposits/human materials)

(iii) Deposits with, or without, placed artefacts or other objects and substances;

(iv) Distinctive kinds of mortuary 'architecture' and modes of access (surface deposition, simple pits (closed/open), pits with timber structures (closed/open), free-standing timber structures);

(v) Post-depositional practices (eg spatial reorganisation of human remains, extraction of bones from mortuary deposits, and the addition of new bones or artefacts).

Viewed in this way, it is apparent that there are relatively few *exclusive* patterns or sequences of practice to be found in earlier Neolithic mortuary evidence in the Middle and Upper Thames Valley, or indeed more widely. Even so, some distinctive practical strategies and forms of signification can be discerned in this evidence.

First, it is apparent that individual and multiple burials of articulated bodies in simple pits, as, for example, at Radley (Fig. 15.2; Barclay and Bradley 1999, 31-4) were not unusual, and that in some cases these were accompanied by sets of artefacts suggesting formal burial, expression of 'fixed' identities (cf Thomas 1991) and possibly the intention *not* to exhume or reorganise the remains at a later date. These burials are discussed in more detail below.

Second, it is likely that provision was made in some contexts for *sequences* of burials (which sometimes involved manipulation of earlier interments). It is possible, for example, to reinterpret the human remains within the linear mortuary structure (5352) at Radley (Fig. 15.4; Barclay and Bradley 1999, 28-31, fig 3.5) in terms of successive burial events, involving the reopening of the chamber and reorganisation or partial extraction of existing skeletal material, culminating in a final male burial. The latter subsequently remained intact as no further bodies were added, possibly in a similar way to the 'flint knapper' burial in the north chamber at Hazleton North (Fig. 15.1; Saville 1990a). These deposits are clearly similar to mortuary deposits found within chambered tombs (discussed above) and beneath non-megalithic long barrows prior to their sealing by mound structures (see Kinnes 1992, 98-107; Field 2006, 132-40).

Third, burial events involving articulated bodies (at least at the time that initial depositional events took place) clearly contrast with instances in which disarticulated and usually partial human skeletal material was placed in pits and ditches. At Sutton Courtenay, for example, several complete and fragmentary human skulls and other bones found in pit V, just to the east of the Drayton South cursus (Barclay *et al.* 2003, 16-20; Leeds 1934a), suggest deliberate collection and placement of skeletal material derived from a source elsewhere. The same process is also evident in the case of Cassington pit 7, which contained the disarticulated remains of four adults and two children (Leeds 1934a). The fragmentary human skeletal material found in causewayed enclosure ditches was probably assembled in similar ways. Examples include deposits of human bone at Abingdon (Avery 1982), Staines (Fig. 14.3: Robertson-Mackay 1987, 36-8, 59, fiche 6-20; P Bradley 2004, 118, fig.13.2), and Windmill Hill (Fig. 15.3), including bone deposit 117 at the top of the primary fill in the outer ditch (Whittle *et al.* 1999, 89-90, 345-6), and bone deposit 630 in the secondary silts of the inner ditch (ibid., 110, 346).

There may, however, have been significant contrasts in the forms and purposes of depositional acts in pits in comparison with ditch contexts, especially in terms of the relative visibility and accessibility of deposited materials. It is usually assumed that pits provided very constrained arenas for observing placed objects and materials, and that these were quickly sealed ('closed') and thus literally embedded in the ground, whereas ditches (both unsilted and silted) provided more visually and physically accessible 'open' surfaces for displaying materials at significant points (eg in liminal contexts at entrances, such as the Trench 42-6 deposit at Staines; Robertson-Mackay 1987, 36-8; Fig. 14.3). In most cases, however, it is uncertain whether pits were immediately backfilled or left open for periods of time, while it is possible that materials placed in ditches may have been covered rather than left exposed. In any case, the issue of visibility may be less important than contrasts in the temporalities of

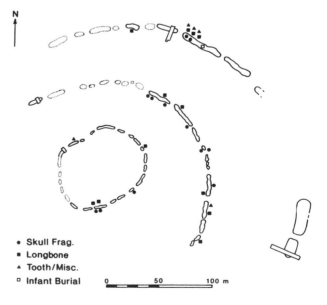

- • Skull Frag.
- ■ Longbone
- ▲ Tooth/Misc.
- □ Infant Burial

0   50   100 m

Fig. 15.3 Human skeletal material in the excavated ditch segments at Windmill Hill

construction and deposition. Pit digging is a purposeful process intended in some cases specifically to accommodate depositional acts (ie there is a process of mutual signification, reinforced by the 'fixing' of materials sealed by backfilling). In contrast, the deposition of materials in ditches most often involved returns to 'old' places, and social actions that were secondary to the initial creation of enclosures, with potential reference to the 'past', narratives of people and events, and prescriptive reification or renewal of cosmological schemes.

Fourth, mortuary deposits in some cases appear to have been accessed at various intervals after initial burial events in order to reorganise and sometimes recover human bone and other objects. It is important to recognise, however, that such actions may have had no connection with the original intentions, beliefs or social identities of those who buried the dead in the first place. The 'disturbed' and incomplete nature of many early Neolithic mortuary deposits, in all contexts, may well be an outcome of several different kinds of practice rather than the reflection of just one complex mortuary process. Disarticulated and partial deposits in both tombs and non-monumental contexts, for example, may be the result of management and extraction activities by the direct descendants of the dead, acting in accordance with religious beliefs and recognised ritual strategies, within a generation or two of deposition. They could also, however, be the result of later activities by people, whether distantly related or not, more interested in generic 'ancestral' materials, emblems of things past, the medicinal properties of ancient body substances, and perhaps even acts of iconoclasm or desecration. In this light, fragmentary human remains found in pits (eg Dorchester-on-Thames pit 3003: Whittle *et al.* 1992, 153) could be interpreted in several different ways, for example: (i) as final depositional events, using selected human remains derived from primary mortuary settings as symbolic media in a new context (eg in votive acts, rites of passage, statements of belonging, claims to land); (ii) as individual graves created with the expectation that they would later be reopened by the relatives of the dead for circulation, dispersal of remains, and/or reinstallation in new depositional contexts (eg as part of long-term mortuary and other ritual processes); or (iii) as individual graves reopened by people with no direct relationship to the dead but wishing to obtain valued materials as symbolic media or resources for consumption in a range of possible social contexts. These interpretative possibilities apply just as easily to all other kinds of 'collective' and/or 'disturbed' mortuary deposits.

In some ways the most striking outcome of this review of early Neolithic mortuary practices in the Middle and Upper Thames Valley is the sheer number and variety of single articulated inhumation burials. The evidence from monuments and especially collective burial deposits has always dominated interpretations of mortuary practices

and their social significance, yet it is increasingly apparent that single graves were both relatively common and involved practices such as artefact deposition that are more usually associated with Beaker period and early Bronze Age burials. The evidence for such burials in the Middle and Upper Thames region is summarised in Table 15.1 and illustrated in Figure 15.2. It is worth noting that while there is now widespread evidence for earlier Neolithic flat graves and other kinds of articulated individual burials at a wide range of sites in southern Britain (see Kinnes 1979, 126-27), including recent discoveries near the Blackwall Tunnel, London (associated with a Carinated Bowl and flint knife; Coles *et al.* 2008), and at Thanet Way, Kent (Clark and Rady 2008, 10-11), the majority of well-recorded burials of these kinds and nearly all those with radiocarbon dates are located within the present study area.

The evidence from these graves raises important questions about the relationships between collective and individual burial, disarticulated and articulated human remains, the absence and presence of artefacts, and the chronologies of distinctive mortuary practices. In addition, like the recent reappraisal of chambered tombs (cf Whittle, Barclay, Bayliss 2007), the widespread presence of single graves in the 4th millennium cal BC highlights problems in conventional interpretations of early Neolithic mortuary rituals, which are usually represented in terms of 'ancestor worship', egalitarian ethics or ideologies, collective identities and 'dividual' personhood (cf Shanks and Tilley 1982; Thorpe 1984; Bradley 1984a; Barrett 1988; Thomas 1988; 1999, 131-51, 2000; King 2001; 2003; Fowler 2004; Darvill 2004,140-65; Jones 2005; Kirk 2006).

The depositional characteristics of earlier Neolithic single graves are very diverse, and there is often doubt about stratigraphic contexts and relationships. The Pangbourne burial, for example, may have been a flat grave but the evidence is inconclusive and other possibilities, such as a ditch context, are equally as likely (A Barclay pers. comm.). The nature of depositional practices is also often ambiguous, although in some cases these may have been more complex than simple one-off burial events: the pre-enclosure burial at Windmill Hill, for example, was probably left exposed for some time in an open pit (Whittle *et al.* 1999, 79-80).

The wider monumental and landscape contexts of these burials, and their chronological relationships with other depositional practices, are also little understood. Only at Radley is there detailed evidence for the spatio-temporal setting of single inhumation graves (Fig. 15.4; cf Barclay 1999c, fig. 9.12). There are three burials with radiocarbon age ranges spanning the period *c* 3800-3100 cal BC (5354, 5355, 5356: Barclay and Bradley 1999, 31-4; Garwood 1999b, 275-6) located close together some 200 m to the east of the Abingdon causewayed enclosure, and *c* 80 m to the north-west of the linear mortuary structure. It is possible that these formed

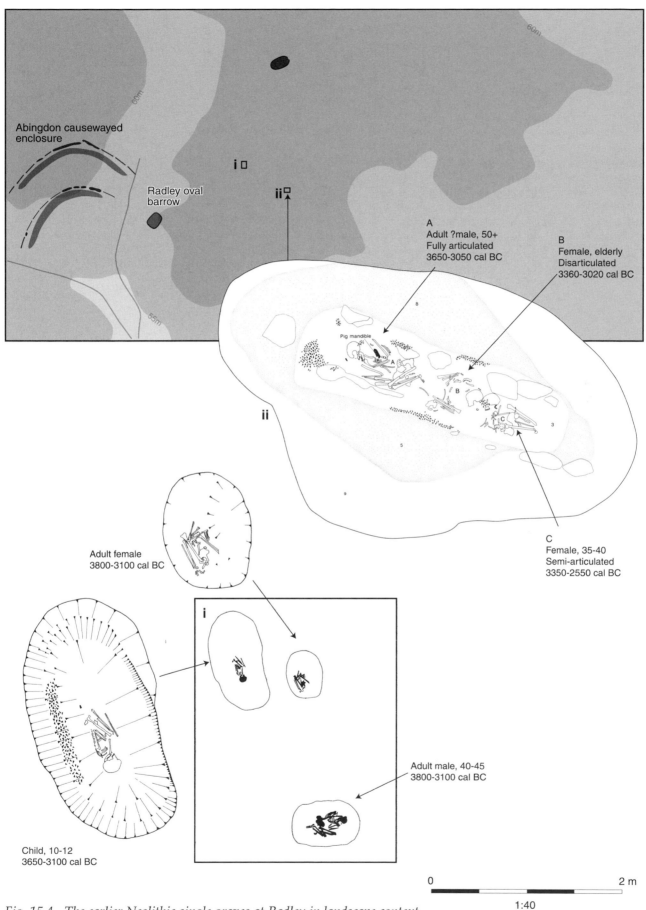

Abingdon causewayed
enclosure

Radley oval
barrow

A
Adult ?male, 50+
Fully articulated
3650-3050 cal BC

B
Female, elderly
Disarticulated
3360-3020 cal BC

Pig mandible

C
Female, 35-40
Semi-articulated
3350-2550 cal BC

Adult female
3800-3100 cal BC

Adult male, 40-45
3800-3100 cal BC

Child, 10-12
3650-3100 cal BC

0   2 m

1:40

Fig. 15.4   The earlier Neolithic single graves at Radley in landscape context

Table 15.1: Earlier Neolithic single inhumation graves in the Middle and Upper Thames Valley

	Context	Sex/age	Artefacts	Radiocarbon dating cal BC (95% confidence)	Reference
Whiteleaf	2-post mortuary structure, disturbed/moved	♂ Adult		3760-3640	Childe and Smith 1954; Hey *et al.* 2007
Mount Farm 602	Pit within ring ditch	♂	4 flint blades, 2 blade fragments	3640-3370 3370-2890	Lambrick forthcoming
Shepperton G10	Base of ring ditch G	♀ 30-40 years		3600-3340	Jones 1990; 2008
Shepperton G8	Primary fill of ring ditch G	? 25-35 years			Jones 1990; 2008
Park Brow 1	?Timber mortuary structure and cairn	♂? *c* 16 years		3700-3500	Richards 1986-90
Park Brow 2	?Timber mortuary structure and cairn	♀ *c* 30 years		3650-3500	Richards 1986-90
Park Brow 3	?Timber mortuary structure and cairn	♂ *c* 40 years		3710-3620	Richards 1986-90
Windmill Hill 707	Pit, predates outer enclosure	♂ 35-45 years	Flint flake Pig scapula in fill	1. 3640-3490 or 3420-3380 2. 3610-3580 or 3520-3340	Whittle *et al.* 1999
Radley 5356	Pit	♀ Aged		3800-3100	Barclay and Bradley 1999
Radley 5354	Pit, possible coffin	Child: 10-12 years	Flint blade-like flakes	3650-3100	Barclay and Bradley 1999
Radley 5355	Pit	♂ 40-45 years	3 flint blade-like flakes	3380-3090	Barclay and Bradley 1999
Abingdon, Curtis Gravel Pit	Pit	♂? Young adult?	Serrated blade, core-rejuvenation flake, 2 blade-like flakes, burnt pebble		Wallis *et al.* 1992
ERL, Dorney, 5588	Pit, near ring ditch 5579	♀ 25-30 years	Fish vertebra (Pike)	3370-2930 Sheep/goat mandible	Allen 2000
ERL, Dorney, 5991	Pit, near ring ditch 5579	Child: 5 years		3330-3220 or 3120-2900	Allen 2000
ERL, Dorney, 5125	Pit, near ring ditch 5361	♂ *c* 30 years	25 sherds of early Neolithic pottery		Allen 2000
Lambourn, secondary burial	Sarsen cist? in east end of mound	♀ 35-45 years	2 marine shells, also flint flakes and chalk objects 'nearby'	3300-2880	Wymer 1966; Schulting 2000
Pangbourne	Pit or ditch	♀ 'Old'	Decorated bowl, antler, deer bones, pig molar		Piggott 1929
Goring, Burial 62	Upper ditch fill	Child: 8-9 years		3100-2890	Allen 1995
Yarnton 9469	Pit	♂ Adult	2 abraded sherds		G Hey pers. comm.
Staines F331	Pit within enclosure (?Neolithic)	♀ 30-40			Robertson-Mackay 1987

a small cemetery, but it is equally likely that they are unrelated and widely separated in time (5355, in particular, may be significantly later than the other burials). Another flat grave, but of less certain date, was found between the two ditches of the causewayed enclosure (Avery 1982, 12). Bodies were also placed in the linear mortuary structure (discussed above), and cranial fragments were deposited in secondary contexts late in the causewayed enclosure ditch fills and in the oval barrow phase 3 and 4 ditch segments. The chronology of burial and depositional events is imprecise, but it now appears probable that *all* the dated earlier Neolithic

mortuary deposits are significantly later than the construction and early use of the enclosure. Recent redating and analysis of the Abingdon enclosure suggests construction of both earthwork circuits within the period *c* 3650-3500 cal BC and probably *c* 3650-3600 cal BC (Whittle, Bayliss, Healy, Hey *et al.* forthcoming) whereas burials 5354 and 5356 probably belong to the period *c* 3540-3340, the linear mortuary deposits and burial 5355 to the period *c* 3400-3100 cal BC, while the scattered cranial fragments were probably all finally deposited after *c* 3400 cal BC (although these may have been redeposited).

The Middle and Upper Thames Valley evidence is exceptionally important more widely as it provides a strong chronological framework for interpreting earlier Neolithic single graves and articulated inhumation burials for the first time (Table 15.1). It is especially striking that a broad contrast exists between earlier single inhumation burials, which are found in primary contexts in a range of funerary monument settings, and mostly lack grave goods (eg Whiteleaf, Shepperton and Park Brow, dating to the period *c* 3750-3500 cal BC), and later single graves which occur mainly in pit contexts, and which are often associated with placed objects, mainly lithic artefacts and animal remains (eg at Windmill Hill, Mount Farm, Radley, Dorney and Goring: dating to the period *c* 3600-2900 cal BC, and mostly *c* 3400-2900 cal BC). These age ranges can be compared with the recent chronological framework proposed for the construction and use of chambered tombs in the period *c* 3750-3400 cal BC (Whittle, Barclay, Bayliss *et al.* 2007, 125-27).

In this light, and considering recent reassessments of the chronologies of other monument categories such as earthen long barrows (Field 2006, 18-21, appendix), causewayed enclosures (Whittle, Bayliss and Healy, forthcoming) and cursus monuments (Barclay and Bayliss 1999), earlier Neolithic mortuary practices can be distinguished with reference to at least three broad chronological phases:

4000-3700 cal BC: Human remains dating to the very earliest Neolithic in Britain now appear to be very scarce and to consist almost entirely of small bone fragments, such as the cremated material in the postholes of the timber building at Yarnton, dating to *c* 3850-3700 cal BC (Bayliss and Hey in prep.), and possibly the human skull fragments from the precairn midden at Hazleton North, dating to *c* 3940-3690 cal BC (Meadows *et al.* 2007, 51, 61, table 1). It is also now apparent that evidence for monumental architecture in this period is very limited and ambiguous, especially as virtually all the radiocarbon dates on short-life sample materials from secure contexts associated with construction events or mortuary deposits belong to the period *c* 3750-3400 cal BC (Field 2006, 18-21, app.; Whittle, Barclay, Bayliss *et al.* 2007; cf Schulting 2000 for a discussion of possible earlier dates). In this context, it would appear that neither prominent monuments, nor the dead, however represented, had a significant presence in the earliest Neolithic landscapes in Britain. There is certainly no *a priori* reason, therefore, to assume that the dead were given a central role as symbolic media in the initial creation of 'farming societies' (cf King 2001). This runs counter to what has become an orthodox vision of the formation of early Neolithic cultural identities, new forms of social agency, and the consolidation of new social organisations, technologies and material culture, especially in relation to the celebration of ancestors (cf Bradley 1984c, 15-20; Barrett 1988; Thomas 2000, 655-58). Indeed, it is now tempting to revive the idea of a 'formative Neolithic' (cf Kinnes 1988; Sheridan 2007; Bayliss *et al.* 2008), in which new kinds of materials, technologies and social relationships were created in ways that were *not* realised immediately through monument building, nor through complex depositional practices involving human bodies.

3750-3400 cal BC: The considerable evidence for monument construction and mortuary practices from *c* 3800 cal BC, and especially after 3700 cal BC, thus contrasts radically with the earliest Neolithic evidence, suggesting a transformation in beliefs and social strategies that gave the dead a new, special and prominent presence in the cultural landscape. This seems to have been realised in many different ways in terms of architectural forms, the nature and sequencing of mortuary practices, and the extent to which human bodies and body parts were drawn upon as symbolic media or resources, both in funerary and non-funerary contexts. It is also important to note the occurrence of burnt human bone in a wide range of depositional contexts at this time, including tombs, pits and ditch fills (discussed in more detail below). It might appear, in this light, that articulated and disarticulated bodies and/or unburnt and burnt remains, represent contrasting traditions of mortuary practice, yet the presence of these corporeal materials in the same kinds of depositional contexts, sometimes side by side, suggests a continuum of variation, part of which may also have been structured temporally. Articulated burials, for example, could be seen as bodies which had, for whatever reason, not been subject to further mortuary treatment or other actions leading to disarticulation, cremation, and/or dispersal.

The distinctions apparent in the mortuary evidence do not, therefore, seem to be a simple matter of contrasting traditions in the treatment of the dead, especially as many initial depositional acts, at least at monument sites, involved complete articulated bodies. Instead, we seem to be faced with different attitudes and strategies in the ways that such events were either 'fixed' in people's minds, for example by material preservation or curation of corpses or dramatic acts of dissolution (ie cremation), or were left 'open' to forms of practical and symbolic qualification, augmentation and incorporation through *subsequent* actions. Chambered tombs, from this perspective, can be seen as architectural forms designed specifically to facilitate certain kinds of subsequent ritual action, whereas the building of earthen long mounds and other unchambered structures could be seen as a means of bringing such actions to a close. Variation in mortuary deposits, in this context, could have resulted from several different social processes, probably in combination, including long-term transformations in the wider cultural milieu of death ritual and mortuary symbolism, changing social rationales and histories at specific locales over time, the realisation of specific short-lived social and political agenda in the performance of ritual acts and construction projects, and local cultural traditions and symbolic repertoires.

The mortuary 'role' of causewayed enclosures may also be clearer in the light of this evidence. The close connection often imagined between enclosures, death and burial (eg Mercer 1980; Thorpe 1984; Edmonds 1993) is based on rare and mainly fragmentary skeletal remains. There is, however, little direct evidence to show that inhumation burials took place within these enclosures: the Windmill Hill grave (Fig. 15.2), for example, was situated outside the two inner ditches and probably sealed under the third (Whittle 1990; Whittle *et al.* 1999, 79-81), while other graves (eg at Abingdon and Staines) appear to be isolated burial events that probably post-date the main periods of construction and use at each site (eg the burial of a child in the middle fills of the Goring enclosure ditch, dating to 3100-2890 cal BC, BM-2835: 4360±45 BP; Ambers and Housley 1995). Where stratigraphic or dating evidence is available, this usually shows that burials occurred later rather than earlier at these sites (eg at Offham Hill, Sussex; Drewett 1977). The suggestion that bodies were left exposed for excarnation purposes, or buried in pits for later exhumation, is based on evidence that could just as easily be explained as the outcome of depositional acts using materials derived from mortuary sites elsewhere. This argument also applies to placed deposits of human remains in ditches. Rather than mortuary settings in their own right, or places through which the dead passed (Edmonds 1993, 116-19), the very limited and inconsistent presence of human skeletal material suggests that these places were only occasional repositories for human remains, possibly for specific votive purposes or other ritual acts. Bones and bodies at causewayed enclosure sites, in this view, were symbolic media or substances believed to have certain qualities and powers, rather than celebrations or emblems of particular people: indeed, it is arguable whether the 'dead', as such, were represented or presenced at enclosure sites at all.

3400-2900 cal BC. It is apparent that many earlier Neolithic single graves belong to the period after chambered tombs went out of use, especially after *c* 3400-3300 cal BC (not 3000 cal

BC, contra Thomas 2000, 665). These graves have sometimes been interpreted as variations on the wider theme of 'complex' mortuary practices (eg Thorpe 1984), either as an *alternative* to tomb deposition, or as one part of an extended mortuary process that *eventually* did lead, after decomposition, exhumation, disarticulation and sorting, to secondary tomb burial (with at least implicit reference to recent Merina mortuary practices; Bloch 1981a). These interpretations, given the apparent temporal separation of tomb-related mortuary practices and most single grave interments, and the evidence for primary deposition of complete bodies within chambered tombs (Whittle, Barclay, Bayliss *et al.* 2007; cf Thomas 1999, 146-49), no longer appear to be convincing. Instead, single graves, especially with artefacts, seem to represent a new emphasis on individual identities (however stereotypical, ideal and relational; ibid., 151-56) in a cultural landscape structured around cursus monuments, other long enclosures and pit circles rather than tombs, long mounds and causewayed enclosures. Complex single graves of this period and the early 3rd millennium cal BC are discussed in more detail below.

This reinterpretation of both the chambered tomb and 'flat grave' evidence allows for a wider reassessment both of the significance of early Neolithic mortuary practices in relation to cultural identity and concepts of personhood, and also the formal and spatio-temporal structuring of the ritual performances involved. Julian Thomas' (2000) reappraisal of Neolithic mortuary practices makes a strong case for recognising, in the circulation of bones, a 'general economy of human remains', akin to gift exchange systems in which transactions of objects or materials were a means of creating social relationships as well as making the dead participants in the lived world (ibid., 660-62). In this process, the circulation and redeposition of skeletal remains were a means of dispersing and incorporating the dead throughout the landscape, so that tombs were not so much abodes of the ancestors but rather liminal places of transformation where 'categories of personhood were dissolved and recreated' (ibid., 662).

This is a convincing interpretation of tombs and other mortuary contexts containing disarticulated remains of the period *c* 3750-3400 cal BC, but it is suggested here that this must be contextualised with reference to the presence of the 'untransformed' dead (articulated individual burials) and of monuments that celebrated and fixed their presence in the Neolithic landscape. It now seems clear that there was no simple temporal progression in these practices, from earlier collective burials and transformative/dispersive mortuary practices that gave the dead a pervasive presence in social life, to later single graves that remained complete and which distanced the dead from the living, fixing them both in space and as part of recognisable descent lines (a view sustained by Thomas 2000, 663-65). Instead, throughout the period in which open-ended transformative and dispersive practices were in play, there was just as much emphasis on the memorialisation and social distancing of the dead, and the celebration and concretisation of their individual and collective identities through the burial of bodies, bones and other materials beneath or beside earthen mounds of various shapes and sizes. Moreover, as suggested above, it is best to see this not as a dichotomy of opposed practices but as two emphases within a continuum of variation. Decisions to keep open or to close places of mortuary deposition did not reflect separate funerary traditions, even at a local scale, but were made with reference to the *same* diverse set of practices, rationales, strategies and beliefs that made sense of and guided the treatment of the dead and their physical remains in all social contexts.

Thomas' (2000, 663-65; cf Barrett 1988; 1994) discussion also brings fresh critical attention to the concept of 'ancestors' in the earlier Neolithic, and the assumed relationship between tombs and ancestor rites. Although he is careful to note that the idea of collectivity construed with reference to ancestors 'in the present', and the creation of individual identities with reference to descent through time, are not mutually exclusive, he suggests that there *was* a profound shift of emphasis over time. In the earlier Neolithic, he argues, the presence of the ancestors was distributed across the landscape through a multiplicity of ritual acts and social transactions involving human bones. In contrast, after 3000 cal BC, new concerns with descent and perhaps tenurial rights came to the fore with efforts to install the dead permanently at specific locations. The discussion above shows that there was no such straightforward temporal progression, and suggests that the simple 'ancestors to ancestry' explanatory framework is no longer tenable, either in cultural or chronological terms (contra Barrett 1988). Indeed, it is arguable whether the idea of 'ancestors' is a useful concept for understanding this kind of evidence, at least in the way that it has been used generically to refer to every conceivable kind of practice which gave prominence to the dead, mortuary deposition, managed human remains and the past (cf Whitley 2002). At the very least, uncritical use of the term has led to the conflation of quite different practices and their significance under the same heading (eg the manipulation of bodies within tombs and the carrying out of processions along cursus monuments are often interpreted as if their 'meaning' was exactly the same and reducible to a single idea; ie ancestors). The evidence from both single graves and collective burials in the Middle and Upper Thames Valley, as elsewhere in Britain, suggests that the relationship between the dead and the living was far more complex than such a stereotypical characterisation implies.

Similar criticisms can be made of recent interpretations of personhood in this period (eg see Jones 2005; Kirk 2006; cf Fowler 2004). Although there is little question that archaeological evidence can be used to reveal distinctive ways of 'being human', and different kinds of subjectivity in the past (Kirk 2006, 333), the ideal-type distinction made between 'our' constructions of individuality and 'their' supposed fragmented and dispersed senses of relational personhood is misleading. It is easy to recognise in our own lives that our senses of self and identity are also multivariate, situational and relational, whilst expressions of individuality or 'permanent', discrete kinds of personhood are just as pervasive in 'other' cultural worlds as ours. Perhaps most unhelpful in much of the recent literature on personhood is the tendency to build interpretations of relational identity and 'dividuality' on only one aspect of the evidence – disarticulated human remains – and to use this to generalise about life in the Neolithic, while ignoring the considerable evidence for quite different kinds of mortuary treatment of 'individual bodies'. In fact, in cross-cultural terms it is striking how widely mortuary rituals and deposits serve to communicate ideas about *unchanging* kinds of personhood and not fluid and relational identities. This involves the selective, salient determination of 'what is really important' in peoples' lives and their identities (ideal, inherited and achieved), and a process of symbolic distillation and synthesis that represents these facets of identity in as unambiguous a way as possible. In this light, it is especially ironic that the disarticulated and collective skeletal deposits in early Neolithic tombs and other contexts, which have been used as the basis of arguments that personhood in this period was relational and fluid, were probably created in the first place either to assert particular unchanging and reducible kinds of moral and sacred identity or personhood, or as substances to be used strategically in ways that had nothing to do with expressions of personhood at all.

EXCEPTIONAL EVENTS: COMPLEX BURIALS IN THE LATE 4TH-EARLY 3RD MILLENNIA CAL BC

In the light of the preceding discussion it is possible to reassess the unusual group of middle or late Neolithic complex burials within the study area, all with artefacts and found in pits central to large mounds. All three sites are in the Upper Thames Valley (Table 15.2; Fig. 15.5): Newnham Murren, Wallingford (Moorey 1982), Linch Hill Corner, Stanton Harcourt XXI (ring ditch 1: Grimes 1943-4, 34-44; 1960, 154-64; Barclay 1995b, 99), and at Radley (oval barrow, grave 2126: Bradley 1992; Barclay and Bradley 1999, 20; Garwood 1999b, 278). Also relevant to this discussion is the burial (grave 602) within an ovate ring ditch at Mount Farm near Dorchester-on-Thames (Lambrick 2010), which has features similar to the other three burials, although

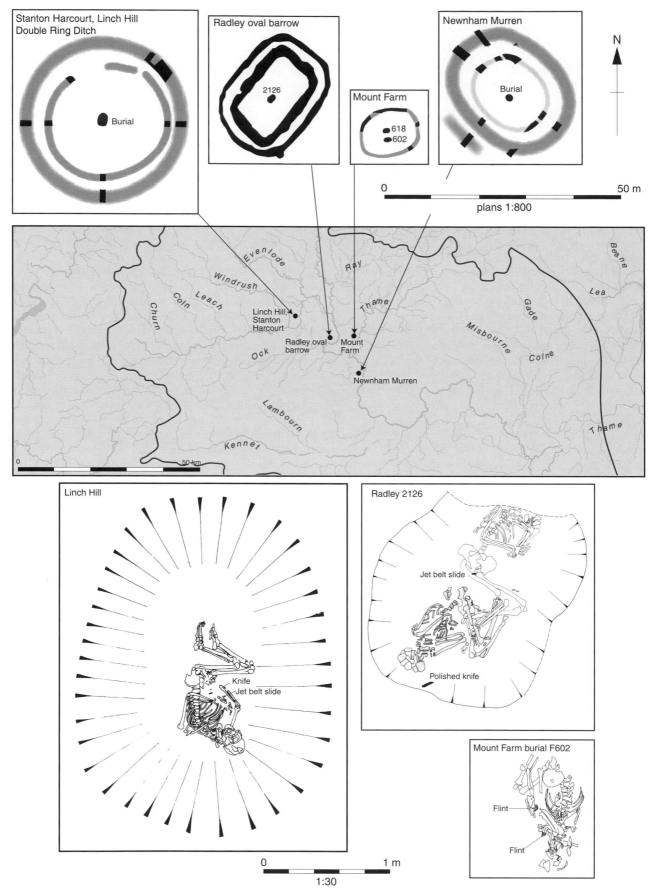

Fig. 15.5   Middle/late Neolithic complex burials in the Middle and Upper Thames Valley: Linch Hill, Radley oval barrow Grave 2126, Mount Farm Grave 602, and Newnham Murren

Table 15.2: Middle/late Neolithic complex burials in the Middle and Upper Thames Valley

	Context	Sex/age	Artefacts	Radiocarbon dating cal BC (95% confidence)	Reference
Mount Farm 602	Pit within ring ditch	♂ 30+ years	4 flint blades, 2 blade fragments	3640-3370 BC 3370-2890 BC	Lambrick 2010
Newnham Murren	Pit at the centre of double ring ditch	♀ 25-35 years	2 flint flakes (one serrated); sherd of Abingdon Ware		Moorey 1982
Stanton Harcourt	Pit at the centre of double ring ditch	♀ Young adult	Polished flint knife; jet belt slider		Grimes 1943-4, 1960; Barclay 1995a, 1995b
Radley oval barrow: grave 2126	Pit central to oval barrow	♀ 30-35 years ♂ 30-35 years	Polished flint knife; jet belt slider; also possible arrowhead?	2880-2560 BC 2470-2190 BC	Bradley 1992; Barclay and Bradley 1999; Garwood 1999a

the dating evidence is ambiguous and it may well be considerably earlier (it is included in Table 15.2 for comparative purposes).

These burials have much in common: in each case they consist of (or in the case of the Radley double burial include) an adult female; all are associated with lithic objects, including polished flint knives in two cases; and two of the burials were associated with very rare jet belt sliders (Fig. 15.6). It is also

Linch Hill Corner

Radley Oval Barrow Grave 2126

```
0          50          100 m
```

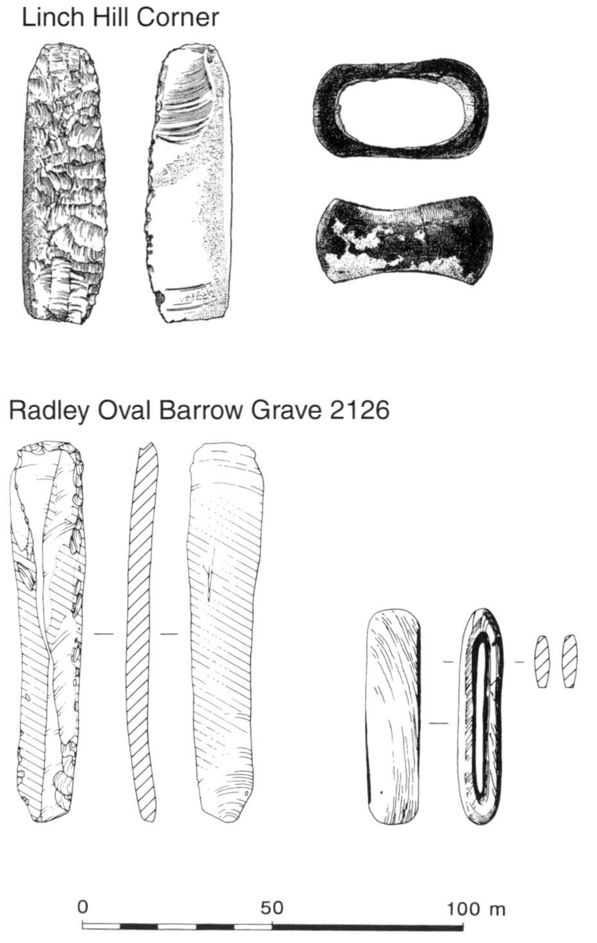

Fig. 15.6   Middle/late Neolithic complex burials: polished knives and jet belt sliders

notable that all three graves were located at the centre of mounds with multiple ditches (Fig. 15.5). At Newnham Murren and Stanton Harcourt these consisted of large circular monuments with concentric double ditches, although it is uncertain whether the two ditches (and the probable recut in the outer ditch at Newnham Murren; Moorey 1982, 57-8, figs 29 and 30) represent coherent monument designs or sequences of mound enlargement or reuse. If they were multiphase monuments it is unclear which, if either, of the ditches the burials were associated with. In both cases, the inner ditch circuit was broken by wide gaps allowing access to the interior, while the outer circuits were continuous, suggesting closure and/or impermeable boundaries. Several alternative interpretations are possible, although it is tempting to view both sites as open arenas subsequently chosen as places for significant burial events, which were memorialised by the construction of massive mound structures built using material from the outer ditches. At Radley, in contrast, the rectangular mound probably predated the grave, although it is not impossible that the Phase 4/5 outer ditch circuit was contemporary with the burial event (Barclay and Bradley 1999, 20-1; Garwood 1999b, 278). From this perspective it is likely that all three burial events represent reuse or appropriation of 'old' monuments which were already significant places in the landscape.

The dating of these burials is problematic. Most discussions of the chronology and cultural contexts of these graves focus on artefact associations and the relative dating of burial and monument types, based largely on the evidence from Duggleby Howe and other sites in Yorkshire (Kinnes 1979, figs 6.2-3; Harding 1997; Thomas 1999, 151-53). Central to Kinnes' definition of a series of artefact sets (Stages A-F) is the 'sequence' from inhumation to cremation graves identified at Duggleby Howe, and the seriation of associated grave goods (though see Loveday 2002). The single grave assemblages from the Upper Thames have been ascribed to Kinnes' Stage D, but it is notable that the particular combination of polished flint knife and jet belt slider is not replicated elsewhere. Indeed, in wider terms, the diverse artefact assemblages found with Neolithic single burials are impossible to date with any precision (Barclay and Wallis 1999) and could in some contexts include curated objects such as heirlooms (cf Woodward 2002). It is worth noting that flint knives and belt sliders were also apparently placed as offerings in the river Thames, although there is again no direct dating evidence for the depositional events involved (see Chapter 14). Absolute dating evidence, unfortunately, is thin and ambiguous. The radiocarbon dates for the Radley grave are inconsistent (ie the age ranges do not overlap even at two standard deviations), both with one another and with the only other directly comparable radiocarbon-dated burial in Britain at Whitegrounds, North Yorkshire (dated to 3500-2910 cal BC: Brewster 1992; Manby *et al.* 2003, 53, fig. 20).

The possible relationship between the three burials discussed here and the Mount Farm grave (cf Barclay 1995c, 107) is difficult to judge. The two radiocarbon dates for the Mount Farm burial are inconsistent and (like the Whitegrounds date) do not overlap with those for Radley, while the relationship between the Mount Farm grave and the ovate ring ditch that encircles it is uncertain. The *un*polished flint knife in the Mount Farm grave, however, is of a type common in middle Neolithic contexts, and is similar to the polished examples from Radley and Linch Hill Corner. The only additional information relevant to dating these burials is stratigraphic: at Linch Hill Corner, a small ring ditch (1a) with a central Beaker grave cut both of the ditches of the late Neolithic monument, perhaps very soon after primary silting had taken place (Grimes 1943-4). Even if the Beaker burial is regarded as relatively early (it has been interpreted as a Step 3 Middle-style vessel: Barclay 1995c, 110, table 21), this would suggest a date for the burial and double ring ditch in the mid-3rd millennium cal BC at the earliest (in line with the later radiocarbon date for the Radley burial). In the light of this conflicting evidence, it is possible to suggest several alternative dates for these burials with significantly different implications for how they can be interpreted, including the following scenarios:

(i) 3600-3400 cal BC: the three burials are contemporary with the earlier date for the Mount Farm grave, which should be included as part of the group. This would suggest not only that all the other radiocarbon dates and relative dating evidence for these burials are incorrect but that an otherwise unrecognised 'rich burial' tradition of individual inhumation burial existed alongside collective burials in tombs.

(ii) 3400-3000 cal BC: the burials belonged to the tradition of single inhumation burial that became most common once collective depositional practices had declined (see the previous section). These were at the 'richer' end of a spectrum of variation in the way that individual identities were represented in

funerary ritual and mortuary deposition. This interpretation is consistent with the Whitegrounds and later Mount Farm radiocarbon dates.

(iii) 3000-2600 cal BC: they are exceptionally rare late Neolithic complex burials, marking attempts to bring significant individual identities and related cultural and political agenda to the fore, in the context of (and perhaps in opposition to) collective ideologies represented by henge construction and collective ceremonial practices. The earlier of the Radley burial radiocarbon dates is consistent with this interpretation. The similarities among the graves, depositional practices and monuments suggest a fairly narrow time frame for these burials, perhaps predating the Dorchester-on-Thames cremation cemeteries (see below). If so, they are more likely to belong to the period *c* 3000-2800 cal BC than 2800-2600 cal BC.

(iv) 2600-2100 cal BC: the burials were a variant of late/final Neolithic single grave practices otherwise most closely associated with Beaker ceramics. The later date for the Radley grave and the stratigraphic evidence from Stanton Harcourt perhaps support this interpretation, although this would mean that the other dating evidence, both absolute and relative, is incorrect and that there is no connection between these and either the Mount Farm or Whitegrounds burials.

The first and last of these scenarios appear least likely given that they require rejection of much of the direct and indirect dating evidence available for the graves. Even if, however, these possibilities are disregarded this still leaves a 600-800 year time span, encompassing major social and cultural changes, within which the burial events could have taken place. There is little question that complex inhumation burials of these kinds are of considerable importance for an understanding of middle/late Neolithic funerary practices in the Thames Valley and more widely in Britain, but it is apparent that new dating evidence is needed to resolve the chronological impasse outlined here and to establish their proper social and cultural context.

A TIME AND A PLACE FOR THE CREMATION CEMETERY

Of all the diverse kinds of Neolithic mortuary practices evident in the Middle and Upper Thames Valley, the cremation cemeteries at Dorchester-on-Thames (Atkinson *et al.* 1951; Whittle *et al.* 1992, 195), and the more recent discoveries at Imperial College Sports Ground in the Colne Valley (Barclay *et al.* 2009), are in some ways the most difficult to interpret in relation to other aspects of cultural life in this period. This is because of the great rarity of similar sites elsewhere in Britain, the variety of the practices and monument contexts represented, and the lack of consistent dating evidence. The closest, oft-cited, parallels are the numerous cremated bone deposits at Stonehenge (Phase 2: Cleal *et al.* 1995, 154-55, 163-64; Parker Pearson *et al.* 2009) and at Duggleby Howe in North Yorkshire (Mortimer 1905, 23-30; Kinnes 1979; Kinnes *et al.* 1983), together with a few examples of smaller groups of cremation 'burials' from a number of pit circle, ring ditch and henge monuments, including sites at Barford, Warwickshire (Oswald 1969), Llandegai A, Gwynedd (Harding 2003, 113), Sarn-y-Bryn Caled 2, Powys (Gibson 1994, 159-61), and West Stow, Suffolk (West 1990).

Cremation burial is itself especially challenging in interpretative terms not only because of the relative rarity, diversity and episodic character of this practice in the British Neolithic, but also because cremation can be characterised or understood in several different ways (cf Downes 1999): as a kind of mortuary treatment that 'prepared' bodies for depositional acts of various kinds, as a transformative ritual process, and as a performative 'ceremonial' event with considerable potential for dramatic choreography and sensory (especially visual) impact. It should also be noted that while the cremated bone deposits at Dorchester-on-Thames are unusually numerous, cremation and the deposition of burnt human bone were in fact widespread practices during the Neolithic.

There are numerous instances of cremated and charred human bone being found in small quantities in earlier Neolithic contexts (Smith and Brickley 2009, 57-60), including chambered tombs such as West Kennet (Piggott 1962) and Ascott-under-Wychwood (Galer 2007, 206-7), in constructional features beneath long mounds (eg at Sales Lot; Smith and Brickley 2009, 58), and in pit contexts (such as the cremated remains of an adult female in the top of a pit to the east of the longhouse at Yarnton, dated to 3655-3535 cal BC: G Hey pers. comm.). Cremation deposits are also known in secondary contexts at earlier Neolithic monuments, such as the small subrectangular mortuary structure at New Wintles Farm, Eynsham, where several pits containing tiny amounts of cremated human bone cut ditch fills containing pottery dating to the mid to late 4th millennium cal BC (Fig. 12.20; Kenward 1982). Similar small deposits of burnt bone have been recorded in later Neolithic pits (eg at Yarnton Sites 3 and 7; G Hey pers. comm.) and in henge ditches (eg Wyke Down, Dorset: Barrett *et al.* 1991, 96; Harding 2003, 28). The cremation cemeteries in the Upper Thames Valley can thus be seen as unusually formalised and concentrated realisations of more extensive kinds of mortuary practices that routinely involved the burning of bodies, and the deposition of burnt human bone in a wide range of monumental and other settings in the landscape during the 4th and earlier 3rd millennia cal BC.

The earliest well-dated cremation *cemetery* in the Thames Valley has been found recently at the

Imperial College Sports Ground site in the Colne Valley (Barclay *et al.* 2009), where two adjacent small ring ditches (one penannular) were foci for a series of at least six interments of cremated human remains in small pits, in most cases consisting of single individuals ranging from young children to adults (Fig. 15.7). All six of the radiocarbon-dated cremated bone deposits belong to the period *c* 3200-

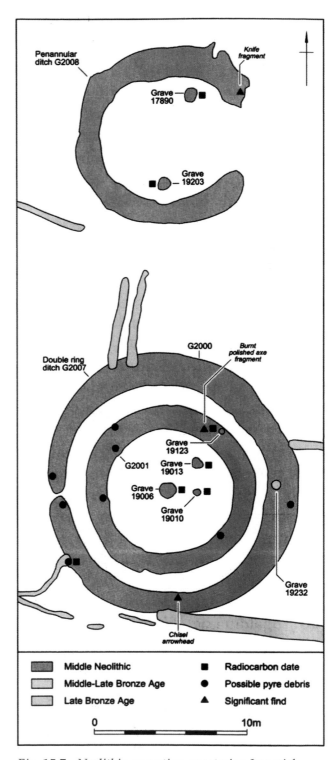

Fig. 15.7 Neolithic cremation cemeteries: Imperial College Sports Ground site plan

Table 15.3: The Dorchester-on-Thames monuments and cremation cemeteries. (Data from Atkinson et al. 1951 and Whittle et al. 1992.)

Site	Type of monument	Number of cremation deposits	Dating evidence for cremation deposits
I	Multi-phased ring ditch	4	?Grooved Ware sherd
II	Multi-phased segmented ring ditch	21	Bone pins; flint fabricator and plano-convex knife; stone macehead
III	Cursus	-	
IV	Penannular enclosure	25	?Petit-tranchet arrowhead
V	Penannular enclosure	21	
VI	Penannular enclosure	49	Flint fabricator; possible petit-tranchet arrowhead
XI	Multi-phased ring ditch	1	*TPQ:* 3310-2660 cal BC
			TPQ: 3090-2780 cal BC
XII	Beaker barrow	-	
XIII	Big Rings henge	-	
XIV	Ring ditch	1	
Site 1	Long 'mortuary' enclosure	-	
Site 2	Penannular enclosure	28	*TPQ:* 2920-2630 cal BC
Site 3	Post circle	6	2950-2200 cal BC
			2950-2200 cal BC
			2300-1500 cal BC
			?Grooved Ware sherd

2900 cal BC. The southern site comprised two concentric ring ditches, in some respects comparable to some of the multiphased ring ditches at Dorchester-on-Thames, although it is possible that the outer ditch is an Early Bronze Age elaboration of the earlier monument (with redeposited ancient pyre debris in the later ditch fills).

The Dorchester-on-Thames cremation cemeteries appear to be somewhat later in date than the Imperial College Sports Ground burials. These sites had a prominent presence in British Neolithic studies for a short time in the 1950s as the basis for Piggott's definition of a 'Dorchester Culture' (Piggott 1954, 351-64), which he regarded as one of the indigenous 'secondary Neolithic' cultural groups (which included the 'Rinyo-Clacton' and 'Peterborough' cultures) that existed in parallel with intrusive earlier Beaker communities. The decline of culture history, and recognition of the supposed unusual and 'unrepresentative' character of cremation deposits in the middle/late Neolithic from the 1960s, however, sidelined the Dorchester-on-Thames sites in processual interpretations of Neolithic cultural systems, which did not favour generalisations based on 'atypical' categories of evidence, or relegated them to the category of local or regional oddities. Reconsiderations of the evidence have been slow in coming (see Harding 2003, 27-8, 113-14), and have been prompted mainly by new work on the Dorchester-on-Thames complex (notably: Whittle *et al.* 1992; Loveday 1999) and by some publications or reinterpretations of evidence from other sites, especially Stonehenge (Cleal *et al.* 1995; Parker Pearson *et al.* 2009) and Duggleby Howe (Loveday 2002).

The monument contexts and sizes of the Dorchester-on-Thames cremation cemeteries are summarised in Table 15.3 (see also Fig. 12.22). The spatial organisation of these cemeteries is discussed above. In total there are 156 recorded deposits of burnt human bone from nine sites, all of them small circular ditched or pit circle monuments which in most cases probably demarcated enclosures rather than mounds. In contrast, cremation burials seem to be absent from the linear monuments and from the Big Rings henge (although neither the cursus nor the henge enclosure have been extensively excavated; Thomas 1999, 195). Of the seven sites with multiple cremated bone deposits, five had more than 20 interments, suggesting recognisable 'cemetery' locales at which a succession of similar depositional events took place, while two sites had less than ten interments. In five cases, mortuary deposition took place in and around small penannular enclosures consisting of linked pits that in most cases probably once held timber posts (Sites IV, V, VI, 2, and possibly Site I, Phase 2; cf Gibson 1992); in one case, cremated bone deposits were found within a larger, circular segmented pit and bank enclosure (conceivably a penannular earthwork; Site II, Phase 3); and in one case cremated human bone deposits were found in the post settings of a burnt timber circle (Site 3).

It is evident that the architectural settings of the 'cremation burials' shared several features, especially penannular enclosure designs, segmented pit construction methods and/or post settings (whilst still displaying considerable variety in architectural design), and that all of the cemeteries with the possible exception of Site 3 represent phases of activity post-dating monument construction (Whittle *et al.* 1992). Post settings, for example, appear to have been removed or already decayed *in situ* by the time burial events took place, while earlier pits and other features were already at least partially silted (ibid.; Thomas 1999, 194-95). It is likely, therefore, that all seven cremation cemeteries were closely related in terms of mortuary practices, funerary ritual and reuse of earlier monuments of similar kinds, and are thus *broadly* contemporaneous. It is impossible, however, to determine the duration of the activities involved. All the burials could have taken place within a single generation, for example, or they could represent more episodic events spanning two or three centuries (cf Atkinson *et al.* 1951, 66; Thomas 1999, 195).

The chronology of the Dorchester-on-Thames cemeteries is still uncertain. The radiocarbon dating evidence is restricted to samples from just three sites, none of the dates are from cremated human bone samples, and few are from stratigraphic contexts directly associated with depositional events. *Termini post quos* for groups of cremation burials are provided by the radiocarbon date on antler from Site 2 (2920-2630 cal BC) and by the dates on two antler picks from Site XI, ditch 1 (3310-2660 cal BC; 3090-2780 cal BC), but in both cases the antler deposits appear to be far removed stratigraphically and temporally from the episodes of cremated human bone deposition. In the case of Site 3, although the radiocarbon-dated samples come from contexts more closely associated with the cremation deposits, they all derive from oak charcoal, are all imprecise and provide conflicting age ranges (2950-2200 cal BC; 2950-2200 cal BC; 2300-1500 cal BC). The artefact associations are also not very helpful for precise dating purposes, although Kinnes, for example, places them broadly within his Stage E (1979, fig. 3.3), post-dating individual inhumation burials associated with flint knives and belt sliders.

It is notable that the Big Rings henge at Dorchester-on-Thames was not used for cremation burials, while the ring ditch that it superseded, Site XIV, did produce a single deposit of cremated bone. It is possible, therefore, that the henge enclosure was constructed after the cremation cemeteries had been abandoned, although it is equally possible that funerary deposition was simply excluded from this monument. Unfortunately, the dating of the Big Rings henge is itself uncertain, although the early Beaker burial at Site XII, which post-dates the henge, suggests that construction must have taken place by *c* 2300 cal BC and probably some time before 2400 cal BC.

Overall, therefore, taking into account the radiocarbon dates, stratigraphic evidence and artefact associations, the cremation cemeteries at Dorchester-on-Thames are most likely to date to the period *c* 2900-2500 cal BC (and probably in the middle or later part of this range given the sources of the radiocarbon samples and possible old wood effects in the case of some or all of the charcoal samples). This is broadly consistent with the dating evidence for the cremated bone deposits at Stonehenge, most of which probably belong to Phase 2 of the monument,

c 3000-2600 cal BC (Cleal *et al.* 1995, 115, 153; Harding 2003, 67-8, fig. 50d), although there is good evidence that such burials took place at Stonehenge over a much longer period (Parker Pearson *et al.* 2009).

A range of flint, stone and bone artefacts were recovered from approximately 10% of the cremated bone deposits at Dorchester-on-Thames. Six artefact types can be defined: bone pins, a macehead, petit tranchet arrowheads, and flint fabricators, knives and flakes (Fig. 12.22). Flint flakes are the most common type and occur with all other types. Bone pins are the second most common type and occur with everything except arrowheads. Knives occur only with bone points and flint flakes. Only one macehead is known, found alongside a bone pin, flint flake and a fabricator. It is notable that many artefacts show significant heat damage and that in some cases only small fragments were present: it is likely that these objects were placed on the cremation pyres, and that many more pyre goods perished during the cremation process or were simply not collected for burial after cremation. It is also possible that some objects such as bone pin fragments and calcined flint flakes have been mistaken for cremated human bone.

The symbolic significance of the funerary artefacts found with the cremations is difficult to assess, especially as those recovered may not be representative of the full burial assemblages that originally accompanied bodies to their funerary pyres. Even so, patterns of both association and separation suggest that some of the artefacts were used to represent age and gender categories or other social roles and identities. Arrowheads, for example, were not found with bone pins or knives: this partly parallels the exclusivity of bone pins and arrowheads in placed deposits within Durrington Walls South Circle and their opposed placement in postholes on either side of the entrance to the timber circle (Richards and Thomas 1984). At Dorchester-on-Thames Site 2 grave goods tended to be found only with the cremations of adults, and the same could be true of Sites I and II (Whittle *et al.* 1992; Atkinson *et al.* 1951). There are also differences between the various sites at Dorchester-on-Thames: cremation burials with bone pins and flint knives, for example, were restricted to Sites I, II and 2, while arrowheads only came from Sites IV and VI.

The particular meanings attached to these arrangements of funerary artefacts, however, are elusive, and the specific nature of the ideal 'community of the dead' represented in the Dorchester-on-Thames cemeteries remains unknown. The social organisation of funerary rituals, their frequency and temporal ordering, and their relationships to depositional events, are all uncertain and clearly open to several alternative interpretations. Loveday's (2002, 140-44) reassessment of the depositional contexts and sequences of burials at Duggleby Howe and at Dorchester-on-Thames Sites IV, V and VI, for example, suggests that burial events at cremation 'cemeteries' took place within extremely short periods of time. This raises questions, he argues, about the assumed temporal separation of inhumation and cremation burials, and also the sheer number of cremated individuals represented, pointing to the possibility that the cremations may have resulted from acts of human sacrifice. Although there is no *a priori* reason to dismiss the possibility of such practices, the Dorchester-on-Thames evidence is not easily reconcilable with this interpretation: in particular, the evidence for very short duration rather than longer duration depositional sequences is arguable at best, while the apparent separate treatment of individual cremated bodies and their furnishing with grave goods suggests acts that celebrated lives or identities, rather than denied, destroyed or consumed them (cf discussions of human sacrifice in Carrasco 1999; Davies 1997; Green 2001; and Taylor 2002).

The ritual process suggested by the archaeological evidence also suggests a complex sequence of practices that led to final deposition within the Dorchester-on-Thames cemeteries. There is no evidence for *in situ* pyre sites, which suggests that acts of cremation took place somewhere other than at the places of burial, while the small size of the excavated cremated bone deposits (Atkinson *et al.* 1951; Whittle *et al.* 1992) suggests selective collection and/or division and dispersal of the cremated remains from pyre sites (the evidence from Stonehenge Phase 2 is very similar; cf Cleal *et al.* 1995, 115, 153; McKinley 1995; Parker Pearson *et al.* 2009). This is more in keeping with depositional practices of a devotional kind, involving the incorporation of parts to represent wholes (eg of individuals or the groups to which they belonged), using substances and materials derived from people to convey significant relationships, qualities or powers, perhaps in terms of corporate belonging to a moral community, cult membership, 'gifts' to gods or as expressions of faith. Fragmentation and multiple deposits of parts of the same bodies in several different locations might also have been a way to use the resource of bodily substances widely, to achieve different ends in different contexts, and/or to disperse the presence of the significant dead spatially and thus integrate or bind together different parts of the cultural landscape with reference to those people, their sacred identities and their social relationships.

There is certainly little question that despite (or perhaps because of) their relative frequency at Dorchester-on-Thames, these cremation burials were significant events, representing special treatment of special people or their corporeal substance, conducted at special places in the later Neolithic landscape. It is striking, in this context, that the few parallels for these cremation cemeteries are all associated with regionally important monuments or centres, and that they seem in most cases to have reused existing monuments (eg at Stonehenge), perhaps involving deliberate allusions to the past or

even intentional appropriation of ancient monuments as part of a political strategy. It is worth noting, in this context, that while there are only a few single inhumation burials of likely middle Neolithic date in the Upper and Middle Thames Valley (Table 15.2), the total of 156 cremation deposits from Dorchester-on-Thames alone is roughly double the number of Beaker burials known in the region. There is no straightforward socio-demographic explanation for this. Although Parker Pearson *et al.* (2009) argue that the Stonehenge burials mark 'royal' funerary events, it is likely that such acts changed in significance during the early to mid-3rd millennium cal BC, and that a complex history of cultural and political transformations is represented in the sequence of changes in ceremonial architecture and depositional practices at both Stonehenge and Dorchester-on-Thames (Loveday 1999; Garwood 1999b, 295-98; Thomas 1999, 192-95).

BEAKER PERIOD AND EARLY BRONZE AGE FUNERARY PRACTICES, 2500-1800 CAL BC

In many respects the prehistory of the later 3rd and early to mid-2nd millennia cal BC is still written primarily from the perspective of the dead, or at least of those who conducted funerals and burial events, and built the funerary monuments – round barrows and related architectural forms – that came to dominate large parts of the landscape (Fig. 14.24). Until recently, however, the interpretative challenges posed by the sheer richness, diversity and complexity of the evidence have been underestimated, especially with regard to the meanings and social and political purposes of funerary ritual and monument-building. In particular, it is now evident that the cultural and political landscapes of the time, the salience and significance of funerary events which took place within them, and the fields of discourse which these events brought into being, changed radically during this period (Garwood 2007a). It is no longer possible, therefore, to treat all round barrows and ring ditches as simple variations on a single architectural theme, or to interpret burials as if they conformed to just one system of signification and representation. In this light, no single all-embracing interpretative framework can be used to interpret the diverse range of funerary practices evident in the Middle and Upper Thames Valley during the Beaker period and early Bronze Age. Instead, it is far more rewarding to explore particular facets of the funerary evidence in cultural, spatial and chronological context, in order to tease out some of the specific meanings of funerary rituals and their importance in the social and cultural lives of those who performed them.

The following sections will focus, first, on the nature of early Beaker burial events in the period *c* 2500-2100 cal BC, and second, on complex sequences of funerary events and 'cemetery' barrows in the period *c* 2200-1800 cal BC. This is followed by discussion of the nature of early Bronze Age mortuary practices and particularly 'elite' burial events in the period *c* 1900-1500 cal BC. In each period it is evident that different categories of people received very different kinds of mortuary and funerary treatment. There were contrasts between those who did and those who did not merit formal burial, those buried with elaborate sets of artefacts and those lacking grave goods, different gender categories, and different age groups (especially evident among different age-sets among the very young; see Garwood 2007c). It is also striking how socio-religious themes and political strategies that guided burial location and modes of display changed over time, and how, at different times, distinctive kinds of temporality were expressed in the spatial articulation of 'historical' narratives concerning the dead and the construction of individual 'biographies'. The Middle and Upper Thames Valley has a major contribution to make to studies of all these aspects of Beaker period and early Bronze Age funerary archaeology, at a national as well as regional scale, not least because of the richness and diversity of the evidence, and the very high quality of recent excavation reports and interpretative syntheses (eg Barclay and Halpin 1999; A J Barclay *et al.* 1995; Cleal 2005; Lambrick and Allen 2004). The sites referenced in the following discussion are in Oxfordshire unless otherwise indicated.

Radical departures: Beaker funerary ritual and the late Neolithic ceremonial landscape

Since the late 19th century, Beaker graves and funerary artefact assemblages have figured prominently in virtually all discussions of late Neolithic and early Bronze Age society, sometimes with little reference to other funerary traditions, and to the virtual exclusion of other kinds of evidence. The interpretative literature is continually being expanded but some persistent themes routinely dominate interpretative debates, notably the typology and chronology of Beakers and artefact sets (eg Clarke 1970; Lanting and van der Waals 1972; Case 1977; 1993; 1995; Kinnes *et al.* 1991; Boast 1995; Needham 2005), the Continental origins and diffusion of Beaker ceramics and Beaker-related practices (eg Clark 1970; Case 2001; R Bradley 2007, 142-53; Needham 2007), social change (eg Shennan 1982; Braithwaite 1984; Thorpe and Richards 1984), and – especially in last 30 years – the social and symbolic significance of Beaker graves (eg Burgess and Shennan 1976; Case 1977; Thorpe and Richards 1984; Thomas 1991, 2000; Mizoguchi 1993; 1995; Barrett 1994, 86-108; Lucas 1996; Brück 2004a; Healy and Harding 2004; Jones 2005).

All too often, however, the Beaker funerary evidence is treated in isolation, as if the traditions of practice represented, and the symbolic meanings evoked, had 'lives' of their own, disengaged from other uses of Beakers, and from other fields of social practice. Indeed, it could be argued that the intense and sustained level of attention devoted to Beaker graves has slewed our perceptions of the wider cultural and political contexts of Beaker funerary events and their significance (Gibson 2007). Only rarely have there been concerted attempts to make sense of the political context of early Beaker burials (eg Thorpe and Richards 1984), the relationships between funerary and non-funerary Beakers (eg Gibson 1982; Case 1993; 1995), or the diverse uses and varied significance of Beaker and other contemporary ceramics in multiple contexts of social action (eg Healy 1995). We should now, perhaps, recognise a social world in which the presence of Beakers was less pervasive, and their importance far more socially specific and contingent than is usually portrayed (see R Bradley 2007, 142-53, for an interpretative discussion that embraces the funerary evidence without giving it primacy). At the same time, insufficient attention has been paid to the (supposed) durability and consistency of Beaker funerary practice as a traditional mode of cultural discourse and representation. Indeed, the assumed long-term coherence of the symbolic schemes and the kinds of personhood construed in late Neolithic, Beaker period and early Bronze Age burial practices (eg Brück 2004a) appears overstated once we recognise how radically the material, social, cultural and landscape contexts of these practices were transformed over time (Needham 2005; Garwood 2007a).

At the very least, we should distinguish between early Beaker (*c* 2500-2100 cal BC) and late Beaker funerary practices (*c* 2150-1750 cal BC). Early Beaker burial events took place, at first, in cultural landscapes that appear in many parts of southern Britain to have been articulated around open ceremonial monuments, many of which were already ancient, some very large, and concentrated in groups, while places of formal burial of any kind were largely or entirely absent. In this world, Beaker inhumation burials were plainly a departure from existing mortuary practices, and represented – at least in terms of the presence of distinctive grave goods and prominent mortuary architecture -- the only consistent mode of complex funerary representation involving formal burial of the dead within built structures. In contrast, late Beaker burial events took place in landscapes pervaded by the presence of the dead and their monuments and by frequent funerary display, at a time when many earlier ceremonial monuments were either marginalised or simply abandoned. Moreover, Beaker funerary practices in this cultural world – insofar as they were at all consistent – represented just one mode of body treatment, deposition and material association amongst many. This period is marked by the contemporaneity of inhumation and cremation practices, several distinctive kinds of grave assemblages, and an extraordinary diversity of monumental architecture, mortuary structures and furniture.

Although there is still considerable room for debate about Beaker chronology and the dating of individual Beaker graves, Needham's (2005) reassessment of the evidence at a national scale offers a framework for constructing more convincing chronological schemes for Beaker burials both regionally and locally. A review of the evidence from the Middle and Upper Thames Valley, based partly on Needham's chronology and partly on evaluations of the radiocarbon dates and artefact associations from individual graves, reveals some striking patterns in the frequency, geographical distribution and location of Beaker burials (Fig. 15.8). It is apparent that early graves are very rare, especially before *c* 2250 cal BC, and that most are clustered in small areas, often located close to late Neolithic ceremonial monuments (see below). This kind of spatial pattern, especially the rare presence and clustering of early burials, is closely paralleled in other regions, including the west Midlands (Garwood 2007b) and south-east England (Garwood in prep.).

Also notable is the high degree of consistency in the categories of people represented (nearly all are adults, the majority male) and to some extent in grave layouts (Fig. 15.9). Most of the adult male burials, for example, consist of crouched inhumations on their left sides, heads to north or north-west, facing east, with nearly all grave goods at the head, in front of the body and at the feet (particularly Beakers). These include Radley 4A (Barclay 1999d, 153-56), Radley 4660 and Radley 950 (Barclay 1999a, 58-65), Stanton Harcourt XXI, ring ditch 1a (Linch Hill Corner: Grimes 1943-4, 34-44; 1960, 154-64; A J

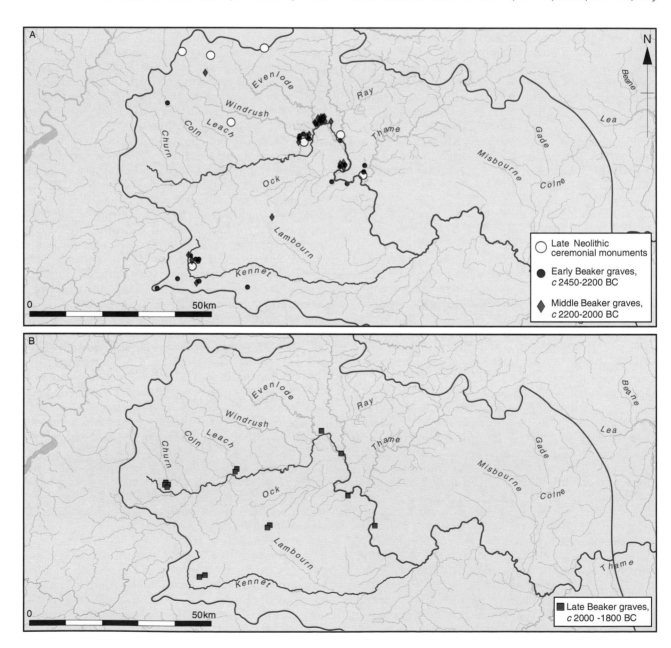

Fig. 15.8   Distribution of (A) earlier and (B) later Beaker graves in the Middle and Upper Thames Valley

404

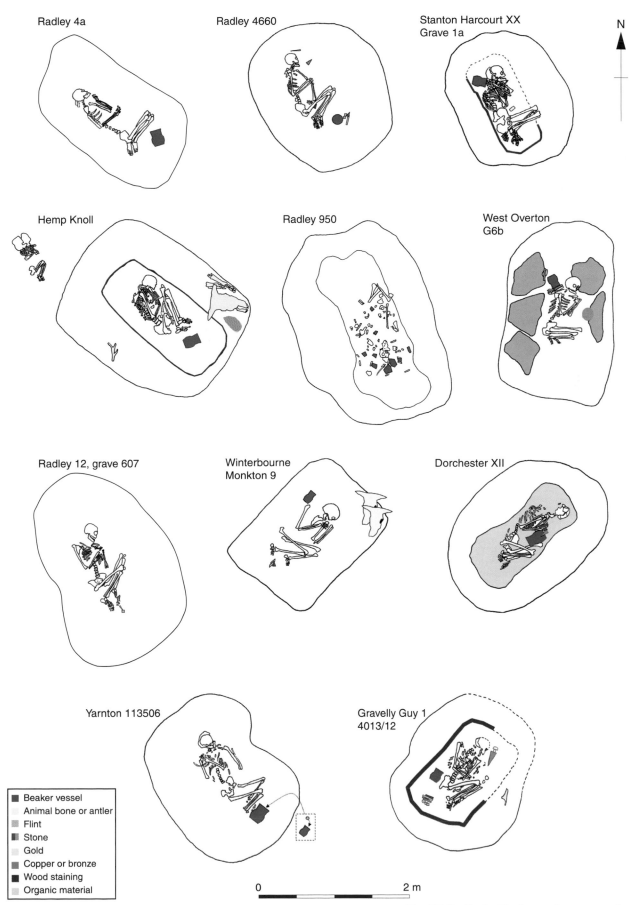

Radley 4a

Radley 4660

Stanton Harcourt XX
Grave 1a

N

Hemp Knoll

Radley 950

West Overton
G6b

Radley 12, grave 607

Winterbourne
Monkton 9

Dorchester XII

Yarnton 113506

Gravelly Guy 1
4013/12

■ Beaker vessel
  Animal bone or antler
■ Flint
■ Stone
  Gold
■ Copper or bronze
■ Wood staining
  Organic material

0   2 m

Fig. 15.9   Early Beaker male graves: plans

Barclay *et al.* 1995, 99), Yarnton 113506 (G Hey, pers. comm.), Hemp Knoll, Wiltshire (Robertson-Mackay 1980), West Overton G6b, Wiltshire (Smith and Simpson 1966), and Lambourn 17, Berkshire (Case 1956a). Radley burial 607 also shares most of these attributes although it lacks a Beaker (Barclay 1999a, 97-110). Other less datable burials, such as Eynsham 15 (Leeds 1938) and Cassington 5 (Leeds 1934a; Case and Sturdy 1959), may also fit this pattern. There are, in addition, a few well-equipped adult male burials probably dating to the period *c* 2250-2000 cal BC, lying on their left sides, but with their heads to the north-east or east, facing south-east, and with grave goods as often behind the body as in front. These include the burials at Dorchester-on-Thames XII (Whittle *et al.* 1992, 175-84) and Gravelly Guy X6 (Lambrick and Allen 2004, 51-61).

The artefacts found in adult male graves appear to evoke a consistent range of themes while still suggesting 'individualistic' assemblages of objects (sometimes including unique items). These were placed in spatial arrangements that are often similar to others but never exactly alike. This suggests recognition of certain widely accepted and valued qualities relating to deportment, social practice or body symbolism, but without necessary conformity to normative 'rules' of deposition. This variation might also relate to how specific aspects of individuals' biographies were represented in funerals, or perhaps different agenda among the mourners who brought grave goods with them to each burial event. Artefacts in these graves, besides Beakers, nearly all include weaponry or weapon components such as metal daggers and barbed and tanged flint arrowheads (Fig. 15.10). The few exceptions to this are either burials with very few objects, such as Radley 607 (with a copper awl), or especially unusual burials such as the central adult male at West Overton G6b (also with an awl, together with several stone, flint and antler tools). The presence of weaponry might well have evoked perceived male virtues related to violence, strength and courage, while other non-weapon burials perhaps emphasised valued crafts, (re-) productivity or perhaps 'magical' transformations of materials. These distinctions are broadly consistent with two of the Beaker male social 'types' proposed by Case (1977), and the possible sacralised stereotypes suggested by Thomas (1991). Even so, direct representation of person-kinds in grave goods is doubtful (except, perhaps in the gendered selection of suitable items) because of the way that materials used in ritual often act as substitutes for other things, evoking abstract or metaphorical meanings rather than references to the empirical or social nature of the objects themselves (ibid.; cf Bloch 2005, 21).

Early burials of women are far rarer and less consistent in layout (Fig. 15.11): these include burials at the Gene Function Centre ring ditch, Oxford (Boston *et al.* 2003), Mount Farm 618

(Lambrick 2010; A Barclay, pers. comm.), Stanton Harcourt 1054 (Lambrick and Allen 2004, 51-61) and flat grave II 2 (Barclay 1995b, 80-1), and possibly Cassington 1 and 10 (Leeds 1934a; Case and Sturdy 1959), Cassington ring ditch (Bradford 1951) and Lower Slaughter, Gloucestershire (Darvill 1987, 86). The burial of a young adult female with a copper awl at Spring Road Municipal Cemetery, Abingdon (grave 3037; Allen and Kamash 2008, 9, fig. 6), dated to 2460-2200 cal BC, lacks a Beaker but is otherwise very similar to female Beaker graves (and makes an interesting contrast with the young adult male burial with an awl in grave 607 at Radley Barrow 12; Barclay 1999a, 97-110). Also lacking Beakers, but definitely belonging to the period *c* 2400-2000 cal BC, are two female burials at Cresswell Field, Yarnton (graves 8775 and 8785; G Hey pers. comm.).

Unlike adult males, female burials almost never have their heads oriented in a northerly direction, and are more likely to lie on their right sides than left, but otherwise they do not appear to share common depositional characteristics in terms of orientation or positioning of artefacts. It is also notable that while all the burials with large artefact sets are those of males, female graves contain very few items that were selected from an extremely limited range of categories (Beaker, flint scraper, copper alloy awl). These patterns have been recognised by Gibbs at a national scale (1989, 72-133), and observed by Sofaer Derevenski (2002, 198-200) at a local scale in the Upper Thames Valley (although there was no attempt to distinguish between early Beaker and later burial).

The significance of the differences between male and female body treatment and grave goods is clearly open to debate, but there is little question that while certain adult males were the subjects of highly prominent and materially elaborate forms of funerary deposition, women appear not to have been to the same extent. This view does have to be treated with considerable caution as a range of highly valued organic artefacts, such as textiles and wooden and leather items may have been placed in the graves of women more often than men. Even so, the smaller size and greater simplicity of women's pit-graves, their secondary positions in relation to males in burial sequences, and their relatively simple surviving artefact sets, does still suggest status differences relating to a particular ideology of adult male primacy and dominance in both cosmological and political order (cf Mizoguchi 1993). Furthermore, while most adult male graves exhibit some coherence in mortuary practices and modes of funerary display, suggesting replication and perhaps explicit referencing of previous burials, the rarity and diverse treatment of adult women suggests relatively episodic funerary events that evoked more contextual and event-contingent concerns rather than an accepted gender-specific genre of funerary symbolism. Indeed, the only

Fig. 15.10 (opposite) Artefacts in early Beaker male graves

Hemp Knoll

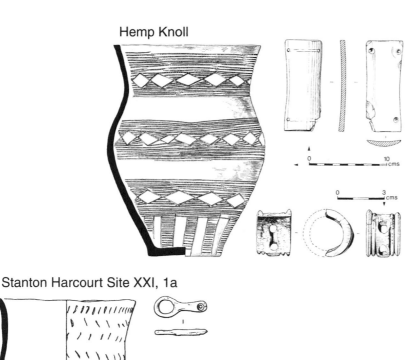

West Overton G6b

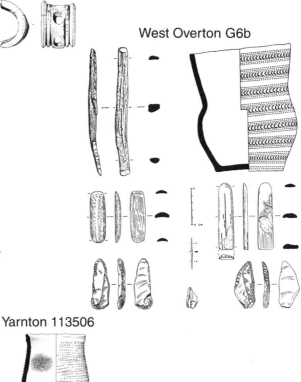

Stanton Harcourt Site XXI, 1a

Yarnton 113506

Radley 4660

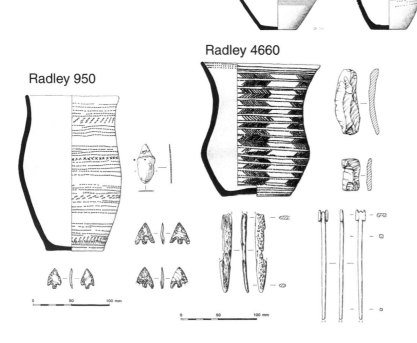

Radley 950

Radley 4A

consistent practice in female body deposition appears to be one that deferred to more consistent male practices: that is, a need to orientate female bodies in a 'not-male' direction.

There is no reason, in this light, to recognise complex differentiation of female identities in mortuary contexts (contra Sofaer Derevenski 2002, 200-2). Instead, these burials appear to have been rare, occasional celebrations of significant women, whose identities in death were constructed partly with reference to male-dominated funerary discourses rather than conscious evocation of specific types of female personhood. This is not to say, of course, that these women and their life stories were in any way insignificant, nor that such burials were unimportant in social or political terms, but rather that we need to situate them within the broader range of early Beaker funerary representation in order to make sense of their variety and particular characteristics as symbolic media.

Well-dated child burials belonging to the period 2500-2100 cal BC are less common even than adult

female burials, but a large proportion of those known in southern Britain have been found within the study area (Fig. 15.12), including the burials in Radley grave 919 (Barclay 1999a, 55-8), the primary burial at Lambourn 17, Berkshire (Case 1956a), Cresswell Field, Yarnton child grave 8620, beside the burial of the woman in grave 8775 (G Hey pers. comm.), the satellite infant burial close to the central adult male at Hemp Knoll (Robertson-Mackay 1980), and the multiple child burials around the central adult male burial at West Overton G6b (Smith and Simpson 1966). A recent evaluation of child burials of this period in southern Britain has revealed some striking contrasts in the way that different age groups were treated (Garwood 2007c). Children less than four years old were mostly buried with adults and older children, often in satellite positions or within grave pits in positions similar to those of artefacts. The Hemp Knoll case provides a good example: the body of a three-year old was placed on the deturfed old land surface close to the primary grave pit containing an adult

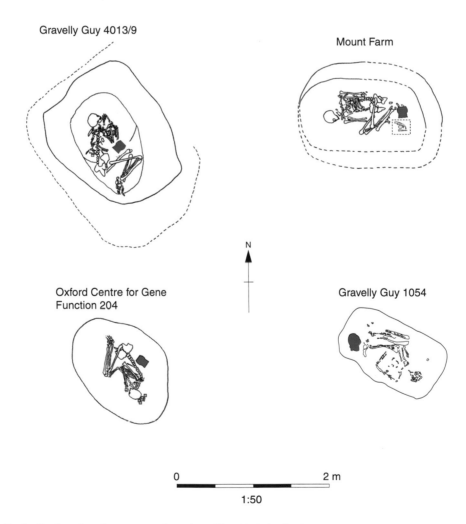

Fig. 15.11 Early Beaker female graves: plans (see Fig. 15.9 for key)

Fig. 15.12 (opposite) Early Beaker child graves: plans (see Fig. 15.9 for key)

408

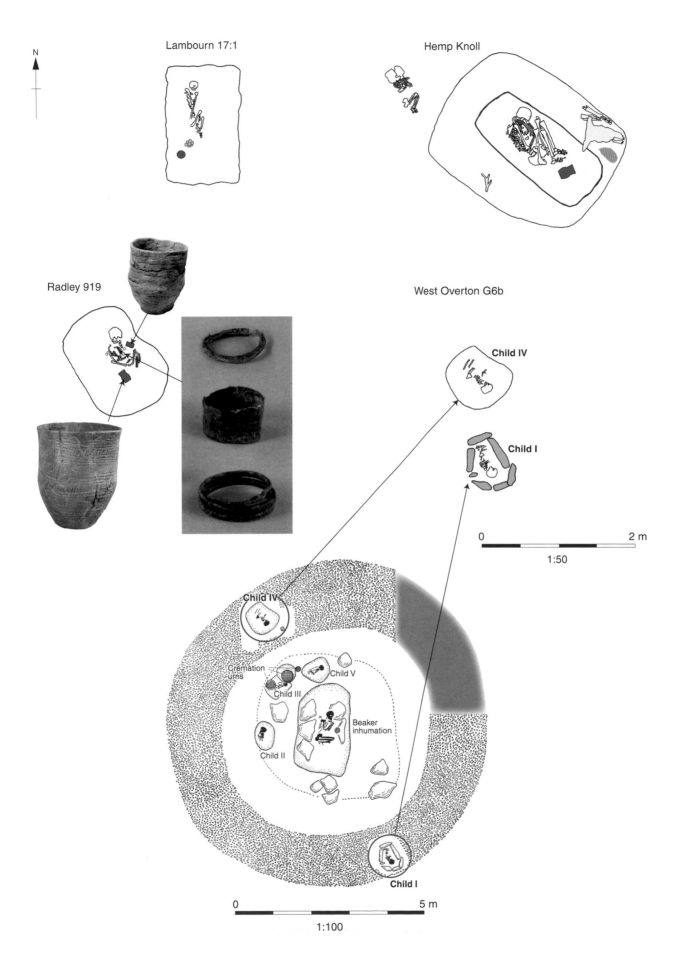

N

Lambourn 17:1

Hemp Knoll

Radley 919

West Overton G6b

Child IV

Child I

0   2 m

1:50

Child IV

Cremation
urns

Child V

Child III

Beaker
inhumation

Child II

Child I

0   5 m

1:100

male with several artefacts. The depositional events took place within a short time of one another: both bodies were aligned in the same direction, and both the grave pit and child's body were sealed directly beneath the mound (Robertson-Mackay 1980, 143). The treatment of young children in this way suggests they were present in burial contexts in ways that referred to the older person present, and in ways that paralleled the deposition of artefacts. As such they may have acted in the same way as artefacts: for example, as votive offerings or gifts embodying certain statuses, qualities or powers.

The burials of children in the four- to eight-year old age group are very different: they consist mostly of primary burials with artefacts, spatially organised in ways very similar to the layout of adult graves. These burials suggest a concern with inherited identities and potential adult roles among children who had reached an age where adult potentiality had become manifest. Given the prominence of adult males in early Beaker graves discussed above, and the rarity of female burials, it

is possible that these were boys rather than girls. It is notable, in this context, that the Radley 919 burial of a four- to five-year old child was oriented with head to the north-west, and with a set of objects (including two Beakers, one containing the body of a neonate) arranged around the body in a way very similar to that in contemporary adult male burials. The rarity of these child graves, however, also suggests that special circumstances lay behind the burial: the breaking of a descent line, for example, might have needed redressive ritual action to deal with anxieties related to kinship-based concepts of cosmological order.

A final aspect of early Beaker graves to consider is their spatial distribution. There are several intriguing features of the evidence. It is apparent that most of these burials are clustered close to or within preexisting ceremonial monument groups, suggesting deliberate attempts to make use of cultural spaces or landscape settings that were already resonant with religious or political significance (see Fig. 15.14). This observation has

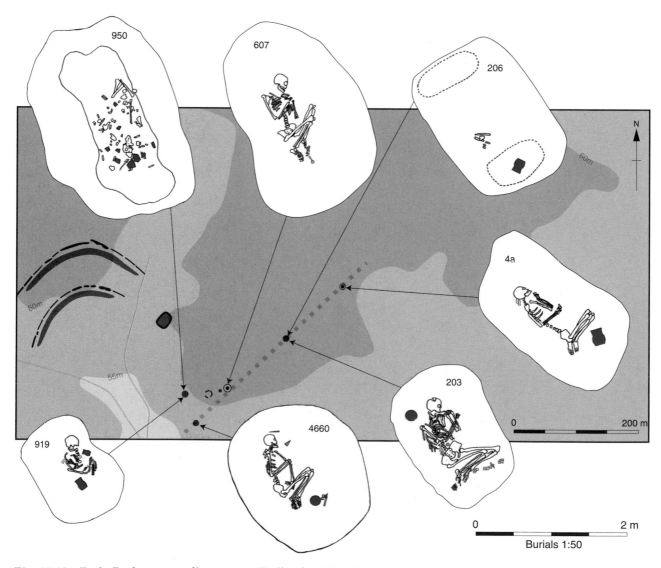

Fig. 15.13   Early Beaker grave alignment at Radley (see Fig. 15.9 for key)

relevance to previous interpretations which identify a range of social tensions in the later 3rd millennium cal BC (eg 'old' versus 'new'; 'communal ceremony' versus 'individualising' burial practices), and explain these as expressions of opposed ideological structures such as 'ritual authority' and 'prestige goods' systems (cf Shennan 1982; Braithwaite 1984; Thorpe and Richards 1984). As Thomas has noted, however, the nature of social and cultural change differed considerably from one area to another, with quite local articulations of old and new (Thomas 1999). Highly generalised

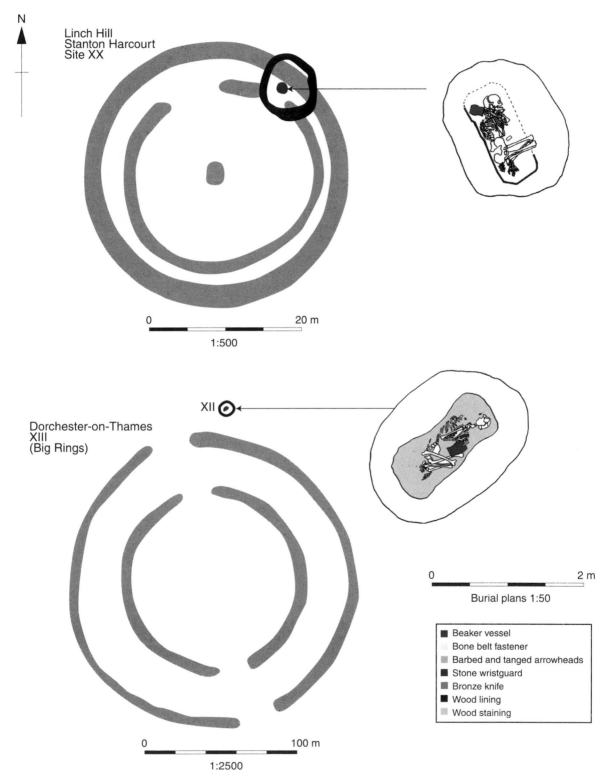

Fig. 15.14   Beaker graves and earlier monuments at Stanton Harcourt XX (Linch Hill Corner) and Dorchester-on-Thames Sites XII and XIII

abstract models of mutually exclusive ideologies that pervaded all aspects of social life, fail to take account of the great diversity of practices, beliefs and values which probably existed in any one community in this period. The Thames Valley evidence certainly suggests a more complex situation than we would expect if starkly opposed belief systems, and their adherents, were simply in contention.

Even so, there are aspects of the evidence which point to especially salient fields of social discourse in which Beaker funerary events seem to have played a prominent part. Despite the copresence of both older and newer monuments alongside Beaker graves within the relatively small areas occupied by ceremonial monument groups, attempts at integration or inter-referencing in terms of architectural or burial forms, locations or orientations, appear inconsistent and ambiguous. At Radley, for example, the line of early Beaker-associated burials of Phase 4 (Fig. 15.13) is not orientated towards any of the earlier monuments but runs between and past them (Garwood 1999b), yet elsewhere there are Beaker graves positioned immediately adjacent to earlier monuments, including the Big Rings henge at Dorchester-on-Thames (Fig. 15.14; Site XII; Whittle *et al.* 1992) and the late Neolithic ring ditch at Linch Hill Corner, Stanton Harcourt (Site XXI, 1: Barclay 1995b, 99-100). Although the evidence is inconclusive, it is tempting to suggest that these contrasting strategies were related to differing perceptions of the things of the past which were evident in the contemporary landscape (cf Bradley 2002).

In some cases, especially where 'ancient monuments' such as long mounds and causewayed enclosures (eg at Radley) were no longer places for social acts in the present, or were even perceived to belong to a past beyond 'social time', referencing seems to have been more allusive than direct, perhaps intended to situate present practices in the setting of a naturalised or distanced order of things, though in such a way that the new was unconstrained by that past world. In these cases, neither the past times imagined nor the places associated with them could be perceived to be a threat to the beliefs or social agenda reified in Beaker burials. In contrast, architectural structures which were still in use for ceremonial purposes, which evoked still powerful meanings, emotions, and visions of the cosmos and cultural identity, could have been foci for social actions (such as rituals) that asserted systems of authority or religious commitment in opposition to those expressing new values and beliefs. In these cases, the positioning of Beaker graves suggests deliberate attempts to appropriate and reformulate the meanings of significant places by rewriting, rejecting or overturning the recent social and religious past. At the very least, burial acts and memorials could obstruct the traditional choreographies of ceremonial performances, and perhaps contaminate them symbolically by incorporating within their performance spaces alien materials

(bodies with Beakers) representative of a different world view. We may be seeing strategic actions by groups intent on making such places their own, as a means of demonstrating social or political dominance, or as expressions of alternative beliefs in situations where religious ideas or cult affiliations had become politicised.

It is very important to note, however, that it was not the existence of monuments in themselves that prompted these strategies, but rather recognition of the kinds of social performances that would or could take place within and around them. This may help explain why some late Neolithic communal ceremonial monuments within the study area were apparently targets for 'iconoclastic' burial acts, and others were not. Equally, where Beaker graves are absent from areas occupied by earlier monuments, this may be because these places were avoided by communities adopting new Beaker-associated practices, or because those practices were successfully excluded from existing monuments by those committed to 'orthodox' religious traditions who were able to sustain their authority in the face of new ideas (cf Thorpe and Richards 1984, 75-80).

Communities of the dead, single graves and mortuary symbolism, 2100-1800 cal BC

In the last two centuries of the 3rd millennium cal BC new themes emerged in funerary ritual and symbolism that maintained only certain aspects of existing practices. In particular, there seems to have been an emphasis on references to the past, physical relationships among the dead and the living, and collective identities. This is marked, in particular, by the reopening of earlier graves and vertical sequences of interments in central grave pits (Fig. 15.15): as, for example, at Gravelly Guy ring ditch X6 (Lambrick and Allen 2004, 51-61), Cassington barrow (Bradford 1951) and Lambourn 17 (Case 1956a). The same concerns seem also to have been realised in repeated constructional and depositional events giving rise to some increasingly large monuments, often containing the remains of a number of individuals, including Radley 12 (Fig. 15.17; Barclay and Halpin 1999) and probably North Stoke double ring ditch (Leeds 1936). The presence of objects that may have been old at the time of burial, in this context, may also have served as a means to reference the past (eg the wristguard fragment in Beaker burial 9551 at Cotswold Community College; Powell *et al.* 2010). At the same time, there is evidence for considerable diversity and individuality in burial assemblages, partly enabled by the adoption of new artefact types for use in graves, notably ceramics such as Food Vessels (from *c* 2100 cal BC) and Collared Urns (from *c* 2000 cal BC).

The relative frequency and cultural significance of monuments where successive construction and burial episodes took place, in comparison with single-phase funerary monuments, remain uncer-

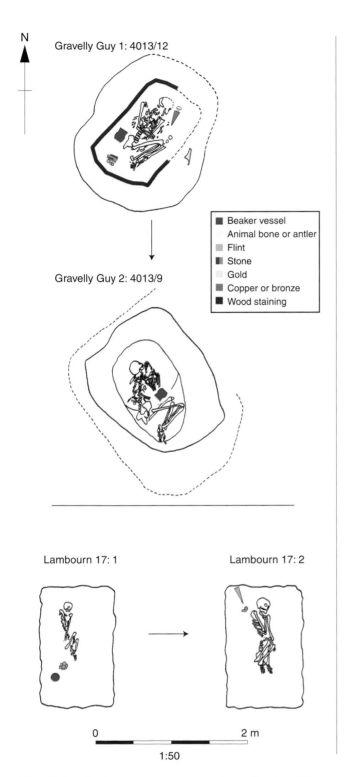

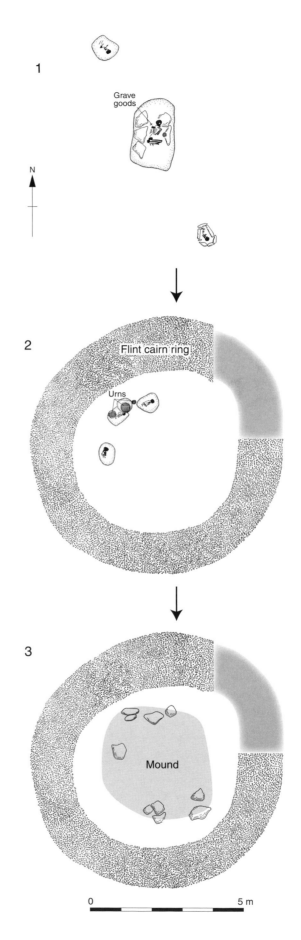

Fig. 15.15 Beaker grave sequences: Gravelly Guy X6 and Lambourn 17 (see Fig. 15.9 for key)

Fig. 15.16 West Overton G6b: plan, showing the arrangement and sequence of burials and monument construction phases

tain. It is has been suggested that multiphase mounds in this period served to assert the community's place in the landscape (or at least the place of the ideal community of the dead), through forms of symbolic expression that emphasised 'growth' (as mounds were enlarged) and ideas of group origins linked to significant 'ancestral' places (Garwood 2007a). The nature of burials at multiphase round barrow sites also seems consistent with ideas of community and continuity, especially in the way that many different age and gender categories may all be present at one site (eg at Radley 12 these included, after the phase 1 adult male burial, an adult, a young adult and an infant in succession: Fig. 15.17; cf Barclay 1999a, 97-102). The multiple burial events at some open arena sites in this period, such as pond barrows, also appear to represent a

tradition of practice that involved several age and sex categories (eg the several mature adult women and children around Radley pond barrow 4866; ibid., 115-28).

It is important, in this context, to note that even though a relatively greater number of burials is recorded from this period in comparison with the period before 2100 cal BC, they must still represent only a small proportion of the wider population and were thus never 'routine' burials. Indeed, it is possible that the deposition of many bodies at these sites represented significant acts of renewal or replenishment in themselves, even 'offerings' to ancestors or deities, rather than formal acts of individual burial. A striking instance of this is the well-preserved infant 'burial' (605/B), interred alongside a Food Vessel at the end of the central grave burial sequence at Radley 12 (Fig. 15.17), which appears to have consisted of only the separated upper half of the child's body (Barclay 1999a, 102, fig. 4.52). Indeed, child burials in this period probably all served specific symbolic purposes (of several kinds, defined by age category) that were largely unrelated to life experiences and everyday identities (Garwood 2007c). At West Overton G6b (Fig. 15.16), two child burials were positioned in diametrically opposed positions, on either side of a central adult male burial with a Beaker assemblage, and sealed by a flint ring cairn that surrounded the central burial (Smith and Simpson 1966). It is likely, given their shared stratigraphic position, symmetrical spatial setting of the graves, and the close similarities between the two children in terms of grave layout (both lying on their right sides with their heads to the south-east), that they were interred at the same time as each other and probably the adult male as well (although there is no precise dating evidence to be certain of this). This striking arrangement of human bodies has clear implications for our understanding of the temporality of funerary practices and the management of corpses if not actual deaths.

These observations reinforce the view that these individuals must have had special significance for the living, especially in the way they were valued for mortuary deposition at monument sites. In societies concerned with the continuity of kin groups in the ancestral landscape, the presence of ancestors, and ideas of renewal (especially if life itself is believed to be a 'limited resource'), there is often a strong belief in the need to install or reinvest (corporeal) sources of regeneration to ensure future reproduction and growth (Bloch and Parry 1982; cf Garwood 2007a; 2007c).

The geographical incidence of multiphased monuments, 'cemetery barrows' and related funerary practices may, however, have been uneven both inter- and intraregionally. In central and southern Wessex and parts of eastern England, for example, numerous multiphased monuments with concentric ring ditches have been excavated and are well-represented in aerial photographic

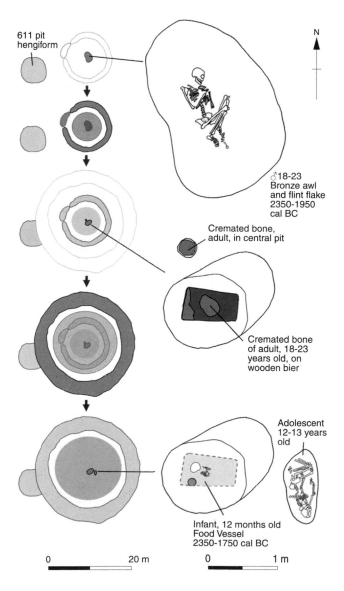

611 pit hengiform

N

♂18-23 Bronze awl and flint flake 2350-1950 cal BC

Cremated bone, adult, in central pit

Cremated bone of adult, 18-23 years old, on wooden bier

Adolescent 12-13 years old

Infant, 12 months old Food Vessel 2350-1750 cal BC

0   20 m   0   1 m

Fig. 15.17   Barrow Hills Barrow 12: constructional and burial sequence. New constructional and depositional events are shown in purple

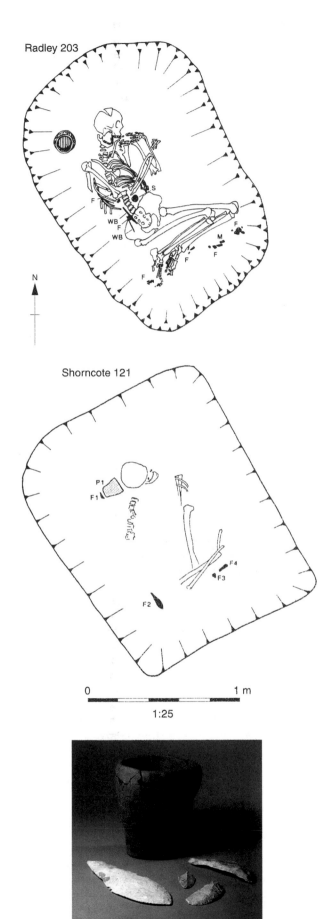

Fig. 15.18 *Later Beaker single graves: Radley 203 and Shorncote 121*

surveys. In these areas they appear to be widespread, occur in pairs or dispersed groups, and were sometimes enlarged on such a scale that they would have dominated very large tracts of the contemporary landscape. In the Middle and Upper Thames Valley, in contrast, these long-lived elaborate monuments seem to be rarer, more scattered and mostly smaller and with fewer burials than in other regions. It is possible, therefore, that there was continuing emphasis on single event acts of burial and mound-building rather than ancestral monuments associated with traditions of reuse and elaboration. It is notable, in this context, that multi-phased sites do not figure prominently in most of the major round barrow groups in the study area: at Stanton Harcourt, for example, there is only one definite example (Gravelly Guy X6; Barclay 1995b, fig. 39); at Radley possibly three, in a dispersed linear arrangement, though none with more than three or four secondary burials (Barrows 12, 14, 15: Barclay and Halpin 1999, figs 1.2 and 1.11); and there is none at Standlake (Catling 1982, fig. 48). One exception to this pattern is North Stoke, where aerial photographs indicate the presence of numerous multi-ring ditches, including at least two with three or more concentric ditch circuits (eg Case 1982a, fig. 33). One of the double ditched sites, excavated by Leeds in 1933, had a series of child burials at the centre, though the contextual details are vague and dating evidence is lacking (Leeds 1936, 16-18).

There is no question that most of the later Beaker graves known in the region, dating to the period *c* 2150-1800 cal BC, are not found in multiphase 'cemetery barrows'. Instead, they occur either in single graves, sometimes at the centre of ring ditches (Fig. 15.18), such as Radley 203 (Barclay 1999a, 135-41) and Shorncote 121 (Barclay and Glass 1995, 24-31), in small groups that were probably not associated with mounds (eg the three inhumations at Overton Down site X/XI; Fowler 2000, 82-6), or in larger and more extensive flat cemeteries (eg at Cassington and Eynsham: Leeds 1934a, 269-75; 1938, 21-6). The dating of many of these sites is imprecise, and it is possible that the great apparent diversity of practices relates to change over time, as well as increasingly localised funerary customs. Certainly, the strong gendered distinctions among earlier Beaker modes of burial do not seem to have been sustained in any consistent or widespread way after 2100 cal BC (cf Gibbs 1989). Overall, therefore, there seems to have been far less conformity to set rules of body treatment and funerary ritual in Food Vessel-associated and later Beaker graves in comparison with earlier Beaker-associated burials. At the same time, the cultural referencing and specific social and political purposes of these burial categories seem to have been very diverse, although arguably sharing a general concern with evoking the past.

At first sight, the Beaker flat cemeteries of this period are perhaps especially difficult to interpret. The relatively large number of burial deposits in the main groups at Cassington (11) and Eynsham (15) is not paralleled elsewhere in England, while dating evidence is limited and the reliability of the original anatomical analyses of skeletal remains is uncertain. Even so, it is possible to discern some general patterns of practice shared by the two sites (see Fig. 15.19). It is notable, for example, that the majority of burials were mature adult males in both cases, and that at Eynsham, at least, there was particular emphasis on the over-40 age group for both men and women. There is also evidence for similar spatial ordering within the cemetery areas, with distinct linear groups of burials oriented NW-SE at both sites: at Cassington eight of the burials occur in an elongated group some 25 m long and 5 m wide, while at Eynsham there are five burials located in a much narrower band approximately 22 m long aligned on a large post setting. It is also evident that most of the women and children at both sites were buried at the end of, and just to one side of, the linear groups of graves. Other gendered distinctions in body treatment, if they are apparent at all, seem to be cemetery-specific and to lack consistency (cf Gibbs 1989). In the main group at Eynsham, for example, the women were buried on their right sides and men on their left, yet the majority of both male and female burials were all oriented with heads to the north-west; at Cassington there seems to be no pattern of body orientation or posture differentiation at all.

Although the precise dating of the cemeteries is uncertain, it is clear that there are no early Beakers or related artefacts at either site, while among the Beakers present are several that fall roughly in the later part of Needham's (2005) chronology, between 2100 and 1800 cal BC. It is possible that these clusters of burials were flat cemetery counterparts of the large groups of burials found at some contemporary 'cemetery barrows' (such as Barnack, Cambridgeshire: Donaldson 1977). The lack of prominent monuments, however, suggests closer parallels with 'open arena' sites such as Radley pond barrow 4886, and especially the Down Farm pond barrow in Dorset where an alignment of pits, some containing cremation burials in pottery vessels, extended eastwards from the 'pond' hollow (Barrett *et al.* 1991, 136-8). Shared alignments in the structuring of practices is perhaps best understood as the realisation of symbolic schemes that referenced celestial phenomena or orientations, or perhaps significant landmarks, in order to convey an idea of a fixed and timeless order to things (cf Owoc 2001a). The linear arrangements of graves at Cassington and Eynsham are also intriguing in chronological and social terms: they recall the earlier alignment of graves associated with Beakers at Radley (Garwood 1999b), while at the same time

they prefigure the striking linear organisation of barrow groups evident in many parts of southern Britain after 1850 cal BC. Although continuity of lineally organised practices and their meaning from one phase to the next is unlikely, as these clearly took on very different forms and were realised in different monumental contexts over time, it is still tempting to interpret the linear arrangements of burials at Cassington and Eynsham in terms of successive funerary events that reified concerns with belonging, descent, history, linear order and/or significant 'pathways', real or symbolic.

Similar concerns with past and present order can also be identified across the wider range of late Beaker single burials, both in clearly monumentalised contexts (ie with ring ditches and mounds) and in less prominent 'flat grave' forms. The contents of these graves suggest considerable cultural conservatism marked by practices that consciously reproduced long-established funerary traditions, often in the context of a rapidly changing funerary landscape marked by the elaboration of ancient mounds and the development of new clusters of monuments. The self-conscious selection of historically significant or even 'archaic' material symbols (such as Beakers), and the enactment of 'traditional' funerary performances, suggest deliberate attempts to use the past as a resource in contemporary social or political discourses (eg at Radley; Garwood 1999b). A similar concern is also evident in burial acts sited close to ancient architectural structures such as the West Kennet Avenue (eg beside stones 5A, 22B, 25B, 29A, and probably 18B and 25A; Smith 1965a). Elsewhere, similar burial events took place in landscape and monument contexts where earlier graves and mounds appear to have been relatively rare. This is especially apparent in the areas at the upper end of the Thames Valley at Shorncote (Barclay and Glass 1995), Lechlade (Thomas and Holbrook 1998), and Cotswold Community (Powell *et al.* 2010). It is possible in these cases that funerary and mound-building events, involving 'ancient' modes of inhumation burial and Beaker pots, served as deliberate attempts to lay claim to land or other rights by asserting 'age old' traditions of belonging and identity. What at first sight appear to be very similar kinds of 'Beaker single graves' may, on closer inspection, have been guided by quite different social and political agenda: in some contexts as a means of resisting changing values or new expressions of status distinctions by reference to traditional authority; in other settings as a means of laying present and future claim to certain kinds of identity, belonging and ownership, by legitimising them with reference to the *same* symbols of tradition and 'ancientness'.

At the same time, there were burial events that seem to have been less concerned with referring to past traditions, or the cultural values and identities associated with them, at least in the decisions made *not* to include Beaker vessels in burial assemblages.

416

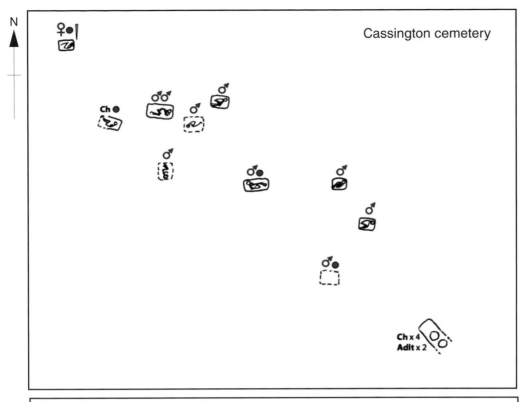

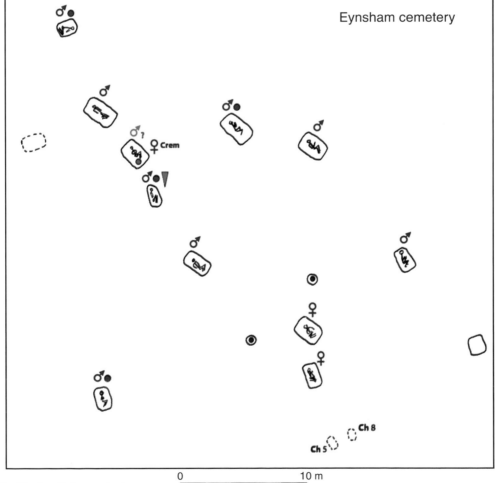

*Fig. 15.19 The Beaker flat cemeteries
at Cassington (top) and Eynsham (bottom)*

At Radley 3, for example, a crouched male inhumation associated with an East Kennet-type flat riveted dagger, dating to *c* 2200-2100 cal BC, was placed at the centre of a large ring ditch situated beside an earlier Beaker monument (Barclay 1999d, 152-53; Garwood 1999b, 304). Another early Aylesford-type bronze dagger placed on top of a primary cremation burial beneath a mound at Hinton (North Bishopstone), Wiltshire (Greenwell site 287; 1890, 57-8; cf Gerloff 1975, cat. 99) may be a very early example of a dagger grave with a cremation, dating on typo-chronological grounds to *c* 2100-1850 cal BC (if the dagger was not an heirloom).

The complex treatment of the dead and the diversity of funerary practices and forms of monumentality in the period 2100-1800 cal BC seem mainly to have been driven by concerns with descent, the reproduction of social groups, community, perceived relationships between timeless domains, historical pasts and the present, and empowerment and authority. Yet it is also apparent that material realisations of these concerns in funerary rituals, depositional acts and monumental architecture, and the degree of cultural and political importance attached to these, were expressed in many different ways in the social landscapes that existed during this period.

EARLY BRONZE AGE BURIALS, MONUMENTS AND LANDSCAPE, 1900-1500 CAL BC

There have been relatively few general interpretative surveys of early Bronze Age funerary practices at either a national or regional scale in the British Isles, especially for the period after 1850/1800 cal BC when Beaker graves disappear from the archaeological record. It is noteworthy, for example, that the most recent detailed description of grave types and chronology is now over 25 years old (Burgess 1980, 79-117, revised in Burgess 1986; cf Needham's (1996) chronological framework). Furthermore, most discussions of the social and cultural significance of burials and burial categories (eg Bradley 1984a, 73-89; Clarke *et al.* 1985; Barrett 1988; 1990) pay relatively little attention to the contextual detail of depositional events (though see Barrett 1994, 113-31; Woodward 2000, 101-22). There has also been a widespread if questionable assumption that the kinds of interpretative approaches used to make sense of Beaker graves (eg Thomas 1991; 1999, 156-62; Mizoguchi 1993; Last 1998) are also broadly relevant to early Bronze Age inhumation burials (and to some extent cremations; cf Barrett 1994, 119-23), despite the very different monumental and cultural landscape contexts of burial events after 1900 cal BC.

Although there has been renewed research interest in the last decade on the representation of social and cultural identities in the early Bronze Age (eg Brück 2004a; 2004b; Healy and Harding 2004; Jones 2005; cf Sørensen 2004), and the role of

funerary artefacts as symbolic media (Woodward 2002), this work focuses mostly on inhumations, makes no strong distinctions between Beaker and later burials, and relies on a very narrow range of case studies. At present, therefore, the whole range of early Bronze Age funerary practices remains relatively little understood, at least in modern terms, while some of the most distinctive and widespread kinds of burials have attracted virtually no recent research interest at all (most notably Food Vessel and Collared Urn cremation graves).

The limited nature of contextual analyses in recent research has been exacerbated by problems of dating, imprecise chronological frameworks and uneven patterns of site investigation. In the Middle and Upper Thames Valley it is apparent that whilst most round barrows probably date to the early Bronze Age, many excavated burials consist of undated, unaccompanied cremation deposits (eg at Stanton Harcourt: Barclay 1995c, 110). This situation is repeated at most of the round barrow groups investigated along the Thames Valley, with the partial exception of Radley. This pattern is less immediately apparent, however, on the chalklands of north Wiltshire and Berkshire where round barrow excavations, primarily in the 19th century, suggest a higher incidence of artefact-associated burials. It is difficult, however, to gauge how representative the results of early excavations on the chalklands are in comparison with more recent investigations on the river gravels. In part, this is because the chalkland sites were generally well-preserved standing mounds with intact burials, sometimes on the old land surfaces, rather than plough-truncated ring ditches. Moreover, the sites targeted by early diggers were usually the most prominent in local landscape terms, and the most architecturally distinctive in external appearance which, during the early Bronze Age, seem to have been associated with elaborately furnished burials more often than less impressive mound structures.

There is no question that the distribution of round barrow investigations is geographically patchy across the region, and the quality of information very uneven. As far as early records are concerned, for example, most of the known investigations in the Avebury district were reported either by Hoare (1812) or Merewether (1851b) and are extremely limited with regard to detailed contextual information. In contrast, the excavations undertaken by Greenwell in north Wiltshire at Aldbourne, and along the Berkshire Downs, provide far more detailed accounts of funerary deposits and grave architecture (Greenwell 1890). More recently, the most intensively investigated part of the study area is the section of the Upper Thames Valley between the Thame and Windrush tributaries, with significant numbers of early Bronze Age burials excavated at Dorchester-on-Thames, Radley, Oxford, Cassington, Stanton Harcourt and Standlake. Yet in other parts of the region with numerous round barrow and ring ditch sites, such as the Kennet Valley, uplands such as the Chilterns (Dyer 1961) and Cotswolds (Darvill 1987, 95-108), and the Middle Thames and Surrey Downs (Needham 1987, 105-8; Grinsell 1987), there are very few examples of recorded funerary deposits even where recent excavations have taken place (eg at sites in the Lower Kennet: Lobb and Rose 1996, 77-9). In this context, claims about the relative distributions, dating and social significance of early Bronze Age burials in different parts of the study area should be treated with considerable caution.

The diversity and complexity of early Bronze Age funerary practices

It is perhaps ironic that recent research devoted to early Bronze Age funerary practices should be so limited given that this period is marked by such diverse burial types, architecture, artefact sets and other kinds of material deposits. It is clearly no coincidence that this material diversity and complexity, even idiosyncrasy, is perceived to be analytically challenging to the point of unpatterned intractability. This perception has a very long history, with origins in the observations of anti-quarian excavators of burial mounds in the 19th century. Greenwell (1890, 64), for example, reflecting on the diversity of burial rites, material deposits, grave architecture and monument forms among the round barrows of Berkshire and the other areas he explored, commented ruefully that: "indeed, so varied are the circumstances attending interments, that it would be scarcely wrong to say that no two burials are in every respect alike".

At a detailed level of contextual analysis, it is possible that the almost limitless diversity of burial practices reflects a more fundamental condition of early Bronze Age funerary ritual. It is possible, for example, that this constituted a 'performative' cultural milieu in which prevailing values and aesthetics encouraged highly creative and innovative means of representing personal identities, qualities and biographies in death (Garwood 1991). The practical outcomes of such a field of funerary discourse may well have included both conscious acts of variance in funerary customs (eg in order to emphasise local identity, or to articulate more spatially extensive social networks) and purposeful, explicit, changes in funerary rituals over time (eg in order to sustain, or create new social distinctions, by making things 'different again'). It is likely, in this context, that the social or religious distinctions that were most salient in such performances, whether relating to age, gender, kinship, descent, political status, cult or caste categories, also changed over time (conceivably at different tempos). From this perspective, it is not that the evidence is necessarily intractable, but rather that our studies so far have been neither precise enough in spatio-temporal terms, nor sensitive enough in contextual terms, to reveal consistent series of practices at appropriate social, spatial and temporal scales of analysis.

While a brief glance at the kinds of evidence from the Middle and Upper Thames study area demonstrates the sheer variety of burial categories and funerary architecture, at the same time it is possible to identify examples of similar series of ritual actions or repeated architectural forms suggestive of more widely shared practices and meanings. At a very basic level, for example, it is possible to identify two kinds of variation in burial deposits and their physical settings: first, between 'open' arenas for repeated funerary activities or access to burials, and 'closed' funerary deposits that were sealed by solid architectural structures such as mounds and banks; second, between 'containment' of human remains in cists, pits and pots, and 'exposure' of corpses or cremations on the ground surface and in pits open to view prior to mound construction. The different conditions of visibility, accessibility, manipulability and temporality afforded by these modes of treating the dead clearly allowed for different kinds of performance, engagement with corporeal remains, representation of relationships among different interments, and memorialisation of the dead through architectural structures (eg immediate/personalised in comparison with delayed/distanced or generalised). It is important to note that these practices were not exclusive from site to site, or between phases of monument use, but rather allowed for different kinds of funerary representation in particular combinations.

Funerary deposition in 'open' arena and premound contexts

Exposed mortuary deposits in open arenas, a feature especially of some late 3rd millennium cal BC 'permeable' monument sites (Bradley 1998b, 139-46; cf Garwood 2007b, 144-47) appear to be very rare in the early Bronze Age of the Thames Valley, although a few sites are known where multiple interments took place, either prior to mound construction or in permanently open settings. It is possible that some of these burials were visible or accessible after initial deposition, at least for a time. It is difficult in most cases, however, to be sure about the temporalities of burial sequences or the degree to which mortuary materials were exposed to view or easily revisited (eg upright urns, for example, could have had wooden lids, creating cist-like structures which were only later sealed, either deliberately or through erosion processes). Without fine-grained contextual information from burials of these kinds, it is safest to consider 'exposed' and 'contained' mortuary deposits found in open settings together.

In some cases, it seems clear that series of mortuary and other rituals took place in open settings that were later monumentalised. At Cassington, for example, there is evidence for a complex series of depositional and constructional acts in an open area defined by a shallow ring ditch:

these included a pit grave containing an adult male inhumation, with an infant in the fills above, and a small stake-built 'hut' built on top of the filled pit, four cremated bone deposits close by (three in a line of pits, one of which was in an upright Collared Urn, another consisting of a rare example of a probable foetus burial), and several separate areas of burning (Atkinson 1946-7). Apart from the pit grave deposits, the sequence of depositional acts and burning events is unknown, although the funerary arena appears to have been left open until the hut was erected, partially burnt, and the whole area sealed soon after by a large gravel mound. A similar line of pits containing cremated human bone deposits is known from Radley, where five pits, one containing an upright Collared Urn with the bones of an adult and subadult, and three more containing

single adult burials, is located near the west end of the linear barrow group, just north-east of Ring Ditch 801 (Barclay 1999a, 128-33). In this case, the setting of the linear 'cremation cemetery' was left open, with no evidence for a mound. An alignment of eight pits at Yarnton Site 7 included one containing the cremation burial of an adult male (4439; G Hey pers. comm.). The pits contained Beaker pottery, flint, fired clay, cremated human bone, burnt stone and wood charcoal. Oak sapwood from the cremation deposit yielded a date of 2140-1960 cal BC (OxA- 12110: 3682±28 BP) and oak sapwood from the upper fill of the pit a date of 2140-1910 cal BC (OxA-12040: 3645±28 BP; Bayliss and Hey in prep.). The only other 'hut' structure from the study area was found at the centre of a large ring ditch at Clifton Hampden: this

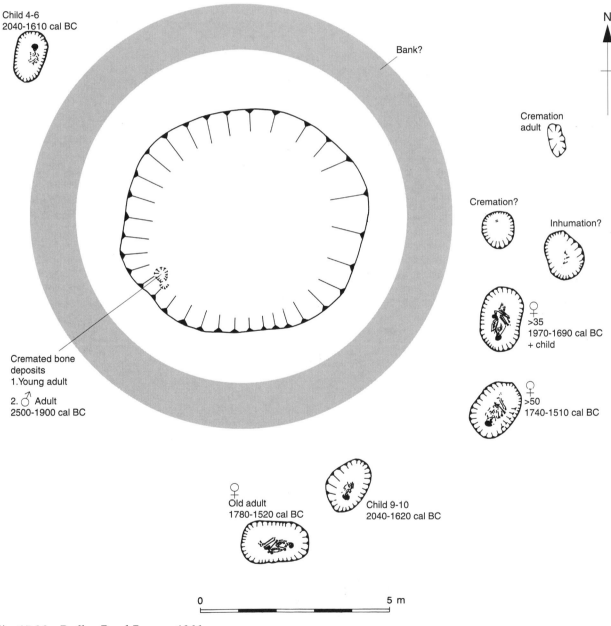

Fig. 15.20   Radley Pond Barrow 4866

surrounded a central cremation burial but there was no other evidence for funerary deposits (Leeds 1936, 15-16).

The occurrence of groups of early Bronze Age burials in 'open' settings at both open and mound sites is certainly far more widespread and more complex, in terms of depositional settings and associated symbolic referents, than is generally assumed. There has, however, been no attempt to review the available evidence at any geographical scale or to identify distinctive kinds of practices. In a few rare cases there is evidence for the construction of open arenas that intentionally or not became foci for subsequent series of burials, such as Radley pond barrow 4866 (Fig. 15.20; Barclay 1999a, 115-28). In contrast, burials of burnt bodies in 'secondary' contexts (often in urns) are far more common, especially in pits cut into round barrow mounds, berms, ditch silts and banks. This practice occurred throughout the period and in all parts of the study area. Early excavators made frequent reference to secondary urn burials in mounds (eg at Avebury G43, excavated by Merewether; see Cleal 2005 for a summary of round barrow excavations in the Avebury area), and there are numerous recent well-documented examples elsewhere in the region (Fig. 15.21), such as Whiteleaf barrow, Buckinghamshire (Childe and Smith 1954, 215, 228-9; Hey *et al.* 2007), Field Farm ring ditch 417, Berkshire (Butterworth and Lobb 1992, 7-13); Burn Ground 2, Hampnett, Gloucestershire (Grimes 1960); City Farm Site 3 (Case *et al.* 1964-5, 6-21), and Radley 12 (Barclay 1999a, 99). In all these cases, old mounds were treated as open stages for funerary rituals and acts of burial, sometimes repeated on several occasions. In some instances, burials took place in prominent elevated positions high up on mound structures, as if making especially assertive statements about the relationship between the burial event/dead person and things of the past, or perhaps to draw visual attention to relationships with the wider landscape or significant landmarks. In other instances, burials took place in more hidden settings (eg in partially filled ditches, as at Radley 12) or in peripheral settings (eg around the edges of eroded mounds, as at Field Farm and possibly City Farm 3), as if expressing a degree of subordination or humility in relation to what the mound was believed to signify, or perhaps in some cases secrecy or obscuration. Elsewhere, cremation graves of this period can occur in open spaces close to round barrows, such as the scattered burials at Radley (some with Collared Urns: 4245, 4321, 4700; Barclay 1999a, 128-33) and City Farm pit 4/6 (Case *et al.* 1964-5, 30), as well as more ancient monuments, such as the cremation burial with a miniature Collared Urn (pit 2) at the south end of the North Stoke bank barrow (Case 1982a, 68, fig. 34).

It is notable that the amounts of cremated human bone present in depositional contexts, especially in secondary burials, are often very small and cannot possibly represent the remains of complete bodies.

As post-depositional decay and disturbance cannot account for the absence of such large parts of these bodies, it has been suggested that many cremation 'burials' in fact were no more than partial or token deposits (eg at Radley: Boyle 1999, 176). This raises the possibility of deliberate selection and parcelling of portions of burnt bodies for dispersal across several areas of social action and perhaps multiple depositional contexts. Rather than formal 'individual' burials, the dis-integration of the cremated dead and the materials that resulted could be interpreted as a means of representing 'dividual' social identities and their roles in several different social contexts (cf Brück 2004a; 2004b), as 'fragmentation' practices concerned with the referencing and networking of identities, relations and events through the dispersal of broken objects (cf Chapman 2000), or as the production of significant, valued corporeal substances embodying sacred qualities, resources or forces for use in 'votive' or 'sacrificial' acts (cf Garwood 2007c).

Indeed, depositional practices involving human remains could perhaps be viewed as just one dimension of a much broader cultural repertoire involving the deliberate, ritualised deposition of cultural materials in many different kinds of social settings. This is perhaps most apparent in the widespread placement of ceramic vessels or sherds, unaccompanied by human remains, in both monumental and non-monumental contexts in this period. Examples include the Aldbourne cup in one of the postholes forming part of the Charnham Lane post circle near Hungerford, Berkshire (Ford 1991), the Biconical Urn placed in an isolated pit (1047) at Yarnton Site 1 (G Hey pers. comm.), and the miniature vessel placed in the ditch silts of the Latton Lands oval enclosure (Powell and Laws, in prep; the shape and size of this monument is reminiscent of twin barrows enclosed by single ditches, although in this case there was no evidence for internal mounds or burials). It is conceivable that deposits of animal bones, lithic artefacts, unworked stones, and burnt plant remains at round barrow sites could all be interpreted in similar ways, although so far there have been no comparative studies of these materials, and no attempt to synthesise the evidence to investigate the full range of non-funerary depositional acts even at a site-specific level.

The presence of burial deposits that were left exposed and open to view prior to their incorporation in mound structures is also difficult to demonstrate with confidence, except where these were placed directly on the old land surface. Unambiguous examples of this kind of practice are extremely rare and mainly belong to the latter part of the early Bronze Age. These include the central cremation burials at sites such as Stanton Harcourt XVI.1, associated with a complex late Wessex 'male' burial assemblage including an incense cup, Camerton-Snowshill dagger, perforated whetstone, awl, bone pin and several beads (Harden and Treweeks 1945); West Overton 4, Wiltshire (associated with a knife-

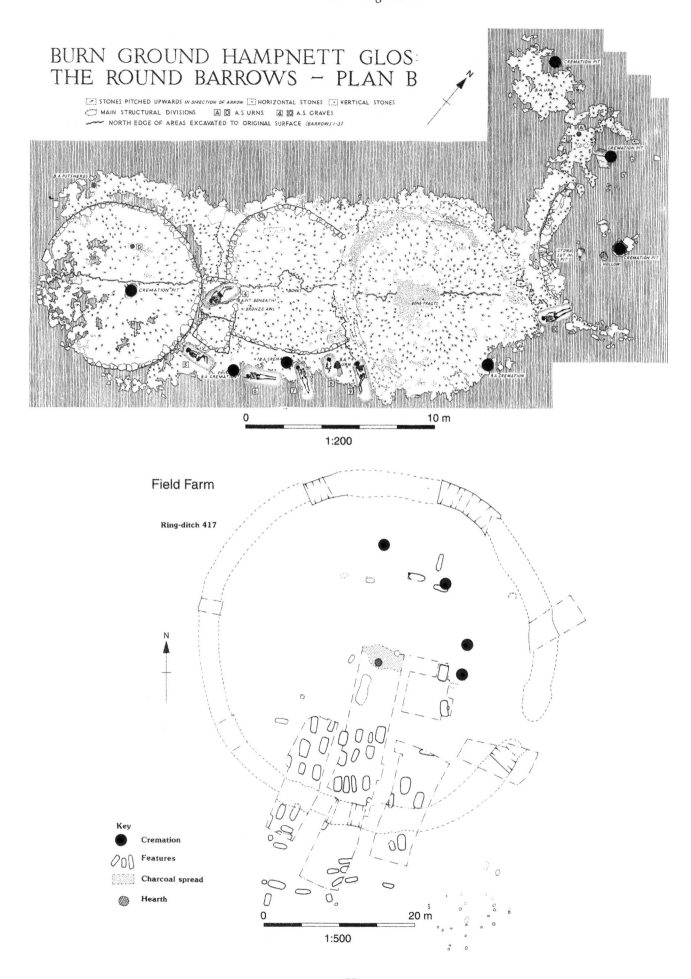

BURN GROUND HAMPNETT GLOS:
THE ROUND BARROWS ~ PLAN B

STONES PITCHED UPWARDS *IN DIRECTION OF ARROW* HORIZONTAL STONES VERTICAL STONES
MAIN STRUCTURAL DIVISIONS A D A.S. URNS 4 10 A.S. GRAVES
NORTH EDGE OF AREAS EXCAVATED TO ORIGINAL SURFACE *(BARROWS 1-3)*

0   10 m
1:200

Field Farm

Ring-ditch 417

N

Key
● Cremation
Features
Charcoal spread
Hearth

0   20 m
1:500

422

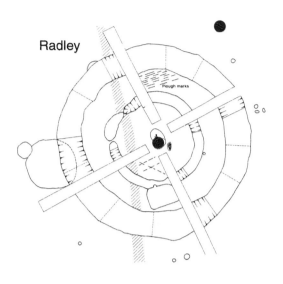

Radley

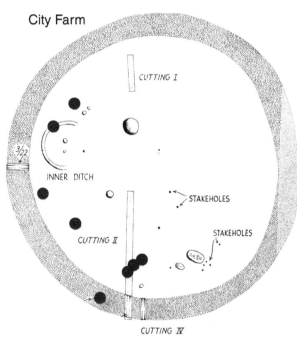

City Farm

CUTTING I

INNER DITCH

STAKEHOLES

STAKEHOLES

CUTTING II

CUTTING IV

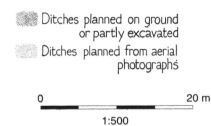

Ditches planned on ground
or partly excavated

Ditches planned from aerial
photographs

0   20 m

1:500

Fig. 15.21 (opposite and above) Plans of round barrows with secondary cremations (marked by red dots)

dagger; Hoare 1812, 90), and Aldbourne 6, Wiltshire (associated with a large 'female' Aldbourne-series burial assemblage including an Aldbourne cup and cover, knife-dagger, two awls, and several beads and other ornaments: Greenwell 1890, 50-3; cf Gerloff 1975, cat. 278). The only earlier example known from the study area is an otherwise unique mortuary deposit at Avebury G23c (unlocated; reported by Merewether 1851b), comprising a centrally positioned grape cup surrounded by a circle of 12 supine inhumations placed radially with their feet towards the centre (Cleal 2005, 125).

Funerary deposition in 'closed' primary contexts sealed by mounds

In contrast to the display of mortuary deposits in open settings, most primary burials sealed beneath or within mounds were already contained in pit graves or built structures (such as coffins, cists or ceramic vessels) that appear to have been quickly if not immediately 'closed' to further scrutiny by being covered by pit backfill or mound construction layers. The diversity of containers is very great indeed. Wooden boxes, probably portable coffins (rather than timber chambers built into grave pits), are known from Aldbourne 14 (Greenwell 1890, 57) and Roundway 5a, Wiltshire (Gerloff 1975, cat. 267), in both cases with knife daggers placed on top of the heaped cremated bone deposits. A log coffin has also been recorded at West Overton G1, Wiltshire (containing an extended inhumation with an unusual association of a small bronze dagger, a pin and a flanged axe: Hoare 1812, 90; cf Gerloff 1975, cat. 271, plate 52H; Needham *et al.* 2010). Sarsen and other stone-built cists have been recorded on the Wiltshire and Berkshire Downs, both rectangular in shape (eg housing the primary burial in an upright Collared Urn at Lambourn 9: Case 1956a, 21) and circular (eg at the centre of the mound 'extension' at Lambourn 18, containing a cremation burial with a copper alloy awl and jet amulet; ibid., 25-6), in Surrey (eg at the Hallams and Junction Pit; Needham 1987, 107-8), and on the Cotswolds (eg at both Snowshill and Naunton, Gloucestershire: Darvill 1987, 99, 101). There are also a few cases where the compactness of the cremated bone deposits suggests that these were contained in leather or fabric bags, such as the central burial at Hodcott Down A (Richards 1986-90, 12).

Most common of all is the containment of cremation burials within upright pottery vessels, or beneath inverted vessels. Numerous examples of such practices, associated above all with Collared Urns, have been recorded throughout the study area since the 18th century. Only in a few cases, however, have these burials been recorded with sufficient attention to the complexities of fill sequences or the precise nature of depositional acts. Examples include the urned cremations at Radley (see Barclay 1999a, 128-33; Boyle 1999, 175-83), the double cremation burial of a man and woman, with three segmented faience beads, beneath an inverted Collared Urn at the centre of Ring Ditch 23 at East Molesey, Hurst Park, Surrey (Andrews and Crockett 1996, 61-4, figs 32 and 33), and the cremation burial of an adult with a bead necklace, awl, shale ring and other objects beneath an inverted Collared Urn (pot 919) at Field Farm ring ditch 417, Berkshire (Butterworth and Lobb 1992, 48-9).

Finally, there are, of course, large numbers of both unaccompanied and accompanied inhumation and cremation burials in 'closed' contexts, placed directly in pits and sealed by backfill deposits and mound structures. Most of the primary burials excavated by Greenwell at Aldbourne, for example, were probably of this kind (Sites 276-86; Greenwell 1890, 46-57), while well-documented examples excavated recently include the cremation burials at the centres of Radley barrow 1 and ring ditch 801 (Barclay 1999a, 46-52). As in the case of burials within containers, however, it is often not possible to judge the temporal intervals between burials, pit-filling and construction events, and it is possible that in some cases bodies or cremated bones were left exposed for at least short periods, or that sealed burial pits were foci for mound building only some time after funerals had taken place.

Satellite burials and complex early Bronze Age funerary architecture

An intriguing aspect of many early Bronze Age funerary events is the presence of satellite burials and artefacts that were deposited at the same time or shortly after primary burials took place. Although the majority of examples known from the study area were recorded in the 19th century, there is no reason in most cases to doubt the contextual details provided by the excavators. At Preshute 1a (the Manton barrow), for example, a patch of clay soil containing 'degraded bone' laid on the old land surface, and a miniature vessel placed at the base of the mound fabric as it was being built, were positioned on either side of an exceptionally richly furnished female inhumation burial (Cunnington 1907). At Aldbourne 6, fragments of cremated human bone, associated with an Aldbourne cup, were scattered on the old land surface to the north of a deturfed area on which another deposit of burnt bones with a large set of fine artefacts had been placed (Greenwell 1890, 50-3). At Lambourn (Greenwell site 289), a miniature vessel was placed on the old land surface close to a pit containing a cremation burial with a stone battle axe, antler hammer, incense cup and small dagger (ibid., 60-1). In each of these cases, portions of human bodies and/or pottery vessels were carefully placed with reference to central burial deposits, as votive or sacrificial acts, or as symbolic statements in their own right. Recognition of this kind of practice reinforces the idea, discussed above, that burials should not be distinguished from the wider range of depositional acts at round barrow sites, but rather seen as just one of many ways of expressing meaning through material objects and substances.

There is, in this context, surprisingly little evidence for complex early Bronze Age funerary architecture associated with primary and satellite burial groups, and little suggestion that long periods of time elapsed between interments and mound construction. At Ogbourne St Andrew G6, Wiltshire, a primary burial pit containing an inhumation burial was filled directly by sarsen stones and covered by a large sarsen cairn, which also housed two satellite burials, both consisting of cremation deposits in upright Collared Urns (Cleal 2005, 129-30). Although it is conceivable that the sarsen cairn remained exposed and accessible for some time, there is nothing to suggest that ritual performances took place on or around this structure. A similar large cairn at Aldbourne 8 was the setting for a major burning event, which left a layer of burnt material that extended from the top of the cairn south-eastwards onto the old land surface around its base (Greenwell 1890, 54-5). The cairn and burnt material were covered, probably not long after the fire, by a massive chalk layer derived from the ditch, although again the temporal interval between these events is unknown. The stakehole circle and inner structure at Hodcott Down A (Fig. 15.25) might have delineated an area for continuing ritual action after the central burial took place, but equally these could have been used for the duration of just one funerary ceremony (Richards 1986-90, 12).

In general, therefore, there is little indication that primary burials and the premound built structures associated with them were foci for repeated visits for ritual performances or depositional acts. Instead, the construction of mounds shortly after burial events, and the care taken over shaping external mound forms, suggests that the monumental architecture that memorialised the dead became the principle medium for guiding understanding and articulating meanings. Mounds appear to have been designed both as an act of physical and semantic 'closure' (Last 2007a) that excluded further actions and reinterpretations of the dead (which would be possible if there was continued access to the dead or direct referencing of mortuary deposits), while at the same time being a means of making 'definitive' and impressive state-ments about the dead and their place in the cultural landscape (Garwood 2007a, 47-8; cf Sørensen 2004, 169). In this light, it is possible to recognise a prevailing mode of cultural representation in early Bronze Age funerary ritual that increasingly emphasised singularity, finality and conclusion (rather than repetition and continuation). At the same time, the individual dead were delivered safely into the past but also given a prominent physical presence as visible 'history', conveyed through the surface forms of funerary architecture that evoked memories of the things housed within.

Burning events, pyres, and funerary display

Although burning events at round barrow sites are evident throughout this period, only in a few cases is there reason to believe these represent *in situ* acts of cremation. At Farncombe Down, Berkshire, for example, several burnt patches and ash deposits sealed by the turf stack were interpreted as evidence for the burning of scrub vegetation prior to monument construction, largely because there was no sign of cremated bone (Rahtz 1962). The most convincing identifications of cremation pyres rest on evidence for localised burnt areas, charcoal deposits and burnt bone fragments on the surface of buried soils, all in proximity to cremation burials and sealed by mounds. It is striking that all the well-documented examples from the study area seem to date to a late stage in the early Bronze Age (after 1750 cal BC, which is consistent with the chronology of cremation pyres more widely in southern Britain: Garwood 2007a). Several of these are associated with late Wessex 'male' artefact sets like those at Stanton Harcourt XVI.1 (Harden and Treweeks 1945), Hodcott Down A (Richards 1986-90), Stancombe Down, Lambourn (Greenwell site 289: 1890, 60-1); Aldbourne 13 (Greenwell 1890, 55-6) and possibly Aldbourne 3 (Greenwell 1890, 48-9). In other cases they consist of cremations with few or no grave goods, as at Swell 5 (a male cremation burial with a bone pin; Darvill 1987, 106-7), Lambourn 1 (with a knife-dagger and miniature vessel; Case 1956a, 19) and Childrey (an unaccompanied cremation burial; Greenwell 1890, 63). Details of depositional processes and the spatial organisation of pyres and subsequent burials are often missing from early accounts, although it is evident in most cases that pyres and burials were usually positioned very close together, or else the burials were placed on top of burnt areas (eg Stanton Harcourt XVI.1; Fig. 15.25) or in pits that cut through pyre remains (eg Hodcott Down A; Fig. 15.25).

The dating and character of cremation pyres beneath mound structures accord closely with the wider picture of short-lived funerary rituals at round barrow sites after 1750 cal BC: visually striking, but transient and soon brought to an end by monument-building events. The qualities of finality and conclusiveness exhibited in this stage of the burial process reinforce the idea that later early Bronze Age funerary ritual was concerned especially with dramatic display (cf Barrett 1990), and with demonstrating closure through the fiery dissolution of the corpse and the embodiment of corporeal remnants, fuel residues and places of burning within mounds. These practices might have been especially important in social and political contexts where dynastic succession, and the inheritance of aristocratic titles and rights, necessitated unambiguous expressions of both endings and new beginnings. The destruction of the body by fire offered vivid testimony to the transformed condition of things past.

The elite dead: power and identity

Implicit in much of the preceding discussion is recognition that the burials found at round barrow sites in the period *c* 1900-1500 cal BC represent a very small, select part of the early Bronze Age population. The special mortuary treatment given to these people, culminating in formal burial and often individual memorialisation through mound-building, has inevitably been interpreted as evidence for significant social differentiation in terms of status and identity. This evidence has been used to support many interpretations of social ranking in this period: these give particular emphasis to ideas such as 'chiefdom' social structures, alliance networks and prestige goods systems, peer-polity interaction, dynastic narratives, elite social display and forms of sacred authority, (eg Renfrew 1973; Shennan 1982; Bradley 1984a, 75-89; Braithwaite 1984; Garwood 1991; Barrett 1994, 105-7; Needham 2000b; Fleming 2004). These interpretations are usually so deeply interwoven with discussions of the 'Wessex' rich grave phenomenon (Piggott 1938; cf Burgess 1980, 98-111, 122-31; Clarke *et al.* 1985) that it is very difficult to investigate early Bronze Age funerary practices without recourse to generalisations about 'chiefly' or 'elite' culture.

There is no question, of course, that at least some burials in this period were provided with especially lavish material associations in the form of highly valued, visually striking grave goods. These may include finely made bronze artefacts (such as daggers and awls), necklaces and other ornaments made of exotic materials (such as gold, jet, amber, and faience), non-local stone objects (eg maceheads and battle axes) and rare composite objects made from several materials (such as halberd pendants and gold-mounted amber and shale buttons), alongside a range of small enigmatic ceramic vessels ('incense cups', 'pygmy cups', etc). Terms such as 'rich burials' or 'elite graves' have been widely used to characterise these interments, although there is clearly great variation in the size, diversity and material richness of artefact sets. This variation and the existence of several distinct kinds of grave layout and artefact assemblage may, however, be indicative not just of a single hierarchy of social 'classes' but of several modes of social and cultural differentiation (eg with reference to cult affiliation, ethnic origins, marriage status, and so forth; cf Woodward 2000, 101-22). Moreover, there was also undoubted change over time in the composition of grave assemblages, their contexts of deposition (see: Gerloff 1975; Burgess 1980; Bradley 1984a), and thus their specific meanings and relative social significance. It would clearly be unwise, therefore, to treat all these burials as part of a unitary funerary tradition with a single scheme of meaning.

It is surprising, despite some significant recent discussions of the construction of identities and ideal social 'types' in early Bronze Age burial events (eg Woodward 2000, 101-22; Brück 2004a; Sørensen 2004), and new thinking about the symbolic references and aesthetics of funerary representation (eg Treherne 1995; Needham 2000b; Woodward 2002), that there has been little recent contextual or comparative analysis of 'rich graves' in Britain. In the case of the Middle and Upper Thames Valley study area, for example, there are only a few short syntheses of the evidence from Oxfordshire (Bradley 1986b, 38-9), Gloucestershire (Darvill 1987, 99-103), and the Marlborough Downs (Cleal 2005, 122-24), together with some occasional comparative discussion in site reports (eg Barclay 1999d, 324-25; Healy 1999, 326-28).

At a large spatial scale, and allowing for geographical biases in terms of site preservation and investigation, it is evident that the distribution of burials with Wessex-related artefacts is extremely uneven (Fig. 15.22). There are relatively large numbers of these burials on the north Wiltshire and Berkshire Downs (notably around Avebury, Aldbourne and Lambourn), but relatively few elsewhere, except for a small but significant concentration at Barrow Hills, Radley, with occasional examples in other parts of the region, such as the well-known late Wessex burials at Stanton Harcourt (Harden and Treweeks 1945) and Snowshill, Gloucestershire (Greenwell 1890, 70-2). Recent discoveries of relatively rich burials at ring ditch sites in low-lying river valley situations, however, suggest that these graves were distributed more widely than was once assumed: examples include Field Farm ring ditch 417, Burghfield, in the Kennet Valley (Butterworth and Lobb 1992), and ring ditch 23 at East Molesey, in the Middle Thames Valley (Andrews and Crockett 1996, 61-4, figs 32 and 33).

The monumental and landscape contexts of rich grave deposition are considerably more difficult to assess. There does seem to be a general relationship between linear barrow groups and the presence of lavishly furnished burials, which often make up a high proportion of the overall number of burials at these sites. At Radley, for example, four of the nine barrows excavated along the main 12-barrow alignment contained fine objects (Fig. 15.23), two being 'Wessex'-style burials in having sheet gold in one of the graves (barrow 2) and a distinctive late Wessex artefact set in the other (barrow 1: Barclay 1999b;

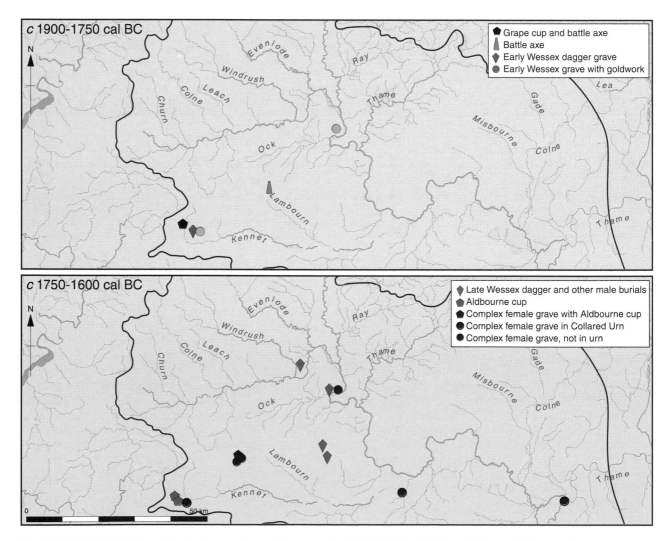

Fig. 15.22   *Distribution of early Bronze Age rich graves in the Middle and Upper Thames Valley*

1999c). The cremation burial in pit E at barrow 16 (the probable twin barrow just off the main alignment at the east end) also falls in this category, associated with a knife-dagger, awl and necklace with jet or shale, amber and faience beads. Yet it is also apparent from Radley and other sites that not all primary burials at round barrow sites were necessarily accompanied by grave goods (which might in part relate to changing fashions of funerary display over time; see below), while some especially rich grave assemblages have been found in isolated monument contexts (most famously, within the study area, the Manton Barrow near Avebury; Cunnington 1907; Fig. 15.24). In other words, there was clearly no simple deterministic relationship between linear round barrow groups and the presence of fine artefacts or complex burial assemblages.

The chronological distribution of rich graves, and the presence or absence of particular grave types, also shows some markedly uneven patterns in the Middle and Upper Thames. Most striking of all is the almost complete absence of early Wessex-style graves from most parts of the region, with the exception of the Avebury district, and their relative rarity even there in comparison with the Stonehenge area (see Cleal 2005). Male inhumation burials with classic early Wessex artefact sets, including objects such as Armorico-British daggers, have not been recorded anywhere in the study area, while the uncertainties surrounding the dating of miniature vessels and knife-daggers

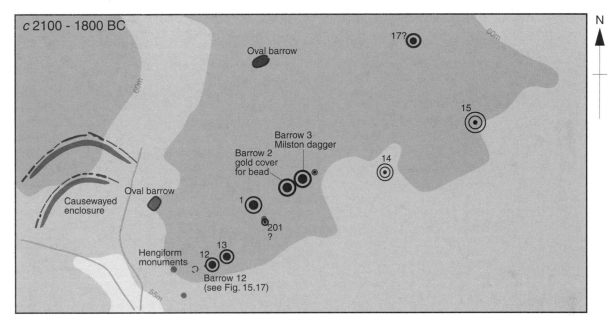

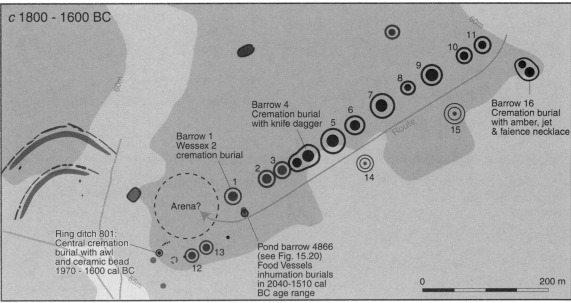

Fig. 15.23   Barrow Hills, Radley: the early Bronze Age barrow alignment and rich graves

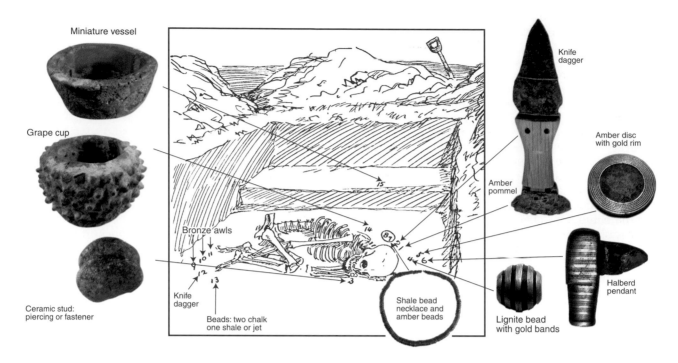

Fig. 15.24   The Manton Barrow Wessex 1 female rich grave

makes it difficult to assign most graves with such objects to the earlier part of the early Bronze Age. The possibility that some objects in graves may, in any case, have been heirlooms (Woodward 2002) deposited some time after their period of manufacture, further complicates interpretation of funerary deposits that lack corroborative radiocarbon dating evidence.

We are left, therefore, with very few burials that seem to date to the period *c* 1950-1750 cal BC. The recently dated inhumation burial in the tree-trunk coffin at West Overton G1 certainly falls within this range (Needham *et al.* 2010), and those with grape cups recorded from Avebury 23c and Winterbourne Monkton G1 probably belong to this period (Cleal 2005), together with the inhumation with satellite cremation burials at Ogbourne St Andrew G6 (ibid.). The cremation burials from Radley 2 (Barclay 1999b, 149-52) and Radley 4 (ibid., 154-56), and possibly Stancombe Down, Lambourn (Greenwell site 289: 1890, 60-1), also belong to the earlier part of the early Bronze Age. It is possible that the cremation burial of an adult and child at Avebury G55 (Smith 1965b), with a Collared Urn, accessory vessel, awl, bone pendant and fossil beads is also early, especially if the possible sheet gold bead-cover found in an unlocated barrow in the same area (G56) came from this burial (Cleal 2005, 129). The only exceptionally rich early Wessex grave from the study area, however, is the primary inhumation burial of a woman in the Manton Barrow (Preshute G1a: Cunnington 1907). The body, possibly wrapped in linen, was surrounded by an array of fine objects (Fig. 15.24), including a necklace consisting of over 150 amber and shale

beads, an amber disc and a halberd pendant, both with sheet gold mounts, two knife-daggers, one with an amber pommel, a grape cup, an incense cup, and several other items. This burial can be placed firmly among a group of lavish early Wessex female graves (Gerloff's Wilsford series; 1975, 197-98), which can be interpreted plausibly as those of very 'high status' individuals, perhaps 'royal' in character (cf Woodward 2000, 101-22; Garwood forthcoming).

In contrast to the rare occurrence of early graves with fine artefacts, there is a relative abundance of later burials with artefacts such as urns, miniature vessels, knife-daggers, awls, beads and other ornaments or dress fittings. In some cases, the grave goods may consist simply of a ceramic urn as container and a knife-dagger (eg at Naunton, Gloucestershire: Darvill 1987, 101) or just several beads (eg at West Overton G19: Cleal 2005, 129), but there are also examples of lavishly furnished burials. These are extremely diverse in terms of grave architecture and the specific sets of objects present, suggesting a concern with individuality and the portrayal of personalised social and political biographies through the assembly of artefact sets (Thomas 1991; Sørensen 2004). Yet the shared aesthetics of funerary display in acts of cremation, and recurring themes in the selection, combination and arrangement of artefacts, especially with respect to gendered identities (Gibbs 1989; Garwood forthcoming), are striking. There is no question that male and female stereotypes and distinctions were given special prominence in those cases when elaborate assemblages of objects were buried with cremated human remains.

Well-known examples of male graves (Figs 15.25-26) include Stanton Harcourt XVI.1 (Harden and Treweeks 1945; A J Barclay *et al*. 1995), Hodcott Down A, Berkshire (Richards 1986-90), Beedon Hill, Berkshire (Gerloff 1975, cat. 180), Snowshill, Gloucestershire (Greenwell 1890, 70-2), and probably Radley 1 (despite the relatively early radiocarbon date; Barclay 1999b, 141-48). The male sex of the cremated body was identified positively in all three of the burials which were excavated in the 20th century. The artefact sets include weapons such as Camerton-Snowshill daggers (at Stanton Harcourt, Hodcott Down, Beedon Hill and Snowshill), a spearhead and stone battle axe (Snowshill), dress fittings or ornaments such as ring-headed bone pins (Stanton Harcourt and Radley) and a crutch-headed bronze pin (Snowshill), and other objects commonly associated with late Wessex male burials such as a perforated whetstone (Stanton Harcourt), bone tweezers (Radley), and miniature vessels (Stanton Harcourt and Beedon Hill). These items suggest a concern with personal appearance but fairly restrained ornamentation, and 'male' attributes associated with violence and warrior prowess (cf Treherne 1995).

Positive identifications of female burials in the study area are rarer and less certain (eg Radley 16, pit E: Barclay and Halpin 1999, 164), but more widely there do appear to be consistent associations between females and Collared Urns, beads, other ornaments, awls, knife-daggers, and/or Aldbourne cups (Gerloff 1975, 197-234; Garwood forthcoming). Examples of such burials in the study area (Fig. 15.27) include Aldbourne 6 (with an Aldbourne cup and lid, a complex necklace of amber, faience, lignite and fossil beads, a bronze knife and two awls, a lignite or shale ring, pendant and conical button, and a polished haemetite pebble; a second Aldbourne cup lay on old land surface nearby: Greenwell 1890, 50-3), Aldbourne 12 (with an Aldbourne cup and bead necklace; Greenwell 1890, 56-70); Field Farm ring ditch 417, pit 524 (with a Collared Urn, amber and faience beads, shale ring, and bronze awl and rod; Butterworth and Lobb 1992), and Radley 16, pit E (with bronze knife-dagger, awl, and shale, amber and faience beads; Barclay and Halpin 1999, 164). The composition of these assemblages again indicates a concern with appearance, but with far more vivid display

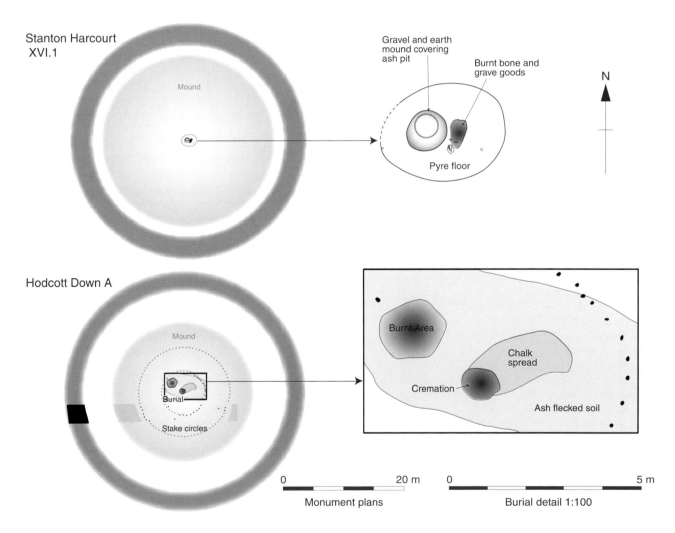

Fig. 15.25   Stanton Harcourt XVI.1 and Hodcott Down A: burials and monument settings

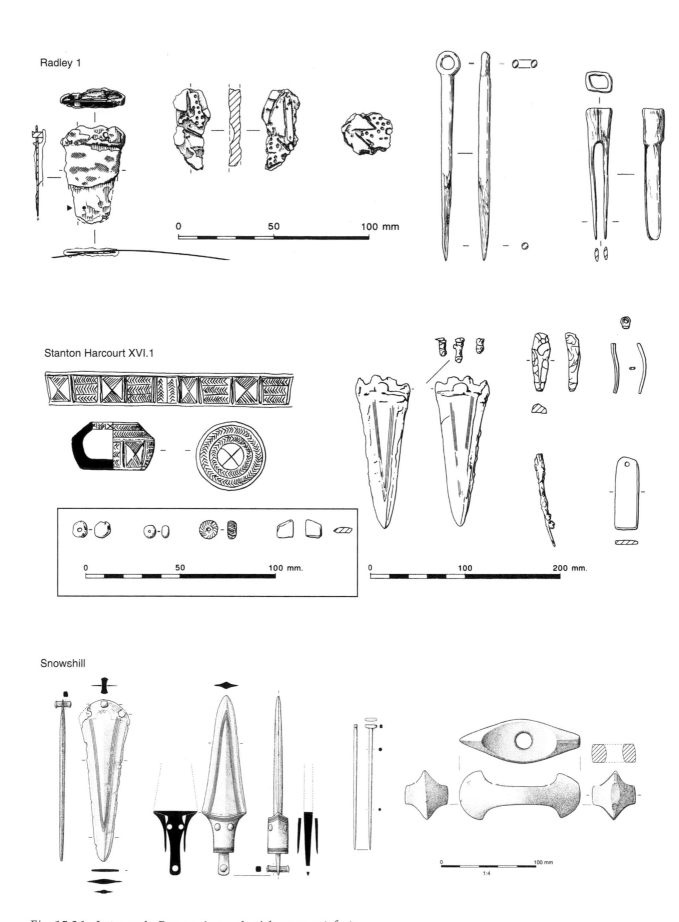

Fig. 15.26   Later early Bronze Age male rich grave artefacts

Aldbourne 6

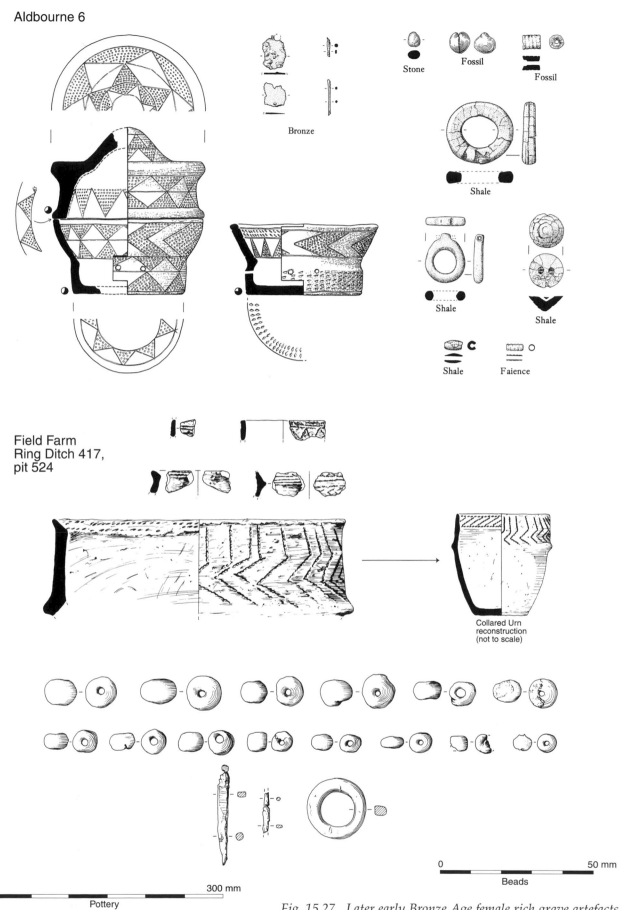

Stone

Fossil

Fossil

Bronze

Shale

Shale

Shale

Shale

Faience

Field Farm
Ring Ditch 417,
pit 524

Collared Urn
reconstruction
(not to scale)

0   300 mm
Pottery

0   50 mm
Beads

Fig. 15.27   Later early Bronze Age female rich grave artefacts

(through colourful and lustrous necklaces) than males, together with items that seem to be dress fittings, such as shale rings and buttons, and others of unknown purpose such as miniature vessels and awls which seem to have held symbolic significance especially (but not exclusively) for women.

Although the dating of many of the burial events marked by these artefact assemblages is understood only imprecisely, it seems likely from the evidence available that there were rapid changes of fashion in funerary aesthetics and material culture, and that the frequency of 'rich graves', in proportion to less well-furnished and unaccompanied burials, varied over time. This might help to explain the occurrence of 'short-run' grave series with similar contents, depositional arrangements and styles of funerary architecture (eg burials with Aldbourne cups). The modes of representation and symbolic referents in these series of burials had only brief periods of salience or relevance before being supplanted by new kinds of funerary display.

This pattern may be supported by the evidence from Barrow Hills, the only linear round barrow group in the region (indeed the country) providing reliable evidence for a long sequence of funerary and monument-building events in linear – and essentially chronological – succession (Garwood 1999b). The apparent survival of remnant mound structures and preserved old land surfaces beneath nearly all the monuments excavated along the main alignment (barrows 1-7 and 11; see Barclay 1999b for site descriptions), means that different degrees of plough damage cannot be used to account for the presence or absence of funerary deposits. Those in pits would not have been disturbed, while those placed on old land surfaces would have had a high chance of survival or would at least have retained some material presence in the buried soil. In this light, it is notable that the earliest barrows (3-1, 4) and the probably latest barrow (11) had primary burials with artefacts, while the other excavated monuments in the middle of the alignment either had primary unaccompanied cremation burials (barrows 5 and 7) or no burial at all (barrow 6). This suggests that while there was continuity in the building sequence and formal designs of mounds, there were changes over time in the social salience and symbolic significance of burial acts, at least in terms of the need to include artefacts in funerary deposits. Again, we seem to be glimpsing a high degree of variation in the nature of graves, ceremonial display and monument construction, and in changes in these over time, which hitherto have often been conflated or ignored because of perceptions of early Bronze Age funerary practices

as essentially variations upon the same themes.

It is clear that each burial and each mound added to a line of monuments served to project a developing narrative, in one direction referring to things ancient or out of time, in the other direction alluding to a history without end as the next place in line was always in principle there to be taken (Garwood 1999b; 2003; 2007a). This does not, however, mean that a single story was being told at each stage. In 'writing' each new chapter of an idealised tale of dynastic origins, glory, heroes' lives and historical events, the resonance, salience and even content of such narratives and myths will have changed. The stories told when the first mounds were built would not have been the same as those told at the last. In this light, changes in acts of burial and in the material culture of death that we may now discern in the course of the early Bronze Age should be seen as expressions of altered visions of society past and present, and of different expectations of how funerary displays would be interpreted and valued.

The evidence from early Bronze Age linear round barrow cemeteries in many ways epitomises the much longer term character and significance of mortuary practices and burial deposition during the whole period from the 4th to the early 2nd millennium cal BC. The treatment of the bodies of the dead, their presence and material properties in ritual acts, and the built structures designed to house or memorialise them, were always meaningful and often extremely significant for forging, reproducing and ending critical social, moral and political relationships, amongst both the living and dead. At the same time, mortuary practices, the performance of funerary rituals and construction of monumental architecture were hugely creative and sometimes innovative affairs with aesthetic and dramatic qualities that were distinctly their own. To reduce these extraordinarily rich, diverse and evocative modes of cultural expression to the unitary empirical category of 'burials' misses entirely their significance for understanding the complexity and changing qualities of cultural life in the past. In this light, the variety, scale and detail of the funerary evidence available from the Upper and Middle Thames Valley, a region which encompasses many diverse and contrasting prehistoric landscapes, provides exceptional insights into the changing presence of the dead in British prehistory and the particular ways in which people in the past 'made' the dead – as corporeal artefacts or substances that were embodiments, mediations and translations of their beliefs and values.

Chapter 16 – Meaningful materials: procurement, production and exchange

by Alistair Barclay and Philippa Bradley

INTRODUCTION

This chapter deals with the material culture of the hunter-gatherers of the 10th to 5th millennia cal BC and the early farming communities of the 4th to mid 2nd millennia cal BC. Hunter-gatherer communities had craft industries based on the working of lithics (mostly flint but also chert, quartzite etc), bone and antler, wood and probably basketry, and almost certainly leather. The start of the 4th millennium cal BC witnessed the addition of new technologies in the form of potting and the exploitation of lithics on a larger scale, with the setting up of organised extraction sites and the grinding and polishing of stone. Throughout the Neolithic period we see the appearance of more specialised artefacts, many of which could have been made for display, as symbols of power and prestige. These could have been used by important individuals during their lives, perhaps at particular ceremonies, and/or have accompanied them at death. They include objects that were made to a very high standard in terms of skill and quality which would, therefore, have stood out from other objects within the same group (for example, a finely decorated pot or an edge-polished flint blade). They could be fashioned from exotic and rare materials such as an unusual rock (eg amber or shale). Towards the middle of the 3rd millennium cal BC, we see the introduction of metals, first copper and gold and then bronze from mainland Europe. It is likely that a number of these objects were imported. The working of metals would have required specialist knowledge of the sources and working of raw materials and the manufacture of finished objects. Such skill and knowledge would have been highly prized, conferring prestige upon the craftsman and upon the wealthy individuals who possessed the objects they made; it is not surprising that much of the evidence for these objects derives from rich individual burials. This chapter deals with the key categories of finds, the range and types of artefacts produced and changes in material culture over time.

Meaningful materials

It is important when discussing the material culture of these communities to try to see beyond our own, early 21st-century preconceptions. It is likely that material culture would have been used to communicate and express ideas and information in a more overt way in the past than we may think of it doing today. In contemporary Western society, objects are often seen as mute and inert, whereas in non-industrial societies they may be imbued with more special significance, perhaps representing the soul or essence of a particular person, and playing an active role in social reproduction (Tilley 1996, 247). Like people, particular objects may have been seen to have had a life or biography starting with birth (production), social life (exchange, circulation and use), death (consumption, destruction and discard) and even regeneration (recycling of Beaker pottery for grog, the reworking of a flint axe to produce other tools and the melting down of metal-work to produce new objects). Objects may also have been seen to prolong life through deliberate acts of curation, as heirlooms or personal adornments. The personal history of a particular object would have been important, especially so with more prestigious objects made from rare and/or exotic materials. In the case of bronzework, for example, it is easy to see how the esoteric knowledge required to transform stone into shiny metal would have conferred particular prestige, and the fact that some composite objects would have required the skills of more than one person to make them (for example, bronze daggers with hilts of horn, bone pommels and sheaths of leather, wood and textile) would have enhanced their significance. Who made them and for whom they were made would have been important, as would their history thereafter which would have attached meaning to a particular object, as well as memories of how and when it was used. Prestigious objects may have had long use-lives that mirrored that of their owner. Other materials which were used in everyday life probably had a shorter life-cycle. Important people may have marked themselves out through the personal display of fine objects, while at a more subtle level, social groups may have been distinguished by the wearing of a particular type of bead or by the way they fashioned, decorated and tempered pots.

It is thought that communities of the 10th to mid 2nd millennia cal BC generally had mobile or semisedentary life-styles. The temporality of habitation was almost certainly based around seasonal movement of people, and gatherings to mark particular events. Certain types of material culture may have been created for particular short-stay activities (making weapons for hunting), for seasonal use or for longer-term projects (the building of monuments), and then either kept, replaced, recycled or discarded as appropriate.

Exchange

Outside our region it is clear that exchange of raw materials was occurring as early as the Mesolithic (Care 1979, 99-100), and although there is little evidence within the Thames Valley itself, it is likely that such exchange would have taken place in this area too.

Different spheres of exchange may have existed across much of Britain, connecting it to Ireland and mainland Europe. The small-scale societies that probably inhabited our study area may have been involved in several spheres of exchange in which goods (materials and tools, clothing and food, animals and people) would have circulated between neighbouring communities. Throughout this period, there is strong evidence that only certain goods were appropriate for exchange. Thus axes and lithic material appear to have been moved across significant distances, and the same is true of materials such as gold, copper, shale, jet, shell, iron pyrites and amber. Unfortunately, we know very little about organic materials. Perhaps surprisingly, pottery appears rarely to have been involved in any system of exchange outside the community. Only a few pots can be demonstrated to have moved between communities and, even in these cases, this could have been the result of the movement of people such as itinerant craftsmen.

Hunter-gatherer communities would also have been virtually self-sufficient in the skills and knowledge necessary to manufacture all their material needs (shelters, clothing, tools, utensils and weapons; Fig. 16.1). While most of these materials could have been procured locally, in certain parts of the Thames Valley exchange would have been essential as there are only very limited sources of good lithic material. Other items such as sea shells, amber and jet would also have been exchanged over long distances ultimately deriving from coastal communities. Unfortunately, we know very little about social and group identity at this time as there are few recorded burials. However, it is likely that clothing, appearance and subtle differences in material culture would have been used to mark out any differences.

The early non-metal-using farming communities of the 4th and early 3rd millennia cal BC would also have been largely self-sufficient in the skills and materials necessary for their everyday needs. Each community would have contained people capable of making and firing pottery, preparing leather, working bast (vegetable fibres, including flax which may have been used to make textiles and cord; wool is likely to have become available only in the Bronze Age; for a possible early example from barrow 1, Barrow Hills, dated to 2040-1680 cal BC (OxA-1886: 3520±70 BP) see Wallis and Hedges 1999), and stitching clothing, working wood, bark and bone and knapping flint for tools and weapons. With the notable exception of jadeite axes from mainland Europe, there is little evidence for specialist craftsmen or for centralised production centres in the early part of this period. Specialised goods do occur and, outside this region, centres for the production of prestigious object were established. Flint mines and stone extraction sites were set up in various parts of Britain and a number of these sites were engaged in the production of particular types of artefact (axes and knives) which were then exchanged across much of Britain. Personal items

Fig. 16.1 Flint knapping

Fig. 16.2   Bone and shale objects: top: belt slider, perforated disc and wingheaded pin from Barrow Hills, Radley; centre: perforated bones, shells, and beads from West Kennet; bottom left: shale bead from Yarnton; bottom right: shale bead from Eyford

Fig. 16.3 (overleaf)   Early metalwork in the Thames Valley

The earliest metalwork from secure contexts in Britain occurs in Beaker-associated grave deposits. The Thames Valley includes some important examples of this early metalwork which consists of tools and ornaments in copper and gold. The earliest well-dated copper objects are a group of rings from a child's grave found in the barrow cemetery at Radley near Abingdon (1). Other early copper finds include the neck ring from Yarnton (2) recovered when two ring ditches were dug away in the 19th century to provide ballast for a railway embankment.

2

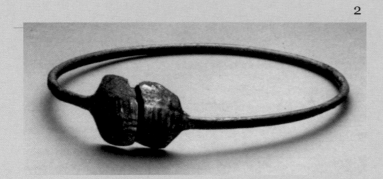

1

Flat axes of copper and bronze are probably slightly later in date, although since they have generally been recovered as stray finds or from contexts such as river deposits which are difficult to date, the precise date of their introduction is unclear. Daggers and knives, however, are known from a number of well-dated burial contexts including important examples from a Beaker burial at Dorchester-on-Thames. Analysis of one of the rivets from a knife dagger associated with this burial showed that it was made of tin-bronze, and the grave group thus forms one of a small number that could bridge the transition from an earlier copper-using industry to that of tin-bronze.

5

6

4

THE THAMES VALLEY

Daggers of later type are known from a number of burials in the Thames Valley, including an example from **Gravelly Guy** which provides evidence of the rarely preserved organic elements of these implements. Analysis has shown that it had a horn hilt and an antler pommel (3), and, when new, it would surely have been a striking object.

The working of metals would have required specialist knowledge which may have been highly prized, conferring prestige upon both the craftsman and the wealthy individuals who possessed the objects they made. It is not surprising that much of the evidence for these objects derives from rich individual burials.

It is easy to see objects such as the Beaker period gold basket 'earrings' from Barrow Hills (1) as high status items. The status of at least some early metalwork is, however, underlined most clearly by rather later finds from the only exceptionally rich early Wessex grave in the study area: the inhumation burial of a woman in the Manton Barrow. The burial was associated with an array of fine objects including an amber disc (4) and a halberd pendant (5), both with sheet gold mounts, a bead with gold bindings (6), and two knife-daggers, one with an amber pommel (7). This burial can be placed firmly among a group of lavish early Wessex female graves which can be interpreted plausibly as those of very high status, perhaps even royal, individuals.

7

3

made from shale and jet, including specialised forms of beads and belt sliders, have been found from sites in the Thames Valley (Fig. 16.2). These objects are likely to have been exchanged as finished objects.

Amongst the later metal-using, farming communities of the late 3rd and early 2nd millennia cal BC, there is a marked increase in the exchange of exotic goods and materials. Trinkets of gold and copper occur mostly in Beaker graves (Fig. 16.3), while other objects appear to copy Continental forms. The earliest Beaker pottery (Fig. 16.4 upper) is stylistically similar to vessels found on the Continental mainland, although many are made from local materials. Other specialised products exchanged across Britain at this time include flint daggers, stone wristguards and objects made from jet and shale, in particular rings, fasteners and buttons (see below).

Amber had been used and exchanged as a semiprecious stone for thousands of years before the early Bronze Age. However, its distribution, circulation and disposal seems to take on a new intensity during the early part of the 2nd millennium cal BC.

Deposition and discard

It has long been recognised that much of the material culture that gets recovered, either as mixed assemblages or individual objects, entered the archaeological record as part of a series of intentional acts of deposition. Our study area includes two very different types of depositional environment. In the river catchment of the Upper Thames, there is a variety of monuments and monument complexes which acted as foci for various formal acts of deposition, either within the monuments themselves, or in graves or pits. In the Middle and Lower Thames, the river and its foreshore rather than graves and pits appear to have acted as the main focus for votive deposits (axes of stone and metal, human and animal remains, antler and stone maceheads, flint and metal knives and daggers, pots, belt sliders and wristguards; Fig. 14.35). The practice of generating accumulations of material culture either as spreads or middens was also important.

The hunter-gatherer communities of the Upper and Middle Thames appear not to have buried their dead in formal graves, and rarely made formal pit deposits, but there is evidence for discard near or at watery places; tree-throw holes were sometimes utilised and middens were created (Chap. 10). The later farming communities also followed these practices, developing some, but they also invented new types of site (monuments) which were often used as arenas for consumption and formal discard. The hunter-gatherer practice of using tree-throw holes as places of deposition appears to have been gradually replaced during the

Fig. 16.4   Reconstructed Beakers from (top and upper centre) Barrow Hills; (lower centre) Drayton and (bottom) Gravelly Guy

0   100 mm

438

4th millennium cal BC by formal pit digging, which may partly reflect the shift of habitation from a natural, woodland environment to a humanly created landscape of woodland clearings (Chaps. 11 and 14). For the metal-using farming communities of the late 3rd and early 2nd millennia, elaborate funerary rituals and burials became more important in the upper reaches of the Thames and Kennet Valleys, while in the Middle and Lower Thames some of the objects used as grave-goods were still deposited in the river (Fig. 14.37; Chaps. 13 and 14). There is evidence, too, that the river was also a place to dispose of the dead. Single and multiple find hoards also become a feature of the archaeological record. Perhaps the clearest example of this is the single or multiple axehead deposits made by the early stone, and later metal-using, farming communities.

RAW MATERIALS

Flint and stone

A range of stone sources was exploited in the early prehistoric period, the Neolithic and Bronze Age being understood better than the Mesolithic. In the Thames Valley a wide variety of raw materials would have been available, the most widely used of which is flint. Holgate (1988a, 61-64) has summarised the range of lithic resources within the Thames basin. There is little evidence for the sources of flint that were exploited before the Neolithic period, and it is assumed that deposits of good-quality surface material would have been enough to satisfy the Mesolithic population, although small-scale shallow surface workings could also have been used. It is only during the Neolithic and Bronze Age that evidence exists for the large-scale mining of flint. In the region, the claim of flint mines at Peppard Common (Peake 1913) has been dismissed (Field 2004); other possible examples in Buckinghamshire and Wiltshire have seen little archaeological investigation and their status thus remains unclear. River gravels and other superficial deposits such as the Plateau Drift would have provided additional sources of flint (Pringle 1926; Arkell 1947). Good-quality Chalk flint comes from the Chilterns to the east of the region and the Berkshire Downs and Marlborough Downs to the south-west.

Other raw materials would have been brought into the region, some as implements such as polished axes which, once broken, would themselves have then been a source of good-quality stone. Cherts, including Portland chert, quartzite (although this is difficult to source and some is probably from the Thames gravels) and other imported materials are also occasionally encountered. A barbed and tanged arrowhead made from chert from the Clifton Down or Black Rock Limestone, which outcrops in the Mendips, was recovered from a possible Iron Age enclosure ditch

Fig. 16.5   Shale necklace and lip stud from the Manton Barrow (Preshute G1a)

at Northmoor, Standlake (Devaney 2005, 106). A single piece of Portland chert was found at the Eton Rowing Course (Lamdin-Whymark in prep.) and some Greensand or cretaceous chert flakes and black chert, possibly Portland, was used for a knife at the causewayed enclosure at Staines (Robertson-Mackay 1987, 95). Perhaps the most studied of stone artefacts is the axe, the sources, distribution and use of which have been extensively discussed (see, for example, Clough and Cummins 1979, 8). Numerous examples of reworked axes exist. At Yarnton, for example, an axe made of Cornish Group I stone was made into a rubber.

Exotic stone from further afield has been found in the Thames Valley, including shale (Figs 16.2 and 16.5) and jet objects (Fig. 15.6), amber, and axes from a range of sources. These artefacts indicate contacts with mainland Europe as well as north Yorkshire and the Dorset coast.

Shell

Marine and fossil shells were used in prehistory mainly as decorative pendants or parts of necklaces. Shells provide evidence for coastal contacts within the region. Worked shells have been recovered from long cairns in the Cotswolds (eg a perforated dog whelk from Nympsfield (Kennard 1938, 210) and a deposit of 70 shells from a ring ditch at Dorchester-on-Thames (Whittle *et al.* 1992, 166)). Shells were also found at the West Kennet long barrow (Piggott 1962, 51-3), and fragments of scallop shell and possibly of a clam shell were found associated with Peterborough Ware at the Cotswold Community site (Powell *et al.* 2010).

Clay

It is generally assumed that most prehistoric pottery was locally made and this appears to be backed up by what limited analysis there has been (Barclay *et al.* in prep.). There is rare evidence from Yarnton for the existence of specialist potters and for the exchange of Beaker pots or potting materials over relatively short distances of 10-20 km. Perhaps the best example of this are the two similar Wessex/Middle Rhine Beakers from Dorchester-on-Thames and Yarnton that were almost certainly made by the same person.

Organic materials

A wide range of organic materials would have been used for both everyday items and more specialised objects. Sadly, little of this material has survived within the Thames Valley, other than from a few waterlogged sites and as material recovered from the river Thames and its tributaries. Wood, textiles, fibres, fur, leather, feathers, horn, antler and bone would probably all have been routinely worked. Complex composite organic objects utilising several different materials have been found indicating a sophisticated understanding of these resources (Figs 16.3 and 16.6). Antler was used for a variety of purposes, including the production of 'maceheads', some decorated (Loveday *et al.* 2007), finds of which are concentrated in the Middle Thames (Figs 14.35 and 14.37). Indirect evidence for textiles, fibres and mineralised wood comes from corroded metal artefacts such as daggers, awls and knives, mostly from graves. Occasionally, evidence for textiles and fibres has been identified as impressions on the bases of pots.

The use of wood as a building material can be inferred from the remains of monuments themselves but little direct evidence has survived on most archaeological sites. From rare survivals of waterlogged sites we have a fairly good understanding of prehistoric woodworking techniques and woodland management practices. Reeds, withies and other materials would probably also have been used fairly widely. These would have been abundant along the edges of the Thames and its tributaries. Other indirect evidence for the use of organic materials can be gained through usewear analysis of worked flint and the study of residues on pottery.

Metals

It is assumed that many of the earliest metal objects (Fig. 16.3) would have been exchanged as finished pieces. Copper could have come from mainland Britain or the Continent, while gold may have entered mainland Britain from Ireland (for example, the gold 'earrings' at Barrow Hills; Barclay and Halpin 1999, 155, 183-6).

PRODUCTION AND CRAFTSMANSHIP

Working stone and flint

A wide variety of methods were used to shape stone and flint objects, including knapping (Fig. 16.1), grinding and pecking. Other techniques such as polishing were used to finish roughed-out artefacts. The extent of such working implies that more than just practical considerations were taken into account, as only the cutting edge of an axe really requires polishing to produce an efficient tool. However, axes were frequently polished all over, sometimes enhancing the pattern or colour of the flint or stone to greater effect (Fig. 14.35).

Pecking and grinding to produce a finished surface leaves little archaeological trace, although a number of polissoirs are known (see below). Amongst the largest stones to have been worked in this way are those used in monuments such as Stonehenge and Avebury. The stones at Stonehenge were worked using woodworking techniques, such as mortise and tenon joints, and there is some evidence that the stones were finished in a manner mimicking adze marks more common in woodworking (Cleal *et al.* 1995, 207, plate 5, Whittle 1997a, 148-9, fig. 1). In contrast to Stonehenge, in the Thames Valley stone for substantial monuments was obtained relatively locally: oolitic limestone at Rollright (Fig. 12.39 and 14.7); conglomerate for the Devil's Quoits at Stanton Harcourt (Fig. 14.22) and sarsen at Avebury (Fig. 12.37; Lambrick 1988; A J Barclay *et al.* 1995; Burl 2000). Although there is little evidence for the shaping of the stones at these sites, obtaining the stones would still have required detailed knowledge of the locality and the available resources. It would also have required immense effort to move and erect them. Some selection of raw materials for tomb building has been identified at Hazleton North, perhaps reflecting the different communities that constructed the monument (Barclay 1997, 155-6).

Knowledge of materials and craftsmanship

It is clear from artefacts and architecture that prehistoric communities were extremely knowledgeable of the raw materials available to them, and were capable of working them efficiently. Whilst it seems likely that many communities would have had efficient flint knappers, certain artefacts, such as daggers, axes and discoidal knives, seem to have been produced by specialist craftsmen at centres such as Grimes Graves (Saville 1981, 67, 70). A flint dagger from Shorncote, Gloucestershire is almost identical to one from Ystradfellte, Brecknock (Bradley 1995, 44), and may have been made by the same knapper. Other prestigious artefacts such as chisel- and barbed and tanged-arrowheads, plano-convex knives and edge-polished knives (Fig. 16.7) may have been made by more highly-skilled and specialised knappers. Many of these artefacts may

Fig. 16.6 Bone tools: (right) tranchet axehead in a modern haft and (left) barbed antler point from the Thames at London

Fig. 16.8   Tranchet axes from the Eton Rowing Course

Fig. 16.7 (opposite)   Flintwork from the Neolithic to the early Bronze Age: top left: Bullhead flint from Grooved Ware pits at Barrow Hills; top right: Neolithic worked flint from Yarnton including an edge-polished knife, scrapers, an oblique arrowhead and a flake from a polished stone axe; bottom left: early Bronze Age knives from Yarnton; bottom right: dagger from a Beaker burial at Shorncote

have been intended for display only, and some of the arrowheads would have been far too thin to have been used. The Shorncote dagger has areas of light polish which may have been the final finishing of the object but may equally have resulted from the artefact being drawn in and out of a sheath, perhaps during display; its very fine condition suggests that some sort of protective cover or sheath was used, although no trace of this was visible archaeologically in the grave (Fig. 16.7; Bradley 1995, 25, 44). Usewear analysis of the Irthlingborough and West Cotton daggers has shown that the artefacts were not used but seem to have been kept in sheaths (Grace 1990, 11), adding support to the possible evidence from Shorncote.

Rarely do we have evidence for the craftsmen themselves other than the artefacts they produced but at Hazleton North the so-called 'flint-knapper' burial provides a fascinating insight. Here a male burial in the northern entrance had a hammerstone by one hand and a reduced core by the other (Saville 1990a, 263, fig. 234).

Raw materials were especially selected for their knapping or working qualities and for their appearance. Attractive stone was frequently chosen for maceheads and axes (see below). Bullhead flint was transported throughout the region from its source in the Reading Beds in the south-east, perhaps because of its attractive appearance. It was recovered from various features at Barrow Hills, including, for example, a very rich Grooved Ware-associated artefact assemblage from a pit (Fig. 16.7; Bradley 1999, 218). Fine jadeite and nephrite axes have been recovered from the river Thames (Fig. 14.35; Cotton and Green 2004, 127-129, fig. 6, no. 14) and an example was found near the Staines causewayed enclosure (Field and Woolley 1983). Some of these axes would have been too fine to have been functional tools but may also have held symbolic or other meanings for their users.

Lithic assemblages and their analysis

Flint is amongst the most enduring legacy that past communities have left archaeologists (Fig. 16.7). Certain sites have yielded literally thousands of pieces that enable us to gain an understanding of the use and exploitation of this raw material. In the past, approaches to flint assemblages were based on typological categorisation of tools and waste. Now, through advances in microwear and usewear analyses (Brown 1989), it can be seen that pieces traditionally thought of as 'waste' are in fact important elements of the contemporary tool kit that had been used in a variety of ways. Retouching was not, therefore, always necessary to produce a tool and, indeed, towards the end of the Bronze Age, was reserved for particular objects where secondary working was required for functional reasons (Brown and Bradley 2006).

If analysis includes technologically-based considerations, in addition to those of typology, greater

insights can be gained into lithic assemblages. The context of deposition of complete assemblages of artefacts can be explored, allowing a more detailed picture of artefact creation, use and deposition to be built up. Usewear and microwear studies allow us to explore the use of organic resources that do not readily survive, such as wood, grasses and other vegetable matter.

Mesolithic flintworking techniques

During the Mesolithic, great care was taken to shape cores in order to produce blades suitable for working into microlithic points (Figs 16.1, 10.9 and 10.13). These would have been set in wooden hafts, several together, to form barbed points for hunting although other activities are also indicated at sites such as Thatcham (see below). Towards the end of the Mesolithic these points became very small. An example from the ditch of a Neolithic enclosure at Yarnton, Oxfordshire measures only a few millimetres in length (Bradley and Cramp in prep.). The skill of the knapper in producing such small items cannot be overestimated. Evidence from Thatcham, Berkshire has shown that the majority of the microliths from the site were not used as projectile points for hunting (Grace 1992, 62) so a wider range of activities should be envisaged.

Mesolithic tool kits typically included burins used for working bone and antler. Small, neatly-worked scrapers, piercing tools, serrated and denticulated blades were also used. A range of heavy tools are also found, including axes, adzes, picks and shafthole implements (Figs 16.8-9). These tools would have had a variety of uses including felling trees and working wood, digging and butchery tasks.

Neolithic flintworking techniques

At the beginning of the Neolithic, new forms and techniques of working flint were adopted (Fig. 16.7). Traditionally, polishing has been seen as one

Fig. 16.9 Stone maceheads from the Eton Rowing Course

of the key indicators of Neolithic assemblages together with the introduction of tool types such as leaf-shaped arrowheads and knives, but polished axes have been found in Irish and Welsh sites in secure Mesolithic contexts (Woodman 1978). Nevertheless, the widespread adoption of polishing, new artefact forms and an emphasis towards finer secondary working rather than careful core reduction, can be seen, together with the use of ceramics, as cultural markers of the Neolithic. Early Neolithic assemblages are frequently blade-based, but flakes tend to broaden with time (Ford *et al.* 1984), blades being used for particular tool types such as serrated and retouched flakes. Evidence for the manufacture of leaf-shaped arrowheads has recently been excavated at the Eton Rowing Course (Lamdin-Whymark in prep.). Evidence for the use of arrowheads, and for warfare in the Neolithic is fairly thin, but there are several examples of arrowheads embedded in skeletons (Fig. 16.10) including one individual at Ascott-under-Wychwood (Cramp 2007, 305, 310-11); further afield similar evidence comes from Fengate (Pryor 1976) and the West Kennet long barrow (Piggott 1962, 25; see Cramp 2007 for a review of the evidence).

Middle Neolithic assemblages are characterised by a variety of new arrowhead types: chisel, oblique and *petit tranchet* forms, knives including discoidal polished types, and maceheads. Many of the arrowheads were extremely finely retouched and may never have been intended for use, as, for example, in the case of chisel arrowheads of various forms from Durrington Walls (Wainwright and Longworth 1971). Brown (1991, 104) has argued that some transverse arrowheads, which have only been minimally retouched into a rough arrowhead shape, were symbolic items. An extremely large and roughly-shaped chisel arrowhead was recovered from the ditch of the Neolithic long enclosure at Yarnton, Oxfordshire (Bradley and Cramp in prep.), and another example came from a Neolithic pit at Terminal Five, Heathrow (Cramp 2006).

Edge polished and discoidal knives, often extensively worked, are also found at this time (Fig. 15.6). Examples have been recovered from individual burials (eg Barrow Hills (Bradley 1999, 224), Mount Farm (Bradley 2010), Linch Hill, Oxfordshire (Grimes 1960), and Five Knolls, Bedfordshire (Dunning and Wheeler 1931; Thomas 1962, 29, fig. 2)). A similar knife came from the secondary fills of the Millbarrow, Wiltshire long barrow (Pollard 1994,

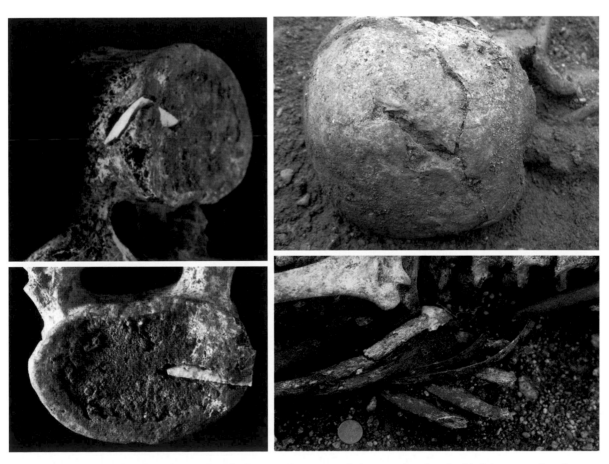

Fig. 16.10   Violence in the Neolithic and early Bronze Age: upper left: arrowhead embedded in a vertebra from Ascott-under-Wychwood; upper right: injury to the skull of a woman from a Beaker burial at the Oxford Centre for Gene Function; lower right: arrow head among the vertebrae and ribs of a skeleton from Barrow Hills, Radley

43, fig. 18). An early study of discoidal knives shows them clustering around Avebury and the Upper and Lower Thames (Clark 1928). Finds from the Thames are still being made, including, for example, a knife from Ewell (Field and Cotton 1987, 87, fig. 4.10). An edge polished knife was recovered from a scatter of worked flint, pottery and animal bone at Yarnton (Fig. 16.7; Bradley and Cramp in prep.), and a similar example came from the west chamber of the West Kennet long barrow (Piggott 1962, 48, fig. 15).

Other polished artefacts that appear at this time are maceheads, several examples of which have been found in the region. These artefacts are frequently carefully worked, and sometimes very attractive flint or stone was used, as, for example, in the case of maceheads from Dorchester-on-Thames and London (Fig. 12.42). A fragmentary flint macehead was recovered from a pit containing Peterborough Ware and other worked flint at Yarnton, Oxfordshire (Roe in prep.). This artefact seems to have broken and several of the pieces were reworked into other tools. At Cam, Gloucestershire an ovoid stone macehead was recovered from a pit containing Fengate Ware, worked flint, daub and animal bone (Smith 1968). A broken chalk macehead came from the long barrow at West Kennet (Piggott 1962, 48-9, fig. 16). This had broken in antiquity and the excavator suggested it may have been used as a pendant. Windmill Hill produced numerous maceheads (Pollard and Whittle 1999, 338-9, fig. 218, no. 1).

Bronze Age flintworking techniques

Bronze Age flintworking is again characterised by a change in arrowhead type, the barbed and tanged form replacing transverse and leaf-shaped types (Fig. 8.18). Very fine forms were produced, some with serrated edges akin to examples from mainland Europe, from Breton graves for example (Clarke *et al.* 1985, 136, figs 4.70, 4.73) which, in some instances, suggest the work of individual craftsmen. Examples of this type are relatively rare in Britain, but have been found in other parts of the country, for example at Queens Low, Staffordshire, Breach Farm, Glamorgan and Manchester airport (Bradley in prep.; Grimes 1938; F Wenban-Smith pers. comm.). A serrated bone barbed and tanged arrowhead was found on the foreshore at Chambers Wharf, Bermondsey and is likely to be early Bronze Age in date (Cotton and Green 2004, 138-9, figs 12-3). Some of these very fine, thin arrowheads must have been for display purposes as they would have been too fragile for use; the bone example may also have been symbolic.

At Barrow Hills a quiver of five arrows appears to have been deposited with a warrior who seems to have been killed, for a small arrowhead was found close to his spine (Bradley 1999, 141, fig 4.77; Fig. 16.10). The arrowheads provide an interesting contrast in this grave: those deposited in the quiver were finely made but the arrowhead that was the cause of death is extremely crude. If this artefact had been found alone, it would probably have been interpreted as a late type and not contemporary with the other arrowheads (Bradley 1999, 143, F99). This burial also had several other groups of flint artefacts which seem to have been deposited in bags or other containers (Barclay and Halpin 1999, 140, fig. 4.76).

At Holloway Lane, Hillingdon, six barbed and tanged arrowheads were found in an aurochs skeleton (Fig. 14.33), providing evidence for trophy hunting and perhaps the existence of an elite warrior class (Cotton *et al.* 2006). Interestingly at Holloway Lane the authors believe that the arrowheads were matched pairs defined by their size and shape (Cotton *et al.* 2006). At Yarnton six barbed and tanged arrowheads were found in a small group in a burial together with a very fine Beaker pot, inside which was a smaller pot and a flint scraper. The arrowheads may have been originally deposited in a bag or other container. They were all quite finely worked and seem to have been made by a single knapper. Another group of fine barbed and tanged arrowheads came from the rich burial 31 at Lambourn (Case 1956a, 22).

A range of neatly retouched knives, scrapers including so-called 'thumbnail' types, and fabricators were also used at this time. Characteristic early Bronze Age flintworking includes extensive, invasive retouching (Fig. 16.7). The emphasis on display items and the skill of the knapper seem to have been important at this time. Flint daggers epitomise the skill of the knapper and are likely to have been made in several specialised centres of production. Fine examples of daggers have been found at Shorncote, Glos (Fig. 16.7; Bradley 1995), Lambourn (barrow 17; Case 1956a), a flint dagger and a faceted hammerstone were recovered from a Beaker grave at Amesbury, Wiltshire (Clarke 1970, 445), and a number have been recovered from the river Thames (Fig. 14.35; see Chapter 14).

Stone working

Relatively little is known about the use of stone other than flint during the Mesolithic. Evidence exists for the exploitation and exchange of certain resources such as Portland chert, a little of which has been found in the Thames Valley (see above). At Thatcham soft ochreous sandstone found in the gravels could have been used as a pigment although there was no obvious sign of wear on the pieces recovered (Wymer 1962, 353; Healy *et al.* 1992, 47). Other worked stone was found at Thatcham: a piece of gritty quartzite had been flaked into a rough disc, a fragment of abraded sandstone may also have been worked, there was a small possible limestone bead, and numerous naturally-holed flints (Wymer 1962, 338, 353). The latter may have been collected and used as weights or for some other purpose. At Wawcott a chert core, a piece of worked slate and a piece of sandstone possibly used as a rubber were recovered (Froom 1976, 158, 160). These stones may have come from sources in Devon and the Vale of Pewsey (Froom 1976, 158).

During the Neolithic a wider range of stone was used for domestic, funerary and 'prestige' artefacts, and for architecture. Raw materials were chosen for a variety of reasons. Often these seem to be purely functional, as material for items such as querns, pin polishers, axe polishers and rubbers, but some contexts in which stone-working is evidenced suggests that this activity could have deeper significance. For example, the large axe polishing grooves on the stones of the West Kennet long barrow and avenue (Piggott 1962, 19-20, plate xiii; Gillings *et al.* 2000, 433) and at Fyfield (Malone 2001, 224, fig. 161) imply either that the act of axe polishing was important in the rituals that took place, or that the place itself imbued the axe with special properties. A portable axe polisher was recovered from a pit at Wallingford which also contained Fengate Ware pottery, worked flint including several small flakes and chips from a polished implement (Richmond 2005, 79, 89, fig. 5). It is likely that the small chips actually derived from an axe whilst it was being polished (Bradley 2005, 87).

Attractive stone was often chosen for slightly more exotic items such as jadeite for axes and a range of coloured, patterned flints and hard stones such as gneiss for maceheads. The distance over which some of this material was brought would have significantly enhanced its prestige. It is of note that some very hard and difficult to work stone such as flint and gneiss were used to make some of the most attractive maceheads. A macehead of banded greenish-grey metamorphosed sandstone from Dorchester-on-Thames would have been a striking object. It had been burnt, probably during a cremation rite, and was found with a flint fabricator, a flint flake and a bone 'skewer' pin (Fig. 12.42; Atkinson *et al.* 1951, 115-116, fig. 31, no. 149).

Stone querns, pin polishers and rubbers are relatively well known from sites in the Thames Valley. A range of imported sandstones were chosen for their abrasive properties, although to some extent locally available materials were used. Some sites provide good evidence for a wide range of stone materials. At the causewayed enclosure at Staines, for example, materials from as far away as the Lake District and North Wales were used, alongside more locally available stone (Robertson-Mackay 1987, 118-9, table 23). The relatively common reuse of such items indicates the importance of good raw materials, and the importance of increasing the longevity of objects that may have been seen as special in some way. At Barrow Hills, Radley a fragmentary Group 1 (Cornish) greenstone axe, reused as a rubber or grinder, was found in a pit associated with Grooved Ware, flint and animal bone (Barclay and Halpin 1999, 77). Quartzitic pebble hammers, a range of rubbers, a grinder, abraded pebbles and saddle quern fragments were recovered from the Hazleton North long cairn

(Saville 1990b, 176-8). A fragmentary quernstone was recovered from the long barrow at Burn Ground, Gloucestershire (Grimes 1960, fig. 32). Small assemblages of worked stone, including saddle querns, rubbers, smoothers and hammerstones were recovered from the long barrows at Ascott-under-Wychwood and Wayland's Smithy (Roe 2007, 315-18; Whittle 1991, 86, fig. 11, nos 9-10, 87). Interestingly, at Ascott-under-Wychwood the largest piece of saddle quern had been incorporated into the inner wall of the monument; this practice has also been noted at Burn Ground and Wayland's Smithy (Roe 2007, 318). An extensive assemblage of worked stone was recovered from the excavations at Windmill Hill which included rubbers, quernstones and pounders as well as a large number of imported axes (Pollard and Whittle 1999, 338-341).

Stone axes have been widely studied (Clough and Cummins 1979; Clough and Cummins 1988; Bradley 1990; Bradley and Edmonds 1993). The range of raw materials used has been extensively examined and detailed distribution maps plotted. The very special nature of certain axes has been well documented: a jadeite axe was deposited under the Sweet Track as a foundation deposit (Coles and Coles 1986, 59-60), chalk axes were buried at Woodhenge (Cunnington 1929, 112-3), and axes were deposited in the mounds of long barrows as at Skendleby and Stanwick (Bradley 2007). The latter site provides a rare link with the wood used to construct the long barrow as the damaged edge of the flint axe left a signature on the wood debris found in the ditches (Taylor 2007). In the Thames Valley there is some evidence for the special treatment of flint and stone axes: at Hazleton North a polished axe fragment was found in close association with a skull wedged between two orthostats, and was interpreted as probably having formed part of the grave goods (Saville 1990a, 165). At Wayland's Smithy the butt of a ground stone axe came from the fill of the primary barrow, contemporary with the secondary barrow (Whittle 1991, 86, fig. 11, no. 4, 87). At Barrow Hills, Radley an extensively worked flint axe fragment may have been placed within the fill of a linear mortuary structure as a grave offering (Barclay and Halpin 1999, 28-31, fig. 3.8, F6).

An enormous number of stone and flint axes have been dredged from the river Thames (Adkins and Jackson 1978; Holgate 1988a), many of which are very fine examples and may never have been intended for use (Fig. 14.35; see Chapter 14). The treatment of these artefacts may be akin to the foundation deposits described above.

Flint and stone maceheads of mid to late Neolithic date have been recovered from sites in the Thames Valley and from the river itself (Fig. 16.9). These examples are made of a variety of raw materials and some seem to have been deposited in formalised ways (see Chapter 14 and above).

The introduction of Beaker pottery brought with it a new set of stone implements that are frequently found in graves, as stray finds, or have been dredged from rivers, particularly the Thames. Often these items are made from stone from exotic sources, and some may have been display or ceremonial items. Elements of stone can be seen to fit into a wider package of grave goods, as, for example, in the case of stone wristguards and flint arrowheads associated with archery.

In the early Bronze Age a range of worked stone implements is generally found in graves which have, however, come from other contexts. These artefacts include shafthole implements (battle axes and axe hammers; Fig. 16.11), wristguards (Fig. 15.10), whetstones and 'sponge' fingers. Many of these artefacts have been very finely worked and may have been display items. A variety of battle axes and axe hammers come from the region (Roe 1979). Important finds include a battle axe from the East Kennet Barrow (G1c), which was found with a late style Beaker and a dagger (Clarke 1970, 446). At

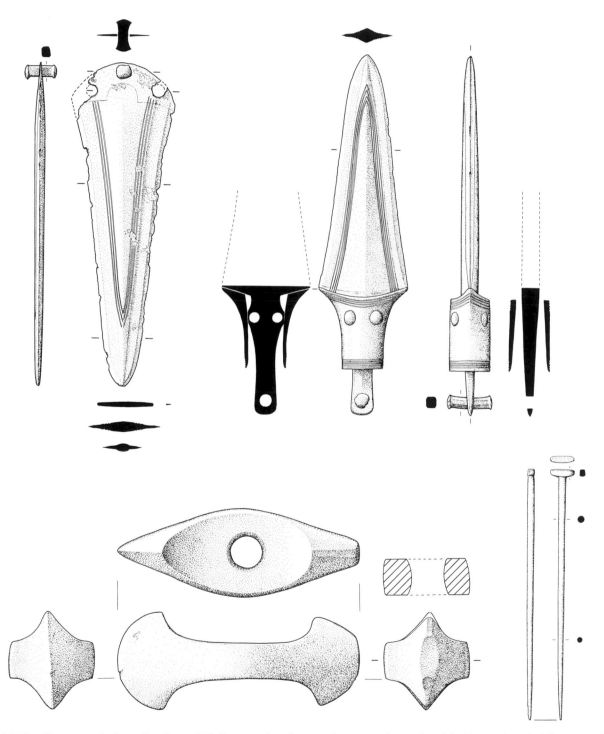

Fig. 16.11   Grave goods from the Snowshill Barrow: top: bronze dagger and spearhead; bottom; stone battle axe and bronze pin

Snowshill, Gloucestershire a picrite (Group 12) battle axe was found with a riveted bronze dagger, a bronze spearhead and a bronze pin (Fig. 16.11; Evens *et al.* 1972, 263; Greenwell 1890, 70-72). Further examples are known from Lambourn (Kinnes and Longworth 1985, 129) and Avebury (Keiller *et al.* 1941). Shafthole implements have also been recovered from the river Thames and may have been deposited with some formality (see Chapter 14).

Small whetstones, sometimes perforated, have been found in early Bronze Age graves and may have been part of a personal tool kit. Within the region examples have been recovered from Stanton Harcourt (Barclay 1995b, 97, fig. 52, 6) and Aldbourne, where the object was perforated (Greenwell 1890). Whetstones of 'sponge finger' type have been found at Gravelly Guy, Stanton Harcourt in a Beaker burial (Roe 2004, 91). Artefacts of this type are usually thought to have been used as whetstones or as leather-working tools. They are relatively rare with examples from outside the region in Wiltshire, Yorkshire and Wales (Roe 2004, 91, table 2.9).

An archer's personal equipment would have included a wristguard, a number of notable examples of which have been found in the Thames Valley. These generally accompany relatively rich burials. From the Thames Valley examples include wristguards from Sonning (Leeds 1939, 266), Gravelly Guy (Roe 2004, 90-1) and Stanton Harcourt (Case 1963), Cotswold Community, Shorncote (Powell *et al.* 2010), Dorchester-on-Thames (Whittle *et al.*1992) and Aldbourne (Kinnes and Longworth 1985, 128, no. 1). A recent study of the sources of these artefacts has shown that raw material selection was of importance (Woodward *et al.* 2006, 541-2). This study also showed that few of these artefacts had been used, suggesting that they were prestigious display items (ibid. 2006, 541).

Amber

Amber was used from at least early post-glacial times. However, although its distribution extends across Britain, finds of Mesolithic and Neolithic amber are rare (Beck and Shennan 1991, 65-9, figs 5.1-2). An amber bead was recovered from a middle Neolithic pit at Cranford Lane, Hillingdon (Hunt 1998, 578). Analysis by Beck and Shennan (1991) concluded that the vast majority of the objects they sampled are of Baltic amber. It is, however, difficult to determine the immediate source of amber since such material, which is chemically indistinguishable from the Baltic amber from northern Europe, occurs naturally along the eastern shores of England and Scotland. Nonetheless, its very scarcity in this country perhaps makes its importation more likely (Beck and Shennan 1991, 37), particularly in the early Bronze Age. Although a few finds of amber come from Beaker burials, the vast majority of finds are of early Bronze Age date and come from dagger graves, associated with Collared Urn

burials. By far the largest concentration of amber is centred on Wessex, but the Upper Thames has a few notable finds with necklaces of amber, and sometimes other beads coming from Barrow Hills, Radley (Fig. 14.26; Barclay and Halpin 1999, 164-5, fig. 5.12), Aldbourne, Wilts (G1; Greenwell 1890, 46-48; Grinsell 1957, 206), and Avebury (West Overton, G 23; Piggott 1938, 104; Grinsell 1957, 153). Small numbers of beads were found at Ashville, Abingdon (Parrington 1978, 27-8), Aldbourne G6 (Greenwell 1890, 50-53; Grinsell 1957, 147), Marshfield, barrow III (Gettins *et al.* 1954, 26-7, 37), and Stanton Harcourt, Barrow 4 (Harden and Treweeks 1945, 29).

At Field Farm, Burghfield 15 amber beads were found inside a large Collared Urn, together with two faience beads, two fragmentary copper alloy awls, a shale ring and a miniature Collared Urn vessel (Mepham 1992, 48 and fig. 18: 5). Six of the beads were found in a linear arrangement suggesting that they were originally part of a necklace; it seems likely that the two faience beads also came from this necklace (Mepham 1992, 48). The most noteworthy amber finds, however, come from the Manton barrow G1a, Preshute, just outside Marlborough (Beck and Shennan 1991, 167). These include a gold bound amber disc with a V-perforation, an amber pommel and five small beads (Fig. 16.3; Annable and Simpson 1964, 47; Cunnington 1908, 1-20; Grinsell 1957, 187-8; Piggott 1938, 105).

Shale, lignite and jet

Shale, lignite and jet appear to have been worked sporadically from the Mesolithic (Darvill 1987, 41). However, in the Middle and Upper Thames, there is little evidence for its use before the Neolithic. From the Neolithic onwards most shale and jet was probably imported as finished objects. Beads occur throughout the Neolithic and Bronze Age, while other items such as belt sliders, rings, buttons and amulets appear to have had short currencies. A small number of simple round or flattened oval beads are known from long barrows and causewayed enclosures (Fig. 16.2). Six beads of shale, jet and lignite were recovered from the chambers of the West Kennet long barrow (Piggott 1962, 51-3, fig. 18). Single beads came from chambered cairns at Notgrove (Clifford 1936; Clarke *et al.* 1985, 235) and Eyford, Gloucestershire (Kinnes and Longworth 1985, 109; Clarke *et al.* 1985, 234): both of these appear to have been included as grave goods. A shale bead was recovered from the middle ditch at Windmill Hill (Smith 1965a, fig. 58). A jet bead or pendant was found together with Grooved Ware in a pit at Yarnton (Fig. 16.2; Sheridan in prep.). At the Eton Rowing Course a single shale bead came from a Neolithic context (F Roe pers. comm.).

Several examples of middle Neolithic belt sliders of jet or shale have been recovered from sites in the Thames Valley. At Linch Hill and Barrow Hills, Radley belt sliders accompanied a male and a female inhumation burial respectively (Figs 16.2 and 15.6; Grimes 1960, 156; Barclay and Halpin 1999, 20, fig. 3.3, J1). Edge polished knives accompanied the female burials at Linch Hill and Radley (Grimes 1960, 156; Barclay and Halpin 1999, 20, fig. 33, F2). Within the region two other finds of belt sliders have been made although their contexts are less secure than those of the examples just cited. At Newbury a jet belt slider was recovered from a thick peat deposit and was associated with bones of red deer and cave bear (McInnes 1968, 140, fig. 29, no. 1, 142). Finally a jet belt slider was recovered from a dump of dredgings beside the Thames at Basildon, Berkshire (McInnes 1968, 140, fig. 29, no. 1a, 142).

A jet belt ring was associated with a Northern/Middle Rhine Beaker at Tolley's pit, Cassington (Clarke 1970, 311, no. 240, 439). A fine jet button came from a Beaker burial at Lambourn 31 (Clarke 1970, 388, no. 892). It was found with a male inhumation, a Beaker, six barbed and tanged arrowheads, an end scraper, a strike-a-light and two knives (Clarke 1970, 445).

A shale ring, associated with amber and faience beads, was found with an early Bronze Age burial at Field Farm, Berkshire, although the ring itself was considered too large to have been part of the necklace (Mepham 1992, 48). A small jet bead of uncertain form was found with bones at Childrey, Berkshire; it is likely to have come from a disturbed cremation in a round barrow (Longworth 1984, 263). A ring, pendant, V-perforated button and a fragmentary bead, all made of jet or shale were recovered from the burial at Aldbourne IV, Wiltshire (Greenwell 1890; Kinnes and Longworth 1985, 126-7). An extraordinary find from the Manton barrow, Preshute included a jet or shale necklace of 150 small circular beads (Fig. 16.5). This was a very rich burial which was accompanied by a range of amber, stone and bronze artefacts and two pottery accessory vessels (see above; Cunnington 1908).

As noted above, an early Bronze Age cremation at Barrow Hills, Radley contained a necklace of 14 beads including oblate, long and short fusiform types of jet or shale (Fig. 14.26; Barclay and Halpin 1999, 164-5, fig. 5.12).

An interesting group of finds from a cremation burial at Ashville included a jet or lignite ring and an axe pendant; beads of amber and bone were also recovered (Balkwill 1978, 26, fig. 26 nos 2-5, 28). A shale ring comparable to the example from Aldbourne (see above) was recovered from barrow 18 at Lambourn. A jet amulet or pendant was also found with this burial (Case 1956a, 26, fig. 8). At Stanton Harcourt a Wessex culture cremation contained a rich finds assemblage which included three beads of amber, jet and fossil sponge (Barclay 1995b, 97, fig. 52, 5a-c). A perforated shale whetstone was also recovered (Barclay 1995b, 97, fig. 52, 6)

Shells, fossils and other natural materials

Perforated and polished marine and fossil shells have been found at a number of sites of Neolithic and Bronze Age date. By the wrists of an inhumation burial in the Lambourn long barrow were two polished and perforated dog whelk shells, possibly the remains of a bracelet or necklace (Wymer 1965-6, 8). Other similar examples have been found at the Nympsfield (Kennard 1938, 191, 210) and West Kennet long barrows (Piggott 1962, 51-3, fig. 18, no. 19). At West Kennet shells of several species (periwinkle, cowrie, and dog whelk) were perforated and presumably used in necklaces or as pendants, as was an unperforated *Dentalium* shell (Fig. 16.2).

A deposit of 70 marine shells was recovered from the lower fills of ring ditch XIV at Dorchester-on-Thames (Whittle *et al.* 1992, 166) although no information is available as to whether these had been modified or not. Fragments of a scallop shell and possibly of a clam shell were also found at Cotswold Community (Powell *et al.* 2010).

At Aldbourne G4 two fossils, a bivalve and an unmodified encrinoid cast, were found together with beads of amber, shale and faience (Fig. 15.27; Kinnes 1994, 42-3, nos 9, 13). The bivalve had been polished but the naturally holed encrinoid could have been used as a bead in its unmodified state. A small piece of polished haematite was also recovered from the same grave group (Kinnes 1994, 42-3, no. 12). Another fossil encrinite used as a bead was found with jet or shale, amber and stone beads in the Manton barrow, Preshute (Cunnington 1908, 9). Several fossil echinoids were recovered from the excavations at Ascott-under-Wychwood, one of which is believed to have been deliberately placed in the southern outer passage (Roe 2007, 316-17, fig. 13.2, no.1).

At Notgrove a naturally perforated stone was found in the central passage (Clifford 1936, 130, fig. 3). Other natural materials that are occasionally found in Beaker burials include iron pyrites which was probably used as part of a fire making kit (cf Cave-Browne 1992). In the Thames Valley examples of pyrites have been found at Barrow Hills, Radley (Barclay and Halpin 1999, 140, 143, fig. 4.79, S4) and Lambourn (Case 1956a, 23, 24, fig. 6).

Faience

A few finds of segmented, spherical or elongated-spherical faience beads have been found in the Thames Valley. Faience is a blue glass-like material, glazed with copper salts, made by firing ground quartz, the manufacture of which would not have presented any technical problems for anyone capable of smelting copper (Renfrew and Newton 1979, 300-301). One complete faience bead and a fragmentary second example were recovered from a Collared Urn at Field Farm, Burghfield (Mepham 1992, 48). These were associated with amber beads and are likely to have formed a necklace (Mepham

1992, 48). Three faience beads, also from the fill of a Collared Urn, were found at Hurst Park, East Molesey (Laidlaw 1996, 91, fig. 52, nos 2-4). A single segmented faience bead came from an amber and shale bead necklace from barrow 16, Barrow Hills, Radley (Fig. 14.26; Barclay and Halpin 1999, fig. 5.12). A possibly Bronze Age faience bead came from a cremation deposit along the Newbury pipeline (Timby *et al.* 2005). However, this was thought to be Romano-British and its dating is uncertain. Necklaces of amber, faience and jet typify Wessex culture burials at the end of early Bronze Age, and can be paralleled at Upton Lovell G1, Wilsford G3 and Amesbury G48, Wiltshire (Annable and Simpson 1964, 108, 112).

Organic materials

Woodworking

There is very little direct evidence for the use of wood, bark and resin during this period in the Thames Valley. In the Upper Thames this is partly because, even on the floodplain of the Thames, the valley was dry land, and even ditches and pits do not provide wet environments for the preservation of organic material. Conditions in the Middle Thames, however, were more conducive to water-logging. Without doubt, wood would have been an important material for making tools, utensils, structures and boats. Comparisons with sites elsewhere, in the Fens (Pryor 1998), the Somerset Levels (Coles and Coles 1986), and Cumbria (Darbyshire 1874) provide reminders of what is often lost from the archaeological record.

In the Middle Thames, sites at Runnymede and Manor Farm, Horton, have produced organic finds. At Horton five or six fragmentary birch-bark containers were recovered from the base of the ditch of an oval barrow (Fig. 16.12; Ford and Pine 2003, 20). These vessels, although badly decayed, were probably fairly substantial and may have had lids; one example seems to have been smaller and may have been a bowl (Ford and Pine 2003, 20). They were constructed from strips of birch bark secured with lime bast fibres (Cartwright 2003, 54). Little evidence was recovered for the function of these containers but a split fragment of animal bone was recovered from the interior surface of one (Cartwright 2003, 54). Fragments of worked wood including a possible spear were recovered from the same length of ditch as the birch-bark containers (Ford and Pine 2003, 22). Wooden piles and a fragment of worked birch were recovered from Neolithic layers at Runnymede Bridge (Heal 1991, 140-1, plates 17-18); the latter may have been stitched.

Indirect evidence for the use of wood has been recovered from burials in the region where wooden trays and coffins survive as soil stains or deposits of charred material. At Barrow Hills, Radley evidence for wooden coffins, biers or trays was recovered from Beaker flat grave 950 and early Bronze Age

barrows 2, 12 and 15 (Barclay and Halpin 1999, 59, 149, 318, 161). The remains of a wooden coffin or lining were also identified at Gravelly Guy (Lambrick and Allen 2004, 54, plate 2.3) and Linch Hill (Grimes 1960, 159, fig. 66). Wood has also been identified in the corrosion products of Bronze artefacts. At Barrow Hills, for example, an awl and a knife-dagger retained traces of wood (Watson 1999, 138, 144). However, these provide relatively limited information about the construction of these artefacts. A possible wooden scabbard with associated fragments of leather was identified at Gravelly Guy (Watson 2004, 87), but these preserved organics were too decayed for precise identification to be made.

An early Neolithic mineralised wooden container was discovered at the bottom of a large pit adjacent to the longhouse at Yarnton; it might have been a small tub (Fig. 16.12; Hey in prep.). The cremated remains of a woman were found at the top of the same feature, bones from which were dated to 3655-3535 cal BC (OxA-14479: 4867±35 BP and SUERC-5689: 4775±35 BP). The same site produced evidence of an early Bronze Age bark container (1880-1620 cal BC; OxA-8929: 3415±40 BP) in a shallow pit near to a palaeochannel, which has possible stitch marks around one edge (Taylor in prep.). A number of early to mid Bronze Age waterholes have also yielded waterlogged wood, including a log ladder (1750-1520 cal BC; OxA-8673: 3365±40 BP) and a bowl (Fig. 16.13; 1680-1430 cal BC; OxA-9779: 3258±39 BP; Hey in prep.). Log ladders seem to have been commonly used to access deep waterholes, particularly where these had been cut into sand or gravel (Taylor in prep.). Although a number of variations occur, mainly with forks at the top or bottom, the alder ladder from Yarnton appears to be of a very simple design with four steps, *c* 70 mm deep, surviving, and evidence that further steps had existed above and below. The wooden bowl had been manufactured using a bronze palstave with a blade 55 mm wide and 7 mm deep, and then finished very finely on the interior, with a smaller tool leaving facets 32 mm wide and 2 mm deep. 'Bruising' scrapes on the interior seem to have been the result of scraping out; further residue appears to lie within the cut marks (ibid.).

Just outside the study area, in the Lower Thames Valley, are two important finds from the river Thames. An alder wood club or beater of early Neolithic date was recovered from the Thames foreshore at Chelsea (Fig. 16.12; Webber with Ganiaris 2004, 125-6, fig. 14.1). It may have been used to kill or stun animals or wildfowl; it could also have been used as an efficient weapon. A perhaps even more remarkable find is the anthropomorphic carved wooden idol from Dagenham (Fig. 16.12; Coles 1990, 320, plate 29). This was found in a peat deposit, approximately 30 m away from the skeleton of a large animal, possibly a deer (Coles 1990, 320). It was made from

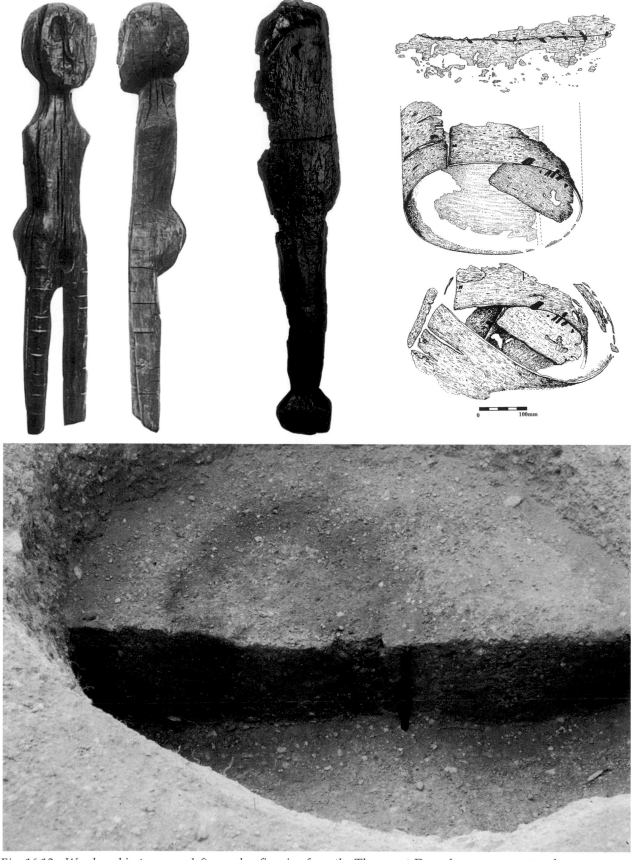

Fig. 16.12 *Wooden objects: upper left: wooden figurine from the Thames at Dagenham; upper centre: beater or 'club' from the Thames at Chelsea; upper right: birch bark container from Horton; bottom: mineralised wooden bucket from Yarnton* in situ

Fig. 16.13   Early Bronze Age wood and bark objects from Yarnton: from top to bottom: wooden bowl; weaving sword; log ladder; part of a bark vessel

yew (although originally identified as pine; J Cotton pers. comm.) and has been radiocarbon dated to 2360-2140 cal BC (OxA-1721: 4310-4080 cal BP; Coles 1990, 326).

Worked bone, horn and antler

Although bone and antler was worked in the Mesolithic period, the evidence from the Upper and Middle Thames Valley is rather sparse. To a large extent this is the result of poor preservation and the fact that a number of Mesolithic sites are located on acidic soils. There are a few finds of bone and antler tools, including antler mattocks, from the Eton Rowing Course (Allen *et al.* in prep.) and from the river Thames and its foreshore ((Fig. 10.15; Cotton and Green 2004, 126-7).

Sites along the Kennet Valley have produced a range of worked bone and antler. At Thatcham for example there is evidence for Mesolithic bone and antler working (Wymer 1962, 351-2). Here a range of tools and weapons, including pins, bodkins, spear-heads and arrowheads, of both bone and antler was recovered (Wymer 1962, 351-2, plate L).

The evidence for bone and antler working in the Neolithic and early Bronze Age is better. Objects can be divided into heavy tools for digging, quarrying and building and smaller tools for craft and manufacture and personal dress items.

Heavy tools, such as antler picks and rakes and ox scapula shovels have been found on monuments in the Upper and Middle Thames (eg Hazleton North, Levitan 1990; Dorchester-on-Thames, Atkinson *et al.* 1951; Barrow Hills, Radley, Barclay and Halpin 1999; Manor Farm, Horton, Ford and Pine 2003). Picks and rakes would have required the collection of red deer antler which, with little modification, could then be put to use as simple digging tools. Bruce Levitan has described their design in detail in his discussion of such implements from Hazleton North (1990, 205-9). Not surprisingly, these tools have been found either placed or discarded within the ditches of long cairns, causewayed enclosures, ring ditches and henges. Antler picks were also sometimes deposited in Beaker graves, albeit largely outside the Thames Valley (Clarke 1970).

A variety of small bone and antler tools including knives, chisels, gouges, combs, awls, pins and points have also been recovered from a wide range of sites. Some of these tools appear to have had special functions. Bone implements were used for knapping flint either as hammers or for pressure flaking, as, for example, at Barrow Hills, Radley (Barclay, Serjeantson and Wallis 1999, 235-6) and Stanton Harcourt field XV (Hamlin 1963, 21-3). Bone tools were also used in the manufacture of pottery. Ribs and other bones were, for example, probably used to finish, smooth and burnish surfaces, and a variety of bone implements were used to decorate vessels. The grooves, dots, and stamps found on early Neolithic decorated styles were probably created using a bone tool kit (Avery 1982, 29). The same is true of some

types of middle Neolithic Impressed Wares, on which small mammal bones were used, and the articular surfaces in particular, to create distinct patterns. The grooved lines and ovals on late Neolithic pottery would have been created by a variety of bone points. Some Beaker pottery was also decorated using bone tools, and it has been argued that bone and antler spatulae, frequent finds in Beaker graves, could have been used to burnish pottery. Rarely, bone combs or notched stamps used to decorate comb-impressed vessels have been found, including an example from the Marlborough Downs (Cleal 1992c). Simpson has reviewed the evidence for comb impressions on Beaker pottery and found that limpet and cockle shells could also have been used to produce comb-like impressions (2004, 210, fig. 4).

Bone awls, points and pins have been found in numerous late Neolithic pits within the region (Figs 16.2 and 12.22; see Barclay, Serjeantson and Wallis 1999, 235 for a summary of the evidence); these are often of fairly simple form but can sometimes be made of unusual species. For example, a possible awl from a pit at Barrow Hills, Radley containing Grooved Ware, worked flint and stone artefacts was made from a white-tailed eagle bone (Barclay, Serjeantson and Wallis 1999, 235).

Modified and perforated boars' tusks have come from a number of sites in the region, including Mount Farm and Barrow Hills, Radley (Barclay, Serjeantson and Wallis 1999, 236, fig. 4.6, WB1). A splinter of a boar's tusk knife or point came from the secondary filling at West Kennet chambered tomb (Piggott 1962, 50). Two boar's tusk points or fragments came from barrow IV, Aldbourne (Kinnes and Longworth 1985, 127, nos 27-8).

Chisels, gouges and knives have been found at a number of early Neolithic sites (eg Abingdon (Avery 1982, 42-3), Windmill Hill (Smith 1965a), West Kennet (Piggott 1962) and the Eton Rowing Course (T Allen pers. comm.). It is likely that such tools had a longer currency since edge-polished bone knives have been found associated with Grooved Ware in the Middle Thames.

A bone scoop made from a limb bone of an aurochs was found in a pit containing Grooved Ware, worked flint and animal bone at Lower Mill Farm, Stanwell (Jones and Ayres 2004, 151). Other similar examples have been found at West Kennet, Windmill Hill and Stonehenge (Jones and Ayres 2004, 151). Although their function is unknown, they may have been used for skinning.

Personal items such as dress pins, beads, and belt fasteners occur throughout the Neolithic and early Bronze Age. Bone beads of simple rounded or cylindrical form occur in some early Neolithic funerary deposits including West Kennet (Fig. 16.2; Piggott 1962, 49-50, fig. 17, 52, fig. 18) and Hazleton North (Saville 1990b, 178, 180, fig. 177). Skewer pins came from the late Neolithic cremation deposits at Dorchester-on-Thames (Fig. 12.42; Atkinson *et al.* 1951) and also from an earlier context at the Sale's

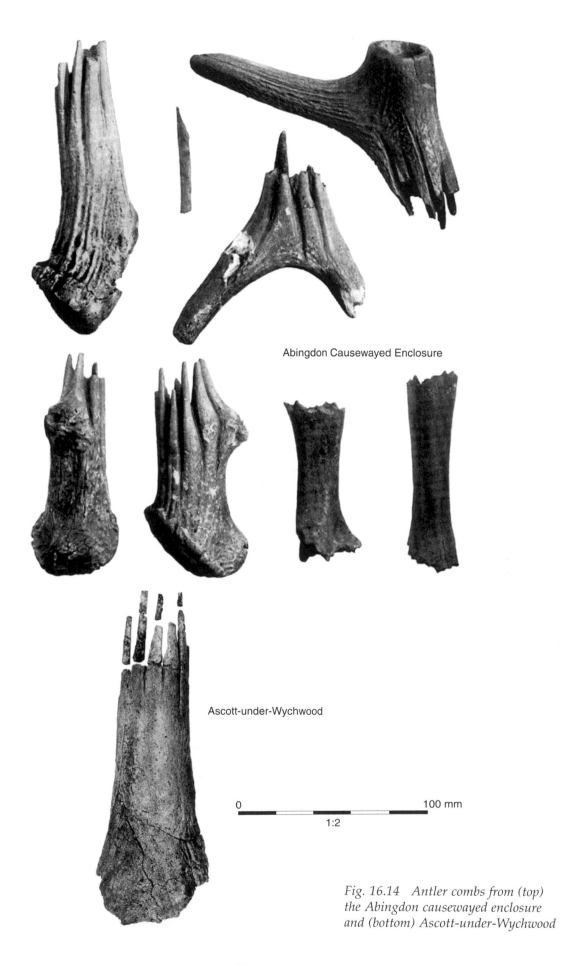

Abingdon Causewayed Enclosure

Ascott-under-Wychwood

0   100 mm

1:2

Fig. 16.14   Antler combs from (top)
the Abingdon causewayed enclosure
and (bottom) Ascott-under-Wychwood

Lot barrow (O'Neill 1966). There is evidence for bone bead manufacture at Windmill Hill (Smith 1965a). Pierced bone phalanges have been recovered from numerous sites including the chambered tomb at West Kennet (Piggott 1962; Fig. 16.2). In the later Neolithic and early Bronze Age, bone beads are scarcer, perhaps as other materials such as shale, jet, amber and faience became more popular. A perforated circular bone disc was found in a Beaker flat grave at Barrow Hills, Radley (Fig. 16.2; Barclay and Halpin 1999, 57, 4.14, WB2). Contemporary parallels for this object have not been found but it is likely to have functioned as a button, toggle or pendant (Barclay, Serjeantson and Wallis 1999, 236).

Bone pins for fastening either clothing or hair occur in the later Neolithic/early Bronze Age. The long skewer pins which occur as grave goods within the cemeteries at Dorchester-on-Thames (Fig. 12.42; Atkinson *et al.* 1951, 114, nos 140-1, 146) have already been mentioned. Other bone pins occur in graves, including the unique winged-headed pin from a Beaker grave at Barrow Hills, Radley (Fig. 16.2; Needham 1999b, 236, fig.4.23, WB4). Needham argues that this pin could have been a copy of metal ones found in mainland Europe. Bone belt fasteners include examples from a Beaker burial at Linch Hill Corner, Stanton Harcourt (Fig. 15.10; Grimes 1960, 161, fig. 67) and a probable cremation burial at Wytham near Oxford (Kinnes and Longworth 1985, 132). Belt fasteners similar to the Linch Hill Corner example have been found in other areas, including, for example, Wessex (A303 road improvements; Leivers and Moore 2008, 27, fig. 15). Other bone objects which occur in some early Bronze Age cremation deposits include pins, ring-headed pins and tweezers (Barrow Hills, Radley: Barclay and Halpin 1999, 147-8, figs 4.82-3; Aldbourne Barrow X: Kinnes and Longworth 1985, 128).

A number of antler combs have been found in Neolithic contexts in the area (Fig. 16.14). Most of these were recovered from the Abingdon cause-wayed enclosure, where around 15 were discovered in the excavations of the 1930s, but one also came from Ascott-under-Wychwood long barrow and another from the recent excavations at Windmill Hill (Avery 1982; Benson and Whittle 2007; Whittle *et al.* 1999). These combs may have been used for grooming or during hide preparation to dehair pelts (Serjeantsen pers. comm.). Antler maceheads have been found, although these are all from the London and Lower Thames foreshore (Fig. 14.35). They seem to belong to the second half of 4th millennium (Loveday *et al.* 2007).

Evidence for bone weaponry or display items is quite rare but a number of objects have been found within the region. A rare bone barbed and tanged arrowhead has been recovered from the river Thames at Bermondsey (see above, Cotton and Green 2004, 138-9, figs 12-13) and is assumed to be a copy of Beaker flint arrowheads. Examples of bone daggers would also appear to copy flint and metal

examples (Gerloff 1975, plate 28, nos 347-351). Complex bone and horn hilts and pommels have been found in Beaker contexts, which exemplify the craftsmanship of the makers. A fine example came from a Beaker grave at Gravelly Guy, Oxfordshire (Fig. 16.3; Gerloff 2004, 84-5), detailed examination of which showed it to have had a horn hilt and an antler pommel (Watson 2004, 86-7; plate 2.8, fig. 2.20). At Barrow Hills, Radley a dagger had an antler shaft with a possible contrasting pommel of horn (Watson 1999, 155). At Foxley Farm, Eynsham a dagger with a bone pommel came from a Beaker grave (Clarke 1970, 447).

Textiles, fibres, leather and resin

The materials discussed in this section are rarely preserved on archaeological sites, except, occasionally, on waterlogged sites. In the Thames Valley chance preservation, usually in corrosion products of metal artefacts or in other exceptional circumstances, has enabled some information to be gleaned allowing us to build up a picture of the types of organic materials used in prehistory. Traces of fabric were identified on a bronze knife from Lambourn (barrow 1: Case 1956a, 19). At Barrow Hills, Radley a small piece of textile was also identified on a flat riveted knife-dagger from barrow 1. It was possible to say that this piece of textile was probably of animal origin and had been plain woven (Wallis and Hedges 1999, 145). A coarse thread running between the rivet holes of the knife-dagger was also identified. Hairs were preserved in the corrosion products on another knife-dagger from the central cremation in barrow 4, Barrow Hills, Radley (Watson 1999, 155, 5.6). A possible decorated sheath fragment, originally believed to be leather, was also recovered from barrow 1, Barrow Hills, Radley (Barclay, Needham and Wallis 1999, 145). During earlier excavations at the same site traces of a possible leather sheath were found under the knife-dagger in barrow 3 (Barclay and Halpin 1999, 153). Another fragmentary sheath was identified at Stanton Harcourt (Barclay 1995b, 97).

Evidence for the use of mastic for hafting has been identified from the Mesolithic onwards but rarely survives (Aveling 1997, 84). Mastic, probably made using resin from birch bark (although analysis using infrared spectroscopy could not confirm this identification), was, however, found on a flint flake from the Mesolithic site at Thatcham (Site III), and has been dated to 8640 - 8260 cal BC (OxA-2848; 9200±90; Roberts et al. 1998). A small piece of the same material was found nearby (Wymer 1962, 353). Traces of animal fats and beeswax were identified on barbed and tanged arrowheads found in an aurochs skeleton at Holloway Lane, Harmondsworth (Cotton *et al.* 2006), which are presumably the remains of mastic used for hafting. Although no analysis was undertaken, the Shorncote dagger bears faint marks between its notches which may indicate where bindings held the haft in place

(Bradley 1995). Traces of a glutinous substance, possibly fish skin or leather, were noted by Martin Atkins on some of the barbed and tanged arrowheads from barrow 31, Lambourn (Case 1956a, 21). Again, this is likely to have been the remains of hafting materials. The same material was also noted on a group of flints, including a flint dagger, from barrow 17 (Case 1956a, 23, 24, fig. 6, no. 5).

What may be charred fibres have been found in Mesolithic peats at Culham Reach (Wessex Archaeology unpubl. excavations), which may derive from clothing or other textiles.

NEW TECHNOLOGIES

Pottery: a novel technology

Pottery production was a novel technology, introduced at the start of the 4th millennium cal BC. It was used to make containers for the cooking and serving of food, and was no doubt tied to new and perhaps more formal ways of sharing food. Its uptake seems to have been quite rapid as similar vessels can be found across most of Britain and Ireland with clear antecedents in the neighbouring areas of mainland Europe. Currently the evidence points to the importation of ideas and a transfer of skills rather than long distance exchange of vessels. Within the study area there are a number of important assemblages of early date (Barclay and Case 2007; Smith and Darvill 1990). Pottery was much more rarely used for making other small objects such as 'spoons' and beads. The earliest pottery assemblage of known date occurs at Ascott-under-Wychwood and can be placed within the 39th-38th centuries cal BC.

The place of potting within the community

As discussed above it is likely that most pottery production was organised by individual households or families as there remains scant evidence that pottery was a specialised craft or the result of centralised production. In fact there is only slight evidence that pots were ever moved over more than relatively short distances.

Pottery production was probably undertaken as a seasonal activity by semisedentary communities that shifted between locales on a cyclical, perhaps seasonal basis (Barclay and Case 2007). Our present understanding of habitation practices of the 4th to early 2nd millennia cal BC is based on a model of impermanent and episodic settlement (see Chapter 11). This suggests that pottery would have to have been carried or stored as people moved from place to place. A 'site' assemblage may thus simply reflect the pottery discarded at that place either through deliberate or accidental action rather than providing an accurate representation of the full range of pottery in use. In the early Neolithic pottery appears to have been accumulated in occupation or midden deposits at both open sites and monuments. Pottery was also placed in pit deposits and as votive deposits within watery places. It was in the period from the mid 3rd millennium to the 2nd millennium cal BC that pottery was, for the first time, deliberately placed in graves.

The analysis of pottery fabrics in the Upper and Middle Thames nearly always concludes that materials for potting were obtained locally. This has been demonstrated at any number of sites (eg Yarnton, the Eton Rowing Course, Ascott and Hazleton: Barclay *et al.* in prep; Barclay and Case 2007, and Smith and Darvill 1990). There is often evidence that a variety of clay sources and tempers were used at any one time. Choice of temper also reflects the availability of resources such as flint, quartzite or shell/limestone. These materials were sometimes used in the same periods, the particular temper in use depending on where the sites in question are located and the nature of local geological deposits. Like other areas of the country, there were, however, changes in the choice of temper over time. In the early Neolithic most pottery was flint-, shell/limestone- or sand-tempered, while the middle Neolithic saw increased use of quartzite and the first use of grog (ceramic fragments obtained by crushing fired pots). Late Neolithic Grooved Ware tends to be either shell- or grog-tempered, while the use of hard materials like flint and quartzite was very rare. The use of shell-temper in Woodlands- and Clacton-style vessels, and of grog in vessels belonging to the Durrington style seems also to reflect deliberate choices (Barclay 1999b). In the Beaker period and the early Bronze Age grog was predominantly used. Because changes in temper seem to coincide with cultural and stylistic change, it is generally argued that the temper was chosen not just for technological reasons. Some temper types such as flint and quartzite would have been highly visible, while others such as grog would have been invisible. The use of a variety of local temper types could have been a way of expressing identity, especially were pots where used in large social gatherings such as communal feasts.

Potting materials may have been procured while other routine tasks of Neolithic life were being undertaken within the landscape, with materials being gathered from multiple sources. As such it may have been scheduled to take place at certain times of the year and to have been carried out by certain members of the community (Barclay 2007). There would have been a need to replace old and broken pots and pots that had gone bad or sour. It is possible, also, that social circumstance sometimes required the making of fresh pots. It is likely that the use-life of pots was short because of the semipermanent nature of settlement, and that the risk of breakage was high because of the cycle of shifting residence, the lack of permanent storage, and the predominant use of vessels for cooking and serving, in addition to accidental breakage due to other factors such as the presence of children and animals

(Arnold 1985, 153; Rice 1987, 297-8 and fig. 9.4).

The evidence for non-local pots and specialist products is slight but includes two very fine Wessex/Middle Rhine Beakers both of which were recovered from single graves (Fig. 15.10). One came from a flat grave at Yarnton, and the other was from a Beaker barrow placed just outside the Big Rings henge at Dorchester-on-Thames. The Beakers are not identical: they differ in height and only one is decorated around the base. However, the profile and firing are similar and, more significantly, the decoration is almost identical. What this probably means is that the pots co-existed, with a strong possibility that one person or group of people were involved in the production of the two vessels. The sites are some 20 km apart. Interestingly the Yarnton Beaker held a smaller vessel that had been tempered with ironstone inclusions suggesting that it too was a non-local product. This Beaker is likely to derive from north Oxfordshire or even Northamptonshire. Another Beaker from Yarnton with rusticated finger-tip decoration is very similar to a vessel from a grave at Foxley Farm, Eynsham. Here we have evidence that either the potter or the pot moved a distance of 7 km along the valley.

Development of pottery production and decoration (Fig 8.18)

The pottery of the earliest Neolithic consists of a range of round-based bowls and cups. Occasionally vessels are thin-walled and well made but coarser vessels occur too. Rims tend to be simple and sometimes squared in profile. Shoulders, where present, can be angular and sometimes elaborately stepped or enhanced with a slight lip or lip and groove. Vessel profiles tend to be open with tall concave necks and relatively low shoulders. It is possible, based on limited radiocarbon evidence, to divide these assemblages into early and later groups, a division which may reflect developments in pottery style which include the adoption of features such as rolled rims. Early assemblages include Ascott-under-Wychwood and Canon Hill, Maidenhead and later assemblages include Hazleton North, Cherhill, Eton Rowing Course Area 6 and Staines Road, Shepperton (Barclay forthcoming; Barclay and Case 2006). In chronological terms the early assemblages appear to belong to the period 4000-3800 cal BC and the later assemblages to the period 3800-3650 cal BC.

After about 3650 cal BC there is a development towards the manufacture of vessels with more upright necks and less angular shoulders that are often set higher up the vessel profile. In some assemblages shoulders are lost all together. Rims become heavier. New bowl forms occur and vessels are sometimes lugged or decorated.

The Plain and Decorated Bowl styles represent subsequent developments of the Bowl tradition in the middle centuries of the 4th millennium cal BC. The Decorated Bowl style appears at much the same time as causewayed enclosures and the two are often found in association. Highly decorated pottery is, in fact, rarely found in any other context (Barclay 2002). The use of terms such as Abingdon Ware to describe assemblages generally masks their complex character. Cleal (1992d, 303) has argued that the use of such type-site terminology should be abandoned or at least not given such primary importance. Whilst there may never have been an Abingdon Ware, it is certainly possible to recognise an Abingdon Style. A better and more sympathetic approach to early Neolithic pottery would be to classify and quantify vessel types in a standardised way as advocated by Cleal (1992d). At present finer detail, and the similarities between different assemblages, is perhaps masked by attempts to classify entire assemblages as belonging to a particular style. Smith (1965a, 223-7, vessels 194, 198-9, 201) was able to identify several Abingdon Ware style vessels at Windmill Hill, while at Abingdon it is possible to recognise vessels more typical of the decorated assemblage from Windmill Hill. At Staines some of the decorated pottery appears more like the Mildenhall style vessels that occur at Orsett (Robertson-Mackay 1987, fig. 48: p1. 36; Kinnes 1978), while other vessels are more like Abingdon Ware and others more like those from the open site at Runnymede (Avery 1982; Kinnes 1991). A similar argument came be made for the pottery from the probable enclosure at Maiden Bower (Piggott 1931, 90, fig. 6).

Peterborough Ware (or Impressed Ware) is perhaps the least understood of the Neolithic pottery styles (Figs 14.13 and 14.35), and unlike Grooved Ware or Beakers there has been no serious attempt at typological analysis. It appears to belong to a middle Neolithic period, although its origins are not well defined. It probably developed sometime after the main phase of causewayed enclosures, appearing sometime in the 36th century cal BC and becoming more widespread from about 3300 cal BC until at least 2900 cal BC (Barclay 2007 and see also Gibson and Kinnes 1997). Within the study area, early assemblages of Peterborough Ware are associated with the cursus at Drayton and with occupation deposits at Yarnton and Runnymede (Barclay *et al*. in prep.). These early assemblages (termed Ebbsfleet Ware) are defined by round bodied bowls and jars, which are often only minimally decorated. By about 3300 cal BC this style had developed into a range of cups, bowls and jars.

Assemblages include a variety of vessel forms, and although bowls are most numerous other types such as jars, dishes and cups also occur (Barclay *et al*. in prep.). The size range is similar to that of earlier Neolithic pottery with rim diameters ranging from 50-400 mm. Of the three defined substyles (Ebbsfleet, Mortlake and Fengate) more variation is perhaps found within Mortlake Ware assemblages. A variety of forms also occurs within the Fengate substyle but rarely with the Ebbsfleet.

Large assemblages of Peterborough Ware have been recovered from the Thames Valley, and paradoxically the largest is from the filling of the chambers within the West Kennet long barrow. This assemblage is surprisingly varied and includes a wide variety of vessel forms. Other relatively large assemblages come from Yarnton, from pit deposits at Lake End Road West near Maidenhead and from the ditches of the Windmill Hill causewayed enclosure (Smith 1965a).

Ebbsfleet Ware (especially 'early' Ebbsfleet) is found as a component of surface middens at a number of sites located close to rivers (eg Drayton and Runnymede) and at the type-site of Ebbsfleet itself (Burchell and Piggott 1939). It is also found associated with some cursus sites, notably Dorchester-on-Thames and Drayton, at the Staines causewayed enclosure and at both long barrows and long cairns in secondary contexts. So-called 'early' Ebbsfleet Ware is found at a number of Cotswold-Severn cairns where it is generally recovered from secondary contexts associated with the blocking or closing down of these monuments (Darvill 1982, 22, fig. 4). Very rarely is Ebbsfleet Ware recovered from either pit deposits or from watery contexts (Lawrence 1929, fig. 1.2).

Mortlake Ware is frequently found in pit deposits, at cursus sites and in the ditches of some Neolithic monuments (Figs 14.13 and 14.35). It is the most common substyle found in watery contexts. It is sometimes found with either Ebbsfleet or Fengate Ware and more rarely with Clacton style Grooved Ware (eg Gravelly Guy: Cleal in Lambrick and Allen 2004).

Fengate Ware is frequently found in pit deposits. It is rarely found in watery contexts with the notable exception of two bowls from the Thames at Wandsworth and Mortlake, respectively (Smith 1918, 11, figs 9-10; Lawrence 1929, 84, fig. 1.3) or in association with monuments. However, one interesting deposit is the complete bowl from the base of the ditch of an oval barrow at Horton (Ford and Pine 2003).

The majority of the known Grooved Ware sites are found on the low-lying gravel terraces close to the river Thames as well as along the Colne Valley. Nearly all of these sites have been excavated in advance of mineral extraction (Barclay 1999b; Barclay 2007). Concentrations of Grooved Ware are thus largely a product of archaeological fieldwork as a response to gravel extraction and other forms of development. Even so, there is a marked difference between sites in the Colne Valley and Middle Thames and those in the Upper Thames. In the Colne Valley, Grooved Ware pits seem to be less numerous and more scattered and isolated (Barclay 1999b). In contrast, at Yarnton excavation on the floodplain revealed a major Neolithic landscape including an important range of Grooved Ware associated contexts (Hey 1994; in prep.).

All three southern Grooved Ware substyles as defined by Wainwright and Longworth (1971, 235-

68) have been found in this region (Barclay 1999b). There are, to some extent, similarities between the Woodlands and Clacton Substyles within this region and the two styles seem to merge (Jones 1976). The chronological evidence for Grooved Ware fits into the framework suggested by Garwood (1999a) with Clacton predating Woodlands.

There are no dates directly associated with the Durrington Walls substyle. At Radley many fragments from a plain Grooved Ware bowl were stratified above placed deposits of antler and cattle limbs in the ditch fill of a hengiform monument. The animal bone produced two radiocarbon determinations – 2580-2040 cal BC and 2870-2200 cal BC (BM-2712-3: 3860±80 BP and 3950±80 BP respectively) – which provide a *terminus post quem* for the deposition of this vessel (Barclay and Halpin 1999; Garwood 1999b).

The Durrington Walls style is represented by assemblages comprising plain cordoned jars or cordoned jars with decorated panels. Plain cordon vessels have been recovered from a number of sites including Abingdon Common (Balkwill 1978), Barton Court Farm (Whittle 1986), Abingdon, Wytham (unpubl.) and Yarnton (Barclay *et al.* in prep.). These assemblages have affinities with much larger assemblages recovered from henge and palisade enclosure sites in Wessex (Longworth 1979; Hamilton and Whittle 2002; 1999). Assemblages of decorated jars from Yarnton, Thrupp and Stanton Harcourt (Thomas and Wallis 1982; Barclay 2002) can all be paralleled within the assemblage from Durrington Walls (Wainwright and Longworth 1971). A number of pit groups from Yarnton appear to contain vessel sets in which a variety of jars and bowls are represented (Barclay *et al.* in prep.).

Barclay (2002) has noted a dichotomy between the predominantly shell-tempered, open tub-shaped forms of the Woodlands/Clacton substyles and the grog-tempered closed bucket shaped forms of the Durrington Walls substyle. This division between the substyles also extends to decoration. With the Woodlands/Clacton substyles decoration is ordered horizontally around the vessel wall. In contrast, decoration on most Durrington Walls vessels is divided vertically by cordons and panels.

One remarkable vessel from the Upper Thames belongs to a relatively small group of pots that are decorated with spiral or concentric motifs (Fig. 16.15). This vessel from Radley is decorated with a spiral motif that has been compared with the horned and spectacle-linked spirals found in passage grave art (eg Pierowall Quarry, Westray, Orkney: Sharples 1984, 102-5, figs 27-9) as well as portable objects and in particular a Maesmore-type macehead (Cleal 1999; Eogan and Richardson 1982, 126; Barclay 2002).

Highly decorated Beaker pottery (Fig. 16.4) with all its associations has provided an attractive group of material for research. Over the last 100 years much time and energy has been spent trying to unravel a workable typology, while more recent

Fig. 16.15 Grooved Ware decorative motifs: top: sherds from Barrow Hills; centre: macehead from Knowth, Co. Meath, Ireland; bottom: decorated stone from Pierowall Quarry, Westray, Orkney

studies have emphasised new concerns such as gender association, social context and materiality (Gibbs 1989; Mizoguchi 1995). Typological work has focused on Beakers from funerary contexts, while work on domestic assemblages has not received the same degree of attention (Case 1993; Needham 2005). Beaker typology and chronology has been a subject of intense debate since Clarke (1970) published his corpus of pottery. Much of this work has been undertaken by Case (1977) who subsumed the work of both Clarke and the sequence of Lanting and van der Waals into a tripartite chronology of early, middle and late Beakers. More recently, based on the results of the British Museum dating programme, he has suggested that his tripartite division is no longer valid (Case 1993) and a new typological scheme has been put forward by Needham (2005) which tries to sequence Beakers by radiocarbon and material associations.

Within the Upper and Middle Thames Valley Beaker pottery has been recovered from a variety of contexts. Initially most, but certainly not all pottery of this type was recovered from graves (see Clarke 1970; Case 1956c and Gibson 1982). Changes in excavation strategy towards larger scale excavations, which often explore landscapes as well as

sites, are beginning to produce a number of assemblages from domestic contexts, although the quality of the assemblage is largely dependent upon the method of deposition. An important factor in recovery bias is whether material was deliberately placed in pits.

At Yarnton a contrast can be made between the assemblage recovered from occupation deposits and other features on the lower lying gravel deposits, and a much larger and better preserved assemblage recovered from pit deposits on the higher gravel terrace (Barclay *et al.* in prep.). Similar contrasts can also be seen at Drayton (Barclay *et al.* 2003) and to some extent at the Eton Rowing Course (Barclay forthcoming). In the Middle Thames in particular pit digging and the formal placing of pit deposits seems to have been a relatively uncommon practice.

Over the last 20 years a significant number of non-funerary assemblages have been recovered in the Upper and Middle Thames Valley, where large-scale excavation ahead of gravel extraction has produced many new sites (eg Eton Rowing Course, Drayton, Yarnton and sites in the Colne Valley: Allen *et al.* in prep.; Barclay *et al.* 2003, 83-9; Barclay *et al.* in prep.). These sites are characterised by pits and occupation deposits. It is apparent that the same styles of Beaker vessels that occur in these deposits were also placed in graves. In other words, funerary Beakers were generally selected from a wider repertoire of domestic vessels. There are vessels that occur in non-funerary deposits that are rarely found in graves. Included here are the large, often rusticated vessels (pot Beakers) that are occasionally found in pit deposits. Yarnton has several examples of this type of vessel, one of which is a much bigger version of a vessel that occurred in a grave at Foxley Farm (Barclay *et al.* in Hey in prep.). Yarnton also produced a few examples of plain vessels which again were rarely selected for grave deposition.

It would appear that Beaker pottery was used in a variety of contexts from the outset, and there is no longer any reason to suggest that the pottery was, at first, a high status style which only subsequently was used in domestic contexts. Unlike other types of Neolithic pottery it does not have a strong association with the use of monuments. A number of early pit assemblages are now known from the Upper Thames gravels, the Cotswolds and the Marlborough Downs (Barclay and Lupton 1999), and the broad range of vessel shapes mirrors what is recovered from grave deposits. Some of these assemblages contain vessels with all-over finger-nail impressions that can be identified perhaps as a coarse ware. Even these vessels, however, can be identified in funerary contexts (eg Linch Hill, Stanton Harcourt and Mount Farm, Berinsfield: Grimes 1960; Lambrick 2010).

Outside the core area of Beaker activity, Beaker pits are relatively scarce in the Upper Thames. Similarly, as has been mentioned, hardly any Beaker pit deposits are known from the Middle Thames Valley, although slightly more material has been recovered from the Essex side of the Thames estuary.

Associations with monuments are rare. Few monuments can be considered to be contemporary with Beaker activity, although a series of henge monuments in the Upper Thames may have been constructed during the initial phases of Beaker usage. The addition of a stone circle, the Devil's Quoits, to one of these henges at Stanton Harcourt almost certainly occurred during the Beaker period. At Avebury spreads of Beaker pottery occurred at some earlier monument sites, although this may only reflect secondary domestic activity around sites that were no longer of ceremonial importance (Hamilton and Whittle 1999).

There is evidence for the placing of Beakers as possibly votive deposits within monuments. The best example is the collection of fragmentary vessels from the secondary filling of the burial chambers of the West Kennet long barrow (Piggott 1962, 34; fig. 14). In the Upper Thames Valley, a number of henges have produced scraps of Beaker pottery but rarely in large quantities (A J Barclay *et al.* 1995; Whittle *et al.* 1992; Saville 1983). Elsewhere within the study area, Beaker pottery occurs quite commonly as secondary material albeit never in significant quantities, sometimes amounting to no more than a handful of small sherds.

A small number of Beakers and Beaker sherds have been recovered from the river Thames (Clarke 1970). There are also a great number of flint daggers from the Thames (Fig. 14.35) and to a lesser extent other objects with Beaker associations such as axe-hammers (Needham 1987). A high concentration of flint daggers occurs in the same area as other Neolithic river finds, including Beakers. Elsewhere flint daggers are found in Beaker graves from around Avebury and from Northamptonshire (Clarke 1970; Clarke 1935). However, the region with the highest concentration of Beaker burials, the Oxford area of the Upper Thames, has failed to produce a single example. Thus, certain objects found in graves in one region were deposited in watery contexts in another. A similar pattern occurs with Peterborough Ware-associated objects in the middle Neolithic. It would appear also that in some areas certain objects were not selected for burial. This argument not only applies to flint daggers, but also to other types of objects and materials such as jet beads, metal rings, pins, armlets and earrings (Needham 1988).

The use of so-called Food Vessels overlaps the use of Beaker pottery during the later centuries of the 3rd millennium cal BC. Unlike Beakers, this type of pottery has been found mostly in funerary contexts, predominantly in the barrow cemeteries of the Upper Thames Valley. They occur with both inhumation and cremation burials. These vessels tend to be plain or carry minimal impressed decoration (Fig. 14.26). Occasionally vessels occur in fabrics that are as fine as some Beaker pottery. Collared Urns are related to Food Vessels but appear slightly later, around the end of the 3rd millennium cal BC. They are more widely distributed in the Upper and Middle Thames Valley than Food Vessels, and are found in both funerary and domestic contexts. Their overall shape, however, suggests that they had a restricted function, perhaps for cooking and for storage rather than for serving food. Other specialised pots known as accessory vessels (eg Fig. 15.27: Aldbourne cup), miniature and cup-like, occur predominately in 'Wessex Culture' grave assemblages and more rarely in pit and ceremonial contexts. Some show heat damage from either having been used to burn material, perhaps incense, or from being placed on cremation pyres. This was certainly the case at a barrow at Stanton Harcourt where a small accessory cup (see Fig. 15.26) had been hard fired to a whitish grey colour and heat had caused the surface to spall (Barclay 1995b, 97-9). There is evidence that Food Vessels and Collared Urns were also occasionally treated in the same way (Barclay 2002), and while many were used as urns to contain cremated human remains, others were destroyed on the pyre along with the body and any other grave offerings. The end of the early Bronze Age period is marked by the appearance of so-called Biconical Urns, a type of pottery that is also found across the Channel. This type of pottery is occasionally found in late round barrows (eg Radley Barrow 14: Barclay and Halpin 1999, 159-160 and figs 5.8-9), in pits and occupation deposits and, most significantly, associated with the earliest timber round houses (eg Yarnton). Along with some rare examples of Collared Urns, it is the only type of early prehistoric pottery to carry possible potters' signatures, an example of which was found at Yarnton (Barclay *et al.* in prep.).

The first metalwork

The Upper Thames Valley contains a significant concentration of early metalwork (Fig. 16.3) belonging to the period 2500-1750 cal BC or Burgess' stages I-III/IV (Needham 1996). This metalwork takes the form of axes, small tools and personal ornaments and occurs in three types of context: burials, hoards and watery deposits. The selective deposition of metalwork from this area has been discussed by both Bradley (1990) and Needham (1988) and part of this discussion builds on their ideas.

Metal was used either to make all or part of an object. Many weapons and tools were composite artefacts with handles and in some cases sheaths made from organic materials such as horn, bone, wood, leather and antler (Fig. 16.3). More rare are composite objects that involve more than one metal or metal alloy. Little is known of the non-metal parts of composite objects, although a few examples of bone or antler pommels and traces of horn hilts have been found (see below).

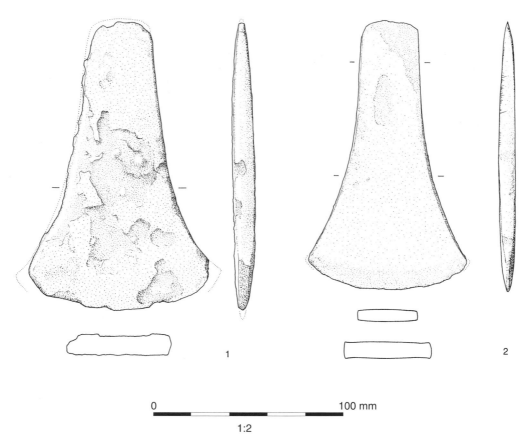

0   100 mm

1:2

Fig. 16.16   Early Bronze Age, bronze flat axeheads from Oddington

Metalworking appeared in Britain around the mid 3rd millennium cal BC at a time of major social transformation (Needham 1996). Profound changes in the archaeological record occurred at this time, major monuments were altered and embellished, individual burials with rich grave assemblages appeared along with new forms of material culture. Metalwork is found across Britain and Ireland, although it is notable that concentrations of early metalwork occur in certain regions.

The earliest metalwork from secure contexts occurs in Beaker-associated grave deposits. Of the 70 Beaker graves recorded from a core area (defined as between Standlake and North Stoke) within the Upper Thames Valley, no less than 14 have produced metalwork. Six graves contain awls, five contain daggers, one contains a copper neck ring, one gold earrings and one copper rings. Radiocarbon dating obtained for burials at Radley indicates that some of these objects may belong to the earliest metal-working traditions (Needham 1999a).

The earliest metalwork includes objects and small tools of gold and copper (Needham 1999a; 1996). The earliest known copper objects are a group of rings from a child's grave found in the barrow cemetery at Radley near Abingdon (Fig. 16.3). Other early copper finds include a neck ring from Yarnton (Fig. 16.3; Clarke *et al.* 1985, 270-1 and plate 7.24) and a copper awl from Spring Road, Abingdon (Northover 2008, 54). From the edge of the Middle

Thames Valley on the Chiltern Hills comes a spiral-headed pin of central European metal (Clarke *et al.* 1985, 84). From the Cotswolds comes a possible basket earring of copper found with a Beaker possibly of Wessex/Middle Rhine type in a secondary grave inserted into the Sale's Lot, Withington early Neolithic long cairn (Darvill 1986; O'Neil 1966).

Probably of slightly later date are the flat axes of copper and bronze (Fig. 16.16). Since flat axes are generally found in contexts that are difficult to date (eg river deposits and as stray finds or possibly hoards) and are only rarely associated with graves, the precise date of their appearance within this sequence is unclear, although it is possible that they appeared somewhat later than the objects just mentioned (Needham 1996). In the Upper Thames Valley early flat axes occur in areas separate from those in which Beaker burials occur. Two axe hoards are recorded from Oddington (Fig. 16.16) and Hawling in the Cotswolds and another from near the church at Cholsey near the Thames at Wallingford (Needham and Saville 1981). A further example comes from Beckley east of Oxford (Leeds 1939, 244). In contrast, a number of axes are known from the Middle Thames Valley (Needham 1987, 97-9, fig. 5.1-2).

Both Bradley and Needham have noted that the two groups of metalwork – small objects such as rings on the one hand and axes on the other – generally occur in mutually exclusive contexts and, although the evidence is slight, the find spots of axes and axe hoards do seem to be peripheral to the main area of Beaker burials in the Upper Thames region (Fig. 14.38). In the Middle Thames Valley, the pattern is slightly different for there are more finds of axes than Beaker burials (Needham 1987). However, at least one Beaker vessel has been dredged from the Thames, and the same stretch of river has also produced metalwork and numerous flint daggers (see Chapter 14), battleaxes and at least one example of a bone dagger (cf Gerloff 1975).

Daggers and knives are known from a number of burial contexts and have also been recovered from the river Thames. In the Oxford area, early copper daggers have been recovered from Beaker burials at Radley (grave 4660: Barclay and Halpin 1999, 60-2; Needham in Barclay and Halpin 1999, 63), Dorchester-on-Thames (Whittle *et al*. 1992, 180) and Sutton Courtenay (Gerloff 1975, 29). The Beaker burial at Dorchester contained a copper tanged dagger and a riveted knife-dagger. The later copper blade has never been analysed, although one of its three rivets was found to be of tin-bronze (Whittle *et al*. 1992, 181). This is an important grave group, and one of a small number that could bridge the transition from an earlier copper-using industry to that of tin-bronze (Needham 1999a, 188).

Daggers of later type occur at Radley, Gravelly Guy, Stanton Harcourt and at Foxley Farm, Eynsham. Four of the excavated barrows (1, 3, 4 and 14) at Radley contained riveted knife blades. In contrast only one of the Beaker burials at Foxley Farm contained a dagger and, likewise, at Stanton Harcourt, only one dagger is known from all the excavated Beaker burials, while a second dagger comes from a Wessex Culture grave (Barclay 1995b, 89-93, 97-9).

On the edge of the region is the important inhumation grave group from a barrow at Snowshill, Gloucestershire that was excavated by Greenwell (1890, 70-72) in the 19th century (Fig. 16.11). This grave contained a bronze dagger associated with a bronze socketed and tanged spearhead, a bronze crutch headed pin and a stone battle axe (Gerloff 1975, 101). A somewhat similar dagger occurs with a Wessex Culture grave at Stanton Harcourt. This burial was also a rich grave group containing an accessory cup, pins of bone and bronze, a whetstone and beads (Harden and Treweeks 1945; Barclay 1995b, 97-9). There are other important grave assemblages with daggers from the Berkshire Downs (Lambourn and Aldbourne: Gerloff 1975). Other daggers of this type are known from the river Thames (Needham 1981). A curved strip of worked gold sheet from the Hamel, Oxford (Palmer 1980) could have been part of a gold-covered dagger pommel, similar to examples recovered from elsewhere in Britain (eg Ridgeway barrow 7, Dorset and Blackwaterfoot, Arran: Clarke *et al*. 1985. 113, 126, figs 4.40 and 4.59).

Personal metal ornaments (Fig. 16.3) are rare and include the early copper rings from Radley, the spiral-headed pin from Sewell, the neck ring from Yarnton, gold basket 'earrings' and gold bead covers from Radley, and a possible copper 'earring' from Sale's Lot (O'Neil 1966), a bronze crutch-headed pin from Snowshill (Fig. 16.11; Kinnes and Longworth 1985, cat. no. 297) and a bronze bracelet from Shorncote (Barclay and Glass 1995).

Another common tool made from metal is the awl of copper or bronze. These tools are a common metal find in Beaker and early Bronze Age burials in the Upper Thames Valley. They are thought to have been used for a variety of functions which could have included the stitching of leatherwork, the decoration of objects and, it has been suggested, the tattooing of human skin. Gibbs (1989), in her study of gender patterning in the later Neolithic and early Bronze Age, found that awls were more common in female graves. Clues about further types of tools can also be found on the organic objects which they made. A palstave and a smaller bronze blade were used to make a wooden bowl at Yarnton (Taylor in prep.). In the absence of other evidence for these types, little can be said about them.

Glossary

aggradation	build-up by the deposition of sediment
aminostratigraphy	living organisms contain amino acid molecules that exist in two geometric forms (enantiomers, or mirror images) L (laevo) and D (dextro). In life L forms are dominant but on death the proteins slowly degrade and L forms convert to D forms. Thus the increase in the proportion of D amino acids can be used to estimate the age of fossils and, by extension, the rocks containing them. Aminostratigraphy is the element of stratigraphy that deals with the distribution of fossils with similar amino acid D/L values in the stratigraphic record, and the organization of strata into units on the basis of the fossils they contain
arboreal	of, or relating to, trees
Aurignacian	an Upper Palaeolithic culture of Europe and south-west Asia, dating from 34,000 to 23,000 BP. It is considered to represent the first appearance of anatomically modern humans in the region
bedding structures	structures within a deposit, formed during deposition and often characteristic of the depositional environmental (e.g. ripple marks, dune bedding, cross-bedding, trough bedding, parallel bedding)
biomass	the total living biological material in a given area
biostratigraphy	the element of stratigraphy that deals with the distribution of fossils in the stratigraphic record and the organisation of strata into units on the basis of their contained fossils
biozone	a *biostratigraphic* unit
boreal	of, or relating to, the north; describes a region that has a northern temperate climate, with cold winters and warm summers; especially used of forests dominated by coniferous species such as spruce, fir, larch and pine
chaîne opératoire	the different stages of (usually stone) tool production, from the acquisition of raw material to the abandonment of the tool
chronostratigraphy	the element of stratigraphy that deals with the relative time relations and ages of rock bodies; it makes use of *stratigraphic* principles, *biostratigraphy*, isotope geology and radiometric techniques. Figure 1.1 of the present volume a presents a simplified chronostratigraphic sequence for the Thames Valley
clast	a rock fragment or grain resulting from the breakdown of larger rocks
col	a high pass in mountains or hills
Coleoptera	beetles
colluvium (colluvial)	the mixture of soil or rock fragments eroded from a hillslope and deposited at its foot
Creswellian	a British Upper Palaeolithic culture named after the type site of Creswell Crags in Derbyshire
crop out	to be exposed at the surface
cryoturbation	disturbance and rearrangement of soil due to freeze/thaw processes
debitage	the sharp-edged waste material left over after the creation of a stone tool
doline	a sinkhole or natural depression in surface topography, often roughly circular, formed by water dissolving limestone
erratic	a rock or rock fragment transported by a glacier and deposited on a rock bed of different formation
facies	all lithological and palaeontological features of a given rock that reflect the environmental conditions in which it was deposited
Fennoscandian	of Fennoscandia: Norway, Sweden and Finland
fissioned subgroups	human groups that have split from larger groups due to internal fissioning forces (eg stress and conflict)
fluvial	of, or relating to, a river or stream
fluvial dissection	incision and erosion of a landscape by streams and rivers to form valleys and hills
foraminifera	very small, single-celled amoeboid creatures inhabiting marine environments studied in living or fossil form as environmental indicators
fossiliferous	containing fossils

glacial	relating to, or derived from, a glacier or ice sheet; associated with a *glaciation*
glacial maximum	the time of maximum extent of the ice sheets during a *glaciation*
glaciation	an 'Ice Age'; a period when a sustained reduction in global temperature allows the expansion of continental and polar ice sheets and mountain glaciers
glacigenic	caused by *glacial* processes
glacio-eustatic	global change in sea level associated with the effects of *glaciation*; sea levels fall when water is locked up in ice, and rise when it melts
glaciofluvial	material moved by glaciers and subsequently sorted and deposited by streams flowing from the melting ice sheets
glaciolacustrine	relating to *glacial* and *proglacial* lakes
Gravettian	a European Upper Palaeolithic culture dating from 28,000 to 23,000 BP
hiatus	a gap in the *stratigraphic* record caused by an interruption in deposition or by erosion of strata
Holocene	the Holocene Epoch is the most recent geological period that began approximately 11,500 calendar years ago (about 9800 BC) and continues to the present. It started late in the retreat of the *Pleistocene* glaciers and is associated with warmer conditions. The Holocene is an *interglacial* period and there is no reason to believe that it represents a permanent end to the Pleistocene
hominin	human. Technically the term *hominin* is now used by biologists for modern and extinct human species and is recognised as a subgroup of the family *hominid*, which covers not only humans but all great apes
ice-wedge casts	fossil ice wedges (created in frozen ground) infilled with sediment
imbrication	overlapping of edges, as in roof tiles or shingles; in a geological sense the long axes of particles lie parallel to each other
interfluve	a region of higher land between two rivers within the same drainage system
interglacial	a period of warmer temperatures between *glaciations* associated with melting of ice sheets, rise in sea level and the immigration of warm-loving plants and animals
interstadial	a period of warmer temperatures during a *glaciation* of insufficient duration or intensity to be considered an *interglacial*
intraformational	within a formation, or unit, of strata
isostacy	equilibrium in the earth's crust such that forces tending to elevate landmasses are balanced by forces tending to depress landmasses
isostatic rebound	the rising of landmasses formerly depressed by the weight of ice sheets
lag gravel	residual accumulations of particles that are coarser than material that has blown or been washed away (see *loess*)
laminated	arranged in thin sheets or layers
Late Glacial Interstadial	a brief period of warm conditions towards the end of the last *glaciation*
lithology	the gross physical character of a rock or rock formation
lithostratigraphy	The element of stratigraphy that deals with the description and nomenclature of the rocks of the Earth based on their lithology and their stratigraphic relations
Loch Lomond stadial	conditions after the *Late Glacial Interstadial*
loess	a windblown deposit of fine-grained silt or clay
magnetic reversal	a periodic reversal of the Earth's magnetic polarity in which the North Pole becomes the South Pole and vice versa. The orientation of the Earth's magnetic field at the time of deposition of sedimentary rocks or on the cooling of igneous rocks is preserved in the rock
Mammal Asssemblage Zone	a grouping of mammal species that is characteristic of a particular time period and applied in *biostratigraphy*
marine transgression	a relative rise in sea level resulting in the influx of the sea over previously dry land
megafauna	species of animals whose average adult weight exceeds 44 kg
multiproxy	using information from a variety of sources as a substitute for direct evidence or information
obligate	restricted to a particular condition of life or environmental contexts
orogenic	the process of mountain formation especially by folding and faulting of the earth's crust
ostracods	small crustaceans, typically around 1 mm in size, often found in fossil form; a good indicator of past environmental conditions in water bodies
palaeobiology	the study of ancient organisms from fossil remains
palaeobotany	*Palaeo* is a prefix derived from Greek that denotes an ancient form of something. Palaeobotany is the recovery and identification of plant remains from geological and archaeological contexts, and their use for biological reconstruction of past environments

palaeocurrent	a former direction of flow in a river or stream
palaeoenvironment	the past environment of an area during a given period of its history
Palaeogene	the Palaeogene is a geological period dating from around 65 to around 23 million years ago. It is notable as an important period for the evolution of mammals following the mass extinction of dinosaurs at the end of the preceding Cretaceous period
palaeontology	the study of prehistoric life forms on Earth through the study of plant and animal fossils
palaeosol	an ancient soil horizon (indicating a former landsurface), usually buried beneath other rocks or recent soil horizons
palynology	the study of *palynomorphs*, often (although not exclusively) pollen
palynomorphs	microscopic organic fossils found in rock or soil deposits
pedogenic	soil building processes
periglacial	an area at the edge of an ice sheet, not buried by ice but subject to severe freezing
Pleistocene	the penultimate geological epoch prior to the *Holocene*. It spans the period of climatic fluctuations informally known as the Ice Age but includes numerous warm *interglacials* as well as evidence for *glaciation*. Formerly dated from 1.8 million to 11,500 years BP. The International Commission on Stratigraphy has recently agreed that its base be extended to 2.6 million years ago (see *Quaternary*)
Pliocene	The geological epoch, traditionally extending from 5.3 million years to 2.6 million years BP, immediately preceding the *Pleistocene*. Its top was formerly dated at 1.8 million years BP but has recently been lowered to 2.6 million years to accommodate changes agreed by the International Commission on Stratigraphy (see *Quaternary* and *Pleistocene*)
polygenetic	having many distinct sources or origins
proglacial lake	a lake at the face of an ice sheet or glacier formed from its meltwater, or created by the damming effect of the ice sheet
Quaternary	the Quaternary Period is a geological time interval that is dated from the end of the Pliocene Epoch roughly 2.6 million years ago to the present. It includes two geological subdivisions, the *Pleistocene* and the *Holocene*. Its base was formerly dated at 1.8 million years BP, but the International Commission on Stratigraphy has recently agreed that it be redefined as the interval of oscillating climatic extremes (glacial and interglacial episodes) that was initiated at about 2.6 million years ago
sandur	(plural sandar) is a glacial outwash plain formed of sediments deposited by meltwater at the terminus of a glacier
solifluction	the slow downhill movement of soil or other material, usually in areas underlain by frozen ground
stadial	a period of cold temperatures during an *interglacial* of insufficient duration or intensity to be considered a *glaciation*
stratigraphy	is the description of all rock bodies forming the Earth's crust and their organisation into distinctive, useful, mappable units based on their inherent properties or attributes in order to establish their distribution and relationship in space and their succession in time, and to interpret geologic history. It is based on the principle that strata normally represent a chronological sequence of events with the earliest at the bottom and the most recent at the top. It is fundamental to geology and archaeology in order to understand the succession of events. NB that in many river terrace sequences such as the Thames, the highest terraces in the 'staircase' are the oldest because the river has cut down through time
syncline	a trough in folded strata: a fold in rocks in which the rocks dip inwards from both sides
taxa	plural of taxon; a name designating an organism or group of organisms
thermal optimum	warmest period (of an *interglacial*)
thermophilous	literally 'heat-loving'; an organism that grows best at elevated temperatures
till	sediment deposited by a glacier, consisting of sand, clay, gravel and boulders mixed together
Younger Dryas	a return, during the last *glaciation*, to severe cold. The period is named after an evergreen subshrub *Dryas octopetala* whose pollen is abundant in sediments from that time

Bibliography

Abbott, W L 1890 Notes on some Pleistocene sections in and around London, *Proc Geol Ass* **11**, 473-80

Adkins, R, and Jackson, R, 1978 *Neolithic stone and flint axes from the river Thames*, Brit Mus Occ Pap **1**, London

Ahlström, T, 2003 Grave or ossuary? Osteological finds from a recently excavated passage tomb in Falbygden, Sweden, in Burenhult and Westergaard 2003, 253-69

Aiello, L C, and Wheeler, P, 2003 Neanderthal thermoregulation and the glacial climate, in *Neanderthals and modern humans in the European landscape during the Last Glaciation: archaeological results of the Stage 3 Project* (eds T van Andel and W Davies), 147-66, Cambridge

Akerman, J W, 1855 Notes of antiquarian researches in the summer and autumn of 1854, *Archaeologia* **35**, 175-86

Aldhouse-Green, H S, 2000 *Paviland Cave and the Red Lady: a definitive report*, Bristol

Aldhouse-Green, H S, and Pettitt, P B, 1998 Paviland Cave: contextualizing the 'Red Lady', *Antiquity* **278**, 756-72

Allen, G W G 1984 *Discovery from the air* (eds J S Bradford and O S G Crawford), Aerial Archaeology **10**, Hertford

Allen, J R L, and Allen, S A, 1997 A stratified prehistoric site from the Kennet floodplain at Ufton Nervet, Berkshire, *Berkshire Archaeol J* **75**, 1-8

Allen, M J, 1992 Landscape history: the molluscan evidence, in Gingell 1992, 145-9

Allen, M J, 1995 Before Stonehenge, in Cleal *et al.* 1995, 41-62

Allen, M J, 2005 Beaker settlement and environment on the chalk downs of southern England, *Proc Prehist Soc* **71**, 219–246

Allen, M J, and Gardiner, J, 2002 A sense of time: cultural markers in the Mesolithic of southern England, in *Inscribed landscapes: marking and making place* (eds B David and M Wilson), 139-53, Honolulu

Allen, M J, and Gardiner, J, 2009 If you go down to the woods today. A re-evaluation of the chalkland postglacial woodland: implications for prehistoric communities, in *Land and people: papers in memory of John G Evans* (eds M J Allen, N Sharples and T O'Connor), Prehistoric Society Research Paper **2**, 49-66, Oxford

Allen, M J, Gardiner, J, Sheridan, A and McOmish, D, forthcoming The British Chalcolithic: place and polity in the later 3rd millennium BC, Prehistoric Society Research Paper **4**, Oxford

Allen, M J, and Healy, F, 1992 Discussion in Healy *et al.* 1992, 70-3

Allen, S, 2005 Mesolithic hunter-gatherer exploitation of the Marlborough Downs, in Brown *et al.* 2005, 95-102

Allen, T, 1977 Interglacial sea level change: evidence for brackish water sedimentation at Purfleet, Essex, *Quaternary Newsletter* **22**, 1-3

Allen, T G, 1995 *Lithics and landscape: archaeological discoveries on the Thames Water pipeline at Gatehampton Farm, Goring, Oxfordshire 1985-92*, Thames Valley Landscapes **7**, Oxford

Allen, T G, 2000 Eton Rowing Course at Dorney Lake: the burial traditions, *Tarmac Papers* **4**, 65-106

Allen, T G, 2005 Dorney, Eton Rowing Course excavations, 2003: sixth interim report, *S Midlands Archaeology* **35**, 23-30

Allen, T G, Barclay, A, and Cromarty, A M, forthcoming *Opening the wood, making the land. The archaeology of a Middle Thames landscape: the Eton rowing course at Dorney and the Maidenhead, Eton and Windsor flood alleviation channel, Mesolithic to earlier Bronze Age*, Thames Valley Landscapes, Oxford

Allen, T G, Barclay, A, and Lamdin-Whymark, H, 2004 Opening the wood, making the land: landscape in the Dorney area of the Middle Thames Valley, in Cotton and Field 2004, 82-98

Allen, T G, Darvill, T C, Green, L S, and Jones, M U, 1993 *Excavations at Roughground Farm, Lechlade, Gloucestershire: a prehistoric and Roman landscape*, Thames Valley Landscapes: the Cotswold Water Park **1**, Oxford

Allen, T G, Hayden, C and Lamdin-Whymark, H, 2009 *From Bronze Age enclosure to Anglo Saxon settlement: archaeological excavations at Taplow hillfort, Buckinghamshire*, Thames Valley Landscapes **30**, Oxford

Allen, T G, and Kamash, Z, 2008 *Saved from the grave: Neolithic to Saxon discoveries at Spring Road municipal cemetery, Abingdon, Oxfordshire, 1990-2000*, Thames Valley Landscapes **28**, Oxford

Allen, T G, and Lamdin-Whymark, H, 2006 Little Wittenham, *S Midlands Archaeol* **36**, 46-7

Allen, T G, and Robinson, M A, 1993 *The prehistoric landscape and Iron Age enclosed settlement at Mingies Ditch, Hardwick-with-Yelford, Oxfordshire*, Thames Valley Landscapes **2**, Oxford

Ambers, J and Housley, R, 1995 Radiocarbon dating, in Allen 1995, 112-3

Ames, R E, 1993 A Mesolithic assemblage from Moor Farm, Holyport, near Maidenhead, *Berkshire Archaeol J* **74**, 1-8

Andrews, P, Cook, J, Currant, A, and Stringer, C (eds) 1999 *Westbury Cave: the Natural History Museum excavations, 1976-1984*, Bristol

Andrews, P, and Crockett, N, 1996 *Three excavations along the Thames and its tributaries*, Wessex Archaeol Rep **10**, Salisbury

Annable, F K, and Simpson, D D A, 1964 *Guide catalogue of the Neolithic and Bronze Age collections in Devizes Museum*, Devizes

Anon, 2005 An important Mesolithic site at Bletchingley, *Surrey Archaeol Soc Bull* **384**, 1-2

Antoine, P, Limondin Lozouet, N, Chaussé, C, Lautridou, J-P, Pastre, J-F, Auguste, P, Bahain, J-J, Falguères, C, and Galehb, B, 2007 Pleistocene fluvial terraces from northern France (Seine, Yonne, Somme): synthesis, and new results from interglacial deposits, *Quaternary Science Reviews* **26**, 2701-23

Arkell, W J, 1947 *The geology of Oxford*, Oxford

Armit, I, Murphy, E, Nelis, E, and Simpson, D, 2003 *Neolithic settlement in Ireland and western Britain*, Oxford

Arnold, D, 1985 *Ceramic theory and cultural process*, Cambridge

Ashbee, P, 1960 *The Bronze Age round barrow in Britain*, London

Ashbee, P, 1966, The Fussell's Lodge long barrow excavations 1957, *Archaeologia* **100**, 1-80

Ashbee, P, 1970 *The earthen long barrow in Britain*, London

Ashbee, P, 1978 Amesbury Barrow 51, excavations 1969, *Wiltshire Archaeol Mag* 70-71, 1-60

Ashbee, P, Smith, I F, and Evans, J G, 1979 Excavation of three long barrows near Avebury, Wiltshire, *Proc Prehist Soc* **45**, 207-300

Ashton, N M, 1998 The spatial distribution of the flint artefacts and human behaviour, in *Excavations at the Lower Palaeolithic site at East Farm, Barnham, Suffolk, 1989-94* (eds N M Ashton, S G Lewis and S Parfitt), 251-8, London

Ashton, N, 2001 One step beyond. Flint shortage above the Goring Gap: the example of Wolvercote, in *A Very Remote Indeed: papers on the Palaeolithic presented to Derek Roe* (eds S Milliken and J Cook), 199-206, Oxford

Ashton, N M, 2002 The absence of humans from Last Interglacial Britain, in *Le dernier interglaciaire et les occupations humaines du Paléolithique moyen* (eds W Roebroeks and A Tuffreau), 93-103, Lille

Ashton, N M, Cook, J, Lewis, S G, and Rose, J, (eds), 1992 *High Lodge: excavations by G de G Sieveking, 1962-68*, London

Ashton, N, Jacobi, R, and White, M J, 2003 The dating of Levallois sites in west London, *Quaternary Newsletter* **99**, 25-32

Ashton, N, and Lewis, S, 2002 Deserted Britain: declining populations in the British late middle Pleistocene, *Antiquity* **76**, 388-96

Ashton, N M, Lewis, S G and Parfitt, S 1998 *Excavations at the Lower Palaeolithic site at East Farm, Barnham, Suffolk 1989-94*, British Museum Press, London

Ashton, N, Lewis, S, Parfitt, S, Candy, I, Keen, D, Kemp, R, Penkman, K, Thomas, G, Whittaker, J and White, M J, 2005 Excavations at the Lower Palaeolithic site at Elveden, Suffolk, UK *Proc Prehist Soc* **71**, 1-62

Ashton, N, Lewis, S, Parfitt, S, and White, M, 2006 Riparian landscapes and human habitat preferences during the Hoxnian (MIS 11) Interglacial, *Journal of Quaternary Science* **21**, 497-505

Ashton, N M, and McNabb, J, 1994 Bifaces in perspective, in *Stories in stones* (eds N M Ashton and A David), Lithic Studies Society Occasional Paper **4**, 182-91, London

Ashton, N M, and McNabb, J, 1996 The flint Industries from the Waechter excavation, in, *Excavations at Barnfield Pit, Swanscombe, 1968-72* (eds B Conway, J McNabb and N Ashton), British Museum Occasional Paper **94**, 201-36, London

Atkinson, R J C, 1942 Archaeological sites on Port Meadow, Oxford, *Oxoniensia* **7**, 24-35

Atkinson, R J C, 1946-7 A middle Bronze Age barrow at Cassington, Oxon, *Oxoniensia* **11-12**, 5-26

Atkinson, R J C, 1949 A henge monument at Westwell, near Burford, Oxon, *Oxoniensia* **14**, 84-7

Atkinson, R J C, 1951 The excavations at Dorchester, Oxon., 1946-51, *Archaeological Newsletter* **4**, 56-9

Atkinson, R J C, 1965 Wayland's Smithy, *Antiquity* **39**, 126-33

Atkinson, R J C, Piggott, C M, and Sandars, N K, 1951 *Excavations at Dorchester, Oxon*, Oxford

Austin, L A, Bergman, C A, Roberts, M B and Wilhelmsen, K H, 1999 Archaeology of the excavated areas, in *Boxgrove: a Middle Pleistocene hominid site at Eartham Quarry, Boxgrove, West Sussex* (eds M B Roberts and S A Parfitt), 313-78, London

Aveling, L, 1997 Mesolithic 'mastics': a sticky problem, *Lithics* **17-18**, 84-5

Avery, M, 1982 The Neolithic causewayed enclosure, Abingdon, in Case and Whittle 1982, 10-50

Ayres, K, and Powell, A, 2003 Animal bone, in Barclay *et al.* 2003, 158-63

Baker, A, Smart, P L, and Edwards, R L, 2007 Mass spectrometric dating of flowstones from Stump Cross Caverns and Lancaster Hole, Yorkshire: palaeoclimate implications, *Journal of Quaternary Science* **11**, 107-14

Balaresque, P, Bowden, R G, Adams, S M, Leung, H-Y, King, T E, Rosser, Z H, Goodwin, J, Moisan, J-P, Richard, C, Millward, A, Demaine, A G, Barbujani, G, Previdere, C, Wilson, I J, Tyler-Smith, C, Jobling, M A, 2010 A predominantly Neolithic origin for European paternal lineage, *PLoS Biol* **8 (1)**, (http://www.plosbiology.org/article/info:doi/10.1371/journal.pbio.1000285; checked July 2010)

Balkwill, C, 1978 The Bronze Age features, the ring-ditches and their neighbourhood, and Appendix 1: a pit with Grooved Ware from Abingdon, in Parrington 1978, 25-33

Barber, A, and Bateman, C, 2003 Farmoor to Blunsden Thames Water Pipeline (Faringdon to Kingston Hill section), *S Midlands Archaeol* **33**, 57-8

Barber, J, 2000 Death in Orkney: a rare event, in *Neolithic Orkney in its European context* (ed. A Ritchie), 185-7, Cambridge

Barber, M, 2002 *Bronze and the Bronze Age: metal-work and society in Britain c 2500–800 BC*, Stroud

Barclay, A J and Wallis J, 1999 The jet/shale belt slider, in Barclay and Halpin 1999, 234

Barclay, A J, 1995a Affinities and design of the monument, in A J Barclay *et al*. 1995, 70-7

Barclay, A J, 1995b A review of Neolithic and Bronze Age sites in the Devil's Quoits area, in A J Barclay *et al*. 1995, 78-105

Barclay, A J, 1995c The ceremonial complex in its local and national context, in A J Barclay *et al*. 1995, 106-15

Barclay, A J, 1997 The portal dolmens of the north east Cotswolds: symbolism, architecture and the transformation of the earliest Neolithic, in *O Neolítico atlántico e as orixes do megalitismo*, Actas do Coloquio Internacional, Santiago de Compostella, 1-6 de Abril de 1996, (ed. A Rodríguez Casal), 151-159, Santiago de Compostella

Barclay, A J, 1999a Final Neolithic/early Bronze Age, in Barclay and Halpin 1999, 35-148

Barclay, A J, 1999b Grooved Ware from the Upper Thames, in Cleal and MacSween 1999, 9-22

Barclay, A J, 1999c Discussion, in Barclay and Halpin 1999, 275-329

Barclay, A J, 1999d Summary and reassessments of monuments excavated before 1983-4, in Barclay and Halpin 1999, 149-66

Barclay, A J, 2000 Spatial histories of the Neolithic: a study of the monuments and material culture of central southern England, unpubl. PhD thesis, Univ. Reading

Barclay, A J, 2002 Ceramic lives, in *Prehistoric Britain: the ceramic basis* (eds A Woodward and J D Hill), 85-95, Oxford

Barclay, A J, 2007 Connections and networks: a wider world and other places, in Benson and Whittle 2007, 331-44

Barclay, A J, forthcoming, earlier prehistoric pottery, in T G Allen *et al*. forthcoming

Barclay, A J, and Bayliss, A, 1999 Cursus monuments and the radiocarbon problem, in Barclay and Harding 1999, 11-29

Barclay, A J, Beavan, N, Bradley, P, Chaffey, G, Challinor, D, McKinley, J I, Powell, A, and Marshall, P, 2009 New evidence for mid-late Neolithic burial from the Colne Valley, West London, *PAST* **63**, 4-6

Barclay, A J, and Bradley, P, 1999 Mesolithic and earlier Neolithic activity, in Barclay and Halpin 1999, 17-34

Barclay, A J, and Brereton, S, 2003 Gazetteer of cursus and related monuments in the Upper Thames Valley, in Barclay *et al*. 2003, 215-32

Barclay, A J, Bradley, R, Hey, G, and Lambrick, G, 1996 The earlier prehistory of the Oxford region in the light of recent research, *Oxoniensia* **61**, 1-20

Barclay, A J, and Case, H, 2007 The early Neolithic pottery and fired clay, in Benson and Whittle 2007, 263-281

Barclay, A J, Doherty, C, and Edwards, E, in prep. The prehistoric pottery, in Hey in prep.

Barclay, A J, and Glass, H, with Parry, C, 1995 Excavations of Neolithic and Bronze Age ring ditches, Shorncote Quarry, Somerford Keynes, Gloucestershire, *Trans Bristol Gloucestershire Archaeol Soc* **113**, 21-60

Barclay, A J, Gray, M, and Lambrick, G, 1995 *Excavations at the Devil's Quoits, Stanton Harcourt, Oxfordshire, 1972-3 and 1988*, Thames Valley Landscapes: the Windrush Valley **3**, Oxford

Barclay, A J, and Halpin, C, 1999 *Excavations at Barrow Hills, Radley, Oxfordshire 1: the Neolithic and Bronze Age monument complex*, Thames Valley Landscapes **11**, Oxford

Barclay, A J, and Harding, J (eds), 1999 *Pathways and ceremonies: the cursus monuments of Britain and Ireland*, Neolithic Studies Group Seminar Papers **4**, Oxford

Barclay, A J, and Hey, G, 1999 Cattle, cursus monuments and the river: the development of ritual and domestic landscapes in the Upper Thames Valley, in Barclay and Harding 1999, 67-76

Barclay, A J, Lambrick, G, Moore, J, and Robinson, M, 2003 *Lines in the landscape: cursus monuments in the Upper Thames Valley*, Thames Valley Landscapes **15**, Oxford

Barclay, A J and Lupton, A 1999 The early prehistoric period, in *Excavations alongside Roman Ermin Street, Gloucestershire and Wiltshire: the archaeology of the A419/A417 Swindon to Gloucester Road Scheme, 2* (A Mudd, R J Williams and A Lupton), 513-17, Oxford

Barclay, A J, and McKeague, P, 1996 A Bronze Age barrow at 24A St Michael's Street, Oxford, in The excavation of two Bronze Age barrows, Oxford (A Parkinson, A Barclay, and P McKeague), *Oxoniensia* **61**, 57-61

Barclay, A J, Needham, S, and Wallis, J, 1999 ?Sheath, in Barclay and Halpin 1999, 145

Barclay, A J, Serjeantson, D, and Wallis, J, 1999 Worked bone and antler, in Barclay and Halpin 1999, 235-236

Barclay, A J, and Thomas, R, 1995 Prehistoric features, in *Two Oxfordshire Anglo-Saxon cemeteries: Berinsfield and Didcot* (eds A Boyle, A Dodd, D Miles and A Mudd), Thames Valley Landscapes **8**, 11, Oxford

Barclay, G J, Maxwell, G S, Simpson, I A, and Davidson, D A, 1995 The Cleaven Dyke: a Neolithic cursus/bank barrow in Scotland, *Antiquity* **69**, 317-26

Barfield, L, and Hodder, M, 1987 Burnt mounds as saunas, and the prehistory of bathing, *Antiquity* **61**, 370-9

Barker, C, 1985 The long mounds of the Avebury region, *Wiltshire Archaeol Nat Hist Mag* **79**, 7-38

Barnatt, J, 1999 Taming the Land: Peak District farming and ritual in the Bronze Age, *Derbyshire Archaeol J* **119**, 19-78.

Barnatt, J, and Collis, J, 1996 *Barrows in the Peak District*, Sheffield

Barnes, I, Boismier W A, Cleal, R M J, Fitzpatrick, A P, and Roberts, M R, 1995 *Early settlement in Berkshire: Mesolithic-Roman occupation sites in the Thames and Kennet Valleys*, Wessex Archaeol Rep **6**, Salisbury

Barnes, I, Butterworth C A, Hawkes, J W, and Smith, L, 1997 *Excavations at Thames Valley Park, Reading, 1986-88*, Wessex Archaeol Rep **14**, Salisbury

Barnes, I, and Cleal, R M J, 1995 Neolithic and Bronze Age settlement at Weir Bank Stud Farm, Bray, in Barnes *et al.* 1995, 1-51

Barrett, J C, 1988 The living, the dead and the ancestors: Neolithic and early Bronze Age mortuary practices, in Barrett and Kinnes 1988, 30-41

Barrett, J C, 1990 The monumentality of death: the character of early Bronze Age mortuary mounds in southern England, *World Archaeol* **22**, 179-89

Barrett, J C, 1991 Towards an archaeology of ritual, in Garwood *et al.* 1991, 1-9

Barrett, J C, 1994 *Fragments from antiquity: an archaeology of social life in Britain, 2900-1200 BC*, Oxford

Barrett, J C, Bradley, R, and Green, M, 1991 *Landscape, monuments and society: the prehistory of Cranborne Chase*, Cambridge

Barrett, J C, and Kinnes, I (eds), 1988 *The archaeology of context in the Neolithic and Bronze Age: recent trends*, Sheffield

Barton, R N E, 1992 *Hengistbury Head, Dorset, 2: the late Upper Palaeolithic and early Mesolithic sites*, Oxford University Committee for Archaeology Monograph **34**, Oxford

Barton, R N E, 1997 *Stone Age Britain*, London

Barton, R N E, 1999 The lateglacial or Late and Final Upper Palaeolithic colonization of Britain, in *The archaeology of Britain* (eds I Ralston and J Hunter), 13-34, London

Barton, R N E, and Froom, F R, 1986 The long blade assemblage from Avington VI, Berkshire, in *The Palaeolithic of Britain and its nearest neighbours: recent trends* (ed. S N Collcutt), 80-84, Sheffield

Barton, R N E, Berridge, P J, Bevins, R E, and Walker, M J, 1995 Persistent places in the Mesolithic landscape: an example from the Black Mountain uplands of south Wales, *Proc Prehist Soc* **61**, 81-116

Barton, R N E, Jacobi, R, Stapert, D, and Street, M, 2003 The Late-glacial reoccupation of the British Isles and the Creswellian, *Journal of Quaternary Science* **18**, 631-43

Bassinot, F C, Labeyrie, L D, Vincent, E, Quidelleur, X, Shackleton, N J and Lancelot, Y 1994, The astronomical theory of climate and the age of the Brunhes-Matuyama magnetic reversal, *Earth and Planetary Science Letters* **126**, 91-108

Barton, N, and Roberts, A, 2004 The Mesolithic period in England: current perspectives and new research, in Saville 2004, 339-58

Bateman, T, 1848 *Vestiges of the antiquities of Derbyshire*, London

Bateman, T, 1861 *Ten years diggings in Celtic and Saxon grave hills in the counties of Derby, Stafford and York*, London and Derby

Bates, M R, Bates, C R, Gibbard, P L, Macphail, R I, Owen, F, Parfitt, S A, Preece, R C, Roberts, M B, Robinson, J E, Whittaker, J E and Wilkinson, K N, 2000 Late Middle Pleistocene deposits at Norton Farm on the West Sussex coastal plain, southern England, *Journal of Quaternary Science* **15**, 61-89

Bates, M R, Keen, D H and Lautridou, J-P, 2003 Pleistocene marine and periglacial deposits of the English Channel, *Journal of Quaternary Science* **18**, 319-37

Bates, M R, and Whittaker, K, 2004 Landscape evolution in the Lower Thames Valley: implications for the archaeology of the earlier Holocene period, in Cotton and Field 2004, 50-70

Bayliss, A and Bronk Ramsey, C, 2004 Pragmatic Bayesians: a decade of integrating radiocarbon dates into chronological models, in *Tools for constructing chronologies: crossing interdisciplinary boundaries* (eds C E Buck and A Millard), 25-42, London

Bayliss, A, Bronk Ramsey, C, Galer, D, McFadyen, L, van der Plicht, J, and Whittle, A, 2007 Interpreting the chronology: the radiocarbon dating programme, in Benson and Whittle 2007, 221-36

Bayliss, A, Bronk Ramsey, C, van der Plicht, J, and Whittle, A, 2007 Bradshaw and Bayes: towards a timetable for the British Neolithic, *Cambridge J Archaeol* **17 (1) (suppl)**, 1-28

Bayliss, A, and Healy, F, 2007 Radiocarbon dates, in Hey *et al.* 2007, 68-70

Bayliss, A, and Hey, G, in prep. The scientific dating, in Hey in prep.

Bayliss, A, McAvoy, F, and Whittle, A W R, 2007 The world recreated: redating Silbury Hill in its monumental landscape, *Antiquity* **81**, 26-53

Bayliss, A, and Whittle, A, (eds), 2007 Histories of the dead: building chronologies for five southern British long barrows, *Cambridge Archaeol J* **17 (1) (suppl.)**, 1-147

Bayliss, A, Whittle, A, and Healy, F, 2008 Timing, tempo and temporality in the Neolithic of southern Britain, in *Between Foraging and Farming: an extended broad spectrum of papers presented to Lendert Louwe Kooijmans* (eds H Fokkens, B J Cikes, A van Gijn, J P Kleijne, H H Ponjee and C G Slapp Endel), Analecta Praehistorica Leidensia **40**, 25-42, Leiden

Bayliss, A, Whittle, A, and Wysocki, M, 2007 Talking about my generation: the date of the West Kennet long barrow, *Cambridge Archaeol J* **17 (1) (suppl.)**, 85-101

Beck, C, and Shennan, S, 1991 *Amber in prehistoric Britain*, Oxbow Monograph **8**, Oxford

Bell, A M, 1894a Palaeolithic remains at Wolvercote, Oxfordshire, I and II, *Antiquary* **30**, 148-152 and 192-8

Bell, A M, 1894b On the Pleistocene gravels at Wolvercote near Oxford, *Report of the British Association for 1893*, 663-4, Oxford

Bell, A M, 1904 Implementiferous sections at Wolvercote (Oxfordshire), *Quarterly Journal of the Geological Society* **60**, 120-32

Bell, C, 1992 *Ritual theory, ritual practice*, Oxford

Bell, F G, 1968 Weichselian glacial floras in Britain, unpubl. PhD thesis, Univ. Cambridge

Bell, F G, 1969 The occurrence or southern steppe and halophyte elements in Weichselian (Last Glacial) floras from southern Britain, *New Phytologist* **68**, 913-22

Bell, M, and Walker, M J C, 1992 *Late Quaternary environmental change: physical and human perspectives*, Harlow

Bender, B, 1998 *Stonehenge: making space*, Oxford

Benson, D, and Fasham, P, 1972 Field work at Chastleton, *Oxoniensia* **37**, 1-9

Benson, D, and Miles, D, 1974 *The Upper Thames valley: an archaeological survey of the river gravels*, OAU Survey **2**, Oxford

Benson, D, and Whittle, A, 2007 *Building memories: the Neolithic Cotswold long barrow at Ascott-Under-Wychwood, Oxfordshire*, Oxford

Biddulph, K, 2006 Neolithic to early Bronze Age Buckinghamshire: a resource assessment, http://www.buckscc.gov.uk/assets/content/bcc/docs/archaeology/A_ST_Bucks_4_Neo-EBA_Bucks_resource_assessment_final.pdf (checked July 2010)

Binford, L R, 1985 Human ancestors: changing views of their behaviour, *Journal of Anthropological Archaeology* **4**, 292-327

Bird, D, 2006, Surrey Archaeological Research Framework, 2006, unpubl. report, Surrey County Council and Surrey Archaeological Society, Guildford

Bird, J, and Bird, D G, 1987 *The archaeology of Surrey to 1540*, Guildford

Bishop, W W, 1958 The Pleistocene geology and geomorphology of three gaps in the Middle Jurassic escarpment, *Phil Trans Roy Soc London B* **241**, 255-306

Blair, K G, 1923 Some coleopterous remains from the peat-bed at Wolvercote, Oxfordshire, *Transactions of the Royal Entomological Society of London* **71**, 558-63

Blezard, R G, 1966 Field meeting at Aveley and West Thurrock, *Proc Geol Ass* **77**, 273-6

Bloch, M, 1981a *Placing the dead: tombs, ancestral villages, and kinship organisation in Madagascar*, London

Bloch, M, 1981b Tombs and states, in *Mortality and immortality: the anthropology and archaeology of death* (eds S C Humphreys, and H King), 137-47, London

Bloch, M, 1986 *From blessing to violence: history and ideology in the circumcision ritual of the Merina of Madagascar*, Cambridge

Bloch, M, 1998 Why trees are good to think with: towards an anthropology of the meaning of life, in *The social life of trees: anthropological perspectives on tree symbolism* (ed. L Rival), 39-56, Oxford

Bloch, M, 2005 *Essays on cultural transmission*, Oxford

Bloch, M, and Parry, J (eds), 1982 *Death and the regeneration of life*, Cambridge

Boast, R, 1995 Fine pots, pure pots, Beaker pots, in *'Unbaked Urns of Rudely Shape': essays on British and Irish pottery* (eds I Kinnes and G Varndell), Oxbow Monograph **55**, 69-80, Oxford

Bocherens, H, Billiou, D, Mariotti, M, Toussaint, M, Patou-Mathis, M, Bonjean, D and Otte, M, 1999 Palaeolenvironment and palaeodietary implications of isotopic biochemistry of last interglacial Neanderthal and mammal bones in Scladina cave (Belgium), *J Archaeol Sci* **26**, 599-607

Boismier, W A, 1995 An analysis of worked flint artefact concentrations from Maidenhead Thicket, Maidenhead, in, *Early settlement in Berkshire* (eds I Barnes, W A Boismier, R M J Cleal, A P Fitzpatrick, and M R Roberts), Wessex Archaeol Rep **6**, 52-64, Salisbury

Boismier, W A, and Mepham, L N, 1995 Excavation of a Mesolithic site at Windmill Hill, Nettlebed, Oxon, *Oxoniensia* **60**, 1-19

Boismier, W, Schreve, D C, White, M J, Robertson, D A, Stuart, A J, Etienne, S, Andrews, J, Coope, G R, Field, M, Green, F M L, Keen, D H, Lewis, S G, French, C A, Rhodes, E, Schwenninger, J-L, Tovey, K and O'Connor, S, 2003 A Middle Palaeolithic site at Lynford Quarry, Mundford, Norfolk: Interim statement, *Proc Prehist Soci* **69**, 315-24

Bonner, D, 1994 An interim report on archaeological investigations on land adjacent to Walton Lodge Lane, Aylesbury, unpubl. report, Buckinghamshire County Archaeological Service, Aylesbury

Bonney, D J, 1964 All Cannings: Rybury Camp, *Wilts Archaeol Nat Hist Mag* **59**, 185

Bonsall, C, and Smith, C, 1989 Late Palaeolithic and Mesolithic bone and antler artefacts from Britain: first reactions to accelerator dates, *Mesolithic Miscellany* **10 (1)**, 33-38

Bonsall, C, and Smith, C, 1990 Bone and antler technology in the British Late Palaeolithic and Mesolithic: the impact of accelerator dating, in *Contributions to the Mesolithic in Europe* (eds P M Vermeersch and P Van Peer), 359-68, Leuven

Booth P, 1997 A prehistoric-early Roman site near Lock Crescent, Kidlington, *Oxoniensia* **62**, 21-49

Booth, P, and Hayden, C, 2000 A Roman settlement at Mansfield College, *Oxoniensia* **65**, 291-331

Booth, P, and Simmonds, A, 2009 *Appleford's earliest farmers: archaeological work at Appleford Sidings, Oxfordshire*, Oxford Archaeology Occas Pap **17**, Oxford

Boston, C, Bowater, C, Boyle, A, and Holmes, A, 2003 Excavation of a Bronze Age barrow at the proposed Centre for Gene Function, South Parks Road, Oxford, 2002, *Oxoniensia* **68**, 179-200

Bowen, D Q (ed.), 1999 *A revised correlation of Quaternary deposits in the British Isles*, Geological Society Special Report **23**, London

Bowen, D Q, Hughes, S A, Sykes, G A and Miller, G H, 1989 Land-sea correlations in the Pleistocene based on isoleucine epimerization in non-marine molluscs, *Nature* **340**, 49-51

Bowen, D Q, Rose, J, McCabe, A M, 1986 Correlation of Quaternary glaciations in England, Ireland, Scotland and Wales, *Quaternary Science Reviews*, **5**, 299-340

Bowler, D and Robinson, M, 1980 Three round barrows at King's Weir, Wytham, Oxon, *Oxoniensia* **45**, 1-8

Bowman, S G E, Ambers, J C, and Leese, M N, 1990 Re-evaluation of British Museum radiocarbon dates issued between 1980 and 1984, *Radiocarbon* **32**, 59-79

Boyle, A, 1999, Human remains, in Barclay and Halpin 1999, 171-83

Boyle, A, Jennings, D, Miles, D, and Palmer, S, 1998 *The Anglo-Saxon cemetery at Butler's Field, Lechlade, Gloucestershire, 1: prehistoric and Roman activity and Anglo-Saxon grave catalogue*, Thames Valley Landscapes **10**, Oxford

Bradford, J P, 1951 Excavations at Cassington, Oxon, *Oxoniensia* **16**, 1-4

Bradley, P and Hey, G, 1993 A Mesolithic site at New Plantation, Fyfield and Tubney, Oxfordshire, *Oxoniensia* **58**,1-26

Bradley, P, 1995 Worked flint, in A J Barclay *et al.* 1995, 43-5

Bradley, P, 1999 Worked flint, in Barclay and Halpin 1999, 211-228

Bradley, P, 2004 Causewayed enclosures: monumentality, architecture, and spatial distribution of artefacts – the evidence from Staines, Surrey, in Cotton and Field 2004, 115-23

Bradley, P, 2005 Worked flint, in Richmond 2006, 85-8

Bradley, P, 2010 Worked flint from Mount Farm, Oxfordshire, in Lambrick 2010 webarchive, http://library.thehumanjourney.net/

Bradley, P, and Cramp, K, in prep. The worked flint, in Hey in prep.

Bradley, P, 2007 The worked flint, in Harding and Healy 2007

Bradley, P, in prep. Worked flint from Kings Low and Queens Low, Staffordshire, in *Kings Low and Queens Low* (ed. G Lock)

Bradley, R, 1984a *The social foundations of prehistoric Britain: themes and variations in the archaeology of power*, London

Bradley, R, 1984b Regional systems in Neolithic Britain, in Bradley and Gardiner 1984, 514

Bradley, R, 1984c The bank barrows and related monuments of Dorset in the light of recent fieldwork, *Proc Dorset Natur Hist Archaeol Soc* **105**, 15–20

Bradley, R, 1986a A reinterpretation of the Abingdon causewayed enclosure, *Oxoniensia* **51**, 18387

Bradley, R, 1986b The Bronze Age in the Oxford area: its local and regional significance, in Briggs *et al.* 1986, 38-48

Bradley, R, 1990 *The passage of arms: an archaeological analysis of prehistoric hoards and votive deposits*, Cambridge

Bradley, R, 1991 The evidence of earthwork monuments, in Barrett *et al.* 1991, 35-58

Bradley, R, 1992 The excavation of an oval barrow beside the Abingdon causewayed enclosure, Oxfordshire, *Proc Prehist Soc* **58**, 12742

Bradley, R, 1993 *Altering the earth: the origins of monuments in Britain and continental Europe*, Soc Antiq Scotland Monograph **8**, Edinburgh

Bradley, R, 1998a Interpreting enclosures, in Edmonds and Richards 1998, 188-203

Bradley, R, 1998b *The significance of monuments: on the shaping of human experience in Neolithic and Bronze Age Europe*, London

Bradley, R, 2000 *An archaeology of natural places*, London

Bradley, R, 2002 *The past in prehistoric societies*, London

Bradley, R, 2003 A life less ordinary: the ritualisation of the domestic sphere in later prehistoric Europe, *Cambridge Archaeol J* **13 (1)**, 5-23

Bradley, R, 2004 Domestication, sedentism, property and time: materiality and the beginnings of agriculture in northern Europe, in *Rethinking materiality* (eds E DeMarrais, C Gosden and C Renfrew), 107-15, Cambridge

Bradley, R, 2005 *Ritual and domestic life in prehistoric Europe*, London

Bradley, R, 2007 *The prehistory of Britain and Ireland*, Cambridge

Bradley, R, and Chambers, R, 1988 A new study of the cursus complex at Dorchester-on-Thames, *Oxford J Archaeol* **7**, 271-89

Bradley, R, and Edmonds, M, 1993 *Interpreting the axe trade: production and exchange in Neolithic Britain*, Cambridge

Bradley, R, and Fraser, E, 2010 Bronze Age barrows on the heathlands of southern England: construction, forms and interpretations, *Oxford J Archaeol* **29**, 15-33

Bradley, R, and Gardiner, J (eds), 1984 *Neolithic studies: a review of some current research*, BAR Brit. Ser. **133**, Oxford

Bradley, R, and Gordon, K, 1988 Human skulls from the river Thames: their dating and significance, *Antiquity* **62**, 503-09

Bradley, R, and Holgate, R, with Ford, S, 1984 The Neolithic sequence in the Upper Thames Valley, in Bradley and Gardiner 1984, 107-34

Bradley, R, and Keith-Lucas, M, 1975 Excavation and pollen analysis on a bell barrow at Ascot, Berkshire, *J Archaeol Science* **2**, 95-108

Brady, K, and Lamdin-Whymark, H, in press Excavation of a Neolithic to Roman landscape at Horcott Pit, near Fairford, Gloucestershire, 2003, *Trans Bristol Gloucestershire Archaeol Soc*

Bradley, R, Over, L, Startin D W A, and Weng, R, 1975-6 The excavation of a Neolithic site at Cannon Hill, Maidenhead, Berkshire, *Berkshire Archaeol J* **68**, 5-19

Braithwaite, M, 1984 Ritual and prestige in the prehistory of Wessex, *c* 2200-1400 BC: a new dimension to the archaeological evidence, in *Ideology, power and prehistory* (eds D Miller and C Tilley), 93-110, Cambridge

Branch, N P, and Green, C P, 2004 Environmental history of Surrey, in *Aspects of archaeology and history in Surrey: towards a research framework for the county* (eds J Cotton, G Crocker, and A Graham), 1-18, Guildford

Brandon, A, and Sumbler, M G, 1988 An Ipswichian fluvial deposit at Fulbeck, Lincolnshire and the chronology of the Trent terraces, *Journal of Quaternary Science* **3**, 127-33

Bratlund, B, 1999 Taubach revisited, *Jahrbuch des Romish-Germanischen Zentralmuseums Mainz* **46**, 61-174

Brewster T C M, 1992 *The excavation of the Whitegrounds Barrow, Burythorpe*, 2nd edn, Malton

Bridgland, D R, 1980 A reappraisal of Pleistocene stratigraphy in north Kent and eastern Essex, and new evidence concerning the former courses of the Thames and Medway, *Quaternary Newsletter* **32**, 15-24

Bridgland, D R, 1983a The Quaternary fluvial deposits of north Kent and eastern Essex. Unpubl. PhD thesis, City of London Polytechnic

Bridgland, D R, 1983b Problems in the application of lithostratigraphic classification to Pleistocene terrace deposits, *Quaternary newsletter* **55**, 1-8

Bridgland, D R, 1988a The Pleistocene fluvial stratigraphy and palaeogeography of Esssex, *Proc Geol Ass* **99**, 291-314

Bridgland, D R, 1988b The Quaternary derivation of quartzites used by Palaeolithic Man in the Thames Basin for Tool manufacture. British Archaeological Reports, British Series, **189**, 187-98

Bridgland, D R, 1994 *Quaternary of the Thames*, London

Bridgland, D R, 1995 The Quaternary sequence of the eastern Thames basin: problems of correlation, in *The Quaternary of the lower reaches of the Thames: field guide* (eds D R Bridgland, P Allen and B A Haggart), 35-49, Durham

Bridgland, D R, 2000 River terrace systems in north-west Europe: an archive of environmental change, uplift and early human occupation, *Quaternary Science Reviews* **19**, 1293-303

Bridgland, D R, Allen, P, Blackford, J, Parfitt, S and

Preece, R, 1995 New work on the Aveley silts and sands: A13 road improvement, Purfleet Road, Aveley, in *The Quaternary of the lower reaches of the Thames: field guide* (eds D R Bridgland, P Allen and B A Haggart), 201-16, Durham

Bridgland, D R, and D'Olier, B, 1995 The Pleistocene evolution of the Thames and Rhine drainage systems in the southern North Sea Basin, in *Island Britain: a Quaternary perspective* (ed. R C Preece), Geological Society Special Publication **96**, 27-45, London

Bridgland, D R, and Harding, P, 1993 Middle Pleistocene Thames terrace deposits at Globe Pit, Little Thurrock, and their contained Clactonian industry, *Proc Geol Ass* **104**, 263-83

Bridgland, D R, and Harding, P, 1994 Lion Pit tramway cutting, West Thurrock, in *Quaternary of the Thames* (ed. D R Bridgland), 237-51, London

Bridgland, D R, and Harding, P, 1995 Lion Pit Tramway Cutting (West Thurrock; TQ 598783), in *The Quaternary of the lower reaches of the Thames: field guide* (eds D R Bridgland, P Allen and B A Haggart), 217-29, Durham

Bridgland, D R, Preece, R C, Roe, H M, Tipping, R M, Coope, G R, Field, M H, Robinson, J E, Schreve, D C and Crowe, K, 2001 Middle Pleistocene interglacial deposits at Barling, Essex, England: evidence for a longer chronology for the Thames terrace sequence, *Journal of Quaternary Science* **16**, 813-40

Briggs, D J, 1973 Quaternary deposits of the Evenlode valley and adjacent areas, unpubl. Ph.D. thesis: Univ. Bristol.

Briggs, D J, 1976 River terraces of the Oxford area, in *Field guide to the Oxford region* (ed. D A Roe), 8-15, Oxford

Briggs, D J, 1988 The environmental background to human occupation in the Upper Thames valley during the Quaternary period, in *Non-flint stone tools and the Palaeolithic occupation of Britain* (eds R J MacRae and N Moloney), BAR Brit. Ser. **189**, 167-86

Briggs, D J, Coope, G R, and Gilbertson, D D, 1985 *The chronology and environmental framework of early Man in the Upper Thames Valley*, BAR Brit. Ser. **137**, Oxford

Briggs, D J, and Gilbertson, D D, 1973 The age of the Hanborough Terrace of the River Evenlode, Oxfordshire, *Proc Geol Ass* **84**, 155-173

Briggs, D J, and Gilbertson, D D, 1974 Recent studies of Pleistocene deposits in the Evenlode valley and adjacent areas of the Cotswolds. *Sound (Journal of the Plymouth Polytechnic Geological Society)* **3**, 7-22

Briggs, D J, and Gilbertson, D D, 1980 Quaternary processes and environments in the Upper Thames basin, *Trans Inst Brit Geog* **5**, 53-65

Briggs, G, Cook, J, and Rowley, T, 1986 *The archaeology of the Oxford region*, Oxford

Brossler, A, Early, R, and Allen, C, 2004 *Green Park (Reading Business Park), phase 2 excavations:*

Neolithic and Bronze Age sites, Thames Valley Landscapes **19**, Oxford

Brown, A G, 1995 The Mesolithic and later flint artefacts, in T G Allen 1995, 65-84

Brown, A G, 1989 Use-wear analysis of surface material – can it really be done? *Lithics* **10**, 33-6

Brown, A G, 1991 Structured deposition and technological change among the flaked stone artefacts from Cranbourne Chase, in *Papers on the prehistoric archaeology of Cranbourne Chase* (eds J Barrett, R Bradley and M Hall), Oxbow Monograph **11**, 101-133, Oxford

Brown, A G, and Bradley, P, 2006 Worked flint, in *Late Bronze Age habitation on a Thames Eyot at Wallingford: the archaeology of the Wallingford Bypass* (A M Cromarty, A Barclay, G Lambrick and M Robinson), Thames Valley Landscapes **22**, 58-70, Oxford

Brown, G, Field, D, and McOmish, D, 2005 *The Avebury landscape: aspects of the field archaeology of the Marlborough Downs*, Oxbow Books, Oxford

Brown, J A, 1887 *Palaeolithic man in North-West Middlesex*, London

Brown, J A, 1889 On the discovery of *Elephas Primigenius* associated with flint implements at Southall, *Proc Geol Ass* **10**, 361-72

Brown, J A, 1895 Notes on the high-level river drift between Hanwell and Iver, *Proc Geol Ass* **14**, 153-73

Brown, L, 1978 A survey of the condition of Oxfordshire long barrows, *Oxoniensia* **43**, 241-5

Brown, T, 1997 Clearances and clearings: deforestation in Mesolithic/Neolithic Britain, *Oxford J Archaeol* **16**, 133-46

Brown, T, 2009 *The environment and aggregate related archaeology*, Oxford

Brück, J (ed.), 2001 *Bronze Age landscapes: tradition and transformation*, Oxford

Brück, J, 1999a What's in a settlement? Domestic practice and residential mobility in early Bronze Age southern England, in *Making places in the prehistoric world: themes in settlement archaeology* (eds J Brück and M Goodman), 52-75, London

Brück, J, 1999b Ritual and rationality: some problems of interpretation in European archaeology, *European Journal of Archaeology* **2 (3)**, 313-44

Brück, J, 2000 Settlement, landscape and social identity: the early/middle Bronze Age transition in Wessex, Sussex and the Thames Valley, *Oxford J Archaeol* **19 (3)**, 273-300

Brück, J, 2004a Material metaphors: the relational construction of identity in early Bronze Age burials in Ireland and Britain, *J Social Archaeol* **4 (3)**, 307-33

Brück, J, 2004b Bronze Age burial practices in Scotland and beyond: differences and similarities, in *Scotland in ancient Europe* (eds I Shepherd and G Barclay), 179-88, Edinburgh

Bryant, I D, 1983 Facies sequences associated with some braided river deposits of late Pleistocene age from southern Britain, *International*

Association of Sedimentologists, Special Publications **6**, 267-75

Buck, C E, Cavanagh W G, and Litton, C D, 1996 *Bayesian approach to interpreting archaeological data*, Chichester

Buck, C E, Kenworthy, J B, Litton, C D, and Smith, A F M, 1991 Combining archaeological and radiocarbon information: a Bayesian approach to calibration, *Antiquity* **65 (249)**, 808-821

Buckingham, C M, Roe, D A and Scott, K, 1996 A preliminary report on the Stanton Harcourt channel deposits (Oxfordshire, England): geological context, vertebrate remains and palaeolithic stone artefacts, *Journal of Quaternary Science* **11**, 397-415

Buckley, V (ed.), 1990 *Burnt offerings: international contributions to burnt mound archaeology*, Dublin

Bull, A J, 1942 Pleistocene chronology, *Proc Geol Assoc* **52**, 1-45

Burchell, J P T, 1957 A temperate bed of the last interglacial period at Northfleet, Kent, *Geological Magazine* **94**, 212-214

Burchell, J P T, and Piggott, S, 1939 Decorated prehistoric pottery from the bed of the Ebbsfleet, North Fleet, Kent, *Antiq J* **19**, 405-20

Burenhult, G, and Westergaard, S (eds), 2003 *Stones and bones: formal disposal of the dead in Atlantic Europe during the Mesolithic-Neolithic interface, 6000-3000 BC*, BAR Int. Ser. **1201**, Oxford

Burgess, C, 1980 *The age of Stonehenge*, London

Burgess, C, 1986 'Urnes of no small variety': Collared Urns reviewed, *Proc Prehist Soc* **52**, 339-51

Burgess, C, and Shennan, S, 1976 The Beaker phenomenon: some suggestions, in *Settlement and economy in the 3rd and 2nd millennia BC* (eds C Burgess and R Miket), BAR Brit. Ser. **33**, 309-27, Oxford

Burl, A, 2000 *The stone circles of Britain, Ireland and Brittany*, New Haven and London

Butler, C, 2005 *Prehistoric flintwork*, Stroud

Butterworth, C A, and Lobb, S J 1992 *Excavations in the Burghfield area, Berkshire*, Wessex Archaeol Rep **1**, Salisbury

Cain, A J, 1982 Subfossil mollusca, in Case and Whittle 1982, 47

Cambridge, P, 1977 Whatever happened to the Boytonian? A review of the marine Plio-Pleistocene of the southern North Sea Basin, *Bulletin of the Geological Society of Norfolk* **29**, 23-45

Campbell, J B, 1977 *The Upper Palaeolithic in Britain*, Oxford

Campbell, J B, and Sampson, C G, 1971 *A new analysis of Kent's Cavern, Devonshire, England*, University of Oregon Anthropological Papers **3**, Oregon

Candy, I, and Schreve, D, C 2007 Land–sea correlation of Middle Pleistocene temperate sub-stages using high-precision uranium-series dating of tufa deposits from southern England, *Quaternary*

Science Reviews **26**, 1223-35

Canham, R, 1978 Excavations at London (Heathrow) Airport 1969, *Trans London and Middlesex Archaeol Soc* **29**, 1-44

Carbonell, E, Mosquera, M, Rodríguez, X P, Sala, R and van der Made, J, 1999 Out of Africa: the dispersal of the earliest technical systems reconsidered, *Journal of Anthropological Archaeology* **18**, 119-36

Care, V, 1979 The production and distribution of Mesolithic axes in southern England, *Proc Prehist Soc* **45**, 93-102

Carew, T, Bishop, B, Meddens, F, and Ridgeway, V, 2006 *Unlocking the landscape: archaeological investigations at Ashford Prison, Middlesex*, Pre-Construct Archaeol Monogr **5**, Great Dunham

Carrasco, D, 1999 *City of sacrifice: the Aztec empire and the role of violence in civilization*, Boston

Carter, R J, 2001 New evidence for seasonal human presence at the early Mesolithic site of Thatcham, Berkshire, England, *J Archaeol Sci* **28**, 1055-60

Cartwright, C, 2003 The bark vessels and associated wood fragments, in Ford and Pine 2003, 52-59

Case, H J, 1952-3 Mesolithic finds in the Oxford area, *Oxoniensia* **17-18**, 1-13

Case, H J, 1956a The Lambourn Seven barrows, *Berkshire Archaeol J* **55**, 15-31

Case, H J, 1956b The Neolithic causewayed camp at Abingdon, Berks, *Antiq J*, **36**, 1130

Case, H J, 1956c Beaker pottery from the Oxford region, *Oxoniensia* **21**, 121

Case, H J, 1963 Notes on the finds and on ring-ditches in the Oxford region, *Oxoniensia* **28**, 19-52

Case, H J, 1973 A ritual site in NE Ireland, in *Megalithic graves and ritual*, (eds G Daniel and P Kjaeruns), 173-96, Copenhagen

Case, H J, 1977 The Beaker culture in Britain and Ireland, in *Beakers in Britain and Europe* (ed. R Mercer), BAR Int. Ser. **26**, 71-101, Oxford

Case, H J, 1982a The linear ditches and southern enclosure, North Stoke, in Case and Whittle 1982, 60-75

Case, H J, 1982b Cassington 1950-2: late Neolithic pits and the Big Enclosure, in Case and Whittle 1982, 118-51

Case, H J, 1986 The Mesolithic and Neolithic in the Oxford Region, in Briggs *et al.* 1986, 18-37

Case, H J, 1993 Beakers: deconstruction and after, *Proc Prehist Soc* **59**, 24168

Case, H J, 1995 Some Wiltshire Beakers and their contexts, *Wilts Hist Archaeol Mag* **88**, 1-17

Case, H J, 2001 The Beaker culture in Britain and Ireland: groups, European contacts and chronology, in *Bell Beakers today: pottery, people, culture, symbols in prehistoric Europe* (ed. F Nicolis), 61-77, Trento

Case, H J, 2004a Bell Beaker and Corded Ware Culture burial associations: a bottom-up rather than top-down approach, in Gibson and Sheridan, 2004, 201-14

Case, H J, 2004b Beaker burial in Britain and Ireland: a role for the dead, in *Graves and funerary rituals during the late Neolithic and early Bronze Age in Europe (2700-2000 BC)*, (eds M Besse and J Desideri), BAR Int. Ser. **1284**, 195-201, Oxford

Case, H J, Bayne, N, Steele, S, Avery, G, and Stermeister, H, 1964-5 Excavations at City Farm, Hanborough, Oxon., *Oxoniensia* **29-30**, 1-98

Case, H J, and Sturdy, D, 1959 Archaeological notes, *Oxoniensia* **24**, 98-102

Case, H J, and Whittle, A W R (eds), 1982 *Settlement patterns in the Oxford region: excavations at the Abingdon causewayed enclosure and other sites*, CBA Res Rep **44**, London

Catling, H W, 1982 Six ring-ditches at Standlake, in Case and Whittle 1982, 88-102

Catt, J A, 1991 Late Devensian glacial deposits and glaciations in eastern England and the adjoining offshore region, in *Glacial deposits in Great Britain and Ireland* (eds J Ehlers, P L Gibbard and J Rose), 61-8, Rotterdam

Cave-Browne, P, 1992 The use of iron pyrites for the creation of fire, *Lithics* **13**, 52-60

Cave, A J E, 1938 Appendix on human bone, in Donovan 1938, 162-4

Chandler, R H, 1914 The Pleistocene deposits of Crayford, *Proc Geol Ass* **25**, 61-71

Chandler, R H, 1916 The implements and cores of Crayford, *Proceedings of the Prehistoric Society of East Anglia* **2**, 240-248

Chapman, J, 2000 *Fragmentation in archaeology*, London

Chatterton, R, 2006 Ritual, in *Mesolithic Britain and Ireland: new approaches*, (eds C Conneller, and G M Warren), 101-20, Stroud

Cheshire, D A, 1981 A contribution towards a glacial stratigraphy of the lower Lea valley, and implications for the Anglian Thames, *Quaternary Studies*, **1**, 27-69

Cheshire, D A, 1983a Till lithology in Hertfordshire and west Essex, in *Diversion of the Thames* (ed. J Rose), 50-9, Cambridge

Cheshire, D A, 1983b Westmill. In *Diversion of the Thames* (ed. J Rose), 120-132, Cambridge

Cheshire, D A, 1983c Hoddesdon, St Albans Sand and Gravel Co. Quarry and Hoddesdon Nursery Pits, in *Diversion of the Thames* (ed. J Rose), 140-148, Cambridge

Cheshire, D A, 1986 The lithology and stratigraphy of the Anglian deposits of the Lea Basin, unpubl. PhD thesis, Hatfield Polytechnic

Chesterman, J T, 1977 Burial rites in a Cotswold long barrow, *Man* **12**, 22-32

Childe, V G, 1931 The forest cultures of northern Europe: a study in evolution and diffusion, *J Royal Anthropological Institute* **61**, 325-48

Childe, V G, and Smith, I F, 1954 The excavation of a Neolithic barrow on Whiteleaf Hill, Bucks, *Proc Prehist Soc* **20**, 212-30

Chisham, C, 2004 Mesolithic human activity and environmental change: a case study of the

Kennet Valley, Unpubl. PhD thesis, Univ. Reading

Chisham, C, 2006 Thames and Solent research framework: the Upper Palaeolithic and Mesolithic of Berkshire, http://thehuman journey.net/pdf_store/sthames/phase3/County/Upper%20Palaeolithic%20&%20Mesolithic/Upper%20Palaeolithic%20&%20Mesolithic%20Berkshire.pdf (checked July 2010)

Churchill, D M, 1962 The stratigraphy of the Mesolithic Sites III and V at Thatcham, Berkshire, England, *Proc Prehist Soc* **28**, 362-70

Churchill, S E, and Smith, F H, 2000 Makers of the early Aurignacian of Europe, *American Journal of Physical Anthropology (yearbook)* **113**, 61-115

Clapham, A J, 1995 Plant remains, in Barnes *et al.* 1995, 35-45; 84-5

Clark, J G D, 1928 Discoidal polished flint knives: their typology and distribution, *Proc Prehist Soc E Anglia* **6**, 40-54

Clark, J G D, 1940 *Prehistoric England*, London

Clark, J G D, 1966 The invasion hypothesis in British archaeology, *Antiquity*, **40 (159)**, 172-89

Clark, J G D, Higgs, E S, and Longworth, I H, 1960 Excavations at the Neolithic site of Hurst Fen, Mildenhall, Suffolk, 1954, 1957 and 1958, *Proc Prehist Soc* **26**, 202-45

Clark, P, and Rady J, 2008 The prehistoric period, in *At the great crossroads: prehistoric, Roman and medieval discoveries on the Isle of Thanet, 1994-95* (eds P Bennett, P Clark, A Hicks, J Rady and I Riddler), Canterbury Archaeological Trust Occasional Paper **4**, 9-100, Canterbury

Clark, J G D, and Rankine, W F, 1939 Excavations at Farnham, Surrey, 1937-38, *Proc Prehist Soc* **5**, 61-118

Clarke, D L, 1970 *Beaker pottery of Great Britain and Ireland*, Cambridge

Clarke, D L, 1976a Mesolithic Europe: the economic basis, in *Problems in economic and social archaeology* (eds G de G Sieveking, I H Longworth and K E Wilson), 449-81, London

Clarke, D L, 1976b The beaker network: social and economic models, *Glockenbechersymposion Oberried 1974* (eds J N Lanting and J D van der Waals), 459-77, Bussum

Clarke, D V, Cowie, T G, and Foxon, A, 1985 *Symbols of power at the time of Stonehenge*, Edinburgh

Clarke, R, 1935 The flint-knapping industry at Brandon, *Antiquity* **9**, 38-56

Cleal, R M J, 1992a Summary, in Gingell 1992, 151-3

Cleal, R M J, 1992b The Neolithic and Beaker pottery, in Gingell 1992, 61-70

Cleal, R M J, 1992c The Dean Bottom Beaker pit assemblage, in Gingell 1992, 111-2

Cleal, R M J, 1992d Significant form: ceramic styles in the earlier Neolithic of southern England, in *Vessels for the ancestors: essays on the Neolithic of Britain and Ireland in honour of Audrey Henshall* (eds N Sharples and A Sheridan), 286–304, Edinburgh

Cleal, R M J, 1999 Prehistoric pottery, in Barclay and Halpin 1999, 195-210

Cleal, R M J, 2005 'The small compass of a grave': early Bronze Age burial in and around Avebury and the Marlborough Downs, in Brown *et al.* 2005, 115-32

Cleal, R M J, and Allen, M, 1995 The visual envelope, in Cleal *et al.* 1995, 34-40

Cleal, R M J and MacSween, A (eds), 1999 *Grooved Ware in Britain and Ireland*, Neolithic Studies Group Seminar Papers **3**, Oxford

Cleal, R M J, Walker, K E and Montague, R, 1995 *Stonehenge in its landscape: 20th-century excavations*, Engl Heritage Archaeol Rep **10**, London

Clifford, E M, 1936 Notgrove long barrow, Gloucestershire, *Archaeologia* **86**, 119-61

Clough, T H McK, and Cummins, W A, 1979 *Stone axe studies*, CBA Res Rep **23**, London

Clough, T H McK, and Cummins, W A, 1988 *Stone axe studies 2*, CBA Res Rep **67**, London

Coles, B, 1990 Anthropomorphic wooden figures from Britain and Ireland, *Proc Prehist Soc* **56**, 315-33

Coles, B, 2006 *Beavers in Britain's past*, Oxford

Coles, J M, and Coles, B, 1986 *Sweet Track to Glastonbury: the Somerset Levels in prehistory*, London

Coles, S, Ford, S and Taylor, A, 2008, An early Neolithic grave and occupation, and an Early Bronze Age hearth on the Thames foreshore at Yabsley Street, Blackwall, London, *Proc Prehist Soc* **74**, 215–33

Collins, D, 1969 Culture traditions and environment of early man, *Current Anthropology* **10**, 267-316

Collins, D, 1978 *Early man in west Middlesex: the Yiewsley Palaeolithic sites*, London

Colls, K, 2002 Witney, Downs Road, *S Midlands Archaeol* **32**, 40

Connah, G, 1965 Excavations at Knap Hill, Alton Priors, *Wilts Archaeol Nat Hist Mag* **60**, 1-23

Conneller, C, 2004 Becoming deer: corporeal transformations at Star Carr, *Archaeological Dialogues* 11 (1), 37-56

Conneller, C, 2005 Moving beyond sites: Mesolithic technology in the landscape, in *Mesolithic studies at the beginning of the 21st century* (eds N Milner and P Woodman), 42-55, Oxford

Conneller, C, and Warren, G, 2006 *Mesolithic Britain and Ireland: new approaches*, Stroud

Conway, B, McNabb, J and Ashton, N, (eds), 1996 *Excavations at Barnfield Pit, Swanscombe, 1968-72*, British Museum Press Occasional Paper **94**, London

Conway, B, and Waechter, J d'A, 1977 Lower Thames and Medway valleys: Barnfield Pit, Swanscombe, in *South east England and the Thames Valley: guide book for excursion A5, X INQUA Congress* (eds E R Shephard-Thorne and J J Wymer), 38-44, Norwich

Coombs, J A, 1873 On a recently exposed section at Battersea, *Proc Geol Ass* **3**, 33-8

Coope, G R, 1982 Coleoptera from two Late Devensian sites in the Lower Colne Valley, West London, England, *Quaternary Newsletter* **38**, 1-6

Coope, G R, 2001 Biostratigraphical distinction of interglacial coleopteran assemblages from southern Britain attributed to Oxygen Isotope Stages 5e and 7, *Quaternary Science Reviews* **20**, 1717-22

Coope, G R, and Angus, R B, 1975 An ecological study of a temperate interlude in the middle of the last glaciation, based on fossil Coleoptera from Isleworth, Middlesex, *Journal of Animal Ecology* **44**, 365-391

Coope, G R, Gibbard, P L, Hall, A R, Preece, R C, Robinson, J E, and Sutcliffe, A J, 1997 Climatic and environmental reconstruction based on fossil assemblages from Middle Devensian (Weichselian) deposits of the River Thames at South Kensington, central London, UK, *Quaternary Science Reviews* **16**, 1163-1195

Copley, M S, Berstan, R, Dudd, S N, Aillaud, S, Mukherjee, A J, Straker, V, Payne, S and Evershed, R P, 2005b Processing of milk products in pottery vessels through British prehistory, *Antiquity* **79**, 895-908

Copley, M S, Berstan, R, Dudd, S N, Docherty, G, Mukherjee, A J, Straker, V, Payne, S, and Evershed, R P, 2003 Direct chemical evidence for widespread dairying in prehistoric Britain, *Proc National Acad Sci USA* **100**, 1524-9

Copley, M S, Berstan, R, Mukherjee, A J, Dudd, S N, Straker, V, Payne, S and Evershed, R P, 2005a Dairying in antiquity III: evidence from absorbed lipid residues dating to the British Neolithic, *J Archaeol Sci* **32**, 523-546

Copley, M S and Evershed, R P, 2007 Organic residue analysis, in Benson and Whittle 2007, 285-8

Cotton, J, 2004 Surrey's early past: a survey of recent work, in *Aspects of archaeology and history in Surrey: towards a research framework for the county* (eds J Cotton, C Crocker and A Graham), 19-38, Guildford

Cotton, J, Elsden, N, Pipe, A, Rayner, L, 2006 Taming the wild: a final Neolithic/earlier Bronze Age aurochs deposit from west London, in *Animals in the Neolithic of Britain and Europe* (eds D Serjeantson and D Field), Neolithic Studies Group Seminar Papers 7, 149-67, Oxford

Cotton, J, and Field, D, 2004 *Towards a new stone age: aspects of the Neolithic in south-east England*, CBA Res Rep **137**, York

Cotton, J, and Green, A, 2004 Further prehistoric finds from Greater London, *Trans London and Middlesex Archaeol Soc* **55**, 119-151

Cotton, J, Mills, J and Clegg, G, 1986 *Archaeology of West Middlesex: the London borough of Hillingdon from the earliest hunters to the late medieval period*, Uxbridge

Cotton, J, and Williams, D, 1997 Two early Bronze Age flat axes from Woldingham and South Nutfield, *Surrey Archaeol Collect* **84**, 181-4

Cotton, J, and Wood, B, 1996 Recent prehistoric finds from the Thames foreshore and beyond in Greater London, *Trans London Middlesex Archaeol Soc* **47**, 1-3

Cowie, R, 2008 Evidence for Neolithic and Bronze Age activity at Ashford Hospital, *Surrey Archaeol Collect* **94**, 71-90

Cram, C L, 1982 Animal bones, in Case and Whittle 1982, 43-7

Cramp, K, 2006 Flint, in Lewis *et al.* 2006, CD Rom, section 3

Cramp, K, 2007 The Flint, in Benson and Whittle 2007, 289-314

Cranshaw, S, 1983 *Handaxes and cleavers: selected Anglian Acheulean industries*, BAR Brit. Ser. **113**, Oxford

Crawford, O G S, 1935 Rectangular enclosures: a note on Mr Leeds' paper, *Antiq J* **15**, 77-8

Crockett, A 2001 The archaeological landscape of Imperial College sports ground, part 1: prehistoric *London Archaeol* **9 (11)**, 295-99

Cromarty, A M, Barclay, A, Lambrick, G, and Robinson, M A, 2006 *Late Bronze Age ritual and habitation on a Thames eyot at Whitecross Farm, Wallingford: the archaeology of the Wallingford Bypass, 1986-92*, Thames Valley Landscapes **22**, Oxford

Cross, S, 2003 Irish Neolithic settlement architecture – a reappraisal, in Armit *et al.* 2003, 195-202

Cuenca, C, 2006 Banbury, Banbury Booster 876F, *S Midlands Archaeol* **36**, 35-9

Cunliffe, B, and Renfrew, C (eds), 1997 *Science and Stonehenge*, Proc Brit Acad **92**, Oxford

Cunnington, M E, 1907 Notes on the opening of a Bronze Age barrow at Manton, near Marlborough, *The Reliquary and Illustrated Archaeologist* **13**, 28-46

Cunnington, M E, 1908 Notes on the opening of a Bronze Age barrow at Manton near Marlborough, *Wilts Archaeol Nat Hist Mag* **35**, 1-20

Cunnington, M E, 1909-10 Notes on the barrows on King's Play Down, Heddington, *Wilts Archaeol Nat Hist Mag* **36**, 311-7

Cunnington, M E, 1911-12 Knap Hill Camp, *Wiltshire Archaeol Nat Hist Mag* **37**, 42-65

Cunnington, M E, 1929 *Woodhenge*, Devizes

Cunnington, M E, 1931 The 'Sanctuary' on Overton Hill, near Avebury, *Wiltshire Archaeol Mag* **45**, 300-35

Curle, A O, 1924 Two late Neolithic vessels from the Thames, *Antiq J* **4**, 149-50

Currant, A P, 1987 Late Pleistocene Saiga antelope *Saiga tatarica* on Mendip, *Proceedings of the University of Bristol Spelaeological Society* **18**, 74-80

Currant, A P, 1991 A Late Glacial Interstadial mammal fauna from Gough's cave, Cheddar, Somerset, England, in *The Late Glacial in north-west Europe: human adaptation and environmental change at the end of the Pleistocene* (eds N Barton, A J Roberts and D A Roe), CBA Research Report **77**, 48-50, London

Currant, A P, 2004 The Late Glacial Interstadial human occupation site at Gough's Cave, Cheddar, Somerset, in *The Quaternary Mammals of southern and eastern England: field guide* (ed. D C Schreve), 93-100, London

Currant, A P, and Jacobi, R M, 2001 A formal mammalian biostratigraphy for the Late Pleistocene of Britain, *Quaternary Science Reviews* **20**, 1707-1716

Currant, A, and Jacobi, R, 2002 Human presence and absence in Britain during the early part of the Late Pleistocene, in *Le Dernier Interglaciaire et les occupations humaines du Palaeolithique* (eds W Roebroeks and A Tuffreau), 105-113, Lille

Curwen, C, 1930 Neolithic camps, *Antiquity* **4**, 22-54

D'Errico, F, Zilhao, J, Julien, M, Baffier, D, Pelegrin, J, Conard, N J, Demars, P-Y, Hublin, J-J, Mellars, P, Mussi, M, Svoboda, J, Taborin, Y, Vega Toscano, L G, and White, R, 1998 Neanderthal acculturation in Western Europe? A critical review of the evidence and its interpretation, *Current Anthropology* **39 (2)**, Supplement: the Neanderthal problem and the evolution of human behavior, S1-S44

Darbyshire, R D, 1874 Notes on the discoveries in Ehrenside Tarn, Cumberland, *Archaeologia* **44**, 273-92

Dark, P, 2000 Revised 'absolute' dating of the early Mesolithic site of Star Carr, North Yorkshire, in the light of changes in the early Holocene tree-ring chronology, *Antiquity* **74** 304-7

Dark, P, and Gent, H, 2001 Pests and diseases of prehistoric crops: a yield 'honeymoon' for early grain crops in Europe?', *Oxford J Archaeol* **20 (1)**, 59-78

Darvill, T C, 1982 *The megalithic chambered tombs of the Cotswold-Severn region*, Highworth

Darvill, T C, 1986 Prospects for dating Neolithic sites and monuments in the Cotswolds and adjacent areas, in *Archaeological results from accelerator dating* (eds J Gowlett and R E M Hedges), Oxford Comm Archaeol Monogr **11**, 119-24, Oxford

Darvill, T C, 1987 *Prehistoric Gloucestershire*, Gloucester

Darvill, T C, 1996 Neolithic buildings in England, Wales and the Isle of Man, in Darvill and Thomas 1996, 77-112

Darvill, T C, 1997 Ever increasing circles: the sacred geographies of Stonehenge in its landscape, in Cunliffe and Renfrew 1997, 167-202

Darvill, T C, 2004 *Long barrows of the Cotswolds and surrounding areas*, Stroud

Darvill, T C, 2006 Early prehistory, in *Twenty-five years of archaeology in Gloucestershire: a review of new discoveries and new thinking in Gloucestershire, South Gloucestershire and Bristol, 1979-2004* (eds N Holbrook, N, and J Jürica), Bristol and Gloucestershire Archaeological Report **3**, 5-60, Cirencester

Darvill, T C, and Thomas, J, 1996 *Neolithic houses in northwest Europe and beyond* Neolithic Studies Group Seminar Papers **1**, Oxbow Monograph **57**, Oxford

David, A, 1998 Two assemblages of later Mesolithic microliths from Seamer Carr, North Yorkshire: fact and fancy, in *Stone Age archaeology: essays in honour of John Wymer*, (eds N Ashton, F Healy, and P Pettit), 196-204, Oxford

Davies, D, 1997 *Death, ritual and belief*, London

Davies, P, Rob, J G, and Ladbrook, D, 2005 Woodland clearance in the Mesolithic: the social aspects, *Antiquity* **79**, 280-8

Dawkins, W B, 1872 *The British Pleistocene Mammalia, Part V: British Pleistocene Ovidae Ovibos moschatus; BLAINVILLE*, London

Dawkins, W B, 1880 *Early man in Britain and his place in the Tertiary Period*, London

Day, S P, 1991 Post-glacial vegetational history of the Oxford region, *New Phytologist* **119**, 445-70

de Lumley, H, 1969 A Palaeolithic camp site near Nice, *Scientific American* **220**, 42-50

Dennell, R, 1982 *European economic prehistory*, London

Dennell, R, and Roebroeks, W, 1996 The earliest colonization of Europe: the short chronology revisited, *Antiquity* **70**, 535-42

Devaney, R, 2005 A green barbed and tanged arrowhead from Oxfordshire, *Lithics* **26**, 106

Dewey, H, and Bromehead, C E N, 1915 *The geology of the country around Windsor and Chertsey*, London

Dewey, H, and Bromehead, C E N, 1921 *The geology of south London*, London

Dewey, H, Bromehead, C E N, Chatwin, C P and Dines, H P, 1924 *The geology of the country around Dartford*, London

Díaz-Andreu, M, Lucy, S, Babić, S and Edwards, D N (eds) 2005 *The archaeology of identity: approaches to gender, age status, ethnicity and religion*, London

Dimbleby, G W, 1958 Pollen, in Wymer 1958, 25-33

Dixon, P, 1988 The Neolithic settlements on Crickley Hill, in *Enclosures and defences in the Neolithic of western Europe*, (eds C Burgess, P Topping, C Mordant and M Madison), BAR Int Ser. **403**, 75-88, Oxford

Dodd, A (ed.), 2003 *Oxford before the university*, Thames Valley Landscapes **17**, Oxford

Donaldson, P, 1977 The excavation of a multiple round barrow at Barnack, Cambridgeshire, 1974-1976, *Antiq J* **57**, 197-231

Donovan, H E, 1938 Adlestrop Hill barrow, Gloucestershire, *Trans Bristol Gloucester Archaeol Soc* **60**, 152-64

Downes, J, 1999 Cremation: a spectacle and a journey, in *The loved body's corruption: archaeological contributions to the study of human mortality* (eds J Downes, and T Pollard), 19–29, Glasgow

Drewett, P, 1977 The Excavation of a Neolithic causewayed enclosure on Offham Hill, East Sussex, *Proc Prehist Soc* **43**, 201-42

Duigan, S L, 1955 Plant remains from the gravels of the Summertown-Radley terrace near

Dorchester, Oxfordshire, *Quarterly Journal of the Geological Society of London* **111**, 225-38

Duigan, S L. 1956 Interglacial plant remains from the Wolvercote Channel, Oxford, *Quarterly Journal of the Geological Society of London* **112**, 363-72

Dunning, G C and Wheeler, R E M, 1931 A barrow at Dunstable, Bedfordshire, *Archaeol J* **88**, 193-217

Dunning, G C, 1932 Bronze Age settlements and a Saxon hut near Bourton-on-the-Water, Gloucestershire, *Antiq J* **12**, 279-93

Dyer, J F, 1961 Barrows of the Chilterns. *Archaeol J* **116**, 1-24

Edmonds, M, 1993 Interpreting causewayed enclosures in the past and the present, in *Interpretative archaeology* (ed. C Tilley), 99-142, Oxford

Edmonds, M, 1999 *Ancestral geographies of the Neolithic: landscapes, monuments and memory*, London

Edmonds, M, and Richards, C, 1998 *Understanding the Neolithic of North-west Europe*, Glasgow

Edwards, C J, Bollongino, R, Scheu, A, Chamberlain, A, tresset, A, Vigne, J-D, Baird, J, Larson, G, Ho, S Y W, Heupink, T H, Shapiro, B, Freeman, A R, Thomas, M G, Arbogast, R-M, Arndt, B, Bartosiewicz, L, Benecke, N, Budja, M, Chaix, L, Choyke, A M, Coqueugniot, E, Döhle, H-J, Göldner, H, Hartz, S, Helmer, D, Herzig, B, Hongo, H, Mashkour, M, Özdogan, M, Pucher, E, Roth, G, Schade-Lindig, S, Schmölcke, U, Schulting, R J, Stephan, E, Uerpmann, H-P, Vörös, I, Voytek, B, Bradley, D G and Burger, J, 2007 Mitochondrial DNA analysis shows a Near Eastern Neolithic origin for domestic cattle and no indication of domestication of European aurochs, *Proc Roy Soc London B* **274**, 1377–85

Ehrenberg, M R, 1977 *Bronze Age spearheads from Berks, Bucks and Oxon*. BAR Brit. Ser. **34**, Oxford

Ehrenberg, M R, 1980 The occurrence of Bronze Age metalwork in the Thames: an investigation, *Trans London Middlesex Archaeol Soc* **31**, 1-15

Ellaby, R, 1987 The Upper Palaeolithic and Mesolithic in Surrey, in Bird and Bird 1987, 53-69

Ellaby, R, 2004 Food for thought: a late Mesolithic site at Charlwood, Surrey, in Cotton and Field 2004, 12-23

Ellis, C J, Allen, M J, Gardiner, J, Harding, P, Ingrem, C, Powell, A, and Scaife, R G, 2003 An early Mesolithic seasonal hunting site in the Kennet Valley, Southern England, *Proc Prehist Soc* **69**, 107-36

Ellison, R, Woods, M A, Allen, D J, Forster, A, Pharaoh T C and King, C, 2004 *Geology of London: special memoir for 1:50,000 geological sheets 256 (North London), 257 (Romford), 270 (South London) and 271 (Dartford) (England and Wales)*, Brit. Geol. Survey, Keyworth, Nottingham

Eogan, G, 1986 *Knowth and other passage-tombs of Ireland*, London

Eogan, G, and Richardson, H, 1982 Two maceheads from Knowth, County Meath, *J Roy Soc Antiq Ir* **112**,123-138

Evans, C and Hodder, I, 2006 *A woodland archaeology: Neolithic sites at Haddenham*, Cambridge

Evans, C, Pollard, P, and Knight, M, 1999 Life in woods: tree-throws, 'settlement' and forest cognition *Oxford J Archaeol* **18** (3), 241-54

Evans, J A, Chenery, C A and Fitzpatrick, A P, 2006, Bronze Age childhood migration of individuals near Stonehenge revealed by Strontium and Oxygen isotope tooth enamel analysis, *Archaeometry* **48** (2), 309-21

Evans, J G, 1971 Habitat change on the calcareous soils of Britain: the impact of Neolithic man, in *Economy and settlement in Neolithic and early Bronze Age Britain and Europe* (ed. D D A Simpson), 27-73, Leicester

Evans, J G, 1972 *Land snails in archaeology*, London

Evans, J G, 1991 Synthesis of the environmental evidence, in Needham 1991, 363-8

Evans, J G, Limbrey, S, and Macphail, R, 2007 The environmental setting, in Benson and Whittle 2007, 55-77

Evans, J G, Limbrey, S, Maté, I, and Mount, R, 1993 An environmental history of the upper Kennet valley, Wiltshire, for the last 10,000 years, *Proc Prehist Soc* **59**, 139-95

Evans, J G, Rouse, A J, and Sharples, N M, 1988 The landscape setting of causewayed camps: some recent work on the Maiden Castle enclosure, in Barrett and Kinnes 1988, 73-84

Evans, J G, and Smith, I F, 1983 Excavations at Cherhill, North Wiltshire, 1967, *Proc Prehist Soc* **49**, 43-117

Evans, M, 1995 The Mollusca from the henge, in A J Barclay *et al.* 1995

Evans, P, 1971 *Towards a Pleistocene time scale. The Phanerozoic time scale: A supplement*, Geological Society Special Publication **5/2**, London

Evans, S J, 1897 *Ancient stone implements, weapons and ornaments of Great Britain*, 2nd edn, London

Evens, E D, Smith, I F, and Wallis, F S, 1972 The petrological identification of stone implements from south-western England, *Proc Prehist Soc* **38**, 235–75

Exon, S, Gaffney, V, Woodward, A, and Yorston, R, 2000 *Stonehenge landscapes: journeys through real and imagined worlds*, Oxford

Fairbairn, A S, 2000 *Plants in Neolithic Britain and beyond*, Neolithic Studies Group Seminar Papers **5**, Oxford

Farizy, C, and David, F, 1992 Subsistence and behavioral patterns of some middle Paleolithic local groups, in *The Middle Paleolithic: adaptation, behavior and variability* (eds H Dibble and P A Mellars), University of Pennsylvania University Museum Monograph **72**, 87-96, Philadelphia

Farley, M E, 1978 Excavations at Low Farm, Fulmer, Bucks 1: the Mesolithic occupation, *Rec Buckinghamshire* **20**, 601-616

Farley, M E, 2007 Upper Palaeolithic and Mesolithic Buckinghamshire 38,000-4000 BC, http://thehumanjourney.net/pdf_store/sthames /phase3/County/Upper%20Palaeolithic%20&

%20Mesolithic/Upper%20Palaeolithic%20&%20 Mesolithic%20Buckinghamshire.pdf (checked July 2010)

Featherstone, R, and Bewley, R, 2000 Recent aerial reconnaissance in north Oxfordshire, *Oxoniensia* **65**, 13-26

Feblot-Augustin, J, 1999 Raw material transport patterns and settlement systems in the European Lower and Middle Palaeolithic: continuity, change and variability, in *The Middle Palaeolithic occupation of Europe* (eds W Roebroeks and C Gamble), 193-214, Leiden

Field, D, 1989 Tranchet tools and Thames picks: Mesolithic core tools from the west London Thames, *Trans London Middlesex Archaeol Soc* **40**, 1-25

Field, D, 1998 Round barrows and the harmonious landscape: placing early Bronze Age burial monuments in south-east England, *Oxford J Archaeol* **17**, 309-26

Field, D, 2004 Sacred geographies in the Neolithic of south-east England, in Cotton and Field 2004, 153-63

Field, D, 2006 *Earthen long barrows: the earliest monuments in the British Isles*, Stroud

Field, D, and Cotton, J, 1987 Neolithic Surrey: a survey of the evidence, in Bird and Bird 1987, 71-96

Field, M, Huntley, B, and Muller, H, 1994 Eemian climatic fluctuations observed in a European pollen record, *Nature* **371**, 779-783

Field, N H, Matthews, C L and Smith, I F, 1964 New Neolithic sites in Dorset and Bedfordshire, with a note on the distribution of Neolithic storage pits in Britain, *Proc Prehist Soc* **15**, 352-81

Field, D, and Woolley, A, 1983 A jadeite axe from Staines Moor, *Surrey Archaeol Collect* **74**, 141-5

Finlayson, C, Giles Pacheco, F, Rodriguez-Vidal, J, Fa, D A, Maria Gutierrez Lopez, J, Santiago Perez, A, Finlayson, G, Allue, E, Baena Preysler, J, Caceres, I, Carrion, J S, Fernandez Jalvo, Y, Gleed-Owen, C P, Jimenez Espejo, F J, Lopez, P, Antonio Lopez Saez, J, Antonio Riquelme Cantal, J, Sanchez Marco, A, Giles Guzman, F, Brown, K, Fuentes, N, Valarino, C Λ, Villalpando, A, Stringer, C B, Martinez Ruiz, F, and Sakamoto, T, 2006 Late survival of Neanderthals at the southernmost extreme of Europe, *Nature* **443**, 850-3

Fitzpatrick, A, 2003 The Amesbury Archer, *Curr Archaeol* **184**, 146-52

Fleming, A, 1971 Territorial patterns in Bronze Age Wessex, *Proc Prehist Soc* **37**, 352-81

Fleming, A, 2004 Hail to the chiefdom? The quest for social archaeology, in *Explaining social change: studies in honour of Colin Renfrew* (eds J Cherry, C Scarre, and S Shennan), 141-47, Cambridge

Foley, R, and Lahr, M M, 1997 Mode 3 technologies and the evolution of modern humans, *Cambridge Archaeol J* **7**, 3-36

Ford, S, 1987a *East Berkshire archaeological survey*, Berkshire County Council Department of Highways and Planning Occas Pap **1**, Reading

Ford, S, 1987b Flint scatters and prehistoric settlement patterns in south Oxfordshire and east Berkshire, in *Lithic analysis in later British prehistory* (eds A Brown and M Edmonds), BAR Brit. Ser. **162**, 101-35, Oxford

Ford, S, 1991 An early Bronze Age pit circle from Charnham Lane, Hungerford, Berkshire, *Proc Prehist Soc* **57**, 179-81

Ford, S, 1991-3 Excavations at Eton Wick, *Berks Archeaol J* **74**, 27-36

Ford, S, 1992 The nature and development of prehistoric settlement and land-use in the Middle Thames Region (8000-500 BC), with special reference to the evidence from lithic artefacts, unpubl. PhD thesis, Univ. Reading

Ford, S, 1997 Loddon Valley (Berkshire) field-walking survey, *Berkshire Archaeol J* **75**, 11-33

Ford, S, 2002, *Charnham Lane, Hungerford, Berkshire: archaeological investigations, 1988–97*, TVAS Monograph **1**, Reading

Ford, S, Bradley, R, Hawkes, J, and Fisher, P, 1984 Flint-working in the metal age, *Oxford J Archaeol* **3 (2)**, 157-73

Ford, S, Lowe, J, and Pine, J, 2006 Early Bronze Age, Roman and medieval boundaries and trackways at Howbery Park, Crowmarsh Gifford, Oxfordshire, *Oxoniensia* **71**, 197-210

Ford, S, with Entwistle, R, and Taylor, K, 2003 *Excavations at Cippenham, Slough, Berkshire, 1995-7*, TVAS Monograph **3**, Reading

Ford, S, and Pine, J, 2003 Neolithic ring ditches and Roman landscape features at Horton (1989-1996), in *Prehistoric, Roman and Saxon sites in eastern Berkshire: excavations, 1989-1997* (ed. S Preston), 12-85, Reading

Ford, S, and Taylor, K, 2004 Neolithic occupation at Cippenham, Slough, Berks, in Cotton and Field 2004, 99-104

Forstén, A, 1996 Climate and the evolution of *Equus* (Perissodactyla, Equidae) in the Plio-Pleistocene of Eurasia, in Neogene and Quaternary Mammals of the Palaearctic (eds A Nadachowski and L Werdelin), *Acta Zoologica Cracoviensa* **39**, 161-6

Fowler, C, 2004 *The archaeology of personhood*, London

Fowler, P J, 2000 *Landscape plotted and pieced: landscape history and local archaeology in Fyfield and Overton, Wiltshire*, London

Francis, E A, 1970 Quaternary, in Geology of Durham County (ed. G Hickling), *Transactions of the Natural History Society of Northumberland* **41**, 134-52

Franks, J W, 1960 Interglacial deposits at Trafalgar Square, London, *New Phytologist* **59**, 145-52

Franks, J W, Sutcliffe, A J, Kerney, M P, and Coope, G R, 1958 Haunt of elephant and rhinoceros: the Trafalgar Square of 100,000 years ago: new discoveries, *Illustrated London News* 14th June, 1011-13

Froom, F R, 1963a An axe of Dorset chert from a Mesolithic site at Kintbury, *Berkshire Archaeol J* **61**, 1-3

Froom, F R, 1963b The Mesolithic around Hungerford, *Trans Newbury District Field Club* **11 (2)**, 62-87

Froom, F R, 1965 An investigation into the Mesolithic around Hungerford part IV-V: excavations at Wawcott IV, *Trans Newbury District Field Club* **11 (3)**, 45-51

Froom, F R, 1972 A Mesolithic site at Wawcott, Kintbury, *Berkshire Archaeol J* **66**, 23-44

Froom, F R, 1976 *Wawcott III: a stratified Mesolithic succession*, BAR Brit. Ser. **27**, Oxford

Froom, R, Cook, J, Debenham, N, and Ambers, J, 1993 Wawcott XXX: an interim report on a Mesolithic site in Berkshire, in *Stories in stone* (eds N Ashton and A David), Lithic Studies Soc Occas Pap **4**, 206-12, Oxford

Fulford, M, and Nichols, E, 1992 *Developing landscapes of lowland Britain. The archaeology of the British river gravels: a review*, Soc Antiq London Occ Pap **14**, London

Funnell, B M, 1995 Global sea-level and the peninsularity of late Cenozoic Britain, in *Island Britain: a Quaternary perspective* (ed. R C Preece), Geological Society Special Publication **96**, 3-13, London

Gaffney, V and Tingle, M, 1989, *The Maddle Farm Project: an integrated survey of prehistoric and Roman landscapes on the Berkshire Downs*, BAR Brit. Ser. **200**, Oxford

Gale, R, 2004 Charcoal from later Neolithic/early Bronze Age, Iron Age and early Roman contexts, in Lambrick and Allen 2004, 445-456

Galer, D, 2007 The human remains, in Benson and Whittle 2007, 189-220

Gamble, C S, 1986 *The Palaeolithic settlement of Europe*, Cambridge

Gamble, C S, 1987 Man the shoveller, in *The Pleistocene Old World* (ed. O Soffer), 82-96, London

Gamble, C S, 1995 The earliest occupation of Europe: the environmental background, in, *The Earliest occupation of Europe* (eds W Roebroeks and T van Kolfschoten), 279-95, Leiden

Gamble, C S, 1996 Hominid behaviour in the Middle Pleistocene: an English perspective, in *The English Palaeolithic reviewed* (eds C S Gamble and A J Lawson), 63-71, Old Sarum

Gamble, C S, 1999 *The Palaeolithic societies of Europe*, Cambridge

Gamble, C, Davies, W, Pettitt, P and Richards, M, 2004 Climate change and evolving human diversity in Europe during the last glacial, *Phil Trans Roy Soc of London B* **359**, 243-54

Gao, C, Keen, D H, Boreham, S, Coope, G R, Pettit, M E, Stuart, A J and Gibbard, P L, 2000 Last interglacial and Devensian deposits of the River Great Ouse at Woolpack Farm, Fenstanton, Cambridgeshire, UK, *Quaternary Science Reviews* **19**, 787-810

Gardiner, J, 1988 The composition and distribution of Neolithic surface flint scatters in central southern England, unpubl. PhD thesis, Univ. Reading

Gardiner, J, 1990 Flint procurement and Neolithic axe production on the South Downs: a re-assessment, *Oxford J Archaeol* **9 (2)**, 119-40

Gardiner, J, 2006 Thames and Solent research framework: the Mesolithic in Hampshire, http://thehumanjourney.net/pdf_store/sthames/phase3/County/Upper%20Palaeolithic%20&%20Mesolithic/Upper%20Palaeolithic%20&%20Mesolithic%20Hampshire.pdf (checked July 2010)

Garrow, D, 2006 *Pits, settlement and deposition during the Neolithic and early Bronze Age in East Anglia*, BAR Brit. Ser. **414**, Oxford

Garrow, D, Beadsmoore, E, and Knight, M, 2006 Pit clusters and the temporality of occupation: an earlier Neolithic site at Kilverstone, Thetford, Norfolk, *Proc Prehist Soc* **72**, 139-158

Garton, D, 1987 Buxton, *Curr Archaeol* **103**, 250-253

Garton, D, 1991 Neolithic settlement in the Peak District: perspective and prospect, in *Recent development in the archaeology of the Peak District* (eds R Hodges and K Smith), 3-22, Sheffield

Garwood, P, 1991 Ritual tradition and the reconstitution of society, in Garwood *et al.* 1991, 10-32

Garwood, P, 1999a Grooved Ware chronology, in Cleal and MacSween 1999, 145-76

Garwood, P, 1999b Discussion, in Barclay and Halpin 1999, 275-309

Garwood, P, 2003 Round barrows and funerary traditions in late Neolithic and Bronze Age Sussex, in *The archaeology of Sussex to AD 2000* (ed. D Rudling), 47-68, Great Dunham

Garwood, P, 2007a Before the hills in order stood: chronology, time and history in the interpretation of early Bronze Age round barrows, in Last 2007b, 30-52, Oxford

Garwood, P, 2007b Late Neolithic and early Bronze Age funerary monuments and burial traditions in the West Midlands, in *The undiscovered country: the earlier prehistory of the west Midlands* (ed. P Garwood), 134-165, Oxford

Garwood, P, 2007c Vital resources, ideal images and virtual lives: children in early Bronze Age funerary ritual, in *Children and social identity in the ancient world* (eds S E E Crawford and G B Shepherd), Institute of Archaeology and Antiquity Multidisciplinary Series **1**, 63-82, Oxford

Garwood, P, forthcoming The image of the dead princess: constructing gendered identities in early Bronze Age funerary ritual, in *Dress* (ed. M Harlow), Institute of Archaeology and Antiquity Multidisciplinary Series **2**, Oxford

Garwood, P, in prep. The Neolithic and early Bronze Age of south-east England: an assessment of the evidence, South East England Regional Research Framework

Garwood, P, Jennings, D, Skeates, R, and Toms, J (eds), 1991 *Sacred and profane: proceedings of a* conference on archaeology, ritual and religion, Oxford, 1989 Oxford Univ. Committee for Archaeol Monogr **32**, Oxford

Gascoyne, M, Currant, A P and Lord, T, 1981 Ipswichian fauna of Victoria Cave and the marine palaeoclimatic record, *Nature* **294**, 652-654

Gates, T, 1975 *The Middle Thames valley: an archaeological survey of the river gravels*, Berkshire Archaeol Comm Publ **1**, Reading

Gaudzinski, S, 1999 The faunal record of the Lower and Middle Palaeolithic of Europe: remarks on human interference, in *The Middle Palaeolithic occupation of Europe* (eds W Roebroeks and C Gamble), 215-233, Leiden

Gaudzinski, S, and Roebroeks, W, 2000 Adults only: reindeer hunting at the Middle Palaeolithic site of Salzgitter-Lebenstedt, Northern Germany, *Journal of Human Evolution* **38**, 497-521

Geertz, C, 1973 *The interpretation of cultures*, New York

Geneste, J-M, 1989 Economie des resources lithiques dans le Moustérien du sud-ouest de la France, in *L'Homme de Neanderthal, Vol. 6: la subsistence* (ed. M Otte), 75-97, Liege

Gerloff, S, 1975 *The early Bronze Age daggers of Great Britain and a reconsideration of the Wessex culture*, Prähistorische Bronzefunde **6 (2)**, Munich

Gerloff, S, 2004 The dagger from grave 4013/12, in Lambrick and Allen 2004, 82-86

Gettins, G L, Taylor, H, and Grinsell, L, 1954 The Marshfield Barrows, *Trans Bristol Gloucestershire Archaeol Soc* **72**, 23-44

Gibbard, P L, 1974 Pleistocene stratigraphy and vegetation history of Hertfordshire, unpubl. PhD thesis, Univ. Cambridge

Gibbard, P L, 1977 Pleistocene history of the Vale of St Albans, *Phil Trans Roy Soc London B* **280**, 445-83

Gibbard, P L, 1979 Middle Pleistocene drainage in the Thames Valley, *Geological Magazine* **116**, 35-44

Gibbard, P L, 1982 Terrace stratigraphy and drainage history of the Plateau Gravels of north Surrey, south Berkshire and north Hampshire, England, *Proc Geol Ass* **93**, 369-84

Gibbard, P L, 1985 *The Pleistocene history of the Middle Thames Valley*, Cambridge

Gibbard, P L, 1988 The history of the great north-west European rivers during the past three million years, *Phil Trans Roy Soc London B* **318**, 559-602

Gibbard, P L, 1994 *The Pleistocene history of the Lower Thames Valley*, Cambridge

Gibbard, P L, 1995a The formation of the Strait of Dover, in *Island Britain: a Quaternary perspective* (ed. R C Preece), Geological Society Special Publication **96**, 15-26, London

Gibbard, P L, 1995b Palaeogeographical evolution of the Lower Thames Valley, in *The Quaternary of the lower reaches of the Thames: field guide* (eds D R Bridgland, P Allen and B A Haggart), 5-34, Durham

Gibbard, P L, 2007 Palaeogeography: Europe cut adrift, *Nature* **448**, 259-60

Gibbard, P L, and Aalto, M M, 1977 A Hoxnian interglacial site at Fisher's Green, Stevenage, Hertfordshire, *New Phytologist* **78**, 505-23

Gibbard, P L, Bryant, I D, and Hall, A R, 1986 A Hoxnian interglacial doline infilling at Slade Oak Lane, Denham, Buckinghamshire, *Geological Magazine* **123**, 27-43

Gibbard, P L, Coope, G, R, Hall, A R, Preece, R C, and Robinson, J E, 1982 Middle Devensian river deposits beneath the 'Upper Floodplain' terrace of the river Thames at Kempton Park, Sunbury, Surrey, England, *Proc Geol Ass* **93**, 275-290

Gibbard, P L, and Hall, A R, 1982 Late Devensian river deposits in the lower Colne Valley, West London, England, *Proc Geol Ass* **93**, 291-300

Gibbard, P L, and Lewin, J, 2003 The history of the major rivers of southern Britain during the Tertiary, *Journal of the Geological Society* **160**, 829-46

Gibbard, P L, and Pettit, M, 1978 The palaeobotany of interglacial deposits at Sugworth, Berkshire, *New Phytologist* **81**, 465-77

Gibbard, P L, and Stuart, A J, 1975 Flora and vertebrate fauna of the Barrington Beds, *Geological Magazine* **112**, 493-501

Gibbard, P L, West, R G, Zagwijn, W H, Balson, P S, Burger, A W, Funnell, B M, Jeffrey, D H, de Jong, J, van Kolfschoten, T, Lister, A M, Meijer, T, Norton, P E P, Preece, R C, Rose, J, Stuart, A J, Whiteman, C A and Zalasiewicz, J A, 1991, Early and Middle Pleistocene correlations in the southern North Sea basin, *Quaternary Science Reviews* **10**, 25-32

Gibbard, P L, Whiteman, C A, and Bridgland, D R, 1988 A preliminary report on the stratigraphy of the Lower Thames Valley, *Quaternary Newsletter* **56**, 1-8

Gibbs, A V, 1989 Sex, gender and material culture patterning in later Neolithic and early Bronze Age England, unpubl. PhD thesis, Univ. Cambridge

Gibson, A M, 1982 *Beaker domestic sites: a study of the domestic pottery of the late 3rd and early 2nd millennia BC in the British Isles*, BAR Brit. Ser. **107**, Oxford

Gibson, A M, 1992, Possible timber circles at Dorchester on Thames, *Oxford J Archaeol* **11** (1), 85-91

Gibson, A M, 1994 Excavations at the Sarn-y-bryn-caled cursus complex, Welshpool, Powys, and the timber circles of Great Britain and Ireland, *Proc Prehist Soc* **60**, 143-223

Gibson, A M, 2005 *Stonehenge and timber circles*, 2nd edition, Stroud

Gibson, A M, 2007 A Beaker veneer? Some evidence from the burial record, in *From Stonehenge to the Baltic: living with cultural diversity in the third millennium BC* (eds L Larsson and M Parker Pearson), BAR Int. Ser. **1692**, 47-64, Oxford

Gibson, A M, and Kinnes, I, 1997 On the urns of a dilemma: radiocarbon and the Peterborough problem, *Oxford J Archaeol* **16**, 65–72

Gibson, A M, and Sheridan, A, 2004 *From sickles to circles: Britain and Ireland at the time of Stonehenge*, Stroud

Gilbertson, D D, 1976 Non-marine molluscan faunas of terrace gravels in the Upper Thames Basin, in D A Roe (ed.), *Field Guide to the Oxford Region*, Quaternary Research Association, Oxford, 16-19.

Gilchrist, R, 1999 *Gender and archaeology: contesting the past*, London

Gillings, M, Pollard, J, and Wheatley, D, 2000 Avebury and the Beckhampton Avenue, *Curr Archaeol* **167**, 428-433

Gillings, M, Pollard, J, Wheatley, D, and Peterson, R, 2008 *The landscape of the megaliths*, Oxford

Gingell, C, 1992 *The Marlborough Downs: a later Bronze Age landscape and its origins*, Wiltshire Archaeological and Natural History Society Monograph **1**, Stroud

Godwin, H, 1975 *The history of the British flora*, Cambridge

Goudie, A S and Hart, M G 1975 Pleistocene events and forms in the Oxford region, in *Oxford and its region* (eds C G Smith and D I Scargill), 3-13, Oxford

Gowlett, J A J, and Hallos, J, 2000 Beeches Pit: overview of the Archaeology, in *The Quaternary of Norfolk and Suffolk: field guide* (eds S G Lewis, Whiteman, C A and R C Preece), 197-206, London

Gowlett, J A J, Hedges, R E M, Law, I A and Perry, C, 1987 Radiocarbon dates from the Oxford AMS system: Archaeometry datelist 5, *Archaeometry* **29 (1)**, 125-55

Grace, R, 1990 The limitations and applications of use wear analysis, in *The interpretative possibilities of microwear studies*, Proceedings of the International Conference on Lithic Use-Wear Analysis, 1989, Uppsala, Sweden (eds B Gräslund, H Knutsson, K Knutsson and J Taffinder), AUN **14**, 9-14, Uppsala

Grace, R, 1992 Use wear analysis, in Healy *et al.* 1992, 53-63

Gray, H St G, 1935 The Avebury excavations, *Archaeologia* **84**, 99-162

Gray, M, and Lambrick, G, 1995 The excavations of 1972-3 and 1988, in A J Barclay *et al.* 1995, 7-49

Green, C P, Field, M H, Keen, D H, Wells, J M, Schwenninger, J-L, Preece, R C, Schreve, D C, Canti, M G, and Gleed-Owen, C P, 2006 Marine Isotope Stage 9 environments of fluvial deposits at Hackney, North London, UK, *Quaternary Science Reviews* **25**, 89-113

Green, C P, Gibbard, P L, and Bishop, B J, 2004 Stoke Newington: geoarchaeology of the Palaeolithic 'floor', *Proc Geol Ass* **115**, 193-208

Green, C P, McGregor, D F M and Evans, A, 1982 Development of the Thames drainage system in Early and Middle Pleistocene times, *Geological Magazine* **119**, 281-90

Green, C, and Rollo-Smith, S, 1984 The excavation of eighteen round barrows near Shrewton, Wiltshire, *Proc Prehist Soc* **50**, 255-318

Green, M, 2000 *A landscape revealed: 10,000 years on a chalkland farm*, Brimscombe Port

Green, M, 2001 *Dying for the gods: human sacrifice in Iron Age and Roman Britain*, Stroud

Greenwell, W G, 1890 Recent researches in barrows in Yorkshire, Wiltshire, Berkshire etc, *Archaeologia* **5**, 1-72

Greig, J R A, 1982 Past and present lime woods of Europe, in *Archaeological aspects of woodland ecology* (eds M Bell and S Limbrey), BAR Int. Ser. **146**, 23-55, Oxford

Greig, J R A, 1991 The botanical remains, in Needham 1991, 234-61

Grigson, C, 1982 Porridge and pannage: pig husbandry in Neolithic England, *Archaeological aspects of woodland ecology* (eds M Bell and S Limbrey), BAR Int. Ser. **146**, 297-314, Oxford

Grigson, C, 1983 Mesolithic and Neolithic animal bones, in Excavations at Cherhill, North Wiltshire, 1967, (J G Evans and I F Smith), *Proc Prehist Soc* **49**, 64-70

Grigson, C, 1989 The animal remains, in Excavation of an early prehistoric site at Stratford's Yard, Chesham (ed. B Stainton), *Rec Buckinghamshire* **31**, 49-74

Grimes, W F, 1938 A barrow on Breach Farm, Llanbleddian, Glamorgan, *Proc Prehist Soc* **4**, 107-21

Grimes, W F, 1943-4 Excavations at Stanton Harcourt, Oxon, 1940, *Oxoniensia* **8**, 19-63

Grimes, W F, 1960 *Excavation on defence sites, 1939-1945, 1: mainly Neolithic – Bronze Age*, Ministry of Works Archaeological Report **3**, London

Grinsell, L, 1936 The Lambourn chambered long barrow, *Berkshire Archaeol J* **40**, 59-62

Grinsell, L, 1957 List of Wiltshire barrows, in *A history of Wiltshire, part 1* (eds R B Pugh and E Crittall), Victoria County Histories, 134-246, Oxford

Grinsell, L, 1987 Surrey barrows 1934-1986: a reappraisal, *Surrey Archaeol Collect* **78**, 1-41

Grootes, P M, Stuiver, M, White, J W C, Johnsen, S, and Jouzel, J, 1993 Comparison of oxygen isotope records from the GISP2 and GRIP Greenland ice cores, *Nature* **366**, 552-4

Grün, R, and Schwarcz, H P, 2000 Revised open system U-series/ESR age calculations for teeth from Stratum C at the Hoxnian Interglacial type locality, England, *Quaternary Science Reviews* **19**, 1151-4

Gupta, S, Collier, J S, Palmer-Felgate, A, and Potter G, 2007 Catastrophic flooding origin of shelf valley systems in the English Channel, *Nature* **448**, 342-5

Guthrie, R D, 1990 *Frozen fauna of the Mammoth Steppe*, Chicago

Guttman, E B, 2005 Midden cultivation in prehistoric Britain: arable crops in gardens *World Archaeol* **37 (2)**, 224-39

Haak, W, Forster, P, Bramanti, B, Matsumura, S, Brandt, G, Tänzer, M, Villems, R, Renfrew, C, Gronenborn, D, Alt, K W, Burger, J, 2005 Ancient DNA from the first European farmers in 7500-year-old Neolithic sites, *Science* **310**, 1016-18

Hallos, J, 2005 15 minutes of fame: Exploring the temporal dimension of Middle Pleistocene lithic technology, *Journal of Human Evolution* **49**, 155-79

Halpin, C, 1984 Blewbury, *Oxford Archaeological Unit Newsletter* **11**, 1-2

Halsted, J, 2008 Chessvale Bowling Club, Chesham, Buckinghamshire: excavations, 2003-4, *Rec Buckinghamshire* **48**, 1-36

Hamblin, R J O, Moorlock, and B S P, Rose, J, 2000 A new glacial stratigraphy for eastern England, *Quaternary Newsletter* **92**, 35-43

Hamilton, J, Hedges, R J M, and Robinson, M, 2009 Rooting for pigfruit: pig feeding in Neolithic and Iron Age Britain compared, *Antiquity* **83**, 998-1011

Hamilton, M, and Whittle, A, 1999 Grooved Ware of the Avebury area: style, contexts and meanings, in Cleal and MacSween 1999, 36-47

Hamlin, A, 1963 Excavations of ring-ditches and other sites at Stanton Harcourt, *Oxoniensia* **28**, 152

Hardaker, T, 2001 New Lower Palaeolithic finds from the Upper Thames, in *A very remote period indeed: papers on the Palaeolithic presented to Derek Roe* (eds S Milliken and J Cook, 180-98, Oxford

Harden, D B, and Treweeks, R C, 1945 Excavations at Stanton Harcourt, Oxon, 1940, II, *Oxoniensia* **10**, 16-41

Harding, A, with Lee, G E, 1987 *Henge monuments and related sites of Great Britain*, BAR Brit. Ser. **175**, Oxford

Harding, J, 1991 Using the unique as the typical: monuments and the ritual landscape, in Garwood *et al.* 1991, 32027

Harding, J, 1997 Interpreting the Neolithic: the monuments of North Yorkshire, *Oxford J Archaeol* **16 (3)**, 279-96

Harding, J, 2003 *Henge monuments of the British Isles*, Stroud

Harding, J, 2006 Pit-digging, occupation and structured deposition on Rudston Wold, eastern Yorkshire, *Oxford J Archaeol* **25 (2)**, 109-126

Harding, J, and Barclay, A, 1999 An introduction to the cursus monuments of Britain and Ireland, in Barclay and Harding 1999, 1-8

Harding, J, and Healy, F, 2007 *The Raunds Area Project: a Neolithic and Bronze Age landscape in Northamptonshire*, London

Hare, F K, 1947 The geomorphology as a part of the Middle Thames, *Proc Geol Ass* **58**, 294-339

Harrison, S, 2003 The Icknield Way: some queries, *Archaeol J* **160**, 1-22

Hassall, T, 1986 Archaeology of Oxford city, in Briggs *et al.* 1986, 115-34

Haughey, F, 2000 The Mesolithic on the tidal Thames: a proleptic viewpoint, in *Mesolithic lifeways: current research in Britain and Ireland* (ed.

R Young), Leicester Archaeol Monogr **7**, 221-31, Leicester

Hayden, C, and Stafford, E 2006 *The prehistoric landscape at White Horse Stone, Boxley, Kent*, CTRL Integrated Site Report Series, Archaeology Data Service, http://ads.ahds.ac.uk/catalogue/projArch

Hays, J D, Imbrie, J, and Shackleton, N J, 1976 Variations in earth's orbit: pacemaker of the ice ages, *Science* **194**, 1121-1132

Heal, V, 1991 The technology of the worked wood and bark, in Needham 1991, 140-147

Healy, F, 1988 *The Anglo-Saxon cemetery at Spong Hill, North Elmham, part VI: occupation during the 7th to 2nd millennia BC*, EAA **39**, Gressenhall

Healy, F, 1993 Lithic material, in *Excavations at Jennings Yard, Windsor, 1986-87* (eds J W Hawkes, and M J Heaton), Wessex Archaeol Rep **3**, 9-15

Healy, F, 1995 Pits, pots and peat: ceramics and settlement in East Anglia, in *'Unbaked urns of rudely shape': essays on British and Irish pottery* (eds I Kinnes and G Varndell), 173-84, Oxford

Healy, F, 1999 The complex in its wider context, in Barclay and Halpin 1999, 325-29

Healy, F, 2004a Gravelly Guy in the context of the Stanton Harcourt ceremonial complex, in Lambrick and Allen 2004, 64-5

Healy, F, 2004b Hambledon Hill and its implications, in *Monuments and material culture*, (eds R Cleal and J Pollard), 15-38, East Knoyle

Healy, F, and Harding, J, 2004 Reading a burial: the legacy of Overton Hill, in Gibson and Sheridan 2004, 176-93

Healy, F, and Harding, J, 2007 A thousand and one things to do with a round barrow, in Last 2007b, 53-71

Healy, F, Heaton, M, and Lobb, S J, 1992 Excavations at a Mesolithic site at Thatcham, Berkshire, *Proc Prehist Soc* **58**, 41-76

Hearne, C M, and Adam, N, 1999 Excavation of an extensive late Bronze Age settlement at Shorncote Quarry, near Cirencester, 1995-6, *Trans Bristol and Gloucestershire Archaeol Soc* **117**, 35-73

Hedges, R E M, Housely, R A, Bronk-Ramsey, C R and Klinken, G J van, 1991 Radiocarbon dates from the Oxford AMS system: Archaeometry Datelist 13, *Archaeometry* **34**, 279-96

Hedges, R E M, Housley, R A, Pettitt, P B, Bronk Ramsey, C and Van Klinken, G J, 1996 Radiocarbon dates from the Oxford AMS System: Archaeometry Datelist 21 (Thatcham), *Archaeometry* **38 (1)**, 181-207

Hedges, R E M, Housley, R, Law, I A, and Bronk-Ramsay, C, 1989 Radiocarbon dates from the Oxford AMS system: Archaeometry datelist 9, *Archaeometry* **31**, 207-34

Hedges, R E M, Saville, A and O'Connell, T 2008 Characterising the diet of individuals at the Neolithic chambered tomb of Hazleton North, Gloucestershire, England using stable isotopic analysis, *Archaeometry* **50 (1)**, 114-28

Helbaek, H, 1952 Early crops in southern England,

Proc Prehist Soc **18**, 194-23

Helms, M, 1998 *Ulyssees' sail: an ethnographic odyssey of power, knowledge and geographical distance*, Princeton

Herne, A, 1988 A time and a place for the Grimston Bowl, in Barrett and Kinnes 1988, 2-29

Hey, G, (ed.) in prep. *Yarnton: Neolithic and Bronze Age settlement and landscape*, Thames Valley Landscapes, Oxford

Hey, G, 1994 Yarnton: recent work, *PAST* **17**, 8

Hey, G, 1996 Yarnton Floodplain, *S Midlands Archaeol* **26**, 67

Hey, G, 1997 Neolithic settlement at Yarnton, Oxfordshire, in *Neolithic landscapes* (ed. P Topping), Oxbow Monograph **86**, 99-111, Oxford

Hey, G, 2001 Whispering Knights, Rollright, Oxfordshire, unpubl. report, The Rollright Trust, Stratford-upon-Avon

Hey, G, 2009 The Devil's Work, *British Archaeology* July-August, 24-9

Hey, G, and Barclay, A, 2007 The Thames Valley in the late 5th and early 4th millennium cal BC: the appearance of domestication and the evidence for change, in Whittle and Cummings 2007, 399-422

Hey, G, Dennis, C, and Mayes, A, 2007 Archaeological investigations on Whiteleaf Hill, Princes Risborough, Buckinghamshire, 2002-5, *Rec Buckinghamshire* **47 (2)**, 1-80

Hey, G and Lacey, M, 2001 *Evaluation of archaeological decision-making processes and sampling strategies*, Oxford

Hey, G, Mulville, J, and Robinson, M, 2003 Diet and culture in southern Britain: the evidence from Yarnton, in *Food, culture and identity in the Neolithic and early Bronze Age* (ed. M Parker Pearson), BAR Int. Ser. **1117**, 79-88, Oxford

Hey, R W, 1965 Highly quartzose pebble gravels in the London Basin, *Proc Geol Ass* **76**, 403- 20

Hey, R W, 1980 Equivalents of the Westland Green Gravels in Essex and East Anglia, *Proc Geol Ass* **91**, 279-90

Hey, R W, 1986 A re-examination of the Northern Drift of Oxfordshire. *Proc Geol Ass* **97**, 291-302

Hey, R W, 1991 Pre-Anglian deposits and glaciations in Britain, in *Glacial deposits in Great Britain and Ireland* (eds J Ehlers, P L Gibbard and J Rose), 13-16, Rotterdam

Hey, R W, and Brenchley, P J, 1977 Volcanic pebbles from Pleistocene gravels in Norfolk and Essex, *Geological Magazine*, **114**, 219-25

Hill, J D, 1995 *Ritual and rubbish in the Iron Age of Wessex*, BAR Brit. Ser. **242**, Oxford

Hingley, R, 1980 The Upper Thames Valley survey, *CBA Group 9 Newsletter* **10**, 141-3

Hinton, M A C, 1901 Excursion to Grays Thurrock, *Proc Geol Ass* **17**, 141-44

Hinton, M A C, and Kennard, A S, 1900 Contributions to the Pleistocene geology of the Thames Valley 1: The Grays Thurrock Area Pt 1, *The Essex Naturalist* **11**, 336-370

Hoare, R C, 1812 *The ancient history of Wiltshire I*, facsimile edn, 1975, London

Hodder, I (ed.), 1982 *Symbolic and structural archaeology*, Cambridge

Hodder, I, 1990 *The domestication of Europe: structure and contingency in Neolithic societies*, Oxford

Holgate, R, 1988a *Neolithic settlement of the Thames Basin*, BAR Brit. Ser. **194**, Oxford

Holgate, R, 1988b The flints, in Lambrick 1988, 85-90

Holgate, R, 1995 Early prehistoric settlement of the Chilterns, in *Chiltern archaeology: recent work. A handbook for the next decade* (ed. R Holgate), 3-16, Dunstable

Holgate, R, 2004a Flintwork, in Lambrick and Allen 2004, 93-9

Holgate, R, 2004b Managing change: the Mesolithic-Neolithic transition in south-east England, in Cotton and Field 2004, 24-8

Holgate, R, Bradley, P, and Wallis, J, 2003 Worked flint, in Barclay *et al.* 2003, 126-34

Hollin, J T, 1971 Ice sheet surges and interglacial sea levels, UnpubL. PhD thesis, Univ. Princeton

Hollin, J T, 1977 Thames interglacial sites, Ipswichian sea levels and Antarctic ice surges, *Boreas* **6**, 33-52

Holmes, T V, 1892 The new railway from Grays Thurrock to Romford: sections between Upminster and Romford, *Journal of the Geological Society, London*, **48**, 365-72

Holyoak, D T, 1980 The late Pleistocene sediments and biostratigraphy of the Kennet Valley, England, unpubl. PhD thesis, Univ. Reading

Holyoak, D T, 1983 The colonisation of Berkshire, England, by land and fresh-water mollusca since the Late Devensian, *Journal of Biogeography* **10**, 483–96

Horton, A, 1977 Nettlebed, in *South east England and the Thames Valley: guide book for excursion A5, X INQUA Congress* (eds E R Shephard-Thorn and J J Wymer), 16-18, Birmingham

Horton, A, 1983 Nettlebed, in *Diversion of the Thames* (ed. J Rose), 63-65, Cambridge

Horton, A, and Whittow, J B, 1977 Oakley Wood pit, Benson, in *South east England and the Thames Valley: guide book for excursion A5, X INQUA Congress* (eds E R Shephard-Thorn and J J Wymer), 18-22, Birmingham

Horton, A, Worssam, B C, and Whittow, J B, 1981 The Wallingford Fan Gravel, *Phil Trans Roy Soc London B* **293**, 215-55

Hosfield, R, 2005 Individuals among palimpsest data: fluvial landscapes in southern England, in *The hominid individual in context: archaeological investigations of Lower and Middle Palaeolithic landscapes, locales and artefacts* (eds C Gamble and M Porr), 220-43, London

Housley, R, Gamble, C, Street, M, and Pettitt, P B, 1997 Radiocarbon evidence for the Lateglacial human recolonisation of Northern Europe, *Proc Prehist Soc* **63**, 25-54

Howell, L, and Durden, T, 1996 A Grooved Ware pit on the Seven Barrows, All Weather Gallop, Sparsholt, Oxfordshire, *Oxoniensia* **61**, 21-5

Humphrey, C, and Laidlaw, J, 1994 *The archetypal*

actions of ritual: a theory of ritual illustrated by the Jain rite of worship, Oxford

Hunt, A J, 1998 *Gazetteer of archaeological investigations in England* **5**, Bournemouth

Insoll, T, 2004 *Archaeology, ritual, religion*, London

Jackson, D A, 1976 The excavation of Neolithic and Bronze Age sites at Aldwincle, Northamptonshire, 1969-71, *Northamptonshire Archaeol* **11**, 12-70

Jackson, D A, 1977 Further excavations at Aldwincle Northamptonshire, 1969-71, *Northamptonshire Archaeol* **12**, 9-54

Jacobi, R, 1978 The Mesolithic of Sussex, in *The archaeology of Sussex lo AD 1500* (ed. P Drewett), CBA Research Report **29**, 15–22, London

Jacobi, R, 1981 The last hunters in Hampshire, in *The archaeology of Hampshire* (eds S J Shennan and R T Schadla Hall), Hampshire Field Club and Archaeological Society Monograph **1**, Winchester, 10–25

Jacobi, R, 1986 The contents of Dr Harley's Showcase, in *The Palaeolithic of Britain and its nearest neighbours: recent studies* (ed. S N Collcutt), 62-8, Sheffield

Jacobi, R, 1987 Lessons of context and contamination in dating the Upper Palaeololithic, in *Archaeological results from accelerator dating* (eds J Gowlett and R Hedges), 81-6, Oxford

Jacobi, R, 1987b Misanthropic miscellany: musings on British early Flandrian archaeology and other flights of fancy, in *Mesolithic northwest Europe: recent trends* (eds P Rowley-Conwy, M Zvelebil and H P Blankholm), 163-168, Sheffield

Jacobi, R, 1990 Leaf-points and the British early Upper Palaeolithic, in *Feuille de pierre: les industries à pointes foliacées du Paléolithique supérieur européen* (ed. J Kozlowski), 271-289, Liège

Jacobi, R, 1991 The Creswellian, Creswell and Cheddar, in *The Late Glacial in north-west Europe: human adaptation and environmental change at the end of the Pleistocene* (eds R N E Barton, A J Roberts and D Roe), CBA Res Rep **77**, London, 128-40

Jacobi, R, 1999 Some observations on the British earlier Upper Palaeolithic, in *Dorothy Garrod and the progress of the Palaeolithic: studies in the prehistoric archaeology of the Near East and Europe* (eds W Davies and R Charles), 35-40, Oxford

Jacobi, R, 2004 The Late Upper Palaeolithic lithic collection from Gough's Cave, Cheddar, Somerset and human use of the cave, *Proc Prehist Soc* **70**, 1-92

Jacobi, R, 2007 A collection of early Upper Palaeolithic artefacts from Beedings, near Pulborough, West Sussex and the context of similar finds from the British Isles, *Proc Prehist Soc* **73**, 229-325

Jacobi, R, and Pettitt, P B, 2000 An Aurignacian Point from Uphill Quarry (Somerset) and the earliest settlement of Britain by *Homo sapiens sapiens*, *Antiquity* **74**, 513-18

James, W, 2003 *The ceremonial animal: a new portrait of anthropology*, Oxford

Jeffery, D H, de Jong, J, van Kolfschoten, T, Lister, A M, Meijer, T, Norton, P E P, Preece, R C, Rose, J, Stuart, A J, Whiteman, C A, and Zalasiewicz, J A, 1991 Early and Early Middle Pleistocene correlations in the southern North Sea basin, *Quaternary Science Reviews* **10**, 23-52

Jessen, K, and Helbaek, K, 1944 Cereals in Great Britain and Ireland in prehistoric and early historic times, *Det Kongelige Danska Videnskabernes Selskab, Biologiske Skrifter* **3**, 1-68

Johnston, R, 1999 An empty path? Processions, memories and the Dorset Cursus, in Barclay and Harding 1999, 39-48

Jones, A, 2005 Lives in fragments? Personhood and the European Neolithic, *J Social Archaeol* **5 (2)**, 193-224

Jones, G, 2000 Evaluating the importance of cultivation and collecting in Neolithic Britain, in Fairbairn 2000, 79-84

Jones, M K, 1978 The plant remains, in Parrington 1978, 93-110

Jones, M U, 1976 Neolithic pottery found at Lechlade, Glos., *Oxoniensia* **41**, 1-5

Jones, P, 1990 Neolithic field monuments and occupation at Staines Road Farm, Shepperton, *Surrey Archaeol Soc Bull* **252**, 6-8

Jones, P, 2008 *A Neolithic ring ditch and later prehistoric features at Staines Road Farm, Shepperton*, Woking

Jones, P, and Ayres, K, 2004 A bone 'scoop' and Grooved Ware vessel from a pit in the Lower Coln Valley, Surrey, in Cotton and Field 2004, 148-153

Jordan, P, 2006 Analogy, in Conneller and Warren 2006, 83-100

Keeley, L H, 1980 *Experimental determination of stone tool uses*, Chicago

Keen, D H, 1990 Significance of the record provided by Pleistocene fluvial deposits and their included molluscan faunas for palaeoenvironmental reconstruction and stratigraphy: cases from the English Midlands, *Palaeogeography, Palaeoclimatology, Palaeoecology* **80**, 25-34

Keen, D H, 1995 Raised beaches and sea-levels in the English Channel in the Middle and Late Pleistocene: problems of interpretation and implications for the isolation of the British Isles, in *Island Britain: a Quaternary Perspective* (ed. R C Preece), Geological Society Special Publication **96**, 63-74, London

Keen, D H, 2001 Towards a late Middle Pleistocene non-marine molluscan biostratigraphy, *Quaternary Science Reviews* **20**, 1657–65

Keen, D H, Hardaker, T, and Lang, A T O, 2006 A Lower Palaeolithic industry from the Cromerian (MIS 13) Baginton Formation of Waverley Wood and Wood Farm Pits, Bubbenhall, Warwickshire, UK, *Journal of Quaternary Science* **21**, 457-70

Keiller, A and Piggott, S, 1939 Badshot long

barrow, in *A survey of the prehistory of the Farnham District (Surrey)*, (eds K P Oakley, W F Rankine and A W G Lowther), 133-49, Guildford

Keiller, A, Piggott, S, and Wallis, F S, 1941 First report of the Sub-Committee of the South-Western Group of Museums and Art Galleries on the petrological identification of stone axes, *Proc Prehist Soc* **7**, 50–72

Keith-Lucas, D M, 1997 Pollen, in Barnes *et al.* 1997, 99-106

Keith-Lucas, D M, 2000 Pollen analysis of sediments from Moor Farm, Staines Moor, Surrey, *Surrey Archaeol Collect* **87**, 85-93

Keith-Lucas, M, 1997 Pollen, in Barnes *et al.* 1997, 99-106

Keith-Lucas, M, 2000 Pollen analysis of sediments from Moor Farm, Staines Moor, Surrey, *Surrey Archaeol Collect* **87**, 85-93

Keith-Lucas, M, 2002 Pollen at Charnham Lane, Hungerford, in Ford 2002,

Kemp, R A, 1985 The decalcified Lower Loam at Swanscombe, Kent: a buried Quaternary soil, *Proc Geol Ass* **96**, 343-55

Kemp, R A, 1995 The Middle and Upper Loam at Northfleet, in *The Quaternary of the Lower Reaches of the Thames: field guide* (eds D R Bridgland, P Allen and B A Haggart), 165-6, Durham

Kennard, A S, 1938 Notes on the shell ornament, in The excavation of the Nympsfield long barrow, Gloucestershire (E M Clifford), *Proc Prehist Soc* **4**, 210

Kennard, A S, 1942a Discussion on Pleistocene chronology, *Proc Geol Ass* **53**, 24-5

Kennard, A S, 1942b Faunas of the High Terrace at Swanscombe, *Proc Geol Ass* **53**, 105

Kennard, A S, 1944 The Crayford Brickearths, *Proc Geol Ass* **55**, 121-69

Kenward, R, 1982 A Neolithic burial enclosure at New Wintles Farm, Eynsham, in Case and Whittle 1982, 51-4

Kerney, M P, 1959 Pleistocene non-marine mollusca of the English interglacial deposits, unpubl. PhD thesis, Univ. London

Kerney, M P, 1971 Interglacial deposits at Barnfield Pit, Swanscombe, and their molluscan fauna, *Quarterly Journal of the Geological Society of London* **127**, 69-86

Kerney, M P, and Cameron, R A D, 1979 *A field guide to the land snails of Britain and north-west Europe*, London

Kerney, M P, Gibbard, P L, Hall, A R, and Robinson, J E, 1982 Middle Devensian river deposits beneath the 'Upper Floodplain' terrace of the River Thames at Isleworth, West London, *Proc Geol Ass* **93**, 385-93

Kerney, M P, and Sieveking, G de G, 1977 Northfleet, in *South East England and the Thames Valley: guide book for excursion A5, X INQUA Congress, Birmingham* (eds E R Shephard-Thorne and J J Wymer), 44-6, Norwich

King, J E, 1962 Report on animal bones, in Wymer 1962, 355-60

King, M P, 2001 Life and death in the 'Neolithic': dwelling-scapes in southern Britain, *European J Archaeol* **4 (3)**, 323-45

King, M P, 2003 Living with the dead: reconsidering the 'Mesolithic'/'Neolithic' transition in Britain and Ireland, in Burenhult and Westergaard 2003, 191-205

King, W B R, and Oakley, K P, 1936 The Pleistocene succession in the lower part of the Thames valley, *Proc Prehist Soc* **1**, 52-76

Kinnes, I A, 1978 The earlier prehistoric pottery, in Excavations at a Neolithic causewayed enclosure, Orsett, Essex, 1975, *Proc Prehist Soc* **44**, 259-68

Kinnes, I A, 1979 *Round barrows and ringditches in the British Neolithic*, Brit Mus Occas Pap **7**, London

Kinnes, I A, 1981 Dialogues with death, in *The archaeology of death* (eds R Chapman, I Kinnes, and K Randsborg), 83-91, Cambridge

Kinnes, I A, 1988 The cattleship Potemkin: the first Neolithic in Britain, in *The archaeology of context in the Neolithic and Bronze Age: recent trends* (eds J Barrett and I Kinnes), 2-9, Sheffield

Kinnes, I A, 1991 The Neolithic pottery, in Needham 1991, 157-61

Kinnes, I A, 1992 *Nonmegalithic long barrows and allied structures in the British Neolithic*, Brit Mus Occas Pap **52**, London

Kinnes, I A, 1994 *British Bronze Age metalwork: A17-30 Beaker and Bronze Age grave groups*, London

Kinnes, I A, Gibson, A, Ambers, J, Bowman, S, Leese, M and Boast, R, 1991 Radiocarbon dating and British Beakers: the British Museum programme, *Scottish Archaeol Rev* **8**, 35-68

Kinnes, I A, and Longworth, I H, 1985 *Catalogue of the excavated prehistoric and Romano-British material in the Greenwell collection*, London

Kinnes, I A, Schadla-Hall, T, Chadwick, P and Dean, P, 1983 Duggleby Howe reconsidered, *Archaeol J* **140**, 83-108

Kirk, T, 2006 Materiality, personhood and monumentality in early Neolithic Britain, *Cambridge Archaeol J* **16 (3)**, 333-47

Kohn, M, and Mithen, S, 1999 Handaxes: products of sexual selection?, *Antiquity* **73**, 518-26

Kuhn, S L, 1995 *Mousterian lithic technology: an ecological perspective*, Princeton

Kytmannow, T, 2008 *Portal dolmens in the landscape: the chronology, morphology and landscape setting of the portal dolmens of Ireland, Wales and Cornwall*, BAR Brit. Ser. **455**, Oxford

Lacaille, A D, 1939 The Palaeolithic contents of the gravels of East Burnham, Bucks, *Antiquaries Journal* **19**, 166-81

Lacaille, A D, 1940 The Palaeoliths from the gravels of the Lower Boyn Hill Terrace around Maidenhead, *Antiq J* **20**, 245-71

Lacaille, A D, 1963 Mesolithic industries beside Colne Waters in Iver and Denham, Buckinghamshire, *Rec Buckinghamshire* **17 (3)**, 143-181

Lacaille, A D, and Oakley, K P, 1936 The Palaeolithic sequence at Iver, Bucks, with an appendix on the geology, *Antiq J* **16**, 421-43

Laidlaw, M, 1996 Faience beads, in *Three excavations along the Thames and its tributaries, 1994: Neolithic to Saxon settlement and burial in the Thames, Colne and Kennet Valleys* (P Andrews and A Crockett), Wessex Archaeol Rep **10**, 91, Salisbury

Lambrick, G, 1988 *The Rollright Stones: megaliths, monuments and settlement in the prehistoric landscape*, London

Lambrick, G, 1992 The development of late prehistoric and Roman farming on the Thames gravels, in Fulford and Nichols 1992, 78-105

Lambrick, G, 2010 *Neolithic to Saxon settlement at Mount Farm, Berinsfield, Dorchester*, OA Occasional Paper **19**, Oxford, http:// library.thehuman journey.net/ (checked July 2010)

Lambrick, G, and Allen, T G, 2004 *Gravelly Guy, Stanton Harcourt, Oxfordshire: the development of a prehistoric and Romano-British community*, Thames Valley Landscapes **21**, Oxford

Lambrick, G, with Bradley, P and Healy, F, 2004 Structures and features, in Lambrick and Allen 2004, 35-65

Lambrick, G, and McDonald, A, 1985 The archaeology and ecology of Port Meadow and Wolvercote Common, Oxford, in *Archaeology and nature conservation* (ed. G Lambrick), 95-110, Oxford

Lambrick, G, and Robinson, M, 1979 *Iron Age and Roman riverside settlements at Farmoor, Oxfordshire*, CBA Res Rep **32**, Oxford

Lambrick, G, with Robinson, M 2009 *The Thames through time. The archaeology of the gravel terraces of the Upper and Middle Thames: the Thames Valley in late prehistory, 1500 BC-AD 50*, Thames Valley Landscapes **29**, Oxford

Lamdin-Whymark, H, 2007 Testpitting results, in Norton 2007

Lamdin-Whymark, H, 2008 *The residue of ritualised action: Neolithic depositional practices in the Middle Thames Valley*, BAR Brit. Ser. **466**, Oxford

Lamdin-Whymark, H, forthcoming Lateglacial flint from prehistoric Ebbsfleet, in Prehistoric Ebbsfleet (E Stafford), Oxford

Lamdin-Whymark, H, in prep. The flint from Eton Rowing Course, in Allen *et al.* in prep

Lamdin-Whymark, H, Brady, K, and Smith, A, forthcoming Excavation of a Neolithic to Roman landscape at Horcott Pit, near Fairford, Gloucestershire, 2002-3, *Trans Bristol and Gloucestershire Archaeol Soc*

Lane Fox, A, 1872 On the discovery of Palæolithic implements in association with *Elephas primigenius* in the gravels of the Thames Valley at Acton, *Quarterly Journal of the Geological Society* **28**, 449-65

Lanting, J N, and van der Waals, J D, 1972 British Beakers as seen from the Continent, *Helinium* **12**, 20-56

Larson, G, Albarella, U, Dobney, K, Rowley-Conwy, P. Schibler, J, Tresset, A, Vigne, J-D, Edwards, C J, Schlumbaum, A, Dinu, A, Balaçsescu, A, Dolman, G, Tagliazozzo, A, Manaseryan, N, Miracle, P, Van Wijngaardeb-Bakker, L, Masseti, M, Bradley, D G and Cooper A,2007, Ancient DNA, pig domestication, and the spread of the Neolithic into Europe', *Proceedings of the National Academy of Sciences*, **104 (39)**, 15276-81

Last, J, 1996 Neolithic houses: a central European perspective, in Darvill and Thomas 1996, 27-40

Last, J, 1998 Books of life: biography and memory in a Bronze Age barrow, *Oxford J Archaeol* **17**, 43-53

Last, J, 1999 Out of line: cursuses and monument typology in eastern England, in Barclay and Harding 1999, 86-97

Last, J, 2007a Covering old ground: barrows as enclosures, in Last 2007, 156-75

Last, J (ed.), 2007b *Beyond the grave: new perspectives on round barrows*, Oxford

Lawrence, G F, 1929 Antiquities from the Middle Thames, *Archaeol J* **86**, 69-98

Leach, A L, 1905 Excursion to Crayford and Erith, *Proc Geol Ass* **19**, 137-41

Leary, J, Darvill, T, and Field, D (eds), 2010 *Round mounds and monumentality in the British Neolithic and beyond*, Neolithic Studies Group Seminar Paper **10**, Oxford

Leary, J, and Field, D, in press *The story of Silbury Hill*, English Heritage, London

Lee, H W, 2001 *A study of Lower Palaeolithic stone artefacts from selected sites in the Upper and Middle Thames Valley, with particular reference to the R J MacRae Collection*, BAR Brit. Ser. **319**, Oxford

Lee, J R, Hamblin, R J O, Moorlock, B S P, and Rose, J, 2004 Dating the earliest lowland glaciation of eastern England: a pre-MIS-12 early Middle Pleistocene Happisburgh Glaciation, *Quaternary Science Reviews* **23**, 1551-66

Lee, J R, Rose, J, Candy, I, and Barendregt, R W, 2005 Sea-level changes, river activity, soil development and glaciation around the western margins of the southern North Sea Basin during the Early and early Middle Pleistocene: evidence from Pakefield, Suffolk, UK, *Journal of Quaternary Science* **21**, 155-79

Leeds, E T, 1927 A Neolithic site at Abingdon, Berks., *Antiq J* **7**, 438-64

Leeds, E T, 1928 A Neolithic site at Abingdon, Berks (second report), *Antiq J* **8**, 461-77

Leeds, E T, 1934a Recent Bronze Age discoveries in Berkshire and Oxfordshire, *Antiq J* **14**, 264-76

Leeds, E T, 1934b Rectangular enclosures of the Bronze Age in the Upper Thames Valley, *Antiq J* **14**, 414-16

Leeds, E T, 1936 Round barrows and ring-ditches in Berkshire and Oxfordshire, *Oxoniensia* **1**, 723

Leeds, E T, 1938 Beakers of the Upper Thames district, *Oxoniensia* **3**, 7-30

Leeds, E T, 1939 Mesolithic and Neolithic; Bronze

Age, in *The Victoria history of the county of Oxford*, vol. 1, (ed. L F Salzman), 238-250, London

Leeds, E T, 1940 New discoveries of Neolithic pottery in Oxfordshire, *Oxoniensia* **5**, 1-12

Leeson, M D, 1891 The Saiga antelope in Britain, *Geological Magazine* **8**, 94

Leivers, M, and Moore, C, 2008 *Archaeology of the A303 Stonehenge improvements*, Salisbury

Leroi-Gourhan, A, 1986 Pollen analysis of sediment samples from Gough's Cave, Cheddar, *Proceedings of the University of Bristol Spelaeological Society* **17**, 141-44

Levitan, B, 1990 The non-human vertebrate remains, in Saville 1990a, 199-218

Levitan, B, and Serjeantson, D, 1999 Animal bone, in Barclay and Halpin 1999, 236-41

Lewis, I M, 1985 *Social anthropology in perspective*, Cambridge

Lewis, J, 1991 A Late Glacial and early Postglacial site at Three Ways Wharf, Uxbridge, England: interim report, in *The Late Glacial in north-west Europe:* human adaptation and environmental change at the end of the Pleistocene (eds N Barton, A J Roberts and D A Roe), CBA Res Rep **77**, 246-55

Lewis, J, forthcoming Hunter-gatherers and first farmers: 500,000 to 1700 BC, in *Excavations at Heathrow Terminal 5* (J Lewis *et al.*)

Lewis, J, Brown, F, Batt, A, Cooke, N, Barrett, J, Every, R, Mepham, L, Brown, K, Cramp, K, Lawson, A J, Roe, F, Allen, S, Petts, D, McKinley, J I, Carruthers, W, Challinor, D, Wiltshire, P, Robinson, M, Lewis, H A, and Bates, M R, 2006 *Landscape evolution in the Middle Thames Valley: Heathrow Terminal 5 Excavations 1, Perry Oaks*, Framework Archaeology Monograph **1**, Oxford and Salisbury

Lewis, S, Maddy, D, Buckingham, C, Coope, G R, Field, M, Keen, D, Pike, A, Roe, D, Scaife, R, and Scott, K, 2005 Pleistocene fluvial sediments, palaeontology and archaeology of the upper River Thames at Latton, Wiltshire, England, *Journal of Quaternary Science* **20**, 1-25

Limbrey, S, and Robinson, S, 1988 Dryland to wetland: soil resources in the Upper Thames Valley, in *The exploitation of wetlands* (eds P Murphy and C French) BAR Brit. Ser. **186**, 129-144

Lister, A M, 1989 Mammalian faunas and the Wolstonian debate, in *West Midlands: field guide* (ed. D H Keen), 5-12, Cambridge

Lister, A M, 1992 Mammalian fossils and Quaternary biostratigraphy, *Quaternary Science Reviews* **11**, 329-44

Lister, A M, 1995 Sea-levels and the evolution of island endemics: the dwarf red deer of Jersey, in *Island Britain: a Quaternary perspective* (ed. R C Preece), Geological Society Special Publication **96**, 151-72

Lister, A M, 1998 The age of the Early Pleistocene mammal faunas from the 'Weybourne Crag' and Cromer Forest-bed Formation (Norfolk, England), in *The dawn of the Quaternary* (eds P L

Gibbard and T van Kolfschoten), Mededelingen Nederlands Instituut voor Toegepaste Geowetenschappen TNO **60**, 271-80

Lister, A M and Brandon, A, 1991 A pre-Ipswichian cold stage mammalian fauna from the Balderton Sand and Gravel, Lincolnshire, England, *Journal of Quaternary Science* **6**, 139-57

Lister, A M, Keen, D H, and Crossling, J, 1990 Elephant and molluscan remains from the basal levels of the Baginton-Lillington Gravels at Snitterfield, Warwickshire, *Proc Geol Ass* **101**, 202-12

Lister, A M, and Sher, A V, 2001 The origin and evolution of the woolly mammoth, *Science* **294**, 1094–7

Lobb, S J, 1995 Excavation at Crofton causewayed enclosure, *Wiltshire Hist Archaeol Mag* **88**, 18-25

Lobb, S J, and Rose, P G, 1996 *Archaeological survey of the Lower Kennet Valley, Berkshire*, Wessex Archaeol Rep **9**, Salisbury

Longworth, I H, 1979 The Neolithic and Bronze Age pottery in G J Wainwright, *Mount Pleasant, Dorset: excavations 1970-1971*, Reports of the Research Committee of the Society of Antiquaries of London **37**, 75-124, London

Longworth, I H, 1984 *Collared Urns of the Bronze Age in Great Britain and Ireland*, Cambridge

Loveday, R, 1999 Dorchester-on-Thames: ritual complex or ritual landscape?, in Barclay and Harding 1999, 49-66

Loveday, R, 2002 Duggleby Howe revisited, *Oxford J Archaeol* **21**, 135-46

Loveday, R, 2006 *Inscribed across the landscape: the cursus enigma*, Stroud

Loveday, R, Gibson, A, Marshall, P D, Bayliss, A, Bronk Ramsey, C and van der Plicht, H, 2007 The antler maceheads dating project, *Proc Prehist Soc* **73**, 381-92

Lowe, J, and Walker, M J C, 1997 *Reconstructing Quaternary environments*, 2nd edn, Harlow

Lucas, G, M, 1996 Of death and debt: a history of the body in Neolithic and Bronze Age Yorkshire, *J European Archaeol* **4**, 99-118

Lynch, F, 1993 *Excavations in the Brenig Valley: a Mesolithic and Bronze Age landscape in north Wales*, Cambrian Archaeol Monogr **5**, Bangor

Lynch, F, and Waddell, J, 1993 Discussion of stake circle barrows, in Lynch 1993, 76-85

MacRae, R J, 1982 Palaeolithic artefacts from Berinsfield, Oxfordshire, *Oxoniensa* **47**, 1-11

MacRae, R J, 1988 Belt, shoulder-bag or basket: an enquiry into handaxe transport and flint sources, *Lithics* **9**, 2-8

MacRae, R J, 1991 New Lower Palaeolthic finds from gravel pits in central southern England, *Lithics* **12**, 2-20

MacRae, R J, and Moloney, N (eds), 1988 *Non-flint stone tools and the Palaeolithic occupation of Britain*, BAR Brit. Ser. **189**, Oxford

Maddy, D, 1997 Uplift driven valley-incision and river terrace formation in southern England,

Journal of Quaternary Science **12**, 539-45

Maddy, D, Lewis, S G, and Green, C P, 1991 A review of the stratigraphic significance of the Wolvercote Terrace of the Upper Thames Valley, *Proc Geol Ass* **102**, 217-25

Maddy, D, Lewis, S G, and Scaife, R G, 1997 Upper Pleistocene deposits at Cassington, Oxfordshire, in *The Quaternary of the South Midlands and the Welsh Marches: field guide* (eds S G Lewis and D Maddy), 107-14, London

Maddy, D, Lewis, S G, Scaife, R G, Bowen, D Q, Coope, G R, Green, C P, Hardaker, T, Keen D H, Rees-Jones, J, Parfitt, S, and Scott, K, 1998 The Upper Pleistocene deposits at Cassington, near Oxford, England, *Journal of Quaternary Science* **13**, 205-31

Malim, T, 2000 The ritual landscape of the Neolithic and Bronze Age along the middle and lower Ouse valley, in *Prehistoric, Roman, and post-Roman landscapes of the Great Ouse Valley* (ed. M Dawson), CBA Res Rep **119**, 57-88, London

Malone, C, 2001 *Neolithic Britain and Ireland*, Stroud

Manby, T G, King, A, and Vyner, B E, 2003 The Neolithic and Bronze Ages: a time of agriculture, in *The archaeology of Yorkshire: an assessment at the beginning of the 21st century* (eds T G Manby, S Moorhouse and P Ottaway), Yorkshire Archaeological Society Occasional Paper **3**, York, 35-113

Mania, D, 1991 The zonal division of the Lower Palaeolithic open-air site at Bilzingsleben, *Anthropologie* **29**, 17-24

Marston, A T, 1937 The Swanscombe skull, *Journal of the Royal Anthropological Institute* **67**, 339-406

McBrearty, S, and Brooks, S, 2000 The revolution that wasn't: a new interpretation of the origin of modern human behaviour, *Journal of Human Evolution* **39**, 453-565

McFadyen, L, 2007, Neolithic architecture and participation: practices of making at long barrow sites, in Last 2007b, 22-9

McFadyen, L, Benson, D, and Whittle, A, 2007 The pre-barrow contexts, in Benson and Whittle 2007, 27-31

McGregor, D F M, and Green, C P, 1978 Gravels of the Thames as a guide to Pleistocene catchment changes, *Boreas*, **7**, 197-203

McInnes, I, 1968 Jet sliders in late Neolithic Britain, in *Studies in Ancient Europe: Essays Presented to Stuart Piggott* (eds J M Coles and D D A Simpson), 137-44, Leicester

McKinley, J I, 1995 Human bone, in Cleal *et al.* 1995, 451-63

McMillan, A A, Hamblin, R J O, Merritt, J W, 2005 *An overview of the lithostratigraphic framework for the Quaternary and Neogene deposits of Great Britain (Onshore)*, British Geological Survey Research Report **RR/04/04**, Nottingham

McNabb, J, 1992 The Clactonian: British Lower Palaeolithic flint technology in biface and non-biface assemblages, Unpubl. PhD Thesis, Univ. London

McNabb, J, 1996 More from the cutting edge: further discoveries of Clactonian bifaces, *Antiquity* **70**, 428-36

McNabb, J, and Ashton, N M 1995 Thoughtful flakers: a reply to Mithen, *Cambridge Archaeol J* **5**, 289-98

McOmish, D, 2005 Bronze Age land allotment on the Marlborough Downs, in Brown *et al.* 2005, 133-6

McPherron, S P, 1994 A reduction model for variability in Acheulian biface morphology, unpubl. PhD thesis, Univ. Pennsylvania

Meadows, J, Barclay, A, and Bayliss, A, 2007 A short passage of time: the dating of the Hazleton long cairn revisited, *Cambridge Archaeol J* **17 (1) (suppl)**, 45-64

Mellars, P, 1974 The Palaeolithic and Mesolithic, in *British Prehistory: a new outline* (ed. C Renfrew), 41-99, London

Mellars, P, 1976 Settlement patterns and industrial variability in the British Mesolithic, in *Problems in economic and social archaeology* (eds G Sieveking, I H Longworth and K Wilson), 375-99, London

Mellars, P, 1996a *The Neanderthal legacy*, Princeton

Mellars, P, 1996b The emergence of biologically modern populations in Europe: a social and cognitive 'revolution'? *Proc Brit Acad* **88**, 179-201

Mellars, P, 1999 The Neanderthal problem continued, *Current Anthropology* **40**, 341-63

Mellars, P, and Dark, P (eds), 1998 *Star Carr in context: new archaeological and palaeoecological investigations at the early Mesolithic site of Star Carr, North Yorkshire*, Cambridge

Mellars, P, and Gibson, K, 1996 *Modelling the early human mind*, Cambridge

Mellars, P, and Stringer, C, 1989 *The human revolution: behavioural and biological perspectives in the origins of modern humans*, Edinburgh

Mepham, L, 1992 Objects within Urn 919, in Butterworth and Lobb 1992, 48-50

Mercer, R J, 1980 *Hambledon Hill: a neolithic landscape*, Edinburgh

Merewether, J, 1851a The excavation of Silbury Hill, in *Memoirs illustrative of the history and antiquities of Witshire, communicated at the annual meeting of the Archaeological Institute of Great Britain and Ireland held at Salisbury, July, 1849*, 73-81, London

Merewether, J, 1851b Diary of the examination of barrows and other earthworks in the neighbourhood of Silbury Hill and Avebury, in *Memoirs illustrative of the history and antiquities of Witshire, communicated at the annual meeting of the Archaeological Institute of Great Britain and Ireland held at Salisbury, July, 1849*, 82-112, London

Metcalf, P, and Huntingdon, R, 1991 *Celebrations of death: the anthropology of mortuary ritual*, 2nd edn, Cambridge

Miles, D, 1986 *Archaeology at Barton Court Farm, Abingdon, Oxon*, Oxford Archaeological Unit Report **3**, CBA Research Report **50**, Oxford

Miles, D, Palmer, S, Lock, G, Gosden, C and Cromarty, A M, 2003 *Uffington White Horse and its landscape: investigations at White Horse Hill, Uffington, 1989–95, and Tower Hill, Ashbury, 1993–4*, Thames Valley Landscapes Monograph **18**, Oxford

Millard, L, 1965 A Mesolithic industry from Bolter End, *Rec Buckinghamshire* **17**, 343-9

Milner, N, 2006 Subsistence, in *Mesolithic Britain and Ireland: new approaches* (eds C Conneller and G Warren), 61-82, Stroud

Milner, N, Craig, O E, Bailey, G N, Pederson, K, and Anderson, S H, 2004 Something fishy in the Neolithic? A re-evaluation of stable isotope analysis of Mesolithic and Neolithic coastal populations, *Antiquity* **78**, 9-22

Milner, N, and Miracle P T, 2002 Introduction; patterning data and consuming theory, in *Consuming patterns and patterns of consumption* (eds P Miracle and N Milner), 1-6, Cambridge

Milner, N, and Woodman, P, 2005 *Mesolithic Studies at the beginning of the 21st century*, Oxford

Miracle, P, 2002 Mesolithic meals from Mesolithic middens, in *Consuming patterns and patterns of consumption* (eds P Miracle and N Milner), 65-88, Cambridge

Mitchell, G F, Penny, L F, Shotton F W, and West, R G, 1973 *A correlation of Quaternary deposits in the British Isles*, Special Report of the Geological Society of London **4**, Edinburgh

Mitchell, J C, 1995 Studying biface utilisation at Boxgrove: Roe deer butchery with replica handaxes, *Lithics* **16**, 64-9

Mithen, S, 1994 Technology and society during the Middle Pleistocene: hominid group size, social learning and industrial variability, *Cambridge Archaeol J* **4**, 3-32

Mithen, S, 1996 *The prehistory of the mind*, London

Mithen, S, 1999 Hunter-gatherers of the Mesolithic, in *The archaeology of Britain* (eds J Hunter and I Ralston), 35-57, London

Mizoguchi, K, 1993 Time in the reproduction of mortuary practices, *World Archaeol* **25**, 223-35

Mizoguchi, K, 1995 The materiality of Wessex Beakers, *Scottish Archaeol Rev* **9**, 175-86

Moffatt, A J, 1986 Quartz signatures in Plio-Pleistocene gravels in the northern part of the London basin, in *Clast lithological analysis* (ed. D R Bridgland), Quaternary Research Association Technical Guide **3**, 117-28, Cambridge

Moffett, L, 1999 The prehistoric use of plant resources, in Barclay and Halpin 1999, 243-246.

Moffett, L, 2004 The evidence for crop-processing products from the Iron Age and Romano-British periods and some earlier prehistoric plant remains, in Lambrick and Allen 2004, 421-44

Moffett, L, Robinson, M A and Straker, V, 1989 Cereals, fruit and nuts: charred plant remains from Neolithic sites in England and Wales and the Neolithic economy, in *The beginnings of agriculture* (eds A Milles, D Williams and N Gardener), BAR Int. Ser. **496**, 243-61, Oxford

Moore, J and Jennings, D, 1992 *Reading Business Park: a Bronze Age landscape*, Thames Valley Landscapes: the Kennet Valley **1**, Oxford

Moore, J, and Scott, E (eds), 1997 *Invisible people and processes: writing gender and childhood into European archaeology*, Leicester

Moorey, P R S, 1982 A Neolithic ring-ditch and Iron Age enclosure at Newnham Murren, near Wallingford, in Case and Whittle 1982, 55-9

Morgan, F de M, 1959a The excavation of a long barrow at Nutbane, Hants, *Proc Prehist Soc* **25**, 15-51

Morgan, F de M, 1959b The radiocarbon dating of Nutbane long barrow, *Antiquity* **33**, 289

Morris, J, 1838 On the deposits containing Carnivora and other Mammalia in the valley of the Thames, *Magazine of Natural History* **2**, 539-48

Mortimer, J R, 1905 *Forty years researches in British and Saxon burial mounds of East Yorkshire*, London

Mukherjee, A J, Berstan, R, Copley, M S, Gibson, A M and Evershed, R P, 2007 Compound-specific stable carbon isotopic detection of pig product processing in British late Neolithic pottery, *Antiquity* **81**, 743-54

Mullin, D, forthcoming The flint, in *Excavations at Oxford Castle: Oxford's western quarter from the mid-Saxon period to the late 18th century*, (A Norton, J Munby and D Poore), Oxford

Mulville, J, in prep. Animal foods from Yarnton floodplain, in Hey in prep.

Mulville, J, and Grigson, C, 2007 The animal bones, in Benson and Whittle 2007, 237-253

Murphy, P, 1982 Impressions of plant remains, in Case and Whittle 1982, 47-9

Murton, J B, Baker, A, Bowen, D Q, Caseldine, C J, Coope, G R, Currant, A P, Evans, J G, Field, M H, Green, C P, Hatton, J, Ito, M, Jones, R L, Keen, D H, Kerney, M P, McEwan, R, McGregor, D F M, Parish, D, Schreve, D C, Smart, P L, and York, L L, 2001 A late Middle Pleistocene temperate-periglacial-temperate sequence (Oxygen Isotope Stages 7-5e) near Marsworth, Buckinghamshire, UK, *Quaternary Science Reviews* **20**, 1787-825

Neal, D, Wardle, A, and Hunn, J, 1990 *Excavation of the Iron Age, Roman and medieval settlement at Gorhambury, St Albans*, English Heritage Archaeological Report **14**, London

Needham, S P, 1981 *The Bulford-Helsbury manufacturing tradition: the production of Stogursey socketed axes during the later Bronze Age in southern Britain*, British Museum Occasional Paper 13, London

Needham, S P, 1987 The Bronze Age, in Bird and Bird 1987, 97-138

Needham, S P, 1988 Selective deposition in the British early Bronze Age, *World Archaeol* **20 (2)**, 22949

Needham, S P, 1991 *Excavation and salvage at Runnymede Bridge, 1978: the late Bronze Age waterfront site*, London

Needham, S P, 1992 Holocene alluviation and interstratified archaeological evidence in the Thames valley at Runnymede Bridge, in Needham and Macklin 1992, 249-60

Needham, S P, 1996 Chronology and periodisation in the British Bronze Age, *Acta Archaeologica* **67** 121-40

Needham, S P, 1999a Radley and the development of early metalwork in Britain, in Barclay and Halpin 1999, 186-8

Needham, S P, 1999b Winged-headed pin, in Barclay and Halpin 1999, 236

Needham, S P, 2000a *The passage of the Thames: Holocene environment and settlement at Runnymede*, London

Needham, S P, 2000b Power pulses across a cultural divide: cosmologically driven acquisition between Armorica and Wessex, *Proc Prehist Soc* **66**, 151-207

Needham, S P, 2005 Transforming Beaker culture in north-west Europe: processes of fusion and fission, *Proc Prehist Soc* **71**, 159-70

Needham, S P, 2007 Isotopic aliens: Beaker movement and cultural transmisions, in *From Stonehenge to the Baltic: living with cultural diversity in the third millennium BC* (eds L Larsson and M Parker Pearson), BAR Int. Ser. **1692**, 41-6, Oxford

Needham, S P, and Macklin, M G, 1992 *Alluvial archaeology in Britain*, Oxbow Monograph **27**, Oxford

Needham, S, Parker Pearson, M, Tyler, A, Richards, M, and Jay, M, 2010 A first 'Wessex 1' date from Wessex, *Antiquity* **84**, 363-73

Nehlich, O, Montgomery, J, Evans, J, Schade-Lindig, S, Pichler, S L, Richards, M P and Alt, K W, 2009 Mobility or migration: a case study from the Neolithic settlement of Nieder-Mörlen (Hessen, Germany), *J Archaeol Sci* **36**, 1791-1799

Needham, S P, and Saville, A, 1981, Two early Bronze Age flat bronze axeheads from Oddington, *Trans Bristol Gloucestershire Archaeol Soc* **99**, 15-20

Needham, S P, and Spence, T, 1996 *Refuse and disposal at Area 16 East, Runnymede*, London

Network Archaeology, 2005 Chalgrove to East Ilsley gas pipeline: archaeological watching brief and excavations, unpubl. report, Oxford Sites and Monuments Record

Newton, E T, 1882 On the occurrence of *Spermophilus* beneath the glacial till of Norfolk, *Geological Magazine* **9**, 51-4

Northover, P, 2008 Analysis of a copper awl, in Allen and Kamash 2008, 54

Norton, A, 2007 Extension Areas 1 and 2, Tubney Wood Quarry, Tubney, Oxfordshire: archaeological test-pitting report, post-excavation assessment and revised project design, unpubl. report, Oxford Archaeology

O'Connell, M, 1990 Excavations during 1979-1985 of a multiperiod site at Stanwell, *Surrey Archaeol Collect* **80**, 2-62

O'Drisceoil, D A, 1988 Burnt mounds: cooking or bathing, *Antiquity* **62**, 671-80

O'Neil, H E, 1957 Condicote earthwork, a henge monument, Gloucestershire, *Trans Bristol Gloucestershire Archaeol Soc* **76**, 141-6

O'Neil, H E, 1966 Sale's Lot long barrow, Withington, Gloucestershire, *Trans Bristol Gloucestershire Archaeol Soc* **85**, 5-35

O'Sullivan, A, 1996 Neolithic, Bronze Age and Iron Age woodworking techniques, in *Trackway excavations in the Mountdillon Bogs, County Longford, 1985-1991* (B Raftery), Irish Archaeological Wetland Unit Transactions **3**, 291-342, Dublin

Oakley, K P, 1939 Geology and Palaeolithic studies, in *A survey of the prehistory of the Farnham District (Surrey)* (eds W F Rankine, A W G Lowther and K P Oakley), 3-58, Guildford

Oakley, K, 1949 *Man the tool-maker,* 1st edn, London

Ohel, M Y, 1979 The Clactonian: an independent complex or an integral part of the Acheulean?, *Current Anthropology* **20**, 685-726

Osborne, P J, 1969 An insect fauna of Late Bronze Age date from Wilsford, Wiltshire, *J Animal Ecology* **38 (3)**, 555-66

Osborne, P J, 1980 The Late Devensian-Flandrian transition depicted by serial insect faunas from West Bromwich, Staffordshire, England, *Boreas* **9**, 139-147

Osborne, P J, 1989 Insects, in *Wilsford Shaft: excavations, 1960-62* (eds P Ashbee, M Bell, and E Proudfoot), Engl Heritage Archaeol Rep **11**, , 96-99 and fiche C1-7, London

Oswald, A, 1969 Excavations for the Avon/Severn Research Committee at Barford, Warwickshire, *Trans Birmingham Warwickshire Archaeol Soc* **83**, 1-64

Oswald, A, Dyer, C, and Barber, M, 2001 *The creation of monuments: Neolithic causewayed enclosures in the British Isles*, London

Owen, R, 1856 Description of a fossil cranium of the musk-buffalo [*Bubalus moschatus,* Owen; *Bos moschatus* (Zimm. and Gmel.), Pallas; *Bos Pallasii,* De Kay; *Ovibos Pallasii,* II. Smith and Bl.] from the 'Lower-level Drift' at Maidenhead, Berkshire, *Quarterly Journal of the Geological Society* **12**, 124-31

Owoc, M A, 2001a Bronze Age cosmologies: the construction of time and space in south-western funerary/ritual monuments, in *Holy ground: theoretical issues relating to the landscape and material culture of ritual space objects* (eds A T Smith and A Brookes), BAR Int. Ser. **956**, 27-38, Oxford

Owoc, M A, 2001b The times, they are a changin': experiencing continuity and development in the early Bronze Age rituals of southwestern Britain, in Brück 2001, 193-206

Owoc, M A, 2002 Munselling the mound: the use of soil colour as metaphor in British Bronze Age funerary ritual, in *Colouring the past: the significance of colour in archaeological research* (eds A Jones and G MacGregor), 127-40, Oxford

Palmer, N, 1980 A Beaker burial and medieval tenements in the Hamel, *Oxoniensia* **45**, 124-34

Palmer, S, 1872-5 On the antiquities found in the peat of Newbury, *Trans Newbury District Field Club* **2**, 123-34

Palmer, S, 1975 A Palaeolithic site at North Road, Purfleet, Essex, *Transactions of the Essex Archaeological Society* **7**, 1-13

Parfitt, S A, Ashton, N M, Lewis, S G, Abel, R L, Coope, G R, Field, M H, Gale, R, Hoare, P G, Larkin, N R, Lewis, M D, Karloukovski, V, Maher, B A , Peglar, S M, Preece, R C, Whittaker, J E, and Stringer C B, 2010 Early Pleistocene human occupation at the edge of the boreal zone in northwest Europe, *Nature* **466**, 229-33

Parfitt, S, Barendregt, R, Breda, M, Candy, I, Collins, M, Coope, G R, Durbidge, P, Field, M, Lee, J, Lister, A, Mutch, R, Penkman, K, Preece, R, Rose, J, Stringer, C, Symmons, R, Whittaker, J, Wymer, J, and Stuart, A, 2005 The earliest record of human activity in northern Europe, *Nature* **438**, 1008-12

Parfitt, S A, Owen, F J and Keen, D H, 1998 Pleistocene stratigraphy, vertebrates and Mollusca, Black Rock, Brighton, in *The Quaternary of Kent and Sussex: field Guide* (eds J B Murton, C A Whiteman, M R Bates, D R Bridgland, A J Long, M B Roberts and M Waller), 146-150, London

Parker Pearson, M, 1999 *The archaeology of death and burial*, Stroud

Parker Pearson, M, 2000 Ancestors, bones and stones in Neolithic and early Bronze Age Britain and Ireland, in *Neolithic Orkney in its European Context* (ed. A Ritchie, A), 203-14, Cambridge

Parker Pearson, M, Chamberlain, A, Jay, M, Marshall, P, Pollard, J, Richards, C, Thomas, J, Tilley, C, and Welham, K, 2009 Who was buried at Stonehenge? *Antiquity* **83**, 23-39

Parker Pearson, M, and Ramilisonina, 1998 Stonehenge for the ancestors: the stones pass on the message, *Antiquity* **72**, 308-26

Parker Pearson, M, and Richards, C, 1994 Ordering the world: perceptions of architecture, space and time, in *Architecture and order: approaches to social space* (eds M Parker Pearson and C Richards), 1-37, London

Parker, A G, 1995a Late Quaternary environmental change in the Upper Thames Basin, central-southern England, unpubl. DPhil thesis, Univ. Oxford

Parker, A G, 1995b Pollen analysis, in The excavation of a late Bronze Age/early Iron Age site at Eight Acre Field, Radley (A Mudd), *Oxoniensia* **60**, 50-53

Parker, A, 1999 Pollen and sediments of Daisy Banks Fen, in Barclay and Halpin 1999, 254-67

Parker, A G, forthcoming The pollen, in T G Allen *et al.* forthcoming

Parker, A G, Goudie, A S, Anderson, D E, Robinson, M A, and Bonsall, C, 2002 A review of the mid-Holocene elm decline in the British Isles, *Progress in Physical Geography* **26**, 1-45

Parker, A G, and Robinson, M A, 2003 Palaeoenvironmental investigations on the Middle Thames at Dorney, UK, in *Alluvial archaeology in Europe* (eds A J Howard, M Macklin and D G Passmore), 43-60, Rotterdam

Parkinson, A, Barclay, A, and McKeague, P, 1996 The excavation of two Bronze Age barrows, Oxford, *Oxoniensia* **61**, 41-64

Parrington, M, 1978 *The excavation of an Iron Age settlement, Bronze Age ring-ditches and Roman features at Ashville Trading Estate, Abingdon, Oxfordshire, 1974-76*, CBA Res Rep **28**, London

Paterson, T T, 1937 Studies on the Palaeolithic succession in England 1: the Barnham Sequence, *Proc Prehist Soc* **3**, 87-135

Paterson, T T, 1944 Core, culture and complex in the Old Stone Age, *Proc Preh Soc* **11**, 1-19

Paterson, T T, and Tebbutt, C F, 1947 Studies in the Palaeolithic succession in England III: palae-oliths from St. Neots, Huntingdonshire, *Proc Preh Soc* **13**, 37-46

Peake, A E, 1913 An account of a flint factory with some new types of flints excavated at Peppard Common, Oxon, *Archaeol J* **70**, 3368

Peake, A E, 1917 A prehistoric site at Kimble S. Bucks, *Proc Prehist Soc E Anglia* **2 (3)**, 437-58

Peake, H J E, 1936 A beaker and a four-legged bowl from Inkpen, Berks, *Antiq J* **XVI**, 97-8

Peake, H J E, and Crawford, OGS, 1922 A flint factory at Thatcham, Berks., *Proc Prehist Soc E Anglia* **3**, 499-514

Pearson, N, and Shanks, M, 2001 *Theatre/archae-ology*, London

Pettitt, P B, 2000a Neanderthal extinction: radio-carbon chronology, problems, prospects and an interprctation of the existing data, *Revue d'Archéométrie* supplement (proceedings of the 3rd international radiocarbon in archaeology conference, Lyon), 165-77

Pevzner, M, Vangengeim, E, and Tesakov, A, 2001 Quaternary subdivisions of eastern Europe based on vole evolution, *Bolletino della Società Paleontologica Italiana* **40**, 269-74

Piggott, S, 1929 Neolithic pottery and other remains from Pangbourne, Berks and Caversham, Oxon, *Proc Prehist Soc E Anglia* **6**, 30-9

Piggott, S, 1931 The Neolithic pottery of the British Isles, *Archaeol J* **88**, 67-158

Piggott, S, 1938 The early Bronze Age in Wessex, *Proc Prehist Soc* **4**, 52-106

Piggott, S, 1954 *Neolithic cultures of the British Isles,* Cambridge

Piggott, S, 1962 *The West Kennet long barrow: excava-tions, 1955-56*, London

Piggott, S, 1989 *Ancient Britons and the antiquarian imagination: ideas from the Renaissance to the Regency*, London

Pike, A W G, Eggins, S, Grün, R, Hedges, R E M,

and Jacobi, R M, 2005 U-series dating of the Late Pleistocene mammalian fauna from Wood Quarry (Steetley), Nottinghamshire, UK, *Journal of Quaternary Science* **20**, 59-65

Pike, K, and Godwin, H, 1953 The interglacial at Clacton-on-Sea, Essex, *Quarterly Journal of the Geological Society of London* **108**, 261-72

Pine, J, and Ford, S, 2003 Excavation of Neolithic, late Bronze Age, early Iron Age and early Saxon features at St Helen's Avenue, Benson, Oxfordshire, *Oxoniensia* **68**, 131-78

Pine, J, and Preston, S, 2004 *Iron Age and Roman settlement and landscape at Totterdown Lane, Horcott near Fairford, Gloucestershire*, TVAS Monograph **6**, Reading

Pitts, M, 2001 Excavating the Sanctuary: new investigations on Overton Hill, Avebury, *Wiltshire Archaeol Mag* **94**, 1-23

Pitts, M, and Roberts, M B, 1997 *Fairweather Eden: life in Britain half a million years ago as revealed by the excavations at Boxgrove*, London

Pitts, M, and Whittle, A, 1992 The development and date of Avebury, *Proc Prehist Soc* **58**, 203-12

Plot, R, 1677 *The natural history of Oxford-shire, being an essay toward the natural history of England*, Oxford and London

Pocock, T I, 1908 *The geology of the country around Oxford*, Memoir of the Geological Survey of Great Britain, London

Pollard, J, 1992 The Sanctuary, Overton Hill, Wiltshire: a reassessment, *Proc Prehist Soc* **58**, 213-26

Pollard, J, 1994 The worked flint, and Appendix 2: dating, associations and contexts of flint polished-edge blade knives, in Excavations at Millbarrow Neolithic chambered tomb, Winterbourne Monkton, North Wiltshire (A Whittle), *Wiltshire Archaeol Natur Hist Mag* **87**, 40-44 and 51-2

Pollard, J, 1995 Inscribing space: formal deposition at the later Neolithic monument of Woodhenge, Wiltshire, *Proc Prehist Soc* **61**, 137-56

Pollard, J, 1999 These places have their moments: thoughts on settlement practices in the British Neolithic, in *Making places in the prehistoric world: themes in settlement archaeology* (eds J Brück and M Goodman), 76-93, London

Pollard, J, 2001, The aesthetics of depositional practice, *World Archaeol* **33 (2)**, 315-33

Pollard, J, 2004 A 'movement of becoming': realms of existence in the early Neolithic of southern Britain, in *Stories from the landscape: archaeologies of inhabitation* (ed. A M Chadwick), BAR Int. Ser. **1238**, 55-69, Oxford

Pollard, J, 2005 Memory, monuments or middens in the Avebury landscape, in Brown *et al.* 2005, 103-14

Pollard, J, 2006 A community of beings: animals and people in the Neolithic of Southern Britain, in *Animals in the Neolithic of Britain and Europe* (eds D Serjeantson and D Field), Neolithic Studies Groups Seminar Papers **7**, 135-48, Oxford

Pollard, J, and Cleal, R, 2004 Dating Avebury, in *Monuments and material culture: papers in honour of an Avebury archaeologist, Isobel Smith* (eds R Cleal and J Pollard), 120-9, East Knoyle

Pollard, J, and Reynolds, A, 2002 *Avebury: the biography of a landscape*, Stroud

Pollard, J, and Whittle, A, 1999 Other finds, in Whittle *et al.* 1999, 338-43

Poore, D, and Wilkinson, D R P, 2001 *Beaumont Palace and the White Friars: excavations at the Sackler Library, Beaumont Street, Oxford*, OAU Occ Pap **9**, Oxford

Pope, M, 2002 The significance of biface-rich assemblages: an examination of behavioural controls on lithic assemblage formation in the Lower Palaeolithic, Unpubl. PhD Thesis, Univ. Southampton

Pope, M, and Roberts, M B, 2005 Observations on the relationship between Palaeolithic individuals and artefact scatters at the Middle Pleistocene site of Boxgrove, UK, in *The hominid individual in context: archaeological investigations of Lower and Middle Palaeolithic landscapes, locales and artefacts* (eds C Gamble and M Porr), 81-97, London

Powell, K, and Laws, G, in prep. A late Neolithic/early Bronze Age enclosure and Iron Age and Romano-British settlement at Latton Lands, *Wiltshire Archaeol Mag*

Powell, K, Smith, A, and Laws, G, 2010 *Evolution of a farming community in the Upper Thames Valley: excavation of a prehistoric, Roman and post-Roman landscape at Cotswold Community, Gloucestershire and Wiltshire*, Thames Valley Landscapes Monograph **31**, Oxford

Powell, T G E, 1973 Excavation of the chambered cairn at Duffryn Ardudwy, Merioneth, Wales, *Archaeologia* **104**, 1-49

Preece, R C (ed.), 1995a *Island Britain: a Quaternary perspective*, Geological Society Special Publication **96**, London

Preece, R C, 1995b Mollusca from interglacial sediments at three critical sites in the Lower Thames, in *The Quaternary of the lower reaches of the Thames: field guide* (eds D R Bridgland, P Allen and B A Haggart), 53-62, Durham

Preece, R C, 1999 Mollusca from the Last Interglacial fluvial deposits of the River Thames at Trafalgar Square, London, *Journal of Quaternary Science* **14**, 77-89

Preece, R C, 2001 Molluscan evidence for differentiation of interglacials within the 'Cromerian Complex', *Quaternary Science Reviews* 20, 1643-56

Preece, R C, and Day, S P, 1994 Comparison of Post-glacial molluscan and vegetational successions from a radiocarbon-dated tufa sequence in Oxfordshire, *J Biogeography* **21** 4, 63-78

Preece, R C, and Parfitt, S A, 2000 The Cromer Forest-bed Formation: New thoughts on an old problem, in, *The Quaternary of Norfolk and Suffolk: field guide* (eds S G Lewis, C A Whiteman and R C Preece), 1-27, London

Prestwich, J, 1856 Note on the Gravel near

Maidenhead, in which the skull of the musk buffalo was found, *Quarterly Journal of the Geological Society* **12**, 131-3

Pringle, J, 1926 *The geology of the county around Oxford*, 2nd edn, London

Pryor, F, 1974 *Excavations at Fengate, Peterborough, England: the 1st report*, Royal Ontario Mus Archaeol Monogr **3**, Toronto

Pryor, F, 1976 A Neolithic multiple burial from Fengate, Peterborough, *Antiquity* **50**, 232-33

Pryor, F, 1985 The discussion, in *Archaeology in the Lower Welland Valley 2*, (eds F Pryor, C French, D Crowther, D Gurney, G Simpson and M Taylor), EAA **27 (2)**, 298-312, Cambridge

Pryor, F, 1998 *Etton: excavations at a Neolithic causewayed enclosure near Maxey, Cambridgeshire, 1982-7*, Engl Heritage Archaeol Rep **18**, London

Pryor, F, 2004 *Britain BC*, London

Rackham, O, 1987 *The history of the countryside*, London

Radcliffe, F, 1960 Excavations at Logic Lane, Oxford, *Oxoniensia* **26-7**, 38-69

Rahtz, P, 1962 Farncombe Down barrow, Berkshire, *Berkshire Archaeol J* **60**, 1-24

Rankine, W F, 1953 Mesolithic research in east Hampshire: the Hampshire Greensand, *Proc Hampshire Field Club* **18**, 157–72

Rankine, W F, and Dimbleby, G W, 1960 Further investigations at a Mesolithic site at Oakhanger, Selborne, Hants, *Proc Prehist Soc* **27**, 246–62

Ray, K, and Thomas, J, 2003 In the kinship of cows: the social centrality of cattle in the earlier Neolithic of southern Britain, in *Food, culture and identity in the Neolithic and early Bronze Age* (ed. M Parker Pearson), BAR Int. Ser. **1117**, 37-51, Oxford

Reading, H G (ed), 1978 *Sedimentary environments and facies*, Oxford

Reid, C, 1899 *The origin of the British Flora*, London

Renfrew, C, 1973 Monuments, mobilisation and social organisation in Neolithic Wessex, in *The explanation of culture change* (ed. C Renfrew), 539-58, London

Renfrew, C, 1976 Megaliths, territories and populations, in *Acculturation and continuity in Atlantic Europe* (ed. S J de Laet), 198-200, Bruges

Renfrew, C, and Cherry, J F (eds), 1986 *Peer polity interaction and socio-political change*, Cambridge

Renfrew, C and Newton, R G, 1979 British faience beads reconsidered, in *Probems in European prehistory* (C Renfrew), 293-303, Edinburgh

Reynier, M J, 1998 Early Mesolithic settlement in England and Wales: some preliminary observations, in *Stone Age archaeology: essays in honour of John Wymer*, (eds N Ashton, F Healy, and P Pettit), 174–84, Oxford

Reynier, M J, 2000 Thatcham revisited: spatial and stratigraphic analysis of two sub-assemblages from Site III and its implications for early Mesolithic typo-chronology in Britain, in *Mesolithic lifeways: current research from Britain and Ireland* (ed. R Young), Leicester University Archaeol Monograph **7**, 33–46, Leicester

Reynier, M J, forthcoming an early Mesolithic stone assemblage from Marsh Benham, Berkshire, UK, *Berkshire Archaeol J*

Rice, P M, 1987 *Pottery analysis: a sourcebook*, Chicago

Richards, C, 1996 Monuments as landscape: creating the centre of the world in late Neolithic Orkney, *World Archaeol* **28**, 190-208

Richards, C, 1998 Centralising tendencies? A re-examination of social evolution in late Neolithic Orkney, in Edmonds and Richards 1998, 516-32

Richards, C, and Thomas, J, 1984 Ritual activity and structured deposition in Neolithic Wessex, in Bradley and Gardiner 1984, 189-218

Richards, J, 1978 *The archaeology of the Berkshire Downs: an introductory survey*, Berkshire Archaeol Comm Publ **3**, Reading

Richards, J, 1986-90 Death and the past environment: the results of work on barrows on the Berkshire Downs, *Berkshire Archaeol J* **73**, 142

Richards, J, 1990 *The Stonehenge Environs Project*, Engl Heritage Archaeol Rep **16**, London

Richards, M P, 2000 Human consumption of plant foods in the British Neolithic: direct evidence from bone stable isotopes, in Fairbairn 2000, 123-35

Richards, M P, Pettitt, P B, Trinkhaus, E, Smith, F H, Paunovic, M, and Karanic, I, 2000 Neanderthal diet at Vindija and Neanderthal predation: the evidence from stable isotopes, *Proceedings of the National Association for Science (USA)* **97**, 7663-6

Richards, M P, Schulting, R J and Hedges, R, 2003 Sharp shift in diet at onset of Neolithic, *Nature* **425**, 366

Richmond, A, 2006 Excavation of a Peterborough Ware pit at Wallingford, Oxfordshire, *Oxoniensia* **70**, 79-96

Richmond, A, Rackham, J, and Scaife, R, 2006 Excavations of a prehistoric stream-side site at Little Marlow, Buckinghamshire, *Rec Buckinghamshire* **46**, 65-118

Riding, J B, Head, M J, and Moorlock, B S P, 2000 Reworked palynomorphs from the Red Crag and Norwich Crag formations (Early Pleistocene) of the Ludham Borehole, Norfolk, *Proc Geol Ass* **111**, 161-71

Riding, J B, Moorlock, B S P, Jeffery, D H, and Hamblin, R J O, 1997 Reworked and indigenous palynomorphs from the Norwich Crag Formation (Pleistocene) of eastern Suffolk: implications for provenance, palaeogeography and climate, *Proc Geol Ass* **108**, 25-38

Ripoll, S, Munoz, F, Bahn, P, and Pettitt, P B, 2004 Palaeolithic cave engravings at Creswell Crags, England, *Proc Prehist Soci* **70**, 93-105

Robb, J, and Miracle, P, 2007 Beyond 'migration' versus 'acculturation': new models for the spread of agriculture, in Whittle and Cummings 2007, 99-115

Roberts, A J, Barton, R N E, and Evans, J, 1998 Early Mesolithic mastic, radiocarbon dating and analysis of organic residues from Thatcham III, Star Carr and Lackford Heath, in *Stone Age Archaeology: essays in honour of John Wymer* (eds N M Ashton, F Healy, and P B Pettit), Lithic Studies Occas Pap **6**, Oxbow Monogr **102**, 185-92, Oxford

Roberts, M B 1996a "Man the Hunter" Returns at Boxgrove, *British Archaeology* **18**, 8-9.

Roberts, M B, 1996b And then came speech and clothing, *British Archaeology* **19**, 8-9

Roberts, M B, and Parfitt, S A (eds), 1999 *Boxgrove: a Middle Palaeolithic Pleistocene hominid site at Eartham Quarry, Boxgrove, West Sussex*, London

Roberts, M B, Stringer, C, and Parfitt, S, 1994 A hominid tibia from Middle Pleistocene sediments at Boxgrove, *Nature* **369**, 311-13

Roberts, M R, 1995 Excavations at Park Farm, Binfield, Berkshire 1990: an Iron Age and Romano-British settlement and two Mesolithic flint scatters, in Barnes *et al.* 1995, 93-132

Robertson-Mackay, M E, 1980 A 'head and hooves' burial beneath a round barrow, with other Neolithic and Bronze Age sites, on Hemp Knoll, near Avebury, Wiltshire, *Proc Prehist Soc* **46**, 123-76

Robertson-Mackay, R, 1987 The Neolithic cause-wayed enclosure at Staines, Surrey: excavations, 1961-63, *Proc Prehist Soc* **53**, 23-128

Robinson, M A, 1981 Investigations of palaeoenvironment in the Upper Thames Valley, unpubl. PhD thesis, Univ. London

Robinson, M A, 1988 The significance of tubers of *Arrhenatherum elatius* (L.) Beauv. from Site 4, excavation 15/11, in Lambrick 1988, 102

Robinson, M A, 1991 The Neolithic and late Bronze Age insect assemblages, in Needham 1991, 277-326

Robinson, M A, 1992a Environmental archaeology of the river gravels: past achievements and future directions, in Fulford and Nichols 1992, 47-62

Robinson, M A, 1992b Environment, archaeology and alluvium on the river gravels of the South Midlands, in Needham and Macklin 1992, 197-20

Robinson, M A, 1993 The pre-Iron Age environment and finds, in Allen and Robinson 1993, 7-19

Robinson, M A, 1995 Plant and invertebrate remains, in The excavation of a late Bronze Age/early Iron Age site at Eight Acre Field, Radley (A Mudd), *Oxoniensia* **60**, 41-50

Robinson, M A, 1999a Land and freshwater mollusca, in *Excavations alongside Roman Ermin Street, Gloucestershire and Wiltshire: the archaeology of the A419/A417 Swindon to Gloucester Road Scheme, 2* (A Mudd, R J Williams and A Lupton), 494-500, Oxford

Robinson, M A, 1999b The prehistoric environmental sequence of the Barrows Hill area, in Barclay and Halpin 1999, 269-74

Robinson, M A, 1999c Land snails, in Barclay and Halpin 1999, 241-43

Robinson, M A, 2000a Coleopteran evidence for the Elm Decline, Neolithic activity in woodland, clearance and use of the landscape, in Fairbairn 2000, 27-36

Robinson, M A, 2000b Middle Mesolithic to late Bronze Age insect assemblages and an early Neolithic assemblage of waterlogged macroscopic plant remains, in Needham 2000a, 146-67

Robinson, M A, 2000c Further consideration of Neolithic charred cereals, fruit and nuts, in Fairbairn 2000, 85-90

Robinson, M A, 2002 Waterlogged macroscopic plant and insect remains, in Shorncote Quarry: excavations of a late prehistoric landscape in the upper Thames Valley, 1997 and 1998 (M Brossler, M Gocher, G Laws, and M Roberts) *Trans Bristol and Gloucestershire Archaeol Soc* **120**, 74-78

Robinson, M A, 2003 Palaeoenvironmental studies, in Barclay *et al.* 2003, 163-78

Robinson, M A, 2006 Macroscopic plant and invertebrate remains, in Cromarty *et al.* 2006, 216-22

Robinson, M A, 2009 Waterlogged macroscopic plant and invertebrate remains, in Booth and Simmonds 2009, 99-105

Robinson, M A, in prep. The archaeobotanic remains, in Hey in prep.

Robinson, M A, and Lambrick, G H, 1984 Holocene alluviation and hydrology in the Upper Thames Basin, *Nature* **308**, 809-14

Robinson, M A, and Lambrick, G, 2009 Living off the land: farming, water, storage and waste, in Lambrick with Robinson 2009, 237-92

Robinson, M A, and Wilson, R, 1987 A survey of environmental archaeology in the south Midlands, in *Environmental archaeology: a regional review 2* (ed. H C M Keeley), Historic Buildings and Monuments Commission for Engl Occas Pap **1**, 16-100, London

Roe, D A, 1968 British Lower and Middle Palaeolithic handaxe groups, *Proc Prehist Soc* **34**, 1-82

Roe, D A, 1981 *The Lower and Middle Palaeolithic periods in Britain: the archaeology of Britain*, London

Roe, D A, 1986 The Palaeolithic period in the Oxford Region, in Briggs *et al.* 1986 1-17

Roe, D A, 1994 The Palaeolithic archaeology of the Oxford Region, *Oxoniensia* **59**, 1-15

Roe, F, 1968 Stone maceheads and the latest Neolithic cultures of the British Isles, in *Studies in ancient Europe: essays presented to Stuart Piggott* (eds J M Coles and D D A Simpson), 145-72, Leicester

Roe, F, 1979 Typology of stone implements with shaftholes, in Clough and Cummins 1979, 23-48

Roe, F, 2004 Stone artefacts from Grave 4013/12, in Lambrick and Allen 2004, 90-94

Roe, F, 2007 The worked stone objects, in Benson and Whittle 2007, 316-318

Roe, F, in prep. The worked stone, in Hey in prep.

Roebroeks, W, Conard, N J, and van Kolfschoten, T, 1992 Dense forests, cold steppes, and the Palaeolithic settlement of northern Europe, *Current Anthropology* **33**, 551-86

Roebroeks, W, and Speleers, B, 2002 Last inter-glacial (Eemian) occupation of the North European Plain and adjacent areas, in *Le Dernier Interglaciaire et les occupations humaines du Palaeolithique moyen* (eds W Roebroeks and A Tuffreau), 31-9, Lille

Roebroeks, W, and van Kolfschoten, T, 1994 The earliest occupation of Europe: a short chronology, *Antiquity* **68**, 489-503

Rolleston, G, 1884 *Scientific papers and addresses* (ed. W Turner), Oxford

Rose, J, 1987 Status of the Wolstonian glaciation in the British Quaternary, *Quaternary Newsletter*, **53**, 1-9

Rose, J, 1989 Tracing the Baginton-Lillington Sands and Gravels from the West Midlands to East Anglia, In *West Midlands, Field Guide* (ed. D H Keen), 102-10, Cambridge

Rose , J, and Allen P, 1977 Middle Pleistocene stratigraphy in south-east Suffolk, *Journal of the Geological Society of London* **133**, 83-102

Rose, J, Allen, P, and Hey, R W, 1976 Middle Pleistocene stratigraphy in southern East Anglia *Nature* **263**, 492-4

Rose, J, Moorlock, B S P, and Hamblin, R J O, 2001 Pre-Anglian fluvial and coastal deposits in Eastern England: lithostratigraphy and palaeoenvironments, *Quaternary International* **70**, 5-22

Rose, J, Whiteman, C A, Allen, P, and Kemp, R A, 1999 The Kesgrave Sands and Gravels: 'pre-glacial' Quaternary deposits of the River Thames and its tributaries between Goring and Cromer, *Proc Geol Ass* **110**, 23-31

Rowe, P J, Atkinson, T C, and Turner, C, 1999 U-series dating of Hoxnian interglacial deposits at Marks Tey, Essex, England, *Journal of Quaternary Science* **14**, 693-702

Ruggles, C, 1999 *Astronomy in prehistoric Britain and Ireland*, Yale

Salter, A E, 1905 On the superficial deposits of central and parts of southern England. *Proc Geol Ass* **19**, 1-56

Sandford, K S, 1924 The river gravels of the Oxford District, *Quarterly Journal of the Geological Society of London* **80**, 113-79

Sandford, K S, 1925 The fossil elephants of the Upper Thames basin, *Quarterly Journal of the Geological Society of London* **81**, 62-86

Sandford, K S, 1926 Pleistocene deposits, in *The Geology of the Country around Oxford* (ed. J Pringle), Memoir of the Geological Survey of Great Britain, 104-72, London

Sandford, K S, 1932 The Pleistocene succession in England, *Geological Magazine* **69**, 17-18

Saville, A, 1980 *Archaeological sites in the Avon and Gloucestershire Cotswolds: an extensive survey of a rural archaeological resource with special reference to plough damage*, Committee for Rescue Archaeology in Avon, Gloucestershire and Somerset Report **5**, Bristol

Saville, A, 1981 *Grimes Graves, Norfolk: excavations, 1971-72, 2: the flint assemblage*, London

Saville, A, 1983 Excavations at Condicote Henge monument, Gloucestershire 1977, *Trans Bristol Gloucestershire Archaeol Soc* **101**, 21-47

Saville, A, 1984 Palaeolithic and mesolithic evidence from Gloucestershire, in *Archaeologyy in Gloucestershire*, (ed. A Saville), 59-79, Cheltenham

Saville, A, 1989 Rodmarton long barrow, Gloucestershire, 1988, *Trans Bristol and Gloucestershire Archaeol Soc* **107**, 189-93

Saville, A, 1990a *Hazleton North: the excavation of a Neolithic long cairn of the Cotswold-Severn group*, English Heritage Report **13**, London

Saville, A, 1990b Stone, bone and fired clay, in Saville 1990a, 177-181

Saville, A (ed.), 2004 *Mesolithic Scotland and its neighbours*, Edinburgh

Scaife, R, 1992 Plant macrofossils and pollen analysis, in Healy *et al.* 1992, 64-70

Scaife, R, 1999 Pollen from Latton Roman Pond, in *Excavations alongside Roman Ermin Street, Gloucestershire and Wiltshire, The archaeology of the A419/A417 Swindon to Gloucester Road Scheme* 2 (eds A Mudd, R J Williams, and A Lupton), 510-12, Oxford

Scaife, R, 2000 Palynology and palaeoenvironment, in Needham 2000a, 168-87

Schechner, R, 1994 Ritual and performance, in *Companion encyclopaedia of anthropology* (ed. T Ingold), 613-47, London

Schreve, D C, 1997 Mammalian biostratigraphy of the later Middle Pleistocene in Britain, unpubl. PhD thesis, Univ. London

Schreve, D C, 2001a Differentiation of the British late Middle Pleistocene interglacials: the evidence from mammalian biostratigraphy, *Quaternary Science Reviews* **20**, 1693-705

Schreve, D C, 2001b Mammalian evidence from fluvial sequences for complex environmental change at the oxygen isotope substage level, *Quaternary International* **79**, 65-74

Schreve, D C, 2004a The mammalian fauna of Barnfield Pit, Swanscombe, Kent, in *The Quaternary mammals of southern and eastern England: field guide* (ed. D C Schreve), 29-48, London

Schreve, D C, 2004b The mammalian fauna of the penultimate (MIS 7) interglacial in the lower Thames valley, in *The Quaternary mammals of southern and eastern England: field guide* (ed. D C Schreve), 69-79, London

Schreve, D C, 2006 The taphonomy of a Middle Devensian (MIS 3) vertebrate assemblage from Lynford, Norfolk, UK, and its implications for Middle Palaeolithic subsistence strategies, *Journal of Quaternary Science* **21**, 543-65

Schreve, D C, and Bridgland, D R, 2002 Correlation of English and German Middle Pleistocene fluvial sequences based on mammalian biostratigraphy, *Netherlands Journal of Geosciences* **81**, 357-73

Schreve, D C, Bridgland, D R, Allen, P, Blackford, J J, Gleed-Owen, C P, Griffiths, H I, Keen, D H, and White, M J, 2002 Sedimentology, palaeontology and archaeology of late Middle Pleistocene River Thames terrace deposits at Purfleet, Essex, UK, *Quaternary Science Reviews* **21**, 1423-64

Schreve, D C, Bridgland, D R, Allen, P, Keen, D H, White, M J, Blackford, J J, Coope, G R, Field, M H, Juby, C, Kemp, R A, Gleed-Owen, C P, Cooper, J H, and Green, F M L, in prep. Late Middle Pleistocene River Thames terrace deposits at Aveley, Essex, UK: a multiproxy framework for the penultimate (MIS 7) interglacial

Schreve, D C, Harding, P, White, M J, Bridgland, D R, Allen, P, Clayton, F, and Keen, D H, 2006 A Levallois knapping site at West Thurrock, Lower Thames, UK: its Quaternary context, environment and age, *Proc Prehist Soc* **72**, 21-52

Schulting, R J, 2000 New AMS dates from the Lambourn long barrow and the question of the earliest Neolithic in southern England: repacking the Neolithic package, *Oxford J Archaeol* **19**, 25-35

Schulting, R J, and Richards, M P, 2000 The use of stable isotopes in studies of subsistence and seasonality in the British Mesolithic, in *Mesolithic lifeways: current research from Britain and Ireland* (ed. R Young), Leicester Archaeology Monographs **7**, 55-65, Leicester

Schwarcz, H P, 1984 Uranium series determinations on stalagmite samples from Bacon Hole, in A P Currant, C B Stringer and S N Colcutt, Bacon Hole Cave, in *Field guide. Wales: Gower Preseli, Fforest Fawr*, (eds D Q Bowen and A Henry), 43, Cambridge

Scott, K, 1980 Two hunting episodes of Middle Palaeolithic Age at La Cotte de Saint-Brelade, Jersey (Channel Islands), *World Archaeology* **12 (2)**, 137-52

Scott, K, and Buckingham, C, 1997 Quaternary fluvial deposits and palaeontology at Stanton Harcourt, Oxfordshire, in *The Quaternary of the south Midlands and the Welsh Marches: field guide* (eds S G Lewis and D Maddy), 115-26, London

Scott, K, and Buckingham, C M, 2001 A river runs through it: a decade of research at Stanton Harcourt, in *A very remote period indeed: papers on the Palaeolithic presented to Derek Roe* (eds S Milliken and J Cook), 207-13, Oxford

Scott, R, 2006 The early Middle Palaeolithic of Britain, Unpubl. PhD thesis, Univ. Durham

Scourse, J D, Austin, W E N, Sejrup, H P, and Ansari, M H, 1999 Foraminiferal isoleucine epimerization determinations from the Nar Valley Clay, Norfolk, UK: implications for Quaternary correlations in the southern North Sea basin, *Geological Magazine* **136**, 543-60

Seddon, M B, and Holyoak, D T, 1985 Evidence of sustained regional permafrost during deposition of fossiliferous Late Pleistocene sediments at Stanton Harcourt, Oxfordshire, *Proc Geol Ass* **96**, 53-73

Serjeantson, D, 2003 Review of environmental archaeology in southern Britain. Animal bones, Neolithic and early Bronze Age (4000 BC-1500 BC): the development of agriculture and animal husbandry, unpubl. report, Univ. Southampton and Engl Heritage Centre for Archaeol

Serjeantson, D, 2006 Food or feast at Neolithic Runnymede, in *Animals in the Neolithic of Britain and Europe* (eds D Serjeantson and D Field), Neolithic Studies Groups Seminar Papers **7**, 113-34, Oxford

Shackleton, N J, 1987 Oxygen isotopes, ice volume and sea level, *Quaternary Science Reviews* **6**, 1835-90

Shackleton, N J, and Opdyke, N D, 1973 Oxygen isotope and palaeomagnetic stratigraphy of equatorial Pacific core V28-238: oxygen isotope temperatures and ice volumes on a 10^5 and 10^6 year scale, *Quaternary Research* **3**, 39-55

Shand, P, Henderson, E, Henderson, R, and Barclay, A, 2003 Corporation Farm, Wilsham Road, Abingdon: a summary of the Neolithic and Bronze Age excavations, 1971-4, in Barclay *et al.* 2003, 31-40

Shanks, M, and Tilley, C, 1982 Ideology, symbolic power and ritual communication: a reinterpretation of Neolithic practices, in Hodder 1982, 129-54

Sharples, N, 1984 Excavations at Pierowall Quarry, Westray, Orkney, *Proc Soc Antiq Scot*, **114**, 75-125

Shell, C A and Pierce, C W, 1998-99 Avebury: ground penetrating radar investigations in the West Kennet Avenue, *National Trust Annual Archaeol Rev*, 58

Shennan, S, 1982 Ideology, change and the European early Bronze Age, in Hodder 1982, 155-61

Sheridan, A, 2007 From Picardie to Pickering and Pencraig Hill? New information on the 'Carinated Bowl Neolithic' in northern Britain, in Whittle and Cummings 2007, 441-92

Sheridan, A, in prep. Shale, in Hey in prep.

Sheridan, R, Sheridan, D, and Hassell, P, 1967 Rescue excavation of a Mesolithic site at Greenham Dairy Farm, Newbury, 1963, *Trans Newbury District Field Club* **11 (4)**, 66-73

Sherlock, R L, and Noble, A H, 1912 On the glacial origin of the Clay-with-flints of Buckinghamshire, and on the former course of the Thames, *Quarterly Journal of the Geological Society of London* **68**, 199-212

Sherlock, R L, and Pocock, R M, 1924 *The geology of the country around Hertford*, London

Shotton, F W, 1973a A mammalian fauna from the Stretton Sand at Stretton-on-Fosse, South Warwickshire, *Geological Magazine* **109**, 473-6

Shotton, F W, 1973b The English Midlands, in *A correlation of Quaternary deposits in the British Isles* (eds G F Mitchell, L F Penny, F W Shotton and R G West), Special Report of the Geological Society of London **4**, 18-22, Edinburgh

Shotton, F W, 1973c General Principles governing the subdivision of the Quaternary System, in *A correlation of Quaternary deposits in the British Isles* (eds G F Mitchell, L F Penny, F W Shotton and R G West), Special Report of the Geological Society of London **4**, 1-7, Edinburgh

Shotton, F W, 1983 Interglacials after the Hoxnian in Britain, in *Quaternary glaciations in the northern hemisphere* (eds D J Easterbrook, P Hansliêk, K-D Jäger and F W Shotton), UNESCO International Geological Correlation Programme, Project 73/1/24, Report **7**, 203-13, Prague

Shotton, F W, Goudie, A S, Briggs, D J, and Osmaston, H A, 1980 Cromerian Interglacial deposits at Sugworth, near Oxford, England, and their relation to the plateau drift of the Cotswolds and the terrace sequence of the Upper and Middle Thames, *Phil Trans Roy Soc London B* **289**, 55–86

Shotton, F W, Keen, D H, Coope, G R, Currant, A P, Gibbard, P L, Aalto, M, Peglar, S M, and Robinson, J E, 1993 The Middle Pleistocene deposits of Waverly Wood pit, Warwickshire, England, *Journal of Quaternary Science* **8**, 293-325

Shotton, F W, and Williams, R E G, 1971 Birmingham University radiocarbon dates V, *Radiocarbon* **13**, 141-56

Shrubsole, O A, 1884 On certain less familiar forms of Palaeolithic flint implements from the gravel at Reading, *The Journal of the Anthropological Institute of Great Britain and Ireland* **14**, 192-200

Shrubsole, O A, 1890 On the valley-gravels about Reading, with especial reference to the Palaeolithic implements found in them, *Quarterly Journal of the Geological Society of London* **46**, 582-94

Shrubsole, O A, and Whitaker, W, 1902 Excursion to Reading, *Proc Geol Ass* **17**, 381-2

Sidell, J, and Wilkinson, K, 2004 The central London Thames: Neolithic river development and floodplain archaeology, in Cotton and Field 2004, 38-49

Simpson, D D A, 1996 'Crown' antler maceheads and the later Neolithic in Britain, *Proc Prehist Soc* **62**, 293-303

Simpson, D D A, 2004 Making an impression: Beaker combs, in *Monuments and material culture: papers in honour of an Avebury archaeologist, Isobel Smith* (eds R Cleal and J Pollard), 207-214, East Knoyle

Singer, R, Gladfelter, B G, and Wymer, J J, 1993 *The Lower Paleolithic site at Hoxne, England*, Chicago

Slade, C F, 1963-4 A late Neolithic site at Sonning, Berkshire, *Berkshire Archaeol J* **61**, 420

Smith, A J, 1989 A catastrophic origin for the palaeovalley system of the eastern English Channel, *Marine Geology* **64**, 65-75

Smith, I and Darvill, T, 1990 The prehistoric pottery, in Saville 1990a, 141-52

Smith, I F, 1965a *Windmill Hill and Avebury: excavations by Alexander Keiller, 1925-1939*, Oxford

Smith, I F, 1965b Excavation of a bell barrow, Avebury G55, *Wiltshire Archaeol Mag* **60**, 24-46

Smith, I F, 1968 Report on the late Neolithic pits at Cam, Gloucestershire, *Trans Bristol Gloucestershire Archaeol Soc* **87**, 16-20

Smith, I F, 1972 Ring ditches in eastern and central Gloucestershire, in *Archaeology and the landscape: essays for L V Grinsell* (ed. P J Fowler), 157-67, London

Smith, I F, and Simpson, D D A, 1966 Excavation of a round barrow on Overton Hill, North Wiltshire, *Proc Prehist Soc* **32**, 122-55

Smith, L, 1997 Bronze Age, in Barnes *et al.* 1997, 24-8

Smith, M, and Brickley, M B, 2006 The date and sequence of use of Neolithic funerary monuments: new AMS dating evidence from the Cotswold-Severn, *Oxford J Archaeol* **25 (4)**, 335-55

Smith, M, and Brickley, M, 2009 *People of the long barrows: life, death and burial in the earlier Neolithic*, Stroud

Smith, R A, 1911 A palaeolithic industry at Northfleet, Kent, *Archaeologia* **62**, 515-2

Smith, R A, 1918 Specimens from the Layton Collection in Brentford Public Library, *Archaeologia* **69**, 1-30

Smith, R A, 1924 Two prehistoric vessels, *Antiq J* **4**, 127-30

Smith, W G, 1894 *Man the primeval savage: his haunts and relics from the hill-tops of Bedfordshire to Blackwall*, London

Snelling, A J R, 1975 A fossil molluscan fauna at Purfleet, Essex, *Essex Naturalist* **33**, 104-8

Sofaer Derevenski, J, 2002 Engendering context: context as gendered practice in the early Bronze Age of the Upper Thames Valley, UK, *European J Archaeol* **5 (2)**, 191-211

Sørensen, M L S, 2004 Stating identities: the use of objects in rich Bronze Age graves, in *Explaining social change: essays in honour of Colin Renfrew* (eds J Cherry, C Scarre, and S Shennan), 167-76, Cambridge

Soressi, M, and Hays, M A, 2003 Manufacture, transport and use of Mousterian bifaces: a case study from the Perigord (France), in *Multiple approaches to the study of bifacial technologies* (eds M Soressi and H Dibble), 125-148, Pennsylvania

Speleers, B, 2000 The relevance of the Eemian for the study of the Palaeolithic occupation of Europe, *Geologie en Mijnbouw/Netherlands Journal of Geosciences* **79**, 283-91

Spikins, P, 2000 Ethno-facts or ethno-fiction? Searching for the structure of settlement patterns, in *Mesolithic lifeways: current research in Britain and Ireland* (ed. R Young), Leicester

Archaeol Monogr **7**, 105-18, Leicester

Spurrell, F C J, 1880a On the discovery of the place where Palaeolithic implements were made at Crayford, *Quarterly Journal of the Geological Society of London* **36**, 544-8

Spurrell, F C J, 1880b On implements and chips from the floor of a Palaeolithic Workshop, *Archaeol J* **38**, 294-9

Stainton, B, 1989 Excavation of an early prehistoric site at Stratford's Yard, Chesham, *Rec Buckinghamshire* **31**, 49-74

Startin, W, and Bradley, R, 1981 Some notes on work organisation and society in prehistoric Wessex, in *Astonomy and society in the period 4000-1500 BC*, (eds C Ruggles and A Whittle), BAR Brit. Ser. **88**, Oxford, 289-96

Stevens, J, 1882 On the earliest known traces of man in the Thames Drift at Reading, *Transactions of the Berkshire archaeological and architectural Society*, 1-18

Stone, S, 1857 Account of certain (supposed) British and Saxon remains recently discovered at Standlake, in the County of Oxford, *Proc Soc Antiq London* **4**, 92-3

Stopp, M P, 1993 Taphonomic analysis of the faunal assemblage, in *The Lower Palaeolithic site at Hoxne, England* (eds R Singer, B G Gladfelter and J J Wymer), 138-149, Chicago and London

Stringer, C B, and Gamble, C, 1993 *In search of the Neanderthals*, London

Stringer, C B, Currant, A P, Schwarcz, H P, and Collcutt, S N, 1986 Age of Pleistocene faunas from Bacon Hole, Wales, *Nature* **320**, 59-62

Stringer, C, and Hublin, J-J, 1999 New age estimates for the Swanscombe hominid, and their significance for human evolution, *Journal of Human Evolution* **37**, 873-7

Stuart, A J, 1980 The vertebrate fauna from the interglacial deposits at Sugworth, near Oxford, *Phil Trans Roy Soc London B* **289**, 87-97

Stuart, A J, 1982 *Pleistocene vertebrates of the British Isles*, London

Stuart, A J, 1995 Insularity and Quaternary vertebrate faunas in Britain and Ireland, in *Island Britain: a Quaternary perspective* (ed. R C Preece), Geological Society Special Publication **96**, 111-126, London

Stuart, A J, and Lister, A M, 2001 The mammalian faunas of Pakefield/Kessingland and Corton, Suffolk: evidence for a new temperate episode in the British early Middle Pleistocene, *Quaternary Science Reviews* **20**, 1677-92

Stukeley, W, 1740 *Stonehenge: a temple restor'd to the British druids*, London

Stukeley, W, 1743 *Abury, a temple of the British Druids, with some others, described*, London

Sumbler, M G, 1983a A new look at the type Wolstonian glacial deposits of central England, *Proc Geol Ass* **94**, 23-31

Sumbler, M G, 1983b The type Wolstonian sequence: some further comments, *Quaternary Newsletter* **40**, 36-9

Sumbler, M G, 1995 The terraces of the rivers Thame and Thames and their bearing on the chronology of glaciation in central and eastern England, *Proc Geol Ass* **106**, 93-106

Sumbler, M G, 2001 The Moreton Drift: a further clue to the glacial chronology in central England, *Proc Geol Ass* **112**, 13-28

Sumbler, M G, Barron, A J M, and Morigi, A N, 2000 *Geology of the Cirencester district*, Memoir of the British Geological Survey (Sheet 235), England and Wales

Sutcliffe, A J, 1964 The mammalian fauna, in *The Swanscombe skull* (ed. C D Ovey), Occasional Papers of the Royal Anthropological Institute **20**, 85-111

Sutcliffe, A J, 1975 A hazard in the interpretation of glacial-interglacial sequences, *Quaternary Newsletter* **17**, 1-3

Sutcliffe, A J, and Kowalski, K, 1976 Pleistocene rodents of the British Isles, *Bulletin of the British Museum (Natural History), Geology*, **27/2**, 33-147

Sutcliffe, A J, Currant, A P, and Stringer, C B, 1987 Evidence of sea-level change from coastal caves with raised beach deposits, terrestrial faunas and dated stalagmites, *Progress in Oceanography* **18**, 243-71

Sutcliffe, A J, Lord, T C, Harmon, R S, Ivanovich, M, Rae, A and, Hess, J W, 1985 Wolverine in northern England at about 83,000 yr BP: faunal evidence for climatic change during Isotope Stage 5, *Quaternary Research* **24,** 73-86

Tambiah, S J, 1979 *A performative approach to ritual*, Oxford

Taylor, J, 1995 The excavation of ring ditch XXII, 6, 1979, in A J Barclay *et al*. 1995, 46-49

Taylor, M, 1988 Some preliminary thoughts on coppicing and pollarding at Etton, in *The exploitation of wetlands* (eds P Murphy and C French), BAR Brit. Ser. **186**, 93-100, Oxford

Taylor, M, 2007 The wood, in Harding and Healy 2007

Taylor, M, in prep. The wood, in Hey in prep.

Taylor, T, 2002 *The buried soul: how humans invented death*, London

Terberger, T, and Street, M, 2002 Hiatus or continuity? New results for the question of Pleniglacial settlement in Central Europe, *Antiquity* **76**, 691-8

Thieme, H, 1997 Lower Palaeolithic hunting spears from Germany, *Nature* **385**, 807-10

Thieme, H, 2005 The Lower Palaeolithic art of hunting: the case of Schoningen 13 II-4, Lower Saxony, Germany, in *The hominid individual in context: archaeological investigations of Lower and Middle Palaeolithic landscapes, locales and artefacts* (eds C Gamble and M Porr), 115-32, London

Thomas, A and Holbrook, N, 1998 Excavations at the Memorial Hall, Lechlade, 1995, in Boyle *et al*. 1998, 282-88

Thomas, J, 1988 The social significance of Cotswold-Severn burial rites, *Man* **(NS) 23**, 540-59

Thomas, J, 1991 Reading the body: Beaker funerary practice in Britain, in Garwood *et al.* 1991, 33-42

Thomas, J, 1993 The politics of vision and the archaeologies of landscape, in *Landscape: politics and perspectives* (ed. B Bender), 19-48, Oxford

Thomas, J, 1996 Neolithic houses in mainland Britain and Ireland: a sceptical view, in Darvill and Thomas 1996, 1-12

Thomas, J, 1999 *Understanding the Neolithic*, London

Thomas, J, 2000 Death, identity and the body in Neolithic Britain, *J Roy Anthropol Inst* **6**, 653-68

Thomas, J, 2001 Glaston, *Curr Archaeol* **173**, 180-4

Thomas, J, and Tilley, C, 1993 The axe and the torso: symbolic structures, in *Interpretive archaeology* (ed. C Tilley), 225-325, Oxford

Thomas, J, and Whittle, A, 1986 Anatomy of a tomb: West Kennet revisited, *Oxford J of Archaeol* **5 (2)**, 129-56

Thomas, K D, 1982 Neolithic enclosures and woodland habitats on the South Downs in Sussex, England, in *Archaeological aspects of woodland ecology*, (eds M Bell amd S Limbrey), BAR Int. Ser. **146**, 147-70, Oxford

Thomas, N, 1962 A gazetteer of Neolithic and Bronze Age sites and antiquities in Bedfordshire, *Bedfordshire Archaeol J* **11**, 16-33

Thomas, R, and Wallis, J, 1982 Recent work on Neolithic and early Bronze Age sites in the Abingdon area, *CBA Regional Group 9 Newsletter* **12**, 181-4

Thompson, G B, 1999 The analysis of wood charcoals from selected pits and funerary contexts, in Barclay and Halpin 1999, 269-74

Thorpe, I J, 1984 Ritual, power and ideology: a reconstruction of earlier Neolithic rituals in Wessex, in *Neolithic Studies* (eds R Bradley, and J Gardiner), BAR Brit. Ser. **133**, 41-60, Oxford

Thorpe, I J, and Richards, C, 1984 The decline of ritual authority and the introduction of Beakers into Britain, in Bradley and Gardiner 1984, 67-84

Thurnham, J, 1860a Examination of a chambered long barrow at West Kennet, Wiltshire, *Archaeologia* **38**, 405-21

Thurnham, J, 1860b Examination of barrows on the downs of north Wiltshire in 1853-57, *Wilstshire Archaeol Nat Hist Soc Mag* **6**, 317-36

Thurnham, J, 1871 On ancient British barrows, especially those of Wiltshire and the adjoining counties, *Archaeologia*, **43**, 285-544

Tilley, C, 1989 Interpreting material culture, in *The meaning of things* (ed. I Hodder), 185-213, London

Tilley, C, 1994 *A phenomenology of landscape*, Oxford

Tilley, C, 1996 *An ethnography of the Neolithic: early prehistoric societies in southern Scandinavia*, Cambridge

Tilley, C, 1999 *Metaphor and material culture*, Oxford

Timby, J, Stansbie, D, Norton, A and Welsh, K, 2005 Excavations along the Newbury Reinforcement Pipeline: Iron Age-Roman activity and a Neolithic pit group, *Oxoniensia* **70**, 203-307

Tipping, R, 2004 Interpretative issues concerning the driving forces of vegetation change in the early Holocene of the British Isles, in Saville 2004, 45-53

Tomlinson, M E, 1929 The drifts of the Stour-Evenlode watershed and their extension into the valleys of the Warwickshire Stour and Upper Evenlode, *Proceedings of the Birmingham Natural History and Philosophical Society* **15**, 157-196

Treacher, L, 1904 On the occurrence of stone implements in the Thames Valley between Reading and Maidenhead, *Man* **10**, 17-19

Treherne, P, 1995 The warrior's beauty: the masculine body and self-identity in Bronze Age Europe, *J European Archaeol* **3 (1)**, 105-44

Tresset, A and Vigne, J-D, 2007 Substitution of species, techniques and symbols at the Mesolithic-Neolithic transition in western Europe, in Whittle and Cummings 2007, 189-210

Trimmer, W K, 1813 An account of some organic remains found near Brentford, Middlesex, *Phil Trans Roy Soc London* **103**, 131-137

Turner, A, 1992 Large carnivores and earliest European hominids: changing determinants of resource availability during the Lower and Middle Pleistocene, *Journal of Human Evolution* **22**, 109-26

Turner, C, 1968 A Lowestoftian Late Glacial flora from the Pleistocene deposits at Hoxne, Suffolk, *New Phytologist* **67**, 327-32

Turner, C, 1983 Nettlebed interglacial deposits, in *Diversion of the Thames: field guide* (ed. J Rose), 66-8, Cambridge

Turner, C (ed.), 1996a *The early Middle Pleistocene in Europe*, Rotterdam

Turner, C, 1996b A brief survey of the early Middle Pleistocene in Europe, in *The early Middle Pleistocene in Europe* (ed. C Turner), 295-317, Rotterdam

Turner, C, and Kerney, M P, 1971 A note on the age of the freshwater beds of the Clacton Channel, *Quarterly Journal of the Geological Society of London* **127**, 87-93

Turner, V, 1967 *The forest of symbols: aspects of Ndembu ritual*, Ithaca

Turner, V, 1974 *Drama, fields and metaphors*, Ithaca

Turner, V, 1982 *From ritual to theatre*, New York

Turner, V, 1990 Are there universals of performance in myth, ritual and drama? in *By means of performance* (eds R Schechner and W Appel), 8-18, Cambridge

TVAS, 2010 TVAS News: Oxford, Thames Valley Archaeological Services, http://www.tvas.co.uk/news/oxford-2.html (checked July 2010)

Tyldesley, J A, 1986a *The Wolvercote Channel handaxe assemblage: a comparative study*, BAR Brit. Ser. **153**, Oxford

Tyldesley, J A, 1986b A reassessment of the handaxe assemblage recovered from the Wolvercote Channel, in *The Palaeolithic of Britain and its nearest neighbours: recent studies* (ed. S N Collcutt), 23-25, Sheffield

Tyldesley, J A, 1987 *The bout coupé handaxe: a typological problem.* BAR Brit. Ser. **170**, Oxford

Tylor, A, 1869 On Quaternary gravels, *Quarterly Journal of the Geological Society of London* **25**, 57-100

van Andel, T, 2003 Glacial environments I: the Weichselian climate in Europe between the end of the OIS5 interglacial and the Last Glacial maximum, in *Neanderthals and modern humans in the European landscape during the Last Glaciation: archaeological results of the Stage 3 project* (eds T van Andel and W Davies), 9-20, Cambridge

van Gennep, A, 1909 *The rites of passage,* (reprinted 1960), London

Vera, F W M, 2000 *Grazing ecology and forest history,* Wallingford

Verdery, K, 1999 *The political lives of dead bodies: reburial and postsocialist change,* New York

Verpoorte, A, 2006 Neanderthal energetics and spatial behaviour *Before Farming* (online version) **2006/3,** article 2

von Koenigswald, W, 1992 Various aspects of migrations in terrestrial mammals in relation to Pleistocene faunas of central Europe, in Mammalian migration and dispersal events in the European Quaternary (eds W von Koenigswald and L Werdelin), *Courier Forschungsinstitut Senckenberg* **153**, 39-47

Vyner, B, 1984 The excavation of a Neolithic cairn at Street House, Loftus, Cleveland, *Proc Prehist Soc* **50**, 151-95

Waechter, J d' A, 1970 Swanscombe, 1969, *Proceedings of the Royal Anthropological Institute for 1969,* 83-5

Wainwright, G J, and Longworth, I, 1971 *Durrington Walls: excavations, 1966-1968,* London

Wallis, J, Gledhill, A, and Eeles, R, 1992 Investigations of prehistoric features east of Peep O Day Lane, south of Abingdon, *CBA Group 9 Newsletter* **22**, 68-73

Wallis, J, and Hedges, J W, 1999 Textile, in Barclay and Halpin 1999, 145

Warren, G M, 2006 Technology, in *Mesolithic Britain and Ireland: new approaches,* (eds C Conneller, and G M Warren), 13-34, Stroud

Warren, S H, 1911 Palaeolithic wooden spear from Clacton, *Quarterly Journal of the Geological Society of London* **67**, cxix

Warren, S H, 1924 The elephant bed of Clacton-on Sea, *Essex Naturalist* **21**, 32-40

Warren, S H, 1926 The classification of the Lower Palaeolithic with especial reference to Essex, *Proceedings and Transactions of the South-Eastern Union of Scientific Societies* 1926, 38–50

Watson, A, 2001 Round barrows in a circular world: monumentalising landscapes in early Bronze Age Wessex, in Brück 2001, 207-16

Watson, J, 1999 Organics, in Barclay and Halpin 1999, 138, 144-5, 155

Watson, J, 2004 Organic material associated with the dagger from grave 4013/12, in Lambrick and Allen 2004, 86-87

Webber, M, with Ganiaris, H, 2004 The Chelsea club: a Neolithic wooden artefact from the river Thames in London, in Cotton and Field 2004, 124-127

Wenban-Smith, F F, 1995 The Ebbsfleet Valley, Northfleet (Baker's Hole), in *The Quaternary of the lower reaches of the Thames* (eds D R Bridgland, Allen, P and Haggart, B A), 147-164, Durham

Wenban-Smith, F F, Allen, P, Bates, M R, Parfitt, S A, Preece, R C, Stewart, J R, Turner, C and Whittaker, JE, 2006 The Clactonian elephant butchery site at Southfleet Road, Ebbsfleet, UK, *Journal of Quaternary Science* (2006) **21** (5), 471-83

Wessex Archaeology, 1994-5 *The English Rivers Palaeolithic Project Report 1: regions 7 (Thames) and 10 (Warwickshire),* Salisbury

Wessex Archaeology, 2002 A303 Archaeological surveys: archaeological evaluation report: Areas R and T, unpubl. report for Highways Agency (Ref. 50527.1b), Wessex Archaeology, Salisbury

Wessex Archaeology, 2005 Preferred Area 4, Denham, Buckinghamshire: archaeological evaluation report, unpublished client report 50692.08, Wessex Archaeology, Salisbury

West, R G, 1956 The Quaternary deposits at Hoxne, Suffolk, *Phil Trans Roy Soc London B,* **239**, 265-356

West, R G, 1969 Pollen analyses from interglacial deposits at Aveley and Grays, Essex, *Proc Geol Ass* **80**, 271-82

West, R G, 1977 *East Anglia: X INQUA Congress excursion guide,* Norwich

West, R G, 1980a *The preglacial Pleistocene of Norfolk and Suffolk,* Cambridge

West, R G, 1980b Pleistocene forest history in East Anglia, *New Phytologist* **85**, 571-622

West, S, 1990 *West Stow: The prehistoric and Romano-British occupations,* EEA **48**, Bury St Edmunds

Westaway, R, Maddy, D, and Bridgland, D R, 2002 Flow in the lower continental crust as a mechanism for the Quaternary uplift of southeast England: constraints from the Thames terrace record, *Quaternary Science Reviews,* **21**, 559–603

Wheeler, A, 1969 *The fishes of the British Isles and north west Europe,* London

Whitaker, W, 1860 Geology of Reading, *The Geologist* **3**, 390-1

Whitaker, W, 1889 *The geology of London and parts of the Thames Valley* **1**, Memoir of the Geological Survey of Great Britain, London.

White, M J, 1997 The earlier Palaeolithic occupation of the Chilterns (southern England): reassessing the sites of Worthington G. Smith, *Antiquity* **71**, 912-31

White, M J, 1998a On the significance of Acheulean

biface variability in southern Britain, *Proc Prehist Soc* **64**, 15-44

White, M J, 1998b Twisted ovate bifaces in the British Lower Palaeolithic: some observations and implications, in *Stone Age archaeology: essays in honour of John Wymer* (eds N Ashton, Healy, F and Pettit, P), 98-104, Oxford

White, M J, 2000 The Clactonian question: on the interpretation of core-and-flake assemblages in the British Lower Palaeolithic, *Journal of World Prehistory* **14**, 1-63

White, M J, 2006 Axeing cleavers: reflections on broad-tipped large cutting tools in the British Lower and Middle Palaeolithic, in *Axe Age: Acheulean toolmaking, from quarry to discard* (eds N Goren-Inbar and G Sharon), 385-386, London

White, M J, and Ashton, N M, 2003 Lower Palaeolithic core technology and the origins of the Levallois method in NW Europe, *Current Anthropology* **44**, 598-609

White, M J, and Jacobi, R M, 2002 Two sides to every story: *bout coupé* handaxes revisited, *Oxford Journal of Archaeology* **21**, 109-33

White, M J, and Plunkett, S J, 2004 *Miss Layard excavates: a Palaeolithic site at Foxhall Road, Ipswich, 1903-1905*, Liverpool

White, M J, and Schreve, D C, 2000 Island Britain – Peninsula Britain: palaeogeography, colonization, and the Lower Palaeolithic settlement of the British Isles, *Proc Prehist Soc* **66**, 1-28

White, M, Scott, R, and Ashton, N, 2006 The early Middle Palaeolithic in Britain: archaeology, settlement history and human behaviour, *Journal of Quaternary Science* **21**, 525-42

Whiteman, C A, 1983 Great Waltham, In *Diversion of the Thames, Field Guide* (ed. J Rose), 163-9, Cambridge

Whiteman, C A 1990 Early and Middle Pleistocene stratigraphy and soils in Central Essex, England, unpubl. PhD thesis, Univ. London

Whiteman C A, and Rose, J, 1992 Thames River Sediments of the British Early and Middle Pleistocene, *Quaternary Science Reviews*, **11**, 363-76

Whitley, J, 2002 Too many ancestors, *Antiquity* **76**, 119-26

Whittle, A, 1986 The Neolithic finds, in Miles, D, *Archaeology at Barton Court Farm, Abingdon, Oxon*, OAU Rep **3** and CBA Res Rep **50**, Oxford and London

Whittle, A, 1990 A model for the Mesolithic-Neolithic transition in the upper Kennet valley, north Wiltshire, *Proc Prehist Soc* **56**, 101-10

Whittle, A, 1991 Wayland's Smithy, Oxfordshire: excavations at the Neolithic tomb in 1962-63 by R J C Atkinson and S Piggott, *Proc Prehist Soc* **57** (**2**), 61-101

Whittle, A, 1993 The Neolithic of the Avebury area: sequence, environment, settlement and monuments, *Oxford J Archaeol* **12 (1)**, 29-54

Whittle, A, 1994 Excavations at Millbarrow chambered tomb, Winterbourne Monkton, north Witlshire, *Wiltshire Archaeol Mag* **87**, 1-53

Whittle, A, 1996 *Europe in the Neolithic*, Cambridge

Whittle, A, 1997a Remembered and imagined belongings: Stonehenge in its traditions and structures of meaning, in Cunliffe and Renfrew 1997, 145-66

Whittle, A, 1997b *Sacred mound, holy rings. Silbury Hill and the West Kennet palisade enclosures: a later Neolithic complex in north Wiltshire*, Oxbow Books Monograph **74**, Oxford

Whittle, A, 2003 *The archaeology of people: dimensions of Neolithic life*, London

Whittle, A, Atkinson, R J C, Chambers, R, and Thomas, N, 1992 Excavations in the Neolithic and Bronze Age complex at Dorchester-on-Thames, Oxfordshire, 1947-1952 and 1981, *Proc Prehist Soc* **58**, 143-201

Whittle, A, Barclay, A, Bayliss, A, McFadyen, L, Schulting, R, and Wysocki, M, 2007 Building for the dead: events, processes and changing world-views from the 38th to the 34th centuries cal BC in southern Britain, *Cambridge Archaeol J* **17 (1) (suppl.)**, 123-47

Whittle, A, Barclay, A, McFadyen, L, Benson, D, and Gallery, D, 2007 Place and time: building and remembrance, in Benson and Whittle 2007, 327-64

Whittle, A, Bayliss, A and Healy, F, forthcoming *Gathering time: dating the early Neolithic enclosures of Southern Britain and Ireland*, Oxford

Whittle, A, Bayliss, A, and Wysocki, M, 2007 Once in a lifetime: the date of the Wayland's Smithy long barrow, *Cambridge Archaeol J* **17 (1) (suppl.)**, 103-21

Whittle, A, Bayliss, A, Healy, F, Hey, G, Robertson-Mackay, R, Allen T and Ford, S, forthcoming The Thames Valley, in Whittle *et al.* forthcoming

Whittle, A, and Cummings, V, 2007 *Going over: the Mesolithic-Neolithic transition in North-West Europe*, Proc Brit Acad **144**, 399-422, London

Whittle, A, Davies, J J, Dennis, I, Fairbairn, A S, and Hamilton, M A, 2000 Neolithic activity and occupation outside Windmill Hill causewayed enclosure, Wiltshire: survey and excavation, 1992-93, *Wiltshire Archaeol and Natur Hist Mag* **93**, 131-80

Whittle, A, and Pollard, J, 1998 Windmill Hill causewayed enclosure: the harmony of symbols, in Edmonds and Richards 1998, 231-47

Whittle, A, Pollard, J, and Grigson, C, 1999 *The harmony of symbols: the Windmill Hill causewayed enclosure*, Oxford

Whittle, A, Rouse, A J, and Evans, J G, 1993 A Neolithic downland monument in its environment: excavations at the Easton Down long barrow, Bishops Cannings, north Wiltshire, *Proc Prehist Soc* **59**, 197-239

Williams, D F, 1982 Petrological analysis of pottery, in Avery 1982, 33-5

Williams, D, 2004 Franks' Sandpit, Betchworth, Surrey: a site of special significance?, in Cotton and Field 2004, 164-7

Wintle, W, 2008 Geophysical survey at Dorchester on Thames 2008, unpubl. report, Univ. Oxford

Wise, P, 1993 Waverley Wood Farm Pit, *Curr Archaeol* **133**, 12-14

Wood, S V Jun., 1868 On the pebble-beds of Middlesex, Essex and Herts, *Quarterly Journal of the Geological Society of London* **24**, 464-72

Woodman, P C, 1978 *The Mesolithic in Ireland*, BAR Brit. Ser. **58**, Oxford

Woodward, A, 2000 *British barrows: a matter of life and death*, Stroud

Woodward, A, 2002 Beads and beakers: heirlooms and relics in the British early Bronze Age, *Antiquity* **76**, 1040-47

Woodward, A, Hunter, J, Ixer, R, Roe, F, Potts, P J, Watson, J S, and Jones, M C, 2006 Beaker age bracers in England: sources, function and use, *Antiquity* **80** (**309**), 530-543

Woodward, A, and Woodward, P, 1996 The topography of some barrow cemeteries in Bronze Age Wessex, *Proc Prehist Soc* **62**, 275-91

Wooldridge, S W, and Linton, D L, 1955 *Structure, surface and drainage in south-east England*, 2nd edn, London

Wymer, J J, 1958 Excavations at Thatcham, Berks 1958, *Trans Newbury District Field Club* **10**, 31-48

Wymer, J J, 1962 Excavations at the Maglemosian sites at Thatcham, Berkshire, England, *Proc Prehist Soc* **28**, 329-361

Wymer, J J, 1964 Excavations at Barnfield Pit, 1955-1960, in *The Swanscombe skull* (ed. C D Ovey), Occasional Papers of the Royal Anthropological Institute **20**, 19-60

Wymer, J J, 1965-6 Excavation of the Lambourn long barrow, 1964 *Berkshire Archaeol J* **62**, 1-16

Wymer, J J, 1968 *Lower Palaeolithic archaeology in Britain as represented by the Thames Valley*, London

Wymer, J J, 1977 *A Gazetteer of Mesolithic sites in England and Wales*, CBA Research Report **20**, London

Wymer, J J, 1983 The Lower Palaeolithic site at Hoxne, *Proceedings of the Suffolk Institute of Archaeology and History* **35**, 169-89

Wymer, J J, 1985 *Palaeolithic sites of East Anglia*, Norwich

Wymer, J J, 1988 Palaeolithic archaeology and the British Quaternary sequence, *Quaternary Science Reviews* **7**, 79-98

Wymer, J J, 1991 *Mesolithic Britain*, Princes Risborough

Wymer, J J, 1999 *The Lower Palaeolithic occupation of Britain*, Old Sarum

Wymer, J J, Lewis, S G, and Bridgland, D R, 1991 Warren Hill, Mildenhall, Suffolk (TL 744743), in *Central East Anglia and the Fen Basin: field guide* (eds S G Lewis, C A Whiteman and D R Bridgland), 50-7, London,

Wysocki, M, and Whittle, A, in prep. On the people of the long barrows: human skeletal remains from West Kennet, Wayland's Smithy and Fussell's Lodge

Yates, D, 1999 Bronze Age field systems in the Thames Valley, *Oxford J Archaeol* **18** (**2**), 157-70

Yates, D, 2001 Bronze Age agricultural intensification in the Thames Valley and Estuary, in Brück 2001, 65-82

York, J, 2002 The life cycle of Bronze Age metalwork from the Thames, *Oxford J Archaeol* **21**, 77-92

Zagwijn, W H, 1985 An outline of the Quaternary stratigraphy of the Netherlands, *Geologie en Mijnbouw* **64**, 17-24

Zagwijn, W H, 1996 The Cromerian Complex Stage of the Netherlands and correlation with other areas in Europe, in *The early Middle Pleistocene in Europe* (ed. C Turner), 145-72, Rotterdam

Zalasiewicz, J A, and Gibbard, P L, 1988 The Pliocene to early Middle Pleistocene of East Anglia: an overview, in *Pliocene-Middle Pleistocene of East Anglia: field guide* (eds P L Gibbard and J A Zalasiewicz), 1-31, Cambridge

Zeuner, F E, 1945 *The Pleistocene period*, Ray Society Publication **130**, London

Zeuner, F E, 1959 *The Pleistocene period*, 2nd edn, London

Zienkiewicz, L, 1999 Pottery: early Neolithic including Ebbsfleet, in Whittle *et al.* 1999, 258-92

Zvelebil, M, 1994 Plant use in the Mesolithic and its role in the transition to farming, *Proc Prehist Soc* **60**, 35-74

Index

Hungerford (Berks) 319
hunting 30, 39, 51, 56, 85, 102, 115, 127, 131, 139,
     143, 196, 199, 208-11, 218-19, 245-6
Hurley (Berks) 137
Hurst Park (East Molesey, Surrey) 451
huts 39, 197, 215, 217, 420
Hyaena Den (Wookey Hole, Somerset) 127
hyaenas, spotted 68, 113, 122
hydrology 161, 174-6, 196, 208

ice core, Greenland 137
ice sheets 41-2, 109, 118, 144
ice-wedge casts 9
Icknield Way 222
identity 395, 402, 406, 408
Iffley (Oxon) 114
Ilford (London) 89, 91
Imperial Sports Ground (Hillingdon, London)
     255, 261, 277-8, 281, 310, 398-400
Inkpen (Berks) 317
insects 75, 90, 123, 142, 161, 176-7, 180-1, 184-5,
     187-8
interglacials 1, 10, 19-20, 50, 63, 65, 67, 87-9, 100,
     104, 109
invasion hypothesis 313
Ipswichian Interglacial 1, 63, 65, 87, 89, 94, 103-4,
     109-10, 112-14, 118
Iron Age 189
Irthlingborough (Northants) 444
Isleworth (London) 125
Ismaili Centre (South Kensington, London) 123-4
isostatic rebound 41
isotopic analysis 199, 289
Iver (Bucks) 160, 205
ivory 131, 139

Jennings Yard (Windsor, Berks) 205, 218
Jerzmanovician 131
jet 277, 280, 397, 423, 425, 427, 434, 438-9, 449-50,
     456, 461
Joint Mitnor Cave Mammal Assemblage-Zone 113
juniper 142
Jurassic Way 222

Keble College (Oxford) 302, 370
Kempton Park Gravel 103-5, 112, 118, 123-4
Kempton Park Quarry (Sunbury, Surrey) 123
Kempton Park Terrace 112, 123
Kennet Valley 193, 196, 203
Kennyland's (Berks) 38
Kensington Road (Reading, Berks) 114
Kent's Cavern (Devon) 25-6, 127, 139
Kesgrave Formation 18, 43
Kesgrave Gravels 38
Kettlebury (Surrey) 208
Kew Bridge (London) 118-19
Kidmore Road Gravel Pit (Caversham, Berks) 53
kill/butchery sites 148
Kimble Farm (Turville, Bucks) 205
King Barrows Ridge (Wilts) 284
King's Men (Oxon) 156, 161, 300, 306, 337
King's Play Down (Wilts) 268

King's Weir (Oxon) 186
Knap Hill (Wilts) 161, 285, 287, 289, 353
knife-daggers 421, 423, 425, 427-9, 451, 456, 463
knives 167, 169, 312, 315, 354, 370, 379, 401, 429,
     434, 439, 445-6, 450, 454, 456
  copper alloy 312, 379, 438, 440, 463
  lithic 167, 169, 243, 277, 279-80, 315, 317, 354,
     370, 390, 397-8, 401, 434, 438-9, 443, 445-6
     discoidal 169, 440, 445-6
     edge-polished 169, 440, 443, 445-6, 450
     plano-convex 315, 400, 440
     polished 256, 397
Knowth (Co. Meath, Ireland) 379
Krukowski microburin 140

La Cotte de St Brelade (Jersey) 102
ladder, log 323, 451, 453
Lake District 253, 447
Lake End Road (Berks) 373, 375
Lambourn (Berks) 160, 166, 171, 205, 270-1, 321,
     363, 367-8, 379-80, 384, 392, 412-13, 423-6, 446,
     449-50, 456-7
landbridge, between Britain and mainland Europe
     3, 25, 28, 51, 109, 127, 174, 180, 195
landscape
  open 56, 98, 102, 107, 122, 142, 185-7, 221, 223,
     245, 328, 355
  sacred 332, 341, 344, 372
landscape archaeology 160
Langdale (Cumbria) 30
Langford (Oxon) 289
Langley Silt Complex 103
last glacial maximum 3, 122, 137, 151
late Neolithic 169, 183
late Neolithic/early Bronze Age 311-12
Latton Lands (Wilts) 95, 363, 421
Lavender Pit (Iver, Bucks) 125
Lavenham (Suffolk) 105
leaf and blade point industries 131
leather 162, 423, 440, 449, 451, 456-7, 463
Lechlade (Glos) 166, 295, 416
Leeds, E T 158, 291
Lehringen (Germany) 115
lemmings 28, 47, 51, 93, 107
Lent Rise Pits (Burnham, Bucks) 72
Levallois
  cores 77, 85, 91-5, 98-100
  flakes 77, 85, 93
  industry 65, 67-8, 77, 80, 85, 92-4, 98-9, 102, 125
  points 77, 85, 88, 99
  technique 65, 77, 88, 99, 102
levees 175
LiDAR 163, 165
Liff's Low (Derbys) 379
lignite 429, 449-50
lime 187
liminality 302
Linch Hill Corner (Oxon) 280, 303, 395-6, 398, 404,
     411-12, 445, 449-51, 456, 460
Lincombian 127
Linearbandkeramik 227, 231
linen 428